国際介護保険
―介護保険の国際化―
用語辞典

編著
住居広士・澤田 如

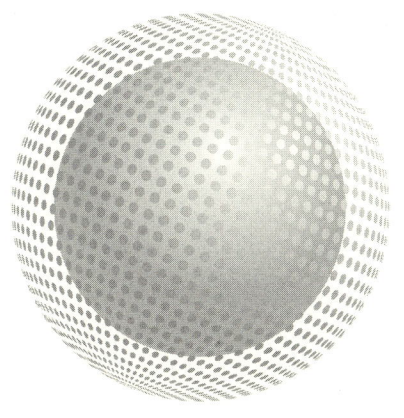

大学教育出版

編著者のことば

　2000年度に実施された日本の介護保険制度により、それまで提供されていなかった新しい介護サービスが創造・展開してきている。日本では少子高齢社会からさらに人口減少長寿社会を迎えて、介護保険制度の変革に拍車がかかっている。日本で初めて福祉・介護職に国家資格を創設した1987年の社会福祉士及び介護福祉士法から激変の時代を迎えて、20年ぶりの2007年にそれが改正され、2008年から国際的な看護・介護人材の受け入れも始まった。

　そのような変革の中で、国際的にも介護保険に関して学術交流を深めながら実践しなければ、介護サービスを必要としている世界中の人々の手元には届かない状況になってきている。その歴史的過程において、オランダでは1968年に介護保険の前身となる特別医療保険が施行されている。オーストリアでは、1993年に介護手当制度が成立している。ドイツでは、1994年4月にドイツ国内で5番目となる介護保険制度の法律が成立し、1995年4月からは在宅サービス、1996年7月からは施設サービスが実施されている。それらに大きな影響を受けて、日本では1997年に介護保険法が成立し、2000年度から介護保険制度が実施されている。2005年、さらに2011年には、その介護保険法が改正されている。アジア諸国でも、いくつかの介護改革が行われている。例えば、韓国ではいわゆる韓国介護保険法である老人長期療養保険法が2007年4月に成立している。2008年7月からは、韓国介護保険制度が実施されて、療養保護士として介護職の国家資格も養成されている。中国では、2002年から国家標準として養老護理員の介護人材の養成が試行されている。日本は2008年の経済連携協定（EPA）の発効で、インドネシアとフィリピンから外国人看護・介護候補者を受け入れている。

　近年では人口の高齢化率が世界で最も高いとされる日本の超高齢社会における介護保険が国際的なスタンダードとして創設・展開していく時代を迎えている。世界に向けてその国際学術交流を展開するためには、学問的共通基盤として介護保険に関する用語の標準化と専門性の架け橋となる『国際介護保険用語辞典』を刊行することにより共通性を持った専門的な国際学術交流が可能となる。

　本辞典の特色・構成は、以下のようになっている。

　第1部の「英和」の部分では、Encyclopedia of Elder Care や Encyclopedia of Social Work など、海外で刊行された数多くの文献等から高齢者福祉、医療、看護、

介護福祉、リハビリテーション、教育、保育等の領域から介護保険に関連して重要となる約7,400語を国際的に検証して改めて翻訳・校閲した。

同じく第1部の「和英」の部分では、上記の文献・領域等に加え、介護福祉用語辞典、社会福祉辞典などの文献等から日本の介護保険および介護福祉等に関連する用語を専門的に検証して改めて翻訳・校閲した。また著者らの理論と実践に基づいて、介護保険や介護福祉等について国際的に英語で学術交流する際よく使用する可能性があると思われる用語も付け加え、約9,400語を収録した。

第2部では、第1部の「和英」の部分において掲載した約9,400語の中から、最重要と思われる684語に関して、日本語だけではなく、英語でもできる限り名詞句にて解説した。この辞典を用いて英語ならびに多言語から日本の介護保険や介護福祉等ついて学ぼうとしている世界の人々のために、ローマ字によるよみがなも表記した。

第3部では、米国や英国、ドイツなど、国際的に用いられている重要な専門用語を国内外の文献等や筆者らの理論と実践の中から新たに検証し、それらを翻訳・校閲して収録した。これらの用語によって、国際的にも学術交流が深めていくことができるように架け橋を構築したのである。

本辞典の付録においては、第2部で取り上げた684語に対して、近年の人口の高齢化と少子化により、その翻訳・校閲の必要性が近未来に高まると予測される先進国と開発途上国を含めた10カ国語（インドネシア語／韓国語／スペイン語／タガログ語／中国語／ドイツ語／ヒンディ語／フランス語／ベトナム語／ポルトガル語）の翻訳・校閲も記した。国際的に介護保険や介護福祉等の分野で活躍する世界の人々に活用されることを願っている。

本辞典では、定訳化しつつある医療・介護用語や官庁などが用いている制度、法令、官庁局名等の翻訳・校閲は、できる限り参照しながら、検証して翻訳・校閲した。しかし、その他の用語に関してはかなりの部分で検証し改めて翻訳・校閲した。その翻訳・校閲の適正化については今後の改訂版を重ねることで最善の翻訳・校閲にむけた尽力を継続する所存である。

また、本辞典に収録した専門用語を翻訳・校閲するにあたっては、近未来には含まれるべきであろう用語が追記されていないこともあると思う。新たな長寿活力社会にも貢献できるような国際介護保険用語辞典になるように、今後とも世界の関係者からのご指導・ご鞭撻をお願い申し上げる。

本辞典の編集・出版にあたりいろいろご指導・ご協力を賜った国際的な執筆者の皆様と翻訳・校閲協力・関係者の皆様に、心からお礼申し上げる。また、今回の出版にご尽力頂いた大学教育出版の佐藤守社長ならびに根気強く編集作業を助けてくださっ

た安田愛様を初め、編集部の皆様に心から感謝申し上げる。
　本辞典は、平成 22 年および平成 23 年度独立行政法人日本学術振興会科学研究費補助金（研究成果公開促進費・学術図書）の助成を受けて刊行した．国際介護保険用語辞典による国際的な用語の標準化と専門性を構築することで、介護保障を必要とする世界の人々のために介護保険の国際化が実現することを祈念申し上げる。

2012 年 1 月 27 日

編著者　住居広士

澤田　如

Preface

Since the long-term care insurance system was implemented in Japan in 2000, long-term care services that were not available are now being created and launched. The transformation of the Japanese system of long-term care insurance is accelerating as the country turns into a "longevity society" with an aging populace, and a declining population due to the falling birthrate. Facing this era of radical change, in 2007 the Japanese government revised the Certified Social Worker and Care Worker Act of 1987, which had established the first national qualification for social services and long-term care professions in Japan. As a result of this revision, since 2008 non-Japanese nursing and care professionals have been able to work more easily in Japan.

Amid reforms of this sort, we have now arrived at a situation where nursing services cannot be adequately provided to the people who need them around the world unless international academic exchange on long-term care insurance is conducted in greater depth. As part of the historic process, the Netherlands enacted special health insurance, the predecessor of long-term care insurance, in 1968; Austria implemented the system of care allowance in 1993; and Germany, enacted its fifth law on long-term care insurance in April 1994, followed by the creation of home care services in April 1995 and facility-based services in July 1996. Greatly influenced by these actions, Japan passed the Long-Term Care Insurance Act in 1997 and implemented a long-term care insurance system in 2000. The Long-Term Care Insurance Act was then amended in 2005 and again in 2011. Long-term care reform is also being carried out in other Asian countries. For example, South Korea enacted its Long-Term Elderly Care Insurance Act in April 2007, implemented a long-term care insurance program in July 2008, and has been training nursing care workers toward acquiring national certification. Since 2002, China has been trialing a scheme to ensure that workers who care for the elderly meet a national standard. For its part, Japan has been accepting foreign nurse and care-worker candidates from the Philippines and Indonesia since the Economic Partnership Agreements (EPA) with these countries came into force in 2008.

We are now at the dawn of a new era in which the system of long-term care insurance developed and launched in "longevity society" Japan—the country with the fastest rate of population aging—is recognized as the global standard. In order to expand Japan's academic exchange in this area with the rest of the world, an academic common ground needs to be created through the standardization of international terminology on long-term care insurance and also the publication of a dictionary of long-term care insurance terminology that may build a bridge between several specialized fields. Based on this common ground, specialized international exchanges then become possible.

The features and structure of this dictionary are as follows.

For the English-Japanese section of Part 1, toward their retranslation and revision we evaluated 7,400 relevant, key long-term care insurance terms from numerous internationally published works in the fields of elder care, medicine, nursing, long-term care, social services, rehabilitation, education, childcare, and so forth. These works included the Encyclopedia of Elder Care and the Encyclopedia of Social Work.

Similarly, for the Japanese-English section of Part 1, we evaluated for retranslation and review the terms relevant to long-term care insurance and care services found in works such as the Dictionary of Care and Welfare Terms and Dictionary of Social Welfare, in addition to the works and fields mentioned above. We also included terms that might commonly be used internationally in English when discussing long-term care insurance or care and welfare, based on the reasoning and experience of the authors and editors. In total, about 9,400 terms were included.

For Part 2, we selected 684 of the 9,400 terms included in the Japanese-English section of Part 1 that we had determined to be especially important and explained in both Japanese and English how the term is used as a noun phrase in a sentence. For those native speakers of English or other languages who are trying to learn about long-term care insurance or care and welfare in Japan by using this dictionary, we have also listed phonetic transcriptions of Japanese words in the Roman alphabet.

For Part 3, we evaluated important technical terms found in domestic and international papers published in countries such as the United States, the United Kingdom, and Germany, and also from the authors' own theories and practices, in order to translate or revise them and include them in the dictionary. Our aim with these translations is to build a linguistic bridge to enable further exchange and collaboration among academics from around the world.

In the Appendix, we listed in 10 languages (Indonesian, Korean, Spanish, Tagalog, Chinese, German, Hindi, French, Vietnamese, and Portuguese) translations of the 684 terms featured in Part 2. These languages from both industrialized and developing countries were selected as they are used in countries where the need for translations and reviews of these terms is expected to increase in the near future due to their aging populations and declining birthrates. It is our hope that individuals—Japanese and non-Japanese alike—who are working internationally on long-term care insurance issues and providing long-term care services will be able to take full advantage of this section.

In this dictionary, medical and nursing terms that are becoming standard– as well as terms for systems, laws, and names of entities such as government agencies–were retranslated and revised while referencing source materials as much as possible. However, a significant number of other terms were evaluated with an eye toward creating new translations and revised versions. Efforts to make as perfect translations as possible and revisions will continue in updated future editions of this dictionary.

Also, we may have inadvertently excluded some terms that may be included in this dictionary. We would like to ask all our colleagues and users worldwide to continue to provide us with their support and guidance as we endeavor to make this an international dictionary applicable in a new era of long-term care insurance.

We would also like sincerely thank all the international authors who provided their guidance and cooperation in editing and publishing this dictionary and to all other individuals involved in the translation and proofreading. We are particularly grateful to President Mamoru Sato of University Education Press (UEP), who has worked unceasingly for the publication of this dictionary, and also to Ai Yasuda and others in the UEP editorial office, for their tireless efforts in the printing process.

This dictionary was published with financial assistance from 2010 and 2011 Grants-in-Aid for Publication of Scientific Research Results and Scientific Literature, provided by the Japan Society for the Promotion of Science. By standardizing global terminology and helping to developing expertise around the world, we hope that the International Dictionary of Long-Term Care Insurance Terms will contribute to the globalization of long-term care insurance, which is essential for people throughout the world who need advanced and secured long-term care.

January 27, 2012
Hiroshi Sumii and Yuki Sawada
Authors and Editors

国際介護保険用語辞典
― 介護保険の国際化 ―

目　次

編著者のことば …………………………………………………………… i
本辞典の特色と構成 ……………………………………………………… xii
凡　例 ……………………………………………………………………… xiii

第1部　介護保険・介護福祉等関連用語 ……………………………… 1
　　　英　和 …………………………………………………………… 2
　　　和　英 …………………………………………………………… 78

第2部　介護保険・介護福祉等関連の重要用語―和英解説 ………… 221

第3部　諸外国における介護福祉等関連用語 ………………………… 269
　　1．英　国（イギリス）における介護福祉等関連用語
　　　　英　和 ………………………………………………………… 270
　　　　和　英 ………………………………………………………… 276
　　2．豪　州（オーストラリア）における介護福祉等関連用語
　　　　英　和 ………………………………………………………… 285
　　　　和　英 ………………………………………………………… 289
　　3．大韓民国（韓国）における介護福祉等関連用語
　　　　韓　日 ………………………………………………………… 294
　　　　日　韓 ………………………………………………………… 298
　　4．独　逸（ドイツ）における介護福祉等関連用語
　　　　独　和 ………………………………………………………… 305
　　　　和　独 ………………………………………………………… 309
　　5．米　国（アメリカ）における介護福祉等関連用語
　　　　英　和 ………………………………………………………… 314
　　　　和　英 ………………………………………………………… 325

付　録　介護保険・介護福祉等関連の重要用語 ― 10カ国語翻訳一覧別（言語別）
　　　　………………………………………………………………341
　　　1．インドネシア語 ………………………………………342
　　　2．韓国語 …………………………………………………350
　　　3．スペイン語 ……………………………………………357
　　　4．タガログ語 ……………………………………………365
　　　5．中国語 …………………………………………………373
　　　6．ドイツ語 ………………………………………………380
　　　7．ヒンディ語 ……………………………………………387
　　　8．フランス語 ……………………………………………394
　　　9．ベトナム語 ……………………………………………401
　　　10．ポルトガル語 …………………………………………408

引用・参考文献一覧 …………………………………………………416

本辞典の特色と構成

第1部：介護保険・介護福祉等関連用語

英和

Encyclopedia of Elder Care や Encyclopedia of Social Work 等海外で刊行された文献等から、高齢者福祉、医療、看護、介護福祉、リハビリテーション、教育、保育等の領域に関連して重要となる約7,400用語を国際的に検証して改めて翻訳・校閲した。

和英

Encyclopedia of Elder Care や Encyclopedia of Social Work 等の海外の文献に加え、介護福祉用語辞典（ミネルヴァ書房）や社会福祉辞典（大月書店）等国内の文献をもとに、高齢者介護福祉・介護保険・保健・医療・福祉ならびに隣接領域等に関連する用語を専門的に検証して改めて約9,400語を翻訳・校閲した。それらの中でも介護保険や介護福祉等に関連する理論と実践上で重要用語と思われる684語には「†」マークを付した。

第2部：介護保険・介護福祉等関連の重要用語 ── 和英解説

介護保険・介護福祉等に関連する用語を理解できるよう、また国際的にも介護保険等に関して学術交流を深めていくのに重要である用語として、第1部の「和英」において「†」マークを付した684語については日本語および英語で簡約文の名詞句にて概説した。また、この辞典を用いて英語ならびに多言語から日本の介護保険や介護福祉等について学ぼうとしている世界の人々のために、日本語の用語にはローマ字によるよみがなを入れた。

第3部：諸外国における介護福祉等関連用語　（五十音順）

1. 英国（イギリス）における介護福祉等関連用語－英和・和英
   イギリスで用いられている高齢者福祉、医療、看護、介護福祉ならびに隣接領域に関連する重要な専門用語の約500語を翻訳・校閲して、収録した。
2. 豪州（オーストラリア）における介護福祉等関連用語－英和・和英
   オーストラリアで用いられている高齢者福祉、医療、看護、介護福祉ならびに隣接領域に関連する重要な専門用語の約260語を翻訳・校閲し、収録した。

3．大韓民国（韓国）における介護福祉等関連用語－韓日・日韓
韓国で用いられている高齢者福祉、医療、看護、介護福祉ならびに隣接領域に関連する重要な専門用語の約360語を翻訳・校閲し、収録した。
4．独逸（ドイツ）における介護福祉等関連用語－独和・和独
ドイツで用いられている高齢者福祉、医療、看護、介護福祉ならびに隣接領域に関連する重要な専門用語の約300語を翻訳・校閲し、収録した。
5．米国（アメリカ）における介護福祉等関連用語－英和・和英
アメリカで用いられている高齢者福祉、医療、看護、介護福祉ならびに隣接領域に関連する重要な専門用語の約720語を翻訳・校閲し、収録した。

付録：介護保険・介護福祉等関連の重要用語― 10カ国語翻訳一覧（言語別）
第2部の「介護保険・介護福祉等関連の重要用語和英解説」において取り上げた684用語を、インドネシア語、韓国語、スペイン語、タガログ語、中国語、ドイツ語、ヒンディ語、フランス語、ベトナム語、ポルトガル語の10カ国語（五十音順）に翻訳・校閲し、表記した。

凡　例

第1部：介護保険・介護福祉等関連用語
　英和
1．各用語は、基本的には米式綴りを採用し、アルファベット順に配列した。本辞典で扱われる用語で英式の綴りが採用されている用語には、以下のようなものがある。

　　　　例）米式　　　　　英式
　　　　　　behavioral　　behavioural
　　　　　　labor　　　　　labour

2．同じ綴りで大文字・小文字の相違がある時は、大文字を先に配列した。
3．用語内にかっこ（「　」等）、ハイフン（－）、中黒記号（・）等を使用した場合は、それらを配列上無視した。
4．団体・組織名等は自称の一般名称で表記し、略称は、コロン（：）の後に示した。
5．略称が一般的表記である場合は、それも挙げた。
　　　　例）OECD
6．1つの用語に翻訳・校閲等を1つ以上記載する場合は、セミコロン（；）の後に

示した。
7. [ ]には、その用語の簡約の説明を表記した。
8. 引用・参考文献は、可及的に原則として巻末に示した。

> 和 英

1. 各用語は、現代かなづかいにより五十音順に配列した。
2. 拗音（ようおん）・促音（そくおん）等を表す小字（ぁ，ぃ，ぅ，ぇ，ぉ．ゃ，ゅ，ょ，っ）は1字とみなし、長音（ー）は配列上無視した。
    例）「スーパービジョン」は「すぱびじょん」として配列している。
3. 濁音・半濁音は配列上無視したが、同位置にあっては、清音、濁音、半濁音の順に配列した。
4. 用語内にかっこ（「　」等）、ハイフン（-）、中黒記号（・）等を使用した場合は、それらを配列上無視した。
5. 日本語の各用語には、（　）内に平仮名でよみがなを付した。
    例）介護福祉（かいごふくし）
6. 外国語の各用語は、片仮名によって示し、（　）内に平仮名でよみがなを付した。
    例）アセスメント（あせすめんと）
7. 外国語の略語等は、A（えー）、B（びー）、C（しー）等と平仮名でよみがなや日本語名称等を付して、上記の原則に従って配列した。
    例）ADL（えーでぃーえる）
    ただし、PET（ぺっと）、WAM NET（わむねっと）と一般名で読んで配列したものもある。
8. ギリシャ文字を含む各用語には、α（あるふぁ）、β（べーた）等と平仮名でよみがなを付して、上記の原則に従って配列した。
    例）αグルコシダーゼ阻害薬（あるふぁぐるこしだーぜそがいやく）
9. 漢数字、洋数字を含む各用語には、1（いち）、2（に）、3（さん）等と平仮名でよみがなを付して、上記の原則に従って配列した。
    例）一型糖尿病（いちがたとうにょうびょう）
10. 団体・組織名等は自称の一般名称で表記し、略称は、コロン（：）の後に示した。
11. 1つの用語に翻訳・校閲等を1つ以上記載する場合は、セミコロン（；）の後に示した。
12. 〈　〉を付した用語は、略語や、〈　〉内の用法でも同様に使われる場合等を示す。
13. 同義語・対等語等がある用語は、その翻訳を別記し、矢印（⇒）をもってその翻

訳がある項目を示した。

　　　例）オージオグラム　⇒　オーディオグラム
14. 引用・参考文献は、可及的に原則として巻末に示した。

第2部：介護保険・介護福祉等関連の重要用語 ― 和英解説

1. 各用語は、現代かなづかいにより五十音順に配列した。
2. 拗音・促音等を表す小字（ぁ，ぃ，ぅ，ぇ，ぉ，ゃ，ゅ，ょ，っ）は1字とみなし、長音（ー）は配列上無視した。

　　　例）「アルツハイマー病」は「あるつはいまびょう」として配列している。
3. 濁音・半濁音は配列上無視したが、同位置にあっては、清音、濁音、半濁音の順に配列した。
4. 外国語の略称等は、A（えー）、B（びー）、C（しー）、D（でぃー）等と読んで上記の原則に従って配列した。
5. 各用語には、【　】内に次の「ローマ字綴り表」に示すヘボン式ローマ字綴りにより、よみがなを付した。

　　　例）介護福祉【kaigo fukushi】

ローマ字綴り表

	あ	い	う	え	お	ま	み	む	め	も
	a	i	u	e	o	ma	mi	mu	me	mo
	か	き	く	け	こ	や		ゆ		よ
	ka	ki	ku	ke	ko	ya		yu		yo
五十音	さ	し	す	せ	そ	ら	り	る	れ	ろ
	sa	shi	su	se	so	ra	ri	ru	re	ro
	た	ち	つ	て	と	わ	ゐ		ゑ	を
	ta	chi	tsu	te	to	wa	i		e	wo
	な	に	ぬ	ね	の	ん				
	na	ni	nu	ne	no	n				
	は	ひ	ふ	へ	ほ					
	ha	hi	fu	he	ho					
	が	ぎ	ぐ	げ	ご	ば	び	ぶ	べ	ぼ
濁音	ga	gi	gu	ge	go	ba	bi	bu	be	bo
半濁音	ざ	じ	ず	ぜ	ぞ	ぱ	ぴ	ぷ	ぺ	ぽ
	za	ji	zu	ze	zo	pa	pi	pu	pe	po
	だ	ぢ	づ	で	ど					
	da	ji	zu	de	do					

拗音	きゃ		きゅ		きょ		ぎゃ		ぎゅ		ぎょ
	kya		kyu		kyo		gya		gyu		gyo
	しゃ		しゅ	しぇ	しょ		じゃ		じゅ		じょ
	sha		shu	she	sho		jya		jyu		jyo
	ちゃ		ちゅ	ちぇ	ちょ		びゃ		びゅ		びょ
	cya		cyu	che	cyo		bya		byu		byo
	にゃ		にゅ		にょ		ぴゃ		ぴゅ		ぴょ
	nya		nyu		nyo		pya		pyu		pyo
	ひゃ		ひゅ		ひょ		てぃ		とぅ		
	hya		hyu		hyo		ti		tu		
	みゃ		みゅ		みょ		でぃ		どぅ		
	mya		myu		myo		di		du		
	りゃ		りゅ		りょ		ふぁ	ふぃ		ふぇ	ふぉ
	rya		ryu		ryo		fa	fi		fe	fo

注意：(1) 促音の「っ（ッ）」は、子音を重ねて表示した。

　　　例）ベッド【beddo】

　　(2) 長音の「o」や「u」等は記入せず、母音の上に長音符号 (-) を付した。

　　　例）パーキンソン病　【pākinson byō】

6．団体・組織名は自称の一般名称で表記し、略称は、コロン（：）の後に示した。

7．外国人名には、《　》内に姓と名のイニシャルを原語と略語で付した。

　　　例）アロイス・アルツハイマー　《Alzheimer, A.》

8．同義語、対等語等がある用語は、その解説を別記し、矢印（→）をもってその解説がある用語を示した。

　　　例）入れ歯　→　義歯

9．引用・参考文献は、可及的に原則として巻末に示した。

第3部：諸外国における介護福祉等関連用語

英和　韓日　独和

1．イギリス、オーストラリア、アメリカにおける各用語は、基本的には米式綴りを採用し、アルファベット順に配列した。本辞典で扱われる用語で英式の綴りが採用されている用語には、以下のようなものが含まれる。

　　　例）米式　　　　　英式
　　　　　aging　　　　ageing
　　　　　center　　　　centre
　　　　　immunization　immunisation
　　　　　labor　　　　 labour
　　　　　organization　organisation

　　　　　　　program　　　　　　　programme
2．韓国における用語は、韓国語の基準で配置した。
3．ドイツにおける用語は、ドイツ語のアルファベット順に配置した。
4．ドイツ語では、男性名詞・女性名詞・中性名詞は明確に区別されるため、本辞典では男性名詞（masculine・masklinum）には〔M〕、女性名詞（feminine・femininum）には〔F〕、中性名詞（neuter・neutrum）には〔N〕を付した。男性名詞・女性名詞が同形の場合には〔M・F〕と付した。また、名詞の複数形（plural・pluralis）には〔Pl〕を付した。
5．用語内にかっこ（「　」等）、ハイフン（－）、中黒記号（・）等を使用した場合は、それらを配列上無視した。
6．団体・組織名等は自称の一般名称で表記し、略称は、コロン（：）の後に示した。
7．1つの用語に翻訳・校閲等を1つ以上記載する場合は、セミコロン（；）の後に示した。
8．略称が一般的である場合は、それらも挙げた。
　　　　例）YMCA
9．[　]には、その用語の簡約の説明を表記した。
10．引用・参考文献は、可及的に原則として巻末に示した。

　|和　英|日　韓|和　独|
1．各用語は、現代かなづかいにより五十音順に配列した。
2．拗音・促音等を表す小字（ぁ,ぃ,ぅ,ぇ,ぉ,ゃ,ゅ,ょ,っ）は1字とみなし、長音（ー）は無視した。
　　　　例）「高齢者ホーム」は「こうれいしゃほむ」として配列している。
3．濁音・半濁音は配列上無視したが、同位置にあっては、清音、濁音、半濁音の順に配列した。
4．用語内にかっこ（「　」等）、ハイフン（－）、中黒記号（・）等を使用した場合は、それらを配列上無視した。
5．日本語の各用語には、（　）内に平仮名でよみがなを付した。
　　　　例）入院保険（にゅういんほけん）
6．外国語の各用語は、片仮名によって示し、（　）内に平仮名でよみがなを付した。
　　　　例）メディケア（めでぃけあ）
7．団体・組織名等は自称の一般名称で表記し、略称は、コロン（：）の後に示した。
8．1つの用語に翻訳・校閲等を1つ以上記載する場合は、セミコロン（；）の後に

示した。

9．イギリス、オーストラリア、アメリカにおける各用語の英語翻訳は、基本的には米式綴りを採用したが、英式の綴りが採用されているものもある（上記参照）。

10．ドイツ語では、男性名詞・女性名詞・中性名詞は明確に区別されるため、本辞典では男性名詞（masculine・masklinum）には〔M〕、女性名詞（feminine・femininum）には〔F〕、中性名詞（neuter・neutrum）には〔N〕を付した。男性名詞・女性名詞が同形の場合には〔M・F〕と付した。また、名詞の複数形（plural・pluralis）には〔Pl〕を付した。

11．引用・参考文献は、可及的に原則として巻末に示した。

付録：介護保険・介護福祉等関連の重要用語—10カ国語翻訳一覧（言語別）

1．各用語は、現代かなづかいにより五十音順に配列した。
2．拗音(ようおん)・促音(そくおん)等を表す小字（ぁ，ぃ，ぅ，ぇ，ぉ，ゃ，ゅ，ょ，っ）は1字とみなし、長音（ー）は無視した。

　　例）「アルツハイマー病」は「あるつはいまびょう」として配列している。

3．濁音・半濁音は配列上無視したが、同位置にあっては、清音、濁音、半濁音の順に配列した。
4．外国語の略称等は、A（えー）、B（びー）、C（しー）、D（でぃー）等と読んでで上記の原則に従って配列した。
5．団体・組織名等は自称の一般名称で表記し、略称は、コロン（：）の後に示した。
6．英語が公用語の1つであったり、英語を話す人口が多い国（例：フィリピン共和国）では、母国語等に翻訳されないまま英語で用いられるのが一般的な用語がある。

　　例）menu

そのような場合は、本辞典でも英語のまま表記した。

7．中国語訳で翻訳に用いられている「、」記号は、「頓号（ドゥン　ハォ）」と呼ばれ、3つ以上並列する名詞の間によく使われる符号であり、名詞間の並列関係を表すものである。
8．ドイツ語では、男性名詞・女性名詞・中性名詞は明確に区別されるため、本辞典では男性名詞（masculine・masklinum）には〔M〕、女性名詞（feminine・femininum）には〔F〕、中性名詞（neuter・neutrum）には〔N〕を付した。男性名詞・女性名詞が同形の場合には〔M・F〕と付した。また、名詞の複数形（plural・pluralis）には〔Pl〕を付した。
9．引用・参考文献は、可及的に原則として巻末に示した。

第1部
介護保険・介護福祉等関連用語

ENGLISH - JAPANESE

A

abandoning elderly 棄老
Abbreviated Injury Scale：AIS 簡易損傷スケール
abdominal breathing 腹式呼吸
abdominal pain 腹痛
abdominal respiration 腹式呼吸
abdominal ultrasound 腹部超音波検査
abdominal x-ray 腹部X線写真
abdominalgia 腹痛
abdominocentesis 腹部穿刺
abduction 外転
abduction block 外転防止ブロック
abduction gait 外転歩行
Abel position アベル体位
ability 能力
abiotic synthesis 非生物合成
able body poor 身体障害のない貧困者
abnormal behavior 異常行動
abnormal eating habit 異食行為
abnormal gait 異常歩行
Abnormal Involuntary Movement Scale：AIMS
　異常不随意運動評価尺度
abnormal posture 異常姿勢
above-elbow amputation 上腕切断
above-knee amputation 大腿切断
above-knee prosthesis 大腿義足
Abraham Harold Maslow マズロー，アブラハム　H.
abrasion 擦り傷；摩耗
abrasion resistance 摩耗抵抗
absolute alcohol 無水アルコール
absolute humidity 絶対湿度
absolute muscle strength 絶対筋力
absolute poverty 絶対的貧困
absolute refractory period 絶対不応期
absolute threshold 絶対閾
absolute threshold of hearing 最小可聴値
absorption 吸収；吸着
absorption atelectasis 吸収性無気肺
absorption factor 吸収係数
absorption rate 吸収速度
absorption rate constant 吸収速度定数
absorption ratio 吸収率
absorption train 吸収装置
abstinence from alcohol 禁酒
abstinence from smoking 禁煙
abuse 虐待
abused child 被虐待児童
abused elderly 被虐待高齢者；被虐待老人

acalculia 計算不能症
acamprosate アカンプロセート
acceptable daily intake 許容一日摂取量
acceptance 受容；受理
acceptance of disability 障害の受容
access 利便
access to care 介護へのアクセス
accessibility 利便性
accessory respiratory muscle 補助呼吸筋
accident 災害
accident compensation 災害補償
accident insurance 災害保険
accidental extubation 偶発抜管；事故抜管
accidental ingestion 誤飲
accidents in the home 家庭内事故
accountability 説明責任；アカウンタビリティ
accreditation 認可；認定
accreditation standards 認可基準
accreditation survey 認定調査
acculturation 文化変容
acupressurist 指圧師
Accupril アキュプリル
acetabular fracture 寛骨臼骨折
Acetaminophen アセトアミノフェン
acetate 酢酸塩
acetic acid 酢酸
Achilles tendon アキレス腱
Achilles tendon lengthening アキレス腱延長術
acid 酸
acid anhydride 酸無水物
acid-base balance 酸塩基平衡
acid-base regulation 酸塩基調節
acidemia アシデミア；酸血症
acidity 酸度；酸性度
acidosis アシドーシス；酸血症
acid-suppressive medication 制酸剤
acquired blindness 中途失明
acquired disability 中途障害
acquired hearing impairment 中途聴覚障害
acquired immune deficiency syndrome：AIDS
　後天性免疫不全症候群；エイズ
acquired sensory impairment 中途知覚障害
acquired visual impairment 中途視覚障害
acquisitive prescription 取得時効
acraturesis 排尿不能症；排尿無力症
acromegaly 先端巨大症；末端肥大症
acronym and definition 略語と定義
act 行為；法
actin アクチン

英語	日本語
actinic injury	光線損傷
actinotherapy	光線療法
action	作用；行為
action potential：AP	活動電位
action research	実践研究；アクションリサーチ
active assisted exercise	自動介助運動
active carbon	活性炭素
active charcoal	活性炭
active exercise	自動訓練
active immunity	能動免疫
active life expectancy	活動的平均余命
active listening	傾聴
active movement	自動運動
active oxygen	活性酸素
active permeation	能動透過
active range of motion：AROM	自動可動域
active self-neglect	意図的自己放任
active transport	能動輸送；活性輸送
activities of daily living：ADL	日常生活活動
activity	アクティビティ；活動
activity limitation	活動制限
activity services	アクティビティサービス
activity theory	活動理論
Actonel	アクトネル
actual expenditure	実支出
actual income	実収入
actual wage	実質賃金
acute anterior poliomyelitis	急性灰白髄炎；急性脊髄前角炎
acute bronchiolitis	急性細気管支炎
acute coronary syndrome	急性冠症候群
acute epidural hematoma	急性硬膜外血腫
acute gastritis	急性胃炎
acute gastrointestinal bleed	急性消化管出血
acute interstitial pneumonia	急性間質性肺炎
acute laryngotracheitis	急性喉頭気管炎
acute leukemia	急性白血病
acute lung injury	急性肺損傷；急性肺傷
acute lymphoblastic leukemia	急性リンパ芽球性白血病
acute lymphocytic leukemia	急性リンパ性白血病
acute lymphoid leukemia：ALL	急性リンパ性白血病
acute myelocytic leukemia：AML	急性骨髄性白血病
acute myelogenous leukemia：AML	急性骨髄性白血病
acute myeloid leukemia	急性骨髄性白血病
acute myocardial infarction	急性心筋梗塞
acute phase	急性期
acute phase of rehabilitation	急性期リハビリテーション
acute pneumonia	急性肺炎
acute posthemorrhagic anemia	急性出血後貧血
acute pulmonary edema	急性肺水腫
acute pyelonephritis	急性腎盂腎炎
acute reference dose	急性参照用量
acute respiratory distress syndrome：ARDS	急性呼吸窮迫症候群
acute respiratory failure	急性呼吸不全
acute respiratory insufficiency	急性呼吸不全
acute urinary retention	急性尿閉症
acyclovir	アシクロビル
adalimumab	アダリムマブ
adaptation	適応；順応
adaptive enzyme	適応酵素
addiction	依存症
addictive drug	習慣性薬物
Addison's disease	アディソン病
addition	加算；付加
addition mutation	付加変異
addition polymer	付加重合体
addition polymerization	付加重合
additional benefit	上乗せ給付
additional pension	付加年金
additional service	上乗せサービス
addition-deletion mutation	付加欠失型突然変異
adduction	内転
adefovir dipivoxil	アデホビルピボキシル
adenoma	腺腫
adephagia	暴食
adequacy	適切
adhesive capsulitis	肩関節周囲炎
adiaphoria	不応性；無関心
adipose tissue	脂肪組織
adipositas	肥満症
adjustment	適応
adjustment mechanism	適応機制
ADL（activities of daily living）	日常生活動作
administration	運営；投与；アドミニストレーション
Administrative Affairs	行政事務
administrative cost	管理運営費；事務費
administrative inspection	行政監査
administrative plan	行政計画
administrative reform	行政改革
administrator	施設長
admission	入院；入所
admission decision	入院決定；入所決定
admission for medical care and custody	医療保護入院
adolescent depression	思春期うつ病
adolescent emaciation	思春期やせ症
adolescent mental health	思春期精神保健
adolescent nausea	思春期拒食症
adolescent psychology	青年期心理学
adopted child	養子
adoption	養子縁組
adrenocorticosteroid	副腎皮質ステロイド
adrenocorticosteroid enema	副腎皮質ホルモン注腸

介護保険・介護福祉等関連用語 英和

adult children　アダルトチルドレン
adult day care　老人デイケア；成人デイケア
adult day care center　老人デイケアセンター；成人デイケアセンター
adult day center　老人デイセンター；成人デイセンター
adult day health care　老人デイヘルスケア；成人デイヘルスケア
adult day services center　老人デイサービスセンター；成人デイサービスセンター
adult disease　成人病
adult education　成人教育
adult foster care home　成人養護施設
adult guardian　成年後見人
adult guardianship　成年後見
adult guardianship system　成年後見制度
Adult Manifest Anxiety Scale　成人用顕現性不安尺度
adult-onset　成人発症
adult-onset rheumatoid arthritis：AORA　成人発症関節リウマチ
adult protective services　成人保護サービス
adult respiratory distress syndrome　成人呼吸窮迫症候群
adult T-cell leukemia：ATLL　成人Ｔ細胞白血病・リンパ腫
advanced cardiac life support　二次救命心肺蘇生法・処置
advanced cardiovascular life support：ACLS　二次心肺蘇生法
advanced life support：ALS　二次救命処置；生命サポートサービス
advanced practice nurse　高度専門看護師
adverse drug reaction：ADR　薬剤副作用
adverse selection　逆選択
Advil　アドビル
advisory committee　審議会
advisory council　諮問機関
Advisory Council on Social Security　社会保障審議会
advocacy　アドボカシー
advocacy activity　擁護活動
advocate　アドボケーター；代弁者
aeration　エアレーション
aerial infection　飛沫感染；空気感染
against medical advice：AMA　医学指示拒否
aged society　高齢社会
ageism　年齢差別；エイジズム
agency　機関
age-related disease　加齢性疾患
age-related macular degeneration　加齢黄斑変性
aggressive behavior　攻撃的行動
aging　加齢；老化
aging index　老年化指数
aging population　高齢化

aging society　高齢化社会
agnosia　失認
agonist　動筋
agoraphobia　広場恐怖症
agraphia　失書；失書症
agreement　同意書
Aid to the Permanently and Totally Disabled：APTD　完全・永続的重度障害者扶助
air bronchogram　気管支透亮像
air conditioning　空調
air curtain　エアカーテン
air embolism　空気塞栓症
air filter　空気ろ過装置；エアフィルタ
air insufflation　通気
air leak　エアリーク；空気漏れ
air mattress　エアーマット
air pollution　空気汚染；大気汚染
air sampler　エアサンプラ
air sampling　エアサンプリング
air shower　エアシャワー
air sleeping pad　エアーパッド
air trapping　エアトラッピング
airborne bacteria　空中細菌；空中浮遊菌
airborne infection　空気感染
airborne infection isolation：AII　空気感染隔離
airborne microbe sampler　空中細菌測定器；空中浮遊菌測定器
airborne particle　空中塵埃；浮遊粒子
airborne precaution　空気予防策
airborne transmission　空気伝播；空気感染
airplane splint　肩外転装具
airway　気道；エアウェイ
airway burn　気道熱傷
airway cleaning　気道洗浄；気道クリーニング
airway closure　気道閉鎖；気道虚脱；エアウェイクロージャ
airway collapse　気道虚脱
airway conductance　気道コンダクタンス
airway maintenance　気道確保
airway management　気道管理
airway obstruction　気道閉塞
airway occlusion　気道閉塞
airway pressure　気道内圧
airway pressure-time curve　気道内圧時間曲線
airway resistance　気道抵抗
airway stenosis　気道狭窄
airway stent　気道ステント
akathisia　静座不能；アカシジア
alarm　警報
albuminuria　蛋白尿
alcohol　アルコール
alcohol-based handrub　擦式アルコール製剤
alcohol consumption　アルコール消費

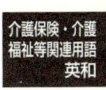

alcohol-containing antiseptic handrub 擦式アルコール製剤
alcohol-related psychosis アルコール幻覚症
alcoholic encephalopathy アルコール性脳障害
alcoholic hallucinosis アルコール幻覚症
alcoholic hepatitis アルコール性肝炎
alcoholic psychosis アルコール精神病
alcoholics アルコール中毒
alcoholism アルコール依存症
Aldactazide アルダクタジド
Aldactone アルダクトン
alendronate アレンドロネート
alert safety system 警報安全システム；アラーム
alexia 失読
algesia 痛覚；痛覚過敏〈症〉
alignment アライメント
alkalemia アルカリ血症
alkalosis アルカローシス；アルカリ血症
allergic bronchitis アレルギー性気管支炎
allergic pruritus アレルギー性そう痒症
allergic reaction アレルギー反応
allergic rhinitis アレルギー性鼻炎
allergy アレルギー
Alli アリ
alliance 同盟
allocated money 配分金
allocation 配分
allocation plan 配分計画；割当計画
allograph 代筆
allotted charge 分担金
allowance 手当
all-you-can-eat buffet バイキング食；食べ放題ブッフェ
Alma-Ata Declaration アルマ・アタ宣言
almshouse 養老院；救貧院
alpha-blocker α 遮断剤
alpha-glucosidase inhibitor α-グルコシダーゼ阻害薬
alternate three-point gait 交互三点歩行
alternative medicine オルタナティブ・メディスン；代替医療
alternative work schedule 交代制勤務
alveolar air 肺胞気
alveolar air equation 肺胞気式
alveolar cell 肺胞上皮細胞
alveolar collapse 肺胞虚脱
alveolar damage 肺胞傷害
alveolar dead space 肺胞死腔
alveolar edema 肺胞水腫；肺胞浮腫
alveolar epithelial cell 肺胞上皮細胞
alveolar epithelium 肺胞上皮
alveolar gas exchange 肺胞ガス交換
alveolar hypoventilation 肺胞低換気

alveolar hypoxia 肺胞性低酸素
alveolar lavage 肺胞洗浄
alveolar macrophage 肺胞マクロファージ；肺胞大食細胞
alveolar membrane 肺胞膜
alveolar pressure 肺胞内圧
alveolar recruitment 肺胞リクルートメント
alveolar space 肺胞腔
alveolar structure 肺胞構築
alveolar surface tension 肺胞表面張力
alveolar surfactant 肺胞サーファクタント；肺胞表面活性物質
alveolar ventilation 肺胞換気
alveolar-arterial oxygen tension difference 肺胞気・動脈血酸素分圧較差
alveolar-capillary barrier 肺胞・毛細血管関門；肺胞・毛細血管障壁
alveolus 肺胞
Alzheimer's disease アルツハイマー病
Ambien アンビエン
ambivalence アンビバレンス；両面価値
ambulance 救急車
ambulation 歩行
ambulation activity 歩行動作
ambulatory care 外来ケア；日帰り介護
ambulatory clinic 外来診療所
ambulatory health care services 通院医療
ambulatory medicine 外来診療
ambulatory rehabilitation 外来リハビリテーション；通所リハビリテーション
amenity アメニティ
American Indian アメリカインディアン
amino acid アミノ酸
Amiodarone アミオダロン
Amitriptyline アミトリプチリン
Amlodipine アムロジピン
ammonia アンモニア
ammonia detoxification アンモニア解毒
amnesia 健忘症
amniocentesis 羊水診断
ampholyte 両性電解質
amphoteric electrolyte 両性電解質
amphoteric surface active agent 両性界面活性剤
amputation 切断
amputation for peripheral vascular disease 血管原性切断
amputation stump 断端；切断端
amylase アミラーゼ
amylum でんぷん
amyotrophic lateral sclerosis；ALS 筋萎縮性側索硬化症
anabolism 同化作用
anaerobe 嫌気性菌

anaerobic exercise　無酸素訓練
anaerobic threshold：AT　無酸素性作業閾値
Anafranil　アナフラニール
anakinra　アナキンラ
anal dilator　肛門拡張器
anal endosonography　肛門管超音波検査
anal manometry　肛門内圧測定
anal mucosal electrosensitivity　肛門粘膜電流感覚閾値
anal speculum　肛門鏡
anal sphincter muscle　肛門括約筋
anal stage　肛門期
anal stimulator　肛門刺激装置
analgesic　鎮痛剤
analgesic drug　鎮痛薬
analysis　分析
analysis of defenses　防衛の分析
analysis of variance：ANOVA　分散分析
analytical psychology　分析心理学
anaphylactic shock　アナフィラキシーショック
anaplastic thyroid cancer　甲状腺未分化癌
Anaprox　アナプロックス
anarchism　無政府主義
anatomical position　解剖学的肢位
androgen　アンドロゲン
androgen deprivation therapy：ADT　アンドロゲン除去療法
anemia　貧血
anesthesia　麻酔；触覚消失
anesthetic　麻酔剤
anethole trithione　アネトールトリチオン
aneurysm　動脈瘤
aneurysmectomy　動脈瘤切除
aneurysmorrhaphy　動脈瘤縫縮術
angina attack　狭心症発作
angina pectoris　狭心症
angiogram　血管造影
angioplasty　血管形成術
angiotensin　アンジオテンシン
angiotensin-converting-enzyme inhibitor：ACE inhibitor　アンジオテンシン変換酵素阻害薬
angiotensin II receptor antagonist　アンジオテンシンII受容体拮抗薬
animal assisted activity：AAA　動物介在活動
animal assisted therapy：AAT　動物介在療法
animal food product　動物性食品
animal therapy　動物療法
anionic surface active agent　陰イオン界面活性剤
anisakis　アニサキス
ankle joint　足継手
ankle-brachial index：ABI　足関節上腕血圧比
ankle-foot orthosis：AFO　短下肢装具
ankylosing　強直性

ankylosing spondylitis　強直性脊椎炎
ankylosis　強直
annual survey　年次調査
annually managed expenditure：AME　各年管理歳出
anode　陽極
anomie　アノミー
anorectal manometry　肛門直腸内圧測定法
anorectal prolapse　直腸肛門脱
anorexia　拒食症
anorexia nervous　神経性食欲不振症
anoscope　肛門鏡
anoscopy　肛門鏡検査
anosmia　嗅覚消失症
anosognosia　病態失認
anoxemia　無酸素血症；低酸素血症
anoxia　無酸素症；低酸素症；酸素欠乏症
antacid　制酸剤
antagonism　拮抗
antagonist　拮抗筋
antalgic gait　有痛性歩行；疼痛回避性歩行
antegrade colonic enema：ACE　順行性洗腸
anterior spinal artery syndrome　前脊髄動脈症候群
anterograde amnesia　前向性健忘
anteroom　前室
anthelmintic　駆虫剤
antianemia drug　貧血治療薬
antianxiety medication　抗不安薬
antibacterial agent　抗菌薬；抗菌物質
antibacterial and deodorization material　抗菌・防臭素材
antibacterial drug　抗菌薬
antibacterial spectrum　抗菌スペクトル
antibiotic　抗生物質；抗生剤
antibiotic resistant infection　抗生物質耐性菌感染
antibody　抗体
antibody titer　抗体価
antibody valence　抗体結合価
anticancer drug　抗癌薬
anticoagulant　抗凝固剤
antidepressant　抗うつ剤
antidiabetic　抗糖尿病薬
antidiscrimination education　同和教育
antidiuresis　抗利尿
antidote　解毒剤
antidromic conduction　逆方向性伝導
antiedemic　抗浮腫性
antiemetic　制吐剤
antiepileptic drug　抗てんかん薬
antifungal　抗真菌性
antifungal antibiotic　抗真菌性抗生物質
antigen　抗原
antigenicity　抗原性
antigravity muscle　抗重力筋

antihistamine	抗ヒスタミン剤
antiinflammatory drug	抗炎症薬
antiinflammatory medication	抗炎症薬
antimicrobial	抗菌
antimicrobial agent	抗菌薬；抗菌物質
antimicrobial resistance	抗菌薬抵抗性
antimicrobial soap	抗菌性石鹸；抗菌剤入り石鹸
antimicrobial spectrum	抗菌スペクトル
antioxidant	抗酸化物
antioxidant agent	抗酸化薬
antioxidant therapy	抗酸化療法
antioxidant vitamin	抗酸化ビタミン
anti-Parkinsonian drug	抗パーキンソン病薬
antiplatelet agent	抗血小板薬
antipodagric	抗痛風薬
antipruritic	鎮痒剤
antipruritic drug	鎮痒薬
antipsoriatic drug	抗乾癬薬
antipsychotic	抗精神病剤
antipsychotic drug	抗精神病薬
antipyretic	下熱剤；解熱薬
antipyretic drug	下熱薬
antisepsis	生体消毒；消毒
antiseptic	防腐剤
antiseptic agent	生体消毒薬
antiseptic handrub	擦式手指消毒
antiseptic handwash	手洗い消毒
antiserum	抗血清
antithrombotic drug	抗血栓薬
antithyroid	抗甲状腺剤
antithyroid drug	抗甲状腺薬
antitussive drug	鎮咳薬
antiviral	抗ウイルス
antiviral drug	抗ウイルス薬
anuria	無尿症
anus	肛門
anxiety	不安症
anxiety neurosis	不安神経症
anxiolytic	抗不安剤
anxiolytic medication	抗不安薬
aortic stenosis	大動脈弁狭窄症
apathy	感情鈍麻
aperture color mode	開口色モード
apex beat	心尖拍動
aphasia	失語；失語症
aphonia	失声；失声症
aplastic anemia	再生不良性貧血
apnea	無呼吸；呼吸停止
apnea–hypopnea index：AHI	無呼吸低呼吸指数
apnea index	無呼吸指数
apneic spell	無呼吸発作
apneic threshold	無呼吸閾値
apneusis	持続性吸息
apolipoprotein	アポリポ蛋白
apoplexy	脳卒中
appeal	不服申し立て；異議申し立て
appeal system	不服申し立て制度；異議申し立て制度
appetite	食欲
appetite center	食欲中枢
applicant	申請者
applicants on the waiting list	待機者
applying pad	当て枕
appointment	予約
appointment of curator of minor	未成年保佐人の選任
appointment of guardian	後見人の選任
appointment of guardian of minor	未成年後見人の選任
apprentice	見習生
apprentice system	徒弟制度
apprenticeship	養成訓練制度；職場実習型訓練制度
apprenticeship period	見習い期間
apprenticeship system	徒弟制度
approach to the critically injured patient	重症外傷患者へのアプローチ
apraxia	失行
apraxia of speech	発語失行
apron	エプロン；前掛け
aptitude test	適正検査
aquatic exercise	アクアエクササイズ
arch support	アーチサポート：ふまず支え
area services	エリアサービス
Aricept	アリセプト
arm sling	アームスリング；腕吊り
arm support	アームサポート
armrest	アームレスト；肘置き
Arnold-Chiari malformation	アーノルド・キアリ奇形
arrhythmia	不整脈
arsenic poisoning	ヒ素中毒
art therapy	芸術療法
arterial blood	動脈血
arterial blood gas	動脈血ガス
arterial blood gas analysis	血液ガス分析
arterial blood pressure	動脈圧
arterial blood sampling	動脈血採取
arterial bruit	動脈雑音
arterial carbon dioxide tension	動脈血二酸化炭素分圧
arterial compliance	動脈コンプライアンス
arterial conduit	動脈グラフト
arterial continuous murmur	動脈連続雑音
arterial desaturation	動脈血飽和度低下
arterial disease	動脈疾患
arterial distensibility	動脈伸展性
arterial embolism	動脈塞栓
arterial-mixed venous oxygen content difference	動脈・混合静脈酸素較差

介護保険・介護福祉等関連用語 英和

arterial occlusive disease：AOD　動脈閉塞疾患
arterial oxygen saturation　動脈血酸素飽和度
arterial oxygen tension　動脈血酸素分圧
arterial partial pressure of carbon dioxide：PaCO2　動脈血炭酸ガス分圧
arterial pulse　動脈拍動
arterial puncture　動脈穿刺
arterial remodeling　動脈再構築
arterial resistance　動脈抵抗
arterial systolic murmur　動脈収縮期雑音
arterial to end-tidal carbon dioxide tension difference　動脈・呼気終末二酸化炭素分圧較差
arterial tonometry　動脈トノメトリー
arterial tree　動脈樹
arterial valve　動脈弁
arteriogenesis　動脈新生
arteriography　動脈造影
arteriole　細動脈
arteriosclerosis　動脈硬化
arteriosclerosis obliterans　閉塞性動脈硬化症
arteriosclerotic heart disease：ASHD　動脈硬化性心疾患
arteriospasm　動脈攣縮
artery　動脈
arthralgia　関節痛
arthritis　関節炎
arthrokinematic approach：AKA　関節運動学的アプローチ
articles of incorporation　定款
articulation disorder　構音障害
articulation training　構音訓練
artificial anus　人工肛門
artificial bladder　人工膀胱
artificial cochlea　人工内耳
artificial feeding　人工栄養
artificial fiber　人造繊維
artificial heart　人工心臓
artificial heart valve　人工心臓弁
artificial hybrid organ　ハイブリッド人工臓器
artificial lens　人工レンズ
artificial limb　義肢
artificial lung　人工肺
artificial organ　人工臓器
artificial respiration　人工呼吸
artificial respirator　人工呼吸器
artificial teeth　義歯
artificial ventilation　人工換気；人工呼吸
as needed：PRN　必要時
asepsis　無菌
aseptic barrier　無菌的遮蔽；無菌的被覆
aseptic intermittent catheterization：AIC　無菌的間欠導尿法
aseptic procedure　無菌操作

Asian American　アジア系アメリカ人
Asperger syndrome　アスペルガー症候群
aspergillosis　アスペルギルス症
asphyxia　窒息；仮死
aspiration　吸入
aspiration cytology　吸引細胞診
aspiration pneumonia　誤嚥性肺炎；嚥下性肺炎
aspirin　アスピリン
aspirin therapy　アスピリン療法
assessed value　評価額
assessment　アセスメント；評価
assessment item　アセスメント項目；評価項目
Assessment of Motor and Process Skills：AMPS　運動技能・プロセス技能評価
assessment of urinary incontinence　失禁アセスメント
assessment tool　アセスメントツール
assign　配置
assignment　割り当てられた仕事
assimilation　同化
assist mode　補助様式；補助モード
assistance　介助；援助；扶助
assistance dog　介助犬
assistant　援助者；介助員
assistant administrator　副施設長
assistant director of nursing　副看護師長
assistant mover　補助動筋
assisted coughing　咳嗽介助
assisted suicide　自殺幇助
assistive device　支援機器
assistive exercise　介助訓練
assistive technology　補助技術
associated movement　連合運動
asthenopia　眼精疲労
asthma　喘息
asthmatic attack　喘息発作
astigmatism　乱視
astringent　収斂剤
asylums　保護施設
asymptomatic carrier　無症候性保有者；無症候性キャリア
at bedtime　就寝時
ataxia　運動失調；運動失調症
ataxic gait　失調性跛行；失調歩行
atheroma　アテローマ；粉瘤；粥腫
athetosis　アテトーシス；アテトーゼ
athletic injury　スポーツ外傷
Ativan　アチバン
atom　原子
atomic bomb　原子爆弾
atomic bomb survivor　被爆者
atopic cough　アトピー咳嗽
atopic dermatitis　アトピー性皮膚炎

atopy　アトピー
atrial fibrillation　心房細動
atrial septal defect　心房中隔欠損症
atrium　心房
atrophic gastritis　萎縮性胃炎
atrophic vaginitis　萎縮性膣炎
atrophy　萎縮
attendance allowance　付添手当
attendant　付添人
attention deficit hyperactivity disorder：ADHD
　注意欠陥・多動性障害
attitudes toward care　介護姿勢
attorney-at-law　弁護士
attorney-in-fact　代理人
attributable risk　寄与危険
attributable risk percent：ARP　寄与危険割合
attribution　帰属
atypical antipsychotic　非定型抗精神病薬
atypical mycobacteria　非定型抗酸菌症
atypical psychosis　非定型精神病
audible pedestrian traffic signal　視覚障害者用信号機
audiogram　オーディオグラム
audiology assessment　聴覚的評価
audiometer　オーディオメーター
audiometry　聴力検査
audit of financial accounts　会計監査
auditory agnosia　聴覚失認
auditory deficit　聴覚障害
auditory disability　聴覚障害
auditory disorder　聴覚障害
auditory hallucination　幻聴
auditory impairment　聴覚障害
auditory sense　聴覚
auditory-verbal center　聴覚音声センター
auditory-verbal therapist　聴覚音声セラピスト
aural hematoma　耳血腫
authority　権力
autism　自閉症
autism spectrum disorder：ASD　自閉症スペクトラム障害
autoclave　オートクレーブ；高圧蒸気滅菌
autogenic training　自律訓練法
autoimmune hepatitis　自己免疫性肝炎
autoimmunity　自己免疫
autolysis　自己溶解
automated auditory brainstem response　自動聴性脳幹反応
automated auditory brainstem response evaluation　自動聴性脳幹反応評価
automated endoscope reprocessor：AER　自動内視鏡洗浄装置
automated external defibrillator　自動体外式除細動器
automatic peritoneal dialysis　自動腹膜透析

automatism　自動症
automobile allowance　自動車手当て
autonomic dysfunction　自律神経機能障害
autonomic dysreflexia　自律神経過反射
autonomic hyperreflexia　自律神経過反射
autonomic nerve　自律神経
autonomic nerve disorder　自律神経障害
autonomic nervous system　自律神経系
autonomous choice　自主選択性
autonomy　オートノミー；自律
autophobia　単独恐怖症
autopsy　剖検；死体解剖；検死
autoreceptor　自己受容体
autoregulation　自己調節；自動調節
autosomal dominant　常染色体優性
autosomal dominant disorder　常染色体優性遺伝病
autosomal dominant inheritance　常染色体優性遺伝
autosomal recessive　常染色体劣性
autosomal recessive disorder　常染色体劣性遺伝病
autosomal recessive inheritance　常染色体劣性遺伝
autosome　常染色体
average length of stay：ALOS　平均在院日数
average life span　平均寿命
aversion therapy　嫌悪療法
aversive stimulus　嫌悪刺激
Avodart　アボダート
avoidance conditioning　回避条件づけ
avoidance learning　回避学習
awake　覚醒
awakening drug　覚醒剤
awakening recovery center　薬物更生施設
axilla　腋窩
axillary artery　腋窩動脈
axillary crutch　松葉杖
axillary osmidrosis　腋臭；わきが
axillary temperature　腋窩温
axis　軸
axonal degeneration　軸索変性
ayurvedic medicine　アユルベーダ医学
Azathioprine　アザチオプリン
azotemia　高窒素血症

B

baby boom　ベビーブーム
baby boom generation　ベビーブーム世代；団塊世代
baby boomer　ベビーブーマー
babysitter　ベビーシッター
bachelor of social work：BSW　ソーシャルワーク学士号
back knee　反張膝
back support　バックサポート

英語	日本語
backrest	バックレスト；背もたれ
bacteremia	菌血症
bacterial pneumonia	細菌性肺炎
bactericidal action	殺菌作用
bacteriostatic action	静菌作用
bacterium	感染菌；細菌
bacteriuria	細菌尿
balance	バランス
balance billing	差額請求
balloon catheter	バルーンカテーテル
balloon expulsion test	バルーン排出試験
balloon retaining test	バルーン保持試験
balneotherapy	温泉療法
bandage	包帯
bar soap	固形石鹸
Baraclude	バラクルード
barium contrast radiography	バリウム造影
barium enema	バリウム注腸造影
barium meal	バリウムがゆ
barium small bowel enema	逆行性バリウム小腸造影
Barthel index	バーセル指数
basal body temperature	基礎体温
basal metabolic rate：BMR	基礎代謝率；基礎代謝量
basal metabolism	基礎代謝
basic allowance	基本手当
basic anxiety	基本的不安
basic care fee	基本介護費
basic color term	基本色名
basic daily fee	日額利用料
basic food group	基礎食品
basin method	ベイスン法
basket forceps	バスケット鉗子
bath board	バスボード
bathing	入浴
bathing activity	入浴動作
bathing assistance	入浴介助
bathing equipment	入浴用具
bathing services	入浴サービス
bathroom	浴室
beadhouse	養老院
Beck Depression Inventory：BDI	ベック抑うつ評価尺度
Becker muscular dystrophy	ベッカー型筋ジストロフィー
bed lift	ベッドリフト
bed mobility	起居動作
bed rest	臥床
bedpan	差し込み便器；便器
bedridden	寝たきり
bedridden period before death：BPbd	最終臥床期間
bedridden status	寝たきり状態
bedside commode	移動トイレ；ポータブルトイレ
bedside rail	ベッド柵
bedside table	床頭台
Beers criteria	ビアーズ基準；高齢者薬剤処方基準
behavior assessment	行動アセスメント
behavior disorder	行動障害
behavior modification	行動変容法
behavior modification approach	行動変容アプローチ
behavior pattern	行動パターン
behavior rehearsal	行動リハーサル
behavior science	行動科学
behavior therapy	行動療法
behavioral and psychological symptoms of dementia：BPSD	認知症に伴う行動障害と精神症状
behavioral language	行動言語
behavioral observation	行動観察
behavioral science	行動科学
behavioral symptom	行動障害
behaviorism	行動主義
Bell's palsy	ベル麻痺
below-elbow amputation	前腕切断
below-knee amputation	下腿切断
beneficence	善行
beneficiary	受益者
benefit	給付
benefit in kind	現物給付
benefit level	給付水準
benefit management services	給付管理業務
benefit period	給付期間
benefits priority list	給付優先リスト
benefits standards	給付基準
benicar	ベニカー
benign prostatic hyperplasia	前立腺肥大症
Benztropine	ベンズトロピン
bereavement	死別
Berg Balance Scale	バーグバランス評価
Bertolotti's syndrome	ベルトロッティ症候群
best practice	最善の治療
beta-amyloid peptide	ベータアミロイドペプチド
beta-blocker	ベータブロッカー
beta-carotene	ベータカロチン
beta receptor blockage	ベータ受容体遮断薬
Biestek's 7 principles	バイスティックの7原則
biguanide	ビグアニド
Bill of Rights	権利章典
billing period	請求対象期間
billing statement	請求書
Binet Intelligence Test	ビネー式知能検査
binge drinking	ビンジ・ドリンキング；酒浸し；酒浸り
Binswanger's disease	ビンスワンガー病
bioburden	バイオバーデン
bioclean system	バイオクリーンシステム
bioelectromagnetic	生体電磁気学
bioengineering	生体工学

bioethics 生命倫理
biofeedback バイオフィードバック
biofeedback therapy バイオフィードバック療法
biofilm バイオフィルム
biohazard mark バイオハザードマーク；感染性医療廃棄物表示
biologic response modifier 生物学的応答調節物質
biological age 生物年齢
biological clean room バイオクリーン病室；生物学的クリーンルーム
biological indicator バイオロジカルインジケータ；生物学的インジケータ
biological paradigm 生物学パラダイム
biological rhythm 生体リズム
biological therapy 生物学的治療法
biomechanics 生体力学
biomedical ethics 生命・医療倫理
biopsy 生検
biopsy forceps 生検鉗子
biotin ビオチン
bipolar disorder 双極性障害；躁うつ病
bipolar I disorder 双極Ⅰ型障害；躁うつ病
bipolar II disorder 双極Ⅱ型障害
birth certificate 出生証明書
birth palsy 分娩麻痺
birth rate 出生率
bisphosphonate drug ビスフォスフォネート製剤
bitter 苦味
bladder hypotonia 低緊張性膀胱
bladder training 排尿訓練
bleeding 出血
blended diet ミキサー食
blennorrhoea alveolaris 歯槽膿漏
Blessed Orientation-Memory-Concentration Test ブレスト見当識・記憶・集中テスト
blindness 盲
blister 水疱
block contract ブロック契約
blood bank 血液銀行
blood donation 献血
blood plasma 血漿
blood poisoning 敗血症
blood pressure 血圧
blood pressure manometer 血圧計
blood serum 血清
blood sugar 血糖
blood sugar level 血糖値
blood test 血液検査
blood transfusion 輸血
blood urea nitrogen：BUN 血液尿素窒素
bloodborne infection 血液媒介感染
bloodborne pathogen 血液由来病原体
bloodborne virus infection 血中ウイルス感染症；血液媒介ウイルス感染症
bloodstream infection 血流感染
blue-collar worker ブルーカラー
board and care home ボード・アンド・ケアホーム
body-centered psychotherapy 身体指向心理療法；ハコミセラピー
body composition 身体組成
body fluid 体液
body image 身体像
body mass index：BMI ボディマス指数
body mechanics ボディメカニクス
body reflection 身体反射
body substance isolation 生体物質隔離；ボディサブスタンスアイソレーション
body surface isolation 生体表面隔離；ボディサーフェイスアイソレーション
body temperature 体温
boiling sterilization 煮沸消毒
boiling water 沸騰水
bone atrophy 骨萎縮
bone density 骨密度
bone disease 骨疾患
bone mineral density 骨塩量
Boniva ボニバ
borderless ボーダレス
Boston Naming Test ボストン呼称テスト
Bouchard's node ブシャール結節
boundary 境界
boutonniere deformity ボタン穴変形
bovine spongiform encephalopathy：BSE 牛海綿状脳症
bowel and bladder dysfunction 膀胱直腸障害
bowel function 腸機能
bowel incontinence 便失禁
bowel irrigation 腸洗浄
bowel management 排便管理
bowel movement 便通
bowel preparation 腸前処置
bowel training 排便訓練
Bowie-Dick Test ボウィー・ディック・テスト
box joint 箱型継手
boxer's fracture ボクサー骨折
brachial plexus palsy 腕神経叢麻痺
Braden Scale for Predicting Pressure Sore Risk 褥瘡発生予測尺度
Braden Scale for Predicting Pressure Ulcer Risk 褥瘡発生予測尺度
bradycardia 徐脈
bradypnea 徐呼吸
Braille ブライユ式点字；点字
Braille block ブライユ式点字ブロック；点字ブロック
Braille reading ブライユ式触読；触読
Braille typewriter ブライユ式点字タイプライター；

点字タイプライター
Braille writing equipment　ブライユ式点字用具；点字用具
brain death　脳死
brain edema　脳浮腫
brain stem　脳幹
brain tumor　脳腫瘍
brainstorming　ブレーンストーミング
brand name medication　先発薬品
breast cancer　乳癌
breast prosthesis　ブレストプロテーゼ
breast reconstruction　乳房再建術
breast-sparing surgery　乳房温存手術
breathing　呼吸
breathing exercise　呼吸訓練
Brief Fatigue Inventory：BFI　簡易疲労一覧表
Brief Oral Health Status Examination：BOHSE　簡易口腔衛生検査
Brief Pain Inventory：BPI　簡易疼痛調査票
brief therapy　ブリーフセラピー；短期療法
brightness　明るさ
bringing up　養育
Broca's aphasia　ブローカー失語
Broca's area　ブローカー野
bronchial asthma　気管支喘息
bronchial drainage　排痰；気管支ドレナージ
bronchitis　気管支炎
bronchodilator　気管支拡張剤
bronchoscopy　気管支鏡
Brown-Sequard syndrome　ブラウン・セカール症候群
bruise　内出血；打撲傷
Brunnstrom stage　ブルンストローム・ステージ
brushing　ブラッシング
brushing cytology　擦過細胞診
bubble bath　気泡浴
Buddhist social work　仏教社会事業
budget　予算
budget buster　財政破綻；財政つぶし
budgeting　予算編成
bulbar palsy　球麻痺
bulimia　過食症
bulimia nervosa　神経性大食症
bull's eye appearance　標的像所見
bunion　バニオン
burden　負担
burden interview　負担質問票
burden of care　介護負担
burden of health care　医療負担
burden rate　負担率
bureaucracy　官僚制；官僚化；官僚政治
burial　埋葬
burial and funeral assistance　葬祭扶助
burial and funeral benefit　葬祭給付

burial and funeral costs　葬祭費用
burial and funeral expenses allowance　葬祭手当
burn　火傷；熱傷
burnout　バーンアウト
burnout syndrome　燃え尽き症候群；バーンアウト・シンドローム
button aid　ボタンエイド
by mouth：PO　経口
bypass surgery　バイパス手術

C

C bar　Cバー
cabinet　内閣
cable housing　ケーブルハウジング；ケーブル鞘
cadherin　カドヘリン
caffeine　カフェイン
Calan　カラン
calcitonin　カルシトニン
calcium　カルシウム
calcium channel blocker　カルシウム拮抗剤
calcium deficiency　カルシウム欠乏症
calcium pyrophosphate deposition disease　ピロリン酸カルシウム結晶沈着症
caliper　キャリパー
caloric intake　摂取熱量
caloric restriction　カロリー制限
Canadian-type hip disarticulation prosthesis　カナダ式股義足
cancer　癌
cancer patient　癌患者
cancer treatment　癌治療
cancerous growth　悪性腫瘍
candesartan　カンデサルタン
candida albicans　カンジダ・アルビカンス
cane　杖
cane-assisted gait　杖歩行
cannula　カニューレ
capital gains tax　譲渡所得課税
capitalism　資本主義
capitated payment　人頭払い制
capitated plan　人頭制前払い定額制
capsaicin　カプサイシン
carbamazepine　カルバマゼピン
carbohydrate　炭水化物
carbon dioxide　二酸化炭素
carbon monoxide　一酸化炭素
carbon monoxide poisoning　一酸化炭素中毒
carcinogenesis　発癌
carcinomatous pain　癌性疼痛
cardiac dysrhythmia　心臓不整脈
cardiac massage　心臓マッサージ
cardiac nuclear medicine　心臓核医学

cardiac output　心拍出量
cardiac rehabilitation　心臓リハビリテーション
cardiac shock　心原性ショック
cardiac shunt　心シャント
cardiac surgery-related infection　心臓外科関連感染
cardiac surgical intensive care unit　循環器外科集中治療室
cardiogenic pulmonary edema　心原性肺水腫
cardiology　循環器；心臓病学
cardiometabolic risk　心血管・代謝疾患リスク
cardiopulmonary cerebral resuscitation：CPCR　心肺脳蘇生法
cardiopulmonary resuscitation：CPR　心肺蘇生法
cardiothoracic ratio　心胸郭比
cardiovascular disease　心血管疾患
cardiovascular risk　心血管リスク
Cardizem　カルディゼム
care　介護；ケア
care conference　ケアカンファレンス
care coordination　ケアコーディネーション
care equipment　介護用具；介護機器；介護用品
care goal　介護目標；ケア目標
care guideline　ケアガイドライン
care home　ケアハウス
care management　ケアマネジメント
care management model　ケアマネジメントモデル
care mix　ケアミックス
care pathway　ケアパス
care plan　ケアプラン；介護計画
care practice　介護行為
care provider-recipient relationship　介護関係
care skills　介護技術
caregiver　介護者
caregiver burden　介護者負担
caregiver burden interview　介護負担質問票
Caregiver Burden Scale　介護負担尺度
caregiver burnout　介護者の燃え尽き症候群
caregiver strain index：CSI　介護者負担指標
caregiver stress　介護者ストレス
caregivers' rights　介護者の権利
carer's allowance　介護者手当
caring for the dying　看取り
caritas　カリタス
carotid artery stenosis　頸動脈狭窄
carrier　保菌者
case conference　ケースカンファレンス
case control study　症例対照研究；ケースコントロール研究
case-fatality rate　致死率
case investigation　事例調査
case management　ケースマネジメント
case mix　ケースミックス
case mix index：CMI　ケースミック指数

case records　ケース記録
case research　事例研究
case study　事例検討；ケースワーク
case work　個別援助技術
case worker　ケースワーカー
cash benefit　現金給付；金銭給付
cast　ギプス
caster　キャスター；自在輪
castration　去勢
castration anxiety　去勢不安
cataplasm　湿布
cataract　白内障
catastrophic medical expenses　高額医療費
catechol-O-methyltransferase：COMT　カテコール-O-メチルトランスフェラーゼ
catharsis　カタルシス
cathartic method　カタルシス法
catheter　カテーテル
catheter-associated bloodstream infection：CABSI　カテーテル関連血流感染
catheter-associated infection　カテーテル関連感染
catheterization　カテーテル留置法
catheter-related bacteremia　カテーテル由来菌血症
catheter-related bloodstream infection：CRBSI　カテーテル由来血流感染
catheter-related infection　カテーテル由来感染
Caucasians　白色人種
causalgia　カウザルギー
Celebrex　セレブレックス
celecoxib　セレコキシブ
cellulitis　蜂窩織炎
cemetery　墓地
centenarian　100歳代
Center for Disease Control and Prevention：CDC　疾病管理予防センター
Center for Epidemiological Studies Depression Scale：CES-D　抑うつ自己評価尺度
Center for Independent Living：CIL　自立生活センター
Center for Intergenerational Learning of Temple University　テンプル大学世間学習センター
central auditory processing disorder　中枢性聴覚処理障害
central catheter　中心静脈カテーテル；中心カテーテル
central cord syndrome：CCS　中心性頸髄損傷
central nervous system　中枢神経系
central parenteral nutrition　中心静脈栄養法
central sterile and supply department　中央滅菌供給部；中央滅菌材料部
central supply　中央供給
central venous pressure　中心静脈圧
centrifugal sampler　遠心エアサンプラ
cerebellum　小脳

介護保険・介護福祉等関連用語　英和

cerebral anemia 脳貧血
cerebral angiography 脳血管造影
cerebral arteriosclerosis 脳動脈硬化症
cerebral contusion 脳挫傷
cerebral embolism 脳塞栓
cerebral hemorrhage 脳出血
cerebral infarction 脳梗塞
cerebral nerve 脳神経
cerebral palsy：CP 脳性麻痺
cerebral thrombosis 脳血栓
cerebral vascular accident 脳血管障害
cerebrovascular dementia 脳血管性認知症
cerebrovascular disorder：CVD 脳血管障害
certificate 証明書
certification 認定；指定
certification appeal 審査請求
certification standards 認証基準
cervical cancer 子宮頸癌
cervical cord injury 頸髄損傷
cervical dysplasia 子宮頸部異形成
cervical orthosis 頸椎装具
cervical radiculopathy 頸部神経根症
cervical spinal cord injury 頸髄損傷
cervical spine 頸椎
cervical spine collar ネックカラー
cervical spondylosis 変形性頸椎症
cervical traction 頸椎牽引
cervicogenic headache 頸椎性頭痛
chamber pot 寝室用便器
change of position 体位変換
change of residence 住み替え
character 性格；キャラクター
Charcot joint シャルコー関節
charity 慈善
Charity Organization Societies：COS 慈善組織協会
chemical fiber 化学繊維
chemical indicator 化学的インジケータ
chemical restraint 薬物拘束
chemoembolization 化学塞栓
chemotherapy 化学療法
chest compression 胸部圧迫
chest pain 胸痛
chest physical therapy 肺理学療法
chest respiration 胸式呼吸
chest strap 胸廓バンド
chest X-ray：CXR 胸部エックス線
chewing problem 咀嚼問題
Cheyne-stokes psychosis チェーンストークス精神病
Cheyne-stokes respiration チェーンストークス呼吸
chicken pox 水痘
chief チーフ
chief complaint 主訴
child 子供；児童

child abuse 児童虐待
child allowance 児童手当；子供手当
child care allowance 育児手当
child care benefit 育児給付
child care leave 育児休業
child custody 監護権
child day care center 保育所
child disability allowance 障害児福祉手当
child neglect 育児放棄；児童放置；怠慢
child protective services 児童虐待保護サービス
child welfare 児童福祉
child welfare services 児童福祉サービス
childbearing 出産
childbearing age 出産適齢
childhood autism 小児自閉症
childhood disintegrative disorder 小児期崩壊性障害
childhood disorder 児童期障害
childless family 無児家族
children 子供；児童
Children's Aid Society 子供を守る会
children's shelter 児童緊急保護施設
chill 悪寒
Chinese medicine 漢方医学
chiropractic カイロプラクティック
chlordiazepoxide クロルジアゼポキシド
chlordiazepoxide-amitriptyline クロルジアゼポキシド・アミトリプチリン
chlorzoxazone クロルゾキサゾン
cholesterol コレステロール
cholinergic therapy コリン作動性療法
cholinesterase inhibitor コリンエステラーゼ阻害薬
chondroitin sulfate コンドロイチン硫酸
chopped diet 刻み食
Christian social work キリスト教社会事業
chromaticity 色度
chromosomal abnormality 染色体異常
chromosome 染色体
chronic arsenic poisoning 慢性ヒ素中毒
chronic bronchitis 慢性気管支炎
chronic disease 慢性疾患
chronic fatigue syndrome 慢性疲労症候群
chronic illness 慢性病
chronic inflammatory demyelinating polyneuropathy 慢性炎症性脱髄性多発ニューロパチー；慢性炎症性脱髄性多発神経炎
chronic kidney disease 慢性腎臓病
chronic lymphocytic leukemia：CLL 慢性リンパ性白血病
chronic myelocytic leukemia 慢性骨髄性白血病
chronic obstructive airway disease 慢性閉塞性気道疾患
chronic obstructive pulmonary disease：COPD 慢性閉塞性肺疾患

chronic pain	慢性疼痛
chronic pyelonephritis	慢性腎盂腎炎
chronic renal failure	慢性腎不全
chronic stage	慢性期
chronic tension-type headache	慢性緊張型頭痛
chronic unemployment	慢性的失業
chronological age	実年齢；暦年齢
cicatricial contracture	瘢痕拘縮
cimetidine	シメチジン
cinedefecography	シネ排泄造影
cineradiography	X線動画撮影
circadian rhythm	サーカディアン・リズム；概日リズム
circadian variation	日内変動
circle mat	円座
circle of Willis	動脈輪；ウィリス
circular causality	円環的因果律
circumduction	分回し運動
circumduction gait	分回し歩行
citizen	市民
citizen movement	市民運動
citizen participation	市民参加
citizenship	市民権
city hospital	市立病院
Civic Code	民法典
Civil Law	民法；市民法
civil rights	公民権
civil rights movement	公民権運動
civil society	市民社会
civilization	文明
classical conditioning	古典的条件づけ
Classification Code of Technical Aids：CCTA	福祉用具分類コード
classification of medical devices	医療機器分類
classified admission	分類収容
classless society	無階級社会
claudication	跛行
clay work	陶芸
clean	清潔
clean area	清潔区域
clean-contaminated operation	準清潔手術
clean-contaminated wound	準清潔創
clean intermittent catheterization：CIC	清潔間欠導尿法
clean room	クリーンルーム；清浄室
clean surgery	清潔手術
clean wound	清潔創
clean zone	クリーンゾーン
cleaning	掃除；清掃
cleaning equipment	掃除用具
cleanliness class	清浄度クラス
cleanness	清潔
cleanroom	クリーンルーム
clearing technique	クリアリング法
clidinium-chlordiazepoxide	クロルジアゼポキシド・クリジニウム
client	クライアント；患者；クライエント
client-centered therapy	クライアント中心療法；患者中心療法；クライエント中心療法
client-oriented	クライアント本位；利用者本位
clinic	診療所
Clinical Dementia Rating Scale：CDR	臨床的認知症評価尺度
clinical examination	臨床検査
clinical intervention	臨床的介入
clinical interview	臨床的面接
clinical laboratory technologist and technician	臨床検査技師
clinical microbiological technician	臨床細菌検査技師
clinical nurse specialist：CNS	専門看護師
clinical nutritional assessment	臨床栄養アセスメント
clinical pathway	クリニカルパス
clinical pharmacist	臨床薬剤師
clinical psychologist	臨床心理士
clinical psychology	臨床心理学
clinical radiologic technologist	診療放射線技師
clinical respiratory care and services	臨床呼吸治療サービス
clinical skill	クリニカルスキル
clinical trial result	臨床試験結果
clinician	臨床家
Clock Drawing Test：CDT	時計描画テスト
clock position	クロックポジション
clomipramine	クロミプラミン
clonazepam	クロナゼパム
clopidogrel	クロピドグレル
clorazepate	クロラゼプ酸
closed drainage	閉鎖式ドレナージ
closed endotracheal suction tube	閉鎖式気管内吸引チューブ
closed kinetic chain	閉運動連鎖
closed panel	限定名簿制
closed system of urinary drainage system	閉鎖式持続導尿システム
clostridium difficile	クロストリジウムディフィシル菌
clothing allowance	被服手当
clouding of consciousness	意識混濁
clozapine	クロザピン
cluster headache	群発頭痛；群発性頭痛
coating drug	被覆剤
coating flux	被覆フラックス
cocaine	コカイン
cochlear implant	人工内耳
Cochrane review	コクランレビュー
cock-up wrist hand orthosis	手関節背屈保持装具
code of ethics	倫理綱領

介護保険・介護福祉等関連用語 英和

code of ethics for nurses　看護師の倫理綱領
codeine　コデイン
co-dependency　共依存
coder　コーダー
coefficients for diagnosis procedure combination：
　DPC　診断群分類別係数
Cognex　コグネックス
cognition　認知
cognitive behavioral therapy　認知行動療法
cognitive disorder　認知障害
cognitive impairment　認識障害
cognitive paradigm　認知パラダイム
cognitive rehabilitation　認知リハビリテーション
cognitive remediation　認知療法；認知訓練
cognitive restructuring　認知的再構成
cognitive status　認知状態
cognitive therapy　認知療法
cohort analysis　コホート分析
cohort isolation　集団隔離
cohort study　コホート研究
cohorting　コホーティング
co-insurance　共同保険
cold sterilant　冷却滅菌剤
cold sterilization　低温滅菌；冷滅菌
cold stress　寒冷ストレス
cold therapy　寒冷療法
cold zone　警戒区域
collaboration　連携
collagen　コラーゲン
collagen disease　膠原病
collection　徴収
collection agency　回収代行業者；債権回収会社
collection letter　督促状
collective bargaining　団体交渉
collective unconscious　集合的無意識
colon cancer　大腸癌
colon preparation　結腸前処置
colonic lavage　結腸洗浄
colonic mucosal biopsy　結腸粘膜生検
colonic transit study　結腸通過検査
colonization　コロナイゼーション
colonization catheter　細菌定着カテーテル
colonoscope　結腸内視鏡
colonoscopy　結腸内視鏡検査
colony forming unit：CFU　コロニー形成単位
color blindness　色盲
color constancy　恒常性
color matching function　等色関数
color opponent cell　反対色細胞
color weakness　色弱
colorectal cancer screening　大腸癌検診
colorectal polyps　大腸ポリープ
colorimetry　測色

coma　昏睡
comatose　昏睡状態
comfort　安楽
commercial activity　商業的活動
Committee on Dietary Allowances　栄養所要量委員会
Committee on Mental Health　精神医療審査会
commode　移動トイレ；ポータブルトイレ；便器付き椅子
commode chair　コモードチェア
communicable disease　伝染病
communication　コミュニケーション
communication aid　コミュニケーションエイド；意思伝達装置
communication board　コミュニケーションボード
communication disorder　コミュニケーション障害
communication notes　コミュニケーションノート
communicative ability　コミュニケーション能力
community　コミュニティ；地域；地域社会
community-acquired infection　市中感染
community action agency　コミュニティ活動機関
community-based rehabilitation　地域密着型リハビリテーション
community-based service　地域密着サービス
community care　地域ケア；コミュニティケア
community care network　地域ケアネットワーク；コミュニティケアネットワーク
community care system　地域ケアシステム；コミュニティケアシステム
community chest　共同募金
community chest campaign　共同募金活動
community development　地域開発
community difference　地域格差
community health　地域保健
community health and medical care　地域保健医療
community hospital　地域病院；コミュニティ病院
community medical care　地域医療
community nursing　地域看護
community organization：CO　地域活動組織；コミュニティーオーガニゼーション
community rehabilitation　地域リハビリテーション
community residential care　地域居住施設サービス
community social work　コミュニティソーシャルワーク
community welfare　地域福祉
community welfare fund　地域福祉基金
community welfare program　地域福祉事業
community welfare services　地域福祉サービス
community work　コミュニティワーク；地域援助技術
community worker　コミュニティワーカー
commuting for care　通い介護；日帰り介護
commuting for rehabilitation　通いリハビリテーション；日帰りリハビリテーション
companion　伴生種

英語	日本語
compartment syndrome	コンパートメント症候群
compassion fatigue	共感疲労
compensation	補償；代償
compensatory movement	代償運動
competence	コンピテンス
competitive employment	競争的雇用；一般雇用
complaint	苦情
complaints handling	苦情処理
Complaints Resolution Committee	運営適正化委員会
complementary and alternative medicine：CAM	補完代替医療
complementary medicine	補完医療；代替医学
complete blood count：CBC	総血球数
complete survey	全数調査
complex	コンプレックス
compliance	コンプライアンス
compliance rate	遵守率
complication	合併症
composite institute	複合施設
compound fracture	開放性骨折
comprehensive community care	地域包括ケア
comprehensive consultation	総合相談
Comprehensive Geriatric Assessment：CGA	高齢者総合評価
comprehensive health care	包括的医療
comprehensive spending review	包括的支出レビュー
comprehensive surveillance	包括的サーベイランス
compressed recording	圧縮記録
compression fracture	圧迫骨折
compression of morbidity	病的状態の圧縮
compromise	妥協
compromised host	易感染宿主；感染防御能低下宿主
compromised patient	易感染患者；感染防御能低下患者；免疫不全患者
compulsive manipulation of tools	道具の強迫的使用
compulsory admission	強制入所
compulsory education	義務教育
compulsory enrollment	強制加入
compulsory insurance	強制保険
computed tomography：CT	コンピューター断層撮影；CT検査
computerized axial tomography：CAT	コンピューター体軸断層撮影
concentric contraction	求心性収縮
concentric contraction of the visual field	求心性視野狭窄
concentric needle EMG	同心型針電極
concepts of independence	自立の概念
concurrent review	同時期監査
conditional release	仮釈放；仮退院；仮出所
conditional voluntary admission	任意入院
conditioned response	条件反応
conditioned stimulus	条件刺激
conduct disorder	行為障害
conduction aphasia	伝導失語
conductive deafness	伝音難聴
cone	錐体
conference	カンファレンス
Conference on Aging	高齢化委員会
confidentiality	秘密保持；守秘
conflict	葛藤
congenital anomaly	先天異常
congenital hip dislocation	先天性股関節脱臼
congenital hypotonia	先天性筋緊張低下
congenital malformation	先天奇形
congenital muscular dystrophy	先天性筋ジストロフィー
congenital nephrotic syndrome	先天性ネフローゼ症候群
congestion	うっ血
congestive heart failure	うっ血性心不全
congregate home	集合ホーム
congregate housing center	集団住宅センター
congregate meal program	集団給食サービス
conjugal family	夫婦家族
conjunctivitis	結膜炎
consciousness	意識
consensus	合意
consensus building	合意形成
conservatism	保守主義
conservative and corporatist welfare state	保守主義的・コーポラティスト福祉国家
conservative treatment	保存的療法；保存的治療
constant friction joint	定摩擦継手
constipation	便秘
constitution	憲法
Constitution of the World Health Organization	世界保健機関憲章
constructional apraxia	構成失行
constructive disability	構成障害
consultation	コンサルテーション
consultation-liaison psychiatry	コンサルテーションリエゾン精神医学
consumer	消費者
consumer-directed care	消費者重視のケア
consumer education	消費者教育
consumer movement	消費者運動
consumer price index：CPI	消費者物価指数
consumer protection	消費者保護
consumer rights group	消費者権利グループ
consumerism	消費者主義；消費者運動
consumption tax	消費税
contact infection	接触感染
contact method	接触法
contact plate	接触寒天培地；接触培地

介護保険・介護福祉等関連用語 英和

contact precaution　接触予防策
contact reflection　接触反射
contact transmission　接触伝播
contaminated area　汚染区域
contaminated operation　汚染手術
contaminated wound　汚染創
contamination　汚染
contamination control　コンタミネーションコントロール
contestable market　競争可能な市場
contextual factor　背景因子
continence　自制
contingency　随伴性
contingent fee　成功報酬
continuative passive motion：CPM　持続他動運動
continuing care　継続的ケア
continuity theory　継続理論
continuous ambulatory peritoneal dialysis：CAPD　連続的携帯式腹膜透析
continuous cold therapy　継続的冷却療法
continuous positive air pressure：CPAP　持続的陽圧気道圧
continuous quality improvement　継続的改善活動
continuous traction　持続牽引
contract　契約
contract document　契約書
contract system　契約制度
contracture　拘縮
contracture prevention　拘縮予防
contrast bath　交代浴
contrast sensitivity　コントラスト感度
contribution in proportion to income　報酬比例拠出
contributory benefit　拠出給付
contributory benefit system　拠出給付制
control and prevention　制御
controlled emotional involvement　統制された情緒的関与
convalescent carrier　回復期保菌者
convalescent home　回復期施設
convalescent rehabilitation　回復期リハビリテーション
conventional　在来型
conventional care　通常介護
conventional medicine　通常医療
conversion disorder　転換性障害
convulsion　痙攣
cooling off　クーリングオフ
coordination　協調
coordination disorder　協調運動障害
coordinator　コーディネーター
co-pay　一部負担金；自己負担金；免責定率負担
co-payment　一部負担金；自己負担金；免責定率負担
coping　コーピング

coping behavior　コーピング行動；対処行動
coping strategy　対処戦略
copy of certificate　証明書の写し
copy of proof　証明書の写し
copycat medication　模倣薬
copyright　著作権
core time　コアタイム
corneal reflex　角膜反射
Cornell medical index：CMI　コーネル・メディカル・インデックス
Cornell Scale for Depression in Dementia：CSDD　コーネル認知症抑うつ尺度
coronary angiography　冠状動脈造影
coronary angioplasty　動脈形成術
coronary artery　冠動脈
coronary artery bypass graft surgery：CABG　冠動脈バイパス手術
coronary artery disease：CAD　冠動脈疾患
coronary care unit：CCU　冠動脈疾患集中治療室
coronary heart disease：CHD　冠動脈性心疾患
corporatist welfare state　コーポラティスト福祉国家
correctional facility　更正施設
corrective orthosis　矯正用装具
corrective shoes　整形靴；靴型装具
corset　コルセット
corticosteroids　コルチコステロイド
cost-benefit　費用便益
cost containment　費用抑制
cost-effective　費用対効果
cost of living　生計費用
cost-of-living adjustment：COLA　生活費用調整
cost-sharing formula　費用負担方式
cost-volume contract　コスト契約
costochondritis　肋軟骨炎
cotton swab　綿棒
cough　咳
cough variant asthma：CVA　咳喘息
Coumadin　クーマディン
council　委員会；協議会；審議会
Council of Economic Advisers：CEA　経済諮問委員会
counseling　カウンセリング
counseling & support　相談援助
counselor　カウンセラー
countertransference　逆転移
county hospital　郡立病院
couple therapy　カップル療法
court assistance　法廷援助
coxarthrosis　変形性股関節症
Cozaar　コザール
cradle　離被架
C-reactive protein　C反応性蛋白
cream-skimming　クリーム・スキミング

cremation 火葬
Creutzfeldt-Jakob disease：CJD ヤコブ病
crime 犯罪
crime by the elderly 老人犯罪
crime victimization 犯罪被害
crimes against the elderly 老人に対する犯罪
criminal code 刑法典
criminal law 刑法
criminal psychology 犯罪心理学
criminology 犯罪社会学
crisis intervention 危機介入
crisis intervention approach 危機介入アプローチ
critical クリティカル；侵襲的
critical failure factor 重要失敗要因；主要失敗要因
critical pathway：CP クリティカルパス
critical success factor：CSF 重要成功要因；主要成功要因
cross contamination 交差汚染
cross infection 交差感染
cross tab クロス集計
cross tabulation クロス集計
cross-sectional area of muscle 筋断面積
cross-sectional survey クロスセクショナルサーベイ
cross-subsidization 内部相互補助
crowding-out theory 閉め出し理論；クラウディング・アウト理論
crude birth rate 普通出生率；粗出生率
crude mortality rate 粗死亡率
crutch 松葉杖；クラッチ
crutch gait 松葉杖歩行
cryotherapy 冷凍療法
crypt hook クリプトフック
crystal arthropathy 結晶関節症
crystal induced arthritis 結晶誘発性関節炎
crystal lens 水晶体
crystallized ability 結晶性能力
crystallized intelligence 結晶性知能
culdocentesis ダグラス窩穿刺
cultural assimilation 文化的同化
cultural barrier 文化的障壁
cultural pattern 文化様式
cumulative effect 蓄積効果
cumulative incidence rate 累積罹患率
curandero クランデロス
curator 保佐人
curator of minor 未成年保佐人
cure キュア
cure vs. care 治療対ケア
Cushing's syndrome クッシング症候群
custodial care 保護型ケア；補助的ケア；療護
custody 監護
Customary, Prevailing and Reasonable：CPR 償還額決定方式

customer 顧客
customer satisfaction：CS 顧客満足
cutaneous pruritus 皮膚掻痒感
cyanamide シアナミド
cyanosis チアノーゼ
cyclobenzaprine シクロベンザプリン
cyclosporine シクロスポリン
cyclothymic disorder 気分循環障害
Cymbalta シンバルタ
CYP-3A シップスリーA
cystocele 膀胱瘤
cystometrography 膀胱内圧測定
cystometry 膀胱内圧測定
cystoscopy 膀胱鏡検査

D

daily money management：DMM 日常的金銭管理
daily treatment 日常的処遇
damper ダンパー
danger to others：DTO 他害行為
danger to self or others 自傷他害
dark adaptation 暗順応
dark/light adaptation 暗明順応
Darvon ダーボン
database データベース
day care デイケア；通所介護
day care center デイケアセンター；通所介護施設
day home デイホーム
day services デイサービス
day services center デイサービスセンター
daylighting 採光
dead on arrival：DOA 来院時心停止
deaf-mute 聾唖者
deafness 聾
death 死
death certificate 死亡診断書
death rate 死亡率
death tax 相続税
death with dignity 尊厳死
Death with Dignity Act 尊厳死法
deceased 故人；死者；死亡者
decentralization 分権化；地方分権
decibel：dB デシベル
decision for the placement 配置決定
decision-making 意思決定
decision-making meeting 判定会議
Declaration of Alma-Ata アルマ・アタ宣言
Declaration of Helsinki ヘルシンキ宣言
Declaration of the Rights of the Child 児童権利宣言
Declaration on the Rights of Disabled Persons 障害者の権利宣言
Declaration on the Rights of Mentally Retarded

Persons 知的障害者の権利宣言
decompression 除圧
deconditioning prevention 弱化予防
decongestant 充血除去剤
decontaminate hands 手指の汚染除去
decontamination procedure 汚染除去処理
decubitus 褥瘡；床ずれ
decubitus ulcer 褥瘡；床ずれ
deductible 定額自己負担；免責定額負担
deduction 控除
deductive method 演繹法
deductive reasoning 演繹推論
deemed status みなし指定
deemed status accreditation みなし指定認定
deep brain stimulation 脳深部刺激療法
deep sensation 深部感覚
deep vein thrombosis 深部静脈血栓症
defamation 名誉毀損
defecation 排便
defecation disorder 排便障害
defecography 排便造影検査
defecometry 排便内圧検査
defense 防衛
defense mechanism 防衛機制
defined contribution 確定拠出年金
deformity 変形
degeneration 変性
degenerative disease 変性疾患
deglutition pneumonia 嚥下性肺炎
degree of freedom of motion 動作の自由度
dehydration 脱水症
dehydroepiandrosterone：DHEA デヒドロエピアンドロステロン
deinstitutionalization 脱施設化；脱施設
deliberate self-harm 故意的自傷行為；計画的自傷行為
delinquent tax collection organization 税金滞納整理機構
delirium せん妄
Delirium Rating Scale せん妄評価尺度
delirium tremens 振戦せん妄
delusion 妄想
delusion of persecution 被害妄想
delusional disorder 妄想性障害
demands ディマンズ
demented elderly 痴呆性老人
dementia 認知症；痴呆
Dementia Rating Scale 認知症評価尺度
Demerol デメロール
democracy 民主主義
democratic socialism 民主社会主義
democratic society 民主主義社会
democratization 民主化
demographic dependency ratio 人口学的従属人口比率
demographic statistics 人口統計
demographic transition theory 人口転換論
demonology 悪霊学
demyelinating disease 脱髄疾患
demyelination 脱髄
denarian 10代
denervation 脱神経；除神経
denial 否認
denial of illness 疾病否認
dental disease 歯科疾患
dental floss デンタルフロス
dental hygienist 歯科衛生士
dentist 歯科医師
dentistry 歯科
denture 入れ歯；義歯
Denver Developmental Screening Test：DDST デンバー式発達スクリーニング検査
Departmental Expenditure Limit：DEL 省庁別歳出限度額
dependency allowance 扶養手当
Dependency and Indemnity Compensation：DIC 軍人遺族手当
dependency ratio 従属人口指数
dependent 被扶養者
dependent health care coverage 家族療養費
dependent population 従属人口
dependent variable 従属変数
depersonalization disorder 離人症
depopulation 過疎
depopulation 少子化
depopulation and aging 少子高齢化
depreciation 減価償却
Deprenyl デプレニール
depression うつ病；抑うつ
depressive neurosis 抑うつ神経症
depressive state うつ状態
depressurized room 陰圧室
deregulation 規制緩和
dermatologist 皮膚科専門医
dermatology 皮膚科学
dermatomyositis 皮膚筋炎
dermatophyte 皮膚糸状菌
designation of curator of minor 未成年保佐人の指定
designation of guardian 後見人の指定
designation of guardian of minor 未成年後見人の指定
designation system for teeth and areas of the oral cavity 歯及び口腔部位の名称システム
desipramine デシプラミン
detergent 洗剤
detergent allergy 洗剤アレルギー
detrusor-sphincter dyssynergia：DSD 排尿筋括約

筋協調不全
developed country　先進国
developing country　発展途上国；開発途上国
development　発達
developmental age　発達年齢
developmental delay　発達遅延
developmental disorder　発達障害
developmental psychopathology　発達精神病理学
developmental quotient：DQ　発達指数
developmental stage　発達段階
developmental test　発達検査
developmental theory　発達理論
deviant behavior　逸脱行動
deviate sexual intercourse　性的逸脱行為
deviation　逸脱
device-related infection　器材関連感染
dexterity　巧緻性
dextromethorphan　デキストロメトルファン
diabetes food exchange list　糖尿病交換表
diabetes medication　糖尿病薬
diabetes mellitus：DM　糖尿病
diabetic coma　糖尿病性昏睡
diabetic ketoacidosis：DKA　糖尿病性ケトアシドーシス
diabetic nephropathy　糖尿病性腎症
diabetic neuropathy　糖尿病性神経症
diabetic retinopathy　糖尿病性網膜症
diagnosis　診断
diagnosis of dementia　認知症の診断
diagnosis procedure combination：DPC　診断群分類
Diagnostic and Statistical Manual of Mental Disorders：DSM　精神障害の診断と統計の手引き
diagnostic criteria for clinical diagnosis of brain death　脳死判定基準
diagnostic imaging　画像診断
diagnostic related groups-prospective payment system：DRG-PPS　診断群別所定報酬支払方式
dialysis　透析
dialysis therapy　透析療法
diaper　おむつ
diaphragm　横隔膜
diarrhea　下痢
diary　日誌
diastolic pressure　拡張期血圧
diathermy　ジアテルミー
diazepam　ジアゼパム
dichromatic reflection model　二色性反射モデル
dietary fiber　食物繊維
dietary habit　食習慣
dietary life　食生活
dietary prescription　栄養処方
dietary restriction　食事制限
dietary supplement　栄養補助食品

diethylstilbestrol：DES　ジエチルスチルベストロール
dietitian　栄養士
differential culture　分離培養
differentiated welfare state　分化した福祉国家
difficult urination　排尿困難
diffuse axonal injury：DAI　びまん性軸索損傷
digestion　消化
digestion and absorption　消化吸収
digestive disease　消化器疾患
digital anorectal examination　肛門直腸指診
digital examination　指診
digital rectal examination　直腸指診
digital subtraction angiography　デジタル血管造影
dignity　尊厳
digoxin　ジゴキシン
dilemma　ジレンマ
diltiazem　ジルチアゼム
diminished capacity　心身耗弱
diminished responsibility　限定責任能力
diphtheria　ジフテリア
diplegia　両麻痺
direct care staff　介護職員；介護従事者；介護担当者
direct contact infection　直接接触感染
direct contact transmission　直接接触感染
direct contract model　直接契約モデル
direct language　直接言語
direct light reflex　直接対光反射
direct social work practice　直接援助技術
direct tax　直接税
direct treatment　直接処遇
director　役員
director of nursing　看護師長
dirty area　不潔区域
dirty behavior　不潔行為
dirty utility room　汚物室；不潔物収納室
dirty wound　不潔創
dirty/infected operation　不潔・感染手術
disability　障害
disability allowance　障害者手当
disability freeze　障害凍結
disability insurance：DI　障害保険
disability living allowance　障害者生活手当；障害者生活支援手当
disability movement　障害者運動
disability pension　障害年金
disability rights movement　障害者権利運動
disability standards for education　教育における障害基準
disability study　障害学
disabled abuse　障害者虐待
disabled parking permit　障害者駐車許可証
disabled sports　障害者スポーツ
disarticulation　関節離断

介護保険・介護福祉等関連用語　英和

disaster benefit　災害給付
disaster prevention　防災
discharge　退院
discharge from the facility　退所
discharge from the hospital　退病院
discharge information　退所時情報
discharge planning　退院計画
disciplinary punishment　懲戒
discoloration　変色
discomfort index　不快指数
Discomfort Scale for Dementia of the Alzheimer's Type : DS-DAT　アルツハイマー型認知症不快評価尺度
discount price　割引料金
discrimination　差別
discriminative stimulus　弁別刺激
disease　疾患；疾病；病気
disease management : DM　疾患管理；疾病管理；病気管理
disease-modifying antirheumatic drug : DMARD　疾患修飾性抗リウマチ薬
disengagement　離脱；遊離
disengagement theory　離脱理論
disinfectant　消毒剤
disinfection　消毒
disinhibition　脱抑制
disorder of environmental origin　環境由来疾患
disorder of executive function　遂行機能障害
disorders of the heart function　心臓機能障害
disorders of the kidney function　腎臓機能障害
disorders of the small intestinal function　小腸機能障害
disorientation　見当識障害；失見当識
dispatch worker　派遣労働者
dispensary　医務室
disperser　微生物飛散者；ディスパーサ
disposable　ディスポーザブル；使い捨て
disposable income　可処分所得
disposal　廃棄；処理
disposal of garbage and swill　生ごみ処理
disseminated intravascular coagulation　播種性血管内凝固症候群
dissemination of information　情報提供
dissociated sensory disturbance　解離性感覚障害
dissociative disorder　解離性障害
dissociative identity disorder　解離同一性障害
distal　遠位；末梢
distal end　遠位端；末端部
distal latency　遠位潜時
distal radius fracture　橈骨遠位端骨折
distance education　遠隔教育
distance learning　遠隔学習
distractibility　転導性

district court　地方裁判所
disturbance of balance　平衡機能障害
disturbance of consciousness　意識障害
disturbance of thermoregulation　体温調節障害
disturbance of urinary storage　蓄尿異常
disulfiram　ジスルフィラム
disuse　廃用
disuse atrophy　廃用萎縮
disuse bone atrophy　廃用性骨萎縮
disuse muscle atrophy　廃用性筋萎縮
disuse syndrome　廃用症候群
diuretic　利尿剤
diversional occupational therapy　気晴し的作業療法
diversity　多様性
diversity and inclusion　多様性と包括性
diverticular disease　憩室疾患
divisions of labor　分業
divorce　離婚
divorce certificate　離婚証明書
dizziness　めまい
DNR〈Do Not Resuscitate〉蘇生処置拒否；蘇生措置拒否
Do Not Resuscitate : DNR　蘇生処置拒否；蘇生措置拒否
DOA〈dead on arrival〉来院時心停止
doctor　医師
doctor appointment　診療予約
doctor referral services　医師紹介サービス
doctor's home visit　往診
doctor's office visit　通院
domestic violence:DV　家庭内暴力；ドメスティック・バイオレンス
dominant inheritance　優性遺伝
donation　寄付
donepezil　ドネペジル
donor　ドナー
donor card　ドナーカード
door　ドア
dopamine　ドーパミン
dopamine receptor blockade　ドーパミン受容体遮断
dopamine receptor D2 blockade　D2ドーパミン受容体拮抗剤
Doral　ドラール
dorsiflexion　背屈
dosage modification　投薬量の調整
double bag technique　二重袋手技
double bind theory　ダブルバインド仮説；二重拘束説
double bucket system　二重バケツ法；ニバケツ法
double contrast roentgenography　二重X線造影法
double stance phase　同時定着時期
double support　両脚支持
double support period　両脚支持期
doughnut phenomenon　ドーナツ現象

Down Syndrome　ダウン症候群
downsize　軽量化
drain　ドレーン；排水管
drama therapy　ドラマセラピー
drape　ドレープ；覆布
drastic medicine　劇薬
dream analysis　夢分析
dressing　更衣；ドレッシング
dressing activity　更衣動作
dressing change　包帯交換
dressing room　更衣室；脱衣場
dressing skill　着衣スキル
drip infusion cholecystography　点滴静脈性胆管胆嚢造影
drooling　流涎
droplet infection　飛沫感染
droplet nuclei　飛沫核
droplet precaution　飛沫予防策
droplet transmission　飛沫伝播
dropout　ドロップアウト
drug　薬
drug abuse　薬物乱用
drug allergy　薬物アレルギー
drug dependence　薬物依存
drug free　薬物のない
drug-induced acute pancreatitis　薬剤性急性膵炎
drug-induced chronic pancreatitis　薬剤性慢性膵炎
drug-induced hepatitis　薬剤性肝炎
drug-induced liver disease　薬剤性肝疾患
drug-induced lupus　薬剤性ループス
drug-induced lupus erythematosus　薬剤性エリテマトーデス
drug-induced osteoporosis　薬剤性骨粗鬆症
drug-induced pancreatitis　薬剤性膵炎
drug-induced Parkinsonism　薬剤性パーキンソニズム
drug-induced psychosis　薬剤因性精神病；薬剤性精神病
drug-induced Schizophrenia　薬剤性統合失調症
drug-induced suffering　薬害
drug-induced thrombocytopenia　薬剤起因性血小板減少症
drug-induced thrombocytopenic purpura　薬剤性血小板減少性紫斑病
drug intoxication　薬物中毒
drug price controls　薬価規制
drug rash　薬疹
drug tariff standards　薬価基準
drunkenness　酩酊
dry heat　乾性温熱
dry heat sterilization　乾熱滅菌
dry mouth　ドライマウス；口腔乾燥症
dual-energy X-ray　二重エネルギーX線
dual-energy X-ray absorptiometry：DEXA　二重エネルギーX線吸収測定法

Duchenne muscular dystrophy　デュシェンヌ型筋ジストロフィー
duloxetine　デュロキセチン
dumbbell　亜鈴
dumping syndrome　ダンピング症候群
Dupuytren's contracture　デュピュイトラン拘縮
durable medical equipment：DME　耐久医療機器
dutasteride　デュタステリド
duty of confidentiality　守秘義務
D-value　D値
dying　臨終
dynamic computed tomography　動的コンピューター断層撮影
dynamic stability　動的安定性
dysarthria　構音障害
dysarthria training　構音訓練
dysautonomia　自律神経失調；自律神経障害
dyschezia　排便障害
dysesthesia　異常知覚
dysexecutive syndrome　遂行機能障害症候群
dyskinesia　ジスキネジア；運動障害
dyslipidemia　脂質異常症
dyspareunia　性交疼痛症
dysphagia　嚥下障害
dysphagia of swallowing function　嚥下機能障害
dysplasia　形成不全
dyspnea　呼吸困難
dystonia　ジストニア

E

ear, nose and throat evaluation　耳鼻咽喉検査
ear, nose and throat specialist　耳鼻咽喉専門医
early ambulation　早期離床
early detection　早期発見
early intervention　早期介入
early-onset Alzheimer's disease　早発性アルツハイマー病
Early Speech Perception Test　初期発話知覚テスト
earmarked revenue　特定財源
earmarked taxation　目的税
earned income tax credit：EITC　勤労所得税額控除
earnings test　所得調査
eastern philosophies　東洋哲学
easy fatigability　易疲労性
eating　食事動作
eating assistance　食事介護；食事援助；食事介助；食事ケア
eating disorder　摂食障害；食行動の異常
eating habit　食習慣
eating tool　食事用具
Eaton-Lambert syndrome　イートン・ランバート症

候群
eccentric contraction　遠心性収縮
eccrine gland　エクリン腺
echocardiogram　心エコー図
echocardiography　心エコー
eco map　エコマップ
ecological approach　エコロジカルアプローチ
ecological psychology　生態学的心理学
ecology　生態学
economic growth　経済成長
economic growth rate　経済成長率
economic system　経済体制
ecosystem　エコシステム
ectopic kidney　異所性腎
ectopic pregnancy　子宮外妊娠
ectopic rhythm　異所性リズム
ectopic sebaceous gland　異所性皮脂腺
ectopic ureter　異所性尿管
ectopic ureterocele　異所性尿管瘤
eczema　湿疹
edema　浮腫
Eden Alternative　エデン・オルタナティブ
edentulism　無歯症
education　教育
educational aid　教育扶助
educational benefit　教育給付
educational expenses　教育費
educational maintenance allowance　教育補助手当て；教育維持手当
educational meeting　教育ミーティング
educational rehabilitation　教育的リハビリテーション
effective demand　有効需要
effective width of doorway　開口有効幅員
Effexor　エフェクサー
effleurage　軽擦法
effort angina　労作性狭心症
effort respiration　努力呼吸
ego　自我；エゴ
ego analysis　自我分析
ego identity　自我同一性
EKG〈electrocardiogram〉　イーケージー；エーカーゲー
elasticity　弾力性
elbow bathing　肘浴
elbow disarticulation prosthesis　肘義手
elbow fracture　肘骨折
Eldepryl　エルデプリル
elder abuse　高齢者虐待；老人虐待
elder abuse and neglect　高齢者虐待・ネグレクト
Elder Abuse Prevention Act　高齢者虐待防止法
elder abuse prevention activity　高齢者虐待防止活動
elderly　高齢者
elderly abuse　高齢者虐待；老人虐待

elderly health　老人保健
elderly household　高齢者世帯
elderly housing　高齢者住宅
elderly legal assistance program　高齢者法律支援プログラム
elderly mistreatment　高齢者虐待
elderly-onset rheumatoid arthritis：EORA　高齢発症関節リウマチ
elderly population　老年人口；高齢者人口
elderly remarriage　老人再婚
elective abortion　人工妊娠中絶
elective cardiac catheterization　待機的心臓カテーテル検査
Electra complex　エレクトラ・コンプレックス
electric aspirator　電動吸引器
electric bed　電動ベッド
electric Braille writer　電動ブライユ式点字タイプライター；電動点字タイプライター
electric records　電子記録
electric toothbrush　電動歯ブラシ
electric upper limb prosthesis　電動義手
electric wheelchair　電動車いす
electrocardiogram：EKG　心電図
electroconvulsive therapy：ECT　電気けいれん療法
electrode　電極
electrodermal responding　皮膚電位反応
electrodiagnosis：EDX　電気診断法
electroencephalogram：EEG　脳波；脳電図
electrogoniometer　電気関節角度計
electromyogram：EMG　筋電図
electromyography　筋電図検査
electromyography of anal sphincter　肛門括約筋筋電図検査
electron beam computed tomography　電子ビームCT；コンピューター断層撮影
electron beam sterilization　電子線滅菌
electronic endoscopy　電子内視鏡検査
electronic health records　電子カルテ；電子健康記録；エレクトロニックヘルスレコード
electrophysiology　電気生理学
electroshock therapy　電気ショック療法
electrostimulation　電気刺激
electrostimulator　電気刺激装置
electrotherapy　電気療法
eletriptan　エレトリプタン
elevation　挙上；補高
eligibility of employee pension　年金受給資格
elimination of thresholds　段差の解消
embolism　塞栓
emergency alarm system　緊急通報装置
emergency assistance：EA　緊急扶助
emergency call　緊急通報
emergency call services　緊急通報サービス

emergency call system　緊急通報システム
emergency contact information　緊急連絡先
emergency first aid　応急手当
emergency medical services　救急医療
emergency medical technician：EMT　救急救命士
emergency planning　防災対策
emergency room：ER　救急救命室；救急外来
emerging infectious disease　新興感染症
EMG〈electromyography〉　イーエムジー
EMG biofeedback　EMGバイオフィードバック
emigrant　出移民
emollient　軟化剤
emotion　情動
emotional abuse　心理的虐待
emotional dependency　精神的依存
emotional disturbance　情緒障害
emotional incontinence　感情失禁
empathic understanding　共感の理解
empathy　共感
emphysema　気腫
emphysematous pyelonephritis　気腫性腎盂腎炎
empiric therapy　経験の治療；経験主義的治療
employee　被用者；従業員
employee insurance　被用者保険；厚生保険
employee pension　被用者年金；厚生年金
employee rules and regulations　就業規則
employee satisfaction：ES　従業員満足度
employees health insurance　被用者健康保険
employees pension fund：EPF　厚生年金基金
employees' pension insurance　厚生年金保険
Employment Act　雇用法
employment adjustment　雇用調整
employment agreements and contracts　雇用契約
employment assistance　就労支援
employment insurance　雇用保険
employment insurance system　雇用保険制度
employment period　雇用期間
employment rate　雇用率
Employment Security Law　職業安定法
empowerment　エンパワメント
empowerment approach　エンパワメントアプローチ
empty-chair technique　エンプティ・チェアー法
empty nest syndrome　空の巣症候群
enalapril　エナラプリル
enamel　エナメル質
Enbrel　エンブレル
encoding disturbance　記銘力障害
encounter group　エンカウンターグループ
endarteritis　動脈内膜炎
end-bearing socket　断端負荷ソケット
endemic　地域の；地域の流行の；風土病
endocrine　内分泌
endocrine disease　内分泌疾患

endocrinologist　内分泌医
endocrinology　内分泌学
end-of-life care　エンド・オブ・ライフケア；終末期ケア
endogenous　内因性
endogenous infection　内因性感染；内因性感染症
endogenous psychosis　内因性精神病
endorectal coil　直腸内コイル
endorectal ultrasonography　経直腸の超音波検査法
endoscope　内視鏡
endoscopic retrograde cholangiopancreatography　内視鏡の逆行性胆道膵管造影
endoscopic ultrasonography　内視鏡の超音波検査
endoscopy　内視鏡検査
endosonography　内視鏡超音波検査
endotoxin test　エンドトキシンテスト
endotracheal anesthesia　気管内麻酔
end-stage renal disease：ESRD　末期腎不全
endurance　持久性；耐久性
endurance exercise　持久訓練
enema　浣腸
energy　エネルギー
energy expenditure　エネルギー消費
energy requirement　エネルギー必要量
energy storing prosthetic foot　エネルギー蓄積足部
enervation　無気力
enforcement notice　強制通告；執行通告
Engel's coefficient　エンゲル係数
enlarging reading device　拡大読書器
enmeshment　纏綿状態
enrollee　登録者；入会者；加入者
enrollment　登録；入会；加入
enrollment restriction　登録制約；入会制限；加入制約
entacapone　エンタカポン
entecavir　エンテカビル
enteral tube　外部チューブ
enteric-coating　腸溶コーティング
enterocele　小腸瘤
enterovirus　エンテロウイルス
entrapment neuropathy　絞扼神経障害
enuresis　遺尿症
environmental control system：ECS　環境制御装置
environmental factor　環境因子
environmental hazards　環境危険物質
environmental maintenance　環境整備
environmental pollution　環境汚染
environmental problem　環境問題
environmental protection agency　環境保護機関
environmental rights　環境権
environmental sampling　環境調査
environmental surveillance　環境サーベイランス
epidemic　流行性；流行
epidemic keratoconjunctivitis：EKC　流行性角結膜炎

介護保険・介護福祉等関連用語　英和

epidemiological study　疫学調査
epidemiology　疫学
epidural analgesia　硬膜外鎮痛法
epidural hematoma　硬膜外血腫
epilepsy　てんかん
epileptic seizure　てんかん発作
episodic memory　エピソード記憶
e-prescription　電子処方
Equal Employment Opportunity Laws　男女雇用機会均等法
equal participation of women and men　男女共同参画
equal rights　平等権
equality of opportunity　機会の平等
equality of result　結果の平等
equilibrium　平衡
equinovarus foot　内反尖足
equipment　用具；機器；道具
equity　公平
erectile dysfunction：ED　勃起不全
erection　勃起
erector spinae　脊柱起立筋
ergometer　エルゴメーター
ergonomics　エルゴノミクス；人間工学
Eros　エロス
erosion　びらん
erythrocyte sedimentation rate：ESR　赤血球沈降速度；赤沈値
erythropoietin　エリスロポエチン
esophageal manometry　食道内圧検査
esophageal motility disorder　食道運動障害
esophageal phase　食道相
esophagus　食道
essential amino acid　必須アミノ酸
essential hypertension　本態性高血圧
essential nutrition　必要栄養素
estate planning　エステートプランニング
estate tax　遺産税
estazolam　エスタゾラム
esteem needs　自我の欲求
esterase　エステラーゼ
estimated daily intake　推定一日摂取量
estrogen　エストロゲン
estrogen replacement therapy：ERT　エストロゲン補充療法
etanercept　エタネルセプト
ethical code　倫理規程
ethics　倫理
ethics in research　研究倫理
ethnic discrimination　民族差別
ethnic minority　少数民族
ethnicity　エスニシティ
ethopropazine　エトプロパジン

ethylene oxide gas sterilization　エチレンオキサイドガス滅菌；エチレンオキシドガス滅菌；酸化エチレンガス滅菌
etiquette　エチケット
eugenic operation　優性手術
eugenic protection　優性保護
eugenics　優生学
eurhythmia　整脈
euthanasia　安楽死
evacuation site　避難場所
evaluation　評価
evaluation criteria　評価項目
evening care　イブニングケア
event-related potential：ERP　事象関連電位
eversion　外がえし；外反
every 2 hours：Q2H　二時間毎
every 3 hours：Q3H　三時間毎
every 4 hours：Q4H　四時間毎
every 6 hours：Q6H　六時間毎
every 8 hours：Q8H　八時間毎
every day：QD　日毎
every hour：QH　一時間毎
every morning：QAM　毎朝
every night：QHS　毎日就寝時間毎
every other day：QOD　一日おき
evidence-based care：EBC　根拠に基づくケア；根拠に基づく介護
evidence-based community planning　根拠に基づく地域計画
evidence-based medicine：EBM　根拠に基づく医療
evidence-based nursing　根拠に基づく看護
Evista　エビスタ
evoked electromyogram　誘発筋電図
evoked potential　誘発電位
examination fee　受験手数料
excessive daytime sleepiness　日中過眠
excessive drooling　過剰な流涎
excretion　排泄
excretion care　排泄介護；排泄ケア
excretion disorder　排泄障害
excretion exercise　排泄訓練
excretion tool　排泄用具
Exelon　エクセロン
exercise　運動；訓練；体操
exercise capacity　運動耐容能
exercise instructor　運動専門士
exercise load　運動負荷
exercise physiology　運動生理
exercise prescription　運動処方
exercise strength　運動強度
exercise test　運動試験
exercise tolerance test：ETT　運動負荷テスト
exercises for maintaining muscle　筋力維持訓練

exfoliative cytology　剥離細胞診
existential therapy　実存的療法
existentialism　実存主義
exit-site infection　出口部感染
exogenous　外因性
exogenous hormone　外因性ホルモン
exogenous infection　外因性感染
exorcism　悪魔払い
expenses for bringing up a child　養育費出
experience rating　病歴価格決定方式
experiential self　経験自己
expert　専門家
exploring electrode　探査電極
exposure　曝露
expressions of desires　意思の伝達
extended care　延長介護
extended childcare　延長保育
extended family　拡大家族
extension　伸展
extension contracture　伸展拘縮
extension shoe　補高靴
external frame of reference　外的照合枠
external rotation　外旋
extinction　消去現象
extinctive prescription　消滅時効
extraversion　外向性
eye bank　アイバンク
eye disease　眼病
eye drop　点眼液
eye goggle　保護用眼鏡

F

F wave　F波
Fabianism　フェビアン主義
face cleaning　洗顔
face sheet　フェイスシート
facial paralysis　顔面神経麻痺；顔面麻痺
facial reflection　表情反応
facilitation technique　促通手技
facility　施設
facility administration　施設運営
facility-based services　施設基盤型サービス
facility management　施設管理
facility volunteer　施設ボランティア
facioscapulohumeral muscular dystrophy　顔面肩甲上腕型筋ジストロフィー
factor analysis　因子分析
failure to thrive：FTT　成長障害
fainting　失神
fall　転倒
fall incident　転倒事故
fall risk　転倒危険度

falling asleep　入眠
falls prevention　転倒予防
famciclovir　ファムシクロビル
familial adenomatous polyposis：FAP　家族性大腸腺腫症；家族性大腸ポリポーシス
family　家族
family allowance　家族手当
family-based care　家族中心ケア
family benefit　家族給付
family budget　家計
family care allowance　介護休業手当金
family care leave　介護休業
family caregiver　家族介護者
Family Caregiver Burden Scale　家族介護負担感尺度
family case work　ファミリー・ケースワーク
family case worker　家族ケースワーカー
family composition　家族構成
family court　家庭裁判所
family disorganization　家族解体
family doctor　家庭医
family doctor's function　家庭医機能
family education　家族指導
family function　家族機能
family history　家族歴
family homeostasis　家族ホメオスタシス
family in need of public assistance　要保護家族
family issue　家族問題
family labor　家内労働
family life cycle　家族周期
family myth　家族神話
family of orientation　定位家族
family of procreation　生殖家族；創設家族
family-oriented care　家族指向ケア
family plan　家族計画
family policy　家庭政策
family-provided care　家族介護
family relationship　家族関係
family rule　家族ルール
family social work　家族ソーシャルワーク；ファミリー・ソーシャルワーク
family social worker　家族ソーシャルワーカー
family structure　家族構造；世帯構造
family support　家族支援；ファミリー・サポート
family support center　家族支援センター；ファミリー・サポート・センター
family system　家族システム
family system theory　家族システム理論
family systems approach　家族システムズアプローチ
family therapy　家族療法
family welfare　家庭福祉
Famvir　ファムビル
fango therapy　鉱泥療法
fantasy wandering　ファンタジー徘徊

介護保険・介護福祉等関連用語 英和

fasciculation potential 線維束自発電位
fasciitis 筋膜炎
fasting blood sugar 空腹時血糖
fat 脂肪
fatal familial insomnia 致死性家族性不眠症
fatherless family 母子家庭
fatigue 疲労
fat-soluble vitamin 脂溶性ビタミン
fatty acid 脂肪酸
fault tree analysis 故障の木解析
feather allergy 羽毛アレルギー
fecal chymotrypsin test 糞便キモトリプシン試験
fecal examination 糞便検査；検便
fecal impaction 宿便
fecal incontinence 便失禁
fecal occult blood test：FOBT 便潜血検査
fece 排泄物
feces sampling 採便
federal government 連邦政府
fee 利用料
feeding activity 食事動作
feeding restriction 摂食制限
fee-for-service：FFS 出来高払い
Feeling Tone Questionnaire：FTQ 感情気分質問票
feet フィート
feminism フェミニズム
feminist social work フェミニスト・ソーシャルワーク
feminist theory フェミニズムの理論
feminization of poverty 貧困の女性化
femoral neck fracture 大腿骨頸部骨折
Ferguson Report ファーガソンレポート
fetal alcohol spectrum disorder 胎児性アルコール・スペクトラム障害
fetal alcohol syndrome 胎児性アルコール症候群
fetal disorder 胎児期障害
feudal society 封建社会
feudalistic thought 封建思想
fever 発熱
fever of unknown origin 不明熱
feverfew フィーバーフュー
fiber 繊維
fiber type grouping 線維タイプグループ化
fibrillation potential 線維自発電位
fibrin フィブリン
fiduciary abuse specialist team：FAST 経済的虐待専門家チーム
field of microscope 顕微鏡視野
filling-in フィリングイン
filtration sterilization ろ過滅菌
financial asset 金融資産
financial capability index 財政力指数
financial management 財務管理
financial stability fund 財政安定化基金

financial statement 財務諸表
financial welfare 財政福祉
finasteride フィナステリド
finding abnormality 異常発見
fines for default 過怠金
finger agnosia 手指失認
finger ladder 指はしご
finger print plate method フィンガープリント法
finger streak plate method フィンガーストリーク法
fingernail 手指爪
fingerspelling 指文字
Fire Department 消防署
fire prevention 防火対策
fire risk 火災危険度
firefighter 消防士
first aid 救急法
fiscal year 会計年度
fitness フィットネス
fitting 適合
fitting evaluation 適合判定
five major nutrients 五大栄養素
five-stage hierarchy of needs 欲求の5段階説
five times daily：5D 一日5回
five times weekly：5W 週五回
fixation 固着
fixator 固定器
fixator muscle 固定筋
fixed amount system 定額制
fixed charge 定額負担
fixed charge rate 定率負担
fixed dystonia 固定ジストニア
flaccid 弛緩
flaccid paralysis 弛緩性麻痺
flame-resistant material 防炎素材
flame sterilization 火炎滅菌
flash pulmonary edema フラッシュ肺水腫
flashback フラッシュバック現象
flat rate benefit 均一給付
flat rate contribution 均一拠出
flavor 風味
Flexeril フレクセリル
flexibility 柔軟性
flexibility exercise 柔軟体操
flexion 屈曲
flexion contracture 屈曲拘縮
flextime フレックスタイム
floating particle 空中浮遊塵埃；空中塵埃；浮遊微粒子
Flomax フロマックス
floppy infant フロッピーインファント
flora 常在菌
flossing teeth 歯間歯磨き
fluid 水分
fluid ability 流動性能力

fluid balance	水分バランス
fluid intake	水分摂取
fluid intake and output	水分出納
fluid intelligence	流動性知能
flu-like symptom	風邪のような症状
fluorescein endoscopy	蛍光内視鏡検査
fluoride	フッ素
fluoroscopy	X線透視検査
fluoxetine	フルオキセチン
fluvoxamine	フルボキサミン
focal	巣状；限局性
focal infection	病巣感染
focus	照準
focus of colonization	細菌増殖の病巣
focusing	フォーカシング
fogging	噴霧
folk medicine	民間療法
folktale	民話
follicular thyroid cancer	濾胞性甲状腺癌
follow-up	フォローアップ
follow-up study	追跡調査
follow-up visit after discharge	退所後訪問指導
food	食物
food-borne infection	食物媒介感染
food contamination	食品汚染
food exchange list for diabetes	糖尿病食品交換表
food inspector	食品衛生監視員
food intake	摂食
food poisoning	食中毒
food preparation	食品調理
food-related disorder	食物関連障害
food safety & sanitation supervisor	食品衛生管理者
food sanitation	食品衛生
foot bath	足浴
foot drop	尖足
foot plate	足板
foot problem	足の問題
foot rest	フットレスト
foot slap	フットスラップ
foot support	フットサポート
footboard	フットボード
footwear	履物
force plate	床反力計
forced crying	強制泣き
forced laughing	強制笑い
forceps	鉗子
forceps biopsy	鉗子生検
Fordism	フォード主義
foreign care worker	外国人介護労働者
foreign-born elderly	外国生まれ高齢者
forensic anthropologist	司法人類学者；法医人類学者
forensic anthropology	司法人類学；法医人類学
forensic autopsy	司法解剖
forensic nurse	司法看護；法医看護師
forensic nursing	司法看護学；法医看護学
forensic pathologist	司法病理学者；法医病理学者
forensic pathology	司法病理学；法医病理学
forensic psychiatric nursing	司法精神看護；法医精神看護
forensic psychologist	司法心理学者；法医心理学者
forensic psychology	司法心理学；法医心理学
forensic social work	司法福祉；法医福祉
forequarter amputation	肩甲胸廓間切断；フォークオーター切断
forequarter amputation prosthesis	肩甲胸廓間切断用義手
forgetfulness	物忘れ
formal care	フォーマルケア
formal network	フォーマルネットワーク
formal sector	フォーマルセクター
formal service	フォーマルサービス
formulary	処方集
for-profit organization	営利団体；民間営利組織
Fosamax	フォサマックス
four food groups	四つの食品群
four-legged cane	四脚杖
four-point gait	四点歩行
four times daily：QID	一日四回
four times weekly：4W	週四回
four-year nursing school	看護系大学
Fowler's position	ファーラー位
fracture	骨折
fracture management	骨折管理
frail child	虚弱児
frail elderly	虚弱高齢者；虚弱老人
frail joint	動揺関節
frailty	虚弱
frame	フレーム
Frankel classification	フランケル分類
fraternity	友愛
fraud	詐欺
free access	フリーアクセス
free medical care	無償医療
free of charge	無料
free rider	フリーライダー
freeter	フリーター
frequent bowel movements	頻便
friction lock joint	摩擦ロック継手
friendly society	友愛組合
friendly visiting	友愛訪問
friendly visitor	友愛訪問員
fringe benefit	付加給付
front wheel folding walker	折りたたみ前輪歩行器
frontal lobe dysfunction	前頭葉障害
frontal lobe syndrome	前頭葉症状
front-temporal dementia	前頭側頭型認知症

介護保険・介護福祉等関連用語 英和

front-wheel walker 前輪歩行器
frovatriptan フロバトリプタン
frozen gait すくみ足
frozen shoulder 凍結肩
frustration フラストレーション；欲求不満
frustration tolerance フラストレーション耐性；
　欲求不満耐性
Fukuyama type congenital muscular dystrophy
　福山型先天性筋ジストロフィー
full-body bath 全身浴
full-body sponge bath 全身清拭
full denture 総入れ歯
full participation and equality 完全参加と平等
full-time employment 正規雇用
full-time equivalent：FTE 常勤換算
function 機能
Functional Activities Questionnaire：FAQ 機能的
　活動質問票
functional age 機能年齢
functional approach 機能的アプローチ
functional assessment 機能評価
Functional Assessment Inventory：FAI 機能評価票
Functional Assessment of Cancer Therapy：FACT
　癌治療機能評価
Functional Assessment of Chronic Illness
　Therapy：FACIT 慢性疾患療法機能評価
functional brace 機能的装具
functional differentiation 機能分化
functional electrical stimulation：FES 機能的電気
　刺激
functional exercise 機能訓練
functional independence 機能的自立
Functional Independence Measure：FIM 機能的
　自立度評価法
functional localization 機能局在
functional magnetic resonance imaging：fMRI
　機能的MRI
functional maintenance 機能維持
functional occupational therapy 機能的作業療法
functional position 機能肢位
functional prognosis 機能予後
functional reconstruction 機能再建
functional recovery 機能回復
functional residual capacity 機能の残気量
Functional Status Questionnaire：FSQ 機能状態
　質問票
functional training 機能訓練
functionalism 機能主義；機能心理学
fundamental human rights 基本的人権
fundamental position 基本肢位
fundamental rights at work 労働基本権
funding-holding 基金所持
funeral expenses 葬祭費用

fungal endophthalmitis 真菌性眼内炎
fungal infection 真菌感染
fungemia 真菌血症
furosemide フロセミド
future of care ケアの未来

G

gabapentin ガバペンチン
Gabitril ガビトリル
Gabriel needle ガブリエル針
GAD〔generalized anxiety disorder〕 全般性不安障害
Gaffky table ガフキー号数
gait 歩行；歩容
gait ability 歩行能力
gait analysis 歩行分析
gait apraxia 歩行失行
gait assessment 歩行機能評価
gait cycle 歩行周期
gait difficulty 歩行困難
gait disability 歩行障害
gait disorder 歩行障害
gait disturbance 歩行障害
gait pattern 歩行パターン
gait training 歩行練習；歩行訓練
gait velocity 歩行速度
galantamine ガランタミン
gallstone 胆石
gambling ギャンブル
gamma sterilization ガンマ線滅菌
gangrene 壊疽
garbage 生ごみ
Garden classification system of fracture ガーデン
　骨折分類
gargling うがい
gas sterilization ガス滅菌
gastrectomy 胃切除術
gastric cancer 胃癌
gastric lavage 胃洗浄
gastric ulcer 胃潰瘍
gastritis 胃炎
gastroenterologist 消化器内科医
gastroenterology 消化器病学
gastroesophageal reflex disease：GERD
　胃食道逆流症
gastrografin enema ガストログラフィン注腸
gastrointestinal physiology 消化管生理学
gastrostomy 胃瘻；胃瘻造設
gastrostomy tube 胃瘻チューブ
gatch bed ギャッチベッド
gauze ガーゼ
gay elder 老年期ゲイ
gender 性別；ジェンダー

gender difference　性差
gender-equal society　男女共同参画社会
gender identity disorder：GID　性同一性障害
gender-related development index：GDI
　ジェンダー開発指数
gender role　性役割
gender track　ジェンダー・トラック
gene　遺伝子
general account　一般会計
general administrative field　一般行政部門
general bathtub　一般浴槽
general bed　一般病床
general condition survey　概況調査
general health education　一般健康教育
general hospital　一般病院
general household survey：GHS　一般世帯調査；
　総合世帯調査
general medical clinic　一般診療所
general practitioner：GP　一般医
general practitioner fundholder　予算保持一般医
generalized anxiety disorder：GAD　全般性不安障害
generation　世代
generation boundary　世代間境界
generatively　生殖性；次世代育成能力
generic drug　後発医薬品
generic social work　ジェネリックソーシャルワーク
genetic diagnosis　遺伝子診断
genetic testing　遺伝子検査
genetics　遺伝学
genital hygiene　陰部清拭
genital stage　性器期
genomic imprinting　ゲノム刷り込み；ゲノムインプ
　リティング；遺伝刷り込み
genuineness　真実性
geographic adjustment factor：GAF　地域差調整係数
geriatric care　高齢者ケア
geriatric care expenditures　療養費出
geriatric care management　高齢者ケアマネジメント
geriatric case management　高齢者ケースマネジメ
　ント
geriatric case manager　高齢者ケースマネジャー
geriatric dentistry　高齢者歯科学分野
Geriatric Depression Scale：GDS　老年期うつ尺度；
　老年うつ病スケール
geriatric disease　老年病
geriatric evaluation and management program
　高齢者評価・マネジメントプログラム
geriatric hospital　老人病院
geriatric intensive care unit　老人集中治療室
geriatric medical care　老人医療
geriatric medicine　老人医療
Geriatric Medicine Fellowship Program　高齢者医
　療フェローシッププログラム

geriatric mental health care　老人精神保健
geriatric nursing　高齢者看護；老人看護
geriatric syndrome　老年症候群
geriatrician　高齢者専門医
geriatrics　老年医学
germicide　殺菌剤
gerontological social work　老年社会福祉学
gerontology　老年学
gerontophobia　老人恐怖症
Gerstmann syndrome　ゲルストマン症候群
gestalt therapy　ゲシュタルト療法
gestational diabetes　妊娠糖尿病
Get-up and Go Test　起立・歩行検査
giant cell arteritis：GCA　巨細胞性動脈炎
gingiva　歯肉
Gini coefficient　ジニ係数
ginkgo biloba　銀杏
glare　まぶしい光
glasses　メガネ
glaucoma　緑内障
global aging　世界的老化
Global Assessment of Functioning：GAF　全体的
　機能評価
Global Assessment Scale：GAS　全体の評価尺度
global standards　グローバルスタンダード
globalization　グローバリゼーション
glossopharyngeal breathing　舌咽呼吸
glossopharyngeal neuralgia　舌咽神経痛
glove juice method　グローブジュース法
glucocorticoid　糖質グルココルチコイド
Glucophage　グルコファージ
glucosamine　グルコサミン
glucose　ブドウ糖；グルコース
glucose anhydride　グルコース無水物
glucose level　糖値
glucose-non-fermentative bacteria　ブドウ糖非発酵菌
glucose tolerance test　ブドウ糖負荷試験
glutaraldehyde　グルタルアルデヒド
gluteus maximus muscle　大臀筋
goal　目標
goal of care　ケア目標
goal setting　目標設定
goiter　甲状腺腫
gold sodium thiomalate　金チオリンゴ酸ナトリウム
gonarthrosis　変形性膝関節症
goniometer　関節角度計
gout　痛風
gouty arthritis　痛風性関節炎
gown technique　ガウンテクニック
grab bar　移動バー
grace period　猶予期間
grandparenting　孫育て
grant-in-aid　助成金；補助金；交付金

介護保険・介護
福祉等関連用語
英和

grant-in-aid for scientific research　科学研究費補助金
grating　グレーチング
Graves' disease　グレーブス病
Great Depression　世界大恐慌
greater trochanter　大転子部
greater trochanter fracture　大転子部骨折
greater trochanteric pain syndrome　大腿骨転子疼痛症候群
greatest happiness for the greatest number　最大多数の最大幸福
Gresham's Law　グレシャムの法則
Grievance Committee of the National Health Insurance　国保連苦情処理委員会
grievances and complaints resolution　苦情解決
grip strength　握力
gross domestic product：GDP　国内総生産
gross motor function　粗大運動能力
gross national product：GNP　国民総生産
gross national welfare：GNW　国民総福祉
ground reaction force　床反力
group counseling　グループカウンセリング
group dynamics　グループダイナミクス
group exercise　グループ運動
group home　グループホーム
group living　グループリビング
group model　グループモデル
group practice　グループ診療
group pressure　集団圧力
group psychotherapy　集団精神療法
group recreation　グループレクリエーション
group supervision　グループスーパービジョン
group therapy　集団療法
group treatment　集団処遇
group work　グループワーク；集団援助技術
group worker　グループワーカー
growth hormone　成長ホルモン
guaiac test　グアヤック検査
guarantee　保証
guarantor　保証人
guardian　後見人；保護者
guardian of minor　未成年後見人
guide dog　盲導犬
Guide to Physical Therapist Practice　理学療法士の実践ガイド
guidelines　ガイドライン
Guillain-Barre syndrome：GBS　ギラン・バレー症候群
gum disease　歯周病
gustation　味覚
gymnastics　体育
gynecologist　婦人科医
gynecology　婦人科学

H

H reflex　H 反射
H wave　H 波
habilitation　ハビリテーション
Haglund's deformity　ハグルンド奇形
hair　髪
hair removal　除毛
haircut　散髪
halazepam　ハラゼパム
half-body bath　半身浴
half-life　ハーフライフ
half lotus sitting position　半跏趺坐
hallucination　幻覚
hallux valgus　外反母趾
halo orthosis　ハロー装具
haloperidol decanoate　デカン酸ハロペリドール
halo-vest orthosis　ハローベスト
Hamilton Rating Scale for Depression：HamD　ハミルトンうつ病評価尺度
hand　手部；ハンド
hand antisepsis　手指消毒
hand bath　手浴
hand hygiene　手指衛生；手指消毒
hand wash　手洗い
handedness　利き手
handicap　社会的不利；ハンディキャップ
handrail　手すり；ハンドレール
handrail installation　手すりの設置
handrim　ハンドリム
Hansen's disease　ハンセン病
Hansen's disease control policy　ハンセン病対策
harness　ハーネス
Harris-Benedict caloric intake equation　ハリス・ベネディクト基礎エネルギー消費量算定式
Harris-Benedict equation　ハリス・ベネディクト算定式
Hartnup disease　ハートナップ病
Hartnup disorder　ハートナップ症
Harvard Medical Malpractice Study　ハーバード医療過誤研究
Hasegawa Dementia Scale：HDS　長谷川式簡易認知症スケール
Hasegawa Dementia Scale-Revised：HDS-R　長谷川式簡易認知症スケール改訂版
Hashimoto disease　橋本病
Hashimoto's thyroiditis　橋本甲状腺炎；橋本病
hay fever　花粉症
Hazard Analysis Critical Control Point system：HACCP　ハサップ
Hazardous Material　危険物；危険有害物質
HBV〈hepatitis B〉　B型肝炎

HDL〈high-density Lipoprotein〉 エッチディーエルコレステロール	hearing aid used in connection with implant 人工内耳
head trauma 頭部外傷	hearing level 聴力レベル
headache 頭痛	hearing loss：HL 難聴
Headache Classification Committee of the International Headache Society 国際頭痛学会頭痛分類委員会	hearing test 聴力検査
	heart 心臓
	heart catheterization 心臓カテーテル法
health 健康；保健	heart disease 心疾患
health and welfare 保健福祉	heart failure 心不全
health and welfare agency 保健福祉機関	heart rate 心拍数
health behavior 健康行動	heartburn 胸やけ
health behavior theory 健康行動理論	heat exhaustion 熱疲弊；熱疲労
health belief model 健康信念モデル	heat rash あせも
health care ヘルスケア	heat retention うつ熱
health care cost containment 医療費抑制策	heat stroke 熱射病；熱中症
health care proxy 医療委任状	heat therapy 温熱療法
health care reform 医療制度改革	heating, ventilation and air-conditioning：HVAC 空気調和
health center 保健センター	
health condition 健康状態	Heberden's nodes ヘバーデン結節
health counseling 健康相談	Heimlich Maneuver ハイムリッヒ法
health culture 健康文化	Helicobacter pylori ヘリコバクター・ピロリ
health education 健康教育	Heller's syndrome ヘラー症候群
health education guidelines 健康教育ガイドライン	hematemesis 吐血
health examination 健康診断	hematochezia 血便
health food 健康食品	hematocrit ヘマトクリット
health guidance 保健指導	hematology 血液学
health handbook 健康手帳	hematoma 血腫
health indicator 健康指標	hematuria 血尿
health industry 健康産業	hemianopia 半盲
health insurance 健康保険	hemiarthroplasty 人工骨頭置換術
health insurance benefit 健康保険給付	hemipelvectomy 片側骨盤切断
health insurance society 健康保険組合	hemipelvectomy prosthesis 片側骨盤用義足
health insurance system 医療保険制度	hemiplegia 片麻痺
health maintenance 健康維持	hemodialysis 血液透析
health management 健康管理	hemoglobin：Hb ヘモグロビン
health observation 健康観察	hemolytic anemia 溶血性貧血
health planning 医療計画	hemophilia 血友病
health policy 医療政策	hemophilic arthropathy 血友病性関節症
health profession 医療専門	hemoptysis 喀血
health professional 医療専門職	hemorrhagic bullae 出血性水疱
health professional shortage area 医療専門職不足地域	hemorrhagic stroke 出血性卒中
	hemorrhaging 大出血
health promotion ヘルスプロモーション；健康増進	hemostasis 止血
health-related quality of life 健康関連QOL	Hendrich's Fall Risk Assessment Tool ヘンドリック転倒危険度評価ツール
health-related services 医療関連サービス	
health risk management 健康危機管理	heparin ヘパリン
healthy carrier 健康保菌者	hepatic arterial infusion 肝動脈動注療法
healthy control 健康対照者	hepatitis 肝炎
healthy person 健常者	hepatitis A A型肝炎
healthy volunteer 健康ボランティア；健常人	hepatitis A virus A型肝炎ウイルス
hearing 聴力	hepatitis B B型肝炎
hearing ability 聴力	hepatitis B Virus B型肝炎ウイルス
hearing aid 補聴器	hepatitis C C型肝炎

hepatitis C virus　C型肝炎ウイルス
hepatitis D　D型肝炎
hepatitis D virus　D型肝炎ウイルス
hepatitis E　E型肝炎
hepatitis E virus　E型肝炎ウイルス
hepatologist　肝臓専門医
hepatology　肝臓病学
Hepsera　ヘプセラ
herbal medicine　漢方薬
Herceptin　ハーセプチン
hereditary disease　遺伝病
hereditary nonpolyposis colorectal cancer：HNCC
　家族性非ポリポーシス大腸癌
hernia of the intervertebral disc　椎間板ヘルニア
heroin　ヘロイン
heroin dependence　ヘロイン依存
herpes zoster　帯状疱疹
hertz　ヘルツ
heterotopic bone formation　異所性骨化
hiatus hernias　裂孔ヘルニア
hibernating myocardium　冬眠心筋
hibernation　冬眠
hidden cultural barrier　隠れた文化的障壁
hierarchical society　階級社会
hierarchy of needs　ニーズの階層
high altitude cerebral edema　高所脳浮腫
high altitude pulmonary edema　高所肺水腫
high deductible health insurance plan　高免責額医
　療保険
high density lipoprotein　高比重リポたんぱく質
high density lipoprotein cholesterol　HDLコレステ
　ロール
high dependency unit　高度治療室
high economic growth　高度経済成長
high efficiency particulate air filter　超高性能フィル
　タ；超高性能ろ過空気フィルタ
high level disinfection　高水準消毒
high touch surface　高頻度接触面
higher apprenticeships　高等養成訓練制度
higher brain dysfunction　高次脳機能障害
higher brain function　高次脳機能
highly advanced medical technology：HAMT
　高度先進医療
hindquarter amputation　ハインドクオーター切断
hip disarticulation prosthesis　股義足
hip fracture　股関節骨折
hip-knee-ankle-foot orthosis：HKAFO　骨盤帯付長
　下肢装具
Hippocratic Oath　ヒポクラテスの誓い
Hispanics　ラテンアメリカ系人
histamine H1 receptor blocker　ヒスタミンH1受容
　体遮断薬
histamine H2 receptor blocker　ヒスタミンH2受容
　体遮断薬
histamine receptor blocker　ヒスタミン受容体遮断薬
HIV infection　ヒト免疫不全ウイルス感染
Hoehn-Yahr stage　Yahr重症度
holiday sharing　祝日補助
holiday　祝日
holism　全体論
holistic medicine　全人的医療；ホリスティック医療
holistic rehabilitative intervention　包括的リハビリ
　テーションアプローチ
holter electrocardiogram　ホルター心電図
home assistance　在宅扶助
home care　在宅ケア；在宅介護；訪問介護
home care assessment　在宅ケアアセスメント
home care medicine　在宅医学
home care services　在宅ケアサービス
home dialysis therapy　在宅透析療法
home elevator　ホームエレベーター
home fire　自宅火災
home health　在宅看護；訪問看護
home health aide　在宅介護士；訪問介護士
home health care　在宅看護ケア；訪問看護ケア
home health care agency　在宅看護ケア機関；訪問
　看護ケア機関
home health medication management　訪問薬剤管
　理指導
Home Health Nurses Association　訪問看護協会
home health services　ホームヘルスサービス
home help　ホームヘルプ
home help services　ホームヘルプサービス
home helper　ホームヘルパー
home helping　生活援助
home improvement　住宅改善
home modification　住宅改修；住宅改造
home modification allowance　住宅改修手当
home modification benefit　住宅改修給付
home oxygen therapy：HOT　在宅酸素療法
home parenteral nutrition：HPN　在宅中心静脈栄養
home repair scam　家屋修理詐欺
home safety　住宅安全
home treatment　在宅治療
homeless　ホームレス；路上生活者
homelessness　帰る家がない
homemaker　家事援助者
homemaker services　家事援助
homemaker services provider　家事サービス提供者
homeopathic remedies　ホメオパシックレメディーズ
homeostasis　ホメオスタシス
homosexuality　同性愛
honorary position　名誉職
hooked probe　鉤ゾンデ
hormone　ホルモン
hormone receptor test　ホルモン受容体検査

hormone replacement therapy　ホルモン補充療法
Horner syndrome　ホルネル症候群
horticultural therapy　園芸療法
hospice　ホスピス
hospice care　ホスピスケア
hospital　病院
hospital accreditation　病院機能評価
hospital-acquired infection　院内感染；病院感染
hospital-acquired pneumonia　病院感染肺炎；院内肺炎
hospital-based services　病院基盤型サービス
hospital environment　病院環境
hospital infection　病院感染；院内感染
Hospital Infection Control Practices Advisory Committee：HICPAC　病院感染管理実践諮問委員会
hospital information system　病院情報システム
hospital insurance：HI　入院保険
hospital level of care　入院治療レベル
hospital stay　在院
hospital transfer　転院
hospital volunteer　病院ボランティア
hospitalism　ホスピタリズム
hospitalization　入院
hospitalization with consent　同意入院
hostile work environment　劣悪的職場環境
hostile work environment harassment　職場環境悪化型セクハラ
host-parasite relationship　宿主・寄生体関係
hot air sterilizer　乾熱滅菌器
hot biopsy　ホットバイオプシー
hot compress　温湿布
hot foment　温罨法
hot pack　ホットパック
hot water disinfection　熱水消毒
hot zone　危険区域；汚染区域
house fire　家屋火災
housebound　閉じこもり
housebound elderly　閉じこもり老人；閉じこもり高齢者
housebound syndrome　閉じこもり症候群
household　世帯
household budget　家計
household in need of public assistance　要保護世帯
households on public assistance　被保護者世帯
housekeeper　家政婦
housekeeping　家事；家事労働；家政
housing assistance　住宅扶助
housing for the aged　老人向け住宅
housing for the elderly　高齢者向け住宅
housing loan　住宅ローン
housing policy　住宅政策
hubbard tank　ハバードタンク
hue　色相

hue cancellation　色相キャンセレーション
human dignity　人間の尊厳
human engineering　人間工学
human epidermal growth factor receptor-2：HER2　ヒト上皮増殖因子受容体2型
Human Genome Project　ヒトゲノムプロジェクト
human immunodeficiency virus：HIV　ヒト免疫不全ウイルス
human lymphocyte antigen　ヒト白血球抗原
human poverty index　人間貧困指数
human resources　人的資源
human rights　人権
human rights advocacy　権利擁護
Human Rights Watch：HRW　ヒューマン ライツ・ウォッチ [国際人権擁護団体]
human science　人間科学
humanistic and existential therapy　人間学的・実存的療法
Humira　ヒュミラ
humoral regulation　液性調節
Huntington's chorea　ハンチントン舞踏病
Huntington's disease　ハンチントン病
hydralazine　ヒドララジン
hydrocodone　ヒドロコドン
hydrocollator　ハイドロコレーター
hydrogen peroxide gas plasma sterilization　過酸化水素ガスプラズマ滅菌
hydrotherapy　水治療法
hydroxychloroquine　ハイドロキシクロロキン
hygiene　衛生
hygiene laboratory technician　衛生検査技師
hygienic hand washing　衛生的手洗い
hygienics　衛生学
hygroscopic fiber　吸湿性繊維
hyperacusis　聴覚過敏
hyper-aged and depopulating society　超少子高齢社会
hyperalgesia　温痛覚過敏
hyperalimentation　高カロリー輸液
hypercapnia　高炭酸ガス血症
hypercholesterolemia　高コレステロール血症
hyperemia　充血
hyperesthesia　感覚過敏；触覚過敏
hyperextension　過伸展
hyperglycemia　高血糖症
hyperglycemic hyperosmolar nonketotic coma：HHNKC　糖尿病性高血糖性高浸透圧性昏睡
hyperkeratosis　過角化症
hyperkinesia　多動；運動亢進
hyperlipidemia　高脂血症
hyperosmolar hyperglycemic syndrome：HHS　高血糖高浸透圧症候群
hypersalivation　唾液分泌過多

介護保険・介護福祉等関連用語 英和

hypertension 高血圧	ileus 腸閉塞；イレウス
hyperthermia 高体温	illegal employment 不法就労
hyperthyroidism 甲状腺機能亢進症	illegal residence 不法滞在
hypertonia 緊張亢進；筋緊張亢進	illness behavior 病気行動
hypertrophic cardiomyopathy 肥大型心筋症	illness experience 病体験；病経験
hypertrophy 肥大	illusion 錯覚
hyperuricemia 高尿酸血症	imbalance 不均衡
hypesthesia 感覚鈍麻；触覚鈍麻	imipramine イミプラミン
hypnosis 催眠	imitation 模倣
hypnotherapy 催眠療法；ヒプノセラピー	Imitrex イミトレックス
hypnotic 睡眠剤	immigrant 移民
hypnotic drug 睡眠薬	immigrant elder 高齢移民
hypochondria 心気症	immobility 不動性
hypoglycemia 低血糖	immobilization 不動
hypokinesis 運動低下	immune system 免疫システム
hyponatremia 低ナトリウム血症	immunity 免疫
hypotension 低血圧	immunization 予防接種
hypothermia 低体温	immunoassay fecal occult blood test 免疫化学的便潜血検査
hypothyroidism 甲状腺機能低下症	
hypotonia 緊張低下；筋緊張低下	immunocompromised host 抵抗力減弱宿主；免疫低下宿主；免疫不全者
hypotonic dehydration 低張性脱水	
hypovolemic shock 循環血液量減少性ショック	immunocompromised patient 抵抗力減弱患者；免疫低下患者；免疫不全患者
hypoxemia 低酸素血症	
hysteria ヒステリー	immunodeficiency 免疫不全症
hysterosalpingography 子宮卵管造影	immunoglobulin：Ig 免疫グロブリン
	immunoglobulin A：IgA 免疫グロブリン A
I	immunoglobulin E：IgE 免疫グロブリン E
	immunoglobulin G：IgG 免疫グロブリン G
Ia reciprocal inhibition Ia 相反抑制	immunoglobulin M：IgM 免疫グロブリン M
IADL〈instrumental activities of daily living〉手段的日常生活活動	immunologic fecal occult blood test 免疫学的便潜血検査
iatrogenesis 医原病	immunoscintigraphy 免疫シンチグラフィー
iatrogenic 医原性	immunosuppressed 免疫抑制；免疫不全
ibandronate イバンドロネート	immunotherapy 免疫療法
Ibuprofen イブプロフェン	impaired fasting glucose：IFG 空腹時高血糖
ice bag 氷嚢	impaired glucose tolerance：IGT 耐糖能異常
ice pack アイスパック	impairment 機能障害；インペアメント
ice pillow 氷枕	impairment of balance function 平衡障害
Icelandic roll on silicone socket：ICEROSS シリコン製内ソケット	impingement インピンジメント；陰萎
	implantable defibrillator 植込み型除細動器
icing アイシング	imposition system 賦課方式
ICU〈intensive care unit〉集中治療室	impotence インポテンツ
ICU-acquired infection 集中治療室感染；ICU 感染	imprinting 刷り込み
ideal body weight：IBW 基準体重比	improvement 向上
ideational apraxia 観念失行	impulse インパルス
identification 身分証明書	in vitro diagnostic reagent 体外診断薬
identity アイデンティティ	in vitro diagnostic test 体外診断検査
identity crisis 同一性危機	inactivation factor 不活性化係数
identity theft 個人情報窃盗	inanimate surface 無生物表面
ideomotor apraxia 観念運動失行	inapparent infection 不顕性感染
idiopathic thrombocytopenic purpura：ITP 特発性血小板減少性紫斑病	inappropriate prescription for elderly 高齢者に対する薬剤不適切投与
ignorance 無知	inattention 注意障害

inching technique　インチング法
incidence　罹患；発生
incidence rate　罹患率；発生率
incinerator　焼却炉
inclusion　インクルージョン
inclusive evaluation　包括評価
income limit　所得制限
income redistribution　所得再分配
income security　所得保障
income tax　所得税
income test　所得テスト
incomplete cervical cord injury　不全頸髄損傷
incomplete quadriplegia　不全四肢麻痺
incongruence　不一致
incontinence　失禁
incontinence care　失禁ケア
incremental threshold　増分閾
incubation carrier　潜伏期保菌者
indemnity　賠償
independence　自立
independence center　自立センター
independence support　自立支援
independent living：IL　自立生活
independent living aid　自立生活器具
independent living skill　自立生活スキル
independent source of revenue　自主財源
independent variable　独立変数
Inderal　インデラル
indicator　インジケータ；指標
indigenous bacterial flora　常在細菌叢
indirect contact infection　間接接触感染
indirect contact spread　間接接触伝播
indirect language　間接言語
indirect social work　間接援助技術
indirect tax　間接税
indirect treatment　間接処遇
indiscrimination　無差別
individual family session　個別家族セッション
individual management　個別管理
individual psychology　個人心理学
individual quota　個人割当
individual retirement account：IRA　個人退職年金勘定
individual treatment　個別処遇
individualism　個人主義
individualization　個別化
individualized care　個別介護；個人ケア
individualized education program　個別教育プログラム
Indocin　インドシン
indomethacin　インドメタシン
indoor climate　室内気候
indoor relief　院内救助

inductive logic programming　帰納論理プログラミング
inductive method　帰納法
inductive reasoning　帰納推理
industrial accident compensation　労災補償
indwelling catheter　留置カテーテル
inequality　不平等
infant　幼児
infant mortality rate　乳児死亡率
infection　感染
infection clinical nurse specialist　感染専門看護師
infection control　感染制御；感染管理；感染対策
infection control and prevention　感染制御・予防；感染管理・予防；感染対策・予防
infection control committee　感染制御委員会；感染管理委員会；感染対策委員会
infection control doctor　感染制御医師；感染管理医師；感染対策医師
infection control nurse　感染制御看護師；感染管理看護師；感染対策看護師
infection control practitioner　感染制御専門家；感染管理専門家；感染対策専門家
infection control program　感染制御プログラム；感染管理プログラム；感染対策プログラム
infection control team　感染制御チーム；感染管理チーム；感染対策チーム
infection prevention　感染予防
infection surveillance　感染症サーベイランス
infectious disease　感染症
infectious medical waste　感染性医療廃棄物
infectious waste　感染性廃棄物
infective endocarditis　感染性心内膜炎
inflamed gum　歯肉炎
infliximab　インフリキシマブ
influenza　インフルエンザ
Influenza vaccine　インフルエンザワクチン
influenza virus　インフルエンザウイルス
informal　インフォーマル
informal care　インフォーマルケア；私的介護
informal group　インフォーマルグループ
informal network　インフォーマルネットワーク
informal resources　インフォーマル資源
informal sector　インフォーマルセクター
informal services　インフォーマルサービス
informal system　インフォーマルシステム
information network　情報ネットワーク
information system　情報システム
information technology：IT　情報技術
informationalized society　情報化社会
informed choice　インフォームド・チョイス
informed consent：IC　インフォームド・コンセント
infrared therapy　赤外線療法
infusate-related bloodstream infection　注入器材関連血流感染；注入剤関連血流感染

ingrown toenail 陥入爪
inhalation 吸息；吸入
inherently governmental activity 政府固有活動
inheritance 相続
inhibitor 阻害因子
inhibitor for rehabilitation リハビリテーション中止基準
initial cost 初期費用
initial intake 初期面接
injection 注射
injection plug インジェクションプラグ
injury 傷害
inner-city phenomenon インナーシティ現象
innocuous drug 無害の薬剤
inpatient 入院患者
inpatient hospice 入院型緩和ケア
insanity 心身喪失
insight 洞察
insight into disease 病識
insight therapy 洞察療法
insomnia 不眠症
inspection 査察
inspector 査察指導員
institutional care 施設ケア；施設介護
institutional care services 施設ケアサービス；施設介護サービス
institutional training 施設実習
institutional welfare 施設福祉
institutionalism 施設主義
instrumental activities of daily living：IADL 手段的日常生活活動；手段的 ADL
insulin インスリン
insulin-dependent diabetes mellitus：IDDM インスリン依存性糖尿病
insulin self-injection インスリン自己注射
insurance 保険
insurance agency 保険機関
insurance benefit 保険給付
insurance card 保険証
insurance company 保険会社
insurance doctor 保険医
insurance period 保険期間
insurance premium 保険料
insurance premium rate 保険料率
intake インテーク
intake conference インテークカンファレンス
intake interview インテーク面接；受理面接
integrated delivery system：IDS 統合供給システム
integrated education 統合教育
integrated health care delivery system 統合医療供給システム
integrated setting 統合された環境
integrated welfare state 統合された福祉国家

integration インテグレーション
integration of the public pension schemes 公的年金一元化
integumentary system 外皮
integumentary system 外皮系
intellectual age 知能年齢
intellectual level 知的水準
intellectual property 知的財産
intellectual property right 知的所有権
intellectualization 知性化
intelligence 知能
intelligence quotient：IQ 知能指数
intelligence test 知能検査
intelligent prosthesis インテリジェント義足
intensity-duration curve：I-D curve 強さ・時間曲線
intensive care management 集中的ケアマネジメント
intensive care unit：ICU 集中治療室
intensive reform plan 集中改革プラン
intercostal neuralgia 肋間神経痛
interdisciplinary 学際的
interdisciplinary team：IDT 多職種チーム
interest group 利益団体
interface インターフェイス
interface reflection 界面反射
interferon インターフェロン
interferon alfa インターフェロンα
interferon beta インターフェロンβ
interferon gamma インターフェロンγ
intergenerational care 世代間ケア
intergenerational redistribution 世代間再分配
intergenerational relations 世代間関係
intergenerational support 世代間扶養
interim order 仮命令
intermediary 中間支払機関
intermediate disinfection 中水準消毒剤
intermediate facility 中間施設
intermittent claudication 間歇〈間欠〉性跛行
intermittent leave 断続的休暇
intermittent pneumatic compression 間欠的空気圧迫治療
intermittent positive-pressure breathing therapy IPPB 療法；間欠的陽圧呼吸法
intermittent traction 間歇〈間欠〉牽引
intermittent urethral catheterization 間欠導尿
internal environment 内部環境
internal frame of reference 内的照合枠
internal medicine 内科
internal rotation 内旋
International Bill of Human Rights 国際人権憲章
International Classification of Diseases：ICD 国際疾病分類
International Classification of Disease, 10th revision：ICD-10 国際疾病分類第 10 版

International Classification of Functioning, Disability and Health：ICF　国際生活機能分類
International Classification of Impairments, Disabilities and Handicaps：ICIDH　国際障害分類
International Council on Social Welfare：ICSW　国際社会福祉協議会
International Covenant on Civil and Political Rights　市民的及び政治的権利に関する国際規約
International Covenant on Economic, Social and Cultural Rights　社会的及び文化的権利に関する国際規約
International Covenant on Human Rights　国際人権規約
international health　国際保健
international health and welfare　国際保健福祉
International Labour Organization：ILO　国際労働機関
International Longevity Center　国際長寿センター
international medicine　国際医療
International Organization for Standardization：ISO　国際標準化機構
International Psychogeriatric Association　国際老年精神学会
International Standard：IS　国際規格
international welfare　国際福祉
International Women's Year：IWY　国際婦人年
international year　国際年
International Year of Biodiversity：IYB　国際生物多様性年
International Year of Chemistry：IYC　国際化学年
International Year of Disabled Persons：IYDP　国際障害者年
International Year of Older Persons：IYOP　国際高齢者年
International Year of Sanitation：IYS　国際衛生年
International Year of the Child　国際児童年
International Year of the Family　国際家族年
interpersonal helping skill　対人援助技術
interpersonal relationship　対人関係
interpersonal relationship skill　対人関係スキル
interpretation　解釈
intertrochanteric fracture　転子間骨折
intervention　介入；インターベンション
intervention study　介入研究
interventional angiography　介入的血管造影
interventional radiology：IVR　介入的画像診断；画像診断の介入治療
interview　インタビュー；面接
interview survey　面接調査
intestinal string　腸ひも
intraarterial　動脈内
intraarterial digital subtraction angiography　動脈内デジタルサブトラクション

intramuscular　筋肉内
intraocular lens：IOL　眼内レンズ
intraocular pressure　眼内圧
intraoperative endoscopy　術中内視鏡検査
intraoperative ultrasonography　術中超音波検査
intratracheal foreign body　気管内異物
intratracheal injection　気管内注入
intravascular catheter　血管内留置カテーテル
intravascular catheter-related infection　血管内留置カテーテル関連感染症
intravascular ultrasound　血管内超音波法
intravenous　点滴
intravenous hyperalimentation：IVH　中心静脈高カロリー輸液法
intravenous pyelogram：IVP　経静脈腎盂造影
intravenous therapy　点滴治療
intrinsic motivation　内発的動機づけ
intrinsic sphincter deficiency：SD　内因性括約筋不全
Intron A　イントロンA
introversion　内向性
inversion　内がえし
investigation questionnaire　質問紙調査
invisible hand　見えざる手
involuntary admission　強制入所
involuntary hospitalization　強制入院
involuntary movement　不随意運動
iodine　ヨウ素
iontophoresis　イオン導入法
IQ（intelligence quotient）　知能指数
IQ test　IQテスト
iron　鉄分
iron deficiency　鉄分欠乏症
iron deficiency anemia　鉄分欠乏貧血症
irrational belief　非合理的信念
irritability　いらいら
ischemic colitis　虚血性腸炎
ischemic heart disease：IHD　虚血性心疾患
ischemic stroke　虚血性発作
ischial weight-bearing　坐骨支持
ISO International Classification for Standards：ICS　ISO国際規格分類
isoarea map　等面積図；分布図
isocarboxazid　イソカルボキサジド
isokinetic contraction　等運動性収縮
isokinetic exercise　等運動性運動
isolation　隔離
isolation precaution　隔離予防策
isolation room　隔離病室；隔離室
isolator　アイソレータ；隔離装置
isometric contraction　等尺性収縮
isometric exercise　等尺性訓練
Isoptin　イソプチン
isotonic contraction　等張性収縮

介護保険・介護福祉等関連用語・英和

isotonic exercise　等張性訓練
isovolumetric　等容
isovolumetric contraction　等容収縮；等容性収縮
isovolumetric contraction time：ICT　等容収縮時間；等容性収縮時間
isovolumetric relaxation　等容弛緩
isovolumetric relaxation time：IRT　等容弛緩時間
isovolumic　等容
isovolumic contraction　等容収縮；等容性収縮
isovolumic contraction time：ICT　等容収縮時間；等容性収縮時間
isovolumic relaxation　等容弛緩
isovolumic relaxation time：IRT　等容弛緩時間
itching　搔痒感
items of intermediate assessment　中間評価項目

J

jacuzzi　泡風呂；気泡風呂
jaundice　黄疸
job placement program　職業安定プログラム
job seeker　求職者
job seeker's benefit　求職者給付
job training　職業訓練
joint　関節；継手
joint contracture　関節拘縮
joint family　複合家族
joint moment　関節モーメント
joint prosthesis　関節補綴
joint replacement　関節置換術
joint stiffness　関節拘縮
judicial review　司法審査
judo orthopedist　柔道整復師
Jungian psychology　ユング心理学
juvenile　少年；若年性
juvenile classification office　少年鑑別所
juvenile delinquency　少年犯罪；非行
juvenile delinquent　非行少年
juvenile diabetes　若年性糖尿病
juvenile idiopathic arthritis　若年性特発性リウマチ
juvenile myoclonic epilepsy　若年性ミオクローヌスてんかん
juvenile Parkinsonism　若年性パーキンソン病
juvenile polyps　若年性ポリープ
juvenile probation officer　少年保護司
juvenile reformatory school　少年院
juvenile rheumatoid arthritis　若年性関節リウマチ

K

Katz ADL index　カッツ ALD インデックス
Kegel exercise　ケーゲル体操
Kelly pad　ケリーパッド

Kenny Self-Care Evaluation　ケニー式セルフケア評価
Keratosis　角化症
keratotic lesions　角化性病変
kernicterus　核黄疸
key person　キーパーソン
keyhole surgery　鍵穴手術
Keynesian Welfare State　ケインズ主義的福祉国家
kidney　腎臓
kidney cancer　腎癌
kidney disease　腎疾患
kidney failure　腎不全
kidney stone　腎結石
kindergarten　幼稚園
kinematic analysis　運動学的分析
Kineret　キネレット
kinesiology　運動学
kinesthesia　運動感覚
kinesthetic sense　運動覚
kinetics　運動力学
kinship care　親族ケア
Klebsiella pneumonia　クレブシエラ肺炎
Klenzak ankle joint　クレンザック足継手
Klonopin　クロノピン
Kluver-Bucy syndrome　クリューバー・ビューバー・ビューシー症候群
knee-ankle-foot orthosis：KAFO　長下肢装具
knee disarticulation prosthesis　膝義足
knee extension assist　膝用伸展補助装置
knee giving way　膝折れ
knee joint　膝継手
knee orthosis：KO　膝装具
knee pad　膝当て
knee replacement　膝関節置換術
knuckle bender　ナックルベンダ；MP屈曲補助装置
Kohs Block Design Test　コース立方体組み合わせテスト
Kondylen Bettung Munster transtibial　KBM式下腿義足
Korean War veteran　朝鮮戦争退役軍人
Korsakoff's psychosis　コルサコフ精神病
kyphosis　後弯

L

labeling　ラベリング
labetalol　ラベタロール
labile hypertension　動揺性高血圧症
labor economics　労働経済学
Labor Federation of Government Related Organizations　政府関係法人労働組合連合
labor force　労働力
labor force population　労働力人口
labor management　労務管理

labor market	労働市場
labor policy	労働政策
labor problem	労働問題
labor relation	労使関係
labor union	労働組合
labor welfare	労働福祉；福祉労働
labyrinthitis	内耳炎
lacunar dementia	まだら認知症
lacunar stroke	ラクナ梗塞
laissez faire	自由放任主義
Lamictal	ラミクタール
laminar air flow：LAF	層流
lamivudine	ラミブジン
lamotrigine	ラモトリギン
language	言語
laparoscopic surgery	腹腔鏡手術；腹腔鏡下手術
large intestine polyps	大腸ポリープ
laser doppler flowmetry	レーザードップラー血流測定
laser surgery	レーザー手術
laser therapy	レーザー治療
Lasix	ラシックス
last will	遺言書
late marriage	晩婚化
late phase rehabilitation	維持期リハビリテーション
latency	潜時
latency period	潜伏期
latent autoimmune diabetes in adults：LADA 成人潜在性自己免疫性糖尿病	
latent content	潜在内容
latent infection	潜伏感染
late-onset Alzheimer's disease	遅発性アルツハイマー病
lateral whip	外側ホイップ
later-life activity	高齢期活動
Latino elder	ラテンアメリカ系高齢者
lavage cytology	洗浄細胞診
law of effect	効果の法則
law violation	法令違反
lawmaker	立法者
laxative	緩下剤
LDL〈low-density lipoprotein〉	エルディーエルコレステロール
lead poisoning	鉛中毒
leadership	リーダーシップ
League of Nations：LON	国際連盟
lean body mass：LBM	除脂肪体重
learned helplessness	学習性無力感
learned helplessness theory	学習性無力感理論
learning ability	学習能力
learning disability：LD	学習障害
learning disability screening	LDスクリーニングテスト
learning paradigm	学習パラダイム
learning theory	学習理論
least developed country：LDC	最貧国
leather work	革細工
leave benefit	休業給付
leave of absence：LoA	休暇
leaving care	リービングケア
leflunomide	レフルノミド
left lateral recumbent	左側臥位
left-right disorientation	左右失認
left ventricular hypertrophy	左心室肥大
leg length	脚長
leg length inequality	脚長不同
leg rest	レッグレスト
legal assistance	法律支援
legal capacity	権利能力
legal employment	合法就労
legal guardian	法定代理人
legal issue	法的問題
legal obligation	法的義務
legal reception services	法定代理受領サービス
legally designated communicable disease	法定伝染病
leg-support	レッグサポート
leisure	余暇
leisure guidance	余暇指導
leisure program	レジャープログラム；余暇プログラム
lending of welfare equipments	福祉用具貸与
length of stay：LOS	入院期間；入所期間
leprosy	ハンセン病；癩
leprosy control policy	ハンセン病対策
lesbian elder	レスビアン高齢者
leukemia	白血病
level of consciousness	意識レベル
level of dementia	痴呆度
levodopa	レボドパ
Lewy body dementia	レビー小体型認知症
liberal	自由主義者
liberal welfare state	自由主義的福祉国家
libido	リビドー
Librax	リブラックス
Librium	リブリウム
licensed clinical social worker：LCSW	有資格臨床ソーシャルワーカー
licensed heath care practitioner：LHCP	有資格医療福祉職
licensed nurse	有資格看護師
licensed social worker	有資格ソーシャルワーカー
lidocaine	リドカイン
life course	ライフコース
life cycle	ライフサイクル；生活周期
life design	ライフデザイン
life event	ライフイベント
life expectancy	平均余命

介護保険・介護福祉等関連用語 英和

life extension	生延長
life functioning	生活機能
life history	生活歴
life insurance	生命保険
life insurance premium	生命保険料
life model	生活モデル；ライフモデル
life needs	生活ニーズ
life review	ライフレビュー；回想
life satisfaction	生活満足度
life skills training	生活技能訓練
life space	生活空間
life space crisis intervention	生活空間危機介入
life span	寿命
life stage	ライフステージ
life structure	生活構造
life style	ライフスタイル
life table	生命表
lifelong education	生涯教育
lifelong employment	終身雇用
lifelong employment system	終身雇用制度
lifelong housing	生涯住宅
lifelong learning	生涯学習
lifelong pension	終身年金
lifelong sports	生涯スポーツ
lifelong wages	生涯賃金
life-prolonging treatment	延命治療
life-span development	生涯発達
lifestyle	生活習慣；ライフスタイル
lifestyle-related disease	生活習慣病
life-sustaining treatment	延命治療
lift	リフト
lift bus	リフトバス
lifting platform	段差解消機
light adaptation	明順応；光順応
light reflex	対光反射
light/dark adaptation	明・暗順応
lighting	照明
lightness	明度
lightness constancy	明度の恒常性
limb-girdle muscular dystrophy	肢帯型筋ジストロフィー
limb kinetic apraxia	肢節運動失行
Limbitrol	リンビトロール
limbs	四肢
limited assistance	部分援助；部分介助；一部介助
line sepsis	留置カテーテル感染；留置カテーテル敗血症
linear causality	直線的因果律
link nurse	リンクナース；連携看護師
lip reading	読話；読唇術
lipid	脂質
lipid storage disease	脂質蓄積症
lipoprotein	リポタンパク
lipoprotein receptor-related protein：LRP	リポタンパク受容体関連蛋白
liquid diet	流動食
liquid soap	液体石鹸
lisinopril	リジノプリル
list of disability grading	身体障害者障害程度等級表
literacy program	リテラシープログラム
literature review	文献レビュー
lithium	リチウム
liver	肝臓
liver cancer	肝癌
liver cirrhosis	肝硬変
liver function test：LFT	肝機能検査
liver spots	肝斑
living assistance services	生活援助
living donor liver transplantation	生体肝移植
living environment	生活環境；住環境
living trust	生前信託
living will	リビングウィル；尊厳死宣言書
local administration	地方行政
local allocation tax	地方交付税
local authority association	地方自治体連合
local autonomy	地方自治
local governing authority	地方行政府
local government	地方自治体
local public entity	地方公共団体
locked facility	閉鎖施設
locked-in syndrome	閉じこめ症候群
locked unit	閉鎖病棟
locomotion	移動
locomotion activity	移動動作
Lofstrand crutch	ロフストランド杖
logotherapy	ロゴセラピー
loneliness	孤独
long-distance care	遠距離介護
long-distance medicine	遠距離医療
longevity	長寿
longevity science	長寿科学
longitudinal arch	縦アーチ
longitudinal study	縦断的調査
long-term care	長期ケア；長期介護
long-term care costs	介護費用
long-term care facility	介護施設
long-term care industry	長期ケア市場
long-term care needs	介護ニーズ
long-term care ombudsman	介護オンブズマン
long-term care services	介護サービス
long-term goal	長期目標
long-term memory	長期記憶
long-term volunteer	長期ボランティア
loperamide	ロペラミド
Lopressor	ロプレッサー
lorazepam	ロラゼパム

lordosis 前弯
losartan ロサルタン
loss of appetite 食欲不振；食欲低下
loss of smell 嗅覚低下
loss of taste 味覚低下
loss of touch sensation 触知覚低下
lost experience 喪失体験
lotus position 蓮華座
Lou Gehrig's disease ルー・ゲーリッグ病
love belonging needs 社会的欲求
low back pain 腰痛
low birth weight infant 低出生体重児
low-density lipoprotein：LDL　LDLコレステロール
low-fat diet 低脂肪食
low floor bus 低床バス
low frequency current therapy 低周波療法
low income 低所得
low income class 低所得層
low income country 低所得国
low income family 低所得家庭
low income household 低所得世帯
low level disinfection 低水準消毒
low temperature burn 低温火傷
low vision ロービジョン
low-wage labor 低賃金労働
low-wage labor market 低賃金労働市場
lower esophageal sphincter：LES 下部食道括約筋
lower esophageal sphincter dysfunction 下部食道括約筋機能障害
lower extremity 下肢
lower extremity orthosis 下肢装具
lower gastrointestinal 下部消化管
lower limb amputation 下肢切断
lower limb prosthesis 義足
lower motor neuron 下位運動ニューロン
lower social stratum 下層社会
lumbago 腰痛症
lumbago exercise 腰痛体操
lumbar puncture 腰椎穿刺
lumbar radiculopathy 腰髄神経症
lumbar spinal cord injury 腰髄損傷
lumbar traction 腰椎牽引
lumbar vertebrae 腰椎
lumbosacral orthosis 腰仙椎装具
lumbrical bar 虫様筋バー
luminance 輝度
lumpectomy 乳腺腫瘍摘出術
lung cancer 肺癌
lung capacity 肺活量
lung transplant 肺移植
lung volume reduction surgery 肺容量減少手術
lupus ループス
lutein ルテイン

Luvox ルボックス
luxatio coxae congenita 先天性股関節脱臼
luxation 脱臼
lycopene リコピン
Lyrica リリカ
Lysosomal storage disease ライソゾーム病；リソソーム病；リソソーム蓄積病

M

MacArthur Competence Assessment Tool for Treatment：MacCAT-T マッカーサー治療同意判断能力評価表
macro level マクロレベル
macrocytic anemia 大球性貧血
macular degeneration 黄斑変性
mad-cow disease 狂牛病
Madelung deformity マーデルング変形
magic hand マジック・ハンド
magnesium マグネシウム
magnetic resonance angiography：MRA 磁気共鳴血管撮影
magnetic resonance imaging：MRI 磁気共鳴装置
magnetic stimulation 磁気刺激
magnifying endoscopy 拡大内視鏡検査
mail survey 郵送調査法
mainstreaming メインストリーミング
maintenance メインテナンス
major depression うつ病
malacia 軟化症；異食症
maladjusted behavior 不適応行動
maladjustment 不適応
maladjustment disorder 適応障害
malignant rheumatoid arthritis 悪性関節リウマチ
malignant tumor 悪性腫瘍
mallet finger マレット指；槌指
malnutrition 栄養不良；栄養失調
malposition 不良肢位
malposture 不良姿勢
malpractice 不正行為
malpractice insurance 医療過誤保険
maltreatment マルトリートメント
mammogram マンモグラム
mammography マンモグラフィ
managed care マネジドケア
managed care plan マネジドケアプラン
managed competition マネジドコンペティション
managed cost マネジドコスト
managed health care マネジドヘルスケア
management system マネジメントシステム
mandatory retirement 定年退職
mandatory retirement system 定年制
mania マニア；狂気

manic depressive psychosis　躁うつ病
manic depressive psychosis in the elderly　老年期躁うつ病
Manifest Anxiety Scale　顕在性不安尺度
manifest content　顕在内容
manometry　検圧法
manual attendant-controlled wheelchair　介助用車いす
manual Braille writer　手動ブライユ式点字タイプライター；手動点字タイプライター
manual cleaning　用手洗浄
manual therapy　徒手療法
mapping technique　マッピング技法
marasmus　マラスムス
marginal village　限界集落
marijuana　大麻
marital deduction　配偶者控除；夫婦間控除
marital property agreement　夫婦財産契約
marital relationship　夫婦関係
marital therapy　夫婦療法
market economy　市場経済
market failure　市場の失敗
market mechanism　市場原理
market success　市場の成功
market testing　市場検定
Marplan　マープラン
marriage　結婚
marriage certificate　婚姻証明書
Marriot Seniors Volunteerism Study　マリオットシニアボランティア調査
Martin-Gruber anastomosis　マーチングリューバー吻合
Maslow's hierarchy of needs　マズローの欲求段階；マズローの欲求5段階説
mass communication　マスコミ
mass media　マスメディア
mass society　大衆社会
massage　マッサージ
massage therapy　マッサージ療法
masseur　按摩師［男性］
masseuse　按摩師［女性］
mastectomy　乳房切断術
master of social work：MSW　ソーシャルワーク修士号
mastication　咀嚼
masticatory disorder　咀嚼機能障害
masticatory disturbance　咀嚼障害
masticatory myositis　咀嚼筋炎
masturbation　マスターベーション
mat　マット
mat activity　床上動作
mat exercise　マット訓練
material abuse　物質的虐待

material culture　物質文化
maternity　母性
maternity allowance　出産手当；出産手当金
maternity assistance　出産扶助
maternity leave　産休
maternity neurosis　育児ノイローゼ
maternity protection　母性保護
matrix metalloprotease enzyme　マトリックスメタロプロテアーゼ酵素
mattress　マットレス
mattress pad　マットレスパッド
mature　円熟
Maxalt　マクサルト
maximal gait velocity　最大歩行速度
maximum conduction velocity：MCV　最大伝導速度
maximum muscle strength　最大筋力
maximum oxygen consumption　最大酸素消費量
maximum resting pressure：MRP　最大静止圧
maximum squeeze pressure：MSP　最大随意収縮圧
maximum tolerable volume　最大耐容量
McGill Pain Questionnaire：MPQ　マクギル疼痛質問表
meal　食事
meal delivery services　配食サービス
meal management　食事管理
meal preparation　食事準備
meal services　食事サービス
meal tray services　配膳
means test　資産調査；収入調査；ミーンズテスト
measles　麻疹
measurement of body temperature　体温測定
mechanical cleaning　機械洗浄
mechanical diet　機械食
mechanical soft diet　機械食
medial single hip joint system　内側単股継手システム
medial whip　内側ホイップ
medical anthropologist　医療人類学者
medical anthropology　医療人類学
medical assistance　医療扶助
medical care benefit　医療給付；療養給付
medical care expenses　医療費；療養費
medical certificate of the cause of death　死体検案書
medical check-up　健康チェック
medical coder　診療情報管理士系
medical device　医療機器；医療器具；医療用具；医療器材
medical director　医長
medical economic　医療経済
medical economic index　医療経済指数
medical education system　医師養成制度
medical equipment　医療機器；医療器具；医療用具
medical error　医療事故；医療ミス

medical ethics 医療倫理	medicine and welfare 医療福祉
medical fee 診療報酬	medicine ball メディシンボール
medical history 既往歴；治療歴	medulla oblongata 延髄
medical home care 在宅医療	medullary thyroid cancer 甲状腺髄様癌
medical home care services 在宅医療サービス	megaloblastic anemia 巨赤芽球性貧血
medical industrial complex 医療産業複合体	meiosis 減数分裂
medical insurance 医療保険	melanocyte メラニン細胞
medical insurance system 医療保険制度	melatonin メラトニン
medical interview 医療面接	melena 下血；メレナ
medical issue 医事問題	memantine メマンティン
medical leave 傷病休暇	membrane filter メンブランフィルタ
medical malpractice 医療過誤	memorial hospital 記念病院
medical malpractice liability insurance 医療過誤補償保険	memory 記憶
	memory disorder 記憶障害
medical malpractice suit 医療過誤訴訟	memory disturbance 記銘障害
medical marijuana 医療大麻	Memory Impairment Screen：MIS 記憶障害検査
medical model 医学モデル	memory retention 記銘力
medical model of disability 障害の医学モデル	Meniere's disease メニエール病
Medical Outcomes Study 36-Item Short-Form Health Survey：MOS SF-36 Health Survey 36項目健康調査票	meningeal leukemia 髄膜白血病
	meningitis 髄膜炎
	menopausal disorder 更年期障害
medical personnel 医療関係者	menopause 閉経；メノポーズ；更年期
medical practice 医療行為；医業；医行為	mental abuse 精神的虐待
Medical Practitioners' Registration Act 医師登録法	mental age：MA 精神年齢
medical profession 医療専門	mental and behavioral disorder 精神および行動の障害
medical professional 医療専門職	
medical records 医療記録	mental capacity assessment 意思能力評価
medical rehabilitation 医学的リハビリテーション	mental competency 精神の適応力
medical rehabilitation services 更生医療	mental disability 精神障害
medical resources 医療資源	mental health 精神保健
medical security 医療保障	mental health and welfare 精神保健福祉
medical security program 医療保障プログラム	mental health care メンタルヘルスケア
medical service plan 医療サービス計画	mental health clinic メンタルヘルスクリニック
medical social services 医療ソーシャルサービス	Mental Health Committees 精神医療審査会
medical social work 医療ソーシャルワーク；メディカルソーシャルワーク	mental health counselor 精神保健カウンセラー
	mental health services 精神保健サービス
medical social worker 医療ソーシャルワーカー	mental illness 精神病
medical specialist 専門医	mental retardation：MR 知的障害；精神遅滞；発達遅滞
medical staff 医療職員；医療従事者	
medical supply 医療品	mentally disabled 精神障害者
medical thermometer 体温測定器	menu 献立
medical waste 医療廃棄物	meralgia paresthetica 知覚過敏性大腿痛
medically needy 医療困窮対象者	mercury poisoning 水銀中毒
medically underserved area 無医地区；無医村；医療サービス不足地域；医療過疎地域	Meridia メリディア
	merit goods メリット財
medication 薬剤	merosin-deficient congenital muscular dystrophy メロシン欠損型先天性筋ジストロフィー
medication adherence 服薬アドヒアランス	
medication compliance 服薬遵守	mesmerize メスメリズム
medication error 誤薬；投薬過誤	metabolic disease 代謝性疾患
medication interaction 薬物相互作用	metabolic disorder 代謝異常
medication management 薬剤管理；服薬管理	metabolic equivalent of task：MET 代謝当量；メッツ
medication restriction 投薬制限	metabolic inhibitor 代謝阻害剤
medicine 医療	metabolic syndrome メタボリック症候群

介護保険・介護福祉等関連用語・英和

metabolism　代謝
metacognition　メタ認知
metal craft　金工細工
metamer　条件等色対
metamerism　条件等色
metaphor　メタファー
metastasis　転移
metatarsal bar　メタタルザルバー
metaxalone　メタキサロン
metered-dose inhaler　定量噴霧式吸入器
metformin　メトホルミン
methicillin-resistant staphylococcus aureus：
　MRSA　メチシリン耐性黄色ブドウ球菌
methocarbamol　メトカルバモール
methotrexate　メトトレキサート
methylprednisolone　メチルプレドニゾロン
metolazone　メトラゾン
metoprolol　メトプロロール
metropolitan area　大都市圏
mezzo level　メゾレベル
micro balloon　微小バルーン
micro level　ミクロレベル
microangiography　微小血管造影
microbial sampling　環境微生物調査
microbial substitute　菌交代現象
microclimate of sleeping floor　寝床気候
micro-expressions　微表情
microorganism contamination　微生物汚染
microwave therapy　極超短波療法
micturition center　排尿中枢
micturition disorder　排尿障害
MID〈multi-infarct dementia〉　多発梗塞性認知症
mid swing　遊脚中期
middle age　中年
middle-class consciousness　中流意識
mid-stance phase　立脚中期
Midtown Manhattan Study　ミッドタウンマンハッタン調査
midwife　助産師
migraine headache　偏頭痛
migrant care worker　外国人介護労働者
migrant work　出稼ぎ
mild cognitive impairment：MCI　軽度認知障害
miliary tuberculosis　粟粒結核症
Milwaukee brace　側弯症装具
minced meal　ミンチ食
mind-body medicine　心身医学
mineral　ミネラル；無機質
mineral deficiency　ミネラル欠乏症
mineral excess　過剰ミネラル
mineral supplementation　ミネラル補給
Mini Mental State Examination：MMSE　ミニメンタルステータス試験

Mini Nutritional Assessment：MNA　簡易栄養状態アセスメント
mini stroke　ミニ脳卒中
minimal brain damage：MBD　微細脳機能損傷
minimal erythema dose：MED　最小紅斑量
minimally invasive surgery　最小侵襲手術
minimum cost of living　最低生活費
Minimum Data Set：MDS　ミニマムデータセット
minimum standard　最低水準
minimum standard of living　最低生活
minimum wage　最低賃金
minimum wage system　最低賃金制度
Minipress　ミニプレス
Minnesota Multiphasic Personality Inventory：
　MMPI　ミネソタ多面人格目録
minor　未成年者；未成年
minor brain damage：MBD　微細脳損傷
minor child　未成年の子供
minor registry　未成年者登記簿
minority　少数派；マイノリティ
minority group　少数派グループ
minutes　議事録
miosis　縮瞳
Mirapex　ミラペックス
mirror writing　鏡像書記
misdiagnosis　誤診
misuse　誤用
misuse syndrome　誤用症候群
mitochondrial disease　ミトコンドリア病
mitral regurgitation　僧帽弁閉鎖不全
mitral stenosis　僧帽弁狭窄症
mixed dementia　混合型認知症
mixed hearing loss　混合性難聴
Miyake Paired Verbal Association Learning Test
　三宅式記銘力検査
mobile arm support　万能腕動作支持器
mobile room air cleaner　可動式室内空気清浄機
mobility　移動性；可動性
mobility aid　移動関連福祉用具；移動補助具；歩行補助機器
mobility skill　移動技能
mobilization　モビライゼーション；受動術
modeling　モデリング
modernization　近代化；現代化
modernization theory　近代化論
Modified Ashworth Scale　改訂アッシュワース尺度
modified Barthel index　改訂バーセル指数
Modified Water Swallow Test　改訂水飲みテスト
modular prosthesis　モジュラー義肢
modular seating system　モジュラー式座位保持システム
modular wheelchair system　モジュラー車いす
module　モジュール

Mohs surgery　モース術
moist heat sterilization　湿熱滅菌
moist heating　湿性温熱
monetary needs　貨幣的ニーズ
money management　金銭管理
monitoring　モニタリング
monitoring measurement　モニター測定
monoamine oxidase inhibitor　モノアミン酸化酵素阻害薬
monochromatic light　単色光
monoplegia　単麻痺
monopolization　業務独占
monosaccharide　単糖類
monosaccharide anhydride　単糖無水物
monosynaptic reflex　単シナプス反射
monthly charge　月割賦課
monthly premium　月額保険料
monthly：1M　毎月
mood　気分
mood disorder　気分障害
moral hazard　モラルハザード
morale　モラール
moratorium　モラトリアム
morbidity compression　病的状態の圧縮；傷病平均年数の圧縮
morbilli　麻疹
morgue　遺体安置所
Morita therapy　森田療法
morphine　モルヒネ
morphine dependence　モルヒネ依存
mortality rate　死亡率
mothball　防虫剤
motherhood　母性
motherless family　父子家庭
mother-to-child transmission　母子感染
motion analysis　動作分析
motion control　運動制御
motivation　動機
motor age　運動年齢
motor age test　動年齢テスト
motor aphasia　運動性失語；運動失語
motor apraxia　運動失行
motor assessment　運動評価
motor ataxia　運動失調；運動失調症
motor development　運動発達
motor developmental evaluation　運動発達評価
motor evoked potential　運動誘発電位
motor function　運動機能
motor impairment　運動障害
motor impersistence　運動維持困難
motor learning　運動学習
motor nerve　運動神経
motor nerve conduction velocity　運動神経伝導速度

motor neuron　運動ニューロン
motor neuron disease　運動ニューロン疾患
motor paralysis　運動麻痺
motor point　運動点
motor point block　運動点ブロック；モーターポイントブロック
motor skill　運動技能
motor unit　運動単位
motor unit action potential：MUAP　運動単位活動電位
motor vehicle accident　自動車事故
mourning　喪
mouth-to-mouth breathing　口対口人工呼吸
mouth-to-nose breathing　口対鼻人工呼吸
mouton　ムートン
movement　運動；動作
movement analysis　運動分析
movement disorder　運動障害
movement during swallowing　嚥下運動
movement dysfunction　運動障害
movement-related functional limitation　運動制限
moving around by wheelchair　車いすの移動
moving expenses　転勤費用
mucocutaneous lymph node syndrome　川崎病
mucopolysaccharidosis　ムコ多糖症
muffled voice　含み声
multidimensional functional assessment　多次元的機能評価
multidimensional poverty index：MPI　多次元貧困指数
multi-drug resistance：MDR　多剤耐性
multi-drug resistant tuberculosis：MDR-TB　多剤耐性結核
multi-infarct dementia　多発梗塞性認知症
Multilevel Assessment Instrument：MAI　多段階評価
multimodal therapy　多面の療法
Multiphasic Environmental Assessment Procedure：MEAP　包括的環境要因調査票
multiple cerebral infarction　多発性脳梗塞
multiple disabilities　重複障害
multiple handicapped　重複障害者
multiple handicapped child　重複障害児
multiple handicaps　重複障害
multiple interviews　重複面接
multiple organ dysfunction syndrome：MODS　多臓器不全症候群
multiple organ failure　多臓器不全
multiple personality disorder　多重人格障害
multiple sclerosis：MS　多発性硬化症
multiple system atrophy：MSA　多系統萎縮症
multipotent　多分化能；多能
multipotent adult progenitor cell　成人型多能性体性幹細胞

multipotent drug　強力な薬
multipurpose senior center　高齢者多目的福祉センター
multivariate analysis　多変量解析
mumps　流行性耳下腺炎
municipal court　自治体裁判所
Munsell color system　マンセル表色系
murder　殺人
muscle　筋
muscle biopsy　筋生検
muscle contracture　筋拘縮；筋拘縮症
muscle cramp　筋クランプ；筋痙攣
muscle endurance　筋持久力
muscle fatigue　筋疲労
muscle fiber conduction velocity　筋線維伝導速度
muscle fiber type　筋線維タイプ
muscle hypertonia　筋緊張亢進
muscle hypertrophy　筋肥大
muscle hypotonia　筋緊張低下
muscle maintenance　筋力維持
muscle reeducation　筋再教育
muscle relaxant　筋弛緩剤
muscle strength　筋力
muscle strength measurement　筋力測定
muscle strengthening exercise　筋力強化訓練
muscle tonus　筋緊張
muscular atrophy　筋萎縮
muscular dystrophy　筋ジストロフィー
muscular strengthening　筋力強化
muscular weakness　筋力低下
musculoskeletal disease　筋骨格疾患
musculoskeletal system　筋骨格系
music therapy　音楽療法
mutations of genes　遺伝子の突然変異
mutual aid　相互扶助
mutual aid association　共済組合
mutual aid pension　共済年金
mutual aid system　共済制度
myalgic encephalomyelitis　筋痛性脳脊髄炎
myasthenia gravis：MG　重症筋無力症
mycosis　真菌症
myelodysplastic syndrome　骨髄異形成症候群
myelopathy　脊髄症
myocardial infarction　心筋梗塞
myocardial ischemia　心筋虚血
myoclonic seizure　ミオクロニー発作
myoclonus　ミオクローヌス
myoclonus epilepsy　ミオクローヌスてんかん
myodesopsia　飛蚊症
myoelectric upper limb prosthesis　筋電義手
myofascial pain syndrome：MPS　筋筋膜性疼痛症候群
myofascial release　筋膜リリース

myoglobin　ミオグロビン
myopathy　ミオパチー
myositis　筋炎
myositis ossificans　骨化性筋炎
myotonia　ミオトニア
myotonic dystrophy　筋強直性ジストロフィー

N

nail　爪
naltrexone　ナルトレキソン
Namenda　ナメンダ
Naprosyn　ナプロシン
naproxen　ナプロキセン
narcissistic caregiver　自己愛性介護者
narcissistic personality disorder　自己愛性人格障害
narcotic　麻薬
narcotic addicted　麻薬中毒者
narcotic addicted infant　麻薬中毒乳児
narcotic addiction　麻薬中毒
narcotics　ナルコティクス
Nardil　ナルジル
narrative approach　ナラティブ・アプローチ
narrative therapy　ナラティブ・セラピー
nasal　経鼻
nasal tube feeding　経鼻経管栄養
National Association of Social Workers code of ethics　全米ソーシャルワーカー協会の倫理綱領
national burden rate　国民負担率
National Cancer Institute　国立がん研究センター
national census　国勢調査
national hospital　国立病院
national income：NI　国民所得
national minimum　ナショナルミニマム
national minimum standards　国家最低基準
national minimum wage　国家最低賃金
national minimum wage compliance officer　国家最低賃金監督官
national responsibility　国家責任
national service framework：NSF　サービスフレームワーク
nationalism　国家主義；ナショナリズム
nationality　国籍
Native American　アメリカ先住民
natural disaster　天災；自然災害
natural fiber　天然繊維
naturally occurring retirement community　自然発生的退職者コミュニティ
nausea　嘔気；吐き気
near-infrared　近赤外線
nebulizer　ネブライザー
neck distortion　頸椎捻挫
necrosis　壊死

nectar liquid diet　ネクター状液体食
need for public assistance　要保護性
needle biopsy　針生検
needle cytology　穿刺細胞診
needle electromyogram　針筋電図
needle puncture　針穿刺
needlestick　針刺し
needlestick injury　針刺し事故；針刺し創
needs　ニーズ
needs assessment　ニーズ・アセスメント
needs-response principle　必要即応の原則
needs survey　ニーズ調査
needy person　困窮者
negative mold　陰性モデル
negative pressure pulmonary edema　陰圧性肺水腫
negative punishment　負の罰
negative reinforcement　負の強化
neglect　ネグレクト；放棄；怠慢
neighborhood association　町内会
neoconservatives　新保守主義
Neonatal Behavior Assessment Scale　新生児行動評価
neonatal intensive care unit：NICU　新生児集中治療室
neonatal mortality rate　新生児死亡率
neonate　新生児
nephrectomy　腎摘除
nephritic syndrome　ネフローゼ症候群
nephrologist　腎臓専門医
nephrology　腎臓学
nerve block　神経ブロック
nerve conduction velocity：NCV　神経伝導速度
nerve entrapment　神経絞扼
nervous tissue　神経組織
net balance of the settled account　実質収支
net national welfare　国民福祉指標
net profit and loss　純損益
network　ネットワーク
network model　ネットワークモデル
networking　ネットワーキング
neuralgia　神経痛
neurocirculatory asthenia　神経循環無力症
neurodegenerative disease　神経変性疾患
neurodevelopmental approach　神経発達的アプローチ
neurofeedback　ニューロフィードバック
neurogenic bladder　神経因性膀胱
neurogenic muscle atrophy　神経原性筋萎縮
neurogenic pulmonary edema　神経原性肺水腫
neurogenic shock　神経原性ショック
neurological condition　神経学的状態
neurological examination　神経学的検査
neurologist　神経学者
neurology　神経学

neuromuscular disease　神経筋疾患
neuromuscular facilitation technique　神経筋促通法
Neurontin　ニューロンチン
neuro-oncologist　神経腫瘍医
neuro-oncology　神経腫瘍学
neuropathic pain　神経原性疼痛
neuropathy　神経障害；ニューロパチー
neurophysiological approach　神経生理学的アプローチ
neurophysiologist　神経生理学者
neurophysiology　神経生理学
neuropsychological evaluation　神経心理学的評価
neuropsychological test　神経心理学的検査
neuropsychologist　神経心理学者
neuropsychology　神経心理学
neurosis　神経症；ノイローゼ
neurosurgical care unit　脳神経外科集中治療室
neurotic disorder　神経症性障害
neutral position　中間位；中立位
new daily persistent headache：NDPH　新規発症持続性連日性頭痛
new federalism　新連邦主義
New York Heart Association functional classification　ニューヨーク心臓協会心機能分類
newborn infant period　幼児期
Niacin　ナイアシン
niche　ニッチ
nidus　病巣
night blindness　夜盲
night care　ナイトケア
night shift　夜勤
night-time delirium　夜間せん妄
night watchman state　夜警国家
nightmare　悪夢
Nishimura Dementia Scale：NMS　N式精神機能検査
nitrate　硝酸塩
nitrogen dioxide　二酸化窒素
nitroglycerin：NG　ニトログリセリン
no added salt：NAS　無塩
no added salt diet　無塩食
nocturia　夜尿症
noise　騒音
nominal wage　名目賃金
nonagenarian　90代
non-atherosclerotic coronary artery disease　非アテローム性冠動脈疾患
non-cancer patient　非癌疾患患者
non-contributory benefit　無拠出給付
non-contributory pension　無拠出年金
non-contributory retirement pension　無拠出退職年金
non-countable asset　算入不可能資産
non-critical　ノンクリティカル；非侵襲的
non-discrimination and equality　無差別平等

non-distribution constraint　非配分の原則
non-esterified fatty acid　遊離脂肪酸
non-governmental organization：NGO　非政府組織
non-insulin-dependent diabetes mellitus：NIDDM　インスリン非依存性糖尿病
non-invasive diagnostic test　非侵襲性検査
non-judgmental attitude　非審判的態度
nonmaleficence principle　無害性原理
non-monetary needs　非貨幣的ニーズ
non-partisan voter　無党派層
non-payment　滞納
non-payment of premium　保険料滞納
non-penal fine　過料
non-prescription drug　非処方箋薬
non-pressure bedding　無圧布団
non-profit advocacy　非営利アドボカシー
non-profit organization：NPO　非営利組織
non-rapid eye movement〈NREM〉sleep　ノンレム睡眠
non-slip　滑り止め；ノンスリップ
non-slip mat　滑り止めマット；ノンスリップマット
non-slip tape　滑り止めテープ；ノンスリップテープ
non-small cell lung cancer：NSCLC　非小細胞肺癌
non-steroidal antiinflammatory drug：NSAID　非ステロイド系抗炎症薬
non-tuberculous mycobacterial infection　非結核性抗酸菌症
non-verbal communication　非言語的コミュニケーション
non-weight bearing brace　体重免荷装具
non-weight-bearing orthosis　免荷装具
normal blood pressure　正常血圧
normal curve　正規曲線
normal flora　正常細菌叢
normal pressure hydrocephalus　正常圧水頭症
normal temperature　平熱
normal value　正常値
normalization　ノーマライゼーション
normocytic anemia　正球性貧血
norovirus　ノロウイルス
Norpramin　ノルプラミン
nortriptyline　ノルトリプチリン
Norvasc　ノルバスク
nosocomial infection　院内感染；病院感染
nostalgia　ノスタルジア
not applicable：N/A　非該当
Not in Education, Employment or Training：NEET　ニート
notarial deed　公正証書
notary public　公証人
nothing by mouth〈nulla per os〉：NPO　絶食
nuclear cardiology　核心臓学
nuclear family　核家族

nuclear heart scan　核心臓スキャン
nuclear scanning　核スキャン
number of patients receiving medical care　受療数
Numeric Rating Scale：NRS　数値評価スケール
nurse　看護師
nurse aide　看護助手
nurse assistant　看護補助員
nursery rhyme　童謡
nursing　看護
nursing home　ナーシングホーム
nursing notes　介護日誌；看護日誌
nursing personnel　看護関係者
nursing profession　看護専門
nursing professional　看護専門職
nursing records　介護記録
nursing shortage　看護師不足
nursing staff　看護職員；看護従事者
nutrient　栄養素
nutrient intake　栄養摂取量
nutrition　栄養
nutrition care management　栄養ケアマネジメント
nutrition care plan　栄養ケア計画
nutrition improvement　栄養改善
nutrition screening initiative：NSI　栄養スクリーニング推進財団
nutrition services　栄養サービス
nutrition therapy　食事療法
nutritional assessment　栄養評価
nutritional disturbance　栄養障害
nutritional education　栄養指導
nutritional intake　栄養摂取
nutritional management　栄養管理
nutritional problem　栄養問題
nutritional requirement　栄養必要量
nutritional screening　栄養スクリーニング
nutritional status　栄養状態
nutritional support　栄養補給
nutritive value of foods　栄養価

O

obesity　肥満
obesity hypoventilation syndrome　肥満低換気症候群
obesity index　肥満指数
oblate　オブラート
observation　観察
observation unit　経過観察病棟
obsessive compulsive disorder：OCD　強迫性障害
obsessive compulsive disorder medication　強迫性障害薬
obstructive sleep apnea　閉塞型睡眠時無呼吸
obstructive sleep apnea syndrome：OSAS　閉塞型睡眠時無呼吸症候群

英語	日本語
occipital neuralgia	後頭神経痛
occult blood test	潜血試験
occupancy rate	占床率
occupational assistance	生業扶助
occupational change	転職
occupational disease	職業病
occupational exposure	職業曝露；業務上曝露
occupational group insurance	職域保険
occupational infection	職業感染
occupational injury	労働災害
Occupational Safety and Health Administration：OSHA	労働安全衛生庁
occupational therapist：OT	作業療法士
occupational therapy	作業療法
octogenarian	80代
odynophagia	嚥下痛
OECD〈Organization for Economic Co-operation and Development〉	経済協力開発機構
Oedipus complex	エディプス・コンプレックス
Oedipus phase	エディプス期
offenders rehabilitation	更生保護
office automation	OA化
official development assistance：ODA	政府開発援助
off-the-job-training：OFF-JT	職場外訓練
ointment	軟膏
olanzapine	オランザピン
old-age	老年期
old-age assistance：OAA	老齢扶助
old-age disorder	高齢期障害
old-age employees' pension	老齢厚生年金
old-age insurance	老齢保険
old-age pension	老齢年金
old-age reserve account	老齢積立口座
older worker	高年齢労働者
oldness	老い
oliguria	乏尿
olmesartan	オルメサルタン
ombudsman	オンブズマン
ombudsperson	オンブズパーソン
oncologist	腫瘍医
oncology	腫瘍学
one-handed activity	片手動作
online education	通信教育
on-site assessment	訪問調査
on-site evaluation	訪問調査
on-site interview	訪問面接
on-site survey	訪問調査
on-the-job-training：OJT	職場訓練
onychia	爪炎
onychodystrophy	爪ジストロフィー
onychogryphosis	爪甲鉤弯症
onychomycosis	爪真菌症；爪白癬
open biopsy	直視下生検
open drainage system	開放式ドレナージ法
open enrollment period	開放登録期間
open facility	開放施設
open fracture	開放性骨折
open kinetic chain	開運動連鎖
open-panel	開放名簿制
operant conditioning	オペラント条件づけ
operant technique	オペラント技法
operating room：OR	手術室
operating suite	手術衣
operating theater	手術室
operation gown	手術用ガウン
operation room registered nurse：OR RN	手術室看護師
ophthalmologist	眼科医
ophthalmology	眼科学
opiate addiction	アヘン中毒
opiate dependence	アヘン依存
opinion poll	世論調査
opinion survey	意識調査
opioid medication	オピオイド薬
opioid-related disorder	アヘン類関連障害
opponens bar	対立バー
opponens splint	対立装具
opponent color	反対色
opportunistic infection	日和見感染
optional categorically needy	選択的制度困窮対象者
optional enrollment	任意加入
optometrist	検眼医；眼鏡士
optometry	検眼
oral and maxillofacial surgeon	口腔顎顔面外科医
oral and maxillofacial surgery	口腔顎顔面外科
oral appliance	口内装置
oral apraxia	口腔失行
oral cancer	口腔癌
oral cavity	口腔
oral disease	口腔疾患
oral health	口腔衛生
oral health assessment	口腔保健アセスメント
oral health care	口腔ケア
oral hygiene	口腔清掃行動
oral intake	経口摂取
oral medication	内服薬
oral propulsive phase	口腔相
oral rehydration therapy	経口補液療法
oral stage	口唇期
oral status	口腔状態
oral temperature	口腔温
oral thermometry	口腔検温
oral transmission	経口感染
organ donation	臓器提供
organ transplantation	臓器移植
organic mental disorder	器質性精神疾患

介護保険・介護福祉等関連用語 英和

organization 組織
Organization for Economic Co-operation and Development：OECD 経済協力開発機構
organizational socialization 組織社会化
orientation 見当識
orlistat オルリスタット
orthodontic appliance 矯正装置
orthopedics 整形外科
orthopnea 起座呼吸
orthoptist：ORT 視能訓練士
orthosis 装具；補装具
orthosis and prosthesis 義肢装具
orthostatic hypotension 起立性低血圧
orthotic treatment 装具療法
orthotics 装具学
ossification of the posterior longitudinal ligament：OPLL 後縦靱帯骨化症
osteoarthritis：OA 変形性関節症
osteomalacia 骨軟化症
osteopenia 骨欠乏症；骨減少性
osteoporosis 骨粗鬆症
ostomate オストメイト
ostomy aid ストーマ用品
OT〈occupational therapist〉 作業療法士
otitis media 中耳炎
otolaryngologist 耳鼻咽喉科医
otolaryngology 耳鼻咽喉学
ototoxic substance 聴器毒性物質
Ottawa Charter for Health Promotion オタワ憲章
out of bed 離床
out of pocket 自費支払い
outbreak アウトブレイク；集団発生；大発生
Outcome and Assessment Information Set：OASIS 在宅ケアアセスメント；オアシス
outdoor relief 院外救助
out-of-pocket 自己支払い
outpatient 通院患者
outpatient care 外来ケア
outpatient care 外来ケア；日帰り介護
outpatient clinic 外来診療所
outpatient medicine 外来診療
outpatient rate 通院者率
outpatient rehabilitation 通所リハビリテーション；外来リハビリテーション
outreach アウトリーチ
ovarian cancer 卵巣癌
over work weakness 過用性筋力低下
overbed table オーバーベッドテーブル
overcompensation 過補償
overeating 過食
overflow incontinence 溢流性尿失禁
overgrowth 過重成長
overkill オーバーキル

overpayment of premium 過誤納額
overpopulation 過密人口
overprotection 過保護
over-the-counter medication 市販薬
overuse 過用
overuse syndrome 過用症候群
own house 持ち家
owner's payment 事業主負担金
oxycodone オキシコドン
OxyContin オキシコンチン
oxygen 酸素
oxygen concentrator 酸素濃縮器
oxygen consumption 酸素消費
oxygen intake 酸素摂取
oxygen therapy 酸素療法
ozone オゾン

P

pacemaker ペースメーカー
Pacific Islander 太平洋諸島出身者
pad パッド
paid time off：PTO 有給休暇
paid voluntary 有償ボランタリ
paid volunteer 有償ボランティア
pain 疼痛
pain clinic ペインクリニック
pain control 疼痛管理
Pain Disability Assessment Scale：PDAS 疼痛生活障害評価尺度
pain disorder 疼痛性障害
pain management 疼痛マネジメント；疼痛管理
pain medication 疼痛薬
pajamas パジャマ
palliative 緩和
palliative care 緩和ケア
palliative care bed 緩和ケア病床
palliative care unit 緩和ケア病棟
palmar flexion 掌屈
palpation 触診
palpitation 動悸
palsy 麻痺
Pamelor パメロール
pancreas 膵臓
pancreatic cancer 膵臓癌
pancreatitis 膵炎
panel heater パネルヒーター
panic disorder パニック障害
pantothenic acid パントテン酸
paper diaper 紙おむつ
Papez circuit パペッツ回路
papillary thyroid cancer 甲状腺乳頭癌
paradigm パラダイム

paradoxical directive　逆説的指示
paradoxical incontinence　奇異性尿失禁
paradoxical intention　逆説的志向
paraffin bath　パラフィン浴
parallel bar　平行棒
Paralympics　パラリンピック
paralysis　麻痺
paralytic side　麻痺側
paranoia　偏執病
paraparesis　不全対麻痺
paraphasia　錯語
paraphrenia　パラフレニー
paraplegia　対麻痺
parasite single　パラサイト・シングル
parasympathetic nerve　副交感神経
parent-centered　保護者中心
parent-child relationship　親子関係
parent group　親の会
parental authority　親権
parental leave　育児休業
parental leave allowance　育児休業手当金
parenteral feeding　非経口栄養
parenteral nutrition　静脈栄養法
parenthood tax rebate　扶養者税額控除
parenting　子育て
parenting support　子育て支援
paresis　不全麻痺；麻痺
paresis　麻痺；不全麻痺
Pareto optimum　パレート最適
Parkinsonism　パーキンソニズム
Parkinson's disease　パーキンソン病
Parkinson's syndrome　パーキンソン症候群
Parnate　パルネート
parole officer　保護司
paroxysmal supraventricular tachycardia　発作性上室頻拍症
partial affairs association　一部事務組合
partial bath　部分浴
partial hepatectomy　部分肝切除
partial pension　部分年金
partial sponge bath　部分清拭
participant　参加者；加入者
participation　参加；加入
participation restriction　参加制約；加入制約
particle counter　パーティクルカウンタ；空中塵埃測定器；空中浮遊微粒子測定器
partner dog　介助犬
part-time staff　非常勤職員
part-time work　パートタイム労働
part-time worker　パートタイム労働者
passive exercise　他動運動
passive range of motion　他動可動域
paste meal　ペースト食

pasteurization　低温殺菌；パスツリゼーション
pasteurizer　低温殺菌器
patellar tendon bearing ankle-foot orthosis　PTB式短下肢装具
patellar tendon bearing transtibial prosthesis　PTB式下腿義足
paternalism　父性的温情主義；パターナリズム
pathogenic organism　病原体
pathological bone fracture　病的骨折
pathology test　病理検査
patient　患者
patient advocacy　患者擁護
patient-centered medicine　患者中心医療
patient-controlled analgesia：PCA　自己調節鎮痛法
patient-provider relationship　患者・提供者間関係
patient records　患者記録；カルテ
patient safety　患者の安全
patient satisfaction survey　患者満足度調査
patient survey　患者調査
patient's instructions for use　使用上の注意
patients' rights　患者の権利
Paxil　パキシル
Paxipam　パキシパム
payment fund　支払基金
payroll deduction　給与天引
peace　平和
peace movement　平和運動
peace study　平和学
pectus excavatum　漏斗胸
pediatric　小児科
pediatric advanced life support　小児に対する二次救命心肺蘇生法・処置
pediatric endoscopy　小児内視鏡検査
pediatric home health　小児在宅医療
pediatrician　小児科医
peer counseling　ピアカウンセリング
peer group　ピアグループ
peer group supervision　ピアグループスーパービジョン
peer relationship　仲間関係
peer supervision　ピアスーパービジョン
peer support　ピアサポート
Pegasys　ペガシス
pegboard　ペグボード
pegylated interferon　ペグインターフェロン
pelvic band　骨盤帯
pelvic floor relaxation　骨盤底弛緩
pelvic fracture　骨盤骨折
penal code　刑法典
penal regulation　罰則
penalty　罰金
pendulum test　振り子試験
penicillin　ペニシリン

介護保険・介護福祉等関連用語　英和

pension 年金
pension benefit 年金給付
pension benefits standards 年金給付基準
Pension Benefits Standards Act 年金給付基準法
pension fund 年金基金
pension insurance system 年金保険制度
pension mathematics 年金数理
pension reserve fund 年金積立基金
pension system 年金制度
pensionable age 年金受給資格年齢；支給開始年齢
pensioner 年金受給者
people's capitalism 人民資本主義
peptic ulcer 消化性潰瘍
peracetic acid 過酢酸
percentage of patients receiving annual dental exams 歯科検診受療率
percentage of patients receiving medical care 受療割合
perception 知覚
percussion パーカッション
percutaneous endoscopic gastrostomy：PEG 経皮内視鏡的胃瘻造設術
percutaneous ethanol injection 経皮的エタノール注入療法
percutaneous implantable electrode 経皮的埋め込み電極
percutaneous infection 経皮感染
percutaneous transhepatic cholangiodrainage 経皮経肝的胆管ドレナージ
percutaneous transluminal coronary angioplasty 経皮経管的冠動脈形成術
percutaneous transluminal coronary recanalization 経皮経管的冠動脈再開通術
performance principle 業績主義
peri〈perineal〉care 陰部洗浄
periarteritis nodosa 結節性動脈周囲炎
perinatal mortality rate 周産期死亡率
perindopril ペリンドプリル
perineal〈peri〉care 陰部洗浄
perineum 会陰
period of apprenticeship 見習い期間
period of employment 雇用期間
period of insurance 保険期間
periodic health evaluation：PHE 定期的健康診断
periodic leg movement 周期性四肢運動
periodic leg movement disorder：PLMD 周期性四肢運動異常症
periodic limb movement disorder 周期性四肢運動障害
periodontal disease 歯周病
periodontitis 歯周病
periodontium 歯周組織
peripheral arterial disease：PAD 末梢動脈疾患

peripheral edema 末梢浮腫
peripheral facial nerve palsy 末梢性顔面神経麻痺
peripheral nerve 末梢神経
peripheral nerve palsy 末梢神経麻痺
peripheral neuropathy 末梢神経障害
peripheral parenteral nutrition：PPN 末梢静脈栄養法
peripheral vascular disease 末梢循環障害
peripheral vestibular dysfunction 末梢前庭機能不全
peripheral vision 周辺視野
peristalsis 蠕動運動
peritoneal dialysis：PD 腹膜透析
peritoneal lavage 腹腔洗浄
peritoneography 腹膜造影
permanent domicile 本籍
permanent tooth 永久歯
permissible exposure limit：PEL 許容曝露濃度
pernicious anemia 悪性貧血
perseveration 保続症
persistent activity 持続活性
persistent disturbance of consciousness 遷延性意識障害
person bringing up 養育者
person in need of public assistance 要保護者
personal assistance services 個人支援サービス
personal care 身体介護
personal care services 対人ケアサービス
personal change 個人内変動
personal-controlled analgesia：PCA 患者調節鎮痛法
personal emergency device 個人の救助器具
personal guardianship 身上監護
personal hygiene 整容；個人衛生
personal hygiene activity 整容動作
personal hygiene assistance 整容介助
personal information 個人情報
Personal Information Protection Act 個人情報保護法
personal insurance 私的保険
personal pension 個人年金；私的年金
personal pension premium 個人年金保険料
personal pension scheme 個人年金プラン
personal protective equipment：PPE 個人防御用装備；個人防護用器材
personal social services 対人社会サービス
personality 人格；性格；パーソナリティ
personality disorder 人格障害
personality inventory 人格検査質問紙
personality test 人格検査；性格検査
personnel costs 人件費用
personnel expenditures 人件費出
pervasive developmental disorder：PDD 広汎性発達障害
pes planus 扁平足
pessary ペッサリー
pest house 隔離病院

英語	日本語
PET	ペット
petition	陳情
phacoemulsification	水晶体乳化吸引術
phallic stage	男根期
phantom limb pain	幻肢痛
phantom limb sensation	幻肢
pharmaceutical costs	薬剤費
pharmaceutical inspection	薬事監視
pharmaceutical inspector	薬事監視員
pharmaceutical services	調剤サービス
pharmacist	薬剤師
pharmacodynamic change	薬理学的変化
pharmacokinetic change	薬物動態的変化
pharmacotherapy	薬物療法
pharmacy	薬局
pharyngeal passage time	咽頭通過時間
pharyngeal phase	咽頭相
pharynx	咽頭
phenelzine	フェネルジン
phenol block	フェノールブロック
phenomenology	現象学
philanthropy	博愛事業
philanthropy	フィランソロピー
philological research	文献研究
philological study	文献検討
PHN：post-herpetic neuralgia	帯状疱疹後神経痛
phobia	恐怖症
photoaging	光老化
photodynamic therapy	光線力学療法
photophobia	羞明
photopigment	感光色素
photoreceptor	視細胞
physiatrist	リハビリテーション医
physical abuse	身体的虐待
physical activity	身体活動量
physical aggression	身体的攻撃
physical barrier	物理的障壁
physical conditioning	身体調整
physical contact	スキンシップ
physical deconditioning	身体デコンディショニング
physical dependence	身体依存
physical disability	身体障害
physical exercise for Parkinson's disease	パーキンソン体操
physical fitness	体力
physical function	身体機能
physical independence	身辺自立
physical medicine	物理医学
physical performance test：PPT	身体機能検査
physical restraint	身体拘束
physical therapist：PT	理学療法士
physical therapy	理学療法
physically weak	虚弱
physician	医師；医者
physician-assisted suicide	医師自殺幇助
physician fee	治療報酬
physician referral services	医師紹介サービス
physician rounds	回診
physiological needs	生理的欲求
Pick's disease	ピック病
Picture Speech Intelligibility Evaluation：SPINE	絵画音声了解度検査
pillow	枕
pilocarpine hydrochloride	塩酸ピロカルピン
pinch	つまみ
pink noise protocol	ピンクノイズプロトコル
placebo effect	プラセボ効果
placement	配置
planning	プランニング
plantar flexion	底屈
plasma glucose	血漿グルコース
plastic orthosis	プラスチック装具
plasticity	可塑性
platform crutch	プラットホームクラッチ；肘台付杖
Plavix	プラビックス
play therapy	遊戯療法
pleasure principle	快楽原則
plug-fit socket	差込ソケット
pneumococcal meningitis	肺炎球菌性髄膜炎
pneumococcal pneumonia	肺炎球菌性肺炎
pneumococcal vaccination	肺炎球菌予防接種
pneumonia	肺炎
pneumonia in the elderly	老人性肺炎
pocket infection	ポケット感染
podiatric medicine	足病
podiatrist	足病医
podiatry	足治療
point gait	動作歩行
point of maximum intensity	最強点
point-of-service	自由診療；受診選択
policymaker	政策立案者
poliomyelitis	灰白髄炎
poliomyelitis	ポリオ
pollakiuria	頻尿
pollution	公害
polyarticular gout	多関節性痛風
polyester allergy	ポリエステルアレルギー
polymyalgia rheumatica	リウマチ性多発筋痛症
polyneuropathy	多発ニューロパチー
polypharmacy	多剤処方；多剤併用
polyps	ポリープ
polysynaptic reflex	多シナプス反射
polyunsaturated fatty acid：PUFA	多価不飽和脂肪酸
polyuria	多尿
poor	貧困者
poor family	貧困家庭

介護保険・介護福祉等関連用語 英和

poor relief　救貧事業
poorhouse　救貧院
popular sovereignty　国民主権
population aging　高齢化
population dynamics　人口動態
population explosion　人口爆発
population movement　人口移動
population projection　将来推計人口
position　体位
positioning　ポジショニング；体位設定
positive discrimination　肯定的差別
positive finding　陽性所見
positive mold　陽性モデル
positive punishment　正の罰
positive reinforcement　正の強化
positive sharp wave　陽性鋭波
positive symptom　陽性症状
positron emission tomography：PET　陽電子放射断層撮影法；ペット；ポジトロン・エミッション・トモグラフィー；ポジトロンCT
post-assessment　事後評価
post-evaluation　事後評価
post-fall syndrome　転倒後症候群
post-herpetic neuralgia：PHN　帯状疱疹後神経痛
post-infection cough　感染後咳そう
post-modern　ポストモダン
post-nasal drip syndrome：PNDS　後鼻漏症候群
post-polio syndrome：PPS　ポリオ後症候群
post-traumatic stress disorder：PTSD　外傷後ストレス障害
post-viral fatigue syndrome　ウイルス感染後疲労症候群
postmortem care　死後処置
postoperative infection　術後感染
postural drainage　体位排痰法；体位ドレナージ
postural exercise　姿勢訓練
postural reaction　姿勢反応
postural reflex　姿勢反射
posture　姿勢
potable water　飲料水
potential need　潜在ニード
pouch　パウチ
poverty　貧困
poverty among the elderly　老人貧困
poverty index　貧困指数
poverty level　貧困水準
poverty line　貧困線
powdered drug　散剤
power　力；能力；権力
power rehabilitation　パワーリハビリテーション
practice manual　業務マニュアル
pramipexole　プラミペキソール
prazosin　プラゾシン

pre-assessment　事前評価
preconscious　前意識
predation　略奪
prednisone　プレドニゾン
pre-evaluation　事前評価
preferential　優先的
preferential rights　先取特権
pregabalin　プレガバリン
prehension　把持
prehension orthosis　把持装具
preimplantation genetic diagnosis　着床前診断
prejudice　偏見
prejudice against the elderly　高齢者に対する偏見
preliminary survey　予備調査
premature atrial contraction：PAC　心房期外収縮
premature infant　未熟児
premature ventricular contraction：PVC　心室期外収縮
premium reduction　保険料減免
premiums on a per capita basis　被保険者均等割
prenatal diagnosis　出生前診断
preoperative anxiety　術前不安
preoperative bowel cleaning　術前腸管処置
preoperative bowel preparation　術前腸管処理；術前腸管準備；術前腸管洗浄
prepaid group practice：PGP　前払い型グループ診療
prepaid medical practice　前払い制診療
prerequisite criteria　必要前提基準
presbycusis　老年性難聴
presbyopia　老眼
prescription　処方箋
prescription medication program　処方薬剤プログラム
presenile dementia　初老期認知症
presenile depression　初老期うつ病
pressure　圧迫
pressure group　圧力団体
pressure ulcer　褥瘡；圧迫潰瘍
pressure ulcer prevention　褥瘡予防
pressure ulcer prevention and treatment　褥瘡予防と治療
Pressure Ulcer Scale for Healing：PUSH　褥瘡治癒過程スケール
pressure ulcer treatment　褥瘡治療
pressure wave　圧波
pressure zone　内圧帯
pressurized room　陽圧室
presyncope　意識消失発作
prevalence　有病
prevalence rate　有病率
prevalence survey　流行調査
prevention　予防
prevention of contracture　拘縮予防
prevention of dementia　認知症の予防

prevention of elder abuse	高齢者虐待防止
prevention of infection	感染予防
prevention of lumbago	腰痛予防
prevention of pressure ulcer	褥瘡予防
preventive benefit	予防給付
preventive care	予防ケア
preventive gerontology	予防老年学
preventive services	予防サービス
preventive treatment	予防処置
preventive vaccination	予防接種
prevocational	職業前
price indexation	物価スライド
primary afferent fiber	一次求心性線維
primary bacteremia	原発性菌血症
primary biliary cirrhosis	原発性胆汁性肝硬変
primary blood stream infection	原発性血流感染
primary care	プライマリ・ケア
primary care physician：PCP	プライマリ・ケア医；かかりつけ担当医；かかりつけ医
primary caregiver	主介護者
primary doctor	主治医；かかりつけ医
primary health care：PHC	プライマリ・ヘルス・ケア
primary open angle glaucoma：POAG	原発開放隅角緑内障
primary poverty	第一次貧困
primary prevention	一次予防
primary process	一次過程
primary progressive aphasia	原発性進行性失語
primary progressive nonfluent aphasia	原発性進行性非流暢性失語
primary stimulus	原刺激
prime mover	主動筋
primitive reflex	原始反射
principle of acceptance	受容の原則
principle of beneficence	善行原理
principle of client self-determination	自己決定の原則
principle of competition	競争原理
principle of confidentiality	秘密保持の原則
principle of controlled emotional involvement	統制された情緒的関与の原則
principle of equalization of income and expenditure	収支相等の原則
principle of individualization	個別化の原則
principle of justice	公正原理
principle of less eligibility	劣等処遇の原則
principle of nonmaleficence	無害性原理
principle of private/public dichotomy	公私分離の原則
principle of purposeful expression of feelings	意図的な感情表現の原則
principle of respect for autonomy	自立性尊重原理
principle of self-help	自助原則
principle of supplementary nature of public assistance	補足性の原理
print disabled	印刷字が読めない障害
prison	刑務所
prisoner	服役囚
privacy	プライバシー
privacy protection	プライバシー保護
private activity	民間活動；私的活動
private activity bond	民間活動債
private assistance	私的扶助
private association	民間団体
private enterprise	民間企業
private facility	民間施設
private foundation	民間助成団体
private home	民間ホーム
private hospital	民間病院；私立病院
private insurance	民間保険
private investment	民間投資
private long-term care insurance	民間介護保険
private medical insurance	民間医療保険
private organization	民間機関
private pension	民間年金
private program	民間事業
private program provider	民間事業者
private room	個室
private school corporation	学校法人
private sector	民間セクター
private services	民間サービス
private social welfare	民間社会福祉
private social welfare organization	民間社会福祉団体
private social welfare program	民間社会福祉事業
private support	私的扶養
private welfare	民間福祉
private welfare activity	民間福祉活動
privatization	民営化；プライバタイゼーション
privatization of Social Security	社会保障の民営化
probation and parole officer	保護監察官
probation and parole system	保護監察制度
probation officer	保護司
probationary employment period	試用期間
probe	プローブ
problem behavior	問題行動
problem-oriented system：POS	問題指向型システム
problem solving	問題解決
problem solving approach	問題解決アプローチ
problem solving process	問題解決過程
proctography	直腸造影
proctoscope	直腸鏡
proctoscopy	直腸鏡検査
proctosigmoidoscope	直腸S状結腸鏡
proctosigmoidoscopy	直腸S状結腸鏡検査
productive aging	プロダクティブ・エイジング
productive welfare	生産の福祉
profession	専門

professional	専門職
professional association	専門職団体
professional practice examination	実技試験
professional social work	社会福祉専門職；福祉専門職
professionalism	専門性
professionalization	専門化
progeria	早老症
progesterone therapy	プロゲステロン療法
prognosis	予後
prognosis prediction	予後予測
progressive bulbar palsy	進行性球麻痺
progressive muscular dystrophy：PMD	進行性筋ジストロフィー
progressive myoclonus epilepsy	進行性ミオクローヌスてんかん
progressive resistance exercise	漸増抵抗訓練
progressive systemic sclerosis	全身性進行性硬化症
projection	投影
projective method	投影法
projective test	投影検査
prokinetic medication	胃運動促進薬
prolonged stretching	持続伸長
promotion of social participation	社会参加促進
pronation	回内
proof of employment letter	在職証明書
proof of immunization	予防接種証明書
proof of work experience	実務経験証明書
property division	財産分与
property tax	資産税
prophylactic medication	予防内服；予防投与
proportional mortality indicator：PMI	死亡割合
proportional mortality rate	死因別死亡割合
propoxyphene	プロポキシフェン
propranolol	プロプラノロール
proprietary medicine	特許売薬
proprioception	固有感覚
proprioception deficit	固有受容性欠陥
proprioceptive neuromuscular facilitation：PNF	固有受容性神経筋促通法
Proscar	プロスカー
ProSom	プロサム
prosopagnosia	相貌失認
prospective payment system	包括払い制度
prospective review	予見的監査
prospective study	予見的研究
prostate cancer	前立腺癌
prostate disease	前立腺疾患
prostate specific antigen	前立腺特異抗原
prostatitis	前立腺炎
prosthesis	義肢
prosthesis fitting	義肢装着
prosthetic	義肢学；補綴
prosthetic equipment	補助器具
prosthetic training	義肢訓練
prosthetist and orthotist：PO	義肢装具士
prostitution	売春
protection	援護
protection of human rights	人権尊重
protective clothing	感染防御衣
protective custody	保護拘置
protective environment：PE	防護環境
protective isolation	予防隔離
protective measure	保護処分
protective services	保護局
protein	たんぱく質
protein energy	たんぱく質エネルギー
protein-energy malnutrition：PEM	たんぱく質・エネルギー低栄養状態
proton pump inhibitor	プロトンポンプ阻害薬
provider	事業者；提供者；供給者；供給主体；売り手
provisional collection	仮徴収
proximal	近位
proximal end	近位端
proximal tibia fracture	脛骨近位部骨折
proxy decision maker	意思決定代理者
Prozac	プロザック
prudent lay person	常識的素人
pruritus	かゆみ
pseudobulbar paralysis	仮性球麻痺
pseudodementia	仮性認知症
pseudomonas pneumonia	緑膿菌性肺炎
psychiatric day care	精神科デイケア
psychiatric day care center	精神科デイケアセンター
psychiatric disorder	精神障害
psychiatric drug	精神薬
psychiatric home health care	精神科訪問看護ケア
psychiatric hospital	精神病院
psychiatric medication	精神薬
psychiatric patient	精神病患者
psychiatric rehabilitation	精神科リハビリテーション
psychiatric social worker：PSW	精神科ソーシャルワーカー；精神保健ソーシャルワーカー
psychiatrist	精神科医
psychiatry	精神医学
psychic trauma	心的外傷
psychoactive drug	精神作用剤
psychoanalysis	精神分析
psychoanalyst	精神分析家
psychoanalytic paradigm	精神分析的のパラダイム
Psychoanalytic therapy	精神分析療法
psychoanalytical psychotherapy	精神分析的心理療法
psychodrama	心理劇
psychodrama therapy	心理劇療法
psychodynamics	心理力動論
psychogenesis	心因

psychogenic reaction	心因反応
psychological abuse	心理的虐待；精神的虐待
psychological assessment	心理評価
psychological dependence	精神依存
psychological test	心理テスト；心理検査
psychological therapy	精神療法
psychology	心理学
psychopathologist	精神病理学者
psychopathology	精神病理学
psychosexual development	心理性的発達理論
psychosexual stages	心理・性的段階
psychosis	精神病
psychosocial assessment	心理社会評価
psychosomatic disease：PSD	心身症
psychotherapy	心理療法；精神療法
psychotic behavior	精神病的行動
psychotropic	向精神剤
psychotropic drug	向精神薬
PT〈physical therapist〉	理学療法士
PTSD〈post-traumatic stress disorder〉	ピーティーエスディ；外傷後ストレス障害
ptyalism	流唾症
public assistance	公的扶助
public assistance fraud	不正受給
public assistance recipient	公的扶助受給者
public assistance standards	公的扶助基準
public businesses account	公営企業等会計部門
public choice theory	公共選択理論
public economics	公共経済学
public guardian	公の後見人
public health	公衆衛生
public health care insurance	公的医療保険
public health care insurance system	公的医療保険制度
Public Health Service Act	公衆衛生法
public housing	公営住宅
public intervention	公的介入
public opinion	世論
public opinion poll	世論調査
public pawnshop	公益質屋
public pension	公的年金
public pension plan subscription process	公的年金制度加入経過
public pension system	公的年金制度
public policy	公共政策
public/private dichotomy	公私分離
public-private competition	官民競争
public prosecutor	検察官
public relief	公的救済
public responsibility	公的責任
public services	公的サービス
public support	公助
public transportation	公共交通機関
public utility	公益事業
public vocational training	公共職業訓練
public welfare	公共福祉
public work	公共事業
puerperal fever	産褥感染症；産褥熱
puerperal sepsis	産褥熱
pulley	滑車
pulmonary aspiration	誤嚥
pulmonary atelectasis	無気肺
pulmonary atresia	肺動脈閉鎖症
pulmonary disease	肺疾患
pulmonary edema	肺水腫
pulmonary embolus	肺塞栓
pulmonary emphysema	肺気腫
pulmonary function test	肺機能検査
pulmonary nocardiosis	肺ノカルジア症
pulmonary rehabilitation	呼吸リハビリテーション
pulmonary tuberculosis	肺結核
pulp pinch	指腹つまみ
pulse	脈拍
pulse oximeter	パルスオキシメータ
punch biopsy	パンチバイオプシー；狙い撃ち組織診
pupillary light reflex	瞳孔対光反射
pureed diet	ピューレ食
pureed solids	ピューレ状
purine metabolism inhibitor	プリン代謝阻害剤
purposeful expression of feelings	意図的な感情表現
purposeful wandering	意図的徘徊
pursed lip breathing	口すぼめ呼吸
push up workout	腕立て伏せ運動
pyelography	腎盂造影
pyelonephritis	腎盂腎炎
pyorrhea	歯槽膿漏
pyramidal tract	錐体路
pyrazinamide	ピラジナミド
pyrogen	パイロジェン；発熱物質
pyrogen test	パイロジェンテスト；発熱物質テスト
pyrophosphate deposition disease	ピロリン酸沈着症
pyuria	膿尿

Q

quad cane	四脚杖
quadragenarian	40代
quadriceps femoris	大腿四頭筋
quadrilateral socket	四辺形ソケット
quadriplegia	四肢麻痺
qualitative investigation	質的調査
qualitative research	質的研究
quality affordable health care	手頃で質の良いケア
quality control：QC	品質管理活動
quality home care	質の良い在宅介護

quality home health care 質の良い在宅看護ケア
quality improvement：QI 改善活動
quality nursing home care 質の良いナーシングホームケア
quality of care ケアの質；介護の質
quality of life assessment QOL 評価
quality of life：QOL 生活の質
quality of medical care 医療の質
quality of service：QoS サービスの質
quality of well-being：QWB 健康福祉の質
quantitative investigation 量的調査
quantitative research 量的研究
quasi-market 準市場；疑似的市場
quasi-medical practice 医業類似行為
quazepam クアゼパム
questionnaire 質問紙；調査票
questionnaire method 質問紙法
quiet sleep 安眠
quinapril キナプリル
quinine sulfate 硫酸キニーネ
quinquagenarian 50代
quota restriction 割当制限
quota share 比例分配

R

racial and ethnic difference 人種的・民族的差異
racial discrimination 人種差別
racism 人種差別主義
radial artery 橈骨動脈
radial artery aneurysm 橈骨動脈瘤
radial artery cannulation 橈骨動脈カニューレ挿入法
radial artery catheter 橈骨動脈カテーテル
radial deviation 橈屈
radiation emergency medical management 緊急被ばく医療管理
radiation therapy 放射線治療
radiculopathy 神経根症
radioactive iodine 放射性ヨウ素
radioallergosorbent test 放射性アレルゲン吸着試験
radiography X線撮影
radioisotope 放射性同位体
radionuclide angiography 放射性核種血管造影
rage 狂気
raloxifene ラロキシフェン
ramelteon ラメルテオン
ramp 傾斜路
random assignment 無作為割当
random sampling 無作為抽出
range of motion：ROM 関節可動域
range of motion exercise 関節可動域訓練
range of motion testing：ROM-T 関節可動域テスト
rapid eye movement〈REM〉sleep レム睡眠

rapport ラポール；信頼関係
rate of population aging 高齢化率
ratio of the elderly population 老年人口比率
rational-emotive therapy 論理情動療法
rationalization 合理化
Raven's colored progressive matrices レーブン色彩マトリックス検査
Razadyne ラザダイン
reach out リーチ・アウト
reacher リーチャー
reaction formation 反動形成
reaction time 反応時間
reactive psychosis 反応性精神病
reading assistance 代読
reading glasses 読書眼鏡
real expenditure 実支出
real income 実収入
reality orientation リアリティ・オリエンテーション；現実見当識
reality orientation training：ROT 現実見当識訓練
reality principle 現実原則
reanalysis of problems 再課題分析
rearfoot varus deformity 後足部内反変形
reassessment 再アセスメント
recap リキャップ
receptive attitude 受容的態度
re-certification 再指定
recessive inheritance 劣性遺伝
recipient 受給者；利用者
reciprocal walking frame 交互式歩行器
reciprocating gait orthosis 交互歩行装具
reclining wheelchair リクライニング型車いす
recognition 再認；認識
recommended dietary allowance：RDA 栄養所要量；推奨量
recording style 記録様式
records 記録
recovery phase rehabilitation 回復期リハビリテーション
recreation レクリエーション
recreation program レクリエーションプログラム
recreational activity レクリエーション活動
rectal 直腸内
rectal biopsy 直腸生検
rectal examination 直腸診
rectal irrigation 直腸洗浄
rectal prolapse 直腸脱
rectocele 直腸瘤
red blood cell：RBC 赤血球
Red Cross 赤十字
red feather community chest movement 赤い羽根募金
rediscovery of poverty 貧困の再発見

redistribution 再分配	relative metabolic rate：RMR エネルギー代謝率
redness 発赤	relative risk 相対危険
re-education of sensation 知覚再教育	relaxation リラクセーション
re-emerging infectious diseases 再興感染症	relief institution 救護施設
reemployment arrangements 再雇用	religion 宗教
reevaluation 再評価	religious corporation 宗教法人
reference daily intake：RDI 基準一日摂取量	relocation stress 転居ストレス
reference electrode 基準電極	Relpax レルパックス
reference group 準拠集団	remaining function 残存能力
reference group theory 準拠集団論	remaining sense 残存感覚
referendum 国民投票	remaining sense of pain 痛覚残留
referral fee 紹介料	remarriage 再婚
referral services 紹介サービス	remedial model 治療モデル
referred pain 関連痛	remedial order 改善命令
reflex 反射	Remicade レミケード
reflex movement 反射運動	reminiscence therapy 回想法
reflex sympathetic dystrophy：RSD 反射性交感神経性ジストロフィー	Reminyl レミニール
	remission 寛解
reframing リフレーミング	remote area medicine 遠隔地医療
refugee 難民	remote care 遠隔ケア
refugee relief program 難民救済	remote medical system 遠隔医療システム
refugee services 難民サービス	remote medicine 遠隔医療
refuse disposal 廃棄物処理	renal failure 腎不全
regeneration medicine 再生医療	renal function 腎機能
regional gap 地域格差	renewal 更新
registered dietitian 管理栄養士	renewal application 更新申請
registered nurse 登録看護師	rental housing 賃貸住宅
registration number 登録番号	repetitive saliva swallowing test：RSST 反復唾液嚥下テスト
regression 退行	
regression behavior 退行行動	report 報告
regular diet 普通食；常食	repression 抑圧
rehabilitation リハビリテーション	reputation 名誉；評判
rehabilitation approach リハビリテーションアプローチ	Requip レキップ
	rescue breathing 人工呼吸
rehabilitation center 通所リハビリテーションセンター	research institution 研究所
	resident 入所者；ナーシングホーム利用者；住民
rehabilitation engineering リハビリテーション工学	resident bacteria 常在菌
rehabilitation equipment リハビリテーション機器	resident flora 常在細菌叢；常在菌
Rehabilitation International：RI 国際障害者リハビリテーション協会	resident movement 住民運動
	resident participation 住民参加
rehabilitation medicine リハビリテーション医学	resident tax 住民税
rehabilitation nurse リハビリテーション看護師	residential care 居住ケア
rehabilitation nursing リハビリテーション看護	residential care work レジデンシャル・ケアワーク
rehabilitation prescription リハビリテーション処方	residential environment 居住環境
rehabilitation program リハビリテーションプログラム	residential facility 入所施設
Rehabilitation Specialty's Handbook リハビリテーション専門手引書	residential social work レジデンシャル・ソーシャルワーク
rehabilitative care リハビリテーション介護	residual function 残存機能
rehydration 水分補給	residual functional capacity 残存能力
reimbursement 償還払い	residual functional capacity assessment 残存能力評価
reinforcer 強化子	
Reiter's syndrome ライター症候群	residual sensation 残尿感
reiterative reflection 反復反射	residual urine 残尿

介護保険・介護福祉等関連用語 英和

resistance 抵抗	Reuter centrifugal sampler RCS サンプラ
resistance exercise 抵抗訓練	revascularization 血行再建術
resistance training 抵抗訓練	reverse mortgage リバースモーゲージ
Resource-Based Relative Value Scale：RBRVS 診療報酬支払相対評価スケール方式	reverse mortgage program リバースモーゲージプログラム
respiration 呼吸	reversed isolation 逆隔離；保護隔離
respirator レスピレーター	ReVia レビア
respirator dependent quadriplegia 人工呼吸器依存四肢麻痺	Revised Children's Manifest Anxiety Scale：RCMAS 改訂版児童用顕在性不安尺度
respiratory disease 呼吸器疾患	Revised Wechsler Adult Intelligence Scale：WAIS-R 改定版ウェクスラー成人知能検査
respiratory disorder 呼吸障害	
respiratory exercise 呼吸練習	Revised Wechsler Memory Scale：WMS-R 改定版ウェクスラー記憶検査
respiratory failure 呼吸不全	
respiratory functional disorder 呼吸機能障害	Rey figure copy Rey 複雑図形検査
respiratory infection 呼吸器感染	rheumatic disorder リウマチ
respiratory isolation 気道感染隔離	rheumatoid arthritis：RA 関節リウマチ
respiratory organ 呼吸器	rheumatologist リウマチ専門医
respiratory paralysis 呼吸麻痺	rheumatology リウマチ学
respiratory therapy 呼吸療法	rhinitis 鼻炎
respiratory training 呼吸訓練	Riemenbugel method リーメンビューゲル法
respite care レスパイトケア	rifampin リファンピン
respite care services レスパイトケアサービス	right lateral recumbent 右側臥位
respondent behavior レスポンデント行動	righting reaction 立ち直り反応
response cost レスポンス・コスト	rights 権利
response hierarchy 反応階層	rights of caregivers 介護者の権利
responsibility 責任	rights of patients 患者の権利
rest home レストホーム	rights of residents ナーシングホーム利用者の権利
resting energy expenditure：REE 安静時エネルギー消費量	rigid scope 硬性鏡
	rigid sigmoidoscopy 硬性 S 状結腸鏡検査
restless legs syndrome：RLS むずむず脚症候群；不穏下肢症候群	rigidity 固縮；強剛
	rigor mortis 死後硬直
restraining tie 抑制帯	Rilutec リルテック
restraint 拘束；抑制	riluzole リルゾール
restricted mobility 運動制限	ring lock 輪止め
restrictive services 制限的サービス	risedronate リセドロン酸
restroom トイレ	risk リスク
retina 網膜	risk assessment リスクアセスメント
retinal sensitivity 網膜感度	risk control リスク管理
retirement 退職；引退	risk factor 危険因子
retirement allowance 退職手当	risk management リスクマネジメント；危機管理
retirement earnings test 退職所得調査	risk prevention 危険防止
retirement test 退職検査；退職調査	risk-sharing plan リスク共有プラン
retroactive indication 遡及適用	risky shift リスキー・シフト
retroactive premium payment 保険料遡及賦課	Risperdal リスパダール
retrograde amnesia 逆行性健忘	risperidone リスペリドン
retrograde pyelography 逆行性腎盂造影	ritual 儀式
retroperitoneal hematoma 後腹膜血腫	rivastigmine リバスチグミン
retrospective charge 遡及賦課	Riverhead Behavioural Memory Test リバーミード行動記憶検査
retrospective review 回顧的監査	
retrospective study 回顧的調査；後ろ向き調査；後ろ向き研究	rizatriptan リザトリプタン
	Robaxin ロバキシン
return to work 職業復帰	rod 桿体
reuse 再使用	roentgen レントゲン

介護保険・介護福祉等関連用語 英和

role	役割
role behavior	役割行動
role conflict	役割葛藤
role distance	役割距離
role expectation	役割期待
role perception	役割認知
role performance	役割遂行
role play	ロールプレイ；役割演技
role playing	ロールプレイング；役割演技
role theory	役割理論
room climate	室内気候
root avulsion injury	神経根引き抜き損傷
ropinirole	ロピニロール
Rorschach Inkblot Test	ロールシャッハ・インクブロット・テスト
Rorschach Test	ロールシャッハ・テスト
rotational vestibulo-ocular reflex	回転前庭動眼反射
rotator cuff injury	腱板損傷；肩腱板損傷
rotator strap	回旋帯
roundback	後弯
routes of infection	感染経路
routine health examination	定期健診
Rozerem	ロゼレム
rubbing method	擦式法；ラビング法
rubeola	麻疹
running cost	ランニングコスト
rural elder	農村部の高齢者
rural society	農村社会
rural village	農村

S

saccharide	糖質
sacral region	仙骨部
sadist	サディスト
safekeeping	保管
safety confirmation	安否確認
safety confirmation system	安否確認システム
safety control	安全管理
safety control system	安全管理体制；安全管理システム
safety education	安全指導
safety issue	安全問題
safety needs	安全の欲求
safety net	セーフティネット；安全ネット
salary calculator	給与計算
saliva	唾液
saliva functioning	唾液機能
salmonella	サルモネラ菌
salmonella food poisoning	サルモネラ食中毒
salt	食塩
salty	塩味
salvation army	救世軍
sample survey	標本調査；抽出調査
sampling	標本抽出
sampling design	標本抽出法
sampling error	標本誤差；抽出誤差
sampling method	抽出法
sand bag	砂嚢
sand play technique	箱庭療法
sanding	サンディング
sanitization	サニテーション
santeria	サンテリア
saponated cresol solution	クレゾール石鹸液
sarcopenia	サルコペニア
satellite system	サテライト方式
satisfaction	満足
satisfaction in caregiving	介護満足感
satisfaction measurement	満足度測定
saturated vapor	飽和蒸気
saturation	彩度
scabies	疥癬
scam	詐欺
scapulohumeral rhythm	肩甲上腕リズム
schema	スキーマ
schizoaffective disorder	分裂感情障害
schizophrenia	統合失調症；精神分裂症
school absenteeism	不登校
school counselor	スクールカウンセラー
school infirmary	保健室
school nurse	養護教諭
school of social work	社会福祉士養成施設
school social worker	スクールソーシャルワーカー
science	科学
scintigraphy	シンチグラフィー
scoliosis	側弯
scotopic luminance	暗所視輝度
scratching	ひっかく
screening	スクリーニング；検診
scrub method	スクラブ法
seasonal work	季節労働
seating aid	座位補助具
seating system	座位保持装置
Sebivo	セビボ
second opinion	セカンドオピニオン
secondary disorder	二次障害
secondary infection	二次感染
secondary medical service area	二次医療圏
secondary physician	副主治医
secondary poverty	第二次貧困
secondary prevention	二次予防
secondary process	二次過程
secondary stress on caregivers	介護者における二次的ストレス
secondhand smoke	受動喫煙
secrecy obligation	秘密保持義務

security 保障
sedative-hypnotic drug 鎮静催眠薬
Seddon's classification セドンの分類
seeing eye dog 盲導犬
seizure disorder 発作異常
seizure medication 発作薬
selective abstraction 選択的抽出
selective dissemination of information：SDI
　選択的情報提供
selective optimization with compensation
　選択的最適化論
selective serotonin reuptake inhibitor：SSRI
　選択的セロトニン再取り込み阻害薬
selective services 選別的サービス
selectivism 選別主義
selegiline セレギリン
selenium セレニウム
self-actualization 自己実現
self-advocacy movement 自己擁護運動；セルフア
　ドボカシー運動
self-assisted exercise 自己他動運動
self-awareness 自己覚知
self-care セルフケア
self-care management セルフケアマネジメント
self-care plan セルフケアプラン
self-catheterization 自己導尿
self-concept 自己概念
self-control セルフコントロール
self-control theory 自己コントロール理論
self-determination 自己決定
self-efficacy 自己効力感
self-employed health insurance deduction 自営業
　者健康保険控除
self-employment 自営業
self-esteem 自尊心
self-evaluation 自己評価
self-expression 自己表現
self-government association 自治会
self-harm：SH 自傷行為
self-hatred 自己嫌悪
self-help 自助
self-help activity 当事者活動
self-help device 自助具
self-help group：SHG セルフヘルプグループ
self-help group for families 家族会
self-identity 自己同一性
self-improvement 自己改善
self-infection 自己感染
self-injury 自傷行為
self-instructional training 自己教示訓練
self-invested personal pension 自己投資型個人年金
self-maintenance 自己調整
self-medication 自己治療

self-medication セルフメディケーション
self-neglect 自己放任
self-poisoning 自家中毒
self-protection type 自己防衛型
self-realization 自己実現
self-reliant living assistance services 自立生活援助
self-responsibility 自己責任
self-restraint 自制
semantic dementia：SD 意味性認知症
semantic memory 意味記憶
semicritical セミクリティカル；半侵襲的
semi-Fowler's position セミファーラー位
semi-private room 二人部屋；準個室
senile deafness 老人性難聴
senile dementia 老人性認知症；老年認知症
senile dementia of the Alzheimer's type：SDAT
　アルツハイマー型認知症
senile depression 老人性うつ病
senile plaque 老人斑
senility 老衰
senior center 高齢者福祉センター；シニアセンター
senior citizens club 老人クラブ；敬老会
Senior Companion Program シニアコンパニオンプ
　ログラム
senior housing シニア住宅
senior volunteer シニアボランティア
senium 老年期
sense 感覚
sense of hearing 聴覚
sense of shame 羞恥心
sense of sight 視覚
sense of smell 嗅覚
sense of taste 味覚
sense of touch 触覚
sense of value 価値観
sensitivity test 感受性試験
sensorineural deafness 感音難聴
sensory aphasia 感覚性失語
sensory change 知覚能力の変移
sensory disorder 感覚障害
sensory disturbance 感覚障害
sensory enhancement 感覚強化法
sensory function 感覚機能
sensory impairment 知覚障害
sensory integration 感覚統合
sensory nerve 感覚神経
sensory nerve conduction velocity 感覚神経伝導速度
sensory paralysis 感覚麻痺；知覚麻痺
sensory substitution 感覚代行
Sentencing Project 判決監視プロジェクト
separation 分離
separation anxiety 分離不安
separation anxiety disorder 分離不安障害

sepsis 敗血
septic shock 敗血症性ショック
septicemia 敗血症
septuagenarian 70代
serial section 連続切片
serologic test for syphilis 血清学的梅毒検査
serotonin セロトニン
serotonin norepinephrine reuptake inhibitor：SNRI セロトニン・ノルアドレナリン再取り込み阻害薬
sertraline セルトラリン
service area サービス提供圏
service code サービスコード
service coordination サービス調整
service dog 介助犬；補助犬
service level サービス水準
setting plate sampling 落下菌測定法
settlement house 隣保館
severance package 退職手当
severe acute respiratory syndrome：SARS サーズ；重症急性呼吸器症候群
sex chromosome 性染色体
sex discrimination 性差別
sexagenarian 60代
sexual abuse 性的虐待
sexual activity 性行為
sexual assault nurse examiner 性暴力被害者支援看護職
sexual division of labor 性別役割分業
sexual dysfunction 性機能障害
sexual harassment セクシャルハラスメント
sexual health セクシュアルヘルス
sexual minority 性的マイノリティ
sexual orientation disturbance 性指向障害
sexual violence 性的暴力
sexuality セクシュアリティ
sexually transmitted disease：STD 性行為感染症；性感染症
share of cost 負担金分担
sharps injury 鋭利物損傷
shave biopsy 薄片生検
sheltered employment 保護雇用
shingles 帯状疱疹
shock ショック
shoe horn 靴べら
shoe horn brace：SHB 靴べら式装具
short leg brace：SLB 短下肢装具
short opponens hand orthosis 短対立装具
short stump 短断端
short wave diathermy 超短波療法
shortness of breath 息切れ
short-term goal 短期目標
short-term memory 短期記憶
short-term volunteer 短期ボランティア

shoulder disarticulation prosthesis 肩義手
shoulder dislocation 肩関節脱臼
shoulder-hand syndrome 肩手症候群
shoulder impingement syndrome 肩インピンジメント症候群
shoulder subluxation 肩関節亜脱臼
shoulder suspension system 肩吊り帯
shoulder wheel 肩輪転器
shower chair シャワーいす；シャワーチェア
shower wheelchair シャワー用車椅子
Shy-Drager syndrome：SDS シャイ・ドレーガー症候群
sialorrhea 流涎症
sibling conflict 兄弟〈姉妹〉間葛藤
sibling rivalry 兄弟〈姉妹〉間競争
sibutramine シブトラミン
sick leave 傷病休暇；疾病休暇
sickness and injury allowance 傷病手当
sickness benefit 疾病給付
sickness impact profile：SIP 疾病影響プロファイル
sickness insurance 疾病保険
side effect 副作用
side pinch 横つまみ
siderail サイドレール
sigmoid colon S状結腸
sigmoidoscopy S状結腸鏡検査
sign language 手話
sign language interpreter：SLI 手話通訳士
significant change 著変
significant difference 有意差
signs of disease 病気の兆候
silent aspiration 不顕性誤嚥
silent infection 不顕性感染
silent killer サイレント・キラー
silent myocardial ischemia 無症候性心筋虚血
Silesian bandage シレジアバンド
silicone soft liner シリコン製ソフトライナー
simple bathtub 簡易浴槽
Sims' position シムス位
simultaneous contrast effect 同時対比効果
single axis joint 単軸継手
single-parent family 一人親家庭
single parent home 母子家庭／父子家庭
single-payer 統合支払い
single photon emission computed tomography：SPECT 単一フォトン断層撮影
single-use device 単回使用器材
sinobronchial syndrome 副鼻腔気管支症候群
sinopulmonary infection 経気道感染
sinus headache 副鼻洞性頭痛
sit to stand 立ち上がり
sit-to-stand exercise 立ち上がり運動
site investigation 訪問調査

介護保険・介護福祉等関連用語 英和

site investigator 訪問調査員	social barrier 社会的障壁
sitting exercise 座位訓練	social capital 社会資本
situational reflection 状況反射	social care 社会的養護
six basic food groups 6つの基礎食品群	social case work ソーシャルケースワーク
six times weekly：6W 週6回	social cognitive theory 社会認知理論
Sjogren's syndrome シェーグレン症候群	social consciousness 社会意識
Skelaxin スケラキシン	social democratic welfare state 社会民主主義的福祉国家
skeletal muscle 骨格筋	
skeleton 骨格	social diagnosis 社会診断
skilled nursing home スキルドナーシングホーム；高度看護施設	social functioning ability：SFA 社会生活力
	social group 社会集団
skin 皮膚	social hand washing 社会の手洗い；日常的手洗い
skin antiseptic 皮膚消毒	social hospitalization 社会的入院
skin barrier 皮膚保護剤	social inclusion 社会的統合；ソーシャルインクルージョン；社会的受容；社会的包摂
skin cancer 皮膚癌	
skin disease 皮膚疾患	social insurance 社会保険
skin disorder 皮膚障害	Social Insurance Medical Fee Payments Fund 社会保険診療報酬支払基金
skin pruritus 皮膚搔痒症	
skin rash 発疹	social insurance premium 社会保険料
skin surface culture method 皮膚表面細菌培養法	social interaction 社会的相互作用
skin tear 皮膚損傷	social isolation 社会的隔離
Skinner box スキナー・ボックス	social medicine 社会医学
sleep 睡眠	social model 社会モデル
sleep apnea 睡眠時無呼吸	social model of disability 障害の社会モデル
sleep apnea syndrome：SAS 睡眠時無呼吸症候群	social movement 社会運動
sleep disorder 睡眠障害	social movement theory 社会運動論
sleep disturbance 睡眠障害	social needs 社会ニーズ；社会的要求
sleep-driving 居眠り運転	social network 社会的ネットワーク
sleeplessness 不眠	social order 社会秩序
sleep-related breathing disorder 睡眠関連呼吸障害	social participation 社会参加
	social pathology 社会病理学
sliding scale スライディングスケール；スライド制；伸縮法	social planning 社会計画
	social policy 社会政策
sliding tube スライディングチューブ	social policy analysis 社会福祉政策分析
slight fever 微熱	social problem 社会問題
sling スリング；吊り具	social problem-solving 社会的問題解決
slope スロープ	social program 社会事業
slowly progressive insulin dependent diabetes 緩徐進行性インスリン依存糖尿病	social rehabilitation 社会的リハビリテーション
	social research 社会調査
slum スラム	social resource 社会資源
small cell lung cancer：SCLC 小細胞肺癌	social rights 社会権
small intestinal polyps 小腸ポリープ	social risk 社会的危険
small intestine 小腸	social risk management 社会的リスクマネジメント；ソーシャルリスクマネジメント
smoke alarm 煙感知器	
smoking 喫煙	social role 社会的役割
snare スネアー	social role theory 社会的役割論
snare electrocoagulation スネアー電気凝固	social science 社会科学
snoring いびき	Social Security 社会保障
SNRI〈serotonin-norepinephrine reuptake inhibitor〉セロトニン・ノルアドレナリン再取り込み阻害薬	Social Security Act 社会保障法
	Social Security benefit 社会保障給付
social action ソーシャルアクション	Social Security burden 社会保障負担
social activity 社会活動	Social Security costs 社会保障費用
social adequacy 社会的適応	Social Security system 社会保障制度
social administration 社会福祉管理	

Social Security tax 社会保障税
social services 社会サービス；ソーシャルサービス
social settlement セツルメント
social skill ソーシャルスキル
social skills training：SST 社会生活技能訓練；社会技能訓練；ソーシャルスキル・トレーニング
social solidarity 社会連帯
social structure 社会構造
social support ソーシャルサポート；社会的支援
social support network ソーシャルサポート・ネットワーク；社会的支援ネットワーク
social support services 社会支援サービス
social system 社会体制
social welfare 社会福祉
Social Welfare Administration 社会福祉運営管理
social welfare agency 社会福祉機関
social welfare organization 社会福祉団体
social welfare planning 社会福祉計画
social welfare research 社会福祉調査
social welfare services 社会福祉サービス
social welfare system 社会福祉制度
social withdrawal 引きこもり
social work ソーシャルワーク
social work practicum 社会福祉現場実習
social work profession 社会福祉専門
social work research ソーシャルワークリサーチ
social worker：SW ソーシャルワーカー
socialism 社会主義
socialization 社会化
society-managed health insurance 組合管掌健康保険
sociology 社会学
sociology of the family 家族社会学
sociology of welfare 福祉社会学
socket ソケット
sodium ナトリウム
sodium hypochlorite 次亜塩素酸ナトリウム
sodium intake 塩分摂取
soil-borne infection 土壌感染
soil-resistant material 防汚素材
solar disinfection 日光消毒
solar water disinfection：SODIS 太陽光を利用した飲料水の殺菌法
soldiers' pension 軍人年金；恩給
solid ankle cushion heel foot：SACH サッチ足部
solitary death 孤独死
solitary-living 独居
solitary-living elderly 独居高齢者；独居老人；一人暮らし高齢者；一人暮らし老人
solo practice 単独開業
solo practitioner 単独開業医
solution-focused approach 解決志向的アプローチ
somatic sensation 体性感覚
somatogenesis 身体因

somatosensory evoked potential：SEP 体性感覚誘発電位
somnipathy 睡眠障害
somnolence 傾眠
Sonata ソナタ
sound amplifier 音声増幅器
sour 酸味
source isolation 感染源隔離
source of infection 感染源
spasm 攣縮
spastic 痙性
spastic diplegia 痙直型両麻痺
spastic paralysis 痙性麻痺
spastic paraparesis 痙性対麻痺
spastic quadriplegia 痙直型四肢麻痺
spastic torticollis 痙性斜頸
spastic type 痙直型
spasticity 痙縮；痙性
special account 特別会計
special benefit allowance 特別手当
special care unit 認知症専門病棟；認知症ケア専門病棟
special collection 特別徴収
special disability allowance 特別障害者手当
special education 特殊教育
special education school 特殊教育諸学校
special meal 特別食
special needs education 特別支援教育
special notes 特記事項
special tax rebate 特別税額控除
special therapeutic diet 特別治療食
special volunteer fund 特別ボランティア基金
specialized bathtub 特殊浴槽
specialized bed 特殊寝台
specific developmental disorder：SDD 特異的発達障害
specific disorder of arithmetical skills 特異的算数能力障害
specific reading disorder 特異的読字障害
specific spelling disorder 特異的綴字障害
specimen collection 検体収集
spectral luminous efficiency 分光視感効率
speech 言語能力
speech and language training 言語訓練
speech clarity 言葉の明瞭性
speech disorder 音声機能障害
speech-language-hearing therapist：ST 言語聴覚士
speech-language impediment 言語障害
speech-language rehabilitation 言語聴覚リハビリテーション
speech-language therapy 言語聴覚療法
speech-language training 言語聴覚訓練
speech perception instructional curriculum and

evaluation　発話知覚指導カリキュラムと評価
speech reception threshold：SRT　語音聴取閾値
speech reception threshold test　語音聴取閾値検査
speech therapist　言語療法士
speech therapy　言語療法；言語治療
sphincter disturbance　括約筋障害
sphincteroplasty　括約筋形成術
spina bifida　二分脊椎
spinal canal stenosis　脊柱管狭窄症
spinal cord injury：SCI　脊髄損傷
spinal orthosis　体幹装具
spinal reflex　脊髄反射
spinal tap　脊椎穿刺
spinal X-ray　脊椎X線
spinocerebellar degeneration　脊髄小脳変性症
spiral ankle-foot orthosis　らせん状支柱付き短下肢装具
spiritual care　スピリチュアルケア
spiritual pain　スピリチュアルペイン
Spiritual Well-Being Scale　霊的幸福尺度
spirituality　霊性
spirometry　肺気量測定法
spironolactone　スピロノラクトン
splint　スプリント；副子
split hook and specialized tool　能動フック・作業用手先具
sponge bath　清拭；スポンジバス
spontaneous activity　自発活動
spore　芽胞；胞子
sports facility　スポーツ施設
sports for the elderly　高齢者スポーツ
spouse　配偶者
spouse abuse　配偶者虐待
sprain　捻挫
spray　散布
sprinkler　スプリンクラー
squamous cell carcinoma　扁平上皮癌
squeezing pain　締めつけられるような痛み
ST〈speech-language-hearing therapist〉　言語聴覚士
stability　安定性
stabilizer　立位保持装置；スタビライザー
staff development　職員研修
staffing　職員配置
stagflation　スタグフレーション
stair lift　階段昇降機
stall bar　肋木
stamp agar method　スタンプアガー法；接触培地法
stance phase　立脚期
standard deduction　標準控除
standard deviation：SD　標準偏差
standard for remuneration　標準報酬
standard language test of aphasia：SLTA　標準失語症検査

standard of living　生活水準
standard precaution　標準予防策
standard rate of insurance premium　保険料基準額
standard wheelchair　普通型車椅子
standardization　標準化
standardization of services　サービスの標準化
standardized mortality ratio：SMR　標準化死亡比
standards of care　介護の基準
standards of medical practice　診療の基準；医療の基準
standards of nursing　看護の基準
standards of nursing practice　看護の基準
standing exercise　立位訓練；起立訓練
standing table　起立台
staphylococcal pneumonia　黄色ブドウ球菌性肺炎
staphylococcus aureus　黄色ブドウ球菌
starch　でんぷん
stasis dermatitis　うっ滞性皮膚炎
state of depressed mood　うつ状態
static stability　静的安定性
stationary bicycle　固定自転車；訓練用固定自転車
statistical hypothesis test　統計的仮説検定
statistical research　統計調査
statistical test　統計の検定
statutory instrument　制定法文書
statutory rates of employment　法定雇用率
steam sterilization　蒸気滅菌；高圧蒸気滅菌
stem family　直系家族
step length　歩幅
step-up contribution　段階保険料
step-up elbow hinge　倍動肘ヒンジ継手
stereotype　ステレオタイプ
stereotyped behavior　常同行為
sterilant　滅菌剤
sterility assurance　無菌保証；滅菌保証
sterility assurance level：SAL　無菌性保証レベル；滅菌保証レベル
sterility test　無菌試験
sterilization　滅菌
sterilization process　滅菌工程
sterilization validation　滅菌バリデーション
sterilized water　滅菌水
sterilizer　滅菌器
steroid　ステロイド
stigma　スティグマ
stimulant abuse　物質乱用
stimulation method　刺激法
stirrup　あぶみ
stoma　ストーマ
stoma care　ストーマケア
stomach cancer　胃癌
stool　便

stool extraction	摘便
stool microbiology	糞便細菌検査
stool production	便産生
stool specimen	検便
strained back	ぎっくり腰
straining	いきみ
strangling pain	窒息しそうな痛み
street value	末端価格
strength	ストレングス
strength-based model	ストレングスモデル
strength exercise	強化運動
strength model	ストレングスモデル
strengths perspective	ストレングス視点
streptococcus pneumoniae	肺炎レンサ球菌
stress	ストレス
stress electrocardiogram	負荷心電図
stress incontinence	腹圧性尿失禁
stress inoculation training	ストレス免疫訓練
stressor	ストレッサー
stretcher	ストレッチャー
stretching	ストレッチング
stretching exercise	伸張運動
strict isolation	厳重隔離
stride	ストライド；重複歩
stride length	ストライド長；重複歩長
stride width	歩隔
strike	労働争議
stroke	脳卒中
stroke care unit	脳卒中集中治療室
Stroke Impairment Assessment Set：SIAS	脳卒中機能障害評価法
stroking	軽擦法
structural incrementalism	構造的増分主義
structural reform of Social Security	社会保障構造改革
stubby	スタビー
student nurse	見習い看護師
stump care	断端管理
stump pain	断端神経痛；断端痛
stump sock	断端袋
styling and setting hair	整髪
subacute care facility	亜急性ケア施設
subacute myelopticoneuropathy：SMON	スモン
subarachnoid hemorrhage：SAH	くも膜下出血
subchorionic hematoma	絨毛膜下血腫
subclavian vein catheterization	鎖骨下静脈直接穿刺法
subconscious mind	潜在意識
subcortical arteriosclerotic encephalopathy	動脈硬化性皮質下白質脳症
subcortical vascular dementia	皮質下血管性認知症
subcutaneous：Sub-Q	皮下
subcutaneous bleeding	皮下出血
subdural hematoma	硬膜下血腫
subject	対象者
subjective happiness	主観的幸福感
Subjective Happiness Scale	主観的幸福感尺度
subjective needs	主観的ニーズ
subjective well-being	主観的幸福度
sublingual gland	舌下腺
sublingual tablet	舌下錠
subluxation	亜脱臼
subsidy	補助金
subsidy adjustment	調整交付金
substance-induced psychosis	物質誘発精神病
substance-related disorder	化学物質関連障害
substantivity	持続性
substitute	代役；代用
substitute function	代替機能
substitute medication	代替調剤
substitution	代理
subtrochanteric fracture	大腿骨転子部骨折
subungual hematoma	爪下血腫
successful aging	幸福な老い；サクセスフル・エイジング
suction	サクション
suction biopsy	吸引生検
suction socket	吸着式ソケット
suctioning	吸引
sudden death	突然死
sudden infant death syndrome	乳幼児突然死症候群
Sudeck atrophy	ズデック骨萎縮
sugar	糖分
suicide	自殺
suicide prevention	自殺予防
sulfasalazine	スルファサラジン
sulfonylurea	スルフォニル尿素
sumatriptan	スマトリプタン
summary records	要約記録
sunbathing	日光浴
sundown syndrome	日没症候群
sundowning	日没行動
sunlight disinfection	日光消毒
super-aged society	超高齢社会
supercentenarian	110歳以上
superego	超自我
superficial sensation	表在感覚
superinfection	菌交代症
superstition	迷信
supervisee	スーパーバイジー
supervision	スーパービジョン
supervisor	スーパーバイザー
supination	回外
supplemental coverage	補足適用
Supplemental Social Security Insurance：SMI	補足的医療保険

介護保険・介護福祉等関連用語 英和

supplementary benefit 補足給付	symptomatic anemia 症候性貧血
support 援助；救援；扶養；サポート	symptomatic therapy 対症療法
support bar 支持棒	synchronicity シンクロニシティ
support group サポートグループ；支援グループ	syncope 意識喪失
support system サポートシステム	syndrome 症候群
supportive occupational therapy 支持的作業療法	synergist 共同筋
suppository 坐薬	synergy 共同運動
supraglottic swallow 息こらえ嚥下	synovectomy 滑膜切除術
surface color mode 表面色モード	synthetic detergent 合成洗剤
surface electrode 表面電極	synthetic fiber 合成繊維
surface electromyogram 表面筋電図	syphilis 梅毒
surgery 手術	systematic and rational reconstruction 系統的論理再構成法
surgical hand antisepsis 手術時手指消毒	
surgical intensive care unit 外科系集中治療室	systemic failure 組織的失敗
surgical mask サージカルマスク；外科用マスク	systemic lupus erythematosus：SLE 全身性エリテマトーデス；全身性紅斑性狼瘡
surgical scrub 手術時手洗い	
surgical site infection 手術部位感染；術野感染	systemic success 組織的成功
surgical wound 手術創	systems perspective システム的視点
surgical wound classification 手術創分類	systolic pressure 収縮期圧
surgical wound infection 手術創感染	
surrogate decision 代理決定	**T**
surveillance サーベイランス；監視	
survey 監査	tablet 錠剤
surveyor 監査官	tachycardia 頻脈
survivors' pension 遺族年金	tachypnea 頻呼吸
survivors' allowance 遺族給付	tacrine タクリン
suspension frame 懸垂フレーム	tactile floor tile 点字ブロック
suspension system 懸垂装置	tai chi 太極拳
swab collection 拭き取り採取；スワブ採取	talipes calcaneus 踵足変形
swab method 拭き取り法；スワブ法	talipes valgus 外反足
swallowing 嚥下	tamsulosin タムスロシン
swallowing difficulty 嚥下困難	tannin タンニン
swallowing function 嚥下機能	tap water 水道水
swallowing problem 嚥下問題	tardive dyskinesia 遅発性ジスキネジア
swallowing reflex 嚥下反射	targeted surveillance 対象限定サーベイランス
swallowing training 嚥下訓練	task analysis 課題分析
Swan-Ganz catheter スワンガンツカテーテル	task-centered approach 課題中心アプローチ
Swan neck deformity スワンネック変形	task-centered model 課題中心モデル
sweet 甘味	task performance ability 課題遂行能力
swelling 腫脹	tattooing 点墨法
swing phase 遊脚期；遊脚相	tax 税金
swing-through gait 大振り歩行	tax burden 租税負担
swing-to gait 小振り歩行	tax burden ratio 租税負担率
symbiosis 共生	tax code タックスコード
symbiosis society 共生社会	tax deduction 税控除
symbolic barrier 物理的障壁	tax deduction at source 源泉徴収
Syme's amputation サイム切断	tax delinquency 税金滞納
Syme's prosthesis サイム義足	tax-exempt organization 非課税団体
sympathetic muscle nerve activity 筋交感神経活動	tax exemption 免税措置
sympathetic nerve 交感神経	tax-privileged 租税優遇
sympathetic skin response 交感神経皮膚反応	tax rebate 税額控除
sympathy 同情	tax revolt 納税者の反乱
symptom 症状	taxation 租税

taxpayer's revolt　納税者の反乱
Taylor's Manifest Anxiety Scale：TMAS　テイラー顕現性不安尺度
team approach　チームアプローチ
team care　チームケア
team medicine　チーム医療
teamwork　チームワーク
technical aid　補助具
technical aid for the disabled　福祉機器；福祉用具
teeth　歯
Tegretol　テグレトール
telbivudine　テルビブジン
telephone assistance　代理電話
telethon　テレソン
temporary　一時的
temporary aid　一時扶助
temporary allowance　一時給付金
temporary appointment　臨時の任用
temporary assistance　一時扶助
temporary disability allowance　障害者一時給付金；障害一時給付金
temporary disability child allowance　障害児一時給付金
temporary disability leave　一時的身体障害休業制度
temporary employment　一時雇用
temporary protection　一時保護
temporary services　一時的サービス
tendency to fall　易転倒性
tennis elbow　テニス肘
tenodesis　腱固定
tenodesis effect　腱固定効果；テノデーシス作用
tenodesis splint　把持装具
tension-type headache　緊張型頭痛
terminal care　終末期ケア；ターミナルケア；終末期介護
terminal impact　膝のインパクト
terminal stage　終末期
terminal sterilization　最終滅菌
terminal treatment　終末期治療
termination of employment　解雇；雇用終了
tertiary education　第三次教育
tertiary processed food　インスタント食品
testament　遺言書
testator　遺言者
testosterone　テストステロン
tetanus　破傷風
tetany　テタニー
thalassemia　サラセミア
thallium scanning　タリウムスキャン
thanatology　死生学
thematic apperception test：TAT　主題統覚検査
theophylline　テオフィリン

theoretical maximum daily intake　理論最大一日摂取量
theory　理論
theory of planned behavior　計画的行動理論
therapeutic diet　治療食
therapeutic electrical stimulation：TES　治療的電気刺激
therapeutic endoscopy　治療的内視鏡検査
therapeutic exercise　運動療法
therapeutic relationship　援助関係；救援関係
thermometer　体温計
thermoregulation　体温調節
thermotherapy　温熱療法
thiamine deficiency　サイアミン欠乏症
thiazide diuretic　サイアザイド系利尿剤
thiazolidinedione　チアゾリジンジオン系薬剤
thickened diet　とろみ食
thickened liquid　濃厚飲料
thickening agent　嚥下補助剤
Thioredoxin　チオレドキシン
third-party panel　第三者委員
third-party quality endorsement　第三者評価
third-party quality endorsement system　第三者評価制度
third sector　第三セクター
thoracic spinal cord injury　胸髄損傷
thoracocentesis　胸腔穿刺
thought disorder　思考障害
three biggest causes of death　三大死因
three-dimension CT　三次元CT
three-dimensional gait analysis　三次元歩行分析
three-dimensional motion analysis　三次元動作解析
three-generation family　三世代家族
three-jaw chuck pinch　三指つまみ
three major nutrients　三大栄養素
three-point gait　三動作歩行；三点歩行
three times daily：TID　一日三回
three times weekly：3W　週三回
threshold　閾値；段差
throat swab culture　咽頭培養
thrombolytic　血栓溶解剤
thrombolytic therapy　血栓溶解療法
thrombosis　血栓
thumb post　母指支え
thumbprint　親指の指紋
thyroid cancer　甲状腺癌
thyroid disease　甲状腺疾患
thyroid-stimulating hormone：TSH　甲状腺刺激ホルモン
TIA〈transient ischemic attack〉　ティーアイエー；一過性脳虚血発作
tiagabine　チアガビン
tibial plateau　脛骨高原

介護保険・介護福祉等関連用語　英和

Tietze's syndrome	ティーツェ症候群
tile mosaic	タイルモザイク
tilting table	斜面台
Timed Get up and Go Test	起立・歩行動作測定法
time-out	タイムアウト
tinea	白癬
tinea pedis	足白癬
Tinel sign	ティネル徴候
tinnitus	耳鳴
tip pinch	指尖つまみ
tipping lever	テッピングレバー；ティッピングレバー
tissue perfusion	組織灌流
toddler class	幼児クラス
toenail	足指爪
Tofranil	トフラニール
toggle brake	トグルブレーキ
toilet screen	トイレスクリーン
toileting assistance	排泄介助
toileting schedule	排泄スケジュール
tolcapone	トルカポン
tolerable daily intake	耐容一日摂取量
tolerance	耐性；耐容性
tomography	断層撮影
tongue swallowing	舌根沈下
tonic neck reflex	緊張性頸反射
tonometry	眼圧計
tools for eating	食事用具
tooth brushing	歯磨き
tooth loss	歯牙喪失
topical	局所；径皮
topiramate	トピラマート
topographical agnosia	地誌的失認
torsional phacoemulsification	トーショナル水晶体乳化吸引術
total aphasia	全失語
total artificial heart	全置換型人工心臓
total assistance	全援助；全介助
total blindness	全盲
total care	全介護
total cholesterol	総コレステロール
total color blindness	全色盲
total contact socket	全面接触ソケット
total dependence	全面依存
total fertility rate：TFR	合計特殊出産率
total health promotion：THP	トータルヘルスプロモーション
total hip arthroplasty	人工股関節形成術
total hip replacement：THR	人工股関節全置換術
total incontinence	完全性尿失禁
total medical costs	総医療費用
total medical expenditures	総医療費支出
total parenteral nutrition：TPN	完全静脈栄養
total period fertility rate：TPFR	合計特殊出生率
total personal care	全人格的ケア
total purchasing	総合購入
total quality management：TQM	総合的品質経営活動
total surface bearing below-knee prosthesis TSB	下腿義足
toxic psychosis	中毒精神病
trace nutrient	微量栄養素
trachea	気管
tracheostomy	気管切開
traction	牽引
traction treatment	牽引療法
trade school	職業学校
traffic drug	不正薬品
Trail-Making Test	トレイルメイキングテスト
trainer	トレーナー
training	訓練
training benefit	訓練給付
Trandate	トランデート
tranquilizer abuse	トランキライザー乱用
transactional analysis	交流分析
transanal ultrasonography	経肛門的超音波検査
transcranial magnetic stimulation：TMS	経頭蓋磁気刺激
transcutaneous electrical nerve stimulation：TENS	経皮的電気神経刺激
transdermal	経皮
transfemoral prosthesis	大腿義足
transfemoral socket	大腿ソケット
transfer	移乗；トランスファー
transfer & locomotion	移乗・移動
transfer aid	移乗補助具；移乗補助用具；移乗関連用具
transfer assistance	移動介護
transfer bar	移動バー
transfer board	トランスファーボード
transfer exercise	移乗訓練
transfer motion	移乗動作
transfer motion training	移乗動作訓練
transference	転移
transference focused psychotherapy	転移焦点化精神療法
transference neurosis	転移神経症
transhumeral prosthesis	上腕義足
transient bacteria	通過菌
transient flora	一過性細菌叢；一過性菌叢；通過細菌
transient ischemic attack：TIA	一過性脳虚血発作
transintestine nutrition method	経腸栄養法
transit study	腸管移送能検査
transition zone	移行域
transitional care	移行期ケア
transitional facility	中間施設
transitional syndrome	通過症候群
translation into Braille	点訳
translational vestibulo-ocular reflex	併進前庭動眼

反射
transmissible disease 伝染性疾患
transmission-based precaution 感染経路別予防策
transportation 送迎；輸送
transportation and escort services 外出支援
transportation fee 移送費
transportation services 送迎サービス；移送サービス
transportation vehicle 送迎車
transradial prosthesis 前腕義手
transrectal ultrasonography 経直腸的超音波検査
transtheoretical model 汎理論的モデル
transtibial prosthesis 下腿義足
transtibial socket 下腿ソケット
transurethral incision of prostate 経尿道的前立腺切除術
transurethral microwave therapy：TUMT 経尿道的マイクロ波温熱療法
transurethral resection：TURP 経尿道的切除
transverse arch 横アーチ
Tranxene トランゼン
tranylcypromine トラニルシプロミン
trastuzumab トラスツズマブ
trauma トラウマ；外傷
traumatic brain injury：TBI 外傷性脳損傷；脳外傷；頭部外傷
traumatic injury 外傷性損傷
travel-associated legionellosis 旅行感染レジオネラ症
treadmill トレッドミル
treadmill testing トレッドミル負荷試験
treatment based classification 分類処遇
treatment policy 処遇方針
treatment prior to and after delivery 分べん前及び分べん後の処置
tree analysis ツリー図
tree diagram 樹形図
tremor 振戦
Trendelenburg position トレンデレンブルグ体位
Trendelenburg sign トレンデレンブルグ徴候
tricenarian 30代
trick motion トリックモーション
tricyclic antidepressant：TCA 三環系抗うつ剤
trigeminal neuralgia：TN 三叉神経痛
trigger トリガー
trigger point トリガーポイント
triglyceride 中性脂肪
triplegia 三肢麻痺
tripod cane 三脚杖
triptan drug トリプタン製薬
trisomy 21 21トリソミー
tristimulus value 三刺激値
trochanteric bursitis 転子滑液包炎
trochanteric fracture 転子部骨折
true emergency 真性救急

true incontinence 真性尿失禁
truncus 体幹
truth telling 告知
tube feeding 経管栄養；チューブ栄養
tuberculoma 結核腫
tuberculosis 結核
tumor necrosis factor：TNF 腫瘍壊死因子
tumor necrosis factor-alpha inhibitor 腫瘍壊死因子α阻害薬
tunnel infection 皮下トンネル感染
turnover rate 離職率
twenty-four-hour care 24時間ケア
twenty-four-hour on call 24時間連絡体制
twenty-four-hour protective oversight 24時間見守り
twice every month：2M 月二回
two-point gait 二動作歩行
two times daily：BID 一日二回
two times weekly：2W 週二回
Tylenol タイレノール
tympanic membrane 鼓膜
type 1 diabetes 一型糖尿病
type 1 diabetes mellitus 一型糖尿病
type 2 diabetes 二型糖尿病
type 2 diabetes mellitus 二型糖尿病
types and scope of public assistance 保護の種類及び範囲
Tyzeka タイゼカ

U

ulcer 潰瘍
ulceration 潰瘍形成
ulnar deviation 尺側偏位；尺屈
ultra low penetration air filter ULPAフィルター
ultra violet radiation 紫外線照射
ultraclean air 超清浄空気
ultra-honey-thick diet 濃厚蜂蜜状液体食
ultrasonically activated device：USAD 超音波凝固切開装置
ultrasonically guided puncture 超音波誘導穿刺
ultrasonography：US 超音波検査
ultrasound 超音波
ultrasound cardiography 心臓超音波検査
ultrasound therapy 超音波療法
ultraviolet 紫外線
ultraviolet disinfection 紫外線殺菌
ultraviolet rays protection material 紫外線遮蔽素材
ultraviolet therapy 紫外線療法
unaffected side of the body 健側
unauthorized 無認可
unconditional positive regard 無条件の肯定的配慮
unconditioned response 無条件反応
unconditioned stimulus 無条件刺激

英語	日本語	英語	日本語
unconscious	無意識	upper extremity amputation	上肢切断
unconsciousness	無意識	upper extremity orthosis	上肢装具
under arm hair	腋毛	upper gastrointestinal	上部消化管
underarm brace	アンダーアームブレース	upper income class	高所得層
undernutrition	低栄養状態	upper limb prosthesis	義手
underwater exercise	水中運動	urban planning	都市計画
underwear	肌着	urban problem	都市問題
undifferentiated	未分化	urbanism	都市生活
undifferentiated status	未分化状態	urbanization	都市化
unemployment	失業；無職；完全失業	urbanizing society	都市化社会
unemployment benefit	失業給付	uremia	尿毒症
unemployment compensation	失業手当；失業補償	uresiesthesia	尿意
unemployment insurance	失業保険	urethra	尿道
unemployment rate	失業率	urethral catheter	尿道カテーテル
unfair charge	不正請求	urethral catheterization	尿道カテーテル法
unfair labor practice	不当労働行為	urethrocele	尿道瘤
uniform chromaticity scale diagram	均等色度図	urge incontinence	切迫性尿失禁
uniform color space	均等色空間	urgent involuntary hospitalization	緊急措置入院
unilateral neglect	半側無視	uric acid	尿酸
unilateral spatial agnosia	半側空間失認	urinal	尿瓶
unilateral spatial neglect：USN	半側空間無視	urinalysis	尿検査
unincorporated association	任意団体	urinary bottle holder	尿器
uninhibited bladder	無抑制膀胱	urinary disorder	排尿障害
uninsured	無保険者	urinary incontinence	尿失禁
union	組合	urinary management	排尿管理；尿路管理
unique hue	ユニーク色相	urinary retention	尿閉
unit	病棟	urinary storage disorder	蓄尿障害
unit price contract	単価契約	urinary tract	尿路
United Nations Children's Fund：UNICEF	ユニセフ	urinary tract infection：UTI	尿路感染
United Nations Decade of Disabled Persons	国際障害者の10年	urination	排尿
United Nations Declaration of Human Rights	国連人権宣言	urine	尿
		urine collector	収尿器
		urine sampling	採尿
United Nations Educational, Scientific and Cultural Organization：UNESCO	ユネスコ	urocystitis	膀胱炎
		urodynamic test	尿流動態検査
United Nations High Commissioner for Refugees：UNHCR	国際連合難民高等弁務官事務所	urologist	泌尿器科医
		urology	泌尿器科
United Nations：UN	国際連合	urosepsis	尿路由来敗血症
universal access	普遍の利便性	urostomy	尿路ストーマ；ウロストミー
Universal Declaration of Human Rights：UDHR	世界人権宣言	usage cost	利用料
		useful field of view	有効視野
universal precautions	普遍的予防策	utensil	家庭道具；台所道具
universalism	普遍主義	uterine prolapse	子宮脱
unpaid labor	無償労働	utility hand	能動ハンド
unpaid work	無償労働	utilization management：UN	利用管理
unsaturated fatty acid	不飽和脂肪酸	utilization rate	稼動率
unskilled long-term care worker	未熟練介護労働者	utilization review：UR	利用監査
unskilled worker	未熟練労働者		
upper airway cough syndrome	上気道咳嗽候群	**V**	
upper esophageal sphincter：UES	上部食道括約筋		
upper esophageal sphincter dysfunction	上部食道括約筋障害	vaccination	予防接種；ワクチン注射
		vacuum cleaner	掃除機
upper extremity	上肢	vaginal care	膣ケア

valacyclovir バラシクロビル	vertigo めまい
valgus 外反	very premature infant 極低出生体重児
validation バリデーション	vestibular dysfunction 前庭障害
validation therapy バリデーション療法	vestibulo-ocular reflex 前庭動眼反射；前庭眼反射
Valium バリウム	vesting 受給権付与
valproic acid バルプロ酸	veteran 退役軍人
Valtrex バルトレックス	Veterans Disability Pension Program 障害軍人年金プログラム
value 価値	
value added tax：VAT 付加価値税	Veterans Disability Program 障害軍人プログラム
value-for-money：VFM バリューフォーマネー	vibration バイブレーション；振動法
valvular disease 弁膜症	vibrio parahaemolyticus 腸炎ビブリオ
valvular heart disease 心臓弁膜症	vicenarian 20代
vancomycin resistant enterococci：VRE バンコマイシン耐性腸球菌	victim care 犯罪被害者救済
	video endoscopy ビデオ内視鏡検査
vancomycin-resistant enterococcus：VRE バンコマイシン耐性腸球菌	videofluorography：VF 嚥下造影検査
	view of life and death 死生観
variable friction joint 可変摩擦継手	violence 暴力
varicella infection 水痘感染	viral hepatitis ウイルス性肝炎
varicella zoster 水痘帯状疱疹	viral infection ウイルス感染症
varicella zoster virus 水痘帯状疱疹ウイルス	virus ウイルス
varix 静脈瘤	visibly soiled hands 肉眼的に汚染した手指
varus 内反	vision 視力
vascular dementia 血管性認知症	vision loss 視力低下
vascular imaging 血管造影	vision substitution 視覚代行
vasodilator 血管拡張剤	visitation rights 面接交渉権
vasogenic shock 血管原性ショック	visual acuity 視力
vasospastic angina pectoris 冠動脈攣縮性狭心症	visual agnosia 視覚失認
	Visual Analog Scale：VAS 視覚的アナログスケール
Vasotec バソテック	visual deficit 視覚障害
vaulting 伸び上がり歩行	visual disability 視覚障害
vegetable food 植物性食品	visual disorder 視覚障害
vegetative state 植物状態	visual disturbance 視覚障害
vein 静脈	visual field defect 視野障害
venlafaxine ベンラファキシン	visual field restriction 視野狭窄
venous blood 静脈血	visual hallucination 幻視
ventilation 換気	visual impairment 視覚障害
ventricular fibrillation 心室細動	visual limitation 視覚制限
ventricular septal defect: VSD 心室中隔欠損	visual perception 視知覚
ventriculoperitoneal shunting VPシャント；脳室腹腔シャント	visual spatial agnosia 視空間失認
	visually disabled 視覚障害者
verapamil ベラパミル	visually impaired 視覚障害者
verbal aggression 言語的攻撃	vital signs バイタルサイン
verbal apraxia 発語失行	vitamin ビタミン
verbal communication 言語的コミュニケーション；口話	vitamin A deficiency ビタミンA欠乏症
	vitamin B1 deficiency ビタミンB1欠乏症
verbal disorder 言語障害	vitamin B12 deficiency ビタミンB12欠乏症
verbal memory 言語性記憶	vitamin B2 deficiency ビタミンB2欠乏症
Verelan ベレラン	vitamin B6 deficiency ビタミンB6欠乏症
vertebral angiography 椎骨脳底動脈造影	vitamin C deficiency ビタミンC欠乏症
vertebral artery 椎骨動脈	vitamin D deficiency ビタミンD欠乏症
vertebral compression fracture 脊椎圧迫骨折	vitamin E deficiency ビタミンE欠乏症
verteporfin ベルテポルフィン	vitamin K deficiency ビタミンK欠乏症
vertical disease transmission 垂直感染	vocational 職業的
vertical relationship 上下関係	

介護保険・介護福祉等関連用語 英和

vocational counseling 職業カウンセリング
vocational education 職業指導
vocational evaluation 職業評価
vocational rehabilitation 職業的リハビリテーション
vocational training 職業訓練
vocational training facility 職業訓練施設
voice generator 人工喉頭
voice guidance 音声案内
volitional disorder 意欲障害
Volkmann's contracture フォルクマン拘縮
voluntarism ボランティアリズム
voluntary ボランタリ
voluntary bankruptcy 自己破産
voluntary closing hook 随意閉じ式フック
voluntary contraction 随意収縮
voluntary guardianship system 任意後見制度
voluntary insurance 任意保険
voluntary movement 随意運動
voluntary opening hook 随意開き式フック
voluntary work 奉仕
volunteer ボランティア；奉仕員
volunteer activity ボランティア活動
volunteer adviser ボランティアアドバイザー
volunteer center ボランティアセンター
volunteer coordinator ボランティアコーディネーター
volunteer fund ボランティア基金
volunteer group ボランティアグループ
Volunteer Probation Officers Act 保護司法
volunteering 社会奉仕
vomiting 嘔吐
voucher system バウチャー方式

W

wage 賃金
wage disparity 賃金格差
wage indexation 賃金スライド
wage system 賃金体系
waist circumference ウエスト周囲
waiting list 待機者リスト
waiting period 待機期間
waiver 免除
walker 歩行器
walking ability 歩行能力
walking aid 歩行補助具
walking cane 歩行用杖
walking rate 歩行率
wandering 徘徊
warfarin ワルファリン
Wassermann reaction ワッセルマン反応
water-absorbing fiber 吸水性繊維
water cooler 冷水供給装置

water leakage test 水漏れ試験
water pill ウォーターピル
water-soluble bag 水溶性バッグ
water-soluble vitamin 水溶性ビタミン
waterborne infection 水系感染
waterless antiseptic agent 速乾性擦式消毒薬
waterless handwashing product 速乾性手洗い用製剤
waterproof sheet 防水シーツ
weak eye sight 弱視
weakness 虚弱
wearable identification 着用身分証明書
wearing-off phenomenon ウェアリングオフ現象；すり減り現象
Wechsler Adult Intelligence Scale：WAIS ウェクスラー成人知能検査
Wechsler Intelligence Scale ウェクスラー知能検査
Wechsler Intelligence Scale for Children：WISC ウェクスラー児童用知能検査
Wechsler Intelligence Scale for Children-Revised：WISC-R ウェクスラー児童用知能検査改訂版
wedge くさび
wedged insole くさび状足底板
weekly care plan 週間ケア計画
weight-bearing 体重負荷
welfare 福祉
welfare activity 福祉活動
welfare allowance 福祉手当
welfare and recreation 福祉レクリエーション
welfare assistance 福祉援助
welfare backlash 福祉反動
welfare benefit 福祉給付
welfare capitalism 福祉資本主義
welfare culture 福祉文化
welfare education 福祉教育
welfare facility 福祉施設
welfare fund 福祉基金；生活福祉資金
welfare fund loan system 生活福祉資金貸付制度
welfare needs 福祉ニーズ
welfare policy 福祉政策
welfare program 福利厚生
welfare regime 福祉レジーム
welfare services 福祉サービス
welfare staff 福祉職員
welfare state 福祉国家
welfare state in crisis 福祉国家の危機
welfare system 福祉制度；福祉システム
well-being ウェルビーイング
Wellbutrin ウェルブトリン
Werner Syndrome：WS ウェルナー症候群
Wernicke-Korsakoff syndrome ウェルニッケコルサコフ症候群
Wernicke's aphasia ウェルニッケ失語
Wernicke's area ウェルニッケ野

Wernicke's encephalopathy　ウェルニッケ脳症
western aphasia battery：WAB　WAB失語症検査
western medicine　西洋医学
wheel　駆動輪
wheelchair　車いす
wheelchair activity　車いす動作
wheelchair assistance　車いすの介助
wheelchair sports　車いすスポーツ
wheelchair transfer　車いす移乗
wheelchair transfer assistance　車いす移乗援助
wheeze　喘鳴
whiplash　むち打ち
whiplash injury　むち打ち症
whirlpool bath　渦流浴
whirlpool spa　泡風呂；気泡風呂
white blood cell：WBC　白血球
white cane　白杖
white-collar worker　ホワイトカラー
whole-body bathing　全身シャワー浴
WHO's three-step pain ladder　WHO三段階ラダー
widow　寡婦；未亡人
widow benefit　寡婦給付
widower　寡夫
widow's pension　寡婦年金
width　幅員
will　遺言書；意志
Wilson's disease　ウィルソン病
withdrawal symptom　禁断症状
withhold　支払い保留
withholding tax　源泉課税
woodworking　木工
word finding difficulty　喚語困難
word finding disorder　喚語障害
word-for-word reflection　逐語反射
work absence　欠勤
work ability index　労働適応能力指標
work adjustment　作業調整
work capacity　作業能力
work environment　労働環境
work hours　労働時間
work incentive program：WIN　労働奨励計画
work sharing　ワークシェアリング
work tolerance　作業耐性
workability　ワーカビリティ
workaholic　ワーカーホリック；仕事中毒
worker's collective　ワーカーズコレクティブ
workers' compensation insurance　労災保険
working-age population　生産年齢人口
working memory　作業記憶
working population　就業人口
World Health Organization：WHO　世界保健機関
wound care　創傷ケア；ウンドケア
wound classification　創分類

wound dressing　創傷被覆材
wound infection　創感染
wrist joint　手継手
writ　令状
writing exercise　書字訓練
written communication　筆談
written examination　筆記試験

X

Xanthogranulomatous pyelonephritis　黄色肉芽腫性腎盂腎炎
Xenical　ゼニカル
xerosis　乾燥症
xerostomia　口腔乾燥症
X-linked dominant inheritance　X連鎖優性遺伝
X-ray　X線
xy chromaticity diagram　xy色度図

Y

Yatabe-Guilford Personality Test　矢田部・ギルフォード性格検査
yoga　ヨガ
Young Men's Christian Association：YMCA　キリスト教青年会
young population　年少人口
Young Women's Christian Association：YWCA　キリスト教女子青年会

Z

z value　Z値
zaleplon　ザレプロン
Zancolli classification　ザンコリ分類
Zaroxolyn　ザロクソリン
zero position　ゼロ肢位
Zestril　ゼストリル
zinc　亜鉛
zolmitriptan　ゾルミトリプタン
Zoloft　ゾロフト
zolpidem　ゾルピデム
Zomig　ゾーミッグ
zoning　区域分け；ゾーニング
zoonose　人獣共通感染症
zoonosis　人獣共通感染症
Zostavax　ゾスタバックス
Zovirax　ゾビラックス
Zung Self-Rating Depression Scale：SDS　ツング自己評価式抑うつ性尺度
Zutphen Elderly Study　ジュトフェン高齢者研究
Zyprexa　ジプレキサ

介護保険・介護福祉等関連用語 英和

和英
JAPANESE - ENGLISH

あ

ISO国際規格分類（あいえすおーこくさいきかくぶんるい） ISO International Classification for Standards：ICS
ISO国際標準化機構（あいえすおーこくさいひょうじゅんかきこう） ISO；International Organization for Standardization
IADL（あいえーでぃーえる） instrumental activities of daily living
IL運動（あいえるうんどう） independent living movement
†IQ（あいきゅー） intelligence quotient
IQテスト（あいきゅーてすと） IQ test
†ICIDH（あいしーあいでぃーえっち） International Classification of Impairments, Disabilities and Handicaps
†ICF（あいしーえふ） International Classification of Functioning, Disability and Health
†ICD（あいしーでぃー） International Classification of Diseases
ICU（あいしーゆー） intensive care unit
ICU感染（あいしーゆーかんせん） ICU-acquired infection
アイシング（あいしんぐ） icing
アイスパック（あいすぱっく） ice pack
アイソレータ（あいそれーた） isolator
アイデンティティ（あいでんてぃてぃ） identity
アイバンク（あいばんく） eye bank
IPPB療法（あいぴーぴーびーりょうほう） intermittent positive-pressure breathing therapy
アウトブレイク（あうとぶれいく） outbreak
アウトリーチ（あうとりーち） outreach
亜鉛（あえん） zinc
赤い羽根募金（あかいはねぼきん） red feather community chest movement
アカウンタビリティ（あかうんたびりてぃ） accountability
アカシジア（あかしじあ）⇒静座不能
明るさ（あかるさ） brightness
アカンプロセート（あかんぷろせーと） acamprosate
亜急性ケア施設（あきゅうせいけあしせつ） subacute care facility
アキュプリル（あきゅぷりる） Accupril
アキレス腱（あきれすけん） Achilles tendon
アキレス腱延長術（あきれすけんえんちょうじゅつ） Achilles tendon lengthening
アクアエクササイズ（あくあえくささいず） aquatic exercise
アクションシステム（あくしょんしすてむ） action system
アクションリサーチ（あくしょんりさーち） action research
悪性関節リウマチ（あくせいかんせつりうまち） malignant rheumatoid arthritis
悪性腫瘍（あくせいしゅよう） malignant tumor：cancerous growth
悪性貧血（あくせいひんけつ） pernicious anemia
アクチン（あくちん） actin
†アクティビティ（あくてぃびてぃ） activity
アクティビティサービス（あくてぃびてぃさーびす） activity services
アクトネル（あくとねる） Actonel
悪魔払い（あくまばらい） exorcism
悪夢（あくむ） nightmare
あぐら座位（あぐらざい） tailor sitting；crossed leg sitting
悪霊学（あくりょうがく） demonology
握力（あくりょく） grip strength
アグレッシブケースワーク（あぐれっしぶけーすわーく） aggressive casework
アザチオプリン（あざちおぷりん） Azathioprine
アジア系アメリカ人（あじあけいあめりかじん） Asian American
足関節上腕血圧比（あしかんせつじょうわんけつあつひ） ankle-brachial index：ABI
アシクロビル（あしくろびる） acyclovir
足治療（あしちりょう） podiatry
足継手（あしつぎて） ankle joint
アシデミア（あしでみあ） acidemia
アシドーシス（あしどーしす） acidosis
足の問題（あしのもんだい） foot problem
足白癬（あしはくせん） tinea pedis
アスピリン（あすぴりん） aspirin
アスピリン療法（あすぴりんりょうほう） aspirin therapy
アスペルガー症候群（あすぺるがーしょうこうぐん） Asperger syndrome
アスペルギルス症（あすぺるぎるすしょう） aspergillosis
†アセスメント（あせすめんと） assessment
アセスメントシート（あせすめんとしーと） assessment sheet
アセスメントツール（あせすめんとつーる） assessment tool
アセトアミノフェン（あせとあみのふぇん） Acetaminophen

あせも（あせも）heat rash
亜脱臼（あだっきゅう）subluxation
アダリムマブ（あだりむまぶ）adalimumab
アダルトチルドレン（あだるとちるどれん）adult children
アーチサポート（あーちさぽーと）arch support
アチバン（あちばん）Ativan
圧縮記録（あっしゅくきろく）compressed recording
アッシュワース尺度（あっしゅわーすしゃくど）Ashworth Scale
圧波（あつは）pressure wave
圧迫（あっぱく）pressure
圧迫潰瘍（あっぱくかいよう）pressure ulcer
圧迫骨折（あっぱくこっせつ）compression fracture
圧力団体（あつりょくだんたい）pressure group
アディソン病（あでぃそんびょう）Addison's disease
†アテトーシス（あてとーしす）athetosis
†アテトーゼ（あてとーぜ）⇒アテトーシス
アデホビルビボキシル（あでほびるびぼきしる）adefovir dipivoxil
当て枕（あてまくら）applying pad
アテローマ（あてろーま）atheroma
アトピー（あとぴー）atopy
アトピー咳嗽（あとぴーがいそう）atopic cough
アトピー性皮膚炎（あとぴーせいひふえん）atopic dermatitis
アドビル（あどびる）Advil
†アドボカシー（あどぼかしー）advocacy
アドボケーター（あどぼけーたー）advocate
アドミニストレーション（あどみにすとれーしょん）administration
アナキンラ（あなきんら）anakinra
アナフィラキシーショック（あなふぃらきしーしょっく）anaphylactic shock
アナフラニール（あなふらにーる）Anafranil
アナプロックス（あなぷろっくす）Anaprox
アニサキス（あにさきす）anisakis
アネトールトリチオン（あねとーるとりちおん）anethole trithione
アノミー（あのみー）anomie
アーノルド・キアリ奇形（あーのるど・きありきけい）Arnold-Chiari malformation
あぶみ（あぶみ）stirrup
アベル体位（あべるたいい）Abel position
アヘン依存（あへんいぞん）opiate dependence
アヘン中毒（あへんちゅうどく）opiate addiction
アヘン類関連障害（あへんるいかんれんしょうがい）opioid-related disorder
アボダート（あぼだーと）Avodart
アポリポ蛋白（あぽりぽたんぱく）apolipoprotein
甘味（あまみ）sweet

アミオダロン（あみおだろん）Amiodarone
アミトリプチリン（あみとりぷちりん）Amitriptyline
アミノ酸（あみのさん）amino acid
アミラーゼ（あみらーぜ）amylase
アームサポート（あーむさぽーと）arm support
アームスリング（あーむすりんぐ）arm sling
アームレスト（あーむれすと）armrest
アムロジピン（あむろじぴん）Amlodipine
アメニティ（あめにてぃ）amenity
アメリカンインディアン（あめりかいんでぃあん）American Indian
アメリカ先住民（あめりかせんじゅうみん）Native American
アユルベーダ医学（あゆるべーだいがく）ayurvedic medicine
洗い出し法（あらいだしほう）wash method
アライメント（あらいめんと）alignment
アラーム（あらーむ）alarm
アリ（あり）Alli
アリセプト（ありせぷと）Aricept
アルカリ血症（あるかりけつしょう）alkalemia
アルカローシス（あるかろーしす）alkalosis
アルコール（あるこーる）alcohol
アルコール依存症（あるこーるいぞんしょう）alcoholism
アルコール幻覚症（あるこーるげんかくしょう）alcoholic hallucinosis；alcohol-related psychosis
アルコール消費（あるこーるしょうひ）alcohol consumption
アルコール性肝炎（あるこーるせいかんえん）alcoholic hepatitis
アルコール性精神病（あるこーるせいせいしんびょう）alcoholic psychosis
アルコール性脳障害（あるこーるせいのうしょうがい）alcoholic encephalopathy
アルコール中毒（あるこーるちゅうどく）alcoholic
RCSサンプラ（あーるしーえすさんぷら）Reuter centrifugal sampler
アルダクタジド（あるだくたじど）Aldactazide
アルダクトン（あるだくとん）Aldactone
†アルツハイマー型認知症（あるつはいまーがたにんちしょう）senile dementia of the Alzheimer's type：SDAT
アルツハイマー型認知症不快評価尺度（あるつはいまーがたにんちしょうふかいひょうかしゃくど）Discomfort Scale for Dementia of the Alzheimer's Type：DS-DAT
†アルツハイマー病（あるつはいまーびょう）Alzheimer's disease
αグルコシダーゼ阻害薬（あるふぁぐるこしだーぜがいやく）alpha-glucosidase inhibitor
α遮断剤（あるふぁしゃだんざい）alpha-blocker

介護保険・介護福祉等関連用語 和英

アルマ・アタ宣言（あるま・あたせんげん）Declaration of Alma-Ata；Alma-Ata Declaration
亜鈴（あれい）dumbbell
アレルギー（あれるぎー）allergy
アレルギー性気管支炎（あれるぎーせいきかんしえん）allergic bronchitis
アレルギー性掻痒症（あれるぎーせいそうようしょう）allergic pruritus
アレルギー性鼻炎（あれるぎーせいびえん）allergic rhinitis
アレルギー反応（あれるぎーはんのう）allergic reaction
アレンドロネート（あれんどろねーと）alendronate
泡風呂（あわぶろ）jacuzzi；whirlpool spa
アンジオテンシンⅡ受容体拮抗薬（あんじおてんしんつーじゅようたいきっこうやく）angiotensin II receptor antagonist
アンジオテンシン変換酵素阻害薬（あんじおてんしんへんかんこうそがいやく）angiotensin-converting enzyme inhibitor；ACE inhibitor
暗順応（あんじゅんのう）dark adaptation
暗所視輝度（あんしょしきど）scotopic luminance
安静臥床（あんせいがしょう）lying position for rest；bed rest
安静時エネルギー消費量（あんせいじえねるぎーしょうひりょう）resting energy expenditure；REE
安全衛生部（あんぜんえいせいぶ）Industrial Safety and Health Department
安全課（あんぜんか）Safety Division
†安全管理（あんぜんかんり）safety control
安全管理システム（あんぜんかんりしすてむ）safety control system
安全管理体制（あんぜんかんりたいせい）⇒安全管理システム
安全指導（あんぜんしどう）safety education
安全対策課（あんぜんたいさくか）Safety Division
安全ネット（あんぜんねっと）safety net
安全の欲求（あんぜんのよっきゅう）safety needs
安全問題（あんぜんもんだい）safety issue
アンダーアームブレース（あんだーあーむぶれーす）underarm brace
安定性（あんていせい）stability
アンドロゲン（あんどろげん）androgen
アンドロゲン除去療法（あんどろげんじょきょりょうほう）androgen deprivation therapy；ADT
アンビエン（あんびえん）Ambien
安否確認（あんぴかくにん）safety confirmation
安否確認システム（あんぴかくにんしすてむ）safety confirmation system
アンビバレンス（あんびばれんす）ambivalence
†罨法（あんぽう）foment
按摩師（あんまし）masseur［男性］；masseuse［女性］

†安眠（あんみん）quiet sleep
†安眠援助（あんみんえんじょ）support for quiet sleep
暗明順応（あんめいじゅんのう）dark/light adaptation
アンモニア（あんもにあ）ammonia
アンモニア解毒（あんもにあげどく）ammonia detoxification
†安楽（あんらく）comfort
安楽椅子型（あんらくいすがた）rocking chair type
安楽死（あんらくし）euthanasia
†安楽な体位（あんらくなたいい）comfortable position
安楽尿器（あんらくにょうき）comfortable urinary aid

い

胃運動促進薬（いうんどうそくしんやく）prokinetic medication
EGM（いーえむじー）electromyography
EMGバイオフィードバック（いーえむじーばいおふぃーどばっく）EMG biofeedback
胃炎（いえん）gastritis
イオン導入法（いおんどうにゅうほう）iontophoresis
胃潰瘍（いかいよう）gastric ulcer
医学指示拒否（いがくしじきょひ）against medical advice；AMA
医学的リハビリテーション（いがくてきりはびりてーしょん）medical rehabilitation
医学モデル（いがくもでる）medical model
E型肝炎（いーがたかんえん）hepatitis E
E型肝炎ウイルス（いーがたかんえんういるす）hepatitis E virus
胃癌（いがん）gastric cancer；stomach cancer
易感染患者（いかんせんかんじゃ）compromised patient
易感染宿主（いかんせんしゅくしゅ）compromised host
生きがいのある生活（いきがいのあるせいかつ）life worth living
息切れ（いきぎれ）shortness of breath
息こらえ嚥下（いきこらええんげ）supraglottic swallow
閾値（いきち）threshold
いきみ（いきみ）straining
異議申し立て（いぎもうしたて）appeal
異議申し立て制度（いぎもうしたてせいど）appeal system
医業（いぎょう）medical practice
医業類似行為（いぎょうるいじこうい）quasi-medical practice

育児・介護休業給付（いくじ・かいごきゅうぎょうきゅうふ）child and family care leave benefit
育児・介護休業制度（いくじ・かいごきゅうぎょうせいど）child and family care leave system
育児休業（いくじきゅうぎょう）parental leave；child care leave
育児休業手当金（いくじきゅうぎょうてあてきん）parental leave allowance
育児給付（いくじきゅうふ）child care benefit
育児手当（いくじてあて）child care allowance
育児ノイローゼ（いくじのいろーぜ）maternity neurosis
育児放棄（いくじほうき）child neglect
育成医療（いくせいいりょう）medical aid for children with potential disability
育成環境課（いくせいかんきょうか）Child-Rearing Promotion Division
育成支援課（いくせいしえんか）Vocational Training Promotion Division
EKG（いーけーじー）electrocardiogram
医原性（いげんせい）iatrogenic
医原病（いげんびょう）iatrogenesis
医行為（いこうい）medical practice
移行域（いこういき）transition zone
移行期ケア（いこうきけあ）transitional care
遺産税（いさんぜい）estate tax
意志（いし）will
医師（いし）physician；doctor
医事課（いじか）Medical Professions Division
意識（いしき）consciousness
意識混濁（いしきこんだく）clouding of consciousness
†意識障害（いしきしょうがい）disturbance of consciousness
意識消失発作（いしきしょうしつほっさ）presyncope
意識喪失（いしきそうしつ）syncope
意識調査（いしきちょうさ）opinion survey
†維持期リハビリテーション（いじきりはびりてーしょん）late phase rehabilitation
意識レベル（いしきれべる）level of consciousness
意思決定（いしけってい）decision-making
意思決定代理者（いしけっていだいりしゃ）proxy decision maker
医師自殺幇助（いしじさつほうじょ）physician-assisted suicide
医師紹介サービス（いししょうかいさーびす）physician referral services；doctor referral services
意思伝達装置（いしでんたつそうち）communication aid
医師登録法（いしとうろくほう）Medical Practitioners' Registration Act

医師との連携（いしとのれんけい）cooperation with physicians
意思能力評価（いしのうりょくひょうか）mental capacity assessment
意思の伝達（いしのでんたつ）expressions of desires
医師法（いしほう）Medical Practitioners Law
いじめ（いじめ）bullying
医事問題（いじもんだい）medical issue
医者（いしゃ）physician；doctor
†萎縮（いしゅく）atrophy
萎縮性胃炎（いしゅくせいいえん）atrophic gastritis
萎縮性膣炎（いしゅくせいちつえん）atrophic vaginitis
移乗（いじょう）transfer
移乗・移動（いじょう・いどう）transfer & locomotion
移乗関連用具（いじょうかんれんようぐ）transfer aid
移乗訓練（いじょうくんれん）transfer exercise
異常行動（いじょうこうどう）abnormal behavior
異常姿勢（いじょうしせい）abnormal posture
異常知覚（いじょうちかく）dysesthesia
†移乗動作（いじょうどうさ）transfer motion
移乗動作訓練（いじょうどうさくんれん）transfer motion training
異常発見（いじょうはっけん）finding abnormality
異常不随意運動評価尺度（いじょうふずいうんどうひょうかしゃくど）Abnormal Involuntary Movement Scale：AIMS
異常歩行（いじょうほこう）abnormal gait
移乗補助具（いじょうほじょぐ）transfer aid
移乗補助用具（いじょうほじょようぐ）transfer aid
異食行為（いしょくこうい）abnormal eating habit
胃食道逆流症（いしょくどうぎゃくりゅうしょう）gastroesophageal reflex disease：GERD
異所性骨化（いしょせいこっか）heterotopic bone formation
異所性腎（いしょせいじん）ectopic kidney
異所性尿管（いしょせいにょうかん）ectopic ureter
異所性尿管瘤（いしょせいにょうかんりゅう）ectopic ureterocele
異所性皮脂腺（いしょせいひしせん）ectopic sebaceous gland
異所性リズム（いしょせいりずむ）ectopic rhythm
いす座位（いすざい）sitting position
衣生活（いせいかつ）clothing life
医政局（いせいきょく）Health Policy Bureau
胃切除術（いせつじょじゅつ）gastrectomy
胃洗浄（いせんじょう）gastric lavage
移送サービス（いそうさーびす）transportation services
†移送費（いそうひ）transportation fee
イソカルボキサジド（いそかるぼきさじど）

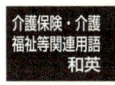

介護保険・介護福祉等関連用語 和英

isocarboxazid
†遺族基礎年金（いぞくきそねんきん）basic survivors' pension
遺族給付（いぞくきゅうふ）survivors' allowance
遺族年金（いぞくねくきん）survivors' pension
イソプチン（いそぷちん）Isoptin
依存症（いぞんしょう）addiction
遺体安置所（いたいあんちじょ）morgue
委託（いたく）assignment
委託事業（いたくぎょう）assignment program
Ia相反抑制（いちえーそうはんよくせい）Ia reciprocal inhibition
一型糖尿病（いちがたとうにょうびょう）type 1 diabetes mellitus；type 1 diabetes
一次過程（いちじかてい）primary process
一時間毎（いちじかんごと）every hour：QH
一次求心性線維（いちじきゅうしんせいせんい）primary afferent fiber
一時給付金（いちじきゅうふきん）temporary allowance
一時雇用（いちじこよう）temporary employment
一時的（いちじてき）temporary
一時的サービス（いちじてきさーびす）temporary services
一時的身体障害休業制度（いちじてきしんたいしょうがいきゅうぎょうせいど）temporary disability leave
一次判定（いちじはんてい）initial assessment；preliminary assessment
一時扶助（いちじふじょ）temporary assistance；temporary aid
一時保護（いちじほご）temporary protection
一次予防（いちじよほう）primary prevention
一日おき（いちにちおき）every other day：QOD；Q2D
一日五回（いちにちごかい）5 times daily：5D；5 times a day
一日三回（いちにちさんかい）3 times daily：TID；3 times a day
一日二回（いちにちにかい）2 times daily：BID；2 times a day
一日四回（いちにちよんかい）4 times daily：QID；4 times a day
一部介助（いちぶかいじょ）limited assistance
一部事務組合（いちぶじむくみあい）partial affairs association
一部負担金（いちぶふたんきん）co-payment
医長（いちょう）medical director
銀杏（いちょう）ginkgo biloba
一過性細菌叢（いっかせいさいきんそう）transient flora
一過性脳虚血発作（いっかっせいのうきょけつほっさ）transient ischemic attack：TIA

一酸化炭素（いっさんかたんそ）carbon monoxide
一酸化炭素中毒（いっさんかたんそちゅうどく）carbon monoxide poisoning
逸脱（いつだつ）deviation
逸脱行動（いつだつこうどう）deviant behavior
一般医（いっぱんい）general practitioner：GP
一般会計（いっぱんかいけい）general account
一般株価指数（いっぱんかぶかしすう）common stock price；price of common stock
一般行政部門（いっぱんぎょうせいぶもん）general administrative field
一般健康教育（いっぱんけんこうきょういく）general health education
一般システム論（いっぱんしすてむろん）general system theory
一般診療所（いっぱんしんりょうしょ）general medical clinic
一般世帯調査（いっぱんせたいちょうさ）general household survey：GHS
一般病院（いっぱんびょういん）general hospital
一般病床（いっぱんびょうしょう）general bed
一般浴槽（いっぱんよくそう）general bathtub
一分間タイムスタディ（いっぷんかんたいむすたでぃ）one-minute time study
溢流性尿失禁（いつりゅうせいにょうしっきん）overflow incontinence
遺伝学（いでんがく）genetics
遺伝子（いでんし）gene
遺伝子検査（いでんしけんさ）genetic testing
遺伝子診断（いでんししんだん）genetic diagnosis
遺伝子の突然変異（いでんしのとつぜんへんい）mutations of genes
遺伝刷り込み（いでんすりこみ）genomic imprinting
易転倒性（いてんとうせい）tendency to fall
遺伝病（いでんびょう）hereditary disease
†移動（いどう）locomotion
†移動介護（いどうかいご）transfer assistance；assistance with transfer
†移動関連福祉用具（いどうかんれんふくしようぐ）mobility aid
移動技能（いどうぎのう）mobility skill
移動性（いどうせい）mobility
†移動トイレ（いどうといれ）commode；bedside commode
移動動作（いどうどうさ）locomotion activity
移動バー（いどうばー）grab bar；transfer bar
移動補助具（いどうほじょぐ）mobility aid
†移動浴槽（いどうよくそう）portable bathtub
意図的自己放任（いとてきじこほうにん）active self-neglect
意図的な感情表現（いとてきなかんじょうひょうげん）purposeful expression of feelings
意図的な感情表現の原則（いとてきなかんじょうひょ

うげんのげんそく）principle of purposeful expression of feelings
意図的徘徊（いとてきはいかい）purposeful wandering
イートン・ランバート症候群（いーとん・らんばーとしょうこうぐん）Eaton-Lambert syndrome
遺尿症（いにょうしょう）enuresis
居眠り運転（いねむりうんてん）sleep-driving
イバンドロネート（いばんどろねーと）ibandronate
いびき（いびき）snoring
易疲労性（いひろうせい）easy fatigability
†衣服（いふく）clothes
衣服圧（いふくあつ）clothing pressure
衣服気候（いふくきこう）clothing climate
†衣服着脱（いふくちゃくだつ）changing clothes
イブニングケア（いぶにんぐけあ）evening care
イブプロフェン（いぶぷろふぇん）Ibuprofen
意味記憶（いみきおく）semantic memory
意味性認知症（いみせいにんちしょう）semantic dementia；SD
イミトレックス（いみとれっくす）Imitrex
イミプラミン（いみぷらみん）imipramine
移民（いみん）immigrant
医務室（いむしつ）dispensary
医薬食品局（いやくしょくひんきょく）Pharmaceutical and Food Safety Bureau
意欲障害（いよくしょうがい）volitional disorder
いらいら（いらいら）irritability
医療（いりょう）medicine
医療委任状（いりょういにんじょう）health-care proxy
医療援助者（いりょうえんじょしゃ）medical support assistant
医療課（いりょうか）Medical Economics Division
医療過誤（いりょうかご）medical malpractice
医療過誤訴訟（いりょうかごそしょう）medical malpractice suit
医療過誤保険（いりょうかごほけん）medical malpractice insurance
医療過誤補償保険（いりょうかごほしょうほけん）medical malpractice liability insurance
医療過疎地域（いりょうかそちいき）medically under-served area
医療関係者（いりょうかんけいしゃ）medical professional
医療監視員（いりょうかんしいん）medical inspector
医療関連サービス（いりょうかんれんさーびす）health-related services
医療機器（いりょうきき）medical device；medical equipment
医療機器分類（いりょうききぶんるい）classification of medical devices；classification of medical equipments
医療器具（いりょうきぐ）medical device；medical equipment
医療器材（いりょうきざい）medical device；medical equipment
医療給付（いりょうきゅうふ）medical care benefit
医療教育制度（いりょうきょういくせいど）medical education system
医療記録（いりょうきろく）medical records
医療計画（いりょうけいかく）health planning
医療経済（いりょうけいざい）medical economic
医療経済指数（いりょうけいざいしすう）medical economic index
医療行為（いりょうこうい）medical practice
医療控除（いりょうこうじょ）deduction for medical care
医療困窮対象者（いりょうこんきゅうたいしょうしゃ）the medically needy
医療サービス委員会（いりょうさーびすいいんかい）Health Services Commission
医療サービス計画（いりょうさーびすけいかく）medical services plan
医療サービスパッケージ（いりょうさーびすぱっけーじ）health services package
医療サービス不足地域（いりょうさーびすぶそくちいき）⇒医療過疎地域
医療産業複合体（いりょうさんぎょうふくごうたい）medical industrial complex
医療資源（いりょうしげん）medical resources
医療事故（いりょうじこ）medical error
医療従事者（いりょうじゅうじしゃ）medical staff
医療受給者証（いりょうじゅきゅうしゃしょう）medical insurance card recipient
†衣料障害（いりょうしょうがい）clothing irritation
医療職員（いりょうしょくいん）medical staff
医療人類学（いりょうじんるいがく）medical anthropology
医療人類学者（いりょうじんるいがくしゃ）medical anthropologist
医療税控除（いりょうぜいこうじょ）tax deduction for medical care
医療政策（いりょうせいさく）health policy
医療制度改革（いりょうせいどかいかく）health-care reform
医療専門（いりょうせんもん）medical profession；health profession
医療専門職（いりょうせんもんしょく）medical professional；health professional
医療専門職不足地域（いりょうせんもんしょくぶそくちいき）health professional shortage area
医療ソーシャルサービス（いりょうそーしゃるさーびす）medical social services
†医療ソーシャルワーカー（いりょうそーしゃるわーかー）

medical social worker
医療ソーシャルワーク（いりょうそーしゃるわーく）
medical social work
医療大麻（いりょうたいま）medical marijuana
医療の基準（いりょうのきじゅん）standards of medical practice
医療の質（いりょうのしつ）quality of medical care
医療の社会化（いりょうのしゃかいか）socialization of medical care；socialization of medicine
医療廃棄物（いりょうはいきぶつ）medical waste
医療費（いりょうひ）medical care expenses；medical expenses
医療費給付（いりょうひきゅうふ）benefit for medical care expenses
医療費控除（いりょうひこうじょ）deduction for medical expenses
医療費税控除（いりょうひぜいこうじょ）tax deduction for medical care expenses
医療費適正化（いりょうひてきせいか）moderation in medical care costs
医療費適正化計画（いりょうひてきせいかけいかく）health expenditure rationalization plan
医療費負担金分担（いりょうひふたんきんぶんたん）share of cost of medical care
医療費抑制策（いりょうひよくせいさく）health care cost containment
医療品（いりょうひん）medical supply
医療複合体（いりょうふくごうたい）integrated health care delivery system
医療福祉（いりょうふくし）medicine and welfare
医療福祉連携（いりょうふくしれんけい）affiliation of medical care and social welfare
医療扶助（いりょうふじょ）medical assistance
医療負担（いりょうふたん）burden of health care
医療法（いりょうほう）Medical Services Law
医療法人（いりょうほうじん）medical corporation
医療保険（いりょうほけん）medical insurance
医療保険課（いりょうほけんか）Health Insurance Division
†医療保険制度（いりょうほけんせいど）health insurance system
医療保険制度の一元化（いりょうほけんせいどのいちげんか）unification of health care insurance programs
医療保護施設（いりょうほごしせつ）medical facility for public assistance recipients
医療保護入院（いりょうほごにゅういん）admission for medical care and custody
医療保障（いりょうほしょう）medical security
医療保障プログラム（いりょうほしょうぷろぐらむ）medical security program
医療ミス（いりょうみす）⇒医療事故
医療面接（いりょうめんせつ）medical interview

医療用具（いりょうようぐ）medical device；medical equipment
医療倫理（いりょうりんり）medical ethics
イレウス（いれうす）ileus
入れ歯（いれば）denture
胃瘻（いろう）gastrostomy
胃瘻チューブ（いろうちゅーぶ）gastrostomy tube
陰圧室（いんあつしつ）depressurized room
陰圧性肺水腫（いんあつせいはいすいしゅ）negative pressure pulmonary edema
陰イオン界面活性剤（いんいおんかいめんかっせいざい）anionic surface active agent
院外救助（いんがいきゅうじょ）outdoor relief
インクルージョン（いんくるーじょん）inclusion
印刷字が読めない障害（いんさつじがよめないしょうがい）print disabled
インジェクションプラグ（いんじぇくしょんぷらぐ）injection plug
インジケータ（いんじけーた）⇒指標
因子分析（いんしぶんせき）factor analysis
インスタント食品（いんすたんとしょくひん）convenience food；tertiary processed food
†インスリン（いんすりん）insulin
インスリン依存性糖尿病（いんすりんいぞんせいとうにょうびょう）insulin-dependent diabetes mellitus；IDDM；Type 1 diabetes
インスリン自己注射（いんすりんじこちゅうしゃ）insulin self-injection
インスリン非依存性糖尿病（いんすりんひいぞんせいとうにょうびょう）non-insulin-dependent diabetes mellitus；NIDDM
陰性モデル（いんせいもでる）negative mold
引退（いんたい）retirement
インターセックス（いんたーせっくす）intersex
インタビュー（いんたびゅー）interview
インターフェイス（いんたーふぇいす）interface
インターフェロン（いんたーふぇろん）interferon
インターフェロンα（いんたーふぇろんあるふぁ）interferon alfa
インターフェロンγ（いんたーふぇろんがんま）interferon gamma
インターフェロンβ（いんたーふぇろんべーた）interferon beta
インターベンション（いんたーべんしょん）intervention
インチング法（いんちんぐほう）inching technique
†インテーク（いんてーく）intake
インテークカンファレンス（いんてーくかんふぁれんす）intake conference
インテーク面接（いんてーくめんせつ）intake interview
インテグレーション（いんてぐれーしょん）integration

インデラル（いんでらる）Inderal
インテリジェント義足（いんてりじぇんとぎそく）intelligent prosthesis
咽頭（いんとう）pharynx
咽頭相（いんとうそう）pharyngeal phase
咽頭通過時間（いんとうつうかじかん）pharyngeal passage time
咽頭培養（いんとうばいよう）throat swab culture
インドシン（いんどしん）Indocin
インドメタシン（いんどめたしん）indomethacin
イントロンA（いんとろんえー）Intron A
院内感染（いんないかんせん）hospital-acquired infection；nosocomial infection
院内救助（いんないきゅうじょ）indoor relief
インナーシティ現象（いんなーしていげんしょう）inner-city phenomenon
インパルス（いんぱるす）impulse
インピンジメント（いんぴんじめんと）impingement
†インフォーマル（いんふぉーまる）informal
インフォーマルグループ（いんふぉーまるぐるーぷ）informal group
インフォーマルケア（いんふぉーまるけあ）informal care
インフォーマルサービス（いんふぉーまるさーびす）informal services
インフォーマル資源（いんふぉーまるしげん）informal resources
インフォーマルシステム（いんふぉーまるしすてむ）informal system
インフォーマルセクター（いんふぉーまるせくたー）informal sector
インフォーマルネットワーク（いんふぉーまるねっとわーく）informal network
インフォームド・コンセント（いんふぉーむど・こんせんと）informed consent：IC
インフォームド・チョイス（いんふぉーむど・ちょいす）informed choice
†陰部清拭（いんぶせいしき）genital hygiene；genital washing
†陰部洗浄（いんぶせんじょう）perineal care；peri care
インフリキシマブ（いんふりきしまぶ）infliximab
インフルエンザ（いんふるえんざ）influenza
インフルエンザウイルス（いんふるえんざういるす）influenza virus
インフルエンザワクチン（いんふるえんざわくちん）Influenza vaccine
†インペアメント（いんぺあめんと）impairment
インポテンツ（いんぽてんつ）impotence
飲料水（いんりょうすい）potable water

う

WeeFIM（うぃーふぃむ）⇒こどものための機能的自立度評価法
ウイルス（ういるす）virus
ウイルス感染後疲労症候群（ういるすかんせんごひろうしょうこうぐん）post-viral fatigue syndrome
ウイルス感染症（ういるすかんせんしょう）viral infection
ウイルス性肝炎（ういるすせいかんえん）viral hepatitis
ウイルソン病（ういるそんびょう）Wilson's disease
ウェアリングオフ現象（うぇありんぐおふげんしょう）wearing-off phenomenon
ウェクスラー児童用知能検査（うぇくすらーじどうようちのうけんさ）Wechsler Intelligence Scale for Children：WISC
ウェクスラー児童用知能検査 改訂版（うぇくすらーじどうようちのうけんさかいていばん）Wechsler Intelligence Scale for Children-Revised：WISC-R
ウェクスラー成人知能検査（うぇくすらーせいじんちのうけんさ）Wechsler Adult Intelligence Scale：WAIS
ウェクスラー知能検査（うぇくすらーちのうけんさ）Wechsler Intelligence Scale
植込み型除細動器（うえこみがたじょさいどうき）implantable defibrillator
ウエスト周囲（うえすとしゅうい）waist circumference
ウェルナー症候群（うぇるなーしょうこうぐん）Werner Syndrome：WS
ウェルニッケ・コルサコフ症候群（うぇるにっけ・こるさこふしょうこうぐん）Wernicke-Korsakoff syndrome
ウェルニッケ失語（うぇるにっけしつご）Wernicke's aphasia
ウェルニッケ脳症（うぇるにっけのうしょう）Wernicke's encephalopathy
ウェルニッケ野（うぇるにっけや）Wernicke's area
ウェルビーイング（うぇるびーいんぐ）well-being
ウェルブトリン（うぇるぶとりん）Wellbutrin
ウォーターピル（うぉーたーぴる）water pill
ウォッシャーステリライザー（うぉっしゃーすてりらいざー）⇒洗浄滅菌器
ウォッシャーディスインフェクター（うぉっしゃーでぃすいんふぇくたー）⇒洗浄消毒器
うがい（うがい）gargling；gargle
牛海綿状脳症（うしかいめんじょうのうしょう）bovine spongiform encephalopathy：BSE
内がえし（うちがえし）inversion
うちわ（うちわ）toe in
うっ血（うっけつ）congestion

介護保険・介護福祉等関連用語和英

うっ血性心不全（うっけつせいしんふぜん）congestive heart failure
うつ状態（うつじょうたい）depressive state；state of depressed mood
うっ滞性皮膚炎（うったいせいひふえん）stasis dermatitis
うつ熱（うつねつ）heat retention
†うつ病（うつびょう）depression
腕立て伏せ運動（うでたてふせうんどう）push up workout
うま味（うまみ）umami
羽毛アレルギー（うもうあれるぎー）feather allergy
ULPAフィルター（うるぱふぃるたー）ultra low penetration air filter
ウロストミー（うろすとみー）urostomy
上乗せ給付（うわのせきゅうふ）additional benefit
上乗せサービス（うわのせさーびす）additional service
運営（うんえい）administration
†運営適正化委員会（うんえいてきせいかいいんかい）Complaints Resolution Committee
運動（うんどう）exercise；movement
運動維持困難症（うんどういじこんなんしょう）motor impersistence
運動覚（うんどうかく）kinesthetic sense；motion sense
運動学（うんどうがく）kinesiology
運動学習（うんどうがくしゅう）motor learning
運動学的分析（うんどうがくてきぶんせき）kinematic analysis
運動感覚（うんどうかんかく）kinesthesia
運動器症候群（うんどうきしょうこうぐん）locomotive syndrome
運動機能（うんどうきのう）motor function
運動技能（うんどうぎのう）motor skill
運動技能・プロセス技能評価（うんどうぎのう・ぷろせすぎのうひょうか）Assessment of Motor and Process Skills：AMPS
†運動器の機能向上（うんどうきのきのうこうじょう）improvement of body functions
運動強度（うんどうきょうど）exercise strength
運動亢進（うんどうこうしん）⇒多動；hyperkinesia
運動試験（うんどうしけん）exercise test；exercise testing
運動失行（うんどうしっこう）motor apraxia
†運動失調（うんどうしっちょう）ataxia
運動失調症（うんどうしっちょうしょう）ataxia
†運動障害（うんどうしょうがい）motor impairment
運動処方（うんどうしょほう）exercise prescription
運動神経（うんどうしんけい）motor nerve；motoneuron
運動神経伝導速度（うんどうしんけいでんどうそくど）motor nerve conduction velocity

運動制御（うんどうせいぎょ）motion control；motor control
運動制限（うんどうせいげん）movement-related functional limitation；restricted mobility
運動性失語（うんどうせいしつご）motor aphasia
運動生理（うんどうせいり）exercise physiology
運動専門士（うんどうせんもんし）exercise instructor
運動耐容能（うんどうたいようのう）exercise capacity
運動単位（うんどうたんい）motor unit
運動単位活動電位（うんどうたんいかつどうでんい）motor unit action potential：MUAP
運動低下（うんどうていか）hypokinesis；hypokinesia
運動点（うんどうてん）motor point
運動点ブロック（うんどうてんぶろっく）motor point block
運動ニューロン（うんどうにゅーろん）motor neuron
運動ニューロン疾患（うんどうにゅーろんしっかん）motor neuron disease
運動年齢（うんどうねんれい）motor age
運動発達（うんどうはったつ）motor development
運動発達評価（うんどうはったつひょうか）motor developmental evaluation
運動評価（うんどうひょうか）motor assessment
運動負荷（うんどうふか）exercise load
運動負荷テスト（うんどうふかてすと）exercise tolerance test：ETT
運動分析（うんどうぶんせき）movement analysis
運動麻痺（うんどうまひ）motor paralysis
運動誘発電位（うんどうゆうはつでんい）motor evoked potential
運動力学（うんどうりきがく）kinetics
†運動療法（うんどうりょうほう）therapeutic exercise
ウンドケア（うんどけあ）⇒創傷ケア

え

エアウェイ（えあうぇい）⇒気道
エアウェイクロージャ（えあうぇいくろーじゃ）⇒気道閉鎖
エアカーテン（えあかーてん）air curtain
エアサンプラ（えあさんぷら）air sampler
エアサンプリング（えあさんぷりんぐ）air sampling
エアシャワー（えあしゃわー）air shower
エアトラッピング（えあとらっぴんぐ）air trapping
†エアーパッド（えあーぱっど）air sleeping pad
エアフィルタ（えあふぃるた）air filter
†エアーマット（えあーまっと）air mattress
エアリーク（えありーく）air leak

エアレーション（えあれーしょん）aeration
永久歯（えいきゅうし）permanent tooth
†エイジズム（えいじずむ）ageism
†エイズ（えいず）AIDS：acquired immune deficiency syndrome
衛生（えいせい）hygiene
衛生学（えいせいがく）hygienics
衛生検査技師（えいせいけんさぎし）hygiene laboratory technician
衛生的手洗い（えいせいてきてあらい）hygienic hand washing
†栄養（えいよう）nutrition
栄養価（えいようか）nutritive value of foods
†栄養改善（えいようかいぜん）nutrition improvement
†栄養管理（えいようかんり）nutritional management
栄養ケア計画（えいようけあけいかく）nutrition care plan
栄養ケアマネジメント（えいようけあまねじめんと）nutrition care management
栄養サービス（えいようさーびす）nutrition services
†栄養士（えいようし）dietitian
栄養失調（えいようしっちょう）malnutrition
栄養指導（えいようしどう）nutritional education；nutritional guidance
栄養士法（えいようしほう）Dietitian Law
栄養障害（えいようしょうがい）nutritional disturbance
栄養状態（えいようじょうたい）nutritional status
栄養処方（えいようしょほう）dietary prescription
†栄養所要量（えいようしょようりょう）recommended dietary allowance：RDA
栄養所要量委員会（えいようしょようりょういいんかい）Committee on Dietary Allowances
栄養スクリーニング（えいようすくりーにんぐ）nutritional screening
栄養スクリーニング推進財団（えいようすくりーにんぐすいしんざいだん）nutrition screening initiative：NSI
栄養摂取（えいようせっしゅ）nutritional intake
栄養摂取量（えいようせっしゅりょう）nutrient intake
†栄養素（えいようそ）nutrient
栄養必要量（えいようひつようりょう）nutritional requirement
栄養評価（えいようひょうか）nutritional assessment
栄養不良（えいようふりょう）malnutrition
栄養補給（えいようほきゅう）nutritional support
栄養補助食品（えいようほじょしょくひん）dietary supplement

栄養問題（えいようもんだい）nutritional problem
営利団体（えいりだんたい）for-profit organization
鋭利物損傷（えいりぶつそんしょう）sharps injury
会陰（えいん）perineum
ALS（えーえるえす）amyotrophic lateral sclerosis
EKG（えーかーげー）electrocardiogram
A型肝炎（えーがたかんえん）hepatitis A
A型肝炎ウイルス（えーがたかんえんういるす）hepatitis A virus
腋窩（えきか）axilla
†腋窩温（えきかおん）axillary temperature
疫学（えきがく）epidemiology
疫学調査（えきがくちょうさ）epidemiological study
腋窩動脈（えきかどうみゃく）axillary artery
腋臭（えきしゅう）axillary osmidrosis；osmidrosis axillae
液性調節（えきせいちょうせつ）humoral regulation
液体石鹸（えきたいせっけん）liquid soap
腋毛（えきもう）under arm hair
エクセロン（えくせろん）Exelon
エクリン腺（えくりんせん）eccrine gland
エゴ（えご）ego
エコシステム（えこしすてむ）ecosystem
エコマップ（えこまっぷ）eco map
エコロジカルアプローチ（えころじかるあぷろーち）ecological approach
†壊死（えし）necrosis
SEKマーク（えすいーけーまーく）SEK mark
SNRI（えすえぬあーるあい）serotonin-norepinephrine reuptake inhibitor
S状結腸（えすじょうけっちょう）sigmoid colon；pelvic colon
S状結腸鏡検査（えすじょうけっちょうきょうけんさ）sigmoidoscopy
エスタゾラム（えすたぞらむ）estazolam
ST（えすてぃー）speech-language-hearing therapist
エステートプランニング（えすてーとぷらんにんぐ）estate planning
エステラーゼ（えすてらーぜ）esterase
エストロゲン（えすとろげん）estrogen
エストロゲン補充療法（えすとろげんほじゅうりょうほう）estrogen replacement therapy：ERT
エスニシティ（えすにしてぃ）ethnicity
壊疽（えそ）gangrene
エタネルセプト（えたねるせぷと）etanercept
エチケット（えちけっと）etiquette
エチレンオキサイドガス滅菌（えちれんおきさいどがすめっきん）ethylene oxide gas sterilization
X線（えっくすせん）X-ray
X線撮影（えっくすせんさつえい）radiography
X線動画撮影（えっくすせんどうがさつえい）

cineradiography
X線透視検査（えっくすせんとうしけんさ）fluoroscopy
X連鎖優性遺伝（えっくすれんさゆうせいいでん）X-linked dominant inheritance
xy色度図（えっくすわいしきどず）xy chromaticity diagram
HDL（えっちでぃーえる）high density lipoprotei
HDLコレステロール（えっちでぃーえるこれすてろーる）high density lipoprotein cholesterol；HDL cholesterol；good cholesterol
H波（えっちは）H wave
H反射（えっちはんしゃ）H reflex
†ADL（えーでぃーえる）activities of daily living
ATP（えーてぃーぴー）adenosine triphosphate
ADP（えーでぃーぴー）adenosine diphosphate
エディプス期（えでぃぷすき）Oedipus phase
エディプス・コンプレックス（えでぃぷす・こんぷれっくす）Oedipus complex
エデン・オルタナティブ（えでん・おるたなてぃぶ）Eden Alternative
エトプロパジン（えとぷろぱじん）ethopropazine
エナメル質（えなめるしつ）enamel
エナラプリル（えならぷりる）enalapril
NMスケール（えぬえむすけーる）Nishimura Dementia Scale：NMS
NGO（えぬじーおー）non-governmental organization
N式精神機能検査（えぬしきせいしんきのうけんさ）Nishimura Dementia Scale：NMS
†NPO（えぬぴーおー）non-profit organization
NPO支援税制（えぬぴーおーしえんぜいせい）NPO tax support system
エネルギー（えねるぎー）energy
エネルギー消費（えねるぎーしょうひ）energy expenditure
エネルギー代謝率（えねるぎーたいしゃりつ）relative metabolic rate；RMR
エネルギー蓄積足部（えねるぎーちくせきそくぶ）energy storing prosthetic foot
エネルギー必要量（えねるぎーひつようりょう）energy requirement
ABCDEモデル（えーびーしーでぃーいーもでる）ABCDE model
エビスタ（えびすた）Evista
エピソード記憶（えぴそーどきおく）episodic memory
APDL（えーぴーでぃーえる）activities parallel to daily living
エフェクサー（えふぇくさー）Effexor
F波（えふは）F wave
エプロン（えぷろん）apron
MID（えむあいでぃー）multi-infarct dementia

MRI（えむあーるあい）magnetic resonance imaging
MRA（えむあーるえー）magnetic resonance angiography
†MRSA（えむあーるえすえい）methicillin-resistant staphylococcus aureus
†MMSE（えむえむえすいー）Mini Mental State Examination
†MMT（えむえむてぃー）Manual Muscle Testing
M波（えむは）M wave
エリアサービス（えりあさーびす）area services
エリスロポエチン（えりすろぽえちん）erythropoietin
LOL（えるおーえる）length of life
エルゴノミクス（えるごのみくす）ergonomics
エルゴメーター（えるごめーたー）ergometer
LD（えるでぃー）learning disability
LDL（えるでぃーえる）low-density lipoprotein
LDLコレステロール（えるでぃーえるこれすてろーる）low-density lipoprotein
LDスクリーニングテスト（えるでぃーすくりーにんぐてすと）learning disability screening
エルデプリル（えるでぷりる）Eldepryl
エレクトラ・コンプレックス（えれくとら・こんぷれっくす）Electra complex
エレトリプタン（えれとりぷたん）eletriptan
エロス（えろす）Eros
遠位（えんい）distal
遠位潜時（えんいせんじ）distal latency
遠位端（えんいたん）distal end
演繹推論（えんえきすいろん）deductive reasoning
演繹法（えんえきほう）deductive method
エンカウンターグループ（えんかうんたーぐるーぷ）encounter group
遠隔医療（えんかくいりょう）remote medicine；telemedicine
遠隔医療システム（えんかくいりょうしすてむ）remote medical system；telemedicine system
遠隔学習（えんかくがくしゅう）distance learning
遠隔教育（えんかくきょういく）distance education
遠隔ケア（えんかくけあ）remote care
遠隔操作用具（えんかくそうさようぐ）aid for extended reach
遠隔地医療（えんかくちいりょう）remote area medicine
円環的因果律（えんかんてきいんがりつ）circular causality
遠距離医療（えんきょりいりょう）long-distance medicine
遠距離介護（えんきょりかいご）long-distance care；long-distance caregiving
†嚥下（えんげ）swallowing

園芸療法（えんげいりょうほう）horticultural therapy
嚥下運動（えんげうんどう）movement during swallowing
嚥下機能（えんげきのう）swallowing function
嚥下機能障害（えんげきのうしょうがい）dysphagia of swallowing function
嚥下訓練（えんげくんれん）swallowing training
†嚥下困難（えんげこんなん）swallowing difficulty
嚥下障害（えんげしょうがい）dysphagia；swallowing disorder；deglutition disorder
†嚥下性肺炎（えんげせいはいえん）aspiration pneumonia；deglutition pneumonia
嚥下造影検査（えんげぞうえいけんさ）videofluorography；VF
嚥下痛（えんげつう）odynophagia
嚥下反射（えんげはんしゃ）swallowing reflex
†嚥下補助剤（えんげほじょざい）thickening agent
嚥下問題（えんげもんだい）swallowing problem
†エンゲル係数（えんげるけいすう）Engel's coefficient
エンゲル法則（えんげるほうそく）Engel's Law
援護（えんご）protection；relief
援護課（えんごか）Relief Division
援護企画課（えんごきかくか）Planning Division of War Victims' Relief
†円座（えんざ）circle mat
塩酸ピロカルピン（えんさんぴろかるぴん）pilocarpine hydrochloride
円熟（えんじゅく）mature
援助（えんじょ）assistance；support
援助関係（えんじょかんけい）therapeutic relationship
援助者（えんじょしゃ）assistant
援助付き雇用（えんじょつきこよう）supported employment
遠心エアサンプラ（えんしんえあさんぷら）centrifugal sampler
遠心性収縮（えんしんせいしゅうしゅく）eccentric contraction
延髄（えんずい）medulla oblongata
エンゼルプラン（えんぜるぷらん）Angel Plan
エンタカポン（えんたかぽん）entacapone
延長介護（えんちょうかいご）extended care；extended long-term care
延長保育（えんちょうほいく）extended childcare
エンテカビル（えんてかびる）entecavir
エンテロウイルス（えんてろういるす）enterovirus
エンド・オブ・ライフケア（えんど・おぶ・らいふけあ）end-of-life care
エンドトキシンテスト（えんどときしんてすと）endotoxin test
†エンパワメント（えんぱわめんと）empowerment

エンパワメントアプローチ（えんぱわめんとあぷろーち）empowerment approach
エンプティ・チェアー法（えんぷてぃ・ちぇあーほう）empty-chair technique
エンブレル（えんぶれる）Enbrel
塩分摂取（えんぶんせっしゅ）sodium intake
延命治療（えんめいちりょう）life-prolonging treatment；life-sustaining treatment

お

オアシス（おあしす）Outcome and Assessment Information Set：OASIS
老い（おい）oldness
OECD（おーいーしーでぃー）Organization for Economic Co-operation and Development
応益原則（おうえきげんそく）benefit principle
†応益負担（おうえきふたん）benefit-received principle
横隔膜（おうかくまく）diaphragma
†嘔気（おうき）nausea
†応急手当（おうきゅうてあて）emergency first aid
黄色肉芽腫性腎盂腎炎（おうしょくにくげしゅせいじんうじんえん）Xanthogranulomatous pyelonephritis
黄色ブドウ球菌（おうしょくぶどうきゅうきん）staphylococcus aureus
黄色ブドウ球菌性肺炎（おうしょくぶどうきゅうきんせいはいえん）staphylococcal pneumonia
往診（おうしん）doctor's home visit
黄疸（おうだん）jaundice
†嘔吐（おうと）vomiting
応能原則（おうのうげんそく）ability-to-pay principle
応能主義（おうのうしゅぎ）ability principle
†応能負担（おうのうふたん）ability-to-pay principle
黄斑変性（おうはんへんせい）macular degeneration
OA化（おーえーか）office automation
大きな政府（おおきなせいふ）big government
大振り歩行（おおぶりほこう）swing-through gait
悪寒（おかん）chill
†起き上がり（おきあがり）getting up
オキシコドン（おきしこどん）oxycodone
オキシコンチン（おきしこんちん）OxyContin
室内気候（おくないきこう）room climate
オージオグラム（おーじおぐらむ）⇒オーディオグラム
オージオメーター（おーじおめーたー）⇒オーディオメーター
OSHA（おーしゃ）⇒労働安全衛生庁
オストメイト（おすとめいと）ostomate
汚染（おせん）contamination
汚染区域（おせんくいき）contaminated area

介護保険・介護福祉等関連用語和英

汚染手術（おせんしゅじゅつ）contaminated operation
汚染除去処理（おせんじょきょしょり）decontamination procedure
汚染創（おせんそう）contaminated wound
オゾン（おぞん）ozone
オタワ憲章（おたわけんしょう）Ottawa Charter for Health Promotion
OT（おーてぃー）occupational therapist
ODA（おーでぃーえー）official development assistance
オーディオグラム（おーでぃおぐらむ）audiogram
オーディオメーター（おーでぃおめーたー）audiometer
オートクレーブ（おーとくれーぶ）autoclave
オートノミー（おーとのみー）autonomy
オーバーキル（おーばーきる）overkill
オーバーベッドテーブル（おーばーべっどてーぶる）overbed table
オピオイド薬（おぴおいどやく）opioid medication
汚物室（おぶつしつ）⇒不潔物収納室
オブラート（おぶらーと）oblate
オペラント技法（おぺらんとぎほう）operant technique
オペラント条件づけ（おぺらんとじょうけんづけ）operant conditioning
†おむつ（おむつ）diaper
†おむつカバー（おむつかばー）diaper cover
†おむつ交換（おむつこうかん）diaper change
†おむつ外し（おむつはずし）diaper removal
親孝行（おやこうこう）filial piety to parents
親子関係（おやこかんけい）parent-child relationship
親の会（おやのかい）parent group
親指の指紋（おやゆびのしもん）thumbprint
オランザピン（おらんざぴん）olanzapine
オーリスタット（おーりすたっと）orlistat
折りたたみ前輪歩行器（おりたたみぜんりんほこうき）front wheel folding walker
オルタナティブ・メディスン（おるたなてぃぶ・めでぃすん）alternative medicine
オルメサルタン（おるめさるたん）olmesartan
温罨法（おんあんほう）hot foment
音楽療法（おんがくりょうほう）music therapy
恩給（おんきゅう）soldiers' pension
温湿布（おんしっぷ）hot compress
音声案内（おんせいあんない）voice guidance
音声機能障害（おんせいきのうしょうがい）speech disorder；speech impairment
音声増幅器（おんせいぞうふくき）sound amplifier
温泉療法（おんせんりょうほう）balneotherapy
温痛覚過敏（おんつうかくかびん）hyperalgesia
温熱療法（おんねつりょうほう）thermotherapy；heat therapy
オンブズパーソン（おんぶずぱーそん）ombudsperson
オンブズマン（おんぶずまん）ombudsman

か

†臥位（がい）lying position
皆医療保険（かいいりょうほけん）universal medical care insurance
皆医療保険制度（かいいりょうほけんせいど）universal medical care insurance system
外因性（がいいんせい）exogenous
外因性感染（がいいんせいかんせん）exogenous infection
外因性ホルモン（がいいんせいほるもん）exogenous hormone
下位運動ニューロン（かいうんどうにゅーろん）lower motor neuron
開運動連鎖（かいうんどうれんさ）open kinetic chain
回外（かいがい）supination
海外協力課（かいがいきょうりょくか）Overseas Cooperation Division
皆介護保険（かいかいごほけん）universal long-term care insurance
皆介護保険制度（かいかいごほけんせいど）universal long-term care insurance system
絵画音声了解度検査（かいがおんせいりょうかいどけんさ）Picture Speech Intelligibility Evaluation：SPINE
階級社会（かいきゅうしゃかい）hierarchical society
概況調査（がいきょうちょうさ）general condition survey
会計監査（かいけいかんさ）audit of financial accounts；audit of financial statements
会計年度（かいけいねんど）fiscal year
解決志向的アプローチ（かいけつしこうてきあぷろーち）solution-focused approach
解雇（かいこ）termination of employment
†介護（かいご）care；long-term care
開口色モード（かいこうしょくもーど）aperture color mode
外向性（がいこうせい）extraversion
開口有効幅員（かいこうゆうこうふくいん）effective width of doorway
介護援助者（かいごえんじょしゃ）care assistant；long-term care assistant
介護オンブズマン（かいごおんぶずまん）long-term care ombudsman
介護型老人ホーム（かいごがたろうじんほーむ）custodial care facility
†介護過程（かいごかてい）care process；process

of care
介護関係（かいごかんけい）care provider-recipient relationship；care provider-client relationship
介護機器（かいごきき）care equipment；care device
†介護技術（かいごぎじゅつ）care skills；skills for long-term care
介護技術講習会（かいごぎじゅつこうしゅうかい）practical skills training for long-term care
†介護休業（かいごきゅうぎょう）family care leave
介護休業制度（かいごきゅうぎょうせいど）family care leave system
介護休業手当金（かいごきゅうぎょうてあてきん）family care allowance
†介護給付（かいごきゅうふ）long-term care insurance benefit
介護給付費納付金（かいごきゅうふひのうふきん）government subsidy to care providers
介護記録（かいごきろく）nursing records
外国生まれ高齢者（がいこくうまれこうれいしゃ）foreign-born elderly
外国人介護労働者（がいこくじんかいごろうどうしゃ）migrant care worker；foreign-born care worker
外国人雇用対策課（がいこくじんこようたいさくか）Foreign Workers' Affairs Division
†介護計画（かいごけいかく）care plan
介護行為（かいごこうい）nursing care practice；long term care practice
介護講習（かいごこうしゅう）practical training for long-term care
介護サービス（かいごさーびす）long-term care services
†介護サービス計画（かいごさーびすけいかく）care services plan
介護サービス情報公開（かいごさーびすじょうほうこうかい）public reporting of long-term care services
介護サービス提供責任者（かいごさーびすていきょうせきにんしゃ）care services manager
介護サービス提供票（かいごさーびすていきょうひょう）service provider report
介護サービスパッケージ（かいごさーびすぱっけーじ）long-term care services package
介護支援サービス（かいごしえんさーびす）care management services
介護支援サービス計画（かいごしえんさーびすけいかく）care management services plan
†介護支援専門員（かいごしえんせんもんいん）care manager
介護事故（かいごじこ）errors in long-term care
介護姿勢（かいごしせい）attitudes toward care
介護施設（かいごしせつ）long-term care facility
介護施設事業者（かいごしせつじぎょうしゃ）institutional care provider
介護実習・普及センター（かいごじっしゅう・ふきゅうせんたー）practice and promotion center for long-term care
†介護指導（かいごしどう）care guidance
†介護者（かいごしゃ）caregiver
介護者ストレス（かいごしゃすとれす）caregiver stress
介護者手当（かいごしゃてあて）carer's allowance
介護者における二次的ストレス（かいごしゃにおけるにじてきすとれす）secondary stress on caregivers
介護者の権利（かいごしゃのけんり）caregivers' rights；rights of caregivers
介護者の燃え尽き症候群（かいごしゃのもえつきしょうこうぐん）caregiver burnout
介護者不安（かいごしゃふあん）anxiety for long-term caregivers
介護者負担（かいごしゃふたん）caregiver burden
介護者負担指標（かいごしゃふたんしひょう）caregiver strain index；CSI
介護従事者（かいごじゅうじしゃ）direct care staff
†介護職員（かいごしょくいん）direct care staff
介護専門（かいごせんもん）direct care profession；care profession
介護専門職（かいごせんもんしょく）direct care professional；care professional
介護相談員（かいごそうだんいん）long-term care advisor；care advisor
介護担当者（かいごたんとうしゃ）direct care staff
介護手当（かいごてあて）long-term care allowance
回顧的監査（かいこてきかんさ）retrospective review
回顧的調査（かいこてきちょうさ）retrospective study
介護手順（かいごてじゅん）procedures of long-term care
†介護ニーズ（かいごにーず）long-term care needs；care needs
介護日誌（かいごにっし）nursing notes
†介護認定審査会（かいごにんていしんさかい）Long-Term Care Certification Committee
介護の基準（かいごのきじゅん）standards of care practice
介護の質（かいごのしつ）quality of care
介護の社会化（かいごのしゃかいか）socialization of care
介護の倫理（かいごのりんり）ethics of long-term care
介護版マネジドケア（かいごばんまねじどけあ）managed long-term care
介護ビジネス（かいごびじねす）long-term care business

介護保険・介護福祉等関連用語 和英

介護費用（かいごひよう）long-term care costs；long-term care expenses
介護費用支払（かいごひようしはらい）payments to care providers
†介護福祉（かいごふくし）care and welfare
†介護福祉士（かいごふくしし）certified care worker；CCW
†介護福祉士国家試験（かいごふくししこっかしけん）National Certification Examination for Care Workers
介護福祉士国家試験・実技試験（かいごふくししこっかしけん・じつぎしけん）National Certification Examination and Practice Examination for Care Workers
†介護福祉士登録（かいごふくししとうろく）Certified Care Worker Registry
介護扶助（かいごふじょ）long-term care assistance
†介護負担（かいごふたん）burden of care；care burden
介護負担質問票（かいごふたんしつもんひょう）Caregiver Burden Interview
介護負担尺度（かいごふたんしゃくど）Caregiver Burden Scale
介護部門（かいごぶもん）direct care section
介護へのアクセス（かいごへのあくせす）access to care
介護放棄（かいごほうき）neglect
†介護報酬（かいごほうしゅう）long-term care insurance payment
†介護保険（かいごほけん）long-term care insurance
介護保険課（かいごほけんか）Long-term Care Insurance Division
†介護保険事業計画（かいごほけんじぎょうけいかく）long-term care insurance plan
介護保険指定事業者（かいごほけんしていじぎょうしゃ）long-term care insurance certified provider
†介護保険審査会（かいごほけんしんさかい）Review Committee on Long-term Care Insurance
†介護保険制度（かいごほけんせいど）long-term care insurance system
†介護保険認定調査（かいごほけんにんていちょうさ）long-term care insurance eligibility assessment
介護保険被保険者（かいごほけんひほけんしゃ）the insured of long-term care insurance
†介護保険法（かいごほけんほう）Long-Term Care Insurance Law
介護保険法施行法（かいごほけんほうしこうほう）Act for Enforcement of the Long-Term Care Insurance Act
介護保険料（かいごほけんりょう）long-term care insurance premium；long-term care premium
介護保険料加算（かいごほけんりょうかさん）additional assistance for long-term care insurance
介護保険料減免制度（かいごほけんりょうげんめんせいど）deduction of long-term care insurance premiums
介護保険料率（かいごほけんりょうりつ）long-term care insurance premium rate；premium rate of long-term care insurance
介護満足感（かいごまんぞくかん）satisfaction in caregiving
†介護目標（かいごもくひょう）care goal
介護モデル（かいごもでる）long-term care model
†介護用具（かいごようぐ）care equipment
介護用品（かいごようひん）care equipment
†介護予防（かいごよぼう）prevention of long-term care
介護予防一般高齢者施策（かいごよぼういっぱんこうれいしゃさく）preventive aged-care approach for the independent
介護予防ケアマネジメント（かいごよぼうけあまねじめんと）preventive care management
介護予防サービス（かいごよぼうさーびす）care-preventive services
†介護予防事業（かいごよぼうじぎょう）preventive long-term care plan
介護予防短期入所生活介護（かいごよぼうたんきにゅうしょせいかつかいご）preventive short-term care accommodation
介護予防特定高齢者施策（かいごよぼうとくていこうれいしゃさく）preventive aged-care approach for the frail
介護予防特定施設入所者生活介護（かいごよぼうとくていしせつにゅうしょしゃせいかつかいご）specific care home for the preventive long-term care
介護予防福祉用具貸与（かいごよぼうふくしようぐたいよ）preventive rental services of welfare equipments
介護予防訪問入浴介護（かいごよぼうほうもんにゅうよくかいご）preventive home bathing care
介護理念（かいごりねん）morality of long-term care
†介護療養型医療施設（かいごりょうようがたいりょうしせつ）long-term health care facility
介護力強化計画（かいごりょくきょうかけいかく）empowerment plan for long-term care
†介護老人福祉施設（かいごろうじんふくししせつ）geriatric welfare facility；welfare facility for aged-care
†介護老人保健施設（かいごろうじんほけんしせつ）geriatric health care facility
介護労働（かいごろうどう）care work
介護労働安定センター（かいごろうどうあんていせん

たー) Care Work Foundation：CWF
†介護労働者（かいごろうどうしゃ）care worker
介護ロボット（かいごろぼっと）care robot
概日リズム（がいじつりずむ）circadian rhythm
解釈（かいしゃく）interpretation
回収代行業者（かいしゅうだいこうぎょうしゃ）⇒債権回収会社
外出支援（がいしゅつしえん）transportation and escort services
†介助（かいじょ）assistance
介助員（かいじょいん）assistant
外傷（がいしょう）trauma
外傷後ストレス障害（がいしょうごすとれすしょうがい）post-traumatic stress disorder：PTSD
外傷性損傷（がいしょうせいそんしょう）traumatic injury
外傷性脳損傷（がいしょうせいのうそんしょう）traumatic brain injury：TBI
介助訓練（かいじょくんれん）assistive exercise
介助犬（かいじょけん）assistance dog；partner dog；service dog
介助用車いす（かいじょようくるまいす）manual attendant-controlled wheelchair
回診（かいしん）physician rounds
†疥癬（かいせん）scabies
外旋（がいせん）external rotation
改善活動（かいぜんかつどう）quality improvement：QI
回旋帯（かいせんたい）rotator strap
改善命令（かいぜんめいれい）remedial order
回想（かいそう）life review；reminiscence
咳嗽介助（がいそうかいじょ）assisted coughing
†回想法（かいそうほう）reminiscence therapy
外側楔付き足底装具（がいそくくさびつきそくていそうぐ）foot orthosis with lateral corrective wedge
外側ホイップ（がいそくほいっぷ）lateral whip
†階段（かいだん）stairs
†階段昇降（かいだんしょうこう）scaling stairs
階段昇降機（かいだんしょうこうき）stair lift
改訂アッシュワース尺度（かいていあっしゅわーすしゃくど）Modified Ashworth Scale
改訂バーセル指数（かいていばーせるしすう）modified Barthel index
改定版ウェクスラー記憶検査（かいていばんうぇくすらーきおくけんさ）Revised Wechsler Memory Scale：WMS-R
改定版ウェクスラー成人知能検査（かいていばんうぇくすらーせいじんちのうけんさ）Revised Wechsler Adult Intelligence Scale：WAIS-R
改訂版児童用顕在性不安尺度（かいていばんじどうようけんざいせいふあんしゃくど）Revised Children's Manifest Anxiety Scale

改訂水飲みテスト（かいていみずのみてすと）Modified Water Swallow Test
外的照合枠（がいてきしょうごうわく）external frame of reference
外転（がいてん）abduction
回転前庭動眼反射（かいてんぜんていどうがんはんしゃ）rotational vestibulo-ocular reflex
外転防止ブロック（がいてんぼうしぶろっく）abduction block
外転歩行（がいてんほこう）abduction gait
ガイドヘルパー（がいどへるぱー）guide helper
ガイドライン（がいどらいん）guidelines
回内（かいない）pronation
介入（かいにゅう）intervention
介入研究（かいにゅうけんきゅう）intervention study
介入的画像診断（かいにゅうてきがぞうしんだん）interventional radiology：IVR
介入的血管造影（かいにゅうてきけっかんぞうえい）interventional angiography
皆年金（かいねんきん）universal pension
皆年金保険（かいねんきんほけん）universal pension insurance
皆年金保険制度（かいねんきんほけんせいど）universal pension insurance system
灰白髄炎（かいはくずいえん）poliomyelitis
開発途上国（かいはつとじょうこく）developing country
外反（がいはん）valgus
外反足（がいはんそく）talipes valgus
外反母趾（がいはんぼし）hallux valgus
外皮（がいひ）integumentary
回避学習（かいひがくしゅう）avoidance learning
外皮系（がいひけい）integumentary system
回避条件づけ（かいひじょうけんづけ）avoidance conditioning
回復期施設（かいふくしせつ）convalescent home
回復期保菌者（かいふくきほきんしゃ）convalescent carrier
†回復期リハビリテーション（かいふくきりはびりてーしょん）recovery phase rehabilitation；convalescent rehabilitation
外部チューブ（がいぶちゅーぶ）enteral tube：ET
解剖学的肢位（かいぼうがくてきしい）anatomical position
開放式ドレナージ法（かいほうしきどれなーじほう）open drainage system
開放施設（かいほうしせつ）open facility
開放性骨折（かいほうせいこっせつ）open fracture；compound fracture
開放登録期間（かいほうとうろくきかん）open enrollment period

開放名簿制（かいほうめいぼせい）open-panel
皆保険（かいほけん）universal insurance
皆保険制度（かいほけんせいど）universal health insurance system
界面反射（かいめんはんしゃ）interface reflection
†潰瘍（かいよう）ulcer
潰瘍形成（かいようけいせい）ulceration
外来ケア（がいらいけあ）outpatient care；ambulatory care
外来時一部負担金（がいらいじいちぶふたんきん）lump sum payment for outpatient
外来診療（がいらいしんりょう）outpatient medicine；ambulatory medicine
外来診療所（がいらいしんりょうしょ）outpatient clinic；ambulatory clinic
外来リハビリテーション（がいらいりはびりてーしょん）outpatient rehabilitation；ambulatory rehabilitation
快楽原則（かいらくげんそく）pleasure principle
解離性感覚障害（かいりせいかんかくしょうがい）dissociated sensory disturbance
解離性障害（かいりせいしょうがい）dissociative disorder
解離同一性障害（かいりどういつせいしょうがい）dissociative identity disorder
カイロプラクティック（かいろぷらくてぃっく）chiropractic
カウザルギー（かうざるぎー）causalgia
カウンセラー（かうんせらー）counselor
カウンセリング（かうんせりんぐ）counseling
ガウンテクニック（がうんてくにっく）gown technique
帰る家がない（かえるいえがない）homelessness
火炎滅菌（かえんめっきん）flame sterilization
家屋火災（かおくかさい）house fire
家屋修理詐欺（かおくしゅうりさぎ）home repair scam
家屋評価（かおくひょうか）house evaluation
科学（かがく）science
過角化症（かかくかしょう）hyperkeratosis
科学研究費補助金（かがくけんきゅうひほじょきん）grant-in-aid for scientific research
化学繊維（かがくせんい）chemical fiber
化学塞栓（かがくそくせん）chemoembolization
化学的インジケータ（かがくてきいんじけーた）chemical indicator
化学物質関連障害（かがくぶっしつかんれんしょうがい）substance-related disorder
化学物質対策課（かがくぶっしつたいさくか）Chemical Hazards Control Division
化学療法（かがくりょうほう）chemotherapy
踵接地（かかとせっち）heel contact
踵バンパー（かかとばんぱー）heel bumper

踵離地（かかとりち）heel off
かがみ肢位（かがみしい）crouch posture
†かかりつけ医（かかりつけい）primary doctor；primary care physician；family doctor
かかりつけ医意見書（かかりつけいいけんしょ）report from the primary doctor
かかりつけ担当医（かかりつけたんとうい）primary care physician
鍵穴手術（かぎあなしゅじゅつ）keyhole surgery
核黄疸（かくおうだん）kernicterus
†核家族（かくかぞく）nuclear family
学際的（がくさいてき）interdisciplinary
学士号（がくしごう）bachelor's degree
学習障害（がくしゅうしょうがい）learning disability；LD；learning disorder
学習性無力感（がくしゅうせいむりょくかん）learned helplessness
学習性無力感理論（がくしゅうせいむりょくかんりろん）learned helplessness theory
学習能力（がくしゅうのうりょく）learning ability
学習パラダイム（がくしゅうぱらだいむ）learning paradigm
学習理論（がくしゅうりろん）learning theory
核心臓学（かくしんぞうがく）nuclear cardiology
核心臓スキャン（かくしんぞうすきゃん）nuclear heart scan
核スキャン（かくすきゃん）nuclear scanning
覚醒（かくせい）awake
覚醒剤（かくせいざい）awakening drug；stimulant
拡大家族（かくだいかぞく）extended family
拡大読書器（かくだいどくしょき）enlarging reading device
拡大内視鏡検査（かくだいないしきょうけんさ）magnifying endoscopy
拡張期血圧（かくちょうきけつあつ）diastolic pressure
確定拠出年金（かくていきょしゅつねんきん）defined contribution
各年管理歳出（かくねんかんりさいしゅつ）annually managed expenditure；AME
角膜反射（かくまくはんしゃ）corneal reflex
隔離（かくり）isolation
隔離室（かくりしつ）isolation room
隔離病院（かくりびょういん）pest house
隔離病室（かくりびょうしつ）isolation room
隔離病棟（かくりびょうとう）isolation unit
隔離予防策（かくりよぼうさく）isolation precaution
隠れた文化的障壁（かくれたぶんかてきしょうへき）hidden cultural barrier
†家計（かけい）household budget；family budget
過誤納額（かごのうがく）overpayment of premium
火災危険度（かさいきけんど）fire risk

過酢酸（かさくさん）peracetic acid
重ね着（かさねぎ）layered clothing
加算（かさん）⇒付加
過酸化水素ガスプラズマ滅菌（かさんかすいそがすぷらずまめっきん）hydrogen peroxide gas plasma sterilization
下肢（かし）lower extremity
†家事（かじ）housekeeping；household work
家事援助（かじえんじょ）homemaker services；chore services
家事援助者（かじえんじょしゃ）homemaker；housekeeper
家事サービス提供者（かじさーびすていきょうしゃ）homemaker services provider
下肢切断（かしせつだん）lower limb amputation
下肢装具（かしそうぐ）lower extremity orthosis
家事手伝い（かじてつだい）domestic helper
家事分担（かじぶんたん）housekeeping assignment
過重成長（かじゅうせいちょう）overgrowth
臥床（がしょう）bed rest
過剰な流涎（かじょうなりゅうぜん）excessive drooling
過剰ミネラル（かじょうみねらる）mineral excess
過食（かしょく）overeating
過食症（かしょくしょう）bulimia
可処分所得（かしょぶんしょとく）disposable income
家事労働（かじろうどう）housekeeping；domestic labor
過伸展（かしんてん）hyperextension
ガストログラフィン注腸（がすとろぐらふぃんちゅうちょう）gastrografin enema
ガス滅菌（がすめっきん）gas sterilization
ガーゼ（がーぜ）gauze
†家政（かせい）housekeeping
仮性球麻痺（かせいきゅうまひ）pseudobulbar paralysis
仮性認知症（かせいにんちしょう）pseudodementia
†家政婦（かせいふ）housekeeper
風邪のような症状（かぜのようなしょうじょう）flu-like symptom
過疎（かそ）depopulation
火葬（かそう）cremation
下層社会（かそうしゃかい）lower social stratum
画像診断（がぞうしんだん）diagnostic imaging
火葬又は埋葬（かそうまたはまいそう）cremation or burial
†家族（かぞく）family
†家族会（かぞくかい）self-help group for families
†家族介護（かぞくかいご）family-provided care
†家族介護者（かぞくかいごしゃ）family caregiver
家族介護負担感尺度（かぞくかいごふたんかんしゃく

ど）Family Caregiver Burden Scale
家族解体（かぞくかいたい）family disorganization
†家族関係（かぞくかんけい）family relationship
家族機能（かぞくきのう）family function
家族給付（かぞくきゅうふ）family benefit
家族計画（かぞくけいかく）family plan
家族ケースワーカー（かぞくけーすわーかー）family case worker
家族ケースワーク（かぞくけーすわーく）family care work
家族構成（かぞくこうせい）family composition
家族構造（かぞくこうぞう）family structure
家族支援（かぞくしえん）family support
家族支援センター（かぞくしえんせんたー）family support center
家族指向ケア（かぞくしこうけあ）family-oriented care
家族システム（かぞくしすてむ）family system
家族システムズアプローチ（かぞくしすてむずあぷろーち）family systems approach
家族システム理論（かぞくしすてむりろん）family system theory
家族指導（かぞくしどう）family education
家族社会学（かぞくしゃかいがく）sociology of the family
家族周期（かぞくしゅうき）family life cycle
家族神話（かぞくしんわ）family myth
家族性大腸ポリポーシス（かぞくせいだいちょうぽりぽーしす）familial adenomatous polyposis：FAP
家族性非ポリポーシス大腸癌（かぞくせいひぽりぽーしすだいちょうがん）hereditary nonpolyposis colorectal cancer：HNCC
家族ソーシャルワーカー（かぞくそーしゃるわーかー）family social worker
家族ソーシャルワーク（かぞくそーしゃるわーく）family social work
家族中心ケア（かぞくちゅうしんけあ）family-based care
家族手当（かぞくてあて）family allowance
家族扶養（かぞくふよう）responsible for family
家族ホメオスタシス（かぞくほめおすたしす）family homeostasis
家族問題（かぞくもんだい）family issue
家族療法（かぞくりょうほう）family therapy
家族療養費（かぞくりょうようひ）dependent health care coverage
家族ルール（かぞくるーる）family rule
家族歴（かぞくれき）family history
可塑性（かそせい）plasticity
下腿義足（かたいぎそく）transtibial prosthesis；below-knee prosthesis
過怠金（かたいきん）fines for default

課題遂行能力（かだいすいこうのうりょく）task performance ability
下腿切断（かたいせつだん）below-knee amputation
下腿ソケット（かたいそけっと）transtibial socket
課題中心アプローチ（かだいちゅうしんあぷろーち）task-centered approach
課題中心モデル（かだいちゅうしんもでる）task-centered model
課題分析（かだいぶんせき）task analysis
肩インピンジメント症候群（かたいんぴんじめんとしょうこうぐん）shoulder impingement syndrome
肩外転装具（かたがいてんそうぐ）airplane splint；shoulder abduction orthosis
肩関節亜脱臼（かたかんせつあだっきゅう）shoulder subluxation
肩関節周囲炎（かたかんせつしゅういえん）adhesive capsulitis；frozen shoulder
肩関節脱臼（かたかんせつだっきゅう）shoulder dislocation
肩義手（かたぎしゅ）shoulder disarticulation prosthesis
肩吊り帯（かたつりたい）shoulder suspension system
肩手症候群（かたてしょうこうぐん）shoulder-hand syndrome
片手動作（かたてどうさ）one-handed activity
片麻痺（かたまひ）hemiplegia
肩輪転子（かたりんてんき）shoulder wheel
カタルシス（かたるしす）catharsis
カタルシス法（かたるしすほう）cathartic method
価値（かち）value
価値観（かちかん）sense of value；conception of value；value system
角化症（かくかしょう）keratosis
角化症病変（かくかしょうびょうへん）keratotic lesions
喀血（かっけつ）hemoptysis；haemoptysis；coughing up of blood
学校法人（がっこうほうじん）private school corporation
滑車（かっしゃ）pulley
活性酸素（かっせいさんそ）active oxygen
活性炭（かっせいたん）active charcoal
活性炭素（かっせいたんそ）active carbon
活性輸送（かっせいゆそう）⇒能動輸送
カッツADLインデックス（かっつえーでぃーえるいんでっくす）Katz ADL index
葛藤（かっとう）conflict
活動（かつどう）activity
活動制限（かつどうせいげん）activity limitation
活動平均余命（かつどうてきへいきんよめい）active life expectancy

活動電位（かつどうでんい）action potential：AP
活動理論（かつどうりろん）activity theory
カップル療法（かっぷるりょうほう）couple therapy
†合併症（がっぺいしょう）complication
滑膜切除術（かつまくせつじょじゅつ）synovectomy
括約筋形成術（かつやくきんけいせいじゅつ）sphincteroplasty
活約筋障害（かつやくきんしょうがい）sphincter disturbance
家庭医（かてい）family doctor
家庭医機能（かていいきのう）family doctor's function
家庭裁判所（かていさいばんしょ）family court
家庭政策（かていせいさく）family policy
家庭相談員（かていそうだんいん）family adviser
家庭道具（かていどうぐ）⇒台所道具
家庭内事故（かていないじこ）home accident；accidents in the home
家庭内暴力（かていないぼうりょく）domestic violence：DV
家庭福祉（かていふくし）family welfare
家庭福祉課（かていふくしか）Family Welfare Division
家庭奉仕（かていほうし）domestic help
家庭奉仕員（かていほうしいん）domestic helper
家庭奉仕員派遣事業（かていほうしいんはけんじぎょう）delivery program of domestic helpers
家庭浴槽（かていよくそう）home bathtub
カテコール-O-メチルトランスフェラーゼ（かてこーる・おると・めちるとらんすふぇらーぜ）catechol-O-methyltransferase：COMT
カテーテル（かてーてる）catheter
カテーテル関連感染（かてーてるかんれんかんせん）catheter-associated infection
カテーテル関連血流感染（かてーてるかんれんけつりゅうかんせん）catheter-associated bloodstream infection：CABSI
カテーテル由来感染（かてーてるゆらいかんせん）catheter-related infection
カテーテル由来菌血症（かてーてるゆらいきんけつしょう）catheter-related bacteremia
カテーテル由来血流感染（かてーてるゆらいけつりゅうかんせん）catheter-related bloodstream infection：CRBSI
カテーテル留置法（かてーてるりゅうちほう）catheterization
ガーデン骨折分類（がーでんこっせつぶんるい）Garden classification system of fracture
可動性（かどうせい）⇒移動性
可動性室内空気清浄機（かどうせいしつないくうきせいじょうき）mobile room air cleaner

稼動率（かどうりつ）utilization rate
カドヘリン（かどへりん）cadherin
家内労働（かないろうどう）family labor
カナダ式股義足（かなだしきこぎそく）Canadian-type hip disarticulation prosthesis
加入（かにゅう）enrollment；participation
加入者（かにゅうしゃ）enrollee；participant
加入制約（かにゅうせいやく）enrollment restriction；participation restriction
カニューレ（かにゅーれ）cannula
ガバペンチン（がばぺんちん）gabapentin
ガビトリル（がびとりる）Gabitril
†寡婦[女性]（かふ）widow
寡夫[男性]（かふ）widower
カフェイン（かふぇいん）caffeine
ガフキー号数（がふきーごうすう）Gaffky table
寡婦給付（かふきゅうふ）widow benefit
カプサイシン（かぷさいしん）capsaicin
下部消化管（かぶしょうかかん）lower gastrointestinal
下部食道括約筋（かぶしょくどうかつやくきん）lower esophageal sphincter；LES
下部食道括約筋機能障害（かぶしょくどうかつやくきんきのうしょうがい）lower esophageal sphincter dysfunction
寡婦税控除（かふぜいこうじょ）tax deduction for widows
家父長制（かふちょうせい）patriarchalism
寡婦年金（かふねんきん）widow's pension
寡婦福祉資金貸与（かふふくししきんたいよ）welfare fund loan for widows
ガブリエル針（がぶりえるしん）Gabriel needle
花粉症（かふんしょう）hay fever
貨幣的ニーズ（かへいてきにーず）monetary needs
可変摩擦継手（かへんまさつつぎて）variable friction joint
芽胞（がほう）spore
過保護（かほご）overprotection
過補償（かほしょう）overcompensation
髪（かみ）hair
†紙おむつ（かみおむつ）paper diaper
過剰人口（かみつじんこう）overpopulation
かゆみ（かゆみ）pruritus
過用（かよう）overuse
†過用症候群（かようしょうこうぐん）overuse syndrome
過用性筋力低下（かようせいきんりょくていか）over work weakness
空の巣症候群（からのすしょうこうぐん）empty nest syndrome
から拭き（からぶき）dry wiping
カラン（からん）Calan
ガランタミン（がらんたみん）galantamine

仮義手（かりぎしゅ）temporary prosthesis of upper limb amputee
仮釈放（かりしゃくほう）conditional release；release on parole
仮出所（かりしゅっしょ）⇒仮釈放
カリタス（かりたす）caritas
仮徴収（かりちょうしゅう）provisional collection
仮命令（かりめいれい）interim order
渦流浴（かりゅうよく）whirlpool bath
過料（かりょう）non-penal fine
カルシウム（かるしうむ）calcium
カルシウム拮抗剤（かるしうむきっこうざい）calcium channel blocker
カルシウム欠乏症（かるしうむけつぼうしょう）calcium deficiency
カルシトニン（かるしとにん）calcitonin
カルディゼム（かるでぃぜむ）Cardizem
カルバマゼピン（かるばまぜぴん）carbamazepine
†加齢（かれい）aging
加齢黄斑変性（かれいおうはんへんせい）age-related macular degeneration
加齢性疾患（かれいせいしっかん）age-related disease
カロリー制限（かろりーせいげん）caloric restriction
革細工（かわざいく）leather work
川崎病（かわさきびょう）mucocutaneous lymph node syndrome
†癌（がん）cancer
眼圧計（がんあつけい）tonometry
簡易栄養状態アセスメント（かんいえいようじょうたいあせすめんと）Mini Nutritional Assessment；MNA
簡易口腔衛生検査（かんいこうくうえいせいけんさ）Brief Oral Health Status Examination；BOHSE
簡易損傷スケール（かんいそんしょうすけーる）Abbreviated Injury Scale；AIS
簡易疼痛調査票（かんいとうつうちょうさひょう）Brief Pain Inventory；BPI
簡易疲労一覧表（かんいひろういちらんひょう）Brief Fatigue Inventory；BFI
簡易浴槽（かんいよくそう）simple bathtub；portable bathtub
肝炎（かんえん）hepatitis
†感音難聴（かんおんなんちょう）sensorineural deafness；sensorineural hearing loss
寛解（かんかい）remission
眼科医（がんかい）ophthalmologist
眼科学（がんかがく）ophthalmology
感覚（かんかく）sense
感覚過敏（かんかくかびん）hyperesthesia
†感覚機能（かんかくきのう）sensory function
感覚強化法（かんかくきょうかほう）sensory

介護保険・介護福祉等関連用語　和英

enhancement
感覚障害（かんかくしょうがい）sensory disturbance；sensory disorder
感覚消失（かんかくしょうしつ）anesthesia
感覚神経（かんかくしんけい）sensory nerve
感覚神経伝導速度（かんかくしんけいでんどうそくど）sensory nerve conduction velocity
感覚性失語（かんかくせいしつご）sensory aphasia
感覚代行（かんかくだいこう）sensory substitution
感覚統合（かんかくとうごう）sensory integration
感覚鈍麻（かんかくどんま）hypesthesia
感覚麻痺（かんかくまひ）sensory paralysis
肝癌（かんがん）liver cancer
癌患者（がんかんじゃ）cancer patient
†換気（かんき）ventilation
肝機能検査（かんきのうけんさ）liver function test；LFT
環境因子（かんきょういんし）environmental factor
環境汚染（かんきょうおせん）environmental pollution
環境危険物質（かんきょうきけんぶっしつ）environmental hazards
環境権（かんきょうけん）environmental rights
環境サーベイランス（かんきょうさーべいらんす）environmental surveillance
眼鏡士（がんきょうし）optometrist
環境制御装置（かんきょうせいぎょそうち）environmental control system；ECS
†環境整備（かんきょうせいび）environmental maintenance；environmental improvement
環境調査（かんきょうちょうさ）environmental sampling
環境微生物調査（かんきょうびせいぶつちょうさ）microbial sampling
環境保護機関（かんきょうほごきかん）environmental protection agency
環境問題（かんきょうもんだい）environmental problem
環境由来疾患（かんきょうゆらいしっかん）disorder of environmental origin
緩下剤（かんげざい）laxative
間欠〈間欠〉牽引（かんけつけんいん）intermittent traction
間歇〈間欠〉性跛行（かんけつせいはこう）intermittent claudication
間欠的空気圧迫療法（かんけつてきくうきあっぱくちりょう）intermittent pneumatic compression
間欠的陽圧呼吸法（かんけつてきようあつこきゅうほう）intermittent positive-pressure breathing therapy
間欠導尿（かんけつどうにょう）intermittent urethral catheterization
†看護（かんご）nursing
監護（かんご）custody

感光色素（かんこうしきそ）photopigment
†肝硬変（かんこうへん）liver cirrhosis
看護課（かんごか）Nursing Division
看護関係者（かんごかんけいしゃ）nursing personnel
看護基礎教育（かんごきそきょういく）basic nursing education
勧告（かんこく）recommendation
看護系大学（かんごけいだいがく）nursing college；college of nursing
監護権（かんごけん）child custody
喚語困難（かんごこんなん）word finding difficulty
†看護師（かんごし）nurse
看護師長（かんごしちょう）director of nursing
看護師の倫理綱領（かんごしのりんりこうりょう）code of ethics for nurses
看護師不足（かんごしぶそく）nursing shortage
看護従事者（かんごじゅうじしゃ）nursing staff
喚語障害（かんごしょうがい）word finding disorder
看護職員（かんごしょくいん）nursing staff
看護助手（かんごじょしゅ）nurse aide
看護専門（かんごせんもん）nursing profession
看護専門職（かんごせんもんしょく）nursing professional
寛骨臼骨折（かんこつきゅうこっせつ）acetabular fracture
看護の基準（かんごのきじゅん）standards of nursing practice；standards of nursing
看護補助員（かんごほじょいん）nurse assistant
監査（かんさ）survey；inspection
監査官（かんさかん）surveyor；inspector
観察（かんさつ）observation
監視（かんし）surveillance
鉗子（かんし）forceps
監視安全課（かんしあんぜんか）Inspection and Safety Division
乾式洗濯（かんしきせんたく）dry cleaning
監視指導・麻薬対策課（かんししどう・まやくたいさくか）Compliance and Narcotics Division
鉗子生検（かんしせいけん）forceps biopsy
カンジダ・アルビカンス（かんじだ・あるびかんす）candida albicans
患者（かんじゃ）patient
患者記録（かんじゃきろく）patient records
患者中心医療（かんじゃちゅうしんいりょう）patient-centered medicine；client-centered medicine
患者中心療法（かんじゃちゅうしんりょうほう）patient-centered therapy；client-centered therapy
患者調査（かんじゃちょうさ）patient survey
患者調節鎮痛法（かんじゃちょうせつちんつうほう）personal-controlled analgesia；PCA
患者・提供者間関係（かんじゃ・ていきょうしゃかん

かんけい） patient-provider relationship
患者の安全（かんじゃのあんぜん） patient safety
患者の権利（かんじゃのけんり） patients' rights；rights of patients
患者満足度調査（かんじゃまんぞくどちょうさ） patient satisfaction survey
患者擁護（かんじゃようご） patient advocacy
感受性試験（かんじゅせいしけん） sensitivity test
感情気分質問票（かんじょうきぶんしつもんひょう） Feeling Tone Questionnaire：FTQ
感情失禁（かんじょうしっきん） emotional incontinence
感情転移（かんじょうてんい） transference
冠状動脈造影（かんじょうどうみゃくぞうえい） coronary angiography
感情鈍麻（かんじょうどんま） apathy
緩徐進行性インスリン依存糖尿病（かんじょしんこうせいいんすりんいぞんとうにょうびょう） slowly progressive insulin dependent diabetes
癌診療連携拠点病院（がんしんりょうれんけいきょてんびょういん） designated cancer hospital
乾性温熱（かんせいおんねつ） dry heat
癌性疼痛（がんせいとうつう） carcinomatous pain
眼精疲労（がんせいひろう） asthenopia
†関節（かんせつ） joint
関節運動学的アプローチ（かんせつうんどうがくてきあぷろーち） arthrokinematic approach：AKA
関節炎（かんせつえん） arthritis
間接援助技術（かんせつえんじょぎじゅつ） indirect social work
関節角度計（かんせつかくどけい） goniometer
†関節可動域（かんせつかどういき） range of motion：ROM
関節可動域訓練（かんせつかどういきくんれん） range of motion exercise
関節可動域テスト（かんせつかどういきてすと） range of motion testing：ROM-T
間接言語（かんせつげんご） indirect language
関節拘縮（かんせつこうしゅく） joint contracture；joint stiffness
間接処遇（かんせつしょぐう） indirect treatment
間接税（かんせつぜい） indirect tax
間接接触感染（かんせつせっしょくかんせん） indirect contact infection
間接接触伝播（かんせつせっしょくでんぱ） indirect contact spread
関節置換術（かんせつちかんじゅつ） joint replacement
関節痛（かんせつつう） arthralgia
関節補綴（かんせつほてつ） joint prosthesis
関節モーメント（かんせつもーめんと） joint moment
†関節リウマチ（かんせつりうまち） rheumatoid arthritis：RA

関節離断（かんせつりだん） disarticulation
†感染（かんせん） infection
完全・永続的重度障害者扶助（かんぜん・えいぞくてきじゅうどしょうがいしゃふじょ） Aid to the Permanently and Totally Disabled：APTD
感染管理（かんせんかんり）⇒感染制御
感染管理委員会（かんせんかんりいいんかい）⇒感染制御委員会
感染管理医師（かんせんかんりいし）⇒感染制御医師
感染管理看護師（かんせんかんりかんごし）⇒感染制御看護師
感染管理専門家（かんせんかんりせんもんか）⇒感染制御専門家
感染管理チーム（かんせんかんりちーむ）⇒感染制御チーム
感染管理・予防（かんせんかんり・よぼう）⇒感染制御・予防
†感染菌（かんせんきん） bacterium；bacteria
感染経路（かんせんけいろ） routes of infection；routes of transmission
感染経路別予防策（かんせんけいろべつよぼうさく） transmission-based precaution
感染源（かんせんげん） source of infection
感染源隔離（かんせんげんかくり） source isolation
感染後咳そう（かんせんごがいそう） post-infection cough
完全参加と平等（かんぜんさんかとびょうどう） full participation and equality
完全失業（かんぜんしつぎょう） unemployment
†感染症（かんせんしょう） infectious disease
感染症サーベイランス（かんせんしょうさーべいらんす） infection surveillance
完全静脈栄養（かんぜんじょうみゃくえいよう） total parenteral nutrition：TPN
感染性医療廃棄物（かんせんせいいりょうはいきぶつ） infectious medical waste
感染制御（かんせんせいぎょ） infection control
感染制御委員会（かんせんせいぎょいいんかい） infection control committee
感染制御医師（かんせんせいぎょいし） infection control doctor
感染制御看護師（かんせんせいぎょかんごし） infection control nurse
感染制御専門家（かんせんせいぎょせんもんか） infection control practitioner
感染制御チーム（かんせんせいぎょちーむ） infection control team
感染制御プログラム（かんせんせいぎょぷろぐらむ） infection-control program
感染制御・予防（かんせんせいぎょ・よぼう） infection control and prevention
感染性心内膜炎（かんせんせいしんないまくえん）

介護保険・介護福祉等関連用語・和英

infective endocarditis
完全性尿失禁（かんぜんせいにょうしっきん）total incontinence
感染性廃棄物（かんせんせいはいきぶつ）infectious waste
感染専門看護師（かんせんせんもんかんごし）infection clinical nurse specialist
感染対策（かんせんたいさく）⇒感染制御
感染対策委員会（かんせんたいさくいいんかい）⇒感染制御委員会
感染対策医師（かんせんたいさくいし）⇒感染制御医師
感染対策看護師（かんせんたいさくかんごし）⇒感染制御看護師
感染対策専門家（かんせんたいさくせんもんか）⇒感染制御専門家
感染対策チーム（かんせんたいさくちーむ）⇒感染制御チーム
感染対策・予防（かんせんたいさく・よぼう）⇒感染制御・予防
感染防御衣（かんせんぼうぎょい）protective clothing
†感染予防（かんせんよぼう）prevention of infection；infection prevention
肝臓（かんぞう）liver
乾燥症（かんそうしょう）xerosis
肝臓専門医（かんぞうせんもんい）hepatologist
肝臓病学（かんぞうびょうがく）hepatology
患側（かんそく）affected part of the body
桿体（かんたい）rod
†浣腸（かんちょう）enema
癌治療（がんちりょう）cancer treatment
癌治療機能評価（がんちりょうきのうひょうか）Functional Assessment of Cancer Therapy：FACT
カンデサルタン（かんでさるたん）candesartan
冠動脈（かんどうみゃく）coronary artery
冠動脈疾患（かんどうみゃくしっかん）coronary artery disease：CAD
冠動脈疾患集中治療室（かんどうみゃくしっかんしゅうちゅうちりょうしつ）coronary care unit：CCU
冠動脈性心疾患（かんどうみゃくせいしんしっかん）coronary heart disease：CHD
肝動脈動注療法（かんどうみゃくどうちゅうりょうほう）hepatic arterial infusion
冠動脈バイパス手術（かんどうみゃくばいぱすしゅじゅつ）coronary artery bypass graft surgery：CABG
冠動脈攣縮性狭心症（かんどうみゃくれんしゅくせいきょうしんしょう）vasospastic angina pectoris
監督課（かんとくか）Inspection Division
眼内圧（がんないあつ）intraocular pressure
眼内レンズ（がんないれんず）intraocular lens：IOL

陥入爪（かんにゅうそう）ingrown toenail
乾熱滅菌（かんねつめっきん）dry heat sterilization
乾熱滅菌器（かんねつめっきんき）hot air sterilizer
観念運動失行（かんねんうんどうしっこう）ideomotor apraxia
†観念失行（かんねんしっこう）ideational apraxia
肝斑（かんぱん）liver spots
眼病（がんびょう）eye disease
カンファレンス（かんふぁれんす）conference
漢方医学（かんぽういがく）Chinese medicine
漢方薬（かんぽうやく）herbal medicine
ガンマ線滅菌（がんませんめっきん）gamma sterilization
官民競争（かんみんきょうそう）public-private competition
官民競争のコスト算定（かんみんきょうそうのこすとさんてい）calculating public-private competition costs
顔面肩甲上腕型筋ジストロフィー（がんめんけんこうじょうわんがたきんじすとろふぃー）facioscapulohumeral muscular dystrophy
顔面シールド付きマスク（がんめんしーるどつきますく）face shield mask
顔面神経麻痺（がんめんしんけいまひ）facial paralysis
顔面麻痺（がんめんまひ）facial paralysis
管理運営費（かんりうんえいひ）administrative cost
†管理栄養士（かんりえいようし）registered dietitian
官僚化（かんりょうか）⇒官僚制
官僚制（かんりょうせい）bureaucracy
寒冷ストレス（かんれいすとれす）cold stress
寒冷地加算（かんれいちかさん）additional cold district allowance
寒冷療法（かんれいりょうほう）cold therapy
関連痛（かんれんつう）referred pain
緩和（かんわ）palliative
†緩和ケア（かんわけあ）palliative care
緩和ケア病床（かんわけあびょうしょう）palliative care bed
緩和ケア病棟（かんわけあびょうとう）palliative care unit

き

奇異性尿失禁（きいせいにょうしっきん）paradoxical incontinence
既往歴（きおうれき）medical history；anamnesis
記憶（きおく）memory
†記憶障害（きおくしょうがい）memory disorder
記憶障害検査（きおくしょうがいけんさ）Memory Impairment Screen：MIS
機械食（きかいしょく）mechanical diet；mechanical soft diet；soft mechanical diet
機械洗浄（きかいせんじょう）mechanical cleaning

機会の平等（きかいのびょうどう）equality of opportunity；equal opportunity
†着替え（きがえ）changing clothes
†気管（きかん）trachea
機関（きかん）agency
機関委任事務（きかんいにんじむ）agency delegated function
気管支炎（きかんしえん）bronchitis
気管支拡張剤（きかんしかくちょうざい）bronchodilator
気管支鏡（きかんしきょう）bronchoscopy
気管支喘息（きかんしぜんそく）bronchial asthma
気管支透亮像（きかんしとうりょうぞう）air bronchogram
気管支ドレナージ（きかんしどれなーじ）bronchial drainage
気管切開（きかんせっかい）tracheostomy
気管内異物（きかんないいぶつ）intratracheal foreign body
気管内注入（きかんないちゅうにゅう）intratracheal injection
気管内麻酔（きかんないますい）endotracheal anesthesia
危機介入（ききかいにゅう）crisis intervention
危機介入アプローチ（ききかいにゅうあぷろーち）crisis intervention approach
危機管理（ききかんり）risk management；crisis management
機器管理サービス（ききかんりさーびす）equipment management services
利き手（きき て）handedness
企業化（きぎょうか）corporatization
企業組合（きぎょうくみあい）corporate union
企業年金（きぎょうねんきん）corporate pension
企業年金国民年金基金課（きぎょうねんきんこくみんねんきんききんか）Corporate Pension and National Pension Fund Division
企業ボランティア（きぎょうぼらんてぃあ）corporate volunteer
起居動作（ききょどうさ）bed mobility
基金所持（ききんほじ）funding-holding
危険因子（きけんいんし）risk factor
危険区域（きけんくいき）hot zone
危険物（きけんぶつ）hazardous material
†危険防止（きけんぼうし）risk prevention
危険有害物質（きけんゆうがいぶっしつ）hazardous material
記号（きごう）signage
†起座位（きざい）sitting position
器材関連感染（きざいかんれんかんせん）device-related infection
起座呼吸（きざこきゅう）orthopnea；orthopnoea
刻み食（きざみしょく）chopped diet

†義歯（ぎし）denture；artificial tooth
義肢（ぎし）prosthesis；limb prosthesis；artificial limb
義肢学（ぎしがく）prosthetic
儀式（ぎしき）ritual
義肢訓練（ぎしくんれん）prosthetic training
義肢装具（ぎしそうぐ）orthosis and a prosthesis
†義肢装具士（ぎしそうぐし）prosthetist and orthotist；PO
義肢装着（ぎしそうちゃく）prosthesis fitting
器質性精神疾患（きしつせいせいしんしっかん）organic mental disorder
気腫（きしゅ）emphysema
義手（ぎしゅ）upper limb prosthesis
気腫性腎盂腎炎（きしゅせいじんうじんえん）emphysematous pyelonephritis
基準一日摂取量（きじゅんいちにちせっしゅりょう）reference daily intake；RDI
基準及び程度の原則（きじゅんおよびていどのげんそく）principle of standards and extent
基準介護（きじゅんかいご）standardized care；standardized long-term care
基準看護（きじゅんかんご）standardized nursing
基準審査課（きじゅんしんさか）Standards and Evaluation Division
基準体重比（きじゅんたいじゅうひ）ideal body weight；IBW
基準電極（きじゅんでんきょく）reference electrode
議事録（ぎじろく）minutes
規制緩和（きせいかんわ）deregulation
季節労働（きせつろうどう）seasonal work
帰属（きぞく）attribution
義足（ぎそく）lower limb prosthesis
基礎控除（きそこうじょ）basic standard deduction
基礎償還点数（きそしょうかんてんすう）basic reimbursement rate
基礎食品（きそしょくひん）basic food group
基礎体温（きそたいおん）basal body temperature
†基礎代謝（きそたいしゃ）basal metabolism
基礎代謝率（きそたいしゃりつ）basal metabolic rate；BMR
基礎代謝量（きそたいしゃりょう）basal metabolic rate；BMR
基礎年金（きそねんきん）basic pension
基礎年金拠出金（きそねんきんきょしゅつきん）contribution for basic pension
基礎年金交付金（きそねんきんこうふきん）grant for basic pension
基礎年金制度（きそねんきんせいど）basic pension system
基礎年金番号（きそねんきんばんごう）basic

介護保険・介護福祉等関連用語 和英

pension number
喫煙（きつえん）smoking
ぎっくり腰（ぎっくりごし）strained back
拮抗（きっこう）antagonism
拮抗筋（きっこうきん）antagonist
輝度（きど）luminance
気道（きどう）airway
気道確保（きどうかくほ）airway maintenance；maintenance of airway
気道感染隔離（きどうかんせんかくり）respiratory isolation
気道管理（きどうかんり）airway management
気道狭窄（きどうきょうさく）airway stenosis
気道虚脱（きどうきょだつ）airway collapse
気道クリーニング（きどうくりーにんぐ）⇒気道洗浄
気道コンダクタンス（きどうこんだくたんす）airway conductance
気道ステント（きどうすてんと）airway stent
気道洗浄（きどうせんじょう）airway cleaning
気道抵抗（きどうていこう）airway resistance
気道内圧（きどうないあつ）airway pressure
気道内圧時間曲線（きどうないあつじかんきょくせん）airway pressure-time curve
気道熱傷（きどうねっしょう）airway burn
気道閉鎖（きどうへいさ）airway closure
気道閉塞（きどうへいそく）airway obstruction；airway occlusion
キナプリル（きなぷりる）quinapril
キネレット（きねれっと）Kineret
記念病院（きねんびょういん）memorial hospital
機能（きのう）function
†機能維持（きのういじ）functional maintenance
機能回復（きのうかいふく）functional recovery
機能局在（きのうきょくざい）functional localization
†機能訓練（きのうくんれん）functional training；functional exercise
機能再建（きのうさいけん）functional reconstruction
機能肢位（きのうしい）functional position
機能主義（きのうしゅぎ）functionalism
†機能障害（きのうしょうがい）impairment；dysfunction
機能状態質問票（きのうじょうたいしつもんひょう）Functional Status Questionnaire：FSQ
帰納推理（きのうすいり）inductive reasoning
機能的アプローチ（きのうてきあぷろーち）functional approach
機能的MRI（きのうてきえむあーるあい）functional magnetic resonance imaging：fMRI
機能的活動質問票（きのうてきかつどうしつもんひょう）Functional Activities Questionnaire：FAQ
機能的作業療法（きのうてきさぎょうりょうほう）functional occupational therapy
機能的残気量（きのうてきざんきりょう）functional residual capacity
機能的自立（きのうてきじりつ）functional independence
機能的自立度評価法（きのうてきじりつどひょうかほう）functional independence measure：FIM
機能的装具（きのうてきそうぐ）functional brace
機能的電気刺激（きのうてきでんきしげき）functional electrical stimulation：FES
機能年齢（きのうねんれい）functional age
機能評価（きのうひょうか）functional assessment
機能評価票（きのうひょうかひょう）Functional Assessment Inventory：FAI
機能分化（きのうぶんか）functional differentiation
帰納法（きのうほう）inductive method
機能予後（きのうよご）functional prognosis
帰納論理プログラミング（きのうろんりぷろぐらみんぐ）inductive logic programming
キーパーソン（きーぱーそん）key person
気晴し的作業療法（きばらしてきさぎょうりょうほう）diversional occupational therapy
寄付（きふ）donation
寄付金税控除（きふきんぜいこうじょ）tax deduction for charity donations
ギプス（ぎぷす）cast
気分（きぶん）mood
気分循環性障害（きぶんじゅんかんせいしょうがい）cyclothymic disorder
気分障害（きぶんしょうがい）mood disorder
気泡風呂（きほうぶろ）⇒泡風呂
気泡浴（きほうよく）bubble bath
基本肢位（きほんしい）fundamental position
基本色名（きほんしきめい）basic color term
基本調査（きほんちょうさ）basic survey
基本手当（きほんてあて）basic allowance
基本的人権（きほんてきじんけん）fundamental human rights；basic human rights
基本的日常生活活動（きほんてきにちじょうせいかつかつどう）basic activities of daily living
基本的不安（きほんてきふあん）basic anxiety
義務教育（ぎむきょういく）compulsory education
記銘障害（きめいしょうがい）memory disturbance：disturbance of memory
†記銘力（きめいりょく）memory retention
記銘力障害（きめいりょくしょうがい）encoding disturbance
逆隔離（ぎゃくかくり）reversed isolation
逆説的志向（ぎゃくせつてきしこう）paradoxical intention
逆説的指示（ぎゃくせつてきしじ）paradoxical directive
逆選択（ぎゃくせんたく）adverse selection

†虐待（ぎゃくたい）abuse
脚長（きゃくちょう）leg length
脚長不同（きゃくちょうふどう）leg length inequality
逆転移（ぎゃくてんい）countertransference
逆方向性伝導（ぎゃくほうこうせいでんどう）antidromic conduction
キャスター（きゃすたー）caster
逆行性健忘（ぎゃっこうせいけんぼう）retrograde amnesia
逆行性腎盂造影（ぎゃっこうせいじんうぞうえい）retrograde pyelography
逆行性バリウム小腸造影（ぎゃっこうせいばりうむしょうちょうぞうえい）barium small bowel enema
†ギャッチベッド（ぎゃっちべっど）gatch bed
キャリパー（きゃりぱー）caliper
ギャンブル（ぎゃんぶる）gambling
キュア（きゅあ）cure
吸引（きゅういん）suctioning
吸引細胞診（きゅういんさいぼうしん）aspiration cytology
吸引生検（きゅういんせいけん）suction biopsy
救援（きゅうえん）support；assistance；help
救援関係（きゅうえんかんけい）therapeutic relationship
休暇（きゅうか）leave of absence：LoA
嗅覚（きゅうかく）sense of smell
嗅覚消失症（きゅうかくしょうしつしょう）anosmia
嗅覚低下（きゅうかくていか）loss of smell
救急医療（きゅうきゅういりょう）emergency medical services；emergency care
救急外来（きゅうきゅうがいらい）emergency room：ER
†救急救命士（きゅうきゅうきゅうめいし）emergency medical technician：EMT
救急救命室（きゅうきゅうきゅうめいしつ）emergency room：ER
救急指定病院（きゅうきゅうしていびょういん）designated emergency hospital
救急車（きゅうきゅうしゃ）ambulance
救急法（きゅうきゅうほう）first aid
休業（きゅうぎょう）⇒休職
休業給付（きゅうぎょうきゅうふ）leave benefit
休業補償（きゅうぎょうほしょう）compensation for leave
救護施設（きゅうごしせつ）relief institution
灸師（きゅうし）moxibustion therapist
吸湿性繊維（きゅうしつせいせんい）hygroscopic fiber
吸収（きゅうしゅう）absorption
吸収係数（きゅうしゅうけいすう）absorption factor
吸収性無気肺（きゅうしゅうせいむきはい）absorption atelectasis
吸収装置（きゅうしゅうそうち）absorption train
吸収速度（きゅうしゅうそくど）absorption rate
吸収速度定数（きゅうしゅうそくどていすう）absorption rate constant
90代（きゅうじゅうだい）nonagenarian
吸収率（きゅうしゅうりつ）absorption ratio
休職（きゅうしょく）leave
求職者（きゅうしょくしゃ）job seeker
求職者給付（きゅうしょくしゃきゅうふ）job seeker's benefit
求心性視野狭窄（きゅうしんせいしやきょうさく）concentric contraction of the visual field
求心性収縮（きゅうしんせいしゅうしゅく）concentric contraction
吸水性繊維（きゅうすいせいせんい）water-absorbing fiber
急性胃炎（きゅうせいいえん）acute gastritis
急性灰白髄炎（きゅうせいかいはくずいえん）acute anterior poliomyelitis
急性間質性肺炎（きゅうせいかんしつせいはいえん）acute interstitial pneumonia
急性冠症候群（きゅうせいかんしょうこうぐん）acute coronary syndrome
急性期（きゅうせいき）acute phase
急性期リハビリテーション（きゅうせいきりはびりてーしょん）acute phase of rehabilitation
救世軍（きゅうせいぐん）salvation army
急性喉頭気管支炎（きゅうせいこうとうきかんしえん）acute laryngotracheitis
急性硬膜外血腫（きゅうせいこうまくがいけっしゅ）acute epidural hematoma
急性呼吸窮迫症候群（きゅうせいこきゅうきゅうはくしょうこうぐん）acute respiratory distress syndrome：ARDS
急性呼吸不全（きゅうせいこきゅうふぜん）acute respiratory failure：acute respiratory insufficiency
急性骨髄性白血病（きゅうせいこつずいせいはっけつびょう）acute myelocytic leukemia：AML；acute myelogenous leukemia：AML；acute myeloid leukemia
急性細気管支炎（きゅうせいさいきかんしえん）acute bronchiolitis
急性参照用量（きゅうせいさんしょうようりょう）acute reference dose
急性出血後貧血（きゅうせいしゅっけつごひんけつ）acute posthemorrhagic anemia
急性消化管出血（きゅうせいしょうかかんしゅっけつ）acute gastrointestinal bleed
急性腎盂腎炎（きゅうせいじんうじんえん）acute pyelonephritis
急性心筋梗塞（きゅうせいしんきんこうそく）acute

介護保険・介護福祉等関連用語・和英

myocardial infarction
急性尿閉（きゅうせいにょうへい）acute urinary retention
急性肺炎（きゅうせいはいえん）acute pneumonia
急性肺傷害（きゅうせいはいしょうがい）⇒急性肺損傷
急性肺水腫（きゅうせいはいすいしゅ）acute pulmonary edema
急性肺損傷（きゅうせいはいそんしょう）acute lung injury
急性白血病（きゅうせいはっけつびょう）acute leukemia
急性リンパ性白血病（きゅうせいりんぱせいはっけつびょう）acute lymphoblastic leukemia；acute lymphocytic leukemia；acute lymphoid leukemia；ALL
吸息（きゅうそく）inhalation
旧措置入所（きゅうそちにゅうしょ）old placement system
吸着式ソケット（きゅうちゃくしきそけっと）suction socket
吸入（きゅうにゅう）inhalation；aspiration
救貧院（きゅうひんいん）almshouse；poorhouse
救貧事業（きゅうひんじぎょう）poor relief project
救貧制度（きゅうひんせいど）poor relief system
給付（きゅうふ）benefit
給付管理業務（きゅうふかんりぎょうむ）benefit management services
給付管理票（きゅうふかんりひょう）benefit management form
給付期間（きゅうふきかん）benefit period
給付基準（きゅうふきじゅん）benefits standards
給付水準（きゅうふすいじゅん）benefit level
給付費審査委員会（きゅうふひしんさいいんかい）Benefit Review Committee
給付優先リスト（きゅうふゆうせんりすと）list of priority benefits
球麻痺（きゅうまひ）bulbar palsy
給与計算（きゅうよけいさん）salary calculator
給与天引（きゅうよてんびき）payroll deduction
灸療法（きゅうりょうほう）moxibustion
QOL（きゅーおーえる）quality of life；QOL
QOL評価（きゅーおーえるひょうか）quality of life assessment
教育（きょういく）education
教育維持手当（きょういくいじてあて）⇒教育補助手当
教育給付（きょういくきゅうふ）educational benefit
教育的リハビリテーション（きょういくてきりはびりてーしょん）educational rehabilitation
教育における障害基準（きょういくにおけるしょうがいきじゅん）disability standards for education
教育費（きょういくひ）educational expenses
教育扶助（きょういくふじょ）educational aid；educational assistance
教育補助手当（きょういくほじょてあて）educational maintenance allowance
教育ミーティング（きょういくみーてぃんぐ）educational meeting
共依存（きょういぞん）co-dependency
境界（きょうかい）boundary
†仰臥位（ぎょうがい）supine position
強化運動（きょうかうんどう）strength exercise
胸郭バンド（きょうかくばんど）chest strap
強化子（きょうかし）reinforcer
†共感（きょうかん）empathy
共感的理解（きょうかんてきりかい）empathic understanding
共感疲労（きょうかんひろう）compassion fatigue
狂気（きょうき）rage
協議会（きょうぎかい）council
狂牛病（きょうぎゅうびょう）mad-cow disease
胸腔穿刺（きょうくうせんし）thoracocentesis
教護院（きょうごいん）home for training and education of juvenile delinquent
強剛（きょうごう）⇒固縮
共済組合（きょうさいくみあい）mutual aid association
共済制度（きょうさいせいど）mutual aid system
共済年金（きょうさいねんきん）mutual aid pension
胸式呼吸（きょうしきこきゅう）chest respiration
狭心症（きょうしんしょう）angina pectoris
狭心症発作（きょうしんしょうほっさ）angina attack
胸髄損傷（きょうずいそんしょう）thoracic spinal cord injury
共生（きょうせい）symbiosis
行政改革（ぎょうせいかいかく）administrative reform
強制加入（きょうせいかにゅう）compulsory enrollment
行政監査（ぎょうせいかんさ）administrative inspection
行政計画（ぎょうせいけいかく）administrative plan
行政指導（ぎょうせいしどう）administrative guidance
行政事務（ぎょうせいじむ）Administrative Affairs
共生社会（きょうせいしゃかい）symbiosis society
矯正装置（きょうせいそうち）orthodontic appliance
強制徴収（きょうせいちょうしゅう）compulsory collection；forcible collection
強制通告（きょうせいつうこく）enforcement notice
強制泣き（きょうせいなき）forced crying
強制入院（きょうせいにゅういん）involuntary

hospitalization；compulsory hospitalization
強制入所（きょうせいにゅうしょ）involuntary admission；compulsory admission
強制保険（きょうせいほけん）compulsory insurance
矯正用装具（きょうせいようそうぐ）corrective orthosis
強制笑い（きょうせいわらい）forced laughing
強制割り当て（きょうせいわりあて）levy
業績主義（ぎょうせきしゅぎ）performance principle
競争可能な市場（きょうそうかのうなしじょう）contestable market
競争原理（きょうそうげんり）principle of competition
鏡像書字（きょうぞうしょじ）mirror writing
競争的雇用（きょうそうてきこよう）competitive employment
兄弟〈姉妹〉間葛藤（きょうだい〈しまい〉かんかっとう）sibling conflict
兄弟〈姉妹〉間競争（きょうだい〈しまい〉かんきょうそう）sibling rivalry
協調（きょうちょう）coordination
協調運動障害（きょうちょううんどうしょうがい）coordination disorder
強直（きょうちょく）ankylosis
強直性（きょうちょくせい）ankylosing
強直性脊椎炎（きょうちょくせいせきついえん）ankylosing spondylitis
胸痛（きょうつう）chest pain
共同運動（きょうどううんどう）synergy
共同筋（きょうどうきん）synergist
協同組合（きょうどうくみあい）cooperative association
共同負担（きょうどうふたん）co-pay
共同募金（きょうどうぼきん）community chest
共同募金活動（きょうどうぼきんかつどう）community chest campaign
共同保険（きょうどうほけん）co-insurance
強迫性障害（きょうはくせいしょうがい）obsessive compulsive disorder
強迫性障害薬（きょうはくせいしょうがいやく）obsessive compulsive disorder medication
胸部圧迫（きょうぶあっぱく）chest compression
胸部エックス線（きょうぶえっくすせん）chest X-ray：CXR
恐怖症（きょうふしょう）phobia
業務独占（ぎょうむどくせん）monopolization
業務マニュアル（ぎょうむまにゅある）practice manual
強力な薬（きょうりょくなくすり）multipotent drug
寄与危険（きよきけん）attributable risk
寄与危険割合（きよきけんわりあい）attributable

risk percent：ARP
局所（きょくしょ）topical：TOP
虚血性心疾患（きょけつせいしんしっかん）ischemic heart disease：IHD
虚血性腸炎（きょけつせいちょうえん）ischemic colitis
虚血性発作（きょけつせいほっさ）ischemic stroke
巨細胞性動脈炎（きょさいぼうせいどうみゃくえん）giant cell arteritis
†虚弱（きょじゃく）frailty；weakness
虚弱高齢者（きょじゃくこうれいしゃ）the frail elderly；the physically frail elderly
虚弱児（きょじゃくじ）the frail child
虚弱老人（きょじゃくろうじん）the frail elderly；the physically frail elderly
居住環境（きょじゅうかんきょう）residential environment
居住ケア（きょじゅうけあ）residential care
拠出給付（きょしゅつきゅうふ）contributory benefit
拠出給付制（きょしゅつきゅうふせい）contributory benefit system
挙上（きょじょう）elevation
拒食症（きょしょくしょう）anorexia
去勢（きょせい）castration
去勢不安（きょせいふあん）castration anxiety
巨赤芽球性貧血（きょせきがきゅうせいひんけつ）megaloblastic anemia
居宅医療（きょたくいりょう）medical home-based care
居宅医療サービス（きょたくいりょうさーびす）medical home-based care services
居宅医療サービス機関（きょたくいりょうさーびすきかん）medical home-based care services agency
居宅医療サービス計画（きょたくいりょうさーびすけいかく）medical home-based care services plan
居宅医療サービス事業者（きょたくいりょうさーびすじぎょうしゃ）medical home-based care services provider
居宅医療サービス事業所（きょたくいりょうさーびすじぎょうしょ）medical home-based care services office
居宅援助（きょたくえんじょ）home-based support
居宅援助サービス（きょたくえんじょさーびす）home-based support services；home-based supportive services
居宅介護（きょたくかいご）home-based care
居宅介護サービス（きょたくかいごさーびす）home-based care services
居宅介護サービス計画（きょたくかいごさーびすけいかく）home-based care services plan

介護保険・介護福祉等関連用語 和英

居宅介護サービス事業者（きょたくかいごさーびすじぎょうしゃ）home-based care services provider
居宅介護サービス事業所（きょたくかいごさーびすじぎょうしょ）home-based care services office
居宅介護支援（きょたくかいごしえん）home-based care management
居宅介護支援事業（きょたくかいごしえんじぎょう）home-based care management program
居宅介護支援事業者（きょたくかいごしえんじぎょうしゃ）home-based care management provider
居宅介護支援事業所（きょたくかいごしえんじぎょうしょ）home-based care management office
居宅サービス（きょたくさーびす）home-based services
居宅サービス計画（きょたくさーびすけいかく）home-based care services plan
居宅サービス事業（きょたくさーびすじぎょう）home-based services program
居宅サービス事業者（きょたくさーびすじぎょうしゃ）home-based services provider
居宅サービス事業所（きょたくさーびすじぎょうしょ）home-based services office
居宅生活援助（きょたくせいかつえんじょ）home-based living support
居宅生活援助サービス（きょたくせいかつえんじょさーびす）home-based living support services；home-based living supportive services
居宅生活援助サービス事業者（きょたくせいかつえんじょさーびすじぎょうしゃ）home-based living support services provider；home-based living supportive services provider
居宅生活援助サービス事業所（きょたくせいかつえんじょさーびすじぎょうしょ）home-based living support services office；home-based living supportive services office
居宅生活援助事業（きょたくせいかつえんじょじぎょう）home-based living support program；home-based living supportive program
居宅生活扶助（きょたくせいかつふじょ）home-based living assistance
居宅生活扶助サービス（きょたくせいかつふじょさーびす）home-based living assistance services
居宅生活扶助サービス事業者（きょたくせいかつふじょさーびすじぎょうしゃ）home-based living assistance services provider
居宅生活扶助サービス事業所（きょたくせいかつふじょさーびすじぎょうしょ）home-based living assistance services office
居宅生活扶助事業（きょたくせいかつふじょじぎょう）home-based living assistance program
居宅扶助（きょたくふじょ）home-based assistance
居宅扶助計画（きょたくふじょけいかく）home-based assistance services plan
居宅扶助サービス（きょたくふじょさーびす）home-based assistance services
居宅扶助サービス計画（きょたくふじょさーびすけいかく）home-based assistance services plan
許容一日摂取量（きょよういちにちせっしゅりょう）acceptable daily intake
許容曝露濃度（きょようばくろのうど）permissible exposure limit：PEL
ギラン・バレー症候群（ぎらん・ばれーしょうこうぐん）Guillain-Barre syndrome：GBS
キリスト教社会事業（きりすときょうしゃかいじぎょう）Christian social work
キリスト教女子青年会（きりすときょうじょしせいねんかい）Young Women's Christian Association：YWCA
キリスト教青年会（きりすときょうせいねんかい）Young Men's Christian Association：YMCA
起立訓練（きりつくんれん）standing exercise
†起立性低血圧（きりつせいていけつあつ）orthostatic hypotension；postural hypotension
起立台（きりつだい）standing table
起立・歩行検査（きりつ・ほこうけんさ）Get-up and Go Test
起立・歩行動作測定法（きりつ・ほこうどうさそくていほう）Timed Get up and Go Test
棄老（きろう）abandoning elderly
†記録（きろく）records
記録様式（きろくようしき）recording style
筋（きん）muscle
近位（きんい）proximal
†筋萎縮（きんいしゅく）muscular atrophy
筋萎縮性側索硬化症（きんいしゅくせいそくさくこうかしょう）amyotrophic lateral sclerosis：ALS
近位端（きんいたん）proximal end
均一給付（きんいつきゅうふ）flat rate benefit
均一拠出（きんいつきょしゅつ）flat rate contribution
禁煙（きんえん）abstinence from smoking
筋炎（きんえん）myositis
緊急措置入院（きんきゅうそちにゅういん）urgent involuntary hospitalization
緊急通報（きんきゅうつうほう）emergency call
緊急通報サービス（きんきゅうつうほうさーびす）emergency call services
緊急通報システム（きんきゅうつうほうしすてむ）emergency call system
緊急通報装置（きんきゅうつうほうそうち）emergency alarm system
緊急被ばく医療管理（きんきゅうひばくいりょうかんり）radiation emergency medical management
緊急扶助（きんきゅうふじょ）emergency assistance：EA

†緊急連絡先（きんきゅうれんらくさき）emergency contact information
筋強直性ジストロフィー（きんきょうちょくせいじすとろふぃー）myotonic dystrophy
筋緊張（きんきんちょう）muscle tonus
筋緊張亢進（きんきんちょうこうしん）muscle hypertonia
筋緊張低下（きんきんちょうていか）muscle hypotonia
筋筋膜性疼痛症候群（きんきんまくせいとうつうしょうこうぐん）myofascial pain syndrome：MPS
筋クランプ（きんくらんぷ）⇒筋痙攣
筋痙攣（きんけいれん）muscle cramp
菌血症（きんけつしょう）bacteremia
筋交感神経活動（きんこうかんしんけいかつどう）sympathetic muscle nerve activity
金工細工（きんこうざいく）metal craft
筋拘縮（きんこうしゅく）muscle contracture
筋拘縮症（きんこうしゅくしょう）muscle contracture
菌交代現象（きんこうたいげんしょう）microbial substitute；microbial substitution
菌交代症（きんこうたいしょう）superinfection
筋骨格疾患（きんこっかくしっかん）musculoskeletal disease
筋骨格系（きんこっかくけい）musculoskeletal system
筋再教育（きんさいきょういく）muscle reeducation
筋弛緩剤（きんしかんざい）muscle relaxant
筋持久力（きんじきゅうりょく）muscle endurance
筋ジストロフィー（きんじすとろふぃー）muscular dystrophy
禁酒（きんしゅ）abstinence from alcohol
筋生検（きんせいけん）muscle biopsy
近赤外線（きんせきがいせん）near-infrared
筋線維タイプ（きんせんいたいぷ）muscle fiber type
筋線維伝導速度（きんせんいでんどうそくど）muscle fiber conduction velocity
†金銭管理（きんせんかんり）money management
金銭給付（きんせんきゅうふ）cash benefit
近代化（きんだいか）modernization
近代化論（きんだいかろん）modernization theory
禁断症状（きんだんしょうじょう）withdrawal symptom
筋断面積（きんだんめんせき）cross-sectional area of muscle
金チオリンゴ酸ナトリウム（きんちおりんごさんなとりうむ）gold sodium thiomalate
緊張型頭痛（きんちょうがたずつう）tension-type headache

緊張亢進（きんちょうこうしん）hypertonia
緊張性頸反射（きんちょうせいけいはんしゃ）tonic neck reflex
緊張低下（きんちょうていか）hypotonia
筋痛性脳脊髄炎（きんつうせいのうせきずいえん）myalgic encephalomyelitis
筋電義手（きんでんぎしゅ）myoelectric upper limb prosthesis
筋電図（きんでんず）electromyogram：EMG
筋電図検査（きんでんずけんさ）electromyography
均等色空間（きんとうしきくうかん）uniform color space
均等色度図（きんとうしきどず）uniform chromaticity scale diagram
筋肉内（きんにくない）intramuscular：IM
筋肥大（きんひだい）muscle hypertrophy
筋疲労（きんひろう）muscle fatigue
筋膜炎（きんまくえん）fasciitis
筋膜リリース（きんまくりりーす）myofascial release
金融資産（きんゆうしさん）financial asset
筋力（きんりょく）muscle strength
筋力維持（きんりょくいじ）muscle maintenance
筋力維持訓練（きんりょくいじくんれん）exercises for maintaining muscle
筋力強化（きんりょくきょうか）muscular strengthening
筋力強化訓練（きんりょくきょうかくんれん）muscle strengthening exercise
筋力測定（きんりょくそくてい）muscle strength measurement
筋力低下（きんりょくていか）muscular weakness
勤労控除（きんろうこうじょ）deduction for employment
勤労者生活課（きんろうしゃせいかつか）Workers' Life Division
勤労者生活部（きんろうしゃせいかつぶ）Workers' Life Department
勤労所得税額控除（きんろうしょとくぜいがくこうじょ）earned income tax credit：EITC
勤労税控除（きんろうぜいこうじょ）tax deduction for employment

＜

クアゼパム（くあぜぱむ）quazepam
グアヤック検査（ぐあやっくけんさ）guaiac test
区域分け（くいきわけ）zoning
空気汚染（くうきおせん）air pollution
空気感染（くうきかんせん）airborne infection
空気感染隔離（くうきかんせんかくり）airborne infection isolation：AII
空気塞栓症（くうきそくせんしょう）air embolism

空気調和（くうきちょうわ）heating, ventilation and air-conditioning：HVAC
空気伝播（くうきでんぱ）airborne transmission
空気予防策（くうきよぼうさく）airborne precaution
空気ろ過装置（くうきろかそうち）air filter
空中細菌（くうちゅうさいきん）airborne bacteria
空中細菌測定器（くうちゅうさいきんそくていき）airborne microbe sampler
空中塵埃（くうちゅうじんあい）airborne particle
空中浮遊菌（くうちゅうふゆうきん）⇒空中細菌
空中浮遊菌測定器（くうちゅうふゆうきんそくてい き）⇒空中細菌測定器
空中浮遊塵埃（くうちゅうふゆうじんあい）⇒空中塵埃
空調（くうちょう）air conditioning
空腹時血糖（くうふくじけっとう）fasting blood sugar
空腹時高血糖（くうふくじこうけっとう）impaired fasting glucose：IFG
くさび（くさび）wedge
くさび状足底板（くさびじょうそくていばん）wedged insole
苦情（くじょう）complaint
†苦情解決（くじょうかいけつ）grievances and complaints resolution
苦情処理（くじょうしょり）grivances and complaints handling
薬（くすり）drug；medication
口すぼめ呼吸（くちすぼめこきゅう）pursed lip breathing
口対口人工呼吸（くちたいくちじんこうこきゅう）mouth-to-mouth breathing
口対鼻人工呼吸（くちたいはなじんこうこきゅう）mouth-to-nose breathing
駆虫剤（くちゅうざい）anthelmintic
靴型装具（くつがたそうぐ）corrective shoes
屈曲（くっきょく）flexion
屈曲拘縮（くっきょくこうしゅく）flexion contracture
クッション（くっしょん）cushion
クッシング症候群（くっしんぐしょうこうぐん）Cushing's syndrome
靴べら（くつべら）shoe horn
靴べら式装具（くつべらしきそうぐ）shoe horn brace：SHB
駆動輪（くどうりん）wheel
国別割当計画（くにべつわりあてけいかく）national allocation plan
クーマディン（くーまでぃん）Coumadin
組合（くみあい）union
組合管掌健康保険（くみあいかんしょうけんこうほけん）society-managed health insurance
†くも膜下出血（くもまくかしゅっけつ）subarachnoid hemorrhage：SAH
クライアント（くらいあんと）client
クライエント（くらいえんと）⇒クライアント
クラウディング・アウト理論（くらうでぃんぐ・あう とりろん）⇒閉め出し理論
クラッチ（くらっち）crutch
クランデロス（くらんでろす）curandero
クリアリング法（くりありんぐほう）clearing technique
クリティカル（くりてぃかる）critical
†クリティカルパス（くりてぃかるぱす）critical pathway：CP
クリニカルスキル（くりにかるすきる）clinical skill
クリニカルパス（くりにかるぱす）clinical pathway
クリプトフック（くりぷとふっく）crypt hook
クリーム・スキミング（くりーむ・すきみんぐ）cream-skimming
クリューバービューシー症候群（くりゅーばーびゅー しーしょうこうぐん）Kluver-Bucy syndrome
クーリングオフ（くーりんぐおふ）cooling off
クリーンゾーン（くりーんぞーん）clean zone
クリーンベンチ（くりーんべんち）clean bench
クリーンルーム（くりーんるーむ）cleanroom
グルコサミン（ぐるこさみん）glucosamine
グルコース無水物（ぐるこーすむすいぶつ）glucose anhydride
グルコファージ（ぐるこふぁーじ）Glucophage
グルタルアルデヒド（ぐるたるあるでひど）glutaraldehyde
グループ運動（ぐるーぷうんどう）group exercise
グループカウンセリング（ぐるーぷかうんせりんぐ）group counseling
グループ診療（ぐるーぷしんりょう）group practice
グループスーパービジョン（ぐるーぷすーぱーびじょ ん）group supervision
グループダイナミクス（ぐるーぷだいなみくす）group dynamics
†グループホーム（ぐるーぷほーむ）group home
グループモデル（ぐるーぷもでる）group model
グループリクリエーション（ぐるーぷりくりえーしょ ん）⇒グループレクリエーション
†グループリビング（ぐるーぷりびんぐ）group living
†グループレクリエーション（ぐるーぷれくりえーしょ ん）group recreation
グループワーカー（ぐるーぷわーかー）group worker
†グループワーク（ぐるーぷわーく）group work
†車いす（くるまいす）wheelchair
車いす移乗（くるまいすいじょう）wheelchair transfer
車いす移乗援助（くるまいすいじょうえんじょ）wheelchair transfer assistance；assistance with wheelchair transfer

車いすから平行棒（くるまいすからへいこうぼう）transfer from wheelchair to parallel bar；wheelchair to parallel bar
†車いすからベッド（くるまいすからべっど）transfer from wheelchair to bed；wheelchair to bed
車いすスポーツ（くるまいすすぽーつ）wheelchair sports
車いす動作（くるまいすどうさ）wheelchair activity
†車いすの移動（くるまいすのいどう）moving around by wheelchair
†車いすの介助（くるまいすのかいじょ）wheelchair assistance；assistance with wheelchair
車の乗降（くるまのじょうこう）getting in and out of the car
グレシャムの法則（ぐれしゃむのほうそく）Gresham's Law
クレゾール石鹸液（くれぞーるせっけんえき）saponated cresol solution
グレーチング（ぐれーちんぐ）grating
クレブシエラ肺炎（くれぶしえらはいえん）Klebsiella pneumonia
グレーブス病（ぐれーぶすびょう）Graves' disease
クレンザック足継手（くれんざっくあしつぎて）Klenzak ankle joint
クロザピン（くろざぴん）clozapine
クロス集計（くろすしゅうけい）cross tabulation
クロスセクショナルサーベイ（くろすせくしょなるさーべい）cross-sectional survey
クロストリジウムディフィシル菌（くろすとりじうむでぃふぃしるきん）clostridium difficile
†クロックポジション（くろっくぽじしょん）clock position
クロナゼパム（くろなぜぱむ）clonazepam
クロノピン（くろのぴん）Klonopin
グローバリゼーション（ぐろーばりぜーしょん）globalization
グローバルスタンダード（ぐろーばるすたんだーど）global standards
クロピドグレル（くろぴどぐれる）clopidogrel
グローブジュース法（ぐろーぶじゅーすほう）glove juice method
クロミプラミン（くろみぷらみん）clomipramine
クロラゼプ酸（くろらぜぷさん）clorazepate
クロルジアゼポキシド（くろるじあぜぽきしど）chlordiazepoxide
クロルジアゼポキシド・アミトリプチリン（くろるじあぜぽきしど・あみとりぷちりん）chlordiazepoxide-amitriptyline
クロルジアゼポキシド・クリジニウム（くろるじあぜぽきしど・くりじにうむ）clidinium-chlordiazepoxide
クロルゾキサゾン（くろるぞきさぞん）chlorzoxazone

軍人遺族手当（ぐんじんいぞくてあて）dependency and indemnity compensation
軍人年金（ぐんじんねんきん）soldiers' pension
群発頭痛（ぐんぱつずつう）cluster headache
郡立病院（ぐんりつびょういん）county hospital
訓練（くんれん）exercise；training
訓練給付（くんれんきゅうふ）training benefit
訓練用仮義肢（くんれんようかりぎし）temporary prosthesis
訓練用仮義足（くんれんようかりぎそく）temporary lower limb prosthesis

け

†ケア（けあ）care
ケアガイドライン（けあがいどらいん）care guideline
ケアカード（けあかーど）care card
ケア環境（けあかんきょう）environment of care
†ケアカンファレンス（けあかんふぁれんす）care conference
ケアコーディネーション（けあこーでぃねーしょん）care coordination
ケアサービス（けあさーびす）care services
†ケアチーム（けあちーむ）care team
ケア付高齢者住宅（けあつきこうれいしゃじゅうたく）elder care housing；aged care home
ケア付住宅（けあつきじゅうたく）adult care housing；aged care home
ケアの質（けあのしつ）quality of care
ケアの未来（けあのみらい）future of care
†ケアハウス（けあはうす）care home
ケアパス（けあぱす）care pathway
†ケアプラン（けあぷらん）care plan
†ケアマネジメント（けあまねじめんと）care management
ケアマネジメント機関（けあまねじめんときかん）care management provider
ケアマネジメントモデル（けあまねじめんともでる）care management model
†ケアマネジャー（けあまねじゃー）care manager
ケアミックス（けあみっくす）care mix
ケア目標（けあもくひょう）care goal
ケアワーカー（けあわーかー）care worker
†ケアワーク（けあわーく）care work
警戒区域（けいかいくいき）cold zone
経過観察病棟（けいかかんさつびょうとう）observation unit
計画的行動理論（けいかくてきこうどうりろん）theory of planned behavior
†経管栄養（けいかんえいよう）tube feeding
経気道感染（けいきどうかんせん）sinopulmonary infection

介護保険・介護福祉等関連用語 和英

経験自己（けいけんじこ）experiential self
経験主義的治療（けいけんしゅぎてきちりょう）⇒経験的治療
経験的治療（けいけんてきちりょう）empiric therapy
経口（けいこう）by mouth；PO；oral
経口感染（けいこうかんせん）oral transmission
経口摂取（けいこうせっしゅ）oral intake
蛍光内視鏡検査（けいこうないしきょうけんさ）fluorescein endoscopy
経口補液療法（けいこうほえきりょうほう）oral rehydration therapy
経肛門的超音波検査（けいこうもんてきちょうおんぱけんさ）transanal ultrasonography
脛骨近位部骨折（けいこつきんいぶこっせつ）proximal tibia fracture
脛骨高原（けいこつこうげん）tibial plateau
経済課（けいざいか）Economic Affairs Division
経済協力開発機構（けいざいきょうりょくかいはつきこう）Organization for Economic Co-operation and Development；OECD
経済計画（けいざいけいかく）economic planning
経済財政諮問会議（けいざいざいせいしもんかいぎ）Council on Economic and Fiscal Policy
経済諮問委員会（けいざいしもんいいんかい）Council of Economic Advisers；CEA
経済政策（けいざいせいさく）economic policy
経済成長（けいざいせいちょう）economic growth
経済成長率（けいざいせいちょうりつ）economic growth rate
経済体制（けいざいたいせい）economic system
経済的虐待専門家チーム（けいざいてきぎゃくたいせんもんかちーむ）fiduciary abuse specialist team；FAST
経済的略奪（けいざいてきりゃくだつ）economic predation
経済連携協定（けいざいれんけいきょうてい）Economic Partnership Agreement；EPA
軽擦法（けいさつほう）effleurage；stroking
憩室疾患（けいしつしっかん）diverticular disease
傾斜路（けいしゃろ）ramp
痙縮（けいしゅく）spasticity
芸術療法（げいじゅつりょうほう）art therapy
経静脈腎盂造影（けいじょうみゃくじんうぞうえい）intravenous pyelogram；IVP
†頸髄損傷（けいずいそんしょう）cervical spinal cord injury；cervical cord injury
痙性（けいせい）spastic
痙性斜頸（けいせいしゃけい）spastic torticollis
痙性対麻痺（けいせいついまひ）spastic paraparesis
形成不全（けいせいふぜん）dysplasia；malformation；deformity

痙性麻痺（けいせいまひ）spastic paralysis
継続的改善活動（けいぞくてきかいぜんかつどう）continuous quality improvement
継続的ケア（けいぞくてきけあ）continuing care
継続的冷却療法（けいぞくてきれいきゃくりょうほう）continuous cold therapy
継続理論（けいぞくりろん）continuity theory
†傾聴（けいちょう）active listening
経腸栄養法（けいちょうえいようほう）transintestine nutrition method
痙直型（けいちょくがた）spastic type
痙直型四肢麻痺（けいちょくがたししまひ）spastic quadriplegia
痙直型両麻痺（けいちょくがたりょうまひ）spastic diplegia
経直腸的超音波検査法（けいちょくちょうてきちょうおんぱけんさほう）transrectal ultrasonography
頸椎（けいつい）cervical spine
頸椎牽引（けいついけんいん）cervical traction
頸椎性頭痛（けいついせいずつう）cervicogenic headache
頸椎装具（けいついそうぐ）cervical orthosis
頸椎捻挫（けいついねんざ）neck distortion
経頭蓋磁気刺激（けいとうがいじきしげき）transcranial magnetic stimulation；TMS
系統的論理再構成法（けいとうてきろんりさいこうせいほう）systematic and rational reconstruction
頸動脈狭窄（けいどうみゃくきょうさく）carotid artery stenosis
軽度認知障害（けいどにんちしょうがい）mild cognitive impairment；MCI
経尿道の切除（けいにょうどうてきせつじょ）transurethral resection；TURP
経尿道的前立腺切除術（けいにょうどうてきぜんりつせんせつじょじゅつ）transurethral incision of prostate
経尿道的マイクロ波温熱療法（けいにょうどうてきまいくろはおんねつりょうほう）transurethral microwave therapy；TUMT
経皮（けいひ）transdermal；TD
経鼻（けいび）nasal；NAS
経皮感染（けいひかんせん）percutaneous infection
経鼻経管栄養（けいびけいかんえいよう）nasal tube feeding
経皮経管的冠動脈形成術（けいひけいかんてきかんどうみゃくけいせいじゅつ）percutaneous transluminal coronary angioplasty
経皮経管的冠動脈再開通術（けいひけいかんてきかんどうみゃくさいかいつうじゅつ）percutaneous transluminal coronary recanalization
経皮経肝的胆管ドレナージ（けいひけいかんてきたんかんどれなーじ）percutaneous transhepatic cholangiodrainage

経皮的埋め込み電極（けいひてきうめこみでんきょく）percutaneous implantable electrode
経皮的エタノール注入療法（けいひてきえたのーるちゅうにゅうりょうほう）percutaneous ethanol injection
経皮的電気神経刺激（けいひてきでんきしんけいしげき）transcutaneous electrical nerve stimulation：TENS
経皮内視鏡的胃瘻造設術（けいひてきないしきょうてきいろうぞうせつじゅつ）percutaneous endoscopic gastrostomy：PEG
頸部神経根症（けいぶしんけいこんしょう）cervical radiculopathy
刑法（けいほう）criminal law
警報（けいほう）alarm
警報安全システム（けいほうあんぜんしすてむ）alert safety system
刑法典（けいほうてん）criminal code；penal code
傾眠（けいみん）somnolence；drowsiness
刑務所（けいむしょ）prison
†契約（けいやく）contract
契約書（けいやくしょ）contract document
契約制度（けいやくせいど）contract system
軽量化（けいりょうか）downsize
痙攣（けいれん）convulsion
敬老（けいろう）respect for the elderly
敬老会（けいろうかい）senior citizens club
敬老の日（けいろうのひ）Respect for the Elderly Day；Respect for the Aged Day
ケインズ主義的福祉国家（けいんずしゅぎてきふくしこっか）Keynesian Welfare State
外科系集中治療室（げかけいしゅうちゅうちりょうしつ）surgical intensive care unit
外科用マスク（げかようますく）surgical mask
†劇薬（げきやく）drastic medicine；violent poison
†下血（げけつ）melena
ケーゲル体操（けーげるたいそう）Kegel exercise
ゲシュタルト療法（げしゅたるとりょうほう）gestalt therapy
ケースエイド（けーすえいど）case aid
ケースエイドワーカー（けーすえいどわーかー）case aid worker
ケース会議（けーすかいぎ）case meeting
†ケースカンファレンス（けーすかんふぁれんす）case conference
ケース記録（けーすきろく）case records
ケースコントロール研究（けーすこんとろーるけんきゅう）case control study
ケースマネジメント（けーすまねじめんと）case management
ケースミックス（けーすみっくす）case mix
ケースミックス指数（けーすみっくすしすう）case mix index：CMI

ケースワーカー（けーすわーかー）case worker
†ケースワーク（けーすわーく）casework
†血圧（けつあつ）blood pressure
血圧計（けつあつけい）blood pressure manometer
血液学（けつえきがく）hematology
血液ガス分析（けつえきがすぶんせき）arterial blood gas analysis
血液銀行（けつえきぎんこう）blood bank
血液検査（けつえきけんさ）blood test
血液対策課（けつえきたいさくか）Blood and Blood Products Division
血液透析（けつえきとうせき）hemodialysis
血液媒介感染（けつえきばいかいかんせん）bloodborne infection
血液由来病原体（けつえきゆらいびょうげんたい）bloodborne pathogen
結核（けっかく）tuberculosis
結核感染症課（けっかくかんせんしょうか）Tuberculosis and Infectious Diseases Control Division
結核腫（けっかくしゅ）tuberculoma
月額保険料（げつがくほけんりょう）monthly premium
結果の平等（けっかのびょうどう）equality of result
血管拡張剤（けっかんかくちょうざい）vasodilator
血管形成術（けっかんけいせいじゅつ）angioplasty
血管原性ショック（けっかんげんせいしょっく）vasogenic shock
血管原性切断（けっかんげんせいせつだん）amputation for peripheral vascular disease
血管性認知症（けっかんせいにんちしょう）vascular dementia
血管造影（けっかんぞうえい）angiogram；vascular imaging
血管内超音波法（けっかんないちょうおんぱほう）intravascular ultrasound
血管内留置カテーテル（けっかんないりゅうちかてーてる）intravascular catheter
血管内留置カテーテル関連感染症（けっかんないりゅうちかてーてるかんれんかんせんしょう）intravascular catheter-related infection
欠勤（けっきん）work absence
血行再建術（けっこうさいけんじゅつ）revascularization
結婚（けっこん）marriage
血腫（けっしゅ）hematoma
血漿（けっしょう）blood plasma
結晶関節症（けっしょうかんせつしょう）crystal arthropathy
血漿グルコース（けっしょうぐるこーす）plasma glucose
結晶性知能（けっしょうせいちのう）crystallized intelligence

結晶性能力（けっしょうせいのうりょく）crystallized ability
結晶誘発性関節炎（けっしょうゆうはつせいかんせつえん）crystal induced arthritis
血清（けっせい）blood serum
血清学的梅毒検査（けっせいがくてきばいどくけんさ）serologic test for syphilis
結節性動脈周囲炎（けっせつせいどうみゃくしゅういえん）periarteritis nodosa
血栓（けっせん）thrombosis
血栓溶解剤（けっせんようかいざい）thrombolytic
血栓溶解療法（けっせんようかいりょうほう）thrombolytic therapy
血中ウイルス感染症（けっちゅうういるすかんせんしょう）bloodborne virus infection
血液尿素窒素（けっちゅうにょうそちっそ）blood urea nitrogen：BUN
結腸洗浄（けっちょうせんじょう）colonic lavage
結腸前処置（けっちょうぜんしょち）colon preparation
結腸通過検査（けっちょうつうかけんさ）colonic transit study
結腸内視鏡（けっちょうないしきょう）colonoscope
結腸内視鏡検査（けっちょうないしきょうけんさ）colonoscopy
結腸粘膜生検（けっちょうねんまくせいけん）colonic mucosal biopsy
血糖（けっとう）blood sugar
血糖値（けっとうち）blood sugar level
血尿（けつにょう）hematuria
血便（けつべん）hematochezia
結膜炎（けつまくえん）conjunctivitis
血友病（けつゆうびょう）hemophilia
血友病性関節症（けつゆうびょうせいかんせつしょう）hemophilic arthropathy
血流感染（けつりゅうかんせん）bloodstream infection
解毒剤（げどくざい）antidote
ケニー式セルフケア評価（けにーしきせるふけあひょうか）Kenny Self-Care Evaluation
下熱剤（げねつざい）antipyretic；antipyretic drug；antipyretic medication
解熱剤（げねつざい）⇒下熱剤
下熱薬（げねつやく）antipyretic drug；antipyretic；antipyretic medication
解熱薬（げねつやく）⇒下熱薬
ゲノムインプリティング（げのむいんぷりてぃんぐ）⇒遺伝刷り込み
ゲノム刷り込み（げのむすりこみ）⇒遺伝刷り込み
KBM式下腿義足（けーびーえむしきかたいぎそく）Kondylen Bettung Munster transtibial
ケーブルハウジング（けーぶるはうじんぐ）cable housing
煙感知器（けむりかんちき）smoke alarm
†下痢（げり）diarrhea
ケリーパッド（けりーぱっど）Kelly pad
ゲルストマン症候群（げるすとまんしょうこうぐん）Gerstmann syndrome
検圧法（けんあつほう）manometry
牽引（けんいん）traction
牽引療法（けんいんりょうほう）traction treatment
減塩食（げんえんしょく）low salt diet；low sodium diet
嫌悪刺激（けんおしげき）aversive stimulus
嫌悪療法（けんおりょうほう）aversion therapy
限界集落（げんかいしゅうらく）marginal village
†幻覚（げんかく）hallucination
減価償却（げんかしょうきゃく）depreciation
検眼医（けんがんい）optometrist
嫌気性菌（けんきせいきん）anaerobe
研究開発振興課（けんきゅうかいはつしんこうか）Research and Development Division
研究所（けんきゅうしょ）research institution
研究倫理（けんきゅうりんり）ethics in research
現金給付（げんきんきゅうふ）cash benefit
献血（けんけつ）blood donation
言語（げんご）language
†健康（けんこう）health
健康保険証（けんこうほけんしょう）health insurance card
健康維持（けんこういじ）health maintenance
†健康観察（けんこうかんさつ）health observation
健康管理（けんこうかんり）health management；health care management
健康関連QOL（けんこうかんれんきゅーおーえる）health-related quality of life
健康危機管理（けんこうききかんり）health risk management
健康教育（けんこうきょういく）health education
健康教育ガイドライン（けんこうきょういくがいどらいん）health education guidelines
肩甲胸廓切断（けんこうきょうかくかんせつだん）forequarter amputation
肩甲胸廓切断用義手（けんこうきょうかくかんせつだんようぎしゅ）forequarter amputation prosthesis
健康局（けんこうきょく）Health Service Bureau
健康行動理論（けんこうこうどうりろん）health behavior theory
健康産業（けんこうさんぎょう）health industry
健康指標（けんこうしひょう）health indicator
健康状態（けんこうじょうたい）health condition；medical condition
肩甲上腕リズム（けんこうじょうわんりずむ）scapulohumeral rhythm

健康食品（けんこうしょくひん）health food
健康診断（けんこうしんだん）health examination；physical examination
健康診断証明書（けんこうしんだんしょうめいしょ）certificate of health examination
健康信念モデル（けんこうしんねんもでる）health belief model
健康増進（けんこうぞうしん）health promotion
健康増進法（けんこうぞうしんほう）Health Promotion Act
健康相談（けんこうそうだん）health counseling
健康対照者（けんこうたいしょうしゃ）healthy control
健康チェック（けんこうちぇっく）medical check-up
健康手帳（けんこうてちょう）health handbook
健康日本21（けんこうにほんにじゅういち）Health Japan 21
健康福祉の質（けんこうふくしのしつ）quality of well-being；QWB
健康フロンティア戦略（けんこうふろんてぃあせんりゃく）Health Frontier Strategic Plan
健康文化（けんこうぶんか）health culture
健康保菌者（けんこうほきんしゃ）healthy carrier
†健康保険（けんこうほけん）health insurance
健康保険給付（けんこうほけんきゅうふ）health insurance benefit
健康保険組合（けんこうほけんくみあい）health insurance society
健康ボランティア（けんこうぼらんてぃあ）⇒健常人
言語訓練（げんごくんれん）speech and language training
†言語障害（げんごしょうがい）speech-language impediment；verbal disorder；speech disturbance
言語性記憶（げんごせいきおく）verbal memory
言語聴覚訓練（げんごちょうかくくんれん）speech-language-hearing training
†言語聴覚士（げんごちょうかくし）speech-language-hearing therapist；ST
言語聴覚リハビリテーション（げんごちょうかくりはびりてーしょん）speech-language-hearing rehabilitation
言語聴覚療法（げんごちょうかくりょうほう）speech-language-hearing therapy
腱固定（けんこてい）tenodesis
言語的攻撃（げんごてきこうげき）verbal aggression
言語的コミュニケーション（げんごてきこみゅにけーしょん）verbal communication
言語能力（げんごのうりょく）language capability
言語療法（げんごりょうほう）speech therapy
言語療法士（げんごりょうほうし）speech therapist

顕在性不安尺度（けんざいせいふあんしゃくど）Manifest Anxiety Scale
顕在内容（けんざいないよう）manifest content
検察官（けんさつかん）public prosecutor
検死（けんし）⇒死体解剖
原子（げんし）atom
幻肢（げんし）phantom limb sensation
幻視（けんし）visual hallucination
原刺激（げんしげき）primary stimulus
幻肢痛（げんしつう）phantom limb pain
現実原則（げんじつげんそく）reality principle
現実見当識（げんじつけんとうしき）reality orientation
現実見当識訓練（げんじつけんとうしきくんれん）reality orientation training；ROT
原子爆弾（げんしばくだん）atomic bomb
原始反射（げんしはんしゃ）primitive reflex
厳重隔離（げんじゅうかくり）strict isolation
現象学（げんしょうがく）phenomenology
健常者（けんじょうしゃ）healthy person
健常人（けんじょうじん）healthy volunteer；healthy subject
検診（けんしん）screening
懸垂装置（けんすいそうち）suspension system
懸垂フレーム（けんすいふれーむ）suspension frame
減数分裂（げんすうぶんれつ）meiosis
減税地震（げんぜいじしん）tax quake
源泉課税（げんせんかぜい）withholding tax
源泉徴収（げんせんちょうしゅう）tax deduction at source
健側（けんそく）unaffected side of the body
現代化（げんだいか）modernization
検体収集（けんたいしゅうしゅう）specimen collection
幻聴（げんちょう）auditory hallucination
限定責任能力（げんていせきにんのうりょく）diminished responsibility
限定名簿制（げんていめいぼせい）closed panel
見当識（けんとうしき）orientation
†見当識障害（けんとうしきしょうがい）disorientation
原発開放隅角緑内障（げんぱつかいほうぐうかくりょくないしょう）primary open angle glaucoma；POAG
原発性菌血症（げんぱつせいきんけつしょう）primary bacteremia
原発性血流感染（げんぱつせいけつりゅうかんせん）primary blood stream infection
原発性進行性失語（げんぱつせいしんこうせいしつご）primary progressive aphasia
原発性進行性非流暢性失語（げんぱつせいしんこうせいひりゅうちょうせいしつご）primary

介護保険・介護福祉等関連用語 和英

113

progressive nonfluent aphasia
原発性胆汁性肝硬変（げんぱつせいたんじゅうせいかんこうへん）primary biliary cirrhosis
腱板損傷（けんばんそんしょう）rotator cuff injury
顕微鏡視野（けんびきょうしや）field of microscope
現物給付（げんぶつきゅうふ）benefit in kind
検便（けんべん）stool specimen
憲法（けんぽう）constitution
健忘症（けんぼうしょう）amnesia
権利（けんり）rights
権利章典（けんりしょうてん）Bill of Rights
権利能力（けんりのうりょく）legal capacity
†権利擁護（けんりようご）human rights advocacy；rights advocacy
権力（けんりょく）authority；power

こ

コアタイム（こあたいむ）core time
故意的自傷行為（こいてきじしょうこうい）deliberate self-harm
誤飲（ごいん）accidental ingestion；ingestion
更衣（こうい）dressing
行為（こうい）act；action；practice
合意（ごうい）consensus
合意形成（ごういけいせい）consensus building
更衣室（こういしつ）dressing room
行為障害（こういしょうがい）conduct disorder
更衣動作（こういどうさ）dressing activity
抗ウイルス（こうういるす）antiviral
抗ウイルス薬（こうういるすやく）antiviral drug；antiviral medication
抗うつ剤（こううつざい）anti-depressant
公営企業職員（こうえいきぎょうしょくいん）local public enterprise personnel
公営企業等会計部門（こうえいきぎょうとうかいけいぶもん）public businesses account
公営住宅（こうえいじゅうたく）public housing
†公益事業（こうえきじぎょう）public utility
公益質屋（こうえきしちや）public pawnshop
†公益法人（こうえきほうじん）public benefit corporation；public service corporation
抗炎症薬（こうえんしょうやく）antiinflammatory drug；antiinflammatory medication
構音訓練（こうおんくんれん）articulation training；dysarthria training
†構音障害（こうおんしょうがい）articulation disorder；dysarthria
公害（こうがい）pollution
高額医療費（こうがくいりょうひ）catastrophic medical expenses
高額介護サービス費（こうがくかいごさーびす）catastrophic long-term care services expenses

高額介護費（こうがくかいごひ）catastrophic long-term care expenses
高額療養費（こうがくりょうようひ）catastrophic health care expenses
効果の法則（こうかのほうそく）law of effect
高カロリー輸液（こうかろりーゆえき）hyperalimentation
交感神経（こうかんしんけい）sympathetic nerve
交感神経皮膚反応（こうかんしんけいひふはんのう）sympathetic skin response
抗乾癬薬（こうかんせんやく）antipsoriatic drug
抗癌薬（こうがんやく）anticancer drug
†後期高齢者（こうきこうれいしゃ）elderly aged 75 and above
後期高齢者医療制度（こうきこうれいしゃいりょうせいど）Health Insurance System for the Elderly Aged 75 and Above
公共経済学（こうきょうけいざいがく）public economics
公共交通機関（こうきょうこうつうきかん）public transportation
抗凝固剤（こうぎょうこざい）anticoagulant
公共事業（こうきょうじぎょう）public work
公共職業安定所（こうきょうしょくぎょうあんていしょ）public employment security office；PESO
公共職業訓練（こうきょうしょくぎょうくんれん）public vocational training
公共政策（こうきょうせいさく）public policy
公共選択理論（こうきょうせんたくりろん）public choice theory
公共福祉（こうきょうふくし）public welfare
抗菌（こうきん）antimicrobial
抗菌剤入り石鹸（こうきんざいいりせっけん）⇒抗菌性石鹸
抗菌スペクトル（こうきんすぺくとる）antimicrobial spectrum；antibacterial spectrum
抗菌性石鹸（こうきんせいせっけん）antimicrobial soap；antibacterial soap
†抗菌・防臭素材（こうきん・ぼうしゅうそざい）antibacterial and deodorization material
抗菌薬（こうきんやく）antimicrobial agent；antibacterial agent；antibacterial drug
抗菌薬抵抗性（こうきんやくていこうせい）antimicrobial resistance
口腔（こうくう）oral cavity
口腔衛生（こうくうえいせい）oral health
口腔温（こうくうおん）oral temperature
口腔顎顔面外科（こうくうがくがんめんげか）oral and maxillofacial surgery
口腔顎顔面外科医（こうくうがくがんめんげかい）oral and maxillofacial surgeon
口腔癌（こうくうがん）oral cancer
口腔乾燥症（こうくうかんそうしょう）xerostomia

† 口腔機能の向上（こうくうきのうのこうじょう）
　improvement of oral functions
† 口腔ケア（こうくうけあ）oral health care
　口腔検温（こうくうけんおん）oral thermometry
　口腔疾患（こうくうしっかん）oral disease
　口腔失行（こうくうしっこう）oral apraxia
　口腔状態（こうくうじょうたい）oral status
　口腔清掃行動（こうくうせいそうこうどう）oral hygiene
　口腔相（こうくうそう）oral propulsive phase
　口腔保健アセスメント（こうくうほけんあせすめんと）oral health assessment
† 合計特殊出生率（ごうけいとくしゅしゅっしょうりつ）total fertility rate：TFR：total period fertility rate：TPFR
　攻撃的行動（こうげきてきこうどう）aggressive behavior
† 高血圧（こうけつあつ）hypertension
　抗血小板薬（こうけっしょうばんやく）antiplatelet agent
　抗血清（こうけっせい）antiserum
　抗血栓薬（こうけっせんやく）antithrombotic drug；antithrombotic medication
　高血糖高浸透圧症候群（こうけっとうこうしんとうあつしょうこうぐん）hyperosmolar hyperglycemic syndrome：HHS
　高血糖症（こうけっとうしょう）hyperglycemia
　抗原（こうげん）antigen
　抗原性（こうげんせい）antigenicity
　後見人（こうけんにん）guardian
　後見人の指定（こうけんにんのしてい）designation of guardian
　後見人の選任（こうけんにんのせんにん）appointment of guardian
　膠原病（こうげんびょう）collagen disease
　孝行（こうこう）piety
　抗甲状腺剤（こうこうじょうせんざい）antithyroid；antithyroid drug；antithyroid medication
　抗甲状腺薬（こうこうじょうせんやく）antithyroid drug；antithyroid；antitussive medication
　交互三点歩行（こうごさんてんほこう）alternate three-point gait
　交互式歩行器（こうごしきほこうき）reciprocal walking frame
　交互歩行装具（こうごほこうそうぐ）reciprocating gait orthosis
　高コレステロール血症（こうこれすてろーるけつしょう）hypercholesterolemia
　交差汚染（こうさおせん）cross contamination
　交差感染（こうさかんせん）cross infection
　抗酸化ビタミン（こうさんかびたみん）antioxidant vitamin
　抗酸化物（こうさんかぶつ）antioxidant

　抗酸化薬（こうさんかやく）antioxidant agent
　抗酸化療法（こうさんかりょうほう）antioxidant therapy
　高脂血症（こうしけつしょう）hyperlipidemia
　高次脳機能（こうじのうきのう）higher brain function
　高次脳機能障害（こうじのうきのうしょうがい）higher brain dysfunction；neuropsychological disorder
　公私分離（こうしぶんり）public/private dichotomy
　公私分離の原則（こうしぶんりのげんそく）principle of private/public dichotomy；principle of separation of public and private interests
　公衆衛生（こうしゅうえいせい）public health
　公衆衛生法（こうしゅうえいせいほう）Public Health Service Act
　後縦靱帯骨化症（こうじゅうじんたいこっかしょう）Ossification of the posterior longitudinal ligament：OPLL
　抗重力筋（こうじゅうりょくきん）antigravity muscle
† 拘縮（こうしゅく）contracture
† 拘縮予防（こうしゅくよぼう）contracture prevention；prevention of contracture
　公助（こうじょ）public-support
　控除（こうじょ）deduction
　甲状腺癌（こうじょうせんがん）thyroid cancer
　甲状腺機能亢進症（こうじょうせんきのうこうしんしょう）hyperthyroidism
　甲状腺機能低下症（こうじょうせんきのうていかしょう）hypothyroidism
　甲状腺刺激ホルモン（こうじょうせんしげきほるもん）thyroid-stimulating hormone：TSH
　甲状腺疾患（こうじょうせんしっかん）thyroid disease
　甲状腺腫（こうじょうせんしゅ）goiter
　甲状腺髄様癌（こうじょうせんずいようがん）medullary thyroid cancer
　甲状腺乳頭癌（こうじょうせんにゅうとうがん）papillary thyroid cancer
　甲状腺未分化癌（こうじょうせんみぶんかがん）anaplastic thyroid cancer
† 公証人（こうしょうにん）notary public
　工場法（こうじょうほう）Factory Act
　高所得層（こうしょとくそう）upper income class
　高所脳浮腫（こうしょのうふしゅ）high altitude cerebral edema
　高所肺水腫（こうしょはいすいしゅ）high altitude pulmonary edema
　更新（こうしん）renewal
　口唇期（こうしんき）oral stage
　抗菌性（こうしんきんせい）antifungal
　抗真菌性抗生物質（こうしんきんせいこうせいぶっし

つ）antifungal antibiotic
更新申請（こうしんしんせい）renewal application
高水準消毒（こうすいじゅんしょうどく）high level disinfection
更生医療（こうせいいりょう）medical rehabilitation services
硬性S状結腸鏡検査（こうせいえすじょうけっちょうきょうけんさ）rigid sigmoidoscopy
厚生科学課（こうせいかがくか）Health Science Division
硬性鏡（こうせいきょう）rigid scope
公正原理（こうせいげんり）principle of justice
抗生剤（こうせいざい）antibiotic
更正施設（こうせいしせつ）correctional facility；rehabilitation facility
構成失行（こうせいしっこう）constructional apraxia
構成障害（こうせいしょうがい）constructive disability
†公正証書（こうせいしょうしょ）notarial deed
向精神剤（こうせいしんざい）psychotropic
抗精神病剤（こうせいしんびょうざい）antipsychotic
向精神薬（こうせいしんやく）psychotropic drug；antipsychotic drug
抗精神病薬（こうせいしんびょうやく）antipsychotic drug；antipsychotic；antipsychotic medication
合成繊維（ごうせいせんい）synthetic fiber
合成洗剤（ごうせいせんざい）synthetic detergent
厚生年金基金（こうせいねんきんききん）employees' pension fund；EPF
厚生年金保険（こうせいねんきんほけん）Employees' Pension Insurance
厚生年金保険法（こうせいねんきんほけんほう）Employees' Pension Insurance Law
†抗生物質（こうせいぶっしつ）antibiotic
抗生物質耐性菌感染（こうせいぶっしつたいせいきんかんせん）antibiotic resistant infection
厚生保険（こうせいほけん）employee insurance；employees' insurance
更生保護（こうせいほご）offenders rehabilitation
厚生労働省（こうせいろうどうしょう）Ministry of Health, Labour and Welfare
厚生労働白書（こうせいろうどうはくしょ）Annual Health, Labour and Welfare Report
公設民営（こうせつみんえい）privatization of public enterprise
光線損傷（こうせんそんしょう）actinic injury
光線力学療法（こうせんりきがくりょうほう）photodynamic therapy
光線療法（こうせんりょうほう）actinotherapy
構造的増分主義（こうぞうてきぞうぶんしゅぎ）structural-incrementalism
†拘束（こうそく）restraint
後足部内反変形（こうそくぶないはんへんけい）rearfoot varus deformity
鉤ゾンデ（こうぞんで）hooked probe
抗体（こうたい）antibody
高体温（こうたいおん）hyperthermia
抗体価（こうたいか）antibody titer
抗体結合価（こうたいけつごうか）antibody valence
交代制勤務（こうたいせいきんむ）alternative work schedule
交代浴（こうたいよく）contrast bath
高炭酸ガス血症（こうたんさんがすけつしょう）hypercapnia
巧緻性（こうちせい）dexterity
高窒素血症（こうちっそけつしょう）azotemia
交通バリアフリー法（こうつうばりあふりーほう）Transportation Accessibility Improvement Law
抗痛風薬（こうつうふうやく）antipodagric
肯定的差別（こうていてきさべつ）positive discrimination
鉱泥療法（こうでいりょうほう）fango therapy
公的医療保険（こうてきいりょうほけん）public health care insurance
公的医療保険制度（こうてきいりょうほけんせいど）public health care insurance system
公的介護保険（こうてきかいごほけん）public long-term care insurance
公的介護保険制度（こうてきかいごほけんせいど）public long-term care insurance system
公的介入（こうてきかいにゅう）public intervention
公的企業（こうてききぎょう）public enterprise
公的救済（こうてききゅうさい）public relief
公的後見人（こうてきこうけんにん）public guardian
公的サービス（こうてきさーびす）public services
公的責任（こうてきせきにん）public responsibility
公的年金（こうてきねんきん）public pension
公的年金一元化（こうてきねんきんいちげんか）integration of the public pension schemes
公的年金制度（こうてきねんきんせいど）public pension system
公的年金制度加入経過（こうてきねんきんせいどかにゅうけいか）public pension plan subscription process
公的扶助（こうてきふじょ）public assistance
公的扶助基準（こうてきふじょきじゅん）public assistance standards
公的扶助受給者（こうてきふじょじゅきゅうしゃ）public assistance recipient
公的扶助費（こうてきふじょひよう）public assistance costs

抗てんかん薬（こうてんかんやく）antiepileptic drug；antiseizure drug
†後天性免疫不全症候群（こうてんせいめんえきふぜんしょうこうぐん）acquired immune deficiency syndrome：AIDS
行動アセスメント（こうどうあせすめんと）behavior assessment
行動科学（こうどうかがく）behavioral science
行動観察（こうどうかんさつ）behavioral observation
行動言語（こうどうげんご）behavioral language
行動主義（こうどうしゅぎ）behaviorism
行動障害（こうどうしょうがい）behavior disorder；behavioral symptom
後頭神経痛（こうとうしんけいつう）occipital neuralgia；C2 neuralgia；Arnold's neuralgia
抗糖尿病薬（こうとうにょうびょうやく）antidiabetic
行動パターン（こうどうぱたーん）behavior pattern
行動変容アプローチ（こうどうへんようあぷろーち）behavior modification approach
行動変容法（こうどうへんようほう）behavior modification
高等養成訓練制度（こうとうようせいくんれんせいど）higher apprenticeships
行動リハーサル（こうどうりはーさる）behavior rehearsal
行動療法（こうどうりょうほう）behavior therapy
高度看護施設（こうどかんごしせつ）skilled nursing home
高度経済成長（こうどけいざいせいちょう）high economic growth
高度先進医療（こうどせんしんいりょう）highly advanced medical technology：HAMT
高度専門看護師（こうどせんもんかんごし）advanced practice nurse
高度治療室（こうどちりょうしつ）high dependency unit
口内装置（こうないそうち）oral appliance
高尿酸血症（こうにょうさんけつしょう）hyperuricemia
更年期（こうねんき）menopause
更年期障害（こうねんきしょうがい）menopausal disorder
高年齢労働者（こうねんれいろうどうしゃ）older worker
抗パーキンソン病薬（こうぱーきんそんびょうやく）anti-Parkinsonian drug；anti-Parkinsonian medication
後発医薬品（こうはついやくひん）generic drug
広汎性発達障害（こうはんせいはったつしょうがい）pervasive developmental disorder：PDD
高比重リポたんぱく質（こうひじゅうりぽたんぱくし

つ）high density lipoprotein
抗ヒスタミン剤（こうひすたみんざい）antihistamine
後鼻漏症候群（こうびろうしょうこうぐん）post nasal drip syndrome：PNDS
高頻度接触面（こうひんどせっしょくめん）high touch surface
抗不安剤（こうふあんざい）anxiolytic
抗不安薬（こうふあんやく）anxiolytic medication；antianxiety medication
高福祉・高負担（こうふくし・こうふたん）high level of welfare, high level of taxation
幸福追求権（こうふくついきゅうけん）the right to the pursuit of happiness
幸福な老い（こうふくなおい）successful aging
後腹膜血腫（こうふくまくけっしゅ）retroperitoneal hematoma
抗浮腫性（こうふしゅせい）antiedemic
公平（こうへい）equity
合法就労（ごうほうしゅうろう）legal employment
硬膜外血腫（こうまくがいけっしゅ）epidural hematoma
硬膜外鎮痛法（こうまくがいちんつうほう）epidural analgesia
硬膜下血腫（こうまくかけっしゅ）subdural hematoma
公民権（こうみんけん）civil rights
公民権運動（こうみんけんうんどう）civil rights movement
高免責額医療保険（こうめんせきがくいりょうほけん）high deductible health insurance plan：HDHP
肛門（こうもん）anus
肛門拡張器（こうもんかくちょうき）anal dilator
肛門括約筋（こうもんかつやくきん）anal sphincter muscle
肛門括約筋電図検査（こうもんかつやくきんきんでんずけんさ）electromyography of anal sphincter
肛門管超音波検査（こうもんかんちょうおんぱけんさ）anal endosonography
肛門期（こうもんき）anal stage
肛門鏡（こうもんきょう）anoscope；anal speculum
肛門鏡検査（こうもんきょうけんさ）anoscopy
肛門刺激装置（こうもんしげきそうち）anal stimulator
肛門直腸指診（こうもんちょくちょうししん）digital anorectal examination
肛門直腸内圧測定法（こうもんちょくちょうないあつそくていほう）anorectal manometry
肛門内圧測定（こうもんないあつそくてい）anal manometry
肛門粘膜電流感覚閾値（こうもんねんまくでんりゅう

かんかくいきち）anal mucosal electrosensitivity
絞扼神経障害（こうやくしんけいしょうがい）entrapment neuropathy
合理化（ごうりか）rationalization
公立病院（こうりつびょういん）public hospital
公立病院改革（こうりつびょういんかいかく）public hospital reform
抗利尿（こうりにょう）antidiuresis
交流分析（こうりゅうぶんせき）transactional analysis
高齢移民（こうれいいみん）immigrant elder
†高齢化（こうれいか）population aging；aging population
高齢化委員会（こうれいかいいんかい）Conference on Aging
高齢化社会（こうれいかしゃかい）aging society
高齢化率（こうれいかりつ）rate of population aging
高齢期活動（こうれいきかつどう）later-life activity
†高齢期障害（こうれいきしょうがい）old-age disorder
†高齢者（こうれいしゃ）elderly
高齢者医療（こうれいしゃいりょう）medical care for the elderly
高齢者医療サービス（こうれいしゃいりょうさービす）medical care services for the elderly
高齢者医療サービス機関（こうれいしゃいりょうさービすきかん）medical care services agency for the elderly
高齢者医療サービス事業者（こうれいしゃいりょうさービすじぎょうしゃ）medical care services provider for the elderly
高齢者医療サービス事業所（こうれいしゃいりょうさービすじぎょうしょ）medical care services office for the elderly
高齢者医療制度（こうれいしゃいりょうせいど）medical care system for the elderly
高齢者医療費（こうれいしゃいりょうひ）medical expenses for the elderly；health care expenditures for the elderly
高齢者医療フェローシッププログラム（こうれいしゃいりょうふぇろーしっぷぷろぐらむ）Geriatric Medicine Fellowship Program
高齢者援助（こうれいしゃえんじょ）support for the elderly
高齢者援助サービス（こうれいしゃえんじょさービす）support services for the elderly；supportive services for the elderly
高齢者援助サービス機関（こうれいしゃえんじょさービすきかん）support services agency for the elderly；supportive services agency for the elderly
高齢者援助サービス事業者（こうれいしゃえんじょさービすじぎょうしゃ）support services provider for the elderly；supportive services provider for the elderly
高齢者援助サービス事業所（こうれいしゃえんじょさービすじぎょうしょ）support services office for the elderly；supportive services office for the elderly
†高齢社会（こうれいしゃかい）aged society
高齢者介護（こうれいしゃかいご）elderly care；geriatric care
高齢者介護機関（こうれいしゃかいごきかん）long-term care agency for the elderly
高齢者介護サービス（こうれいしゃかいごさービす）long-term care services for the elderly
高齢者介護サービス機関（こうれいしゃかいごさービすきかん）long-term care services agency for the elderly
高齢者介護サービス事業者（こうれいしゃかいごさービすじぎょうしゃ）long-term care services provider for the elderly
高齢者介護サービス事業所（こうれいしゃかいごさービすじぎょうしょ）long-term care services office for the elderly
高齢者介護支援（こうれいしゃかいごしえん）elderly care management
高齢者介護支援サービス（こうれいしゃかいごしえんさービす）elderly care management services
高齢者介護支援サービス機関（こうれいしゃかいごしえんさービすきかん）elderly care management services agency
高齢者介護支援サービス事業者（こうれいしゃかいごしえんさービすじぎょうしゃ）elderly care management services provider
高齢者介護支援サービス事業所（こうれいしゃかいごしえんさービすじぎょうしょ）elderly care management services office
高齢者介護事業者（こうれいしゃかいごじぎょうしゃ）long-term care provider for the elderly
高齢者介護施設（こうれいしゃかいごしせつ）long-term care facility for the elderly
高齢者介護放棄（こうれいしゃかいごほうき）elder neglect
高齢者介護保険（こうれいしゃかいごほけん）long-term care insurance for the elderly
高齢者学級（こうれいしゃがっきゅう）educational class for the elderly
高齢者学校（こうれいしゃがっこう）school for the elderly
高齢者看護（こうれいしゃかんご）geriatric nursing
†高齢者虐待（こうれいしゃぎゃくたい）elder abuse；elderly mistreatment
高齢者虐待防止（こうれいしゃぎゃくたいぼうし）prevention of elder abuse

高齢者虐待防止活動（こうれいしゃぎゃくたいぼうしかつどう）elder abuse prevention activity
†高齢者虐待防止法（こうれいしゃぎゃくたいぼうしほう）Elder Abuse Prevention Act
高齢者給食（こうれいしゃきゅうしょく）meal services for the elderly
高齢者共同生活（こうれいしゃきょうどうせいかつ）group living for the elderly
高齢者共同生活援助（こうれいしゃきょうどうせいかつえんじょ）group living support for the elderly
高齢者共同生活支援（こうれいしゃきょうどうせいかつしえん）group living management for the elderly
高齢者共同生活扶助（こうれいしゃきょうどうせいかつふじょ）group living assistance for the elderly
高齢者居住共同体（こうれいしゃきょじゅうきょうどうたい）community living for the elderly；senior living community
高齢者居宅援助（こうれいしゃきょたくえんじょ）home-based support for the elderly
高齢者居宅介護（こうれいしゃきょたくかいご）home-based care for the elderly
高齢者居宅介護支援（こうれいしゃきょたくかいごしえん）home-based care management for the elderly
高齢者居宅生活援助（こうれいしゃきょたくせいかつえんじょ）home-based living support for the elderly
高齢者居宅生活扶助（こうれいしゃきょたくせいかつふじょ）home-based living assistance for the elderly
高齢者居宅扶助（こうれいしゃきょたくふじょ）home-based assistance for the elderly
高齢者ケア（こうれいしゃけあ）；elderly care；geriatric care
高齢者ケアアドバイザー（こうれいしゃけああどばいざー）senior care advisor
高齢者ケア付住宅（こうれいしゃけあつきじゅうたく）elder care housing；aged care home
高齢者ケアマネジメント（こうれいしゃけあまねじめんと）geriatric care management
高齢者ケースマネジメント（こうれいしゃけーすまねじめんと）geriatric case management
高齢者ケースマネジャー（こうれいしゃけーすまねじゃー）geriatric case manager
高齢者雇用（こうれいしゃこよう）employment of older workers；employment of the elderly；hiring older workers
高齢者雇用促進（こうれいしゃこようそくしん）employment promotion for the elderly
高齢者雇用促進対策（こうれいしゃこようそくしんたいさく）employment promotion policy for the elderly

高齢者雇用対策課（こうれいしゃこようたいさくか）Employment Measures for the Elderly Division
高齢者在宅援助（こうれいしゃざいたくえんじょ）home support for the elderly
高齢者在宅介護支援（こうれいしゃざいたくかいごしえん）elderly home care management
高齢者在宅生活援助（こうれいしゃざいたくせいかつえんじょ）home living support for the elderly
高齢者在宅生活扶助（こうれいしゃざいたくせいかつふじょ）home living assistance for the elderly
高齢者在宅扶助（こうれいしゃざいたくふじょ）home assistance for the elderly
高齢者サービス調整チーム（こうれいしゃさーびすちょうせいちーむ）service management team for the elderly
高齢者歯科学分野（こうれいしゃしかがくぶんや）geriatric dentistry
高齢者住宅（こうれいしゃじゅうたく）elderly housing
高齢者住宅政策（こうれいしゃじゅうたくせいさく）housing policy for the elderly
高齢者人口（こうれいしゃじんこう）elderly population
高齢者スポーツ（こうれいしゃすぽーつ）sports for the elderly
高齢者生活福祉センター（こうれいしゃせいかつふくしせんたー）welfare center for the elderly
高齢者生活扶助（こうれいしゃせいかつふじょ）living assistance for the elderly
†高齢者世帯（こうれいしゃせたい）elderly household
高齢者専門医（こうれいしゃせんもんい）geriatrician
高齢者専用賃貸住宅（こうれいしゃせんようちんたいじゅうたく）senior rental housing
高齢者総合評価（こうれいしゃそうごうひょうか）Comprehensive Geriatric Assessment：CGA
高齢者大学（こうれいしゃだいがく）university for the elderly
高齢者多目的福祉センター（こうれいしゃたもくてきふくしせんたー）multipurpose senior center
高齢者に対する偏見（こうれいしゃにたいするへんけん）prejudice against the elderly
高齢者に対する薬剤不適切投与（こうれいしゃにたいするやくざいふてきせつとうよ）inappropriate prescription for elderly
高齢者ネグレクト（こうれいしゃねぐれくと）elder neglect
高齢者の尊厳（こうれいしゃのそんげん）dignity of the elderly
高齢者評価・マネジメントプログラム（こうれいしゃひょうか・まねじめんとぷろぐらむ）geriatric evaluation and management programs

高齢者福祉（こうれいしゃふくし）welfare for the elderly
高齢者福祉サービス（こうれいしゃふくしさーびす）welfare services for the elderly
高齢者福祉センター（こうれいしゃふくしせんたー）senior center
高齢者扶助（こうれいしゃふじょ）assistance for the elderly
高齢者扶助サービス（こうれいしゃふじょさーびす）assistance services for the elderly
高齢者扶助サービス機関（こうれいしゃふじょさーびすきかん）assistance services agency for the elderly
高齢者扶助サービス事業者（こうれいしゃふじょさーびすじぎょうしゃ）assistance services provider for the elderly
高齢者扶助サービス事業所（こうれいしゃふじょさーびすじぎょうしょ）assistance services office for the elderly
高齢者法律援助プログラム（こうれいしゃほうりつえんじょぷろぐらむ）elderly legal assistance program
高齢者保健医療（こうれいしゃほけんいりょう）health care for the elderly
高齢者保健医療サービス（こうれいしゃほけんいりょうさーびす）health care services for the elderly
高齢者保健医療制度（こうれいしゃほけんいりょうせいど）health care system for the elderly
高齢者保健医療費（こうれいしゃほけんいりょうひ）health care expenditures for the elderly；medical expenses for the aged
高齢者保健福祉（こうれいしゃほけんふく）geriatric health and welfare
高齢者保健福祉推進十か年戦略（こうれいしゃほけんふくしすいしんじゅっかねんせんりゃく）Ten-Year Strategy to Promote Health and Welfare for the Aged；Gold Plan
高齢者向け公営住宅（こうれいしゃむけこうえいじゅうたく）public housing for the elderly
高齢者向け住宅（こうれいしゃむけじゅうたく）housing for the elderly
高齢者向け民間サービス（こうれいしゃむけみんかんさーびす）private services for the elderly
高齢者向け優良賃貸住宅（こうれいしゃむけゆうりょうちんたいじゅうたく）high-quality rental housing for the elderly
高齢出産（こうれいしゅっさん）advanced maternal age
高齢・障害者雇用対策部（こうれい・しょうがいしゃこようたいさくぶ）Employment Measures for the Elderly and Persons with Disabilities Department
高齢発症関節リウマチ（こうれいはっしょうかんせつりうまち）elderly-onset rheumatoid arthritis：EORA
口話（こうわ）verbal communication
後弯（こうわん）kyphosis；roundback
†声かけ（こえかけ）verbal encouragement；encouragement
†誤嚥（ごえん）pulmonary aspiration
†誤嚥性肺炎（ごえんせいはいえん）aspiration pneumonia
語音聴取閾値（ごおんちょうしゅいきち）speech reception threshold：SRT
語音聴取閾値検査（ごおんちょうしゅいきちけんさ）speech reception threshold test
コカイン（こかいん）cocaine
股関節骨折（こかんせつこっせつ）hip fracture
股義足（こぎそく）hip disarticulation prosthesis
顧客（こきゃく）customer
顧客満足（こきゃくまんぞく）customer satisfaction：CS
†呼吸（こきゅう）respiration；breathing
呼吸器（こきゅうき）respiratory organ
呼吸器感染（こきゅうきかんせん）respiratory infection
呼吸器疾患（こきゅうきしっかん）respiratory disease
†呼吸機能障害（こきゅうきのうしょうがい）respiratory functional disorder
呼吸訓練（こきゅうくんれん）respiratory exercise；breathing exercise；respiratory training
呼吸困難（こきゅうこんなん）dyspnea
呼吸障害（こきゅうしょうがい）respiratory disorder
呼吸不全（こきゅうふぜん）respiratory failure
呼吸麻痺（こきゅうまひ）respiratory paralysis
呼吸リハビリテーション（こきゅうりはびりてーしょん）pulmonary rehabilitation
呼吸療法（こきゅうりょうほう）respiratory therapy
呼吸練習（こきゅうれんしゅう）respiratory exercise；breathing exercise；respiratory training
国際医療（こくさいいりょう）international medicine
国際衛生年（こくさいえいせいねん）International Year of Sanitation：IYS
国際課（こくさいか）International Affairs Division
国際化学年（こくさいかがくねん）International Year of Chemistry：IYC
国際家族年（こくさいかぞくねん）International Year of the Family：IYF
国際規格（こくさいきかく）International Standard：IS
国際厚生事業団（こくさいこうせいじぎょうだん）

Japan International Corporation of Welfare Services: JICWELS
国際高齢者年（こくさいこうれいしゃねん）International Year of Older Persons：IYOP
†国際疾病分類（こくさいしっぺいぶんるい）International Classification of Diseases：ICD
国際疾病分類第10版（こくさいしっぺいぶんるいだいじゅっぱん）International Classification of Disease, 10th revision：ICD-10
国際児童年（こくさいじどうねん）International Year of the Child：IYC
国際社会福祉協議会（こくさいしゃかいふくしきょうぎかい）International Council on Social Welfare：ICSW
国際障害者年（こくさいしょうがいしゃねん）International Year of Disabled Persons：IYDP
国際障害者の10年（こくさいしょうがいしゃのじゅうねん）United Nations Decade of Disabled Persons
†国際障害分類（こくさいしょうがいぶんるい）International Classification of Impairments, Disabilities and Handicaps：ICIDH
国際人権規約（こくさいじんけんきやく）International Covenant on Human Rights
国際人権憲章（こくさいじんけんけんしょう）International Bill of Human Rights
国際頭痛学会頭痛分類委員会（こくさいずつうがっかいずつうぶんるいいいんかい）Headache Classification Committee of the International Headache Society
†国際生活機能分類（こくさいせいかつきのうぶんるい）International Classification of Functioning, Disability and Health：ICF
国際生物多様性年（こくさいせいぶつたようせいねん）International Year of Biodiversity：IYB
国際長寿センター（こくさいちょうじゅせんたー）International Longevity Center
国際年（こくさいねん）international year
国際年金課（こくさいねんきんか）International Pension Division
†国際標準化機構（こくさいひょうじゅんかきこう）International Organization for Standardization：ISO
国際福祉（こくさいふくし）international welfare
国際婦人年（こくさいふじんねん）International Women's Year：IWY
国際保健（こくさいほけん）international health
国際保健福祉（こくさいほけんふくし）international health and welfare
国際リハビリテーション協会（こくさいりはびりてーしょんきょうかい）Rehabilitation International：RI
国際連合（こくさいれんごう）United Nations：UN

国際連合難民高等弁務官事務所（こくさいれんごうなんみんこうとうべんむかんじむしょ）United Nations High Commissioner for Refugees：UNHCR
国際連盟（こくさいれんめい）League of Nations：LON
国際労働機関（こくさいろうどうきかん）International Labour Organization：ILO
国際老年精神学会（こくさいろうねんせいしんがっかい）International Psychogeriatric Association
国勢調査（こくせいちょうさ）national census
国籍（こくせき）nationality
告知（こくち）truth telling
極超短波療法（ごくちょうたんぱりょうほう）microwave therapy
極低出生体重児（ごくていしゅっしょうたいじゅうじ）very premature infant
国内総生産（こくないそうせいさん）gross domestic product：GDP
コグネックス（こぐねっくす）Cognex
国保連苦情処理委員会（こくほれんくじょうしょりいいんかい）Grievance Committee of the National Health Insurance
国民医療費（こくみんいりょうひ）national medical expenditures；national health expenditures
国民皆医療保険（こくみんかいいりょうほけん）national universal medical insurance
国民介護費（こくみんかいごひ）national long-term care expenditures；national expenditures on long-term care services
国民皆年金（こくみんかいねんきん）universal pension
国民健康づくり運動（こくみんけんこうづくりうんどう）national health promotion movement
国民健康づくり対策（こくみんけんこうづくりたいさく）national health promotion policy
国民健康保険（こくみんけんこうほけん）National Health Insurance
国民健康保険課（こくみんけんこうほけんか）National Health Insurance Division
国民健康保険組合（こくみんけんこうほけんくみあい）National Health Insurance Society
国民健康保険証（こくみんけんこうほけんしょう）National Health Insurance card
国民健康保険制度（こくみんけんこうほけんせいど）National Health Insurance system
国民健康保険法（こくみんけんこうほけんほう）National Health Insurance Act
国民健康保険料（こくみんけんこうほけんりょう）National Health Insurance premiums
国民健康保険料減免（こくみんけんこうほけんりょうげんめん）deduction for National Health Insurance premiums

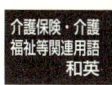

国民健康保険料税減免（こくみんけんこうほけんりょうぜいげんめん）tax deduction for National Health Insurance premiums
国民主権（こくみんしゅけん）popular sovereignty
国民所得（こくみんしょとく）national income；NI
国民生活センター（こくみんせいかつせんたー）National Consumer Affairs Center of Japan
国民総生産（こくみんそうせいさん）gross national product；GNP
国民総福祉（こくみんそうふくし）gross national welfare；GNW
国民投票（こくみんとうひょう）referendum
国民年金（こくみんねんきん）National Pension
国民年金基金（こくみんねんきんききん）National Pension Fund
国民年金の記号番号（こくみんねんきんのきごうばんごう）National Pension registration number
国民年金被保険者の受給金額（こくみんねんきんひほけんしゃのじゅきゅうきんがく）amount of National Pension Insurance benefit
国民年金法（こくみんねんきんほう）National Pension Law
国民年金保険（こくみんねんきんほけん）National Pension Insurance
国民年金保険料（こくみんねんきんほけんりょう）National Pension premiums
国民年金保険料減免（こくみんねんきんほけんりょうげんめん）deduction for National Pension premiums
国民年金保険料税減免（こくみんねんきんほけんりょうぜいげんめん）tax deduction for National Pension premiums
国民福祉指標（こくみんふくししひょう）net national welfare
国民負担率（こくみんふたんりつ）national burden rate
コクランレビュー（こくらんれびゅー）Cochrane review
国立医薬品食品衛生研究所（こくりついやくひんしょくひんえいせいけんきゅうしょ）National Institute of Health Sciences
国立がん研究センター（こくりつがんけんきゅうせんたー）National Cancer Center
国立感染症研究所（こくりつかんせんしょうけんきゅうしょ）National Institute of Infectious Diseases
国立国際医療研究センター（こくりつこくさいいりょうけんきゅうせんたー）National Center for Global Health and Medicine
国立社会保障・人口問題研究所（こくりつしゃかいほしょう・じんこうもんだいけんきゅうしょ）National Institute of Population and Social Security Research

国立循環器病研究センター（こくりつじゅんかんきびょうけんきゅうせんたー）National Cerebral and Cardiovascular Center
国立成育医療研究センター（こくりつせいいくいりょうけんきゅうせんたー）National Center for Child Health and Development
国立精神・神経医療研究センター（こくりつせいしん・しんけいいりょうけんきゅうせんたー）National Center of Neurology and Psychiatry
国立長寿医療研究センター（こくりつちょうじゅいりょうけんきゅうせんたー）National Center for Geriatrics and Gerontology
国立病院（こくりつびょういん）national hospital
国立病院課（こくりつびょういんか）National Hospitals Division
国立保健医療科学院（こくりつほけんいりょうかがくいん）National Institute of Public Health
国連人権宣言（こくれんじんけんせんげん）United Nations Declaration of Human Rights
固形石鹸（こけいせっけん）bar soap
こころのケア（こころのけあ）mental health care
コザール（こざーる）Cozaar
個室（こしつ）private room
鼓室形成術（こしつけいせいじゅつ）tympanoplasty
50代（ごじゅうだい）quinquagenarian
固縮（こしゅく）rigidity
故障の木解析（こしょうのきかいせき）fault tree analysis
故人（こじん）deceased
誤診（ごしん）misdiagnosis
個人衛生（こじんえいせい）personal hygiene
個人ケア（こじんけあ）individualized care
個人支援サービス（こじんしえんさーびす）personal support services
個人主義（こじんしゅぎ）individualism
個人情報（こじんじょうほう）personal information
個人情報窃盗（こじんじょうほうせっとう）identity theft
個人情報保護法（こじんじょうほうほごほう）Personal Information Protection Act
個人心理学（こじんしんりがく）individual psychology
個人退職年金勘定（こじんたいしょくねんきんかんじょう）Individual Retirement Accounts；IRA
個人的救助器具（こじんてきさきゅうじょきぐ）personal emergency device
個人内変動（こじんないへんどう）personal change
個人年金（こじんねんきん）personal pension
個人年金プラン（こじんねんきんぷらん）personal pension scheme
個人年金保険料（こじんねんきんほけんりょう）personal pension premium
個人防御用器材（こじんぼうぎょようきざい）⇒個人

防御用装備
個人防御用装備（こじんぼうぎょようそうび）personal protective equipment：PPE
個人割当（こじんわりあて）individual quota
コスト契約（こすとけいやく）cost-volume contract
コース立方体組み合わせテスト（こーすりっぽうたいくみあわせてすと）Kohs Block Design Test：Kohs Block Test
子育て（こそだて）parenting
子育て支援（こそだてしえん）parenting support
コーダー（こーだー）coder
五大栄養素（ごだいえいようそ）five major nutrients；five essential nutrients
固着（こちゃく）fixation
骨萎縮（こついしゅく）bone atrophy
骨塩量（こつえんりょう）bone mineral density
骨格（こっかく）skeleton
骨格筋（こっかくきん）skeletal muscle
国家最低基準（こっかさいていきじゅん）national minimum standards
国家最低賃金（こっかさいていちんぎん）national minimum wage
国家最低賃金監督官（こっかさいていちんぎんかんとくかん）national minimum wage compliance officer
国家試験・実技試験（こっかしけん・じつぎしけん）National Certification Examination and Practice Examination
骨化性筋炎（こつかせいきんえん）myositis ossificans
国家責任（こっかせきにん）national responsibility
骨欠乏症（こつけつぼうしょう）osteopenia
骨減少性（こつげんしょうせい）⇒骨欠乏症
骨疾患（こつしっかん）bone disease
骨髄異形成症候群（こつずいいけいせいしょうこうぐん）myelodysplastic syndrome
†骨折（こっせつ）fracture
骨折管理（こっせつかんり）fracture management
†骨粗鬆症（こつそしょうしょう）osteoporosis
骨軟化症（こつなんかしょう）osteomalacia
骨盤骨折（こつばんこっせつ）pelvic fracture
骨盤帯（こつばんたい）pelvic band
骨盤帯付長下肢装具（こつばんたいつきちょうかしそうぐ）hip-knee-ankle-foot orthosis：HKAFO
骨盤底弛緩（こつばんていしかん）pelvic floor relaxation
骨密度（こつみつど）bone density
固定筋（こていきん）fixator
固定ジストニア（こていじすとにあ）fixed dystonia
固定自転車（こていじてんしゃ）stationary bicycle
コーディネーター（こーでぃねーたー）coordinator
コデイン（こでいん）codeine
古典的条件づけ（こてんてきじょうけんづけ）

classical conditioning
孤独（こどく）loneliness
孤独死（こどくし）solitary death
子としての義務（ことしてのぎむ）filial duty
†言葉かけ（ことばかけ）verbal encouragement；encouragement
言葉の明瞭性（ことばのめいりょうせい）speech clarity
子供（こども）child；children
子供えん（こどもえん）children's hall
子供手当（こどもてあて）child allowance
子供のための機能的自立度評価法（こどものためのきのうてきじりつどひょうかほう）WeeFIM
子供を守る会（こどもをまもるかい）Children's Aid Society
コーネル認知症抑うつ尺度（こーねるにんちしょうよくうつしゃくど）Cornell Scale for Depression in Dementia：CS
コーネル・メディカル・インデックス（こーねる・めでぃかる・いんでっくす）Cornell medical index：CMI
コーピング（こーぴんぐ）coping
コーピング行動（こーぴんぐこうどう）coping behavior
小振り歩行（こぶりほこう）swing-to gait
個別援助技術（こべつえんじょぎじゅつ）case work
個別化（こべつか）individualization
†個別介護（こべつかいご）individualized care
個別家族セッション（こべつかぞくせっしょん）individual family session
個別化の原則（こべつかのげんそく）principle of individualization
個別管理（こべつかんり）individual-based management
個別教育計画（こべつきょういくけいかく）individualized educational plan
個別教育プログラム（こべつきょういくぷろぐらむ）individualized education program
個別ケア（こべつけあ）individualized care
個別処遇（こべつしょぐう）individual treatment
コホーティング（こほーてぃんぐ）cohorting
コホート研究（こほーとけんきゅう）cohort study
コホート分析（こほーとぶんせき）cohort analysis
コーポラティスト福祉国家（こーぽらてぃすとふくしこっか）corporatist welfare state
鼓膜（こまく）tympanic membrane
†コミュニケーション（こみゅにけーしょん）communication
†コミュニケーションエイド（こみゅにけーしょんえいど）communication aid
コミュニケーション障害（こみゅにけーしょんしょうがい）communication disorder
コミュニケーション能力（こみゅにけーしょんのうり

よく）communicative ability
コミュニケーションノート（こみゅにけーしょんのーと）communication notes
コミュニケーションボード（こみゅにけーしょんぼーど）communication board
コミュニティ（こみゅにてぃ）community
コミュニティオーガニゼーション（こみゅにてぃおーがにぜーしょん）community organization
コミュニティ活動機関（こみゅにてぃかつどうきかん）community action agency
コミュニティケア（こみゅにてぃけあ）community care
コミュニティ再生（こみゅにてぃさいせい）community revitalization
コミュニティソーシャルワーク（こみゅにてぃそーしゃるわーく）community social work
コミュニティワーカー（こみゅにてぃわーかー）community worker
コミュニティワーク（こみゅにてぃわーく）community work
コモードチェア（こもーどちぇあ）commode chair
誤薬（ごやく）medication error
固有感覚（こゆうかんかく）proprioception
固有受容性欠陥（こゆうじゅようせいけっかん）proprioception deficit
固有受容性神経筋促通法（こゆうじゅようせいしんけいきんそくつうほう）proprioceptive neuromuscular facilitation：PNF
誤用（ごよう）misuse
雇用開発課（こようかいはつか）Employment Development Division
雇用期間（こようきかん）employment period；period of employment
雇用均等・児童家庭局（こようきんとう・じどうかていきょく）Equal Employment, Children and Families Bureau
雇用均等政策課（こようきんとうせいさくか）Equal Employment Policy Division
雇用契約（こようけいやく）employment agreements and contracts：contract of employment；employment contract
雇用終了（こようしゅうりょう）⇒解雇
誤用症候群（ごようしょうこうぐん）misuse syndrome
雇用政策課（こようせいさくか）Employment Policy Division
雇用調整（こようちょうせい）employment adjustment
雇用統計課（こようとうけいか）Employment Statistics Division
雇用法（こようほう）Employment Act
雇用保険（こようほけん）employment insurance
雇用保険課（こようほけんか）Employment Insurance Division
雇用保険制度（こようほけんせいど）employment insurance system
雇用保険法（こようほけんほう）Employment Insurance Law
雇用率（こようりつ）employment rate
コラーゲン（こらーげん）collagen
コリンエステラーゼ阻害薬（こりんえすてらーぜそがいやく）cholinesterase inhibitor
コリン作動性療法（こりんさどうせいりょうほう）cholinergic therapy
コルサコフ精神病（こるさこふせいしんびょう）Korsakoff's psychosis
コルセット（こるせっと）corset
コルチコステロイド（こるちこすてろいど）corticosteroids
ゴールドプラン（ごーるどぷらん）Gold Plan
ゴールドプラン21（ごーるどぷらんにじゅういち）Gold Plan 21：Gold Plan for 21st century
†コレステロール（これすてろーる）cholesterol
コロナイゼーション（ころないぜーしょん）colonization
コロニー形成単位（ころにーけいせいたんい）colony forming unit：CFU
婚姻証明書（こんいんしょうめいしょ）marriage certificate
困窮者（こんきゅうしゃ）the needy
根拠に基づく医療（こんきょにもとづくいりょう）evidence-based medicine：EBM；evidence-based practice：EBP
根拠に基づく介護（こんきょにもとづくかいご）evidence-based care：EBC
根拠に基づく看護（こんきょにもとづくかんご）evidence-based nursing
根拠に基づくケア（こんきょにもとづくけあ）evidence-based care：EBC
根拠に基づく地域計画（こんきょにもとづくちいきけいかく）evidence-based community planning
混合型認知症（こんごうがたにんちしょう）mixed dementia
混合性難聴（こんごうせいなんちょう）mixed hearing loss
コンサルテーション（こんさるてーしょん）consultation
コンサルテーションリエゾン精神医学（こんさるてーしょんりえぞんせいしんいがく）consultation-liaison psychiatry
昏睡（こんすい）coma
昏睡状態（こんすいじょうたい）comatose
†献立（こんだて）menu
コンタミネーションコントロール（こんたみねーしょんこんとろーる）contamination control
コンディショナー（こんでぃしょなー）conditioner

コントラスト感度（こんとらすとかんど）contrast sensitivity
コンドロイチン硫酸（こんどろいちんりゅうさん）chondroitin sulfate
コンパートメント症候群（こんぱーとめんとしょうこうぐん）compartment syndrome
コンピテンス（こんぴてんす）competence
コンピューター体軸断層撮影（こんぴゅーたーたいじくだんそうさつえい）computerized axial tomography：CAT
コンピューター断層撮影（こんぴゅーたーだんそうさつえい）computed tomography：CT
コンプライアンス（こんぷらいあんす）compliance
コンプレックス（こんぷれっくす）complex

さ

†座位（ざい）sitting position
サイアザイド系利尿剤（さいあざいどけいりにょうざい）thiazide diuretic
†再アセスメント（さいあせすめんと）reassessment
サイアミン欠乏症（さいあみんけつぼうしょう）thiamine deficiency
在院（ざいいん）hospital stay；hospitalization
災害（さいがい）accident
災害給付（さいがいきゅうふ）disaster benefit
災害保険（さいがいほけん）accident insurance
災害補償（さいがいほしょう）accident compensation
再課題分析（さいかだいぶんせき）reanalysis of problems
最強点（さいきょうてん）point of maximum intensity
細菌（さいきん）bacterium；bacteria
細菌性肺炎（さいきんせいはいえん）bacterial pneumonia
細菌増殖の病巣（さいきんぞうしょくのびょうそう）focus of colonization
細菌定着カテーテル（さいきんていちゃくかてーてる）colonization catheter
細菌尿（さいきんにょう）bacteriuria
座位訓練（ざいくんれん）sitting exercise
債権回収会社（さいけんかいしゅうがいしゃ）collection agency：debt collector
採光（さいこう）daylighting
再興感染症（さいこうかんせんしょう）re-emerging infectious diseases
再雇用（さいこよう）reemployment
再婚（さいこん）remarriage
財産分与（ざいさんぶんよ）property division
座位姿勢（ざいしせい）sitting posture
再指定（さいしてい）re-certification
最終臥床期間（さいしゅうがしょうきかん）bedridden period before death：BPbd
最終滅菌（さいしゅうめっきん）terminal sterilization
再使用（さいしよう）reuse
最小可聴値（さいしょうかちょうち）absolute threshold of hearing
最小紅斑量（さいしょうこうはんりょう）minimal erythema dose：MED
最小侵襲手術（さいしょうしんしゅうしゅじゅつ）minimally invasive surgery
在職証明書（ざいしょくしょうめいしょ）proof of employment letter
財政安定化基金（ざいせいあんていかききん）financial stability fund
再生医療（さいせいいりょう）regeneration medicine
財政つぶし（ざいせいつぶし）⇒財政破綻
財政破綻（ざいせいはたん）budget buster
財政福祉（ざいせいふくし）financial welfare
再生不良性貧血（さいせいふりょうせいひんけつ）aplastic anemia
財政力指数（ざいせいりょくしすう）financial capability index
最善の治療（さいぜんのちりょう）best practice
最大筋力（さいだいきんりょく）maximum muscle strength
最大酸素消費量（さいだいさんそしょうひりょう）maximum oxygen consumption；maximum oxygen intake
最大随意収縮圧（さいだいずいいしゅうしゅくあつ）maximum squeeze pressure：MSP
最大静止圧（さいだいせいしあつ）maximum resting pressure：MRP
最大耐容量（さいだいたいようりょう）maximum tolerable volume：MTV
最大多数の最大幸福（さいだいたすうのさいだいこうふく）the greatest happiness for the greatest number
最大伝導速度（さいだいでんどうそくど）maximum conduction velocity：MCV
最大歩行速度（さいだいほこうそくど）maximal gait velocity；maximum gait speed
在宅医（ざいたくい）home care physician
在宅医学（ざいたくいがく）home care medicine
在宅医療（ざいたくいりょう）medical home care
在宅医療サービス（ざいたくいりょうさーびす）medical home care services
在宅医療推進会議（ざいたくいりょうすいしんかいぎ）Commission for Promotion of Home Care
在宅医療対策（ざいたくいりょうたいさく）medical home care plan
在宅援助（ざいたくえんじょ）home support
†在宅介護（ざいたくかいご）home care

介護保険・介護福祉等関連用語 和英

在宅介護サービス機関（ざいたくかいごさーびすきかん）home care services agency
在宅介護サービス事業者（ざいたくかいごさーびすじぎょうしゃ）home care services provider
在宅介護サービス事業所（ざいたくかいごさーびすじぎょうしょ）home care services office
在宅介護士（ざいたくかいごし）home care aide
在宅介護支援（ざいたくかいごしえん）home care management
在宅介護支援センター（ざいたくかいごしえんせんたー）home care management center
在宅介護相談員（ざいたくかいごそうだんいん）home care advisor
在宅介護福祉士（ざいたくかいごふくしし）certified home care worker
†在宅看護（ざいたくかんご）home health care
在宅看護ケア（ざいたくかんごけあ）home health care
†在宅ケア（ざいたくけあ）home care
在宅ケアアセスメント（ざいたくけああせすめんと）home care assessment
在宅ケアサービス（ざいたくけあさーびす）home care services
在宅ケアサービス機関（ざいたくけあさーびすきかん）home care services agency
在宅ケアサービス事業者（ざいたくけあさーびすじぎょうしゃ）home care services provider
在宅ケアサービス事業所（ざいたくけあさーびすじぎょうしょ）home care services office
在宅ケアプラン（ざいたくけあぷらん）care plan for home care
在宅高齢者介護サービス（ざいたくこうれいしゃかいごさーびす）home care services for the elderly
在宅高齢者福祉サービス（ざいたくこうれいしゃふくしさーびす）in-home welfare services for the elderly
在宅サービス（ざいたくさーびす）home care services
在宅サービス機関（ざいたくさーびすきかん）home care services agency
在宅サービス事業者（ざいたくさーびすじぎょうしゃ）home care services provider
在宅サービス事業所（ざいたくさーびすじぎょうしょ）home care services office
在宅サービス提供者（ざいたくさーびすていきょうしゃ）home care services provider
在宅酸素療法（ざいたくさんそりょうほう）home oxygen therapy：HOT
在宅障害者介護サービス（ざいたくしょうがいしゃかいごさーびす）home care services for the disabled
在宅障害者福祉サービス（ざいたくしょうがいしゃふくしさーびす）in-home welfare services for the disabled
在宅障害者福祉サービス機関（ざいたくしょうがいしゃふくしさーびすきかん）in-home welfare services agency for the disabled
在宅障害者福祉サービス事業者（ざいたくしょうがいしゃふくしさーびすじぎょうしゃ）in-home welfare services provider for the disabled
在宅障害者福祉サービス事業所（ざいたくしょうがいしゃふくしさーびすじぎょうしょ）in-home welfare services agency for the disabled
在宅中心静脈栄養（ざいたくちゅうしんじょうみゃくえいよう）home parenteral nutrition：HPN
在宅治療（ざいたくちりょう）home treatment
在宅透析療法（ざいたくとうせきりょうほう）home dialysis therapy
在宅福祉サービス（ざいたくふくしさーびす）in-home welfare services
在宅福祉サービス機関（ざいたくふくしさーびすきかん）in-home welfare services agency
在宅福祉サービス事業者（ざいたくふくしさーびすじぎょうしゃ）in-home welfare services provider
在宅福祉サービス事業所（ざいたくふくしさーびすじぎょうしょ）in-home welfare services office
在宅福祉対策（ざいたくふくしたいさく）in-home welfare policy
在宅扶助（ざいたくふじょ）home assistance
在宅リハビリテーション（ざいたくりはびりてーしょん）home rehabilitation
在宅療養（ざいたくりょうよう）home health care
在宅療養支援診療所（ざいたくりょうようしえんしんりょうしょ）home health care support clinic
在宅老人介護サービス（ざいたくろうじんかいごさーびす）home care services for the aged
在宅老人福祉サービス（ざいたくろうじんふくしさーびす）in-home welfare services for the aged
財団法人（ざいだんほうじん）incorporated foundation
最低水準（さいていすいじゅん）minimum standard
最低生活（さいていせいかつ）minimum standard of living；minimum living
最低生活費（さいていせいかつひ）minimum cost of living
最低生活保障（さいていせいかつほしょう）guaranteed minimum standard of living
最低賃金（さいていちんぎん）minimum wage
最低賃金制度（さいていちんぎんせいど）minimum wage system
彩度（さいど）saturation
細動脈（さいどうみゃく）arteriole
サイドレール（さいどれーる）siderail
採尿（さいにょう）urine sampling
再認（さいにん）recognition

再認定（さいにんてい）re-certification
座位バランス（ざいばらんす）balance in a sitting position
再評価（さいひょうか）reevaluation
最貧国（さいひんこく）least developed country：LDC
再分配（さいぶんぱい）redistribution
採便（さいべん）feces sampling
座位保持（ざいほじ）maintain a sitting position
座位保持装置（ざいほじそうち）seating system
座位補助具（ざいほじょぐ）seating aid
催眠（さいみん）hypnosis
催眠療法（さいみんりょうほう）hypnotherapy
財務委員会（ざいむいいんかい）Committee of Ways and Means
財務管理（ざいむかんり）financial management
サイム義足（さいむぎそく）Syme's prosthesis
財務諸表（ざいむしょひょう）financial statement
サイム切断（さいむせつだん）Syme's amputatio
在来型（ざいらいがた）conventional
サイレント・キラー（さいれんと・きらー）silent killer
差額請求（さがくせいきゅう）balance billing
差額ベッド（さがくべっど）beds with an extra charge
サーカディアン・リズム（さーかでぃあん・りずむ）⇒概日リズム
詐欺（さぎ）fraud；scam
先取特権（さきどりとっけん）preferential rights
作業記憶（さぎょうきおく）working memory
作業耐性（さぎょうたいせい）work tolerance
作業調整（さぎょうちょうせい）work adjustment
作業テーブル（さぎょうてーぶる）work-table
作業能力（さぎょうのうりょく）work capacity
作業用義手（さぎょうようぎしゅ）work arm
†作業療法（さぎょうりょうほう）occupational therapy
†作業療法士（さぎょうりょうほうし）occupational therapist：OT
錯語（さくご）paraphasia
酢酸（さくさん）acetic acid
酢酸塩（さくさんえん）acetate
サクション（さくしょん）suction
サクセスフル・エイジング（さくせすふる・えいじんぐ）⇒幸福な老い
作話（さくわ）confabulation
鎖骨下静脈直接穿刺法（さこつかじょうみゃくちょくせつせんしほう）subclavian vein catheterization
坐骨支持（ざこつしじ）ischial weight-bearing
査察（ささつ）inspection；survey
査察指導員（ささつしどういん）inspector；surveyor
サージカルマスク（さーじかるますく）⇒外科用マスク

差込ソケット（さしこみそけっと）plug-fit socket
差し込み便器（さしこみべんき）bedpan
左心室肥大（さしんしつひだい）left ventricular hypertrophy
SARS（さーず）⇒重症急性呼吸器症候群
錯覚（さっかく）illusion
擦過細胞診（さっかさいぼうしん）brushing cytology
殺菌剤（さっきんざい）germicide
殺菌作用（さっきんさよう）bactericidal action
擦式アルコール製剤（さっしきあるこーるせいざい）alcohol-containing antiseptic handrub；alcohol-based handrub
擦式手指消毒（さっしきしゅししょうどく）antiseptic handrub
擦式法（さっしきほう）rubbing method
殺人（さつじん）murder
サッチ足部（さっちそくぶ）solid ankle cushion heel foot：SACH
サディスト（さでぃすと）sadist
サテライト方式（さてらいとほうしき）satellite system
里親（さとおや）foster care
里親制度（さとおやせいど）foster care system
里祖父母プログラム（さとそふぼぷろぐらむ）foster grandparent program
サニテーション（さにてーしょん）sanitization
砂嚢（さのう）sand bag
サービスコード（さーびすこーど）service code
サービス水準（さーびすすいじゅん）service level
サービス推進課（さーびすすいしんか）Customer Service Promotion Division
†サービス担当者会議（さーびすたんとうしゃかいぎ）service staff meeting
サービス調整（さーびすちょうせい）service coordination
サービス提供圏（さーびすていきょうけん）service area
サービス提供責任者（さーびすていきょうせきにんしゃ）service manager
サービスの質（さーびすのしつ）quality of service：QoS
サービスの標準化（さーびすのひょうじゅんか）standardization of services
サービスパッケージ（さーびすぱっけーじ）services package
サービス評価（さーびすひょうか）evaluation of services
サービスフレームワーク（さーびすふれーむわーく）national service framework：NSF
サービスメニュー（さーびすめにゅー）service menu
サービス目標（さーびすもくひょう）goal of

services
サービス利用者（さーびすりようしゃ）service recipient
サーベイランス（さーべいらんす）⇒監視
差別（さべつ）discrimination
サポート（さぽーと）support
サポートグループ（さぽーとぐるーぷ）support group
†サポートシステム（さぽーとしすてむ）support system
座薬（ざやく）suppository
左右失認（さゆうしつにん）left-right disorientation
作用（さよう）action
サラセミア（さらせみあ）thalassemia
サルコペニア（さるこぺにあ）sarcopenia
サルモネラ菌（さるもねらきん）salmonella
サルモネラ食中毒（さるもねらしょくちゅうどく）salmonella food poisoning
ザレプロン（ざれぷろん）zaleplon
ザロクソリン（ざろくそりん）Zaroxolyn
酸（さん）acid
酸塩基調節（さんえんきちょうせつ）acid-base regulation
酸塩基平衡（さんえんきへいこう）acid-base balance
参加（さんか）participation；enrollment
三角巾（さんかくきん）sling
三角コーナー（さんかくこーなー）triangle corner
参加者（さんかしゃ）participant；enrollee
参加制約（さんかせいやく）participation restriction；enrollment restriction
三環系抗うつ剤（さんかんけいこううつざい）tricyclic antidepressant：TCA
三脚杖（さんきゃくづえ）tripod cane
産休（さんきゅう）maternity leave
酸血症（さんけつしょう）acidosis
ザンコリ分類（ざんこりぶんるい）Zancolli classification
散剤（さんざい）powdered drug
三叉神経痛（さんさしんけいつう）trigeminal neuralgia：TN
三時間毎（さんじかんごと）every 3 hours：Q3H
三刺激値（さんしげきち）tristimulus value
三次元CT（さんじげんしーてぃー）three-dimension CT
三次元動作解析（さんじげんどうさかいせき）three-dimensional motion analysis
三次元歩行分析（さんじげんほこうぶんせき）three-dimensional gait analysis
三指つまみ（さんしつまみ）three-jaw chuck pinch
三肢麻痺（さんしまひ）triplegia
30代（さんじゅうだい）tricenarian
36項目健康調査票（さんじゅうろくこうもくけんこうちょうさひょう）Medical Outcomes Study 36-Item Short-Form Health Survey：MOS SF-36 Health Survey
産褥感染症（さんじょくかんせんしょう）puerperal fever；childbed fever
産褥熱（さんじょくねつ）puerperal sepsis
三世代家族（さんせだいかぞく）three-generation family
酸素（さんそ）oxygen
酸素欠乏症（さんそけつぼうしょう）⇒無酸素症
酸素消費（さんそしょうひ）oxygen consumption
酸素摂取（さんそせっしゅ）oxygen intake
酸素濃縮器（さんそのうしゅくき）oxygen concentrator
酸素療法（さんそりょうほう）oxygen therapy
残存感覚（ざんぞんかんかく）remaining sense
†残存機能（ざんぞんきのう）residual function
残存能力（ざんぞんのうりょく）remaining function；residual functional capacity
残存能力評価（ざんぞんのうりょくひょうか）residual functional capacity assessment
三大栄養素（さんだいえいようそ）three major nutrients
三大死因（さんだいしいん）three biggest causes of death
暫定居宅サービス計画（ざんていきょたくさーびすけいかく）tentative plan for home-based care services
サンディング（さんでぃんぐ）sanding
サンテリア（さんてりあ）santeria
三点歩行（さんてんほこう）three-point gait
酸度（さんど）acidity
三動作歩行（さんどうさほこう）three-point gait
算入不可能資産（さんにゅうふかのうしさん）non-countable asset
残尿（ざんにょう）residual urine
残尿感（ざんにょうかん）residual sensation
三人移乗法（さんにんいじょうほう）three-person transfer
†散髪（さんぱつ）haircut
散布（さんぷ）spray
酸味（さんみ）sour
酸無水物（さんむすいぶつ）acid anhydride

し

死（し）death
次亜塩素酸ナトリウム（じあえんそさんなとりうむ）sodium hypochlorite
ジアゼパム（じあぜぱむ）diazepam
指圧（しあつ）acupressure
指圧師（しあつし）acupressurist
ジアテルミー（じあてるみー）diathermy

シアナミド（しあなみど）cyanamide
死因別死亡割合（しいんべつしぼうわりあい）proportional mortality rate
自営業（じえいぎょう）self-employment
自営業者健康保険控除（じえいぎょうしゃけんこうほけんこうじょ）self-employed health insurance deduction
シェイピング（しぇいぴんぐ）shaping
シェーグレン症候群（しぇーぐれんしょうこうぐん）Sjogren's syndrome
JCS［日本式昏睡尺度］（じぇーしーえす）Japan Coma Scale
ジエチルスチルベストロール（じえちるすちるべすとろーる）diethylstilbestrol：DES
ジェネリックソーシャルワーク（じぇねりっくそーしゃるわーく）generic social work
支援機器（しえんきき）supportive device；assistive device
支援グループ（しえんぐるーぷ）support group
ジェンダー（じぇんだー）gender
ジェンダー開発指数（じぇんだーかいはつしすう）gender-related development index：GDI
ジェンダー・トラック（じぇんだー・とらっく）gender track
支援費制度（しえんひせいど）support payment system
塩味（しおあじ）salty
歯科（しか）dentistry
自我（じが）ego
歯科医師（しかいし）dentist
歯科医師法（しかいしほう）Dental Practitioners Law
紫外線（しがいせん）ultraviolet
紫外線殺菌（しがいせんさっきん）ultraviolet disinfection
†紫外線遮蔽素材（しがいせんしゃへいそざい）ultraviolet rays protection material
紫外線照射（しがいせんしょうしゃ）ultra violet radiation
紫外線療法（しがいせんりょうほう）ultraviolet therapy
†歯科衛生士（しかえいせいし）dental hygienist
歯科衛生士法（しかえいせいしほう）Dental Hygienists Law
視覚（しかく）sense of sight
四角コーナー（しかくこーなー）square corner
視覚失認（しかくしつにん）visual agnosia
†視覚障害（しかくしょうがい）visual impairment；visual disorder；visual deficit
†視覚障害者（しかくしょうがいしゃ）the visually impaired；the visually disabled；blind person
視覚障害者更生施設（しかくしょうがいしゃこうせいしせつ）rehabilitation facility for the visually

impaired
視覚障害者情報提供施設（しかくしょうがいしゃじょうほうていきょうしせつ）information services facility for the visually impaired
視覚障害者用信号機（しかくしょうがいしゃようしんごうき）audible pedestrian traffic signal；audible traffic signal
視覚制限（しかくせいげん）visual limitation
視覚代行（しかくだいこう）vision substitution
視覚的アナログスケール（しかくてきあなろぐすけーる）Visual Analog Scale：VAS
資格任用制度（しかくにんようせいど）system for appointing a qualified person；system for appointing qualified persons
歯科検診受療率（しかけんしんじゅりょうりつ）percentage of patients receiving annual dental exams
歯科疾患（しかしっかん）dental disease
歯牙喪失（しがそうしつ）tooth loss
C型肝炎（しーがたかんえん）hepatitis C
C型肝炎ウイルス（しーがたかんえんういるす）hepatitis C virus
自家中毒（じかちゅうどく）self-poisoning；autointoxication
自我同一性（じがどういつせい）ego identity
自我の欲求（じがのよっきゅう）esteem needs
自我分析（じがぶんせき）ego analysis
歯科保健課（しかほけんか）Dental Health Division
†弛緩（しかん）flaccid；flaccidity
弛緩性麻痺（しかんせいまひ）flaccid paralysis
歯間歯磨き（しかんはみがき）dental floss；flossing teeth
色覚恒常（しきかくこうじょう）color constancy
磁気共鳴血管撮影（じききょうめいけっかんさつえい）magnetic resonance angiography：MRA
磁気共鳴装置（じききょうめいそうち）magnetic resonance imaging：MRI
磁気刺激（じきしげき）magnetic stimulation
色弱（しきじゃく）color weakness
色相（しきそう）hue
色相キャンセレーション（しきそうきゃんせれーしょん）hue cancellation
色度（しきど）chromaticity
色盲（しきもう）color blindness
子宮外妊娠（しきゅうがいにんしん）ectopic pregnancy
持久訓練（じきゅうくんれん）endurance exercise；endurance training
子宮頸癌（しきゅうけいがん）cervical cancer
子宮頸部異形成（しきゅうけいぶいけいせい）cervical dysplasia
持久性（じきゅうせい）endurance
子宮脱（しきゅうだつ）uterine prolapse

支給要件（しきゅうようけん）requirements for benefits
子宮卵管造影（しきゅうらんかんぞうえい）hysterosalpingography
事業者（じぎょうしゃ）provider
事業所（じぎょうしょ）office；agency
事業主負担金（じぎょうぬしふたんきん）owner's payment
軸（じく）axis
視空間失認（しくうかんしつにん）visual spatial agnosia
軸索変性（じくさくへんせい）axonal degeneration
シクロスポリン（しくろすぽりん）cyclosporine
シクロベンザプリン（しくろべんざぷりん）cyclobenzaprine
刺激法（しげきほう）stimulation method
†止血（しけつ）hemostasis；haemostasis
耳血腫（じけっしゅ）aural hematoma
自己愛性介護者（じこあいせいかいごしゃ）narcissistic caregiver
自己愛性人格障害（じこあいせいじんかくしょうがい）narcissistic personality disorder
†思考障害（しこうしょうがい）thought disorder
自己改善（じこかいぜん）self-improvement
自己概念（じこがいねん）self-concept
†自己覚知（じこかくち）self-awareness
自己感染（じこかんせん）self-infection
ジゴキシン（じごきしん）digoxin
自己教示訓練（じこきょうじくんれん）self-instructional training
†自己決定（じこけってい）self-determination
自己決定の原則（じこけっていのげんそく）principle of client self-determination
自己嫌悪（じこけんお）self-hatred
死後硬直（しごこうちょく）rigor mortis
自己効力感（じここうりょくかん）self-efficacy
自己コントロール理論（じこことろーるりろん）self-control theory
†自己実現（じこじつげん）self-realization；self-actualization
自己支払い（じこしはらい）out-of-pocket
自己受容体（じこじゅようたい）autoreceptor
死後処置（しごしょち）postmortem care
自己責任（じこせきにん）self-responsibility
自己他動運動（じこたどううんどう）self-assisted exercise
自己調整（じこちょうせい）self-maintenance
自己調節（じこちょうせつ）autoregulation
自己調節鎮痛法（じこちょうせつちんつうほう）patient-controlled analgesia；PCA
自己治療（じこちりょう）self-medication
自己同一性（じこどういつせい）self-identity
自己投資型個人年金（じことうしがたこじんねんきん）self-invested personal pension
自己導尿（じこどうにょう）self-catheterization
仕事中毒（しごとちゅうどく）workaholic
自己破産（じこはさん）voluntary bankruptcy
事故抜管（じこばっかん）accidental extubation
事故評価（じこひょうか）accident evaluation
自己評価（じこひょうか）self-evaluation
事後評価（じごひょうか）post evaluation；post assessment
自己表現（じこひょうげん）self-expression
自己負担金（じこふたんきん）co-payment
自己防衛型（じこぼうえいがた）self-protection type；self-defense type
自己放任（じこほうにん）self-neglect
自己免疫（じこめんえき）autoimmunity
自己免疫性肝炎（じこめんえきせいかんえん）autoimmune hepatitis
自己溶解（じこようかい）autolysis
自己擁護運動（じこようごうんどう）self-advocacy movement
視細胞（しさいぼう）photoreceptor
自在輪（じざいりん）caster
自殺（じさつ）suicide
自殺幇助（じさつほうじょ）assisted suicide
自殺予防（じさつよぼう）suicide prevention
資産税（しさんぜい）property tax
資産調査（しさんちょうさ）means test
四肢（しし）limbs；extremities
脂質（ししつ）lipid
†脂質異常症（ししついじょうしょう）dyslipidemia
脂質蓄積症（ししつちくせきしょう）lipid storage disease
支持的作業療法（しじてきさぎょうりょうほう）supportive occupational therapy
支持棒（しじぼう）support bar
四肢麻痺（ししまひ）quadriplegia
死者（ししゃ）deceased
市社会福祉協議会（ししゃかいふくしきょうぎかい）City Council of Social Welfare
歯周組織（ししゅうそしき）periodontium
歯周病（ししゅうびょう）gum disease；periodontal disease；periodontitis
自主財源（じしゅざいげん）independent source of revenue
自主選択性（じしゅせんたくせい）autonomous choice
自主退院（じしゅたいいん）⇒医学指示拒否
思春期うつ病（ししゅんきうつびょう）adolescent depression
思春期拒食症（ししゅんききょしょくしょう）adolescent nausea
思春期精神保健（ししゅんきせいしんほけん）adolescent mental health

思春期やせ症（ししゅんきやせしょう）adolescent emaciation
自助（じじょ）self-help
事象関連電位（じしょうかんれんでんい）event-related potential：ERP
市場経済（しじょうけいざい）market economy
市場検定（しじょうけんてい）market testing
市場原理（しじょうげんり）market mechanism
†自傷行為（じしょうこうい）self-harm：SH；self-injury
自傷他害（じしょうたがい）danger to self or others
市場の失敗（しじょうのしっぱい）market failure
市場の成功（しじょうのせいこう）market success
†自助具（じじょぐ）self-help device
自助原則（じじょげんそく）principle of self-help；self-help principle
指診（ししん）digital examination
ジスキネジア（じすきねじあ）dyskinesia
システム的視点（しすてむてきしてん）systems perspective
ジストニア（じすとにあ）dystonia
ジスルフィラム（じするふぃらむ）disulfiram
姿勢（しせい）posture
自制（じせい）self-restraint；continence
死生学（しせいがく）thanatology
†死生観（しせいかん）view of life and death
姿勢訓練（しせいくんれん）postural exercise
姿勢反射（しせいはんしゃ）postural reflex
姿勢反応（しせいはんのう）postural reaction
施設（しせつ）facility
施設運営（しせつうんえい）facility administration
肢節運動失行（しせつうんどうしっこう）limb kinetic apraxia
†施設介護（しせつかいご）institutional care
施設介護サービス（しせつかいごさーびす）institutional care services
施設環境（しせつかんきょう）institutional environment
施設管理（しせつかんり）facility management
施設基盤型サービス（しせつきばんがたさーびす）facility-based services
施設ケア（しせつけあ）institutional care
施設ケアサービス（しせつけあさーびす）institutional care services
施設ケアプラン（しせつけあぷらん）care plan for institutional care
施設サービス（しせつさーびす）institutional services
施設サービス計画（しせつさーびすけいかく）institutional services plan
施設実習（しせつじっしゅう）institutional training
施設主義（しせつしゅぎ）institutionalism
施設長（しせつちょう）administrator

施設福祉（しせつふくし）institutional welfare
施設福祉サービス（しせつふくしさーびす）institutional welfare services
施設ボランティア（しせつぼらんてぃあ）facility volunteer
慈善（じぜん）charity
自然災害（しぜんさいがい）natural disaster
慈善組織協会（じぜんそしききょうかい）Charity Organization Societies：COS
指尖つまみ（しせんつまみ）tip pinch
自然発生的退職者コミュニティ（しぜんはっせいてきたいしょくしゃこみゅにてぃ）naturally occurring retirement communities
事前評価（じぜんひょうか）pre-evaluation；pre-assessment
歯槽膿漏（しそうのうろう）blennorrhoea alveolaris；alveolar；pyorrhea
持続活性（じぞくかっせい）persistent activity
持続牽引（じぞくけんいん）continuous traction
持続伸張（じぞくしんちょう）prolonged stretching
持続性（じぞくせい）substantivity
持続性吸息（じぞくせいきゅうそく）apneusis
持続他動運動（じぞくたどううんどう）continuative passive motion：CPM
持続的気道陽圧（じぞくてききどうようあつ）continuous positive air pressure：CPAP
†自尊心（じそんしん）self-esteem
死体解剖（したいかいほう）autopsy
肢帯型筋ジストロフィー（したいがたきんじすとろふぃー）limb-girdle muscular dystrophy
死体検案書（したいけんあんしょ）medical certificate of the cause of death
†肢体不自由（したいふじゆう）crippled
肢体不自由児（したいふじゆうじ）crippled child
肢体不自由児更生施設（したいふじゆうじこうせいしせつ）rehabilitation facility for crippled children
肢体不自由児施設（したいふじゆうじしせつ）facility for crippled children
肢体不自由児通園施設（したいふじゆうじつうえんしせつ）day care services facility for crippled children
肢体不自由者（したいふじゆうしゃ）crippled person
肢体不自由児養護学校（したいふじゆうじようごがっこう）special school for crippled children
肢体不自由児療護施設（したいふじゆうじりょうごしせつ）custodial care facility for crippled children
自宅火災（じたくかさい）home fire
自治会（じちかい）self-government association；local self-government
視知覚（しちかく）visual perception
自治事務（じちじむ）autonomous affairs

自治体裁判所（じちたいさいばんしょ）municipal court
市中感染（しちゅうかんせん）community-acquired infection
視聴覚障害者情報提供施設（しちょうかくしょうがいしゃじょうほうていきょうしせつ）information services facility for the visually and auditorially impaired
市町村（しちょうそん）municipality
市町村一般会計（しちょうそんいっぱんかいけい）municipality's general account
市町村介護保険事業計画（しちょうそんかいごほけんじぎょうけいかく）municipality's long-term care insurance program plan
市町村合併（しちょうそんがっぺい）consolidation of municipalities；municipal consolidation
市町村社会福祉協議会（しちょうそんしゃかいふくしきょうぎかい）municipal council of social welfare
市町村特別給付（しちょうそんとくべつきゅうふ）special municipal benefit
市町村保健センター（しちょうそんほけんせんたー）municipal health center
疾患（しっかん）disease
疾患管理（しっかんかんり）disease management：DM
疾患修飾性抗リウマチ薬（しっかんしゅうしょくせいこうりうまちやく）disease-modifying antirheumatic drug：DMARD
†実技試験（じつぎしけん）professional practice examination
失業（しつぎょう）unemployment
失業給付（しつぎょうきゅうふ）unemployment benefit
失業手当（しつぎょうてあて）unemployment compensation；unemployment allowance
失業保険（しつぎょうほけん）unemployment insurance
失業補償（しつぎょうほしょう）unemployment compensation
失業率（しつぎょうりつ）unemployment rate
†失禁（しっきん）incontinence
失禁アセスメント（しっきんあせすめんと）assessment of urinary incontinence；incontinence assessment
失禁ケア（しっきんけあ）incontinence care
失見当識（しつけんとうしき）disorientation
†失語（しつご）aphasia
失行（しっこう）apraxia
†シーツ交換（しーつこうかん）changing bed sheets
執行通告（しっこうつうこく）enforcement notice
失語症（しつごしょう）aphasia
失算（しっさん）acalculia；dyscalculia

湿式洗濯（しつしきせんたく）wet cleaning
†実支出（じっししゅつ）actual expenditure；real expenditure
実質収支（じっしつしゅうし）net balance of the settled account
実質賃金（じっしつちんぎん）actual wage
†実収入（じっしゅうにゅう）actual income；real income
実収入以外の収入（じっしゅうにゅういがいのしゅうにゅう）income other than actual income
失書（しっしょ）agraphia；dysgraphia
失神（しっしん）fainting
湿疹（しっしん）eczema
失声（しっせい）⇒失声症
湿性温熱（しっせいおんねつ）moist heating
失声症（しっせいしょう）aphonia
実践研究（じっせんけんきゅう）action research
実存主義（じつぞんしゅぎ）existentialism
実存的療法（じつぞんてきりょうほう）existential therapy
失調性跛行（しっちょうせいはこう）ataxic gait
失調歩行（しっちょうほこう）⇒失調性跛行
質的研究（しつてきけんきゅう）qualitative research
質的調査（しつてきちょうさ）qualitative investigation
失読（しつどく）alexia
室内気候（しつないきこう）indoor climate
室内歩行（しつないほこう）walk in room
†失認（しつにん）agnosia
湿熱滅菌（しつねつめっきん）moist heat sterilization
実年齢（じつねんれい）chronological age
質の良い在宅介護（しつのよいざいたくかいご）quality home care
質の良い在宅看護ケア（しつのよいざいたくかんごけあ）quality home health care
質の良いナーシングホームケア（しつのよいなーしんぐほーむけあ）quality nursing home care
湿布（しっぷ）cataplasm；poultice
シップスリーA（しっぷすりーえー）CYP-3A
疾病（しっぺい）disease；sickness；illness
疾病影響プロファイル（しっぺいえいきょうぷろふぁいる）sickness impact profile：SIP
疾病管理予防センター（しっぺいかんりよぼうせんたー）Center for Disease Control and Prevention：CDC
疾病休暇（しっぺいきゅうか）sick leave
疾病対策課（しっぺいたいさくか）Specific Diseases Control Division
疾病年金（しっぺいねんきん）sickness pension
疾病否認（しっぺいひにん）denial of illness
疾病保険（しっぺいほけん）sickness insurance

†実務経験証明書（じつむけいけんしょうめいしょ）
  proof of work experience
質問紙（しつもんし）questionnaire
質問紙調査（しつもんしちょうさ）investigation
  questionnaire
質問紙法（しつもんしほう）questionnaire method
指定（してい）designation；certification
指定医制度（していいせいど）designation system
  for medical providers
指定医療機関（していいりょうきかん）designated
  medical care agency
指定居宅介護支援事業者（していきょたくかいごしえ
  んじぎょうしゃ）designated home-based care
  management provider
指定居宅サービス（していきょたくさーびす）
  designated home-based care services
CT検査（しーてぃーけんさ）computed
  tomography：CT
指定情報公表センター（していじょうほうこうひょう
  せんたー）designated public information center
指定の取り消し（していのとりけし）cancellation of
  designation；cancellation of certification
指定病院（していびょういん）designated hospital
私的介護（してきかいご）informal care
私的活動（してきかつどう）private activity
私的年金（してきねんきん）personal pension
私的扶助（してきふじょ）private assistance
私的扶養（してきふよう）private support
私的保険（してきほけん）personal insurance
児童委員（じどういいん）commissioned child
  welfare volunteer
†自動運動（じどううんどう）active movement
指導課（しどうか）Guidance of Medical Service
  Division
自動介助運動（じどうかいじょうんどう）active
  assisted exercise
自動可動域（じどうかどういき）active range of
  motion：AROM
児童館（じどうかん）child welfare residential
  facility；children's house；children's hall
†児童期障害（じどうきしょうがい）childhood
  disorder
児童虐待（じどうぎゃくたい）child abuse
児童虐待防止法（じどうぎゃくたいぼうしほう）
  Child Abuse Prevention Law
児童虐待保護サービス（じどうぎゃくたいほごさーび
  す）child protective services
児童緊急保護施設（じどうきんきゅうほごしせつ）
  children's shelter
自動訓練（じどうくんれん）active exercise
児童憲章（じどうけんしょう）Children's Charter
児童権利宣言（じどうけんりせんげん）Declaration
  of the Rights of the Child

児童厚生施設（じどうこうせいしせつ）children's
  recreational facility
自動思考（じどうしこう）autonomic thought
自動車事故（じどうしゃじこ）motor vehicle
  accident
自動車手当て（じどうしゃてあて）automobile
  allowance
自動症（じどうしょう）automatism
児童自立支援（じどうじりつしえん）independence
  support for children
児童相談員（じどうそうだんいん）advisor for
  children's issues
児童相談所（じどうそうだんしょ）child guidance
  center
自動体外式除細動器（じどうたいがいしきじょさいど
  うき）automated external defibrillator：AED
自動聴性脳幹反応（じどうちょうせいのうかんはんの
  う）automated auditory brainstem response
自動聴性脳幹反応評価（じどうちょうせいのうかんは
  んのうひょうか）automated auditory brainstem
  response evaluation
児童手当（じどうてあて）child allowance
児童手当法（じどうてあてほう）Child Allowance
  Law
自動内視鏡洗浄装置（じどうないしきょうせんじょう
  そうち）automated endoscope reprocessor：
  AER
児童福祉（じどうふくし）child welfare
児童福祉機関（じどうふくしきかん）child welfare
  agency
児童福祉計画（じどうふくしけいかく）child welfare
  plan
児童福祉サービス（じどうふくしさーびす）child
  welfare services
児童福祉司（じどうふくしし）child welfare officer
児童福祉施設（じどうふくししせつ）child welfare
  facility
児童福祉審議会（じどうふくししんぎかい）Advisory
  Council on Child Welfare
児童福祉法（じどうふくしほう）Child Welfare Law
自動腹膜透析（じどうふくまくとうせき）automatic
  peritoneal dialysis
児童放置（じどうほうち）child neglect
シニアコンパニオンプログラム（しにあこんぱにおん
  ぷろぐらむ）Senior Companion Program
シニア住宅（しにあじゅうたく）senior housing；
  senior home
シニアセンター（しにあせんたー）senior center
シニアボランティア（しにあぼらんてぃあ）senior
  volunteer
歯肉（しにく）gingiva
歯肉炎（しにくえん）inflamed gum
ジニ係数（じにけいすう）Gini coefficient

シネ排泄造影（しねはいせつぞうえい）cinedefecography
視能訓練士（しのうくんれんし）orthoptist：ORT
Cバー（しーばー）C bar
自発活動（じはつかつどう）spontaneous activity
支払基金（しはらいききん）payment fund
支払い保留（しはらいほりゅう）withhold
C反応性蛋白（しーはんのうせいたんぱく）C-reactive protein
市販薬（しはんやく）over-the-counter medication
耳鼻咽喉科医（じびいんこうかい）otolaryngologist；ear, nose and throat specialist
耳鼻咽喉学（じびいんこうがく）otolaryngology
耳鼻咽喉検査（じびいんこうけんさ）ear, nose and throat evaluation
自費支払い（じひしはらい）out of pocket
指標（しひょう）indicator
尿瓶（しびん）urinal
指腹つまみ（しふくつまみ）pulp pinch
ジフテリア（じふてりあ）diphtheria
シブトラミン（しぶとらみん）sibutramine
ジプレキサ（じぷれきさ）Zyprexa
†自閉症（じへいしょう）autism
自閉症スペクトラム障害（じへいしょうすぺくとらむしょうがい）autism spectrum disorder：ASD
死別（しべつ）bereavement
四辺形ソケット（しへんけいそけっと）quadrilateral socket
死亡（しぼう）death
脂肪（しぼう）fat
司法解剖（しほうかいぼう）forensic autopsy
司法看護（しほうかんご）forensic nurse
司法看護学（しほうかんごがく）forensic nursing
脂肪酸（しぼうさん）fatty acid
死亡者（しぼうしゃ）deceased
司法審査（しほうしんさ）judicial review
死亡診断書（しぼうしんだんしょ）death certificate
司法心理学（しほうしんりがく）forensic psychology
司法心理学者（しほうしんりがくしゃ）forensic psychologist
司法人類学（しほうじんるいがく）forensic anthropology
司法人類学者（しほうじんるいがくしゃ）forensic anthropologist
司法精神看護（しほうせいしんかんご）forensic psychiatric nursing
脂肪組織（しぼうそしき）adipose tissue
司法病理学（しほうびょうりがく）forensic pathology
司法病理学者（しほうびょうりがくしゃ）forensic pathologist
司法福祉（しほうふくし）forensic social work

死亡率（しぼうりつ）mortality rate；death rate
死亡割合（しぼうわりあい）proportional mortality indicator：PMI
資本主義（しほんしゅぎ）capitalism
しみ抜き（しみぬき）stain removal
市民（しみん）citizen
市民運動（しみんうんどう）citizen movement
市民権（しみんけん）citizenship
市民参加（しみんさんか）citizen participation
市民社会（しみんしゃかい）civil society
市民的及び政治的権利に関する国際規約（しみんてきおよびせいじてきけんりにかんするこくさいきやく）International Covenant on Civil and Political Rights
市民法（しみんほう）Civil Law
事務職員（じむしょくいん）clerical personnel
シムス位（しむすい）Sims' position
事務費（じむひ）administrative cost
閉め出し理論（しめだしりろん）crowding-out theory
シメチジン（しめちじん）cimetidine
締めつけられるような痛み（しめつけられるようないたみ）squeezing pain
諮問委員会（しもんいいんかい）advisory council
シャイ・ドレーガー症候群（しゃい・どれーがーしょうこうぐん）Shy-Drager syndrome：SDS
社会医学（しゃかいいがく）social medicine
社会意識（しゃかいいしき）social consciousness
社会運動（しゃかいうんどう）social movement
社会運動論（しゃかいうんどうろん）social movement theory
社会・援護局（しゃかい・えんごきょく）Social Welfare and War Victims' Relief Bureau
社会化（しゃかいか）socialization
社会科学（しゃかいかがく）social science
社会学（しゃかいがく）sociology
社会活動（しゃかいかつどう）social activity
社会技能訓練（しゃかいぎのうくんれん）social skills training
社会計画（しゃかいけいかく）social planning
社会権（しゃかいけん）social rights
社会構造（しゃかいこうぞう）social structure
社会サービス（しゃかいさーびす）social services
社会参加（しゃかいさんか）social participation
社会参加促進（しゃかいさんかそくしん）promotion of social participation
社会支援サービス（しゃかいしえんさーびす）social support services
社会事業（しゃかいじぎょう）social program
†社会資源（しゃかいしげん）social resources
社会資本（しゃかいしほん）social capital
社会集団（しゃかいしゅうだん）social group
社会就労センター（しゃかいしゅうろうせんたー）

Support of Employment, Living and Participation：SELP
社会主義（しゃかいしゅぎ）socialism
社会診断（しゃかいしんだん）social diagnosis
社会生活技能訓練（しゃかいせいかつぎのうくんれん）social skills training：SST
社会生活力（しゃかいせいかつりょく）social functioning ability：SFA
社会政策（しゃかいせいさく）social policy
社会体制（しゃかいたいせい）social system；social structure
社会秩序（しゃかいちつじょ）social order
社会調査（しゃかいちょうさ）social research
社会の及び文化的権利に関する国際規約（しゃかいておよびぶんかてきけんりにかんするこくさいきやく）International Covenant on Economic, Social and Cultural Rights
社会的介護（しゃかいてきかいご）socialized long-term care
社会的隔離（しゃかいてきかくり）social isolation
社会的危険（しゃかいてききけん）social risk
社会的強者（しゃかいてききょうしゃ）socially advantaged person
社会的支援（しゃかいてきしえん）social support
社会的支援ネットワーク（しゃかいてきしえんねっとわーく）social support network
社会的弱者（しゃかいてきじゃくしゃ）socially disadvantaged person
社会的受容（しゃかいてきじゅよう）⇒社会的統合
社会的障壁（しゃかいてきしょうへき）social barrier
社会的相互作用（しゃかいてきそうごさよう）social interaction
社会的手洗い（しゃかいてきてあらい）social hand washing
社会的適用（しゃかいてきてきおう）social adequacy
社会的統合（しゃかいてきとうごう）social inclusion
社会的入院（しゃかいてきにゅういん）social hospitalization
社会的ネットワーク（しゃかいてきねっとわーく）social network
†社会的不利（しゃかいてきふり）handicap
社会的包摂（しゃかいてきほうせつ）⇒社会的統合
社会的問題解決（しゃかいてきもんだいかいけつほう）social problem-solving
社会的役割（しゃかいてきやくわり）social role
社会的役割論（しゃかいてきやくわりろん）social role theory
社会的要求（しゃかいてきようきゅう）social needs
社会的養護（しゃかいてきようご）social care
社会的欲求（しゃかいてきよっきゅう）love belonging needs
社会的リスクマネジメント（しゃかいてきりすくまねじめんと）social risk management
社会的リハビリテーション（しゃかいてきりはびりてーしょん）social rehabilitation
社会統計課（しゃかいとうけいか）Social Statistics Division
社会ニーズ（しゃかいにーず）social needs
社会認知理論（しゃかいにんちりろん）social cognitive theory
社会病理学（しゃかいびょうりがく）social pathology
†社会福祉（しゃかいふくし）social welfare
社会福祉運営管理（しゃかいふくしうんえいかんり）Social Welfare Administration
社会福祉援助活動（しゃかいふくしえんじょかつどう）social work and welfare activity
社会福祉援助技術（しゃかいふくしえんじょぎじゅつ）social work and welfare practice
社会福祉士及び介護福祉士法（しゃかいふくしおよびかいごふくししほう）Certified Social Worker and Care Worker Act
社会福祉関係八法の改正（しゃかいふくしかんけいはっぽうのかいせい）Revision of the Eight Acts related to Social Welfare
社会福祉管理（しゃかいふくしかんり）social administration
社会福祉管理事務所（しゃかいふくしかんりじむしょ）Social Administration Office
社会福祉機関（しゃかいふくしきかん）social welfare agency
社会福祉基準（しゃかいふくしきじゅん）social welfare standards
社会福祉基礎構造改革（しゃかいふくしきそこうぞうかいかく）Basic Structural Reform of Social Welfare
社会福祉教育（しゃかいふくしきょういく）social work and welfare education
社会福祉協議会（しゃかいふくしきょうぎかい）Council of Social Welfare
社会福祉経営（しゃかいふくしけいえい）social administration
社会福祉計画（しゃかいふくしけいかく）social welfare planning
社会福祉計画法（しゃかいふくしけいかくほう）social welfare planning method
社会福祉現場実習（しゃかいふくしげんばじっしゅう）social work practicum
社会福祉サービス（しゃかいふくしさーびす）social welfare services
†社会福祉士（しゃかいふくしし）certified social worker：CSW
†社会福祉事業（しゃかいふくしじぎょう）social

介護保険・介護福祉等関連用語 和英

welfare services
社会福祉事業団（しゃかいふくしじぎょうだん）social welfare services agency
社会福祉事業法（しゃかいふくしじぎょうほう）Social Welfare Service Law
社会福祉施設（しゃかいふくししせつ）social welfare facility
社会福祉事務所（しゃかいふくしじむしょ）social welfare office
社会福祉事務所職員（しゃかいふくしじむしょしょくいん）social welfare office staff
社会福祉主事（しゃかいふくししゅじ）social welfare officer
社会福祉振興・試験センター（しゃかいふくししんこう・しけんせんたー）Center of Social Welfare Promotion and National Examination
社会福祉水準（しゃかいふくしすいじゅん）level of social welfare
社会福祉政策分析（しゃかいふくしせいさくぶんせき）social policy analysis
社会福祉制度（しゃかいふくしせいど）social welfare system
社会福祉専門（しゃかいふくしせんもん）social work profession
社会福祉専門職（しゃかいふくしせんもんしょく）professional social work
社会福祉専門職団体（しゃかいふくしせんもんしょくだんたい）professional association of social workers
社会福祉団体（しゃかいふくしだんたい）social welfare organization
社会福祉調査（しゃかいふくしちょうさ）social welfare research
社会福祉費用（しゃかいふくしひよう）cost of social welfare
社会福祉法（しゃかいふくしほう）Social Welfare Service Law
社会福祉法人（しゃかいふくしほうじん）social welfare corporation
社会福祉法制（しゃかいふくしほうせい）social welfare registration
社会福祉士養成施設（しゃかいふくしようせいせつ）school of social work
社会法（しゃかいほう）Social Law
社会奉仕（しゃかいほうし）volunteering；voluntary services
†社会保険（しゃかいほけん）social insurance
社会保険業務センター（しゃかいほけんぎょうむせんたー）social insurance operation center
社会保険事務所（しゃかいほけんじむしょ）social insurance office
社会保険審査員（しゃかいほけんしんさいん）social insurance examiner

社会保険審査会（しゃかいほけんしんさかい）Examination Committee of Social Insurance
社会保険診療報酬支払基金（しゃかいほけんしんりょうほうしゅうしはらいききん）Social Insurance Medical Fee Payments Fund
社会保険庁（しゃかいほけんちょう）Social Insurance Agency
社会保険費（しゃかいほけんひ）social insurance expenses
社会保険費用（しゃかいほけんひよう）social insurance costs
社会保険方式（しゃかいほけんほうしき）social insurance system
社会保険料（しゃかいほけんりょう）social insurance premium
社会保険料税控除（しゃかいほけんりょうぜいこうじょ）tax deduction for social insurance premiums
社会保険労務士（しゃかいほけんろうむし）certified social insurance and labor consultant
†社会保障（しゃかいほしょう）Social Security
社会保障給付（しゃかいほしょうきゅうふ）Social Security benefit
社会保障給付費（しゃかいほしょうきゅうふひ）ccosts of Social Security benefit
社会保障構造改革（しゃかいほしょうこうぞうかいかく）structural reform of Social Security system；structural reform of Social Security
†社会保障審議会（しゃかいほしょうしんぎかい）Advisory Council on Social Security
社会保障税（しゃかいほしょうぜい）Social Security tax
社会保障制度（しゃかいほしょうせいど）Social Security system
社会保障制度審議会（しゃかいほしょうせいどしんぎかい）National Advisory Council on the Social Security System
社会保障の民営化（しゃかいほしょうのみんえいか）privatization of Social Security
社会保障費用（しゃかいほしょうひよう）Social Security costs
社会保障負担（しゃかいほしょうふたん）Social Security burden
社会保障法（しゃかいほしょうほう）Social Security Act
社会民主主義的福祉国家（しゃかいみんしゅしゅぎてきふくしこっか）social democratic welfare state
社会モデル（しゃかいもでる）social model
社会問題（しゃかいもんだい）social problem
社会連帯（しゃかいれんたい）social solidarity
†視野狭窄（しやきょうさく）visual field restriction
弱化予防（じゃくかよぼう）deconditioning prevention

弱視（じゃくし）weak eye sight
尺側偏位（しゃくそくへんい）ulnar deviation
若年性関節りうまち（じゃくねんせいかんせつりうまち）juvenile rheumatoid arthritis
若年性糖尿病（じゃくねんせいとうにょうびょう）juvenile diabetes
若年性特発性リウマチ（じゃくねんせいとっぱつせいりうまち）juvenile idiopathic arthritis
若年性パーキンソン病（じゃくねんせいぱーきんそんびょう）juvenile Parkinsonism
若年性ポリープ（じゃくねんせいぽりーぷ）juvenile polyps
若年性ミオクローヌスてんかん（じゃくねんせいみおくろーぬすてんかん）juvenile myoclonic epilepsy；Janz syndrome
†視野障害（しやしょうがい）visual field defect
社団法人（しゃだんほうじん）incorporated association
尺屈（しゃっくつ）ulnar deviation；ulnar flexion
しゃっくり（しゃっくり）hiccups
シャドーイング（しゃどーいんぐ）shadowing
シャドー・ワーク（しゃどー・わーく）shadow work
煮沸消毒（しゃふつしょうどく）boiling sterilization
斜面台（しゃめんだい）tilting table
シャルコー関節（しゃるこーかんせつ）Charcot joint
シャワーいす（しゃわーいす）shower chair
シャワーチェア（しゃわーちぇあ）shower chair
シャワー用車椅子（しゃわーようくるまいす）shower wheelchair
†シャワー浴（しゃわーよく）shower bath
シャンプー（しゃんぷー）shampoo
†収益事業（しゅうえきじぎょう）profit-making business
住環境（じゅうかんきょう）living environment
週間ケア計画（しゅうかんけあけいかく）weekly care plan
週間サービス計画（しゅうかんさーびすけいかく）weekly service plan；weekly care plan
習慣性薬物（しゅうかんせいやくぶつ）addictive drug
周期性四肢運動（しゅうきせいししうんどう）periodic leg movement
周期性四肢運動異常症（しゅうきせいししうんどういじょうしょう）periodic leg movement disorder；PLMD
周期性四肢運動障害（しゅうきせいししうんどうしょうがい）periodic limb movement disorder
宗教（しゅうきょう）religion
従業員（じゅうぎょういん）employee
従業員満足度（じゅうぎょういんまんぞくど）employee satisfaction；ES

就業規則（しゅうぎょうきそく）employee rules and regulations
就業構造（しゅうぎょうこうぞう）employment structure
就業人口（しゅうぎょうじんこう）working population
宗教法人（しゅうきょうほうじん）religious corporation
充血（じゅうけつ）hyperemia
充血除去剤（じゅうけつじょきょざい）decongestant
自由権（じゆうけん）the right of freedom
集合的無意識（しゅうごうてきむいしき）collective unconscious
集合ホーム（しゅうごうほーむ）congregate home
週五回（しゅうごかい）5 times weekly；5W；5 times a week
週三回（しゅうさんかい）3 times weekly；3W；3 times a week
周産期死亡率（しゅうさんきしぼうりつ）perinatal mortality rate
修士号（しゅうしごう）master's degree
収支相等の原則（しゅうしそうとうのげんそく）principle of equalization of income and expenditure
自由主義者（じゆうしゅぎしゃ）liberal
自由主義的福祉国家（じゆうしゅぎてきふくしこっか）the liberal welfare state
収縮期圧（しゅうしゅくきあつ）systolic pressure
重症外傷患者へのアプローチ（じゅうしょうがいしょうかんじゃへのあぷろーち）approach to the critically injured patient
重症急性呼吸器症候群（じゅうしょうきゅうせいこきゅうきしょうこうぐん）severe acute respiratory syndrome；SARS
重症筋無力症（じゅうしょうきんむりょくしょう）myasthenia gravis；MG
重症心身障害（じゅうしょうしんしんしょうがい）severe physical and mental disabilities
重症心身障害児（じゅうしょうしんしんしょうがいじ）the severely mentally and physically disabled child
重症心身障害児施設（じゅうしょうしんしんしょうがいじしせつ）facility for the severely mentally and physically disabled children
重症心身障害児通園事業（じゅうしょうしんしんしょうがいじつうえんじぎょう）day care services program for the severely mentally and physically disabled children
重症心身障害者（じゅうしょうしんしんしょうがいしゃ）the severely mentally and physically disabled
重症心身障害者施設（じゅうしょうしんしんしょうがいしゃしせつ）facility for the severely mentally

介護保険・介護福祉等関連用語　和英

and physically disabled
重症心身障害者通園事業（じゅうしょうしんしんしょうがいしゃつうえんじぎょう）day care services program for the severely mentally and physically disabled
重心（じゅうしん）center of gravity：CG
終身雇用（しゅうしんこよう）lifelong employment
終身雇用制度（しゅうしんこようせいど）lifelong employment system
就寝時（しゅうしんじ）at bedtime：BED
重心図（じゅうしんず）locus of center of gravity
終身年金（しゅうしんねんきん）lifelong pension
自由診療（じゆうしんりょう）point-of-service
†従属人口（じゅうぞくじんこう）dependent population
従属人口指数（じゅうぞくじんこうしすう）dependency ratio
従属変数（じゅうぞくへんすう）dependent variable
10代（じゅうだい）denarian
住宅安全（じゅうたくあんぜん）home safety
†住宅改修（じゅうたくかいしゅう）home modification
住宅改修給付（じゅうたくかいしゅうきゅうふ）home modification benefit
住宅改修手当（じゅうたくかいしゅうてあて）home modification allowance
住宅改善（じゅうたくかいぜん）home improvement
住宅改造（じゅうたくかいぞう）home modification
住宅政策（じゅうたくせいさく）housing policy
住宅扶助（じゅうたくふじょ）housing assistance
住宅ローン（じゅうたくろーん）housing loan
集団圧力（しゅうだんあつりょく）group pressure
集団援助技術（しゅうだんえんじょぎじゅつ）group work
集団隔離（しゅうだんかくり）cohort isolation
集団給食サービス（しゅうだんきゅうしょくさーびす）congregate meal program
集団検診（しゅうだんけんしん）group physical examination：group medical examination
集団住宅センター（しゅうだんじゅうたくせんたー）congregate housing center
集団処遇（しゅうだんしょぐう）group treatment
集団精神療法（しゅうだんせいしんりょうほう）group psychotherapy
縦断的調査（じゅうだんてきちょうさ）longitudinal study
集団発生（しゅうだんはっせい）⇒アウトブレイク
集団療法（しゅうだんりょうほう）group therapy
羞恥心（しゅうちしん）sense of shame
集中改革プラン（しゅうちゅうかいかくぷらん）intensive reform plan
集中治療室（しゅうちゅうちりょうしつ）intensive care unit：ICU

集中的ケアマネジメント（しゅうちゅうてきけあまねじめんと）intensive care management
柔道整復師（じゅうどうせいふくし）judo orthopedist
重度障害児（じゅうどしょうがいじ）the severely disabled child
重度障害者（じゅうどしょうがいしゃ）the severely disabled
重度身体障害児（じゅうどしんたいしょうがいじ）the severely physically disabled child
重度身体障害者（じゅうどしんたいしょうがいしゃ）the severely physically disabled
重度身体障害者更生援護施設（じゅうどしんたいしょうがいしゃこうせいえんごしせつ）rehabilitation and assistance center for the severely disabled
重度身体障害者更生施設（じゅうどしんたいしょうがいしゃこうせいしせつ）rehabilitation facility for the severely physically disabled
重度身体障害者授産施設（じゅうどしんたいしょうがいしゃじゅさんしせつ）sheltered workshop for the severely disabled
重度精神障害児（じゅうどせいしんしょうがいじ）the severely mentally disabled child
重度精神障害者（じゅうどせいしんしょうがいしゃ）the severely mentally disabled
重度知的障害児（じゅうどちてきしょうがいじ）the severely mentally retarded child
重度知的障害者（じゅうどちてきしょうがいしゃ）the severely mentally retarded
柔軟仕上げ剤（じゅうなんしあげざい）softener agent
柔軟性（じゅうなんせい）flexibility
柔軟体操（じゅうなんたいそう）flexibility exercise
週二回（しゅうにかい）2 times weekly：2W：2 times a week
収尿器（しゅうにょうき）urine collector
周辺視野（しゅうへんしや）peripheral vision
自由貿易協定（じゆうぼうえききょうてい）Free Trade Agreement: FTA
自由放任主義（じゆうほうにんしゅぎ）laissez faire：laissez-faire principle
†終末期（しゅうまつき）terminal stage
終末期医療（しゅうまつきいりょう）terminal medical care
†終末期介護（しゅうまつきかいご）terminal care
終末期看護（しゅうまつきかんご）terminal nursing care
終末期ケア（しゅうまつきけあ）terminal care
終末期治療（しゅうまつきちりょう）terminal treatment
住民（じゅうみん）resident
住民運動（じゅうみんうんどう）resident movement
住民基本台帳（じゅうみんきほんだいちょう）basic

resident registration
住民基本台帳カード（じゅうみんきほんだいちょうかード）basic resident registration card
住民参加（じゅうみんさんか）resident participation
住民税（じゅうみんぜい）resident tax
羞明（しゅうめい）photophobia
絨毛膜下血腫（じゅうもうまくかけっしゅ）subchorionic hematoma
重要失敗要因（じゅうようしっぱいよういん）critical failure factor
重要成功要因（じゅうようせいこうよういん）critical success factor；CSF
週四回（しゅうよんかい）4 times weekly；4W；4 times a week
収斂剤（しゅうれんざい）astringent
就労支援（しゅうろうしえん）employment assistance
週六回（しゅうろっかい）6 times weekly；6W；6 times a week
受益権（じゅえきけん）the right to receive benefits
受益者（じゅえきしゃ）beneficiary
受益者請求金（じゅえきしゃせいきゅうきん）charges to beneficiaries
受益者負担（じゅえきしゃふたん）benefit principle
受益者負担の原則（じゅえきしゃふたんのげんそく）beneficiary-to-pay principle
主介護者（しゅかいごしゃ）primary caregiver
手関節背屈保持装具（しゅかんせつはいくつほじそうぐ）cock-up wrist hand orthosis
主観的幸福感（しゅかんてきこうふくかん）subjective well-being；subjective happiness
主観的幸福感尺度（しゅかんてきこうふくかんしゃくど）Subjective Happiness Scale
主観的幸福度（しゅかんてきこうふくど）subjective well-being；subjective happiness
主観的ニーズ（しゅかんてきにーず）subjective needs
受給権（じゅきゅうけん）the right to receive benefits
受給権付与（じゅきゅうけんふよ）vesting
受給者（じゅきゅうしゃ）recipient
需給調整事業課（じゅきゅうちょうせいじぎょうか）Demand and Supply Adjustment Division
受給要件（じゅきゅうようけん）requirements to receive benefits
儒教（じゅきょう）Confucianism
祝日（しゅくじつ）holiday
祝日補助（しゅくじつほじょ）holiday sharing
宿主・寄生体関係（しゅくしゅ・きせいたいかんけい）host-parasite relationship
縮瞳（しゅくどう）miosis
宿便（しゅくべん）fecal impaction

樹形図（じゅけいず）tree diagram
受験手数料（じゅけんてすうりょう）examination fee
授産事業（じゅさんじぎょう）sheltered workshop services
授産施設（じゅさんしせつ）sheltered workshop facility
†主治医（しゅじい）primary doctor；attending doctor
†主治医意見書（しゅじいいけんしょ）doctor's note；report from the primary doctor
手指衛生（しゅしえいせい）hand hygiene
手指失認（しゅししつにん）finger agnosia
手指消毒（しゅししょうどく）hand antisepsis
手指の汚染除去（しゅしのおせんじょきょ）decontaminate hands
手術（しゅじゅつ）surgery
手術衣（しゅじゅつい）operating suite
手術時手指消毒（しゅじゅつじしゅしょうどく）surgical hand antisepsis
手術室（しゅじゅつしつ）operating room；OR；operating theater
手術室看護師（しゅじゅつしつかんごし）operation room registered nurse；OR RN
手術時手洗い（しゅじゅつじてあらい）surgical scrub；surgical hand washing
手術創（しゅじゅつそう）surgical wound
手術創感染（しゅじゅつそうかんせん）surgical wound infection
手術創分類（しゅじゅつそうぶんるい）surgical wound classification
手術部位感染（しゅじゅつぶいかんせん）surgical site infection
手術用ガウン（しゅじゅつようがうん）operation gown
主訴（しゅそ）chief complaint
主題統覚検査（しゅだいとうかくけんさ）thematic apperception test；TAT
手段的ADL（しゅだんてきえーでぃーえる）⇒手段的日常生活動作
†手段的日常生活活動（しゅだんてきにちじょうせいかつかつどう）instrumental activities of daily living；IADL
腫脹（しゅちょう）swelling
†出血（しゅっけつ）bleeding
出血性水疱（しゅっけつせいすいほう）hemorrhagic bullae
出血性卒中（しゅっけつせいそっちゅう）hemorrhagic stroke
術後感染（じゅつごかんせん）postoperative infection
出産（しゅっさん）childbearing；deliver
出産手当（しゅっさんてあて）maternity allowance

介護保険・介護福祉等関連用語和英

出産適齢（しゅっさんてきれい）childbearing age
出産扶助（しゅっさんふじょ）maternity assistance
出生証明書（しゅっしょうしょうめいしょ）birth certificate
出生前診断（しゅっしょうぜんしんだん）prenatal diagnosis；prenatal screening
出生率（しゅっしょうりつ）birth rate
術前腸管処置（じゅつぜんちょうかんしょち）preoperative bowel cleaning
術前腸管処理（じゅつぜんちょうかんしょり）preoperative bowel preparation
術前不安（じゅつぜんふあん）pre-operative anxiety
術中超音波検査（じゅつちゅうちょうおんぱけんさ）intraoperative ultrasonography
術中内視鏡検査（じゅつちゅうないしきょうけんさ）intraoperative endoscopy
術野感染（じゅつやかんせん）⇒手術部位感染
受動喫煙（じゅどうきつえん）secondhand smoke
主動筋（しゅどうきん）prime mover
手動ブライユ式点字タイプライター（しゅどうぶらいゆしきてんじたいぷらいたー）manual Braille writer；manual-type Braille writer
取得時効（しゅとくじこう）acquisitive prescription
ジュトフェン高齢者研究（じゅとふぇんこうれいしゃけんきゅう）Zutphen Elderly Study
守秘（しゅひ）confidentiality
†守秘義務（しゅひぎむ）duty of confidentiality；confidentiality
手部（しゅぶ）hand
寿命（じゅみょう）life span
受容（じゅよう）acceptance
腫瘍医（しゅようい）oncologist
腫瘍壊死因子（しゅようえしいんし）tumor necrosis factor；TNF
腫瘍壊死因子α阻害薬（しゅようえしいんしあるふぁそがいやく）tumor necrosis factor-alpha inhibitor
腫瘍学（しゅようがく）oncology
主要失敗要因（しゅようしっぱいよういん）⇒重要失敗要因
主要成功要因（しゅようせいこうよういん）⇒重要成功要因
受容的態度（じゅようてきたいど）receptive attitude
受容の原則（じゅようのげんそく）principle of acceptance
†手浴（しゅよく）hand bath
受理（じゅり）acceptance
受理面接（じゅりめんせつ）intake interview
受療数（じゅりょうすう）number of patients receiving medical care
受療割合（じゅりょうわりあい）percentage of patients receiving medical care
†手話（しゅわ）sign language
手話援助（しゅわえんじょ）sign language support
手話援助者（しゅわえんじょしゃ）supporter of sign language；sign language supporter
手話通訳士（しゅわつうやくし）sign language interpreter；SLI
手話奉仕（しゅわほうし）sign language volunteer work
手話奉仕員（しゅわほうしいん）sign language volunteer
循環器（じゅんかんき）cardiology
循環器外科集中治療室（じゅんかんきげかしゅうちゅうちりょうしつ）cardiac surgical intensive care unit
循環血液量減少性ショック（じゅんかんけつえききりょうげんしょうせいしょっく）hypovolemic shock
準拠集団（じゅんきょしゅうだん）reference group
準拠集団論（じゅんきょしゅうだんろん）reference group theory
順行性洗腸（じゅんこうせいせんちょう）antegrade colonic enema；ACE
準個室（じゅんこしつ）semi-private room
準市場（じゅんしじょう）quasi-market
遵守率（じゅんしゅりつ）compliance rate
準清潔手術（じゅんせいけつしゅじゅつ）clean-contaminated operation
準清潔創（じゅんせいけつそう）clean-contaminated wound
純損益（じゅんそんえき）net profit and loss
†除圧（じょあつ）decompression
消化（しょうか）digestion
†障害（しょうがい）disability
傷害（しょうがい）injury
障害一時給付金（しょうがいいちじきゅうふきん）temporary disability allowance
障害学（しょうがいがく）disability study
生涯学習（しょうがいがくしゅう）lifelong learning
†障害基礎年金（しょうがいきそねんきん）basic disability pension
生涯教育（しょうがいきょういく）lifelong education
障害軍人年金プログラム（しょうがいぐんじんねんきんぷろぐらむ）Veterans Disability Pension Program
障害軍人プログラム（しょうがいぐんじんぷろぐらむ）Veterans Disability Program
障害厚生年金（しょうがいこうせいねんきん）employee pension for disability
障害高齢者（しょうがいこうれいしゃ）disabled elderly
障害高齢者の日常生活自立度（しょうがいこうれいしゃのにちじょうせいかつじりつど）independence

level of the disabled elderly
紹介サービス（しょうかいさーびす）referral services
障害児（しょうがいじ）disabled child
障害児一時給付金（しょうがいじいちじきゅうふきん）temporary disability child allowance；temporary allowance for the disabled children
障害児医療（しょうがいじいりょう）medical care for the disabled children
障害児介護（しょうがいじかいご）caring for the disabled children；care for the disabled children　disabled children's care
障害児介護支援（しょうがいじかいごしえん）care management for the disabled children
障害児看護（しょうがいじかんご）nursing care for the disabled children
障害児教育（しょうがいじきょういく）education for the disabled children
障害児福祉手当（しょうがいじふくしてあて）child disability allowance
障害児扶助（しょうがいじふじょ）assistance for the disabled children
障害児保育（しょうがいじほいく）nursery for the disabled children
障害者（しょうがいしゃ）the disabled；disabled person
障害者一時給付金（しょうがいしゃいちじきゅうふきん）temporary disability allowance；temporary allowance for the disabled
障害者医療（しょうがいしゃいりょう）medical care for the disabled
障害者運動（しょうがいしゃうんどう）disability movement
障害者援助（しょうがいしゃえんじょ）support for the disabled
障害者介護（しょうがいしゃかいご）caring for the disabled；care for the disabled
障害者介護支援（しょうがいしゃかいごしえん）disability care management
障害者看護（しょうがいしゃかんご）nursing care for the disabled
障害者基本計画（しょうがいしゃきほんけいかく）basic pension for persons with disabilities
障害者基本法（しょうがいしゃきほんほう）Basic Act for Persons with Disabilities
障害者虐待（しょうがいしゃぎゃくたい）disabled abuse；abuse of the disabled
障害者教育（しょうがいしゃきょういく）education for the disabled
障害者ケアマネジメント（しょうがいしゃけあまねじめんと）care management for the disabled；disability care management
障害者権利運動（しょうがいしゃけんりうんどう）disability rights movement
障害者更生センター（しょうがいしゃこうせいせんたー）rehabilitation center for the disabled
障害者更生相談所（しょうがいしゃこうせいそうだんしょ）rehabilitation counseling center for the disabled
障害者雇用（しょうがいしゃこよう）employment of the disabled
障害者雇用促進（しょうがいしゃこようそくしん）employment promotion for the disabled
障害者雇用促進対策（しょうがいしゃこようそくしんたいさく）employment promotion policy for the disabled
障害者雇用促進法（しょうがいしゃこようそくしんほう）Law for Employment Promotion of Persons with Disabilities
障害者雇用対策課（しょうがいしゃこようたいさくか）Employment Measures for Persons with Disabilities Division
障害者雇用率（しょうがいしゃこようりつ）employment rates of the disabled
障害者作業所（しょうがいしゃさぎょうしょ）workshop for the disabled
障害者情報ネットワーク（しょうがいしゃじょうほうねっとわーく）information network for the disabled
障害者職業訓練（しょうがいしゃしょくぎょうくんれん）vocational training for the disabled
障害者職業訓練施設（しょうがいしゃしょくぎょうくんれんしせつ）vocational training facility for the disabled
障害者自立生活（しょうがいしゃじりつせいかつ）independent living for the disabled
障害者自立生活運動（しょうがいしゃじりつせいかつうんどう）independent living movement of the disabled
障害者自立生活センター（しょうがいしゃじりつせいかつせんたー）independent living center for the disabled
障害者自立センター（しょうがいしゃじりつせんたー）independence center for the disabled
障害者スポーツ（しょうがいしゃすぽーつ）disabled sports；sports for the disabled
障害者生活支援手当（しょうがいしゃせいかつしえんてあて）disability living allowance
障害者生活手当（しょうがいしゃせいかつてあて）disability living allowance
障害者税控除（しょうがいしゃぜいこうじょ）tax deduction for the disabled
障害者団体（しょうがいしゃだんたい）organization for the disabled
障害者駐車許可証（しょうがいしゃちゅうしゃきょかしょう）disabled parking permit

障害者手当（しょうがいしゃてあて）disability allowance
障害者の権利宣言（しょうがいしゃのけんりせんげん）Declaration on the Rights of Disabled Persons
障害者の尊厳（しょうがいしゃのそんげん）dignity of the disabled
障害者福祉（しょうがいしゃふくし）welfare for the disabled
障害者福祉相談員（しょうがいしゃふくしそうだんいん）welfare adviser for the disabled
障害者福祉手当（しょうがいしゃふくしてあて）disability welfare allowance
障害者福祉年金（しょうがいしゃふくしねんきん）disability welfare pension
障害者扶助（しょうがいしゃふじょ）assistance for the disabled
障害者プラン（しょうがいしゃぷらん）federal plan for the disabled
障害者向け民間サービス（しょうがいしゃむけみんかんさーびす）private services for the disabled
生涯住宅（しょうがいじゅうたく）lifelong housing
障害児療育（しょうがいじりょういく）care with education for the disabled children
生涯スポーツ（しょうがいすぽーつ）lifelong sports
生涯賃金（しょうがいちんぎん）lifelong wages
障害程度区分（しょうがいていどくぶん）disability levels
障害程度区分の認定（しょうがいていどくぶんのにんてい）certification of disability level
障害等級（しょうがいとうきゅう）disability levels
障害凍結（しょうがいとうけつ）disability freeze
障害認定（しょうがいにんてい）disability certification；certification of disability
障害年金（しょうがいねんきん）disability pension
障害の医学モデル（しょうがいのいがくもでる）medical model of disability
障害の概念（しょうがいのがいねん）concept of the disablement；concept of disability
障害の社会モデル（しょうがいのしゃかいもでる）social model of disability
†障害の受容（しょうがいのじゅよう）acceptance of disability
生涯発達（しょうがいはったつ）life-span development
障害福祉課（しょうがいふくしか）Welfare Division for Persons with Disabilities
障害福祉手当（しょうがいふくしてあて）disability welfare allowance
障害福祉年金（しょうがいふくしねんきん）disability welfare pension
障害保険（しょうがいほけん）disability insurance：DI
障害保健福祉部（しょうがいほけんふくしぶ）Department of Health and Welfare for Persons with Disabilities
障害モデル（しょうがいもでる）model of disability
障害幼児（しょうがいようじ）the disabled infant
紹介料（しょうかいりょう）referral fee
障害老人（しょうがいろうじん）the disabled elderly
消化管生理学（しょうかかんせいりがく）gastrointestinal physiology
消化器疾患（しょうかきしっかん）digestive disease
消化器内科医（しょうかきないかい）gastroenterologist
消化吸収（しょうかきゅうしゅう）digestion and absorption
消化性潰瘍（しょうかせいかいよう）peptic ulcer；peptic ulcer disease
償還額決定方式（しょうかんがくけっていほうしき）customary, prevailing and reasonable：CPR
償還払い（しょうかんばらい）reimbursement
試用期間（しようきかん）probationary employment period
上気道咳症候群（じょうきどうせきしょうこうぐん）upper airway cough syndrome
小規模作業所（しょうきぼさぎょうしょ）small-scale workshop
小規模身体障害者療護施設（しょうきぼしんたいしょうがいしゃりょうごせつ）small-scale custodial facility for the physically disabled
†小規模多機能型居宅介護（しょうきぼたきのうがたきょたくかいご）small-scale multi-functional home-based care services
小規模多機能型サービス（しょうきぼたきのうがたさーびす）small-scale multi-functional services
小規模多機能サービス（しょうきぼたきのうさーびす）small-scale multi-functional services
小規模特別養護老人ホーム（しょうきぼとくべつようごろうじんほーむ）small-scale geriatric welfare home for the aged
蒸気滅菌（じょうきめっきん）steam sterilization；autoclaving
焼却炉（しょうきゃくろ）incinerator
商業的活動（しょうぎょうてきかつどう）commercial activity
状況反射（じょうきょうはんしゃ）situational reflection
消去現象（しょうきょげんしょう）extinction
常勤換算（じょうきんかんさん）full-time equivalent：FTE
掌屈（しょうくつ）palmar flexion
上下関係（じょうげかんけい）vertical relationship

条件刺激（じょうけんしげき）conditioned stimulus
条件等色（じょうけんとうしょく）metamerism
条件等色対（じょうけんとうしょくたい）metamer
条件反応（じょうけんはんのう）conditioned response
症候群（しょうこうぐん）syndrome
症候性貧血（しょうこうせいひんけつ）symptomatic anemia
錠剤（じょうざい）tablet
常在菌（じょうざいきん）resident flora；resident bacteria；flora
常在細菌叢（じょうざいさいきんそう）resident flora；indigenous bacterial flora
小細胞肺癌（しょうさいぼうはいがん）small cell lung cancer；SCLC
硝酸塩（しょうさんえん）nitrate
上肢（じょうし）upper extremity
†少子化（しょうしか）depopulation
少子化社会（しょうしかしゃかい）society with the declining birth rate
常識的素人（じょうしきてきしろうと）prudent layperson
†少子高齢化（しょうしこうれいか）depopulation and aging
少子社会（しょうししゃかい）society with the declined birth rate
上肢切断（じょうしせつだん）upper extremity amputation
上肢装具（じょうしそうぐ）upper extremity orthosis
小舎制（しょうしゃせい）cottage system
照準（しょうじゅん）focus
症状（しょうじょう）symptom
床上動作（しょうじょうどうさ）mat activity
使用上の注意（しようじょうのちゅうい）patient's instructions for use
常食（じょうしょく）regular diet
少数派（しょうすうは）minority
少数派グループ（しょうすうはぐるーぷ）minority group
少数民族（しょうすうみんぞく）ethnic minority；racial minority
脂溶性ビタミン（しようせいびたみん）fat-soluble vitamin
常染色体（じょうせんしょくたい）autosome
常染色体優性（じょうせんしょくたいゆうせい）autosomal dominant
常染色体優性遺伝（じょうせんしょくたいゆうせいいでん）autosomal dominant inheritance
常染色体優性遺伝病（じょうせんしょくたいゆうせいいでんびょう）autosomal dominant disorder
常染色体劣性（じょうせんしょくたいれっせい）autosomal recessive
常染色体劣性遺伝（じょうせんしょくたいれっせいいでん）autosomal recessive inheritance
常染色体劣性遺伝病（じょうせんしょくたいれっせいいでんびょう）autosomal recessive disorder
踵足変形（しょうそくへんけい）talipes calcaneus
小腸（しょうちょう）small intestine
小腸機能障害（しょうちょうきのうしょうがい）disorders of the small intestinal function
象徴的障壁（しょうちょうてきしょうへき）symbolic barrier
省庁別公共サービス協約（しょうちょうべつこうきょうさーびすきょうやく）department public services agreement
省庁別歳出限度額（しょうちょうべつさいしゅつげんどがく）departmental expenditure limits；DEL
小腸ポリープ（しょうちょうぽりーぷ）small intestinal polyps
小腸瘤（しょうちょうりゅう）enterocele
情緒障害（じょうちょしょうがい）emotional disturbance
情緒障害児短期治療施設（じょうちょしょうがいじたんきちりょうせつ）short-term treatment facility for disabled children with emotional disturbance
情動（じょうどう）emotion
常同行為（じょうどうこうい）stereotyped behavior
床頭台（しょうとうだい）bedside table；bedside cabinet
消毒（しょうどく）disinfection
消毒剤（しょうどくざい）disinfectant
譲渡所得課税（じょうとしょとくかぜい）capital gains tax
小児科（しょうにか）pediatric
小児科医（しょうにかい）pediatrician
小児期崩壊性障害（しょうにきほうかいせいしょうがい）childhood disintegrative disorder
小児在宅ケア（しょうにざいたくけあ）pediatric home care
小児在宅医療（しょうにざいたくいりょう）pediatric home health
小児自閉症（しょうにじへいしょう）childhood autism
小児内視鏡検査（しょうにないしきょうけんさ）pediatric endoscopy
小児に対する二次救命心肺蘇生法・処置（しょうににたいするにじきゅうめいしんぱいそせいほう・しょち）pediatric advanced life support
小児慢性特定疾患治療研究事業（しょうにまんせいとくていしっかんちりょうけんきゅうじぎょう）medical aid for specific chronic diseases of children
少年（しょうねん）juvenile
少年院（しょうねんいん）juvenile reformatory

介護保険・介護福祉等関連用語 和英

school
少年鑑別所（しょうねんかんべつしょ）juvenile classification facility
少年犯罪（しょうねんはんざい）juvenile delinquency
少年法（しょうねんほう）Juvenile Law
少年保護司（しょうねんほごし）juvenile probation officer
小脳（しょうのう）cerebellum
消費者（しょうひしゃ）consumer
消費者運動（しょうひしゃうんどう）consumer movement；consumerism
消費者教育（しょうひしゃきょういく）consumer education
消費者権利グループ（しょうひしゃけんりぐるーぷ）consumer rights group
消費者重視ケア（しょうひしゃじゅうしけあ）consumer-directed care
消費者主義（しょうひしゃしゅぎ）consumerism
消費者庁（しょうひしゃちょう）Consumer Affairs Agency
消費者物価指数（しょうひしゃぶっかしすう）consumer price index：CPI
消費者保護（しょうひしゃほご）consumer protection
消費者保護事務所（しょうひしゃほごじむしょ）consumer protection office
消費税（しょうひぜい）consumption tax
消費生活協同組合（しょうひせいかつきょうどうくみあい）consumers' cooperative association
傷病休暇（しょうびょうきゅうか）sick leave；medical leave
傷病手当（しょうびょうてあて）sickness and injury allowance
傷病平均年数の圧縮（しょうびょうへいきんねんすうのあっしゅく）morbidity compression
上部消化管（じょうぶしょうかかん）upper gastrointestinal
上部食道括約筋（じょうぶしょくどうかつやくきん）upper esophageal sphincter：UES
上部食道括約筋機能障害（じょうぶしょくどうかつやくきんきのうしょうがい）upper esophageal sphincter dysfunction
情報開示（じょうほうかいじ）information disclosure
情報化社会（じょうほうかしゃかい）informationalized society
情報技術（じょうほうぎじゅつ）information technology：IT
情報公開（じょうほうこうかい）information disclosure
消防士（しょうぼうし）firefighter
情報システム（じょうほうしすてむ）information system
消防署（しょうぼうしょ）fire department
情報提供（じょうほうていきょう）dissemination of information
情報ネットワーク（じょうほうねっとわーく）information network
静脈（じょうみゃく）vein
†静脈栄養法（じょうみゃくえいようほう）parenteral nutrition
静脈血（じょうみゃくけつ）venous blood
静脈瘤（じょうみゃくりゅう）varix
照明（しょうめい）lighting
証明書（しょうめいしょ）certificate；proof
証明書の写し（しょうめいしょのうつし）copy of certificate；copy of proof
消滅時効（しょうめつじこう）extinctive prescription
将来推計人口（しょうらいすいけいじんこう）population projection
使用率（しようりつ）use rate
条例（じょうれい）ordinance
症例対照研究（しょうれいたいしょうけんきゅう）case control study
上腕義手（じょうわんぎしゅ）transhumeral prosthesis；above-elbow prosthesis
上腕切断（じょうわんせつだん）above-elbow amputation
初期発話知覚テスト（しょきはつわちかくてすと）Early Speech Perception Test
初期費用（しょきひよう）initial cost
初期面接（しょきめんせつ）initial intake
職域保険（しょくいきほけん）occupational group insurance
職員研修（しょくいんけんしゅう）staff development
職員配置（しょくいんはいち）staffing
処遇改善命令（しょぐうかいぜんめいれい）order for improvement of services
処遇方針（しょぐうほうしん）treatment policy
食塩（しょくえん）salt
職業安定局（しょくぎょうあんていきょく）Employment Security Bureau
職業安定プログラム（しょくぎょうあんていぷろぐらむ）job placement program
職業安定法（しょくぎょうあんていほう）Employment Security Law
職業カウンセリング（しょくぎょうかうんせりんぐ）vocational counseling
職業学校（しょくぎょうがっこう）trade school
職業家庭両立課（しょくぎょうかていりょうりつか）Work and Family Harmonization Division
職業感染（しょくぎょうかんせん）occupational infection

職業訓練（しょくぎょうくんれん）vocational training；job training
職業訓練施設（しょくぎょうくんれんしせつ）vocational training facility
職業指導（しょくぎょうしどう）vocational education；vocational guidance
職業前（しょくぎょうぜん）prevocational
職業的（しょくぎょうてき）vocational
†職業的リハビリテーション（しょくぎょうてきりはびりてーしょん）vocational rehabilitation
職業能力開発局（しょくぎょうのうりょくかいはつきょく）Human Resource Development Bureau
職業曝露（しょくぎょうばくろ）occupational exposure
職業病（しょくぎょうびょう）occupational disease
職業評価（しょくぎょうひょうか）vocational evaluation
職業復帰（しょくぎょうふっき）return to work
食行動の異常（しょくこうどうのいじょう）eating disorder
†食事（しょくじ）meal
食事援助（しょくじえんじょ）eating assistance；assistance with eating
†食事介護（しょくじかいご）eating assistance；assistance with eating
†食事介助（しょくじかいじょ）eating assistance；assistance with eating
食事管理（しょくじかんり）meal management
食事ケア（しょくじけあ）eating assistance；assistance with eating
食事サービス（しょくじさーびす）meal services
食事準備（しょくじじゅんび）meal preparation
食事制限（しょくじせいげん）dietary restriction
食事宅配サービス（しょくじたくはいさーびす）delivered meals
†食事動作（しょくじどうさ）eating；feeding activity
食習慣（しょくしゅうかん）eating habit；dietary habit
食事用具（しょくじようぐ）eating tool；tool for eating
†食事療法（しょくじりょうほう）nutrition therapy
触診（しょくしん）palpation
食生活（しょくせいかつ）dietary life
†褥瘡（じょくそう）pressure ulcer；decubitus ulcer；pressure sore
褥瘡治癒過程スケール（じょくそうちゆかていすけーる）Pressure Ulcer Scale for Healing：PUSH
褥瘡治療（じょくそうちりょう）pressure ulcer treatment
褥瘡発生予測尺度（じょくそうはっせいよそくしゃくど）Braden Scale for Predicting Pressure Ulcer Risk；Braden Scale for Predicting Pressure Sore Risk
†褥瘡予防（じょくそうよぼう）prevention of pressure ulcer；pressure ulcer prevention
褥瘡予防と治療（じょくそうよぼうとちりょう）pressure ulcer prevention and treatment
触知覚低下（しょくちかくていか）loss of touch sensation
†食中毒（しょくちゅうどく）food poisoning
食道（しょくどう）esophagus
食道運動障害（しょくどううんどうしょうがい）esophageal motility disorder
食道相（しょくどうそう）esophageal phase
食道内圧検査（しょくどうないあつけんさ）esophageal manometry
職場外訓練（しょくばがいくんれん）off-the-job-training：OFF-JT
職場環境悪化型セクハラ（しょくばかんきょうあっかがたせくはら）hostile work environment harassment
職場訓練（しょくばくんれん）on-the-job-training：OJT
職場実習型訓練制度（しょくばじっしゅうがたくんれんせいど）apprenticeship
食品安全部（しょくひんあんぜんぶ）Department of Food Safety
†食品衛生（しょくひんえいせい）food sanitation
食品衛生監視員（しょくひんえいせいかんしいん）food inspector
食品衛生管理者（しょくひんえいせいかんりしゃ）food safety & sanitation supervisor
食品衛生法（しょくひんえいせいほう）Food Sanitation Law
食品汚染（しょくひんおせん）food contamination
食品調理（しょくひんちょうり）food preparation
†植物状態（しょくぶつじょうたい）vegetative state
†植物性食品（しょくぶつせいしょくひん）vegetable food
食物（しょくもつ）food
食物関連障害（しょくもつかんれんしょうがい）food-related disorder
食物繊維（しょくもつせんい）dietary fiber
食物媒介感染（しょくもつばいかいかんせん）food-borne infection
†食欲（しょくよく）appetite
食欲中枢（しょくよくちゅうすう）appetite center
食欲低下（しょくよくていか）loss of appetite
†食欲不振（しょくよくふしん）loss of appetite
徐呼吸（じょこきゅう）bradypnea
助産師（じょさんし）midwife；maternity nurse
書字訓練（しょじくんれん）writing exercise
除脂肪体重（じょしぼうたいじゅう）lean body mass：LBM

介護保険・介護福祉等関連用語 和英

助成金（じょせいきん）grant-in-aid
女性の社会参加（じょせいのしゃかいさんか）social participation of women
触覚（しょっかく）sense of touch
触覚過敏（しょっかくかびん）⇒感覚過敏
触覚鈍麻（しょっかくどんま）⇒感覚鈍麻
ショック（しょっく）shock
所得再分配（しょとくさいぶんぱい）income redistribution
所得税（しょとくぜい）income tax
所得制限（しょとくせいげん）income limit
所得調査（しょとくちょうさ）earnings test
所得テスト（しょとくてすと）income test
所得保障（しょとくほしょう）income security
†ショートステイ（しょーとすてい）short-stay
ショートステイサービス（しょーとすていさーびす）short-stay services
処方集（しょほうしゅう）formulary
処方箋（しょほうせん）prescription
処方薬剤プログラム（しょほうやくざいぷろぐらむ）prescription medication program
徐脈（じょみゃく）bradycardia
除毛（じょもう）hair removal
処理（しょり）disposal
初老期うつ病（しょろうきうつびょう）presenile depression
†初老期認知症（しょろうきにんちしょう）presenile dementia
シリコン製内ソケット（しりこんせいうちそけっと）Icelandic roll on silicone socket：ICEROSS
シリコン製ソフトライナー（しりこんせいそふとらいなー）silicone soft liner
†自立（じりつ）independence
自律（じりつ）autonomy
自律訓練法（じりつくんれんほう）autogenic training
†自立支援（じりつしえん）independence support
自律神経（じりつしんけい）autonomic nerve
自律神経過反射（じりつしんけいかはんしゃ）autonomic hyperreflexia；autonomous hyperreflexia
自律神経機能障害（じりつしんけいきのうしょうがい）autonomic dysfunction
自律神経系（じりつしんけいけい）autonomic nervous system
自律神経失調（じりつしんけいしっちょう）dysautonomia
自律神経障害（じりつしんけいしょうがい）autonomic nerve disorder
自立生活（じりつせいかつ）independent living：IL
自立生活運動（じりつせいかつうんどう）independent living movement
自立生活援助（じりつせいかつえんじょ）self-reliant living assistance services
自立生活器具（じりつせいかつきぐ）independent living aid
自立生活スキル（じりつせいかつすきる）independent living skill
自立生活センター（じりつせいかつせんたー）Center for Independent Living：CIL；Independent Living Center
自立センター（じりつせんたー）independence center
自律尊重原理（じりつそんちょうげんり）principle of respect for autonomy
†自立度（じりつど）level of independent living
自立の概念（じりつのがいねん）concepts of independence
私立病院（しりつびょういん）private hospital
市立病院（しりつびょういん）city hospital
視力（しりょく）vision；visual acuity
視力障害（しりょくしょうがい）visual disturbance
†視力低下（しりょくていか）vision loss
ジルチアゼム（じるちあぜむ）diltiazem
シルバーホーム（しるばーほーむ）senior home
シルバーライフスタイル（しるばーらいふすたいる）senior lifestyle
事例研究（じれいけんきゅう）case research
†事例検討（じれいけんとう）case study
事例調査（じれいちょうさ）case investigation
シレジアバンド（しれじあばんど）Silesian bandage
ジレンマ（じれんま）dilemma
新医療臨床研修制度（しんいりょうりんしょうけんしゅうせいど）new clinical training system of primary care
心因（しんいん）psychogenesis
心因反応（しんいんはんのう）psychogenic reaction
腎盂腎炎（じんうじんえん）pyelonephritis
腎盂造影（じんうぞうえい）pyelography
心エコー（しんえこー）echocardiography；cardiac ECHO
心エコー図（しんえこーず）echocardiogram
新エンゼルプラン（しんえんぜるぷらん）New Angel Plan for Children
人格（じんかく）personality
人格検査（じんかくけんさ）personality test
人格検査質問紙（じんかくけんさしつもんし）personality inventory
人格障害（じんかくしょうがい）personality disorder
新型特養（しんがたとくよう）unit-based care
腎癌（じんがん）kidney cancer
審議会（しんぎかい）council；advisory committee
†心気症（しんきしょう）hypochondria

腎機能（じんきのう）renal function
新規発症持続性連日性頭痛（しんきはっしょうじぞくせいれんじつせいずつう）new daily persistent headache：NDPH
鍼灸（しんきゅう）acupuncture and moxibustion
心胸郭比（しんきょうかくひ）cardiothoracic ratio
真菌感染（しんきんかんせん）fungal infection
心筋虚血（しんきんきょけつ）myocardial ischemia
真菌血症（しんきんけつしょう）fungemia
心筋梗塞（しんきんこうそく）myocardial infarction
真菌症（しんきんしょう）mycosis
真菌性眼内炎（しんきんせいがんないえん）fungal endophthalmitis
寝具（しんぐ）bedclothes
シンクロニシティ（しんくろにしてぃ）synchronicity
神経因性膀胱（しんけいいんせいぼうこう）neurogenic bladder
神経学（しんけいがく）neurology
神経学者（しんけいがくしゃ）neurologist
神経学的検査（しんけいがくてきけんさ）neurological examination
神経学的状態（しんけいがくてきじょうたい）neurological condition
神経筋疾患（しんけいきんしっかん）neuromuscular disease
神経筋促通法（しんけいきんそくつうほう）neuromuscular facilitation technique
神経原性筋萎縮（しんけいげんせいきんいしゅく）neurogenic muscle atrophy
神経原性ショック（しんけいげんせいしょっく）neurogenic shock
神経原性疼痛（しんけいげんせいとうつう）neuropathic pain
神経原性肺水腫（しんけいげんせいはいすいしゅ）neurogenic pulmonary edema
神経絞扼（しんけいこうやく）nerve entrapment
神経根症（しんけいこんしょう）radiculopathy
神経根引き抜き損傷（しんけいこんひきぬきそんしょう）root avulsion injury
神経腫瘍医（しんけいしゅようい）neuro-oncologist
神経循環無力症（しんけいじゅんかんむりょくしょう）neurocirculatory asthenia
神経症（しんけいしょう）neurosis
神経障害（しんけいしょうがい）neuropathy
神経症性障害（しんけいしょうせいしょうがい）neurotic disorder；neurotic disability
神経心理学（しんけいしんりがく）neuropsychology
神経心理学者（しんけいしんりがくしゃ）neuropsychologist
神経心理学的検査（しんけいしんりがくてきけんさ）neuropsychological test
神経心理学的評価（しんけいしんりがくてきひょうか）neuropsychological evaluation

神経性食欲不振症（しんけいせいしょくよくふしんしょう）anorexia nervous；anorexia
神経性大食症（しんけいせいたいしょくしょう）bulimia nervosa
神経性無食欲症（しんけいせいむしょくよくしょう）anorexia nervosa
神経生理学（しんけいせいりがく）neurophysiology
神経生理学者（しんけいせいりがくしゃ）neurophysiologist
神経生理学的アプローチ（しんけいせいりがくてきあぷろーち）neurophysiological approach
神経組織（しんけいそしき）nervous tissue
神経痛（しんけいつう）neuralgia
神経伝導速度（しんけいでんどうそくど）nerve conduction velocity：NCV
神経発達的アプローチ（しんけいはったつてきあぷろーち）neurodevelopmental approach
神経ブロック（しんけいぶろっく）nerve block
神経変性疾患（しんけいへんせいしっかん）neurodegenerative disease
心血管疾患（しんけっかんしっかん）cardiovascular disease
心血管・代謝疾患リスク（しんけっかん・たいしゃっかんりすく）cardiometabolic risk
心血管リスク（しんけっかんりすく）cardiovascular risk
腎結石（じんけっせき）kidney stone
親権（しんけん）parental authority
人権（じんけん）human rights
心原性ショック（しんげんせいしょっく）cardiac shock
心原性肺水腫（しんげんせいはいすいしゅ）cardiogenic pulmonary edema
人権尊重（じんけんそんちょう）protection of human rights
人件費出（じんけんひしゅつ）personnel expenditures
人件費用（じんけんひよう）personnel costs
人口移動（じんこういどう）population movement
人工栄養（じんこうえいよう）artificial feeding
振興課（しんこうか）Promotion Division
人口学的従属人口比率（じんこうがくてきじゅうぞくじんこうひりつ）demographic dependency ratio
人工換気（じんこうかんき）artificial ventilation
新興感染症（しんこうかんせんしょう）emerging infectious disease
人工血管（じんこうけっかん）artificial blood vessel
人工喉頭（じんこうこうとう）voice generator
人工肛門（じんこうこうもん）artificial anus
人工股関節形成術（じんこうこかんせつけいせいじゅつ）total hip arthroplasty
人工股関節全置換術（じんこうこかんせつぜんちかんじゅつ）total hip replacement：THR

介護保険・介護福祉等関連用語 和英

†人工呼吸（じんこうこきゅう）artificial respiration；rescue breathing；artificial breathing
人工呼吸器（じんこうこきゅうき）artificial respirator
人工呼吸器依存四肢麻痺（じんこうこきゅうきいぞんししまひ）respirator dependent quadriplegia
人工骨頭置換術（じんこうこっとうちかんじゅつ）hemiarthroplasty
人工心臓（じんこうしんぞう）artificial heart
人工心臓弁（じんこうしんぞうべん）artificial heart valve
進行性球麻痺（しんこうせいきゅうまひ）progressive bulbar palsy
進行性筋ジストロフィー（しんこうせいきんじすとろふぃー）progressive muscular dystrophy；PMD
進行性ミオクローヌスてんかん（しんこうせいみおくろーぬすてんかん）progressive myoclonus epilepsy
人工臓器（じんこうぞうき）artificial organ
人口転換論（じんこうてんかんろん）demographic transition theory
人口統計（じんこうとうけい）demographic statistics
人工透析（じんこうとうせき）hemodialysis
人口動態（じんこうどうたい）population dynamics
人口動態・保健統計課（じんこうどうたい・ほけんとうけいか）Vital and Health Statistics Division
人工内耳（じんこうないじ）artificial cochlea；cochlear implant；hearing-aid used in connection with implant
人工妊娠中絶（じんこうにんしんちゅうぜつ）elective abortion
人工肺（じんこうはい）artificial lung
人口爆発（じんこうばくはつ）population explosion
人工膀胱（じんこうぼうこう）artificial bladder
人工レンズ（じんこうれんず）artificial lens
新国民生活指標（しんこくみんせいかつしひょう）People's Life Indicators
新ゴールドプラン（しんごーるどぷらん）New Gold Plan for the Elderly
審査管理課（しんさかんりか）Evaluation and Licensing Division
審査請求（しんさせいきゅう）certification appeal
心疾患（しんしっかん）heart disease
腎疾患（しんしっかん）kidney disease
心室期外収縮（しんしつきがいしゅうしゅく）premature ventricular contraction；PVC
心室細動（しんしつさいどう）ventricular fibrillation
真実性（しんじつせい）genuineness
心室中隔欠損（しんしつちゅうかくけっそん）ventricular septal defect；VSD
寝室用便器（しんしつようべんき）chamber pot

心シャント（しんしゃんと）cardiac shunt
人獣共通感染症（じんじゅうきょうつうかんせんしょう）zoonosis；zoonose
人種差別（じんしゅさべつ）racial discrimination
人種差別主義（じんしゅさべつしゅぎ）racism
人種的・民族的差異（じんしゅてき・みんぞくてきさい）racial and ethnic difference
人種割当（じんしゅわりあて）racial quotas
†身上監護（しんじょうかんご）personal guardianship
寝床気候（しんしょうきこう）microclimate of sleeping floor
心身医学（しんしんいがく）mind-body medicine
心身耗弱（しんしんこうじゃく）diminished capacity
†心身症（しんしんしょう）psychosomatic disease；PSD
心身障害児（しんしんしょうがいじ）the physically and mentally disabled child
心身障害児施設（しんしんしょうがいじしせつ）facility for the physically and mentally disabled children
心身障害児ホームヘルプ（しんしんしょうがいじほーむへるぷ）home help services for the physically and mentally disabled children
心身障害者（しんしんしょうがいしゃ）the physically and mentally disabled
心身障害者施設（しんしんしょうがいしゃしせつ）facility for the physically and mentally disabled
心身障害者ホームヘルプ（しんしんしょうがいしゃほーむへるぷ）home help services for the physically and mentally disabled
心身喪失（しんしんそうしつ）insanity
診診連携（しんしんれんけい）affiliation between outpatient clinics
真性救急（しんせいきゅうきゅう）true emergency
新生児（しんせいじ）neonate；newborn
新生児行動評価（しんせいじこうどうひょうか）Neonatal Behavior Assessment Scale；NBAS
新生児死亡率（しんせいじしぼうりつ）neonatal mortality rate
新生児集中治療室（しんせいじしゅうちゅうちりょうしつ）neonatal intensive care unit；NICU；newborn intensive care unit；intensive care nursery
申請者（しんせいしゃ）applicant
真性尿失禁（しんせいにょうしっきん）true incontinence
申請保護の原則（しんせいほごのげんそく）principle of public assistance based on application
†振戦（しんせん）tremor
振戦せん妄（しんせんせんもう）delirium tremens

心尖拍動（しんせんはくどう）apex beat
心臓（しんぞう）heart
腎臓（じんぞう）kidney
心臓核医学（しんぞうかくいがく）cardiac nuclear medicine
心臓カテーテル法（しんぞうかてーてるほう）heart catheterization
心臓機能障害（しんぞうきのうしょうがい）disorders of the heart function
腎臓機能障害（じんぞうきのうしょうがい）disorders of the kidney function
心臓外科関連感染（しんぞうげかかんれんかんせん）cardiac surgery-related infection
人造繊維（じんぞうせんい）artificial fiber；chemical fiber
心臓超音波検査（しんぞうちょうおんぱけんさ）ultrasound cardiography
腎臓内科医（じんぞうないかい）nephrologist
心臓病学（しんぞうびょうがく）⇒循環器
心臓不整脈（しんぞうふせいみゃく）cardiac dysrhythmia
†心臓弁膜症（しんぞうべんまくしょう）valvular heart disease
心臓マッサージ（しんぞうまっさーじ）cardiac massage
心臓リハビリテーション（しんぞうりはびりてーしょん）cardiac rehabilitation
親族ケア（しんぞくけあ）kinship care
身体依存（しんたいいぞん）physical dependence
身体因（しんたいいん）somatogenesis
身体援助（しんたいえんじょ）physical assistance
†身体介護（しんたいかいご）personal care
身体活動量（しんたいかつどうりょう）amount of physical activity
†身体機能（しんたいきのう）physical function
身体機能検査（しんたいきのうけんさ）physical performance test；PPT
身体拘束（しんたいこうそく）physical restraint；body restraint
身体指向心理療法（しんたいしこうしんりりょうほう）body-centered psychotherapy
身体障害（しんたいしょうがい）physical disability
身体障害高齢者（しんたいしょうがいこうれいしゃ）the physically disabled elderly
身体障害児（しんたいしょうがいじ）the physically disabled child
身体障害児介護支援（しんたいしょうがいじかいごしえん）care management for the physically disabled children
身体障害者（しんたいしょうがいしゃ）the physically disabled
身体障害者医療（しんたいしょうがいしゃいりょう）medical care for the physically disabled

身体障害者運動（しんたいしょうがいしゃうんどう）movement for the physically disabled
身体障害者援助（しんたいしょうがいしゃえんじょ）support for the physically disabled
身体障害者介護（しんたいしょうがいしゃかいご）caring for the physically disabled；care for the physically disabled
身体障害者介護支援（しんたいしょうがいしゃかいごしえん）care management for the physically disabled；disability care management
身体障害者看護（しんたいしょうがいしゃかんご）nursing care for the physically disabled
身体障害者居宅介護（しんたいしょうがいしゃきょたくかいご）home-based care for the physically disabled
身体障害者居宅介護支援（しんたいしょうがいしゃきょたくかいごしえん）home-based care management for the disabled
身体障害者更生援護施設（しんたいしょうがいしゃこうせいえんごしせつ）rehabilitation and assistance center for the physically disabled；rehabilitation facility for persons with disabilities
身体障害者更生基金（しんたいしょうがいしゃこうせいききん）rehabilitation fund for the physically disabled
身体障害者更生施設（しんたいしょうがいしゃこうせいしせつ）rehabilitation facility for the physically disabled；rehabilitation facility for persons with disabilities
身体障害者更生相談所（しんたいしょうがいしゃこうせいそうだんしょ）rehabilitation counseling center for physically disabled
身体障害者雇用（しんたいしょうがいしゃこよう）employment of the physically disabled
身体障害者雇用促進（しんたいしょうがいしゃこようそくしん）employment promotion for the physically disabled
身体障害者雇用促進対策（しんたいしょうがいしゃこようそくしんたいさく）employment promotion policy for the physically disabled
身体障害者雇用率（しんたいしょうがいしゃこようりつ）employment rates of the physically disabled；employment rates for persons with physically disabilities
身体障害者在宅介護支援（しんたいしょうがいしゃざいたくかいごしえん）home care management for the disabled
身体障害者作業所（しんたいしょうがいしゃさぎょうしょ）workshop for the physically disabled
身体障害者社会参加促進センター（しんたいしょうがいしゃしゃかいさんかそくしんせんたー）promotion center of social participation for the

介護保険・介護福祉等関連用語　和英

physically disabled
身体障害者授産施設（しんたいしょうがいしゃじゅさんしせつ）sheltered workshop for the physically disabled
身体障害者障害程度等級表（しんたいしょうがいしゃしょうがいていどとうきゅうひょう）list of disability grading
身体障害者相談員（しんたいしょうがいしゃそうだんいん）advisor for the physically disabled
身体障害者短期入所（しんたいしょうがいしゃたんきにゅうしょ）short-stay for the physically disabled
身体障害者通所授産施設（しんたいしょうがいしゃつうしょじゅさんしせつ）sheltered workshop for the physically disabled
身体障害者デイサービス（しんたいしょうがいしゃでいさーびす）day care services for the physically disabled
身体障害者デイサービスセンター（しんたいしょうがいしゃでいさーびすせんたー）day services center for the physically disabled
身体障害者手帳（しんたいしょうがいしゃてちょう）physical disability certificate handbook
身体障害者福祉（しんたいしょうがいしゃふくし）welfare for the physically disabled
身体障害者福祉作業所（しんたいしょうがいしゃふくしさぎょうしょ）welfare workshop for the physically disabled
身体障害者福祉司（しんたいしょうがいしゃふくしし）welfare officer for the physically disabled
身体障害者福祉審議会（しんたいしょうがいしゃふくししんぎかい）Advisory Council for the Welfare of Physically Disabled Persons
身体障害者福祉センター（しんたいしょうがいしゃふくしせんたー）welfare center for the physically disabled
身体障害者福祉法（しんたいしょうがいしゃふくしほう）Act on Welfare of Physically Disabled Persons
身体障害者福祉ホーム（しんたいしょうがいしゃふくしほーむ）welfare home for the physically disabled
身体障害者扶助（しんたいしょうがいしゃふじょ）assistance for the physically disabled
身体障害者ホームヘルプサービス（しんたいしょうがいしゃほーむへるぶさーびす）home help services for the physically disabled
身体障害者向け民間サービス（しんたいしょうがいしゃむけみんかんさーびす）private services for the physically disabled
身体障害者療護施設（しんたいしょうがいしゃりょうごしせつ）custodial care facility for the physically disabled
身体障害のない貧困者（しんたいしょうがいのないひんこんしゃ）able body poor

身体障害幼児（しんたいしょうがいようじ）physically disabled infant
身体障害老人（しんたいしょうがいろうじん）physically disabled aged person
身体像（しんたいぞう）body image
身体組成（しんたいそせい）body composition
身体調整（しんたいちょうせい）physical conditioning
身体的虐待（しんたいてきぎゃくたい）physical abuse
身体的攻撃（しんたいてきこうげき）physical aggression
身体デコンディショニング（しんたいでこんでぃしょにんぐ）physical deconditioning
身体反射（しんたいはんしゃ）body reflection
診断（しんだん）diagnosis
診断群分類（しんだんぐんぶんるい）diagnosis procedure combination：DPC
診断群分類別係数（しんだんぐんぶんるいべつけいすう）coefficients for diagnosis procedure combination
診断群別所定報酬額支払方式（しんだんぐんべつしょていほうしゅうがくしはらいほうしき）diagnostic related groups-prospective payment system：DRG-PPS
シンチグラフィー（しんちぐらふぃー）scintigraphy
伸張運動（しんちょううんどう）stretching exercise
心的外傷（しんてきがいしょう）psychic trauma
人的資源（じんてきしげん）human resources；manpower
腎摘除（じんてきじょ）nephrectomy
伸展（しんてん）extension
伸展拘縮（しんてんこうしゅく）extension contracture
心電図（しんでんず）electrocardiogram：EKG
振動（しんどう）vibration
人頭制前払い定額制（じんとうせいまえばらいていがくせい）capitated plan
人頭払い制（じんとうばらいせい）capitated payment
心肺蘇生法（しんぱいそせいほう）cardiopulmonary resuscitation：CPR
心肺脳蘇生法（しんぱいのうそせいほう）cardiopulmonary cerebral resuscitation：CPCR
心拍出量（しんはくしゅつりょう）cardiac output
心拍数（しんぱくすう）heart rate
シンバルタ（しんばるた）Cymbalta
深部感覚（しんぶかんかく）deep sensation
深部静脈血栓症（しんぶじょうみゃくけっせんしょう）deep vein thrombosis
心不全（しんふぜん）heart failure
腎不全（じんふぜん）kidney failure；renal failure
身辺自立（しんぺんじりつ）physical independence
心房（しんぼう）atrium
心房期外収縮（しんぼうきがいしゅうしゅく）

premature atrial contraction：PAC
心房細動（しんぼうさいどう）atrial fibrillation
心房中隔欠損症（しんぼうちゅうかくけっそんしょう）atrial septal defect
新保守主義（しんほしゅしゅぎ）neoconservatives
人民資本主義（じんみんしほんしゅぎ）people's capitalism
信用失墜行為の禁止（しんようしっついこういのきんし）prohibition of acts causing discredit；Prohibition of Acts to Damage Impartiality
†信頼関係（しんらいかんけい）rapport
信頼関係の構築（しんらいかんけいのこうちく）building rapport
心理学（しんりがく）psychology
心理劇（しんりげき）psychodrama
心理劇療法（しんりげきりょうほう）psychodrama therapy
心理検査（しんりけんさ）psychological test
心理社会評価（しんりしゃかいひょうか）psychosocial assessment
心理・性的段階（しんり・せいてきだんかい）psychosexual stages
心理・性的発達理論（しんり・せいてきはったつりろん）psychosexual development
心理的虐待（しんりてきぎゃくたい）psychological abuse；emotional abuse
心理テスト（しんりてすと）psychological test
心理評価（しんりひょうか）psychological assessment
診療所（しんりょうしょ）clinic
診療情報管理士系（しんりょうじょうほうかんりしけい）medical coder；diagnostic coder；clinical coder
診療の基準（しんりょうのきじゅん）⇒医療の基準
診療放射線技師（しんりょうほうしゃせんぎし）clinical radiologic technologist
診療報酬（しんりょうほうしゅう）medical fee；medical treatment fee
診療報酬支払相対評価スケール方式（しんりょうほうしゅうしはらいそうたいひょうかすけーるほうしき）Resource-Based Relative Value Scale：RBRVS
診療報酬制度（しんりょうほうしゅうせいど）medical treatment fee system
診療予約（しんりょうよやく）doctor appointment；doctor's appointment
心理力動論（しんりりきどうろん）psychodynamics
心理療法（しんりりょうほう）psychotherapy
新連邦主義（しんれんぽうしゅぎ）new federalism
進路指導教官（しんろしどうきょうかん）school counselor；guidance counselor

す

随意運動（ずいいうんどう）voluntary movement
随意収縮（ずいいしゅうしゅく）voluntary contraction
随意閉じ式フック（ずいいとじしきふっく）voluntary closing hook
随意開き式フック（ずいいひらきしきふっく）voluntary opening hook
膵炎（すいえん）pancreatitis
水銀中毒（すいぎんちゅうどく）mercury poisoning
水系感染（すいけいかんせん）waterborne infection
遂行機能障害（すいこうのうしょうがい）disorder of executive function
遂行機能障害症候群（すいこうきのうしょうがいしょうこうぐん）dysexecutive syndrome
水晶体（すいしょうたい）crystal lens
水晶体乳化吸引術（すいしょうたいにゅうかきゅういんじゅつ）phacoemulsification
†推奨量（すいしょうりょう）recommended dietary allowance：RDA
スイス型膝止め（すいすがたひざとめ）Swiss lock
膵臓（すいぞう）pancreas
膵臓癌（すいぞうがん）pancreatic cancer
錐体（すいたい）cone
錐体路（すいたいろ）pyramidal tract
水中運動（すいちゅううんどう）underwater exercise
垂直感染（すいちょくかんせん）vertical disease transmission
推定一日摂取量（すいていいちにちせっしゅりょう）estimated daily intake
水痘（すいとう）chicken pox
水道課（すいどうか）Water Supply Division
水痘感染（すいとうかんせん）varicella infection
水道水（すいどうすい）tap water
水痘帯状疱疹（すいとうたいじょうほうしん）varicella zoster
水痘帯状疱疹ウイルス（すいとうたいじょうほうしんういるす）varicella zoster virus
随伴性（ずいはんせい）contingency
水分（すいぶん）fluid
水分出納（すいぶんすいとう）fluid intake and output
水分摂取（すいぶんせっしゅ）fluid intake
†水分バランス（すいぶんばらんす）fluid balance
†水分補給（すいぶんほきゅう）rehydration
†水疱（すいほう）blister
髄膜炎（ずいまくえん）meningitis
髄膜白血病（ずいまくはっけつびょう）meningeal leukemia
†睡眠（すいみん）sleep
睡眠関連呼吸障害（すいみんかんれんこきゅうしょうがい）sleep-related breathing disorder
睡眠剤（すいみんざい）hypnotic
睡眠時無呼吸（すいみんじむこきゅう）sleep apnea

睡眠時無呼吸症候群（すいみんじむこきゅうしょうこうぐん）sleep apnea syndrome ; SAS
睡眠障害（すいみんしょうがい）sleep disorder ; somnipathy ; sleep disturbance
睡眠薬（すいみんやく）hypnotic drug ; sleep medicine ; sleeping pill
水溶性バッグ（すいようせいばっぐ）water-soluble bag
水溶性ビタミン（すいようせいびたみん）water-soluble vitamin
スウェーデン式膝装具（すうぇーでんしきひざそうぐ）Swedish knee cage
数値評価スケール（すうちひょうかすけーる）Numeric Rating Scale ; NRS
数理課（すうりか）Actuarial Affairs Division
スキナー・ボックス（すきなー・ぼっくす）Skinner box
スキーマ（すきーま）schema
スキルドナーシングホーム（すきるどなーしんぐほーむ）skilled nursing home
スキンシップ（すきんしっぷ）physical contact
すくみ足（すくみあし）frozen gait
スクラブ法（すくらぶほう）scrub method
スクリーニング（すくりーにんぐ）screening
スクールカウンセラー（すくーるかうんせらー）school counselor
スクールソーシャルワーカー（すくーるそーしゃるわーかー）school social worker
スケラキシン（すけらきしん）Skelaxin
巣状（すじょう）focal
スタグフレーション（すたぐふれーしょん）stagflation
スタッフモデル（すたっふもでる）staff model
スタビー（すたびー）stubby
スタビライザー（すたびらいざー）⇒立位保持装置
スタンプアガー法（すたんぷあがーほう）stamp agar method
†頭痛（ずつう）headache
スティグマ（すてぃぐま）stigma
ズデック骨萎縮（ずでっくこついしゅく）Sudeck atrophy
ステレオタイプ（すてれおたいぷ）stereotype
ステロイド（すてろいど）steroid
ストーマ（すとーま）stoma
ストーマケア（すとーまけあ）stoma care
ストーマ用品（すとーようひん）ostomy aid
ストライド（すとらいど）stride
ストライド長（すとらいどちょう）stride length
†ストレス（すとれす）stress
ストレス免疫訓練（すとれすめんえきくんれん）stress inoculation training
ストレッサー（すとれっさー）stressor
†ストレッチャー（すとれっちゃー）stretcher
ストレッチング（すとれっちんぐ）stretching
ストレングス（すとれんぐす）strength
†ストレングス視点（すとれんぐすしてん）strengths perspective
ストレングスモデル（すとれんぐすもでる）strength model ; strength-based model
スネアー（すねあー）snare
スネアー電気凝固（すねあーでんきぎょうこ）snare electrocoagulation
すのこ（すのこ）sunoko
†スーパーバイザー（すーぱーばいざー）supervisor
†スーパーバイジー（すーぱーばいじー）supervisee
†スーパービジョン（すーぱーびじょん）supervision
†スピリチュアルケア（すぴりちゅあるけあ）spiritual care
スピリチュアルペイン（すぴりちゅあるぺいん）spiritual pain
スピロノラクトン（すぴろのらくとん）spironolactone
スプリンクラー（すぷりんくらー）sprinkler
スプリント（すぷりんと）splint
滑り止め（すべりどめ）non-slip
滑り止めマット（すべりどめまっと）non-slip mat
スポーツ外傷（すぽーつがいしょう）athletic injury ; sports injury
スポーツ施設（すぽーつしせつ）sports facility
スポンジバス（すぽんじばす）sponge bath
スマトリプタン（すまとりぷたん）sumatriptan
住み替え（すみかえ）change of residence ; move
スモン（すもん）subacute myelopticoneuropathy ; SMON
スライディングスケール（すらいでぃんぐすけーる）sliding scale
スライディングチューブ（すらいでぃんぐちゅーぶ）sliding tube
スラム（すらむ）slum
擦り傷（すりきず）abrasion
刷り込み（すりこみ）imprinting
すりつけ板（すりつけいた）barrier-free threshold
すり減り現象（すりへりげんしょう）⇒ウェアリングオフ現象
スリング（すりんぐ）sling
スルファサラジン（するふぁさらじん）sulfasalazine
スルフォニル尿素（するふぉにるにょうそ）sulfonylurea
スロープ（すろーぷ）slope
スワブ採取（すわぶさいしゅ）⇒拭き取り採取
スワブ法（すわぶほう）⇒拭き取り法
スワンガンツカテーテル（すわんがんつかてーてる）Swan-Ganz catheter
スワンネック変形（すわんねっくへんけい）Swan neck deformity

せ

生延長（せいえんちょう）life extension
性格（せいかく）personality；character
性格検査（せいかくけんさ）personality test
税額控除（ぜいがくこうじょ）tax rebate
生活衛生課（せいかつえいせいか）Environmental Health Division
†生活援助（せいかつえんじょ）home helping
†生活環境（せいかつかんきょう）living environment
生活関連活動（せいかつかんれんかつどう）activities parallel to daily living：APDL
生活機能（せいかつきのう）life functioning
生活技能訓練（せいかつぎのうくんれん）life skills training
生活協同組合（せいかつきょうどうくみあい）co-operative union：CO-OP
生活空間（せいかつくうかん）life space；living space
生活空間危機介入（せいかつくうかんききかいにゅう）life space crisis intervention
生活権（せいかつけん）the right to live
生活構造（せいかつこうぞう）life structure
生活支援サービス（せいかつしえんさーびす）living support services
生活習慣（せいかつしゅうかん）lifestyle
†生活習慣病（せいかつしゅうかんびょう）lifestyle-related disease；lifestyle diseases
生活周期（せいかつしゅうき）life cycle
生活水準（せいかつすいじゅん）standards of living
生活相談員（せいかつそうだんいん）life management advisor
生活ニーズ（せいかつにーず）life needs
生活能力（せいかつのうりょく）ability to live
†生活の質（せいかつのしつ）quality of life：QOL
生活費用調整（せいかつひようちょうせい）cost-of-living adjustment：COLA
生活福祉資金（せいかつふくししきん）welfare fund
生活福祉資金貸付制度（せいかつふくししきんかしつけせいど）welfare fund loan system
†生活扶助（せいかつふじょ）daily-needs assistance
生活保護（せいかつほご）public assistance
生活保護基準（せいかつほごきじゅん）public assistance standards；standards of public assistance
生活保護受給者（せいかつほごじゅきゅうしゃ）public assistance recipient
生活保護費用（せいかつほごひよう）public assistance costs
生活保護法（せいかつほごほう）Public Assistance Law
生活満足度（せいかつまんぞくど）life satisfaction
生活モデル（せいかつもでる）life model

†生活歴（せいかつれき）life history
性感染症（せいかんせんしょう）sexually transmitted disease：STD
性器期（せいきき）genital stage
正規曲線（せいききょくせん）normal curve
正規雇用（せいきこよう）full-time employment
性機能障害（せいきのうしょうがい）sexual dysfunction
請求書（せいきゅうしょ）billing statement
正球性貧血（せいきゅうせいひんけつ）normocytic anemia
請求対象期間（せいきゅうたいしょうきかん）billing period
制御（せいぎょ）control and prevention
生業扶助（せいぎょうふじょ）occupational assistance
税金（ぜいきん）tax
税金還付（ぜいきんかんぷ）tax rebate
静菌作用（せいきんさよう）bacteriostatic action
税金滞納（ぜいきんたいのう）tax delinquency
税金滞納整理機構（ぜいきんたいのうせいりきこう）delinquent tax collection organization
整形靴（せいけいぐつ）corrective shoes；orthopedic shoes
整形外科（せいけいげか）orthopedics
生計費用（せいけいひよう）cost of living
†清潔（せいけつ）cleanness
清潔間欠尿法（せいけつかんけつどうにょうほう）clean intermittent catheterization：CIC
清潔区域（せいけつくいき）clean area
清潔手術（せいけつしゅじゅつ）clean surgery
清潔創（せいけつそう）clean wound
生検（せいけん）biopsy
生検鉗子（せいけんかんし）biopsy forceps
制限的サービス（せいげんてきさーびす）restrictive services
性行為（せいこうい）sexual activity
性行為感染症（せいこういかんせんしょう）sexually transmitted disease：STD
税控除（ぜいこうじょ）tax deduction
性交疼痛症（せいこうとうつうしょう）dyspareunia
成功報酬（せいこうほうしゅう）contingent fee；conditional fee
性差（せいさ）gender difference
正座位（せいざい）kneel sitting
政策コミュニティ（せいさくこみゅにてぃ）policy community
政策実施（せいさくじっし）policy implementation
政策立案者（せいさくりつあんしゃ）policymaker
静座不能（せいざふのう）akathisia
性差別（せいさべつ）sex discrimination
制酸剤（せいさんざい）antacid；acid-suppressive medication

介護保険・介護福祉等関連用語 和英

生産的福祉（せいさんてきふくし）productive welfare
生産年齢人口（せいさんねんれいじんこう）working-age population；productive age population
†清拭（せいしき）sponge bath
性指向障害（せいしこうしょうがい）sexual orientation disturbance
正常圧水頭症（せいじょうあつすいとうしょう）normal pressure hydrocephalus
正常血圧（せいじょうけつあつ）normal blood pressure
正常細菌叢（せいじょうさいきんそう）normal flora
清浄室（せいじょうしつ）clean room
正常値（せいじょうち）normal value
清浄度クラス（せいじょうどくらす）cleanliness class
生殖家族（せいしょくかぞく）family of procreation
生殖性（せいしょくせい）generatively
精神医学（せいしんいがく）psychiatry
精神依存（せいしんいぞん）psychological dependence
精神医療審査会（せいしんいりょうしんさかい）Committee on Mental Health
精神および行動の障害（せいしんおよびこうどうのしょうがい）mental and behavioral disorder
精神科医（せいしんかい）psychiatrist
†精神科ソーシャルワーカー（せいしんかそーしゃるわーかー）psychiatric social worker；PSW
成人型多能性体性幹細胞（せいじんがたたのうせいたいせいかんさいぼう）multipotent adult progenitor cell
精神科デイケア（せいしんかでいけあ）psychiatric day care
精神科デイケアセンター（せいしんかでいけあせんたー）psychiatric day care center
精神科訪問看護ケア（せいしんかほうもんかんごけあ）psychiatric home health care
精神科リハビリテーション（せいしんかりはびりてーしょん）psychiatric rehabilitation；psychosocial rehabilitation
成人教育（せいじんきょういく）adult education
成人呼吸窮迫症候群（せいじんこきゅうせっぱくしょうこうぐん）adult respiratory distress syndrome
精神作用剤（せいしんさようざい）psychoactive drug
†精神障害（せいしんしょうがい）psychiatric disorder；mental disability；mental disorder
精神障害高齢者（せいしんしょうがいこうれいしゃ）the mentally disabled elderly
精神障害児（せいしんしょうがいじ）the mentally disabled child
†精神障害者（せいしんしょうがいしゃ）the mentally disabled
精神障害者医療（せいしんしょうがいしゃいりょう）medical care for the mentally disabled
精神障害者運動（せいしんしょうがいしゃうんどう）movement for the mentally disabled
精神障害者援助（せいしんしょうがいしゃえんじょ）support for the mentally disabled
精神障害者介護（せいしんしょうがいしゃかいご）caring for the mentally disabled
精神障害者介護支援（せいしんしょうがいしゃかいごしえん）care management for the mentally disabled
精神障害者看護（せいしんしょうがいしゃかんご）nursing care for the mentally disabled
精神障害者居宅介護（せいしんしょうがいしゃきょたくかいご）home-based care for the mentally disabled
精神障害者居宅介護支援（せいしんしょうがいしゃきょたくかいごしえん）home-based care management for the mentally disabled
精神障害者更生相談所（せいしんしょうがいしゃこうせいそうだんしょ）rehabilitation counseling center for the mentally disabled
精神障害者雇用（せいしんしょうがいしゃこよう）employment of the mentally disabled
精神障害者雇用促進（せいしんしょうがいしゃこようそくしん）employment promotion for the mentally disabled
精神障害者雇用促進対策（せいしんしょうがいしゃこようそくしんたいさく）employment promotion policy for the mentally disabled
精神障害者雇用率（せいしんしょうがいしゃこようりつ）employment rates of the mentally disabled；employment rates for persons with mental disabilities
精神障害者在宅介護支援（せいしんしょうがいしゃざいたくかいごしえん）home care management for the mentally disabled
精神障害者作業所（せいしんしょうがいしゃさぎょうしょ）workshop for the mentally disabled
精神障害者社会適応訓練（せいしんしょうがいしゃしゃかいてきおうくんれん）social skills training for the mentally disabled；social rehabilitation and training for people with mental disorders
精神障害者社会復帰施設（せいしんしょうがいしゃしゃかいふっきしせつ）social rehabilitation and training facility for the mentally disabled；rehabilitation center for the mentally disabled
精神障害者授産施設（せいしんしょうがいしゃじゅさんしせつ）sheltered workshop for the mentally disabled；sheltered workshop for people with mental disorders
精神障害者小規模作業所（せいしんしょうがいしゃし

ょうきほさぎょうしょ）small-scale workshop for the mentally disabled
精神障害者生活訓練施設（せいしんしょうがいしゃせいかつくんれんしせつ）daily living training facility for mentally disabled
精神障害者地域生活援護（せいしんしょうがいしゃちいきせいかつえんご）community living support for the mentally disabled
精神障害者地域生活支援事業（せいしんしょうがいしゃちいきせいかつしえんじぎょう）community living support program for the mentally disabled
精神障害者地域生活支援センター（せいしんしょうがいしゃちいきせいかつしえんせんたー）community living support center for the mentally disabled
精神障害者通所授産施設（せいしんしょうがいしゃつうしょじゅさんしせつ）sheltered workshop for the mentally disabled
精神障害者福祉作業所（せいしんしょうがいしゃふくしさぎょうしょ）welfare workshop for the mentally disabled
精神障害者福祉ホーム（せいしんしょうがいしゃふくしほーむ）welfare home for the mentally disabled；welfare home for people with mental disorders
精神障害者扶助（せいしんしょうがいしゃふじょ）assistance for the mentally disabled
精神障害者向け民間サービス（せいしんしょうがいしゃむけみんかんさーびす）private services for the psychiatric patient
精神障害者療護施設（せいしんしょうがいしゃりょうごしせつ）custodial care facility for the mentally disabled
精神障害の診断と統計の手引き（せいしんしょうがいのしんだんととうけいのてびき）Diagnostic and Statistical Manual of Mental Disorders：DSM
精神・障害保健課（せいしん・しょうがいほけんか）Mental Health and Disability Health Division
精神障害幼児（せいしんしょうがいようじ）mentally disabled infant
精神障害老人（せいしんしょうがいろうじん）mentally disabled elder
成人潜在性自己免疫性糖尿病（せいじんせんざいせいじこめんえきせいとうにょうびょう）latent autoimmune diabetes in adults：LADA
精神遅滞（せいしんちたい）mental retardation：MR
成人デイケア（せいじんでいけあ）adult day care
成人デイケアセンター（せいじんでいけあせんたー）adult day care center
成人T細胞白血病・リンパ腫（せいじんてぃーさいぼうはっけつびょう・りんぱしゅ）adult T-cell leukemia：ATLL

成人デイサービスセンター（せいじんでいさーびすせんたー）adult day services center
成人デイセンター（せいじんでいせんたー）adult day center
精神的依存（せいしんてきいぞん）emotional dependency
精神的虐待（せいしんてきぎゃくたい）psychological abuse；mental abuse；emotional abuse
精神的適応力（せいしんてきてきおうりょく）mental competency
精神年齢（せいしんねんれい）mental age：MA
成人発症（せいじんはっしょう）adult-onset
成人発症関節リウマチ（せいじんはっしょうかんせつりうまち）adult-onset rheumatoid arthritis：AORA
精神病（せいしんびょう）psychosis；mental illness
成人病（せいじんびょう）adult disease
精神病院（せいしんびょういん）psychiatric hospital
精神病的行動（せいしんびょうてきこうどう）psychotic behavior
精神病理学（せいしんびょうりがく）psychopathology
精神病理学者（せいしんびょうりがくしゃ）psychopathologist
精神分析（せいしんぶんせき）psychoanalysis
精神分析家（せいしんぶんせきか）psychoanalyst
精神分析的心理療法（せいしんぶんせきてきしんりりょうほう）psychoanalytical psychotherapy
精神分析的パラダイム（せいしんぶんせきてきぱらだいむ）psychoanalytic paradigm
精神分析療法（せいしんぶんせきりょうほう）psychoanalytic therapy
精神分裂症（せいしんぶんれつびょう）schizophrenia
精神保健（せいしんほけん）mental health
精神保健及び精神障害者福祉に関する法律（せいしんほけんおよびせいしんしょうがいしゃふくしにかんするほうりつ）Health and Welfare Law for the Mentally Disabled
精神保健カウンセラー（せいしんほけんかうんせらー）mental health counselor
精神保健サービス（せいしんほけんさーびす）mental health services
精神保健指定医（せいしんほけんしていい）designated psychiatrist
精神保健ソーシャルワーカー（せいしんほけんそーしゃるわーかー）psychiatric social worker：PSW
精神保健福祉（せいしんほけんふくし）mental health and welfare
†精神保健福祉士（せいしんほけんふくしし）certified

psychiatric social worker：CPSW
精神保健福祉士法（せいしんほけんふくししほう）Certified Psychiatric Social Workers Act
精神保健福祉センター（せいしんほけんふくしせんたー）mental health and welfare center
精神保健福祉相談員（せいしんほけんふくしそうだんいん）advisor for the health and welfare of the mentally disabled；mental health and welfare counselor
精神保健福祉法（せいしんほけんふくしほう）Health and Welfare Law for the Mentally Disabled
成人保護サービス（せいじんほごさーびす）adult protective services
精神薬（せいしんやく）psychiatric medication；psychiatric drug
成人用顕現性不安尺度（せいじんようけんげんせいふあんしゃくど）Adult Manifest Anxiety Scale
成人養護施設（せいじんようごしせつ）adult foster care home
精神療法（せいしんりょうほう）psychotherapy；psychological therapy
性染色体（せいせんしょくたい）sex chromosome
生前信託（せいぜんしんたく）living trust
清掃（せいそう）cleaning
生存権（せいぞんけん）the right to a decent standard of living
生態学（せいたいがく）ecology
生態学的心理学（せいたいがくてきしんりがく）ecological psychology
生体肝移植（せいたいかんいしょく）living donor liver transplantation
生体工学（せいたいこうがく）bioengineering
生体消毒（せいたいしょうどく）antisepsis
生体消毒薬（せいたいしょうどくやく）antiseptic agent
生体電磁気学（せいたいでんじきがく）bioelectromagnetic
生体表面隔離（せいたいひょうめんかくり）body surface isolation
生体物質隔離（せいたいぶっしつかくり）body substance isolation
生体力学（せいたいりきがく）biomechanics；body mechanics
生体リズム（せいたいりずむ）biological rhythm
成長障害（せいちょうしょうがい）failure to thrive：FTT
成長ホルモン（せいちょうほるもん）growth hormone
制定法文書（せいていほうぶんしょ）statutory instrument
静的安定性（せいてきあんていせい）static stability
性的逸脱行為（せいてきいつだつこうい）deviate sexual intercourse
性的虐待（せいてきぎゃくたい）sexual abuse
性的暴力（せいてきぼうりょく）sexual violence
性的マイノリティ（せいてきまいのりてぃ）sexual minority
性同一性障害（せいどういつせいしょうがい）gender identity disorder：GID
制吐剤（せいとざい）antiemetic
生年月日（せいねんがっぴ）date of birth
青年期心理学（せいねんきしんりがく）adolescent psychology
成年後見（せいねんこうけん）adult guardianship
成年後見監督人（せいねんこうけんかんとくにん）supervisor of adult guardian
†成年後見制度（せいねんこうけんせいど）adult guardianship system
成年後見人（せいねんこうけんにん）adult guardian
正の強化（せいのきょうか）positive reinforcement
正の罰（せいのばつ）positive punishment
†整髪（せいはつ）styling and setting hair
政府開発援助（せいふかいはつえんじょ）official development assistance：ODA
政府関係法人労働組合連合（せいふかんけいほうじんろうどうくみあいれんごう）Labor Federation of Government Related Organizations
政府管掌（せいふかんしょう）government administered
政府管掌健康保険（せいふかんしょうけんこうほけん）government administered health insurance；government sponsored health insurance
政府固有活動（せいふこゆうかつどう）inherently governmental activity
生物学的応答調節物質（せいぶつがくてきおうとうちょうせつぶっしつ）biologic response modifier
生物学的治療法（せいぶつがくてきりょうほう）biological therapy
生物学パラダイム（せいぶつがくぱらだいむ）biological paradigm
生物年齢（せいぶつねんれい）biological age
性別（せいべつ）gender
性別役割分業（せいべつやくわりぶんぎょう）sexual division of labor
性暴力被害者支援看護職（せいぼうりょくひがいしゃしえんかんごしょく）sexual assault nurse examiner
整脈（せいみゃく）eurhythmia
生命・医療倫理（せいめい・いりょうりんり）biomedical ethics
生命サポートサービス（せいめいさぽーとさーびす）advanced life support：ALS
†生命の延長（せいめいのえんちょう）extension of maximum life span

生命表（せいめいひょう）life table
生命保険（せいめいほけん）life insurance
生命保険料（せいめいほけんりょう）life insurance premium
†生命倫理（せいめいりんり）bioethics
性役割（せいやくわり）gender role
†整容（せいよう）personal hygiene
西洋医学（せいよういがく）western medicine
整容介護（せいようかいご）personal hygiene care
整容介助（せいようかいじょ）personal hygiene assistance；assistance with personal hygiene
整容動作（せいようどうさ）personal hygiene activity
生理的欲求（せいりてきよっきゅう）physiological needs
政令指定都市（せいれいしていとし）government ordinance city；city designated by government ordinance
世界人権宣言（せかいじんけんせんげん）Universal Declaration of Human Rights：UDHR
世界大恐慌（せかいだいきょうこう）Great Depression
世界的老化（せかいてきろうか）global aging
†世界保健機関（せかいほけんきかん）World Health Organization：WHO
世界保健機関憲章（せかいほけんきかんけんしょう）Constitution of the World Health Organization
セカンドオピニオン（せかんどおぴにおん）second opinion
咳（せき）cough
赤外線療法（せきがいせんりょうほう）infrared therapy
赤十字（せきじゅうじ）Red Cross
脊髄症（せきずいしょう）myelopathy
脊髄小脳変性症（せきずいしょうのうへんせいしょう）spinocerebellar degeneration：spinocerebellar ataxia
†脊髄損傷（せきずいそんしょう）spinal cord injury：SCI
脊髄反射（せきずいはんしゃ）spinal reflex
咳喘息（せきぜんそく）cough variant asthma：CVA
脊柱管狭窄症（せきちゅうかんきょうさくしょう）spinal canal stenosis
脊柱起立筋（せきちゅうきりつきん）erector spinae
†脊椎圧迫骨折（せきついあっぱくこっせつ）vertebral compression fracture
脊椎X線（せきついえっくすせん）spinal X-ray
脊椎穿刺（せきついせんし）spinal tap
責任（せきにん）responsibility
セクシャルハラスメント（せくしゃるはらすめんと）sexual harassment
セクシュアリティ（せくしゅありてぃ）sexuality
セクシュアルヘルス（せくしゅあるへるす）sexual health
ゼストリル（ぜすとりる）Zestril
†世帯（せたい）household
世代（せだい）generation
世代間関係（せだいかんかんけい）intergenerational relations
世代間境界（せだいかんきょうかい）generation boundary
世代間ケア（せだいかんけあ）intergenerational care
世代間再分配（せだいかんさいぶんぱい）intergenerational redistribution
世代間扶養（せだいかんふよう）intergenerational support
世代間紛争（せだいかんふんそう）intergenerational conflict
世帯構造（せたいこうぞう）⇒家族構造
世帯単位の原則（せたいたんいのげんそく）principle of public assistance on a household basis
舌咽呼吸（ぜついんこきゅう）glossopharyngeal breathing
舌咽神経痛（ぜついんしんけいつう）glossopharyngeal neuralgia
舌下錠（ぜっかじょう）sublingual tablet
舌下腺（ぜっかせん）sublingual gland；sublingual
赤血球（せっけっきゅう）red blood cell：RBC
赤血球沈降速度（せっけっきゅうちんこうそくど）erythrocyte sedimentation rate：ESR
舌根沈下（ぜっこんちんか）tongue swallowing
摂取熱量（せっしゅねつりょう）caloric intake
†摂食（せっしょく）food intake
絶食（ぜっしょく）nothing by mouth [nulla per os]：NPO
接触感染（せっしょくかんせん）contact infection
接触寒天培地（せっしょくかんてんばいち）contact plate
†摂食障害（せっしょくしょうがい）eating disorder
摂食制限（せっしょくせいげん）feeding restriction
接触伝播（せっしょくでんぱ）contact transmission
接触培地（せっしょくばいち）contact plate
接触反射（せっしょくはんしゃ）contact reflection
接触法（せっしょくほう）contact method
接触予防策（せっしょくよぼうさく）contact precaution
絶対閾（ぜったいいき）absolute threshold
絶対筋力（ぜったいきんりょく）absolute muscle strength
絶対湿度（ぜったいしつど）absolute humidity
絶対的貧困（ぜったいてきひんこん）absolute poverty

絶対不応期（ぜったいふおうき）absolute refractory period
切断（せつだん）amputation
切断端（せつだんたん）⇒断端
設置基準（せっちきじゅん）requirements for establishment
Z値（ぜっち）z value
切迫性尿失禁（せっぱくせいにょうしっきん）urge incontinence
説明責任（せつめいせきにん）accountability
セツルメント（せつるめんと）social settlement
セドンの分類（せどんのぶんるい）Seddon's classification
ゼニカル（ぜにかる）Xenical
セビボ（せびぼ）Sebivo
セーフティネット（せーふてぃねっと）safety net
セミクリティカル（せみくりてぃかる）semicritical
†セミファーラー位（せみふぁーらーい）semi-Fowler's position
背もたれ（せもたれ）backrest
セルトラリン（せるとらりん）sertraline
セルフアドボカシー運動（せるふあどぼかしーうんどう）⇒自己擁護運動
†セルフケア（せるふけあ）self-care
セルフケアプラン（せるふけあぷらん）self-care plan
セルフケアマネジメント（せるふけあまねじめんと）self-care management
セルフコントロール（せるふこんとろーる）self-control
†セルフヘルプグループ（せるふへるぷぐるーぷ）self-help group；SHG
セルフメディケーション（せるふめでぃけーしょん）self-medication
セレギリン（せれぎりん）selegiline
セレコキシブ（せれこきしぶ）celecoxib
セレニウム（せれにうむ）selenium
セレブレックス（せれぶれっくす）Celebrex
ゼロ肢位（ぜろしい）zero position
セロトニン（せろとにん）serotonin
セロトニン・ノルアドレナリン再取り込み阻害薬（せろとにん・のるあどれなりんさいとりこみそがいやく）serotonin-norepinephrine reuptake inhibitor；SNRI
世論調査（せろんちょうさ）public opinion poll
†繊維（せんい）fiber
前意識（ぜんいしき）preconscious
線維自発電位（せんいじはつでんい）fibrillation potential
線維束自発電位（せんいそくじはつでんい）fasciculation potential
線維タイプグループ化（せんいたいぷぐるーぷか）fiber type grouping

船員保険（せんいんほけん）Seamen's Insurance
船員保険法（せんいんほけんほう）Seamen's Insurance Law
†全援助（ぜんえんじょ）total assistance
遷延性意識障害（せんえんせいいしきしょうがい）persistent disturbance of consciousness
全介護（ぜんかいご）total care
全介助（ぜんかいじょ）total assistance
†洗顔（せんがん）face cleaning；face washing
前期高齢者（ぜんきこうれいしゃ）elderly aged between 65 and 74；young-old
潜血試験（せんけつしけん）occult blood test
善行（ぜんこう）beneficence
善行原理（ぜんこうげんり）principle of beneficence
前向性健忘（ぜんこうせいけんぼう）anterograde amnesia
全国健康福祉祭（ぜんこくけんこうふくしまつり）National Health and Welfare Festival
全国社会福祉協議会（ぜんこくしゃかいふくしきょうぎかい）Japan National Council of Social Welfare
全国有料老人ホーム協会（ぜんこくゆうりょうろうじんほーむきょうかい）Japanese Association of Retirement Housing
全国老人クラブ連合会（ぜんこくろうじんくらぶれんごうかい）Japan Federation of Senior Citizens' Club, Inc
全国老人デイ・ケア連絡協議会（ぜんこくろうじんでい・けあれんらくきょうぎかい）Adult Day-care Liaison Council Japan
仙骨部（せんこつぶ）sacral region
†洗剤（せんざい）detergent
洗剤アレルギー（せんざいあれるぎー）detergent allergy
潜在意識（せんざいいしき）subconscious mind
潜在内容（せんざいないよう）latent content
潜在ニーズ（せんざいにーず）potential needs
潜時（せんじ）latency
全色盲（ぜんしきもう）total color blindness
穿刺細胞診（せんしさいぼうしん）needle cytology
前室（ぜんしつ）anteroom
全失語（ぜんしつご）total aphasia；global aphasia
腺腫（せんしゅ）adenoma
†洗浄（せんじょう）washing
洗浄細胞診（せんじょうさいぼうしん）lavage cytology
洗浄消毒器（せんじょうしょうどくき）washer disinfector
洗浄滅菌器（せんじょうめっきんき）washer sterilizer
占床率（せんしょうりつ）occupancy rate

染色体（せんしょくたい）chromosome
† 染色体異常（せんしょくたいいじょう）chromosomal abnormality；abnormal chromosome
† 全人格的ケア（ぜんじんかくてきけあ）total personal care
先進国（せんしんこく）developed country
全身性エリテマトーデス（ぜんしんせいえりてまとーです）systemic lupus erythematosus；SLE
全身性紅斑性狼瘡（ぜんしんせいこうはんせいろうそう）systemic lupus erythematosus；SLE
† 全身清拭（ぜんしんせいしき）full-body sponge bath
全身性進行性硬化症（ぜんしんせいしんこうせいこうかしょう）progressive systemic sclerosis
全人的医療（ぜんじんてきいりょう）holistic medicine
† 全身浴（ぜんしんよく）full-body bath
全数調査（ぜんすうちょうさ）complete survey
前脊髄動脈症候群（ぜんせきずいどうみゃくしょうこうぐん）anterior spinal artery syndrome
漸増抵抗訓練（ぜんぞうていこうくんれん）progressive resistance exercise
† 尖足（せんそく）foot drop
喘息（ぜんそく）asthma
喘息発作（ぜんそくほっさ）asthmatic attack
全体的機能評価（ぜんたいてききのうひょうか）Global Assessment of Functioning；GAF
全体的評価尺度（ぜんたいてきひょうかしゃくど）Global Assessment Scale；GAS
全体論（ぜんたいろん）holism
† 洗濯（せんたく）laundry
洗濯板（せんたくいた）rubbing board
洗濯機（せんたくき）washing machine
洗濯室（せんたくしつ）laundry room
選択的最適化論（せんたくてきさいてきかろん）selective optimization with compensation
選択的情報提供（せんたくてきじょうほうていきょう）selective dissemination of information；SDI
選択的制度困窮対象者（せんたくてきせいどこんきゅうたいしょうしゃ）optional categorically needy
選択的セロトニン再取り込み阻害薬（せんたくてきせろとにんさいとりこみそがいやく）selective serotonin reuptake inhibitor；SSRI
選択的抽出（せんたくてきちゅうしゅつ）selective abstraction
洗濯用合成洗剤（せんたくようごうせいせんざい）laundry synthetic detergent
洗濯用石鹸（せんたくようせっけん）laundry soap
先端巨大症（せんたんきょだいしょう）acromegaly
全置換型人工心臓（ぜんちかんがたじんこうしんぞう）total artificial heart
前庭眼反射（ぜんていがんはんしゃ）vestibulo-ocular reflex
前庭障害（ぜんていしょうがい）vestibular dysfunction
前庭動眼反射（ぜんていどうがんはんしゃ）vestibulo-ocular reflex
先天異常（せんてんいじょう）congenital anomaly
先天奇形（せんてんきけい）congenital malformation
先天性筋緊張低下（せんてんせいきんきんちょうていか）congenital hypotonia
先天性筋ジストロフィー（せんてんせいきんじすとろふぃー）congenital muscular dystrophy
先天性股関節脱臼（せんてんせいこかんせつだっきゅう）luxatio coxae congenita；congenital hip dislocation
先天性ネフローゼ症候群（せんてんせいねふろーぜしょうこうぐん）congenital nephrotic syndrome
銭湯（せんとう）public bath house
蠕動運動（ぜんどううんどう）peristalsis
前頭側頭型認知症（ぜんとうそくとうがたにんちしょう）front-temporal dementia
前頭葉（ぜんとうよう）frontal lobe
前頭葉障害（ぜんとうようしょうがい）frontal lobe dysfunction
前頭葉症状（ぜんとうようしょうじょう）frontal lobe syndrome
† 洗髪（せんぱつ）shampooing；hair washing
先発薬品（せんぱつやくひん）brand name medication
全般性不安障害（ぜんぱんせいふあんしょうがい）generalized anxiety disorder；GAD
潜伏感染（せんぷくかんせん）latent infection
潜伏期（せんぷくき）latency period
潜伏期保菌者（せんぷくきほきんしゃ）incubation carrier
選別主義（せんべつしゅぎ）selectivism
選別的サービス（せんべつてきさーびす）selective services
喘鳴（ぜんめい）wheeze
全面依存（ぜんめんいぞん）total dependence
洗面器（せんめんき）washbowl
全面接触ソケット（ぜんめんせっしょくそけっと）total contact socket
† せん妄（せんもう）delirium
全盲（ぜんもう）total blindness
せん妄評価尺度（せんもうひょうかしゃくど）Delirium Rating Scale
専門（せんもん）profession
専門医（せんもんい）medical specialist
専門化（せんもんか）professionalization
専門家（せんもんか）expert
専門看護師（せんもんかんごし）clinical nurse specialist；CNS

介護保険・介護福祉等関連用語 和英

専門職（せんもんしょく）professional
専門職団体（せんもんしょくだんたい）professional association
専門性（せんもんせい）professionalism
前立腺炎（ぜんりつせんえん）prostatitis
前立腺癌（ぜんりつせんがん）prostate cancer；carcinoma of the prostate
前立腺疾患（ぜんりつせんしっかん）prostate disease
前立腺特異抗原（ぜんりつせんとくいこうげん）prostate specific antigen
前立腺肥大症（ぜんりつせんひだいしょう）benign prostatic hyperplasia
前輪歩行器（ぜんりんほこうき）front-wheel walker
前弯（ぜんわん）lordosis
前腕義手（ぜんわんぎしゅ）transradial prosthesis；below-elbow prosthesis
前腕切断（ぜんわんせつだん）below-elbow amputation

そ

総医療費支出（そういりょうひしゅつ）total medical expenditures
総医療費用（そういりょうひよう）total medical costs
†総入れ歯（そういれば）full denture
†躁うつ病（そううつびょう）manic depressive psychosis
爪炎（そうえん）onychia
騒音（そうおん）noise
爪下血腫（そうかけっしゅ）subungual hematoma
創感染（そうかんせん）wound infection
臓器移植（ぞうきいしょく）organ transplantation
早期介入（そうきかいにゅう）early intervention
臓器提供（ぞうきていきょう）organ donation
†早期発見（そうきはっけん）early detection
双極Ⅰ型障害（そうきょくⅠがたしょうがい）bipolar Ⅰ disorder
双極性障害（そうきょくせいしょうがい）bipolar disorder
双極Ⅱ型障害（そうきょくⅡがたしょうがい）bipolar Ⅱ disorder
早期離床（そうきりしょう）early ambulation
†装具（そうぐ）orthosis；brace
装具学（そうぐがく）orthotics
装具療法（そうぐりょうほう）orthotic treatment
送迎（そうげい）transportation
送迎サービス（そうげいさーびす）transportation services
送迎車（そうげいしゃ）transportation vehicle
総血球数（そうけっきゅうすう）complete blood count：CBC

総合購入（そうごうこうにゅう）total purchasing
爪甲鉤弯症（そうこうこうわんしょう）onychogryphosis
総合世帯調査（そうごうせたいちょうさ）general household survey
総合相談（そうごうそうだん）comprehensive consultation
総合的品質管理活動（そうごうてきひんしつかんりかつどう）total quality management：TQM
総合病院（そうごうびょういん）comprehensive hospital
相互扶助（そうごふじょ）mutual aid
総コレステロール（そうこれすてろーる）total cholesterol
葬祭給付（そうさいきゅうふ）burial and funeral benefit
葬祭手当（そうさいてあて）burial and funeral expenses allowance
葬祭費出（そうさいひしゅつ）burial and funeral expenses
葬祭費用（そうさいひよう）burial and funeral costs
葬祭扶助（そうさいふじょ）burial and funeral assistance
†掃除（そうじ）cleaning；cleanup
掃除機（そうじき）vacuum cleaner
爪ジストロフィー（そうじすとろふぃー）onychodystrophy
†喪失体験（そうしつたいけん）lost experience
掃除用具（そうじようぐ）cleaning equipment
創傷ケア（そうしょうけあ）wound care
創傷被覆材（そうしょうひふくざい）wound dressing
装飾ハンド（そうしょくはんど）cosmetic hand
装飾用義手（そうしょくようぎしゅ）cosmetic〈non-functional〉upper limb prosthesis
爪真菌症（そうしんきんしょう）onychomycosis
創設家族（そうせつかぞく）family of procreation
相続（そうぞく）inheritance
相続税（そうぞくぜい）death tax
相対危険（そうたいきけん）relative risk
相談援助（そうだんえんじょ）counseling & support
相談センター（そうだんせんたー）advisory center
早発性アルツハイマー病（そうはつせいあるつはいまーびょう）early-onset Alzheimer's disease
増分閾（ぞうぶんいき）incremental threshold
創分類（そうぶんるい）wound classification
相貌失認（そうぼうしつにん）prosopagnosia
僧帽弁狭窄症（そうぼうべんきょうさくしょう）mitral stenosis
僧帽弁閉鎖不全（そうぼうべんへいさふぜん）mitral regurgitation

総務課（そうむか）General Affairs Division
掻痒感（そうようかん）itching
層流（そうりゅう）laminar air flow：LAF
早老症（そうろうしょう）progeria
阻害因子（そがいいんし）inhibitor
遡及適用（そきゅうてきよう）retroactive indication
遡及賦課（そきゅうふか）retrospective charge
†側臥位（そくがい）side-lying position
測色（そくしょく）colorimetry
塞栓（そくせん）embolism
促通手技（そくつうしゅぎ）facilitation technique
足底接地（そくていせっち）foot flat
足底板（そくていばん）insole
足板（そくばん）foot plate
足病（そくびょう）podiatric medicine
足病医（そくびょうい）podiatrist
側面つまみ（そくめんつまみ）lateral pinch
†足浴（そくよく）foot bath
粟粒結核症（ぞくりゅうけっかくしょう）miliary tuberculosis
側弯（そくわん）scoliosis
側弯症装具（そくわんしょうそうぐ）Milwaukee brace
ソケット（そけっと）socket
組織（そしき）organization
組織灌流（そしきかんりゅう）tissue perfusion
組織社会化（そしきしゃかいか）organizational socialization
組織的失敗（そしきてきしっぱい）systemic failure
組織的成功（そしきてきせいこう）systemic success
粗死亡率（そしぼうりつ）crude mortality rate；crude death rate
†咀嚼（そしゃく）mastication；chewing
咀嚼機能障害（そしゃくきのうしょうがい）masticatory disorder
咀嚼筋炎（そしゃくきんえん）masticatory myositis
咀嚼障害（そしゃくしょうがい）mastication disorder；masticatory disturbance
咀嚼問題（そしゃくもんだい）chewing problem
ソーシャルアクション（そーしゃるあくしょん）social action
ソーシャルインクルージョン（そーしゃるいんくるーじょん）social inclusion
ソーシャルケースワーク（そーしゃるけーすわーく）social case work
ソーシャルサービス（そーしゃるさーびす）social services
ソーシャルサポート（そーしゃるさぽーと）social support
ソーシャルサポート・ネットワーク（そーしゃるさぽーと・ねっとわーく）social support network
ソーシャルスキル（そーしゃるすきる）social skills

ソーシャルスキル・トレーニング（そーしゃるすきる・とれーにんぐ）social skills training：SST
ソーシャルリスクマネジメント（そーしゃるりすくまねじめんと）social risk management
†ソーシャルワーカー（そーしゃるわーかー）social worker：SW
ソーシャルワーク（そーしゃるわーく）social work
ソーシャルワーク学士号（そーしゃるわーくがくしごう）Bachelor of Social Work：BSW
ソーシャルワーク修士号（そーしゃるわーくしゅうしごう）Master of Social Work：MSW
ソーシャルワーク博士号（そーしゃるわーくはかせごう）Doctor of Philosophy (PhD) in Social Work
ソーシャルワークリサーチ（そーしゃるわーくりさーち）social work research
ゾスタバックス（ぞすたばっくす）Zostavax
租税（そぜい）taxation
蘇生処置拒否（そせいしょちきょひ）Do Not Resuscitate：DNR
租税負担（そぜいふたん）tax burden
租税負担率（そぜいふたんりつ）tax burden ratio
租税優遇（そぜいゆうぐう）tax-privileged
粗大運動能力（そだいうんどうのうりょく）gross motor function
措置期間（そちきかん）placement period
措置権者（そちけんしゃ）administering authority
†措置制度（そちせいど）client allocation system
†措置費（そちひ）client allocation costs
速乾性擦式消毒薬（そっかんせいさつしきしょうどくやく）waterless antiseptic agent
速乾性手洗い用製剤（そっかんせいてあらいようせいざい）waterless handwashing product
外がえし（そとがえし）eversion
そとわ（そとわ）toe out
ソナタ（そなた）Sonata
ゾーニング（ぞーにんぐ）zoning
その他の衛生材料（そのほかのえいせいざいりょう）other sanitary supplies
ゾビラックス（ぞびらっくす）Zovirax
ゾーミッグ（ぞーみっぐ）Zomig
ソミーブレース（そみーぶれーす）SOMI brace：sterno-occipital-mandibular-immobilizer brace
ゾルピデム（ぞるぴでむ）zolpidem
ゾルミトリプタン（ぞるみとりぷたん）zolmitriptan
ゾロフト（ぞろふと）Zoloft
損害賠償請求権（そんがいばいしょうせいきゅうけん）the right to demand the compensation for damage
尊厳（そんげん）dignity
尊厳死（そんげんし）death with dignity
尊厳死宣言書（そんげんしせんげんしょ）living will
尊厳死法（そんげんしほう）Death with Dignity Act
尊厳のある生活（そんげんのあるせいかつ）life with

介護保険・介護福祉等関連用語 和英

dignity
尊厳の保持（そんげんのほじ）maintenance of the dignity

た

体位（たいい）position
体育（たいいく）gymnastics
体位設定（たいいせってい）positioning
第一号被保険者（だいいちごうひほけんしゃ）the first insured
第一次貧困（だいいちじひんこん）primary poverty
体位ドレナージ（たいいどれなーじ）postural drainage
体位排痰法（たいいはいたんほう）postural drainage
†体位変換（たいいへんかん）change of position
退院（たいいん）discharge
退院計画（たいいんけいかく）discharge planning
退院時清掃（たいいんじせいそう）discharge cleaning
退院調整（たいいんちょうせい）discharge management
大うつ病（だいうつびょう）major depression
体液（たいえき）body fluid
退役軍人（たいえきぐんじん）veteran
†体温（たいおん）body temperature
体温計（たいおんけい）thermometer
†体温測定（たいおんそくてい）measurement of body temperature
体温測定計（たいおんそくていけい）medical thermometer
体温調節（たいおんちょうせつ）thermoregulation
体温調節障害（たいおんちょうせつしょうがい）disturbance of thermoregulation
体外診断検査（たいがいしんだんけんさ）in vitro diagnostic test
体外診断薬（たいがいしんだんやく）in-vitro diagnostic reagent；in-vitro diagnostics
体幹（たいかん）truncus
体幹装具（たいかんそうぐ）spinal orthosis
大気汚染（たいきおせん）air pollution
待機期間（たいききかん）waiting period
待機者（たいきしゃ）applicants on the waiting list
待機者リスト（たいきしゃりすと）waiting list
待機的心臓カテーテル検査（たいきてきしんぞうかてーてるけんさ）elective cardiac catheterization
耐久医療機器（たいきゅういりょうきき）durable medical equipment；DME
耐久性（たいきゅうせい）⇒持久性
大球性貧血（だいきゅうせいひんけつ）macrocytic anemia
太極拳（たいきょくけん）tai chi

体験としての障害（たいけんとしてのしょうがい）experienced illness
†退行（たいこう）regression
退行行動（たいこうこうどう）regression behavior
代行者（だいこうしゃ）agent
対光反射（たいこうはんしゃ）light reflex
第三次教育（だいさんじきょういく）tertiary education
第三者委員（だいさんしゃいいん）third-party panel
第三者評価（だいさんしゃひょうか）third-party quality endorsement；third-party endorsement of quality　third-party certification
第三者評価制度（だいさんしゃひょうかせいど）third-party quality endorsement system；third-party certification program
第三世界（だいさんせかい）the third world
第三セクター（だいさんせくたー）third sector
胎児期障害（たいじきしょうがい）fetal disorder
胎児性アルコール症候群（たいじせいあるこーるしょうこうぐん）fetal alcohol syndrome
胎児性アルコール・スペクトラム障害（たいじせいあるこーる・すぺくとらむしょうがい）fetal alcohol spectrum disorder
代謝（たいしゃ）metabolism
代謝異常（たいしゃいじょう）metabolic disorder
大舎制（だいしゃせい）dormitory system
代謝性疾患（たいしゃせいしっかん）metabolic disease
代謝阻害剤（たいしゃそがいざい）metabolic inhibitor
代謝当量（たいしゃとうりょう）metabolic equivalent of task；MET
大衆社会（たいしゅうしゃかい）mass society
体重負荷（たいじゅうふか）weight-bearing
体重免荷装具（たいじゅうめんかそうぐ）non-weight bearing brace
大出血（だいしゅっけつ）hemorrhaging
退所（たいしょ）discharge from the facility
代償（だいしょう）compensation
代償運動（だいしょううんどう）compensatory movement
対象限定サーベイランス（たいしょうげんていさーべいらんす）targeted surveillance
対象者（たいしょうしゃ）subject
†帯状疱疹（たいじょうほうしん）herpes zoster；shingles
帯状疱疹後神経痛（たいじょうほうしんごしんけいつう）post-herpetic neuralgia；PHN
対症療法（たいしょうりょうほう）symptomatic therapy
退職（たいしょく）retirement
退職検査（たいしょくけんさ）⇒退職調査
退職者医療制度（たいしょくしゃいりょうせいど）

retiree health care system
退職者医療保険制度（たいしょくしゃいりょうほけんせいど）retiree health care insurance system
退職所得調査（たいしょくしょとくちょうさ）retirement earnings test
退職調査（たいしょくちょうさ）retirement test
退職手当（たいしょくてあて）retirement allowance ; severance package ; severance pay
対処行動（たいしょこうどう）coping behavior
退所後訪問指導（たいしょごほうもんしどう）follow-up visit after discharge
退所時情報（たいしょじじょうほう）discharge information
対処戦略（たいしょせんりゃく）coping strategy
対人援助技術（たいじんえんじょぎじゅつ）interpersonal helping skill
対人関係（たいじんかんけい）interpersonal relationship
対人関係スキル（たいじんかんけいすきる）interpersonal relationship skill
対人ケアサービス（たいじんけあさーびす）personal care services
対人社会サービス（たいじんしゃかいさーびす）personal social services
耐性（たいせい）tolerance
体性感覚（たいせいかんかく）somatic sensation
体性感覚誘発電位（たいせいかんかくゆうはつでんい）somatosensory evoked potential : SEP
タイゼカ（たいぜか）Tyzeka
体操（たいそう）exercise
代替医療（だいたいいりょう）alternative medicine
大腿義足（だいたいぎそく）above-knee prosthesis ; transfemoral prosthesis
代替機能（だいたいきのう）substitute function
大腿骨頸部骨折（だいたいこつけいぶこっせつ）femoral neck fracture
大腿骨転子部骨折（だいたいこつてんしぶこっせつ）subtrochanteric fracture
大腿骨転子疼痛症候群（だいたいこつてんしとうつうしょうこうぐん）greater trochanteric pain syndrome
†大腿四頭筋（だいたいしとうきん）quadriceps femoris
大腿切断（だいたいせつだん）above-knee amputation
大腿ソケット（だいたいそけっと）transfemoral socket
代替調剤（だいたいちょうざい）substitute medication
代替・補完医学（だいたい・ほかんいがく）complementary medicine
†大腸癌（だいちょうがん）colon cancer

大腸癌検診（だいちょうがんけんしん）colorectal cancer screening
大腸癌集団検診（だいちょうがんしゅうだんけんしん）group examination for the large bowel cancer
大腸ポリープ（だいちょうぽりーぷ）colorectal polyps ; large intestine polyps
大臀筋（だいでんきん）gluteus maximus muscle
大転子部（だいてんしぶ）greater trochanter
大転子部骨折（だいてんしぶこっせつ）greater trochanter fracture
耐糖能異常（たいとうのういじょう）impaired glucose tolerance : IGT
大動脈弁狭窄症（だいどうみゃくべんきょうさくしょう）aortic stenosis
†代読（だいどく）reading assistance
台所道具（だいどころどうぐ）utensil
大都市圏（だいとしけん）metropolitan area
第二号被保険者（だいにごうひほけんしゃ）the secondary insured
第二次貧困（だいにじひんこん）secondary poverty
滞納（たいのう）non-payment ; nonpayment
大発生（だいはっせい）⇒アウトブレイク
†代筆（だいひつ）allograph
退病院（たいびょういん）discharge from the hospital
太平洋諸島出身者（たいへいようしょとうしゅっしんしゃ）Pacific Islander
代弁者（だいべんしゃ）advocate
大麻（たいま）marijuana
怠慢（たいまん）neglect
タイムアウト（たいむあうと）time-out
代役（だいやく）substitute
代用（だいよう）substitute
耐容一日摂取量（たいよういちにちせっしゅりょう）tolerable daily intake
太陽光を利用した飲料水の殺菌法（たいようこうをりようしたいんりょうすいのさっきんほう）solar water disinfection : SODIS
耐容性（たいようせい）tolerance
代理（だいり）substitution
代理決定（だいりけってい）surrogate decision
代理出産（だいりしゅっさん）surrogacy ; surrogate delivery
代理受領（だいりじゅりょう）legal reception services
対立装具（たいりつそうぐ）opponens splint
対立バー（たいりつばー）opponens bar
†代理電話（だいりでんわ）telephone assistance
代理人（だいりにん）attorney-in-fact
代理判断（だいりはんだん）substituted judgment
体力（たいりょく）physical fitness
タイルモザイク（たいるもざいく）tile mosaic

介護保険・介護福祉等関連用語 和英

タイレノール（たいれのーる）Tylenol
†ダウン症候群（だうんしょうこうぐん）Down syndrome
唾液（だえき）saliva
唾液機能（だえききのう）saliva functioning
唾液分泌過多（だえきぶんぴつかた）hypersalivation
他害行為（たがいこうい）danger to others：DTO：danger to others〈DTO〉behavior
多価不飽和脂肪酸（たかふほうわしぼうさん）polyunsaturated fatty acid：PUFA
多関節性痛風（たかんせつせいつうふう）polyarticular gout
妥協（だきょう）compromise
ダグラス窩穿刺（だぐらすかせんし）culdocentesis
タクリン（たくりん）tacrine
宅老所（たくろうしょ）adult day care center
多系統萎縮症（たけいとういしゅくしょう）multiple system atrophy：MSA
多剤処方（たざいしょほう）polypharmacy
多剤耐性（たざいたいせい）multi-drug resistance：MDR
多剤耐性結核（たざいたいせいけっかく）multi-drug resistant tuberculosis：MDR-TB
多剤併用（たざいへいよう）polypharmacy
多次元的機能評価（たじげんてききのうひょうか）multidimensional functional assessment
多次元貧困指数（たじげんひんこんしすう）multidimensional poverty index：MPI
多シナプス反射（たしなぷすはんしゃ）polysynaptic reflex
多重債務（たじゅうさいむ）multiple debtor
多重人格性障害（たじゅうじんかくせいしょうがい）multiple personality disorder
多職種チーム（たしょくしゅちーむ）interdisciplinary team：IDT
多職種連携（たしょくしゅれんけい）interprofessional work
多職種連携教育（たしょくしゅれんけいきょういく）interprofessional education
多臓器不全（たぞうきふぜん）multiple organ failure
多臓器不全症候群（たぞうきふぜんしょうこうぐん）multiple organ dysfunction syndrome：MODS
多段階評価（ただんかいひょうか）Multilevel Assessment Instrument
†立ち上がり（たちあがり）sit to stand
立ち上がり運動（たちあがりうんどう）sit-to-stand exercise
立ち直り反応（たちなおりはんのう）righting reaction
†脱臼（だっきゅう）luxation；joint dislocation
タックスコード（たっくすこーど）tax code
脱健着患（だっけんちゃくかん）put clothing on the affected side and take the clothing off the unaffected side
脱施設（だつしせつ）deinstitutionalization
脱施設化（だつしせつか）deinstitutionalization
脱脂綿、ガーゼ、その他の衛生材料（だつしめん、がーぜ、そのほかのえいせいざいりょう）absorbent cotton, gauze and other sanitary supplies
脱神経（だつしんけい）denervation
脱髄（だつずい）demyelination
脱髄疾患（だつずいしっかん）demyelinating disease
†脱水症（だっすいしょう）dehydration
脱退一時金（だったいいちじきん）lump-sum withdrawal payments
脱退一時金裁定請求書（だったいいちじきんさいていせいきゅうしょ）claim form for the lump-sum withdrawal payments
脱抑制（だつよくせい）disinhibition
縦アーチ（たてあーち）longitudinal arch
多動（たどう）hyperkinesia；hyperkinesis
†他動運動（たどううんどう）passive exercise
他動可動域（たどうかどういき）passive range of motion
田中ビネー式知能検査（たなかびねーしきちのうけんさ）Tanaka-Binet Intelligence Test：Tanaka Binet Scale of Intelligence
多尿（たにょう）polyuria；excessive urine output
多発梗塞性認知症（たはつこうそくせいにんちしょう）multi-infarct dementia
多発性硬化症（たはつせいこうかしょう）multiple sclerosis：MS
多発性脳梗塞（たはつせいのうこうそく）multiple cerebral infarction
多発ニューロパチー（たはつにゅーろぱちー）polyneuropathy
WHO（だぶりゅえっちおー）World Health Organization
WHO三段階ラダー（だぶりゅえっちおーさんだんかいらだー）WHO's three-step pain ladder
ダブルバインド仮説（だぶるばいんどかせつ）⇒二重拘束説
多分化能（たぶんかのう）multipotent
食べ放題ブッフェ（たべほうだいぶっふぇ）all-you-can-eat buffet
多変量解析（たへんりょうかいせき）multivariate analysis；multivariate statistics
他法との給付調整（たほうとのきゅうふちょうせい）adjustment with other laws
打撲傷（だぼくしょう）bruise
ダーボン（だーぼん）Darvon
†ターミナルケア（たーみなるけあ）terminal care
タムスロシン（たむすろしん）tamsulosin

多面的療法（ためんてきりょうほう）multimodal therapy
多様性（たようせい）diversity
多様性と包括性（たようせいとほうかつせい）diversity and inclusion
タリウムスキャン（たりうむすきゃん）thallium scanning
単一フォトン断層撮影（たんいつふぉとんだんそうさつえい）single photon emission computed tomography：SPECT
単回使用器材（たんかいしようきざい）single-use device
団塊世代（だんかいせだい）⇒ベイビーブーム世代
段階保険料（だんかいほけんりょう）step-up contribution
単価契約（たんかけいやく）unit price contract
†短下肢装具（たんかしそうぐ）ankle-foot orthosis：AFO；short leg brace：SLB
短期記憶（たんききおく）short-term memory
短期ケア施設（たんきけあしせつ）short-term care facility
短期入所ケア（たんきにゅうしょけあ）short-stay care
短期入所療養介護（たんきにゅうしょりょうようかいご）short-stay health care
短期ボランティア（たんきぼらんてぃあ）short-term volunteer
短期目標（たんきもくひょう）short-term goal
短期療法（たんきりょうほう）brief therapy
男根期（だんこんき）phallic stage
段差（だんさ）threshold
†端座位（たんざい）sitting position
段差解消機（だんさかいしょうき）lifting platform
探査電極（たんさでんきょく）exploring electrode
段差の解消（だんさのかいしょう）elimination of thresholds
短時間・在宅労働課（たんじかん・ざいたくろうどうか）Part-Time Work and Home Work Division
単軸継手（たんじくつぎて）single axis joint
単シナプス反射（たんしなぷすはんしゃ）monosynaptic reflex
断酒会（だんしゅかい）drinking giving-up organization；Stop Drinking Alcohol Support Group
男女共同参画（だんじょきょうどうさんかく）equal participation of women and men
男女共同参画社会（だんじょきょうどうさんかくしゃかい）gender-equal society
単色光（たんしょくこう）monochromatic light
男女雇用機会均等法（だんじょこようきかいきんとうほう）Equal Employment Opportunity Laws
炭水化物（たんすいかぶつ）carbohydrate
胆石（たんせき）gallstone

断層撮影（だんそうさつえい）tomography
断続的休暇（だんぞくてききゅうか）intermittent leave
団体交渉（だんたいこうしょう）collective bargaining
短対立装具（たんたいりつそうぐ）short opponens hand orthosis
断端（だんたん）amputation stump
断端管理（だんたんかんり）stump care
断端神経痛（だんたんしんけいつう）stump pain
短断端（たんだんたん）short stump
断端痛（だんたんつう）stump pain
断端負荷ソケット（だんたんふかそけっと）end-bearing socket
断端袋（だんたんぶくろ）stump sock
単糖無水物（たんとうむすいぶつ）monosaccharide anhydride
単糖類（たんとうるい）monosaccharide
単独開業（たんどくかいぎょう）solo practice
単独開業医（たんどくかいぎょうい）solo practitioner
単独恐怖症（たんどくきょうふしょう）autophobia
タンニン（たんにん）tannin
ダンパー（だんぱー）damper
たんぱく質（たんぱくしつ）protein
たんぱく質エネルギー（たんぱくしつえねるぎー）protein energy
たんぱく質・エネルギー低栄養状態（たんぱくしつ・えねるぎーていえいようじょうたい）protein-energy malnutrition：PEM
蛋白尿（たんぱくにょう）albuminuria
ダンピング症候群（だんぴんぐしょうこうぐん）dumping syndrome
単麻痺（たんまひ）monoplegia
弾力性（だんりょくせい）elasticity

ち

チアガビン（ちあがびん）tiagabine
チアゾリジンジオン系薬剤（ちあぞりじんじおんけいやくざい）thiazolidinedione
†チアノーゼ（ちあのーぜ）cyanosis
地域（ちいき）community
地域一般病院（ちいきいっぱんびょういん）community general hospital
地域医療（ちいきいりょう）community medical care
地域医療計画（ちいきいりょうけいかく）community medical care plan
地域援助技術（ちいきえんじょぎじゅつ）community work
地域開発（ちいきかいはつ）community development

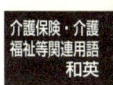

地域格差（ちいきかくさ）community difference；regional gap
地域加算（ちいきかさん）additional payment to community
地域看護（ちいきかんご）community nursing
地域居住施設ケアサービス（ちいききょじゅうしせつけあさーびす）community residential care services
地域居住施設サービス（ちいききょじゅうしせつさーびす）community residential services
地域ケア会議（ちいきけあかいぎ）community care meeting
地域ケアシステム（ちいきけあしすてむ）community care system
地域ケアネットワーク（ちいきけあねっとわーく）community care networks
地域計画（ちいきけいかく）community planning；regional planning；community plan
地域高齢者福祉（ちいきこうれいしゃふくし）community welfare for the elderly
地域高齢者福祉活動（ちいきこうれいしゃふくしかつどう）community welfare activities for the elderly
地域差調整係数（ちいきさちょうせいけいすう）geographic adjustment factor；GAF
地域支援（ちいきしえん）community support
地域支援事業（ちいきしえんじぎょう）community support project
地域社会（ちいきしゃかい）community
地域障害者福祉（ちいきしょうがいしゃふくし）community welfare for the disabled
地域障害者福祉活動（ちいきしょうがいしゃふくしかつどう）community welfare activities for the disabled
地域組織活動（ちいきそしきかつどう）community organization activity
地域病院（ちいきびょういん）community hospital
地域福祉（ちいきふくし）community welfare
地域福祉援助技術（ちいきふくしえんじょぎじゅつ）community welfare work
地域福祉課（ちいきふくしか）Community Welfare and Services Division
地域福祉活動（ちいきふくしかつどう）community welfare activity
地域福祉機関（ちいきふくしきかん）community welfare facility
地域福祉基金（ちいきふくしききん）community welfare fund
地域福祉計画（ちいきふくしけいかく）community welfare planning
地域福祉権利擁護事業（ちいきふくしけんりようごじぎょう）community advocacy services
地域福祉コーディネーター（ちいきふくしこーでぃねーたー）community welfare services coordinator
地域福祉サービス（ちいきふくしさーびす）community welfare services
地域福祉事業（ちいきふくしじぎょう）community welfare program
地域福祉事業者（ちいきふくしじぎょうしゃ）community welfare provider
地域福祉事業所（ちいきふくしじぎょうしょ）community welfare office
地域福祉施設（ちいきふくししせつ）community welfare facility
地域福祉センター（ちいきふくしせんたー）community welfare center
地域包括ケア（ちいきほうかつけあ）comprehensive community care
†地域包括支援センター（ちいきほうかつしえんせんたー）community comprehensive care center
地域保健（ちいきほけん）community health
地域保健医療（ちいきほけんいりょう）community health and medical care
地域保健医療計画（ちいきほけんいりょうけいかく）community health and medical care plan
地域保健法（ちいきほけんほう）Community Health Act
†地域密着サービス（ちいきみっちゃくがたさーびす）community-based care services
地域密着型通所介護（ちいきみっちゃくがたつうしょかいご）community-based day care services
地域密着型通所リハビリテーション（ちいきみっちゃくがたつうしょりはびりてーしょん）ambulatory community-based rehabilitation；community-based and outpatient rehabilitation
地域密着型訪問介護（ちいきみっちゃくがたほうもんかいご）home and community-based care
地域密着型訪問看護ケア（ちいきみっちゃくがたほうもんかんごけあ）home and community-based health care
地域密着型リハビリテーション（ちいきみっちゃくがたりはびりてーしょん）community-based rehabilitation
地域リハビリテーション（ちいきりはびりてーしょん）community rehabilitation
地域連携パス（ちいきれんけいぱす）liaison critical pathway
地域老人福祉（ちいきろうじんふくし）community welfare for the aged
地域老人福祉活動（ちいきろうじんふくしかつどう）community welfare activities for the aged
小さな政府（ちいさなせいふ）small government
†チェーンストークス呼吸（ちぇーんすとーくすこきゅう）Cheyne-stokes respiration
チェーンストークス精神病（ちぇーんすとーくすせい

しんびょう）Cheyne-stokes psychosis
チオレドキシン（ちおれどきしん）Thioredoxin
知覚（ちかく）sensation；perception
知覚過敏性大腿痛（ちかくかびんせいだいたいつう）meralgia paresthetica
知覚再教育（ちかくさいきょういく）re-education of sensation
知覚障害（ちかくしょうがい）sensory impairment
知覚能力の変移（ちかくのうりょくのへんい）sensory change
知覚麻痺（ちかくまひ）sensory paralysis；anesthesia
逐語反射（ちくごはんしゃ）word-for-word reflection
蓄積効果（ちくせきこうか）cumulative effect
蓄尿異常（ちくにょういじょう）urinary storage disturbance
†蓄尿障害（ちくにょうしょうがい）urinary storage disorder
致死性家族性不眠症（ちしせいかぞくせいふみんしょう）fatal familial insomnia
地誌的失認（ちしてきしつにん）topographical agnosia
致死率（ちしりつ）case-fatality rate
知性化（ちせいか）intellectualization
膣ケア（ちつけあ）vaginal care
窒息（ちっそく）asphyxia
窒息しそうな痛み（ちっそくしそうないたみ）strangling pain
知的財産（ちてきざいさん）intellectual property
†知的障害（ちてきしょうがい）mental retardation；MR；intellectual disorder
知的障害高齢者（ちてきしょうがいこうれいしゃ）the mentally retarded elderly；elderly person with mental retardation
知的障害児（ちてきしょうがいじ）the mentally retarded child；child with mental retardation
知的障害児施設（ちてきしょうがいじしせつ）facility for the mentally retarded children
†知的障害者（ちてきしょうがいしゃ）the mentally retarded；person with mental retardation
知的障害者医療（ちてきしょうがいしゃいりょう）medical care for the mentally retarded
知的障害者運動（ちてきしょうがいしゃうんどう）movement for the mentally retarded
知的障害者援助（ちてきしょうがいしゃえんじょ）support for the mentally retarded
知的障害者介護（ちてきしょうがいしゃかいご）caring for the mentally retarded；care for the mentally retarded
知的障害者介護支援（ちてきしょうがいしゃかいごしえん）care management for the mentally retarded

知的障害者居宅介護（ちてきしょうがいしゃきょたくかいご）home-based care for the mentally retarded
知的障害者居宅介護支援（ちてきしょうがいしゃきょたくかいごしえん）home-based care management for the mentally retarded
知的障害者居宅介護支援事業（ちてきしょうがいしゃきょたくかいごしえんじぎょう）home-based care management program for the mentally retarded
知的障害者グループホーム（ちてきしょうがいしゃぐるーぷほーむ）group home for the mentally retarded
知的障害者更生施設（ちてきしょうがいしゃこうせいしせつ）rehabilitation facility for the mentally retarded；rehabilitation facility for people with mental retardation
知的障害者更生相談所（ちてきしょうがいしゃこうせいそうだんしょ）rehabilitation counseling center for the mentally retarded
知的障害者在宅介護支援（ちてきしょうがいしゃざいたくかいごしえん）home care management for the mentally retarded
知的障害者作業所（ちてきしょうがいしゃさぎょうしょ）workshop for the mentally retarded
知的障害者授産施設（ちてきしょうがいしゃじゅさんしせつ）sheltered workshop for the mentally retarded；sheltered workshop for people with mental retardation
知的障害者相談員（ちてきしょうがいしゃそうだんいん）advisor for the mentally retarded；counselor for people with mental retardation
知的障害者短期入所（ちてきしょうがいしゃたんきにゅうしょ）short-stay for the mentally retarded
知的障害者短期入所事業（ちてきしょうがいしゃたんきにゅうしょじぎょう）short-stay program for the mentally retarded
知的障害者デイサービス（ちてきしょうがいしゃでいさーびす）day care services for the mentally retarded
知的障害者デイサービス事業（ちてきしょうがいしゃでいさーびすじぎょう）day care services program for the mentally retarded
知的障害者デイサービスセンター（ちてきしょうがいしゃでいさーびすせんたー）day services center for the mentally retarded
知的障害者の権利宣言（ちてきしょうがいしゃのけんりせんげん）Declaration on the Rights of Mentally Retarded Persons
知的障害者福祉（ちてきしょうがいしゃふくし）welfare for the mentally retarded
知的障害者福祉機関（ちてきしょうがいしゃふくしきかん）welfare agency for the mentally retarded

介護保険・介護福祉等関連用語 和英

知的障害者福祉作業所（ちてきしょうがいしゃふくしさぎょうしょ）welfare workshop for the mentally retarded
知的障害者福祉司（ちてきしょうがいしゃふくしし）welfare officer for the mentally retarded
知的障害者福祉事業所（ちてきしょうがいしゃふくしじぎょうしょ）welfare office for the mentally retarded
知的障害者福祉施設（ちてきしょうがいしゃふくししせつ）welfare facility for the mentally retarded
知的障害者福祉ホーム（ちてきしょうがいしゃふくしほーむ）welfare home for the mentally retarded
知的障害者扶助（ちてきしょうがいしゃふじょ）assistance for the mentally retarded
知的障害者ホームヘルプサービス（ちてきしょうがいしゃほーむへるぷさーびす）home help services for the mentally retarded
知的障害者向け民間サービス（ちてきしょうがいしゃむけみんかんさーびす）private services for the mentally retarded
知的障害幼児（ちてきしょうがいようじ）the mentally retarded infant；the mentally retarded baby；baby with mental retardation
知的障害老人（ちてきしょうがいろうじん）the elderly mentally retarded；elderly with mental retardation
知的所有権（ちてきしょゆうけん）intellectual property right
知的水準（ちてきすいじゅん）intellectual level
†知能（ちのう）intelligence
知能検査（ちのうけんさ）intelligence test
†知能指数（ちのうしすう）intelligence quotient；IQ
知能年齢（ちのうねんれい）intellectual age
遅発性アルツハイマー病（ちはつせいあるつはいまーびょう）late-onset Alzheimer's disease
遅発性ジスキネジア（ちはつせいじすきねじあ）tardive dyskinesia
チーフ（ちーふ）chief
チーフホームヘルパー（ちーふほーむへるぱー）chief home helper
†痴呆（ちほう）dementia
地方行政（ちほうぎょうせい）local administration
地方行政府（ちほうぎょうせいふ）local governing authority
地方公共団体（ちほうこうきょうだんたい）local public entity；local public body；local public authority
地方交付税（ちほうこうふぜい）local allocation tax
地方裁判所（ちほうさいばんしょ）district court
地方自治（ちほうじち）local autonomy
地方自治体（ちほうじちたい）local government
地方自治体連合（ちほうじちたいれんごう）local authority association

地方自治法（ちほうじちほう）Local Autonomy Law
痴呆性高齢者（ちほうせいこうれいしゃ）the demented elderly；elderly with dementia
痴呆性高齢者の日常生活自立度（ちほうせいこうれいしゃのにちじょうせいかつじりつど）independence level of the demented elderly
†痴呆性老人（ちほうせいろうじん）the demented elderly；elderly with dementia
痴呆性老人グループホーム（ちほうせいろうじんぐるーぷほーむ）group home for the demented elderly
†痴呆性老人の日常生活自立度（ちほうせいろうじんのにちじょうせいかつじりつど）independence level of the demented elderly
痴呆対応型共同生活介護（ちほうたいおうがたきょうどうせいかつかいご）group home for the demented
痴呆対応共同生活介護（ちほうたいおうきょうどうせいかつかいご）group home for the demented
痴呆度（ちほうど）level of dementia；stage of dementia
地方分権（ちほうぶんけん）decentralization
†チームアプローチ（ちーむあぷろーち）team approach
チーム医療（ちーむいりょう）team medicine
†チームケア（ちーむけあ）team care
チームケアの確立（ちーむけあのかくりつ）establishment of the team care
チームワーク（ちーむわーく）teamwork
着衣スキル（ちゃくいすきる）dressing skill
着床前診断（ちゃくしょうぜんしんだん）preimplantation genetic diagnosis
†着脱（ちゃくだつ）changing clothes
着用身分証明書（ちゃくようみぶんしょうめいしょ）wearable identification
注意欠陥・多動性障害（ちゅういけっかん・たどうせいしょうがい）attention deficit hyperactivity disorder；ADHD
注意障害（ちゅういしょうがい）inattention
中央供給（ちゅうおうきょうきゅう）central supply
中央滅菌供給部（ちゅうおうめっきんきょうきゅうぶ）central sterile and supply department
中央滅菌材料部（ちゅうおうめっきんざいりょうぶ）central sterile and supply department
中央労働委員会（ちゅうおうろうどういいんかい）Central Labour Relations Commission
中間位（ちゅうかんい）neutral position
中間施設（ちゅうかんしせつ）intermediate facility；transitional facility
中間支払機関（ちゅうかんしはらいきかん）intermediary
中間評価項目（ちゅうかんひょうかこうもく）items of intermediate assessment

中間法人法（ちゅうかんほうじんほう）Non-Profit Mutual Benefit Corporation Law
中国残留孤児（ちゅうごくざんりゅうこじ）Japanese orphans in China
中耳炎（ちゅうじえん）otitis media
注射（ちゅうしゃ）injection
抽出調査（ちゅうしゅつちょうさ）sample survey
抽出法（ちゅうしゅつほう）sampling method
中心暗点（ちゅうしんあんてん）central scotoma
中心カテーテル（ちゅうしんかてーてる）central catheter
中心静脈圧（ちゅうしんじょうみゃくあつ）central venous pressure
中心静脈栄養法（ちゅうしんじょうみゃくえいようほう）central parenteral nutrition
中心静脈カテーテル（ちゅうしんじょうみゃくかてーてる）⇒中心カテーテル
中心静脈高カロリー輸液法（ちゅうしんじょうみゃくこうかろりーゆえきほう）intravenous hyperalimentation：IVH
中心性頸髄損傷（ちゅうしんせいけいずいそんしょう）central cord syndrome：CCS
中水準消毒剤（ちゅうすいじゅんしょうどくざい）intermediate disinfection
中枢神経系（ちゅうすうしんけいけい）central nervous system
中枢性聴覚処理障害（ちゅうすうせいちょうかくしょりしょうがい）central auditory processing disorder
中性脂肪（ちゅうせいしぼう）triglyceride；neutral fat
中性洗剤（ちゅうせいせんざい）neutral detergent
中毒精神病（ちゅうどくせいしんびょう）toxic psychosis
中途視覚障害（ちゅうとしかくしょうがい）acquired visual impairment
中途視覚障害者（ちゅうとしかくしょうがいしゃ）person with acquired visual impairment；the newly blind
中途失明（ちゅうとしつめい）acquired blindness
中途障害（ちゅうとしょうがい）acquired disability；acquired impairment；acquired disorder
中途知覚障害（ちゅうとちかくしょうがい）acquired sensory impairment
中途聴覚障害（ちゅうとちょうかくしょうがい）acquired hearing impaired
中途聴覚障害者（ちゅうとちょうかくしょうがいしゃ）person with acquired hearing impairment
注入器材関連血流感染（ちゅうにゅうきざいかんれんけつりゅうかんせん）infusate-related bloodstream infection
中年（ちゅうねん）middle age

虫様筋バー（ちゅうようきんばー）lumbrical bar
中立位（ちゅうりつい）⇒中間位
中流意識（ちゅうりゅういしき）middle-class consciousness
チューブ栄養（ちゅーぶえいよう）tube feeding
腸炎ビブリオ（ちょうえんびぶりお）vibrio parahaemolyticus
超音波（ちょうおんぱ）ultrasound
超音波凝固切開装置（ちょうおんぱぎょうこせっかいそうち）ultrasonically activated device：USAD
超音波検査（ちょうおんぱけんさ）ultrasonography：US
超音波誘導穿刺（ちょうおんぱゆうどうせんし）ultrasonically guided puncture
超音波療法（ちょうおんぱりょうほう）ultrasound therapy
懲戒（ちょうかい）disciplinary punishment
聴覚（ちょうかく）auditory sense；sense of hearing
聴覚音声セラピスト（ちょうかくおんせいせらぴすと）auditory-verbal therapist
聴覚音声センター（ちょうかくおんせいせんたー）auditory-verbal center
聴覚過敏（ちょうかくかびん）hyperacusis
聴覚失認（ちょうかくしつにん）auditory agnosia
†聴覚障害（ちょうかくしょうがい）auditory impairment；auditory disorder；auditory deficit
聴覚障害者（ちょうかくしょうがいしゃ）the auditorially disabled；the auditory impaired
聴覚障害者更生施設（ちょうかくしょうがいしゃこうせいしせつ）rehabilitation facility for the auditorially impaired
聴覚障害者情報提供施設（ちょうかくしょうがいしゃじょうほうていきょうしせつ）information services facility for the auditorially impaired
聴覚的評価（ちょうかくてきひょうか）audiology assessment
長下肢装具（ちょうかしそうぐ）knee-ankle-foot orthosis：KAFO；long leg brace：LLB
腸管移送able検査（ちょうかんいそうのうけんさ）transit study
長期介護（ちょうきかいご）long-term care
長期記憶（ちょうききおく）long-term memory
長期ケア（ちょうきけあ）long-term care
長期ケア市場（ちょうきけあしじょう）long-term care industry；long-term care markets
長期施設ケア（ちょうきしせつけあ）long-term institutional care
聴器毒性物質（ちょうきどくせいぶっしつ）ototoxic substance
長期入所（ちょうきにゅうしょ）long-term stay
腸機能（ちょうきのう）bowel function
長期ボランティア（ちょうきぼらんてぃあ）

介護保険・介護福祉等関連用語 和英

long-term volunteer
長期目標（ちょうきもくひょう）long-term goal
超高性能フィルタ（ちょうこうせいのうふぃるた）high efficiency particulate air filter
超高齢社会（ちょうこうれいしゃかい）super-aged society
長座位（ちょうざい）long sitting position
調剤サービス（ちょうざいさーびす）pharmaceutical services
調査票（ちょうさひょう）questionnaire
超自我（ちょうじが）superego
長寿（ちょうじゅ）longevity
長寿医療制度（ちょうじゅいりょうせいど）Health Insurance System for Elderly Aged 75 and Above
徴収（ちょうしゅう）collection
長寿科学（ちょうじゅかがく）longevity science
†長寿社会（ちょうじゅしゃかい）longevity society
長寿社会福祉基金（ちょうじゅしゃかいふくしききん）Social Welfare Funds for Longevity Society
超少子高齢社会（ちょうしょうしこうれいしゃかい）hyper-aged and depopulating society
†調整交付金（ちょうせいこうふきん）adjustment subsidy；subsidy adjustment
超清浄空気（ちょうせいじょうくうき）ultraclean air
腸洗浄（ちょうせんじょう）bowel irrigation；intestinal lavage
腸前処置（ちょうぜんしょち）bowel preparation
朝鮮戦争退役軍人（ちょうせんせんそうたいえきぐんじん）Korean War veteran
長対立装具（ちょうたいりつそうぐ）long opponens wrist hand orthosis
超短波療法（ちょうたんぱりょうほう）short wave diathermy
町内会（ちょうないかい）neighborhood association
腸ひも（ちょうひも）intestinal string
†重複障害（ちょうふくしょうがい）multiple disabilities；multiple handicaps
重複障害児（ちょうふくしょうがいじ）multiple handicapped child
重複障害者（ちょうふくしょうがいしゃ）multiple handicapped
重複面接（ちょうふくめんせつ）multiple interviews
†腸閉塞（ちょうへいそく）ileus
腸溶コーティング（ちょうようこーてぃんぐ）enteric-coating
†調理（ちょうり）cooking
調理器具（ちょうりきぐ）cooking tool
調理空間（ちょうりくうかん）cooking space
調理済み（ちょうりずみ）ready-to-serve dish
†調理方法（ちょうりほうほう）cooking recipe

聴力（ちょうりょく）hearing；hearing ability
聴力検査（ちょうりょくけんさ）hearing test；audiometry
†聴力レベル（ちょうりょくれべる）hearing level
直視下生検（ちょくしかせいけん）open biopsy
†直接援助技術（ちょくせつえんじょぎじゅつ）direct social work practice
直接契約モデル（ちょくせつけいやくもでる）direct contract model
直接言語（ちょくせつげんご）direct language
直接処遇（ちょくせつしょぐう）direct treatment
直接処遇職員（ちょくせつしょぐうしょくいん）direct treatment staff
直接税（ちょくせつぜい）direct tax
直接接触感染（ちょくせつせっしょくかんせん）direct contact infection；direct-contact transmission
直接対光反射（ちょくせつたいこうはんしゃ）direct light reflex
直線的因果律（ちょくせんてきいんがりつ）linear causality
直腸Ｓ状結腸鏡（ちょくちょうえすじょうけっちょうきょう）proctosigmoidoscope
直腸Ｓ状結腸鏡検査（ちょくちょうえすじょうけっちょうきょうけんさ）proctosigmoidoscopy
直腸鏡（ちょくちょうきょう）proctoscope
直腸鏡検査（ちょくちょうきょうけんさ）proctoscopy
直腸肛門脱（ちょくちょうこうもんだつ）anorectal prolapse
直腸指診（ちょくちょうししん）digital rectal examination
直腸診（ちょくちょうしん）rectal examination
直腸生検（ちょくちょうせいけん）rectal biopsy
直腸洗浄（ちょくちょうせんじょう）rectal irrigation
直腸造影（ちょくちょうぞうえい）proctography
直腸脱（ちょくちょうだつ）rectal prolapse
直腸内（ちょくちょうない）rectal；REC
直腸内コイル（ちょくちょうないこいる）endorectal coil
直腸内超音波検査法（ちょくちょうないちょうおんぱけんさほう）endorectal ultrasonography
直腸瘤（ちょくちょうりゅう）rectocele
著作権（ちょさくけん）copyright
直系家族（ちょっけいかぞく）stem family
著変（ちょへん）significant change
治療 対 ケア（ちりょう たい けあ）care versus cure
治療食（ちりょうしょく）therapeutic diet
治療的電気刺激（ちりょうてきでんきしげき）therapeutic electrical stimulation；TES
治療的内視鏡検査（ちりょうてきないしきょうけん

さ) therapeutic endoscopy
治療報酬（ちりょうほうしゅう）physician fee
治療モデル（ちりょうもでる）remedial model
治療歴（ちりょうれき）medical history
鎮咳薬（ちんがいやく）antitussive drug
賃金（ちんぎん）wage
賃金格差（ちんぎんかくさ）wage disparity
賃金スライド（ちんぎんすらいど）wage indexation
賃金体系（ちんぎんたいけい）wage system
賃金福祉統計課（ちんぎんふくしとうけいか）Wages and Labour Welfare Statistics Division
陳情（ちんじょう）petition；appeal
鎮静催眠薬（ちんせいさいみんやく）sedative-hypnotic drug
賃貸住宅（ちんたいじゅうたく）rental housing；rental home；rental house
鎮痛剤（ちんつうざい）analgesic
鎮痛薬（ちんつうやく）analgesic drug
鎮痒剤（ちんようざい）antipruritic
鎮痒薬（ちんようやく）antipruritic drug；antipruritic medication

つ

椎間板ヘルニア（ついかんばんへるにあ）hernia of the intervertebral disc；intervertebral disc herniation
椎骨動脈（ついこつどうみゃく）vertebral artery
椎骨脳底動脈造影（ついこつのうていどうみゃくぞうえい）vertebral angiography
追跡調査（ついせきちょうさ）follow-up study
†対麻痺（ついまひ）paraplegia
通院（つういん）doctor's office visit
通院医療（つういんいりょう）ambulatory health care services
通院患者（つういんかんじゃ）outpatient
通院者率（つういんしゃりつ）outpatient rate
通過菌（つうかきん）transient bacteria
痛覚（つうかく）algesia
痛覚残留（つうかくざんりゅう）remaining sense of pain
通過症候群（つうかしょうこうぐん）transitional syndrome
通気（つうき）air insufflation
通常医療（つうじょういりょう）conventional medicine
通常介護（つうじょうかいご）conventional long-term care
†通所介護（つうしょかいご）day care services
通所介護施設（つうしょかいごしせつ）day care services center
†通所リハビリテーション（つうしょりはびりてーしょん）ambulatory rehabilitation；outpatient rehabilitation
通所リハビリテーションセンター（つうしょりはびりてーしょんせんたー）ambulatory rehabilitation center；outpatient rehabilitation center
通信教育（つうしんきょういく）online education；correspondence course
痛風（つうふう）gout
痛風性関節炎（つうふうせいかんせつえん）gouty arthritis
†杖（つえ）cane
†杖歩行（つえほこう）cane-assisted gait
使い捨て（つかいすて）disposable
付添手当（つきそいてあて）attendance allowance
付添人（つきそいにん）attendant
継手（つぎて）joint
月二回（つきにかい）twice every month；2M
月割賦課（つきわりふか）monthly charge
爪先接地（つまさきせっち）toe contact
爪先離地（つまさきりち）toe off
つまみ（つまみ）pinch
爪（つめ）nail
強さ・時間曲線（つよさ・じかんきょくせん）intensity-duration curve；I-D curve
ツリー図（つりーず）tree analysis
ツング自己評価式抑うつ性尺度（つんぐじこひょうかしきよくうつせいしゃくど）Zung Self-Rating Depression Scale；SDS

て

手当（てあて）allowance
†手洗い（てあらい）hand wash
手洗い消毒（てあらいしょうどく）antiseptic handwash
TIA（てぃーあいえー）transient ischemic attack
定位家族（ていいかぞく）family of orientation
低栄養状態（ていえいようじょうたい）undernutrition
TSB下腿義足（てぃーえすびーかたいぎそく）total surface bearing below-knee prosthesis
DOA（でぃーおーえー）dead on arrival
低温殺菌（ていおんさっきん）pasteurization
低温殺菌器（ていおんさっきんき）pasteurizer
低温滅菌（ていおんめっきん）cold sterilization
低温火傷（ていおんやけど）low temperature burn
定額自己負担（ていがくじこふたん）deductible
定額制（ていがくせい）fixed amount system
定額負担（ていがくふたん）fixed charge；fixed price
D型肝炎（でぃーがたかんえん）hepatitis D
D型肝炎ウイルス（でぃーがたかんえんういるす）hepatitis D virus
定款（ていかん）articles of incorporation

介護保険・介護福祉等関連用語 和英

定期健診（ていきけんしん）routine health examination
定期的健康診断（ていきてきけんこうしんだん）periodic health evaluation；PHE
低緊張性膀胱（ていきんちょうせいぼうこう）bladder hypotonia
底屈（ていくつ）plantar flexion；plantarflexion
デイケア（でいけあ）day care
デイケアセンター（でいけあせんたー）day care center
†低血圧（ていけつあつ）hypotension
†低血糖（ていけっとう）hypoglycemia
t検定（てぃーけんてい）t-test
抵抗（ていこう）resistance
抵抗訓練（ていこうくんれん）resistance exercise；resistance training
抵抗力減弱患者（ていこうりょくげんじゃくかんじゃ）immunocompromised patient
抵抗力減弱宿主（ていこうりょくげんじゃくしゅくしゅ）immunocompromised host
デイサービス（でいさーびす）day services
デイサービスセンター（でいさーびすせんたー）day services center
低酸素血症（ていさんそけつしょう）hypoxemia；anoxemia
低酸素症（ていさんそしょう）⇒無酸素症
†T字杖（てぃーじつえ）T-cane
低脂肪食（ていしぼうしょく）low-fat diet
低周波療法（ていしゅうはりょうほう）low frequency current therapy
低出生体重児（ていしゅっしょうたいじゅうじ）low birth weight infant
提出代行者（ていしゅつだいこうしゃ）person submitting application on behalf of the applicant；person authorized to submit applications on behalf of the applicant
低床バス（ていしょうばす）low floor bus
低所得（ていしょとく）low income
低所得家庭（ていしょとくかてい）low income family
低所得高齢者向け賃貸住宅（ていしょとくこうれいしゃむけちんたいじゅうたく）low-income rental housing for the elderly；rental housing for low-income elderly
低所得国（ていしょとくこく）low income country
低所得世帯（ていしょとくせたい）low income household
低所得層（ていしょとくそう）low income class
低水準消毒（ていすいじゅんしょうどく）low level disinfection
Tストラップ（てぃーすとらっぷ）T-strap
ディスパーサ（でぃすぱーさ）⇒微生物飛散器
ディスポーザブル（でぃすぽーざぶる）⇒使い捨て

低体温（ていたいおん）hypothermia
D値（でぃーち）D-value；decimal reduction value；decimal reduction time
低張性脱水（ていちょうせいだっすい）hypotonic dehydration
低賃金労働（ていちんぎんろうどう）low-wage labor
低賃金労働市場（ていちんぎんろうどうしじょう）low-wage labor market
ティーツェ症候群（てぃーつぇしょうこうぐん）Tietze's syndrome
D2ドーパミン受容体拮抗剤（でぃーつーどーぱみんじゅようたいきっこうざい）dopamine receptor D2 blockade
ティッピングレバー（てぃっぴんぐればー）tipping lever
低ナトリウム血症（ていなとりうむけつしょう）hyponatremia
ティネル徴候（てぃねるちょうこう）Tinel sign
定年（ていねん）retirement
定年制（ていねんせい）mandatory retirement system
定年退職（ていねんたいしょく）mandatory retirement
DV（でぃーぶい）domestic violence
デイホーム（でいほーむ）day home
定摩擦継手（ていまさつつぎて）constant friction joint
ディマンズ（でぃまんず）demands
出移民（でいみん）emigrant
剃毛（ていもう）shaving
テイラー顕現性不安尺度（てぃらーけんげんせいふあんしゃくど）Taylor's Manifest Anxiety Scale
定率負担（ていりつふたん）fixed charge rate
定量噴霧式吸入器（ていりょうふんむしききゅうにゅうき）Metered-dose inhaler
テオフィリン（ておふぃりん）theophylline
出稼ぎ（でかせぎ）migrant work
デカン酸ハロペリドール（でかんさんはろぺりどーる）haloperidol decanoate
適応（てきおう）adjustment；adaptation
適応機制（てきおうきせい）adjustment mechanism
適応酵素（てきおうこうそ）adaptive enzyme
適応障害（てきおうしょうがい）maladjustment disorder
適合（てきごう）fitting
適合判定（てきごうはんてい）fitting evaluation
デキストロメトルファン（できすとろめとるふぁん）dextromethorphan
適正検査（てきせいけんさ）aptitude test
出来高払い（できだかばらい）fee-for-service；FFS
†摘便（てきべん）stool extraction
適用（てきよう）adequacy

出口部感染（でぐちぶかんせん）exit-site infection
テクノエイド協会（てくのえいどきょうかい）Association for Technical Aids
テグレトール（てぐれとーる）Tegretol
手頃で質の良いケア（てごろでしつのよいけあ）quality affordable health care
デジタル血管造影（でじたるけっかんぞうえい）digital subtraction angiography
デシプラミン（でしぷらみん）desipramine
デシベル（でしべる）decibel；dB
テストステロン（てすとすてろん）testosterone
†手すり（てすり）handrail
手すりの設置（てすりのせっち）handrail installation
テタニー（てたにー）tetany
データベース（でーたべーす）database
手継手（てつぎて）wrist joint
テッピングレバー（てっぴんぐればー）tipping lever
鉄分（てつぶん）iron
鉄分欠乏症（てつぶんけつぼうしょう）iron deficiency
鉄分欠乏貧血症（てつぶんけつぼうひんけつしょう）iron deficiency anemia
テニス肘（てにすひじ）tennis elbow
テノデーシス作用（てのでーしすさよう）tenodesis effect
†手引き（てびき）hand-assisted escort
デヒドロエピアンドロステロン（でひどろえぴあんどろすてろん）dehydroepiandrosterone；DHEA
デプレニール（でぷれにーる）Deprenyl
デメロール（でめろーる）Demerol
デュシェンヌ型筋ジストロフィー（でゅしぇんぬがたきんじすとろふぃー）Duchenne muscular dystrophy
デュタステライド（でゅたすてらいど）dutasteride
デュピュイトラン拘縮（でゅぴゅいとらんこうしゅく）Dupuytren's contracture
デュロキセチン（でゅろきせちん）duloxetine
テルビブジン（てるびぶじん）telbivudine
テレソン（てれそん）telethon
転移（てんい）metastasis；transference
転移焦点化精神療法（てんいしょうてんかせいしんりょうほう）transference focused psychotherapy
転移神経症（てんいしんけいしょう）transference neurosis
転院（てんいん）hospital transfer
†伝音難聴（でんおんなんちょう）conductive deafness
てんかん（てんかん）epilepsy
点眼液（てんがんえき）eye drop
転換性障害（てんかんせいしょうがい）conversion disorder
てんかん発作（てんかんほっさ）epileptic seizure

電気関節角度計（でんきかんせつかくどけい）electrogoniometer
電気けいれん療法（でんきけいれんりょうほう）electroconvulsive therapy：ECT
電気刺激（でんきしげき）electrostimulation
電気刺激装置（でんきしげきそうち）electrostimulator
電気ショック療法（でんきしょっくりょうほう）electroshock therapy
電気診断法（でんきしんだんほう）electrodiagnosis：EDX
電気生理学（でんきせいりがく）electrophysiology
電極（でんきょく）electrode
転居ストレス（てんきょすとれす）relocation stress
電気療法（でんきりょうほう）electrotherapy
転勤費用（てんきんひよう）moving expenses
天候（てんこう）weather
天災（てんさい）⇒自然災害
†点字（てんじ）Braille
転子滑液包炎（てんしかつえきほうえん）Trochanteric bursitis
電子カルテ（でんしかるて）electronic health records
転子間骨折（てんしかんこっせつ）intertrochanteric fracture
電子記録（でんしきろく）electric records
電子健康記録（でんしけんこうきろく）electronic health records
電子処方（でんししょほう）e-prescription
電子政府（でんしせいふ）cyber government
電子線滅菌（でんしせんめっきん）electron beam sterilization
点字タイプライター（てんじたいぷらいたー）Braille typewriter
電子内視鏡検査（でんしないしきょうけんさ）electronic endoscopy
電子ビームCT（でんしびーむしーてぃー）electron-beam computed tomography
転子部骨折（てんしぶこっせつ）trochanteric fracture
点字ブロック（てんじぶろっく）Braille block；tactile floor tile
点字用具（てんじようぐ）Braille writing equipment
天井走行型リフター（てんじょうそうこうがたりふたー）slide-on-ceiling type of lift
転職（てんしょく）occupational change
伝染性疾患（でんせんせいしっかん）transmissible disease
伝染病（でんせんびょう）communicable disease
伝染病予防法（でんせんびょうよぼうほう）Communicable Diseases Prevention Law
デンタルフロス（でんたるふろす）dental floss
点滴（てんてき）intravenous：IV

173

点滴静脈性胆管胆嚢造影（てんてきじょうみゃくせいたんかんたんのうぞうえい）drip infusion cholecystography
点滴治療（てんてきちりょう）intravenous therapy：IV therapy
転倒（てんとう）fall
転倒危険度（てんとうきけんど）fall risk
電動義手（でんどうぎしゅ）electric upper limb prosthesis
電動吸引器（でんどうきゅういんき）electric aspirator
†電動車いす（でんどうくるまいす）electric wheelchair
転倒後症候群（てんとうごしょうこうぐん）post-fall syndrome
転倒事故（てんとうじこ）fall incident
伝導失語（でんどうしつご）conduction aphasia
転導性（てんどうせい）distractibility
電動歯ブラシ（でんどうはぶらし）electric toothbrush
電動プライユ式点字タイプライター（でんどうぶらいゆしきてんじたいぷらいたー）electric Braille writer
†電動ベッド（でんどうべっど）electric bed
転倒予防（てんとうよぼう）falls prevention
天然繊維（てんねんせんい）natural fiber
デンバー式発達スクリーニング検査（でんばーしきはったつすくりーにんぐけんさ）Denver Developmental Screening Test：DDST
テンプル大学世代間学習センター（てんぷるだいがくせだいかんがくしゅうせんたー）Center for Intergenerational Learning of Temple University
でんぷん（でんぷん）amylum；starch
点墨法（てんぼくほう）tattooing
纏綿状態（てんめんじょうたい）enmeshment
点訳（てんやく）translation into Braille；Braille translation

と

等面積図（とうめんせきず）isoarea map
ドア（どあ）door
トイレ（といれ）restroom
トイレスクリーン（といれすくりーん）toilet screen
同意書（どういしょ）agreement
同一性危機（どういつせいきき）identity crisis
同意入院（どういにゅういん）hospitalization with consent
等運動性運動（とううんどうせいうんどう）isokinetic exercise
等運動性収縮（とううんどうせいしゅうしゅく）isokinetic contraction
投影（とうえい）projection

投影検査（とうえいけんさ）projective test
投影法（とうえいほう）projective method
同化（どうか）assimilation
同化作用（どうかさよう）anabolism
†動悸（どうき）palpitation
動機（どうき）motivation
動筋（どうきん）agonist
橈屈（とうくつ）radial deviation
道具の強迫的使用（どうぐのきょうはくてきしよう）compulsive manipulation of tools
陶芸（とうげい）clay work
統計情報部（とうけいじょうほうぶ）Statistics and Information Department
統計調査（とうけいちょうさ）statistical research；statistical survey
統計的仮説検定（とうけいてきかせつけんてい）statistical hypothesis test
統計的検定（とうけいてきけんてい）statistical test
凍結肩（とうけつがた）frozen shoulder
統合医療供給システム（とうごういりょうきょうきゅうしすてむ）integrated delivery system：IDS
統合教育（とうごうきょういく）integrated education
統合された環境（とうごうされたかんきょう）integrated setting
統合された福祉国家（とうごうされたふくしこっか）integrated welfare state
†統合失調症（とうごうしっちょうしょう）schizophrenia
統合支払い（とうごうしはらい）single-payer
瞳孔対光反射（どうこうたいこうはんしゃ）pupillary light reflex
橈骨遠位端骨折（とうこつえんいたんこっせつ）distal radius fracture
橈骨動脈（とうこつどうみゃく）radial artery
橈骨動脈カテーテル（とうこつどうみゃくかてーてる）radial artery catheter
橈骨動脈カニューレ挿入法（とうこつどうみゃくかにゅーれそうにゅうほう）radial artery cannulation
橈骨動脈瘤（とうこつどうみゃくりゅう）radial artery aneurysm
洞察（どうさつ）insight
洞察療法（どうさつりょうほう）insight therapy
動作の自由度（どうさのじゆうど）degree of freedom of motion
動作分析（どうさぶんせき）motion analysis
動作歩行（どうさほこう）point gait
同時期監査（どうじきかんさ）concurrent review
当事者活動（とうじしゃかつどう）self-help activity
同時対比効果（どうじたいひこうか）simultaneous contrast effect
糖質（とうしつ）saccharide

同時定着時期（どうじていちゃくじき）double stance phase
等尺性訓練（とうしゃくせいくんれん）isometric exercise
等尺性収縮（とうしゃくせいしゅうしゅく）isometric contraction
同情（どうじょう）sympathy
等色関数（とうしょくかんすう）color matching function
同心型針電極（どうしんがたはりでんきょく）concentric needle EMG
同性愛（どうせいあい）homosexuality
糖性グルココルチコイド（とうせいぐるここるちこいど）glucocorticoid
統制された情緒的関与（とうせいされたじょうちょてきかんよ）controlled emotional involvement
統制された情緒的関与の原則（とうせいされたじょうちょてきかんよのげんそく）principle of controlled emotional involvement
†透析（とうせき）dialysis
透析療法（とうせきりょうほう）dialysis therapy
糖値（とうち）glucose level
等張性訓練（とうちょうせいくんれん）isotonic exercise
等張性収縮（とうちょうせいしゅうしゅく）isotonic contraction
†疼痛（とうつう）pain
疼痛回避性歩行（とうつうかいひせいほこう）⇒有痛性歩行
疼痛管理（とうつうかんり）pain management；pain control
疼痛生活障害評価尺度（とうつうせいかつしょうがいひょうかしゃくど）Pain Disability Assessment Scale；PDAS
疼痛性障害（とうつうせいしょうがい）pain disorder
疼痛マネジメント（とうつうまねじめんと）pain management
疼痛薬（とうつうやく）pain medication；pain relief medication；painkiller medication
動的安定性（どうてきあんていせい）dynamic stability
動的コンピューター断層撮影（どうてきこんぴゅーたーだんそうさつえい）dynamic computed tomography
†糖尿病（とうにょうびょう）diabetes mellitus：DM
糖尿病交換表（とうにょうびょうこうかんひょう）food exchange list for diabetes；diabetes food exchange list
糖尿病食品交換表（とうにょうびょうしょくひんこうかんひょう）food exchange list for diabetes；diabetes food exchange list
糖尿病性ケトアシドーシス（とうにょうびょうせいけとあしどーしす）diabetic ketoacidosis：DKA
糖尿病性高血糖性高浸透圧性昏睡（とうにょうびょうせいこうけっとうせいこうしんとうあつせいこんすい）hyperglycemic hyperosmolar nonketotic coma
糖尿病性昏睡（とうにょうびょうせいこんすい）diabetic coma
糖尿病性神経症（とうにょうびょうせいしんけいしょう）diabetic neuropathy
糖尿病性腎症（とうにょうびょうせいじんしょう）diabetic nephropathy
糖尿病性網膜症（とうにょうびょうせいもうまくしょう）diabetic retinopathy
糖尿病薬（とうにょうびょうやく）diabetes medication
動年齢テスト（どうねんれいてすと）motor-age test
頭部外傷（とうぶがいしょう）traumatic brain injury；head trauma
動物介在活動（どうぶつかいざいかつどう）animal assisted activity：AAA
動物介在療法（どうぶつかいざいりょうほう）animal assisted therapy：AAT；animal assisted health care
動物性食品（どうぶつせいしょくひん）animal food product；animal source foods：ASF
動物療法（どうぶつりょうほう）animal therapy
トウブレーク（とうぶれーく）toe-break
糖分（とうぶん）sugar
動脈（どうみゃく）artery
動脈圧（どうみゃくあつ）arterial blood pressure；arterial pressure
動脈樹（どうみゃくき）arterial tree
動脈グラフト（どうみゃくぐらふと）arterial conduit；artery graft
動脈形成術（どうみゃくけいせいじゅつ）coronary angioplasty
動脈血（どうみゃくけつ）arterial blood
動脈血ガス（どうみゃくけつがす）arterial blood gas
動脈血採取（どうみゃくけつさいしゅ）arterial blood sampling
動脈血酸素分圧（どうみゃくけつさんそぶんあつ）arterial oxygen tension；arterial partial pressure of oxygen：PaO2
動脈血酸素飽和度（どうみゃくけつさんそほうわど）arterial oxygen saturation
動脈血炭酸ガス分圧（どうみゃくけつたんさんがすぶんあつ）arterial partial pressure of carbon dioxide：PaCO2
動脈血二酸化炭素分圧（どうみゃくけつにさんかたんそぶんあつ）arterial carbon dioxide tension
動脈血飽和度低下（どうみゃくけつほうわどていか）arterial desaturation

†動脈硬化（どうみゃくこうか）arteriosclerosis
動脈硬化性心疾患（どうみゃくこうかせいしんしっかん）arteriosclerotic heart disease；ASHD
動脈硬化性皮質下白質脳症（どうみゃくこうかせいひしつかはくしつのうしょう）subcortical arteriosclerotic encephalopathy
動脈・呼気終末二酸化炭素分圧較差（どうみゃく・こきしゅうまつにさんかたんそぶんあつかくさ）arterial to end-tidal carbon dioxide tension difference
動脈・混合静脈酸素較差（どうみゃく・こんごうじょうみゃくさんそかくさ）arterial-mixed venous oxygen content difference
動脈コンプライアンス（どうみゃくこんぷらいあんす）arterial compliance
動脈再構築（どうみゃくさいこうちく）arterial remodeling
動脈雑音（どうみゃくざつおん）arterial bruit；arterial murmur
動脈疾患（どうみゃくしっかん）arterial disease
動脈収縮期雑音（どうみゃくしゅうしゅくきざつおん）arterial systolic murmur
動脈新生（どうみゃくしんせい）arteriogenesis
動脈伸展性（どうみゃくしんてんせい）arterial distensibility
動脈穿刺（どうみゃくせんし）arterial puncture
動脈造影（どうみゃくぞうえい）arteriography
動脈塞栓（どうみゃくそくせん）arterial embolism
動脈抵抗（どうみゃくていこう）arterial resistance
動脈トノメトリー（どうみゃくとのめとりー）arterial tonometry
動脈内（どうみゃくない）intraarterial
動脈内デジタルサブトラクション（どうみゃくないでじたるさぶとらくしょん）intraarterial digital subtraction angiography
動脈内膜炎（どうみゃくないまくえん）endarteritis
動脈拍動（どうみゃくはくどう）arterial pulse
動脈閉塞疾患（どうみゃくへいそくしっかん）arterial occlusive disease；AOD
動脈弁（どうみゃくべん）arterial valve
動脈瘤（どうみゃくりゅう）aneurysm；arterial aneurysm
動脈瘤切除（どうみゃくりゅうせつじょ）aneurysmectomy
動脈瘤縫縮術（どうみゃくりゅうほうしゅくじゅつ）aneurysmorrhaphy
動脈輪（どうみゃくりん）circle of Willis
動脈攣縮（どうみゃくれんしゅく）arteriospasm
動脈連続雑音（どうみゃくれんぞくざつおん）arterial continuous murmur
冬眠（とうみん）hibernation
冬眠心筋（とうみんしんきん）hibernating myocardium；myocardial hibernation

同盟（どうめい）alliance；confederation
投薬過誤（とうやくかご）medication error
投薬制限（とうやくせいげん）medication restriction
投薬量の調整（とうやくりょうのちょうせい）dosage modification
投与（とうよ）administration
等容（とうよう）isovolumetric；isovolumic
童謡（どうよう）nursery rhyme
動揺関節（どうようかんせつ）frail joint
等容弛緩（とうようしかん）isovolumetric relaxation；isovolumic relaxation
等容弛緩時間（とうようしかんじかん）isovolumetric relaxation time；IRT；isovolumic relaxation time
等容収縮（とうようしゅうしゅく）isovolumetric contraction；isovolumic contraction
等容収縮時間（とうようしゅうしゅくじかん）isovolumetric contraction time；ICT；isovolumic contraction time
動揺性高血圧症（どうようせいこうけつあつしょう）labile hypertension
等容性収縮（とうようせいしゅうしゅく）isovolumetric contraction；isovolumic contraction
等容性収縮時間（とうようせいしゅうしゅくじかん）isovolumetric contraction time；isovolumic contraction time
東洋哲学（とうようてつがく）eastern philosophy
登録（とうろく）enrollment；registration
登録看護師（とうろくかんごし）registered nurse
登録者（とうろくしゃ）enrollee
登録番号（とうろくばんごう）registration number
同和教育（どうわきょういく）anti-discrimination education
特異的算数能力障害（とくいてきさんすうのうりょくしょうがい）specific disorder of arithmetical skills
特異的綴字障害（とくいてきていじしょうがい）specific spelling disorder
特異的読字障害（とくいてきどくじしょうがい）specific reading disorder
特異的発達障害（とくいてきはったつしょうがい）specific developmental disorder；SDD
特殊教育（とくしゅきょういく）special education
特殊教育諸学校（とくしゅきょういくしょがっこう）special education school
†特殊寝台（とくしゅしんだい）specialized bed；special bed
†特殊浴槽（とくしゅよくそう）specialized bathtub；special bathtub
読書眼鏡（どくしょめがね）reading glasses
読唇術（どくしんじゅつ）lip reading
督促状（とくそくじょう）collection letter

特定活動（とくていかつどう）designated activity
特定財源（とくていざいげん）earmarked revenue
特定疾患（とくていしっかん）intractable disease
特定疾病（とくていしっぺい）intractable disease
特定承認保険医療機関（とくていしょうにんほけんいりょうきかん）certified medical facility for health insurance
特定非営利活動促進法（とくていひえいりかつどうそくしんほう）Law to Promote Specified Non-Profit Activities：NPO Law
特定福祉用具（とくていふくしようぐ）special welfare equipment
特定福祉用具販売（とくていふくしようぐはんばい）certified welfare equipment trade
特定療養費（とくていりょうようひ）specific geriatric care costs
特発性血小板減少性紫斑病（とくはつせいけっしょうばんげんしょうせいしはんびょう）idiopathic thrombocytopenic purpura
特別会計（とくべつかいけい）special account
特別区（とくべつく）special ward
特別支援学級（とくべつしえんがっきゅう）special class for the disabled children
特別支援学校（とくべつしえんがっこう）special school
特別支援教育（とくべつしえんきょういく）special needs education
特別障害者控除（とくべつしょうがいしゃこうじょ）special deduction for the disabled
特別障害者税控除（とくべつしょうがいしゃぜいこうじょ）special tax deduction for the disabled
特別障害者手当（とくべつしょうがいしゃてあて）special disability allowance
特別食（とくべつしょく）special meal
特別税額控除（とくべつぜいがくこうじょ）special tax deduction
特別地域加算（とくべつちいきかさん）additional payment to special region
特別徴収（とくべつちょうしゅう）special collection
†特別治療食（とくべつちりょうしょく）special therapeutic diet
特別手当（とくべつてあて）special benefit allowance
特別ニーズプラン（とくべつにーずぷらん）special needs plan
特別保険料徴収（とくべつほけんりょうちょうしゅう）special premium collection
特別ボランティア基金（とくべつぼらんてぃあききん）special volunteer fund
†特別養護老人ホーム（とくべつようごろうじんほーむ）geriatric welfare home
独立行政法人（どくりつぎょうせいほうじん）independent administrative institution
独立変数（どくりつへんすう）independent variable
トグルブレーキ（とぐるぶれーき）toggle brake
†読話（どくわ）lip-reading；speech-reading
時計描画テスト（とけいびょうがてすと）Clock Drawing Test：CDT
†吐血（とけつ）hematemesis
床ずれ（とこずれ）decubitus；bedsore；pressure sore
都市化（としか）urbanization
都市化社会（としかしゃかい）urbanizing society
都市計画（としけいかく）urban planning
閉じこめ症候群（とじこめしょうこうぐん）locked-in syndrome
閉じこもり（とじこもり）housebound；withdrawal
閉じこもり症候群（とじこもりしょうこうぐん）housebound syndrome；withdrawal syndrome
閉じこもり老人（とじこもりろうじん）housebound elderly
都市生活（としせいかつ）urbanism
都市問題（としもんだい）urban problem
†徒手筋力テスト（としゅきんりょくてすと）Manual Muscle Testing：MMT
徒手療法（としゅりょうほう）manual therapy
土壌感染（どじょうかんせん）soil-borne infection
トーショナル水晶体乳化吸引術（とーしょなるすいしょうたいにゅうかきゅういんじゅつ）torsional phacoemulsification
トータルヘルスプロモーション（とーたるへるすぷろもーしょん）total health promotion：THP
特記事項（とっきこう）special notes
†独居（どっきょ）solitary-living
独居高齢者（どっきょこうれいしゃ）solitary-living elderly
独居障害者（どっきょしょうがいしゃ）solitary living disabled person
特許売薬（とっきょばいやく）proprietary medicine
独居老人（どっきょろうじん）solitary-living elderly
突然死（とつぜんし）sudden death
徒弟制度（とていせいど）apprenticeship system；apprentice system
ドナー（どなー）donor
ドナーカード（どなーかーど）donor card
ドーナツ現象（どーなつげんしょう）doughnut phenomenon
ドネペジル（どねぺじる）donepezil
ドーパミン（どーぱみん）dopamine
ドーパミン受容体遮断（どーぱみんじゅようたいしゃだん）dopamine receptor blockade
トピラマート（とぴらまーと）topiramate
トフラニール（とふらにーる）Tofranil
留置調査（とめおきちょうさ）placement questionnaire

ドメスティック・バイオレンス（どめすてぃっく・ばいおれんす）domestic violence：DV
ドライクリーニング（どらいくりーにんぐ）dry cleaning
ドライシャンプー（どらいしゃんぷー）dry shampoo
ドライブスルー出産（どらいぶするーしゅっさん）drive-through delivery
ドライマウス（どらいまうす）dry mouth
トラウマ（とらうま）trauma
トラスツズマブ（とらすつずまぶ）trastuzumab
トラニルシプロミン（とらにるしぷろみん）tranylcypromine
ドラマセラピー（どらませらぴー）drama therapy
ドラール（どらーる）Doral
トランキライザー乱用（とらんきらいざーらんよう）tranquilizer abuse
トランスファー（とらんすふぁー）transfer
トランスファーボード（とらんすふぁーぼーど）transfer board
トランゼン（とらんぜん）Tranxene
トランデート（とらんでーと）Trandate
トリガー（とりがー）trigger
トリガーポイント（とりがーぽいんと）trigger point
取消（とりけし）revocation
トリックモーション（とりっくもーしょん）trick motion
トリプタン製薬（とりぷたんせいやく）triptan drug
努力呼吸（どりょくこきゅう）effort respiration
トルカポン（とるかぽん）tolcapone
トレイルメイキングテスト（とれいるめいきんぐてすと）Trail-Making Test
ドレッシング（どれっしんぐ）dressing
トレッドミル（とれっどみる）treadmill
トレッドミル負荷試験（とれっどみるふかしけん）treadmill testing
トレーナー（とれーなー）trainer
ドレープ（どれーぷ）drape
ドレーン（どれーん）⇒排水管
トレンデレンブルグ体位（とれんでれんぶるぐたいい）Trendelenburg position
トレンデレンブルグ徴候（とれんでれんぶるぐちょうこう）Trendelenburg sign
ドロップアウト（どろっぷあうと）dropout
とろみ（とろみ）thickened
とろみ食（とろみしょく）thickened diet；altered consistency diet；nectar consistency diet

な

ナイアシン（ないあしん）Niacin
内圧帯（ないあつたい）pressure zone
内因性（ないいんせい）endogenous
内因性括約筋不全（ないいんせいかつやくきんふぜん）intrinsic sphincter deficiency：SD
内因性感染（ないいんせいかんせん）endogenous infection
内因性精神病（ないいんせいせいしんびょう）endogenous psychosis
内科（ないか）internal medicine
内閣（ないかく）cabinet
内向性（ないこうせい）introversion
内耳炎（ないじえん）labyrinthitis
内視鏡（ないしきょう）endoscope
内視鏡検査（ないしきょうけんさ）endoscopy
内視鏡手術（ないしきょうしゅじゅつ）endoscopic
内視鏡超音波検査（ないしきょうちょうおんぱけんさ）endosonography
内視鏡の逆行性胆膵管造影（ないしきょうてきぎゃっこうせいたんどうすいかんぞうえい）endoscopic retrograde cholangiopancreatography
内視鏡の超音波検査（ないしきょうてきちょうおんぱけんさ）endoscopic ultrasonography
内出血（ないしゅっけつ）bruise
内旋（ないせん）internal rotation
内側単股継手システム（ないそくたんこつぎてしすてむ）medial single hip joint system
内側ホイップ（ないそくほいっぷ）medial whip
内的照合枠（ないてきしょうごうわく）internal frame of reference
内転（ないてん）adduction
ナイトケア（ないとけあ）night care
ナイトケア事業（ないとけあじぎょう）night care project
ナイトサービス（ないとさーびす）night services
ナイトホスピタル（ないとほすぴたる）night hospital
内発的動機づけ（ないはつてきどうきづけ）intrinsic motivation
内反（ないはん）varus
内反尖足（ないはんせんそく）equinovarus foot
内部環境（ないぶかんきょう）internal environment
内服薬（ないふくやく）oral medication
†内部障害（ないぶしょうがい）internal disorder
内部障害者更生施設（ないぶしょうがいしゃこうせいしせつ）rehabilitative facility for people with internal disorders
内部相互補助（ないぶそうごほじょ）cross-subsidization
内分泌（ないぶんぴつ）endocrine
内分泌医（ないぶんぴつい）endocrinologist
内分泌学（ないぶんぴつがく）endocrinology
内分泌疾患（ないぶんぴつしっかん）endocrine disease
流し（ながし）sink

中底（なかぞこ）insole
仲間関係（なかまかんけい）peer relationship
ナショナリズム（なしょなりずむ）nationalism
ナショナルミニマム（なしょなるみにまむ）national minimum
ナーシングホーム（なーしんぐほーむ）nursing home
ナックルベンダ（なっくるべんだ）knuckle bender
ナトリウム（なとりうむ）sodium
70代（ななじゅうだい）septuagenarian
ナプロキセン（なぷろきせん）naproxen
ナプロシン（なぷろしん）Naprosyn
生ごみ（なまごみ）garbage
生ごみ処理（なまごみしょり）disposal of garbage and swill
鉛中毒（なまりちゅうどく）lead poisoning
ナメンダ（なめんだ）Namenda
ナラティブ・アプローチ（ならてぃぶ・あぷろーち）narrative approach
ナラティブ・セラピー（ならてぃぶ・せらぴー）narrative therapy
ナルコティクス（なるこてぃくす）narcotics
ナルジル（なるじる）Nardil
ナルトレキソン（なるとれきそん）naltrexone
軟化剤（なんかざい）emollient
軟化症（なんかしょう）malacia
軟膏（なんこう）ointment
軟式洗濯（なんしきせんたく）dry cleaning
†難聴（なんちょう）hearing loss；HL；hearing impairment；hard of hearing
難聴高齢者（なんちょうこうれいしゃ）auditorially impaired elderly
難聴児（なんちょうじ）auditorially impaired child
難聴者（なんちょうしゃ）auditorially impaired
難聴幼児（なんちょうようじ）auditorially impaired infant
難聴幼児通園施設（なんちょうようじつうえんしせつ）day services facility for the auditory loss infants
†難病（なんびょう）incurable disease
難病対策（なんびょうたいさく）policy for incurable diseases
難病認定（なんびょうにんてい）incurable disease certification；certification of incurable disease
難民（なんみん）refugee
難民救済（なんみんきゅうさい）refugee relief program；relief programs for the refugees
難民サービス（なんみんさーびす）refugee services

に

二型糖尿病（にがたとうにょうびょう）type 2 diabetes mellitus；type 2 diabetes

苦味（にがみ）bitter
肉眼的に汚染した手指（にくがんてきにおせんしたしゅし）visibly soiled hands
二酸化炭素（にさんかたんそ）carbon dioxide
二酸化窒素（にさんかちっそ）nitrogen dioxide
二次医療圏（にじいりょうけん）secondary medical service area
二次過程（にじかてい）secondary process
二時間毎（にじかんごと）every 2 hours；Q2H
二次感染（にじかんせん）secondary infection
二次救命処置（にじきゅうめいしょち）advanced life support；ALS
二次救命心肺蘇生法・処置（にじきゅうめいしんぱいそせいほう・しょち）advanced cardiac life support
二次障害（にじしょうがい）secondary disorder；secondary disability
二次心肺蘇生法（にじしんぱいせいほう）advanced cardiovascular life support；ACLS
二次判定（にじはんてい）secondary assessment
21トリソミー（にじゅういちとりそみー）trisomy 21
21世紀における国民健康づくり運動（にじゅういっせいきにおけるこくみんけんこうづくりうんどう）National Health Promotion Movement in the 21st Century；Healthy Japan 21
21世紀福祉ビジョン（にじゅういっせいきふくしびじょん）Welfare Vision for the 21st Century
二重X線造影法（にじゅうえっくすせんぞうえいほう）double contrast roentgenography
二重エネルギーX線（にじゅうえねるぎーえっくすせん）dual-energy X-ray；DEXA
二重エネルギーX線吸収測定法（にじゅうえねるぎーえっくすせんきゅうしゅうそくていほう）dual-energy X-ray absorptiometry；DEXA
二重拘束説（にじゅうこうそくせつ）double-bind theory
20代（にじゅうだい）vicenarian
二重バケツ法（にじゅうばけつほう）double-bucket system
二重袋手技（にじゅうぶくろしゅぎ）double-bag technique
24時間ケア（にじゅうよじかんけあ）twenty-four-hour care
24時間見守り（にじゅうよじかんみまもり）twenty-four-hour protective oversight
24時間連絡体制（にじゅうよじかんれんらくたいせい）24-hour on call
二色性反射モデル（にしょくせいはんしゃもでる）dichromatic reflection model
二次予防（にじよぼう）secondary prevention
†ニーズ（にーず）needs
ニーズ・アセスメント（にーず・あせすめんと）needs assessment

介護保険・介護福祉等関連用語和英

ニーズ調査（にーずちょうさ）needs survey
ニーズの階層（にーずのかいそう）hierarchy of needs
†日常生活活動（にちじょうせいかつかつどう）activities of daily living：ADL
日常生活自立度判定基準（にちじょうせいかつじりつどはんていきじゅん）index of independence in activities of daily living
日常生活用具（にちじょうせいかつようぐ）equipments for daily living activities
日常清掃（にちじょうせいそう）usual cleaning
日常的金銭管理（にちじょうてききんせんかんり）daily money management：DMM
日常的処遇（にちじょうてきしょぐう）daily treatment；daily care
†日内変動（にちないへんどう）circadian variation
日没行動（にちぼつこうどう）sundowning
日没症候群（にちぼつしょうこうぐん）sundown syndrome
日光消毒（にっこうしょうどく）sunlight disinfection；solar disinfection
日光浴（にっこうよく）sunbathing
日誌（にっし）diary
ニッチ（にっち）niche
日中過睡眠（にっちゅうかすいみん）excessive daytime sleepiness
ニート（にーと）Not in Education, Employment or Training：NEET
二動作歩行（にどうさほこう）two-point gait
ニトログリセリン（にとろぐりせりん）nitroglycerin：NG
二分脊椎（にぶんせきつい）spina bifida
日本アイバンク協会（にほんあいばんくきょうかい）Japan Eye Bank Association
日本医師会（にほんいしかい）Japan Medical Association
日本いのちの電話連盟（にほんいのちのでんわれんめい）Federation of Inochi No Denwa Inc
日本介護福祉士会（にほんかいごふくししかい）Japan Association of Certified Care Workers
日本救急救命士協会（にほんきゅうきゅうきゅうめいしきょうかい）Japanese Paramedics Association
日本工業規格（にほんこうぎょうきかく）Japanese Industrial Standards：JIS
日本口腔外科学会（にほんこうくうげかがっかい）Japanese Society of Oral and Maxillofacial Surgeons
日本高齢者虐待防止センター（にほんこうれいしゃくたいぼうしせんたー）Japanese Center for the Prevention of Elder Abuse
日本歯科医師会（にほんしかいしかい）Japan Dental Association

日本式昏睡尺度（にほんしきこんすいしゃくど）Japan Coma Scale：JCS
日本社会福祉士会（にほんしゃかいふくししかい）Japan Association of Certified Social Workers
日本集中治療医学会（にほんしゅうちゅうちりょういがくかい）Japanese Society of Intensive Care Medicine
日本ソーシャルワーカー協会（にほんそーしゃるわーかーきょうかい）Japanese Association of Social Workers
日本尊厳死協会（にほんそんげんしきょうかい）Japan Society for Dying with Dignity
日本WHO協会（にほんだぶりゅえっちおー）WHO Association of Japan
日本版デンバー式発達スクリーニング検査（にほんばんでんばーしきはったつすくりーにんぐけんさ）Japanese Version of Denver Developmental Screening Test：JDDST-R
日本微量栄養素学会（にほんびりょうえいようそがっかい）Japan Trace Nutrients Research Society
日本放射線技師会（にほんほうしゃせんぎしかい）Japan Association of Radiological Technologists：JART
日本薬剤師会（にほんやくざいしかい）Japan Pharmaceutical Association
日本臨床衛生検査技師会（にほんりんしょうえいせいけんさぎしかい）Japanese Association of Medical Technologists：JAMT
日本臨床工学技士会（にほんりんしょうこうがくぎしかい）Japan Association for Clinical Engineering Technologists
入院（にゅういん）hospitalization；admission
入院型緩和ケア（にゅういんがたかんわけあ）inpatient hospice
入院患者（にゅういんかんじゃ）inpatient
入院期間（にゅういんきかん）length of stay：LOS
入院措置（にゅういんそち）involuntary hospital admission
入院治療レベル（にゅういんちりょうれべる）hospital level of care
入院保険（にゅういんほけん）hospital insurance：HI
入院料（にゅういんりょう）admission charge
入会（にゅうかい）enrollment
入会者（にゅうかいしゃ）enrollee
乳癌（にゅうがん）breast cancer
乳児死亡率（にゅうじしぼうりつ）infant mortality rate
入所（にゅうしょ）admission
入所型施設利用者の権利（にゅうしょがたしせつりようしゃのけんり）rights of residents
入所期間（にゅうしょきかん）length of stay：LOS
入所決定（にゅうしょけってい）admission

decision；decision for admission
入所施設（にゅうしょしせつ）residential facility
入所者（にゅうしょしゃ）resident
乳腺腫瘍摘出術（にゅうせんしゅようてきしゅつじゅつ）lumpectomy
乳房温存手術（にゅうぼうおんぞんしゅじゅつ）breast-sparing surgery
乳房再建術（にゅうぼうさいけんじゅつ）breast reconstruction
乳房切断術（にゅうぼうせつじょじゅつ）mastectomy
†入眠（にゅうみん）falling asleep
乳幼児突然死症候群（にゅうようじとつぜんししょうこうぐん）sudden infant death syndrome
†入浴（にゅうよく）bathing
入浴介助（にゅうよくかいじょ）bathing assistance；assistance with bathing
入浴サービス（にゅうよくさーびす）bathing services
ニューヨーク心臓協会心機能分類（にゅーよーくしんぞうきょうかいしんのうぶんるい）New York Heart Association functional classification
入浴動作（にゅうよくどうさ）bathing activity
入浴用具（にゅうよくようぐ）bathing equipment
ニューロパチー（にゅーろぱちー）neuropathy
ニューロフィードバック（にゅーろふぃーどばっく）neurofeedback
ニューロンチン（にゅーろんちん）Neurontin
†尿（にょう）urine
†尿意（にょうい）uresiesthesia
†尿器（にょうき）urinary bottle holder
尿検査（にょうけんさ）urinalysis
尿酸（にょうさん）uric acid
†尿失禁（にょうしっきん）urinary incontinence
尿道（にょうどう）urethra
尿道カテーテル（にょうどうかてーてる）urethral catheter
尿道カテーテル法（にょうどうかてーてるほう）urethral catheterization
尿道瘤（にょうどうりゅう）urethrocele
尿毒症（にょうどくしょう）uremia
尿閉（にょうへい）urinary retention
尿流動態検査（にょうりゅうどうたいけんさ）urodynamic test
尿路（にょうろ）urinary tract
†尿路感染（にょうろかんせん）urinary tract infection: UTI
尿路管理（にょうろかんり）urinary management
尿路ストーマ（にょうろすとーま）urostomy
尿路由来敗血症（にょうろゆらいはいけつしょう）urosepsis
任意加入（にんいかにゅう）optional enrollment；optional entry

任意後見制度（にんいこうけんせいど）voluntary guardianship system；voluntary guardianship
任意団体（にんいだんたい）unincorporated association；unincorporated voluntary association
任意入院（にんいにゅういん）voluntary hospital admission
任意保険（にんいほけん）voluntary insurance
認可（にんか）accreditation；approval
認可基準（にんかきじゅん）accreditation standards
人間科学（にんげんかがく）human science
人間学的・実存的療法（にんげんがくてき・じつぞんてきりょうほう）humanistic and existential therapy
人間工学（にんげんこうがく）human engineering；ergonomics
人間の尊厳（にんげんのそんげん）human dignity
人間貧困指数（にんげんひんこんしすう）human poverty index
認識障害（にんしきしょうがい）cognitive impairment
妊娠糖尿病（にんしんとうにょうびょう）gestational diabetes
認知（にんち）cognition
認知訓練（にんちくんれん）cognitive remediation
認知行動療法（にんちこうどうりょうほう）cognitive behavioral therapy；cognitive behavior therapy
†認知症（にんちしょう）dementia
認知障害（にんちしょうがい）cognitive disorder
認知症介護研究・研修センター（にんちしょうかいごけんきゅう・けんしゅうせんたー）Dementia Care Research and Training Center
認知症介護情報ネットワーク（にんちしょうかいごじょうほうねっとわーく）Dementia Care Information Network
認知症グループホーム（にんちしょうぐるーぷほーむ）group home for the demented；group home for the elderly with dementia
認知症ケア専門病棟（にんちしょうけあせんもんびょうとう）dementia special care unit
†認知症高齢者（にんちしょうこうれいしゃ）the demented elderly
認知症高齢者対策（にんちしょうこうれいしゃたいさく）policy for the elderly with dementia；policy for dementia
†認知症高齢者の日常生活自立度（にんちしょうこうれいしゃのにちじょうせいかつじりつど）independence level of the demented elderly
認知症専門病棟（にんちしょうせんもんびょうとう）special care unit
認知状態（にんちじょうたい）cognitive status

介護保険・介護福祉等関連用語和英

†認知症対応型共同生活介護（にんちしょうたいおうがたきょうどうせいかつかいご）group home for the demented；group home for the elderly with dementia
†認知症対応型通所介護（にんちしょうたいおうがたつうしょかいご）day care services for the demented
認知症度（にんちしょうど）level of dementia；stage of dementia
認知症に伴う行動障害と精神症状（にんちしょうにともなうこうどうしょうがいとせいしんしょうじょう）behavioral and psychological symptoms of dementia：BPSD
認知症の診断（にんちしょうのしんだん）diagnosis of dementia
認知症の人と家族の会（にんちしょうのひととかぞくのかい）Alzheimer's Association Japan
認知症の予防（にんちしょうのよぼう）prevention of dementia
認知症評価尺度（にんちしょうひょうかしゃくど）Dementia Rating Scale
認知症老人（にんちしょうろうじん）the elderly with dementia
認知症老人対策（にんちしょうろうじんたいさく）policy for elderly with dementia
認知症老人の日常生活自立度（にんちしょうろうじんのにちじょうせいかつじりつど）independence level of the demented elderly
認知的・経験的自己理論（にんちてき・けいけんてきじこりろん）cognitive experiential self theory
認知的再構成（にんちてきさいこうせい）cognitive restructuring
認知パラダイム（にんちぱらだいむ）cognitive paradigm
認知リハビリテーション（にんちりはびりてーしょん）cognitive rehabilitation
認知療法（にんちりょうほう）cognitive therapy；cognitive remediation
認定（にんてい）accreditation；certification
認定NPO法人（にんていえぬぴーおーほうじん）approved non-profit corporation
認定看護師（にんていかんごし）certified nurse：CN
認定看護助産師（にんていかんごじょさんし）certified nurse midwife
認証基準（にんていきじゅん）certification standards
認定健康教育士（にんていけんこうきょういくし）certified health education specialist
認定調査（にんていちょうさ）accreditation survey

ね

†寝返り（ねがえり）roll over
ネクター状液体食（ねくたーじょうえきたいしょく）nectar liquid diet
ネグレクト（ねぐれくと）neglect
†寝たきり（ねたきり）bedridden
寝たきり高齢者（ねたきりこうれいしゃ）bedridden elderly
寝たきり高齢者対策（ねたきりこうれいしゃたいさく）policy for the bedridden elderly
寝たきり高齢者予防（ねたきりこうれいしゃよぼう）prevention of becoming bedridden elderly
寝たきり状態（ねたきりじょうたい）bedridden status
†寝たきり度（ねたきりど）bedridden level
寝たきり度判定基準（ねたきりどはんていきじゅん）criteria for bedridden
寝たきり予防（ねたきりよぼう）prevention of becoming bedridden
寝たきり老人（ねたきりろうじん）bedridden elderly
寝たきり老人ゼロ作戦（ねたきりろうじんぜろさくせん）bedridden eradication campaign
寝たきり老人対策（ねたきりろうじんたいさく）policy for the bedridden elderly
寝たきり老人予防（ねたきりろうじんよぼう）prevention of becoming bedridden elderly
ネックカラー（ねっくからー）cervical spine collar
熱射病（ねっしゃびょう）⇒熱中症
†熱傷（ねっしょう）burn
熱水消毒（ねっすいしょうどく）hot water disinfection
熱中症（ねっちゅうしょう）heat stroke
ネットワーキング（ねっとわーきんぐ）networking
ネットワーク（ねっとわーく）network
ネットワークモデル（ねっとわーくもでる）network model
熱疲弊（ねつひへい）heat exhaustion
†寝床（ねどこ）bedding
ネブライザー（ねぶらいざー）nebulizer
ネフローゼ症候群（ねふろーぜしょうこうぐん）nephritic syndrome；Nephrotic syndrome
†年金（ねんきん）pension
年金課（ねんきんか）Pension Division
年金基金（ねんきんききん）pension fund
年金給付（ねんきんきゅうふ）pension benefit
年金給付基準（ねんきんきゅうふきじゅん）pension benefits standards
年金給付基準法（ねんきんきゅうふきじゅんほう）Pension Benefits Standards Act
年金給付水準（ねんきんきゅうふすいじゅん）level of pension benefits

年金局（ねんきんきょく）Pension Bureau
年金支給開始年齢（ねんきんしきゅうかいしねんれい）pensionable age
年金受給資格（ねんきんじゅきゅうしかく）eligibility of employee pension
年金受給資格年齢（ねんきんじゅきゅうしかくねんれい）pensionable age
年金受給者（ねんきんじゅきゅうしゃ）pensioner
年金審議会（ねんきんしんぎかい）National Pension Council
年金数理（ねんきんすうり）pension mathematics
年金制度（ねんきんせいど）pension system
年金積立基金（ねんきんつみたてききん）pension reserve fund
年金手帳（ねんきんてちょう）pension handbook
年金保険（ねんきんほけん）pension insurance
年金保険課（ねんきんほけんか）Pension Insurance Division
年金保険制度（ねんきんほけんせいど）pension insurance system
年金保険料（ねんきんほけんりょう）pension insurance premiums
年金保険料納付（ねんきんほけんりょうのうふ）payment of pension premiums
捻挫（ねんざ）sprain
年次調査（ねんじちょうさ）annual survey
年少人口（ねんしょうじんこう）young population
年齢差別（ねんれいさべつ）ageism

の

ノイローゼ（のいろーぜ）neurosis
脳外傷（のうがいしょう）traumatic brain injury：TBI
脳幹（のうかん）brain stem
†脳血管障害（のうけっかんしょうがい）cerebrovascular disorder：CVD
†脳血管性認知症（のうけっかんせいにんちしょう）cerebrovascular dementia
脳血管造影（のうけっかんぞうえい）cerebral angiography
†脳血栓症（のうけっせんしょう）cerebral thrombosis
濃厚飲料（のうこういんりょう）thickened liquid
†脳梗塞（のうこうそく）cerebral infarction
濃厚蜂蜜状液体食（のうこうはちみつじょうえきたいしょく）ultra-honey-thick diet
納骨・その他葬祭のために必要なもの（のうこつ・そのほかそうさいのためにひつようなもの）cineration and any other things necessary for funerals
脳挫傷（のうざしょう）cerebral contusion
†脳死（のうし）brain death

脳死判定基準（のうしはんていきじゅん）diagnostic criteria for clinical diagnosis of brain death
†脳出血（のうしゅっけつ）cerebral hemorrhage
脳腫瘍（のうしゅよう）brain tumor
脳神経（のうしんけい）cerebral nerve
脳神経外科集中治療室（のうしんけいげかしゅうちゅうちりょうしつ）neurosurgical care unit
脳深部刺激療法（のうしんぶしげきりょうほう）deep brain stimulation
納税者の反乱（のうぜいしゃのはんらん）taxpayer's revolt；tax revolt
†脳性麻痺（のうせいまひ）cerebral palsy：CP
†脳塞栓（のうそくせん）cerebral embolism
脳卒中（のうそっちゅう）stroke：apoplexy
脳卒中機能障害評価法（のうそっちゅうきのうしょうがいひょうかほう）Stroke Impairment Assessment Set：SIAS
脳卒中集中治療室（のうそっちゅうしゅうちゅうちりょうしつ）stroke care unit
農村（のうそん）rural village
農村社会（のうそんしゃかい）rural society
農村部の高齢者（のうそんぶのこうれいしゃ）rural elder
脳電図（のうでんず）⇒脳波
能動透過（のうどうとうか）active permeation
能動ハンド（のうどうはんど）utility hand
能動フック・作業用手先具（のうどうふっく・さぎょうようてさきぐ）split hook and specialized tool
脳動脈硬化症（のうどうみゃくこうかしょう）cerebral arteriosclerosis
能動免疫（のうどうめんえき）active immunity
能動輸送（のうどうゆそう）active transport
膿尿（のうにょう）pyuria
脳波（のうは）electroencephalogram：EEG
脳貧血（のうひんけつ）cerebral anemia
脳浮腫（のうふしゅ）brain edema
能力（のうりょく）ability
能力開発課（のうりょくかいはつか）Human Resources Development Division
能力主義（のうりょくしゅぎ）ability principle
†能力低下（のうりょくていか）disability
能力評価課（のうりょくひょうかか）Vocational Ability Evaluation Division
ノスタルジア（のすたるじあ）nostalgia
伸び上がり歩行（のびあがりほこう）vaulting
伸び率管理制度（のびりつかんりせいど）management system of growth rate
†ノーマライゼーション（のーまらいぜーしょん）normalization
ノルトリプチリン（のるとりぷちりん）nortriptyline
ノルバスク（のるばすく）Norvasc
ノルプラミン（のるぷらみん）Norpramin
ノロウイルス（のろういるす）norovirus

介護保険・介護福祉等関連用語 和英

ノンクリティカル（のんくりてぃかる）non-critical
ノンスリップ（のんすりっぷ）non-slip
ノンスリップテープ（のんすりっぷてーぷ）non-slip tape
ノンスリップマット（のんすりっぷまっと）non-slip mat
†ノンレム睡眠（のんれむすいみん）non-rapid eye movement sleep：NREM sleep

は

歯（は）teeth
肺移植（はいいしょく）lung transplant
†肺炎（はいえん）pneumonia
肺炎球菌性髄膜炎（はいえんきゅうきんせいずいまくえん）pneumococcal meningitis
肺炎球菌性肺炎（はいえんきゅうきんせいはいえん）pneumococcal pneumonia
肺炎球菌予防接種（はいえんきゅうきんよぼうせっしゅ）pneumococcal vaccination
肺炎レンサ球菌（はいえんれんさきゅうきん）streptococcus pneumoniae
バイオクリーンシステム（ばいおくりーんしすてむ）bioclean system
バイオクリーン病室（ばいおくりーんびょうしつ）biological clean room
バイオハザードマーク（ばいおはざーどまーく）biohazard mark
バイオバーデン（ばいおばーでん）bioburden
バイオフィードバック（ばいおふぃーどばっく）biofeedback
バイオフィードバック療法（ばいおふぃーどばっくりょうほう）biofeedback therapy
バイオフィルム（ばいおふぃるむ）biofilm
バイオロジカルインジケータ（ばいおろじかるいんじけーた）biological indicator
†徘徊（はいかい）wandering
背臥位（はいがい）supine position
肺活量（はいかつりょう）lung capacity；vital capacity
†肺癌（はいがん）lung cancer
廃棄（はいき）disposal
†肺気腫（はいきしゅ）pulmonary emphysema
肺機能検査（はいきのうけんさ）pulmonary function test
廃棄物処理（はいきぶつしょり）refuse disposal
廃棄物処理法（はいきぶつしょりほう）Waste Disposal and Public Cleaning Law
配給割当（はいきゅうわりあて）distribution quota
肺気量測定法（はいきりょうそくていほう）spirometry
†バイキング食（ばいきんぐしょく）all-you-can-eat buffet

配偶者（はいぐうしゃ）spouse
配偶者虐待（はいぐうしゃぎゃくたい）spouse abuse
配偶者控除（はいぐうしゃこうじょ）marital deduction
配偶者税控除（はいぐうしゃぜいこうじょ）tax deduction for a spouse
背屈（はいくつ）dorsiflexion；dorsal flexion
背景因子（はいけいいんし）contextual factor
敗血（はいけつ）sepsis
肺結核（はいけっかく）pulmonary tuberculosis
敗血症（はいけつしょう）septicemia；blood poisoning
敗血症性ショック（はいけつしょうせいしょっく）septic shock
肺疾患（はいしっかん）pulmonary disease
売春（ばいしゅん）prostitution
売春防止法（ばいしゅんぼうしほう）Prostitution Prevention Law
賠償（ばいしょう）indemnity；compensation
配食サービス（はいしょくさーびす）meal delivery services；Meals on Wheels
排水管（はいすいかん）drain
肺水腫（はいすいしゅ）pulmonary edema
†バイスティックの7原則（ばいすてぃっくのななげんそく）Biestek's 7 principles
†排泄（はいせつ）excretion；toileting
排泄介護（はいせつかいご）excretion care
†排泄介助（はいせつかいじょ）toileting assistance；assistance with toileting
排泄関連用具（はいせつかんれんようぐ）continence care product
排泄訓練（はいせつくんれん）excretion exercise；toilet training
排泄ケア（はいせつけあ）excretion care
排泄障害（はいせつしょうがい）excretion disorder
排泄スケジュール（はいせつすけじゅーる）toileting schedule
排泄物（はいせつぶつ）fece
排泄用具（はいせつようぐ）excretion tool
配膳（はいぜん）meal tray services
肺塞栓（はいそくせん）pulmonary embolus
†バイタルサイン（ばいたるさいん）vital signs
配置（はいち）placement
配置決定（はいちけってい）decision for the placement；placement decision
倍動肘ヒンジ継手（ばいどうひじひんじつぎて）step-up elbow hinge
肺動脈閉鎖症（はいどうみゃくへいさしょう）pulmonary atresia
梅毒（ばいどく）syphilis
ハイドロキシクロロキン（はいどろきしくろろきん）hydroxychloroquine

ハイドロコレーター（はいどろこれーたー）hydrocollator
†排尿（はいにょう）urination
排尿管理（はいにょうかんり）urinary management
排尿筋括約筋協調不全（はいにょうきんかつやくきんきょうちょうふぜん）detrusor-sphincter dyssynergia；DSD
排尿訓練（はいにょうくんれん）bladder training
†排尿困難（はいにょうこんなん）difficult urination
†排尿障害（はいにょうしょうがい）micturition disorder；dysuria；urinary disorder
排尿中枢（はいにょうちゅうすう）micturition center
排尿不能症（はいにょうふのうしょう）acraturesis
排尿無力症（はいにょうむりょくしょう）⇒排尿不能症
肺ノカルジア症（はいのかるじあしょう）pulmonary nocardiosis
バイパス手術（ばいぱすしゅじゅつ）bypass surgery
ハイブリッド人工臓器（はいぶりっどじんこうぞうき）artificial hybrid organ
バイブレーション（ばいぶれーしょん）⇒振動
配分（はいぶん）allocation
配分金（はいぶんきん）allocated money
配分計画（はいぶんけいかく）allocation plan
†排便（はいべん）defecation
排便管理（はいべんかんり）bowel management
排便訓練（はいべんくんれん）bowel training
†排便障害（はいべんしょうがい）dyschezia；defecation disorder
排便造影検査（はいべんぞうえいけんさ）defecography
排便内圧検査（はいべんないあつけんさ）defecometry
肺胞（はいほう）alveolus
肺胞ガス交換（はいほうがすこうかん）alveolar gas exchange
肺胞換気（はいほうかんき）alveolar ventilation
肺胞気（はいほうき）alveolar air
肺胞気式（はいほうきしき）alveolar air equation
肺胞気・動脈血酸素分圧較差（はいほうき・どうみゃくけつさんそぶんあつこうさ）alveolar-arterial oxygen tension difference
肺胞虚脱（はいほうきょだつ）alveolar collapse
肺胞腔（はいほうこう）alveolar space
肺胞構築（はいほうこうちく）alveolar structure
肺胞サーファクタント（はいほうさーふぁくたんと）⇒肺胞表面活性物質
肺胞死腔（はいほうしこう）alveolar dead space
肺胞傷害（はいほうしょうがい）alveolar damage
肺胞上皮（はいほうじょうひ）alveolar epithelium
肺胞上皮細胞（はいほうじょうひさいぼう）alveolar epithelial cell；alveolar cell
肺胞水腫（はいほうすいしゅ）⇒肺胞浮腫
肺胞性低酸素（はいほうせいていさんそ）alveolar hypoxia
肺胞洗浄（はいほうせんじょう）alveolar lavage
肺胞低換気（はいほうていかんき）alveolar hypoventilation
肺胞内圧（はいほうないあつ）alveolar pressure
肺胞表面活性物質（はいほうひょうめんかっせいぶっしつ）alveolar surfactant
肺胞表面張力（はいほうひょうめんちょうりょく）alveolar surface tension
肺胞浮腫（はいほうふしゅ）alveolar edema
肺胞膜（はいほうまく）alveolar membrane
肺胞マクロファージ（はいほうまくろふぁーじ）alveolar macrophage
肺胞・毛細血管関門（はいほう・もうさいけっかんかんもん）alveolar-capillary barrier
肺胞・毛細血管障壁（はいほう・もうさいけっかんしょうへき）alveolar-capillary barrier
肺胞リクルートメント（はいほうりくるーとめんと）alveolar recruitment
ハイムリッヒ法（はいむりっひほう）Heimlich Maneuver
廃用（はいよう）disuse
†廃用萎縮（はいよういしゅく）disuse atrophy
†廃用症候群（はいようしょうこうぐん）disuse syndrome
廃用性筋萎縮（はいようせいきんいしゅく）disuse muscle atrophy
廃用性骨萎縮（はいようせいこついしゅく）disuse bone atrophy
肺容量減少手術（はいようりょうげんしょうしゅじゅつ）lung volume reduction surgery
肺理学療法（はいりがくりょうほう）chest physical therapy
ハイリスク（はいりすく）high risk
パイロジェン（ぱいろじぇん）pyrogen
パイロジェンテスト（ぱいろじぇんてすと）pyrogen test
パウチ（ぱうち）pouch
バウチャー方式（ばうちゃーほうしき）voucher system
歯及び口腔部位の呼称システム（はおよびこうくうぶいのこしょうしすてむ）designation system for teeth and areas of the oral cavity
博士号（はかせごう）Doctor of Philosophy degree；doctorate degree
パーカッション（ぱーかっしょん）percussion
吐き気（はきけ）nausea
パキシパム（ぱきしぱむ）Paxipam
パキシル（ぱきしる）Paxil
履物（はきもの）footwear

介護保険・介護福祉等関連用語 和英

パーキンソニズム（ぱーきんそにずむ）Parkinsonism
パーキンソン症候群（ぱーきんそんしょうこうぐん）Parkinson's syndrome
パーキンソン体操（ぱーきんそんたいそう）physical exercise for Parkinson's disease
†パーキンソン病（ぱーきんそんびょう）Parkinson's disease
博愛事業（はくあいじぎょう）philanthropy
†白杖（はくじょう）white cane
白色人種（はくしょくじんしゅ）Caucasians
白癬（はくせん）tinea
†白内障（はくないしょう）cataract
バーグバランス評価（ばーぐばらんすひょうか）Berg Balance Scale
薄片生検（はくへんせいけん）shave biopsy
剥離細胞診（はくりさいぼうしん）exfoliative cytology
ハグルンド奇形（はぐるんどきけい）Haglund's deformity
曝露（ばくろ）exposure
派遣労働者（はけんろうどうしゃ）dispatch worker
跛行（はこう）claudication
箱型継手（はこがたつぎて）box joint
箱庭療法（はこにわりょうほう）sand play technique
ハサップ（はさっぷ）Hazard Analysis Critical Control Point system：HACCP
把持（はじ）prehension
把持装具（はじそうぐ）tenodesis splint：prehension orthosis
橋本甲状腺炎（はしもとこうじょうせんえん）Hashimoto's thyroiditis
橋本病（はしもとびょう）Hashimoto disease
パジャマ（ぱじゃま）pajamas
播種性血管内凝固症候群（はしゅせいけっかんないぎょうこしょうこうぐん）disseminated intravascular coagulation
把持用具（はじようぐ）aid for grasping
破傷風（はしょうふう）tetanus
バスケット鉗子（ばすけっとかんし）basket forceps
バスボード（ばすぼーど）bath board
†長谷川式簡易知能評価スケール改訂版（はせがわしきかんいちのうひょうかすけーるかいていばん）Hasegawa's Dementia Scale-Revised：HDS-R
長谷川式簡易認知症スケール（はせがわしきかんいにんちしょうすけーる）Hasegawa's Dementia Scale：HDS
ハーセプチン（はーせぷちん）Herceptin
バーセル指数（ばーせるしすう）Barthel index
バソテック（ばそてっく）Vasotec
パーソナリティ（ぱーそなりてぃ）personality
肌着（はだぎ）underwear

パターナリズム（ぱたーなりずむ）paternalism
八時間毎（はちじかんごと）every 8 hours；Q8H
80代（はちじゅうだい）octogenarian
発癌（はつがん）carcinogenesis
罰金（ばっきん）penalty；fine
†バックサポート（ばっくさぽーと）back support
バックレスト（ばっくれすと）backrest
白血球（はっけっきゅう）white blood cell：WBC；leukocyte
白血病（はっけつびょう）leukemia
発語失行（はつごしっこう）verbal apraxia；apraxia of speech
発生（はっせい）incidence
発生率（はっせいりつ）incidence rate
罰則（ばっそく）penal regulation
発達（はったつ）development
発達検査（はったつけんさ）developmental test
発達指数（はったつしすう）developmental quotient：DQ
†発達障害（はったつしょうがい）developmental disorder；developmental disability
発達障害者支援法（はったつしょうがいしゃしえんほう）Developmental Disabilities Assistance Act
発達精神病理学（はったつせいしんびょうりがく）developmental psychopathology
発達段階（はったつだんかい）developmental stage
発達遅延（はったつちえん）developmental delay
発達年齢（はったつねんれい）developmental age
発達理論（はったつりろん）developmental theory
発展途上国（はってんとじょうこく）developing country
パッド（ぱっど）pad
†発熱（はつねつ）fever
発話知覚指導カリキュラムと評価（はつわちかくしどうかりきゅらむとひょうか）speech perception instructional curriculum and evaluation
パーティクルカウンタ（ぱーてぃくるかうんた）particle counter
パートタイム労働（ぱーとたいむろうどう）part-time work
パートタイム労働者（ぱーとたいむろうどうしゃ）part-time worker
ハートナップ症（はーとなっぷしょう）Hartnup disorder
ハートビル法（はーとびる法）Heart Building Law
バニオン（ばにおん）bunion
パニック障害（ぱにっくしょうがい）panic disorder
ハーネス（はーねす）harness
パネルヒーター（ぱねるひーたー）panel heater
ハーバード医療過誤研究（はーばーどいりょうかごけんきゅう）Harvard Medical Malpractice Study
ハバードタンク（はばーどたんく）hubbard tank
ハビリテーション（はびりてーしょん）habilitation

ハブ（はぶ）hub
ハーフライフ（はーふらいふ）half-life
パペッツ回路（ぱぺっつかいろ）Papez circuit
歯磨き（はみがき）tooth brushing
ハミルトンうつ病評価尺度（はみるとんうつびょうひょうかしゃくど）Hamilton Rating Scale for Depression；HamD
パメロール（ぱめろーる）Pamelor
バラクルード（ばらくるーど）Baraclude
パラサイト・シングル（ぱらさいと・しんぐる）parasite single
バラシクロビル（ばらしくろびる）valacyclovir
ハラゼパム（はらぜぱむ）halazepam
パラダイム（ぱらだいむ）paradigm
パラフィン浴（ぱらふぃんよく）paraffin bath
パラフレニー（ぱらふれにー）paraphrenia
パラリンピック（ぱらりんぴっく）Paralympics
バランス（ばらんす）balance
バリア器材（ばりあきざい）barrier equipment
バリアナーシング（ばりあなーしんぐ）barrier nursing
†バリアフリー（ばりあふりー）barrier free
バリアフリー住宅（ばりあふりーじゅうたく）barrier free home
バリアフリー新法（ばりあふりーしんぽう）New Barrier Free Law
バリアフリーデザイン（ばりあふりーでざいん）barrier free design
バリアフリーマップ（ばりあふりーまっぷ）barrier free map
バリア予防策（ばりあよぼうさく）barrier precaution
バリウム（ばりうむ）Valium
バリウムがゆ（ばりうむがゆ）barium meal
バリウム造影（ばりうむぞうえい）barium contrast radiography
バリウム注腸造影（ばりうむちゅうちょうぞうえい）barium enema
針筋電図（はりきんでんず）needle electromyogram
針刺し（はりさし）needlestick
針刺し事故（はりさしじこ）needlestick injury
はり師（はりし）acupuncturist
はり師・きゅう師（はりし・きゅうし）acupuncture and moxibustion therapist
ハリス・ベネディクト基礎エネルギー消費量算定式（はりす・べねでぃくときそえねるぎーしょうひりょうさんていしき）Harris-Benedict caloric intake equation
ハリス・ベネディクト算定式（はりす・べねでぃくとさんていしき）Harris-Benedict equation
針生検（はりせいけん）needle biopsy
針穿刺（はりせんし）needle puncture
バリデーション（ばりでーしょん）validation

バリデーション療法（ばりでーしょんりょうほう）validation therapy
バリューフォーマネー（ばりゅーふぉーまねー）value-for-money；VFM
パルスオキシメータ（ぱるすおきしめーた）pulse oximeter
バルトレックス（ばるとれっくす）Valtrex
パルネート（ぱるねーと）Parnate
バルプロ酸（ばるぷろさん）valproic acid
†バルーンカテーテル（ばるーんかてーてる）balloon catheter
バルーン排出試験（ばるーんはいしゅつしけん）balloon expulsion test
バルーン保持試験（ばるーんほじしけん）balloon retaining test
パレート最適（ぱれーとさいてき）Pareto optimum
ハロー装具（はろーそうぐ）halo orthosis
ハローベスト（はろーべすと）halo-vest orthosis
パワーリハビリテーション（ぱわーりはびりてーしょん）power rehabilitation
バーンアウト（ばーんあうと）burnout
バーンアウト・シンドローム（ばーんあうと・しんどろーむ）burnout syndrome
半跏趺坐（はんかふざ）half lotus sitting position
半月（はんげつ）cuff
判決監視プロジェクト（はんけつかんしぷろじぇくと）Sentencing Project
バンコマイシン耐性腸球菌（ばんこまいしんたいせいちょうきゅうきん）vancomycin resistant enterococci；VRE
晩婚化（ばんこんか）late marriage
瘢痕拘縮（はんこんこうしゅく）cicatricial contracture；scar contracture
半座位（はんざい）half-sitting position
犯罪（はんざい）crime
犯罪社会学（はんざいしゃかいがく）criminology
犯罪心理学（はんざいしんりがく）criminal psychology
犯罪被害（はんざいひがい）crime victimization
犯罪被害者救済（はんざいひがいしゃきゅうさい）victim care
反射（はんしゃ）reflex
反射運動（はんしゃうんどう）reflex movement
反射性交感神経性ジストロフィー（はんしゃせいこうかんしんけいせいじすとろふぃー）reflex sympathetic dystrophy；RSD
†半身浴（はんしんよく）half-body bath
伴生種（ばんせいしゅ）companion
ハンセン病（はんせんびょう）Hansen's disease；leprosy
ハンセン病対策（はんせんびょうたいさく）Hansen's disease control policy；leprosy control policy

介護保険・介護福祉等関連用語 和英

半側空間失認（はんそくくうかんしつにん）unilateral spatial agnosia
半側空間無視（はんそくくうかんむし）unilateral spatial neglect：USN
半側無視（はんそくむし）unilateral neglect
反対色（はんたいしょく）opponent color
反対色細胞（はんたいしょくさいぼう）color opponent cell
パンチバイオプシー（ぱんちばいおぷしー）punch biopsy
反長膝（はんちょうひざ）back knee
†半調理（はんちょうり）semi-prepared dish
ハンチントン病（はんちんとんびょう）Huntington's disease
ハンチントン舞踏病（はんちんとんぶとうしょう）Huntington's chorea；Huntington's disease
判定会議（はんていかいぎ）decision-making meeting
ハンディキャップ（はんでぃきゃっぷ）handicap
ハンド（はんど）hand
反動形成（はんどうけいせい）reaction formation
パントテン酸（ぱんとてんさん）pantothenic acid
ハンドリム（はんどりむ）handrim
ハンドレール（はんどれーる）handrail
万能腕動作支持器（ばんのううでどうさしじき）mobile arm support
反応階層（はんのうかいそう）response hierarchy
反応時間（はんのうじかん）reaction time
反応性精神病（はんのうせいせいしんびょう）reactive psychosis
反復唾液嚥下テスト（はんぷくだえきえんげてすと）repetitive saliva swallowing test：RSST
反復反射（はんぷくはんしゃ）reiterative reflection
半盲（はんもう）hemianopia
汎理論的モデル（はんりろんてきもでる）transtheoretical model

ひ

ピアカウンセリング（ぴあかうんせりんぐ）peer counseling
ピアグループ（ぴあぐるーぷ）peer group
ピアグループスーパービジョン（ぴあぐるーぷすーぱーびじょん）peer group supervision
ピアサポート（ぴあさぽーと）peer support
ピアーズ基準（ぴあーずきじゅん）Beers criteria：Beers list
ピアスーパービジョン（ぴあすーぱーびじょん）peer supervision
非アテローム性冠動脈疾患（ひあてろーむせいかんどうみゃくしっかん）non-atherosclerotic coronary artery disease
非営利アドボカシー（ひえいりあどぼかしー）non-profit advocacy
非営利組織（ひえいりそしき）non-profit organization：NPO
PHN（ぴーえっちえぬ）post-herpetic neuralgia
BADL（びーえーでぃーえる）basic activities of daily living
†BMI（びーえむあい）body mass index
鼻炎（びえん）rhinitis
ビオチン（びおちん）biotin
皮下（ひか）subcutaneous：Sub-Q
非該当（ひがいとう）not applicable：N/A
†被害妄想（ひがいもうそう）delusion of persecution
日帰り介護（ひがえりかいご）ambulatory care；outpatient care；commuting for care
日帰りリハビリテーション（ひがえりりはびりてーしょん）ambulatory rehabilitation；outpatient rehabilitation；commuting for rehabilitation
皮下出血（ひかしゅっけつ）subcutaneous bleeding
非課税世帯（ひかぜいせたい）tax-exempt household
非課税団体（ひかぜいだんたい）tax-exempt organization
B型肝炎（びーがたかんえん）hepatitis B：HBV
B型肝炎ウイルス（びーがたかんえんういるす）hepatitis B Virus
皮下トンネル感染（ひかとんねるかんせん）tunnel infection
非貨幣的ニーズ（ひかへいてきにーず）non-monetary needs
光老化（ひかりろうか）photoaging
非癌疾患患者（ひがんしっかんかんじゃ）non-cancer patient
引きこもり（ひきこもり）social withdrawal
被虐待高齢者（ひぎゃくたいこうれいしゃ）abused elderly
被虐待児童（ひぎゃくたいじどう）abused child；battered child
被虐待老人（ひぎゃくたいろうじん）abused elderly
ビグアニド（びぐあにど）biguanide
非経口栄養（ひけいこうえいよう）parenteral feeding
髭そり（ひげそり）shaving
非結核性抗酸菌症（ひけっかくせいこうさんきんしょう）non-tuberculous mycobacterial infection
†非言語的コミュニケーション（ひげんごてきこみゅにけーしょん）nonverbal communication
非行少年（ひこうしょうねん）juvenile delinquent
非合理的信念（ひごうりてきしんねん）irrational belief
日毎（ひごと）every day：QD
膝当て（ひざあて）knee pad；anterior knee cap

微細脳機能損傷（びさいのうきのうそんしょう） minimal brain damage：MBD
微細脳損傷（びさいのうそんしょう） minor brain damage：MBD
膝折れ（ひざおれ） knee giving way；giving way of the knee
膝関節置換術（ひざかんせつちかんじゅつ） knee replacement
膝義足（ひざぎそく） knee disarticulation prosthesis
膝座位（ひざい）⇒正座位
膝装具（ひざそうぐ） knee orthosis：KO；knee brace
膝継手（ひざつぎて） knee joint
膝のインパクト（ひざのいんぱくと） terminal impact
膝用伸展補助装置（ひざようしんてんほじょそうち） knee extension assist
P300（ぴーさんびゃく） P300
肘置き（ひじおき） armrest
肘義手（ひじぎしゅ） elbow disarticulation prosthesis
肘骨折（ひじこっせつ） elbow fracture
肘台付杖（ひじだいつきつえ） platform crutch
皮質下血管性認知症（ひしつかけっかんせいにんちしょう） subcortical vascular dementia
肘這い（ひじはい） creeping
非常勤職員（ひじょうきんしょくいん） part-time staff
微小血管造影（びしょうけっかんぞうえい） microangiography
非小細胞肺癌（ひしょうさいぼうはいがん） non-small cell lung cancer：NSCLC
微小バルーン（びしょうばるーん） micro balloon
肘浴（ひじよく） elbow bathing
非処方箋薬（ひしょほうせんやく） non-prescription drug
非侵襲的検査（ひしんしゅうてきけんさ） non-invasive diagnostic test
非審判的態度（ひしんぱんてきたいど） non-judgmental attitude
非審判的態度の原則（ひしんぱんてきたいどのげんそく） principle of non-judgmental attitude
ヒスタミンH2受容体遮断薬（ひすたみんえっちつーじゅようたいしゃだんやく） histamine H2-receptor blocker
ヒスタミンH1受容体遮断薬（ひすたみんえっちわんじゅようたいしゃだんやく） histamine H1-receptor blocker
ヒスタミン受容体遮断薬（ひすたみんじゅようたいしゃだんやく） histamine receptor blocker
ヒステリー（ひすてりー） hysteria
非ステロイド系抗炎症薬（ひすてろいどけいこうえんしょうざい） non-steroidal antiinflammatory drug：NSAID
ビスフォスフォネート製剤（びすふぉすふぉねーとせいざい） bisphosphonate drug
非政府組織（ひせいふそしき） non-governmental organization：NGO
微生物汚染（びせいぶつおせん） microorganism contamination
非生物合成（ひせいぶつごうせい） abiotic synthesis
微生物飛散者（びせいぶつひさんしゃ） disperser
ヒ素中毒（ひそちゅうどく） arsenic poisoning
肥大（ひだい） hypertrophy
肥大型心筋症（ひだいがたしんきんしょう） hypertrophic cardiomyopathy
†ビタミン（びたみん） vitamin
ビタミンE欠乏症（びたみんいーけつぼうしょう） vitamin E deficiency
ビタミンA欠乏症（びたみんえーけつぼうしょう） vitamin A deficiency
ビタミンK欠乏症（びたみんけーけつぼうしょう） vitamin K deficiency
ビタミンC欠乏症（びたみんしーけつぼうしょう） vitamin C deficiency
ビタミンD欠乏症（びたみんでぃーけつぼうしょう） vitamin D deficiency
ビタミンB12欠乏症（びたみんびーじゅうにけつぼうしょう） vitamin B12 deficiency
ビタミンB2欠乏症（びたみんびーつーけつぼうしょう） vitamin B2 deficiency
ビタミンB6欠乏症（びたみんびーろくーけつぼうしょう） vitamin B6 deficiency
ビタミンB1欠乏症（びたみんびーわんけつぼうしょう） vitamin B1 deficiency
左側臥位（ひだりそくがい） Left Lateral Recumbent
ひっかく（ひっかく） scratching
†筆記試験（ひっきしけん） written examination
ピック病（ぴっくびょう） Pick's disease；Pick disease
必須アミノ酸（ひっすあみのさん） essential amino acid
筆談（ひつだん） written communication
必要栄養量（ひつようえいようりょう） essential nutrition
必要時（ひつようじ） as needed：PRN
必要前提基準（ひつようぜんていきじゅん） prerequisite criteria
必要即応の原則（ひつようそくおうのげんそく） needs-response principle
PT（ぴーてぃー） physical therapist
PTSD（ぴーてぃーえすでぃー） post-traumatic stress disorder
非定型抗酸菌症（ひていけいこうさんきんしょう）

atypical mycobacteria
非定型抗精神病薬（ひていけいこうせいしんびょうやく）atypical antipsychotic
非定型精神病（ひていけいせいしんびょう）atypical psychosis
PTB式下腿義足（ぴーてぃーびーしきかたいぎそく）patellar tendon bearing transtibial prosthesis
PTB式短下肢装具（ぴーてぃーびーしきたんかしそうぐ）patellar tendon bearing ankle-foot orthosis
ビデオ内視鏡検査（びでおないしきょうけんさ）video endoscopy
ヒトゲノムプロジェクト（ひとげのむぷろじぇくと）Human Genome Project
ヒト上皮増殖因子受容体2型（ひとじょうひぞうしょくいんしじゅようたい2にがた）human epidermal growth factor receptor-2：HER2
ヒト白血球抗原（ひとはっけっきゅうこうげん）human lymphocyte antigen
ヒト免疫不全ウイルス（ひとめんえきふぜんういるす）human immunodeficiency virus：HIV
ヒト免疫不全ウイルス感染（ひとめんえきふぜんういるすかんせん）HIV infection
ヒドララジン（ひどららじん）hydralazine
一人親家庭（ひとりおやかてい）single-parent family
一人暮らし高齢者（ひとりぐらしこうれいしゃ）solitary-living elderly
一人暮らし障害者（ひとりぐらししょうがいしゃ）solitary-living disabled person
一人暮らし老人（ひとりぐらしろうじん）solitary-living elderly
一人っ子政策（ひとりっこせいさく）one-child policy
ヒドロコドン（ひどろこどん）hydrocodone
避難場所（ひなんばしょ）evacuation site
泌尿器科（ひにょうきか）urology
泌尿器科医（ひにょうきかい）urologist
否認（ひにん）denial
ビネー式知能検査（びねーしきちのうけんさ）Binet Intelligence Test；Binet Test
微熱（びねつ）slight fever
非配分の原則（ひはいぶんのげんそく）non-distribution constraint
被爆者（ひばくしゃ）atomic bomb survivor
微表情（びひょうじょう）micro-expressions
皮膚（ひふ）skin
皮膚科医（ひふかい）dermatologist
皮膚科学（ひふかがく）dermatology
皮膚癌（ひふがん）skin cancer
皮膚筋炎（ひふきんえん）dermatomyositis
被服（ひふく）clothes
被覆剤（ひふくざい）coating drug
被覆材（ひふくざい）coating flux
被服手当（ひふくてあて）clothing allowance
皮膚糸状菌（ひふしじょうきん）dermatophyte
皮膚糸状菌症（ひふしじょうきんしょう）dermatophytosis
皮膚疾患（ひふしっかん）skin disease
皮膚障害（ひふしょうがい）skin disorder
皮膚消毒（ひふしょうどく）skin antiseptic
皮膚掻痒感（ひふそうようかん）cutaneous pruritus
皮膚掻痒症（ひふそうようしょう）skin pruritus
皮膚損傷（ひふそんしょう）skin tear
皮膚電位反応（ひふでんいはんのう）electrodermal responding
ヒプノセラピー（ひぷのせらぴー）⇒催眠療法
皮膚表面細菌培養法（ひふひょうめんさいきんばいようほう）skin surface culture method
皮膚保護剤（ひふほござい）skin barrier
被扶養者（ひふようしゃ）dependent
飛蚊症（ひぶんしょう）myodesopsia；floaters
ヒポクラテスの誓い（ひぽくらてすのちかい）Hippocratic Oath
†被保険者（ひほけんしゃ）insured
被保険者期間（ひほけんしゃきかん）insured period
被保険者均等割（ひほけんしゃきんとうわり）premiums on a per capita basis
被保護者（ひほごしゃ）public assistance recipient
被保護者世帯（ひほごしゃせたい）household on public assistance；household with public assistance；household receiving public assistance
飛沫核（ひまつかく）droplet nuclei
飛沫感染（ひまつかんせん）droplet infection；aerial infection
飛沫伝播（ひまつでんぱ）droplet transmission
飛沫予防策（ひまつよぼうさく）droplet precaution
†肥満（ひまん）obesity
肥満指数（ひまんしすう）obesity index
肥満症（ひまんしょう）adipositas
びまん性軸索損傷（びまんせいじくさくそんしょう）diffuse axonal injury：DAI
肥満低換気症候群（ひまんていかんきしょうこうぐん）obesity hypoventilation syndrome
†秘密保持（ひみつほじ）confidentiality
秘密保持義務（ひみつほじぎむ）secrecy obligation
秘密保持の原則（ひみつほじのげんそく）principle of confidentiality
100歳代（ひゃくさいだい）centenarian
110歳以上（ひゃくじゅっさいいじょう）supercentenarian
日雇労働者（ひやといろうどうしゃ）day laborer；day labor employee
日雇労働者健康保険（ひやといろうどうしゃけんこう

ほけん）Day Laborers Health Insurance
ヒューマン・ライツ・ウォッチ（ひゅーまん・らいつ・うぉっち）Human Rights Watch：HRW［国際人権擁護団体］
ヒュミラ（ひゅみら）Humira
ピューレ状（ぴゅーれじょう）puréed solid
病院（びょういん）hospital
病院環境（びょういんかんきょう）hospital environment
病院感染（びょういんかんせん）hospital infection；hospital-acquired infection
病院感染管理実践諮問委員会（びょういんかんせんかんりじっせんしもんいいんかい）Hospital Infection Control Practice Advisory Committee
病院感染肺炎（びょういんかんせんはいえん）hospital-acquired pneumonia
病院機能評価（びょういんきのうひょうか）hospital accreditation
病院基盤型サービス（びょういんきばんがたさーびす）hospital-based services
病院情報システム（びょういんじょうほうしすてむ）hospital information system
病院退院（びょういんたいいん）discharge from the hospital
病院入院（びょういんにゅういん）hospitalization
病院ボランティア（びょういんぼらんてぃあ）hospital volunteer
評価（ひょうか）assessment；evaluation
評価額（ひょうかがく）assessed value
評価項目（ひょうかこうもく）assessment item；evaluation item
病気行動（びょうきこうどう）illness behavior
病気の兆候（びょうきのちょうこう）signs of disease
病原体（びょうげんたい）pathogenic organism；pathogen
表在感覚（ひょうざいかんかく）superficial sensation
病識（びょうしき）insight into disease
被用者（ひようしゃ）employee
被用者健康保険（ひようしゃけんこうほけん）employees health insurance；employees' health insurance
被用者年金（ひようしゃねんきん）employee pension；employees' pension
被用者保険（ひようしゃほけん）employee insurance；employees' insurance
標準化（ひょうじゅんか）standardization
標準化死亡比（ひょうじゅんかしぼうひ）standardized mortality ratio：SMR
標準給付パッケージ（ひょうじゅんきゅうふぱっけーじ）standard benefits package
標準給付費額（ひょうじゅんきゅうふひがく）cost of standard benefits
標準控除（ひょうじゅんこうじょ）standard deduction
標準失語症検査（ひょうじゅんしつごしょうけんさ）standard language test of aphasia：SLTA
標準年金（ひょうじゅんねんきん）standard pension
標準負担額（ひょうじゅんふたんがく）cost of standard payment
標準偏差（ひょうじゅんへんさ）standard deviation：SD
標準報酬（ひょうじゅんほうしゅう）standard for remuneration
標準予防策（ひょうじゅんよぼうさく）standard precaution
病床規制（びょうしょうきせい）control of hospital bed；hospital bed-control
表情反射（ひょうじょうはんしゃ）facial reflection
病診連携（びょうしんれんけい）affiliation between outpatient clinics and hospitals
病巣（びょうそう）nidus
病巣感染（びょうそうかんせん）focal infection
費用対効果（ひようたいこうか）cost-effective
病態失認（びょうたいしつにん）anosognosia
費用徴収（ひようちょうしゅう）collection of costs
†氷枕（ひょうちん）ice pillow
病的骨折（びょうてきこっせつ）pathological bone fracture
病的状態の圧縮（びょうてきじょうたいのあっしゅく）morbidity compression；compression of morbidity
標の像所見（ひょうてきぞうしょけん）bull's eye appearance
病棟（びょうとう）unit
平等権（びょうどうけん）equal rights
病棟清掃（びょうとうせいそう）cleaning of the patient care unit
†氷嚢（ひょうのう）ice bag
漂白（ひょうはく）bleaching
漂白液（ひょうはくえき）bleach solution
漂白剤（ひょうはくざい）bleaching agent
費用負担方式（ひようふたんほうしき）cost-sharing formula
費用便益（ひようべんえき）cost-benefit
標本誤差（ひょうほんごさ）sampling error
標本抽出（ひょうほんちゅうしゅつ）sampling
標本抽出法（ひょうほんちゅうしゅつほう）sampling design
標本調査（ひょうほんちょうさ）sample survey
表面筋電図（ひょうめんきんでんず）surface electromyogram
表面色モード（ひょうめんしょくもーど）surface color mode

介護保険・介護福祉等関連用語 和英

表面電極（ひょうめんでんきょく）surface electrode
費用抑制（ひようよくせい）cost containment
病理検査（びょうりけんさ）pathology test
病歴価格決定方式（びょうれきかかくけっていほうしき）experience rating
†日和見感染（ひよりみかんせん）opportunistic infection
ピラジンアミド（ぴらじんあみど）pyrazinamide
びらん（びらん）erosion
微量栄養素（びりょうえいようそ）trace nutrient
比例分配（ひれいぶんぱい）quota share
疲労（ひろう）fatigue
広場恐怖症（ひろばきょうふしょう）agoraphobia
ピロリン酸塩沈着症（ぴろりんさんえんちんちゃくしょう）pyrophosphate deposition disease
ピロリン酸カルシウム結晶沈着症（ぴろりんさんかるしうむけっしょうちんちゃくしょう）calcium pyrophosphate deposition disease
ピンクノイズプロトコル（ぴんくのいずぷろとこる）pink noise protocol
†貧血（ひんけつ）anemia
貧血治療薬（ひんけつちりょうやく）antianemia drug
頻呼吸（ひんこきゅう）tachypnea
貧困（ひんこん）poverty
貧困家庭（ひんこんかてい）poor family
貧困指数（ひんこんしすう）poverty index
貧困者（ひんこんしゃ）poor
貧困水準（ひんこんすいじゅん）poverty level
貧困線（ひんこんせん）poverty line
貧困の再発見（ひんこんのさいはっけん）rediscovery of poverty
貧困の女性化（ひんこんのじょせいか）feminization of poverty
品質管理活動（ひんしつかんりかつどう）quality control：QC
ビンジ・ドリンキング（びんじ・どりんきんぐ）binge drinking
ビンスワンガー病（びんすわんがーびょう）Binswanger's disease
頻尿（ひんにょう）polyuria；pollakiuria
†頻便（ひんべん）frequent bowel movements
頻脈（ひんみゃく）tachycardia

ふ

ファーガソンレポート（ふぁーがそんれぽーと）Ferguson Report
ファミリー・ケースワーク（ふぁみりー・けーすわーく）family case work
ファミリー・サポート（ふぁみりー・さぽーと）family support

ファミリー・サポート・センター（ふぁみりー・さぽーと・せんたー）family support center
ファミリー・ソーシャルワーク（ふぁみりー・そーしゃるわーく）family social work
ファムシクロビル（ふぁむしくろびる）famciclovir
ファムビル（ふぁむびる）Famvir
†ファーラー位（ふぁーらーい）Fowler's position
不安症（ふあんしょう）anxiety
不安神経症（ふあんしんけいしょう）anxiety neurosis
ファンタジー徘徊（ふぁんたじーはいかい）fantasy wandering
不一致（ふいっち）incongruence
フィットネス（ふぃっとねす）fitness
フィート（ふぃーと）feet
フィナステリド（ふぃなすてりど）finasteride
フィーバーフュー（ふぃーばーふゅー）feverfew
VPシャント（ぶいぴーしゃんと）ventriculoperitoneal shunting
フィブリン（ふぃぶりん）fibrin
フィランソロピー（ふぃらんそろぴー）philanthropy
フィリングイン（ふぃりんぐいん）filling-in
フィンガーストリーク法（ふぃんがーすとりーくほう）finger streak plate method
フィンガープリント法（ふぃんがーぷりんとほう）finger print plate method
夫婦家族（ふうふかぞく）conjugal family
夫婦関係（ふうふかんけい）marital relationship
夫婦財産契約（ふうふざいさんけいやく）marital property agreement
夫婦療法（ふうふりょうほう）marital therapy
風味（ふうみ）flavor
†フェイスシート（ふぇいすしーと）face sheet
フェイスマスク（ふぇいすますく）face mask
フェネルジン（ふぇねるじん）phenelzine
フェノールブロック（ふぇのーるぶろっく）phenol block
フェビアン主義（ふぇびあんしゅぎ）Fabianism
フェミニスト・ソーシャルワーク（ふぇみにすと・そーしゃるわーく）feminist social work
フェミニズム（ふぇみにずむ）feminism
フェミニズム理論（ふぇみにずむりろん）feminist theory
不応性（ふおうせい）adiaphoria
フォーカシング（ふぉーかしんぐ）focusing
フォークオーター切断（ふぉーくおーたーせつだん）forequarter amputation
フォサマックス（ふぉさまっくす）Fosamax
フォード主義（ふぉーどしゅぎ）Fordism
フォーマルケア（ふぉーまるけあ）formal care
フォーマルサービス（ふぉーまるさーびす）formal service
フォーマルセクター（ふぉーまるせくたー）formal

sector
フォーマルネットワーク（ふぉーまるねっとわーく）formal network
フォルクマン拘縮（ふぉるくまんこうしゅく）Volkmann's contracture；ischemic contracture
†フォローアップ（ふぉろーあっぷ）follow-up
付加（ふか）addition
不快指数（ふかいしすう）discomfort index
付加価値税（ふかかちぜい）value added tax：VAT
付加給付（ふかきゅうふ）fringe benefit；supplement benefit
付加欠失型突然変異（ふかけっしつがたとつぜんへんい）addition-deletion mutation
付加重合（ふかじゅうごう）addition polymerization
付加重合体（ふかじゅうごうたい）addition polymer
負荷心電図（ふかしんでんず）stress electrocardiogram
不活性化係数（ふかっせいかけいすう）inactivation factor
付加年金（ふかねんきん）additional pension
付加変異（ふかへんい）addition mutation
賦課方式（ふかほうしき）imposition system
拭き取り採取（ふきとりさいしゅ）swab collection
拭き取り法（ふきとりほう）swab method
不均衡（ふきんこう）imbalance
腹圧性尿失禁（ふくあつせいにょうしっきん）stress incontinence
幅員（ふくいん）width
服役囚（ふくえきしゅう）prisoner
†腹臥位（ふくがい）prone position
副看護師長（ふくかんごしちょう）assistant director of nursing
腹腔鏡手術（ふくくうきょうしゅじゅつ）laparoscopic surgery
複合家族（ふくごうかぞく）joint family；extended family
副交感神経（ふくこうかんしんけい）parasympathetic nerve
複合施設（ふくごうしせつ）composite institute
腹腔洗浄（ふくこうせんじょう）peritoneal lavage
†副作用（ふくさよう）side effect
†福祉（ふくし）welfare
福祉援助（ふくしえんじょ）welfare assistance
福祉援助者（ふくしえんじょしゃ）welfare assistant
福祉活動（ふくしかつどう）welfare activity
福祉関係者（ふくしかんけいしゃ）welfare personnel
†福祉機器（ふくしきき）technical aid for the disabled
福祉基金（ふくしききん）welfare fund
†腹式呼吸（ふくしきこきゅう）abdominal breathing；abdominal respiration

福祉基準（ふくしきじゅん）welfare standards
福祉基盤課（ふくしきばんか）Welfare Promotion Division
福祉給付（ふくしきゅうふ）welfare benefit
福祉教育（ふくしきょういく）welfare education
福祉行政（ふくしぎょうせい）welfare administration
福祉公社（ふくしこうしゃ）welfare public corporation
福祉国家（ふくしこっか）welfare state
福祉国家の危機（ふくしこっかのきき）welfare state in crisis
福祉コミュニティ（ふくしこみゅにてぃ）community organization for welfare
福祉サービス（ふくしさーびす）welfare services
福祉サービス第三者評価制度（ふくしさーびすだいさんしゃひょうかせいど）third party quality certification system for welfare services
福祉システム（ふくししすてむ）welfare system
福祉施設（ふくししせつ）welfare facility
福祉指標（ふくししひょう）welfare indicator
福祉資本主義（ふくししほんしゅぎ）welfare capitalism
†福祉事務所（ふくしじむしょ）welfare office；public welfare office
福祉事務所所長（ふくしじむしょしょちょう）superintendent of public welfare office
福祉社会（ふくししゃかい）welfare society
福祉社会学（ふくししゃかいがく）sociology of welfare
福祉車両（ふくししゃりょう）welfare vehicle
福祉住環境コーディネーター（ふくしじゅうかんきょうこーでぃねーたー）housing & environment coordinator
福祉情報（ふくしじょうほう）welfare information
福祉職員（ふくししょくいん）welfare staff
福祉人材（ふくしじんざい）welfare manpower
福祉人材情報センター（ふくしじんざいじょうほうせんたー）Social Welfare National Center for Social Service Human Resources
福祉水準（ふくしすいじゅん）level of welfare
福祉政策（ふくしせいさく）welfare policy
福祉制度（ふくしせいど）welfare system
副施設長（ふくしせつちょう）assistant administrator
福祉専門（ふくしせんもん）welfare profession
福祉専門職（ふくしせんもんしょく）professional social work
福祉タクシー（ふくしたくしー）welfare taxi；welfare taxi services
福祉手当（ふくしてあて）welfare allowance
福祉電話（ふくしでんわ）telephone assistive device；assistive listening and technology

介護保険・介護福祉等関連用語　和英

device
福祉ニーズ（ふくしにーず）welfare needs
福祉年金（ふくしねんきん）welfare pension
福祉反動（ふくしはんどう）welfare backlash
福祉文化（ふくしぶんか）welfare culture
福祉ホーム（ふくしほーむ）welfare home
副主治医（ふくしゅじい）secondary physician
†福祉用具（ふくしようぐ）welfare equipment
福祉用具購入（ふくしようぐこうにゅう）purchase of welfare aids；purchase of welfare equipments
福祉用具産業（ふくしようぐさんぎょう）welfare equipment industry
福祉用具専門相談員（ふくしようぐせんもんそうだんいん）welfare equipments advisor
†福祉用具貸与（ふくしようぐたいよ）welfare equipment rentals；lending of welfare equipments
福祉用具貸与サービス（ふくしようぐたいよさーびす）welfare equipment rental services
福祉用具販売（ふくしようぐはんばい）welfare equipments trade
福祉用具プランナー（ふくしようぐぷらんなー）welfare equipments planner
福祉用具分類コード（ふくしようぐぶんるいこーど）Classification Code of Technical Aids：CCTA
福祉用具法（ふくしようぐほう）Welfare Equipment Law
福祉リクリエーション（ふくしりくりえーしょん）⇒福祉レクリエーション
福祉倫理（ふくしりんり）welfare ethics
福祉レクリエーション（ふくしれくりえーしょん）welfare and recreation
福祉レジーム（ふくしれじーむ）welfare regime
福祉労働（ふくしろうどう）labour welfare
副腎皮質ホルモン注腸（ふくじんひしつほるもんちゅうちょう）adrenocorticosteroid enema
腹痛（ふくつう）abdominalgia；abdominal pain
副鼻腔気管支症候群（ふくびこうきかんししょうこうぐん）sinobronchial syndrome
副鼻洞性頭痛（ふくびどうせいずつう）sinus headache
腹部X線写真（ふくぶえっくすせんしゃしん）abdominal x-ray
腹部穿刺（ふくぶせんし）abdominocentesis
腹部超音波検査（ふくぶちょうおんぱけんさ）abdominal ultrasound
腹膜造影（ふくまくぞうえい）peritoneography
腹膜透析（ふくまくとうせき）peritoneal dialysis：PD
含み声（ふくみごえ）muffled voice
服薬アドヒアランス（ふくやくあどひあらんす）medication adherence
服薬管理（ふくやくかんり）medication management
服薬遵守（ふくやくじゅんしゅ）medication compliance
福山型先天性筋ジストロフィー（ふくやまがたせんてんせいきんじすとろふぃー）Fukuyama type congenital muscular dystrophy
福利厚生（ふくりこうせい）welfare program
不潔・感染手術（ふけつ・かんせんしゅじゅつ）dirty/infected operation
不潔区域（ふけつくいき）dirty area
不潔行為（ふけつこうい）dirty behavior
不潔創（ふけつそう）dirty wound
不潔物収納室（ふけつぶつしゅうのうしつ）dirty utility room
不顕性感染（ふけんせいかんせん）silent infection；inapparent infection
不顕性誤嚥（ふけんせいごえん）silent aspiration
父子家庭（ふしかてい）single-father family；motherless family
父子世帯（ふしせたい）single-father household；motherless household
ブシャール結節（ぶしゃーるけっせつ）Bouchard's node
†浮腫（ふしゅ）edema
扶助（ふじょ）assistance
婦人科（ふじんか）gynecology
婦人科医（ふじんかい）gynecologist
婦人科学（ふじんかがく）gynecology
不随意運動（ふずいいうんどう）involuntary movement
不正行為（ふせいこうい）malpractice
不正受給（ふせいじゅきゅう）public assistance fraud
不正請求（ふせいせいきゅう）unfair charge
父性的温情主義（ふせいてきおんじょうしゅぎ）paternalism
不整脈（ふせいみゃく）arrhythmia
不正薬品（ふせいやくひん）traffic drug
不正利得の徴収（ふせいりとくのちょうしゅう）collection of wrongful gain
不全頚髄損傷（ふぜんけいずいそんしょう）incomplete cervical cord injury
不全四肢麻痺（ふぜんししまひ）incomplete quadriplegia
不全対麻痺（ふぜんついまひ）paraparesis
不全麻痺（ふぜんまひ）paresis
二人部屋（ふたりべや）⇒準個室
負担（ふたん）burden
負担質問票（ふたんしつもんひょう）burden interview
負担率（ふたんりつ）burden rate
普通型車椅子（ふつうがたくるまいす）standard wheelchair

普通出生率（ふつうしゅっしょうりつ）crude birth rate
普通食（ふつうしょく）regular diet
普通税徴収（ふつうぜいちょうしゅう）ordinary tax collection
普通石鹸（ふつうせっけん）plain soap
普通徴収（ふつうちょうしゅう）ordinary collection
普通保険料徴収（ふつうほけんりょうちょうしゅう）ordinary premium collection；premium collection
物価スライド（ぶっかすらいど）price indexation
仏教社会事業（ぶっきょうしゃかいじぎょう）Buddhist social work
物質の虐待（ぶっしつてきぎゃくたい）material abuse
物質文化（ぶっしつぶんか）material culture
物質誘発精神病（ぶっしつゆうはつせいしんびょう）substance-induced psychosis
物質乱用（ぶっしつらんよう）stimulant abuse
プッシュアップ（ぷっしゅあっぷ）push up
プッシュオフ（ぷっしゅおふ）push off
フッ素（ふっそ）fluoride
沸騰水（ふっとうすい）boiling water
†フットサポート（ふっとさぽーと）foot support
フットスラップ（ふっとすらっぷ）foot slap
フットボード（ふっとぼーど）footboard
フットレスト（ふっとれすと）foot rest
物理医学（ぶつりいがく）physical medicine
物理的障壁（ぶつりてきしょうへき）physical barrier
不適応（ふてきおう）maladjustment
不適応行動（ふてきおうこうどう）maladjusted behavior
不動（ふどう）immobilization
不登校（ふとうこう）school absenteeism
不動性（ふどうせい）immobility
ブドウ糖（ぶどうとう）glucose
ブドウ糖非発酵菌（ぶどうとうひはっこうきん）glucose-non-fermentative bacteria
ブドウ糖負荷試験（ぶどうとうふかしけん）glucose tolerance test
不当労働行為（ふとうろうどうこうい）unfair labor practice
フードボックス（ふーどぼっくす）food box
ふとん乾燥サービス（ふとんかんそうさーびす）futon mattress drying service
負の強化（ふのきょうか）negative reinforcement
負の罰（ふのばつ）negative punishment
不平等（ふびょうどう）inequality
不服申し立て（ふふくもうしたて）appeal
不服申し立て制度（ふふくもうしたてせいど）appeal system
†部分援助（ぶぶんえんじょ）limited assistance

部分介助（ぶぶんかいじょ）limited assistance
部分肝切除（ぶぶんかんせつじょ）partial hepatectomy
†部分清拭（ぶぶんせいしき）partial sponge bath
部分年金（ぶぶんねんきん）partial pension
†部分浴（ぶぶんよく）partial bath
普遍主義（ふへんしゅぎ）universalism
普遍的予防策（ふへんてきよぼうさく）universal precautions
普遍的利便性（ふへんてきりべんせい）universal access
不法就労（ふほうしゅうろう）illegal employment
不法滞在（ふほうたいざい）illegal residence
不飽和脂肪酸（ふほうわしぼうさん）unsaturated fatty acid
ふまずしん（ふまずしん）shank
踏み切り（ふみきり）push off
不眠（ふみん）sleeplessness；insomnia
不眠症（ふみんしょう）insomnia；sleeplessness
不明熱（ふめいねつ）fever of unknown origin
浮遊微粒子（ふゆうびりゅうし）floating particle
扶養（ふよう）support；sustenance
扶養義務（ふようぎむ）responsibility to support dependents
扶養義務者（ふようぎむしゃ）person responsible for dependent family；person responsible for dependent family members
扶養者税額控除（ふようしゃぜいがくこうじょ）parenthood tax rebate
扶養税控除（ふようぜいこうじょ）tax deduction for dependents
扶養手当（ふようてあて）dependency allowance
†プライバシー（ぷらいばしー）privacy
プライバシー保護（ぷらいばしーほご）privacy protection
プライバタイゼーション（ぷらいばたいぜーしょん）privatization
†プライマリ・ケア（ぷらいまり・けあ）primary care
プライマリ・ケア医（ぷらいまり・けあい）primary care physician；PCP
プライマリ・ヘルス・ケア（ぷらいまり・へるす・けあ）primary health care；PHC
ブライユ式触読（ぶらいゆしきしょくどく）Braille reading
ブライユ式点字（ぶらいゆしきてんじ）Braille
ブライユ式点字タイプライター（ぶらいゆしきてんじたいぷらいたー）Braille typewriter
ブライユ式点字ブロック（ぶらいゆしきてんじぶろっく）Braille block
ブライユ式点字用具（ぶらいゆしきてんじようぐ）Braille writing equipment
ブラウン・セカール症候群（ぶらうん・せかーるしょうこうぐん）Brown-Sequard syndrome

プラスチック装具（ぷらすちっくそうぐ）plastic orthosis
フラストレーション（ふらすとれーしょん）frustration
フラストレーション耐性（ふらすとれーしょんたいせい）frustration tolerance
プラセボ効果（ぷらせぼーこうか）placebo effect
プラゾシン（ぷらぞしん）prazosin
フラッシュ肺水腫（ふらっしゅはいすいしゅ）flash pulmonary edema
フラッシュバック現象（ふらっしゅばっくげんしょう）flashback
ブラッシング（ぶらっしんぐ）brushing
プラットホームクラッチ（ぷらっとほーむくらっち）⇒肘台付杖
プラビックス（ぷらびっくす）Plavix
プラミペキソール（ぷらみぺきそーる）pramipexole
フランケル分類（ふらんけるぶんるい）Frankel classification
プランニング（ぷらんにんぐ）planning
フリーアクセス（ふりーあくせす）free access
振り子試験（ふりこしけん）pendulum test
フリーター（ふりーたー）freeter
ブリーフセラピー（ぶりーふせらぴー）brief therapy
不良肢位（ふりょうしい）malposition
不良姿勢（ふりょうせい）malposture
フリーライダー（ふりーらいだー）free rider
プリン代謝障害剤（ぷりんたいしゃそがいざい）purine metabolism inhibitor
フルオキセチン（ふるおきせちん）fluoxetine
ブルーカラー（ぶるーからー）blue-collar worker
フルボキサミン（ふるぼきさみん）fluvoxamine
ブルンストローム・ステージ（ぶるんすとろーむ・すてーじ）Brunnstrom stage
プレガバリン（ぷれがばりん）pregabalin
フレクセリル（ふれくせりる）Flexeril
ブレスト見当識・記憶・集中テスト（ぶれすとけんとうしき・きおく・しゅうちゅうてすと）Blessed Orientation-Memory-Concentration Test
ブレストプロテーゼ（ぶれすとぷろてーぜ）breast prosthesis
フレックスタイム（ふれっくすたいむ）flextime；flexi- time
プレッサー（ぷれっさー）Lopressor
プレドニゾン（ぷれどにぞん）prednisone
プレハブ住宅（ぷれはぶじゅうたく）prefabricated home
フレーム（ふれーむ）frame
ブレーンストーミング（ぶれーんすとーみんぐ）brainstorming
ブローカー失語（ぶろーかーしつご）Broca's aphasia
ブローカー野（ぶろーかーや）Broca's area

プロゲステロン療法（ぷろげすてろんりょうほう）progesterone therapy
プロザック（ぷろざっく）Prozac
プロサム（ぷろさむ）ProSom
プロスカー（ぷろすかー）Proscar
プロセス・ゴール（ぷろせす・ごーる）process-goal
フロセミド（ふろせみど）furosemide
プロダクティブ・エイジング（ぷろだくてぃぶ・えいじんぐ）productive aging
ブロック契約（ぶろっくけいやく）block contract
フロッピーインファント（ふろっぴーいんふぁんと）floppy infant
プロトンポンプ阻害薬（ぷろとんぽんぷそがいやく）proton pump inhibitor
フロバトリプタン（ふろばとりぷたん）frovatriptan
プローブ（ぷろーぶ）probe
†プロフィール（ぷろふぃーる）profile
プロプラノロール（ぷろぷらのろーる）propranolol
プロポキシフェン（ぷろぽきしふぇん）propoxyphene
フロマックス（ふろまっくす）Flomax
フローリング（ふろーりんぐ）flooring
分化した福祉国家（ぶんかしたふくしこっか）differentiated welfare state
文化的障壁（ぶんかてきしょうへき）cultural barrier
文化的同化（ぶんかてきどうか）cultural assimilation
文化変容（ぶんかへんよう）acculturation
文化様式（ぶんかようしき）cultural pattern
分業（ぶんぎょう）divisions of labor；task allocation；division of tasks
分権化（ぶんけんか）decentralization
文献研究（ぶんけんけんきゅう）philological research
文献検討（ぶんけんけんとう）philological study
文献レビュー（ぶんけんれびゅー）literature review
分光視感効率（ぶんこうしかんこうりつ）spectral luminous efficiency
分散分析（ぶんさんぶんせき）analysis of variance：ANOVA
分析（ぶんせき）analysis
分析心理学（ぶんせきしんりがく）analytical psychology
分担金（ぶんたんきん）allotted charge
分娩介助（ぶんべんかいじょ）assistance with delivery
糞便キモトリプシン試験（ふんべんきもとりぷしんしけん）fecal chymotrypsin test
糞便検査（ふんべんけんさ）fecal examination；feces examination
糞便細菌検査（ふんべんさいきんけんさ）stool microbiology

分娩前および分娩後の処置（ぶんべんぜんおよびぶんべんごのしょち）treatment prior to and after delivery
分娩麻痺（ぶんべんまひ）birth palsy
分回し運動（ぶんまわしうんどう）circumduction；circular movement
分回し歩行（ぶんまわしほこう）circumduction gait
噴霧（ふんむ）fogging
文明（ぶんめい）civilization
分離（ぶんり）separation
分離培養（ぶんりばいよう）differential culture
分離不安（ぶんりふあん）separation anxiety
分離不安障害（ぶんりふあんしょうがい）separation anxiety disorder
粉瘤（ふんりゅう）atheroma
分類収容（ぶんるいしゅうよう）classified admission
分類処遇（ぶんるいしょぐう）treatment based classification
分裂感情障害（ぶんれつかんじょうしょうがい）schizoaffective disorder

へ

閉運動連鎖（へいうんどうれんさ）closed kinetic chain
平均在院日数（へいきんざいいんにっすう）average length of stay：ALOS
†平均寿命（へいきんじゅみょう）average life span
平均世帯人員（へいきんせたいじんいん）average size of households；average household size
平均薬価（へいきんやっか）average price of drugs
†平均余命（へいきんよめい）life expectancy
閉経（へいけい）menopause
平衡（へいこう）equilibrium；balance
平衡機能障害（へいこうきのうしょうがい）disturbance of balance；balance disorder；impaired vestibular function
平衡障害（へいこうしょうがい）impairment of balance function
平行棒（へいこうぼう）parallel bar
閉鎖式気管内吸引チューブ（へいさしきかんないきゅういんちゅーぶ）closed endotracheal suction tube
閉鎖式持続導尿システム（へいさしきじぞくどうにょうしすてむ）closed system of urinary drainage system
閉鎖式ドレナージ（へいさしきどれなーじ）closed drainage
閉鎖施設（へいさしせつ）locked facility
閉鎖病棟（へいさびょうとう）locked unit
併進前庭動眼反射（へいしんぜんていどうがんはんしゃ）translational vestibulo-ocular reflex

ベイスン法（べいすんほう）basin method
閉塞型睡眠時無呼吸（へいそくがたすいみんじむこきゅう）obstructive sleep apnea
閉塞型睡眠時無呼吸症候群（へいそくがたすいみんじむこきゅうしょうこうぐん）obstructive sleep apnea syndrome：OSAS
閉塞性動脈硬化症（へいそくせいどうみゃくこうかしょう）arteriosclerosis obliterans
平熱（へいねつ）normal temperature
平和（へいわ）peace
平和運動（へいわうんどう）peace movement
平和学（へいわがく）peace study
ペインクリニック（ぺいんくりにっく）pain clinic
ペガシス（ぺがしす）Pegasys
僻地医療体制（へきちいりょうたいせい）medical care system for remote areas
ペグインターフェロン（ぺぐいんたーふぇろん）pegylated interferon
ペグボード（ぺぐぼーど）pegboard
ペースト食（ぺーすとしょく）pureed diet
ペースメーカー（ぺーすめーかー）pacemaker
βアミロイドペプチド（べーたあみろいどぺぷちど）beta-amyloid peptide
βカロテン（べーたかろちん）beta-carotene
β受容体遮断薬（べーたじゅようたいしゃだんやく）beta receptor blockage
βブロッカー（べーたぶろっかー）beta-blocker
ベッカー型筋ジストロフィー（べっかーがたきんじすとろふぃー）Becker muscular dystrophy；Benign pseudohypertrophic muscular dystrophy
ベック抑うつ評価尺度（べっくよくうつひょうかしゃくど）Beck Depression Inventory：BDI
ペッサリー（ぺっさりー）pessary
†ベッド（べっど）bed
ペット（ぺっと）PET：positron emission tomography
†ベッドから車いす（べっどからくるまいす）transfer from bed to wheelchair
ベッド柵（べっどさく）bedside rail
ベッド上肢位（べっどじょうしい）bed positioning
ベッドパンウォッシャ（べっどぱんうぉっしゃ）⇒便器洗浄機
†ベッドメーキング（べっどめーきんぐ）bed making
ベッドリフト（べっどりふと）bed lift
ベニカー（べにかー）benicar
ベニシリン（ぺにしりん）penicillin
ヘバーデン結節（へばーでんけっせつ）Heberden's nodes
ヘパリン（へぱりん）heparin
ベビーシッター（べびーしったー）babysitter；nanny
ベビーブーマー（べびーぶーまー）baby boomer
ベビーブーム（べびーぶーむ）baby boom

ベビーブーム世代（べびーぶーむせだい）baby boom generation
ヘプセラ（へぷせら）Hepsera
ヘマトクリット（へまとくりっと）hematocrit
ヘモグロビン（へもぐろびん）hemoglobin；Hb
ヘラー症候群（へらーしょうこうぐん）Heller's syndrome
ベラパミル（べらぱみる）verapamil
ヘリコバクター・ピロリ（へりこばくたー・ぴろり）Helicobacter pylori
ペリンドプリル（ぺりんどぷりる）perindopril
ヘルシンキ宣言（へるしんきせんげん）Declaration of Helsinki
ヘルスケア（へるすけあ）health care
ヘルスプロモーション（へるすぷろもーしょん）health promotion
ヘルツ（へるつ）hertz
ベルテポルフィン（べるてぽるふぃん）verteporfin
ベルトロッティ症候群（べるとろってぃしょうこうぐん）Bertolotti's syndrome
ベル・パッド法（べる・ぱっどほう）bell and pad
ベル麻痺（べるまひ）Bell's palsy
ベレラン（べれらん）Verelan
ヘロイン（へろいん）heroin
ヘロイン依存（へろいんいぞん）heroin dependence
便（べん）stool
便意（べんい）bowel movement
返還請求（へんかんせいきゅう）claims for refund
†便器（べんき）bedpan；toilet
便器洗浄機（べんきせんじょうき）bedpan washer
便器付き椅子（べんきつきいす）commode
変形（へんけい）deformity
変形性関節症（へんけいせいかんせつしょう）osteoarthritis；OA；degenerative joint disease
変形性頸椎症（へんけいせいけいついしょう）cervical spondylosis；cervical osteochondrosis
変形性股関節症（へんけいせいこかんせつしょう）coxarthrosis
変形性膝関節症（へんけいせいしつかんせつしょう）gonarthrosis
偏見（へんけん）prejudice
弁護士（べんごし）attorney-at-law；lawyer
便産生（べんさんせい）stool production
†便失禁（べんしっきん）fecal incontinence；bowel incontinence
偏執病（へんしゅうびょう）paranoia
変色（へんしょく）discoloration
偏頭痛（へんずつう）migraine headache
ベンズトロピン（べんずとろぴん）Benztropine
変性（へんせい）degeneration
変性疾患（へんせいしっかん）degenerative disease
便潜血検査（べんせんけつけんさ）fecal occult blood test：FOBT
片側骨盤切断（へんそくこつばんせつだん）hemipelvectomy
片側骨盤用義足（へんそくこつばんようぎそく）hemipelvectomy prosthesis
便通（べんつう）bowel movement
扁桃腺（へんとうせん）tonsil
ヘンドリック転倒危険度評価ツール（へんどりっくてんとうきけんどひょうかつーる）Hendrich's Fall Risk Assessment Tool
†便秘（べんぴ）constipation
扁平上皮癌（へんぺいじょうがん）squamous cell carcinoma
扁平足（へんぺいそく）pes planus；flat foot；fallen arches
弁別刺激（べんべつしげき）discriminative stimulus
弁膜症（べんまくしょう）valvular disease
†片麻痺（へんまひ）hemiplegia
ベンラファキシン（べんらふぁきしん）venlafaxine

ほ

保育（ほいく）nursery child care
保育園（ほいくえん）nursery school
保育課（ほいくか）Day Care Division
†保育士（ほいくし）certified child care worker
保育所（ほいくしょ）child day care center
保育ニーズ（ほいくにーず）nursery needs
法（ほう）Act；Law
法医看護（ほういかんご）forensic nurse
法医看護学（ほういかんごがく）forensic nursing
法医心理学（ほういしんりがく）forensic psychology
法医心理学者（ほういしんりがくしゃ）forensic psychologist
法医人類学（ほうじんるいがく）forensic anthropology
法医人類学者（ほうじんるいがくしゃ）forensic anthropologists
法医精神看護（ほうせいしんかんご）forensic psychiatric nursing
ボウイー・ディック・テスト（ぼうぃー・でぃっく・てすと）Bowie-Dick Test
法医病理学（ほういびょうりがく）forensic pathology
法医病理学者（ほういびょうりがくしゃ）forensic Pathologist
法医福祉（ほういふくし）forensic social work
防衛（ぼうえい）defense
防衛機制（ぼうえいきせい）defense mechanism
防衛の分析（ぼうえいのぶんせき）analysis of defenses
†防炎素材（ぼうえんそざい）flame-resistant material

†防汚素材（ぼうおそざい）soil-resistant material
蜂窩織炎（ほうかしきえん）cellulitis
防火対策（ぼうかたいさく）fire prevention；fire prevention policy
包括型地域生活支援（ほうかつがたちいきせいかつしえん）assertive community treatment
包括的医療（ほうかつてきいりょう）comprehensive health care；comprehensive medical care
包括的環境要因調査票（ほうかつてきかんきょういんちょうさひょう）Multiphasic Environmental Assessment Procedure；MEAP
包括的サーベイランス（ほうかつてきさーべいらんす）comprehensive surveillance
包括的指示（ほうかつてきしじ）comprehensive order
包括的支出レビュー（ほうかつてきししゅつれびゅー）comprehensive spending review
包括的地域ケアシステム（ほうかつてきちいきけあしすてむ）comprehensive community care system
包括的リハビリテーションアプローチ（ほうかつてきりはびりてーしょんあぷろーち）holistic rehabilitative intervention
包括払い制度（ほうかつばらいせいど）prospective payment system
包括評価（ほうかつひょうか）inclusive evaluation
剖検（ぼうけん）⇒死体解剖
封建思想（ほうけんしそう）feudalistic thought
封建社会（ほうけんしゃかい）feudal society
膀胱炎（ぼうこうえん）urocystitis
膀胱鏡検査（ぼうこうきょうけんさ）cystoscopy
膀胱直腸障害（ぼうこうちょくちょうしょうがい）bowel and bladder dysfunction
膀胱内圧測定（ぼうこうないあつそくてい）cystometrography；cystometry
膀胱瘤（ぼうこうりゅう）cystocele
防護環境（ぼうごかんきょう）protective environment：PE
報告（ほうこく）report
防災（ぼうさい）disaster prevention
防災対策（ぼうさいたいさく）emergency planning
奉仕（ほうし）voluntary work
胞子（ほうし）⇒芽胞
奉仕員（ほうしいん）volunteer
放射性アレルゲン吸着試験（ほうしゃせいあれるげんきゅうちゃくしけん）radioallergosorbent test
放射性核種血管造影（ほうしゃせいかくしゅけっかんぞうえい）radionuclide angiography
放射性同位体（ほうしゃせいどういたい）radioisotope
放射性ヨウ素（ほうしゃせいようそ）radioactive iodine
放射線治療（ほうしゃせんちりょう）radiation therapy
報酬比例拠出（ほうしゅうひれいきょしゅつ）contribution in proportion to income
暴食（ぼうしょく）adephagia
法人（ほうじん）corporation；juridical person
法人税（ほうじんぜい）corporation tax
防水シーツ（ぼうすいしーつ）waterproof sheet
包帯（ほうたい）bandage
包帯交換（ほうたいこうかん）dressing change
防虫剤（ぼうちゅうざい）mothball
法廷援助（ほうていえんじょ）court assistance
法定雇用率（ほうていこようりつ）statutory rates of employment
法定受託事業（ほうていじゅたくじぎょう）statutory functions entrusted
法定代理受領サービス（ほうていだいりじゅりょうさーびす）legal reception services
法定代理人（ほうていだいりにん）legal guardian
法定伝染病（ほうていでんせんびょう）legally designated communicable disease；reportable communicable disease；legal communicable disease
法的義務（ほうてきぎむ）legal obligation
法的問題（ほうてきもんだい）legal issue
乏尿（ぼうにょう）oliguria
防犯対策（ぼうはんたいさく）crime prevention policy
防腐剤（ぼうふざい）antiseptic
訪問栄養食事指導（ほうもんえいようしょくじしどう）home nutrition education services；home-based nutrition education
†訪問介護（ほうもんかいご）home care
訪問介護員（ほうもんかいごいん）home care worker
訪問介護員養成研修（ほうもんかいごいんようせいけんしゅう）home care worker training program
訪問介護計画（ほうもんかいごけいかく）care plan for home care
訪問介護事業（ほうもんかいごじぎょう）home care project
訪問介護事業者（ほうもんかいごじぎょうしゃ）home care provider
訪問介護事業所（ほうもんかいごじぎょうしょ）home care office
訪問介護ステーション（ほうもんかいごすてーしょん）home care nurses station
†訪問看護（ほうもんかんご）home health
訪問看護協会（ほうもんかんごきょうかい）Home Health Nurses Association
訪問看護ケア（ほうもんかんごけあ）home health care
訪問看護計画（ほうもんかんごけいかく）home health plan of care

訪問看護師（ほうもんかんごし）home health nurse
† 訪問看護ステーション（ほうもんかんごすてーしょん）home health nurses station
訪問教育（ほうもんきょういく）educational home visiting
訪問口腔衛生（ほうもんこうくうえいせい）mobile oral health services
訪問歯科衛生（ほうもんしかえいせい）mobile dental hygiene services
訪問歯科衛生指導（ほうもんしかえいせいしどう）mobile dental hygiene and educational services
訪問指導（ほうもんしどう）educational home visit
訪問洗濯サービス（ほうもんせんたくさーびす）home laundry services
訪問調査（ほうもんちょうさ）on-site assessment ; on-site survey ; on-site evaluation
訪問調査員（ほうもんちょうさいん）site investigator
訪問入浴（ほうもんにゅうよく）home bathing
† 訪問入浴介護（ほうもんにゅうよくかいご）home bathing care
訪問入浴サービス（ほうもんにゅうよくさーびす）home bathing services
訪問面接（ほうもんめんせつ）on-site interview
訪問薬剤管理指導（ほうもんやくざいかんりしどう）home health medication management and education
† 訪問リハビリテーション（ほうもんりはびりてーしょん）home care rehabilitation
訪問理美容サービス（ほうもんりびようさーびす）home beauty services ; mobile beauty services
法律支援（ほうりつしえん）legal assistance
法律扶助（ほうりつふじょ）legal aid
暴力（ぼうりょく）violence
法令違反（ほうれいいはん）law violation
飽和蒸気（ほうわじょうき）saturated vapor
歩隔（ほかく）stride width ; step width
保管（ほかん）safekeeping
補完医療（ほかんいりょう）complementary medicine
補完代替医療（ほかんだいたいいりょう）complementary and alternative medicine : CAM
保菌者（ほきんしゃ）carrier
ボクサー骨折（ぼくさーこっせつ）boxer's fracture
墨汁法（ぼくじゅうほう）India ink method
ポケット感染（ぽけっとかんせん）pocket infection
呆け老人を抱える家族の会（ぼけろうじんをかかえるかぞくのかい）Alzheimer's Association Japan
保険（ほけん）insurance
保険医（ほけんい）insurance doctor
保険課（ほけんか）Employees' Health Insurance Division
保険会社（ほけんがいしゃ）insurance company

保険期間（ほけんきかん）period of insurance ; insurance period
保険機関（ほけんきかん）insurance agency
保険給付（ほけんきゅうふ）insurance benefit
保険局（ほけんきょく）Health Insurance Bureau
保健行動（ほけんこうどう）health behavior
† 保健師（ほけんし）public health nurse: PHN
保険事故（ほけんじこ）insured event
保健室（ほけんしつ）school infirmary
保健指導（ほけんしどう）health guidance
† 保険者（ほけんしゃ）insurer
† 保健所（ほけんじょ）public health center
保険証（ほけんしょう）insurance card
保健センター（ほけんせんたー）health center
保健福祉（ほけんふくし）health and welfare
保健福祉機関（ほけんふくしきかん）health and welfare agency
保健福祉基準（ほけんふくしきじゅん）health and welfare standards
保健福祉教育（ほけんふくしきょういく）health and welfare education
保健福祉サービス（ほけんふくしさーびす）health and welfare services
保健福祉事業所（ほけんふくしじぎょうしょ）health and welfare office
保健福祉施策（ほけんふくししさく）policy of health and welfare
保健福祉施設（ほけんふくししせつ）health and welfare facility
保健福祉事務所（ほけんふくしじむしょ）health and welfare office
保健福祉水準（ほけんふくしすいじゅん）level of health and welfare
† 保険料（ほけんりょう）insurance premium
保険料基準額（ほけんりょうきじゅんがく）standard rate of insurance premium
保険料減免（ほけんりょうげんめん）premium reduction
保険料算定基準（ほけんりょうさんていきじゅん）insurance premium rate calculator standard
保険料水準（ほけんりょうすいじゅん）insurance premium level
保険料遡及賦課（ほけんりょうそきゅうふか）retroactive premium payment
保険料滞納（ほけんりょうたいのう）non-payment of premium
保険料徴収（ほけんりょうちょうしゅう）collection of insurance premiums
保険料納付済期間（ほけんりょうのうふずみきかん）period for the premium payment
保険料免除（ほけんりょうめんじょ）immunity from premium contributions
保険料率（ほけんりょうりつ）insurance premium

rate
†歩行（ほこう）gait；ambulation；walk
補高（ほこう）elevation
†歩行器（ほこうき）walker
歩行機能評価（ほこうきのうひょうか）gait assessment
補高靴（ほこうぐつ）extension shoe
歩行訓練（ほこうくんれん）gait training
歩行困難（ほこうこんなん）gait difficulty
歩行失行（ほこうしっこう）gait apraxia
歩行周期（ほこうしゅうき）gait cycle；walking cycle
歩行障害（ほこうしょうがい）gait disability；gait disturbance；gait disorder
歩行速度（ほこうそくど）gait velocity
歩行動作（ほこうどうさ）ambulation activity
歩行能力（ほこうのうりょく）gait ability；ambulation ability；walking ability
歩行パターン（ほこうぱたーん）gait pattern
歩行分析（ほこうぶんせき）gait analysis
歩行補助機器（ほこうほじょききー）⇒移動補助具
歩行補助具（ほこうほじょぐ）walking aid
歩行用杖（ほこうようつえ）walking cane
歩効率（ほこうりつ）walking rate
†歩行練習（ほこうれんしゅう）gait training
保護課（ほごか）Public Assistance Division
保護型介護施設（ほごがたかいごしせつ）custodial care facility
保護型ケア（ほごがたけあ）custodial care
保護監察官（ほごかんさつかん）probation and parole officer
保護監察制度（ほごかんさつせいど）probation and parole system
保護義務者（ほごぎむしゃ）person responsible for protection
保護局（ほごきょく）protective services
保護拘置（ほごこうち）protective custody
保護雇用（ほごこよう）sheltered employment
保護司（ほごし）probation officer；parole officer
保護施設（ほごしせつ）asylums
保護司法（ほごしほう）Volunteer Probation Officers Act
保護者（ほごしゃ）guardian
保護者中心（ほごしゃちゅうしん）parent-centered
保護処分（ほごしょぶん）protective measure
保護の種類及び範囲（ほごのしゅるいおよびはんい）types and scope of public assistance
保護の補足性（ほごのほそくせい）supplementary nature of public assistance
保護用眼鏡（ほごようめがね）eye goggle
保佐監督人（ほさかんとくにん）supervisor of the curator
保佐人（ほさにん）curator

補佐人（ほさにん）court assistant
母子家庭（ほしかてい）single-mother family；fatherless family
母子寡婦福祉（ほしかふふくし）welfare for fatherless families and widows
母子寡婦福祉貸付金（ほしかふふくしかしつけきん）welfare loan for fatherless families and widows
母子寡婦福祉施設（ほしかふふくししせつ）welfare facility for fatherless families and widows；welfare facilities for fatherless families
母子寡婦福祉センター（ほしかふふくしせんたー）welfare center for fatherless families and widows
母子感染（ほしかんせん）mother-to-child transmission
母子健康手帳（ほしけんこうてちょう）maternal and child health handbook
母指支え（ほしささえ）thumb post
母子指導員（ほししどういん）fatherless families advisor
†ポジショニング（ぽじしょにんぐ）positioning
母子世帯（ほしせたい）single-mother household；fatherless household
母子相談員（ほしそうだんいん）advisor for fatherless families
母子手帳（ほしてちょう）maternal and child health handbook
ポジトロン・エミッション・トモグラフィー（ぽじとろん・えみっしょん・ともぐらふぃー）positron emission tomography；PET
ポジトロンCT（ぽじとろんしーてぃー）positron emission tomography；PET
母子福祉（ほしふくし）social services for fatherless families
母子保健課（ほしほけんか）Maternal and Child Health Division
保守主義（ほしゅしゅぎ）conservatism
保守主義的・コーポラティスト福祉国家（ほしゅしゅぎてき・こーぽらてぃすとふくしこっか）the conservative and corporatist welfare state
保証（ほしょう）guarantee；warranty
保障（ほしょう）security
補償（ほしょう）compensation
補償課（ほしょうか）Compensation Division
保証人（ほしょうにん）guarantor
補助器具（ほじょきぐ）prosthetic equipment
補助技術（ほじょぎじゅつ）assistive technology
補助金（ほじょきん）subsidy
補助具（ほじょぐ）technical aid
補助犬（ほじょけん）service dog
補助呼吸筋（ほじょこきゅうきん）accessory respiratory muscle
補助調節換気（ほじょちょうせつかんき）assist and/or controlled mechanical ventilation

補助的ケア（ほじょてきけあ）custodial care
補助動筋（ほじょどうきん）assistant mover
補助様式補助モード（ほじょようしきほじょモード）assist mode
ポストモダン（ぽすともだん）post-modern
ボストン呼称テスト（ぼすとんこしょうてすと）Boston Naming Test：BNT
ホスピス（ほすぴす）hospice
ホスピスケア（ほすぴすけあ）hospice care
ホスピタリズム（ほすぴたりずむ）hospitalism
母性（ぼせい）maternity；motherhood
母性保護（ぼせいほご）maternity protection
補装具（ほそうぐ）orthosis；prosthesis；orthopedic appliance
†補足給付（ほそくきゅうふ）supplementary benefit
保続症（ほぞくせい）perseveration
補足性の原理（ほそくせいのげんり）principle of supplementary nature of public assistance
補足的医療保険（ほそくてきいりょうほけん）Supplemental Social Security Insurance：SMI
補足適用（ほそくてきよう）supplemental coverage
保存的治療（ほぞんてきちりょう）conservative treatment
保存的療法（ほぞんてきりょうほう）⇒保存的治療
†ポータブルトイレ（ぽーたぶるといれ）commode；bedside commode
†ポータブル浴槽（ぽーたぶるよくそう）portable bathtub
ボーダレス（ぼーだれす）borderless
ボタン穴変形（ぼたんあなへんけい）boutonniere deformity
ボタンエイド（ぼたんえいど）button aid
墓地（ぼち）cemetery
†補聴器（ほちょうき）hearing aid
勃起（ぼっき）erection
勃起不全（ぼっきふぜん）erectile dysfunction：ED；male impotence
発作異常（ほっさいじょう）seizure disorder
発作性上室頻拍症（ほっさせいじょうしつひんぱくしょう）paroxysmal supraventricular tachycardia
発作薬（ほっさやく）seizure medication
†発疹（ほっしん）skin rash
†発赤（ほっせき）redness
ホットバイオプシー（ほっとばいおぷしー）hot biopsy
ホットパック（ほっとぱっく）hot pack
補綴（ほてい）prosthetic
ボディサーフェイスアイソレーション（ぼでぃさーふぇいすあいそれーしょん）⇒生体表面隔離
ボディサブスタンスアイソレーション（ぼでぃさぶすたんすあいそれーしょん）⇒生体物質隔離
†ボディメカニクス（ぼでぃめかにくす）body mechanics

ホテルコスト（ほてるこすと）hotel costs
ボード・アンド・ケアホーム（ぼーど・あんど・けあほーむ）board and care home
ボニバ（ぼにば）Boniva
歩幅（ほはば）step length
保父（ほふ）male nursery teacher
保母（ほぼ）certified child care worker
ホームエレベーター（ほーむえれべーたー）home elevator
ホームケア促進事業（ほーむけあそくしんじぎょう）home care promotion plan
ホームプログラム（ほーむぷろぐらむ）home program
ホームヘルスサービス（ほーむへるすさーびす）home health services
†ホームヘルパー（ほーむへるぱー）home helper
ホームヘルプ（ほーむへるぷ）home help
ホームヘルプサービス（ほーむへるぷさーびす）home help services
ホームレス（ほーむれす）homeless
ホメオスタシス（ほめおすたしす）homeostasis
ホメオパシックレメディーズ（ほめおぱしっくれめでぃーず）homeopathic remedies
歩容（ほよう）gait
ボランタリ（ぼらんたり）voluntary
†ボランティア（ぼらんてぃあ）volunteer
ボランティアアドバイザー（ぼらんてぃああどばいざー）volunteer adviser
ボランティア活動（ぼらんてぃあかつどう）volunteer activity
ボランティア基金（ぼらんてぃあききん）volunteer fund
ボランティアグループ（ぼらんてぃあぐるーぷ）volunteer group
ボランティアコーディネーター（ぼらんてぃあこーでぃねーたー）volunteer coordinator
ボランティアセンター（ぼらんてぃあせんたー）volunteer center
ボランティアリズム（ぼらんてぃありずむ）voluntarism
ポリエステルアレルギー（ぽりえすてるあれるぎー）polyester allergy
ポリオ（ぽりお）poliomyelitis
ポリオ後症候群（ぽりおごしょうこうぐん）post-polio syndrome：PPS
ホリスティック医療（ほりすてぃっくいりょう）holistic medicine
ポリープ（ぽりーぷ）polyps
ホルター心電図（ほるたーしんでんず）holter electrocardiogram
ホルネル症候群（ほるねるしょうこうぐん）Horner syndrome
†ホルモン（ほるもん）hormone

ホルモン受容体検査（ほるもんじゅようたいけんさ） hormone receptor test
ホルモン補充療法（ほるもんほじゅうりょうほう） hormone replacement therapy
ホワイトカラー（ほわいとからー） white-collar worker
本籍（ほんせき） permanent domicile；permanent address
本態性高血圧（ほんたいせいこうけつあつ） essential hypertension

ま

毎朝（まいあさ） every morning：QAM
埋葬（まいそう） burial
毎月（まいつき） monthly：1M
毎日就寝時間前（まいにちしゅうしんじかんまえ） every night：QHS
マイノリティ（まいのりてぃ） minority
前払い型グループ診療（まえばらいがたぐるーぷしんりょう） prepaid group practice：PGP
前払い制診療（まえばらいせいしんりょう） prepaid medical practice
マクギル疼痛質問表（まくぎるとうつうしつもんひょう） McGill Pain Questionnaire：MPQ
マクサルト（まくさると） Maxalt
マグネシウム（まぐねしうむ） magnesium
枕（まくら） pillow
マクロレベル（まくろれべる） macro level
孫育て（まごそだて） grandparenting
摩擦ロック継手（まさつろっくつぎて） friction lock joint
マジック・ハンド（まじっく・はんど） magic hand
麻疹（ましん） measles；rubeola；morbilli
麻酔（ますい） anesthesia
麻酔剤（ますいざい） anesthetic
マスコミ（ますこみ） mass communication
マスターベーション（ますたーべーしょん） masturbation
マスメディア（ますめでぃあ） mass media
マズロー, アブラハム ハロルド（まずろー、あぶらはむ はろるど） Abraham Harold Maslow
マズローの欲求段階（まずろーのよっきゅうだんかい） Maslow's hierarchy of needs
まだら認知症（まだらにんちしょう） lacunar dementia
マーチングリューバー吻合（まーちんぐりゅーばーふんごう） Martin-Gruber anastomosis
マッカーサー治療同意判断能力評価表（まっかーさーちりょうどういはんだんのうりょくひょうかひょう） MacArthur Competence Assessment Tool for Treatment：MacCAT-T
末期腎不全（まっきじんふぜん） end-stage renal disease：ESRD
マッサージ（まっさーじ） massage
マッサージ療法（まっさーじりょうほう） massage therapy
末梢循環障害（まっしょうじゅんかんしょうがい） peripheral vascular disease
末梢静脈栄養法（まっしょうじょうみゃくえいようほう） peripheral parenteral nutrition：PPN
末梢神経（まっしょうしんけい） peripheral nerve
末梢神経障害（まっしょうしんけいしょうがい） peripheral neuropathy
末梢神経麻痺（まっしょうしんけいまひ） peripheral nerve palsy
末梢性顔面神経麻痺（まっしょうせいがんめんしんけいまひ） peripheral facial nerve palsy
末梢前庭機能不全（まっしょうぜんていきのうふぜん） peripheral vestibular dysfunction
末梢動脈疾患（まっしょうどうみゃくしっかん） peripheral arterial disease：PAD
末梢浮腫（まっしょうふしゅ） peripheral edema
末端価格（まったんかかく） street value
†マット（まっと） mat
マット訓練（まっとくんれん） mat exercise
マットレス（まっとれす） mattress
マットレスパッド（まっとれすぱっど） mattress pad
†松葉杖（まつばづえ） crutch；axillary crutch
松葉杖歩行（まつばづえほこう） crutch gait
マッピング技法（まっぴんぐぎほう） mapping technique
マーデルング変形（まーでるんぐへんけい） Madelung deformity
マトリックスメタロプロテアーゼ酵素（まとりっくすめたろぷろてあーぜこうそ） matrix metalloprotease enzyme
マニア（まにあ） mania
マネジドケア（まねじどけあ） managed care
マネジドケアプラン（まねじどけあぷらん） managed care plan
マネジドコスト（まねじどこすと） managed cost
マネジドコンペティション（まねじどこんぺてぃしょん） managed competition
マネジドヘルスケア（まねじどへるすけあ） managed health care
マネジメントシステム（まねじめんとしすてむ） management system
†麻痺（まひ） paralysis；palsy；paresis
麻痺側（まひそく） paralytic side
まぶしい光（まぶしいひかり） glare
マープラン（まーぷらん） Marplan
摩耗抵抗（まもうていこう） abrasion resistance
麻薬（まやく） narcotic；narcotic drug
麻薬中毒（まやくちゅうどく） narcotic addiction

麻薬中毒者（まやくちゅうどくしゃ）narcotic addicted
麻薬中毒乳児（まやくちゅうどくにゅうじ）narcotic addicted infant
マラスムス（まらすむす）marasmus
マリオットシニアボランティア調査（まりおっとしにあぼらんてぃあちょうさ）Marriot Seniors Volunteerism Study
マルトリートメント（まるとりーとめんと）maltreatment
マレット指（まれっとゆび）mallet finger
慢性炎症性脱髄性多発神経炎（まんせいえんしょうせいだつずいせいたはつしんけいえん）chronic inflammatory demyelinating polyneuropathy
慢性炎症性脱髄性多発ニューロパチー（まんせいえんしょうせいだつずいせいたはつにゅーろぱちー）chronic inflammatory demyelinating polyneuropathy
慢性関節リウマチ（まんせいかんせつりうまち）rheumatoid arthritis；RA
慢性期（まんせいき）chronic stage
慢性気管支炎（まんせいきかんしえん）chronic bronchitis
慢性緊張型頭痛（まんせいきんちょうがたずつう）chronic tension-type headache
慢性骨髄性白血病（まんせいこつずいせいはっけつびょう）chronic myelocytic leukemia
慢性疾患（まんせいしっかん）chronic disease
慢性疾患療法機能評価（まんせいしっかんりょうほうきのうひょうか）Functional Assessment of Chronic Illness Therapy；FACIT
慢性腎盂腎炎（まんせいじんうじんえん）chronic pyelonephritis
慢性腎臓病（まんせいじんぞうびょう）chronic kidney disease
慢性腎不全（まんせいじんふぜん）chronic renal failure
慢性的失業（まんせいてきしつぎょう）chronic unemployment
慢性疼痛（まんせいとうつう）chronic pain
慢性ヒ素中毒（まんせいひそちゅうどく）chronic arsenic poisoning
慢性病（まんせいびょう）chronic Illness
慢性疲労症候群（まんせいひろうしょうこうぐん）chronic fatigue syndrome
慢性閉塞性気道疾患（まんせいへいそくせいきどうしっかん）chronic obstructive airway disease
慢性閉塞性肺疾患（まんせいへいそくせいはいしっかん）chronic obstructive pulmonary disease；COPD
慢性リンパ性白血病（まんせいりんぱせいはっけつびょう）chronic lymphoid leukemia；CLL
マンセル表色系（まんせるひょうしょくけい）Munsell system
満足（まんぞく）satisfaction
満足度測定（まんぞくどそくてい）satisfaction measurement
マンモグラフィ（まんもぐらふぃ）mammography
マンモグラム（まんもぐらむ）mammogram

み

見えざる手（みえざるて）invisible hand
ミオクロニー発作（みおくろにーほっさ）myoclonic seizure
ミオクローヌス（みおくろーぬす）myoclonus
ミオクローヌスてんかん（みおくろーぬすてんかん）myoclonus epilepsy
ミオグロビン（みおぐろびん）myoglobin
ミオトニア（みおとにあ）myotonia
ミオパチー（みおぱちー）myopathy
味覚（みかく）gustation；sense of taste
味覚低下（みかくていか）loss of taste
†ミキサー食（みきさーしょく）blended diet
右側臥位（みぎそくがい）right lateral recumbent
ミクロレベル（みくろれべる）micro level
未熟児（みじゅくじ）premature infant
未熟練介護労働者（みじゅくれんかいごろうどうしゃ）unskilled long-term care worker
未熟練労働者（みじゅくれんろうどうしゃ）unskilled worker
水治療法（みずちりょうほう）hydrotherapy
水漏れ試験（みずもれしけん）water leakage test
水を必要としない消毒薬（みずをひつようとしないしょうどくやく）⇒速乾性擦式消毒薬
水を必要としない手洗い用製剤（みずをひつようとしないてあらいようせいざい）⇒速乾性手洗い用製剤
未成年（みせいねん）minor；under age
未成年後見監督人（みせいねんこうけんかんとくにん）supervisor of guardian of minor
未成年後見人（みせいねんこうけんにん）guardian of minor
未成年後見人の指定（みせいねんこうけんにんのしてい）designation of guardian of minor
未成年後見人の選任（みせいねんこうけんにんのせんにん）appointment of guardian of minor
未成年者（みせいねんしゃ）minor；under age
未成年者登記簿（みせいねんしゃとうきぼ）minor registry
未成年の子供（みせいねんのこども）minor child
未成年保佐人（みせいねんほさにん）curator for minors
未成年補佐人（みせいねんほさにん）court assistant for minors
ミッドタウンマンハッタン調査（みっどたうんまんはったんちょうさ）Midtown Manhattan Study

ミトコンドリア病（みとこんどりあびょう）mitochondrial disease
看取り（みとり）care for the dying
みなし指定（みなししてい）deemed status
みなし指定認定（みなしていにんてい）deemed status accreditation
見習い看護師（みならいかんごし）student nurse
見習い期間（みならいきかん）period of apprenticeship；apprenticeship period
見習生（みならいせい）apprentice
ミニ脳卒中（みにのうそっちゅう）mini stroke
ミニプレス（みにぷれす）Minipress
ミニマムデータセット（みにまむでーたせっと）Minimum Data Set：MDS
ミニメンタルステータス試験（みにめんたるすてーたすしけん）Mini Mental State Examination：MMSE
ミネソタ多面人格目録（みねそたためんじんかくもくろく）Minnesota Multiphasic Personality Inventory：MMPI
†ミネラル（みねらる）mineral
ミネラル欠乏症（みねらるけつぼうしょう）mineral deficiency
ミネラル補給（みねらるほきゅう）mineral supplementation
身の回りの世話（みのまわりのせわ）self-care
未分化（みぶんか）undifferentiated
未分化状態（みぶんかじょうたい）undifferentiated status
身分証明書（みぶんしょうめいしょ）identification
未亡人（みぼうじん）widow
耳鳴（みみなり）tinnitus
†脈拍（みゃくはく）pulse
三宅式記銘力検査（みやけしききめいりょくけんさ）Miyake Paired Verbal Association Learning Test
ミラペックス（みらぺっくす）Mirapex
民営化（みんえいか）privatization
民間医療保険（みんかんいりょうほけん）private medical insurance
民間営利組織（みんかんえいりそしき）for-profit organization
民間介護保険（みんかんかいごほけん）private long-term care insurance
民間活動（みんかんかつどう）private activity
民間活動債（みんかんかつどうさい）private activity bond
民間機関（みんかんきかん）private organization
民間企業（みんかんきぎょう）private enterprise
民間サービス（みんかんさーびす）private service
民間事業（みんかんじぎょう）private program
民間事業者（みんかんじぎょうしゃ）private program provider

民間施設（みんかんしせつ）private facility
民間社会福祉（みんかんしゃかいふくし）private social welfare
民間社会福祉事業（みんかんしゃかいふくしじぎょう）private social welfare program
民間社会福祉団体（みんかんしゃかいふくしだんたい）private social welfare organization
民間助成団体（みんかんじょせいだんたい）private foundation
民間セクター（みんかんせくたー）private sector
民間団体（みんかんだんたい）private association
民間投資（みんかんとうし）private investment
民間年金（みんかんねんきん）private pension
民間非営利組織（みんかんひえいりそしき）private non-profit organization
民間病院（みんかんびょういん）private hospital
民間福祉（みんかんふくし）private welfare
民間福祉活動（みんかんふくしかつどう）private welfare activity
民間保険（みんかんほけん）private insurance
民間ホーム（みんかんほーむ）private home
民間療法（みんかんりょうほう）folk medicine
民主化（みんしゅか）democratization
民主社会主義（みんしゅしゃかいしゅぎ）democratic socialism
民主主義（みんしゅしゅぎ）democracy
民主主義社会（みんしゅしゅぎしゃかい）democratic society
ミーンズテスト（みーんずてすと）means test
民生委員（みんせいいいん）welfare commission volunteer
民生委員の協力（みんせいいいんのきょうりょく）cooperation of commission volunteers
民生委員法（みんせいいいんほう）Welfare Commission Volunteers Act
民族差別（みんぞくさべつ）ethnic discrimination；race discrimination
ミンチ食（みんちしょく）minced meal
民法（みんぽう）Civil Law
民法典（みんぽうてん）Civic Code
民話（みんわ）folktale

む

無意識（むいしき）unconsciousness；unconscious
無医村（むいそん）medically underserved area
無医地区（むいちく）medically underserved area
無塩（むえん）no added salt：NAS
無塩食（むえんしょく）no added salt diet：NAS diet
無階級社会（むかいきゅうしゃかい）classless society

介護保険・介護福祉等関連用語 和英

無害性原理（むがいせいげんり）nonmaleficence principle；principle of nonmaleficence
無害の薬剤（むがいのやくざい）innocuous drug
無関心（むかんしん）adiaphoria
無機質（むきしつ）mineral
無気肺（むきはい）pulmonary atelectasis
無拠出給付（むきょしゅつきゅうふ）non-contributory benefit
無拠出給付制（むきょしゅつきゅうふせい）non-contributory benefit system
無拠出退職年金（むきょしゅつたいしょくねんきん）non-contributory retirement pension
無拠出年金（むきょしゅつねんきん）non-contributory pension
無気力（むきりょく）enervation
無菌（むきん）asepsis
無菌試験（むきんしけん）sterility test
無菌性保証レベル（むきんせいほしょうれべる）⇒滅菌保証レベル
無菌操作（むきんそうさ）aseptic procedure；aseptic technique
無菌的間欠導尿法（むきんてきかんけつどうにょうほう）aseptic intermittent catheterization：AIC
無菌的遮蔽（むきんてきしゃへい）aseptic barrier
無菌的被覆（むきんてきひふく）⇒無菌的遮蔽
無菌保証（むきんほしょう）sterility assurance
無限責任中間法人（むげんせきにんちゅうかんほうじん）unlimited liability non-profit mutual benefit corporation
無呼吸（むこきゅう）apnea
無呼吸閾値（むこきゅういきち）apneic threshold
無呼吸指数（むこきゅうしすう）apnea index
無呼吸低呼吸指数（むこきゅうていこきゅうしすう）apnea-hypopnea index：AHI
無呼吸発作（むこきゅうほっさ）apneic spell
ムコ多糖症（むこたとうしょう）mucopolysaccharidosis
無作為抽出（むさくいちゅうしゅつ）random sampling
無作為割当（むさくいわりあて）random assignment
無差別（むさべつ）indiscrimination
無差別平等（むさべつびょうどう）non-discrimination and equality
無酸素血症（むさんそけつしょう）anoxemia
無酸素症（むさんそしょう）anoxia
無酸素性訓練（むさんそせいくんれん）anaerobic exercise
無酸素性作業閾値（むさんそせいさぎょういきち）anaerobic threshold：AT
無児家族（むじかぞく）childless family
無歯症（むししょう）edentulism
無償医療（むしょういりょう）free medical care；free health care
無条件刺激（むじょうけんしげき）unconditioned stimulus
無条件の肯定的配慮（むじょうけんのこうていてきはいりょ）unconditional positive regard
無条件反応（むじょうけんはんのう）unconditioned response
無症候性キャリア（むしょうこうせいきゃりあ）asymptomatic carrier
無症候性心筋虚血（むしょうこうせいしんきんきょけつ）silent myocardial ischemia
無症候性保菌者（むしょうこうせいほきんしゃ）asymptomatic carrier
無償労働（むしょうろうどう）unpaid labor；unpaid work
無職（むしょく）unemployment；jobless
無水アルコール（むすいあるこーる）absolute alcohol
むずむず脚症候群（むずむずあししょうこうぐん）⇒レストレスレッグス症候群
無政府主義（むせいふしゅぎ）anarchism
無生物表面（むせいぶつひょうめん）inanimate surface
無知（むち）ignorance
むち打ち（むちうち）whiplash
むち打ち症（むちうちしょう）whiplash injury
六つの基礎食品群（むっつのきそしょくひんぐん）six basic food groups
無党派層（むとうはそう）non-partisan voter
ムートン（むーとん）mouton
無尿症（むにょうしょう）anuria
無認可（むにんか）unauthorized
胸やけ（むねやけ）heartburn
無年金者（むねんきんしゃ）unqualified person for public pension
無保険者（むほけんしゃ）uninsured
無抑制膀胱（むよくせいぼうこう）uninhibited bladder
無料（むりょう）free of charge

め

明・暗順応（めい・あんじゅんのう）light/dark adaptation
明順応（めいじゅんのう）light adaptation
迷信（めいしん）superstition
酩酊（めいてい）drunkenness
明度（めいど）lightness
明度の恒常性（めいどのこうじょうせい）lightness constancy
名目賃金（めいもくちんぎん）nominal wage
名誉（めいよ）reputation
名誉毀損（めいよきそん）defamation

名誉職（めいよしょく）honorary position
メインストリーミング（めいんすとりーみんぐ）mainstreaming
メインテナンス（めいんてなんす）maintenance
メガネ（めがね）glasses
メスメリズム（めすめりずむ）mesmerize
メゾレベル（めぞれべる）mezzo level
メタキサロン（めたきさろん）metaxalone
メタタルザルバー（めたたるざるばー）metatarsal bar
メタ認知（めたにんち）metacognition
メタファー（めたふぁー）metaphor
†メタボリック症候群（めたぼりっくしょうこうぐん）metabolic syndrome
メチシリン耐性黄色ブドウ球菌（めちしりんたいせいおうしょくぶどうきゅうきん）methicillin-resistant staphylococcus aureus：MRSA
メチルプレドニゾロン（めちるぷれどにぞろん）methylprednisolone
†滅菌（めっきん）sterilization
滅菌器（めっきんき）sterilizer
滅菌工程（めっきんこうてい）sterilization process
滅菌剤（めっきんざい）sterilant
滅菌水（めっきんすい）sterilized water
滅菌バリデーション（めっきんばりでーしょん）sterilization validation
滅菌保証（めっきんほしょう）⇒無菌保証
滅菌保証レベル（めっきんほしょうれべる）sterility assurance level：SAL
メッツ（めっつ）metabolic equivalent of task：MET
メディカルソーシャルワーク（めでぃかるそーしゃるわーく）medical social work
メディカルレター（めでぃかるれたー）medical letter
メディシンボール（めでぃしんぼーる）medicine ball
メトカルバモール（めとかるばもーる）methocarbamol
メトトレキサート（めととれきさーと）methotrexate
メトプロロール（めとぷろろーる）metoprolol
メトホルミン（めとほるみん）metformin
メトラゾン（めとらぞん）metolazone
メニエール病（めにえーるびょう）Meniere's disease
メノポーズ（めのぽーず）menopause
めまい（めまい）dizziness；vertigo
メマンティン（めまんてぃん）memantine
メラトニン（めらとにん）melatonin
メラニン細胞（めらにんさいぼう）melanocyte
メリット財（めりっとざい）merit goods
メリディア（めりでぃあ）Meridia

メレナ（めれな）⇒下血
メロシン欠損型先天性筋ジストロフィー（めろしんけっそんがたせんてんせいきんじすとろふぃー）merosin-deficient congenital muscular dystrophy
綿（めん）cotton
免疫（めんえき）immunity
免疫化学的便潜血検査（めんえきかがくてきべんせんけつけんさ）immunoassay fecal occult blood test
免疫学的便潜血検査（めんえきがくてきべんせんけつけんさ）immunologic fecal occult blood test
免疫グロブリン（めんえきぐろぶりん）immunoglobulin：Ig
免疫グロブリンE（めんえきぐろぶりんいー）immunoglobulin E：IgE
免疫グロブリンA（めんえきぐろぶりんえー）immunoglobulin A：IgA
免疫グロブリンM（めんえきぐろぶりんえむ）immunoglobulin M：IgM
免疫グロブリンG（めんえきぐろぶりんじー）immunoglobulin G
免疫システム（めんえきしすてむ）immune system
免疫シンチグラフィー（めんえきしんちぐらふぃー）immunoscintigraphy
免疫不全症（めんえきふぜんしょう）immunodeficiency
免疫抑制（めんえきよくせい）immunosuppressed
免疫療法（めんえきりょうほう）immunotherapy
免荷装具（めんかそうぐ）non-weight-bearing orthosis
免除（めんじょ）waiver
免税措置（めんぜいそち）tax exemption measure
免責定額負担（めんせきていがくふたん）deductible
免責定率負担（めんせきていりつふたん）co-payment
面接（めんせつ）interview
面接交渉権（めんせつこうしょうけん）visitation rights
面接調査（めんせつちょうさ）interview survey：personal interview survey
メンタルヘルスクリニック（めんたるへるすくりにっく）mental health clinic
メンタルヘルスケア（めんたるへるすけあ）mental health care
メンブランフィルタ（めんぶらんふぃるた）membrane filter
綿棒（めんぼう）cotton swab

も

喪（も）mourning
盲（もう）blindness

介護保険・介護福祉等関連用語 和英

盲学校（もうがっこう）school for the blind
盲教育（もうきょういく）education for the blind
盲高齢者（もうこうれいしゃ）blind elderly
盲児（もうじ）blind child
盲児施設（もうじしせつ）facility for the blind children
盲者（もうしゃ）blind person
盲者施設（もうしゃしせつ）facility for the blind persons
盲人（もうじん）blind person
盲人ガイドヘルパー（もうじんがいどへるぱー）guide helper for the blind
盲人ガイドヘルプ（もうじんがいどへるぷ）guidance for the blind
盲人施設（もうじんしせつ）facility for the blind
盲人ホーム（もうじんほーむ）home for the blind
†妄想（もうそう）delusion
妄想性障害（もうそうせいしょうがい）delusional disorder
盲導犬（もうどうけん）guide dog；seeing-eye dog
網膜（もうまく）retina
網膜感度（もうまくかんど）retinal sensitivity
盲幼児（もうようじ）blind infant
盲聾唖児（もうろうあじ）deaf-blind and mute child
盲聾唖児施設（もうろうあじしせつ）facility for deaf-blind children
盲聾唖者（もうろうあしゃ）deaf-blind and mute
盲聾唖幼児（もうろうあようじ）deaf-blind and mute infant
盲聾児（もうろうじ）deaf-blind child
盲聾者（もうろうしゃ）deaf-blind person
盲老人（もうろうじん）blind elderly
盲老人ホーム（もうろうじんほーむ）long-term care home for the elderly blind
盲聾幼児（もうろうようじ）deaf-blind infant
†燃え尽き症候群（もえつきしょうこうぐん）burnout syndrome
目的税（もくてきぜい）earmarked taxation
目標（もくひょう）goal
目標設定（もくひょうせってい）goal setting
モジュラー義肢（もじゅらーぎし）modular prosthesis
モジュラー車いす（もじゅらーくるまいす）modular wheelchair system
モジュラー式座位保持システム（もじゅらーしきざいほじしすてむ）modular seating system
モジュール（もじゅーる）module
モース術（もーすじゅつ）Mohs surgery
持ち家（もちいえ）own house
木工（もっこう）woodworking
モデリング（もでりんぐ）modeling
モニター測定（もにたーそくてい）monitoring measurement

†モニタリング（もにたりんぐ）monitoring
モノアミン酸化酵素阻害薬（ものあみんさんかこうそそがいやく）monoamine oxidase inhibitor
物忘れ（ものわすれ）forgetfulness
モビライゼーション（もびらいぜーしょん）mobilization
模倣（もほう）imitation
模倣薬（もほうやく）copycat medication
モラトリアム（もらとりあむ）moratorium
モラール（もらーる）morale
モラルハザード（もらるはざーど）moral hazard
森田療法（もりたりょうほう）Morita therapy
モールド型座位保持装置（もーるどがたざいほじそうち）molded seating system
モルヒネ（もるひね）morphine
モルヒネ依存（もるひねいぞん）morphine dependence
問題解決（もんだいかいけつ）problem solving
問題解決アプローチ（もんだいかいけつあぷろーち）problem solving approach
問題解決過程（もんだいかいけつかてい）problem solving process
†問題行動（もんだいこうどう）problem behavior
問題指向型システム（もんだいしこうがたしすてむ）problem-oriented system；POS

や

夜間学校（やかんがっこう）night school
†夜間せん妄（やかんせんもう）night-time delirium
夜間装具（やかんそうぐ）night orthosis
夜間対応型訪問介護（やかんたいおうがたほうもんかいご）night home care
夜間病院（やかんびょういん）night hospital
夜間保育（やかんほいく）night care for children
夜勤（やきん）night shift
役員（やくいん）director
薬害（やくがい）drug-induced suffering
†薬剤（やくざい）medication
†薬剤管理（やくざいかんり）medication management
†薬剤師（やくざいし）pharmacist
薬剤性エリテマトーデス（やくざいせいえりてまとーです）drug-induced lupus erythematosus
薬剤性肝炎（やくざいせいかんえん）drug-induced hepatitis
薬剤性肝疾患（やくざいせいかんしっかん）drug-induced liver disease
薬剤性急性膵炎（やくざいせいきゅうせいすいえん）drug-induced acute pancreatitis
薬剤性血小板減少症（やくざいせいけっしょうばんげんしょうしょう）drug-induced thrombocytopenia

薬剤性血小板減少性紫斑病（やくざいせいけっしょうばんげんしょうせいしはんびょう）drug-induced thrombocytopenic purpura
薬剤性骨粗鬆症（やくざいせいこつそしょうしょう）drug-induced osteoporosis
薬剤性膵炎（やくざいせいすいえん）drug-induced pancreatitis
薬剤性精神病（やくざいせいせいしんびょう）drug-induced psychosis
薬剤性統合失調症（やくざいせいとうごうしっちょうしょう）drug-induced Schizophrenia
薬剤性パーキンソニズム（やくざいせいぱーきんそにずむ）drug-induced Parkinsonism
薬剤性慢性膵炎（やくざいせいまんせいすいえん）drug-induced chronic pancreatitis
薬剤性ループス（やくざいせいるーぷす）drug-induced lupus
薬剤費（やくざいひ）pharmaceutical costs
薬剤副作用（やくざいふくさよう）adverse drug reaction：ADR
薬事監視（やくじかんし）pharmaceutical inspection
薬事監視員（やくじかんしいん）pharmaceutical inspector
薬事法（やくじほう）Pharmaceutical Affairs Law
薬疹（やくしん）drug rash
薬物アレルギー（やくぶつあれるぎー）drug allergy
薬物依存（やくぶついぞん）drug dependence；drug addiction
薬物更生施設（やくぶつこいせいしせつ）awakening recovery center；awakening drug rehab center
薬物拘束（やくぶつこうそく）chemical restraint
薬物相互作用（やくぶつそうごさよう）medication interaction
薬物中毒（やくぶつちゅうどく）drug intoxication
薬物動態的変化（やくぶつどうたいてきへんか）pharmacokinetic change
薬物のない（やくぶつのない）drug free
薬物乱用（やくぶつらんよう）drug abuse；substance abuse
†薬物療法（やくぶつりょうほう）pharmacotherapy
薬理学的変化（やくりがくてきへんか）pharmacodynamic change
役割（やくわり）role
役割演技（やくわりえんぎ）role playing
役割葛藤（やくわりかっとう）role conflict
役割期待（やくわりきたい）role expectation
役割距離（やくわりきょり）role distance
役割行動（やくわりこうどう）role behavior
役割遂行（やくわりすいこう）role performance
役割認知（やくわりにんち）role perception
役割理論（やくわりりろん）role theory
夜警国家（やけいこっか）night watchman state；minimal state
火傷（やけど）burn
ヤコブ病（やこぶびょう）Creutzfeldt-Jakob disease：CJD
矢田部・ギルフォード性格検査（やたべ・ぎるふぉーどせいかくけんさ）Yatabe-Guilford Personality Test
薬価基準（やっかきじゅん）drug tariff standards；drug tariff
薬価規制（やっかきせい）drug price controls
薬局（やっきょく）pharmacy
夜尿症（やにょうしょう）nocturia；nycturia
病体験（やまいたいけん）illness experience
夜盲（やもう）night blindness
ヤール重症度（やーるじゅうしょうど）Hoehn-Yahr stage

ゆ

遺言者（ゆいごんしゃ）testator
遺言書（ゆいごんしょ）will；testament；last will
友愛（ゆうあい）fraternity
友愛組合（ゆうあいくみあい）friendly society
友愛訪問（ゆうあいほうもん）friendly visiting
友愛訪問員（ゆうあいほうもんいん）friendly visitor
有意差（ゆういさ）significant difference
遊脚期（ゆうきゃくき）swing phase
遊脚中期（ゆうきゃくちゅうき）mid swing
有給休暇（ゆうきゅうきゅうか）paid time off：PTO
遊戯療法（ゆうぎりょうほう）play therapy
優遇措置（ゆうぐうそち）preferential placement
有限責任中間法人（ゆうげんせきにんちゅうかんほうじん）limited liability non-profit mutual benefit corporation
有効視野（ゆうこうしや）useful field of view
有効需要（ゆうこうじゅよう）effective demand
有資格医療福祉職（ゆうしかくいりょうふくししょく）licensed heath care practitioner：LHCP
有資格看護師（ゆうしかくかんごし）licensed nurse
有資格ソーシャルワーカー（ゆうしかくそーしゃるわーかー）licensed social worker
有資格臨床ソーシャルワーカー（ゆうしかくりんしょうそーしゃるわーかー）licensed clinical social worker：LCSW
有償ボランタリ（ゆうしょうぼらんたり）paid voluntary
有償ボランティア（ゆうしょうぼらんてぃあ）paid volunteer
優性遺伝（ゆうせいいでん）dominant inheritance
優生学（ゆうせいがく）eugenics
優性手術（ゆうせいしゅじゅつ）eugenic operation
優性保護（ゆうせいほご）eugenic protection

優生保護法（ゆうせいほごほう）Eugenic and Maternal Protection Law
優先座席（ゆうせんざせき）priority seat
優先的（ゆうせんてき）preferential
郵送調査法（ゆうそうちょうさほう）mail survey
有痛性歩行（ゆうつうせいほこう）antalgic gait
誘発筋電図（ゆうはつきんでんず）evoked electromyogram
誘発電位（ゆうはつでんい）evoked potential
有病（ゆうびょう）prevalence
有病率（ゆうびょうりつ）prevalence rate；morbidity
猶予期間（ゆうよきかん）grace period
遊離脂肪酸（ゆうりしぼうさん）non-esterified fatty acid
†有料老人ホーム（ゆうりょうろうじんほーむ）private residential home for the elderly
床清掃（ゆかせいそう）floor cleaning
浴衣（ゆかた）bathrobe
床反力（ゆかはんりょく）ground reaction force；floor reaction force
床反力計（ゆかはんりょくけい）force plate
床面レベル（ゆかめんれべる）floor level
輸血（ゆけつ）blood transfusion
輸送（ゆそう）transportation
ユートピア（ゆーとぴあ）Utopia
ユニーク色相（ゆにーくしきそう）unique hue
ユニセフ（ゆにせふ）United Nations Children's Fund：UNICEF
†ユニットケア（ゆにっとけあ）unit-based care
ユニバーサルデザイン（ゆにばーさるでざいん）universal design
†ユニバーサルファッション（ゆにばーさるふぁっしょん）universal fashion
ユネスコ（ゆねすこ）United Nations Educational, Scientific and Cultural Organization：UNESCO
指はしご（ゆびはしご）finger ladder
指文字（ゆびもじ）fingerspelling
夢分析（ゆめぶんせき）dream analysis
揺りいす（ゆりいす）rocking chair
ユング心理学（ゆんぐしんりがく）Jungian psychology

よ

陽圧室（ようあつしつ）pressurized room
養育（よういく）bringing up
養育医療（よういくいりょう）medical aid for premature infants
養育者（よういくしゃ）person bringing up
養育費出（よういくひしゅつ）expenses for bringing up a child
養育費用（よういくひよう）costs for bringing up a child
養育費用平均（よういくひようへいきん）average cost of bringing up a child
†要援護高齢者（ようえんごこうれいしゃ）support-required elderly
†要介護（ようかいご）long-term care-required
†要介護者（ようかいごしゃ）long-term care recipient
要介護状態（ようかいごじょうたい）long-term care status
要介護状態区分（ようかいごじょうたいくぶん）category of long-term care status
†要介護度（ようかいごど）long-term care classification levels
†要介護認定（ようかいごにんてい）certification of long term care-required；long-term care-required certification
要介護認定基準（ようかいごにんていきじゅん）certification standards for long-term care insurance benefits
要介護認定の取消し（ようかいごにんていのとりけし）cancellation of certification of long-term care-required
要介護寝たきり老人（ようかいごねたきりろうじん）bedridden long-term care recipient
陽極（ようきょく）anode
用具（ようぐ）equipment
溶血性貧血（ようけつせいひんけつ）hemolytic anemia
養護学校（ようごがっこう）school for the physically and mentally disabled children；school for the disabled children
擁護活動（ようごかつどう）advocacy activity
養護教諭（ようごきょうゆ）school nurse
養護施設（ようごしせつ）residential care home for children；children's home
養護児童（ようごじどう）child in need of protection
†養護老人ホーム（ようごろうじんほーむ）residential home for the elderly
養子（ようし）adopted child
幼児（ようじ）infant
†要支援（ようしえん）long-term assistance-required
養子縁組（ようしえんぐみ）adoption
†要支援者（ようしえんしゃ）long-term assistance recipient
†要支援認定（ようしえんにんてい）certification of long-term assistance-required；long-term assistance-required certification
要支援認定の取消し（ようしえんにんていのとりけし）cancellation of certification of long-term assistance-required

幼児期（ようじき）newborn infant period
幼児クラス（ようじくらす）toddler class
用手洗浄（ようしゅせんじょう）manual cleaning
腰髄神経根症（ようずいしんけいこんしょう）lumbar radiculopathy
羊水診断（ようすいしんだん）amniocentesis；amniotic fluid test
腰髄損傷（ようずいそんしょう）lumbar spinal cord injury
陽性鋭波（ようせいえいは）positive sharp wave
養成訓練制度（ようせいくんれんせいど）apprenticeship
陽性症状（ようせいしょうじょう）positive symptom
陽性所見（ようせいしょけん）positive finding
陽性モデル（ようせいもでる）positive mold
腰仙椎装具（ようせんついそうぐ）lumbosacral orthosis
ヨウ素（ようそ）iodine
幼稚園（ようちえん）kindergarten
腰椎（ようつい）lumbar vertebra；lumbar vertebrae
腰椎牽引（ようついけんいん）lumbar traction
腰椎穿刺（ようついせんし）lumbar puncture
腰痛（ようつう）low back pain
†腰痛症（ようつうしょう）lumbago；low back pain
†腰痛体操（ようつうたいそう）lumbago exercise；exercise for low back pain
†腰痛予防（ようつうよぼう）prevention of lumbago；lumbago prevention
陽電子放射断層撮影法（ようでんしほうしゃだんそうさつえいほう）positron emission tomography；PET
要介護家族（ようかいごかぞく）family in need of public assistance
要介護者（ようかいごしゃ）person in need of public assistance
要介護性（ようかいごせい）the need for public assistance
要介護世帯（ようかいごせたい）household in need of public assistance
要約記録（ようやくきろく）summary records
養老院（ようろういん）almshouse；beadhouse
余暇（よか）leisure
ヨガ（よが）yoga
余暇指導（よかしどう）leisure education；leisure guidance；guidance for leisure
余暇プログラム（よかぷろぐらむ）⇒レジャープログラム
余暇利用（よかりよう）use of leisure time
抑圧（よくあつ）repression
抑うつ（よくうつ）depression
抑うつ型（よくうつがた）depression type

抑うつ自己評価尺度（よくうつじこひょうかしゃくど）Center for Epidemiological Studies Depression Scale；CES-D
抑うつ神経症（よくうつしんけいしょう）depressive neurosis
浴室（よくしつ）bathroom
†抑制（よくせい）restraint
抑制帯（よくせいたい）restraining tie
†浴槽（よくそう）bathtub
浴比（よくひ）bath ratio
予見的監査（よけんてきかんさ）prospective review
予見的研究（よけんてきけんきゅう）prospective study
予後（よご）prognosis
横アーチ（よこあーち）transverse arch
横つまみ（よこつまみ）side pinch
予後予測（よごよそく）prognosis prediction
予算（よさん）budget
予算編成（よさんへんせい）budgeting
予算保持一般医（よさんほじいっぱんい）general practitioner fundholder
四時間毎（よじかんごと）every 4 hours；Q4H
欲求の5段階説（よっきゅうのごだんかいせつ）five-stage hierarchy of needs
欲求不満（よっきゅうふまん）frustration
欲求不満耐性（よっきゅうふまんたいせい）frustration tolerance
四つの食品群（よっつのしょくひんぐん）four food groups；four basic food groups
四つ這い（よつばい）crawling
四つ這い移動（よつばいいどう）creeping
予備調査（よびちょうさ）preliminary survey
予防（よぼう）prevention；precaution
予防隔離（よぼうかくり）protective isolation
†予防給付（よぼうきゅうふ）preventive benefit
予防ケア（よぼうけあ）preventive care
予防サービス（よぼうさーびす）preventive services
予防処置（よぼうしょち）preventive treatment
予防接種（よぼうせっしゅ）immunization；preventive vaccination；vaccination
予防接種証明書（よぼうせっしゅしょうめいしょ）proof of immunization；certificate of immunization
予防投与（よぼうとうよ）prophylactic medication
予防内服（よぼうないふく）prophylactic medication
予防老年学（よぼうろうねんがく）preventive gerontology
嫁姑葛藤（よめしゅうとめかっとう）conflict between mothers-in-law and daughters-in-law；conflict between mothers-in-law and brides
予約（よやく）appointment
与薬（よやく）assistance with the self-administration of medication

世論（よろん）public opinion
世論調査（よろんちょうさ）public opinion poll
†四脚杖（よんきゃくづえ）quad cane；four-legged cane
40代（よんじゅうだい）quadragenarian
四点歩行（よんてんほこう）four-point gait
401Kプラン（よんまるいちけーぷらん）401K plan

ら

癩（らい）leprosy
来院時心停止（らいいんじしんていし）dead on arrival：DOA
ライソゾーム病（らいぞーむびょう）Lysosomal storage diseases
ライター症候群（らいたーしょうこうぐん）Reiter's syndrome
ライフイベント（らいふいべんと）life event
ライフコース（らいふこーす）life course
†ライフサイクル（らいふさいくる）life cycle
†ライフスタイル（らいふすたいる）life style
ライフステージ（らいふすてーじ）life stage；stages of life
ライフデザイン（らいふでざいん）life design
ライフモデル（らいふもでる）life model
†ライフレビュー（らいふれびゅー）life review；reminiscence
ラクナ梗塞（らくなこうそく）lacunar stroke
ラザダイン（らざだいん）Razadyne
ラシックス（らしっくす）Lasix
らせん状支柱付き短下肢装具（らせんじょうしちゅうつきたんかしそうぐ）spiral ankle-foot orthosis
落下菌測定法（らっかきんそくていほう）setting plate sampling
ラテンアメリカ系高齢者（らてんあめりかけいこうれいしゃ）Latino elder
ラテンアメリカ系人（らてんあめりかけいじん）Hispanics
ラビング法（らびんぐほう）⇒擦式法
ラベタロール（らべたろーる）labetalol
ラベリング（らべりんぐ）labeling
†ラポール（らぽーる）rapport
ラミクタール（らみくたーる）Lamictal
ラミブジン（らみぶじん）lamivudine
ラメルテオン（らめるておん）ramelteon
ラモトリギン（らもとりぎん）lamotrigine
ラロキシフェン（らろきしふぇん）raloxifene
乱視（らんし）astigmatism
卵巣癌（らんそうがん）ovarian cancer
ランニングコスト（らんにんぐこすと）running cost

り

リアリティ・オリエンテーション（りありてぃ・おりえんてーしょん）reality orientation
リウマチ（りうまち）rheumatic disorder；rheumatism
リウマチ学（りうまちがく）rheumatology
リウマチ性多発筋痛症（りうまちせいたはつきんつうしょう）polymyalgia rheumatica
リウマチ専門医（りうまちせんもんい）rheumatologist
利益団体（りえきだんたい）interest group
理学療法（りがくりょうほう）physical therapy；physiotherapy
†理学療法士（りがくりょうほうし）physical therapist：PT
理学療法士の実践ガイド（りがくりょうほうしのじっせんがいど）Guide to Physical Therapist Practice
罹患（りかん）incidence
罹患率（りかんりつ）incidence rate
罹患率調査（りかんりつちょうさ）incidence survey
リキャップ（りきゃっぷ）recap
リクライニング型車いす（りくらいにんぐがたくるまいす）reclining wheelchair
リクリエーション（りくりえーしょん）⇒レクリエーション
リクリエーション活動（りくりえーしょんかつどう）⇒レクリエーション活動
リクリエーションプログラム（りくりえーしょんぷろぐらむ）⇒レクリエーションプログラム
リコピン（りこぴん）lycopene
離婚（りこん）divorce
離婚者（りこんしゃ）divorced person
離婚証明書（りこんしょうめいしょ）divorce certificate
リザトリプタン（りざとりぷたん）rizatriptan
リジノプリル（りじのぷりる）lisinopril
履修時間（りしゅうじかん）curriculum hours
離床（りしょう）out of bed
離職率（りしょくりつ）turnover rate
離人症（りじんしょう）depersonalization disorder
リスキー・シフト（りすきー・しふと）risky shift
リスク（りすく）risk
リスクアセスメント（りすくあせすめんと）risk assessment
リスク管理（りすくかんり）risk control
リスク共有プラン（りすくきょうゆうぷらん）risk-sharing plan
リスクマネジメント（りすくまねじめんと）risk management
リストラ（りすとら）restructuring
リスパダール（りすぱだーる）Risperdal

リスペリドン（りすぺりどん）risperidone
リセドロン酸（りせどろんさん）risedronate
リソソーム蓄積病（りそそーむちくせきびょう）⇒ライソゾーム病
リソソーム病（りそそーむびょう）⇒ライソゾーム病
リーダーシップ（りーだーしっぷ）leadership
離脱（りだつ）disengagement
離脱理論（りだつりろん）disengagement theory
リーチ・アウト（りーち・あうと）reach out
リチウム（りちうむ）lithium
リーチャー（りーちゃー）reacher
†立位（りつい）standing position
立位訓練（りついくんれん）standing exercise
立位保持装置（りついほじそうち）stabilizer
立脚期（りっきゃくき）stance phase
立脚中期（りっきゃくちゅうき）mid-stance phase
リッチモンドに帰れ（りっちもんどにかえれ）back to Richmond
立法者（りっぽうしゃ）lawmaker；legislator
リテラシープログラム（りてらしーぷろぐらむ）literacy program
リドカイン（りどかいん）lidocaine
†利尿剤（りにょうざい）diuretic
リバスチグミン（りばすちぐみん）rivastigmine
リバースモーゲージ（りばーすもーげーじ）reverse mortgage
リバースモーゲージプログラム（りばーすもーげーじぷろぐらむ）reverse mortgage program
†リハビリテーション（りはびりてーしょん）rehabilitation
リハビリテーションアプローチ（りはびりてーしょんあぷろーち）rehabilitation approach
リハビリテーション医（りはびりてーしょんい）physiatrist
†リハビリテーション医学（りはびりてーしょんいがく）rehabilitation medicine
†リハビリテーション介護（りはびりてーしょんかいご）rehabilitative care
リハビリテーション看護（りはびりてーしょんかんご）rehabilitation nursing
リハビリテーション看護師（りはびりてーしょんかんごし）rehabilitation nurse
リハビリテーション機器（りはびりてーしょんきき）rehabilitation equipment
リハビリテーション工学（りはびりてーしょんこうがく）rehabilitation engineering
リハビリテーション処方（りはびりてーしょんしょほう）rehabilitation prescription
リハビリテーション専門手引書（りはびりてーしょんせんもんてびきしょ）Rehabilitation Specialty's Handbook
リハビリテーションソーシャルワーカー（りはびりてーしょんそーしゃるわーかー）social worker for rehabilitation
リハビリテーションソーシャルワーク（りはびりてーしょんそーしゃるわーく）social work in rehabilitation
リハビリテーション中止基準（りはびりてーしょんちゅうしきじゅん）inhibitor for rehabilitation
リハビリテーションプログラム（りはびりてーしょんぷろぐらむ）rehabilitation program
リバーミード行動記憶検査（りばーみーどこうどうきおくけんさ）Riverhead Behavioural Memory Test
離被架（りひか）cradle
リビドー（りびどー）libido
リビングウィル（りびんぐうぃる）⇒尊厳死宣言書
リービングケア（りーびんぐけあ）leaving care
リファンピン（りふぁんぴん）rifampin
リフター（りふたー）lifter
リフト（りふと）lift
リフトバス（りふとばす）lift bus
リブラックス（りぶらっくす）Librax
リブリウム（りぶりうむ）Librium
リフレーミング（りふれーみんぐ）reframing
利便（りべん）access
利便性（りべんせい）accessibility
リポタンパク（りぽたんぱく）lipoprotein
リポタンパク受容体関連蛋白（りぽたんぱくじゅようたいかんれんたんぱく）lipoprotein receptor-related protein；LRP
リーメンビューゲル法（りーめんびゅーげるほう）Riemenbugel method
略語と定義（りゃくごとていぎ）acronym and definition
略奪（りゃくだつ）predation
流行（りゅうこう）epidemic
流行性（りゅうこうせい）epidemic
流行性角結膜炎（りゅうこうせいかくけつまくえん）epidemic keratoconjunctivitis；EKC
流行性耳下腺炎（りゅうこうせいじかせんえん）mumps
硫酸キニーネ（りゅうさんきにーね）quinine sulfate
流涎（りゅうぜん）drooling
流涎症（りゅうぜんしょう）sialorrhea；polysialia；ptyalism
流唾症（りゅうだしょう）ptyalism
†留置カテーテル（りゅうちかてーてる）indwelling catheter
留置カテーテル感染（りゅうちかてーてるかんせん）indwelling catheter infection
留置カテーテル敗血症（りゅうちかてーてるはいけつしょう）line sepsis
†流動食（りゅうどうしょく）liquid diet
†流動性知能（りゅうどうせいちのう）fluid intelligence

流動性能力（りゅうどうせいのうりょく）fluid ability
療育（りょういく）care and education
療育医療（りょういくいりょう）medical care and education for the disabled children
療育指導（りょういくしどう）care and education for the disabled children
利用監査（りようかんさ）utilization review：UR
利用管理（りようかんり）utilization management：UN
両脚支持（りょうきゃくしじ）double support
両脚支持期（りょうきゃくしじき）double support period
療護（りょうご）custodial care
良肢位（りょうしい）proper functional position
利用者（りようしゃ）recipient；client；resident
利用者支払（りようしゃしはらい）client payment
利用者評価（りようしゃひょうか）client evaluation；recipient evaluation
利用者負担金（りようしゃふたんきん）charges for recipients
利用者本位（りようしゃほんい）client-oriented；person-oriented
両性界面活性剤（りょうせいかいめんかっせいざい）amphoteric surface active agent
両性電解質（りょうせいでんかいしつ）ampholyte；amphoteric electrolyte
量的研究（りょうてきけんきゅう）quantitative research
量的調査（りょうてきちょうさ）quantitative investigation
寮母（りょうぼ）dormitory matron
両麻痺（りょうまひ）diplegia
両面価値（りょうめんかち）ambivalence
療養型病床群（りょうようがたびょうしょうぐん）long-term health care beds；a group of beds for long-term health care
療養給付（りょうようきゅうふ）long-term health care benefits
療養費（りょうようひ）long-term health care expenses
療養費支出（りょうようひしゅつ）long-term health care expenditures
療養病床（りょうようびょうしょう）long-term health care bed
療養費用補償（りょうようひようほしょう）compensation for long-term health care costs
料理道具（りょうりどうぐ）cooking utensil
†利用料（りようりょう）usage cost；fee
緑内障（りょくないしょう）glaucoma
緑膿菌性肺炎（りょくのうきんせいはいえん）pseudomonas pneumonia
旅行感染レジオネラ症（りょこうかんせんれじおねらしょう）travel-associated legionellosis
リラクセーション（りらくせーしょん）relaxation
リラクゼーション（りらくぜーしょん）⇒リラクセーション
リリカ（りりか）Lyrica
リルゾール（るぞーる）riluzole
リルテック（るてっく）Rilutek
理論（りろん）theory
理論最大一日摂取量（りろんさいだいいちにちせっしゅりょう）theoretical maximum daily intake
リンクナース（りんくなーす）⇒連携看護師
臨時的任用（りんじてきにんよう）temporary appointment
臨終（りんじゅう）dying；death
臨床栄養アセスメント（りんしょうえいようあせすめんと）clinical nutritional assessment
臨床家（りんしょうか）clinician
臨床検査（りんしょうけんさ）clinical examination
臨床検査技師（りんしょうけんさぎし）clinical laboratory technologist and technician
臨床工学技士（りんしょうこうがくぎし）clinical engineering technologist
臨床呼吸治療サービス（りんしょうこきゅうちりょうさーびす）clinical respiratory care and services
臨床細菌検査技師（りんしょうさいきんけんさぎし）clinical microbiological technician
臨床試験（りんしょうしけん）clinical trial
臨床試験結果（りんしょうしけんけっか）clinical trial result
臨床心理学（りんしょうしんりがく）clinical psychology
臨床心理士（りんしょうしんりし）clinical psychologist
臨床的介入（りんしょうてきかいにゅう）clinical intervention
臨床的認知症評価尺度（りんしょうてきにんちしょうひょうかしゃくど）Clinical Dementia Rating Scale：CDR
臨床的面接（りんしょうてきめんせつ）clinical interview
臨床薬剤師（りんしょうやくざいし）clinical pharmacist
リンス（りんす）rinse
リンビトロール（りんびとろーる）Limbitrol
隣保館（りんぽかん）settlement house
倫理（りんり）ethics
倫理規程（りんりきてい）ethical code
倫理綱領（りんりこうりょう）code of ethics

る

累積罹患率（るいせきりかんりつ）cumulative incidence rate

ルー・ゲーリッグ病（るー・げーりっくびょう）Lou Gehrig's disease
ルテイン（るていん）lutein
ループス（るーぷす）lupus
ルボックス（るぼっくす）Luvox

れ

冷あん法（れいあんぽう）cold compress
冷却滅菌剤（れいきゃくめっきんざい）cold sterilant
冷湿布（れいしっぷ）cold pack
令状（れいじょう）writ
冷水供給装置（れいすいきょうきゅうそうち）water cooler
霊性（れいせい）spirituality
霊的幸福尺度（れいてきこうふくしゃくど）Spiritual Well-Being Scale
冷凍療法（れいとうりょうほう）cryotherapy
レイ複雑図形検査（れいふくざつずけいけんさ）Rey figure copy
冷滅菌（れいめっきん）cold sterilization
レキップ（れきっぷ）Requip
暦年齢（れきねんれい）chronological age
レクリエーション（れくりえーしょん）recreation
レクリエーション活動（れくりえーしょんかつどう）recreational activity
レクリエーションプログラム（れくりえーしょんぷろぐらむ）recreation program
レーザー手術（れーざーしゅじゅつ）laser surgery
レーザー治療（れーざーちりょう）laser therapy
レーザードップラー血流測定（れーざーどっぷらーけつりゅうそくてい）laser doppler flowmetry
レジデンシャル・ケアワーク（れじでんしゃる・けあわーく）residential care work
レジデンシャル・ソーシャルワーク（れじでんしゃる・そーしゃるわーく）residential social work
レジャープログラム（れじゃーぷろぐらむ）leisure program
レストホーム（れすとほーむ）rest home
レストレスレッグス症候群（れすとれすれっぐすしょうこうぐん）restless legs syndrome：RLS
レスパイトケア（れすぱいとけあ）respite care
レスパイトケアサービス（れすぱいとけあさーびす）respite care services
レズビアン（れすびあん）lesbian
レズビアン（れずびあん）⇒レスビアン
レスビアン高齢者（れすびあんこうれいしゃ）lesbian elder
レズビアン高齢者（れずびあんこうれいしゃ）⇒レスビアン高齢者
レスピレーター（れすぴれーたー）respirator
レスポンス・コスト（れすぽんす・こすと）response cost
レスポンデント行動（れすぽんでんとこうどう）respondent behavior
劣悪的職場環境（れつあくてきしょくばかんきょう）hostile work environment
レッグサポート（れっぐさぽーと）leg-support
レッグレスト（れっぐれすと）leg rest
裂孔ヘルニア（れっこうへるにあ）hiatus hernia；hiatal hernia
劣性遺伝（れっせいいでん）recessive inheritance
劣等処遇の原則（れっとうしょぐうのげんそく）principle of less eligibility
レビア（れびあ）ReVia
レビー小体型認知症（れびーしょうたいがたにんちしょう）Lewy body dementia
レフルノミド（れふるのみど）leflunomide
レーブン色彩マトリックス検査（れーぶんしきさいまとりっくすけんさ）Raven's colored progressive matrices
レボドパ（れぼどぱ）levodopa
レミケード（れみけーど）Remicade
レミニール（れみにーる）Reminyl
†レム睡眠（れむすいみん）rapid eye movement〈REM〉sleep
レルパックス（れるぱっくす）Relpax
連携（れんけい）collaboration
連携看護師（れんけいかんごし）link nurse
連携・協働高齢者ヘルスケアチーム（れんけい・きょうどうこうれいしゃへるすけあちーむ）geriatric interdisciplinary health care team
蓮華座（れんげざ）lotus position
連合運動（れんごううんどう）associated movement
攣縮（れんしゅく）spasm
連続切片（れんぞくせっぺん）serial section
連続的携帯式腹膜透析（れんぞくてきけいたいしきふくまくとうせき）continuous ambulatory peritoneal dialysis：CAPD
連帯債務（れんたいさいむ）joint and several obligation
連帯責任（れんたいせきにん）joint and several liability
連帯納付義務（れんたいのうふぎむ）joint and several obligation for payments
レントゲン（れんとげん）x-ray；roentgen
連邦政府（れんぽうせいふ）federal government

ろ

†聾（ろう）deafness
聾唖学校（ろうあがっこう）school for the deaf mute
聾唖高齢者（ろうあこうれいしゃ）the deaf-mute

elderly
聾唖児（ろうあじ）the deaf-mute child
聾唖児施設（ろうあじしせつ）facility for the deaf-mute children
聾唖者（ろうあしゃ）the deaf-mute；deaf-mute person
聾唖幼児（ろうあようじ）the deaf-mute child
聾唖老人（ろうあろうじん）the deaf-mute elderly
†老化（ろうか）aging
聾学校（ろうがっこう）school for the deaf
†老眼（ろうがん）presbyopia
老健局（ろうけんきょく）Health and Welfare Bureau for the Elderly
老研式活動能力指標（ろうけんしきかつどうのうりょくしひょう）Tokyo Metropolitan Institute of Gerontology index of competence：TMIG-IC
聾高齢者（ろうこうれいしゃ）the aged deaf；the deaf elderly
労災管理課（ろうさいかんりか）Workers' Compensation Administration Division
労災保険（ろうさいほけん）workers' compensation insurance
労災保険業務室（ろうさいほけんぎょうむしつ）Compensation Operation Office
労災補償（ろうさいほしょう）industrial accident compensation
労災補償部（ろうさいほしょうぶ）Worker's Compensation Department
労作性狭心症（ろうさせいきょうしんしょう）effort angina
労使関係（ろうしかんけい）labor relation
聾者（ろうしゃ）the deaf
老人医療（ろうじんいりょう）geriatric medicine；geriatric medical care
老人医療サービス（ろうじんいりょうさーびす）medical care services for the aged
老人医療受給対象者（ろうじんいりょうじゅきゅうたいしょうしゃ）target population of geriatric medicine
老人医療制度（ろうじんいりょうせいど）medical care system for the aged
老人医療費（ろうじんいりょうひ）medical care expenditures for the aged；medical expenses for the aged
老人援助（ろうじんえんじょ）support for the aged
老人介護（ろうじんかいご）elderly care；caring for the elderly
老人介護機関（ろうじんかいごきかん）long-term care agency for the aged
老人介護サービス（ろうじんかいごさーびす）long-term care services for the aged
老人介護サービス機関（ろうじんかいごさーびすきかん）long-term care services agency for the aged

老人介護サービス事業者（ろうじんかいごさーびすぎょうしゃ）long-term care services provider for the aged
老人介護サービス事業所（ろうじんかいごさーびすぎょうしょ）long-term care services office for the aged
老人介護支援（ろうじんかいごしえん）elderly care management
老人介護支援センター（ろうじんかいごしえんせんたー）care management center for the aged
老人介護事業所（ろうじんかいごじぎょうしょ）long-term care office for the aged
老人介護施設（ろうじんかいごしせつ）long-term care facility for the aged
老人学級（ろうじんがっきゅう）educational class for the aged
老人学校（ろうじんがっこう）school for the aged
老人看護（ろうじんかんご）geriatric nursing
老人虐待（ろうじんぎゃくたい）elder abuse
老人休養ホーム（ろうじんきゅうようほーむ）rest home for the aged；recreational home for the aged；rest home for the elderly
老人共同生活（ろうじんきょうどうせいかつ）group living for the aged
老人共同生活支援（ろうじんきょうどうせいかつしえん）group living support for the aged
老人恐怖症（ろうじんきょうふしょう）gerontophobia
老人居宅介護（ろうじんきょたくかいご）home-based care for the aged
老人居宅介護支援（ろうじんきょたくかいごしえん）home-based care management the aged
老人居宅介護支援センター（ろうじんきょたくかいごしえんせんたー）home-based care management center for the aged
老人居宅生活扶助（ろうじんきょたくせいかつふじょ）home-based living assistance for the aged
老人クラブ（ろうじんくらぶ）senior citizens club；old people's club
老人ケア付住宅（ろうじんけあつきじゅうたく）elder care housing；aged care home
老人雇用（ろうじんこよう）employment of the aged
老人雇用促進（ろうじんこようそくしん）employment promotion for the aged
老人雇用促進対策（ろうじんこようそくしんたいさく）employment promotion policy for the aged
老人雇用率（ろうじんこようりつ）employment rates of the aged；employment rates for older people
老人再婚（ろうじんさいこん）elderly remarriage；remarriage in old age
老人在宅介護支援（ろうじんざいたくかいごしえん）elderly home care management

老人在宅介護支援センター（ろうじんざいたくかいごしえんせんたー）home care management center for the aged
老人在宅生活支援センター（ろうじんざいたくせいかつしえんせんたー）living management center for the aged
老人集中治療室（ろうじんしゅうちゅうちりょうしつ）geriatric intensive care unit
老人診療報酬制度（ろうじんしんりょうほうしゅうせいど）geriatric medical fee system
†老人性うつ病（ろうじんせいうつびょう）senile depression
老人精神保健（ろうじんせいしんほけん）geriatric mental health care
老人精神保健制度（ろうじんせいしんほけんせいど）geriatric mental health care system
老人精神保健対策（ろうじんせいしんほけんたいさく）policy of geriatric mental health care
†老人性難聴（ろうじんせいなんちょう）senile deafness；presbycusis；senile hearing loss
老人性認知症（ろうじんせいにんちしょう）senile dementia
老人性認知症疾患センター（ろうじんせいにんちしょうしっかんせんたー）Senile Dementia Center
老人性肺炎（ろうじんせいはいえん）pneumonia in the elderly
老人世話付住宅（ろうじんせわつきじゅうたく）elder care housing；aged care home
老人総合相談センター（ろうじんそうごうそうだんせんたー）comprehensive counseling center for the aged
老人大学（ろうじんだいがく）college for the elderly；university for the aged
老人短期入所（ろうじんたんきにゅうしょ）short-stay for the aged
老人短期入所施設（ろうじんたんきにゅうしょしせつ）short-stay facility for the aged
老人デイケア（ろうじんでいけあ）adult day care
老人デイケアセンター（ろうじんでいけあせんたー）adult day care center
老人デイサービスセンター（ろうじんでいさーびすせんたー）adult day services center
老人デイセンター（ろうじんでいせんたー）adult day center
老人デイヘルスケア（ろうじんでいへるすけあ）adult day health care
老人に対する犯罪（ろうじんにたいするはんざい）crimes against the elderly
老人の尊厳（ろうじんのそんげん）dignity of the aged
老人斑（ろうじんはん）senile plaque
老人犯罪（ろうじんはんざい）crime by the elderly；criminal offense by elderly

老人病院（ろうじんびょういん）geriatric hospital
老人貧困（ろうじんひんこん）poverty among the elderly
老人福祉（ろうじんふくし）welfare for the aged
老人福祉機関（ろうじんふくしきかん）welfare agency for the aged
老人福祉サービス（ろうじんふくしさーびす）welfare services for the aged
老人福祉事業（ろうじんふくしじぎょう）welfare program for the aged
老人福祉事業者（ろうじんふくしじぎょうしゃ）welfare provider for the aged
老人福祉事業所（ろうじんふくしじぎょうしょ）welfare office for the aged
老人福祉施策（ろうじんふくししさく）welfare policy for the aged
老人福祉施設（ろうじんふくししせつ）geriatric welfare facility；welfare facility for the elderly
老人福祉指導主事（ろうじんふくししどうしゅじ）social worker for the elderly；welfare supervisor for the elderly
老人福祉制度（ろうじんふくしせいど）welfare system for the aged；welfare system for the elderly；elderly welfare system
老人福祉センター（ろうじんふくしせんたー）welfare center for the aged
老人福祉相談員（ろうじんふくしそうだんいん）welfare adviser for the aged
老人福祉法（ろうじんふくしほう）Welfare Law for the Elderly
老人扶助（ろうじんふじょ）assistance for the aged
老親扶養（ろうしんふよう）responsible for an aging parent；responsible for aging parents
老人扶養（ろうじんふよう）responsible for the age
老人扶養控除（ろうじんふようこうじょ）deduction for elderly dependents
老人扶養税控除（ろうじんふようぜいこうじょ）tax deduction for elderly dependents
老人訪問看護ケア（ろうじんほうもんかんごけあ）home health care for the aged
老人保健（ろうじんほけん）elderly health
老人保健医療（ろうじんほけんいりょう）medical and health care for the aged
老人保健医療計画（ろうじんほけんいりょうけいかく）medical and health care plan for the aged
老人保健医療サービス（ろうじんほけんいりょうさーびす）medical and health care services for the aged
老人保健医療制度（ろうじんほけんいりょうせいど）medical and health care system for the aged
老人保健医療対策（ろうじんほけんいりょうたいさく）policy of health and medical care of the

elderly
老人保健課（ろうじんほけんか）Division of the Heath for the Elderly
老人保健計画（ろうじんほけんけいかく）health plan for the aged
老人保健サービス（ろうじんほけんさーびす）health services for the aged；elderly health services
老人保健サービス計画（ろうじんほけんさーびすけいかく）health services plan for the aged
老人保健事業（ろうじんほけんじぎょう）health programs for the aged
†老人保健施設（ろうじんほけんしせつ）geriatric health care facility
老人保健制度（ろうじんほけんせいど）health care systems for the aged
老人保健福祉（ろうじんほけんふくし）health and welfare for the aged
老人保健福祉機関（ろうじんほけんふくしきかん）health and welfare agency for the aged
老人保健福祉局（ろうじんほけんふくしきょく）Health and Welfare Bureau for the Elderly
老人保健福祉計画（ろうじんほけんふくしけいかく）Health and Welfare Plan for the Aged
老人保健福祉圏域（ろうじんほけんふくしけんいき）welfare administration district and health-welfare of the aged
老人保健福祉サービス計画（ろうじんほけんふくしさーびすけいかく）health and welfare services plan for the aged；health and welfare plan for the aged
老人保健福祉事業（ろうじんほけんふくしじぎょう）health and welfare program for the aged
老人保健福祉事業者（ろうじんほけんふくしじぎょうしゃ）health and welfare provider for the aged
老人保健福祉事業所（ろうじんほけんふくしじぎょうしょ）health and welfare office for the aged
老人保健福祉施設（ろうじんほけんふくしせつ）geriatric health and welfare facility
老人保健福祉制度（ろうじんほけんふくしせいど）health and welfare system for the aged
老人保健法（ろうじんほけんほう）Health and Medical Services Law for the Elderly
老人ホーム（ろうじんほーむ）care home for the aged
老人ホームヘルプ（ろうじんほーむへるぷ）home help for the aged
老人ホームヘルプサービス（ろうじんほーむへるぷさーびす）home help services for the aged
老人向け公営住宅（ろうじんむけこうえいじゅうたく）public housing for the aged
老人向け住宅（ろうじんむけじゅうたく）housing for the aged
老人向け民間サービス（ろうじんむけみんかんさーびす）private services for the aged
老人無職世帯（ろうじんむしょくせたい）aged retiree household
老衰（ろうすい）senility
労働安全衛生庁（ろうどうあんぜんえいせいちょう）Occupational Safety and Health Administration
労働安全衛生法（ろうどうあんぜんえいせいほう）Industrial Safety and Health Act
労働衛生課（ろうどうえいせいか）Industrial Health Division
労働環境（ろうどうかんきょう）work environment；labor environment
労働基準局（ろうどうきじゅんきょく）Labour Standards Bureau
労働基本権（ろうどうきほんけん）fundamental rights at work
労働組合（ろうどうくみあい）labor union
労働経済学（ろうどうけいざいがく）labor economics；labour economics
労働災害（ろうどうさいがい）occupational injury；industrial accident
労働時間（ろうどうじかん）work hours
労働市場（ろうどうしじょう）labor market
労働市場センター業務室（ろうどうしじょうせんたーぎょうむしつ）Labour Market Center Operations Office
労働奨励計画（ろうどうしょうれいけいかく）work incentive program；WIN
労働政策（ろうどうせいさく）labor policy
労働争議（ろうどうそうぎ）strike；strike action
労働適応能力指標（ろうどうてきおうのうりょくひょう）work ability index：WAI
労働福祉（ろうどうふくし）labour welfare
労働保険徴収課（ろうどうほけんちょうしゅうか）Labour Insurance Contribution Levy Division
労働問題（ろうどうもんだい）labor problem
労働力（ろうどうりょく）labor force
労働力人口（ろうどうりょくじんこう）labor force population
漏斗胸（ろうときょう）pectus excavatum
朗読奉仕（ろうどくほうし）reading volunteer services
朗読奉仕員（ろうどくほうしいん）reading volunteer
老年医学（ろうねんいがく）geriatrics
老年うつ病スケール（ろうねんうつびょうすけーる）Geriatric Depression Scale：GDS
老年学（ろうねんがく）gerontology
老年化指数（ろうねんかしすう）aging index
老年期（ろうねんき）old-age；senescence；senium
老年期うつ尺度（ろうねんきうつしゃくど）Geriatric Depression Scale：GDS

老年期ゲイ（ろうねんきげい）gay elder
老年期躁うつ病（ろうねんきそううつびょう）manic depressive psychosis in the elderly
老年社会福祉学（ろうねんしゃかいふくしがく）gerontological social work
老年者控除（ろうねんしゃこうじょ）deduction for the aged
老年者税控除（ろうねんしゃぜいこうじょ）tax deduction for the seniors
老年症候群（ろうねんしょうこうぐん）geriatric syndrome
老年人口（ろうねんじんこう）elderly population
老年人口比率（ろうねんじんこうひりつ）ratio of the elderly population
老年性難聴（ろうねんせいなんちょう）presbycusis
†老年認知症（ろうねんにんちしょう）senile dementia
老年病（ろうねんびょう）geriatric disease
労務管理（ろうむかんり）labor management
老齢加算（ろうれいかさん）supplemental payment to the aged
†老齢基礎年金（ろうれいきそねんきん）basic old-age pension
老齢厚生年金（ろうれいこうせいねんきん）old-age employees' pension
高齢者介護（ろうれいしゃかいご）elderly care：caring for the elderly
†老齢年金（ろうれいねんきん）old-age pension
†老齢福祉年金（ろうれいふくしねんきん）old-age welfare pension
老齢扶助（ろうれいふじょ）old-age assistance
老齢保険（ろうれいほけん）old-age insurance
老老介護（ろうろうかいご）elder to elder care：elderly care provided by elderly
聾唖人（ろうあうじん）the deaf-mute elderly
ろ過滅菌（ろかめっきん）filtration sterilization
六時間毎（ろくじかんごと）every 6 hours：Q6H
60代（ろくじゅうだい）sexagenarian
肋軟骨炎（ろくなんこつえん）costochondritis
肋木（ろくぼく）stall bar
ロゴセラピー（ろごせらぴー）logotherapy
ロコモティブシンドローム（ろこもてぃぶしんどろーむ）locomotive syndrome
ロサルタン（ろさるたん）losartan
路上生活者（ろじょうせいかつしゃ）homeless
ロゼレム（ろぜれむ）Rozerem
肋間神経痛（ろっかんしんけいつう）intercostal neuralgia
ロバキシン（ろばきしん）Robaxin
ロービジョン（ろーびじょん）low vision
ロピニロール（ろぴにろーる）ropinirole
ロフストランド杖（ろふすとらんどづえ）Lofstrand crutch

ロペラミド（ろぺらみど）loperamide
濾胞性甲状腺癌（ろほうせいこうじょうせんがん）follicular thyroid cancer
ロラゼパム（ろらぜぱむ）lorazepam
ロールシャッハ・インクブロット・テスト（ろーるしゃっは・いんくぶろっと・てすと）Rorschach Inkblot Test
ロールシャッハ・テスト（ろーるしゃっは・てすと）Rorschach Test
†ロールプレイ（ろーるぷれい）role play
ロールプレイング（ろーるぷれいんぐ）role playing
論理情動療法（ろんりじょうどうりょうほう）rational-emotive therapy

わ

YMCA（わいえむしーえー）Young Men's Christian Association
YWCA（わいだぶりゅしーえー）Young Women's Christian Association
ワーカーズコレクティブ（わーかーずこれくてぃぶ）worker's collective
ワーカビリティ（わーかびりてぃ）workability
ワーカーホリック（わーかーほりっく）workaholic
ワークシェアリング（わーくしぇありんぐ）work sharing
和式便器（わしきべんき）squat toilet
WAC法（わっくほう）Well Aging Community Law：WAC Law
ワッセルマン反応（わっせるまんはんのう）Wassermann reaction
輪止め（わどめ）ring lock
WAB失語症検査（わぶしつごしょうけんさ）western aphasia battery：WAB
ワムネット（わむねっと）WAM NET：welfare and medical service network system
割当計画（わりあてけいかく）⇒配分計画
割当雇用（わりあてこよう）employment quota
割当制（わりあてせい）quota system
割当制限（わりあてせいげん）quota restriction
割り当てられた仕事（わりあてられたしごと）assignment
割引料金（わりびきりょうきん）discount price
ワルファリン（わるふぁりん）warfarin
腕神経叢麻痺（わんしんけいそうまひ）brachial plexus palsy

第2部
介護保険・介護福祉等関連の重要用語
― 和英解説 ―

IQ 【aikyū】 intelligence quotient
知能指数のこと。
A term that refers to the "intelligence quotient."
ICIDH 【aishīaidīecchi】 International Classification of Impairments, Disabilities and Handicaps
国際障害分類のこと。
A term that refers to the "International Classification of Impairments, Disabilities and Handicaps."
ICF 【aishīefu】 International Classification of Functioning, Disability and Health
国際生活機能分類のこと。
A term that refers to the "International Classification of Functioning, Disability and Health."
ICD 【aishīdī】 International Classification of Diseases
国際疾病分類のこと。
A term that refers to the "International Classification of Diseases."
アクティビティ 【akutibiti】 activity
「活動」という意味。
A term that refers to recreation, action or movement.
アセスメント 【asesumento】 assessment
観察や情報収集から得られた利用者の状況を分析し、利用者のニーズとそれを阻害する要因を明確化し、評価することこと。
The act of evaluating the status of an individual, clarifying his or her needs, and identifying the underlying causes of each need based on observations and information obtained.
アテトーシス 【atetōshisu】 athetosis
錐体外路性の付随運動の１つで、ゆっくりとねじれるような規則性のない動きが連続して起こっている状態。
A symptom that is characterized by involuntary, convoluted writhing and continuous movements of the hands and feet typically caused by lesions in the corpus striatum of the brain.
アテトーゼ 【atetōze】 athetosis
→アテトーシス参照
A symptom that is characterized by involuntary, convoluted writhing and continuous movements of the hands and feet typically caused by lesions in the corpus striatum of the brain.
アドボカシー 【adobokashī】 advocacy
代弁機能や権利擁護により、利用者の社会資源に対して、柔軟な対応や改良を求めていくこと。
An individual or organization that advocates on behalf of others to influence organizations, governments or societies to improve social resources.
アルツハイマー型認知症 【arutsuhaimā gata ninchi shō】 senile dementia of the Alzheimer's type: SDAT
老年期にアルツハイマー病様の脳の変性によって発症する認知症の一種。
One type of dementia that occurs in old age, resulting from the formation of plaques or nerve tangles in the brain of Alzheimer's patients.
アルツハイマー病 【arutsuhaimā byō】 Alzheimer's disease
アロイス・アルツハイマー《Alzheimer, A.》が、1907年に脳内に特有の神経原線維変化と老人斑が見られる認知症を報告した病気。
A progressive and degenerative disease of the brain which causes the irreversible loss of neurons; reported by Alois Alzheimer in 1907.
安全管理 【anzen kanri】 safety control
介護をする上で、要介護者などに危害を及ぼさないように安全に管理すること。
The management of safety in order to reduce the risk of harm to patients while providing care.
罨法 【anpō】 foment
冷水・温水、薬剤などを身体の一部分に当てることにより、炎症や痛みをおさえること。
The application of warm or cold liquids, or medications to the body to relieve inflammation and pain.
安眠 【anmin】 quiet sleep
心地よい安らかな眠りのこと。
A term that refers to blissful and peaceful sleep.
安眠援助 【anmin enjo】 support for quiet sleep
心地よく安眠できるように援助すること。
Support for blissful and peaceful sleep.

安楽 【anraku】 comfort
身体的、精神的、社会的に不快がなく満足した安らかな状態のこと。
A peaceful state having no physical, mental or social discomfort.

安楽な体位 【anraku na taii】 comfortable position
身体的にも、精神的にも苦痛がないリラックスした姿勢のこと。
A relaxed position having no physical discomfort or mental pain.

意識障害 【ishiki shōgai】 disturbance of consciousness
精神活動が阻害されて、その機能の低下が認められる状態で、物事を正しく理解することなどができないこと。
A change in cognition or a perceptual disturbance that causes a lack of awareness about the environment.

維持期リハビリテーション 【ijiki rihabiritēshon】 late phase rehabilitation
急性期から回復期を経過した後に、機能や能力を維持するために継続的に行うリハビリテーションのこと。
A rehabilitation program designed to assist patients to attain and maintain their highest level of functioning during the late stage.

萎縮 【ishuku】 atrophy
一旦、正常の大きさに発育した器官、組織が負傷や病気などで縮小すること。
A reduction in the size of an organ or body part due to injury or disease.

移乗動作 【ijō dōsa】 transfer motion
利用者が対象物から別の対象物に乗り移る動作。
An individual moving from one object (e.g., chair/wheelchair) to another.

移送費 【isōhi】 transportation fee
医師の指示によって、緊急入院などが必要な患者を移送したとき、その交通費があとから医療保険で支給される、その費用のこと。
When a patient is transferred to a hospital for emergency hospitalization as per doctor's order, the travelling and life support costs are paid by the health insurance.

遺族基礎年金 【izoku kiso nenkin】 basic survivors' pension
国民年金保険、または老齢基礎年金の加入者が死亡したとき、その死亡者の遺族に支給される基礎的な年金。
A pension benefit that is paid to eligible dependents upon the death of a person who had enrolled in the National Pension Insurance or Basic Old-Age Pension.

移動 【idō】 locomotion
身体の重心が移ることにより位置が変化すること。
A change in position due to movement of the body.

移動介護 【idō kaigo】 transfer assistance
要介護者などが一人で移動が困難な場合に、介護者や福祉用具などを利用して移動すること。
A movement undertaken by an immobile or partially immobile individual, with the help of care workers or welfare aids.

移動関連福祉用具 【idō kanren fukushi yōgu】 mobility aid
高齢者や障害者などで移動が困難な場合に、その能力低下の度合を軽減するために用いる福祉用具。
A device specifically designed to aid in the movement of elderly or impaired people.

移動トイレ 【idō toire】 commode
移動可能な携帯用の便器のこと。
A chair-like movable and portable toilet with a container below the toilet.

移動浴槽 【idō yokusō】 portable bathtub
体力の低下や寝たきりなどで、浴槽までの移動が困難な要介護者などが入浴するための可動できる浴槽。
A bathtub that can be easily transported and carried for bathing services for immobile or bedridden individuals requiring care.

衣服 【ifuku】 clothes
主として身体躯幹部を被覆するもの。
Mainly, materials used to cover the body.

衣服着脱 【ifuku chakudatsu】 changing clothes
衣服を着たり脱いだりすること。
Replacing soiled clothes for clean ones.

衣料障害 【iryō shōgai】 clothing irritation
衣服によって身体に障害を起こすこと。

Physical imperfections caused by clothing.

医療ソーシャルワーカー 【iryō sōsharu wākā】 medical social worker
病院や診療所などで、患者や家族の抱える生活上の問題などの相談援助を行う保健医療分野のソーシャルワーカー。
A person from the health care field who usually works in a hospital or clinic and delivers psychosocial, emotional and counseling support to individuals and/or their families with multiple problems in their daily life.

医療保険制度 【iryō hoken seido】 health insurance system
疾病、負傷、死亡または分娩などの医療に対して、保険者が保険給付を行う制度。
A system in which the insurer provides insurance benefits to beneficiaries for medical treatment of diseases, injuries, death or childbirth and so forth.

インスリン 【insurin】 insulin
ランゲルハンス島β細胞から分泌される血糖を低下させるホルモン。
A natural hormone secreted by the islets of Langerhans in the pancreas that reduces the levels of blood sugar.

インテーク 【intēku】 intake
ケースワークの過程において、最初の面接段階のこと。
An initial casework screening interview that helps to gather basic information and evaluate the needs of the interviewee.

インフォーマル 【infōmaru】 informal
「非公式」「形にとらわれない」「普段着の」などの意味。
A term that refers to something not officially recognized; not formal and/or casual.

陰部清拭 【inbu seishiki】 genital hygiene
陰部を拭いて清潔にすること。
The washing practices involved in maintaining a healthy environment in the genital region.

陰部洗浄 【inbu senjō】 perineal care
陰部を洗い流して清潔にすること。
Washing and cleaning of the genital and rectal areas.

インペアメント 【inpeamento】 impairment
→機能障害参照
A reduction or worsening of a physical or mental ability due to aging, disease and/or injury.

うつ病 【utsu byō】 depression
主に気分障害を伴う精神病で、心が落ち込む抑うつ状態が長く続き、さまざまな心身症状が現れてくる精神障害。
A psychosomatic symptom, mainly a mood disorder resulting in prolonged extreme sadness, despair and anxiousness, which also causes some physical symptoms.

運営適正化委員会 【unei tekiseika iin kai】 Complaints Resolution Committee
福祉サービスの利用で苦情が発生した場合、それを解決する機関。
An organization that resolves any reported complaints regarding welfare services.

運動器の機能向上 【undōki no kinō kōjō】 improvement of body functions
介護保険制度での予防給付による選択的サービスの1つで、介護予防のために運動訓練などを行うこと。
One of the selective services provided by the long-term care insurance system whereby a beneficiary conducts motion exercise for care prevention.

運動失調 【undō shicchō】 ataxia
筋肉の協調が欠けているため、運動機能が混乱してバランスを崩すこと。
A neurological sign or symptom that results in loss of coordination of the muscle movements.

運動障害 【undō shōgai】 motor impairment
運動器に関する身体機能の障害により引き起こされ、自分の思い通りに身体を動かすことが困難な状態。
A loss or limitation of function in voluntary movement or mobility resulting from dysfunction within the motor system.

運動療法 【undō ryōhō】 therapeutic exercise
運動障害や運動不足などに対して、体操・運動を行う治療の方法。
A method of performing therapeutic exercise for motility disorders and lack of exercise.

エアーパッド 【eā paddo】 air sleeping pad
体位変換などに使用するもので、ポンプで空気を送り込むことで寝返りをさせることができるもの。

An inflatable pad that is used for changing position by inflating air with a pump.
エアーマット 【eā matto】 air mattress
褥瘡になりやすい圧迫部位への圧力を減圧するために使用される空気マット。
An inflatable mattress that is used to reduce and relieve pressure on tissues to prevent ulcers from forming.
エイジズム 【eijizumu】 ageism
意識のうちに潜む高齢に対する差別意識。
Stereotyping and discrimination on the basis of age, especially prejudice against the elderly.
エイズ 【eizu】 AIDS
→後天性免疫不全症候群参照
→ see【kōtensei meneki fuzen shōkōgun】
栄養 【eiyō】 nutrition
生物における生命の営みのうち、体外から取り入れたたんぱく質や脂質、炭水化物、ミネラル、ビタミンなどのこと。
Intake of materials by an organism required for survival, such as proteins, fats, carbohydrates, vitamins and minerals.
栄養改善 【eiyō kaizen】 nutrition improvement
介護保険制度での予防給付による選択サービスの1つで、低栄養の予防・改善のための栄養教育。
One of the selective services provided by the long-term care insurance system that helps educate and improve the nutritional uptake of the beneficiaries.
栄養管理 【eiyō kanri】 nutritional management
食生活にかかわる個人または集団の栄養状態の管理の総称。
A generic term for assisting an individual or a group of individuals with a balanced dietary intake.
栄養士 【eiyō shi】 dietitian
栄養士法第1条に規定された専門職で、「都道府県知事の免許を受けて、栄養士の名称を用いて栄養の指導に従事することを業とする者」のこと。
According to the Dietitian Law (Article 1), a dietitian is "a person, designated by the prefecture governor, who engages in nutritional guidance using the name of dietitian."
栄養所要量 【eiyō shoyōryō】 recommended dietary allowance: RDA
集団の大部分（約98%）にとって十分となる栄養素量。
The daily dietary intake levels of essential nutrients considered necessary to meet the requirements of most healthy people (98%).
栄養素 【eiyōso】 nutrient
食物から摂取され、生体が生命を維持し、成長および発育するために必要な物質。
An essential substance taken in from foods to help the body grow, repair and sustain itself.
腋窩温 【ekikaon】 axillary temperature
わきの下である腋窩における体温のこと。
A method of measuring body temperature by holding the thermometer under the armpit.
壊死 【eshi】 necrosis
身体の細胞や組織の死。
The death of body cells and tissues.
ADL 【ēdīeru】 activities of daily living
→日常生活活動参照
→ see【nichijō seikatsu katsudō】
NPO 【enupīō】 non-profit organization
特定非営利活動法人のこと。
An organization which uses surplus revenues for self-preservation rather than distributing them as profit.
MRSA 【emuāruesuē】 methicillin-resistant staphylococcus aureus
抗生物質のメチシリンに耐性ができた黄色ブドウ球菌のこと。
A type of staph bacteria called Staphylococcus aureus that is resistant to the antibiotic methicillin and causes several infections that are difficult to treat.
MMSE 【emuemuesuī】 Mini Mental State Examination
1975年にフォルスタインら《Folstein, M. F. et al.》が開発した、記憶能力や構成能力などによって認知症の程度

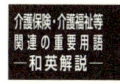

を簡易に評価する方法。
A brief test, created by Folstein, S. E., et al. in 1975, widely used to screen for dementia and to assess cognitive/mental status including memory and orientation.

MMT 【emuemutī】 Manual Muscle Testing
ロバート・ロベット《Lovett. R.》が開発した抗重力の筋力検査法（徒手筋力テスト）。
A method of examining muscle power by using an electronic device developed by Robert Lovett.

嚥下 【enge】 swallowing
飲食物を口腔で食塊にし、その食塊ならびに口咽腔の分泌物を咽頭と食道を通じて胃まで送る過程。
A process of sending alimentary bolus and oropharyngeal cavity juice through the pharynges/throat.

嚥下困難 【enge konnan】 swallowing difficulty
嚥下の障害のため、口腔中の飲食物が飲み下せない状態。
A state where an individual is unable to swallow food and drink due to a disorder.

嚥下性肺炎 【enge sei haien】 aspiration pneumonia
異物、通常は食物片、胃内容物または吐物の気管支への流入に従う気管支肺炎。
Bronchopneumonia caused by inhaling a foreign substance into the bronchial tree, such as vomit or a piece of food.

嚥下補助剤 【enge hojozai】 thickening agent
誤嚥防止のために、のどごしを良くしたり、食物を塊にまとめやすくしたりするために加えられる増粘剤。
A substance that is added to liquid and food to increase the viscosity and improve the bolus formation during the digestive process.

エンゲル係数 【engeru keisū】 Engel's coefficient
家計支出に占める食料費の割合。
The proportion of income spent on food in family expenditure.

円座 【enza】 circle mat
丸くなったドーナツ型の敷物。
A round donut-shaped mat.

エンパワメント 【enpawamento】 empowerment
本来持っている能力を十分に発揮できない状態にある個人・グループに対して、自身の強さを目覚し、自己決定能力を高められるように支援し、自らが抱える問題を主体的に解決しようとする力を持てるように援助する過程。
A process or set of processes that help to increase the political, social, economic, and/or spiritual strength of people who don't have confidence in their own abilities, so they can increase their capability to make decisions to solve their own problems.

応益負担 【ōeki futan】 benefit-received principle
サービス利用者の所得状況を考慮せず、一律にサービスの利用状況に応じた費用負担を決める方式のこと。
The idea that the cost burden should be proportional to the amount of benefit or number of services that the individual receives, irrespective of income or wealth level.

嘔気 【ōki】 nausea
嘔吐に先立ち起こる咽頭から胃部にかけての漠然とした不快感（吐き気）のこと。
A vague feeling of uneasiness or discomfort of the throat or upper stomach with an involuntary urge to vomit.

応急手当 【ōkyū teate】 emergency first aid
応急処置をするまでにしておく手当のこと。
The initial care or treatment provided to a sick or injured person until definitive medical treatment can be applied.

嘔吐 【ōto】 vomiting
胃の内容物が逆流して食道、口腔をへて外へ排出される現象。
The expulsion of the contents of one's stomach through the throat and mouth.

応能負担 【ōnō futan】 ability-to-pay principle
サービス利用者の所得状況を把握し、その所得状況に応じ支払い状況を判断し、必要負担額を決める方式のこと。
A method to decide the necessary amount of money that should be paid according to an individual's level of income or wealth.

起き上がり 【okiagari】 getting up
寝ている状態（臥位）から座位になるまでの動作。

A movement that occurs when one arises from a sleeping position (supine position) to a sitting position.

おむつ　【omutsu】　diaper
排泄物を吸収して陰部の汚染を防ぎ、清潔に保つためのもの。
An absorbent garment used to absorb bodily waste, avoiding infection of the genitals and maintaining cleanliness.

おむつカバー　【omutsu kabā】　diaper cover
おむつから排泄物が漏れて汚染することを防ぐもの。
A cloth cover used to prevent leaks of bodily waste from a diaper.

おむつ交換　【omutsu kōkan】　diaper change
排泄物を吸収して陰部の汚染を防ぎ、清潔に保つためにおむつをとりかえること。
An act of changing diapers in order to remove the absorbed bodily waste avoiding infection of the genitals and maintaining cleanliness.

おむつ外し　【omutsu hazushi】　diaper removal
おむつを当てている状態から、おむつを使用せず、排泄できる状態に移行すること、またはそのための援助のこと。
A term used for providing assistance with toileting or implementing a scheduled toileting program to help incontinent people become continent so they no longer need to wear diapers.

臥位　【ga i】　lying position
横たわって寝ている姿勢のこと。
A body position in which the body is in a flat or horizontal position.

介護　【kaigo】　care
心身に不自由が生じ身の回りのことが自分自身でできなくなった時に、その人の世話をすること。
A variety of services provided to aid people when they are unable to care for themselves due to physical and/or mental impairments.

介護過程　【kaigo katei】　care process
利用者のニーズを中心にした介護を行うために必要とされる一連の課題達成プロセスのこと。
A process of accomplishing a suit of assignments which are necessary to provide nursing care with a focus on an individual's needs.

介護技術　【kaigo gijutsu】　care skills
介護に関する専門的知識を基にして、実践する介護行為のこと。
The special techniques related to nursing care, especially for long-term care patients.

介護休業　【kaigo kyūgyō】　family care leave
介護の必要な家族がいる労働者が、その介護のために休業できる制度。
A system that permits an employee to be absent from his or her job to take care of a family member who requires care.

介護給付　【kaigo kyūfu】　long-term care insurance benefit
介護保険制度において、要介護認定の結果、被保険者が要介護（1～5）と認定された要介護者に対する給付。
The benefits provided to individuals who are classified into "care-required (level 1 to 5)" based on the results of an on-site assessment of each individual's physical and mental status under the long-term care insurance system.

介護計画　【kaigo keikaku】　care plan
要支援者・要介護者に対して介護サービスを適切に提供するために記した具体的な計画書。
A set of actions the nursing staff will implement to aid an individual to meet his or her medical and non-medical needs.

介護サービス計画　【kaigo sābisu keikaku】　care services plan
介護計画、ケアプランのこと。
A term that refers to care plans.

介護支援専門員　【kaigo shien senmon in】　care manager
要介護者などの介護ニーズを満たし、介護サービスの提供と連絡・調整する専門職。
A professional who is responsible for the assessment, development, coordination and implementation of care plans for elderly and disabled persons.

介護指導　【kaigo shidō】　care guidance
高齢者や障害者を介護している家族などに、介護に関する知識や技術を直接指導したり、助言したりすること。
An act of providing direct guidance and suggestions about long-term care to families who take care of the

elderly and disabled.

介護者 【kaigo sha】 caregiver
身体上または精神上の疾患や障害がある者に対して介護を行う看護師や介護士などのこと。
A person such as a nurse or care worker, responsible for the supervision, prevention and treatment of physical or psychological illness and disability.

介護職員 【kaigo shokuin】 direct care staff
介護を仕事としている職員のこと。
Nursing staff responsible for providing direct care for the sick and disabled.

介護ニーズ 【kaigo nīzu】 long-term care needs
身体上または精神上の障害により日常生活を営むことができない場合、その充足を求める身体的・精神的・社会的な要求、欲求、必要という意味。
The physical, mental and social needs, wants and demands of people with difficulties in their daily life due to physical and psychological disorders.

介護認定審査会 【kaigo nintei shinsa kai】 Long-Term Care Certification Committee
被保険者が介護保険の給付を受けるために、介護サービスが必要か必要でないのか、必要であるならどの程度必要なのか、要介護状態・要支援状態の審査判定の業務を行う市町村に設置された機関。
A group of health care experts officially delegated to review the applications to determine whether or not the applicant qualifies for long-term care insurance benefits, and if so, how much and what kind of benefits are to be provided. They take into account the result of physical, psychological and social assessments and a report from the applicant's doctor.

介護福祉 【kaigo fukushi】 care and welfare
社会福祉分野の専門的な教育を受けた者が、加齢や心身障害などにより社会生活上に困難を持つ人や援助を必要とする人に対して、直接的な介護や生活援助を中軸として、身体的側面・精神心理的側面・社会的側面から援助すること。
An act of providing direct care and assistance by a person with knowledge and skills in providing care to people who have difficulties in their social life or require care, by looking into their physical, mental, psychological and social aspects of their needs.

介護福祉士 【kaigo fukushi shi】 certified care worker: CCW
身体や精神に障害がある人たちの介護を業務とする専門の国家資格を持った職種。
An individual who has acquired a national qualification for caring and assisting persons with a physical and/or mental disability.

介護福祉士国家試験 【kaigo fukushi shi kokka shiken】 National Certification Examination for Care Workers
介護福祉士として必要な知識および技能に関する国家試験。
A national objective test provided to assess and evaluate the knowledge and skills of the applicant as a certified care worker.

介護福祉士登録 【kaigo fukushi shi tōroku】 Certified Care Worker Registry
介護福祉士となるために、国家試験に合格してから登録すること。
The registration program that requires all certified care workers to be registered after passing the National Certification Examination for Care Workers, to perform care worker tasks. It ensures that they meet the qualifications for a certified care worker.

介護負担 【kaigo futan】 burden of care
寝たきりや認知症などの要介護者などを介護している介護者やその家族の身体的、精神的、経済的な負担。
The physical, mental and financial burden on the caregivers providing care for the bedridden and/or demented person.

介護報酬 【kaigo hōshū】 long-term care insurance payment
介護サービス事業者が介護サービスを提供した場合、その対価として介護保険から9割、利用者からは残りの1割が自己負担として事業者に支払われる報酬のこと。
The long-term care insurance system pays the service providers 90% of the charges and the individual pays the remaining 10% co-insurance.

介護保険 【kaigo hoken】 long-term care insurance
認知症や寝たきりなどで要介護や要支援状態になったときに、必要な介護サービスを提供し、その費用を保障するための保険。
A national insurance that covers certain health care costs and expenses, and provides services for those

individuals who may require long-term care due to dementia or being bedridden.

介護保険事業計画 【kaigo hoken jigyō keikaku】 long-term care insurance plan
介護保険法により、市区町村と都道府県は3年ごとに、5年間を一期として、見直して策定する事業計画。
As per Long-Term Care Insurance Law, it is the 5-year action plan for long-term care insurance that must be reviewed every three years by both municipal and prefectural governments in Japan.

介護保険審査会 【kaigo hoken shinsa kai】 Review Committee on Long-Term Care Insurance
保険者からの保険給付に関する決定、また保険料その他の徴収に関する決定への不服に対する審査請求を審理・裁決する、各都道府県に設置される機関。
A committee formed in each prefecture whose purpose is to monitor the use, delivery and cost-effectiveness of long-term care services provided to long-term care insurance beneficiaries and to review the appeal of the decision of the committee.

介護保険制度 【kaigo hoken seido】 long-term care insurance system
地方自治体が介護を必要とする40歳以上の中高齢者などに介護サービスを提供する社会保険制度。
A social insurance program that provides health care services to persons aged 40 years and above if they qualify for the benefits.

介護保険認定調査 【kaigo hoken nintei chōsa】 long-term care insurance eligibility assessment
要介護認定の申請または更新のために、30日以内に行う調査。
An assessment of the functional and cognitive status of an applicant performed within 30 days of applying for long-term care insurance benefits.

介護保険法 【kaigo hoken hō】 Long-Term Care Insurance Law
要支援・要介護状態となった高齢者などに必要な介護サービスを提供することなどを定めた法律。
A law that established the provision of long-term care services for the elderly who are in need of assistance or care.

介護目標 【kaigo mokuhyō】 care goal
介護計画を方向づける目標のこと。
A goal that will give direction for the care plan.

介護用具 【kaigo yōgu】 care equipment
介護に関連する福祉用具のこと。
A device for nursing care.

介護予防 【kaigo yobō】 prevention of long-term care
要支援状態になる可能性のある者、あるいは要支援の状態にある者が、要介護状態にならないように行う介護サービス。
A system of health care which provides services designed to prevent individuals from being "care-" or "assistance-" required under long-term care insurance.

介護予防事業 【kaigo yobō jigyō】 preventive long-term care plan
介護予防するために市町村で実施する介護保険制度による地域支援事業の中の1つの事業。
One of the community support plans developed and implemented by municipal governments that is involved in setting up preventative measures to ensure that their residents do not become weak and frail.

介護療養型医療施設 【kaigo ryōyōgata iryō shisetsu】 long-term health care facility
医療と介護の必要性が高い要介護者向けの医療型の介護保険施設。
A type of long-term care insurance-covered health care facility designed for people who require regular medical attention and nursing supervision/care.

介護老人福祉施設 【kaigo rōjin fukushi shisetsu】 geriatric welfare facility
特別養護老人ホームが介護保険制度で指定されて介護保険施設として機能した時の名称。
An inclusive term for a certified long-term care insurance facility that provides nursing and welfare services for the elderly.

介護老人保健施設 【kaigo rōjin hoken shisetsu】 geriatric health care facility
介護保険法に基づく施設サービスの1つ。
A type of long-term care insurance-covered health care facility designed for elderly people who require regular medical attention and rehabilitation.

介護労働者 【kaigo rōdō sha】 care worker
介護サービスにたずさわる労働者。
A worker involved in the delivery of direct care services.

介助　【kaijo】　assistance
生活の基本場面において高齢者や障害者が、ある行為を実際に行う時に、生活主体の必要に応じて行われる他者（介護職や家族など）による補完・代替的な行為。
The supplemental or alternative help supplied by people such as care workers and family members to people such as the elderly and disabled, based on their daily needs.

疥癬　【kaisen】　scabies
疥癬虫という非常に微細なダニが皮膚に寄生することにより起こる皮膚病。
A skin disease caused by tiny invisible parasites that burrow under the host's skin causing severe itching.

回想法　【kaisō hō】　reminiscence therapy
過去の経験について振り返って考え、それを他の人に話したり、評価をしたりするという心理学的援助の1つの方法。
One of the psychotherapeutic techniques which reviews, discusses and assesses the experience or events of the individual's life.

階段　【kaidan】　stairs
異なる高さの所への段差のある昇降路。
A series of steps leading from one level to another.

階段昇降　【kaidan shōkō】　scaling stairs
階段を昇ったり降りたりすること。
Climbing up and down stairs.

回復期リハビリテーション　【kaifukuki rihabiritēshon】　recovery phase rehabilitation
発症直後の急性期を過ぎて、その後の約半年程度のリハビリテーション。
Rehabilitation provided approximately six months following the time of the onset of problems and acute phase of rehabilitation.

潰瘍　【kaiyō】　ulcer
皮膚や粘膜において限局的に組織がただれてえぐれた状態。
A partial break in the skin accompanied by the disintegration of tissues.

かかりつけ医　【kakaritsuke i】　primary doctor
身近に健康相談をしたり、病気に対する医療などを行ったりする医師。
A medical doctor who offers health consultation to a person with an undiagnosed health concern and orders medical care/treatments as necessary.

核家族　【kaku kazoku】　nuclear family
夫婦とその未婚の子どもからなる家族の基礎単位のこと。
A basic unit of family that consists of two married parents and their unmarried children.

家計　【kakei】　household budget
家庭生活の経済的運営のこと。
A term that refers to household economy.

家事　【kaji】　housekeeping
健康的で安全、なおかつ快適に家庭生活を営むための一連の労働。
A series of acts such as vacuuming rooms and disposing of rubbish to maintain a healthy, safe and comfortable environment for living.

家政　【kasei】　housekeeping
生活の変化に対応しながら、家庭経営、食生活、衣生活、住生活などを運営し、一家の暮らしをうまくまとめていくこと。
The maintenance and management of household affairs such as dealing with financial, nutritional and clothing matters, in response to changes in the environment.

家政婦　【kasei fu】　housekeeper
家事労働のうち、主に家政管理以外の生活手段（物）を整えたり、家族員（人）と関わったりする仕事を、その家の家族（主に主婦）に代わって行うことを職業とする女性のこと。
A woman who is employed to perform the domestic work and is responsible for the maintenance and cleaning of the household on behalf of her employers, mainly housewives.

家族　【kazoku】　family
夫婦関係や親子・兄弟などの血縁関係によって結ばれている親族関係から構成されている小集団。
A small group of individuals of common ancestry; composed of relatives who are related by marriage or

blood, such as a husband and wife, siblings, parents and their children.

家族会 【kazoku kai】 self-help group for families
障害者・要介護者、難病患者などを身内に持ち、共通した問題を抱えている家族同士が集まって組織した団体。
A group or organization formed by family members who have a common problem such as having a family member with a disability, the need for long-term care or an incurable and difficult-to-treat disease.

家族介護 【kazoku kaigo】 family-provided care
高齢者や障害者など介護を必要としている人に対して、家族がその介護を担うこと。
A family caring for the elderly or handicapped relative who is in need of care.

家族介護者 【kazoku kaigo sha】 family caregiver
介護を担っている家族のこと。
A family member who provides care for his or her family.

家族関係 【kazoku kankei】 family relationship
夫婦関係、親子関係、兄弟関係、嫁姑関係など家族集団内の構成員相互の人間関係の総称。
An inclusive term for mutual relationships of individuals in one family group, such as the relationship between a husband and wife, parents and their children, siblings, mother-in-laws and daughter-in-laws and so forth.

合併症 【gappei shō】 complication
1つの病気が起こることで、他の病気も一緒に起こること。
A medical condition in which one disease occurs with another at the same time.

寡婦 【kafu】 widow
一般的には夫に先立たれた女性のこと。
In general, it refers to a bereaved woman.

紙おむつ 【kami omutsu】 paper diaper
吸収性の高い紙を層状に重ねたおむつ。
A diaper layered with high absorbent paper.

過用症候群 【kayō shōkōgun】 overuse syndrome
過度の運動や訓練により生じる運動機能の低下や障害。
A group of body impairments that occur due to excessive exercise or training.

加齢 【karei】 aging
一般的に年齢を重ねること。
In general, the process of getting older.

癌 【gan】 cancer
悪性腫瘍のこと。
A group of diseases characterized by uncontrolled cell growth.

感音難聴 【kanon nanchō】 sensorineural deafness
内耳から聴神経を伝って大脳の聴覚中枢までの経路上に起こった難聴。
A type of hearing loss caused by lesions somewhere in the inner ear, central auditory nerve that runs from the ear to the brain, or the brain itself.

感覚機能 【kankaku kinō】 sensory function
人間の外部環境および内部環境に関する情報を受容器で受けて、中枢神経系に伝える機能のこと。
An ability to sense stimuli in both the internal and external environment and send the stimuli to the central nervous system.

換気 【kanki】 ventilation
生活空間を対象とした空気の入れ換えのこと。
The exchange of air or gasses in a room to provide high air quality.

環境整備 【kankyō seibi】 environmental maintenance
安全で快適な生活空間を整えること。
The arrangement of a safe and pleasant living space.

看護 【kango】 nursing
日本介護協会（1973年）の定義によると、看護とは、健康のあらゆるレベルにおいて、個人が健康的に正常な日常生活ができるように援助すること。
According to the Japan Care Services Association (1973), "nursing" is to provide assistance with all aspects of health to help a person be able to lead a healthy and normal daily life.

肝硬変 【kankō hen】 liver cirrhosis
肝臓の炎症が繰り返し起き、肝臓が硬くなって十分に働かなくなってしまう病気のこと。
A liver disease caused by repeated episodes of inflammation or hardening of the liver preventing proper function.

看護師 【kango shi】 nurse
保健師助産師看護師法によると、「厚生労働大臣の免許を受けて、傷病者若しくはじよく婦に対する療養上の世話、又は診療の補助を行うことを業とするものである」（第5条）と定義されている者。
According to the Public Health Nurse, Midwife and Nurse Law (Article 5) a nurse is "a person who has obtained a formal permission from the Minister of Health, Labour and Welfare in Japan, being a professional in providing nursing care and support for medical treatments."

関節 【kansetsu】 joint
結合する2つまたはそれ以上の骨の骨端間に一定の間隙が存在して完全に分離し、両骨が可動的に結合した組織。
An area that connects two or more bones, which is separated by short and tough fibers of cartilage for the purpose of body part motion.

関節可動域 【kansetsu kadō iki】 range of motion : ROM
関節を他動的あるいは自動的に運動させた場合の可動範囲のこと。
The degree of movement that a joint can move voluntarily or involuntarily.

関節リウマチ 【kansetsu riumachi】 rheumatoid arthritis : RA
多発性の関節炎を主症状とする原因不明の慢性全身性疾患。
A chronic, autoimmune and systemic inflammatory disorder that principally attacks synovial joints that can also affect other internal organs.

感染 【kansen】 infection
何らかの病原微生物が人体の組織や臓器に入り込み、そこで増殖を続ける状態。
A state whereby a host organism is infected by a pathogenic organism often resulting in a diseased state.

感染菌 【kansen kin】 bacterium
感染により病気を引き起こす病原菌のこと。
A single celled organism/pathogen that can cause sickness upon infection.

感染症 【kansen shō】 infectious disease
生体に感染を引き起こす病原菌が組織に侵入・定着して、その炎症により細胞障害や機能障害を起こした状態のこと。
A disease caused by infectious agents such as bacteria, viruses and so forth, causing tissue damage and impairing host function.

感染予防 【kansen yobō】 prevention of infection
病原体が体内に侵入・定着・増殖することを予防すること。
An act of preventing infectious agents from entering/settling/growing in the body.

浣腸 【kanchō】 enema
直腸や結腸へ液体を入れて、大腸内の便やガスを排除すること。
A method of eliminating stool and gas inside the colon by inserting liquids into the rectum and colon.

観念失行 【kannen shikkō】 ideational apraxia
認知機能は十分に保たれており、運動をする機能にも異常がないのに、物を正しく操作することができないこと。
A neurological disorder characterized by the inability to plan for a specific movement and perform learned complex tasks involving the use of objects in the proper order in the absence of motor and sensory impairment.

管理栄養士 【kanri eiyō shi】 registered dietician
栄養士法第1条2に規定される専門職のことで、厚生労働大臣より免許を受け、健康の保持促進のための栄養指導や施設における給食管理などを行う者のこと。
According to the Dietitian Law (Article 1), a registered dietitian is a person designated by the Minister of Health, Labour and Welfare, who designs meal plans, engages in nutrition guidance and supervises food preparation for individuals at a facility for promoting health.

緩和ケア 【kanwa kea】 palliative care
終末期を迎える患者に対して、医療上のいわゆる治療中心の医学的対応だけではなく、精神面でのサポートを主体とする接し方を取り入れたケア。
The specialized care for individuals that have a terminal illness ; mainly provides mental and emotional

support in addition to some medical treatments.
記憶障害　【kioku shōgai】　memory disorder
記憶の一連の過程のどこかに障害が起こること。
Disturbances that appear somewhere in encoding information and in the retention of acquired information or in the recall of information.
着替え　【kigae】　changing clothes
着ている衣服を脱ぎ、別の衣服を着ること。
An act of removing clothes one is wearing and putting on other clothes.
気管　【kikan】　trachea
呼吸運動によりとりこまれた空気を肺から出し入れする導管の一部。
The windpipe that connects the pharynx to the lungs.
危険防止　【kiken bōshi】　risk prevention
介護事故など、要介護者などに危害や損失が起こらないように防ぐ工夫をすること。
The ideas or methods to avoid and decrease the chance of an unfavorable injury or event occurring in nursing practices.
起座位　【kiza i】　sitting position
ベッド上でベッドアップなどにより上半身を起こした姿勢。
The posture of a person whose upper body is lifted off the bed.
義歯　【gishi】　denture
抜けたり、欠けたりした歯の代わりになる人工的な入れ歯のこと。
A partial or complete set of artificial teeth used for one or more missing teeth.
義肢装具士　【gishi sōgu shi】　prosthetist and orthotist: PO
1987年義肢装具士法によって国家資格化された専門職。
A health care professional who has skills and knowledge in making and fitting artificial parts of the human body and is nationally qualified by the Artificial Limb Fitters Law of 1987.
基礎代謝　【kiso taisha】　basal metabolism
身体的、精神的に安静な状態で生きていくために必要とされる最小のエネルギー消費量のこと。
The minimum amount of energy consumption required by a person in a physically and mentally resting state.
機能維持　【kinō iji】　functional maintenance
身体運動を行うための種々の機能を、現在のレベルで維持させること。
An act of attaining or maintaining the highest level of physical function.
機能訓練　【kinō kunren】　functional training
病気や加齢などで心身機能が低下した人に、健康の維持と増進を図り、日常生活の自立を助け、介護予防などを目的に訓練を行うこと。
A type of exercise provided to individuals with decreased physical ability due to illness or aging, and which involves maintaining and improving health and physical function to independently carry out activities performed in daily life and preventing them from requiring long-term care.
機能障害　【kinō shōgai】　impairment
世界保健機関（WHO）の国際障害分類（1980年）によれば、「心理的、生理的、解剖的な構造又は機能の何らかの喪失又は異常」のこと。
According to International Classification of Impairments, Disabilities and Handicaps (ICIDH) created by World Health Organization (WHO) in 1980, it refers to "any reduction or abnormality of psychological, physiological, or anatomical structure or function."
記銘力　【kimei ryoku】　memory retention
新たに知覚し、体験したことなどを記憶の中に取り入れ、とどめておく能力。
The ability to memorize and recall new information and experiences.
虐待　【gyakutai】　abuse
不当にあるいは不適切に対応することで、むごい待遇や残酷な取り扱いをすること。
A term used to describe improper or inappropriate acts/treatment toward a person.
ギャッチベッド　【gyacchi beddo】　gatch bed
背上げや膝上げなどの機能がついた特殊寝台と呼ばれるベッド。
A bed that has features such as lifting an individual's back and knees.

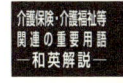

救急救命士 【kyūkyū kyūmei shi】 emergency medical technician: EMT
重度の意識状態にある傷病者を病院に搬送中、医師の指示の下、応急処置をすることができる名称独占の専門職。
A professional who is trained to provide emergency medical services in conjunction with a doctor while transporting a critically ill patient to a hospital.

仰臥位 【gyōga i】 supine position
上肢を体幹側に付けて、下肢は伸展して仰向けで寝ている姿勢。
A lying down position with the face up, upper limbs near the body and lower limbs folded.

共感 【kyōkan】 empathy
一般には、他人の感情などを自分も同じように感じたり理解したりすること。
In general, understanding of and sympathizing with others emotions similarly.

虚弱 【kyojaku】 frailty
体力がなく心身が弱いこと。
Weakening of the mind and body due to the loss of physical strength.

起立性低血圧 【kiritsu sei teiketsuatsu】 orthostatic hypotension
臥位から座位、立位へと急な体位の変換によって生じる血圧の低下。
A form of decreased blood pressure due to sudden changes in body positions such as the supine to the standing position.

記録 【kiroku】 records
サービスなどに関する実践の過程・結果・評価などの事実を書き記すこと。
Writing down the facts about the client such as his or her previous history, assessment results and other health care related information.

筋萎縮 【kin ishuku】 muscular atrophy
骨格筋が疾患や不動化などにより量的に減少すること。
The loss of skeletal muscle mass in a quantitative manner due to disease or limb immobilization.

緊急連絡先 【kinkyū renraku saki】 emergency contact information
急病や災害などの緊急時に連絡する相手先のこと。
A list of emergency phone numbers and other information of people who can be contacted in case of any emergency like sudden illness or accidents.

金銭管理 【kinsen kanri】 money management
実際に金銭を保管しておくことや、適正に金銭を管理すること。
Managing and budgeting a money source appropriately.

苦情解決 【kujō kaiketsu】 grievances and complaints resolution
サービス利用者などから申し出された不平や不満に対して、これを処理して解決すること。
A process or set of processes to solve complaints and dissatisfaction reported by an individual.

くも膜下出血 【kumomakuka shukketsu】 subarachnoid hemorrhage : SAH
くも膜下腔内に出血した血液が混入すること。
Bleeding into the subarachnoid space.

クリティカルパス 【kuritikaru pasu】 critical pathway : CP
必要な治療や検査、看護などの内容を、入院後の時間の経過とともに示した治療の予定表。
An algorithm that documents the medical and nursing procedures including treatments and diagnostic tests during a patient's hospitalization.

グループホーム 【gurūpu hōmu】 group home
日常生活で障害を持つ人を、小規模の家族的な集団生活で自立支援を行う地域密着型サービス。
A small community-based facility or supervised home-like residence for impaired people with similar needs who cannot live alone without proper supervision.

グループリビング 【gurūpu ribingu】 group living
おおむね60歳以上の比較的健康な高齢者が、親族以外の人とともに共同の場で生活をする居住形態。
A type of residential facility for relatively healthy people aged 60 and above in which residents live with people other than family members.

グループレクリエーション 【gurūpu rekuriēshon】 group recreation
複数の要介護者などとレクリエーションをグループで行うこと。
An act of performing some type of recreation in a group with multiple members.

グループワーク 【gurūpu wāku】 group work
意図的なグループ経験を通じて援助するソーシャルワークの援助技術の1つ。
One of the techniques in social work through which individuals work in groups assisted by a staff member, who guides their interaction in the program.

車いす 【kuruma isu】 wheelchair
移動に用いられる車輪つきのいす。
A chair having wheels used for the movement of an impaired individual.

車いすからベッド 【kuruma isu kara beddo】 transfer from wheelchair to bed
利用者が車いすからベッドへ移乗すること。
An individual moving from wheelchair to bed.

車いすの移動 【kuruma isu no idō】 moving around by wheelchair
車いすを用いて目的とする場所へ行くこと。
Traveling to a destination with a person using a wheelchair.

車いすの介助 【kuruma isu no kaijo】 wheelchair assistance
利用者が車いすで移動や移乗する際に手助けをすること。
Assistance provided to the individual while moving around by wheelchair or moving to the wheelchair.

クロックポジション 【kurokku pojishon】 clock position
物の配置などを時計の文字盤に見立てた位置。
Noting the position of an object or item using the positions shown on the clock face.

ケア 【kea】 care
一般的に、気遣うこと、その人が願っているように助けること。
In general, the term refers to helping individuals based on their wishes and needs.

ケアカンファレンス 【kea kanfarensu】 care conference
利用者の援助過程で、適切なケアを行うためにケアに携わる者が集まり、討議する会議のこと。
A meeting of health care professionals who are involved in the care of patients to discuss appropriate care for the patients.

ケアチーム 【kea chīmu】 care team
利用者の自立支援をするために多種多様なメンバーで構成するチームのこと。
A team formed by a variety of health care professionals to provide care to maximize and maintain the highest level of independence.

ケアハウス 【kea hausu】 care home
老人ホームの一種で、自由な環境で自立支援する共同住宅。
One type of residential care setting where a number of elderly people live and have access to various services for independent living.

ケアプラン 【kea puran】 care plan
支援を必要とする人に対するサービスの供給システムの計画。
A plan or sequence of actions undertaken by the caregivers to aid an individual to meet his or her medical and non-medical needs.

ケアマネジメント 【kea manejimento】 care management
利用者が抱える社会生活上の複数のニーズの解決や充足のために、適切な社会資源を結びつける一連の方法。
A multi-step process which coordinates necessary social services with resource providers on behalf of an individual to resolve and fulfill his or her multiple social needs.

ケアマネジャー 【kea manejā】 care manager
→介護支援専門員参照
A professional who is responsible for the assessment, development, coordination and implementation of care plans for elderly and disabled persons.

ケアワーク 【kea wāku】 care work
ケアに基づく対人援助サービスであり、その技術を意味している。
A term that refers to the techniques of providing personal support based on a sense of responsibility to provide care for other people.

経管栄養 【keikan eiyō】 tube feeding
消化管に開口部からチューブを挿入して流動食を与える栄養補給法。
A nutrient supply method that gives liquid nutrition to a person who cannot take food or drink through

swallowing by inserting a catheter in the opening of the digestive tract.
頸髄損傷　【keizui sonshō】　cervical spinal cord injury
脊髄の中で頸髄が外傷により障害され、完全あるいは不全の麻痺を生じる障害。
An injury to the cervical spinal cord that may result in partial or total paralysis.
傾聴　【keichō】　active listening
話の内容とそれに伴う情緒的な側面を受容的に聞くこと。
A communication skill that requires the listener to listen to the emotional undertone of what a person is saying and comprehend, interpret and evaluate what the listener hears.
契約　【keiyaku】　contract
相互に意思表示して、約束することを合意した取り決めのこと。
A written or verbal agreement made by one party to another.
劇薬　【gekiyaku】　drastic medicine
人または、動物の身体にこれが吸収された場合、たとえ微量でも危害を与えるか、与えるおそれのあるもの。
A drug that is specified as harmful or can cause harm to humans or animals if administered.
下血　【geketsu】　melena
肛門より排出される血液のこと。
The discharge of black, tarry, bloody stools containing decomposed blood.
ケースカンファレンス　【kēsu kanfarensu】　case conference
事例を検討するための会議や検討会のこと。
A meeting or investigation performed to analyze a case.
ケースワーク　【kēsu wāku】　casework
利用者と援助者との直接的ならびに、個別的な対人間関係を通した援助技術のこと。
The social work that involves directly and interpersonally working with individuals who need support.
血圧　【ketsuatsu】　blood pressure
血流によって血管壁に及ぼす内圧のこと。
The pressure exerted by the flow of blood on the walls of the arteries.
下痢　【geri】　diarrhea
便の水分量が増加し液状またはそれに近い便を一日数回〜数十回排泄する症状。
A condition in which an individual has frequent and liquid bowel movements.
幻覚　【genkaku】　hallucination
現実には存在しないものがあたかも存在するかのように知覚されるもの。
Perceiving something that does not exist.
健康　【kenkō】　health
WHOによると、「身体的、精神的ならびに社会的に完全に良好な状態であり、単に病気や虚弱がないことに留まるものではない」こと。
According to World Health Organization (WHO), it refers to "a state of complete physical, psychological and social well-being and not merely the absence of disease or infirmity."
健康観察　【kenkō kansatsu】　health observation
健康の状態を評価して把握すること。
Monitoring and evaluating the health status.
健康保険　【kenkō hoken】　health insurance
事業所に使用される者を被保険者とする強制医療保険。
A mandatory insurance that provides health insurance coverage to almost all workers.
言語障害　【gengo shōgai】　speech-language impediment
話す・聞いて理解する・書く・読むといった言語能力が障害されること。
A communication disorder that affects the ability to talk, understand, write and read.
言語聴覚士　【gengo chōkaku shi】　speech-language-hearing therapist
言語障害や聴覚障害のためにコミュニケーションをとることが難しくなった人に対するリハビリテーションを行う専門職。
A professional who provides speech therapy to people who have difficulties with communication caused by speech and hearing impairments.
見当識障害　【kentō shiki shōgai】　disorientation
見当識が障害され、自分のいる場所や現在の時間などがわからなくなること。

A state where orientation is damaged and the person does not recognize time, location and persons.

権利擁護　【kenri yōgo】　human rights advocacy
利用者への権利侵害からの保護・救済。
The protection and advocacy of the rights of persons.

公益事業　【kōeki jigyō】　public utility
公益を目的として行う事業。
An organization that supplies necessities to the public.

公益法人　【kōeki hōjin】　public benefit corporation
公益事業をする人の集まりや財産を中心とした集まりに与えられる法的な人格。
A corporation involved in providing services to benefit the public.

構音障害　【kōon shiyōgai】　articulation disorder
発語器官の障害により正しく明瞭に声を出して発音できないこと。
An inability to pronounce particular sounds correctly due to speech impairments.

後期高齢者　【kōki kōrei sha】　elderly aged 75 and above
老年人口を区分した時の75歳以上の高齢者のこと。
Persons aged 75 and above.

抗菌・防臭素材　【kōkin - bōshū sozai】　antibacterial and deodorization material
繊維製品に抗菌剤を付加し、細菌の増加を抑制し悪臭の発生を防ぐ抗菌防臭加工された素材。
A fabric or material that contains antibacterial and anti-odor chemicals that kill and / or slow down the growth of bacteria and decreases odor production.

口腔機能の向上　【kōkū kinō no kōjō】　improvement of oral functions
介護保険制度での予防給付による選択サービスの1つで、口腔の機能を向上させる訓練。
One of the selective services provided by the long-term care insurance system that offers an exercise program for improving the function of the mouth.

口腔ケア　【kōkū kea】　oral health care
口腔内を清潔にすることによって、口腔内の状態を改善すること。
Any measures taken to improve or maintain one's oral cavity by brushing, flossing and cleaning.

合計特殊出生率　【gōkei tokushu shusshō ritsu】　total fertility rate: TFR
1人の女性が生涯に産む平均の子どもの数。
The average number of children born to one woman in her lifetime.

高血圧　【kō ketsuatsu】　hypertension
動脈血圧が正常より高い状態にあること。
High blood pressure; a condition in which the arterial blood pressure is higher than normal.

拘縮　【kōshuku】　contracture
関節を動かさないことにより、関節自体が固くなり動きが悪くなった状態のこと。
Stiffness of the joints as a result of lack of joint movements that limits full extension.

拘縮予防　【kōshuku yobō】　contracture prevention
関節の可動域の低下を招かないように予防すること。
Preventing the deterioration of joint mobility.

公証人　【kōshōnin】　notary public
民事に関する公正証書を作成する者。
A public officer who creates notarized civil affairs related documents.

公正証書　【kōsei shōsho】　notarial deed
公正人が作成する、遺言や金銭の貸借に関する証書。
A legal document such as a living will or promissory notes created by the notary public.

抗生物質　【kōsei busshitsu】　antibiotic
微生物によって作られ、微生物、その他の生活細胞の発育などの機能を阻止する物質。
A compound or substance derived from special microorganisms that fight bacterial infections by killing or slowing down their growth, for example, penicillin or streptomycin.

拘束　【kōsoku】　restraint
抑制すること。
The act of restraining: constricted or controlled.

後天性免疫不全症候群 【kōten sei meneki fuzen shōkōgun】 acquired immune deficiency syndrome : AIDS
自己組織以外を排除する免疫機能が不全を起こす症状を引き起こすウイルスに感染すると起こる症候群の略称。
A term used for an infectious disease caused by the human immunodeficiency virus (HIV) that progressively reduces the effectiveness of the immune system.

高齢化 【kōrei ka】 population aging
総人口に占める高齢者の割合が高くなること。
The increase in the proportion of elderly people in the total population.

高齢期障害 【kōrei ki shōgai】 old-age disorder
加齢ならびに老化に伴って高齢期に起こる障害。
A health complication that occurs in older people due to aging-related changes in their functioning.

高齢者 【kōrei sha】 elderly
一般には65歳以上の人のこと。
In general, it refers to persons aged 65 and above.

高齢社会 【kōrei shakai】 aged society
老年人口比率（総人口の中で65歳以上の高齢者を占める割合）が14%を超えた社会。
A society with more than 14% of the population aged 65 and above.

高齢者虐待 【kōrei sha gyakutai】 elder abuse
高齢者に対する身体的、心理的、経済的、性的、放棄による虐待。
The physical, emotional, financial or sexual mistreatment or neglect of older people.

高齢者虐待防止法 【kōrei sha gyakutai bōshi hō】 Elder Abuse Prevention Act
高齢者の虐待が深刻な場合に、高齢者の保護の措置、養護者の負担の軽減を図ることなどを目的として定めた法律（2005年成立）。
A law established in 2005 calling for increased national responsibility in protecting the elderly from abuse and neglect, and also relieving caregiver stress.

高齢者世帯 【kōrei sha setai】 elderly household
65歳以上の者のみで構成する世帯。
A household consisting entirely of persons above the age of 65.

声かけ 【koe kake】 verbal encouragement
→言葉かけ参照
An act of providing verbal encouragement or cueing.

誤嚥 【goen】 pulmonary aspiration
食物や水、睡液などが誤って食道でなく気道に入ってしまうこと。
An act in which food, liquid or saliva accidentally enters into the airways instead of the esophagus.

誤嚥性肺炎 【goen sei haien】 aspiration pneumonia
→嚥下性肺炎参照
Bronchopneumonia caused by inhaling a foreign substance into the bronchial tree, such as vomit or a piece of food.

呼吸 【kokyū】 respiration
外界から酸素を取り入れ、体内で排出された二酸化炭素を排泄する働きのこと。
A natural act of inhaling and exhaling that exchanges oxygen and carbon dioxide.

呼吸機能障害 【kokyū kinō shōgai】 respiratory functional disorder
呼吸器の病気による酸素と二酸化炭素の交換をする機能の障害。
A disability of function in exchanging oxygen and carbon dioxide caused by a respiratory disease.

国際疾病分類 【kokusai shippei bunrui】 International Classification of Diseases: ICD
世界保健機関（WHO）が定めた疾病や死因に関する国際的統計の分類基準。
The international classification codes concerning disease or cause of death issued by the World Health Organization (WHO).

国際障害分類 【kokusai shōgai bunrui】 International Classification of Impairments, Disabilities and Handicaps: ICIDH
1980年に世界保健機関（WHO）から出された障害の概念およびそれに基づく分類。
A common framework for classifying the consequences of disease issued by World Health Organization (WHO) in 1980.

国際生活機能分類 【kokusai seikatsu kinō bunrui】 International Classification of Functioning, Disability and Health: ICF
世界保健機関 (WHO) が2001年に提唱した改訂版の国際障害分類。
The revised version of International Classification of Impairments, Disabilities and Handicaps (ICIDH) approved by World Health Organization (WHO) in 2001.

国際標準化機構 【kokusai hyōjun ka kikō】 International Organization for Standardization: ISO
1947年に成立された各国の標準化機関から、160か国以上参加しており電気分野以外の工業分野の国際標準規格を策定する連合体。
An international organization funded in 1947 and made up of approximately 160 countries, that determines the standards that should be applied for both technical and non-technical fields, except electric/electronic engineering.

骨折 【kossetsu】 fracture
骨が外力によって変形や破壊が生じること。
A complete or incomplete break in a bone due to an excessive external force.

骨粗鬆症 【kotsu soshōshō】 osteoporosis
全身にわたる骨量の減少などにより骨の脆弱性が増し、痛みや骨折を起こしやすくなった状態。
A condition of reduced bone mass in which bones become prone to fracture due to a reduction in bone density.

言葉かけ 【kotoba kake】 verbal encouragement
依頼関係を形成するための大切なコミュニケーションの1つ。
One of the important types of communication required to build rapport.

個別介護 【kobetsu kaigo】 individualized care
個人の尊重と尊厳を重視し、サービス利用者の個性に注目した介護を行うこと。
Care which is planned to meet the needs of a patient with respect and dignity.

コミュニケーション 【komyunikēshon】 communication
知覚、感情、思考などを表出し、身振り、記号、言語などを媒体としてその内容を伝達する行為。
An act of transmitting information such as thoughts, messages and feelings as by gestures, signals and language.

コミュニケーションエイド 【komyunikēshon eido】 communication aid
発声・発語が困難な場合に、意思伝達の補助・代替手段として用いる機器や用具。
An instrument or tool used as an aid or alternative medium for communication when verbalization is difficult.

コレステロール 【koresuterōru】 cholesterol
細胞膜、胆汁酸、各種ホルモンなどの原材料となる脂質の一種。
A lipid that is used to produce essential substances such as cell membrane, bile acids and hormones.

献立 【kondate】 menu
食品の正しい選択や調理法、料理の種類などを決める食事計画のこと。
The process of menu planning that includes applying the knowledge of food, nutrients, cooking methods and recipes.

座位 【zai】 sitting position
上半身は直立位、上肢は体幹に沿って垂らし、臀部と大腿後面を支持面として体重を支える姿勢。
A position where the upper half of the body is in the standing position with the upper limbs hanging parallel and the body weight is put on the rear of the hips and thighs, which are used as a supporting surface.

再アセスメント 【sai asesumento】 reassessment
計画通りにサービスの提供がされているなどを確認して、新たな課題に対して計画を立てるための再評価。
Re-evaluation for confirming whether the services are provided as previously planned and creating a care plan for new issues.

在宅介護 【zaitaku kaigo】 home care
家庭やその人の住み慣れた場で、生活の質を維持しつつ暮らしを継続できるよう、保健・医療・福祉からの支援を提供するサービス。
A form of health and supportive care provided in the client's home by health care professionals from medical and welfare perspectives so that the client could continue to live at home and maintain the same

quality of life.

在宅看護　【zaitaku kango】　home health
看護師などが在宅で療養する患者に対するサービス。
A form of health care services provided by health care professionals, such as nurses, in the patient's home.

在宅ケア　【zaitaku kea】　home care
→在宅介護参照
→ see【zaitaku kaigo】

作業療法　【sagyō ryōhō】　occupational therapy
身体または精神に障害のある者に対して、主体的な生活の獲得を図るために行うリハビリテーションの一種。
A type of rehabilitation therapy that improves health and independence by enabling individuals with physical and mental disability to perform purposeful activities.

作業療法士　【sagyō ryōhō shi】　occupational therapist
理学療法士及び作業療法士法（1965年）によれば、「身体又は精神に障害のある者に対し、主としてその応用的動作能力又は社会適応能力の回復を図るため、手芸、工作、その他の作業を行わせること」を医師の指示により実施する専門職。
According to the Physical Therapists and Occupational Therapists Law (established in 1965), it refers to a health professional who provides therapy, primarily handcraft, under the direction of the doctor for individuals with physical and mental disabilities to promote the recovery of social skills and adaptive behavior skills.

サービス担当者会議　【sābisu tantō sha kaigi】　service staff meeting
ケアプラン作成や変更時に開催する会議。
A meeting of health care professionals held at the time of creating or changing care plans.

サポートシステム　【sapōto shisutemu】　support system
病気や障害、老齢となって生活が難しくなった時の支援の仕組み。
A network of persons that provides individuals with practical or emotional support after becoming sick, disabled or aged.

残存機能　【zanzon kinō】　residual function
心身に備わる全機能のうち、障害を受けた機能以外に残された機能。
The remaining capacity to function after a disease or illness has affected the individual.

散髪　【sanpatsu】　haircut
伸びた髪の毛を切って、整えること。
An act of cutting and setting the extended hair.

紫外線遮蔽素材　【shigaisen shahei sozai】　ultraviolet rays protection materials
紫外線を吸収または拡散する物質を付与して遮蔽率を向上させた素材。
A material that contains ultraviolet blockers or absorbers to block or absorb ultraviolet rays.

歯科衛生士　【shika eisei shi】　dental hygienist
歯科医師の指導の下に歯石の除去、虫歯予防のための薬物塗布、歯磨き指導などを行い、歯科診療の補助を行う国家資格の専門職。
A specialist in oral hygiene with a national qualification to provide dental services such as teeth cleaning, applying medication and educating patients on oral hygiene under the supervision of a dentist.

視覚障害　【shikaku shōgai】　visual impairment
長期的、または永続的に視覚機能が低下した状態。
The long term or permanent impairment of vision.

視覚障害者　【shikaku shōgai sha】　the visually impaired
視覚機能が先天的または後天的な原因により永続的に機能低下している人。
A person whose visual functioning is permanently deteriorating because of a hereditary disease or due to some acquired disease or injury.

弛緩　【shikan】　flaccid
筋緊張が低下した状態で、筋に発生する張力がゆるむ状態のこと。
A state where muscle tone is diminished and tension on muscle is loosened.

止血　【shiketsu】　hemostasis
出血を止めること。

The biological processes involved in forming a blood clot to stop bleeding.
思考障害　【shikō shōgai】　thought disorder
精神疾患により生じる思考障害のこと。
A pattern of disabled language or thought processing that can occur due to psychotic mental illness.
自己覚知　【jiko kakuchi】　self-awareness
援助者が自分の価値観や判断基準、感情、行動の傾向などについて自己理解すること。
An awareness of oneself including one's value, judgment standard, feelings and behaviors.
自己決定　【jiko kettei】　self-determination
個人が生活していく上で、自己責任をもって自己選択し決定すること。
The act of deciding what to do or think without external compulsion and to be responsible for that decision.
自己実現　【jiko jitsugen】　self-actualization
個人が自分の生活や人生において、自らが目標とする生き方を実現すること。
The act of developing or achieving one's full potential and life goals.
脂質異常症　【shishitsu ijō shō】　dyslipidemia
血液中のコレステロールや中性脂肪が異常値を示すこと。
An abnormal quantity of lipids within the blood.
自傷行為　【jishō kōi】　self-harm: SH
自己の肉体の一部を傷つける行為。
An act of injuring one's own body.
自助具　【jijogu】　self-help device
何らかの身体障害などを持っている人が日常生活を行えるように工夫して用いる道具の総称。
A collective term for the tools used by people with physical or mental disorders to conduct daily life activities.
死生観　【shiseikan】　view of life and death
生と死に対する考え方。
An approach toward life and death.
施設介護　【shisetsu kaigo】　institutional care
介護保険法にもとづき、要介護状態の高齢者などを対象とした施設サービス。
A facility-based service geared towards the elderly who are in need of continuous care under long-term care insurance.
自尊心　【jisonshin】　self-esteem
自分自身に誇りを持ち、また自分の尊厳を意識することによって、自分の品位を保とうとする心理または態度。
Philosophy or attitude of retaining one's dignity and self awareness.
肢体不自由　【shitai fu jiyū】　crippled
骨・関節系・神経系・筋系、血管系、運動制御に関係する中枢神経系などの運動器の機能障害によって生じる身体運動能力の低下による障害。
A functional damage to the bone, joint, nerve, muscle, blood vessel and/or central nerve system that regulates motor function, caused by injury or illness.
実技試験　【jitsugi shiken】　professional practice examination
筆記試験に合格した者に限り受験することができ、介護技術などに関する専門的技能を試す介護福祉士国家試験の2次試験。
A hands-on practical exam that can be taken after a written test and is designed to evaluate the knowledge, skills and abilities required to become a certified care worker.
失禁　【shikkin】　incontinence
排泄機能の調節ができずに自分の意思に関係なく尿または便を排泄すること。
An involuntary excretion of urine or passage of stool as a result of the inability to control bladder or bowel movements.
失語　【shitsugo】　aphasia
脳血管障害や頭部外傷などで大脳の言語に関わる部分が損傷されて生じる言語障害。
A partial or total loss of the ability to produce and comprehend language caused by an illness or injury to the related part of the brain.

シーツ交換 【shītsu kōkan】 changing bed sheets
利用者が臥床した状態で、快適に寝心地のよい寝床になるようにシーツを整える技術。
A technique of making an occupied bed to make an individual feel comfortable to sleep.

実支出 【jisshishutsu】 actual expenditure
消費支出と非消費支出を合計した支出で生活形成のための費用になる支出。
The sum of expenditures of individuals or nations on consumption and non-consumption expenses for daily life.

実収入 【jisshūnyū】 actual income
実質的に家庭の鈍財産高（資産－負債）を増加させる収入のこと。
The income of individuals or nations after paying income taxes and adjusting for inflation.

失認 【shitsunin】 agnosia
視覚・聴覚・触覚などの機能は保有しているが、それを正しく認識できない状態。
The inability to recognize common objects, persons, sounds, shapes or odor while the major senses of sight, hearing, smell, touch and taste are not defective nor is there any significant memory loss.

実務経験証明書 【jitsumu keiken shōmei sho】 proof of work experience
実務経験を証明する書類。
A document that proves his or her professional work experience or qualification.

自動運動 【jidō undō】 active movement
自分の意見と力で目的とする身体の部位を動かすこと。
The movements of intended parts of the body with one's own will and strength.

児童期障害 【jidō ki shōgai】 childhood disorder
6～12歳の時期の児童期に、日常生活において適応上の困難をきたしている状態。
A disorder which commonly occurs in children between the ages of 6 to 12 and causes difficulty in daily life.

自閉症 【jihei shō】 autism
脳機能の発達の遅れなどによるもので、公汎性発達障害から定義された症候群。
A disorder in the neural development that can lead to impaired social interaction and communication and is a term used to describe a diagnostic category called pervasive developmental disorders (PDD).

社会資源 【shakai shigen】 social resources
個人や集団が社会生活上のニーズを充足するための施設、設備、資金、物資、人材、技能などの総称。
A generic term for the facilities, equipment, capital, products or skills used to fulfill the needs of the social life of an individual or group.

社会的不利 【shakai teki furi】 handicap
機能障害あるいは能力低下の結果として社会で受ける不利益のこと。
Social disadvantages as a result of functional disabilities or impairments of one's ability.

社会福祉 【shakai fukushi】 social welfare
社会関係の困難を生活面から把握して個人の最低生活を援助すること。
The various social services and assistance provided to people with social difficulties after determining and confirming the needs for every aspect of daily life.

社会福祉士 【shakai fukushi shi】 certified social worker
専門的知識・技術を持って、福祉に関する相談に応じ、助言、指導、福祉サービスを提供する者または医師その他の保健医療サービスを提供する者その他の関係者との連絡および調整その他の援助を行うこと（「相談援助」）を業とする者（社会福祉士法及び介護福祉士法第2条）。
A person with the expertise and techniques to provide advice, education, referrals to other professionals who provide health and welfare services such as physicians and health care personnel, and coordinate those services (Article 2 of the Social Worker and Care Worker Law).

社会福祉事業 【shakai fukushi jigyō】 social welfare services
社会福祉を目的として計画し活動する事業のこと。
A field which includes the planning and implementation of activities aimed at improving the quality of life for individuals, groups and communities.

社会保険 【shakai hoken】 social insurance
強制的保険技術を利用して社会政策を実現しようとする経済保障政策。
A mandatory insurance program that aims to materialize social policies.

社会保障　【shakai hoshō】　Social Security
国民が生きている限り人間らしく暮らすために、国の責任で、国民の生活の安定や健康の確保を目的に生活を保障する制度。
A system that aims to provide social protection based on the state's responsibility so that all Japanese people can enjoy the decent minimum standard of living.

社会保障審議会　【shakai hoshō shingi kai】　Advisory Council on Social Security
厚生労働省の付属機関で、社会保障に関する厚生労働大臣の諮問機関。
The affiliated organization of the Ministry of Health, Labour and Welfare that has the power or duty to advise on the Social Security system.

視野狭窄　【shiya kyōsaku】　visual field restriction
目に見える範囲が狭くなること。
A medical condition where one's sight in scope becomes narrow.

視野障害　【shiya shōgai】　visual field defect
目で見える範囲に障害があること。
A medical condition where one or more blind spots exist in the normal field of vision.

シャワー浴　【shawā yoku】　shower bath
シャワーで行う入浴方法。
A way of bathing through a shower.

収益事業　【shūeki jigyō】　profit-making business
収益を得る目的で行う事業のこと。
The business that aims to make a profit.

従属人口　【jūzoku jinkō】　dependent population
扶養する人たちである生産年齢人口に対して、扶養される人たちのこと。
A group of people who do not work and rely on others.

住宅改修　【jūtaku kaishū】　home modification
日常生活の自立、事故の防止、介護負担の軽減を図るため障害や加齢に応じて住宅を改修すること。
An act of reforming one's house in response to disorders, impairments or increasing age, with the aim of improving independent living, preventing accidents and reducing the burden of care.

終末期　【shūmatsuki】　terminal stage
人の生涯における終焉が明らかに近づいた時期。
A period in one's life when the end of life is close.

終末期介護　【shūmatsuki kaigo】　terminal care
人生の終末期を迎えた人への介護。
The supportive nursing care of people who are terminally ill.

主治医　【shujii】　primary doctor
主となってその患者の医療を行い、責任を持つ医師。
A medical doctor who takes the main responsibility for a patient's health and provides diagnosis, medical advice and treatments for the patient.

主治医意見書　【shujii iken sho】　doctor's note
介護保険制度利用のための要介護認定、要支援認定の判定に用いられる主治医の意見書。
A descriptive written report created by the applicant's doctor, used to determine the eligibility for long-term care insurance benefits.

手段的日常生活活動　【shudan teki nichijō seikatsu dōsa】　instrumental activities of daily living: IADL
自立した社会生活をおくるための家事や薬の管理、買い物、電話の使い方、金銭の管理などの応用的な活動のこと。
A term that refers to a series of life functions necessary for independent living in a community setting such as preparing meals, taking medications, shopping for groceries, using the telephone and managing money.

出血　【shukketsu】　bleeding
血管が損傷し血液が血管外へ流出すること。
Occurs when a blood vessel is damaged and blood flows outside of the vessel.

守秘義務　【shuhi gimu】　duty of confidentiality
福祉専門職をはじめ医師や弁護士など、それぞれの職業の分野において、職務上知り得た個人情報を一切漏らしてはいけないこと。

The duty that requires all health care professionals such as doctors and attorneys to respect the confidentiality of their patients/clients and not to divulge any information obtained during the course of consultation/treatment.

手浴 【shuyoku】 hand bath
手をお湯につけて洗うこと。
Washing one's hands by putting them in hot water.

手話 【shuwa】 sign language
主に手の動きによって意思を伝える言語で、聴覚障害者にとり自立生活のために重要なコミュニケーション手段。
The important means of communication employing signs made mainly with hands, used usually by individuals with hearing impairments.

除圧 【joatsu】 decompression
身体の一部を極端に圧迫することを軽減すること。
An act of reducing extreme compression occurring in any part of the body.

障害 【shōgai】 disability
障害者基本法の定義では、「継続的に日常生活又は社会生活に相当な制限を受ける」こと。
According to the Basic Act for Persons with Disabilities, it refers to any people who suffer from a substantial limitation in daily or social life.

障害基礎年金 【shōgai kiso nenkin】 basic disability pension
原則、国民年金保険（基礎年金）に加入中の人、または、60歳以上65歳未満で国民年金保険に加入していた人が、病気やけがで一定の障害状態になった時に支給される年金。
A form of pension provided when people who are enrollees of the Basic Pension program or enrollees of the National Pension Insurance program aged between 60 and 64 become disabled and are unable to work due to an illness or disability.

障害の受容 【shōgai no juyō】 acceptance of disability
自己の身体障害を客観的かつ現実的に認め、受け入れること。
Realizing and accepting one's own physical disorder objectively and realistically.

小規模多機能型居宅介護 【shōkibo takinō gata kyotaku kaigo】 small-scale multi-functional home-based care services
25人以下の登録制となっている事業所において、自宅に住む要介護高齢者などに対して「通所」を中心に、自宅への「訪問」や宿泊施設での「泊まり」を組み合わせている地域密着型サービス。
A type of community-based day care facility that is small but provides a wide range of services such as day care, home care and institutional care for up to 25 elderly people who live at home.

少子化 【shōshi ka】 depopulation
社会の中で、子どもの数と割合が低下していること。
A reduction in the number and percentage of children in society.

少子高齢化 【shōshi kōrei ka】 depopulation and aging
出生率の低さから子どもが年々減少する一方、高齢者は年々増加していく状態。
A condition where the number of children decreases and the number of elderly increases every year.

静脈栄養法 【jōmyaku eiyō hō】 parenteral nutrition
静脈血管内に直接的に栄養素を投与する方法。
A method of providing the essential nutrients and fluids directly inside the venous vessels.

職業的リハビリテーション 【shokugyō teki rihabiritēshon】 vocational rehabilitation
精神・身体障害者の持っている能力を活かした職業につけるように援助する、また、それが継続できるように職業訓練や職業指導などを行うリハビリテーション。
The teaching of life and work skills that will be needed to get and/or keep a job for individuals who suffer from mental or physical disorders, but who still have the ability to function.

食事 【shokuji】 meal
生きるために必要な栄養素を摂取するために、食物を摂取すること。
Eating food items that provide nutrients necessary for survival.

食事介護 【shokuji kaigo】 eating assistance
心身のさまざまな障害により、自力で食事できない人に、必要な援助を行うこと。
An act of providing necessary assistance to individuals who cannot eat on their own due to various types of physical and mental disabilities.

食事介助　【shokuji kaijo】　eating assistance
→食事介護参照
An act of providing necessary assistance to individuals who cannot eat on their own due to various types of physical and mental disabilities.

食事動作　【shokuji dōsa】　eating
食事に関連する一連の動作。
An action related to consuming food.

食事療法　【shokuji ryōhō】　nutrition therapy
ある種の栄養障害や、生理的ないし病的状態に対し、その是正を図るために行う栄養治療法。
An intervention that aims to treat certain kinds of malnutrition or illness.

褥瘡　【jokusō】　pressure ulcer
身体の一部に長時間外力が加わって、血液が遮断され、皮膚に発赤や潰瘍、壊死などをきたした状態のこと。
A wound or skin breakdown due to prolonged pressure applied to the skin.

褥瘡予防　【jokusō yobō】　prevention of pressure ulcer
褥瘡の作りやすい原因を軽減して、発生や進行の予防を図ること。
An act of reducing the risk of developing and progressing pressure ulcers.

食中毒　【shoku chūdoku】　food poisoning
食物中の細菌や化学物質を経口的に摂取して起こる急性の胃腸炎などの病気の総称。
A generic term for health problems caused by eating improperly stored, prepared or managed food that may be contaminated by a harmful pathogen.

食品衛生　【shokuhin eisei】　food sanitation
飲食物を原因とする健康障害を防いで健康を守るようにするための取り組みのこと。
A set of protocols that should be used in the production and preparation of food products to remove the risk of introducing contaminating pathogens.

植物状態　【shokubutsu jōtai】　vegetative state
大脳が機能停止するため、意識障害を伴う重度の寝たきりとなるが、脳幹の機能が保たれた状態。
A state where the brainstem function is maintained but the larger brain functions have stopped so that the person's consciousness is damaged and they become bedridden.

植物性食品　【shokubutsu sei shokuhin】　vegetable food
穀類、芋類、野菜類、海藻類、きのこ類、種実類などの植物から成る食品。
Any kind of plants such as cereals, potatoes, vegetables, seaweed, mushrooms, nuts and seeds.

食欲　【shokuyoku】　appetite
食べ物や飲み物を食したいという欲求のこと。
A physical desire to eat or drink.

食欲不振　【shokuyoku fushin】　loss of appetite
食事時間がきても食欲が湧かないこと。
A feeling of no desire to eat even at mealtime.

ショートステイ　【shōto sutei】　short-stay
在宅の要介護者などが一時的に入所して、施設の介護を受けるサービス。
The provision of short-term or temporary care provided at a nursing facility for those who are sick or disabled and live at home.

初老期認知症　【shorō ki ninchi shō】　presenile dementia
老年期前期の40歳以上64歳以下に発症する脳の変性で生じる認知症。
Dementia caused by organic deterioration in the brain, occurring between the ages of 40 to 64.

自立　【jiritsu】　independence
主体的で他者に依存していないこと。
Being independent, mainly not depending on others.

自立支援　【jiritsu shien】　independence support
自立の過程において、その権利が十分に発揮できない個人に対して行う援助者の支援のこと。
Support given by health care professionals to individuals who cannot live independently.

自立度　【jiritsu do】　level of independent living
どの程度日常生活において自立しているのかを判定する尺度。
Criteria for determining the independent level of daily living.

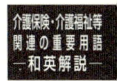

視力低下 【shiryoku teika】 vision loss
視力が低下した状態。
A decrease in one's vision.

事例検討 【jirei kentō】 case study
課題をもつある事象についてその状況を明らかにし、原因を考え、解決方法などを検討すること。
An investigation of an individual or an event to determine causes and solutions for a positive outcome.

心気症 【shinki shō】 hypochondria
心身の些細な不調にとらわれ、医学的検査で問題がないにもかかわらずその不調にこだわり、重大な病気の徴候ではないかと恐れ、それを執拗に他人に訴え続ける状態。
A disorder characterized by excessive preoccupation or repetitive complaints about having a serious illness, even when there is not any medical evidence to prove the presence of an illness.

人工呼吸 【jinkō kokyū】 artificial respiration
自分で呼吸できない人に対して緊急的に対象者の気道を確保して人工的に呼吸を補助すること。
An act of supporting respiration in emergency cases to individuals who cannot breath on their own.

身上監護 【shinjō kango】 personal guardianship
判断能力の不十分な成年者の日常生活を整える支援。
A legal support service for those who lack the mental capacity to make decisions to carry out the activities of daily living.

心身症 【shinshin shō】 psychosomatic disease: PSD
身体症状を主とするが、その診断や治療に、心理的因子についての配慮が特に重要な意味を持つ病態。
A disease in which physiological changes are facilitated by psychological stressors and may require to take into account those stressors for diagnosis and treatment.

振戦 【shinsen】 tremor
身体の一部または全身の規則的な不随意運動のこと。
A repetitive and involuntary movement of one or more parts of the body.

心臓弁膜症 【shinzō benmaku shō】 valvular heart disease
心臓の4つの弁のいずれかに障害が起こる心臓病。
A heart disease that involves one or more of the four valves of the heart.

身体介護 【shintai kaigo】 personal care
自立生活が困難な高齢者や障害者に対して、介護する人が、直接に身体に触れて介助すること。
An act of providing direct care and assistance to aged or impaired people who have difficulties with activities of daily living.

身体機能 【shintai kinō】 physical function
身体動作などの活動を行うための能力。
The ability of the body to perform mobility tasks.

信頼関係 【shinrai kankei】 rapport
→ラポール参照
A trusting and intimate relationship between the care provider and the care recipient.

推奨量 【suishō ryō】 recommended dietary allowance: RDA
集団の大部分（約98％）にとって十分となる栄養素量のこと。
The daily dietary intake levels of essential nutrients considered necessary to meet the requirements of most healthy people (98%).

水分バランス 【suibun baransu】 fluid balance
身体への水分の供給と損失の代謝のこと。
The balance between the amount of water taken into the body and the amount lost from the body.

水分補給 【suibun hokyū】 rehydration
身体で損失した水分を補うこと。
Restoring lost water to the body.

水疱 【suihō】 blister
表皮下に細胞液がたまり、小さな豆状になった状態。
A fluid filled pocket in the upper layers of the skin called the epidermis.

睡眠 【suimin】 sleep
眠ること。

A state characterized by reduced or absent consciousness whereby the mind and body are resting.

頭痛　【zutsū】　headache
　頭部の痛み。
　A pain in the head area.

ストレス　【sutoresu】　stress
　心身の負担になる刺激によって、生体内部に生じる緊張状態、または歪みのこと。
　An intense physical and/or psychological type of tension caused by strong external stimuli, both physiological and psychological.

ストレッチャー　【sutorecchā】　stretcher
　移動の困難な人を寝かせたまま移送する担架車のこと。
　A medical cart used for moving injured or immobile people from one place to another.

ストレングス視点　【sutorengusu shiten】　strengths perspective
　クライエントの持つ力に焦点を当て、それを引き出し強化して、最大限に発揮できるよう支援を行うこと。
　A method which helps individuals recognize their strengths and abilities to cope or overcome their personal issues and challenges.

スーパーバイザー　【sūpābaizā】　supervisor
　スーパーバイジーに対してスーパービジョンを行う指導者のこと。
　An individual who supervises, oversees, directs and evaluates the performance and activities of a supervisee.

スーパーバイジー　【sūpābaijī】　supervisee
　スーパーバイザーから指導をうける者。
　An individual who is directed by a supervisor.

スーパービジョン　【sūpābijon】　supervision
　指導者から被指導者への指導・監督による対人援助法。
　A process of directing and overseeing the performance and activity of an individual or a group of individuals.

スピリチュアルケア　【supirichuaru kea】　spiritual care
　身体面のみならず、自己存在や価値観より内面から魂の叫びに関わるケア。
　Care that focuses not only the physical aspects, but also on the mind and spirit of the individual.

生活援助　【seikatsu enjo】　home helping
　住み慣れた地域で心身の健康を保ちながら過ごせる家庭生活を、衣・食・住・その他において支援すること。
　An act of assisting people living in the community to maintain their physical, mental and emotional health by helping with their clothing, nutritional and housing issues.

生活環境　【seikatsu kankyō】　living environment
　生活において人間と関わる周囲の事象や状態のこと。
　A wide range of circumstances, objects or conditions by which one is surrounded.

生活習慣病　【seikatsu shūkan byō】　lifestyle-related disease
　生活習慣と深く関わり、加齢とともに増加する病気。
　A disease deeply related to one's lifestyle and which worsens with age.

生活の質　【seikatsu no shitsu】　quality of life : QOL
　個人にとって生活の質的側面を問う場面に使われる概念。
　A concept used to measure the general well-being of individuals.

生活扶助　【seikatsu fujo】　daily-needs assistance
　生活困窮のために最低限度の生活を営むことが難しい者に対して、飲食物費、被服費、移送費、光熱水費、家具・什器費、加算など、日常生活の需要を満たすために設定されている扶助。
　A type of assistance provided to low income people who have difficulty maintaining the minimum standard of living of paying for their daily expenses such as food/drink, transportation, utility bills, clothes and household appliances.

生活歴　【seikatsu reki】　life history
　現在に影響を及ぼしている過去の生活における出来事の記録。
　Records of the series of events that have happened in the past and still affect a person's life.

清潔　【seiketsu】　cleanness
　衛生的にきれいに保つこと。

Keeping oneself or surroundings clean and sanitized.

清拭　【seishiki】　sponge bath
入浴できないような介護者などの身体を、温湯や石鹸を用いてタオルなどで拭いて清潔に保つこと。
An act of washing the body with a wet cloth or sponge using warm water and soap to maintain the cleanliness of the body for those who cannot take a bath.

精神科ソーシャルワーカー　【seishinka sōsharu wākā】　psychiatric social worker
精神障害者とその家族の抱える問題に対する相談援助者。
A person who helps people with mental disorders and their family deal with their problems.

精神障害　【seishin shōgai】　psychiatric disorder
精神疾患の総体、精神状態の偏りや異常のことを総称したもの。
A generic term for any pattern of psychological symptoms that causes a disruption and abnormality in an individual's thinking, feeling, moods and so forth.

精神障害者　【seishin shōgai sha】　the mentally disabled
精神保健および精神障害者福祉に関する法律（第5条）によれば、統合失調症、精神作用物質による急性中毒又はその依存症、知的障害、精神物質その他の精神疾患を有する者のこと。
According to the Act on Mental Health and Welfare for the Mentally Disabled (Article 5), it refers to a person with schizophrenia or a person who suffers from acute poisoning by psychotropic agents or addiction, mental retardation, intellectual disabilities and/or other related conditions.

精神保健福祉士　【seishin hoken fukushi shi】　certified psychiatric social worker: CPSW
1997年に制定された精神保健福祉領域のソーシャルワーカーの名称独占の国家資格。
The national licensing system of social workers for mental health services, established in 1997.

成年後見制度　【seinen kōken seido】　adult guardianship system
判断能力の不十分な成年者が損害を受けないように、その諸権利を守るとともに社会的に支援する制度。
The system that protects and supports judgment-impaired adults who have some difficulty in protecting their rights.

整髪　【seihatsu】　styling and setting hair
くしやブラシを使用して、髪の毛をとかして整えること。
Arranging and designing the hair by using a comb and brush.

生命の延長　【seimei no enchō】　extension of maximum life span
生命の維持期間を最大限に引き延ばすこと。
Reversing the process or reducing the rate of aging to extend the maximum amount of time a person or a group of people can survive between birth and death.

生命倫理　【seimei rinri】　bioethics
生命に関わる倫理のこと。
Ethical issues related to life.

整容　【seiyō】　personal hygiene
顔を洗ったり、歯を磨いたり、髪を整えたり、髭を剃るなどの身だしなみのこと。
A set of practices such as washing face and hair, brushing teeth or shaving, associated with ensuring good health and cleanliness.

世界保健機関　【sekai hoken kikan】　World Health Organization : WHO
国連の専門機関の1つで、保健分野における国際機関。
One of the specialized organizations of the United Nations, acting as an authority on public health.

脊髄損傷　【sekizui sonshō】　spinal cord injury : SCI
脊髄が損傷を受けた状態。
Damage or trauma to the spinal cord.

脊椎圧迫骨折　【sekitsui appaku kossetsu】　vertebral compression fracture
脊椎椎体が外力を受け、つぶれた状態になる骨折。
A situation where the bones in the spine called vertebrae are broken or compressed due to trauma.

世帯　【setai】　household
同一の住居で生活し、生計を同じくする者の集団のこと。
A basic residential unit consisting of the members of a family who live together and share the same living accommodation.

摂食　【sesshoku】　food intake
口から食物を取り入れること。
Oral intake of food.

摂食障害　【sesshoku shōgai】　eating disorder
口から食物を取り入れることの支障。
A disorder of taking in food.

セミファーラー位　【semi fārā i】　semi-Fowler's position
背臥位から上半身を約20～30度挙上し、股関節と膝関節を軽く屈曲した姿勢。
A body posture when lying in a supine position with both legs either bent or straight and the head at approximately 20 to 30 degrees.

セルフケア　【serufu kea】　self-care
基本的には自分自身で自己の健康状態の維持、生命の安全、自立に向けた取り組みを行うこと。
It basically refers to any personal health maintenance activities performed by a person with the intention of maintaining health, protecting life and becoming independent.

セルフヘルプグループ　【serufu herupu gurūpu】　self-help group: SHG
共通の問題を抱える人やその家族により、自発的に結成された当事者グループで、メンバー同士で助け合いながら問題の解決のために活動するグループ。
A group or organization formed by people or families having a common problem or situation and where activities are conducted to overcome and resolve problems by helping each other.

繊維　【seni】　fiber
細くて長い糸状の素材のこと。
An elongated filament; threadlike structure.

全援助　【zen enjo】　total assistance
重度な心身の障害のために、全面的な全介助を要する状態。
A state where an individual is totally dependent due to physical and mental disabilities.

洗顔　【sengan】　face cleansing
肌の汚れを取り除いて清潔に保つために顔を洗うこと。
Washing an individual's face to keep skin clean.

洗剤　【senzai】　detergent
個体の表面に付着した汚れを除去して清浄にする目的で用いられる物質の総称。
A substance used to remove the dirt and stains in the laundry.

洗浄　【senjō】　washing
洗い流すことによって、汚れをきれいに除去して清潔にすること。
Removing and cleaning the dirt by flushing it with water and detergent.

染色体異常　【senshokutai ijō】　chromosomal abnormality
染色体の数と構造に異常が起こること。
Abnormality in the number of chromosomes and/or its structure.

全人格的ケア　【zenjinkaku teki kea】　total personal care
すべてのニーズを捉えて総合的にケアを提供すること。
An act of providing necessary care for meeting all aspects of the needs of the person.

全身清拭　【zenshin seishiki】　full-body sponge bath
清拭の種類の1つで、全身を拭く清拭方法のこと。
A type of bathing including wiping the whole body with a wet cloth or sponge.

全身浴　【zenshin yoku】　full-body bath
首から下の全身を浴槽に浸ける入浴方法のこと。
A type of bathing where the whole body below the neck is dipped in the bathtub.

尖足　【sensoku】　foot drop
足関節が足裏側に曲がる底屈位を示す変形。
A condition where a person has difficulty pointing their toes upward.

洗濯　【sentaku】　laundry
着用時に付着した衣類の汚れを洗って除去し、衣類を再び清潔・快適にすること。
An act of washing soiled clothing, towels and bed linen.

洗髪　【senpatsu】　shampooing
頭髪を清潔に保つために行う身体の清潔援助法の1つ。
An act of washing the hair and scalp with various liquid or cream preparations of soap.

せん妄　【senmō】　delirium
幻覚や妄想などを伴う意識混濁により混乱する状態。
A confused state where the individual can suffer from drowsiness, disorientation and hallucination.

総入れ歯　【sō ireba】　full denture
歯が1本もない場合に、抜けたり欠けたりした歯の代わりに人工的な歯を入れること。
A complete set of artificial teeth used when there are no teeth left.

躁うつ病　【sō utsu byō】　manic depressive psychosis
気分が高揚する躁状態と、ふさいでいるうつ状態を繰り返す精神病。
A mental disorder characterized by repeated episodes of mania and depression.

早期発見　【sōki hakken】　early detection
自覚症状がない時に病気や障害を発見すること。
An act of finding a disease before it is fully developed.

装具　【sōgu】　orthosis
体幹の機能障害の軽減などを目的として使用する補助具。
An orthopedic device designed to support and improve movement of an injured or weak part of the body.

掃除　【sōji】　cleaning
掃いたり拭いたりしてゴミや汚れをなくすこと。
An act of removing dirt, dust, stains or impurities by sweeping or wiping.

喪失体験　【sōshitsu taiken】　lost experience
大切なものを失う経験をすること。
The experience of losing important things.

側臥位　【sokuga i】　side-lying position
横向きで、下肢を伸展させた姿勢。
A posture in which a person lies on one side with both legs straight.

足浴　【sokuyoku】　foot bath
足の一部をお湯に浸けて洗うこと。
Washing one's feet by putting them in hot water.

咀嚼　【soshaku】　mastication
消化の第一段階で、口腔へ取り組んだ食物を歯の表面で噛み、切り、砕いて細かくし、睡液と混ぜ合わせて咽頭へ送り込みやすくすること。
The first step of digestion in which food is crushed and ground by teeth, mixed with digestive enzymes and then sent down the throat.

ソーシャルワーカー　【sōsharu wākā】　social worker
社会福祉専門職者としての一定の教育・訓練を受け、専門的価値や理論および技術を習得し、社会福祉実践（ソーシャルワーカー）を実践する者の総称。
A generic term for a person with education, training, values, knowledge, theory and skills in social work; involved in social welfare services.

措置制度　【sochi seido】　client allocation system
法律などに従って判断を下して処分する制度。
A system of assigning each individual to a particular facility/service for all their needs according to the regulations.

措置費　【sochi hi】　client allocation costs
措置制度に基づく福祉サービスの提供にかかる費用。
All costs that are paid for allocating an individual to a particular facility/service, including the cost of labor, operations, maintenance, in-service education and so forth.

体位変換　【taii henkan】　change of position
身体の姿勢の向きを変えること。
To change the orientation of one's physical posture.

体温　【taion】　body temperature
身体の各部位において保持される温度。

体温測定　【taion sokutei】　measurement of body temperature
身体の生理的変化を観察する方法の1つとして、体温を測定すること。
An act of measuring body temperature as one of the methods for observing physiological changes.

退行　【taikō】　regression
精神・生理的機能や機構あるいは状態が、未発達・未分化な時点まで逆戻りしてしまうこと。
Reversion to earlier patterns of feeling or behavior, or stages of mental and physiological functioning.

帯状疱疹　【taijō hōshin】　herpes zoster
水痘ウイルスが再発して帯状の発疹が出る症状。
A viral disease characterized by a blistering skin rash caused by the varicella-zoster virus.

大腿四頭筋　【daitai shitōkin】　quadriceps femoris
膝関節の伸展と大腿を挙上する下肢の大腿前面にわたる筋。
A muscle group located on the front part of the thigh and is an extensor muscle of the knee.

大腸癌　【daichō gan】　colon cancer
大腸にできる癌。
Large intestine (colorectal) cancer.

代読　【daidoku】　reading assistance
文章を読むことができなくなった時、利用者に代わって読む援助。
Reading on behalf of individuals who have difficulty with reading.

代筆　【daihitsu】　allograph
利用者に代わって手紙・書類などを書くこと。
Writing letters/other documents on behalf of individuals who cannot write.

代理電話　【dairi denwa】　telephone assistance
電話のやりとりが困難な人に代わり電話をすること。
Making a call on behalf of individuals who have difficulty communicating by phone.

ダウン症候群　【dauns hōkōgun】　Down Syndrome
突然変異で21番染色体が3本と過剰となる21トリソミーにより起こる先天性の症候群。
A congenital disorder caused by the inheritance of three #21 chromosomes.

立ち上がり　【tachiagari】　sit to stand
座位姿勢から立位姿勢をとるまでの姿勢転換動作のこと。
The movement of changing position from a sitting to a standing position.

脱臼　【dakkyū】　luxation
何らかの外的因子などにより、関節面の相互の位置関係が失われている状態。
A displacement or misalignment of a joint due to some external cause.

脱水症　【dassui shō】　dehydration
身体の体液、特に細胞外液が失われた状態。
An excessive loss of body fluids, especially extracellular fluids.

他動運動　【tadō undō】　passive exercise
他人の力や器械器具の力を借りて身体を動かす運動。
Fitness performed with the assistance of a person or equipment which moves a part of the body.

ターミナルケア　【tāminaru kea】　terminal care
それ以上延命の治療が困難になった終末期において提供されるケア。
Supportive care provided to individuals with a terminal illness during the terminal phase.

短下肢装具　【tan kashi sōgu】　ankle-foot orthosis: AFO
膝関節より遠位部の下肢に使用する装具。
An appliance used for the lower leg and foot to support the ankle.

端座位　【tanza i】　sitting position
ベッドなどの端から膝関節より先の両下腿を垂らした座位姿勢のこと。
A body position with both lower legs hanging over the edge of the bed or seat.

チアノーゼ　【chianōze】　cyanosis
低酸素血症により、皮膚および粘膜が青みを帯びた状態。
The appearance of a blue coloration of the skin due to hypoxemia.

地域包括支援センター 【chiiki hōkatsu shien sentā】 community comprehensive care center
地域支援事業の中の1つである包括的支援事業を実施する機関。
A community-based organization implementing comprehensive support operations.

地域密着サービス 【chiiki micchaku gata sābisu】 community-based care service
要介護状態になっても、地域に密着して生活が継続できるように2005年の介護保険法改正で創設されたサービス。
A type of service established by Long-Term Care Insurance Law in 2005 which aims to promote independent living for people in need of long-term care in the community.

チェーンストークス呼吸 【chēn sutōkusu kokyū】 Cheyne-stokes respiration
呼吸の変化が周期的に起こる生命の危機を従う異常呼吸。
An abnormal breathing pattern marked by alternating periods of decreased and increased breathing.

蓄尿障害 【chikunyō shōgai】 urinary storage disorder
尿を蓄えて保持することが障害されること。
A disorder that causes an inability to store urine.

知的障害 【chiteki shōgai】 mental retardation: MR
知的機能の障害が発達期に現れ、日常生活に支障が生じているために何らかの特別の援助を必要とする状態にあるもの。
A mental impairment that has occurred during the development stage and requires some kind of assistance in daily living activities.

知的障害者 【chiteki shōgai sha】 the mentally retarded
知的な障害のある者。
A person with intellectual difficulties.

知能 【chinō】 intelligence
知能の定義は多様であるが、単に記憶あるいは学習した知識経験を応用することではなく、自分にとって新しい課題事態を解決する能力。
Although it has been defined in different ways, it is not only the ability to apply learned knowledge and experience, but also the capacity to solve new problems.

知能指数 【chinō shisū】 intelligence quotient: IQ
知能の程度を精神年齢と生活年齢の比の指数で示した知能検査結果に基づく指標。
An index derived from the results of an intelligence test, expressed as the ratio of the mental age in months to chronological age, multiplied by 100.

痴呆 【chihō】 dementia
→認知症参照
A serious loss of cognitive/intellectual abilities.

痴呆性老人 【chihō sei rōjin】 the demented elderly
→認知症高齢者参照
An elderly person suffering from dementia.

痴呆性老人の日常生活自立度 【chihō sei rōjin no nichijō seikatsu jiritsu do】 independence level of the demented elderly
→認知症高齢者の日常生活自立度参照
A criteria for determining the independent level of daily living of elderly people suffering from dementia, established by the Ministry of Welfare (currently known as the Ministry of Health, Labour and Welfare) in 1993.

チームアプローチ 【chīmu apurōchi】 team approach
さまざまな職種がチームを編成してアプローチすること。
An approach made by a team composed of members with varied qualifications, skills and experiences that contribute to the improvement of a patient's care.

チームケア 【chīmu kea】 team care
保健・医療・福祉などの専門職が、連携・協働しながら利用者のケアをすること。
The act of taking care of the clients by an association or cooperation of health/medical care and long-term care professionals.

着脱 【chakudatsu】 changing clothes
衣服を着たり脱いだりする行為のこと。
An act of wearing and removing clothes.

聴覚障害 【chōkaku shōgai】 auditory impairment
聞き取りに支障を伴う聴覚の障害。
A disability or impairment of hearing.

長寿社会 【chōju shakai】 longevity society
健康を保ちつつ、楽しみながら積極的に生きる肯定的な高齢者像を希求する意図を背景とした社会。
A society who has the intention of maintaining the health of elderly people while they live happily, actively and positively.

調整交付金 【chōsei kōfu kin】 adjustment subsidy
すべての市町村が介護サービスを円滑に安定的に提供できるように、国から交付される財源。
A federal governmental subsidy paid to municipal governments to support the provision and delivery of a steady long-term care service.

重複障害 【chōfuku shōgai】 multiple disabilities
障害が重複している状態、すなわち単一の障害ではなく2種類以上の障害を併せもつ状態。
Having not only one impairment but a combination of two or more impairments at the same time.

腸閉塞 【chō heisoku】 ileus
腸管がふさがり内容物が通過できなくなる状態。
Being unable to eliminate feces or pass gas because of a partial or complete blockage of the intestine.

調理 【chōri】 cooking
生野菜や生肉などの食品素材にさまざまな加熱、非加熱操作を加えて、食物にすること。
The act of converting commodities such as raw plant or animal materials into edible foods using heating or non-heating processes.

調理方法 【chōri hōhō】 cooking recipe
栄養の目的にかなうように食材に施される料理の方法。
A set of instructions for cooking food.

聴力レベル 【chōryoku reberu】 hearing level
聞こえの能力である聴力の程度を表す尺度。
A scale showing the level of hearing ability.

直接援助技術 【chokusetsu enjo gijutsu】 direct social work practice
人と人の関わりによる直接的な対人関係を基盤とした援助の方法。
A method of delivering direct support/therapy though a worker-client relationship based on bonding.

対麻痺 【tsui mahi】 paraplegia
両側下肢が麻痺している状態。
Paralysis of the lower part of the body.

通所介護 【tsūsho kaigo】 day care service
送迎を受ける日帰り介護で、デイサービスと呼ばれる居宅介護サービス。
A community-based center that provides care, supervision and transportation to persons who require assistance with daily living activities.

通所リハビリテーション 【tsūsho rihabiritēshon】 ambulatory rehabilitation
日帰りのリハビリテーション介護で、デイケアと呼ばれる居宅介護サービス。
A type of home-based care service in which individuals travel to a so-called "day care center" to have rehabilitation therapy.

杖 【tsue】 cane
支柱に握り部分を取り付けた歩行を補助する福祉用具。
A slender walking aid which has a hand grip on the support bar.

杖歩行 【tsue hokō】 cane-assisted gait
杖をついて歩くこと。
Ambulation with a stick or cane.

手洗い 【tearai】 hand wash
手指をこすりあわせて流水であらうこと。
An act of washing hands using soap and running water.

低血圧 【tei ketsuatsu】 hypotension
血圧が正常よりも低下して、拍出量が低下した状態。
Blood pressure below normal, causing decreased cardiac output.

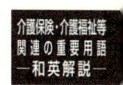

低血糖 【tei kettō】 hypoglycemia
血液中のブドウ糖の量が、正常よりも低下した状態。
A state where the blood sugar levels drop below normal.

T字杖 【tī ji tsue】 T-cane
歩行補助杖の1つで握り手がT字型をした単脚杖。
One type of walking stick which has a T-shaped grip.

摘便 【teki ben】 stool extraction
直腸下部に便が硬くて詰まっている時に、指先で便をかき出すこと。
Extraction of impacted stool in the lower rectum using a finger.

手すり 【tesuri】 handrail
手で支えることにより転倒防止や移動、車いすへの移乗を助けるために壁などに取り付けた棒。
A narrow rail, attached to the wall, side of a stairway and so forth, used to avoid fall incidents while providing stability and support when moving around or transferring to a wheelchair.

手引き 【tebiki】 hand-assisted escort
障害者または視覚障害者に対して誘導するときに用いる介助法の1つ。
One of the methods used for guiding impaired people by using a hand.

伝音難聴 【denon nanchō】 conductive deafness
鼓膜から中耳までの間で、音が振動として伝わっていく部分の障害により起こる難聴。
A hearing impairment caused by a defect in the part of the ear that conducts sound, specifically the area between the eardrum and middle ear.

点字 【tenji】 Braille
指先の触覚だけで読める特殊な触読文字。
Special reading and writing tool for the blind that is made up of tactile dots and can be read only with the sense of touch.

電動車いす 【dendō kuruma isu】 electric wheelchair
電動モーターで駆動する車いす。
A wheelchair operated by an electric motor.

電動ベッド 【dendō beddo】 electric bed
リモートコントロール（リモコン）により、電気で高さ調節や体位変換を行う調節機能がついたベッド。
A bed with electric height, head and foot adjustment features that can be controlled by a remote control.

動悸 【dōki】 palpitation
普段意識しない心臓の脈拍を不快に感じる自覚症状。
Abnormal pulsation of the heart which is usually not noticeable to the individual.

統合失調症 【tōgō shicchō shō】 schizophrenia
生活環境から入る情報をうまく総合しきれない認知障害、幻覚や妄想などが出現し、対人接触の障害をきたす精神病。
A psychological disorder including cognitive impairment where information obtained from one's surroundings cannot be synthesized properly, occurring as fantasies and delusions, and can affect interpersonal contacts.

透析 【tōseki】 dialysis
医療行為の1つで、腎不全の患者の血液中の老廃物や余分な水分を人工的にろ過し、血液をきれいにすること。
One of the medical practices that removes the waste and excess water from the blood of a patient suffering from renal failure.

疼痛 【tōtsū】 pain
身体的な痛み。
An unpleasant sensation occurring in the body.

糖尿病 【tōnyō byō】 diabetes mellitus: DM
血液中の糖成分が慢性的に高くなり、尿に放出される代謝異常の病態。
A disease of metabolic abnormality where glucose in the blood increases chronically and gets discharged in the urine.

動脈硬化 【dōmyaku kōka】 arteriosclerosis
動脈の退行性病変によって、動脈壁が肥厚・硬化あるいは変形した状態。
A chronic disease in which thickening, hardening or changing in the shape of the artery walls result in

impaired blood circulation.

特殊寝台　【tokushu shindai】　specialized bed
特殊な機能を備えた寝台のこと。
A bed equipped with special features.

特殊浴槽　【tokushu yokusō】　specialized bathtub
一般的な浴槽では入浴が困難な利用者が入浴できるように開発された特殊な浴槽。
A special bathtub for a person who has difficulties bathing in a general bathtub.

特別治療食　【tokubetsu chiryō shoku】　special therapeutic diet
特定の病気に対し、一人ひとりの患者の状況に応じて栄養素の制限などを考慮して調整され、病気の治療を目的に与えられる食事。
A special diet designed to optimize the nutritional needs of the individual by taking into account the pre-existing medical condition and nutritional needs in order to treat a variety of diseases and disorders.

特別養護老人ホーム　【tokubetsu yōgo rōjin hōmu】　geriatric welfare home
65歳以上で、身体上または、精神上著しい障害があるために常時の介護を必要とし、かつ、居宅においてこれを受けることが困難なものを入所させる施設。
A facility which provides a wide range of care to people aged 65 and above, who have physical and psychological disorders, and require continuous care but can't be cared for at home or in the community.

読話　【dokuwa】　lip-reading
聴覚障害者のコミュニケーションの1つで、相手の表情や口の動きから音声言語を読み取ること。
A method of understanding the speech of others by visually interpreting the facial expression and movements of the lips and mouth.

吐血　【toketsu】　hematemesis
消化管系、特に食道や胃から出血した血液を吐出するか、また吐物に血液が混込する状態。
The vomiting of blood or coffee-ground material due to hemorrhage in the gastrointestinal system.

徒手筋力テスト　【toshu kinryoku tesuto】　Manual Muscle Testing: MMT
ロバート・ロベット《Lovett. R.》が開発した抗重力の筋力検査法。
A method of examining muscle power by using an electronic device developed by Robert Lovett.

独居　【dokkyo】　solitary-living
家族や親族などとともに住まず、一人で暮らしていること。
Leading life independently without any family or relatives.

内部障害　【naibu shōgai】　internal disorder
内臓機能に障害があること。
The improper functions of the internal organs.

難聴　【nan chō】　hearing loss
会話音や物音など身のまわりの音が聞き分けにくくなること。
A wide range of hearing difficulties in determining the sounds and conversations in one's surroundings.

難病　【nan byō】　incurable disease
「不治の病」などと難治性疾患について一般に使われてきた言葉。
A term commonly used in Japan for a disease that is difficult to cure.

ニーズ　【nīzu】　needs
必要、欲求、要求などのこと。
A term that refers to necessity, requirement and demand.

日常生活活動　【nichijō seikatsu katsudō】　activities of daily living: ADL
一人の人間が生きるために行う、基本的かつ各人共通の、毎日繰り返される身体活動群。
The basic activities of everyday life that individuals perform such as eating, toileting, bathing, dressing and transferring.

日内変動　【nichinai hendō】　circadian variation
生物体内の働きが周期的に変動している生体リズムにおける24時間の周期。
The biochemical and physiological or behavioral processes that occur during a 24-hour cycle.

入眠　【nyūmin】　falling asleep
疲れを取り、エネルギーを蓄えるために眠りに入ること。
Being in a state of sleep to relieve fatigue and gain energy.

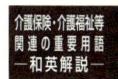

入浴　【nyūyoku】　bathing
日常的な生活行為の1つで、浴槽に体の一部あるいは全身を浸けること。
One of the activities of daily living, in which one's body is wholly or partially washed.

尿　【nyō】　urine
血液中の老廃物などが腎臓で濾過されて抽出された水分。
A liquid byproduct of the body after the body fluids have been filtered through the kidneys.

尿意　【nyō i】　uresiesthesia
膀胱内に尿が留まった時に大脳に起きる感覚。
A sensation produced in one's brain at the time when urine is stored in the bladder.

尿器　【nyō ki】　urinary bottle holder
トイレへの移動動作が困難な場合に、尿を集めるための容器。
A urine collection container that is used when a patient has difficulty in moving to the rest room.

尿失禁　【nyō shikkin】　urinary incontinence
本人の意思に関係なく尿が出てしまうこと。
Involuntary urination from one's body due to the loss of bladder control.

尿路感染　【nyōro kansen】　urinary tract infection
尿が腎臓で作られ、尿管を通って膀胱に留まり、尿道から排出されるまでの尿路におこる感染病。
An infection that occurs in the urinary tract, commonly associated with bacterial and yeast infections.

認知症　【ninchi shō】　dementia
脳のさまざまな器質的疾患のために生じた後天性の回復不可能な知能の欠損状態。
A defect of one's acquired intellectual ability which cannot be recovered due to various diseases or injuries of the brain.

認知症高齢者　【ninchi shō kōrei sha】　the demented elderly
認知症を発症している高齢者のこと。
An elderly person suffering from dementia.

認知症高齢者の日常生活自立度　【ninchi shō kōrei sha no nichijō seikatsu jiritsu do】　independence level of the demented elderly
厚生省（当時）が1993年に定めた認知症高齢者の日常生活自立度を決める際の判定基準。
A criteria for determining the independent level of daily living of elderly people suffering from dementia, established by the Ministry of Welfare (currently known as the Ministry of Health, Labour and welfare) in 1993.

認知症対応型共同生活介護　【ninchi shō taiō gata kyōdō seikatsu kaigo】　group home for the demented
認知症のある要介護者に対して介護サービスを提供する地域密着型サービス。
A community-based home which provides supervision and care for people who suffer from dementia.

認知症対応型通所介護　【ninchi shō taiō gata tsūsho kaigo】　day care services for the demented
認知症の要介護者に対して、通所介護で介護サービスを提供する地域密着型サービス。
A community-based care service for people with dementia who are in need of care.

寝返り　【negaeri】　roll over
普通に寝ている状態から右側もしくは左側へ転がること。
Rolling over on one's left or right side while sleeping.

寝たきり　【netakiri】　bedridden
日常生活において何らかの介護を要する要介護状態。
An individual who cannot leave the bed due to severe impairment or illness.

寝たきり度　【netakiri do】　bedridden level
障害高齢者の日常生活自立度判定基準の略称。
The abbreviation for criteria for determining the independent level of daily living of elderly people suffering from disabilities.

熱傷　【nesshō】　burn
高熱の液体、気体、固体などによって起こる皮膚および粘膜のやけど。
Injuries to skin due to liquids, gases or solids that come into contact with the skin and or mucosa.

寝床　【nedoko】　bedding
寝るために用いる布団や枕、寝巻のこと。
Materials used for sleeping such as a futon, mattress, pillow and pajamas.

年金 【nenkin】 pension
本人や遺族に給付を行うことで所得の保障をして、生涯にわたって支給され生活を支える保険金。
An insurance benefit paid to people or their family members, which is paid throughout their lives to safeguard their income.

脳血管障害 【nō kekkan shōgai】 cerebrovascular disorder :CVD
脳の血管が詰まったり破れたりすることによって、脳が器質的に損傷され、損傷された場所によって半身麻痺、意識障害、言語障害などが見られる疾患群の総称。
An inclusive term for a group of brain dysfunctions caused by blockage or the bursting of blood vessels in the brain, which may cause paralysis, impaired consciousness, speech impairment and so forth depending on the parts of the brain damaged.

脳血管性認知症 【nō kekkan sei ninchi shō】 cerebrovascular dementia
脳血管の障害に起因した認知症の総称。
A type of dementia caused by cerebrovascular disease.

脳血栓症 【nō kessen shō】 cerebral thrombosis
脳の血管内壁に少しずつ異物が付着（粥状硬化）するため、やがて血管が狭窄し最終的に詰まってしまう病態。
A medical condition in which a foreign body slowly adheres to the inner wall of a blood vessel in the brain and eventually blocks the vessel.

脳梗塞 【nō kōsoku】 cerebral infarction
脳の血管が詰まり、それより先の脳に血液が流れなくなりその流域の脳細胞が死んでしまう病態。
A medical condition in which the blood vessel in the brain is blocked, causing a disturbance in blood supply to the brain.

脳死 【nō shi】 brain death
脳幹を含む全脳機能が完全に失われた状態。
A state where all functions of the brain including the brainstem lose their functionality.

脳出血 【nō shukketsu】 cerebral hemorrhage
脳の血管が損傷することで、出血した病態。
A medical condition in which blood vessels in the brain are ruptured and cause bleeding.

脳性麻痺 【nō sei mahi】 cerebral palsy: CP
発達途上の脳に種々の原因が加わって、非進行性の病変を生じ、その結果主として永続的な中枢運動障害をもたらした状態の総称。
An inclusive term for a group of conditions that can cause the development of an immature brain and produce non-progressive lesions, which can result in a permanent central impairment of motions.

脳塞栓 【nō sokusen】 cerebral embolism
心臓や頸動脈などで形成された血栓などが血流によって脳内に運ばれ脳の動脈を詰まらせる病態。
An obstruction of the cerebral artery by an embolus such as a blood clot formed inside a blood vessel, that is carried by the bloodstream to the brain where it blocks the artery.

能力低下 【nōryoku teika】 disability
ある物事をなし得る能力が、低下すること。
Decline in one's capabilities to achieve something.

ノーマライゼーション 【nōmaraizēshon】 normalization
すべての子供、障害者、高齢者などが一人の人間として人格を尊重され、一人の市民としての権利を保障されて、地域社会で主体的な生活が送ることができる社会を目指すこと。
Aiming to build a society where all children, disabled and elderly people will be respected as individual human beings, their rights as citizens will be safeguarded and they would be able to lead independent lives in society.

ノンレム睡眠 【nonremu suimin】 non-rapid eye movement sleep：NREM sleep
急速眼球運動（REM）を伴わない睡眠。
The phase of sleep without rapid eye movement (REM).

肺炎 【haien】 pneumonia
病原菌などさまざまな原因によって起こる肺実質の炎症の総称。
An inclusive term for an inflammatory condition of the lung caused by organisms such as viruses and bacteria and can result in the alveolar filling with fluid.

徘徊 【haikai】 wandering
目的もなく当てもなく歩き回る状態。
A state of walking around without any purpose.

肺癌 【hai gan】 lung cancer
肺にできた上皮性の悪性腫瘍。
An epithelial malignant tumor that forms in the lungs.

肺気腫 【hai kishu】 pulmonary emphysema
肺が過膨張して呼気を十分に吐ききれず、肺に空気がたまってしまう慢性の疾患。
A chronic lung condition in which the alveoli in the lung may be over-inflated and stretched and making it difficult to exhale air.

バイキング食 【baikingu shoku】 all-you-can-eat buffet
さまざまな料理をテーブルに並べてセルフサービスで好きなだけ食べる食事。
A meal where a variety of dishes are set out on the table or sideboard for self-service.

バイスティックの7原則 【baisutikku no nana gensoku】 Biestek's 7 principles
米国のバイスティック《Biestek, F.P》が、援助者とクライエントの基本的な関係として明示した7つの原則。
Seven principles of the casework relationship between workers and clients identified by Biestek, F. P from the United States of America.

排泄 【haisetsu】 excretion
体内の不要な物を対外に排出すること。
An act of excreting bodily waste.

排泄介助 【haisetsu kaijo】 toileting assistance
身体的・精神的・社会的な障害により排泄行為が自分でできなくなった人に対して支援すること。
Providing support to a person who cannot egest independently due to a physical/mental/social disability.

バイタルサイン 【baitaru sain】 vital signs
生命維持を示す徴候。
Signs that include the heart beat, blood pressure, temperature and breathing rate that show sustainment of life.

排尿 【hainyō】 urination
老廃物を含んだ血液が腎臓でろ過され、老廃物が尿となり、尿管を通り膀胱に運ばれ、尿道から体外へ排出されること。
An act of eliminating urine from the urinary bladder after removing waste from the blood by the kidneys and passing it down to the ureters, bladder and urethra.

排尿困難 【hainyō konnan】 difficult urination
膀胱に貯留された尿が出にくくなることや、または、残尿のある状態。
A condition in which a person has difficulties ejecting urine from the bladder or is unable to empty the bladder completely.

排尿障害 【hainyō shōgai】 urinary disorder
頻尿、排尿困難、尿失禁など排尿が障害されること。
A disorder characterized by frequent urination, difficult urination or incontinence.

排便 【haiben】 defecation
便を体外に排出すること。
An act of eliminating feces from the digestive tract via the anus.

排便障害 【haiben shōgai】 dyschezia
便秘、下痢など、便を排泄することが障害されること。
A disorder in defecation such as constipation or diarrhea.

廃用萎縮 【haiyō ishuku】 disuse atrophy
廃用症候群の一症状で、身体の低活動により生じる骨・筋の萎縮。
A wasting or diminution in the size of bones or muscles occurring as a result of low activity.

廃用症候群 【haiyō shōkōgun】 disuse syndrome
身体の不活動により引き起こされる身体機能の低下の多様な症状。
Various symptoms of decline in the body's functions as a result of immobilization of the affected body parts.

パーキンソン病 【pākinson byō】 Parkinson's disease
振戦・固縮・無動の三大徴候が見られ、不随意運動を伴う中枢神経疾患。

A degenerative disease that affects the central nervous system impairing motor skills and is characterized by the three cardinal motor symptoms of tremors, rigidity and akinesia.

白杖 【hakujō】 white cane
視覚障害者らが障害物などを探索するため、さらには、障害者であることを他者に表示して安全歩行するために補助する白い杖。
A special cane for individuals who are blind or have low vision that makes it easier for those people to feel obstacles and alerts others that this person is visually impaired.

白内障 【hakunai shō】 cataract
眼球の水晶体が濁ること。
A clouding or loss in the transparency of the lens in the eye.

長谷川式簡易認知症スケール改訂版 【hasegawa shiki kani ninchi shō sukēru kaitei ban】 Hasegawa's dementia scale-revised: HDS-R
認知症のスクリーニング用に、1974年に長谷川和夫らによって開発された高齢者用知能評価スケールの代表的なもの。
A rating scale for dementia: a set of items developed by Kazuo Hasegawa in 1974 for assessing the cognitive status of the elderly.

バックサポート 【bakku sapōto】 back support
車いすの使用者の背部が寄りかかる部位で、いわゆる背もたれの部分。
A backrest on the wheelchair which provides support and positioning.

発達障害 【hattatsu shōgai】 developmental disorder
一般的には発達期に起こる、知的障害、自閉症、学習障害、脳性麻痺、てんかんなどの障害のこと。
A group of disorders that usually occur during childhood, including intellectual disability, autism, learning disability, cerebral palsy and epilepsy.

発熱 【hatsu netsu】 fever
筋収縮や疾患などにより熱の産生が増し、末梢血管収縮により熱放散が抑えられる状態。
A state characterized by an elevation of body temperature above normal due to muscle contradiction or disease, and where heat dissipation is reduced due to the contraction of surrounding blood vessels.

バリアフリー 【baria furī】 barrier free
公共建築物や交通機関などの物理的な障壁に加え、制度的な障壁、文化・情報面、精神的な障壁などのあらゆる面における障壁の除去という意味の用語。
A term that refers to the elimination of not only the structural and architectural boundaries found in public and transportation facilities, but also the political, cultural, informational and emotional biases found in various situations.

バルーンカテーテル 【barūn katēteru】 balloon catheter
尿を自動的に体外のバッグに蓄尿されるように、膀胱に挿入する管のこと。
A tube inserted in the urinary bladder in order to withdraw or introduce fluid.

半身浴 【hanshin yoku】 half-body bath
浴槽内の水位を胸の下からへその上あたりまでにして、入浴すること。
Taking a bath by maintaining the water level in the bathtub at below one's chest.

半調理 【han chōri】 semi-prepared dish
調理の過程で、切断、粉砕、混合、調合といった下処理のみを行い、加熱を途中でやめるなど最後まで調理をしてしまわない調理の手法。
A technique of cooking by performing only the pre-process like cutting, crushing, mixing and heating and not doing the cooking completely.

BMI 【bīemuai】 body mass index
身長と体重の計算式で肥満の状況を表す1つの指数。
An indicator for determining obesity status calculated from an individual's height and weight.

被害妄想 【higai mōsō】 delusion of persecution
自分が他者から害を加えられるという内容の根拠のない念慮。
A false belief and thought of being hurt by others that is maintained in spite of evidence against it.

非言語的コミュニケーション 【hi gengo teki komyunikēshon】 non-verbal communication
視線、表情、態度、身振りなどの非言語的手段により、送り手と受け手が互いに自分の訴え、考え、感情などのやりとりをすること。

The process of exchanging information such as opinions, thoughts and emotions with others through eye contact, facial expressions, attitudes and gestures.

ビタミン　【bitamin】　vitamin
微量の摂取で効果を示し、人体の生命維持、成長、生殖のために必須の栄養素。
Any of various organic components required in minute amounts for maintaining good health, growth and reproduction of the human body.

筆記試験　【hikki shiken】　written examination
筆記にて行われる介護福祉士国家試験のこと。
A national written examination of certified care workers.

被保険者　【hi hoken sha】　the insured
保険制度において、保険金を支払い、給付を受ける権利を持っている人。
A person having rights to receive benefits from the insurance provider due to paying insurance premiums.

肥満　【himan】　obesity
脂肪組織が過剰に蓄積して体重が標準よりも超過した状態。
A medical condition caused by excessive accumulation of body fat causing one's weight to exceed his or her ideal body weight.

秘密保持　【himitsu hoji】　confidentiality
クライエントが専門的援助関係の中で打ち明ける秘密の情報を保全すること。
An ethical principle associated with professionals, of maintaining information of the client by not disclosing it to anyone who is not authorized to have access.

氷枕　【hyō chin】　ice pillow
氷と水を入れたゴム製の枕のこと。
A rubber pillow which holds ice and water.

氷囊　【hyōnō】　ice bag
ゴムの袋に氷と水を入れたもの。
A thin waterproof rubber bag to hold ice and water.

日和見感染　【hiyorimi kansen】　opportunistic infection
生体に常在して病原性を示さなかった微生物が生体に感染症を発症させること。
An infection caused by pathogens that do not normally infect a healthy host.

貧血　【hinketsu】　anemia
何らかの原因で、血液の単位容積中の赤血球または血色素量が減少した状態。
A state where a number of red blood cells or quantity of hemoglobin measured in unit volume is reduced below normal levels.

頻便　【hinben】　frequent bowel movements
便を頻回にわたって排泄する状態。
A state where stool is excreted frequently.

ファーラー位　【fārā i】　Fowler's position
ベッド上で上半身を約45度起こした体位。
A body posture in which the upper half of the body is elevated approximately 45 degrees on the bed.

フェイスシート　【feisu shīto】　face sheet
利用者の氏名、性別、年齢、職業、学歴など、属性に関する情報が記載されている用紙。
A document that contains information about the client such as name, gender, age, occupation and highest education level.

フォローアップ　【forō appu】　follow-up
立案した介護サービス計画（ケアプラン）に基づく介護サービスが、利用者およびその家族と一緒に設定した目標に向かって適切に適用されているか評価して確認すること。
An act of confirming and evaluating whether health care services provided based on the care goals and plan created by health care professionals along with clients and their family are appropriate.

腹臥位　【fukuga i】　prone position
うつ伏せで上肢は体幹側に置き、下肢を伸展させた姿勢。
A body posture where one lies on the stomach, puts the upper extremities on the trunk and extends the lower extremities.

副作用 【fuku sayō】 side effect
治療効果を期待する作用（主作用）以外に現れる作用のこと。
A secondary effect of a drug or treatment in addition to the intended effects.

福祉 【fukushi】 welfare
快い生活やよりよい暮らしの幸福のあり方。
A living blessed with a pleasurable lifestyle and better livelihood.

福祉機器 【fukushi kiki】 technical aid for the disabled
要介護者などの生活を支援するために作られた機械全般のこと。
A general device made for supporting the life of a person in need of nursing care.

腹式呼吸 【fuku shiki kokyū】 abdominal respiration
横隔膜を上下させることで腹部の運動による呼吸。
Breathing that occurs primarily by moving the diaphragm up or down.

福祉事務所 【fukushi jimu sho】 welfare office
社会福祉行政の中心的な機関。
A central organization of social welfare policies.

福祉用具 【fukushi yōgu】 welfare equipment
心身の機能が低下し日常生活を行う上で支障のある者に対して、日常生活をより便利かつ補助する道具。
A device which assists and makes daily life activities convenient for those whose physical and mental functions are reduced and face difficulties in performing daily life activities.

福祉用具貸与 【fukushi yōgu taiyo】 welfare equipment rentals
福祉用具の中の日常生活用具を公費により給付あるいは貸与されること。
Renting and leasing devices for daily life activities at the government's expense.

浮腫 【fushu】 edema
臨床的にはいわゆる「むくみ」で、細胞間隙に体液が過剰に貯留する状態。
An abnormal and excessive accumulation of liquid in the cellular intervals as a result of clinical swellings.

フットサポート 【futto sapōto】 foot support
車いすを構成する一部で、足部を支えるもの。
A constituting part of the wheelchair which supports the leg.

部分援助 【bubun enjo】 limited assistance
利用者の行動を部分的に援助すること。
An act of partially assisting the individual's actions.

部分清拭 【bubun seishiki】 partial sponge bath
病気やけが、体力の低下が著しいなどで入浴できない時、50〜55℃のお湯を準備し、タオルまたはウォッシュクロスを固く絞って身体の一部分を拭くこと。
An act of wiping a part of the body by soaking a towel or wash cloth in water that is 50-55°C (122-131°F) when bathing is not possible due to illness or injury or when body strength is remarkably low.

部分浴 【bubun yoku】 partial bath
病気やけが、体力の低下が著しいなどで入浴できない時、身体の一部だけを湯につけて洗うこと。
An act of washing only some part of the body when bathing is not possible due to illness or injury or when body strength is remarkably low.

プライバシー 【puraibashī】 privacy
他者と区別された自分の領域であり、私事、私的秘密といった意味。
An area or condition which is separated or secured from the presence or view of other people; personal things; personal secrets.

プライマリ・ケア 【puraimari kea】 primary care
厚生労働省によれば、「個人や家庭が最初に接する保健医療システムであり、医師は初期患者の問題を的確に把握して、適切な指示や緊急に必要な処置の実施や他の適切な医師へ紹介を行い、個人や家庭の継続的な健康の保持、慢性疾患の継続的な治療やリハビリテーションについて、いわゆる主治医としての役割を果たすもの」と定義している。
According to the Ministry of Health, Labour and Welfare, it refers to a health care system by medical doctors/physicians who help maintain good health and provide the first consultation for a person or a group of people with a health concern as well as diagnosing, providing appropriate orders and emergency medical treatments, referring to specialists or providing continuous treatments and rehabilitation.

プロフィール 【purofīru】 profile
簡単な人物紹介のこと。
A simple biography.

平均寿命 【heikin jumyō】 average life span
死亡の状況が将来も変わらないと仮定した場合に、統計的に計算される0歳児の平均余命のこと。
The length of time a new born is expected to live between birth and death, assuming mortality trends stay constant.

平均余命 【heikin yomei】 life expectancy
各年齢の個人が平均してあと何年生きられるかを示す指標の1つ。
One indicator which shows how long an individual in each age group will live on average.

ベッド 【beddo】 bed
睡眠や横になるための寝台。
A piece of furniture used for sleeping and reclining.

ベッドから車いす 【beddo kara kuruma isu】 transfer from bed to wheelchair
要介護者などがベッドから車いすへ移動する時の動作。
The action when a person moves to a wheelchair from the bed.

ベッドメーキング 【beddo mēkingu】 bed making
利用者にとって快適で寝心地のよいベッドを作るためのベッド上の整備。
Restoring a bed to an unslept-in condition so that individuals can feel comfortable.

便器 【benki】 bedpan
排泄した尿や便を、衛生的に収集する用具。
A bowl shaped like a toilet seat that collects excreted urine and stool in a sanitary manner.

便失禁 【ben shikkin】 fecal incontinence
自分の意思ではなく無意識の便の漏れ。
Unconscious leakage of feces.

便秘 【benpi】 constipation
大腸の機能的、器質的異常により発生し、異常に長く腸内に糞便が貯留したり、排便が遠のいたりして不快感と苦痛を伴う状態。
A state of discomfort or pain occurring due to feces accumulating inside the intestine and difficulties occurring with defecation.

片麻痺 【hen mahi】 hemiplegia
障害された大脳半球側とは反対側の上下肢に運動麻痺が生じる状態。
Paralysis affecting only one side of the body opposite to the affected cerebral hemisphere.

保育士 【hoiku shi】 certified child care worker
専門的知識および技術を持って、児童の保育および児童の保護者に対する保育に関する指導を行うことを業とする者。
A person who has specialized knowledge and techniques to provide care to children and instructions regarding childcare to their parents.

防炎素材 【bōen sozai】 flame-resistant material
火源を近づけた時に燃えないか、または燃えても広がらない素材のこと。
A material which does not burn even when in close contact with a fire source or if it burned does not spread the fire.

防汚素材 【bōo sozai】 soil-resistant material
食物のシミや汚れなどが付きにくくした素材、または、付いた汚れが洗濯などで落ちやすくした素材のこと。
A material which is difficult to stain and can be washed easily.

訪問介護 【hōmon kaigo】 home care
訪問介護員（ホームヘルパー）や介護福祉士が要介護者などの自宅を訪問して排泄・入浴・食事などに関する身体介護や、買物・料理・洗濯・掃除などの生活援助、日常生活全般にわたる相談助言などのサービスを提供すること。
A form of care service provided in the individual's home by home helpers or certified care workers, providing assistance related to activities of daily living such as toileting, bathing and eating and instrumental activities of daily living such as shopping, cooking, washing and cleaning.

訪問看護 【hōmon kango】 home health
訪問看護が必要と主治医が認めた場合、要介護者の自宅に訪問看護ステーションの看護師などが訪問し、療養上

の世話または必要な診療の補助を行うこと。
Health care or supportive care provided in the patient's home by licensed nurses when his or her attending physician believes the patient requires care and orders those services.

訪問看護ステーション 【hōmon kango sutēshon】 home health nurses station
看護師、准看護師、保健師などが配置されている訪問事業所のこと。
An area or station where nursing staff congregate and carry out their administrative duties.

訪問入浴介護 【hōmon nyūyoku kaigo】 home bathing care
要介護者の自宅に訪問し、浴槽を提供して入浴の介護を行い、身体の清潔の保持や心身機能の維持向上を図るサービス。
A service whereby a nurse will visit the home of clients with a bathtub and provide bathing assistance to maintain the cleanliness of the body.

訪問リハビリテーション 【hōmon rihabiritēshon】 home care rehabilitation
要介護者・要支援者に対して、理学療法士・作業療法士・言語聴覚士などが主治医の指示のもと、各家庭に出かけていき、リハビリテーションや指導などを提供するサービス。
A service whereby physical, occupational and speech therapists will go to an individual's home and provide rehabilitation and education.

保健師 【hoken shi】 public health nurse：PHN
保健所、保健センター、病院、一般企業などで、住民や社員に対し、保健指導業務などを行う国家資格の専門職。
A specialized professional who has a special national qualification for offering health guidance for citizens. They are usually employees of public health centers, hospitals, private or sector organizations.

保険者 【hoken sha】 the insurer
保険制度を運営し、保険料を徴収し、事故が発生したら、それに対して被保険者に保険給付（サービスを提供）する者。
A person running an insurance system, collecting insurance premiums and providing the insurance benefits to the insured in case of an accident.

保健所 【hoken jo】 public health center
地域における住民の疾病の予防、公衆衛生の向上・増進を図ることを目的としている機関。
A public agency aimed to prevent disease and promote and improve public health in the community.

保険料 【hoken ryō】 insurance premium
保険事業に要する費用にあてるために被保険者が拠出する料金。
A periodic payment made by the insured to the company in order to cover the expenses required for carrying insurance business.

歩行 【hokō】 gait
両方の下肢を交互に出して移動すること。
A movement of walking by alternately moving both of the lower extremities.

歩行器 【hokō ki】 walker
左右のフレームとこれを連結する中央のパイプからなり、利用者はその間に立って歩行を行う用具。
A three-sided walking tool configured of left and right frames joined by a middle pipe that allows the user to stand and walk in the center of the frame.

歩行練習 【hokō renshū】 gait training
歩行が何らかの原因で障害された場合に、平行棒・松葉杖・杖の使用や、理学療法士・作業療法士などによる介助や指導下で、リハビリ室や室外で歩く基本的動作の練習のこと。
An act of practicing the basic movements for walking inside or outside of a rehabilitation room with the support of physical/occupational therapists, parallel bars, crutches or a cane.

ポジショニング 【pojishoningu】 positioning
安定したリラクゼーションが得られる姿勢、位置取りのこと。
An act of placing or arranging the body into a position in which a person feels comfortable and relaxed.

補足給付 【hosoku kyūfu】 supplementary benefit
所得に応じて負担限度額を設定し、低所得者の負担が重くならないように、基準費用額と負担限度額との差額を給付すること。
An income-tested benefit provided to low income people for determining the difference between what they can afford and how much the service actually costs, to minimize their financial burden.

ポータブルトイレ 【pōtaburu toire】 commode
室内用で、持ち運びができる腰掛け便器。
A portable toilet chair used inside the room.

ポータブル浴槽 【pōtaburu yokusō】 portable bathtub
居室などで入浴を容易に行うことができる携帯用の簡易浴槽。
A simple portable bathtub through which bathing can be done easily in the room.

補聴器 【hochō ki】 hearing aid
音を大きくする機能を持ち、難聴者の補装具。
A hearing-impaired person's equipment which has the function of increasing the volume of the sound.

発疹 【hosshin】 skin rash
血流量の減少、色素の沈着や減少または欠如、炎症、腫瘍の真皮内への浸潤、表皮の肥厚などが生じる状態。
An eruption of the skin causing symptoms such as decreased blood flow, loss of or decreased pigment deposition, skin cancer, inflammation and hyperplasia of the epidermis.

発赤 【hosseki】 redness
鮮紅色を呈し、圧迫すると退色し、圧迫をやめると再びもとの色にもどる紅斑が皮膚に生じること。
Red spots on the skin that disappear when pressure is applied and reappear when pressure is relieved.

ボディメカニクス 【bodi mekanikusu】 body mechanics
骨格や筋、内臓を含めた姿勢や動作などの力学的相互関係を科学的に考えた生体力学。
The study of posture and movement of bones, muscle and internal organs and the relationship between them; also known as biomechanics.

ホームヘルパー 【hōmu herupā】 home helper
要支援・要介護高齢者、障害者、難病患者などの自宅に訪問して排泄・入浴・食事などに関する身体介護や買物・調理・洗濯・掃除などの生活援助、さらに日常生活全般にわたる相談助言などのサービスを提供する専門職。
A care professional who visits the home of elderly and disabled people in need of care; offers support for patients with incurable or difficult-to-treat diseases, provides assistance with activities of daily living such as toileting/bathing/eating and with instrumental activities of daily living such as shopping/cooking/washing/cleaning and so forth, and also provides consultation related to their overall daily lifestyle.

ボランティア 【borantia】 volunteer
現代社会のさまざまな問題を解決・予防するため、労力や金品の提供を自由意志によって行うこと。
Any type of practice on behalf of others such as providing assistance, money or goods without wanting to receive anything in return.

ホルモン 【horumon】 hormone
内分泌腺から直接血液やリンパ液中に分泌される微量な物質。
A trace substance secreted directly into the blood and lymph nodes from the endocrine glands.

マット 【matto】 mat
大きさや形状など色々なサイズの敷物。
A flat piece of fabric or carpet of various sizes, designs and colors.

松葉杖 【matsubazue】 crutch
怪我などにより下肢が不自由な者の歩行を補助するための木製またはアルミ製の補助具。
A support tool, either wooden or aluminum, used by people with a leg injury as an aid in ambulation.

麻痺 【mahi】 paralysis
神経系の異常によって起こった筋力低下や知覚の消失、あるいは運動などの障害。
Weakening of muscular strength, loss of sensory perception or damage in movements and so forth, usually caused by abnormalities in one's nervous system.

ミキサー食 【mikisā shoku】 blended diet
元来は分粥食をミキサーでブレンドしたものでブレンダー食ともいう流動食のこと。
A type of diet in which foods have been blended into a smooth consistency.

ミネラル 【mineraru】 mineral
生体に必要な無機成分の1つ。
One of naturally occurring compounds that is required by the body for healthy functioning.

脈拍 【myaku haku】 pulse
心臓の拍動を表す動脈の圧力の変動。
It represents the tactile arterial palpation of the heartbeat.

メタボリック症候群 【metaborikku shōkōgun】 metabolic syndrome
内臓脂肪型肥満に加えて、高血糖、高血圧、脂質異常症のうち2つ以上がある場合に診断される症候群。
A set of any two or more of the following signs in the same person meet the criteria for the metabolic syndrome: abdominal obesity, high blood sugar, high blood pressure and dyslipidemia.

滅菌 【mekkin】 sterilization
ある場(器材、身体、食材など)からすべての微生物を排除し、無菌的すなわち細菌のいない状態にすること。
An act of removing or killing all living pathogenic organisms from the surface of instruments, body and food.

妄想 【mōsō】 delusion
実際にあり得ない思考内容や観念。
A false or deceptive belief and thought.

燃え尽き症候群 【moetsuki shōkōgun】 burnout syndrome
極度の心身の疲労と感情の枯渇を主とする症候群。
A syndrome principally involving extreme physical and mental fatigue and depletion of emotions.

モニタリング 【monitaringu】 monitoring
クライエントの問題が解決に向かっているかどうかを見極める段階のこと。
A stage of carefully observing whether a client's difficulties are being resolved.

問題行動 【mondai kōdō】 problem behavior
行動が問題とされる行為。
An action or reaction of a person that is troublesome or disruptive.

夜間せん妄 【yakan senmō】 night-time delirium
幻覚や妄想などを伴う意識混濁により混乱する状態。
A confused state due to clouded consciousness accompanied by hallucination and delusion.

薬剤 【yakuzai】 medication
生物学的作用を要する薬を調合したもの。
A medicine or compound which exerts a biological effect.

薬剤管理 【yakuzai kanri】 medication management
適切に薬の服用ができるように、薬の保存から服薬などに対応すること。
The monitoring of medications an individual takes to confirm that the individual is complying with the medication regimen.

薬剤師 【yakuzai shi】 pharmacist
調剤、医薬品の供給、その他薬事衛生をつかさどる国家資格を有する専門職。
A health care professional in medicine with a national qualification to assist people with understanding what and how the medications they are taking will work.

薬物療法 【yakubutsu ryōhō】 pharmacotherapy
薬剤を用いて病気の症状などを抑えること。
The treatment of a disease or disorder by administering medications.

有料老人ホーム 【yūryō rōjin hōmu】 private residential home for the elderly
食事などの提供その他日常生活上必要な便宜を供与することを目的とする施設であって、老人福祉施設でないもの。
A facility aiming at providing some help with activities of daily living such as bathing, as well as instrumental activities of daily living such as preparing meals. It is different from a geriatric welfare facility that provides continuous nursing care.

ユニットケア 【yunitto kea】 unit-based care
長期ケア施設などに入所している要介護者などをケアする際に、少人数のグループに分けてケアすること。
An act of providing care in small groups for people in need of care in long-term care facilities.

ユニバーサルファッション 【yunibāsaru fasshon】 universal fashion
年齢、体型、サイズ、障害に関わらず、すべての生活者に機能的かつ美的なファッション商品を推奨し、提供しようとするもの。
An idea that means to provide functional and fashionable items such as clothing and foot wear to as many individuals as possible regardless of age, body shape, size and ability.

要援護高齢者 【yō engo kōrei sha】 support-required elderly
日常生活を営むのに支障があり援助、保護、介護などが必要な高齢者。
An elderly person who has difficulties in carrying out his or her daily living activities and is in need of

support, protection and care.

要介護　【yō kaigo】　long-term care-required
介護保険制度において被保険者が、市町村の介護認定審査会で要介護状態であると要介護認定されること。
A person who is classified into the "care-required (level 1 to 5)" based on the results of an on-site assessment of each individual's physical and mental status under the long-term care insurance system.

要介護者　【yō kaigo sha】　long-term care recipient
介護保険法によれば、要介護状態に該当する者。
According to Long-Term Care Insurance Law (Article 7), it refers to a person who qualifies and receives the long-term care benefits from long-term care insurance.

要介護度　【yō kaigo do】　long-term care classification levels
介護保険制度における要支援状態と要介護状態の区分。
The classification levels of benefits under long-term care insurance.

要介護認定　【yō kaigo nintei】　certification of long term care-required
要介護状態にあるか否かを、全国一律の基準にもとづいて公平かつ客観的に認定すること。
An act of equally and objectively assessing and classifying an applicant into one of five levels (care-required level 1 to 5 for long-term care benefits under long-term care insurance) based the classification standards.

養護老人ホーム　【yōgo rōjin hōmu】　residential home for the elderly
65歳以上の者であって、環境上の理由、および経済的理由により居宅において養護を受けるのが困難な者を入所させ、養護するとともに、その他の援助を行うことを目的とする施設（老人福祉法第11）。
A facility which provides supportive care to people aged 65 and above and require continuous care, but can't be cared for at home or in the community due to some environmental and financial issues (Article 11 of the Welfare Law for the Elderly).

要支援　【yō shien】　long-term assistance-required
介護保険制度において、被保険者が市町村の介護認定審査会で要支援状態であると認定されること。
A person who is classified into "assistance-required (level 1 and 2)" based on the results of an on-site assessment of each individual's physical and mental status under the long-term care insurance system: in need of long-term assistance.

要支援者　【yō shien sha】　long-term assistance recipient
介護保険法にて、要支援状態に該当するもの（第7条）。
According to Long-Term Care Insurance Law (Article 7), it refers to a person who qualifies and receives preventive care from long-term care insurance.

要支援認定　【yō shien nintei】　certification of long-term assistance-required
要支援状態にあるか否かを、全国一律の基準にもとづいて公平かつ客観的に認定すること。
An act of equally and objectively assessing and classifying an applicant into either "assistance-required" level 1 or 2 for preventive care benefits under long-term care insurance based on the classification standards.

腰痛症　【yōtsū shō】　lumbago
腰部とその周辺にさまざまな疼痛を伴う疾患。
A condition where pain is experienced in the lower back and surrounding parts of the body.

腰痛体操　【yōtsū taisō】　lumbago exercise
腰痛に対する治療あるいは予防するための体操。
A type of nonsurgical treatment or exercise to prevent lower back pain.

腰痛予防　【yōtsū yobō】　prevention of lumbago
腰痛を引き起こさないように予防すること。
An act of reducing the risk of developing lower back pain.

抑制　【yokusei】　restraint
身体拘束ともいわれ、転落や転倒などの防止、また点滴や経管栄養の管を抜くことを防ぐため、強制的に行動を制限する行為。
Also called a physical restraint, an act of limiting the movements of an individual forcefully in order to avoid fall incidents, rollover or to avoid removal of tubes used for intravenous drips or feeding.

浴槽　【yokusō】　bathtub
入浴の際に使用する湯船のこと。

A bathtub used for taking a bath.

予防給付　【yobō kyūfu】　preventive benefit
介護保険制度において、要介護認定の結果、被保険者が要支援1または2と認定された要支援者に対する給付。
The benefits provided to individuals who are classified into the "assistance-required (level 1 and 2)" based on the results of an on-site assessment of each individual's physical and mental status under the long-term care insurance system.

四脚杖　【yonkyaku tsue】　quad cane
支柱の先端が4本に分かれている杖。
A cane that has a four-legged rectangular base of support for providing extra stability.

ライフサイクル　【raifu saikuru】　life cycle
人の出生から死亡までを1周期とした人生の過程のこと。
The cycle of life; the period from birth to death.

ライフスタイル　【raifu sutairu】　life style
衣、食、住、交際、余暇活動などを含めた生活の仕方。
A method of living including clothing, food, housing, entertainment and leisure activities.

ライフレビュー　【raifu rebyū】　life review
自分の人生を振り返り、語ることで、自分の歩んできた人生の意味を見いだし、自己を肯定できるようになること。
Looking back at one's life and reviewing the meaning of how one has lived his or her life.

ラポール　【rapōru】　rapport
援助する側とされる側の間に結ばれる親近感や信頼感に溢れた援助関係。
A trusting and intimate relationship between the care provider and the care recipient.

理学療法士　【rigaku ryōhō shi】　physical therapist：PT
医師の指示の下に理学療法を行う専門職。
A health care professional who provides physical therapy under the supervision of a medical doctor.

立位　【ritsu i】　standing position
立っている姿勢のこと。
A body position in which the body is raised upright on the feet.

利尿剤　【rinyō zai】　diuretic
腎臓の機能単位であるネフロンの尿細管や集合管に作用し、体内のナトリウム水分の排泄である利尿を促す薬。
A medication used to increase the excretion of sodium moisture from the body by using the convoluted tubules of the nephron.

リハビリテーション　【rihabiritēshon】　rehabilitation
何らかの障害によって、一度失われた機能の回復を目指すこと。
The action of restoring the skills and abilities of an individual who has had an illness or injury so they can attain maximum self-sufficiency and function as normal as possible.

リハビリテーション医学　【rihabiritēshon igaku】　rehabilitation medicine
疾患に伴う障害に対して、心身の機能維持や向上を目指す医療分野のリハビリテーションのこと。
Rehabilitation in the medical field that aims to maintain or restore the body function that was lost through injury or illness.

リハビリテーション介護　【rihabiritēshon kaigo】　rehabilitative care
介護を必要とする人々に対するリハビリテーション理念に基づいた介護の実践。
Care provided to people in need based on the principle of rehabilitative care.

留置カテーテル　【ryūchi katēteru】　indwelling catheter
尿を排泄する目的で尿道から膀胱内に留置するカテーテル。
A flexible plastic tube inserted from the urethra into the bladder to withdraw urine.

流動食　【ryūdō shoku】　liquid diet
流動体、または口腔内ですみやかに流動体になり、消化されやすく、残渣のない刺激の少ない食物のこと。
Mild food in liquid or strained form that has no residue and is easy to swallow and digest.

流動性知能　【ryūdō sei chinō】　fluid intelligence
新しいことを学習したり覚えたりするような、経験の影響を受けることが少ない知能。
The ability to learn and recognize new things and is independent of acquired knowledge and experience.

利用料 【riyō ryō】 usage cost
介護サービスの利用者が負担する料金。
The quantity of payment given by a recipient for long-term care services.

レクリエーション 【rekuriēshon】 recreation
生活の中のゆとりとやすらぎ、楽しみを創造していくさまざまな活動の総称。
An inclusive term for various activities for getting comfort, peace and enjoyment in one's life.

レム睡眠 【remu suimin】 rapid eye movement sleep：REM sleep
急速眼球運動のことで、眠っているのに眼球が激しく動いている睡眠状態のこと。
A sleeping condition where the eyes move quickly during sleep.

聾 【rō】 deafness
両耳の聴力レベルが約100dB（デシベル）以上の聴覚障害のこと。
A loss of ability to hear sounds greater than 100 dB (decibels) in both ears.

老化 【rōka】 aging
生物に時の経過とともに起こる変化のうち、成熟期以降の現象。
The biological changes that occur in humans after they reach the age of maturity.

老眼 【rōgan】 presbyopia
中年以降で近くのものが見えにくくなる遠視のこと。
An aging medical condition where the eye shows decreased ability to focus on close objects.

老人性うつ病 【rōjin sei utsu byō】 senile depression
老年期に発症するうつ病。
Depression that occurs in elderly people.

老人性難聴 【rōjin sei nanchō】 senile deafness
加齢に伴い、徐々に高音部の聞こえが悪くなり、次第に中音部、低音部に及ぶ難聴。
A loss of the ability to hear high frequencies, followed by a loss in ability to hear mid and low frequencies due to aging.

老人保健施設 【rōjin hoken shisetsu】 geriatric health care facility
病状がほぼ安定して、入院治療よりも看護・介護・リハビリテーションが必要な高齢者を対象とする施設。
A facility targeting elderly people whose health condition is in a stable stage and who require nursing care or rehabilitation rather than acute hospital treatment.

老年認知症 【rōnen ninchi shō】 senile dementia
老年期に好発し進行性認知症を主症状とする脳の変性疾患。
A disease caused by the degeneration of brain cells, often associated with old age and is the predominant symptom of progressive dementia.

老齢基礎年金 【rōrei kiso nenkin】 basic old-age pension
老齢を理由に支給される国民年金。
The national pension available to the elderly.

老齢年金 【rōrei nenkin】 old-age pension
→老齢基礎年金参照
The national pension available to the elderly.

老齢福祉年金 【rōrei fukushi nenkin】 old-age welfare pension
国民年金保険が始まった1961年には、すでに保険料を納付できない年齢に達していた人に支給される年金。
The pension that is paid to a person who had reached a certain age and retired where the premiums cannot be paid when National Pension Insurance was implemented in 1961.

ロールプレイ 【rōru purei】 role play
シナリオを作り、話す人、聴く人、観察する人を決めて演じてもらう手法。
A technique that uses scenarios to explore the different genres of practice such as writer, speaker, listener or observer.

第３部

諸外国における介護福祉等関連用語

1．英国（イギリス）における介護福祉等関連用語【英　和】

Accident and Emergency：A&E　救急医療
accountability　説明責任
Additional Voluntary Contributions：AVCs　任意付加保険料
Adjudicating Medical Authorities：AMAs　医療裁定局
Adjudication Officer：AO　裁定官
Advisory Programmers　就業助言
after-care　病後の介護
age addition　年齢加算
almshouse　養老院；救貧院
appropriate personal pensions：APP　適格個人年金
Artisans and Labourers Dwelling Act　職人および労働者住居法
Artisans and Labourers Dwelling Improvement Act　職人および労働者住居改善法
associated philanthropy　博愛協会
attendance allowance　付添い手当金
Audit Commission　監査委員会；自治体監査委員会
Back to Work Bonus　職場復帰ボーナス
Barclay Report　バークレイ報告書
basic pension　基礎年金
bed blocker　ベッドを塞ぐ人
benefit in kind　現物給付
best value：BV　ベストバリュー
Best Value Programme　最高の価値計画
Beveridge Report　ベヴァリッジ報告書
binary system　二元的システム
Blind Persons Law　盲人法
Blue Badge Scheme　ブルー・バッジ・スキーム
Board of Poor Law Guardians　貧民保護委員会
British Association of Social Workers：BASW　英国ソーシャルワーカー協会
budgeting loan　生活資金一時貸付金
Building Society　建築協会
capping　収入・支出権限制限
Care Standard Act　ケア基準法
Care Standards Commission　ケア基準委員会
Career Development Locus　キャリア開発融資
Carers Act　介護者法
Carers National Association　全英介護者協会
Carers National Association：CAN　全英家族介護者協会
Carers Recognition and Service Act　介護評価サービス法
cash benefit　現金給付
Central Association for Mental Welfare　精神福祉全英連合会
Central Council for Education and Training in Social Work：CCETSW　中央ソーシャルワーク教育研修協議会
Certificate in Social Service：CSS　ソーシャルサービス資格
Certificate in Social Work：CSW　認定ソーシャルワーカー
Certificate of Qualification in Social Work：CQSW　ソーシャルワーク認定資格
Certificate of Secondary Education：CSE　中等教育資格
charitable trust　慈善トラスト
Charitable Uses Act　慈善用途法
charity　慈善
charity hospital　慈善病院
Charity Organization Society：COS　慈善組織協会
charity school　慈善学校
child abuse and neglect　児童虐待
child benefit　児童給付
Child Benefit Act　児童手当法
child care officer　児童保護官
Child Care Tax Credit：CCTC　保育タックスクレジット
child deprivation　児童剥奪
child minding　保育ママ
Child Poverty Action Group：CPAG　児童貧困行動グループ
child protection　児童保護
Child Support Act　児童支援法
Child Support Agency：CSA　児童援護エイジェンシー
ChildLine　無料子ども電話相談事業
Children Act 1989　1989年児童法
Children's Act　児童法
children's allowances　児童手当
Children's Legal Center　児童法律センター
Citizen Advice Bureau　市民アドバイスビューロー
Citizens Advice Bureau　市民相談所
Citizens' Chapter　市民憲章
citizenship　市民権
Civil Service Benevolent Fund　公務員済生基金
cold weather payment　暖房費補助
commercial system　営利システム
Commission for Health Improvement：CHI　保健医療改善委員会
Commission for Racial Equality　人種平等委員会
Commission for Social Care Inspection：CSCI　ソーシャルケア査察委員会
Commissions for Care Standards　ケア基準委員会
commonality　共同性
community　地域社会
Community Care：Agenda for Action　コミュニティケア行動計画指針

community care grant　地域ケア支援一時金
Community Care-Policy Guidance　コミュニティケア政策要綱
community care reform　コミュニティケア改革
community mental health team　地域精神保健チーム
Community Service Volunteers　地域サービス・ボランティア
complaints procedure　苦情処理手続き
Comprehensive Health Services and Rehabilitation　包括的保健サービスおよびリハビリテーション
Comprehensive Spending Review　包括的支出見直し
Compulsory Competitive Tendering：CCT　強制競争入札
consortium　合同委員会
constant attendance allowance：CAA　常時付き添い手当
contact out　適用除外
continuing education　継続教育
contract culture　契約文化
contributory benefits　拠出制給付
Contributory Pensions Act　拠出年金法
cost of Social Security　社会保障給付費
council tax　カウンシル税
council tax benefit　カウンシル税給付金
Country and County Borough Councils　州および特別市会
Court of Appeal　控訴院
crisis loan　災害避難貸付金
Critical Association　批判的共同社会論
custody　保護
CVS　民間福祉協議会
day nursery　保育所
decentralized pluralism　分権的多元主義
Department for Education and Employment　教育・雇用省
Department of Social Security：DDS　社会保障省
Diploma in Social Work　ソーシャルワーク資格
direct payment　直接支払い制度
Direction on Choice　選択指導書
Disability Discrimination Act 1995　1995 年障害者差別禁止法
disability living allowance：DLA　障害者生活手当金
disability working allowance　障害者就労手当金
Disabled Person Act 1986　1986 年障害者法
Disabled Persons Tax Credit：DPTC　障害者タックスクレジット
District Health Authorities：DHAs　地域保健当局
domestic help　家事援助
domiciliary service　在宅サービス
dual polity　二重政体
Economic and Social Research Council　経済社会研究委員会
Education Act　教育法

efficiency scrutinies　能率監査
Elberfeld system　エルバーフェルト制度
Elizabethan Poor Law　エリザベス救貧法 [貧民救助法]
Employment and Training Act　雇用および訓練法
enabling　条件整備
enabling authority　条件整備型自治体 [条件整備団体]
End Physical Punishment of Children　児童への体罰禁止
Enterprise Allowance Scheme　起業援助手当制度
enterprise zone　企業地域制度
Environment Protection Act　環境保護法
Equal Opportunities Commission　機会平等委員会
European Union　ヨーロッパ連合
Exceptionally Severe Disablement Allowance：SDA　特別重度障害手当
Fabianism　フェビアン主義
Factory Act　工場法
fair rent　公正家賃
family credit　家族クレジット；世帯給付
Family Health Services　家庭保健サービス
family income supplement　家族所得補足給付；世帯所得補足金
family support　家族支援
Favored Goods　公的サービス
Financial Management Initiative：FMI　財務管理イニシアチブ
five giant evil　5 つの巨人
Foundation Trust：FT　ファンデーショントラスト
freehold　自由保有権
Free-Standing Additional Voluntary Contributions：FSAVC　付加保険料
Friendly Society　友愛組合
from-cradle-to-grave　ゆりかごから墓場まで
full employment　完全雇用
funding scheme　積立方式
funeral payment　死亡一時金
General National Vocational Qualification：GNVQ　一般国家職業資格
general practitioner：GP　一般医；家庭医
general practitioner fundholding　予算保持一般医
General Social Care Council：GSCC　総合社会ケア協議会
General Vocational Qualification：GNVQ　英国総合職業資格
Genuinely-seeking-the Job Clause　挙証責任条項
Gilbert's Act　ギルバート法
Golden Rule　黄金律；行動規範
governance　組織統治
graduated pension：GP　段階制年金
Grant Maintained Schools：GMSs　政府助成校
Griffith Report　グリフィス報告書
Guaranteed Minimum Pension：GMP　最低保障年金

英国
英和

guardian's allowance　保護者手当金
guardians benefit　保護者手当
Guild of Help　援助ギルド
Health and Social Care Act　医療介護法
health authority　保健当局
Health Boards　保健局
Health Care Assistant：HCA　医療介護士
health visitor　保健師
Help for the Unemployed in Seeking Work　職探し援助
Help Scheme for Becoming Self-Employment　自営業促進
higher education　高等教育
Higher Education Funding Councils　高等教育資金協議会
home nursing　在宅看護
Homes Fit for Heroes　英雄のための住居
House of Commons　下院
House of Lords　上院
Housing Association　住民協会
housing benefit　住宅給付；住宅補助金制度
Housing Green Paper　住宅緑書
housing inspector　住宅検査官制度
Housing of Working Class Act　勤労者階級住宅法
Housing, Town and Country Planning Act　住宅・都市計画法
Idiot Act　白痴法
Improving Management in Government-The Next Steps　ネクスト・ステップス改革
incapacity benefit　労働不能給付；就労不能手当
income maintenance　所得維持；所得保障
income-related benefit　所得関連給付
income support　所得補助
income support for mortgage interest payments　住宅ローン利補助制度
individual learning account　個人学習口座
indoor-relief　院内救済
industrial death benefit　業務災害死亡給付
industrial injuries benefit　労災給付
Industrial Injuries Disablement Pension　業務災害障害年金
Industry Training Board：ITB　産業別訓練委員会
Industry Training Organization：ITO　産業別訓練組織
informal system　インフォーマル・システム
Inner Urban Area Act　都心地域法
In-Service Course in Social Care：ICSC　ソーシャルケアコース
internal market　内部市場
invalid care allowance　障害者介護手当金
invalidity benefit　障害給付
Job Center　ジョブセンター
Job Club　就職相談会
Job Creation Programme　雇用機会創出計画

Job Interview Guarantee Scheme：JIG　ジョブ・インタビュー・ギャランティー
Job Introduction Scheme　職業紹介事業
Job Release Scheme　高齢者早期退職制度
job search seminar　職探しセミナー
jobfinders grant　求職活動手当金
jobseeker's allowance　求職者手当金
jobshops　ジョブショップ
jobstart allowance　就労開始手当
leasehold　借地〈家〉権
lifelong education　生涯教育
local authority　地方当局
Local Authority Planning Statement：LAPS　地方自治体計画報告
Local Authority Social Service Act　地方自治体社会サービス法
local devolution　地方分権化
Local Education Authority　地方教育局
local governance　地方統治
local government　地方政府
Local Government Act　地方政府法
Lodging House Act　下宿法
Lords Spiritual　聖職者議員
Lords Temporal　世俗議員
lower earnings limit　最低稼得収入額
Lunacy Act　精神異常法
luncheon club　昼食クラブ
maltreatment　不適切処遇
managerialism　経営管理主義
Manpower Services Commission：MSC　マンパワー・サービスコミッション
marginal accountability　限界の財政責任
maternity allowance：MA　出産手当
maternity grant　出産一時金
maternity service　妊婦サービス
Meals on Wheels：MoW　ミールズ・オン・ウィール；食事配達サービス
Mechanics' Institutes　職工学院
Medical Appeal Tribunals：MAT　医療不服審査会
Mental Capacity Act 2005　2005年意思決定能力法
Mental Deficiency Act　精神欠陥法
Mental Health Act　精神保健法
Mental Health Core Group　精神保健中核グループ
Mental Illness Specific Grants：MISG　精神障害特別補助金
metropolitan area　大都市圏
model of an extension ladder　繰り出し梯子モデル
Modernizing Social Services　社会サービスの近代化
money purchase　拠出建て
Moodie Report　ムーディ報告書
multilateral school　多課程制学校
National Assistance Act　国民扶助法
National Care Commission　政府ケア審議会

National Care Service Committee：NCSC　全英ケア基準委員会
National Care Strategy　全英介護者戦略
National Centre for Volunteering：NCV　全英ボランティア活動センター
National Council for Social Services：NCSS　全英社会福祉協議会
National Council for the Single Woman and Her Dependents：NCSWD　家族を扶養する単身女性全英協議会
National Council for Vocational Qualification：NCVQ　全英職業資格協会
National Council for Voluntary Organization：NCVO　全英民間組織協議会
National Disability Council　全英障害協議会
National Economic Development Council：NEDC　全英国民経済発展委員会
National Health Service：NHS　全英国民保健サービス
National Health Service Act　全英国民保健サービス法
National Health Service Improvement Plan：NHSIP　全英国民保健サービス改善計画
National Health Service Trust：NHS Trust　全英国民保健サービストラスト
National Health Services and Community Care Act　全英国民保健サービス・コミュニティケア法
National Institute for Health and Clinical Excellence：NICE　英国立最適保健医療研究所
national insurance　国民保険
National Insurance Fund　英国国民保険基金
National Lotteries Control Board：NLCB　英国国営宝くじ委員会
national lottery　英国国営宝くじ
National Minimum Wage　英国最低賃金制度
National Minimum Wage Act 1998　1998年全国最低賃金法
National Parks and Countryside Act　英国国立公園および田園地域法
National Service Framework：NSF　全英サービスフレームワーク
National Society for the Prevention of Cruelty to Children：NSPCC　全英児童虐待防止協会
National Vocational Qualification：NVQ　職業能力評価制度
needs-led　ニーズ主導
neighborhood movement　隣友運動
new philanthropy　新たな博愛
New Poor Law　改正救貧法
New Public Management：NPM　新公共管理；ニュー・パブリック・マネジメント
New Town Act　新都市開発法
NHS Executive　英国国民保健サービス執行委員会

non-contributory benefit　無拠出制給付
non-contributory retirement pension　無拠出退職年金
Nurseries and Child-Minders Regulation Act　保育所及びチャイルドマインダー法
nursing auxiliary：NA　看護介護士
occupational pension　職域年金
Occupational Pension Regulatory Authority：OPRA　職域年金管理委員会
Occupational Pensions Board　職域年金委員会
Offenders Rehabilitation Act　更生保護法
Old Persons Act　老年金法
one-parent benefit　ひとり親給付
operational strategy：OS　オペレーショナル・ストラテジー
opting-out　オプト・アウト；免除規定
outdoor-relief　院外救済
owner-occupation　持家
panel　審査会
parallel bars theory　平行棒理論
parliament　議会
patch-based system　パッチ基盤システム
paternalism　家父長主義
pay-as-you-earn：PAYE　源泉徴収
payroll giving　給料天引き寄付
People's Capitalism　人民資本主義
performance　役割遂行
Performance Assessment Framework：PAF　業績評価枠組み
personal allowance　個人手当
personal pension plan　個人年金プラン
personal pension schemes　個人年金政策
personal social services：PSS　対人社会サービス；人的社会サービス
philanthropy　博愛事業
place of safety order　安全措置命令
poll tax　人頭税
Poor Law　救貧法
popular capitalism　民衆資本主義
post qualifying studies：PQS　認定後研修
postcode lottery　郵便番号宝くじ
Practice Teaching Award　実習教員資格
Preliminary Certificate in Social Care：PCSC　初級ソーシャルケア資格
primary care group：PCG　プライマリ・ケアグループ
Primary Care Trust：PCT　プライマリ・ケアトラスト
privatisation　民営化
privatisation policy　民営化政策
provider　事業者
providing authority　サービス提供団体
Provisional Collection of Taxes Act　暫定課税徴収法
public choice　公共選択
Public Expenditure Survey Committee：PESC　公共支出調査委員会

purchaser　購入者
purchaser-provider split　購入者・提供者分離
Qualifications and Curriculum Authority：QCA　資格・カリキュラム当局
quasi-market　準市場；疑似的市場
rate support grant　地方税支援補助金
RCC　農村地域協議会
Regional Commission for Care Standard　地域ケア基準委員会
Regional Health Authorities　地方保健当局
Registered Home Tribunal　施設登録審査会
Registered Homes Act　施設登録法；登録ホーム法
Rent Act　家賃法
rent allowance　家賃手当
Rent Assessment Committee　家賃査定委員会
rent rebate　家賃補助；家賃減額
rent tribunal　家賃審判所
replacement rate　就業換算率
Report of Wood Committee　ウッド委員会報告
residential home　老人ホーム；入所施設
residential service　施設サービス
respite care　レスパイトケア
retirement pension　退職年金
revenue support grant　歳入援助交付金
rolling back　守備範囲の見直し
Royal Commission on Long Term Care　長期介護に関する王立委員会
Rural District Councils　村部市会
salary-related　給与建て
Salvation Army　救世軍
Scottish General Vocational Qualification：GSVQ　スコットランド総合職業資格
Scottish Vocational Education Council：SCOTVEC　スコットランド職業教育協会
Scottish Vocational Qualification：SVQ　スコットランド職業資格
secondary education　中等教育
Seebohm Report　シーボーム報告書
separate spheres model　公私分離モデル
Severe Disablement Allowance　重度障害者手当金
Sex Discrimination Act　性別差別禁止法
sheltered house　シェルタード・ハウス
sheltered housing　シェルタード・ハウジング
sickness benefit　疾病給付
single assessment：SAP　シングルアセスメント
skill center　技能センター
Skills Training Agency：STA　技能訓練局
social advocacy　社会的代弁
Social Care Institute for Excellence：SCIE　最良社会ケア研究所
social exclusion　社会的排除
social fund　社会基金
social housing　社会住宅

Social Insurance and Allied Services　社会保険および関連サービス
social policy　社会政策
Social Security　社会保障
Social Security Administration Act　社会保障管理法
Social Security Appeal Tribunals：SSAT　社会保障不服審査会
Social Security Contributions and Benefits Act　社会保障料および給付法
Social Security Pension Act　社会保障年金法
Social Service Department：SSD　社会福祉サービス部
social services　社会サービス
Social Services Inspectorate　社会サービス監査部
Social Services Inspectorate Standard　社会サービス監査基準
Special Temporary Employment Programme：STEP　特別臨時雇用事業
Special Transitional Grant　特別移行補助金
Speenhamland system　スピーナムランド制度
Standard Accountability　基準型財政責任
Standard Housing Benefit　標準住宅給付制度
Standard Spending Assessments　標準支出額
star rating　星評価；スターレイティング
State Earnings-Related Pension Scheme：SERPS　国家収入関連年金制度
state retirement pension　国家退職年金
statutory maternity pay：SMP　法定出産給与
statutory sick pay　法定傷病給付
statutory system　決定システム
Strategic Health Authorities　戦略的保健当局
Street Warden　街頭ウォーデン
subsistence minimum　生存最低限水準
supplementary benefit　補足給付
symbiotic relationship　共生関係
tax expenditure　租税支出
Temporary Short-Time Working Compensation Scheme　臨時短期就労補償事業
total purchasing　包括購入
Town and Country Planning Act　都市農村計画法
Toynbee Hall　トインビーホール
trade club　労働者クラブ
Training Agency：TA　職業訓練機関
Training and Enterprise Councils：TEC　職業訓練・企業協議会
Training for Work　就労訓練
training in industry scheme　企業内訓練事業
Training Opportunities Scheme：TOPS　職業訓練事業
Training Organization for Personal Social Service：TOPPS　対人社会サービス研修機構
Travel to Interview Scheme：TIS　地方面接支援
treasury grant　国庫補助

treasury supplement　国庫補足
unitary authority　地方自治制度
unitary development　単一開発計画
Universities Funding Council：UFC　大学資金協議会
University for Industry　産業大学
University Grants Committee：UGC　大学補助金委員会
upper earning limit：UEL　最高稼得収入額
Urban Development Corporation　都市開発公社
Urban District Councils　市部郡会
urban regeneration　都市再生
value for money：VFM　支出に見合う価値
Vocational Training and Education　職業教育訓練政策
voluntary activity　自発的行為
voluntary association　民間協会
voluntary organization　民間組織団体
voluntary sector　民間部門
voluntary social services　民間福祉
voluntary system　民間非営利団体システム
VSO　海外民間サービス
war pension　戦争年金
warden　管理人 [シルバーハウジング]
Warfare State　戦争国家
welfare pluralism　福祉多元主義
Welfare State　福祉国家
Welfare to Work　福祉から労働へ
White Paper Caring for People　コミュニティケア白書
Widowed Mother's Allowance：WMA　母子手当金
widow's benefit　寡婦給付
widow's payment：WPT　寡婦一時金
widow's pension：WP　寡婦年金
With Respect to Old Age　高齢者への尊敬の念を持って
Wolfenden Report　ウルフェンデン報告
work house　労役場
Workers Educational Association：WEA　労働者教育委員会
Workhouse Test Act　労役場テスト法
Working Family Tax Credit：WFTC　就労家族タックスクレジット
working for patients　患者のための活動
Youth Opportunities Programme：YOPs　若年者雇用機会事業
Youth Training Scheme：YTS　若年者訓練プログラム

英国
英和

1. 英国（イギリス）における介護福祉等関連用語【和　英】

新たな博愛（あらたなはくあい）　new philanthropy
安全措置命令（あんぜんそちめいれい）　place of safety order
5つの巨人（いつつのきょじん）　five giant evil
一般医（いっぱんい）　general practitioner：GP
一般国家職業資格（いっぱんこっかしょくぎょうしかく）　General National Vocational Qualification：GNVQ
医療介護士（いりょうかいごし）　Health Care Assistant：HCA
医療介護法（いりょうかいごほう）　Health and Social Care Act
医療裁定局（いりょうさいていきょく）　Adjudicating Medical Authorities：AMAs
医療不服審査会（いりょうふふくしんさかい）　Medical Appeal Tribunals：MAT
院外救済（いんがいきゅうさい）　outdoor-relief
院内救済（いんないきゅうさい）　indoor-relief
インフォーマルシステム（いんふぉーまるしすてむ）　informal system
ウッド委員会報告（うっどいいんかいほうこく）　Report of Wood Committee
ウルフェンデン報告（うるふぇんでんほうこく）　Wolfenden Report
英国国営くじ（えいこくこくえいたからくじ）　national lottery
英国国営宝くじ委員会（えいこくこくえいたからくじいんかい）　National Lotteries Control Board：NLCB
英国国民保険基金（えいこくこくみんほけんききん）　National Insurance Fund
英国国民保健サービス執行委員会（えいこくこくみんほけんさーびすしっこういいんかい）　NHS Executive
英国国立公園および田園地域法（えいこくこくりつこうえんおよびでんえんちいきほう）　National Parks and Countryside Act
英国国立最適保健医療研究所（えいこくこくりつさいてきほけんいりょうけんきゅうしょ）　National Institute for Health and Clinical Excellence：NICE
英国最低賃金制度（えいこくさいていちんぎんせいど）　national minimum wage
英国総合職業資格（えいこくそうごうしょくぎょうしかく）　General Vocational Qualification：GNVQ
英国ソーシャルワーカー協会（えいこくそーしゃるわーかーきょうかい）　British Association of Social Workers：BASW
英雄のための住居（えいゆうのためのじゅうきょ）　Homes Fit for Heroes
営利システム（えいりしすてむ）　commercial system

エリザベス救貧法（えりざべすきゅうひんぽう）　Elizabethan Poor Law［貧民救助法］
エルバーフェルト制度（えるばーふぇるとせいど）　Elberfeld system
援助ギルド（えんじょぎるど）　the Guild of Help
黄金律（おうごんりつ）　the Golden Rule
オプト・アウト（おぷと・あうと）　opting-out
オペレーショナル・ストラテジー（おぺーれーしょん・すとらてじー）　operational strategy：OS
海外民間サービス（かいがいみんかんさーびす）　VSO
介護者法（かいごしゃほう）　Carers Act
介護評価サービス法（かいごひょうかさーびすほう）　Carers Recognition and Service Act
改正救貧法（かいせいきゅうひんぽう）　New Poor Law
街頭ウォーデン（がいとううぉーでん）　Street Warden
下院（かいん）　House of Commons
カウンシル税（かうんしるぜい）　council tax
カウンシル税給付金（かうんしるぜいきゅうふきん）　council tax benefit
家事援助（かじえんじょ）　domestic help
家族クレジット（かぞくくれじっと）　family credit
家族支援（かぞくしえん）　family support
家族所得補足給付（かぞくしょとくほそくきゅうふ）　family income supplement
家族を扶養する単身女性全英協議会（かぞくをふようするたんしんじょせいぜんえいきょうぎかい）　National Council for the Single Woman and Her Dependents：NCSWD
家庭医（かてい）　general practitioner：GP
家庭保健サービス（かていほけんさーびす）　Family Health Services
寡婦一時金（かふいちじきん）　widow's payment：WPT
寡婦給付（かふきゅうふ）　widow's benefit
家父長主義（かふちょうしゅぎ）　paternalism
寡婦年金（かふねんきん）　Widow's Pension：WP
環境保護法（かんきょうほごほう）　Environment Protection Act
看護士（かんごかいごし）　nursing auxiliary：NA
監査委員会（かんさいいんかい）　Audit Commission
患者のための活動（かんじゃのためのかつどう）　working for patients
完全雇用（かんぜんこよう）　full employment
管理人（かんりにん）　warden［シルバーハウジング］
議会（ぎかい）　parliament
機会平等委員会（きかいびょうどういいんかい）　Equal Opportunities Commission
起業援助手当制度（きぎょうえんじょてあてせいど）

Enterprise Allowance Scheme
企業地域制度（きぎょうちいきせいど） enterprise zone
企業内訓練事業（きぎょうないくんれんじぎょう） training in industry scheme
疑似的市場（ぎじてきしじょう） quasi-market
基準型財政責任（きじゅんがたざいせいせきにん） standard accountability
基礎年金（きそねんきん） basic pension
技能訓練局（ぎのうくんれんきょく） Skills Training Agency：STA
技能センター（ぎのうせんたー） skill center
キャリア開発融資（きゃりあかいはつゆうし） Career Development Locus
救急医療（きゅうきゅういりょう） Accident and Emergency：A&E
求職活動手当金（きゅうしょくかつどうてあてきん） jobfinders grant
求職者手当金（きゅうしょくしゃてあてきん） jobseeker's allowance
救世軍（きゅうせいぐん） Salvation Army
救貧院（きゅうひんいん） almshouse
救貧法（きゅうひんほう） Poor Law
給与建て（きゅうよだて） salary-related
給料天引き寄付（きゅうりょうてんびききふ） payroll giving
教育・雇用省（きょういく・こようしょう） Department for Education and Employment
教育法（きょういくほう） Education Act
共生関係（きょうせいかんけい） symbiotic relationship
強制競争入札（きょうせいきょうそうにゅうさつ） Compulsory Competitive Tendering：CCT
業績評価枠組み（ぎょうせきひょうかわくぐみ） Performance Assessment Framework：PAF
共同性（きょうどうせい） commonality
業務災害死亡給付（ぎょうむさいがいしぼうきゅうふ） industrial death benefit
業務災害障害年金（ぎょうむさいがいしょうがいねんきん） Industrial Injuries Disablement Pension
拠出制給付（きょしゅつせいきゅうふ） contributory benefits
拠出建て（きょしゅつだて） money purchase
拠出年金法（きょしゅつねんきんほう） Contributory Pensions Act
挙証責任条項（きょしょうせきにんじょうこう） Genuinely-seeking-the Job Clause
ギルバート法（ぎるばーとほう） Gilbert's Act
勤労者階級住宅法（きんろうしゃかいきゅうじゅうたくほう） Housing of Working Class Act
苦情処理手続き（くじょうしょりてつづき） complaints procedure
繰り出し梯子モデル（くりだしてこもでる） model of an extension ladder
グリフィス報告書（ぐりふぃすほうこくしょ） Griffith Report
ケア基準委員会（けあきじゅんいいんかい） Commissions for Care Standards；Care Standards Commission
ケア基準法（けあきじゅんほう） Care Standard Act
経営管理主義（けいえいかんりしゅぎ） managerialism
経済社会研究委員会（けいざいしゃかいけんきゅういいんかい） Economic and Social Research Council
継続教育（けいぞくきょういく） continuing education；further education
契約文化（けいやくぶんか） contract culture
下宿法（げじゅくほう） Lodging House Act
決定システム（けっていしすてむ） statutory system
限界的財政責任（げんかいてきざいせいせきにん） marginal accountability
現金給付（げんきんきゅうふ） cash benefit；direct payment
源泉徴収（げんせんちょうしゅう） pay-as-you-earn：PAYE
建築協会（けんちくきょうかい） Building Society
現物給付（げんぶつきゅうふ） benefit in kind
公共支出調査委員会（こうきょうししゅつちょうさいいんかい） Public Expenditure Survey Committee：PESC
公共選択（こうきょうせんたく） public choice
公私分離モデル（こうしぶんりもでる） separate spheres model
工場法（こうじょうほう） Factory Act
更生保護法（こうせいほごほう） Offenders Rehabilitation Act
公正家賃（こうせいやちん） fair rent
控訴院（こうそいん） Court of Appeal
公的サービス（こうてきさーびす） Favored Goods
合同委員会（ごうどういいんかい） consortium
行動規範（こうどうきはん） the Golden Rule
高等教育（こうとうきょういく） higher education
高等教育資金協議会（こうとうきょういくしきんきょうぎかい） Higher Education Funding Councils
購入者（こうにゅうしゃ） purchaser
購入者・提供者分離（こうにゅうしゃ・ていきょうしゃぶんり） purchaser-provider split
公務員済生基金（こうむいんさいせいききん） Civil Service Benevolent Fund
高齢者早期退職制度（こうれいしゃそうきたいしょくせいど） Job Release Scheme
高齢者への尊敬の念を持って（こうれいしゃへのそんけいのねんをもって） With Respect to Old Age
国民扶助法（こくみんふじょほう） National Assistance Act

国民保険（こくみんほけん） national insurance
個人学習口座（こじんがくしゅうこうざ） individual learning account
個人手当（こじんてあて） personal allowance
個人年金政策（こじんねんきんせいさく） personal pension schemes
国家収入関連年金制度（こっかしゅうにゅうかんれんねんきんせいど） State Earnings-Related Pension Scheme：SERPS
国家退職年金（こっかたいしょくねんきん） state retirement pension
国庫補助（こっこほじょ） treasury grant
国庫補足（こっこほそく） treasury supplement
コミュニティケア改革（こみゅにてぃけあかいかく） community care reform
コミュニティケア行動計画指針（こみゅにてぃけあこうどうけいかくししん） Community Care：Agenda for Action
コミュニティケア政策要綱（こみゅにてぃけあせいさくようこう） Community Care-policy guidance
コミュニティケア白書（こみゅにてぃけあはくしょ） the White Paper Caring for People
雇用および訓練法（こようおよびくんれんほう） Employment and Training Act
雇用機会創出計画（こようきかいそうしゅつけいかく） Job Creation Programme
災害避難貸付金（さいがいひなんかしつけきん） Crisis Loan
最高稼得収入額（さいこうかとくしゅうにゅうがく） upper earning limit：UEL
最高の価値計画（さいこうのかちけいかく） Best Value Programme
在宅看護（ざいたくかんご） home nursing
在宅サービス（ざいたくさーびす） domiciliary service
最低稼得収入額（さいていかとくしゅうにゅうがく） lower earnings limit
裁定官（さいていかん） Adjudication Officer：AO
最低保障年金（さいていほしょうねんきん） Guaranteed Minimum Pension：GMP
歳入援助交付金（さいにゅうえんじょこうふきん） revenue support grant
財務管理イニシアチブ（ざいむかんりいにしあちぶ） Financial Management Initiative：FMI
最良社会ケア研究所（さいりょうしゃかいけあけんきゅうしょ） Social Care Institute for Excellence：SCIE
ソーシャルケアコース（そーしゃるけあこーす） In-Service Course in Social Care：ICSC
サービス提供団体（さーびすていきょうだんたい） providing authority
産業大学（さんぎょうだいがく） University for Industry

産業別訓練委員会（さんぎょうべつくんれんいいんかい） Industry Training Board：ITB
産業別訓練組織（さんぎょうべつくんれんそしき） Industry Training Organization：ITO
暫定課税徴収法（ざんていかぜいちょうしゅうほう） Provisional Collection of Taxes Act
自営業促進（じえいぎょうそくしん） Help Scheme for Becoming Self-Employment
シェルタード・ハウジング（しぇるたーど・はうじんぐ） sheltered housing
シェルタード・ハウス（しぇるたーど・はうす） sheltered house
資格・カリキュラム当局（しかく・かりきゅらむとうきょく） Qualifications and Curriculum Authority：QCA
事業者（じぎょうしゃ） provider
支出に見合う価値（ししゅつにみあうかち） value for money：VFM
施設サービス（しせつさーびす） residential service
施設登録審査会（しせつとうろくしんさかい） Registered Home Tribunal
施設登録法（しせつとうろくほう） Registered Homes Act
慈善（じぜん） charity
慈善学校（じぜんがっこう） charity school
慈善組織協会（じぜんそしききょうかい） Charity Organization Society：COS
慈善トラスト（じぜんとらすと） charitable trust
慈善病院（じぜんびょういん） charity hospital
慈善用途法（じぜんようとほう） Charitable Uses Act
自治体監査委員会（じちたいかんさいいんかい） Audit Commission
実習教員資格（じっしゅうきょういんしかく） Practice Teaching Award
疾病給付（しっぺいきゅうふ） sickness benefit
児童援護エイジェンシー（じどうえんごえいじぇんしー） Child Support Agency：CSA
児童虐待（じどうぎゃくたい） child abuse and neglect
児童給付（じどうきゅうふ） child benefit
児童支援法（じどうしえんほう） Child Support Act
児童手当（じどうてあて） children's allowances
児童手当法（じどうてあてほう） Child Benefit Act
児童剥奪（じどうはくだつ） child deprivation
児童貧困行動グループ（じどうひんこんこうどうぐるーぷ） Child Poverty Action Group：CPAG
児童への体罰禁止（じどうへのたいばつきんし） End Physical Punishment of Children
児童法（じどうほう） Children's Act
児童法律センター（じどうほうりつせんたー） Children's Legal Center
児童保護（じどうほご） child protection

児童保護官（じどうほごかん）child care officer
自発的行為（じはつてきこうい）voluntary activity
市部郡会（しぶぐんかい）Urban District Councils
死亡一時金（しぼういちじきん）funeral payment
シーボーム報告書（しーぼーむほうこくしょ）Seebohm Report
市民アドバイスビューロー（しみんあどばいすびゅーろー）Citizen Advice Bureau
市民憲章（しみんけんしょう）Citizens' Chapter
市民権（しみんけん）citizenship
市民相談所（しみんそうだんしょ）Citizens Advice Bureau
社会基金（しゃかいききん）Social Fund
社会サービス（しゃかいさーびす）social services
社会サービス監査基準（しゃかいさーびすかんさきじゅん）Social Services Inspectorate Standard
社会サービス監査部（しゃかいさーびすかんさぶ）Social Services Inspectorate
社会サービスの近代化（しゃかいさーびすのきんだいか）Modernizing Social Services
社会住宅（しゃかいじゅうたく）social housing
社会政策（しゃかいせいさく）social policy
社会的代弁（しゃかいてきだいべん）social advocacy
社会的排除（しゃかいてきはいじょ）social exclusion
社会福祉サービス部（しゃかいふくしさーびすぶ）Social Service Department：SSD
社会保険および関連サービス（しゃかいほけんおよびかんれんさーびす）Social Insurance and Allied Services
社会保障（しゃかいほしょう）Social Security
社会保障管理法（しゃかいほしょうかんりほう）Social Security Administration Act
社会保障給付費（しゃかいほしょうきゅうふひ）cost of Social Security
社会保障省（しゃかいほしょうしょう）Department of Social Security：DDS
社会保障年金法（しゃかいほしょうねんきんほう）Social Security Pension Act
社会保障不服審査会（しゃかいほしょうふふくしんさかい）Social Security Appeal Tribunals：SSAT
社会保障料および給付法（しゃかいほしょうりょうおよびきゅうふほう）Social Security Contributions and Benefits Act
借地権（しゃくちけん）leasehold
若年者訓練プログラム（じゃくねんしゃくんれんぷろぐらむ）Youth Training Scheme：YTS
若年者雇用機会事業（じゃくねんしゃこようきかいじぎょう）Youth Opportunities Programme：YOPs
州および特別市会（しゅうおよびとくべつしかい）Country and County Borough Councils

就業換算率（しゅうぎょうかんさんりつ）replacement rates
就業助言（しゅうぎょうじょげん）Advisory Programmers
就職相談会（しゅうしょくそうだんかい）Job Club
住宅給付（じゅうたくきゅうふ）housing benefit
住宅協会（じゅうたくきょうかい）Housing Association
住宅検査官制度（じゅうたくけんさかんせいど）housing inspector
住宅・都市計画法（じゅうたく・としけいかくほう）Housing, Town and Country Planning Act
住宅補助金制度（じゅうたくほじょきんせいど）housing benefit
住宅緑書（じゅうたくりょくしょ）Housing Green Paper
住宅ローン金利補助制度（じゅうたくろーんきんりほじょせいど）income support for mortgage interest payments
重度障害者手当金（じゅうどしょうがいしゃてあてきん）severe disablement allowance
収入・支出権限制限（しゅうにゅう・ししゅつけんげんせいげん）capping
自由保有権（じゆうほゆうけん）freehold
就労開始手当（しゅうろうかいしてあて）jobstart allowance
就労家族タックスクレジット（しゅうろうかぞくたっくすくれじっと）Working Family Tax Credit：WFTC
就労訓練（しゅうろうくんれん）Training for Work
就労不能手当（しゅうろうふのうてあて）incapacity benefit
出産一時金（しゅっさんいちじきん）maternity grant
出産手当（しゅっさんてあて）maternity allowance：MA
守備範囲の見直し（しゅびはんいのみなおし）rolling back
準市場（じゅんしじょう）quasi-market
上院（じょういん）House of Lords
障害給付（しょうがいきゅうふ）invalidity benefit
生涯教育（しょうがいきょういく）lifelong education
障害者介護手当金（しょうがいしゃかいごてあてきん）invalid care allowance
障害者就労手当金（しょうがいしゃしゅうろうてあてきん）disability working allowance
障害者生活手当金（しょうがいしゃせいかつてあてきん）disability living allowance：DLA
障害者タックスクレジット（しょうがいしゃたっくすくれじっと）Disabled Persons Tax Credit：DPTC
条件整備（じょうけんせいび）enabling
条件整備型自治体（じょうけんせいびがたじちたい）enabling authority［条件整備団体］

英国和英

常時付き添い手当（じょうじつきそいてあて） constant attendance allowance：CAA
初級ソーシャルケア資格（しょきゅうそーしゃるけあしかく） Preliminary Certificate in Social Care：PCSC
職域年金（しょくいきねんきん） occupational pension
職域年金委員会（しょくいきねんきんいいんかい） Occupational Pensions Board
職域年金管理委員会（しょくいきねんきんかんりいいんかい） Occupational Pension Regulatory Authority：OPRA
職業教育訓練政策（しょくぎょうきょういくくんれんせいさく） Vocational Education and Training
職業訓練機関（しょくぎょうくんれんきかん） Training Agency：TA
職業訓練・企業協議会（しょくぎょうくんれん・きぎょうきょうぎかい） Training and Enterprise Councils：TEC
職業訓練事業（しょくぎょうくんれんじぎょう） Training Opportunities Scheme：TOPS
職業紹介事業（しょくぎょうしょうかいじぎょう） Job Introduction Scheme
職業能力評価制度（しょくぎょうのうりょくひょうかせいど） National Vocational Qualification：NVQ
職工学院（しょくこうがくいん） Mechanics' Institutes
職探し援助（しょくさがしえんじょ） Help for the Unemployed in Seeking Work
職探しセミナー（しょくさがしせみなー） job search seminar
食事配達サービス（しょくじはいたつさーびす） Meals on Wheels：MoW
職人および労働者住居改善法（しょくにんおよびろうどうしゃじゅうきょかいぜんほう） Artisans and Labourers Dwelling Improvement Act
職人および労働者住居法（しょくにんおよびろうどうしゃじゅうきょほう） Artisans and Labourers Dwelling Act
職場復帰ボーナス（しょくばふっきぼーなす） Back to Work Bonus
所得維持（しょとくいじ） income maintenance
所得関連給付（しょとくかんれんきゅうふ） income-related benefit
所得補助（しょとくほじょ） income support
所得保障（しょとくほしょう） income maintenance
ジョブ・インタビュー・ギャランティー（じょぶ・いんたびゅー・ぎゃらんてぃー） Job Interview Guarantee Scheme：JIG
ジョブショップ（じょぶしょっぷ） jobshops
ジョブセンター（じょぶせんたー） Job Center
シングルアセスメント（しんぐるあせすめんと） single assessment：SAP

新公共管理（しんこうきょうかんり） New Public Management：NPM
審査会（しんさかい） panel
人種平等委員会（じんしゅびょうどういいんかい） Commission for Racial Equality
人的社会サービス（じんてきしゃかいさーびす） personal social services：PSS
人頭税（じんとうぜい） poll tax
新都市開発法（しんとしかいはつほう） New Town Act
人民資本主義（じんみんしほんしゅぎ） People's Capitalism
スコットランド職業教育協会（すこっとらんどしょくぎょうきょういくきょうかい） Scottish Vocational Education Council：SCOTVEC
スコットランド職業資格（すこっとらんどしょくぎょうしかく） Scottish Vocational Qualification：SVQ
スコットランド総合職業資格（すこっとらんどそうごうしょくぎょうしかく） Scottish General Vocational Qualification：GSVQ
スターレイティング（すたーれいてぃんぐ） star rating
スピーナムランド制度（すぴーなむらんどせいど） Speenhamland system
生活資金一時貸付金（せいかつしきんいちじかしつけきん） budgeting loan
聖職者議員（せいしょくしゃぎいん） Lords Spiritual
精神心神状況法（せいしんしんじょうほう） Lunacy Act
精神欠陥法（せいしんけっかんほう） Mental Deficiency Act
精神障害特別補助金（せいしんしょうがいとくべつほじょきん） Mental Illness Specific Grants：MISG
精神福祉全英連合会（せいしんふくしぜんえいれんごうかい） Central Association for Mental Welfare
精神保健中核グループ（せいしんほけんちゅうかくぐるーぷ） Mental Health Core Group
精神保健法（せいしんほけんほう） Mental Health Act
生存最低限水準（せいぞんさいていげんすいじゅん） subsistence minimum
政府ケア審議会（せいふけあしんぎかい） National Care Commission
政府助成校（せいふじょせいこう） Grant Maintained Schools：GMSs
性別差別禁止法（せいべつさべつきんしほう） Sex Discrimination Act
世俗議員（せぞくぎいん） Lords Temporal
世帯給付（せたいきゅうふ） family credit
世帯所得補足制度（せたいしょとくほそくせいど） Family Income Supplement
説明責任（せつめいせきにん） accountability

全英介護者協会（ぜんえいかいごしゃきょうかい）
Carers National Association
全英介護者戦略（ぜんえいかいごしゃせんりゃく）
National Care Strategy
全英家族介護者協会（ぜんえいかぞくかいごしゃきょうかい）　Carers National Association：CAN
全英ケア基準委員会（ぜんえいけあきじゅんいいんかい）
National Care Service Committee：NCSC
全英国民経済発展委員会（ぜんえいこくみんけいざいはってんいいんかい）　National Economic Development Council：NEDC
全英国民保健サービス(ぜんえいこくみんほけんさーびす)
National Health Service：NHS
全英国民保健サービス改善計画（ぜんえいこくみんほけんさーびすかいぜんけいかく）　National Health Service Improvement Plan：NHSIP
全英国民保健サービス・コミュニティケア法（ぜんえいこくみんほけんさーびす・こみゅにてぃけあほう）
National Health Services and Community Care Act
全英国民保健サービストラスト（ぜんえいこくみんほけんさーびすとらすと）　National Health Service Trust：NHS Trust
全英国民保健サービス法（ぜんえいこくみんほけんさーびすほう）　National Health Service Act
全英コミュニティケア法(ぜんえいこみゅにてぃけあほう)
National Health Service and Community Act
全英サービスフレームワーク（ぜんえいさーびすふれーむわーく）　National Service Framework：NSF
全英児童虐待防止協会（ぜんえいじどうぎゃくたいぼうしきょうかい）　National Society for the Prevention of Cruelty to Children：NSPCC
全英社会福祉協議会（ぜんえいしゃかいふくしきょうぎかい）　National Council for Social Services：NCSS
全英障害協議会（ぜんえいしょうがいきょうぎかい）
National Disability Council
全英職業資格協会（ぜんえいしょくぎょうしかくきょうかい）　National Council for Vocational Qualification：NCVQ
全英ソーシャルワーカー協会（ぜんえいそーしゃるわーかーきょうかい）　British Association of Social Workers：BASW
全英ボランティア活動センター（ぜんえいぼらんてぃあかつどうせんたー）　National Centre for Volunteering：NCV
全英民間組織協議会（ぜんえいみんかんそしききょうぎかい）　National Council for Voluntary Organization：NCVO
1995年障害者差別禁止法（せんきゅうひゃくきゅうじゅうごねんしょうがいしゃさべつきんしほう）
Disability Discrimination Act 1995
1998年全国最低賃金法（せんきゅうひゃくきゅうじゅうはちねんぜんこくさいていちんぎんほう）
National Minimum Wage Act 1998
1989年児童法（せんきゅうひゃくはちじゅうきゅうねんじどうほう）　Children Act 1989
1986年障害者法（せんきゅうひゃくはちじゅうろくねんしょうがいしゃほう）　Disabled Person Act 1986
戦争国家（せんそうこっか）　Warfare State
戦争年金（せんそうねんきん）　war pension
選択指導書（せんたくしどうしょ）　Direction on Choice
戦略的保健当局（せんりゃくてきほけんとうきょく）
Strategic Health Authorities
総合社会ケア協議会（そうごうしゃかいけあきょうぎかい）　General Social Care Council：GSCC
組織統治（そしきとうち）　governance
ソーシャルケアコース（そーしゃるけあこーす）
In-Service Course in Social Care：ICSC
ソーシャルケア査察委員会（そーしゃるけあささついいんかい）　Commission for Social Care Inspection：CSCI
ソーシャルサービス資格（そーしゃるさーびすしかく）
Certificate in Social Service：CSS
ソーシャルワーク資格（そーしゃるわーくしかく）
Diploma in Social Work：Dip. SW
ソーシャルワーク認定資格（そーしゃるわーくにんていしかく）　Certificate of Qualification in Social Work：CQSW
租税支出（そぜいししゅつ）　tax expenditure
村部市会（そんぶしかい）　Rural District Councils
大学資金協議会（だいがくしきんきょうぎかい）
Universities Funding Council：UFC
大学補助金委員会（だいがくほじょきんいいんかい）
University Grants Committee：UGC
退職年金（たいしょくねんきん）　retirement pension
対人社会サービス（たいじんしゃかいさーびす）
personal social services
対人社会サービス研修機構（たいじんしゃかいさーびすけんしゅうきこう）　Training Organization for Personal Social Service：TOPPS
大都市圏（だいとしけん）　metropolitan area
多課程制学校（たかていせいがっこう）　multilateral school
単一開発計画（たんいつかいはつけいかく）　unitary development
段階制年金（だんかいせいねんきん）　graduated pension：GP
暖房費補助（だんぼうひほじょ）　cold weather payment
地域ケア基準委員会（ちいきけあきじゅんいいんかい）
Regional Commission for Care Standard
地域ケア支援一時金（ちいきけあしえんいちじきん）
community care grant

地域サービス・ボランティア（ちいきさーびす・ぼらんてぃあ） Community Service Volunteers : CSV
地域社会（ちいきしゃかい） community
地域精神保健チーム（ちいきせいしんほけんちーむ） community mental health team
地方政府法（ちいきせいふほう） Local Government Act
地域保健当局（ちいきほけんとうきょく） District Health Authorities : DHAs
地方教育局（ちほうきょういくきょく） Local Education Authority
地方自治制度（ちほうじちせいど） unitary authority
地方自治体計画報告（ちほうじちたいけいかくほうこく） Local Authority Planning Statement : LAPS
地方自治体社会サービス部（ちほうじちたいしゃかいさーびすぶ） Social Services Department : SSD
地方自治体社会サービス法（ちほうじちたいしゃかいさーびすほう） Local Authority Social Service Act
地方税支援補助金（ちほうぜいしえんほじょきん） rate support grant
地方政府（ちほうせいふ） local government
地方当局（ちほうとうきょく） local authority
地方統治（ちほうとうち） local governance
地方分権化（ちほうぶんけんか） local devolution
地方保健当局（ちほうほけんとうきょく） Regional Health Authorities
地方面接支援（ちほうめんせつしえん） travel to interview scheme : TIS
中央ソーシャルワーク教育研修協議会（ちゅうおうそーしゃるわーくきょういくけんしゅうきょうぎかい） Central Council for Education and Training in Social Work : CCETSW
昼食クラブ（ちゅうしょくくらぶ） luncheon club
中等教育（ちゅうとうきょういく） secondary education
中等教育資格（ちゅうとうきょういくしかく） Certificate of Secondary Education : CSE
長期介護に関する王立委員会（ちょうきかいごにかんするおうりついいんかい） Royal Commission on Long Term Care
直接支払い制度（ちょくせつしはらいせいど） direct payment
付添い手当金（つきそいてあてきん） attendance allowance
積立方式（つみたてほうしき） funding scheme
適格個人年金（てきかくこじんねんきん） appropriate personal pensions : APP
適用除外（てきようじょがい） contact out
トインビーホール（といんびーほーる） Toynbee Hall
登録ホーム法（とうろくほーむほう） Registered Homes Act
特別移行補助金（とくべついこうほじょきん） Special Transitional Grant
特別重度障害手当（とくべつじゅうどしょうがいてあて） Exceptionally Severe Disablement Allowance : SDA
特別臨時雇用事業（とくべつりんじこようじぎょう） Special Temporary Employment Programme : STEP
都市開発公社（としかいはつこうしゃ） Urban Development Corporation
都市再生（としさいせい） urban regeneration
都市・農村計画法（とし・のうそんけいかくほう） Town and Country Planning Act
都心地域法（としんちいきほう） Inner Urban Area Act
内部市場（ないぶしじょう） internal market
二元的システム（にじてきしすてむ） binary system
二重政体（にじゅうせいたい） dual polity
ニーズ主導（にーずしゅどう） needs-led
2005年意思決定能力法（にせんごねんいしけっていのうりょくほう） Mental Capacity Act 2005
入所施設（にゅうしょしせつ） residential home
ニューパブリックマネジメント（にゅーぱぶりっくまねじめんと） New Public Management : NPM
任意付加保険料（にんいふかほけんりょう） Additional Voluntary Contributions : AVCs
認定後研修（にんていごけんしゅう） post qualifying studies : PQS
認定ソーシャルワーカー（にんていそーしゃるわーかー） Certificate in Social Work : CSW
妊婦サービス（にんぷさーびす） maternity service
ネクストステップス改革（ねくすとすてっぷかいかく） Improving Management in Government-The Next Steps
年齢加算（ねんれいかさん） age addition
農村地域協議会（のうそんちいききょうぎかい） RCC
能率監査（のうりつかんさ） efficiency scrutinies
博愛協会（はくあいきょうかい） associated philanthropy
博愛事業（はくあいじぎょう） philanthropy
白痴法（はくちほう） Idiot Act
バークレイ報告書（ばーくれいほうこくしょ） Barclay Report
パッチ基盤システム（ぱっちきばんしすてむ） patch-based system
ひとり親給付（ひとりおやきゅうふ） one-parent benefit
批判的共同社会論（ひはんてきききょうどうしゃかいろん） Critical Association
病後の介護（びょうごのかいご） after-care
標準支出額（ひょうじゅんししゅつがく） Standard Spending Assessments
標準住宅給付制度（ひょうじゅんじゅうたくきゅうふせいど） Standard Housing Benefit

貧民救助法（ひんみんきゅうじょほう）Elizabethan Poor Law ［エリザベス救貧法］
貧民保護委員会（ひんみんほごいいんかい）Board of Poor Law Guardians
ファンデーショントラスト（ふぁんでーしょんとらすと）Foundation Trust：FT
フェビアン主義（ふぇびあんしゅぎ）Fabianism
付加保険料（ふかほけんりょう）Free-Standing Additional Voluntary Contributions：FSAVC
福祉から労働へ（ふくしからろうどうへ）Welfare to Work
福祉国家（ふくしこっか）Welfare State
福祉多元主義（ふくしたげんしゅぎ）welfare pluralism
不適切処遇（ふてきせつしょぐう）maltreatment
プライマリ・ケアグループ（ぷらいまり・けあぐるーぷ）primary care group：PCG
プライマリ・ケアトラスト（ぷらいまり・けあとらすと）Primary Care Trust：PCT
ブルー・バッジ・スキーム（ぶるー・ばっじ・すきーむ）Blue Badge Scheme
フレキシブル・ケア・アテンダンス（ふれきしぶる・けあ・あてんだんす）flexible care attendance
フレキシブル・レスパイト（ふれきしぶる・れすぱいと）flexible respite
分権的多元主義（ぶんけんてきたげんしゅぎ）decentralized pluralism
平行棒理論（へいこうぼうりろん）parallel bars theory
ベヴァリッジ報告書（べうぁりっじほうこくしょ）Beveridge Report
ベストバリュー（べすとばりゅー）best value：BV
ベッドを塞ぐ人（べっどをふさぐひと）bed blocker
保育所（ほいくしょ）day nursery
保育所およびチャイルドマインダー法（ほいくしょおよびちゃいるどまいんだーほう）Nurseries and Child-Minders Regulation Act
保育タックスクレジット（ほいくたっくすくれじっと）Child Care Tax Credit：CCTC
保育ママ（ほいくまま）child minding
包括購入（ほうかつにゅう）total purchasing
包括的支出見直し（ほうかつてきししゅつみなおし）Comprehensive Spending Review
包括的保健サービスおよびリハビリテーション（ほうかつてきほけんさーびすおよびりはびりてーしょん）Comprehensive Health Services and Rehabilitation
法定出産給与（ほうていしゅっさんきゅうよ）statutory maternity pay：SMP
法定傷病給付（ほうていしょうびょうきゅうふ）statutory sick pay
保健医療改善委員会（ほけんいりょうかいぜんいいんかい）Commission for Health Improvement：CHI

保健局（ほけんきょく）Health Boards
保健師（ほけんし）health visitor
保健当局（ほけんとうきょく）health authority
保護（ほご）custody
保護者手当（ほごしゃてあて）guardians benefit
保護者手当金（ほごしゃてあてきん）guardian's allowance
母子手当金（ほしてあてきん）widowed mother's allowance：WMA
星評価（ほしひょうか）star rating
補足給付（ほそくきゅうふ）supplementary benefit
マンパワー・サービスコミッション（まんぱわー・さーびすこみっしょん）Manpower Services Commission：MSC
ミールズ・オン・ウィール（みーるず・おん・うぃーる）Meals on Wheels
民営化（みんえいか）privatisation
民営化政策（みんえいかせいさく）privatisation policy
民間協会（みんかんきょうかい）voluntary association
民間組織団体（みんかんそしきだんたい）voluntary organization
民間非営利団体システム（みんかんひえいりだんたいすてむ）voluntary system
民間福祉（みんかんふくし）voluntary social services
民間福祉協議会（みんかんふくしきょうぎかい）CVS
民間部門（みんかんぶもん）voluntary sector
民衆資本主義（みんしゅうしほんしゅぎ）popular capitalism
無拠出制給付（むきょしゅつせいきゅうふ）non-contributory benefit
無拠出退職年金（むきょしゅつたいしょくねんきん）non-contributory retirement pension
ムーディ報告書（むーでぃほうこくしょ）Moodie Report
無料子ども電話相談事業（むりょうこどもでんわそうだんじぎょう）ChildLine
盲人法（もうじんほう）Blind Persons Law
持家（もちいえ）owner-occupation
役割遂行（やくわりすいこう）performance
家賃減額（やちんげんがく）rent rebate
家賃査定委員会（やちんさていいいんかい）Rent Assessment Committee
家賃審判所（やちんしんぱんしょ）rent tribunal
家賃手当（やちんてあて）rent allowance
家賃法（やちんほう）Rent Act
家賃補助（やちんほじょ）rent rebate
友愛組合（ゆうあいくみあい）Friendly Society
郵便番号宝くじ（ゆうびんばんごうたからくじ）postcode lottery
ゆりかごから墓場まで（ゆりかごからはかばまで）

英国和英

from-cradle-to-grave
養老院（ようろういん） almshouse
予算保持一般医（よさんほじいっぱんい） general practitioner（GP）fundholding
ヨーロッパ連合（よーろっぱれんごう） European Union
臨時短期就労補償事業（りんじたんきしゅうろうほしょうじぎょう） Temporary Short-Time Working Compensation Scheme
隣友運動（りんゆううんどう） neighborhood movement
レスパイトケア（れすぱいとけあ） respite care
労役場テスト法（ろうえきじょうてすとほう） Workhouse Test Act
労災給付（ろうさいきゅうふ） industrial injuries benefit
老人ホーム（ろうじんほーむ） residential home
労働者教育委員会(ろうどうしゃきょういくいいんかい) Workers Educational Association：WEA
労働者クラブ（ろうどうしゃくらぶ） trade club
労働不能給付（ろうどうふのうきゅうふ） incapacity benefit
老年年金法（ろうねんねんきんほう） Old Persons Act
労役場（ろええきじょう） work house

2. 豪州（オーストラリア）における介護福祉等関連用語【英　和】

Aboriginal and Torres Strait Islander Health Performance Framework　アボリジニ・トレス海峡島民健康パフォーマンスフレームワーク
Aboriginal Community Controlled Health Services：ACCHS　アボリジニ地域医療サービス
Aboriginal Medical Services：AMS　アボリジニ医療サービス
ACAT：Aged Care Assessment Team　高齢者ケア評価チーム
accommodation bond　施設保証金
accommodation charge　入居料
Accountability Principles 1998　1998 年責任原則
Accreditation Grant Principles 1999　1999 年認証金原則
Activity Therapy Centre　活動セラピーセンター
Advocacy Grant Principles 1997　1997 年擁護許可原則
Age Care Education and Training Incentive program：ACETI　高齢者介護教育・トレーニングプログラム
age pension　老齢年金
Aged and Community Services Australia　豪州高齢者・地域サービス
Aged Care Assessment Service：ACAS　高齢者ケア評価サービス
Aged Care Assessment Team：ACAT　高齢者ケア評価チーム
Aged Care Association Australia　豪州高齢者介護協会
Aged Care Commissioner　高齢者介護調査委員
Aged Care Complaints Investigation Scheme　高齢者介護苦情調査計画
Aged Care Complaints Resolution System：ACCRS　高齢者ケア苦情処理システム
Aged Care Funding Instrument：ACFI　高齢者ケア補助金支給制度
aged care homes for Aboriginal and Torres Strait Islander people　アボリジニ・トレス海峡島民向け老人ホーム
Aged Care Information Line　高齢者ケア情報ライン
Aged Care Reform Strategy　高齢者ケア改革戦略
Aged Care Standards Agency　高齢者ケア基準委員会
Aged Care Standards and Accreditation Agency　高齢者ケア基準・認定エージェンシー
Aged Care Structural Reform　高齢者ケア構造改革
Aged or disabled Persons Care Act　高齢者・障害者介護法
Aged or disabled Persons Home Act　高齢者・障害者住宅法
Aged Person Home Act　高齢者住宅法

Aged Rights Advocacy Service　高齢者権利擁護サービス
Ageing in Place　高齢者一括介護施設
Allocation Principles 1997　1997 年配分原則
Alzheimer's Australia　豪州アルツハイマー病協会
Approval of Care Recipients Principles 1997　1997 年介護受領者原則の承認
Approved Provider Principles 1997　1997 年認可事業者原則
Arthritis Australia　豪州関節炎協会
Assistance with Care and Housing for the Aged：ACHA　高齢者のための介護と住宅援助
attendant allowance　アテンダント手当
Australian Council for Rehabilitation of Disabled　豪州障害リハビリテーション協議会
Australian Council of Trade Union：ACTU　豪州労働組合評議会
Australian Government Directory of Services for Older People 2010　2010 年度豪州政府機関高齢者サービス案内書
Australian Immunisation Handbook　豪州予防接種ハンドブック
Australian Institute of Health and Welfare　豪州保健福祉協会
Australian Institute of Health and Welfare Act 1987　1987 年豪州保健福祉研究所法
Australian Physiotherapy Association　豪州理学治療協会
Beyondblue　全豪うつ病運動
Bladder and Bowel Foundation　膀胱・腸の健康財団
Breast Screen Australia　全豪胸部スクリーン
bulk billing　バルクビリング
Cancer Council of Australia　豪州癌協議会
Care Aggregated Module：CAM　ケア費用集計基準
Carelink Center　ケアリンクセンター
carer allowance　介護者手当
Carer Resource Center　介護者資源センター
carer respite care　介護者レスパイトケア
Carer Respite Center　介護者レスパイトケアセンター
Carers Australia　豪州介護者協会
Carers Victoria　介護者ビクトリア
CareSearch　ケアサーチ
Centre for Grief Education　悲観教育センター
Centrelink　センターリンク
Certification Principles 1997　1997 年認定原則
Charter of Rights and Responsibilities for Community Care　地域ケアの権利と責任憲章
Classification Principles 1997　1997 年分類法原則
Cognitive Dementia and Memory Services：CDAMS　認知症・記憶サービス

豪州英和

Commonwealth Carelink Centres 豪州連邦ケアリンクセンター
Commonwealth Rehabilitation Service 豪州連邦リハビリテーション庁
Commonwealth Respite and Carelink Centres 豪州連邦レスパイト・ケアリンクセンター
Community Aged Care Package：CACP 地域高齢者ケアパッケージ
Community Care Grant Principles 1997 1997年地域ケア許可原則
Community Care Service Finder 地域ケアサービス検索サイト
Community Care Subsidy Principles 1997 1997年地域ケア助成金原則
Community Liaison Advisory Safety Project：CLASP 地域諮問安全プロジェクト
Community Nursing and Health Centre 地域看護・医療センター
Community Option Projects：COP コミュニティ・オプション・プロジェクト
Community Partners Program コミュニティ・パートナー・プログラム
Community Service Orders Scheme 地域サービス計画
Community Visitors Grant Principles 1997 1997年コミュニティ訪問者交付金原則
Community Visitors Scheme コミュニティ訪問客計画
Compassionate Friends 慈悲の友
compensable resident 補償対象入所者
Complaints Investigation Scheme 苦情調査サービス
Compulsory Competitive Tendering：CCT 強制的競争入札制度
concessional resident 割引適用入所者
concessional resident supplement 割引該当入所者補償
conditional adjustment payment 条件付き支払い
Consumer Medicine Information：CMI 消費者医療情報
Continence Aids Assistance Scheme 失禁援助計画
Continence Aids Payment Scheme 失禁援助支払い計画
Continence Foundation of Australia 豪州失禁財団
Council on the Ageing：COTA 高齢者協議会
Council on the Ageing Strategy：COTA Strategy 高齢者協議会運動戦略
daily care fee 日常介護費
Day Therapy Centres デイセラピーセンター
days of grace 保険料払込猶予期間
Delivered Meals Subsidy Act 宅配給食サービス助成法
Dementia and Memory Community Centres 認知症・記憶障害地域センター

Dementia Behaviour Management Advisory Service：DBMAS 認知症行動管理サービス
Department of Health and Ageing 保健老齢局
Diabetes Australia 豪州糖尿病協会
Dietary Guidelines for Older Australians 豪州高齢者用栄養ガイドライン
diversional therapist ダイバージョナルセラピスト
diversional therapy ダイバージョナルセラピー
Documentation Accountability Manual 書類作成改訂マニュアル
Domiciliary Medication Management Review：DMMR 在宅薬剤管理レビュー
domiciliary nursing care benefit 在宅看護給付
Enhanced Primary Care プライマリ・ケア改善プログラム
Ethnic Aged Services 民族高齢者サービス
Extended Aged Care at Home：EACH 長期在宅高齢者ケア
Extended Aged Care at Home Dementia：EACHD 認知症専門長期在宅高齢者ケア
Extra Service Principles 1997 1997年特別サービス原則
Financial Hardship Assistance 財政援助政策
Flexible Care Grant Principles 2008 2008年順応的介護金原則
full pensioner 満額年金受給者
Geriatric Assessment Team：GAT 高齢者評価チーム
Geriatric Evaluation & Management Model of care 高齢者評価・管理プログラム
Glaucoma Australia 豪州緑内障学会
Good Grief グッドグリーフ
Government-subsidised residential aged care facility 政府補助高齢者介護施設
guardian's allowance 保護者手当
Handicapped Child's Allowance 障害児手当
Handicapped Persons Assistance Act 障害者援助法
HealthInsite ヘルスインサイト
Heart Foundation 心臓病財団
high-level care 高度介護
Home and Community Care Act 1985 1985年在宅・地域介護法令
Home and Community Care Program：HACC 在宅・地域ケア計画
Home Medicine Reviews：HMR 在宅医学調査会
Human Rights and Equal Opportunity Commission 人権機会平等委員会
incentive allowance 奨励手当
Independent Living Centre 自立生活センター
independent living unit 自立生活病棟
Information Principles 1997 1997年情報原則
Invalid Pensions Act 障害年金法
Investigation Principles 2007 2007年調査原則
low-level care 低度介護

Meals on Wheels　配食サービス
Medicare Australia　豪州老齢者医療保障制度
Medicare benefits schedule　老年者医療保障制度給付利益帯
Mental Health Foundation　精神保健財団
Mid-Term Review of the Aged Care Reform Strategy　高齢者ケア改革戦略中間検討
mobility allowance　移動手当
multi-purpose services：MPS　多目的サービス
MyHospitals　マイホスピタル
National Aboriginal and Torres Strait Islander National Aged Care Strategy　全豪アボリジニ・トレス海峡島民国家老人介護計画
National Aboriginal Community Controlled Health Organisation　全豪アボリジニ地域コントロール健康組織
National Bowel Cancer Screening Program　全豪腸癌スクリーニングプログラム
National Care Strategy　全豪介護計画
National Carer Counseling Program　全豪介護者カウンセリングプログラム
National Cervical Screening Program　全豪子宮頸部癌スクリーニングプログラム
National Continence Helpline　全豪失禁電話ホットライン
National Continence Management Strategy　豪州失禁管理戦略
National Dementia Helpline　豪州認知症相談ホットライン
National Diabetes Services Scheme：NDSS　全豪糖尿病サービス計画
National Health and Hospitals Network　豪州国民医療・病院ネットワーク
National Medicines Policy：NMP　豪州国家医薬品戦略
National Relay Service　全豪中継サービス
National Respite for Carers Program　全豪介護者レスパイトプログラム
National Service Standard Instrument：NSSI　全豪サービス基準評価表
Occupational Therapists Association of Australia　豪州作業療法士協会
Office of Aged Care Quality and Compliance：OACQC　高齢者ケアの質・コンプライアンスオフィス
Office of Hearing Services　聴力サービス局
Old Age Pensions Act　老齢年金法
Optometrists Association Australia　豪州検眼士協会
Osteoporosis Australia　豪州骨粗鬆症協会
Palliative Care Australia　豪州緩和ケア協会
pensioner concession card　年金受給者割引カード
Personal Care Assessment Instrument　対人ケア評価表

Petrol Sniffing Prevention Program　ガソリン吸引防止プログラム
Pharmaceutical Benefits Scheme　医薬品給付制度
Podiatry Association Council　足病学協会
Point of Care Testing technology　ポイント・オブ・ケア検査技術
pre-entry leave　入所前猶予期間
Privacy Act 1988　1988年プライバシー法
protective commissioner　保護管理官
provisional fee　条件付き料金
PUROBUS Club　プロバス・クラブ
qualifying service　資格審査サービス
Quality Assurance for Aboriginal and Torres Strait Islander Medical Services：QAAMS　アボリジニ・トレス海峡島住民のための医療の質保証
Quality of Care Principles 1997　1997年ケアの質原則
Quality Use of Medicines：QUM　医薬品の品質使用
Quality Use of Medicines Evaluation Program：QUMEP　医薬品の品質使用評価プログラム
Quality Use of Medicines Map：QUMmap　医薬品の品質使用マップ
QUM：Quality Use of Medicines　クム
Records Principles 1997　1997年記録原則
regional health services　地域保健サービス
rehabilitation allowance　リハビリテーション手当
Relative Resource Equity Formula：RREF　相対的資源公平配分方式
remote area allowance　遠隔地手当
resident　施設ケア利用者
resident agreement　施設ケア利用者同意書
Resident Classification Scale：RCS　施設ケア利用者分類基準
residential aged care　高齢者介護住宅
Residential Aged Care Structural Reform Package　高齢者介護施設構造改革パッケージ
Residential Care Standard and Accreditation Agency　施設ケア基準認定機関
Residential Care Subsidy Principles 1997　1997年施設利用者介護助成金原則
Residential Medications Management Review　施設利用者医薬品管理評価
retention amount　差し引き額
Royal District Nursing Services：RDNS　ロイヤル地区看護サービス
Sanctions Principles 1997　1997年制裁原則
security of tenure　保有保障
self-contained cottage　自活コティジ
self-funded retiree　自費年金者
self-management program　自己管理プログラム
sheltered employment allowance　保護雇用手当
sickness allowance　疾病手当
sickness benefit　傷病給付

豪州英和

Social Services Act　社会サービス法
specified care and services　特定介護・サービス
Speech Pathology Australia　豪州言語聴覚病理学会
Standard Aggregated Module：SAM　標準費用基準
Standard Association of Australia　豪州基準協会
Standards Monitoring Team　ケア基準監視チーム
State Grants Home Care Act　州助成在宅法
Statutory Declaration　法令宣言
superannuation pension　退職年金
Telstra Disability Equipment Program　テルストラ障害機器プログラム
Telstra Priority Assistance　テルストラ・プライオリティ援助
University of the Third Age Education:U3A　大学第三期年齢層大学教育
User Right Strategy　利用者権利戦略
User Rights Principles 1997　1997年利用者権利原則
Veterans Affairs Network　退役軍人ネットワーク
veterans home care　退役軍人在宅ケア
Vietnam Veterans Counseling Service：VVCS　ベトナム戦争退役軍人カウンセリングサービス
Vision Australia　ビジョン豪州
vital call system　バイタルコールシステム
Volunteering Australia　ボランティアリング豪州
White Repatriation Health Card　ホワイト帰還者保健カード
Work Adjustment Centre　作業適応センター
Work Preparation Centre　作業準備センター

2. 豪州（オーストラリア）における介護福祉等関連用語 【和　英】

アテンダント手当（あてんだんとてあて）　attendant allowance
アボリジニ医療サービス（あぼりじにいりょうさーびす）Aboriginal Medical Services：AMS
アボリジニ地域医療サービス（あぼりじにちいきいりょうさーびす）　Aboriginal Community Controlled Health Services：ACCHS
アボリジニ・トレス海峡島住民のための医療の質保証（あぼりじに・とれすかいきょうとうじゅうみんのためのいりょうのしつほしょう）　Quality Assurance for Aboriginal and Torres Strait Islander Medical Services：QAAMS
アボリジニ・トレス海峡島民健康パフォーマンスフレームワーク（あぼりじに・とれすかいきょうとうみんけんこうぱふぉーまんすふれーむわーく）　Aboriginal and Torres Strait Islander Health Performance Framework
アボリジニ・トレス海峡島民向け老人ホーム（あぼりじに・とれすかいきょうとうみんむけろうじんほーむ）　Aged care homes for Aboriginal and Torres Strait Islander people
移動手当（いどうてあて）　mobility allowance
医薬品給付制度（いやくひんきゅうふせいど）　Pharmaceutical Benefits Scheme
医薬品の品質使用（いやくひんのひんしつしよう）　Quality Use of Medicines：QUM
医薬品の品質使用評価プログラム（いやくひんのひんしつしようひょうかぷろぐらむ）　Quality Use of Medicines Evaluation Program：QUMEP
医薬品の品質使用マップ（いやくひんのひんしつしようまっぷ）　Quality Use of Medicines Map：QUMmap
ACAT（えーきゃっと）　Aged Care Assessment Team
遠隔地手当（えんかくちてあて）　remote area allowance
介護者資源センター（かいごしゃしげんせんたー）　Carer Resource Center
介護者手当（かいごしゃてあて）　carer allowance
介護者ビクトリア（かいごしゃびくとりあ）　Carers Victoria
介護者レスパイトケア（かいごしゃれすぱいとけあ）　carer respite care
介護者レスパイトケアセンター（かいごしゃれすぱいとけあせんたー）　Carer Respite Center
ガソリン吸引防止プログラム（がそりんきゅういんぼうしぷろぐらむ）　Petrol Sniffing Prevention Program
活動セラピーセンター（かつどうせらぴーせんたー）　Activity Therapy Centre
強制的競争入札制度（きょうせいてききょうそうにゅうさつせいど）　Compulsory Competitive Tendering：CCT
苦情調査サービス（くじょうちょうささーびす）　Complaints Investigation Scheme
グッドグリーフ（ぐっどぐりーふ）　Good Grief
クム（くむ）　QUM：Quality Use of Medicines
ケア基準監視チーム（けあきじゅんかんしちーむ）　Standards Monitoring Team
ケアサーチ（けあさーち）　CareSearch
ケア費用集計基準（けあひようしゅうけいきじゅん）　Care Aggregated Module：CAM
ケアリンクセンター（けありんくせんたー）　Carelink Center
豪州アルツハイマー病協会（ごうしゅうあるつはいまーびょうきょうかい）　Alzheimer's Australia
豪州介護者協会（ごうしゅうかいごしゃきょうかい）　Carers Australia
豪州癌協議会（ごうしゅうがんきょうぎかい）　Cancer Council of Australia
豪州関節炎協会（ごうしゅうかんせつえんきょうかい）　Arthritis Australia
豪州緩和ケア協会（ごうしゅうかんわけあきょうかい）　Palliative Care Australia
豪州基準協会（ごうしゅうきじゅんきょうかい）　Standard Association of Australia
豪州検眼士協会（ごうしゅうけんがんしきょうかい）　Optometrists Association Australia
豪州言語聴覚病理学会（ごうしゅうげんごちょうかくびょうりがっかい）　Speech Pathology Australia
豪州高齢者介護協会（ごうしゅうこうれいしゃかいごきょうかい）　Aged Care Association Australia
豪州高齢者・地域サービス（ごうしゅうこうれいしゃ・ちいきさーびす）　Aged and Community Services Australia
豪州高齢者用栄養ガイドライン（ごうしゅうこうれいしゃようえいようがいどらいん）　Dietary Guidelines for Older Australians
豪州国民医療・病院ネットワーク（ごうしゅうこくみんいりょう・びょういんねっとわーく）　National Health and Hospitals Network
豪州国家医薬品戦略（ごうしゅうこっかいやくひんせんりゃく）　National Medicines Policy：NMP
豪州骨粗鬆症協会（ごうしゅうこつそしょうしょうきょうかい）　Osteoporosis Australia
豪州作業療法士協会（ごうしゅうさぎょうりょうほうしきょうかい）　Occupational Therapists Association of Australia
豪州失禁管理戦略（ごうしゅうしっきんかんりせんりゃく）　National Continence Management Strategy
豪州失禁財団（ごうしゅうしっきんざいだん）

Continence Foundation of Australia
豪州障害リハビリテーション協議会（ごうしゅうしょうがいりはびりてーしょんきょうぎかい） Australian Council for Rehabilitation of Disabled
豪州糖尿病協会（ごうしゅうとうにょうびょうきょうかい） Diabetes Australia
豪州認知症相談ホットライン（ごうしゅうにんちしょうそうだんほっとらいん） National Dementia Helpline
豪州保健福祉協会(ごうしゅうほけんふくしきょうかい) Australian Institute of Health and Welfare
豪州予防接種ハンドブック（ごうしゅうよぼうせっしゅはんどぶっく） Australian Immunisation Handbook
豪州理学治療協会（ごうしゅうりがくちりょうきょうかい） Australian Physiotherapy Association
豪州緑内障学会(ごうしゅうりょくないしょうがっかい) Glaucoma Australia
豪州連邦ケアリンクセンター（ごうしゅうれんぽうけありんくせんたー） Commonwealth Carelink Centres
豪州連邦リハビリテーション庁（ごうしゅうれんぽうりはびりてーしょんちょう） Commonwealth Rehabilitation Service
豪州連邦レスパイト・ケアリンクセンター（ごうしゅうれんぽうれすぱいと・けありんくせんたー） Commonwealth Respite and Carelink Centres
豪州労働組合評議会（ごうしゅうろうどうくみあいひょうぎかい） Australian Council of Trade Union : ACTU
豪州老齢者医療保障制度(ごうしゅうろうれいしゃいりょうほしょうせいど) Medicare Australia
高度介護（こうどかいご） high-level care
高齢者一括介護施設（こうれいしゃいっかつかいごしせつ） Ageing in Place
高齢者介護教育・トレーニングプログラム(こうれいしゃかいごきょういく・とれーにんぐぷろぐらむ) Age Care Education and Training Incentive program : ACETI
高齢者介護苦情調査計画（こうれいしゃかいごくじょうちょうさけいかく） Aged Care Complaints Investigation Scheme
高齢者介護施設構造改革パッケージ（こうれいしゃかいごしせつこうぞうかいかくぱっけーじ） Residential Aged Care Structural Reform Package
高齢者介護住宅（こうれいしゃかいごじゅうたく） residential aged care
高齢者介護調査委員（こうれいしゃかいごちょうさいいん） Aged Care Commissioner
高齢者協議会（こうれいしゃきょうぎかい） Council on the Ageing : COTA
高齢者協議会運動戦略（こうれいしゃきょうぎかいうんどうせんりゃく） Council on the Ageing Strategy : COTA Strategy
高齢者ケア改革戦略（こうれいしゃけあかいかくせんりゃく） Aged Care Reform Strategy

高齢者ケア改革戦略中間検討（こうれいしゃけあかいかくせんりゃくちゅうかんけんとう） Mid-Term Review of the Aged Care Reform Strategy
高齢者ケア基準委員会（こうれいしゃけあきじゅんいいんかい） Aged Care Standards Agency
高齢者ケア基準・認定エージェンシー（こうれいしゃけあきじゅん・にんていえーじぇんしー） Aged Care Standards and Accreditation Agency
高齢者ケア苦情処理システム（こうれいしゃけあくじょうしょりしすてむ） Aged Care Complaints Resolution System : ACCRS
高齢者ケア構造改革（こうれいしゃけあこうぞうかいかく） Aged Care Structural Reform
高齢者ケア情報ライン（こうれいしゃけあじょうほうらいん） Aged Care Information Line
高齢者ケアの質・コンプライアンスオフィス（こうれいしゃけあのしつ・こんぷらいあんすおふぃす） Office of Aged Care Quality and Compliance : OACQC
高齢者ケア評価サービス（こうれいしゃけあひょうかさーびす） Aged Care Assessment Service : ACAS
高齢者ケア評価チーム（こうれいしゃけあひょうかちーむ） Aged Care Assessment Team : ACAT
高齢者ケア補助金支給制度（こうれいしゃけあほじょきんしきゅうせいど） Aged Care Funding Instrument : ACFI
高齢者権利擁護サービス（こうれいしゃけんりようごさーびす） Aged Rights Advocacy Service
高齢者住宅法（こうれいしゃじゅうたくほう） Aged Person Home Act
高齢者・障害者介護法（こうれいしゃ・しょうがいしゃかいごほう） Aged or disabled Persons Care Act
高齢者・障害者住宅法（こうれいしゃ・しょうがいしゃじゅうたくほう） Aged or disabled Persons Home Act
高齢者のための介護と住宅援助（こうれいしゃのためのかいごとじゅうたくえんじょ） Assistance with Care and Housing for the Aged : ACHA
高齢者評価・管理プログラム（こうれいしゃひょうか・かんりぷろぐらむ） Geriatric Evaluation & Management Model of care
高齢者評価チーム（こうれいしゃひょうかちーむ） Geriatric Assessment Team : GAT
コミュニティ・オプション・プロジェクト(こみゅにてぃ・おぷしょん・ぷろじぇくと) Community Option Projects : COP
コミュニティ・パートナー・プログラム（こみゅにてぃ・ぱーとなー・ぷろぐらむ） Community Partners Program
コミュニティ訪問客計画（こみゅにてぃほうもんきゃくけいかく） Community Visitors Scheme
財政援助政策（ざいせいえんじょせいさく） Financial

Hardship Assistance
在宅医学調査会（ざいたくいがくちょうさかい）
　Home Medicine Reviews：HMR
在宅看護給付（ざいたくかんごきゅうふ）domiciliary nursing care benefit
在宅・地域ケア計画（ざいたく・ちいきけあけいかく）Home and Community Care Program：HACC
在宅薬剤管理レビュー（ざいたくやくざいかんりれびゅー）Domiciliary Medication Management Review：DMMR
作業準備センター（さぎょうじゅんびせんたー）Work Preparation Centre
作業適応センター（さぎょうてきおうせんたー）Work Adjustment Centre
差し引き額（さしひきがく）retention amount
資格審査サービス（しかくしんささーびす）qualifying service
自活コテイジ（じかつこていじ）self-contained cottage
自己管理プログラム（じこかんりぷろぐらむ）self-management programs
施設ケア基準認定機関（しせつけあきじゅんにんていきかん）Residential Care Standard and Accreditation Agency
施設ケア利用者（しせつけありようしゃ）resident
施設ケア利用者同意書（しせつけありようしゃどういしょ）resident agreement
施設ケア利用者分類基準（しせつけありようしゃぶんるいきじゅん）Resident Classification Scale：RCS
施設保証金（しせつほしょうきん）accommodation bond
施設利用者医薬品管理評価（しせつりようしゃいやくひんかんりひょうか）Residential Medications Management Review
失禁援助計画（しっきんえんじょけいかく）Continence Aids Assistance Scheme
失禁援助支払い計画（しっきんえんじょしはらいけいかく）Continence Aids Payment Scheme
疾病手当（しっぺいてあて）sickness allowance
自費年金者（じひねんきんしゃ）self-funded retiree
慈悲の友（じひのとも）Compassionate Friends
社会サービス法（しゃかいさーびすほう）Social Services Act
州助成在宅法（しゅうじょせいざいたくほう）State Grants Home Care Act
障害児手当（しょうがいじてあて）Handicapped Child's Allowance
障害者援助法（しょうがいしゃえんじょほう）Handicapped Persons Assistance Act
障害年金法（しょうがいねんきんほう）Invalid Pensions Act
条件付き支払い（じょうけんつきしはらい）conditional adjustment payment
条件付き料金（じょうけんつきりょうきん）provisional fee
消費者医療情報（しょうひしゃいりょうじょうほう）Consumer Medicine Information：CMI
傷病給付（しょうびょうきゅうふ）sickness benefit
奨励手当（しょうれいてあて）incentive allowance
書類作成改訂マニュアル（しょるいさくせいかいていまにゅある）Documentation Accountability Manual
自立生活センター（じりつせいかつせんたー）Independent Living Centre
自立生活病棟（じりつせいかつびょうとう）independent living unit
人権機会平等委員会（じんけんきかいびょうどういいんかい）Human Rights and Equal Opportunity Commission
心臓病財団（しんぞうびょうざいだん）Heart Foundation
精神保健財団（せいしんほけんざいだん）Mental Health Foundation
政府補助高齢者介護施設（せいふほじょこうれいしゃかいごしせつ）Government-subsidised residential aged care facility
1999年認証金原則（せんきゅうひゃくきゅうじゅうきゅうねんにんしょうきんげんそく）Accreditation Grant Principles 1999
1997年介護受領者原則の承認（せんきゅうひゃくきゅうじゅうななねんかいごじゅりょうしゃげんそくのしょうにん）Approval of Care Recipients Principles 1997
1997年記録原則（せんきゅうひゃくきゅうじゅうななねんきろくげんそく）Records Principles 1997
1997年ケアの質原則（せんきゅうひゃくきゅうじゅうななねんけあのしつげんそく）Quality of Care Principles 1997
1997年コミュニティ訪問者交付金原則（せんきゅうひゃくきゅうじゅうななねんこみゅにてぃほうもんしゃこうふきんげんそく）Community Visitors Grant Principles 1997
1997年施設利用者介護助成金原則（せんきゅうひゃくきゅうじゅうななねんしせつりようしゃかいごじょせいきんげんそく）Residential Care Subsidy Principles 1997
1997年情報原則（せんきゅうひゃくきゅうじゅうななねんじょうほうげんそく）Information Principles 1997
1997年制裁原則（せんきゅうひゃくきゅうじゅうななねんせいさいげんそく）Sanctions Principles 1997
1997年地域ケア許可原則（せんきゅうひゃくきゅうじゅうななねんちいきけあきょかげんそく）Community Care Grant Principles 1997
1997年地域ケア助成金原則（せんきゅうひゃくきゅうじゅうななねんちいきけあじょせいきんげんそく）Community Care Subsidy Principles 1997

1997年特別サービス原則（せんきゅうひゃくきゅう
じゅうななねんとくべつさーびすげんそく） Extra
Service Principles 1997
1997年認可事業者原則（せんきゅうひゃくきゅうじゅう
ななねんにんかじぎょうしゃげんそく） Approved
Provider Principles 1997
1997年認定原則（せんきゅうひゃくきゅうじゅうななね
んにんていげんそく） Certification Principles 1997
1997年配分原則（せんきゅうひゃくきゅうじゅうななね
んはいぶんげんそく） Allocation Principles 1997
1997年分類法原則（せんきゅうひゃくきゅうじゅうな
なねんぶんるいほうげんそく） Classification
Principles 1997
1997年擁護許可原則（せんきゅうひゃくきゅうじゅうな
なねんようごきょかげんそく） Advocacy Grant
Principles 1997
1997年利用者権利原則（せんきゅうひゃくきゅうじゅう
ななねんりようしゃけんりげんそく） User Rights
Principles 1997
1998年責任原則（せんきゅうひゃくきゅうじゅうはちね
んせきにんげんそく） Accountability Principles
1998
1985年在宅・地域介護法令（せんきゅうひゃくはち
じゅうごねんざいたく・ちいきかいごほうれい）
Home and Community Care Act 1985
1987年豪州保健福祉研究所法（せんきゅうひゃくはち
じゅうななねんごうしゅうほけんふくしけんきゅうしょ
ほう） Australian Institute of Health and Welfare
Act 1987
1988年プライバシー法（せんきゅうひゃくはちじゅう
はちねんぷらいばしーほう） Privacy Act 1988
全豪アボリジニ地域コントロール健康組織（ぜんごうあ
ぼりじにちいきこんとろーるけんこうそしき）
National Aboriginal Community Controlled
Health Organisation
全豪アボリジニ・トレス海峡島民国家老人介護計画（ぜ
んごうあぼりじに・とれすかいきょうとうみんこっ
かろうじんかいごけいかく） National Aboriginal
and Torres Strait Islander National Aged Care
Strategy
全豪うつ病運動（ぜんごううつびょううんどう）
Beyondblue
全豪介護計画（ぜんごうかいごけいかく） National
Care Strategy
全豪介護者カウンセリングプログラム（ぜんごうかいご
しゃかうんせりんぐぷろぐらむ） National Carer
Counseling Program
全豪介護者レスパイトプログラム（ぜんごうかいごしゃ
れすぱいとぷろぐらむ） National Respite for
Carers Program
全豪胸部スクリーン（ぜんごうきょうぶすくりーん）
Breast Screen Australia
全豪サービス基準評価表（ぜんごうさーびすきじゅん
ひょうかひょう） National Service Standard
Instrument : NSSI
全豪子宮頸部癌スクリーニングプログラム（ぜんごうし
きゅうけいぶがんすくりーにんぐぷろぐらむ）
National Cervical Screening Program
全豪失禁電話ホットライン（ぜんごうしっきんでんわほっ
とらいん） National Continence Helpline
全豪中継サービス（ぜんごうちゅうけいさーびす）
National Relay Service
全豪腸癌スクリーニングプログラム（ぜんごうちょうが
んすくりーにんぐぷろぐらむ） National Bowel
Cancer Screening Program
全豪糖尿病サービス計画（ぜんごうとうにょうびょうさー
びすけいかく） National Diabetes Services
Scheme : NDSS
センターリンク（せんたーりんく） Centrelink
相対的資源公平配分方式（そうたいてきしげんこうへい
はいぶんほうしき） Relative Resource Equity
Formula : RREF
足病学協会（そくびょうがくきょうかい） Podiatry
Association Council
退役軍人在宅ケア（たいえきぐんじんざいたくけあ）
veterans home care
退役軍人ネットワーク（たいえきぐんじんねっとわーく）
Veterans Affairs Network
大学第三期年齢層大学教育（だいがくだいさんきねんれ
いそうだいがくきょういく） University of the
Third Age Education:U3A
退職年金（たいしょくねんきん） superannuation
pension
対人ケア評価表（たいじんけあひょうかひょう）
Personal Care Assessment Instrument
ダイバージョナルセラピー（だいばーじょなるせらぴー）
diversional therapy
ダイバージョナルセラピスト（だいばーじょなるせらぴ
すと） diversional therapist
宅配給食サービス助成法（たくはいきゅうしょくさーび
すじょせいほう） Delivered Meals Subsidy Act
多目的サービス（たもくてきさーびす） multi-
purpose services : MPS
地域看護・医療センター（ちいきかんご・いりょうせん
たー） Community Nursing and Health Centre
地域ケアサービス検索サイト（ちいきけあさーびすけん
さくさいと） Community Care Service Finder
地域ケアの権利・責任憲章（ちいきけあのけんり・せき
にんけんしょう） Charter of Rights and
Responsibilities for Community Care
地域高齢者ケアパッケージ（ちいきこうれいしゃけあぱっ
けーじ） Community Aged Care Package :
CACP
地域サービス計画（ちいきさーびすけいかく）
Community Service Orders Scheme
地域諮問安全プロジェクト（ちいきしもんあんぜんぷろ

じぇくと) Community Liaison Advisory Safety Project：CLASP
地域保健サービス (ちいきほけんさーびす) regional health services
長期在宅高齢者ケア (ちょうきざいたくこうれいしゃけあ) Extended Aged Care at Home：EACH
聴力サービス局 (ちょうりょくさーびすきょく) Office of Hearing Services
デイセラピーセンター (でいせらぴーせんたー) Day Therapy Centres
低度介護 (ていどかいご) low-level care
テルストラ障害機器プログラム (てるすとらしょうがいききぷろぐらむ) Telstra Disability Equipment Program
テルストラ・プライオリティ援助 (てるすとら・ぷらいおりてぃえんじょ) Telstra Priority Assistance
特定介護・サービス (とくていかいご・さーびす) specified care and services
2010年度豪州政府機関高齢者サービス案内書 (にせんじゅうねんどごうしゅうせいふきかんこうれいしゃーびすあんないしょ) Australian Government Directory of Services for Older People 2010
2007年調査原則 (にせんななねんちょうさげんそく) Investigation Principles 2007
2008年順応的介護金原則 (にせんはちねんじゅんのうてきかいごきんげんそく) Flexible Care Grant Principles 2008
入居料 (にゅうきょりょう) accommodation charge
入所前猶予期間 (にゅうしょまえゆうよきかん) pre-entry leave
認知症・記憶サービス (にんちしょう・きおくさーびす) Cognitive Dementia and Memory Services：CDAMS
認知症・記憶障害地域センター (にんちしょう・きおくしょうがいちいきせんたー) Dementia and Memory Community Centres
認知症行動管理サービス (にんちしょうこうどうかんりさーびす) Dementia Behaviour Management Advisory Service：DBMAS
認知症専門長期在宅高齢者ケア (にんちしょうせんもんちょうきざいたくこうれいしゃけあ) Extended Aged Care at Home Dementia：EACHD
年金受給者割引カード (ねんきんじゅきゅうしゃわりびきかーど) Pensioner Concession card
配食サービス (はいしょくさーびす) Meals on Wheels
バイタルコールシステム (ばいたるこーるしすてむ) vital call system
バルクビリング (ばるくびりんぐ) bulk billing
悲観教育センター (ひかんきょういくせんたー) Centre for Grief Education
ビジョン豪州 (びじょんごうしゅう) Vision Australia

標準費用基準 (ひょうじゅんひようきじゅん) Standard Aggregated Module：SAM
プライマリ・ケア改善プログラム (ぷらいまり・けあかいぜんぷろぐらむ) Enhanced Primary Care
プロバス・クラブ (ぷろばす・くらぶ) PUROBUS Club
ベトナム戦争退役軍人カウンセリングサービス (べとなむせんそうたいえきぐんじんかうんせりんぐさーびす) Vietnam Veterans Counseling Service：VVCS
ヘルスインサイト (へるすいんさいと) HealthInsite
ポイント・オブ・ケア検査技術 (ぽいんと・おぶ・けあけんさぎじゅつ) Point of Care Testing technology
膀胱・腸の健康財団 (ぼうこう・ちょうのけんこうざいだん) Bladder and Bowel Foundation
法令宣言 (ほうれいせんげん) Statutory Declaration
保険料払込猶予期間 (ほけんりょうはらいこみゆうよきかん) days of grace
保健老齢局 (ほけんろうれいきょく) Department of Health and Ageing
保護管理官 (ほごかんりかん) protective commissioner
保護雇用手当 (ほごこようてあて) sheltered employment allowance
保護者手当 (ほごしゃてあて) guardian's allowance
補償対象入所者 (ほしょうたいしょうにゅうしょしゃ) compensable resident
保有保障 (ほゆうほしょう) security of tenure
ボランティアリング豪州 (ぼらんてぃありんぐごうしゅう) Volunteering Australia
ホワイト帰還者保健カード (ほわいときかんしゃほけんかーど) White Repatriation Health Card
マイホスピタル (まいほすぴたる) MyHospitals
満額年金受給者 (まんがくねんきんじゅきゅうしゃ) full pensioner
民族高齢者サービス (みんぞくこうれいしゃさーびす) Ethnic Aged Services
リハビリテーション手当 (りはびりてーしょんてあて) rehabilitation allowance
利用者権利戦略 (りようしゃけんりせんりゃく) User Right Strategy
ロイヤル地区看護サービス (ろいやるちくかんごさーびす) Royal District Nursing Services：RDNS
老年者医療保障制度給付利益帯 (ろうねんしゃいりょうほしょうせいどきゅうふりえきたい) Medicare benefits schedule
老齢年金 (ろうれいねんきん) age pension
老齢年金法 (ろうれいねんきんほう) Old Age Pensions Act
割引該当入所者補償 (わりびきがいとうにゅうしょしゃほしょう) concessional resident supplement
割引適用入所者 (わりびきてきようにゅうしょしゃ) concessional resident

3．大韓民国（韓国）における介護福祉等関連用語　【韓　日】

가사활동도우미　家事活動ドウミ
가정도우미　家庭ドウミ
가정봉사사업　家庭奉仕事業
가정봉사원　家政奉仕員
가정봉사원파견사업　家庭奉仕員派遣事業
가정봉사원파견사업소　家庭奉仕員派遣事業所
가정봉사원파견시설　家庭奉仕員派遣施設
가족부양　家族扶養
가족요양비　家族療養費
가족요양비지급신청서　家族療養費支給申請書
가출노인　家出老人
간호보조사　看護補助師
간호조무사　看護助務師
감액노령연금　減額老齢年金
건강보건재정운영국　健康保健財政運営局
건강보험심사평가원　健康保険審査評価院
건강보험재정안정종합대책　健康保険財政安定総合対策
결연사업　結縁事業
경로당　敬老堂
경로당활성화사업　敬老堂活性化事業
경로당활성화협의체　敬老堂活性化協議体
경로대학　敬老大学
경로식당　敬老食堂
경로연금　敬老年金
경로우대　敬老優待
경로우대서비스　敬老優待サービス
경로우대제도　敬老優待制度
경로우대증　敬老優待証
경로우대할인제도　敬老優待割引制度
경로헌장　敬老憲章
경로효친사상　敬老孝親思想
경비노인양로시설　軽費老人養老施設
경비노인요양시설　軽費老人療養施設
경비노인전문요양시설　軽費老人専門療養施設
고려장　高麗葬　[日本でいう姥捨山]
고령사회기본법　高齢社会基本法
고령사회대책기본법　高齢社会対策基本法
고령자고용　高齢者雇用
고령자고용장려금　高齢者雇用奨励金
고령자고용정보센터　高齢者雇用情報センター
고령자고용지원금　高齢者雇用支援金
고령자고용촉진법　高齢者雇用促進法
고령자고용촉진장려금　高齢者雇用促進奨励金
고령자인재은행　高齢者人材銀行
고령자창업지원　高齢者創業支援
고령자취업　高齢者就業
고령자취업알선사업　高齢者就業斡旋事業
고령자취업알선센터　高齢者就業斡旋センター
고령자취업정보　高齢者就業情報
고령자취업지원센터　高齢者就業支援センター

고령친화산업　高齢親和産業
고령친화산업지원센터　高齢親和産業支援センター
고령친화산업진흥법　高齢親和産業振興法
고부갈등　嫁姑葛藤
고용정책기본법　雇用政策基本法
고용차별금지법　雇用差別禁止法
공무원연금　公務員年金
공적노인요양보장추진기획단　公的老人療養保障推進企画団
교통수당　交通手当
국민건강보험공단　国民健康保険公団
국민기초생활수급자　国民基礎生活受給者
국민생활기초생활보장법　国民生活基礎生活保障法
국민연금공단　国民年金公団
국제노인문화예술제　国際老人文化芸術祭
군인연금　軍人年金
기능훈련사　機能訓練士
기탁식품　寄託食品
노령선　老齢線
노령수당　老齢手当
노인 4 고　老人の 4 苦
노인가정도우미사업　老人家庭ドウミ事業
노인간호센터　老人看護センター
노인간호학회　老人看護学会
노인거주복지시설　老人居住福祉施設
노인건강 & 복지연구소　老人健康 & 福祉研究所
노인건강증진프로그램연구소　老人健康増進プログラム研究所
노인건강진단　老人健康診断
노인건강체조경연대회　老人健康体操競演大会
노인공동작업장　老人共同作業場
노인교실　老人教室
노인교육　老人教育
노인권익보호당　老人権益保護党
노인능력은행　老人能力銀行
노인대학　老人大学
노인도우미　老人ドウミ
노인무료급식　老人無料給食
노인문화제　老人文化祭
노인보건복지대책위원회　老人保健福祉対策委員会
노인보건복지종합대책　老人保健福祉総合対策
노인보건의료시설　老人保健医療施設
노인보호전문기관　老人保護専門機関
노인복지관　老人福祉館
노인복지사　老人福祉士
노인복지상담　老人福祉相談
노인복지상담원　老人福祉相談員
노인복지시설연합회　老人福祉施設連合会
노인복지주택　老人福祉住宅
노인복지회관　老人福祉会館

노인부양　老人扶養	노인전문요양시설　老人専門療養施設
노인부양기피현상　老人扶養忌避現象	노인종합복지관　老人総合福祉館
노인상담원　老人相談員	노인주간보호시설　老人昼間保護施設
노인생활과학연구소　老人生活科学研究所	노인주거복지시설　老人住居福祉施設
노인수당　老人手当	노인주거연구소　老人住居研究所
노인수발보장법률제정안　老人スバル保障法律制定案 [スバルはケアという意味]	노인준비교육　老人準備教育
노인수발보험법안　老人スバル保険法案 [スバルはケアという意味]	노인찾기종합센터　家出老人捜索総合センター
노인수발평가관리원　老人スバル評価管理院 [スバルはケアという意味]	노인촌락　老人村
	노인타운　老人タウン
노인승차권제도　老人乗車券制度	노인학교　老人学校
노인아파트　老人アパート	노인학교지도사　老人学校指導師
노인양로시설　老人養老施設	노인학대상담센터　老人虐待相談センター
노인여가　老人余暇	노인헌장　老人憲章
노인여가복지시설　老人余暇福祉施設	노인휴양소　老人休養所
노인요양공동생활가정　老人療養共同生活家庭	노인휴양시설　老人休養施設
노인요양복지시설　老人療養福祉施設	노후생애설계전문가　老後生涯設計専門家
노인요양시설　老人療養施設	단기보호　短期保護
노인요양원　老人療養院	단기보호사업　短期保護事業
노인유휴노동력　老人遊休労働力	단기보호사업소　短期保護事業所
노인의 날　老人の日	단기보호시설　短期保護施設
노인의료복지시설　老人医療福祉施設	달력나이　暦年齢
노인인력활용대책　老人人材活用対策	대한간호복지재단　大韓看護福祉財団
노인자살　老人自殺	대한간호협회　大韓看護協会
노인자살예방센터　老人自殺予防センター	대한노인과학발명협회　大韓老人科学発明協会
노인자원봉사　老人ボランティア	대한노인내과학회　大韓老人内科学会
노인자원봉사단　老人志願奉仕団	대한노인물리치료학회　大韓老人理学治療学会
노인장기요양　老人長期療養	대한노인병원협의회　大韓老人病院協議会
노인장기요양개호보험제도　老人長期療養介護保険制度	대한노인병학회　大韓老人病学会
노인장기요양급여비용심사·지급결정통지서　老人長期療養給付費用審査·支給決定通知書	대한노인복지신문　大韓老人福祉新聞
	대한노인요양병원협회　大韓老人療養病院協会
노인장기요양급여비용심사명세서　老人長期療養給付費用審査明細書	대한노인의학회　大韓老人医学会
	대한노인재활의학회　大韓老人レクリエーション医学会
노인장기요양급여비용심사청구서　老人長期療養給付費用審査請求書	대한노인정신의학회　大韓老人精神医学会
노인장기요양급여비용정산심사결정통지서　老人長期療養給付費用精算審査決定通知書	대한노인회　大韓老人会
	대한노화방지의학회　大韓老化防止医学会
노인장기요양급여비용청구명세서접수증　老人長期療養給付費用請求明細書受付証	대한뇌졸중학회　大韓脳血管障害学会
	대한실버산업협회　大韓シルバー産業協会
노인장기요양보장　老人長期療養保障	대한요양보호사협회　大韓療養保護士協会
노인장기요양보험　老人長期療養保険	대한은퇴자협회　大韓退職者協会
노인장기요양보험법　老人長期療養保険法	대한임상노인의학회　大韓臨床老人医学会
노인장기요양보험법시행규칙　老人長期療養保険法施行規則	대한전인케어복지협회　大韓全人ケア福祉協会
	대한치매학회　大韓認知症学会
노인장기요양보험법시행령　老人長期療養保険法施行令	대한케어복지학회　大韓ケア福祉学会
노인장기요양보험운영센터　老人長期療養保険運営センター	데이·나이트서비스　デイ·ナイトサービス
	두문불출노인　引きこもり老人
노인장기요양보험제도　老人長期療養保険制度	무료노인양로시설　無料老人養老施設
노인장기요양보호종합대책　老人長期療養保護総合対策	무료노인요양시설　無料老人療養施設
	무료노인전문요양시설　無料老人専門療養施設
노인재가복지사업소　老人在宅福祉事業所	무료양로시설　無料養老施設
노인재가복지시설　老人在宅福祉施設	밑반찬배달서비스　おかず配達サービス
노인전문병원　老人専門病院	방문간호경과기록부　訪問看護経過記録簿
	방문간호보조사교육　訪問看護補助師教育
	방문요양　訪問療養

韓国
韓日

배식서비스　配食サービス	장기요양수가　長期療養数価
보건복지부　保健福祉部	장기요양시설　長期療養施設
비전 2030　ビジョン 2030	장기요양심사위원회　長期療養審査委員会
사회복지관　社会福祉館	장기요양심판위원회　長期療養審判委員会
새로마지플랜 2015 (저출산・고령사회 기본계획)　新しく迎えるプラン 2015　[低出産・高齢社会基本計画]	장기요양인정서　長期療養認定書
	장기요양인정점수　長期療養認定点数
	장기요양인정조사표　長期療養認定調査票
선보호・후사회보장　先家庭保護・後社会保障	장기요양판정위원회　長期療養判定委員会
수발　鬚髮	장년봉사단　壮年奉仕団
시군구　市郡区　[日本でいう市区町村]	장애인장기요양보험제도　障害者長期療養保険制度
실버산업육성추진위원회　シルバー産業育成推進委員会	재가노인복지사업　在宅老人福祉事業
실버타운　シルバータウン	재가복지봉사센터　在宅福祉奉仕センター
실비노인복지주택　実費老人福祉住宅	재가복지사업　在家福祉事業
실비양로시설　実費養老施設	저출산・고령사회기본법　低出産・高齢社会基本法
쌍무적 부양　双務的扶養	저출산・고령사회위원회　低出産・高齢社会委員会
야간보호　夜間保護	전국노인건강축제　全国老人健康祭
여성노인사업　女性老人事業	전국노인병원협의회　全国老人病院協議会
요양　療養	전국노인보호전문기관　全国老人保護専門機関
요양급여비용　療養給付費用	전국노인복지관대회　全国老人福祉館大会
요양병원요양비　療養病院療養費	전국노인복지단체연합회　全国老人福祉団体連合会
요양보호　療養保護	전국노인복지단체협의회　全国老人福祉団体協議会
요양보호관리사　療養保護管理士　[日本でいうケアマネジャー]	전국요양보호사협회　全国療養保護士協会
	전국푸드뱅크　全国フードバンク
	정년퇴직자계속고용장려금　定年退職者継続雇用奨励金
요양보호관리사제도　療養保護管理士制度	주・야간 보호　昼・夜間保護
요양보호사　療養保護士	주간보호　昼間保護
요양보호사양성강좌　療養保護士養成講座	주간보호사업　昼間保護事業
요양보호사양성시설　療養保護士養成施設	주간보호사업소　昼間保護事業所
요양보호사양성커리큘럼　療養保護士養成カリキュラム	주간보호시설　昼間保護施設
요양보호사양성표준교과서　療養保護士養成標準教科書	중앙노인보호전문기관　中央老人保護専門機関
요양원　療養院	지역복지협력사업　地域福祉協力事業
우호방문서비스　友好訪問サービス	지역사회복지관　地域社会福祉館
유교사상　儒教思想	지원봉사　志願奉仕
유료노인복지주택　有料老人福祉住宅	지원봉사원육성사업　志願奉仕員育成事業
유료노인양로시설　有料老人養老施設	지원봉사활동　志願奉仕活動
유료노인요양시설　有料老人療養施設	치매・뇌졸증가족교실　認知症・脳血管障害家族教室
유료노인전문요양시설　有料老人専門療養施設	치매전문병원　認知症専門病院
유료양로시설　有料養老施設	케어복지사　ケア福祉士
은퇴농장　退職農場	특례요양비　特例療養費
은퇴이민　退職移民	특별현금급여　特別現金給付
은퇴촌　引退村	편무적 부양　片務的扶養
의료급여법　医療給付法	표준근로계약서　標準勤労契約書
의료급여수급자　医療給付受給者	표준장기요양이용계획서　標準長期療養利用計画書
의료기사등에 관한 법률　医療技師等に関する法律	푸드뱅크　フードバンク
의료보호법　医療保護法	푸드뱅크식품　フードバンク食品
의약분업　医薬分業	한국가톨릭노인복지협의회　韓国カトリック老人福祉協議会
임금피크제　賃金ピーク制	
장기보호시설　長期保護施設	한국갤럽　韓国ギャラップ
장기요양기관　長期療養機関	한국교회노인학교연합회　韓国教会老人学教連合会
장기요양등급　長期療養等級	한국노년유권자연맹　韓国老年有権者連盟
장기요양등급인정　長期療養等級認定	한국노년자원봉사회　韓国老年志願奉仕会
장기요양등급판정위원회　長期療養等級判定委員会	한국노년학연구회　韓国老年学研究所
장기요양보험료　長期療養保険料	한국노인과학학술단체엽합회　韓国老人科学学術団体連
장기요양보호　長期療養保護	

合会
한국노인대학복지협의회　韓国老人大学福祉協議会
한국노인대학연구회　韓国老人大学研究会
한국노인문제연구소　韓国老人問題研究所
한국노인문화센터　韓国老人文化センター
한국노인방송　韓国老人放送
한국노인병연구소　韓国老人病研究所
한국노인보호전문기관　韓国老人保護専門機関
한국노인복지개인시설협회　韓国老人福祉個人施設協会
한국노인복지상담회　韓国老人福祉相談会
한국노인복지선교협의회　韓国老人福祉宣教協議会
한국노인복지센터　韓国老人福祉センター
한국노인복지시설협회　韓国老人福祉施設協会
한국노인복지운동　韓国老人福祉運動
한국노인복지장기요양기관협회　韓国老人福祉長期療養機関協会
한국노인복지중앙회　韓国老人福祉中央会
한국노인복지학회　韓国老人福祉学会
한국노인복지회(한국헬프에이지)　韓国老人福祉会；韓国ヘルプエイジ
한국노인상조회　韓国老人互助会
한국노인생활지원재단　韓国老人生活支援財団
한국노인성교육연구소　韓国老人の性教育研究所
한국노인시설물리치료사협의회　韓国老人施設理学治療士協議会
한국노인여가전문지도자협회　韓国老人余暇専門指導者協会
한국노인연합회　韓国老人連合会
한국노인요양센터　韓国老人療養センター
한국노인요양시설경영연구회　韓国老人療養施設経営研究会
한국노인의 전화　韓国老人の電話
한국노인인권센터　韓国老人人権センター
한국노인인력개발원　韓国老人人材開発院
한국노인인지건강협회　韓国老人認知健康協会
한국노인종합복지관협회　韓国老人総合福祉館協会
한국노인체육협회　韓国老人体育協会
한국노인학대방지정보망　韓国老人虐待防止情報網
한국노인학대연구소　韓国老人虐待研究所
한국노인학대피해상담센터　韓国老人虐待被害相談センター
한국노화학회　韓国老化学会
한국민간자격협회　韓国民間資格協会
한국보건사회연구원　韓国保健社会研究院
한국보건산업진흥원　韓国保健産業振興院
한국보건의료인국가시험원　韓国保健医療人国家試験院
한국사회복지사협회　韓国社会福祉士協会
한국사회복지학회　韓国社会福祉学会
한국사회복지협의회　韓国社会福祉協議会
한국소비자보호원　韓国消費者保護院
한국시니어클럽협회　韓国シニアクラブ協会
한국여가레크리에이션협회　韓国余暇レクリエーション協会

한국요양보호사협회　韓国療養保護士協会
한국요양보호협회　韓国療養保護協会
한국재가노인복지협회　韓国在宅老人福祉協会
한국정년퇴직인협회　韓国定年退職者協会
한국주택협회　韓国住宅協会
한국치매가족정보망　韓国認知症家族情報網
한국치매가족협회　韓国認知症家族協会
한국치매미술치료협회　韓国認知症美術治療協会
한국치매미아방지협회　韓国認知症迷子防止協会
한국치매협회　韓国認知症協会
한국케어사회복지대학협의회　韓国ケア社会福祉大学協議会
한국평생교육노인대학협의회　韓国生涯教育老人大学協議会
한국표준질병・사인분류　韓国標準疾病・死因分類
한국헬프에이지　韓国ヘルプエイジ
한방의　漢方医
환과고독　鰥寡孤独
황혼이혼　熟年離婚
황혼재혼　熟年再婚
효도　親孝行

3．大韓民国（韓国）における介護福祉等関連用語 【日　韓】

新しく迎えるプラン 2015（低出産・高齢社会基本計画）（あたらしくむかえるぷらんにせんじゅうご（ていしゅっさん・こうれいしゃかいきほんけいかく）） 새로마지플랜 2015（저출산・고령사회 기본계획）
家出老人（いえでろうじん） 가출노인
家出老人捜索総合センター（いえでろうじんそうさそうごうせんたー） 노인찾기종합센터
医薬分業（いやくぶんぎょう） 의약분업
医療技師等に関する法律（いりょうぎしとうにかんするほうりつ） 의료기사등에 관한 법률
医療給付受給者（いりょうきゅうふじゅきゅうしゃ） 의료급여수급자
医療給付法（いりょうきゅうふほう） 의료급여법
医療保護法（いりょうほごほう） 의료보호법
引退村（いんたいむら） 은퇴촌
おかず配達サービス（おかずはいたつさーびす） 밑반찬배달서비스
親孝行（おやこうこう） 효도
家事活動ドウミ（かじかつどうどうみ） 가사활동도우미　[日本でいうホームヘルパー]
家政奉仕員（かせいほうしいん） 가정봉사원　[日本でいうホームヘルパー]
家族扶養（かぞくふよう） 가족부양
家族療養費（かぞくりょうようひ） 가족요양비
家族療養費支給申請書（かぞくりょうようひしきゅうしんせいしょ） 가족요양비지급신청서
家庭ドウミ（かていどうみ） 가정도우미　[日本でいうホームヘルパー]
家庭奉仕員派遣事業（かていほうしいんはけんじぎょう） 가정봉사원파견사업
家庭奉仕員派遣事業所（かていほうしいんはけんじぎょうしょ） 가정봉사원파견사업소
家庭奉仕員派遣施設（かていほうしいんはけんしせつ） 가정봉사원파견시설
家庭奉仕事業（かていほうしじぎょう） 가정봉사사업
鰥寡孤独（かんかこどく） 환과고독
韓国カトリック老人福祉協議会（かんこくかとりっくろうじんふくしきょうぎかい） 한국가톨릭노인복지협의회
韓国ギャラップ（かんこくぎゃらっぷ） 한국갤럽
韓国教会老人学教連合会（かんこくきょうかいろうじんがくえんれんごうかい） 한국교회노인학교연합회
韓国ケア社会福祉大学協議会（かんこくけあしゃかいふくしだいがくきょうぎかい） 한국케어사회복지대학협의회
韓国在宅老人福祉協会（かんこくざいたくろうじんふくしきょうかい） 한국재가노인복지협회
韓国シニアクラブ協会（かんこくしにあくらぶきょうかい） 한국시니어클럽협회
韓国社会福祉学会（かんこくしゃかいふくしがっかい） 한국사회복지학회
韓国社会福祉士協会（かんこくしゃかいふくしきょうかい） 한국사회복지사협회
韓国社会福祉協議会（かんこくしゃかいふくしきょうぎかい） 한국사회복지협의회
韓国住宅協会（かんこくじゅうたくきょうかい） 한국주택협회
韓国生涯教育老人大学協議会（かんこくしょうがいきょういくろうじんだいがくきょうぎかい） 한국평생교육노인대학협의회
韓国消費者保護院（かんこくしょうひしゃほごいん） 한국소비자보호원
韓国定年退職者協会（かんこくていねんたいしょくしゃきょうかい） 한국정년퇴직인협회
韓国認知症家族協会（かんこくにんちしょうかぞくきょうかい） 한국치매가족협회
韓国認知症家族情報網（かんこくにんちしょうかぞくじょうほうもう） 한국치매가족정보망
韓国認知症協会（かんこくにんちしょうきょうかい） 한국치매협회
韓国認知症美術治療協会（かんこくにんちしょうびじゅつちりょうきょうかい） 한국치매미술치료협회
韓国認知症迷子防止協会（かんこくにんちしょうまいごぼうしきょうかい） 한국치매미아방지협회
韓国標準疾病・死因分類（かんこくひょうじゅんしっぺい・しいんぶんるい） 한국표준질병・사인분류
韓国ヘルプエイジ（かんこくへるぷえいじ） 한국헬프에이지
韓国保健医療人国家試験院（かんこくほけんいりょうじんこっかしけんいん） 한국보건의료인국가시험원
韓国保健産業振興院（かんこくほけんさんぎょうしんこういん） 한국보건산업진흥원
韓国保健社会研究院（かんこくほけんしゃかいけんきゅういん） 한국보건사회연구원
韓国民間資格協会（かんこくみんかんしかくきょうかい） 한국민간자격협회
韓国余暇レクリエーション協会（かんこくよかれくりえーしょんきょうかい） 한국여가레크리에이션협회
韓国療養保護協会（かんこくりょうようほごきょうかい） 한국요양보호협회
韓国療養保護士協会（かんこくりょうようほごしきょうかい） 한국요양보호사협회
韓国老化学会（かんこくろうかがっかい） 한국노화학회
韓国老人科学学術団体連合会（かんこくろうじんかがくがくじゅつだんたいれんごうかい） 한국노인과학술단체연합회
韓国老人虐待研究所（かんこくろうじんぎゃくたいけんきゅうしょ） 한국노인학대연구소
韓国老人虐待被害相談センター（かんこくろうじんぎゃ

くたいひがいそうだんせんたー）　한국노인학대피해상담센터
韓国老人虐待防止情報網（かんこくろうじんぎゃくたいぼうしじょうほうもう）　한국노인학대방지정보망
韓国老人互助会（かんこくろうじんごじょかい）　한국노인상조회
韓国老人施設理学治療士協議会（かんこくろうじんしせつりがくちりょうしきょうぎかい）　한국노인시설물리치료사협의회
韓国老人人権センター（かんこくろうじんじんけんせんたー）　한국노인인권센터
韓国老人人材開発院（かんこくろうじんじんざいかいはついん）　한국노인인력개발원
韓国老人生活支援財団（かんこくろうじんせいかつしえんざいだん）　한국노인생활지원재단
韓国老人総合福祉館協会（かんこくろうじんそうごうふくしかんきょうかい）　한국노인종합복지관협회
韓国老人体育協会（かんこくろうじんたいいくきょうかい）　한국노인체육협회
韓国老人大学研究会（かんこくろうじんだいがくけんきゅうかい）　한국노인대학연구회
韓国老人大学福祉協議会（かんこくろうじんだいがくふくしきょうぎかい）　한국노인대학복지협의회
韓国老人認知健康協会（かんこくろうじんにんちけんこうきょうかい）　한국노인인지건강협회
韓国老人の性教育研究所（かんこくろうじんのせいきょういくけんきゅうしょ）　한국노인성교육연구소
韓国老人の電話（かんこくろうじんのでんわ）　한국노인의 전화
韓国老人病研究所（かんこくろうじんびょうけんきゅうしょ）　한국노인병연구소
韓国老人福祉運動（かんこくろうじんふくしうんどう）　한국노인복지운동
韓国老人福祉会（かんこくろうじんふくしかい）　한국노인복지회（한국헬프에이지）
韓国老人福祉学会（かんこくろうじんふくしがっかい）　한국노인복지학회
韓国老人福祉個人施設協会（かんこくろうじんふくしこじんしせつきょうかい）　한국노인복지개인시설협회
韓国老人福祉施設協会（かんこくろうじんふくししせつきょうかい）　한국노인복지시설협회
韓国老人福祉宣教協議会（かんこくろうじんふくしせんきょうきょうぎかい）　한국노인복지선교협의회
韓国老人福祉センター（かんこくろうじんふくしせんたー）　한국노인복지센터
韓国老人福祉相談協会（かんこくろうじんふくしそうだんきょうかい）　한국노인복지상담협회
韓国老人福祉中央会（かんこくろうじんふくしちゅうおうかい）　한국노인복지중앙회
韓国老人福祉長期療養機関協会（かんこくろうじんふくしちょうきりょうようきかんきょうかい）　한국노인복지장기요양기관협회
韓国老人文化センター（かんこくろうじんぶんかせんたー）　한국노인문화센터
韓国老人放送（かんこくろうじんほうそう）　한국노인방송
韓国老人保護専門機関（かんこくろうじんほごせんもんきかん）　한국노인보호전문기관
韓国老人問題研究所（かんこくろうじんもんだいけんきゅうしょ）　한국노인문제연구소
韓国老人余暇専門指導者協会（かんこくろうじんよかせんもんしどうしゃきょうかい）　한국노인여가전문지도자협회
韓国老人療養施設経営研究会（かんこくろうじんりょうようしせつけいえいけんきゅうかい）　한국노인요양시설경영연구회
韓国老人療養センター（かんこくろうじんりょうようせんたー）　한국노인요양센터
韓国老人連合会（かんこくろうじんれんごうかい）　한국노인연합회
韓国老年学研究所（かんこくろうねんがくけんきゅうしょ）　한국노년학연구회
韓国老年志願奉仕会（かんこくろうねんしがんほうしかい）　한국노년자원봉사회
韓国老年有権者連盟（かんこくろうねんゆうけんしゃれんめい）　한국노년유권자연맹
看護助務師（かんごじょむし）　간호조무사
看護補助師（かんごほじょし）　간호보조사
漢方医（かんぽうい）　한방의
寄託食品（きたくしょくひん）　기탁식품
機能訓練士（きのうくんれんし）　기능훈련사
軍人年金（ぐんじんねんきん）　군인연금
ケア福祉士（けあふくしし）　케어복지사
軽費老人専門療養施設（けいひろうじんせんもんりょうようしせつ）　경비노인전문요양시설
軽費老人養老施設（けいひろうじんようろうしせつ）　경비노인양로시설
軽費老人療養施設（けいひろうじんりょうようしせつ）　경비노인요양시설
敬老憲章（けいろうけんしょう）　경로헌장
敬老孝親思想（けいろうこうしんしそう）　경로효친사상
敬老食堂（けいろうしょくどう）　경로식당
敬老大学（けいろうだいがく）　경로대학
敬老堂（けいろうどう）　경로당
敬老堂活性化協議体（けいろうどうかっせいかきょうぎたい）　경로당활성화협의체
敬老堂活性化事業（けいろうどうかっせいかじぎょう）　경로당활성화사업
敬老年金（けいろうねんきん）　경로연금
敬老優待（けいろうゆうたい）　경로우대
敬老優待サービス（けいろうゆうたいさーびす）　경로우대서비스
敬老優待証（けいろうゆうたいしょう）　경로우대증
敬老優待制度（けいろうゆうたいせいど）　경로우대제도

敬老優待割引制度（けいろうゆうたいわりびきせいど）경로우대할인제도
結縁事業（けつえんじぎょう）　결연사업
減額老齢年金（げんがくろうれいねんきん）　감액노령연금
健康保険財政安定総合対策（けんこうほけんざいせいあんていそうごうたいさく）건강보험재정안정종합대책
健康保健財政運営局（けんこうほけんざいせいうんえいきょく）건강보건재정운영국
健康保険審査評価院（けんこうほけんしんさひょうかいん）건강보험심사평가원
交通手当（こうつうてあて）　교통수당
公的老人療養保障推進企画団（こうてきろうじんりょうようほしょうすいしんきかくだん）공적노인요양보장추진기획단
公務員年金（こうむいんねんきん）　공무원연금
高麗葬（こうらいそう）　고려장 [日本でいう姥捨山]
高齢社会基本法（こうれいしゃかいきほんほう）　고령사회기본법
高齢社会対策基本法（こうれいしゃかいたいさくきほんほう）　고령사회대책기본법
高齢者雇用（こうれいしゃこよう）　고령자고용
高齢者雇用支援金（こうれいしゃこようしえんきん）　고령자고용지원금
高齢者雇用情報センター（こうれいしゃこようじょうほうせんたー）　고령자고용정보센터
高齢者雇用奨励金（こうれいしゃこようしょうれいきん）　고령자고용장려금
高齢者雇用促進奨励金（こうれいしゃこようそくしんしょうれいきん）　고령자고용촉진장려금
高齢者雇用促進法（こうれいしゃこようそくしんほう）　고령자고용촉진법
高齢者就業（こうれいしゃしゅうぎょう）　고령자취업
高齢者就業斡旋事業（こうれいしゃしゅうぎょうあっせんじぎょう）　고령자취업알선사업
高齢者就業斡旋センター（こうれいしゃしゅうぎょうあっせんせんたー）　고령자취업알선센터
高齢者就業支援センター（こうれいしゃしゅうぎょうしえんせんたー）　고령자취업지원센터
高齢者就業情報（こうれいしゃしゅうぎょうじょうほう）　고령자취업정보
高齢者人材銀行（こうれいしゃじんざいぎんこう）　고령자인재은행
高齢者創業支援（こうれいしゃそうぎょうしえん）　고령자창업지원
高齢親和産業（こうれいしんわさんぎょう）　고령친화산업
高齢親和産業支援センター（こうれいしんわさんぎょうしえんせんたー）　고령친화산업지원센터
高齢親和産業振興法（こうれいしんわさんぎょうしんこうほう）　고령친화산업진흥법
国際老人文化芸術祭（こくさいろうじんぶんかげいじゅつさい）　국제노인문화예술제
国民基礎生活受給者（こくみんきそせいかつじゅきゅうしゃ）　국민기초생활수급자
国民健康保険公団（こくみんけんこうほけんこうだん）　국민건강보험공단
国民生活基礎生活保障法（こくみんせいかつきそせいかつほしょうほう）　국민생활기초생활보장법
国民年金公団（こくみんねんきんこうだん）　국민연금공단
雇用差別禁止法（こようさべつきんしほう）　고용차별금지법
雇用政策基本法（こようせいさくきほんほう）　고용정책기본법
在家福祉事業（ざいけふくしじぎょう）　재가복지사업
在宅福祉奉仕センター（ざいたくふくしほうしせんたー）　재가복지봉사센터
在宅老人福祉事業（ざいたくろうじんふくしじぎょう）　재가노인복지사업
志願奉仕（しがんほうし）　지원봉사
志願奉仕員育成事業（しがんほうしいんいくせいじぎょう）　지원봉사원육성사업
志願奉仕活動（しがんほうしかつどう）　지원봉사활동
市郡区（しぐんく）　시군구 [日本でいう市区町村]
実費養老施設（じっぴようろうしせつ）　실비양로시설
実費老人福祉住宅（じっぴろうじんふくしじゅうたく）　실비노인복지주택
社会福祉館（しゃかいふくしかん）　사회복지관
儒教思想（じゅきょうしそう）　유교사상
熟年再婚（じゅくねんさいこん）　황혼재혼
熟年離婚（じゅくねんりこん）　황혼이혼
障害者長期療養保険制度（しょうがいしゃちょうきりょうようほけんせいど）　장애인장기요양보험제도
女性老人事業（じょせいろうじんじぎょう）　여성노인사업
シルバー産業育成推進委員会（しるばーさんぎょういくせいすいしんいいんかい）　실버산업육성추진위원회
シルバータウン（しるばーたうん）　실버타운
鬢髪（すばる）　수발
先家庭保護・後社会保障（せんかていほご・ごしゃかいほしょう）　선보호・후사회보장
全国フードバンク（ぜんこくふーどばんく）　전국푸드뱅크
全国療養保護士協会（ぜんこくりょうようほごしきょうかい）　전국요양보호사협회
全国老人健康祭（ぜんこくろうじんけんこうさい）　전국노인건강축제
全国老人病院協議会（ぜんこくろうじんびょういんきょうぎかい）　전국노인병원협의회
全国老人福祉館大会（ぜんこくろうじんふくしかんたいかい）　전국노인복지관대회
全国老人福祉団体協議会（ぜんこくろうじんふくしだんたいきょうぎかい）　전국노인복지단체협의회
全国老人福祉団体連合会（ぜんこくろうじんふくしだん

たいれんごうかい） 전국노인복지단체연합회
全国老人保護専門機関（ぜんこくろうじんほごせんもんきかん） 전국노인보호전문기관
壮年奉仕団（そうねんほうしだん） 장년봉사단
双務的扶養（そうむてきふよう） 쌍무적 부양
大韓看護協会（だいかんかんごきょうかい） 대한간호협회
大韓看護福祉財団（だいかんかんごふくしざいだん） 대한간호복지재단
大韓ケア福祉学会（だいかんけあふくしがっかい） 대한케어복지학회
大韓シルバー産業協会（だいかんしるばーさんぎょうきょうかい） 대한실버산업협회
大韓全人ケア福祉協会（だいかんぜんじんけあふくしきょうかい） 대한전인케어복지협회
大韓退職者協会（だいかんたいしょくしゃきょうかい） 대한은퇴자협회
大韓認知症学会（だいかんにんちしょうがっかい） 대한치매학회
大韓脳血管障害学会（だいかんのうけっかんしょうがいがっかい） 대한뇌졸중학회
大韓療養保護士協会（だいかんりょうようごしきょうかい） 대한요양보호사협회
大韓臨床老人医学会（だいかんりんしょうろうじんいがくかい） 대한임상노인의학회
大韓老化防止医学会（だいかんろうかぼうしいがくかい） 대한노화방지의학회
大韓老人医学会（だいかんろうじんいがくかい） 대한노인의학회
大韓老人会（だいかんろうじんかい） 대한노인회
大韓老人科学発明協会（だいかんろうじんかがくはつめいきょうかい） 대한노인과학발명협회
大韓老人精神医学会（だいかんろうじんせいしんいがくかい） 대한노인정신의학회
大韓老人内科学会（だいかんろうじんないかがっかい） 대한노인내과학회
大韓老人病院協議会（だいかんろうじんびょういんきょうぎかい） 대한노인병원협의회
大韓老人病学会（だいかんろうじんびょうがっかい） 대한노인병학회
大韓老人福祉新聞（だいかんろうじんふくししんぶん） 대한노인복지신문
大韓老人理学治療学会（だいかんろうじんりがくちりょうびょういんきょうかい） 대한노인물리치료학회
大韓老人療養病院協会（だいかんろうじんりょうようびょういんきょうかい） 대한노인요양병원협회
大韓老人レクリエーション医学会（だいかんろうじんれくりえーしょんいがくかい） 대한노인재활의학회
退職移民（たいしょくいみん） 은퇴이민
退職農場（たいしょくのうじょう） 은퇴농장
短期保護（たんきほご） 단기보호
短期保護事業（たんきほごじぎょう） 단기보호사업
短期保護事業所（たんきほごじぎょうしょ） 단기보호사업소
短期保護施設（たんきほごしせつ） 단기보호시설
地域社会福祉館（ちいきしゃかいふくしかん） 지역사회복지관
地域福祉協力事業（ちいきふくしきょうりょくじぎょう） 지역복지협력사업
中央老人保護専門機関（ちゅうおうろうじんほごせんもんきかん） 중앙노인보호전문기관
昼間保護（ちゅうかんほご） 주간보호
昼間保護事業（ちゅうかんほごじぎょう） 주간보호사업
昼間保護事業所（ちゅうかんほごじぎょうしょ） 주간보호사업소
昼間保護施設（ちゅうかんほごしせつ） 주간보호시설
昼・夜間保護（ちゅう・やかんほご） 주・야간 보호
長期保護施設（ちょうきほごしせつ） 장기보호시설
長期療養機関（ちょうきりょうようきかん） 장기요양기관
長期療養施設（ちょうきりょうようしせつ） 장기요양시설
長期療養審査委員会（ちょうきりょうようしんさいいんかい） 장기요양심사위원회
長期療養審判委員会（ちょうきりょうようしんぱんいいんかい） 장기요양심판위원회
長期療養数価（ちょうきりょうようすうか） 장기요양수가
長期療養等級（ちょうきりょうようとうきゅう） 장기요양등급
長期療養等級認定（ちょうきりょうようとうきゅうにんてい） 장기요양등급인정
長期療養等級判定委員会（ちょうきりょうようとうきゅうはんていいいんかい） 장기요양등급판정위원회
長期療養認定書（ちょうきりょうようにんていしょ） 장기요양인정서
長期療養認定調査票（ちょうきりょうようにんていちょうさひょう） 장기요양인정조사표
長期療養認定点数（ちょうきりょうようにんていてんすう） 장기요양인정점수
長期療養判定委員会（ちょうきりょうようはんていいいんかい） 장기요양판정위원회
長期療養保険料（ちょうきりょうようほけんりょう） 장기요양보험료
長期療養保護（ちょうきりょうようほご） 장기요양보호
賃金ピーク制（ちんぎんぴーくせい） 임금피크제
低出産・高齢社会委員会（ていしゅっさん・こうれいしゃかいいいんかい） 저출산・고령사회위원회
低出産・高齢社会基本法（ていしゅっさん・こうれいしゃかいきほんほう） 저출산・고령사회기본법
デイ・ナイトサービス（でい・ないとさーびす） 데이・나이트서비스
定年退職者継続雇用奨励金（ていねんたいしょくしゃけいぞくこようしょうれいきん） 정년퇴직자계속고용

韓国
日韓

장려금
特別現金給付 (とくべつげんきんきゅうふ) 特別현금급여
特例療養費 (とくれいりょうようひ) 특례요양비
認知症専門病院 (にんちしょうせんもんびょういん) 치매전문병원
認知症・脳血管障害家族教室 (にんちしょう・のうけっかんしょうがいかぞくきょうしつ) 치매・뇌졸증가족교실
配食サービス (はいしょくさーびす) 배식서비스
引きこもり老人 (ひきこもりろうじん) 두문불출노인
ビジョン2030 (びじょんにせんさんじゅう) 비전2030
標準勤労契約書 (ひょうじゅんきんろうけいやくしょ) 표준근로계약서
標準長期療養利用計画書 (ひょうじゅんちょうきりょうようりようけいかくしょ) 표준장기요양이용계획서
フードバンク (ふーどばんく) 푸드뱅크
フードバンク食品 (ふーどばんくしょくひん) 푸드뱅크식품
片務的扶養 (へんむてきふよう) 편무적 부양
訪問看護経過記録等 (ほうもんかんごけいかきろくぼ) 방문간호경과기록부
訪問看護補助師教育 (ほうもんかんごほじょしきょういく) 방문간호보조사교육
訪問療養 (ほうもんりょうよう) 방문요양
保健福祉部 (ほけんふくしぶ) 보건복지부
無料養老施設 (むりょうようろうしせつ) 무료양로시설
無料老人専門療養施設 (むりょうろうじんせんもんりょうようしせつ) 무료노인전문요양시설
無料老人養老施設 (むりょうろうじんようろうしせつ) 무료노인양로시설
無料老人療養施設 (むりょうろうじんりょうようしせつ) 무료노인요양시설
夜間保護 (やかんほご) 야간보호
友好訪問サービス (ゆうこうほうもんさーびす) 우호방문서비스
有料養老施設 (ゆうりょうようろうしせつ) 유료양로시설
有料老人専門療養施設 (ゆうりょうろうじんせんもんりょうようしせつ) 유료노인전문요양시설
有料老人福祉住宅 (ゆうりょうろうじんふくしじゅうたく) 유료노인복지주택
有料老人養老施設 (ゆうりょうろうじんようろうしせつ) 유료노인양로시설
有料老人療養施設 (ゆうりょうろうじんりょうようしせつ) 유료노인요양시설
嫁姑葛藤 (よめしゅうとめかっとう) 고부갈등
療養 (りょうよう) 요양
療養院 (りょうよういん) 요양원
療養給付費用 (りょうようきゅうふひよう) 요양급여비용

療養病院療養費 (りょうようびょういんりょうようひ) 요양병원요양비
療養保護 (りょうようほご) 요양보호
療養保護管理士 (りょうようほごかんりし) [日本でいうケアマネジャー] 요양보호관리사
療養保護管理士制度 (りょうようほごかんりしせいど) 요양보호관리사제도
療養保護士 (りょうようほごし) 요양보호사
療養保護士養成カリキュラム (りょうようほごしようせいかりきゅらむ) 요양보호사양성커리큘럼
療養保護士養成講座 (りょうようほごしようせいこうざ) 요양보호사양성강좌
療養保護士養成施設 (りょうようほごしようせいしせつ) 요양보호사양성시설
療養保護士養成標準教科書 (りょうようほごしようせいひょうじゅんきょうかしょ) 요양보호사양성표준교과서
暦年齢 (れきねんれい) 달력나이
老後生涯設計専門家 (ろうごしょうがいせっけいせんもんか) 노후생애설계전문가
老人アパート (ろうじんあぱーと) 노인아파트
老人医療福祉施設 (ろうじんいりょうふくししせつ) 노인의료복지시설
老人学校 (ろうじんがっこう) 노인학교
老人学校指導師 (ろうじんがっこうしどうし) 노인학교지도사
老人家庭ドウミ事業 (ろうじんかていどうみじぎょう) 노인가정도우미사업
老人看護学会 (ろうじんかんごがっかい) 노인간호학회
老人看護センター (ろうじんかんごせんたー) 노인간호센터
老人虐待相談センター (ろうじんぎゃくたいそうだんせんたー) 노인학대상담센터
老人休養施設 (ろうじんきゅうようしせつ) 노인휴양시설
老人休養所 (ろうじんきゅうようじょ) 노인휴양소
老人教育 (ろうじんきょういく) 노인교육
老人教室 (ろうじんきょうしつ) 노인교실
老人共同作業場 (ろうじんきょうどうさぎょうじょう) 노인공동작업장
老人居住福祉施設 (ろうじんきょじゅうふくししせつ) 노인거주복지시설
老人権益保護党 (ろうじんけんえきほごとう) 노인권익보호당
老人健康＆福祉研究所 (ろうじんけんこう＆ふくしけんきゅうしょ) 노인건강＆복지연구소
老人健康診断 (ろうじんけんこうしんだん) 노인건강진단
老人健康増進プログラム研究所 (ろうじんけんこうぞうしんぷろぐらむけんきゅうしょ) 노인건강증진프로그램연구소
老人健康体操競演大会 (ろうじんけんこうたいそうきょ

うえんたいかい)　노인건강체조경연대회
老人憲章（ろうじんけんしょう）　노인헌장
老人在宅福祉事業所（ろうじんざいたくふくしじぎょうしょ）　노인재가복지사업소
老人在宅福祉施設（ろうじんざいたくふくししせつ）　노인재가복지시설
老人志願奉仕団（ろうじんしがんほうしだん）　노인자원봉사단
老人自殺（ろうじんじさつ）　노인자살
老人自殺予防センター（ろうじんじさつよぼうせんたー）　노인자살예방센터
老人住居研究所（ろうじんじゅうきょけんきゅうしょ）　노인주거연구소
老人住居福祉施設（ろうじんじゅうきょふくししせつ）　노인주거복지시설
老人準備教育（ろうじんじゅんびきょういく）　노인준비교육
老人乗車券制度（ろうじんじょうしゃけんせいど）　노인승차권제도
老人人材活用対策（ろうじんじんざいかつようたいさく）　노인인력활용대책
老人スバル評価管理院（ろうじんすばるひょうかかんりいん）　노인수발평가관리원 [スバルはケアの意味］
老人スバル保険法案（ろうじんすばるほけんほうあん）　노인수발보험법안
老人スバル保障法律制定案（ろうじんすばるほしょうほうりつせいていあん）　노인수발보장법률제정안
老人生活科学研究所（ろうじんせいかつかがくけんきゅうしょ）　노인생활과학연구소
老人専門病院（ろうじんせんもんびょういん）　노인전문병원
老人専門療養施設（ろうじんせんもんりょうようしせつ）　노인전문요양시설
老人総合福祉館（ろうじんそうごうふくしかん）　노인종합복지관
老人相談員（ろうじんそうだんいん）　노인상담원
老人大学（ろうじんだいがく）　노인대학
老人タウン（ろうじんたうん）　노인타운
老人昼間保護施設（ろうじんちゅうかんほごしせつ）　노인주간보호시설
老人長期療養（ろうじんちょうきりょうよう）　노인장기요양
老人長期療養介護保険制度（ろうじんちょうきりょうようかいごほけんせいど）　노인장기요양개호보험제도
老人長期療養給付費用審査・支給決定通知書（ろうじんちょうきりょうようきゅうふひようしんさ・しきゅうけっていつうちしょ）　노인장기요양급여비용심사・지급결정통지서
老人長期療養給付費用審査請求書（ろうじんちょうきりょうようきゅうふひようしんせいきゅうしょ）　노인장기요양급여비용심사청구서
老人長期療養給付費用審査明細書（ろうじんちょうきりょうようきゅうふひようしんさめいさいしょ）　노인장기요양급여비용심사명세서
老人長期療養給付費用請求明細書受付証（ろうじんちょうきりょうようきゅうふひようせいきゅうめいさいしょうけつけしょう）　노인장기요양급여비용청구명세서접수증
老人長期療養給付費用精算審査決定通知書（ろうじんちょうきりょうようきゅうふひようせいさんしんさけっていつうちしょ）　노인장기요양급여비용정산심사결정통지서
老人長期療養保険（ろうじんちょうきりょうようほけん）　노인장기요양보험
老人長期療養保険運営センター（ろうじんちょうきりょうようほけんうんえいせんたー）　노인장기요양보험운영센터
老人長期療養保険制度（ろうじんちょうきりょうようほけんせいど）　노인장기요양보험제도
老人長期療養保険法（ろうじんちょうきりょうようほけんほう）　노인장기요양보험법
老人長期療養保険法施行規則（ろうじんちょうきりょうようほけんほうせこうきそく）　노인장기요양보험법시행규칙
老人長期療養保険法施行令（ろうじんちょうきりょうようほけんほうせこうれい）　노인장기요양보험법시행령
老人長期療養保護総合対策（ろうじんちょうきりょうようほごそうごうたいさく）　노인장기요양보호종합대책
老人長期療養保障（ろうじんちょうきりょうようほしょう）　노인장기요양보장
老人手当（ろうじんてあて）　노인수당
老人ドウミ（ろうじんどうみ）　노인도우미 [日本でいうホームヘルパー]
老人能力銀行（ろうじんのうりょくぎんこう）　노인능력은행
老人の４苦（ろうじんのしく）　노인４고
老人の日（ろうじんのひ）　노인의 날
老人福祉会館（ろうじんふくしかいかん）　노인복지회관
老人福祉館（ろうじんふくしかん）　노인복지관
老人福祉士（ろうじんふくしし）　노인복지사
老人福祉施設連合会（ろうじんふくししせつれんごうかい）　노인복지시설연합회
老人福祉住宅（ろうじんふくしじゅうたく）　노인복지주택
老人福祉相談（ろうじんふくしそうだん）　노인복지상담
老人福祉相談員（ろうじんふくしそうだんいん）　노인복지상담원
老人扶養（ろうじんふよう）　노인부양
老人扶養忌避現象（ろうじんふようきひげんしょう）　노인부양기피현상
老人文化祭（ろうじんぶんかさい）　노인문화제
老人保健医療施設（ろうじんほけんいりょうしせつ）

韓国
日韓

노인보건의료시설
老人保健福祉総合対策（ろうじんほけんふくしそうごうたいさく）노인보건복지종합대책
老人保健福祉対策委員会（ろうじんほけんふくしたいさくいいんかい）노인보건복지대책위원회
老人保護専門機関（ろうじんほごせんもんきかん）노인보호전문기관
老人ボランティア（ろうじんぼらんてぃあ）노인자원봉사
老人村（ろうじんむら）노인촌락
老人無料給食（ろうじんむりょうきゅうしょく）노인무료급식
老人遊休労働力（ろうじんゆうきゅうろうどうりょく）노인유휴노동력
老人養老施設（ろうじんようろうしせつ）노인양로시설
老人余暇（ろうじんよか）노인여가
老人余暇福祉施設（ろうじんよかふくししせつ）노인여가복지시설
老人療養院（ろうじんりょうよういん）노인요양원
老人療養共同生活家庭（ろうじんりょうようきょうどうせいかつかてい）노인요양공동생활가정
老人療養施設（ろうじんりょうようしせつ）노인요양시설
老人療養福祉施設（ろうじんりょうようふくししせつ）노인요양복지시설
老齢線（ろうれいせん）노령선
老齢手当（ろうれいてあて）노령수당

4. 独逸（ドイツ）における介護福祉等関連用語【独　和】

Allgemeine Ortskrankenkasse：AOK〔F〕　一般地区疾病金庫
Altenbetreuungszentrum〔N〕　高齢者世話センター
Altenheim〔N〕　老人ホーム
Altenhilfe〔F〕　高齢者扶助
Altenpflege〔F〕　高齢者介護
Altenpflegeheim〔N〕　高齢者介護施設
Altenpflegehelfer/in　老人介護ヘルパー
Altenpfleger/in　老人介護士
Altenwerkstätte〔F〕　老人作業所
Altenwohnung〔F〕　老人住宅
alternde Gesellschaft〔F〕　高齢化社会
Alters-und Invaliditätssicherung〔F〕　老齢・障害保障
Altersgeld〔N〕　老齢手当
Alterskasse〔F〕　老齢金庫
Altersrente〔F〕　老齢年金
Alterssicherung〔F〕　老齢保障
ambulante Pflege〔F〕　訪問介護
ambulante Versorgung〔F〕　訪問介助
ambulanter Pflegedienst〔M〕　訪問介護サービス
Angehörige/r　親族
Antrag〔M〕　申請
Arbeiterkrankenversicherungsgesetz〔N〕　労働者疾病保険法
Arbeiterversicherung〔F〕　労働者保険
Arbeiterwohlfahrt-Bundesverbande.V.：AWO〔F〕　労働者福祉連合会
Arbeitnehmer/in　被用者
Arbeitsentgelt〔N〕　労働報酬
Arbeitsgesetzbuch〔N〕　労働法典
Arbeitslose/r　失業者
Arbeitslosengeld〔N〕　失業給付金
Arbeitslosenversicherung〔F〕　失業保険
Arbeitsmarkt〔M〕　労働市場
Arbeitsnebenkosten〔Pl〕　労務付帯経費
Arbeitsunfähigkeit〔F〕　就業不能
Arbeitsunfall〔M〕　労働災害
Arznei〔F〕　医薬品
Arztgutachten〔N〕　医師の専門的意見書
Arzthonorar〔N〕　医師診療報酬
ärztlicher Kunstfehler〔M〕　医療過誤
Ausbildung〔F〕　訓練教育
Ausgleichsfond〔M〕　負担調整基金
Badekur〔F〕　温泉療法
Beanstandung〔F〕　異議
Bedürftigkeitsprüfung〔F〕　ミーンズ・テスト
Begutachtungs-Richtlinie〔F〕　審査指針
Behandlung〔F〕　治療
Behandlungspflege〔F〕　治療の介護

Behinderte/r　障害者
Behindertenheim〔N〕　障害者ホーム
Behindertenhilfe〔F〕　障害者援助
Behindertenpflege〔F〕　障害者介護
Behindertenrente〔F〕　障害年金
Behindertensport〔M〕　障害者スポーツ
Behindertenwerkstätte〔F〕　障害者作業所
Behinderung〔F〕　障害
Beitrag〔M〕　保険料
Beitragsbemessungsgrenze〔F〕　保険料算定限度額
Beitragssatz〔M〕　保険料率
Beratung〔F〕　助言
Betreuer/in　世話人
Betreuung〔F〕　世話
Betriebskrankenkasse〔F〕　企業疾病金庫
Bewohner/in　居住者
Bezirkssozialarbeit〔F〕　地区ソーシャルワーク
Bundesaufsichtsamt〔N〕für das Versicherungswesen：BAV　連邦保険制度監督庁
Bundesgesetzblatt〔N〕　連邦官報
Bundesministerium〔N〕für Arbeit und Soziales：BMAS　連邦労働・社会秩序省
Bundesministerium〔N〕für Familie, Senioren, Frauen und Jugend：BMFSFJ　連邦家庭・高齢者・女性・青少年省
Bundesministerium〔N〕für Gesundheit：BMG　連邦保健省
Bundessozialhilfegesetz：BSHG〔N〕　連邦社会扶助法
Bundesstaat〔M〕　連邦国家
Bundesvereinigung〔F〕der Deutschen Arbeitgeberverbände　ドイツ使用者団体連邦連合会
Bundesversicherungsamt〔N〕　連邦保険庁
Bundesversorgungsgesetz：BVG〔N〕　連邦援護法
Datenschutz〔M〕　データ保護
Demenz〔F〕　認知症
Demenzkranke/r　認知症患者
Deutscher Caritasverband e.V.：DCW〔M〕　ドイツ・カリタス連合会
Deutsches Rotes Kreuz e.V.：DRK〔N〕　ドイツ赤十字社
Diakonisches Werk〔N〕der Evangelischen Kirche in Deutschland e.V.：DW　ドイツ福音主義教会奉仕団：ディアコニー
Empfänger/in　受給者
Ergänzungsleistung〔F〕　補足給付
Ernährung〔F〕　栄養摂取
Fallmanagement〔N〕　ケースマネジメント
Familienversicherte/r　家族被保険者
Familienversicherung〔F〕　家族保険

独逸
独和

Finanzausgleich〔M〕 財政調整
freie Wohlfahrtspflege〔F〕 民間福祉団体
Freiwilliges Soziales Jahr：FSJ〔N〕 任意社会奉仕年
Frontotemporale Demenz〔F〕 前頭側頭型認知症
Gastarbeiter/in 外国人労働者
Gebietskörperschaft〔F〕 地方公共団体
Geldleistung〔F〕 現金給付
Gemeinde〔F〕 市町村
Gemeindeverband〔M〕 市町村連合
Gemeinschaft〔F〕 ゲマインシャフト
gemeinschaftliche Verantwortung〔F〕 連帯責任
Gemeinschaftsaufgabe〔F〕 共同任務
Gemeinwohl〔N〕 公共の福祉
Generationenvertrag〔M〕 世代間契約
Gesellschaft〔F〕 ゲゼルシャフト
Gesellschaftspolitik〔F〕 社会政策
Gesundheitsreformgesetz：GRG〔N〕 医療保障改革法
Gesundheitswesen〔N〕 保健制度
Grundpflege〔F〕 基礎介護
Grundrente〔F〕 基礎年金
Grundsicherung〔F〕 基本保障
Hausarzt/ärztin 家庭医
Haushaltshilfe〔F〕 家事援助
häusliche Krankenpflege〔F〕 在宅看護
häusliche Pflege〔F〕 在宅介護
häusliche Versorgung〔F〕 在宅介助
hauswirtschaftliche Versorgung〔F〕 家事介助
Heilfürsorge〔F〕 医療扶助
Heilverfahren〔N〕 療養
Heimarbeit〔F〕 家内労働
Heimarbeiter/in 家内労働者
Heimarzt/ärztin ホーム医
Heimbeirat〔M〕 ホーム協議会
Heimentgelt〔N〕 ホーム報酬
Heimgesetz：HeimG〔N〕 ホーム法
Heimmindestbauverordnung：Heim-MindBauV〔F〕 ホーム最低建築令
Heimpflege〔F〕 施設介護
Heimvertrag〔M〕 ホーム契約
Hilfsmittel〔N〕 補助具
Hospiz〔N〕 ホスピス
Innungskrankenkasse〔F〕 同業組合疾病金庫
Invaliditäts- und Altersversicherungsgesetz〔N〕 廃疾老齢保険法
Invaliditäts- und Alterssicherung〔F〕 障害・老齢保障
Investitionskostenzuschuss〔M〕 投資助成
Kinder-Berücksichtigungsgesetz：KiBG〔N〕 公的介護保険の保険料に子供数を配慮する法
Kinder- und Jugendhilfegesetz：KJHG〔N〕 児童および少年援助法
Kinderfreibetrag〔M〕 子供控除

Kindergeld〔N〕 子供手当
Kinderkrankenpfleger/in 児童看護師
Kombinationsleistung〔F〕 組み合わせ給付
Körperpflege〔F〕 身体介護
Kostenerstattung〔F〕 費用還付
Krankengeld〔N〕 疾病給付金
Krankenhilfe〔F〕 疾病援助
Krankenkasse〔F〕 疾病金庫
Krankenkassenleistung〔F〕 疾病金庫給付
Krankenpflege〔F〕 看護
Krankenpflegestation〔F〕 看護所
Krankenversicherung〔F〕 疾病保険
Krankenversorgung〔F〕 疾病援護
Krankheit〔F〕 病気
Krankheitsurlaub〔M〕 病気休暇
Kuratorium Deutsche Altershilfe：KDA〔N〕 ドイツ高齢者援助機構
Kurzzeitpflege〔F〕 ショートステイ
Landespflegegesetz〔N〕 州介護法
Leistungs- und Preisvergleichsliste〔F〕 給付と価格の比較リスト
Leistungsbetrag〔M〕 給付額
Leistungsempfänger/in 給付受給者
Lewy-Körper-Demenz〔F〕 レビー小体型認知症
Medicproof [Medizinischer Dienst der Privaten Krankenkassen] メデックプルーフ [民間疾病保険の医療サービス機構]
Medizinischer Dienst〔M〕der Krankenversicherung：MDK 疾病保険医療サービス機構
Medizinischer Dienst〔M〕des Spitzenverbandes Bund der Krankenkassen：MDS 疾病保険医療サービス機構の中央組織
mehrgliedrige Alteneinrichtung〔F〕 高齢者複合施設
mehrgliedrige Einrichtungen〔Pl〕 複合施設
mehrgliedriges Altenheim〔N〕 複合老人ホーム
Mindesteinkommen〔N〕 最低所得
Mindestsicherung〔F〕 最低保障
Mobilität〔F〕 移動
Nachlassgericht〔N〕 遺産裁判所
Nachtpflege〔F〕 ナイトケア
Paritätischer Wohlfahrtsverband-Gesamtverband e.V.：DPWV〔M〕 ドイツ同権福祉事業団
Pflege〔F〕 介護
Pflegebedürftige/r 要介護者
Pflegebedürftigkeit〔F〕 要介護
Pflegebedürftigkeits-Richtlinien：PflRi〔Pl〕 要介護指針
Pflegebeihilfe〔F〕 介護補助
Pflegeberater/in 介護アドバイザー
Pflegeberatung〔F〕 介護相談
Pflegedienst〔M〕 介護サービス
Pflegeeinrichtung〔F〕 介護施設
Pflegefachkraft〔F〕 介護専門職

Pflegegeld〔N〕介護手当
Pflegeheim〔N〕介護ホーム
Pflegehilfsmittel〔N〕介護補助具
Pflegekasse〔F〕介護金庫
Pflegekostenversicherung〔F〕介護費用保険
Pflegekurs〔M〕介護講習
Pflegeleistungs-Ergänzungsgesetz：PflEG〔N〕
　介護給付補完法
Pflegeperson〔F〕介護者
Pflegepersonal〔N〕介護職員
Pflegeplan〔M〕介護計画
Pflegequalitätssicherungsgesetz：PQsG〔N〕
　介護の質の保障法
Pflegequote〔F〕要介護率
Pflegereform〔F〕介護改革
Pflegerentenversicherung〔F〕介護年金保険
Pflegerisiko〔N〕介護リスク
Pflegesachleistung〔F〕介護現物給付
Pflegestatistik〔F〕介護統計
Pflegestufe〔F〕介護等級
Pflegestufe 0〔F〕介護等級0
Pflegestützpunkt〔M〕介護支援拠点
Pflegetagegeldversicherung〔F〕介護期間手当保険
Pflegetätigkeit〔F〕介護活動
Pflegeurlaub〔M〕介護休暇
Pflegevergütung〔F〕介護報酬
Pflegeversicherung〔F〕介護保険
Pflegevertrag〔M〕介護契約
Pflegevertretung〔F〕代替介護
Pflege-Weiterentwicklungsgesetz：PfWG〔N〕
　介護拡張法
Pflegewohngeld〔N〕介護住宅手当
Pflegezeit〔F〕介護時間
Pflegezulage〔F〕介護加算
Pflichtversicherte/r〔F〕強制被保険者
Pflichtversicherung〔F〕義務保険
Praktikant/in　見習生
private Pflege-Pflichtversicherung〔F〕民間介護義務
　保険
private Pflegeversicherung〔F〕民間介護保険
Qualitätssicherung〔F〕質の保障
Rahmenvertrag〔M〕枠組契約
Rehabilitation〔F〕リハビリテーション
Rehabilitationseinrichtung〔F〕リハビリテーション
　施設
Rehabilitationsleistung〔F〕リハビリテーション給付
Rentenversicherung〔F〕年金保険
Rentenversicherungbeitrag〔M〕年金保険料
Rentner/in　年金受給者
Sachleistung〔F〕現物給付
Schwarzarbeit〔F〕闇労働
Schwerbehinderte/r　重障害者
Schwerbehindertengesetz：SchwbG〔N〕重障害者
　保護法
Selbsthilfe〔F〕自助
Selbsthilfegruppe〔F〕自助グループ
Senioren-Wohngemeinschaft〔F〕高齢者住居共同体
Solidarbeitrag〔M〕連帯費用
Solidargemeinschaft〔F〕連帯社会
Solidaritätsprinzip〔N〕連帯性原理
Sozialabgaben〔Pl〕社会保険料分担金
Sozialamt〔N〕社会福祉事務所
Sozialarbeit〔F〕ソーシャルケースワーク
Sozialarbeiter/in　ソーシャルワーカー
Sozialbeamte/in　福祉事務所員
Sozialbeirat〔M〕社会審議会
Sozialbeitrag〔M〕社会保険料
Sozialbericht〔M〕社会報告書
Sozialbudget〔N〕社会予算
soziale Marktwirtschaft〔F〕社会的市場経済
soziale Pflegeversicherung〔F〕公的介護保険
soziale Sicherung〔F〕社会保障
soziale Wohlfahrt〔F〕社会福祉
soziale Wohlfahrtspflege〔F〕社会福祉サービス
sozialer Wohlfahrtsstaat〔M〕社会福祉国家
Sozialgesetzbuch：SGB〔N〕社会法典
Sozialhilfe〔F〕社会扶助
Sozialleistung〔F〕社会給付
Sozialmedizin〔M〕社会保険審査医師
Sozialrecht〔N〕社会権
Sozialstaatsprinzip〔N〕社会国家の原則
Sozialstation〔F〕ソーシャルステーション
Sozialversicherung〔F〕社会保険
Sozialversicherungsträger〔M〕社会保険保険者
Sozialversorgung〔F〕社会援護
stationäre Versorgung〔F〕施設介助
Subsidiaritätsprinzip〔N〕補完性原理
Tagespflege〔F〕デイケア
technisches Hilfsmittel〔N〕技術的な補助具
teilstationäre Pflege〔F〕通所介護
Umlageverfahren〔N〕賦課方式
Unfallversicherung〔F〕労災保険
Unterhaltsberechtigter〔M〕被扶養者
Unterhaltsgeld〔N〕生計手当
Unterhaltspflicht〔F〕扶養義務
Unterstützungskasse〔F〕共済金庫
Unterstützungsverein〔M〕共済組合
Urlaubspflege〔F〕介護休業
vaskuläre Demenz〔F〕脳血管性認知症
Verbrauchsprodukt〔N〕消耗品
Vergütungsvertrag〔M〕報酬契約
Versicherte/r　被保険者
Versicherungsleistung〔F〕保険給付
Versicherungspflicht〔F〕保険加入義務
Versicherungspflichtige/r　保険加入義務者
Versicherungsprinzip〔N〕保険原理

独逸
独和

Versicherungsträger〔M〕 保険者
Versorgungsvertrag〔M〕 介助契約
Verwahrpflege〔F〕 留置介護
vollstationäre Pflege〔F〕 入所施設介護
vollstationäre Pflegeeinrichtung〔F〕 入所介護施設
Wohlfahrtsstaat〔M〕 福祉国家
Wohngemeinschaft〔F〕 住居共同体
Zentralwohlfahrtsstelle〔F〕der Juden in Deutschland e.V.：ZWStdJ ドイツユダヤ人中央福祉所
Zivildienst〔M〕 兵役代替勤務
zugelassene Pflegeeinrichtung〔F〕 認可介護施設
Zuzahlung〔F〕 自己負担

4．独逸（ドイツ）における介護福祉等関連用語 【和　独】

異議（いぎ）　Beanstandung〔F〕
遺産裁判所（いさんさいばんしょ）　Nachlassgericht〔N〕
医師診療報酬（いししんりょうほうしゅう）　Arzthonorar〔N〕
医師の専門的意見書（いしのせんもんてきいけんしょ）　Arztgutachten〔N〕
一般地区疾病金庫（いっぱんちくしっぺいきんこ）　Allgemeine Ortskrankenkasse：AOK〔F〕
移動（いどう）　Mobilität〔F〕
医薬品（いやくひん）　Arznei〔F〕
医療過誤（いりょうかご）　ärztlicher Kunstfehler〔M〕
医療扶助（いりょうふじょ）　Heilfürsorge〔F〕
医療保障改革法（いりょうほしょうかいかくほう）　Gesundheitsreformgesetz：GRG〔N〕
栄養摂取（えいようせっしゅ）　Ernährung〔F〕
温泉療法（おんせんりょうほう）　Badekur〔F〕
介護（かいご）　Pflege〔F〕
介護アドバイザー（かいごあどばいざー）　Pflegeberater/in
介護改革（かいごかいかく）　Pflegereform〔F〕
介護拡張法（かいごかくちょうほう）　Pflege-Weiterentwicklungsgesetz：PfWG〔N〕
介護加算（かいごかさん）　Pflegezulage〔F〕
介護活動（かいごかつどう）　Pflegetätigkeit〔F〕
介護期間手当保険（かいごきかんてあてほけん）　Pflegetagegeldversicherung〔F〕
介護休暇（かいごきゅうか）　Pflegeurlaub〔M〕
介護休業（かいごきゅうぎょう）　Urlaubspflege〔F〕
介護給付補完法（かいごきゅうふほかんほう）　Pflegeleistungs-Ergänzungsgesetz：PflEG〔N〕
介護金庫（かいごきんこ）　Pflegekasse〔F〕
外国人労働者（がいこくじんろうどうしゃ）　Gastarbeiter/in
介護計画（かいごけいかく）　Pflegeplan〔M〕
介護契約（かいごけいやく）　Pflegevertrag〔M〕
介護現物給付（かいごげんぶつきゅうふ）　Pflegesachleistung〔F〕
介護講習（かいごこうしゅう）　Pflegekurs〔M〕
介護サービス（かいごさーびす）　Pflegedienst〔M〕
介護支援拠点（かいごしえんきょてん）　Pflegestützpunkt〔M〕
介護時間（かいごじかん）　Pflegezeit〔F〕
介護施設（かいごしせつ）　Pflegeeinrichtung〔F〕
介護者（かいごしゃ）　Pflegeperson〔F〕
介護住宅手当（かいごじゅうたくてあて）　Pflegewohngeld〔N〕
介護職員（かいごしょくいん）　Pflegepersonal〔N〕
介護専門職員（かいごせんもんしょくいん）　Pflegefachkraft〔F〕

介護相談（かいごそうだん）　Pflegeberatung〔F〕
介護手当（かいごてあて）　Pflegegeld〔N〕
介護等級（かいごとうきゅう）　Pflegestufe〔F〕
介護等級0（かいごとうきゅうぜろ）　Pflegestufe 0〔F〕
介護統計（かいごとうけい）　Pflegestatistik〔F〕
介護年金保険（かいごねんきんほけん）　Pflegerentenversicherung〔F〕
介護の質の保障法（かいごのしつのほしょうほう）　Pflegequalitätssicherungsgesetz：PQsG〔N〕
介護費用保険（かいごひようほけん）　Pflegekostenversicherung〔F〕
介護報酬（かいごほうしゅう）　Pflegevergütung〔F〕
介護保険（かいごほけん）　Pflegeversicherung〔F〕
介護補助（かいごほじょ）　Pflegebeihilfe〔F〕
介護補助具（かいごほじょぐ）　Pflegehilfsmittel〔N〕
介護ホーム（かいごほーむ）　Pflegeheim〔N〕
介護リスク（かいごりすく）　Pflegerisiko〔N〕
介助契約（かいじょけいやく）　Versorgungsvertrag〔M〕
家事援助（かじえんじょ）　Haushaltshilfe〔F〕
家事介助（かじかいじょ）　hauswirtschaftliche Versorgung〔F〕
家族被保険者（かぞくひほけんしゃ）　Familienversicherte/r
家族保険（かぞくほけん）　Familienversicherung〔F〕
家庭医（かていい）　Hausarzt/ärztin
家内労働（かないろうどう）　Heimarbeit〔F〕
家内労働者（かないろうどうしゃ）　Heimarbeiter/in
看護（かんご）　Krankenpflege〔F〕
看護所（かんごしょ）　Krankenpflegestation〔F〕
企業疾病金庫（きぎょうしっぺいきんこ）　Betriebskrankenkasse〔F〕
技術的な補助具（ぎじゅつてきなほじょぐ）　technisches Hilfsmittel〔N〕
基礎介護（きそかいご）　Grundpflege〔F〕
基礎年金（きそねんきん）　Grundrente〔F〕
基本保障（きほんほしょう）　Grundsicherung〔F〕
義務保険（ぎむほけん）　Pflichtversicherung〔F〕
給付額（きゅうふがく）　Leistungsbetrag〔M〕
給付受給者（きゅうふじゅきゅうしゃ）　Leistungsempfänger/in
給付と価格の比較リスト（きゅうふとかかくのひかくりすと）　Leistungs- und Preisvergleichsliste〔F〕
共済金庫（きょうさいきんこ）　Unterstützungskasse〔F〕
共済組合（きょうさいくみあい）　Unterstützungsverein〔M〕
強制被保険者（きょうせいひほけんしゃ）　Pflichtversicherte/r〔F〕

共同任務（きょうどうにんむ）
　Gemeinschaftsaufgabe〔F〕
居住者（きょじゅうしゃ）Bewohner/in
組み合わせ給付（くみあわせきゅうふ）
　Kombinationsleistung〔F〕
訓練教育（くんれんきょういく）Ausbildung〔F〕
ケースマネジメント（けーすまねじめんと）
　Fallmanagement〔N〕
ゲゼルシャフト（げぜるしゃふと）Gesellschaft〔F〕
ゲマインシャフト（げまいんしゃふと）
　Gemeinschaft〔F〕
現金給付（げんきんきゅうふ）Geldleistung〔F〕
現物給付（げんぶつきゅうふ）Sachleistung〔F〕
公共の福祉（こうきょうのふくし）Gemeinwohl〔N〕
公的介護保険（こうてきかいごほけん）soziale
　Pflegeversicherung〔F〕
公的介護保険の保険料に子供数を配慮する法（こうてき
　かいごほけんのほけんりょうにこどもすうをはいりょ
　するほう）Kinder-Berücksichtigungsgesetz : KiBG
　〔N〕
高齢化社会（こうれいかしゃかい）alternde
　Gesellschaft〔F〕
高齢者介護（こうれいしゃかいご）Altenpflege〔F〕
高齢者介護施設（こうれいしゃかいごしせつ）
　Altenpflegeheim〔N〕
高齢者住居共同体（こうれいしゃじゅうきょきょうどう
　たい）Senioren-Wohngemeinschaft〔F〕
高齢者世話センター（こうれいしゃせわせんたー）
　Altenbetreuungszentrum〔N〕
高齢者複合施設（こうれいしゃふくごうしせつ）
　mehrgliedrige Alteneinrichtung〔F〕
高齢者扶助（こうれいしゃふじょ）Altenhilfe〔F〕
子供控除（こどもこうじょ）Kinderfreibetrag〔M〕
子供手当（こどもてあて）Kindergeld〔N〕
財政調整（ざいせいちょうせい）Finanzausgleich〔M〕
在宅介護（ざいたくかいご）häusliche Pflege〔F〕
在宅介助（ざいたくかいじょ）häusliche Versorgung
　〔F〕
在宅看護（ざいたくかんご）häusliche
　Krankenpflege〔F〕
最低所得（さいていしょとく）Mindesteinkommen
　〔N〕
最低保障（さいていほしょう）Mindestsicherung〔F〕
自己負担（じこふたん）Zuzahlung〔F〕
自助（じじょ）Selbsthilfe〔F〕
自助グループ（じじょぐるーぷ）Selbsthilfegruppe
　〔F〕
施設介護（しせつかいご）Heimpflege〔F〕
施設介助（しせつかいじょ）stationäre Versorgung
　〔F〕
市町村（しちょうそん）Gemeinde〔F〕
市町村連合（しちょうそんれんごう）
　Gemeindeverband〔M〕

失業給付金（しつぎょうきゅうふきん）
　Arbeitslosengeld〔N〕
失業者（しつぎょうしゃ）Arbeitslose/r
失業保険（しつぎょうほけん）
　Arbeitslosenversicherung〔F〕
質の保障（しつのほしょう）Qualitätssicherung〔F〕
疾病援護（しっぺいえんご）Krankenversorgung〔F〕
疾病援助（しっぺいえんじょ）Krankenhilfe〔F〕
疾病給付金（しっぺいきゅうふきん）Krankengeld〔N〕
疾病金庫（しっぺいきんこ）Krankenkasse〔F〕
疾病金庫給付（しっぺいきんこきゅうふ）
　Krankenkassenleistung〔F〕
疾病保険（しっぺいほけん）Krankenversicherung
　〔F〕
疾病保険医療サービス機構（しっぺいほけんいりょう
　さーびすきこう）Medizinischer Dienst〔M〕der
　Krankenversicherung : MDK
疾病保険医療サービス機構の中央組織（しっぺいほけん
　いりょうさーびすきこうのちゅうおうそしき）
　Medizinischer Dienst〔M〕des Spitzenverbandes
　Bund der Krankenkassen : MDS
疾病老齢保健法（しっぺいろうれいほけんほう）
　Invaliditäts- und Alterversicherungsgesetz〔N〕
児童および少年援助法（じどうおよびしょうねんえん
　じょほう）Kinder- und Jugendhilfegesetz :
　KJHG〔N〕
児童看護師（じどうかんごし）Kinderkrankenpfleger/
　in
社会援護（しゃかいえんご）Sozialversorgung〔F〕
社会給付（しゃかいきゅうふ）Sozialleistung〔F〕
社会権（しゃかいけん）Sozialrecht〔N〕
社会国家の原則（しゃかいこっかのげんそく）
　Sozialstaatsprinzip〔N〕
社会審議会（しゃかいしんぎかい）Sozialbeirat〔M〕
社会政策（しゃかいせいさく）Gesellschaftspolitik
　〔F〕
社会的市場経済（しゃかいてきしじょうけいざい）
　soziale Marktwirtschaft〔F〕
社会福祉（しゃかいふくし）soziale Wohlfahrt〔F〕
社会福祉国家（しゃかいふくしこっか）sozialer
　Wohlfahrtsstaat〔M〕
社会福祉サービス（しゃかいふくしさーびす）soziale
　Wohlfahrtspflege〔F〕
社会福祉事務所（しゃかいふくしじむしょ）
　Sozialamt〔N〕
社会扶助（しゃかいふじょ）Sozialhilfe〔F〕
社会報告書（しゃかいほうこくしょ）Sozialbericht
　〔M〕
社会法典（しゃかいほうてん）Sozialgesetzbuch :
　SGB〔N〕
社会保険（しゃかいほけん）Sozialversicherung〔F〕
社会保険審査医師（しゃかいほけんしんさいし）
　Sozialmedizin〔F〕

社会保険保険者（しゃかいほけんほけんしゃ）
　Sozialversicherungsträger〔M〕
社会保険料（しゃかいほけんりょう）　Sozialbeitrag
　〔M〕
社会保険料分担金(しゃかいほけんりょうぶんたんきん)
　Sozialabgaben〔Pl〕
社会保障（しゃかいほしょう）　soziale Sicherung〔F〕
社会予算（しゃかいよさん）　Sozialbudget〔N〕
州介護法（しゅうかいごほう）　Landespflegegesetz
　〔N〕
就業不能（しゅうぎょうふのう）　Arbeitsunfähigkeit
　〔F〕
住居共同体（じゅうきょきょうどうたい）
　Wohngemeinschaft〔F〕
重障害者（じゅうしょうがいしゃ）
　Schwerbehinderte/r
重障害者保護法（じゅうしょうがいしゃほごほう）
　Schwerbehindertengesetz：SchwbG〔N〕
受給者（じゅきゅうしゃ）　Empfänger/in
障害（しょうがい）　Behinderung〔F〕
障害者（しょうがいしゃ）　Behinderte/r
障害者援助（しょうがいしゃえんじょ）
　Behindertenhilfe〔F〕
障害者介護（しょうがいしゃかいご）
　Behindertenpflege〔F〕
障害者作業所（しょうがいしゃさぎょうしょ）
　Behindertenwerkstätte〔F〕
障害者スポーツ（しょうがいしゃすぽーつ）
　Behindertensport〔M〕
障害者ホーム（しょうがいしゃほーむ）
　Behindertenheim〔N〕
障害年金（しょうがいねんきん）　Behindertenrente
　〔F〕
障害・老齢保障（しょうがい・ろうれいほしょう）
　Invaliditäts- und Alterssicherung〔F〕
消耗品（しょうもうひん）　Verbrauchsprodukt〔N〕
ショートステイ（しょーとすてい）　Kurzzeitpflege
　〔F〕
助言（じょげん）　Beratung〔F〕
審査指針（しんさししん）　Begutachtungs-Richtlinie
申請（しんせい）　Antrag〔M〕
親族（しんぞく）　Angehörige/r
身体介護（しんたいかいご）　Körperpflege〔F〕
生計手当（せいけいてあて）　Unterhaltsgeld〔N〕
世代間契約（せだいかんけいやく）
　Generationenvertrag〔M〕
世話（せわ）　Betreuung〔F〕
世話人（せわにん）　Betreuer/in
前頭側頭型認知症(ぜんとうそくとうがたにんちしょう)
　Frontotemporale Demenz〔F〕
ソーシャルケースワーク（そーしゃるけーすわーく）
　Sozialarbeit〔F〕

ソーシャルステーション（そーしゃるすてーしょん）
　Sozialstation〔F〕
ソーシャルワーカー（そーしゃるわーかー）
　Sozialarbeiter/in
代替介護（だいたいかいご）　Pflegevertretung〔F〕
地区ソーシャルワーク（ちくそーしゃるわーく）
　Bezirkssozialarbeit
地方公共団体（ちほうこうきょうだんたい）
　Gebietskörperschaft〔F〕
治療（ちりょう）　Behandlung〔F〕
治療的介護（ちりょうてきかいご）
　Behandlungspflege〔F〕
通所介護（つうしょかいご）　teilstationäre Pflege〔F〕
デイケア（でいけあ）　Tagespflege〔F〕
データ保護（でーたほご）　Datenschutz〔M〕
ドイツ・カリタス連合会（どいつ・かりたすれんごうか
　い）　Deutscher Caritasverband e.V.：DCW〔M〕
ドイツ高齢者援助機構（どいつこうれいしゃえんじょき
　こう）　Kuratorium Deutsche Altershilfe：KDA〔N〕
ドイツ使用者団体連邦連合会（どいつしようしゃだんた
　いれんぽうれんごうかい）　Bundesvereinigung〔F〕
　der Deutschen Arbeitgeberverbände
ドイツ赤十字社（どいつせきじゅうじしゃ）
　Deutsches Rotes Kreuz e.V.：DRK〔N〕
ドイツ同権福祉事業団（どいつどうけんふくしじぎょう
　だん）　Paritätischer Wohlfahrtsverband-
　Gesamtverband e.V.：DPWV〔M〕
ドイツ福音主義教会奉仕団（どいつふくいんしゅぎきょ
　うかいほうしだん）　Diakonisches Werk〔N〕 der
　Evangelischen Kirche in Deutschland e.V.：DW
ドイツユダヤ人中央福祉所（どいつゆだやじんちゅうお
　うふくししょ）　Zentralwohlfahrtsstelle〔F〕der
　Juden in Deutschland e.V.：ZWStdJ
同業組合疾病金庫（どうぎょうくみあいしっぺいきんこ）
　Innungskrankenkasse〔F〕
投資助成（とうしじょせい）
　Investitionskostenzuschuss〔M〕
ナイトケア（ないとけあ）　Nachtpflege〔F〕
入所介護施設（にゅうしょかいごしせつ）
　vollstationäre Pflegeeinrichtung〔F〕
入所施設介護（にゅうしょしせつかいご）
　vollstationäre Pflege〔F〕
任意社会奉仕年（にんいしゃかいほうしねん）
　Freiwilliges Soziales Jahr：FSJ〔N〕
認可介護施設（にんかかいごしせつ）　zugelassene
　Pflegeeinrichtung〔F〕
認知症（にんちしょう）　Demenz〔F〕
認知症患者（にんちしょうかんじゃ）　Demenzkranke/r
年金受給者（ねんきんじゅきゅうしゃ）　Rentner/in
年金保険（ねんきんほけん）　Rentenversicherung〔F〕
年金保険料（ねんきんほけんりょう）
　Rentenversicherungbeitrag〔M〕
脳血管性認知症（のうけっかんせいにんちしょう）

独逸
和独

vaskuläre Demenz〔F〕
廃疾老齢保険法（はいしつろうれいほけんほう）
　Invaliditäts- und Altersversicherungsgesetz〔N〕
被扶養者（ひふようしゃ）Unterhaltsberechtigter
　〔M〕
被保険者（ひほけんしゃ）Versicherte/r
費用還付（ひようかんぷ）Kostenerstattung〔F〕
病気（びょうき）Krankheit〔F〕
病気休暇（びょうききゅうか）Krankheitsurlaub〔M〕
被用者（ひようしゃ）Arbeitnehmer/in
賦課方式（ふかほうしき）Umlageverfahren〔N〕
複合施設（ふくごうしせつ）mehrgliedrige
　Einrichtungen〔Pl〕
複合老人ホーム（ふくごうろうじんほーむ）
　mehrgliedriges Altenheim〔N〕
福祉国家（ふくしこっか）Wohlfahrtsstaat〔M〕
福祉事務所員（ふくしじむしょいん）Sozialbeamte/
　in
負担調整基金（ふたんちょうせいききん）
　Ausgleichsfond〔M〕
扶養義務（ふようぎむ）Unterhaltspflicht〔F〕
兵役代替勤務（へいえきだいたいきんむ）Zivildienst
　〔M〕
報酬契約（ほうしゅうけいやく）Vergütungsvertrag
　〔M〕
訪問介護（ほうもんかいご）ambulante Pflege〔F〕
訪問介護サービス（ほうもんかいごさーびす）
　ambulanter Pflegedienst〔M〕
訪問介助（ほうもんかいじょ）ambulante Versorgung
　〔F〕
補完性原理（ほかんせいげんり）Subsidiaritätsprinzip
　〔N〕
保険加入義務（ほけんかにゅうぎむ）
　Versicherungspflicht〔F〕
保険加入義務者（ほけんかにゅうぎむしゃ）
　Versicherungspflichtige/r
保険給付（ほけんきゅうふ）Versicherungsleistung
　〔F〕
保険原則（ほけんげんそく）Versicherungsprinzip
　〔N〕
保険者（ほけんしゃ）Versicherungsträger〔M〕
保健制度（ほけんせいど）Gesundheitswesen〔N〕
保険料（ほけんりょう）Beitrag〔M〕
保険料算定限度額（ほけんりょうさんていげんどがく）
　Beitragsbemessungsgrenze〔F〕
保険料率（ほけんりょうりつ）Beitragssatz〔M〕
補助具（ほじょぐ）Hilfsmittel〔N〕
ホスピス（ほすぴす）Hospiz〔N〕
補足給付（ほそくきゅうふ）Ergänzungsleistung〔F〕
ホーム医（ほーむい）Heimarzt/ärztin
ホーム協議会（ほーむきょうぎかい）Heimbeirat〔M〕
ホーム契約（ほーむけいやく）Heimvertrag〔M〕
ホーム最低建築令（ほーむさいていけんちくれい）

Heimmindestbauverordnung：Heim-MindBauV
　〔F〕
ホーム法（ほーむほう）Heimgesetz：HeimG〔N〕
ホーム報酬（ほーむほうしゅう）Heimentgelt〔N〕
ミーンズ・テスト（みーんず・てすと）
　Bedürftigkeitsprüfung〔F〕
見習生（みならいせい）Praktikant/in
民間介護義務保険（みんかんかいごぎむほけん）
　private Pflege-Pflichtversicherung〔F〕
民間介護保険（みんかんかいごほけん）private
　Pflegeversicherung〔F〕
民間福祉団体（みんかんふくしだんたい）freie
　Wohlfahrtspflege〔F〕
メデックプルーフ［民間疾病保険の医療サービス機構］
　（めでぃっくぷるーふ）Medicproof
　〔Medizinischer Dienst der Privaten
　Krankenkassen〕
闇労働（やみろうどう）Schwarzarbeit〔F〕
要介護（ようかいご）Pflegebedürftigkeit〔F〕
要介護指針（ようかいごししん）
　Pflegebedürftigkeits-Richtlinien：PflRi〔Pl〕
要介護者（ようかいごしゃ）Pflegebedürftige/r
要介護率（ようかいごりつ）Pflegequote〔F〕
リハビリテーション（りはびりてーしょん）
　Rehabilitation〔F〕
リハビリテーション給付（りはびりてーしょんきゅうふ）
　Rehabilitationsleistung〔F〕
リハビリテーション施設（りはびりてーしょんしせつ）
　Rehabilitationseinrichtung〔F〕
留置介護（りゅうちかいご）Verwahrpflege〔F〕
療養（りょうよう）Heilverfahren〔N〕
レビー小体型認知症（れびーしょうたいがたにんちしょ
　う）Lewy-Körper-Demenz〔F〕
連帯社会（れんたいしゃかい）Solidargemeinschaft
　〔F〕
連帯性原理（れんたいせいげんり）
　Solidaritätsprinzip〔N〕
連帯責任（れんたいせきにん）gemeinschaftliche
　Verantwortung〔F〕
連帯費用（れんたいひよう）Solidarbeitrag〔M〕
連邦援護法（れんぽうえんごほう）
　Bundesversorgungsgesetz：BVG〔N〕
連邦家庭・高齢者・女性・青少年省（れんぽうかてい・
　こうれいしゃ・じょせい・せいしょうねんしょう）
　Bundesministerium für Familie, Senioren, Frauen
　und Jugend：BMFSFJ〔N〕
連邦官報（れんぽうかんぽう）Bundesgesetzblatt〔N〕
連邦国家（れんぽうこっか）Bundesstaat〔M〕
連邦社会扶助法（れんぽうしゃかいふじょほう）
　Bundessozialhilfegesetz：BSHG〔N〕
連邦保健省（れんぽうほけんしょう）
　Bundesministerium〔N〕für Gesundheit：BMG
連邦保険制度監督庁（れんぽうほけんせいどかんとくちょ

う） Bundesaufsichtsamt〔N〕für das
　　Versicherungswesen：BAV
連邦保険庁（れんぽうほけんちょう）
　　Bundesversicherungsamt〔N〕
連邦労働・社会秩序省（れんぽうろうどう・しゃかいち
　　つじょしょう） Bundesministerium〔N〕für
　　Arbeit und Soziales：BMAS
労災保険（ろうさいほけん）　Unfallversicherung〔F〕
老人介護士（ろうじんかいごし）　Altenpfleger/in
老人介護ヘルパー（ろうじんかいごへるぱー）
　　Altenpflegehelfer/in
老人作業所（ろうじんさぎょうしょ）　Altenwerkstätte
　　〔F〕
老人住宅（ろうじんじゅうたく）　Altenwohnung〔F〕
老人ホーム（ろうじんほーむ）　Altenheim〔N〕
労働災害（ろうどうさいがい）　Arbeitsunfall〔M〕
労働市場（ろうどうしじょう）　Arbeitsmarkt〔M〕
労働者疾病保険法（ろうどうしゃしっぺいほけんほう）
　　Arbeiterkrankenversicherungsgesetz〔N〕
労働者福祉連合会（ろうどうしゃふくしれんごうかい）
　　Arbeiterwohlfahrt-Bundesverband e.V.：AWO〔M〕
労働者保険（ろうどうしゃほけん）
　　Arbeiterversicherung〔F〕
労働報酬（ろうどうほうしゅう）　Arbeitsentgelt〔N〕
労働法典（ろうどうほうてん）　Arbeitsgesetzbuch
　　〔N〕
労務付帯経費（ろうむふたいけいひ）
　　Arbeitsnebenkosten〔Pl〕
老齢金庫（ろうれいきんこ）　Alterskasse〔F〕
老齢・障害保障（ろうれい・しょうがいほしょう）
　　Alters- und Invaliditätssicherung〔F〕
老齢手当（ろうれいてあて）　Altersgeld〔N〕
老齢年金（ろうれいねんきん）　Altersrente〔F〕
老齢保障（ろうれいほしょう）　Alterssicherung〔F〕
枠組契約（わくぐみけいやく）　Rahmenvertrag〔M〕

独逸
和独

5. 米国（アメリカ）における介護福祉等関連用語 【英　和】

Accreditation Council for Home Care　在宅ケア認定評議会
Activity Department　アクティビティ部
Acute Care of Elders : ACE　高齢者急性期ケア
Administration for Children and Families　児童・家庭局
Administration on Aging : AoA　高齢局
Administration on Developmental Disabilities　発達障害庁
Administrative Procedure Act　行政手続法
adult care home　高齢者ホーム
Adult Education Act　成人教育法
adult foster home　アダルト・フォスターホーム
adult protective services : APS　成人虐待保護サービス
advance directive　医療事前指示書
Advisory Council on Social Security　社会保障諮問委員会
Age Discrimination Act　年齢差別禁止法
Age Discrimination in Employment Act　雇用年齢差別禁止法
Agency for Health Care Policy and Research : AHCPR　医療政策・研究所
Agency for Healthcare Research and Quality : AHRQ　医療研究・品質局
Agency for Toxic Substances and Disease Registry : ATSDR　有害物質・疾病登録局
Aging Network　エイジングネットワーク
aid to the blind　視覚障害者扶助
Aid to the Permanently and Totally Disabled : APTD　完全永久就業不能者扶助
Aids to Families with Dependent Children : AFDC　児童扶養世帯扶助制度
almshouse　養老院
Alzheimer's Association　アルツハイマー協会
Alzheimer's care unit　アルツハイマーケア病棟
Ambulatory Patient Group : APG　外来患者疾病分類
Ambulatory Payment Classification : APC　外来包括支払い分類
American Academy of Audiology　米国聴覚医学
American Academy of Dermatology　米国皮膚科学会
American Academy of Family Physicians : AAFP　米国家庭内科医学会
American Academy of Home Care Physicians　米国在宅医学会
American Academy of Hospice and Palliative Medicine　米国ホスピス・緩和医療学会
American Academy of Neurology　米国神経学会
American Academy of Nursing　米国看護学会
American Academy of Ophthalmology　米国眼学会
American Academy of Otolaryngology-Head and Neck Surgery　米国耳鼻咽喉・頭部・首部外科手術協会
American Academy of Physical Medicine and Rehabilitation　米国身体医学・リハビリテーション学会
American Academy of Professional Coders　米国専門コーダー協会
American Academy of Sleep Medicine　米国睡眠医学学会
American Academy of Wound Management　米国褥瘡学会
American Aging Association　米国老年学会
American Alliance for Health, Physical Education, Recreation and Dance　米国保健・体育・レクリエーション・ダンス連合
American Association for Continuity of Care　米国包括的ケア協会
American Association for Geriatric Psychiatry　米国老年精神医学会
American Association for Homecare　米国在宅ケア協会
American Association for Respiratory Care　米国呼吸ケア学会
American Association of Cardiovascular and Pulmonary Rehabilitation　米国心血管呼吸リハビリテーション学会
American Association of Clinical Endocrinologists　米国臨床内分泌学会
American Association of Dental Schools　米国歯科学教育学会
American Association of Diabetes Educators　米国糖尿病教育者会
American Association of Homes and Services for the Aging : AAHSA　米国高齢者ホーム・サービス協会
American Association of Homes for the Aging　米国高齢者ホーム協会
American Association of Physical Anthropology　米国自然人類学会
American Association of Retired Persons : AARP　米国退職者協会
American Association of Sex Educators, Counselors and Therapists　米国性教育者・カウンセラー・セラピスト協会
American Bar Association　米国法曹協会
American Board of Family Practice　米国家庭医療学会
American Board of Internal Medicine : ABIM　米国

内科専門医機構
American Board of Internal Medicine certification examination　米国内科専門医機構認定試験
American Board of Medical Societies：ABMS　米国専門医協会
American Board of Physical Therapy Specialties：ABPTS　米国理学療法専門協会
American Cancer Society　米国癌協会
American College of Cardiology　米国心臓病学会
American College of Chest Physicians　米国胸部内科医学会
American College of Gastroenterology　米国消化器病学会
American College of Obstetricians and Gynecologists　米国産科婦人科学会
American College of Physicians　米国内科学会
American College of Physicians Clinical Efficacy Assessment Subcommittee　米国内科学会臨床効能評価小委員会
American College of Preventive Medicine：ACPM　米国予防医学会
American College of Radiology：ACR　米国放射線学会
American College of Radiology Breast Imaging Reporting and Data System　米国放射線学会乳房イメージレポート・データシステム
American College of Rheumatology：ACR　米国リウマチ学会
American Council for Headache Education　米国頭痛教育協議会
American Council of the Blind　米国盲人委員会
American Council on Exercise　米国運動協議会
American Dental Association　米国歯科医師会
American Diabetes Association　米国糖尿病協会
American Dietetic Association　米国栄養士会
American Federation for Aging Research　米国加齢研究連合
American Foundation for the Blind　米国盲人財団
American Foundation for Urologic Disease　米国泌尿器疾患財団
American Gastroenterological Association　米国消化器病学会
American Geriatrics Society　米国老年医学会
American Group Psychotherapy Association　米国集団精神療法学会
American Health Care Association　米国医療協会
American Health Information Management Association　米国健康情報管理学会
American Heart Association　米国心臓学会
American Hospital Association：AHA　米国病院協会
American Lung Association　米国肺協会
American Medical Association：AMA　米国医師会
American Medical Directors Association　米国医療ディレクター協会
American Medical Informatics Association　米国医療情報学協会
American Nurses' Association　米国看護師協会
American Occupational Therapy Association　米国作業療法士協会
American Optometric Association　米国眼科医協会
American Organization of Nurse Executives：AONE　米国看護幹部機構
American Osteopathic Association：AOA　米国整骨医協会
American Pain Society　米国疼痛学会
American Parkinson Disease Association　米国パーキンソン病協会
American Physical Therapy Association：APTA　米国理学療法士協会
American Podiatric Medical Association　米国足病医学会
American Psychiatric Association　米国精神医学会
American Psychological Association　米国心理学会
American Public Health Association　米国公衆衛生協会
American Public Welfare Association　米国公衆福祉協議会
American Red Cross　米国赤十字
American Rehabilitation Association　米国リハビリテーション協会
American Rehabilitation Counseling Association　全米リハビリテーションカウンセリング協会
American Society for Geriatric Dentistry　米国老年歯科学会
American Society for Pain Management Nursing　米国疼痛管理看護学会
American Society for Parenteral and Enteral Nutrition：ASPEN　米国静脈経腸栄養学会
American Society for Training and Development：ASTD　米国教育開発学会
American Society of Bioethics and Humanities　米国生命倫理学会
American Society of Clinical Oncology　米国臨床腫瘍学会
American Society of Colon and Rectal Surgeons　米国直腸結腸外科学会
American Society of Consultant Pharmacists　米国顧問薬剤師協会
American Society of Law, Medicine & Ethics　米国法・医学・倫理学会
American Society of Pension Professionals & Actuaries　米国年金専門職・アクチュアリー会
American Society on Aging　米国高齢者学会
American Speech-Language-Hearing Association　米国言語聴覚士学会
American Therapeutic Recreation Association

米国
英和

米国レクリエーション療法協会
American Thoracic Society：ATS　米国胸部疾患学会
Americans with Disabilities Act：ADA　米国障害者法
ancillary nursing personnel　補助看護職員
Any Willing Provider Law　有意志医療機関排除禁止法
Architectural Barriers Act　建築障壁法
Area Agencies on Aging：AAA　地域高齢者局
Arizona long-term care system　アリゾナ州長期ケアシステム
Arthritis Foundation　関節炎財団
Asia-Pacific Institute of Ageing Studies　アジア太平洋老年研究学会
Assembly Bill：AB　下院州議会法案
Assisted Living Facilities Association of America　米国アシステッド・リビング協会
assisted living facility　アシステッド・リビング施設
Association for Gerontology in Higher Education　老年学高等教育協会
Association of American Medical Colleges　米国医科大学協会
Association of Social Work Boards　ソーシャルワーク委員協会
Association of University Programs in Health Administration：AUPHA　衛生行政・大学プログラム協会
benefit in kind　現物給付
Breast and Cervical Cancer Prevention and Treatment Act　乳癌・子宮癌予防・治療法
Breast Imaging Reporting and Data System：BI-RADS　乳房イメージレポート・データシステム
Bureau of Labor Statistics：BLS　労働統計局
Bureau of Prisons　刑務所局
California Work Opportunities and Responsibility to Kids：CalWORKs　カルフォルニア州就労機会・児童責任事業
care resource team　ケア資源チーム
Caregiver's Bill of Rights　介護者の権利章典
Case Management Society of America　米国ケースマネジメント学会
Catastrophic Coverage Act　高額医療費保険法
Catholic Charities　カトリック・チャリティーズ
Catholic Health Association：CHA　カトリック医療協会
Census Information Center　国勢調査情報センター
Center for Information Technology：CIT　情報技術センター
Center for Scientific Review：CSR　科学審査センター
Centers for Disease Control and Prevention：CDC　疾病管理予防センター
Centers for Medicare and Medicaid Services：CMS　メディケア・メディケイド庁
certified geriatric pharmacist　高齢者医療専門薬剤師
certified nurse assistant　認定看護助手

certified occupational therapy assistant　認定作業療法士アシスタント
chaplain services　司祭サービス
charge nurse　責任看護師
chief nursing officer：CNO　最高看護責任者
Child Care and Development Fund：CCDF　児童保護・育成基金
child labor laws　児童労働基準法
Civil Rights Act　公民権法
clinical resource team　臨床資源チーム
Code of Federal Regulations：CFR　連邦規則集
Commission of Dietetic Registration：CDR　栄養士登録委員会
Commission on Accreditation in Physical Therapy Education：CAPTE　理学療法教育認定委員会
Commission on Chronic Illness　慢性疾患委員会
Commission on Income Maintenance Programs　収入維持計画諮問委員会
Committee of Ways and Means　財務委員会
Committee on Economic Security：CES　経済保障委員会
Common Procedure Coding System：CPCS　診療報酬コード体系
community-based mental health care　地域基盤型精神衛生ケア
community-based residential facility　地域基盤型居住施設
Community Health Accreditation Program：CHAP　地域保健医療認定プログラム
Community Health Information Networks：CHIN　地域医療情報ネットワーク
Community Living Assistance and Support Services Program　地域生活援助・支援プログラム
Community Mental Health Center：CMHC　地域精神衛生センター
Community Nursing Organization：CNO　地域看護組織
Community Services Agency：CSA　地域サービス機関
Comprehensive Employment and Training Act　包括的雇用及び訓練法
compression of morbidity　病的状態の圧縮
congregate housing　集団ホーム
Congregate Housing Services Act　集団ホームサービス法
congregate meal　集団給食サービス
Congressional Budget Office　連邦議会予算局
Connecticut Hospice Program　コネティカットホスピスプログラム
conservatorship　後見人制度
Consolidated Budget Office：CBO　議会予算局
Consolidated Omnibus Budget Reconciliation Act：COBRA　包括予算調整強化法

Consumer Driven Health Plan：CDHP　消費者主導型医療保険
Continuing Care Accreditation Commission　継続的ケア認定委員会
Continuing Care Retirement Community：CCRC　継続的ケア提供型退職者コミュニティ
Council on Social Work Education：CSWE　全米ソーシャルワーク教育協議会
Current Population Survey：CPS　人口動態調査
Current Procedural Terminology：CPT　診療報酬共通コード
Deficit Reduction Act：DRA　財政赤字削減法
Defined Benefit Plan　確定給付型年金
Defined Contribution Plan　確定拠出型年金
Delta Society　デルタ協会
Department of Health and Human Services：HHS　保健福祉省
Department of Health, Education and Welfare：HEW　保健教育福祉省
Department of Health Services　保健省
Department of Housing and Urban Development：HUD　住宅都市開発省
Department of Justice　司法省
Department of Social Services　社会サービス省
Department of Transportation　運輸省
Department of Veterans Affairs：VA　退役軍人省
Developmental Disabilities Services and Facilities Act　発達障害サービス・施設法
Diagnosis Related Group：DRG　診断群別支払い方式
Disability Discrimination Act　障害者差別禁止法
Domestic Volunteer Service Act　米国内ボランティア法
Durable Power of Attorney　権限委譲
Durable Power of Attorney for Finances　財務委任状
Durable Power of Attorney for Health Care　医療委任状
Durable Power of Attorney for Health Care Act　医療委任状法
early retirement pension　早期退職年金
early retirement plan　早期退職制度
Economic Bill of Rights　経済権利法
economic dependency ratio　経済的従属人口比率
Economic Opportunity Act：EOA　経済機会法
Elder Life Program　エルダーライフプログラム
Eldercare Locator　高齢者ケア検索サイト
Elderhostel Program　エルダーホステルプログラム；高齢者向け生涯教育プログラム
Elderly Nutrition Program：ENP　高齢者栄養プログラム
Emergency Response Support System　緊急時対策支援システム
Employee Retirement Income Security Act：ERISA　従業員退職所得保障法；エリサ法

Employment Act　雇用法
Environmental Protection Agency：EPA　環境保護庁
Equal Rights Amendment　男女平等憲法修正案
Expanded In-home Services for the Elderly：EISEP　拡大高齢者向け在宅プログラム
Fair Housing Act　公正住宅法
Fair Housing Amendments Act　公正住宅改正法
Fair Labor Standards Act　公正労働基準法
Family and Medical Leave Act：FMLA　家族・医療休暇法
Family Assistance Plan：FAP　家族扶助計画
family council　家族会
Federal Civil Service Retirement System　連邦市民退職サービス制度
Federal Emergency Management Agency　連邦緊急事態管理庁
Federal Emergency Relief Administration：FERA　連邦緊急救済管理局
Federal Housing Administration　連邦住宅管理局
Federal Insurance Contributions Act：FICA　連邦保険拠出法
Federal Poverty Level：FPL　連邦貧困基準
Federal Register　連邦官報
Federal Security Agency　連邦社会保障機関
Federal Student Aid　連邦学資金援助
Federal Wage System　連邦賃金制度
Federally Qualified Health Center：FQHC　連邦政府認可医療センター
Fiduciary Abuse Specialist Team：FAST　金銭無断悪用専門チーム
filial obligation　老親扶養義務
filial responsibility　老親扶養意識
Food and Drug Administration：FDA　食品医薬品局
Food Stamp Program　食糧スタンププログラム
for-profit organization　営利団体
Forum on Long-Term Care Issue in Nursing　看護における長期ケア問題フォーラム
Freedom of Choice Act　選択の自由法
full retirement age：FRA　年金受給年齢
gag rule　ギャグルール
General Accounting Office　会計検査院
general assistance：GA　一般扶助
General Education Development Certificate：GED　高等学校卒業認定証明書
Geriatric Research, Education and Clinical Center：GRECC　老人研究・教育・医療センター
Gerontological Society of America　米国老年学学会
Gray Panthers　グレイパンサーズ
Greater Avenue for Independent：GAIN　拡大自立支援
Group Health Association　グループ医療協会
group hospitalization　団体入院支払い

米国英和

Guaranteed Insurability Option：GIO　給付増額保障特約
Harvard Community Health Plan　ハーバードコミュニティヘルスプラン
Health Care and Education Reconciliation Act　医療・教育調整法
Health Care Financing Administration：HCFA　医療財務庁
Health Care for All Americans Act　国民皆医療法
Health Insurance Association of America：HIAA　全米医療保険協会
Health Insurance Plan of Greater New York　グレータニューヨーク医療保険事業
Health Insurance Portability and Accountability Act　医療保険相互運用性・説明責任法
Health Maintenance Organization：HMO　健康維持組織
Health Maintenance Organization Act：HMO Act　健康維持組織法
Health Resources and Services Administration　医療資源・サービス局
Health Risk Appraisal：HRA　健康危険度評価
Health Services Cost Review Commission　医療費検討協議会
Hill-Burton Act　ヒル・バートン法
Home Care Quality Assurance　在宅ケア品質保証
home health aide　訪問看護助手
Home Health Compare　在宅サービス事業者間比較プログラム
Home Health Quality Initiative　在宅サービスの質改善イニシアティブ
Home Health Resource Groups：HHRG　在宅サービス資源利用度別グループ
Hospital Compare　病院間比較プログラム
Hospital Insurance　入院保険　[メディケア・パートA]
Hospital Physician Organization：HPO　病院医師組織
Hospital Survey and Construction Act　病院検査・建設法
Hours per Resident Day：hprd　一利用者一日あたりの看護・介護時間
House of Representatives Select Committee on Aging　高齢化問題に関する下院特別委員会
House Ways and Means Committee　下院歳入委員会
Housing Act　住宅法
Housing and Community Development Act　住宅・コミュニティ開発法
Hull-House　ハル・ハウス
inaccessible asset　アクセス不可能資産
Indian Health Services：HIS　インディアン衛生局
Individual Practice Association：IPA　開業医組織
Individual Retirement Account：IRA　個人退職口座

Infectious Disease Society of America　米国感染症学会
information and referral　情報・照会サービス
initial certification education　初期認定教育
Institute of Medicine　医学研究所
Integrated Benefit Plan　給付統合型プラン
integrated delivery network：IDN　統合供給ネットワーク
integrated delivery system：IDS　統合供給システム
integrated health care delivery system：IHCDS　統合医療供給システム
intermediate care facility：ICF　中間ケア施設
intermediate nursing facility：INF　中間看護施設
Intermodal Surface Transportation Efficiency Act　総合陸上輸送効率化法
Internal Revenue Service：IRS　内国歳入庁
International Institute for Reminiscence and Life Review　国際回想法学会
International Society for Reminiscence and Life Review　国際回想法学会
Job Opportunities and Basic Skills Training：JOBS　就業機会基本技能訓練
Job Training Partnership Act：JTPA　職業訓練協力法
John E. Fogarty International Center for Advanced Study in the Health Sciences：FIC　フォガーティ国際衛生科学先端研究センター
Johns Hopkins Health System　ジョンズ・ホプキンス医療システム
Joint Commission on Accreditation of Healthcare Organization：JCAHO　医療機関合同認定委員会
Kaiser Family Foundation　カイザーファミリー財団
Kaiser Permanente　カイザーパーマナンテ
Kaiser Plan　カイザープラン
Kennedy-Kassebaum Bill　ケネディ・カセバウム法
Kerr-Mills Bill　カー・ミルズ法案
Kingsley Hall　キングスレー館
ledge practice　会員制診療
licensed practical nurse：LPN　免許実務看護師　[日本でいう准看護師]
licensed vocational nurse：LVN　免許実務看護師　[日本でいう准看護師]
Lifespan Respite Care Act　包括的レスパイトケア法
long-term care　長期ケア
Long-Term Care Evaluation and Accreditation Program：LEAP　介護評価認定プログラム
Long-Term Care Gerontology Center　長期ケア老年学センター
Long-Term Care Ombudsman Program　長期ケア高齢者オンブズマンプログラム
Long-Term Care Residents' Bill of Rights　長期ケア利用者の権利章典
Low Income Home Energy Assistance Program：

LIHEAP 低所得世帯光熱費扶助プログラム
maintenance of effort：MOE 持続的努力要求
Major Diagnostic Category：MDC 主要診断群
Managed Care Organization：MCO マネジドケア組織
Mandatory Categorically Needy 義務的制度困窮対象者
Manpower Development and Training Act 人的資源訓練法
marital deduction 配偶者控除
MassHealth マスヘルス［マサチューセッツ州のメディケイド］
Meals on Wheels ミールズ・オン・ウィール［食事配達サービス］
Medal of Honor Pension 栄誉賞年金
Medi-Cal メディ・カル［カリフォルニア州のメディケイド］
Medicaid メディケイド［低所得者医療扶助制度］
medical saving account：MSA 医療貯金口座
Medical Technology Assessment：MTA 医療技術評価
medically needy 医学上必要な者
Medicare メディケア［老人・障害者医療保険制度］
Medicare Advantage メディケア・アドバンテージ
Medicare Advantage Plan 処方箋薬費保険プラン
Medicare and Medicaid Certification Inspection メディケア・メディケイド認定調査
Medicare and Medicaid-certified nursing home メディケア・メディケイド認定ナーシングホーム
Medicare Appeals System メディケア不服申し立て制度
Medicare Catastrophic Coverage Act メディケア高額医療保障法
Medicare-certified home health agency メディケア認定在宅看護機関
Medicare-certified hospice agency メディケア認定ホスピス機関
Medicare-certified hospital メディケア認定病院
Medicare-certified skilled nursing facility メディケア認定スキルドナーシングホーム；メディケア認定高度看護施設
Medicare Health Maintenance Organization メディケア HMO
Medicare Part A メディケア・パート A ［入院保険］
Medicare Part B メディケア・パート B ［補足的医療保険］
Medicare Part C メディケア・パート C ［メディケア・プラス・チョイス］
Medicare Part D メディケア・パート D ［処方箋薬剤給付保険］
Medicare+Choice メディケア・プラス・チョイス［メディケア・パート C］
Medicare+Choice Program メディケア・プラス・チョイスプログラム
Medicare Prescription Drug Improvement and Modernization Act メディケア処方箋薬剤改善・近代化法
Medicare Supplement Insurance：Medigap メディケア補足保険
Medigap メディギャップ
Medigap Standardization メディケア補足保険標準化
Mental Health Parity Act 精神保健同等法
merit system 実力本位制度
Minimum Data Set：MDS ミニマムデータセット
Minimum Data Set coordinator ミニマムデータ セットコーディネーター
Minimum Monthly Maintenance Needs Allowance：MMMNA 月間最低必要手当
multipurpose senior center 多目的高齢者センター
National Abuse Incidence Study 全米高齢者虐待事例調査
National Adult Day Services Association 全米老人デイサービス協会
National Advisory Council on Long Term Care Case Management 全米長期ケアケースマネジメント諮問委員会
National Advisory Council on Nurse Education and Practice：NACNEP 全米看護師教育実務諮問委員会
National Alliance for Caregiving 全米介護者連合
National Alliance for the Mentally Ill 全米精神病者連合
National Anemia Action Council 全米貧血行動協議会
National Aphasia Association 全米失語症協会
National Asian Pacific Center on Aging 全米アジア・太平洋諸国系高齢者協会
National Assistance Act 国民扶助法
National Association for Continence 全米排泄障害協会
National Association for Home Care：NAHC 全米在宅ケア協会
National Association for Home Care and Hospice 全米在宅ケア・ホスピス協会
National Association for Senior Living Industries 全米高齢者住宅産業協会
National Association for the Advancement of Colored People：NAACP 全米黒人地位向上協会
National Association of Adult Protective Services 全米成人保護サービス協会
National Association of Area Agencies on Aging 全米地域高齢者福祉協会
National Association of Geriatric Education Centers 全米老年医学教育センター
National Association of Insurance Commissioners：NAIC 全米保険監督官協会

National Association of Manufacturers　全米製造者協会
National Association of Professional Geriatric Care Managers　全米高齢者ケアマネジャー協会
National Association of Social Workers：NASW　全米ソーシャルワーカー協会
National Association of Social Workers code of ethics　全米ソーシャルワーカー協会の倫理綱領
National Association of the Deaf　全米聾者協会
National Association State Units on Aging　全米高齢者局
National Bar Association　全米法曹協会
National Bioethics Advisory Commission　全米生命倫理諮問委員会
National Cancer Act　米国癌法
National Cancer Institute：NCI　米国国立癌研究所
National Center for Assisted Living　全米アシステッド・リビングセンター
National Center for Biotechnology Information　米国国立バイオテクノロジー情報センター
National Center for Complementary and Alternative Medicine：NCCAM　米国国立補完代替医療センター
National Center for Environmental Health：NCEH　米国国立環境衛生センター
National Center for Health Statistics：NCHS　米国医療統計センター
National Center for Infectious Diseases：NCID　米国国立感染病センター
National Center for Injury Prevention and Control：NCIPC　米国国立傷害防止センター
National Center for Research Resources：NCRR　米国国立研究資源センター
National Center on Elder Abuse　全米高齢者虐待問題研究所
National Center on Minority Health and Health Disparities：NCMHD　米国国立マイノリティ健康・健康格差センター
National Center on Physical Activity and Disability　米国国立身体活動・障害センター
National Center on Sleep Disorders Research　米国国立睡眠障害研究所
National Cholesterol Education Program　全米コレステロール教育プログラム
National Chronic Care Consortium　米国国立長期ケアコンソーシアム
National Citizens' Coalition for Nursing Home Reform　全米ナーシングホーム改革国民連合協会
National Civilian Community Corps：NCCC　全米市民地域社会協会
National Coalition for Health Professional Education in Genetics　全米遺伝医学専門教育連合
National Commission on Social Security Reform：NCSSR　全米社会保障改革審議会
National Committee for Quality Assurance：NCQA　全米品質保証委員会
National Committee for the Prevention of Elder Abuse　全米老人虐待防止対策委員会
National Conference of Commissioner on Uniform State Laws　統一州法委員全米会議
National Conference of Gerontological Nurse Practitioners　老年専門ナースプラクティショナー全米会議
National Conference on Economic Security　全米経済社会保障会議
National Consumers League　全米消費者連盟
National Council for Therapeutic Recreation Certification：NCTRC　全米レクリエーション療法認定協議会
National Council Licensure Examination-Registered Nurses：NCLEX-RN　全米登録看護師資格試験
National Council of Assisted Living：NCAL　全米アシステッド・リビング協議会
National Council of Senior Citizens：NCSC　全米高齢者国民協議会
National Council on Aging　全米高齢者協議会
National Council on Disability　全米障害者協議会
National Council on Independent Living　全米自立生活協議会
National Crime Victimization Survey：NCVS　全米犯罪被害調査
National Depressive and Manic-Depressive Association　全米うつ病・躁うつ病協会
National Elder Mistreatment Study　全米高齢者虐待調査
National Elderly Nutrition program　全米高齢者栄養プログラム
National Eye Health Education Program　全米眼の健康教育プログラム
National Eye Institute：NEI　米国国立眼病研究所
National Family Caregiver Support Program　全米家族介護者支援プログラム
National Family Caregivers Association　全米家族介護者協会
National Federation of the Blind　全米視覚障害者連合
National Gerontological Nursing Association　全米老年看護学会
National Headache Foundation　全米頭痛財団
National Health and Nutrition Examination Survey：NHANES　全米保健・栄養検査調査
National Health Insurance Act　全米国民医療保険法
National Health Interview Survey　全米健康聞取り調査
National Health Planning and Resources

Development Act　国家医療計画・資源開発法
National Heart, Lung and Blood Institute：NHLBI　米国国立心・肺・血液研究所
National High Blood Pressure Education Program　全米高血圧教育プログラム
National Hospice Organization：NHO　全米ホスピス協会
National Housing Act　全米住宅法
National Human Genome Research Institute：NHGRI　米国国立ヒトゲノム研究所
National Indian Council on Aging：NICOA　全米インディアン高齢者協議会
National Institute for Occupational Safety and Health：NIOSH　米国国立職業安全健康研究所
National Institute of Adult Day Care：NIAD　米国国立成人デイケア研究所
National Institute of Allergy and Infectious Diseases：NIAID　米国国立アレルギー・感染症研究所
National Institute of Arthritis and Musculoskeletal and Skin Diseases：NIAMS　米国国立関節炎・骨格筋・皮膚疾患研究所
National Institute of Biomedical Imaging and Bioengineering：NIBIB　米国国立画像生物医学・生物工学研究所
National Institute of Child Health and Human Development：NICHD　米国国立小児保健発達研究所
National Institute of Dental and Craniofacial Research：NIDCR　米国国立歯科・頭蓋顔面研究所
National Institute of Dental Research　米国国立歯学研究所
National Institute of Diabetes and Digestive and Kidney Diseases：NIDDK　米国国立糖尿病・消化器・腎疾病研究所
National Institute of Environmental Health Sciences：NIEHS　米国国立環境衛生科学研究所
National Institute of General Medical Sciences：NIGMS　米国国立一般医科学研究所
National Institute of Mental Health：NIMH　米国国立精神衛生研究所
National Institute of Neurological Disorders and Stroke：NINDS　米国国立神経疾患・脳卒中研究所
National Institute of Nursing Research：NINR　米国国立看護研究所
National Institute of Occupational Safety and Health　米国国立労働安全衛生研究所
National Institute on Aging：NIA　米国国立高齢化研究所
National Institute on Alcohol Abuse and Alcoholism：NIAAA　米国国立アルコール乱用・依存症研究所
National Institute on Deafness and Other Communication Disorders：NIDCD　米国国立聴覚・伝達障害研究所
National Institute on Disability and Rehabilitation Research　米国国立障害リハビリテーション研究所
National Institute on Drug Abuse：NIDA　米国国立薬物乱用研究所
National Institutes of Health　米国国立衛生研究所
National Institutes of Health Clinical Center：NIHCC　米国国立衛生研究所・臨床センター
National Interfaith Coalition on Aging　全米宗教間相互協力委員会
National League for Nursing　全米看護連盟
National Library of Medicine：NLM　米国国立医学図書館
National Long Term Care Ombudsman Resource Center　全米長期ケアオンブズマン資源センター
National Minimum Drinking Age Act　国家最低飲酒年齢法
National Nosocomial Infections Surveillance System　全米病院感染サーベイランスシステム
National Nurses Week　全米看護師週間
National Nursing Home Survey　全米ナーシングホーム調査
National Nursing Home Week　全米ナーシングホーム週間
National Nursing Staff Development Organization　全米看護職員教育協会
National Opinion Research Center　全米意識調査センター
National Organization of Forensic Social Work　全米司法福祉学会
National Osteoporosis Foundation　全米骨粗鬆症財団
National Parkinson Foundation, Inc.　全米パーキンソン財団
National Patient Safety Foundation　全米患者安全財団
National Pharmaceutical Council　全米医薬品協議会
National Pressure Ulcer Advisory Panel　全米褥瘡諮問委員会
National Quality Guidelines　全米質ガイドライン
National Recreation and Parks Association　全米レクリエーション・公園協会
National Reference Center for Bioethics Literature　全米生命倫理文献図書館
National Rehabilitation Association　全米リハビリテーション協会
National Resource Center on Supportive Housing and Home Modification　全米支援付き住居・住宅改修資源センター
National Resources Planning Board：NRPB　全米資源企画委員会
National Science Foundation　全米科学財団

National Senior Citizens Law Center 全米高齢者国民法律センター
National Seniors Council 全米高齢者評議会
National Stroke Association 全米脳卒中協会
National Therapeutic Recreation Society 全米レクリエーション療法協会
National Voter Registration Act 全米投票者登録法
National Welfare Rights Organization 国民福祉権利組織
Natural Death Act 自然死法
New Deal ニューディール政策
New York Heart Association：NYHA ニューヨーク心臓協会
nonforfeiture value 不没収価格
nursing assistive personnel 看護支援職員
nursing extender 看護補助員
nursing facility 看護施設
nursing home ナーシングホーム
Nursing Home Compare ナーシングホーム間比較プログラム
Nursing Home Quality Initiative ナーシングホームの質の改善イニシアティブ
Nursing Home Reform Act ナーシングホーム改革法
Nursing Hours per Patient Day：nhppd 一患者一日あたりの看護時間
nursing support personnel 看護支援職員
Nutrition Program for the Elderly Act 高齢者栄養管理プログラム法
Nutrition Services Incentive Program 栄養サービスインセンティブプログラム
Occupational Safety and Health Administration 労働安全衛生庁
occupational therapy aide 作業療法士助手
Office of Economic Opportunity 経済機会局
Office of Public Health and Science：OPHS 公衆衛生科学室
Office of the Federal Register 連邦官報事務局
Office of the Surgeon General 公衆衛生総監局
Old-Age and Survivors Insurance：OASI 老齢遺族保険
Old-Age and Survivors Insurance, Disability and Hospital Insurance Trust Fund：OASDHI Trust Fund 老齢遺族障害医療保険信託基金
Old-Age and Survivors Insurance Trust Fund：OASI Trust Fund 老齢遺族保険信託基金
Old-Age, Survivors and Disability Insurance：OASDI 老齢遺族障害保険
Old-Age, Survivors and Disability Insurance Trust Fund：OASDI Trust Fund 老齢遺族障害保険信託基金
Old-Age, Survivors, Disability and Health Insurance：OASDHI 老齢遺族医療保険
old-old オールド・オールド [75歳～84歳の高齢者]

Older Americans Act：OAA アメリカ高齢者法
Older Americans Act Amendments アメリカ高齢者改正法
Older Americans Act Comprehensive Services Amendments アメリカ高齢者包括的サービス改正法
Older Women's League 高齢女性連盟
Older Workers Benefit Protection Act 高齢労働者利益保護法
oldest-old オールデスト・オールド [85歳以上の高齢者]
Olmstead Decision オルムステッド法
Omnibus Budget Reconciliation Act：OBRA 包括予算調整法
On-Lok オンロック
On-Lok Senior Services オンロックシニアサービス
Oncology Nursing Society 腫瘍看護学会
Online Survey, Certification and Reporting：OSCAR 監査・認証オンラインレポート
Online Survey, Certification and Reporting database：OSCAR database 監査・認証オンラインレポートデータベース
open access plan オープンアクセスプラン
Oregon Death with Dignity Act オレゴン州尊厳死法
Oregon Health Decision オレゴン保健会議
Oregon Health Plan オレゴンヘルスプラン [オレゴン州のメディケイド]
Outcome and Assessment Information Set：OASIS 在宅サービス版アウトカム・アセスメント表
pastoral service 牧師サービス
Patient Classification System：PCS 患者分類システム
Patient Dependency Group：PDG 依存度別患者グループ
Patient Protection and Affordable Care Act：PPACA 医療保険改革法；患者の保護と手頃な医療法
Patient Self-Determination Act 患者の自己決定法
Patient's Bill of Rights 患者の権利章典
pay-as-you-go system 賦課方式
payroll tax 給与税
peer-review organization：PRO 同僚審査機関
Pension Benefit Guaranty Corporation 年金給付保証公社
Pension Benefits Standards Act 年金給付基準法
personal care aide 日常生活介護者
personal care home 身体ケアホーム
Personal Responsibility and Work Opportunity Reconciliation Act：PRWORA 自己責任就労機会調整法
Pharmaceutical Assistance to the Aged and Disabled 高齢者・身体障害者向け薬剤援助プログラム
Pharmaceutical Manufacturers Association 製薬工

業協会
pharmaceutical retail-price survey　医薬品価格調査
Physician Hospital Organization：PHO　医師病院組織
Physician Organization：PO　医師組織
Physician Organized Delivery System：PODS　医師組織提供システム
Physician Payment Review Commission：PPRC　診療報酬検討委員会
Physician Practice Management Company：PPMC　開業医総合管理会社
point of service：POS　受診選択プラン
Preferred Provider Arrangement：PPA　選定医療提供協定
Preferred Provider Organization：PPO　選定医療提供組織
Prepaid Group Practice：PGP　前払い型グループ診療
Prescription Drug Coverage　処方箋薬剤給付保険[メディケア・パートD]
Principal Inpatient Diagnostic Cost Group：PIP-DCG　主要入院疾病別費用グループ
Privacy Rules of Health Insurance Portability and Accountability Act　医療保険相互運用性・説明責任法における個人情報保護法
probate court　検認裁判所
Professional Review Organization：PRO　診療審査機構
Professional Standard Review Organization：PSRO　診療報酬支払い審査機構
Programs of All Inclusive Care for the Elderly：PACE　高齢者包括ケアプログラム
Prospective Payment Assessment Commission：Pro-PAC　包括払い方式評価委員会
Prospective Payment System：PPS　所定報酬支払い方式
Public Health Service　公衆衛生局
Public Health Service Act　公衆衛生法
Public Health Service Commissioned Corps　公衆衛生局受託隊
Quality Assurance Committee　質保証委員会
Quality Improvement Organization：QIO　医療の質改善組織
quality indicator　クオリティインジケータ
quality measure　クオリティメジャー
Racial Discrimination Act　人種差別禁止法
Railroad Retirement Act　鉄道退職年金法
registered nurse　登録看護師[日本でいう正看護師]
registered occupational therapist　登録作業療法士
Rehabilitation Act　リハビリテーション法
rehabilitation unit　リハビリテーション病棟
relative value unit：RVU　相対価値単位
Resident Assessment Instrument：RAI　アールエーアイ
Resident Assessment Protocols：RAPs　ラップス
Resident Bill of Rights　ナーシングホーム利用者の権利章典
resident care conference　利用者ケアカンファレンス
resident council　利用者会
residential care　居住施設ケア
residential community care　地域居住施設サービス
Resident's Rights　ナーシングホーム利用者の権利
Resource-Based Relative Value Scale：RBRVS　資源準拠相対評価尺度
Resource-Based Relative Value Scale System　資源準拠相対評価尺度システム
Resource-Based Relative Value System　資源準拠相対評価システム
Resource Utilization Group：RUG　資源利用別グループ
Resource Utilization Groups Version III：RUG-III　資源利用別グループ第3版
respite care　レスパイトケア
rest home　レストホーム
Restless Legs Syndrome Foundation　レストレスレッグス症候群財団
Retired Senior Volunteers Program：RSVP　退職高齢者ボランティアプログラム
retirement community　退職者コミュニティ
retirement home　退職者ホーム
sandwiched generation　サンドイッチ世代
Senate Finance Committee　上院財務委員会
Senate Special Committee on Aging　高齢化問題に関する上院特別委員会
Senate Special Subcommittee on Problems of the Aged and Aging　高齢者・高齢化問題に関する上院議会特別小委員会
Service Corps of Retired Executives：SCORE　退職管理職サービス組合
Servicemen's Readjustment Act　軍人再調整法
Sex Discrimination Act　性差別禁止法
silent generation　サイレント世代[1927年-1945年生まれ]
skilled nursing facility　高度看護施設
Small Business Administration　中小企業局
SNAPforSeniors　スナップ・フォー・シニアーズ
Social Security　社会保障
Social Security Act　社会保障法
Social Security Administration：SSA　社会保障庁
Social Security Amendments　社会保障改正法
Social Security Board：SSB　社会保障委員会
Social Security number　社会保障番号
Social Security tax　社会保障税
Social Services Agency：SSA　社会サービス機関
Social Services block grant：SSBG　社会サービス包

括補助金
Social Services Department ソーシャルサービス部
socialized medicine 医療社会化制度
Society of Surgical Oncology 米国外科腫瘍学会
special focus facility：SFF 特別監視施設
Stand-Alone Prescription Drug Coverage Plan：PDP 単独民間処方薬剤費保険
Standard Nonforfeiture Law 標準不没収価格法
star rating スターレイティング；星評価
state government 州政府
State of the Union 年頭教書
State Units on Aging：SUA 州高齢者局
Stewart B. McKinney Homeless Assistance Act スチュワート・B・マッキニー・ホームレス援助法
Sun City, Arizona アリゾナ州サンシティ
superintendent of nurses 看護管理部長
Supplemental Medical Insurance：SMI 補足的医療保険
Supplemental Security Insurance：SSI 補足的所得保障
Supreme Court of the United States 米国最高裁判所
Surgeon General 公衆衛生局長
swing generation スイング世代 [1900年-1926年生まれ]
Tax Equity and Fiscal Responsibility Act：TEFRA 税負担の公正・財政責任法
Tax Reform Act 税制改革法
Technology-Related Assistance for Individuals with Disability Act 障害者のための技術関連支援法
Telecommunications Act 電気通信法
telecommunications device for the deaf：TDD 聴覚障害者用電気通信機器
Temporary Assistance for Needy Families：TANF 一時的貧困家庭扶助
TennCare テンケア [テネシー州のメディケイド]
traditional indemnity insurance 伝統的医療保険
transitional care planning 遷移性の患者管理立案
Uniform Rights of the Terminally Ill Act 統一末期病者権利法
unlicensed assistive personnel 無免許補助職員
unlicensed nursing personnel 無免許看護職員
Urban Mass Transportation Act 都市大量交通法
U.S. Environmental Protection Agency 米国環境保護庁
U.S. Department of Health and Human Services：HHS 米国保健福祉省
U.S. Department of Health, Education and Welfare：HEW 米国保健教育福祉省
U.S. Department of Health Services 米国保健省
U.S. Department of Housing and Urban Development：HUD 米国住宅都市開発省
U.S. Department of Justice 米国司法省

U.S. Department of Social Services 米国社会サービス省
U.S. Department of Transportation 米国運輸省
U.S. Department of Veterans Affairs：VA 米国退役軍人省
U.S. Food and Drug Administration 米国食品医薬品局
U.S. House of Representatives Select Committee on Aging 高齢化問題に関する米国下院特別委員会
U.S. Preventive Services Task Force：USPSTF 米国予防医療作業部会
U.S. Senate Finance Committee 米国上院財務委員会
U.S. Senate Special Committee on Aging 高齢化問題に関する米国上院特別委員会
U.S. Senate Special Subcommittee on Problems of the Aged and Aging 高齢者・高齢化問題に関する米国上院議会特別小委員会
U.S. Supreme Court 米国最高裁判所
usual customary and reasonable：UCR 慣例的適性治療額
Utilization Review Committee：URC 施設利用調査委員会
utilization review management：URM 施設利用管理
VA hospital 退役軍人病院
veteran benefit 退役軍人給付
Veterans Affairs hospital 退役軍人病院
Veterans Health Administration：VHA 退役軍人健康庁
Veterans Services 退役軍人サービス
Visiting Nurse Associations of America 米国訪問看護師協会
war on cancer 癌との戦い
war on poverty 貧困との戦い
White House Conference on Aging ホワイトハウス高齢者会議
White House Office of National Drug Control Policy ホワイトハウス国家麻薬管理政策局
Women's Health Initiative：WHI 女性の健康イニシアティブ
Workers' Compensation Court 労働者補償裁判所
Workforce Investment Act 総労働力投資法
Wound, Ostomy and Continence Nurses Society 創傷・オストミー・失禁管理看護師協会
Young Men's Christian Association：YMCA キリスト教青年会
young-old ヤングオールド [65歳～74歳の高齢者]
Young Women's Christian Association：YWCA キリスト教女子青年会

5. 米国（アメリカ）における介護福祉等関連用語【和　英】

アクセス不可能資産（あくせすふかのうしさん）inaccessible asset
アクティビティ部（あくてぃびてぃぶ）Activity Department
アジア・太平洋老年研究学会（あじあ・たいへいようろうねんけんきゅうがっかい）Asia-Pacific Institute of Ageing Studies
アシステッド・リビング施設（あしすてっど・りびんぐしせつ）assisted living facility
アダルト・フォスターホーム（あだると・ふぉすたーほーむ）adult foster home
アメリカ人高齢者改正法（あめりかじんこうれいしゃかいせいほう）Older Americans Act Amendments
アメリカ人高齢者法（あめりかじんこうれいしゃほう）Older Americans Act：OAA
アメリカ人高齢者包括的サービス改正法（あめりかじんこうれいしゃほうかつてきさーびすかいせいほう）Older Americans Act Comprehensive Services Amendments
アリゾナ州サンシティ（ありぞなしゅうさんしてぃ）Sun City, Arizona
アリゾナ州長期ケアシステム（ありぞなしゅうちょうきけあしすてむ）Arizona long-term care system
RAI（あーるえーあい）Resident Assessment Instrument；
アルツハイマー協会（あるつはいまーきょうかい）Alzheimer's Association
アルツハイマーケア病棟（あるつはいまーけあびょうとう）Alzheimer's care unit
医学研究所（いがくけんきゅうしょ）Institute of Medicine
医学上必要な者（いがくじょうひつようなもの）medically needy
医師組織（いしそしき）Physician Organization：PO
医師組織提供システム（いしそしきていきょうしすてむ）Physician Organized Delivery System：PODS
医師病院組織（いしびょういんそしき）Physician Hospital Organization：PHO
依存度別患者グループ（いぞんどべつかんじゃぐるーぷ）Patient Dependency Group：PDG
一患者一日あたりの看護時間（いちかんじゃいちにちあたりのかんごじかん）Nursing Hours per Patient Day：nhppd
一時的貧困家庭扶助（いちじてきひんこんかていふじょ）Temporary Assistance for Needy Families：TANF
一利用者一日あたりの看護・介護時間（いちりようしゃいちにちあたりのかんご・かいごじかん）Hours per Resident Day：hprd
一般扶助（いっぱんふじょ）general assistance：GA

医薬品価格調査（いやくひんかかくちょうさ）pharmaceutical retail-price survey
医療委任状（いりょういにんじょう）Durable Power of Attorney for Health Care
医療委任状法（いりょういにんじょうほう）Durable Power of Attorney for Health Care Act
医療機関合同認定委員会（いりょうきかんごうどうにんていいいんかい）Joint Commission on Accreditation of Healthcare Organization：JCAHO
医療技術評価（いりょうぎじゅつひょうか）Medical Technology Assessment：MTA
医療・教育調整法（いりょう・きょういくちょうせいほう）Health Care and Education Reconciliation Act
医療研究・品質局（いりょうけんきゅう・ひんしつきょく）Agency for Healthcare Research and Quality：AHRQ
医療財務庁（いりょうざいむちょう）Health Care Financing Administration：HCFA
医療資源・サービス局（いりょうしげん・さーびすきょく）Health Resources and Services Administration
医療事前指示書（いりょうじぜんしじしょ）advance directive；advanced directive
医療社会化制度（いりょうしゃかいかせいど）socialized medicine
医療政策・研究所（いりょうせいさく・けんきゅうしょ）Agency for Health Care Policy and Research：AHCPR
医療貯蓄口座（いりょうちょちくこうざ）medical saving account：MSA
医療の質改善組織（いりょうのしつかいぜんそしき）Quality Improvement Organization：QIO
医療費検討協議会（いりょうひけんとうきょうぎかい）Health Services Cost Review Commission
医療保険改革法（いりょうほけんかいかくほう）Patient Protection and Affordable Care Act：PPACA
医療保険相互運用性・説明責任法（いりょうほけんそうごうんようせい・せつめいせきにんほう）Health Insurance Portability and Accountability Act
医療保険相互運用性・説明責任法における個人情報保護法（いりょうほけんそうごううんようせい・せつめいせきにんほうにおけるこじんじょうほうほごほう）Privacy Rules of Health Insurance Portability and Accountability Act
インディアン衛生局（いんでぃあんえいせいきょく）Indian Health Services：HIS
運輸省（うんゆしょう）Department of

Transportation
エイジングネットワーク（えいじんぐねっとわーく）
Aging Network
衛生行政・大学プログラム協会（えいせいぎょうせい・だいがくぷろぐらむきょうかい）Association of University Programs in Health Administration : AUPHA
栄養サービスインセンティブプログラム（えいようさーびすいんせんてぃぶぷろぐらむ）Nutrition Services Incentive Program
栄養士登録委員会（えいようしとうろくいいんかい）Commission of Dietetic Registration : CDR
栄誉賞年金（えいよしょうねんきん）Medal of Honor Pension
営利団体（えいりだんたい）for-profit organization
MDS（えむでぃーえす）Minimum Data Set
MDSコーディネーター（えむでぃーえすこーでぃねーたー）MDS〈Minimum Data Set coordinator〉
エリサ法（えりさほう）ERISA : Employee Retirement Income Security Act
エルダーホステルプログラム（えるだーほすてるぷろぐらむ）Elderhostel Program
エルダーライフプログラム（えるだーらいふぷろぐらむ）Elder Life Program
オープンアクセスプラン（おーぷんあくせすぷらん）open access plan
オールデスト・オールド（おーるですと・おーるど）oldest-old [85歳以上の高齢者]
オールド・オールド（おーるど・おーるど）old-old [75歳〜84歳の高齢者]
オルムステッド法（おるむすてっどほう）Olmstead Decision
オレゴン州尊厳死法（おれごんしゅうそんげんしほう）Oregon Death with Dignity Act
オレゴンヘルスプラン（おれごんへるすぷらん）Oregon Health Plan [オレゴン州のメディケイド]
オレゴン保健会議（おれごんほけんかいぎ）Oregon Health Decision
オンロック（おんろっく）On-Lok
オンロックシニアサービス（おんろっくしにあさーびす）On-Lok Senior Services
会員制診療（かいいんせいしんりょう）ledge practice
開業医総合管理会社（かいぎょういそうごうかんりがいしゃ）Physician Practice Management Company : PPMC
開業医組織（かいぎょういそしき）Individual Practice Association : IPA
会計検査院（かいけいけんさいん）General Accounting Office
介護者の権利章典（かいごしゃのけんりしょうてん）Caregiver's Bill of Rights
介護評価認定プログラム（かいごひょうかにんていぷろぐらむ）Long-Term Care Evaluation and

Accreditation Program : LEAP
カイザーパーマナンテ（かいざーぱーまなんて）Kaiser Permanente
カイザーファミリー財団（かいざーふぁみりーざいだん）Kaiser Family Foundation
カイザープラン（かいざーぷらん）Kaiser Plan
外来患者疾病分類（がいらいかんじゃしっぺいぶんるい）Ambulatory Patient Group : APG
外来包括支払い分類（がいらいほうかつしはらいぶんるい）Ambulatory Payment Classification : APC
下院歳入委員会（かいんさいにゅういいんかい）House Ways and Means Committee
下院州議会法案（かいんしゅうぎかいほうあん）Assembly Bill : AB
科学審査センター（かがくしんさせんたー）Center for Scientific Review : CSR
拡大高齢者向け在宅プログラム（かくだいこうれいしゃむけざいたくぷろぐらむ）Expanded In-home Services for the Elderly : EISEP
拡大自立支援（かくだいじりつしえん）Greater Avenue for Independent : GAIN
確定給付型年金（かくていきゅうふがたねんきん）defined benefit plan
確定拠出型年金（かくていきょしゅつがたねんきん）defined contribution plan
家族・医療休暇法（かぞく・いりょうきゅうかほう）Family and Medical Leave Act : FMLA
家族会（かぞくかい）family council
家族扶助計画（かぞくふじょけいかく）family assistance plan : FAP
カトリック医療協会（かとりっくいりょうきょうかい）Catholic Health Association : CHA
カトリック・チャリティーズ（かとりっく・ちゃりてぃーず）Catholic Charities
カー・ミルズ法案（かー・みるずほうあん）Kerr-Mills Bill
カルフォルニア州就労機会・児童責任事業（かるふぉるにあしゅうしゅうろうきかい・じどうせきにんじぎょう）California Work Opportunities and Responsibility to Kids : CalWORKs
環境保護局（かんきょうほごきょく）Environmental Protection Agency : EPA
看護管理部長（かんごかんりぶちょう）superintendent of nurses
看護支援職員（かんごしえんしょくいん）nursing support personnel ; nursing assistive personnel
看護施設（かんごしせつ）nursing facility
看護における長期ケア問題フォーラム（かんごにおけるちょうきけあもんだいふぉーらむ）Forum on Long-Term Care Issue in Nursing
看護補助職員（かんごほじょしょくいん）nursing extender
監査・認証オンラインレポート（かんさ・にんしょうお

んらいんれぽーと）Online Survey, Certification and Reporting：OSCAR
監査・認証オンラインレポートデータベース（かんさ・にんしょうおんらいんれぽーとでーたべーす）Online Survey, Certification and Reporting database：OSCAR database
患者の権利章典（かんじゃのけんりしょうてん）Patient's Bill of Rights
患者の自己決定法（かんじゃのじこけっていほう）Patient Self-Determination Act
患者の保護と手頃な医療法（かんじゃのほごとてごろないりょうほう）Patient Protection and Affordable Care Act：PPACA
患者分類システム（かんじゃぶんるいしすてむ）Patient Classification System：PCS
関節炎財団（かんせつえんざいだん）Arthritis Foundation
完全永久就業不能者扶助（かんぜんえいきゅうしゅうぎょうふのうしゃふじょ）Aid to the Permanently and Totally Disabled：APTD
癌との戦い（がんとのたたかい）War on Cancer
慣例的適性治療額（かんれいてきてきせいちりょうがく）usual customary and reasonable：UCR
議会予算局（ぎかいよさんきょく）Consolidated Budget Office：CBO
義務的制度困窮対象者（ぎむてきせいどこんきゅうたいしょうしゃ）Mandatory Categorically Needy
ギャグルール（ぎゃぐるーる）gag rule
給付増額保障特約（きゅうふぞうがくほしょうとくやく）Guaranteed Insurability Option：GIO
給付統合型プラン（きゅうふとうごうがたぷらん）Integrated Benefit Plan
給与税（きゅうよぜい）payroll tax
行政手続法（ぎょうせいてつづきほう）Administrative Procedure Act
居住施設ケア（きょじゅうしせつけあ）residential care
キリスト教女子青年会（きりすときょうじょしせいねんかい）Young Women's Christian Association：YWCA
キリスト教青年会（きりすときょうせいねんかい）Young Men's Christian Association：YMCA
緊急時対策支援システム（きんきゅうじたいさくしえんしすてむ）Emergency Response Support System
キングスレー館（きんぐすれーかん）Kingsley Hall
金銭無断悪用専門チーム（きんせんむだんあくようせんもんちーむ）Fiduciary Abuse Specialist Team：FAST
クオリティインジケータ（くおりてぃいんじけーた）quality indicator
クオリティメジャー（くおりてぃめじゃー）quality measure

グループ医療協会（ぐるーぷいりょうきょうかい）Group Health Association
グレイパンサーズ（ぐれいぱんさーず）Gray Panthers
グレータニューヨーク医療保険事業（ぐれーたにゅーよーくいりょうほけんじぎょう）Health Insurance Plan of Greater New York
軍人再調整法（ぐんじんさいちょうせいほう）Servicemen's Readjustment Act
ケア資源チーム（けあしげんちーむ）care resource team
経済機会局（けいざいきかいきょく）Office of Economic Opportunity
経済機会法（けいざいきかいほう）Economic Opportunity Act：EOA
経済権利法（けいざいけんりほう）Economic Bill of Rights
経済的従属人口比率（けいざいてきじゅうぞくじんこうひりつ）economic dependency ratio
経済保障委員会（けいざいほしょういいんかい）Committee on Economic Security：CES
継続的ケア提供型退職者コミュニティ（けいぞくてきあていきょうがたたいしょくしゃこみゅにてぃ）Continuing Care Retirement Community：CCRC
継続的ケア認定委員会（けいぞくてきあにんていいいんかい）Continuing Care Accreditation Commission
刑務所局（けいむしょきょく）Bureau of Prisons
月間最低必要手当（げっかんさいていひつようてあて）minimum monthly maintenance needs allowance：MMMNA
ケネディ・カセバウム法（けねでぃ・かせばうむほう）Kennedy-Kassebaum Bill
権限委譲（けんげんいじょう）Durable Power of Attorney
健康維持組織（けんこういじそしき）Health Maintenance Organization：HMO
健康維持組織法（けんこういじそしきほう）Health Maintenance Organization Act：HMO Act
健康危険度評価（けんこうきけんどひょうか）Health Risk Appraisal：HRA
建築障壁法（けんちくしょうへきほう）Architectural Barriers Act
検認裁判所（けんにんさいばんしょ）probate court
現物給付（げんぶつきゅうふ）benefit in kind
高額医療費保険法（こうがくいりょうひほけんほう）Catastrophic Coverage Act
後見人制度（こうけんにんせいど）conservatorship
公衆衛生科学室（こうしゅうえいせいかがくしつ）Office of Public Health and Science：OPHS
公衆衛生局（こうしゅうえいせいきょく）Public Health Service
公衆衛生局受託隊（こうしゅうえいせいきょくじゅたくたい）Public Health Service Commissioned Corps

公衆衛生局長（こうしゅうえいせいきょくちょう） Surgeon General
公衆衛生総監局（こうしゅうえいせいそうかんきょく） Office of the Surgeon General
公衆衛生法（こうしゅうえいせいほう） Public Health Service Act
公正住宅改正法（こうせいじゅうたくかいせいほう） Fair Housing Amendments Act
公正住宅法（こうせいじゅうたくほう） Fair Housing Act
公正労働基準法（こうせいろうどうきじゅんほう） Fair Labor Standards Act
高等学校卒業認定証明書（こうとうがっこうそつぎょうにんていしょうめいしょ） General Education Development Certificate：GED
高度看護施設（こうかんごしせつ） skilled nursing facility
公民権法（こうみんけんほう） Civil Rights Act
高齢化問題に関する下院特別委員会（こうれいかもんだいにかんするかいんとくべついんかい） House of Representatives Select Committee on Aging
高齢化問題に関する上院特別委員会（こうれいかもんだいにかんするじょういんとくべついんかい） Senate Special Committee on Aging
高齢化問題に関する米国下院特別委員会（こうれいかもんだいにかんするべいこくかいんとくべついんかい） U.S. House of Representatives Select Committee on Aging
高齢化問題に関する米国上院特別委員会（こうれいかもんだいにかんするべいこくじょういんとくべついんかい） U.S. Senate Special Committee on Aging
高齢局（こうれいきょく） Administration on Aging：AoA
高齢者医療専門薬剤師（こうれいしゃいりょうせんもんやくざいし） certified geriatric pharmacist
高齢者栄養管理プログラム法（こうれいしゃえいようかんりぷろぐらむほう） Nutrition Program for the Elderly Act
高齢者栄養プログラム（こうれいしゃえいようぷろぐらむ） Elderly Nutrition Program：ENP
高齢者急性期ケア（こうれいしゃきゅうせいきけあ） Acute Care of Elders：ACE
高齢者ケア検索サイト（こうれいしゃけあけんさくさいと） Eldercare Locator
高齢者・高齢化問題に関する上院議会特別小委員会（こうれいしゃ・こうれいかもんだいにかんするじょういんぎかいとくべつしょういいんかい） Senate Special Subcommittee on Problems of the Aged and Aging
高齢者・高齢化問題に関する米国上院議会特別小委員会（こうれいしゃ・こうれいかもんだいにかんするべいこくじょういんぎかいとくべつしょういいんかい） U.S. Senate Special Subcommittee on Problems

of the Aged and Aging
高齢者・身体障害者向け薬剤援助プログラム（こうれいしゃ・しんたいしょうがいしゃむけやくざいえんじょぷろぐらむ） Pharmaceutical Assistance to the Aged and Disabled
高齢者包括ケアプログラム（こうれいしゃほうかつけあぷろぐらむ） Programs of All Inclusive Care for the Elderly：PACE
高齢者ホーム（こうれいしゃほーむ） adult care home
高齢女性連盟（こうれいじょせいれんめい） Older Women's League
高齢労働者利益保護法（こうれいろうどうしゃりえきほごほう） Older Workers Benefit Protection Act
国際回想法学会（こくさいかいそうほうがっかい） International Institute for Reminiscence and Life Review ［旧International Society for Reminiscence and Life Review］
国勢調査情報センター（こくせいちょうさじょうほうせんたー） Census Information Center
国民皆医療法（こくみんかいいりょうほう） Health Care for All Americans Act
国民福祉権利組織（こくみんふくしけんりそしき） National Welfare Rights Organization
国民扶助法（こくみんふじょほう） National Assistance Act
個人退職口座（こじんたいしょくこうざ） Individual Retirement Account：IRA
国家医療計画・資源開発法（こっかいりょうけいかく・しげんかいはつほう） National Health Planning and Resources Development Act
国家最低飲酒年齢法（こっかさいていいんしゅねんれいほう） National Minimum Drinking Age Act
コネティカットホスピスプログラム（こねていかっとほすぴすぷろぐらむ） Connecticut Hospice Program
雇用年齢差別禁止法（こようねんれいさべつきんしほう） Age Discrimination in Employment Act
雇用法（こようほう） Employment Act
最高看護責任者（さいこうかんごせきにんしゃ） chief nursing officer：CNO
財政赤字削減法（ざいせいあかじさくげんほう） Deficit Reduction Act：DRA
在宅ケア認定評価会（ざいたくけあにんていひょうかかい） Accreditation Council for Home Care
在宅ケア品質保証（ざいたくけあひんしつほしょう） Home Care Quality Assurance
在宅サービス事業者間比較プログラム（ざいたくさーびすじぎょうしゃかんひかくぷろぐらむ） Home Health Compare
在宅サービス資源利用度別グループ（ざいたくさーびすしげんりようべつぐるーぷ） Home Health Resource Groups：HHRG
在宅サービスの質改善イニシアティブ（ざいたくさーびすのしつかいぜんいにしあてぃぶ） Home Health

Quality Initiative
在宅サービス版アウトカム・アセスメント表（ざいたくさーびすばんあうとかむ・あせすめんとひょう） Outcome and Assessment Information Set：OASIS
財務委員会（ざいむいいんかい） Committee of Ways and Means
財務委任状（ざいむいにんじょう） Durable Power of Attorney for Finances
サイレント世代（さいれんとせだい） silent generation [1927年-1945年生まれ]
作業療法士助手（さぎょうりょうほうしじょしゅ） occupational therapy aide
サンドイッチ世代（さんどいっちせだい） sandwiched generation
視覚障害者扶助（しかくしょうがいしゃふじょ） aid to the blind
資源準拠相対評価システム（しげんじゅんきょそうたいひょうかしすてむ） Resource-Based Relative Value System
資源準拠相対評価尺度（しげんじゅんきょそうたいひょうかしゃくど） Resource-Based Relative Value Scale：RBRVS
資源準拠相対評価尺度システム（しげんじゅんきょそうたいひょうかしゃくどしすてむ） Resource-Based Relative Value Scale System
資源利用別グループ（しげんりようべつぐるーぷ） Resource Utilization Group：RUG
資源利用別グループ第3版（しげんりようべつぐるーぷだいさんぱん） Resource Utilization Groups Version III：RUG-III
自己責任就労機会調整法（じこせきにんしゅうろうきかいちょうせいほう） Personal Responsibility and Work Opportunity Reconciliation Act：PRWORA
司祭サービス（しさいさーびす） chaplain services
施設利用管理（しせつりようかんり） utilization review management：URM
施設利用調査委員会（しせつりようちょうさいいんかい） Utilization Review Committee：URC
自然死法（しぜんしほう） Natural Death Act
持続的努力要求（じぞくてきどりょくようきゅう） maintenance of effort：MOE
疾病管理予防センター（しっぺいかんりよぼうせんたー） Centers for Disease Control and Prevention：CDC
質保証委員会（しつほしょういいんかい） Quality Assurance Committee
実力本位制度（じつりょくほんいせいど） merit system
児童・家庭局（じどう・かていきょく） Administration for Children and Families
児童扶養世帯扶助制度（じどうふようせたいふじょせいど） Aids to Families with Dependent Children：AFDC

児童保護・育成基金（じどうほご・いくせいききん） Child Care and Development Fund：CCDF
児童労働基準法（じどうろうどうきじゅんほう） child labor laws
司法省（しほうしょう） Department of Justice
社会サービス省（しゃかいさーびすしょう） Department of Social Services
社会サービス包括補助金（しゃかいさーびすほうかつほじょきん） Social Services block grant：SSBG
社会保障（しゃかいほしょう） Social Security
社会保障委員会（しゃかいほしょういいんかい） Social Security Board：SSB
社会保障改正法（しゃかいほしょうかいせいほう） Social Security Amendments
社会保障諮問委員会（しゃかいほしょうしもんいいんかい） Advisory Council on Social Security
社会保障税（しゃかいほしょうぜい） Social Security tax
社会保障庁（しゃかいほしょうちょう） Social Security Administration：SSA
社会保障番号（しゃかいほしょうばんごう） Social Security number
社会保障法（しゃかいほしょうほう） Social Security Act
従業員退職所得保障法（じゅうぎょういんたいしょくしょとくほしょうほう） Employee Retirement Income Security Act：ERISA
就業機会基本技能訓練（しゅうぎょうきかいきほんぎのうくんれん） Job Opportunities and Basic Skills Training：JOBS
州高齢者局（しゅうこうれいしゃきょく） State Units on Aging：SUA
州政府（しゅうせいふ） state government
住宅・コミュニティ開発法（じゅうたく・こみゅにてぃかいはつほう） Housing and Community Development Act
住宅都市開発省（じゅうたくとしかいはつしょう） Department of Housing and Urban Development：HUD
住宅法（じゅうたくほう） Housing Act
集団給食サービス（しゅうだんきゅうしょくさーびす） congregate meal
集団ホーム（しゅうだんほーむ） congregate housing
集団ホームサービス法（しゅうだんほーむさーびすほう） Congregate Housing Services Act
収入維持計画諮問委員会（しゅうにゅういじけいかくしもんいいんかい） Commission on Income Maintenance Programs
受診選択プラン（じゅしんせんたくぷらん） point of service：POS
腫瘍看護学会（しゅようかんごがっかい） Oncology Nursing Society
主要診断群（しゅようしんだんぐん） Major

米国和英

Diagnostic Category : MDC
主要入院疾病別費用グループ（しゅようにゅういんしっぺいべつひようぐるーぷ）Principal Inpatient Diagnostic Cost Group : PIP-DCG
上院財務委員会（じょういんざいむいいんかい）Senate Finance Committee
障害者差別禁止法（しょうがいしゃさべつきんしほう）Disability Discrimination Act
障害者のための技術関連支援法（しょうがいしゃのためのぎじゅつかんれんしえんほう）Technology-Related Assistance for Individuals with Disability Act
消費者主導型医療保険(しょうひしゃしゅどうがたいりょうほけん) Consumer Driven Health Plan : CDHP
情報技術センター（じょうほうぎじゅつせんたー）Center for Information Technology : CIT
情報・照会サービス（じょうほう・しょうかいさーびす）information and referral
初期認定教育（しょきにんていきょういく）initial certification education
職業訓練協力法（しょくぎょうくんれんきょうりょくほう）Job Training Partnership Act : JTPA
食品医薬品局（しょくひんいやくひんきょく）Food and Drug Administration : FDA
食糧スタンププログラム（しょくりょうすたんぷぷろぐらむ）Food Stamp Program
女性の健康イニシアティブ（じょせいのけんこういにしあてぃぶ）Women's Health Initiative : WHI
所定報酬支払い方式（しょていほうしゅうしはらいほうしき）Prospective Payment System : PPS
処方箋薬剤給付保険（しょほうせんやくざいきゅうふほけん）Prescription Drug Coverage : Medicare Part D
処方箋薬費保険プラン（しょほうせんやくひほけんぷらん）Medicare Advantage Plan
ジョンズ・ホプキンス医療システム（じょんず・ほぷきんすいりょうしすてむ）Johns Hopkins Health System
人口動態調査（じんこうどうたいちょうさ）Current Population Survey : CPS
人種差別禁止法（じんしゅさべつきんしほう）Racial Discrimination Act
身体ケアホーム（しんたいけあほーむ）personal care home
診断群別支払い方式（しんだんぐんべつしはらいほうしき）Diagnosis Related Group : DRG
人的資源訓練法（じんてきしげんくんれんほう）Manpower Development and Training Act
診療審査機構（しんりょうしんさきこう）Professional Review Organization : PRO
診療報酬共通コード（しんりょうほうしゅうきょうつうこーど）Current Procedural Terminology : CPT
診療報酬検討委員会（しんりょうほうしゅうけんとういいんかい）Physician Payment Review Commission : PPRC
診療報酬コード体系（しんりょうほうしゅうこーどたいけい）Common Procedure Coding System : CPCS
診療報酬支払い審査機構（しんりょうほうしゅうしはらいしんさきこう）Professional Standard Review Organization : PSRO
スイング世代（すいんぐせだい）swing generation [1900年-1926年生まれ]
スターレイティング（すたーれいてぃんぐ）star rating
スチュワート・B・マッキニー・ホームレス援助法（すちゅわーと・びー・まっきにー・ほーむれすえんじょほう）Stewart B. McKinney Homeless Assistance Act
スナップ・フォー・シニアーズ（すなっぷ・ふぉー・しにあーず）SNAPforSeniors
性差別禁止法（せいさべつきんしほう）Sex Discrimination Act
成人虐待保護サービス（せいじんぎゃくたいほごさーびす）adult protective services : APS
成人教育法（せいじんきょういくほう）Adult Education Act
精神保健同等法（せいしんほけんどうとうほう）Mental Health Parity Act
税制改革法（ぜいせいかいかくほう）Tax Reform Act
税負担の公正・財政責任法（ぜいふたんのこうせい・ざいせいせきにんほう）Tax Equity and Fiscal Responsibility Act : TEFRA
製薬工業協会（せいやくこうぎょうきょうかい）Pharmaceutical Manufacturers Association
責任看護師（せきにんかんごし）charge nurse
遷移性の患者管理立案（せんいせいのかんじゃかんりりつあん）transitional care planning
選択の自由法（せんたくのじゆうほう）Freedom of Choice Act
選定医療提供協定（せんていいりょうていきょうきょうてい）Preferred Provider Arrangement : PPA
選定医療提供組織(せんていいりょうていきょうそしき) Preferred Provider Organization : PPO
全米アジア・太平洋諸国系高齢者協会（ぜんべいあじあ・たいへいようしょこくけいこうれいしゃきょうかい）National Asian Pacific Center on Aging
全米アシステッド・リビング協議会(ぜんべいあしすてっど・りびんぐきょうぎかい) National Council of Assisted Living : NCAL
全米アシステッド・リビングセンター（ぜんべいあしすてっど・りびんぐせんたー）National Center for Assisted Living
全米意識調査センター(ぜんべいいしきちょうさせんたー) National Opinion Research Center
全米遺伝医学専門教育連合（ぜんべいいでんいがくせんもんきょういくれんごう）National Coalition for Health Professional Education in Genetics
全米医薬品協議会（ぜんべいいやくひんきょうぎかい）

National Pharmaceutical Council
全米医療保険協会(ぜんべいいりょうほけんきょうかい)
Health Insurance Association of America：HIAA
全米インディアン高齢者協議会(ぜんべいいんでぃあんこうれいしゃきょうぎかい) National Indian Council on Aging：NICOA
全米うつ病・躁うつ病協会(ぜんべいうつびょう・そううつびょうきょうかい) National Depressive and Manic-Depressive Association
全米介護者連合(ぜんべいかいごしゃれんごう) National Alliance for Caregiving
全米科学財団（ぜんべいかがくざいだん）National Science Foundation
全米家族介護者協会（ぜんべいかぞくかいごしゃきょうかい）National Family Caregivers Association
全米家族介護者支援プログラム（ぜんべいかぞくかいごしゃしえんぷろぐらむ）National Family Caregiver Support Program
全米看護師教育実務諮問委員会（ぜんべいかんごしきょういくじつむしもんいいんかい）National Advisory Council on Nurse Education and Practice：NACNEP
全米看護師週間（ぜんべいかんごししゅうかん）National Nurses Week
全米看護職員教育協会（ぜんべいかんごしょくいんきょういくきょうかい）National Nursing Staff Development Organization
全米看護連盟（ぜんべいかんごれんめい）National League for Nursing
全米患者安全財団(ぜんべいかんじゃあんぜんざいだん) National Patient Safety Foundation
全米経済社会保障会議(ぜんべいけいざいしゃかいほしょうかいぎ) National Conference on Economic Security
全米健康聞取り調査（ぜんべいけんこうききとりちょうさ）National Health Interview Survey
全米高血圧教育プログラム（ぜんべいこうけつあつきょういくぷろぐらむ）National High Blood Pressure Education Program
全米高齢者栄養プログラム（ぜんべいこうれいしゃえいようぷろぐらむ）National Elderly Nutrition Program
全米高齢者虐待事例調査（ぜんべいこうれいしゃぎゃくたいじれいちょうさ）National Abuse Incidence Study
全米高齢者虐待調査（ぜんべいこうれいしゃぎゃくたいちょうさ）National Elder Mistreatment Study
全米高齢者虐待問題研究所（ぜんべいこうれいしゃぎゃくたいもんだいけんきゅうしょ）National Center on Elder Abuse
全米高齢者協議会(ぜんべいこうれいしゃきょうぎかい) National Council on Aging
全米高齢者局（ぜんべいこうれいしゃきょく）National Association State Units on Aging
全米高齢者ケアマネジャー協会（ぜんべいこうれいしゃけあまねじゃーきょうかい）National Association of Professional Geriatric Care Managers
全米高齢者国民協議会（ぜんべいこうれいしゃこくみんきょうぎかい）National Council of Senior Citizens：NCSC
全米高齢者国民法律センター（ぜんべいこうれいしゃこくみんほうりつせんたー）National Senior Citizens Law Center
全米高齢者住宅産業協会（ぜんべいこうれいしゃじゅうたくさんぎょうきょうかい）National Association for Senior Living Industries
全米高齢者評議会(ぜんべいこうれいしゃひょうぎかい) National Seniors Council
全米黒人地位向上協会（ぜんべいこくじんちいこうじょうきょうかい）National Association for the Advancement of Colored People：NAACP
全米国民医療保険法（ぜんべいこくみんいりょうほけんほう）National Health Insurance Act
全米骨粗鬆症財団（ぜんべいこつそしょうしょうざいだん）National Osteoporosis Foundation
全米コレステロール教育プログラム（ぜんべいこれすてろーるきょういくぷろぐらむ）National Cholesterol Education Program
全米在宅ケア協会（ぜんべいざいたくけあきょうかい）National Association for Home Care：NAHC
全米在宅ケア・ホスピス協会（ぜんべいざいたくけあ・ほすぴすきょうかい）National Association for Home Care and Hospice
全米支援付き住居・住宅改修資源センター（ぜんべいしえんつきじゅうきょ・じゅうたくかいしゅうしげんせんたー）National Resource Center on Supportive Housing and Home Modification
全米視覚障害者連合（ぜんべいしかくしょうがいしゃれんごう）National Federation of the Blind
全米資源企画委員会(ぜんべいしげんきかくいいんかい) National Resources Planning Board：NRPB
全米質ガイドライン（ぜんべいしつがいどらいん）National Quality Guidelines
全米失語症協会（ぜんべいしつごしょうきょうかい）National Aphasia Association
全米司法福祉学会（ぜんべいしほうふくしがっかい）National Organization of Forensic Social Work
全米市民地域社会協会（ぜんべいしみんちいきしゃかいきょうかい）National Civilian Community Corps：NCCC
全米社会保障改革審議会（ぜんべいしゃかいほしょうかいかくしんぎかい）National Commission on Social Security Reform：NCSSR
全米宗教間相互協力委員会（ぜんべいしゅうきょうかんそうごきょうりょくいいんかい）National Interfaith Coalition on Aging

全米住宅法（ぜんべいじゅうたくほう）National Housing Act
全米障害者協議会（ぜんべいしょうがいしゃきょうぎかい）National Council on Disability
全米消費者連盟（ぜんべいしょうひしゃれんめい）National Consumers League
全米褥瘡諮問委員会（ぜんべいじょくそうしもんいいんかい）National Pressure Ulcer Advisory Panel
全米自立生活協議会（ぜんべいじりつせいかつきょうぎかい）National Council on Independent Living
全米頭痛財団（ぜんべいずつうざいだん）National Headache Foundation
全米精神病者連合（ぜんべいせいしんびょうしゃれんごう）National Alliance for the Mentally Ill
全米成人保護サービス協会（ぜんべいせいじんほごさーびすきょうかい）National Association of Adult Protective Services
全米製造者協会（ぜんべいせいぞうしゃきょうかい）National Association of Manufacturers
全米生命倫理諮問委員会（ぜんべいせいめいりんりしもんいいんかい）National Bioethics Advisory Commission
全米生命倫理文献図書館（ぜんべいせいめいりんりぶんけんとしょかん）National Reference Center for Bioethics Literature
全米ソーシャルワーカー協会（ぜんべいそーしゃるわーかーきょうかい）National Association of Social Workers：NASW
全米ソーシャルワーカー協会の倫理綱領（ぜんべいそーしゃるわーかーきょうかいのりんりこうりょう）National Association of Social Workers code of ethics
全米ソーシャルワーク教育協議会（ぜんべいそーしゃるわーくきょういくきょうぎかい）Council on Social Work Education：CSWE
全米地域高齢者福祉協会（ぜんべいちいきこうれいしゃふくしきょうかい）National Association of Area Agencies on Aging
全米長期ケアオンブズマン資源センター（せんべいちょうきけあおんぶずまんしげんせんたー）National Long Term Care Ombudsman Resource Center
全米長期ケアケースマネジメント諮問委員会（ぜんべいちょうきけあけーすまねじめんとしもんいいんかい）National Advisory Council on Long Term Care Case Management
全米投票者登録法（ぜんべいとうひょうしゃとうろくほう）National Voter Registration Act
全米登録看護師資格試験（ぜんべいとうろくかんごししかくしけん）National Council Licensure Examination-Registered Nurses：NCLEX-RN
全米ナーシングホーム改革国民連合協会（ぜんべいなーしんぐほーむかいかくこくみんれんごうきょうかい）National Citizens' Coalition for Nursing Home Reform
全米ナーシングホーム週間（ぜんべいなーしんぐほーむしゅうかん）National Nursing Home Week
全米ナーシングホーム調査（ぜんべいなーしんぐほーむちょうさ）National Nursing Home Survey
全米脳卒中協会（ぜんべいのうそっちゅうきょうかい）National Stroke Association
全米排泄障害協会（ぜんべいはいせつしょうがいきょうかい）National Association for Continence
全米パーキンソン財団（ぜんべいぱーきんそんざいだん）National Parkinson Foundation, Inc.
全米犯罪被害調査（ぜんべいはんざいひがいちょうさ）National Crime Victimization Survey：NCVS
全米病院感染サーベイランスシステム（ぜんべいびょういんかんせんさーべいらんすしすてむ）National Nosocomial Infections Surveillance System
全米貧血行動協議会（ぜんべいひんけつこうどうきょうぎかい）National Anemia Action Council
全米品質保証委員会（ぜんべいひんしつほしょういいんかい）National Committee for Quality Assurance：NCQA
全米法曹協会（ぜんべいほうそうきょうかい）National Bar Association
全米保健・栄養検査調査（ぜんべいほけん・えいようけんさちょうさ）National Health and Nutrition Examination Survey：NHANES
全米保険監督官協会（ぜんべいほけんかんとくかんきょうかい）National Association of Insurance Commissioners：NAIC
全米ホスピス協会（ぜんべいほすぴすきょうかい）National Hospice Organization：NHO
全米眼の健康教育プログラム（ぜんべいめのけんこうきょういくぷろぐらむ）National Eye Health Education Program
全米リハビリテーションカウンセリング協会（ぜんべいりはびりてーしょんかうんせりんぐきょうかい）American Rehabilitation Counseling Association
全米リハビリテーション協会（ぜんべいりはびりてーしょんきょうかい）National Rehabilitation Association
全米レクリエーション・公園協会（ぜんべいれくりえーしょん・こうえんきょうかい）National Recreation and Parks Association
全米レクリエーション療法協会（ぜんべいれくりえーしょんりょうほうきょうかい）National Therapeutic Recreation Society
全米レクリエーション療法認証協議会（ぜんべいれくりえーしょんりょうほうにんていきょうぎかい）National Council for Therapeutic Recreation Certification：NCTRC
全米聾者協会（ぜんべいろうしゃきょうかい）National Association of the Deaf
全米老人虐待防止対策委員会（ぜんべいろうじんぎゃくたいぼうしたいさくいいんかい）National

Committee for the Prevention of Elder Abuse
全米老人デイサービス協会（ぜんべいろうじんでいさーびすきょうかい）National Adult Day Services Association
全米老年医学教育センター（ぜんべいろうねんいがくきょういくせんた一）National Association of Geriatric Education Centers
全米老年看護学会（ぜんべいろうねんかんごがっかい）National Gerontological Nursing Association
早期退職制度（そうきたいしょくせいど）early retirement plan
早期退職年金（そうきたいしょくねんきん）early retirement pension
総合陸上輸送効率化法（そうごうりくじょうゆそうこうりつかほう）Intermodal Surface Transportation Efficiency Act
創傷・オストミー・失禁管理看護師協会（そうしょう・おすとみー・しっきんかんりかんごしきょうかい）Wound, Ostomy and Continence Nurses Society
相対価値単位（そうたいかちたんい）relative value unit：RVU
総労働力投資法（そうろうどうりょくとうしほう）Workforce Investment Act
ソーシャルサービス機関（そーしゃるさーびすきかん）Social Services Agency：SSA
ソーシャルサービス部（そーしゃるさーびすぶ）Social Services Department
ソーシャルワーク委員協会（そーしゃるわーくいいんきょうかい）Association of Social Work Boards
退役軍人給付（たいえきぐんじんきゅうふ）veteran benefit
退役軍人健康庁（たいえきぐんじんけんこうちょう）Veterans Health Administration：VHA
退役軍人サービス（たいえきぐんじんさーびす）Veterans Services
退役軍人省（たいえきぐんじんしょう）Department of Veterans Affairs：VA
退役軍人病院（たいえきぐんじんびょういん）VA hospital；Veterans Affairs hospital
退職管理職サービス組合（たいしょくかんりしょくさーびすくみあい）Service Corps of Retired Executives：SCORE
退職高齢者ボランティアプログラム（たいしょくこうれいしゃぼらんてぃあぷろぐらむ）Retired Senior Volunteers Program：RSVP
退職者コミュニティ（たいしょくしゃこみゅにてぃ）retirement community
退職者ホーム（たいしょくしゃほーむ）retirement home
多目的高齢者センター（たもくてきこうれいしゃせんたー）multipurpose senior center
男女平等憲法修正案（だんじょびょうどうけんぽうしゅうせいあん）Equal Rights Amendment

団体入院支払い（だんたいにゅういんしはらい）group hospitalization
単独民間処方薬剤費保険（たんどくみんかんしょほうやくざいひほけん）Stand-Alone Prescription Drug Coverage Plan：PDP
地域医療情報ネットワーク（ちいきいりょうじょうほうねっとわーく）Community Health Information Networks：CHIN
地域看護組織（ちいきかんごそしき）Community Nursing Organization：CNO
地域基盤型居住施設（ちいきききばんがたきょじゅうせつ）community-based residential facility
地域基盤型精神衛生ケア（ちいきききばんがたせいしんえいせいけあ）community-based mental health care
地域居住施設サービス（ちいききょじゅうしせつさーびす）residential community care
地域高齢者局（ちいきこうれいしゃきょく）Area Agencies on Aging
地域サービス機関（ちいきさーびすきかん）Community Services Agency：CSA
地域生活援助・支援プログラム（ちいきせいかつえんじょ・しえんぷろぐらむ）Community Living Assistance and Support Services Program
地域精神衛生センター（ちいきせいしんえいせいせんたー）Community Mental Health Center：CMHC
地域保健医療認定プログラム（ちいきほけんいりょうにんていぷろぐらむ）Community Health Accreditation Program：CHAP
中間看護施設（ちゅうかんかんごしせつ）intermediate nursing facility：INF
中間ケア施設（ちゅうかんけあしせつ）intermediate care facility：ICF
中小企業局（ちゅうしょうきぎょうきょく）Small Business Administration
聴覚障害者用電気通信機器（ちょうかくしょうがいしゃようでんきつうしんききき）telecommunications device for the deaf：TDD
長期ケア（ちょうきけあ）long-term care
長期ケア高齢者オンブズマンプログラム（ちょうきけあこうれいしゃおんぶずまんぷろぐらむ）Long-Term Care Ombudsman Program
長期ケア利用者の権利章典（ちょうきけありようしゃのけんりしょうてん）Long-Term Care Residents' Bill of Rights
長期ケア老年学センター（ちょうきけあろうねんがくせんたー）Long-Term Care Gerontology Center
低所得世帯光熱費扶助プログラム（ていしょとくせたいこうねつひふじょぷろぐらむ）Low Income Home Energy Assistance Program：LIHEAP
鉄道退職年金法（てつどうたいしょくねんきんほう）Railroad Retirement Act
デルタ協会（でるたきょうかい）Delta Society

米国和英

電気通信法（でんきつうしんほう）Telecommunications Act
テンケア（てんけあ）TennCare［テネシー州のメディケイド］
伝統的医療保険（でんとうてきいりょうほけん）traditional indemnity insurance
統一州法委員全米会議（とういつしゅうほういいんぜんべいかいぎ）National Conference of Commissioner on Uniform State Laws
統一末期病者権利法（とういつまっきびょうしゃけんりほう）Uniform Rights of the Terminally Ill Act
統合医療供給システム（とうごういりょうきょうきゅうしすてむ）integrated health care delivery system：IHCDS
統合供給システム（とうごうきょうきゅうしすてむ）integrated delivery system：IDS
統合供給ネットワーク（とうごうきょうきゅうねっとわーく）integrated delivery network：IDN
同僚審査機関（どうりょうしんさきかん）peer-review organization：PRO
登録看護師（とうろくかんごし）registered nurse［日本でいう正看護師］
登録作業療法士（とうろくさぎょうりょうほうし）registered occupational therapist：OTR
特別監視施設（とくべつかんししせつ）special focus facility：SFF
都市大量交通法（としたいりょうこうつうほう）Urban Mass Transportation Act
内国歳入庁（ないこくさいにゅうちょう）Internal Revenue Service：IRS
ナーシングホーム（なーしんぐほーむ）nursing home
ナーシングホーム改革法（なーしんぐほーむかいかくほう）Nursing Home Reform Act
ナーシングホーム間比較プログラム（なーしんぐほーむかんひかくぷろぐらむ）Nursing Home Compare
ナーシングホームの質改善イニシアティブ（なーしんぐほーむのしつかいぜんいにしあてぃぶ）Nursing Home Quality Initiative
ナーシングホーム利用者の権利（なーしんぐほーむりようしゃのけんり）Resident's Rights
ナーシングホーム利用者の権利章典（なーしんぐほーむりようしゃのけんりしょうてん）Resident Bill of Rights
日常生活介護者（にちじょうせいかつかいごしゃ）personal care aide
入院保険（にゅういんほけん）Hospital Insurance；Medicare Part A
乳癌・子宮癌予防・治療法（にゅうがん・しきゅうがんよぼう・ちりょうほう）Breast and Cervical Cancer Prevention and Treatment Act
乳房イメージレポート・データシステム（にゅうぼうめーじれぽーと・でーたしすてむ）Breast Imaging Reporting and Data System：BI-RADS

ニューディール政策（にゅーでぃーるせいさく）New Deal
ニューヨーク心臓協会（にゅうよーくしんぞうきょうかい）New York Heart Association：NYHA
認定看護助手（にんていかんごじょしゅ）certified nurse assistant
認定作業療法士アシスタント（にんていさぎょうりょうほうしあしすたんと）certified occupational therapy assistant
年金給付基準法（ねんきんきゅうふきじゅんほう）Pension Benefits Standards Act
年金給付保証公社（ねんきんきゅうふほしょうこうしゃ）Pension Benefit Guaranty Corporation
年金受給年齢（ねんきんじゅきゅうねんれい）full retirement age：FRA
年頭教書（ねんとうきょうしょ）State of the Union
年齢差別禁止法（ねんれいさべつきんしほう）Age Discrimination Act
配偶者控除（はいぐうしゃこうじょ）marital deduction
発達障害サービス・施設法（はったつしょうがいさーびす・しせつほう）Developmental Disabilities Services and Facilities Act
発達障害庁（はったつしょうがいちょう）Administration on Developmental Disabilities
ハーバードコミュニティヘルスプラン（はーばーどこみゅにてぃへるすぷらん）Harvard Community Health Plan
ハル・ハウス（はる・はうす）Hull-House
病院医師組織（びょういんいしそしき）Hospital Physician Organization：HPO
病院間比較プログラム（びょういんかんひかくぷろぐらむ）Hospital Compare
病院検査・建設法（びょういんけんさ・けんせつほう）Hospital Survey and Construction Act
標準不没収価格法（ひょうじゅんふぼっしゅうかかくほう）Standard Nonforfeiture Law
病的状態の圧縮（びょうてきじょうたいのあっしゅく）compression of morbidity
ヒル・バートン法（ひる・ばーとんほう）Hill-Burton Act
貧困との戦い（ひんこんとのたたかい）war on poverty
フォガティ国際衛生科学先端研究センター（ふぉがーてぃこくさいえいせいかがくせんたんけんきゅうせんたー）John E. Fogarty International Center for Advanced Study in the Health Sciences：FIC
賦課方式（ふかほうしき）pay-as-you-go system
不没収価格（ふぼっしゅうかかく）nonforfeiture value
米国アシステッド・リビング協会（べいこくあしすてっど・りびんぐきょうかい）Assisted Living Facilities Association of America
米国医科大学協会（べいこくいかだいがくきょうかい）Association of American Medical Colleges

米国医師会（べいこくいしかい）American Medical Association：AMA
米国医療協会（べいこくいりょうきょうかい）American Health Care Association
米国医療情報学協会（べいこくいりょうじょうほうがくきょうかい）American Medical Informatics Association
米国医療ディレクター協会（べいこくいりょうでぃれくたーきょうかい）American Medical Directors Association
米国医療統計センター（べいこくいりょうとうけいせんたー）National Center for Health Statistics：NCHS
米国運動協議会（べいこくうんどうきょうぎかい）American Council on Exercise
米国運輸省（べいこくうんゆしょう）U.S. Department of Transportation
米国栄養士会（べいこくえいようしかい）American Dietetic Association
米国家庭医療学会（べいこくかていいりょうがっかい）American Board of Family Practice
米国家庭内科学会(べいこくかていないかいがっかい)American Academy of Family Physicians：AAFP
米国加齢研究連合（べいこくかれいけんきゅうれんごう）American Federation for Aging Research
米国眼科医協会（べいこくがんかいきょうかい）American Optometric Association
米国眼科学会（べいこくがんかがっかい）American Academy of Ophthalmology
米国癌協会（べいこくがんきょうかい）American Cancer Society
米国環境保護庁（べいこくかんきょうほごちょう）U.S. Environmental Protection Agency
米国看護学会（べいこくかんごがっかい）American Academy of Nursing
米国看護幹部機構（べいこくかんごかんぶきこう）American Organization of Nurse Executives：AONE
米国看護師協会（べいこくかんごしきょうかい）American Nurses' Association
米国感染症学会（べいこくかんせんしょうがっかい）Infectious Disease Society of America
米国癌法（べいこくがんほう）National Cancer Act
米国教育開発学会（べいこくきょういくかいはつがっかい）American Society for Training and Development：ASTD
米国胸部疾患学会(べいこくきょうぶしっかんがっかい)American Thoracic Society：ATS
米国胸部内科学会（べいこくきょうぶないかいがくかい）American College of Chest Physicians
米国外科腫瘍学会（べいこくげかしゅようがっかい）Society of Surgical Oncology

米国ケースマネジメント学会（べいこくけーすまねじめんとがっかい）Case Management Society of America
米国健康情報管理学会（べいこくけんこうじょうほうかんりがっかい）American Health Information Management Association
米国言語聴覚士学会（べいこくげんごちょうかくしがっかい）American Speech-Language-Hearing Association
米国公衆衛生協会（べいこくこうしゅうえいせいきょうかい）American Public Health Association
米国公衆福祉協議会（べいこくこうしゅうふくしきょうぎかい）American Public Welfare Association
米国高齢者学会（べいこくこうれいしゃがっかい）American Society on Aging
米国高齢者ホーム協会(べいこくこうれいしゃほーむきょうかい) American Association of Homes for the Aging
米国高齢者ホーム・サービス協会（べいこくこうれいしゃほーむ・さーびすきょうかい）American Association of Homes and Services for the Aging：AAHSA
米国呼吸ケア学会（べいこくこきゅうけあがっかい）American Association for Respiratory Care
米国国立ヒトゲノム研究所（べいこくこくりつひとげのむけんきゅうしょ）National Human Genome Research Institute：NHGRI
米国国立アルコール乱用・依存症研究所（べいこくこくりつあるこーるらんよう・いぞんしょうけんきゅうしょ）National Institute on Alcohol Abuse and Alcoholism：NIAAA
米国国立アレルギー・感染症研究所（べいこくこくりつあれるぎー・かんせんしょうけんきゅうしょ）National Institute of Allergy and Infectious Diseases：NIAID
米国国立医学図書館（べいこくこくりついがくとしょかん）National Library of Medicine：NLM
米国国立一般医科学研究所（べいこくこくりついっぱんいかがくけんきゅうしょ）National Institute of General Medical Sciences：NIGMS
米国国立衛生研究所(べいこくこくりつえいせいけんきゅうしょ）National Institutes of Health
米国国立衛生研究所・臨床センター（べいこくこくりつえいせいけんきゅうしょ・りんしょうせんたー）National Institutes of Health Clinical Center：NIHCC
米国国立画像生物医学・生物工学研究所（べいこくこくりつがぞうせいぶついがく・せいぶつこうがくけんきゅうしょ）National Institute of Biomedical Imaging and Bioengineering：NIBIB
米国国立環境衛生科学研究所(べいこくこくりつかんきょうえいせいかがくけんきゅうしょ）National Institute of Environmental Health Sciences：NIEHS
米国国立環境衛生センター（べいこくこくりつかんきょう

米国和英

うえいせいせんたー) National Center for Environmental Health：NCEH
米国国立癌研究所（べいこくこくりつがんけんきゅうしょ) National Cancer Institute：NCI
米国国立看護研究所（べいこくこくりつかんごけんきゅうしょ) National Institute of Nursing Research：NINR
米国国立関節炎・骨格筋・皮膚疾患研究所（べいこくこくりつかんせつえん・こっかくきん・ひふしっかんけんきゅうしょ) National Institute of Arthritis and Musculoskeletal and Skin Diseases：NIAMS
米国国立感染病センター(べいこくこくりつかんせんびょうせんたー) National Center for Infectious Diseases：NCID
米国国立眼病研究所（べいこくこくりつがんびょうけんきゅうしょ) National Eye Institute：NEI
米国国立研究資源センター（べいこくこくりつけんきゅうしげんせんたー) National Center for Research Resources：NCRR
米国国立高齢化研究所（べいこくこくりつこうれいかけんきゅうしょ) National Institute on Aging：NIA
米国国立歯科・頭蓋顔面研究所（べいこくこくりつしか・とうがいがんめんけんきゅうしょ) National Institute of Dental and Craniofacial Research：NIDCR
米国国立歯学研究所（べいこくこくりつしがくけんきゅうしょ) National Institute of Dental Research
米国国立傷害防止センター（べいこくこくりつしょうがいぼうしせんたー) National Center for Injury Prevention and Control：NCIPC
米国国立障害リハビリテーション研究所（べいこくこくりつしょうがいりはびりてーしょんけんきゅうしょ) National Institute on Disability and Rehabilitation Research
米国国立小児保健発達研究所（べいこくこくりつしょうにほけんはったつけんきゅうしょ) National Institute of Child Health and Human Development：NICHD
米国国立職業安全健康研究所（べいこくこくりつしょくぎょうあんぜんけんこうけんきゅうしょ) National Institute for Occupational Safety and Health：NIOSH
米国国立神経疾患・脳卒中研究所（べいこくこくりつしんけいしっかん・のうそっちゅうけんきゅうしょ) National Institute of Neurological Disorders and Stroke：NINDS
米国国立身体活動・障害センター（べいこくこくりつしんたいかつどう・しょうがいせんたー) National Center on Physical Activity and Disability
米国国立心・肺・血液研究所（べいこくこくりつしん・ぱい・けつえきけんきゅうしょ) National Heart, Lung and Blood Institute：NHLBI
米国国立睡眠障害研究所（べいこくこくりつすいみんしょうがいけんきゅうしょ) National Center on Sleep Disorders Research
米国国立精神衛生研究所（べいこくこくりつせいしんえいせいけんきゅうしょ) National Institute of Mental Health：NIMH
米国国立成人デイケア研究所（べいこくこくりつせいじんでいけあけんきゅうしょ) National Institute of Adult Day Care：NIAD
米国国立聴覚・伝達障害研究所（べいこくこくりつちょうかく・でんたつしょうがいけんきゅうしょ) National Institute on Deafness and Other Communication Disorders：NIDCD
米国国立長期ケアコンソーシアム（べいこくこくりつちょうきけあこんそーしあむ) National Chronic Care Consortium
米国国立糖尿病・消化器・腎疾病研究所（べいこくこくりつとうにょうびょう・しょうかき・じんしっぺいけんきゅうしょ) National Institute of Diabetes and Digestive and Kidney Diseases：NIDDK
米国国立バイオテクノロジー情報センター（べいこくこくりつばいおてくのろじーじょうほうせんたー) National Center for Biotechnology Information
米国国立補完代替医療センター（べいこくこくりつほかんだいたいいりょうせんたー) National Center for Complementary and Alternative Medicine：NCCAM
米国国立マイノリティ健康・健康格差センター（べいこくこくりつまいのりてぃけんこう・けんこうかくさせんたー) National Center on Minority Health and Health Disparities：NCMHD
米国国立薬物乱用研究所（べいこくこくりつやくぶつらんようけんきゅうしょ) National Institute on Drug Abuse：NIDA
米国国立労働安全衛生研究所（べいこくこくりつろうどうあんぜんえいせいけんきゅうしょ) National Institute of Occupational Safety and Health
米国顧問薬剤師協会（べいこくこもんやくざいしきょうかい) American Society of Consultant Pharmacists
米国最高裁判所（べいこくさいこうさいばんしょ) Supreme Court of the United States；U.S. Supreme Court
米国在宅医学会（べいこくざいたくいがくかい) American Academy of Home Care Physicians
米国在宅ケア協会（べいこくざいたくけあきょうかい) American Association for Homecare
米国作業療法士協会(べいこくさぎょうりょうほうしきょうかい) American Occupational Therapy Association
米国産科婦人科学会(べいこくさんかふじんかがっかい) American College of Obstetricians and Gynecologists
米国歯科医師会（べいこくしかいしかい) American

Dental Association
米国歯科学教育学会（べいこくしかがくきょういくがっかい）American Association of Dental Schools
米国自然人類学協会（べいこくしぜんじんるいがくきょうかい）American Association of Physical Anthropology
米国耳鼻咽喉・頭部・首部外科手術協会（べいこくじびいんこう・とうぶ・しゅぶげかしゅじゅつきょうかい）American Academy of Otolaryngology-Head and Neck Surgery
米国司法省（べいこくしほうしょう）U.S. Department of Justice
米国社会サービス省(べいこくしゃかいさーびすしょう）U.S. Department of Social Services
米国住宅都市開発省（べいこくじゅうたくとしかいはつしょう）U.S. Department of Housing and Urban Development：HUD
米国集団精神療法学会(べいこくしゅうだんせいしんりょうほうがっかい）American Group Psychotherapy Association
米国上院財務委員会（べいこくじょういんざいむいいんかい）U.S. Senate Finance Committee
米国障害者法（べいこくしょうがいしゃほう）Americans with Disabilities Act：ADA
米国消化器病学会（べいこくしょうかきびょうがっかい）American College of Gastroenterology；American Gastroenterological Association
米国静脈経腸栄養学会（べいこくじょうみゃくけいちょうえいようがっかい）American Society for Parenteral and Enteral Nutrition：ASPEN
米国褥瘡学会（べいこくじょくそうがっかい）American Academy of Wound Management
米国食品医薬品局（べいこくしょくひんいやくひんきょく）U.S. Food and Drug Administration
米国神経学会（べいこくしんけいがっかい）American Academy of Neurology
米国心血管呼吸リハビリテーション学会（べいこくしんけっかんこきゅうりはびりてーしょんがっかい）American Association of Cardiovascular and Pulmonary Rehabilitation
米国心臓学会（べいこくしんぞうがっかい）American Heart Association
米国心臓病学会（べいこくしんぞうびょうがっかい）American College of Cardiology
米国身体医学・リハビリテーション学会（べいこくしんたいがく・りはびりてーしょんがっかい）American Academy of Physical Medicine and Rehabilitation
米国心理学会（べいこくしんりがっかい）American Psychological Association
米国睡眠医学学会（べいこくすいみんいがくがっかい）American Academy of Sleep Medicine
米国頭痛教育協議会（べいこくずつうきょういくぎかい）American Council for Headache Education
米国性教育者・カウンセラー・セラピスト協会（べいこくせいきょういくしゃ・かうんせらー・せらぴすときょうかい）American Association of Sex Educators, Counselors and Therapists
米国整骨医協会（べいこくせいこついきょうかい）American Osteopathic Association：AOA
米国精神医学会（べいこくせいしんいがくかい）American Psychiatric Association
米国生命倫理学会（べいこくせいめいりんりがっかい）American Society of Bioethics and Humanities
米国赤十字（べいこくせきじゅうじ）American Red Cross
米国専門医協会（べいこくせんもんいきょうかい）American Board of Medical Societies：ABMS
米国専門コーダー協会（べいこくせんもんこーだーきょうかい）American Academy of Professional Coders
米国足病医学会（べいこくそくびょういがくかい）American Podiatric Medical Association
米国退役軍人省（べいこくたいえきぐんじんしょう）U.S. Department of Veterans Affairs：VA
米国退職者協会（べいこくたいしょくしゃきょうかい）American Association of Retired Persons：AARP
米国聴覚医学会（べいこくちょうかくいがくかい）American Academy of Audiology
米国直腸結腸外科学会（べいこくちょくちょうけっちょうげかがっかい）American Society of Colon and Rectal Surgeons
米国疼痛学会（べいこくとうつうがっかい）American Pain Society
米国疼痛管理看護学会（べいこくとうつうかんりかんごがっかい）American Society for Pain Management Nursing
米国糖尿病教育者会（べいこくとうにょうびょうきょういくしゃかい）American Association of Diabetes Educators
米国糖尿病協会(べいこくとうにょうびょうきょうかい）American Diabetes Association
米国内科学会（べいこくないかがっかい）American College of Physicians
米国内科学会臨床効能評価小委員会(べいこくないかがっかいりんしょうこうのうひょうかしょういいんかい）American College of Physicians Clinical Efficacy Assessment Subcommittee
米国内科専門医機構（べいこくないかせんもんいきこう）American Board of Internal Medicine：ABIM
米国内科専門医機構認定試験（べいこくないかせんもんいきこうにんていしけん）American Board of Internal Medicine certification examination
米国内ボランティア法（べいこくないぼらんてぃあほう）

米国
和英

Domestic Volunteer Service Act
米国年金専門職・アクチュアリー会（べいこくねんきんせんもんしょく・あくちゅありーかい）American Society of Pension Professionals & Actuaries
米国肺協会（べいこくはいきょうかい）American Lung Association
米国パーキンソン病協会（べいこくぱーきんそんびょうきょうかい）American Parkinson Disease Association
米国泌尿器疾患財団（べいこくひにょうきしっかんざいだん）American Foundation for Urologic Disease
米国皮膚科学会（べいこくひふかがっかい）American Academy of Dermatology
米国病院協会（べいこくびょういんきょうかい）American Hospital Association：AHA
米国法・医学・倫理学会（べいこくほう・いがく・りんりがっかい）American Society of Law, Medicine & Ethics
米国包括的ケア協会（べいこくほうかつてきけあきょうかい）American Association for Continuity of Care
米国放射線学会（べいこくほうしゃせんがっかい）American College of Radiology：ACR
米国放射線学会乳房イメージレポート・データシステム（べいこくほうしゃせんがっかいにゅうぼういめーじれぽーと・でーたしすてむ）American College of Radiology Breast Imaging Reporting and Data System
米国法曹協会（べいこくほうそうきょうかい）American Bar Association
米国訪問看護師協会（べいこくほうもんかんごしきょうかい）Visiting Nurse Associations of America
米国保健教育福祉省（べいこくほけんきょういくふくししょう）U.S. Department of Health, Education and Welfare：HEW
米国保健省（べいこくほけんしょう）U.S. Department of Health Services
米国保健・体育・レクリエーション・ダンス連合（べいこくほけん・たいいく・れくりえーしょん・だんすれんごう）American Alliance for Health, Physical Education, Recreation and Dance
米国保健福祉省（べいこくほけんふくししょう）U.S. Department of Health and Human Services：HHS
米国ホスピス・緩和医療学会（べいこくほすぴす・かんわいりょうがっかい）American Academy of Hospice and Palliative Medicine
米国盲人委員会（べいこくもうじんいいんかい）American Council of the Blind
米国盲人財団（べいこくもうじんざいだん）American Foundation for the Blind
米国予防医学会（べいこくよぼういがくかい）American College of Preventive Medicine：

ACPM
米国予防医療作業部会（べいこくよぼういりょうさぎょうぶかい）U.S. Preventive Services Task Force：USPSTF
米国リウマチ学会（べいこくりうまちがっかい）American College of Rheumatology：ACR
米国理学療法士協会（べいこくりがくりょうほうしきょうかい）American Physical Therapy Association：APTA
米国理学療法専門協会（べいこくりがくりょうほうせんもんきょうかい）American Board of Physical Therapy Specialties：ABPTS
米国リハビリテーション協会（べいこくりはびりてーしょんきょうかい）American Rehabilitation Association
米国臨床腫瘍学会（べいこくりんしょうしゅようがっかい）American Society of Clinical Oncology
米国臨床内分泌学会（べいこくりんしょうないぶんぴつがっかい）American Association of Clinical Endocrinologists
米国レクリエーション療法協会(べいこくれくりえーしょんりょうほうきょうかい）American Therapeutic Recreation Association
米国老年医学会（べいこくろうねんいがくかい）American Geriatrics Society
米国老年学会（べいこくろうねんがくがっかい）Gerontological Society of America
米国老年学会（べいこくろうねんがっかい）American Aging Association
米国老年歯科学会（べいこくろうねんしかがっかい）American Society for Geriatric Dentistry
米国老年精神医学会（べいこくろうねんせいしんいがくかい）American Association for Geriatric Psychiatry
包括的雇用及び訓練法（ほうかつてきこようおよびくんれんほう）Comprehensive Employment and Training Act
包括的レスパイトケア法（ほうかつてきれすぱいとけあほう）Lifespan Respite Care Act
包括払い方式評価委員会（ほうかつばらいほうしきひょうかいいんかい）Prospective Payment Assessment Commission：Pro-PAC
包括予算調整強化法（ほうかつよさんちょうせいきょうかほう）Consolidated Omnibus Budget Reconciliation Act：COBRA
包括予算調整法（ほうかつよさんちょうせいほう）Omnibus Budget Reconciliation Act：OBRA
訪問看護助手（ほうもんかいごじょしゅ）home health aide
牧師サービス（ぼくしさーびす）pastoral service
保健教育福祉省（ほけんきょういくふくししょう）Department of Health, Education and Welfare：HEW
保健省（ほけんしょう）Department of Health

Services
保健福祉省（ほけんふくししょう）Department of Health and Human Services：HHS
星評価（ほしひょうか）star rating
補助看護職員（ほじょかんごしょくいん）ancillary nursing personnel
補足的医療保険（ほそくてきいりょうほけん）Supplemental Medical Insurance：SMI：Medicare Part B
補足的所得保障（ほそくてきしょとくほしょう）Supplemental Security Insurance：SSI
ホワイトハウス高齢者会議（ほわいとはうすこうれいしゃかいぎ）White House Conference on Aging
ホワイトハウス国家麻薬管理政策局（ほわいとはうすこっかまやくかんりせいさくきょく）White House Office of National Drug Control Policy
前払い型グループ診療（まえばらいがたぐるーぷしんりょう）Prepaid Group Practice：PGP
マスヘルス（ますへるす）MassHealth ［マサチューセッツ州のメディケイド］
マネジドケア組織（まねじどけあそしき）Managed Care Organization：MCO
慢性疾患委員会（まんせいしっかんいいんかい）Commission on Chronic Illness
ミニマムデータセット（みにまむでーたせっと）Minimum Data Set：MDS
ミニマムデータセットコーディネーター（みにまむでーたせっとこーでぃねーたー）Minimum Data Set coordinator
ミールズ・オン・ウィール（みーるず・おん・うぃーる）Meals on Wheels ［食事配達サービス］
無免許看護職員（むめんきょかんごしょくいん）unlicensed nursing personnel
無免許補助職員（むめんきょほじょしょくいん）unlicensed assistive personnel
メディ・カル（めでぃ・かる）Medi-Cal ［カリフォルニア州のメディケイド］
メディギャップ（めでぃぎゃっぷ）Medigap ［メディケア補足保険］
メディケア（めでぃけあ）Medicare ［老人・障害者医療保険制度］
メディケア・アドバンテージ（めでぃけあ・あどばんてーじ）Medicare Advantage
メディケア HMO（めでぃけあえっちえむおー）Medicare HMO：Medicare Health Maintenance Organization
メディケア高額医療保障法（めでぃけあこうがくいりょうほしょうほう）Medicare Catastrophic Coverage Act
メディケア処方箋薬剤改善・近代化法（めでぃけあしょほうせんやくざいかいぜん・きんだいかほう）Medicare Prescription Drug Improvement and Modernization Act

メディケア認定高度看護施設（めでぃけあにんていこうどかんごしせつ）Medicare-certified skilled nursing facility
メディケア認定在宅看護機関（めでぃけあにんていざいたくかんごきかん）Medicare-certified home health agency
メディケア認定スキルドナーシングホーム（めでぃけあにんていすきるどなーしんぐほーむ）Medicare-certified skilled nursing facility
メディケア認定病院（めでぃけあにんていびょういん）Medicare-certified hospital
メディケア認定ホスピス機関（めでぃけあにんていほすぴすきかん）Medicare-certified hospice agency
メディケア・パート A（めでぃけあ・ぱーとえー）Medicare Part A：Hospital Insurance ［入院保険］
メディケア・パート C（めでぃけあ・ぱーとしー）Medicare Part C：Medicare+Choice
メディケア・パート D（めでぃけあ・ぱーとでぃー）Medicare Part D：Prescription Drug Coverage ［処方箋薬剤給付保険］
メディケア・パート B（めでぃけあ・ぱーとびー）Medicare Part B：Supplemental Medical Insurance ［補足的医療保険］
メディケア不服申し立て制度（めでぃけあふくもうしたてせいど）Medicare Appeals System
メディケア・プラス・チョイス（めでぃけあ・ぷらす・ちょいす）Medicare+Choice：Medicare Part C
メディケア・プラス・チョイスプログラム（めでぃけあ・ぷらす・ちょいすぷろぐらむ）Medicare+Choice Program
メディケア補足保険（めでぃけあほそくほけん）Medicare Supplement Insurance：Medigap
メディケア補足保険標準化（めでぃけあほそくほけんひょうじゅんか）Medigap Standardization
メディケア・メディケイド庁（めでぃけあ・めでぃけいどちょう）Centers for Medicare and Medicaid Services：CMS
メディケア・メディケイド認定調査（めでぃけあ・めでぃけいどにんていちょうさ）Medicare and Medicaid Certification Inspection
メディケア・メディケイド認定ナーシングホーム（めでぃけあ・めでぃけいどにんていなーしんぐほーむ）Medicare and Medicaid-certified nursing home
メディケイド（めでぃけいど）Medicaid ［低所得者医療扶助制度］
免許実務看護師（めんきょじつむかんごし）licensed practical nurse：LPN：licensed vocational nurse：LVN ［日本でいう准看護師］
ヤングオールド（やんぐおーるど）young-old ［65歳～74歳の高齢者］
有意志医療機関排除禁止法（ゆういしいりょうきかんはいじょきんしほう）Any Willing Provider Law
有害物質・疾病登録局（ゆうがいぶっしつ・しっぺいと

米国和英

うろくきょく）Agency for Toxic Substances and Disease Registry：ATSDR
養老院（ようろういん）almshouse
ラップス（らっぷす）Resident Assessment Protocols：RAPs
理学療法教育認定委員会（りがくりょうほうきょういくにんていいいんかい）Commission on Accreditation in Physical Therapy Education：CAPTE
リハビリテーション病棟（りはびりてーしょんびょうとう）rehabilitation unit
リハビリテーション法（りはびりてーしょんほう）Rehabilitation Act
利用者会（りようしゃかい）resident council
利用者ケアカンファレンス（りようしゃけあかんふぁれんす）resident care conference
臨床資源チーム（りんしょうしげんちーむ）clinical resource team
レストホーム（れすとほーむ）rest home
レストレスレッグス症候群財団(れすとれすれっぐすしょうこうぐんざいだん）Restless Legs Syndrome Foundation
レスパイトケア（れすぱいとけあ）respite care
連邦学資金援助（れんぽうがくしきんえんじょ）Federal Student Aid
連邦官報（れんぽうかんぽう）Federal Register
連邦官報事務局（れんぽうかんぽうじむきょく）Office of the Federal Register
連邦議会予算局（れんぽうぎかいよさんきょく）Congressional Budget Office
連邦規則集（れんぽうきそくしゅう）Code of Federal Regulations：CFR
連邦緊急救済管理局（れんぽうきんきゅうきゅうさいかんりきょく）Federal Emergency Relief Administration：FERA
連邦緊急事態管理庁（れんぽうきんきゅうじたいかんりちょう）Federal Emergency Management Agency
連邦市民退職サービス制度（れんぽうしみんたいしょくさーびすせいど）Federal Civil Service Retirement System
連邦社会保障機関（れんぽうしゃかいほしょうきかん）Federal Security Agency
連邦住宅管理局（れんぽうじゅうたくかんりきょく）Federal Housing Administration
連邦政府認可医療センター(れんぽうせいふにんかいりょうせんたー）Federally Qualified Health Center：FQHC
連邦賃金制度（れんぽうちんぎんせいど）Federal Wage System
連邦貧困基準（れんぽうひんこんきじゅん）Federal Poverty Level：FPL
連邦保険拠出法（れんぽうほけんきょしゅつほう）Federal Insurance Contributions Act：FICA
老齢遺族保険（ろいれいいぞくほけん）Old-Age and Survivors Insurance：OASI
老人研究・教育・医療センター（ろうじんけんきゅう・きょういく・いりょうせんたー）Geriatric Research, Education and Clinical Center：GRECC
老親扶養意識（ろうしんふようぃしき）filial responsibility
老親扶養義務（ろうしんふようぎむ）filial obligation
労働安全衛生庁（ろうどうあんぜんえいせいちょう）Occupational Safety and Health Administration
労働者補償裁判所(ろうどうしゃほしょうさいばんしょ）Workers' Compensation Court
労働統計局（ろうどうとうけいきょく）Bureau of Labor Statistics：BLS
老年学高等教育協会（ろうねんがくこうとうきょういくきょうかい）Association for Gerontology in Higher Education
老年専門ナースプラクティショナー全米会議（ろうねんせんもんなーすぷらくてぃしょなーぜんべいかいぎ）National Conference of Gerontological Nurse Practitioners
老齢遺族障害医療保険（ろうれいいぞくしょうがいいりょうほけん）Old-Age, Survivors, Disability and Health Insurance：OASDHI
老齢遺族障害医療保険信託基金（ろうれいいぞくしょうがいりょうほけんしんたくききん）Old-Age and Survivors Insurance, Disability and Hospital Insurance Trust Fund：OASDHI Trust Fund
老齢遺族障害保険（ろうれいいぞくしょうがいほけん）Old-Age, Survivors and Disability Insurance：OASDI
老齢遺族障害保険信託基金（ろうれいいぞくしょうがいほけんしんたくききん）Old-Age, Survivors and Disability Insurance Trust Fund：OASDI Trust Fund
老齢遺族保険信託基金（ろうれいいぞくほけんしんたくききん）Old-Age and Survivors Insurance Trust Fund：OASI Trust Fund
YMCA（わいえむしーえー）Young Men's Christian Association [キリスト教青年会]
YWCA（わいだぶりゅしーえー）Young Women's Christian Association [キリスト教女子青年会]

付録
介護保険・介護福祉等関連の重要用語
― 10 カ国語翻訳一覧 ―

1. インドネシア語 (Indonesian)

IQ　IQ
ICIDH　klasifikasi kecacatan secara international
ICF　klasifikasi fungsi hidup secara internasional
ICD　klasifikasi penyakit secara internasional
アクティビティ　aktifitas；kegiatan
アセスメント　assessment
アテトーシス　gerakan spontan abnormal yang tak teratur；memutar sekitar sumbu memanjang tubuh
アテトーゼ　gerakan spontan abnormal yang tak teratur；memutar sekitar sumbu memanjang tubuh.
アドボカシー　advokasi；pembelaan
アルツハイマー型認知症　demensia tipe alzeimer
アルツハイマー病　penyakit alzeimer
安全管理　pengawasan keamanan
罹法　menimbulkan
安眠　tidur nyenyak
安眠援助　membantu untuk tidur nyenyak
安楽　nyaman
安楽な体位　posisi tubuh yang nyaman
意識障害　gangguan kesadaran
維持期リハビリテーション　pemeliharaan fase rehabilitasi
萎縮　athropia
移乗動作　gerakan perpindahan
移送費　biaya transportasi；ongkos kirim
遺族基礎年金　dasar pensiun bagi Akhli Waris
移動　perpindahan
移動介護　bantuan mobilisasi；perpindahan
移動関連福祉用具　alat bantu untuk mobilisasi；perpindahan
移動トイレ　portable toilet
移動浴槽　portable mandi
衣服　pakaian
衣服着脱　mengganti pakaian
衣料障害　hambatan penggunaan pakaian
医療ソーシャルワーカー　pekerja sosial di bidang medis
医療保険制度　sistem asuransi kesehatan
インスリン　insulin
インテーク　masukan；asupan
インフォーマル　informal
陰部清拭　kebersihan genetalia
陰部洗浄　perawatan perineal
インペアメント　penurunan kondisi tubuh
うつ病　depresi
運営適正化委員会　komite yang menangani pengaduan atau komplen．
運動器の機能向上　peningkatan fungsi-fungsi alat gerak

運動失調　gerakan yang tak teratur
運動障害　gangguan pada pergerakan
運動療法　terafi olahraga
エアーパッド　udara pad
エアーマット　tikar udara
エイジズム　ageisme
エイズ　AIDS
栄養　nutrisi；gizi
栄養改善　perbaikan gizi
栄養管理　pengawasan gizi
栄養士　ahli gizi
栄養所要量　jumlah gizi yang dibutuhkan
栄養素　zat nutrisi；zat gizi
腋窩温　temperatur；suhu ketiak
壊死　nekrosis；kematian jaringan
ADL　aktivitas kehidupan sehari-hari
NPO　non-profit organization
MRSA　methicillin-resistant staphylococcus aureus
MMSE　Mini Mental State Examination
MMT　Panduan Pengujian Otot
嚥下　menelan
嚥下困難　kesulitan menelan
嚥下性肺炎　aspirasi pneumonia
嚥下補助剤　obat untuk membantu kelancaran menelan
エンゲル係数　Koefisien Engel
円座　bantal bulat
エンパワメント　pemberdayaan
応益負担　kewajiban penerima
嘔気　mual
応急手当　pertolongan darurat
嘔吐　muntah
応能負担　kesediaan membayar
起き上がり　bangkit
おむつ　popok
おむつカバー　cover popok
おむつ交換　pergantian popok
おむつ外し　membuka popok
臥位　tidur dengan posisi berbaring
介護　perawatan
介護過程　proses keperawatan gerontik
介護技術　teknik perawatan gerontik
介護休業　cuti merawat
介護給付　imbalan perawat gerontik
介護計画　rencana keperawatan gerontik
介護サービス計画　rencana pelayanan keperawatan
介護支援専門員　care manager
介護指導　bimbingan keperawatan
介護者　perawat gerontik；perawat orang cacat

インドネシア語

介護職員　perawat gerontik
介護ニーズ　kebutuhan keperawatan jangka panjang
介護認定審査会　dewan sertifikasi perawatan jangka panjang
介護福祉　perawatan kesejahteraan
介護福祉士　perawat gerontik
介護福祉士国家試験　ujian sertifikasi perawat gerontik
介護福祉士登録　pendaftaran bagi perawat gerontik yang sudah bersertifikat
介護負担　beban perawatan
介護報酬　biaya perawatan jangka panjang
介護保険　asuransi gerontik
介護保険事業計画　rencana proyek asuransi perawatan jangka panjang
介護保険審査会　dewan pengawas asuransi perawatan jangka panjang
介護保険制度　sistem asuransi perawatan
介護保険認定調査　pemeriksa ; peninjau ijin asuransi perawatan gerontik jangka panjang
介護保険法　undang-undang asuransi perawatan gerontik
介護目標　target perawatan gerontik
介護用具　peralatan untuk perawatan gerontik
介護予防　pencegahan perawatan gerontik jangka panjang
介護予防事業　proyek pencegahan perawatan gerontik jangka panjang
介護療養型医療施設　fasilitas ; panti jompo untuk pasien yang memiliki penyakit kronis
介護老人福祉施設　fasilitas ; panti jompo untuk lansia yang ditunjuk oleh sistem asuransi perawatan gerontik
介護老人保健施設　fasilitas ; panti jompo untuk asuhan kesehatan lansia
介護労働者　pekerja perawatan jangka panjang
介助　bantuan
疥癬　gatal
回想法　terapi mengingat kenangan masa lalu
階段　tangga
階段昇降　turun naik tangga
回復期リハビリテーション　pemulihan fase rehabilitasi
潰瘍　radang
かかりつけ医　dokter primer
核家族　Keluarga Berencana ; KB
家計　anggaran rumah tangga
家事　pekerjaan rumah tangga
家政　management rumah tangga
家政婦　pengurus rumah tangga
家族　keluarga
家族会　kelompok mandiri bagi keluarga

家族介護　perawatan oleh keluarga
家族介護者　perawatan keluarga
家族関係　hubungan keluarga
合併症　komplikasi
寡婦　janda
紙おむつ　popok kertas
過剰症候群　sindrom berlebihan
加齢　bertambah usia
癌　kangker
感音難聴　tuli sensorineural
感覚機能　fungsi sensori
換気　ventilasi
環境整備　pemeliharaan lingkungan
看護　keperawatan
肝硬変　pengerutan hati
看護師　perawat
関節　sendi ; persendian
関節可動域　rentang gerak sendi
関節リウマチ　reumatik sendi
感染　infeksi
感染菌　bakteri
感染症　penyakit infeksi
感染予防　pencegahan infeksi
浣腸　enema
観念失行　ideasional apraxia
管理栄養士　ahli gizi bersertifikat
緩和ケア　perawatan paliativ
記憶障害　gangguan memori
着替え　pakaian pengganti
気管　batang tenggorokan ; trakhea
危険防止　pencegahan resiko
起座位　posisi duduk di tempat tidur
義歯　gigi palsu
義肢装具士　bagian ekstermitan buatan
基礎代謝　basal metabolisme
機能維持　pemeliharaan fungsional
機能訓練　latihan fungsional
機能障害　gangguan fungsi tubuh
記銘力　kemampuan mengingat
虐待　penyiksaan
ギャッチベッド　gatch bed
救急救命士　teknis penyelamatan darurat
仰臥位　posisi terlentang
共感　empati
虚弱　pisiknya lemah
起立性低血圧　hipotensi ortostatik ; tekanan darah rendah
記録　catatan perawat
筋萎縮　atropi otot
緊急連絡先　alamat darurat ; emergency adres
金銭管理　manajemen keuangan
苦情解決　pemecahan ; penanggulangan keluhan
くも膜下出血　pendarahan subarachnoid ; lapisan

otak bawah
クリティカルパス　jalur kritis
グループホーム　group home
グループリビング　kelompok hidup
グループレクリエーション　kelompok rekreasi
グループワーク　kelompok kerja sosial
車いす　kursi roda
車いすからベッド　perpindahan dari kursi roda ke tempat tidur
車いすの移動　mobilisasi dengan kursi roda
車いすの介助　bantuan perpindahan ; mobilisasi dengan kursi roda
クロックポジション　clock position
ケア　perawatan
ケアカンファレンス　rapat keperawatan
ケアチーム　team perawatan
ケアハウス　panti jompo
ケアプラン　rencana keperawatan
ケアマネジメント　management perawatan
ケアマネジャー　manager perawatan
ケアワーク　pekerjaan perawat
経管栄養　selang NGT ; selang nutrient ; pipa makanan
頸髄損傷　kerusakan saraf serviks ; tulang belakang
傾聴　mendengarkan dengan seksama ; mendengarkan dengan aktif
契約　kontrak
劇薬　obat berbahaya
下血　keluar darah dari dubur
ケースカンファレンス　rapat yang membahas tentang suatu kasus
ケースワーク　kerja kasus
血圧　tekanan darah
下痢　diare
幻覚　halusinasi
健康　kesehatan
健康観察　observasi kesehatan
健康保険　asuransi kesehatan
言語障害　gangguan bahasa
言語聴覚士　ahli terapi untuk gangguan pendengaran dan gangguan bahasa
見当識障害　gangguan orientasi
権利擁護　advokasi hak-hak
公益事業　utilitas ekonomi publik
公益法人　perusahaan yang memberikan maanfaat untuk publik
構音障害　gangguan artikulasi
後期高齢者　kaum lanjut usia ; gerontik
抗菌・防臭素材　bahan deodorisasi anti bakteri
口腔機能の向上　peningkatan fungsi oral
口腔ケア　perawatan mulut
合計特殊出生率　tingkat kesuburan total
高血圧　hipertensi ; tekanan darah tinggi

拘縮　kontraktur
拘縮予防　pencegahan kontraktur
公証人　notaris
公正証書　akta notaris
抗生物質　antibiotik
拘束　ikatan
後天性免疫不全症候群　sindrom defisiensi imun didapat：AIDS
高齢化　populasi lansia
高齢期障害　gangguan pada gerontik ; usia lanjut
高齢者　gerontik ; usia lanjut
高齢社会　masyarakat usia lanjut ; gerontik
高齢者虐待　penyiksaan terhadap lansia
高齢者虐待防止法　hukum pencegahan penganiayaan lansia
高齢者世帯　rumah tangga lansia
声かけ　komunikasi terapeutik
誤嚥　aspirasi paru
誤嚥性肺炎　aspirsai pneumonia
呼吸　pernapasan
呼吸機能障害　gangguan pernapasan fungsional
国際疾病分類　klasifikasi penyakit secara internasional
国際障害分類　klasifikasi kecacatan secara internasional
国際生活機能分類　klasifikasi fungsi hidup secara internasional
国際標準化機構　organisasi standarisasi secara internasional
骨折　patah tulang ; fraktur
骨粗鬆症　osteoporosis ; pengeroposan tulang
言葉かけ　sapaan
個別介護　perawatan individu
コミュニケーション　komunikasi
コミュニケーションエイド　bantuan komunikasi
コレステロール　kolesterol
献立　menu
座位　posisi duduk
再アセスメント　penilaian kembali
在宅介護　perawatan jangka panjang di rumah
在宅看護　perawatan kesehatan di rumah
在宅ケア　perawatan di rumah
作業療法　terapi okupasional
作業療法士　ahli terapi okupasional
サービス担当者会議　rapat staf bagian pelayanan
サポートシステム　support sistem
残存機能　fungsi residual
散髪　potong rambut
紫外線遮蔽素材　bahan pelindung sinar ultra violet
歯科衛生士　ahli kesehatan gigi
視覚障害　cacat penglihatan
視覚障害者　tuna netra
弛緩　lembek

インドネシア語

止血　hemostasis
思考障害　gangguan berpikir
自己覚知　kesadran diri
自己決定　keputusan diri sendiri
自己実現　realisasi diri
脂質異常症　abnormalisasi livid
自傷行為　mutilasi diri
自助具　perangkat ; alat bantu untuk diri sendiri
死生観　pandangan hidup dan mati
施設介護　fasilitas ; panti jompo
自尊心　rasa harga diri
肢体不自由　kelumpuhan anggota badan bagian bawah
実技試験　ujian praktek ; ujian teknik keperawatan gerontik
失禁　ganguan kontrol buang air besar
失語　tunawicara
シーツ交換　perbeden ; pergantian seprei
実支出　pengeluaran aktual
実収入　pendapatan aktual
失認　kerusakan kognitif
実務経験証明書　surat keterangan pengalaman kerja
自動運動　gerakan aktif
児童期障害　gangguan pada masa kanak-kanak
自閉症　autisme
社会資源　sumberdaya sosial
社会的不利　kurang mendapat pengakuan di masyarakat
社会福祉　kesejahteraan masyarakat
社会福祉士　pekerja sosial bersertifikat
社会福祉事業　usaha kesejahteraan masyarakat
社会保険　asuransi sosial
社会保障　jaminan sosial
社会保障審議会　dewan jaminan sosial
視野狭窄　menyempitnya wilayah pandangan
視野障害　gangguan pandangan
シャワー浴　kamar mandi shower
収益事業　usaha ; proyek yang bertujuan untuk mendapatkan keuntungan
従属人口　penduduk yang tertanggung
住宅改修　renovasi rumah
終末期　tahap terminal
終末期介護　perawatan pada akhir hayat
主治医　dokter yang menangani
主治医意見書　surat pendapat dokter
手段の日常生活活動　instrumental aktivitas sehari-hari
出血　pendarahan
守秘義務　wajib dirahasiakan
手浴　perendaman tangan
手話　bahasa isyarat
除圧　dekompresi
障害　kecacatan

障害基礎年金　pensiunan bagi orang cacat
障害の受容　menerima atas kecacatan dirinya
小規模多機能型居宅介護　rumah pelayanan keperawatan multi fungsi dengan kapasitas kecil
少子化　penurunan tingkat kelahiran
少子高齢化　tingkat kelahiran anak menurun ; tetapi usia lanjut terus bertambah
静脈栄養法　metode pemberian nutrisi ke dalam pembuluh darah balik ; vena
職業的リハビリテーション　rehabilitasi vokasional
食事　makan
食事介護　bantuan perawatan untuk makan
食事介助　bantu perawatan untuk makan
食事動作　gerakan makan
食事療法　terapi melalui nutrisi
褥瘡　dekubitus
褥瘡予防　pencegahan ulkus dekubitus
食中毒　keracunan makanan
食品衛生　sanitasi makanan
植物状態　keadaan tanaman
植物性食品　sayuran
食欲　napsu makan
食欲不振　anorexia ; tidak ada napsu makan
ショートステイ　short stay
初老期認知症　tahap terjadi dimentia ; kepikunan
自立　mandiri
自立支援　dukungan kemandirian
自立度　tingkat kemandirian
視力低下　penurunan ; bekurangnya kemampuan melihat
事例検討　studi kasus
心気症　hypochondria
人工呼吸　napas buatan
身上監護　perwalian pribadi
心身症　penyakit psikomatik
振戦　tremor
心臓弁膜症　penyakit katup jantung
身体介護　perawatan tubuh
身体機能　fungsi fisik
信頼関係　hubungan keprcayaan
推奨量　jumlah diet yang dianjurkan
水分バランス　keseimbangan cairan
水分補給　rehidrasi
水疱　gelembung air
睡眠　tidur
頭痛　sakit kepala
ストレス　stres
ストレッチャー　blankar ; usungan
ストレングス視点　kekuatan perspektif
スーパーバイザー　pengawas
スーパーバイジー　supervisee
スーパービジョン　pengawasan
スピリチュアルケア　perawatan spiritual

345

生活援助　dukungan hidup
生活環境　lingkungan hidup
生活習慣病　penyakit akibat gaya hidup buruk
生活の質　Kualitas hidup
生活扶助　bantuan mata pencaharian
生活歴　sejarah kehidupan；riwayat hidup
清潔　kebersihan
清拭　waslap
精神科ソーシャルワーカー　perawat psikiatrik
精神障害　gangguan kejiwaan
精神障害者　penyandang gangguan jiwa
精神保健福祉士　perawat psikiatrik bersertifikat
成年後見制度　sistem perwalian untuk orang dewasa
整髪　rias rambut
生命の延長　panjang umur
生命倫理　biotika
整容　berdandan
世界保健機関　oraganisasi kesehatan dunia；WHO
脊髄損傷　cedera sumsum tulang belakang
脊椎圧迫骨折　fraktur kompresi sumsum tulang belakang
世帯　rumah tangga
摂食　asupan makanan
摂食障害　gangguan asupan makanan
セミファーラー位　posisi semifowler
セルフケア　perlindungan diri
セルフヘルプグループ　kelompok bantuan mandiri；KSM
繊維　serat；fiber
全援助　bantuan；perawatan total
洗顔　pembersihan wajah
洗剤　detergen
洗浄　pencucian
染色体異常　kromosom abnormal
全人格的ケア　perawatan diri total
全身清拭　mandi seluruh tubuh menggunakan spon
全身浴　mandi seluruh tubuh
尖足　drop kaki
洗濯　mencuci pakaian；laundry
洗髪　keramas；mencuci rambut
せん妄　igauan
総入れ歯　gigi palsu
躁うつ病　manic depresi psikosis
早期発見　deteksi dini
装具　bagian tubuh buatan
掃除　bersih-bersih
喪失体験　kehilangan pengalaman
側臥位　posisi badan ke samping
足浴　perendaman kaki
咀嚼　mengunyah
ソーシャルワーカー　pekerja sosial
措置制度　sistem penempatan untuk klien

措置費　biaya penempatan untuk klien
体位変換　perubahan posisi badan
体温　suhu tubuh
体温測定　pengukuran suhu tubuh
退行　kemunduran
帯状疱疹　herpes zoster
大腿四頭筋　quadriceps femoris muscle
大腸癌　kanker colon
代読　orang yang diberi surat kuasa untuk baca
代筆　allograph
代理電話　agensi telephon
ダウン症候群　Down's syndrome
立ち上がり　berdiri
脱臼　dislokasi
脱水症　dehidrasi
他動運動　gerakan pasif
ターミナルケア　terminal care
短下肢装具　ankle kaki orthosis
端座位　duduk dipinggir tempat tidur
チアノーゼ　cyanosis
地域包括支援センター　pusat bantuan regional yang komprehensif
地域密着サービス　layanan berbasis komunitas peduli
チェーンストークス呼吸　cheyne-stokes respirasi
蓄尿障害　gangguan pengumpulan kemih
知的障害　gangguan intelektual
知的障害者　penyandang gangguan intelektual
知能　intelegensi
知能指数　IQ
痴呆　pikun
痴呆性老人　dementia pada lansia
痴呆性老人の日常生活自立度　tingkat kemandirian hidup sehari-hari pada lansia yang memiliki gangguan dementia
チームアプローチ　tim pendekatan
チームケア　tim perawatan
着脱　memakai dan membuka baju
聴覚障害　gangguan pendengaran
長寿社会　masyarakat yang berusia panjang
調整交付金　penyesuaian subsidi
重複障害　gangguan multi fungsi
腸閉塞　ileus
調理　masak
調理方法　resep makanan
聴力レベル　tingkat auditory
直接援助技術　teknik bantuan langsung；praktek kerja social langsung
対麻痺　paraplesia
通所介護　perawatan harian；rawat jalan
通所リハビリテーション　rehabilitasi harian
杖　tongkat
杖歩行　tongkat,alat bantu jalan

日本語	インドネシア語
手洗い	cuci tangan
低血圧	hypotensi；darah rendah
低血糖	gula darah rendah；hypoglikemia
T字杖	T-cane
摘便	ekstraksi feces
手すり	pegangan
手引き	panduan
伝音難聴	tuli konduktif
点字	hurup braile
電動車いす	kursi roda listrik
電動ベッド	bed elektrik
動悸	palpitasi
統合失調症	skizofrenia
透析	dialisis
疼痛	sakit；nyeri
糖尿病	diabetesmelitus；penyakit gula
動脈硬化	arteriosklerosis；penyempitan pembuluh darah
特殊寝台	gatch bed
特殊浴槽	tempat mandi khusus
特別治療食	terapi diet khusus
特別養護老人ホーム	fasilitas kesejahteraan untuk usia lanjut
読話	membacara gerak bibir
吐血	hematemisis；muntah darah
徒手筋力テスト	manual muscle test：MMT
独居	hidup sendiri
内部障害	hambatan pada bagian dalam
難聴	kehilangan pendengaran
難病	penyakit yang sulit disembuhkan
ニーズ	kebutuhan
日常生活活動	aktivitas sehari-hari
日内変動	variasi sirkandian
入眠	tertidur
入浴	mandi
尿	urine
尿意	urgensi kemih
尿器	pispot
尿失禁	inkontinentia urine
尿路感染	infeksi saluran kemih
認知症	pikun
認知症高齢者	dementia pada lansia
認知症高齢者の日常生活自立度	tingkat kemandirian hidup sehari-hari panda lansia yang mengalami ganguan dementia
認知症対応型共同生活介護	panti jompo untuk orang yang dementia
認知症対応型通所介護	rawat jalan bagi penderita dementia
寝返り	berguling
寝たきり	bedrest
寝たきり度	tingkat bedrest di tempat tidur
熱傷	luka bakar
寝床	tempat tidur
年金	dana pensiun
脳血管障害	gangguan cerbrovaskular
脳血管性認知症	dementia cerebrovascular
脳血栓症	cerebral trombosis
脳梗塞	infeksi cerebral
脳死	kematian otak
脳出血	perdarahan otak
脳性麻痺	kelumpuhan；cerebral palsy
脳塞栓	emboli otak
能力低下	disability；penurunan kemampuan
ノーマライゼーション	normalisasi
ノンレム睡眠	non-rapid eye movement〈NREM〉tidur
肺炎	pneumonia
徘徊	berkeliling
肺癌	kanker paru-paru
肺気腫	emphysema pulmonary
バイキング食	viking's food
バイスティックの7原則	7 prinsip biestek
排泄	ekskresi；pengeluaran
排泄介助	bantuan ekskresi；bantuan eliminasi
バイタルサイン	tanda-tanda vital
排尿	urine
排尿困難	kesulitan berkemih
排尿障害	gangguan kemih
排便	fece
排便障害	gangguan buang air besar
廃用萎縮	atrofi disuse
廃用症候群	sindrom disuse
パーキンソン病	penyakit parkinson
白杖	white cane
白内障	katarak
長谷川式簡易認知症スケール改訂版	skala-revisi dementia ala Hasegawa
バックサポート	membantu tubuh bgian belakang
発達障害	gangguan perkembangan
発熱	demam
バリアフリー	bebas hambatan
バルンカテーテル	balon kateter
半身浴	mandi setengah badan
半調理	teknik memasak setengah jadi
BMI	Body Mass Index：BMI
被害妄想	delusi penganiayaan
非言語的コミュニケーション	komunikasi non verbal
ビタミン	vitamin
筆記試験	ujian tertulis
被保険者	tertanggung
肥満	kegemukan
秘密保持	menjamin kerahasiaan
氷枕	bantal es
氷嚢	kantong es
日和見感染	infeksi opportunistik

貧血　anemia
頻便　sering buang air besar
ファーラー位　posisi fowler
フェイスシート　face sheet ; lembar wajah ;
　　lembaran yang bertuliskan identitas diri pasien.
フォローアップ　tindak lanjut ; follow up
腹臥位　posisi tengkurap ; prone
副作用　efek samping
福祉　kesejahteraan
福祉機器　alat kesejahteraan
腹式呼吸　pernapasan perut
福祉事務所　kantor kesejahteraan sosial
福祉用具　alat kesejahteraan
福祉用具貸与　sewa alat bantu kesejahteraan
浮腫　edema ; bengkak
フットサポート　penyangga kaki pada kursi roda
部分援助　bantuan untuk aktifitas tertentu
部分清拭　mewaslap sebagian tubuh
部分浴　mandi sebagian
プライバシー　privacy
プライマリ・ケア　perawatan primer
プロフィール　profile
平均寿命　rata-rata usia hidup
平均余命　rata-rata harapan hidup
ベッド　tempat tidur
ベッドから車いす　perpindahan dari tempat tidur
　　ke kursi roda
ベッドメーキング　perbeden ; menyiapkan tempat
　　tidur
便器　pispot
便失禁　gangguan kontrol buang air besar
便秘　kontipasi ; sembelit
片麻痺　hemiplegia ; lumpuh sebelah
保育士　perawat anak bersertifikat
防炎素材　bahan tahan api
防汚素材　bahan anti kotor
訪問介護　perawatan home visite
訪問看護　perawatan home visite untuk bagian
　　medis
訪問看護ステーション　pos perawat medis
　　kunjungan rumah
訪問入浴介護　kunjungan perawatan memandikan
訪問リハビリテーション　kunjungan rehabilitasi
保健師　perawat kesehatan masyarakat
保険者　penanggung asuransi
保健所　pusat kesehatan publik
保険料　premi asuransi
歩行　jalan kaki
歩行器　alat bantu jalan
歩行練習　latihan berjalan
ポジショニング　posisi
補足給付　manfaat tambahan
ポータブルトイレ　portable toilet

ポータブル浴槽　portable mandi
補聴器　alat bantu dengar
発疹　bintil-bintil
発赤　kemerahan
ボディメカニクス　mekanika tubuh ; body mekanik
ホームヘルパー　home helper
ボランティア　sukarelawan
ホルモン　hormon
マット　matras
松葉杖　kruk
麻痺　lumpuh ; parslysis
ミキサー食　makanan yang di blender
ミネラル　mineral
脈拍　denyut nadi
メタボリック症候群　metabolik sindrome
滅菌　sterilisasi
妄想　khayalan ; delusi
燃え尽き症候群　sindrom pasca luka bakar
モニタリング　monitoring
問題行動　masalah prilaku
夜間せん妄　mengigau malam hari
薬剤　obat
薬剤管理　manajemen obat-obatan
薬剤師　apoteker
薬物療法　pharmakoteraphi
有料老人ホーム　panti jompo swasta
ユニットケア　unit perawatan
ユニバーサルファッション　universal fashion
要援護高齢者　lansia yang membutuhkan perawatan
要介護　perlu perawatan
要介護者　orang yang perlu perawatan
要介護度　level ; tingkat perlunya perawatan
要介護認定　pengesyahan perlunya perawatan
養護老人ホーム　fasilitas perawatan untuk lansia ;
　　panti jompo
要支援　perlu bantuan jangka panjang
要支援者　orang yang memerlukan dukungan
　　jangka panjang
要支援認定　sertifikat ; pengesahan perlunya
　　bantuan jangka panjang
腰痛症　sakit pinggang
腰痛体操　senam untuk mencegah sakit pinggang
腰痛予防　pencegahan sakit pinggang
抑制　pengekangan
浴槽　bak mandi
予防給付　manfaat pencegahan
四脚杖　quad cane ; tongkat berkaki empat
ライフサイクル　siklus hidup
ライフスタイル　gaya hidup
ライフレビュー　tinjauan hidup
ラポール　hubungan kepercayaan antara pasien dan
　　perawat
理学療法士　ahli terapi fisik

立位　posisi berdiri
利尿剤　diuretik
リハビリテーション　rehabilitasi
リハビリテーション医学　ilmu kedokteran rehabilitashi
リハビリテーション介護　perawatan rehabilitasi
留置カテーテル　kateter permanen
流動食　makanan cair
流動性知能　fluid intelligence
利用料　biaya pemakaian
レクリエーション　rekreasi
レム睡眠　rapid eye movement〈REM〉tidur
聾　tuli
老化　penuaan
老眼　presbiopia
老人性うつ病　depresi senilis
老人性難聴　ganguan pendengaran akibat usia lanjut
老人保健施設　fasilitas kesehatan bagi orang lanjut usia
老年認知症　dimentia pada lansia
老齢基礎年金　pokok pensiun hari tua
老齢年金　uang pensiun
老齢福祉年金　kesejahteraan pensiun hari tua
ロールプレイ　role play

インドネシア語

2. 韓国語（Korean）

IQ　지능지수
ICIDH　국제장애분류
ICF　국제생활기능분류
ICD　국제질병분류
アクティビティ　액티비티
アセスメント　어세스먼트
アテトーシス　아테토시스
アテトーゼ　아테토제
アドボカシー　권리옹호
アルツハイマー型認知症　알츠하이머형 치매
アルツハイマー病　알츠하이머병
安全管理　안전관리
黽法　찜질
安眠　안면
安眠援助　안면원조
安楽　안락
安楽な体位　안락한 체위
意識障害　의식장애
維持期リハビリテーション　유지기 리허빌리테이션
萎縮　위축
移乗動作　갈아타기 동작
移送費　이송비용
遺族基礎年金　유족기초연금
移動　이동
移動介護　이동수발
移動関連福祉用具　이동관련 복지용구
移動トイレ　이동화장실
移動浴槽　이동욕조
衣服　의복
衣服着脱　의복 갈아입기
衣料障害　의류장애
医療ソーシャルワーカー　의료사회복지사
医療保険制度　의료보험제도
インスリン　인슐린
インテーク　인테이크
インフォーマル　인포멀
陰部清拭　음부닦기
陰部洗浄　음부세정
インペアメント　인페어먼트
うつ病　우울증
運営適正化委員会　운영적정화위원회
運動器の機能向上　운동기의 기능향상
運動失調　운동실조
運動障害　운동장애
運動療法　운동요법
エアーパッド　에어패드
エアーマット　에어매트
エイジズム　에이지즘
エイズ　에이즈
栄養　영양

栄養改善　영양개선
栄養管理　영양관리
栄養士　영양사
栄養所要量　영양소요량
栄養素　영양소
腋窩温　겨드랑체온
壊死　회사
ADL　일상생활활동
NPO　비영리법인
MRSA　감염관리
MMSE　엠엠에스이［치매기능검사］
MMT　도수근력테스트
嚥下　연하［삼킴］
嚥下困難　연하곤란
嚥下性肺炎　연하성 폐렴
嚥下補助剤　연하보조제
エンゲル係数　엥겔계수
円座　원좌［뺑 둘러앉음］
エンパワメント　임파워먼트
応益負担　응익부담
嘔気　구토기
応急手当　응급처리
嘔吐　구토
応能負担　응능부담
起き上がり　일어서기
おむつ　기저귀
おむつカバー　기저귀 커버
おむつ交換　기저귀 교환
おむつ外し　기저귀 떼기
臥位　와위
介護　장기요양
介護過程　장기요양과정
介護技術　장기요양기술
介護休業　장기요양휴가
介護給付　장기요양급여
介護計画　장기요양계획
介護サービス計画　장기요양서비스계획
介護支援専門員　장기요양지원전문인
介護指導　장기요양지도
介護者　장기요양자
介護職員　장기요양직원
介護ニーズ　장기요양니즈
介護認定審査会　개호인정심사회
介護福祉　개호복지
介護福祉士　개호복지사
介護福祉士国家試験　개호복지사 국가시험
介護福祉士登録　개호복지사 등록
介護負担　장기요양부담
介護報酬　장기요양수가
介護保険　장기요양보험

介護保険事業計画　장기요양보험사업계획
介護保険審査会　개호보험심사회
介護保険制度　개호보험제도
介護保険認定調査　장기요양인정조사
介護保険法　개호보험법
介護目標　장기요양목표
介護用具　장기요양용구
介護予防　장기요양예방
介護予防事業　장기요양예방사업
介護療養型医療施設　요양형 의료시설
介護老人福祉施設　장기요양노인복지시설
介護老人保健施設　장기요양노인보건시설
介護労働者　장기요양노동자
介助　수발
疥癬　개선[옴]
回想法　회상법
階段　계단
階段昇降　계단승강
回復期リハビリテーション　회복기 리허빌리테이션
潰瘍　궤양
かかりつけ医　주치의
核家族　핵가족
家計　가계
家事　가사
家政　가정
家政婦　가정부
家族　가족
家族会　가족회
家族介護　가족수발
家族介護者　가족수발자
家族関係　가족관계
合併症　합병증
寡婦　과부
紙おむつ　종이 기저귀
過用症候群　과용증후군
加齢　가령
癌　암
感音難聴　감음난청
感覚機能　감각기능
換気　환기
環境整備　환경정비
看護　간호
肝硬変　간경변
看護師　간호사
関節　관절
関節可動域　관절가동영역
関節リウマチ　관절염
感染　감염
感染菌　감염 균
感染症　감염증
感染予防　감염예방
浣腸　관장
観念失行　관념실행

管理栄養士　관리영양사
緩和ケア　완화케어
記憶障害　기억장애
着替え　갈아입기
気管　기관
危険防止　위험방지
起座位　기좌위
義歯　의치
義肢装具士　의지장구사
基礎代謝　기초대사
機能維持　기능유지
機能訓練　기능훈련
機能障害　기능장애
記銘力　기명력
虐待　학대
ギャッチベッド　개치베드
救急救命士　구급구명사
仰臥位　앙와위
共感　공감
虚弱　허약
起立性低血圧　기립성 저혈압
記録　기록
筋萎縮　근위축
緊急連絡先　긴급연락처
金銭管理　금전관리
苦情解決　불평해결
くも膜下出血　지주막하출혈
クリティカルパス　크리티컬 패스
グループホーム　그룹 홈
グループリビング　그룹 리빙
グループレクリエーション　그룹 레크리에이션
グループワーク　그룹워크
車いす　휠체어
車いすからベッド　휠체어에서 침대로
車いすの移動　휠체어의 이동
車いすの介助　휠체어의 수발
クロックポジション　클록 포지션
ケア　케어
ケアカンファレンス　케어 컨퍼런스
ケアチーム　케어 팀
ケアハウス　케어하우스
ケアプラン　케어플랜
ケアマネジメント　케어매니지먼트
ケアマネジャー　케어매니저
ケアワーク　케어워크
経管栄養　경관영양
頸髄損傷　경추손상
傾聴　경청
契約　계약
劇薬　극약
下血　하혈
ケースカンファレンス　케이스 컨퍼런스
ケースワーク　케이스워크

血圧　혈압
下痢　설사
幻覚　환각
健康　건강
健康観察　건강관찰
健康保険　건강보험
言語障害　언어장애
言語聴覚士　언어청각사
見当識障害　견당식장애
権利擁護　권리옹호
公益事業　공익사업
公益法人　공익법인
構音障害　구음장애
後期高齢者　후기고령자
抗菌・防臭素材　항균・방취소재
口腔機能の向上　구강기능의 향상
口腔ケア　구강케어
合計特殊出生率　합계특수출산율
高血圧　고혈압
拘縮　구축 [오므라듦]
拘縮予防　구축예방
公証人　공증인
公正証書　공정증서
抗生物質　항생물질
拘束　구속
後天性免疫不全症候群　후천성면역부전증후군
高齢化　고령화
高齢期障害　고령기 장애
高齢者　고령자
高齢社会　고령사회
高齢者虐待　고령자학대
高齢者虐待防止法　고령자학대방지법
高齢者世帯　고령자세대
声かけ　말 걸기
誤嚥　오연 [잘못 삼킴]
誤嚥性肺炎　오연성 폐렴
呼吸　호흡
呼吸機能障害　호흡기능장애
国際疾病分類　국제질병분류
国際障害分類　국제장애분류
国際生活機能分類　국제생활기능분류
国際標準化機構　국제표준화기구
骨折　골절
骨粗鬆症　골다공증
言葉かけ　말 걸기
個別介護　개별수발
コミュニケーション　커뮤니케이션
コミュニケーションエイド　커뮤니케이션 에이드
コレステロール　콜레스테롤
献立　식단
座位　좌위
再アセスメント　재 어세스먼트
在宅介護　재가장기요양

在宅看護　재가간호
在宅ケア　재가케어
作業療法　작업요법
作業療法士　작업치료사
サービス担当者会議　서비스담당자회의
サポートシステム　서포트 시스템
残存機能　잔존기능
散髪　이발
紫外線遮蔽素材　자외선차폐소재
歯科衛生士　치과위생사
視覚障害　시력장애
視覚障害者　시각장애인
弛緩　이완
止血　지혈
思考障害　사고장애
自己覚知　자기각지
自己決定　자기결정
自己実現　자기실현
脂質異常症　지방질 이상증
自傷行為　자상행위
自助具　자조도구
死生観　사생관
施設介護　시설장기요양
自尊心　자존심
肢体不自由　지체부자유
実技試験　실기시험
失禁　실금
失語　실어
シーツ交換　시트교환
実支出　실비지출
実収入　실수입
失認　실인증
実務経験証明書　실무경험증명서
自動運動　자동운동
児童期障害　아동기 장애
自閉症　자폐증
社会資源　사회자원
社会の不利　사회적 불리
社会福祉　사회복지
社会福祉士　사회복지사
社会福祉事業　사회복지사업
社会保険　사회보험
社会保障　사회보장
社会保障審議会　사회보장심의회
視野狭窄　시야협착
視野障害　시야장애
シャワー浴　샤워
収益事業　수익사업
従属人口　종속인구
住宅改修　주택개량
終末期　종말기
終末期介護　종말기 장기요양
主治医　주치의

主治医意見書　주치의 의견서
手段的日常生活活動　수단적 일상생활활동
出血　출혈
守秘義務　묵비의무
手浴　손 목욕
手話　수화
除圧　제압
障害　장애
障害基礎年金　장애기초연금
障害の受容　장애의 수용
小規模多機能型居宅介護　소규모다기능형거택개호
少子化　출생률감소
少子高齢化　저출산 고령화
静脈栄養法　정맥영양요법
職業的リハビリテーション　직업적 리허빌리테이션
食事　식사
食事介護　식사장기요양
食事介助　식사수발
食事動作　식사동작
食事療法　식사요법
褥瘡　욕창
褥瘡予防　욕창예방
食中毒　식중독
食品衛生　식품위생
植物状態　식물상태
植物性食品　식물성 식품
食欲　식욕
食欲不振　식욕부진
ショートステイ　단기보호
初老期認知症　초로기 치매
自立　자립
自立支援　자립지원
自立度　자립도
視力低下　시력저하
事例検討　사례검토
心気症　심기증
人工呼吸　인공호흡
身上監護　신상감호
心身症　심신증
振戦　진전 [떨림증]
心臓弁膜症　심장판막증
身体介護　신체장기요양
身体機能　신체기능
信頼関係　신뢰관계
推奨量　추천량
水分バランス　수분밸런스
水分補給　수분보급
水疱　물구품
睡眠　수면
頭痛　두통
ストレス　스트레스
ストレッチャー　스트래쳐
ストレングス視点　스트렝스 시점

スーパーバイザー　슈퍼바이저
スーパーバイジー　슈퍼바이지
スーパービジョン　슈퍼비전
スピリチュアルケア　스피리츄얼 케어
生活援助　생활원조
生活環境　생활환경
生活習慣病　생활습관병
生活の質　생활의 질
生活扶助　생활부조
生活歴　생활경험년수
清潔　청결
清拭　닦기
精神科ソーシャルワーカー　정신보건사회복지사
精神障害　정신장애
精神障害者　정신장애인
精神保健福祉士　정신보건복지사
成年後見制度　성년후견제도
整髪　이발
生命の延長　생명의 연장
生命倫理　생명윤리
整容　청결
世界保健機関　세계보건기관
脊髄損傷　척수손상
脊椎圧迫骨折　척추압박골절
世帯　세대
摂食　섭식
摂食障害　섭식장애
セミファーラー位　세미 반좌위
セルフケア　셀프케어
セルフヘルプグループ　셀프 헬프 그룹
繊維　섬유
全援助　전면원조
洗顔　세수
洗剤　세제
洗浄　세정
染色体異常　염색체이상
全人格的ケア　전인격적 케어
全身清拭　전신 닦기
全身浴　전신 목욕
尖足　첨족
洗濯　세탁
洗髪　머리 감기
せん妄　섬망
総入れ歯　틀니
躁うつ病　조울병
早期発見　조기발견
装具　장구
掃除　청소
喪失体験　상실체험
側臥位　측와위
足浴　발 목욕
咀嚼　저작
ソーシャルワーカー　소셜워커

措置制度 조치제도	T字杖 T자 지팡이
措置費 조치비용	摘便 적변
体位変換 체위변환	手すり 손잡이
体温 체온	手引き 안내
体温測定 체온측정	伝音難聴 전음난청
退行 퇴행	点字 점자
帯状疱疹 대상포진	電動車いす 전동휠체어
大腿四頭筋 대퇴사두근	電動ベッド 전동베드
大腸癌 대장암	動悸 동계
代読 대독	統合失調症 정신분열증
代筆 대필	透析 투석
代理電話 대리전화	疼痛 동통
ダウン症候群 다운증후군	糖尿病 당뇨병
立ち上がり 일어서기	動脈硬化 동맥경화
脱臼 탈구	特殊寝台 특수침대
脱水症 탈수증	特殊浴槽 특수욕조
他動運動 타의적 운동	特別治療食 특별치료식
ターミナルケア 터미널 케어	特別養護老人ホーム 특별양호노인홈
短下肢装具 단하지 장구	読話 독순술
端座位 단좌위	吐血 토혈
チアノーゼ 치아노제	徒手筋力テスト 도수근력테스트
地域包括支援センター 지역포괄지원센터	独居 독거
地域密着サービス 지역밀착서비스	内部障害 내부장애
チェーンストークス呼吸 체인스토크스 호흡	難聴 난청
蓄尿障害 소변 저장장애	難病 난치병
知的障害 지적장애	ニーズ 니즈
知的障害者 지적장애인	日常生活活動 일상생활활동
知能 지능	日内変動 일내변동
知能指数 지능지수	入眠 잠들기
痴呆 치매	入浴 목욕
痴呆性老人 치매성 노인	尿 오줌
痴呆性老人の日常生活自立度 치매성 노인의 일상생활 자립도	尿意 요의
	尿器 소변기
チームアプローチ 팀 어프로치	尿失禁 소변실금
チームケア 팀 케어	尿路感染 요로감염
着脱 착탈의	認知症 인지증
聴覚障害 청각장애	認知症高齢者 인지증고령자
長寿社会 장수사회	認知症高齢者の日常生活自立度 인지증고령자의 일상생활자립도
調整交付金 조정교부금	
重複障害 중복장애	認知症対応型共同生活介護 인지증대응형 공동생활개호
腸閉塞 장폐쇄	
調理 조리	認知症対応型通所介護 인지증대응형 통소개호
調理方法 조리방법	寝返り 돌아눕기
聴力レベル 청력수준	寝たきり 와상
直接援助技術 직접원조기술	寝たきり度 와상도
対麻痺 대마비	熱傷 열상
通所介護 주간보호	寝床 침상
通所リハビリテーション 주간리허빌리테이션	年金 연금
杖 지팡이	脳血管障害 뇌혈관장애
杖歩行 지팡이 보행	脳血管性認知症 뇌혈관성 인지증
手洗い 손 씻기	脳血栓症 뇌혈전
低血圧 저혈압	脳梗塞 뇌경색
低血糖 저혈당	脳死 뇌사

脳出血　뇌출혈
脳性麻痺　뇌성마비
脳塞栓　뇌전색
能力低下　능력저하
ノーマライゼーション　노멀라이제이션
ノンレム睡眠　논렘수면
肺炎　폐렴
徘徊　배회
肺癌　폐암
肺気腫　폐기종
バイキング食　뷔페식
バイスティックの7原則　비에스틱의 7대 원칙
排泄　배설
排泄介助　배설수발
バイタルサイン　바이탈사인
排尿　배뇨
排尿困難　배뇨곤란
排尿障害　배뇨장애
排便　배변
排便障害　배변장애
廃用萎縮　폐용성 근 위축
廃用症候群　폐용증후군
パーキンソン病　파킨슨병
白杖　흰 지팡이
白内障　백내장
長谷川式簡易認知症スケール改訂版　하세가와식 간이 인지증스케일 개정판
バックサポート　백 지원
発達障害　발달장애
発熱　발열
バリアフリー　배리어프리
バルンカテーテル　벌룬 도뇨 카테터
半身浴　반신목욕
半調理　반 조리
BMI　BMI [체질량지수]
被害妄想　피해망상
非言語的コミュニケーション　비언어적 커뮤니케이션
ビタミン　비타민
筆記試験　필기시험
被保険者　피보험자
肥満　비만
秘密保持　비밀보지
氷枕　얼음베개
氷囊　얼음주머니
日和見感染　기회감염
貧血　빈혈
頻便　빈변
ファーラー位　반좌위
フェイスシート　페이스 시트
フォローアップ　팔로우 업
腹臥位　복와위
副作用　부작용
福祉　복지

福祉機器　복지기기
腹式呼吸　복식호흡
福祉事務所　복지사무소
福祉用具　복지용구
福祉用具貸与　복지용구대여
浮腫　부종
フットサポート　풋 지원
部分援助　부분원조
部分清拭　부분세정
部分浴　부분목욕
プライバシー　프라이버시
プライマリ・ケア　예방진료
プロフィール　프로필
平均寿命　평균수명
平均余命　평균여명
ベッド　베드
ベッドから車いす　베드에서 휠체어로
ベッドメーキング　침구정리
便器　변기
便失禁　대변실금
便秘　변비
片麻痺　편마비
保育士　보육사
防炎素材　방염소재
防汚素材　오염방지소재
訪問介護　방문요양
訪問看護　방문간호
訪問看護ステーション　방문간호스테이션
訪問入浴介護　방문목욕
訪問リハビリテーション　방문리허빌리테이션
保健師　보건사
保険者　보험사
保健所　보건소
保険料　보험료
歩行　보행
歩行器　보행기
歩行練習　보행연습
ポジショニング　포지셔닝
補足給付　보충급여
ポータブルトイレ　포터블 변기
ポータブル浴槽　포터블 욕조
補聴器　보청기
発疹　발진
発赤　발적
ボディメカニクス　보디 메커닉스
ホームヘルパー　홈 헬퍼
ボランティア　자원봉사
ホルモン　호르몬
マット　매트
松葉杖　지팡이
麻痺　마비
ミキサー食　믹서식
ミネラル　미네랄

韓国語

脈拍　맥박
メタボリック症候群　메타보릭증후군
滅菌　멸균
妄想　망상
燃え尽き症候群　탈진증후군
モニタリング　모니터링
問題行動　문제행동
夜間せん妄　야간섬망
薬剤　약제
薬剤管理　약 관리
薬剤師　약제사
薬物療法　약품요법
有料老人ホーム　유료노인홈
ユニットケア　유니트케어
ユニバーサルファッション　유니버설 패션
要援護高齢者　원호 대상 고령자
要介護　장기요양대상
要介護者　장기요양인정자
要介護度　장기요양등급
要介護認定　장기요양인정
養護老人ホーム　양호노인홈
要支援　지원대상
要支援者　지원대상자
要支援認定　장기요양지원인정
腰痛症　허리통증
腰痛体操　요통체조
腰痛予防　요통예방
抑制　억제
浴槽　욕조
予防給付　예방급여
四脚杖　네발지팡이
ライフサイクル　라이프사이클
ライフスタイル　라이프스타일
ライフレビュー　라이프 리뷰
ラポール　라포르
理学療法士　이학요법사 [물리치료사]
立位　입위
利尿剤　이뇨제
リハビリテーション　리허빌리테이션
リハビリテーション医学　리허빌리테이션 의학
リハビリテーション介護　리허빌리테이션 장기요양
留置カテーテル　유치 도뇨 카테터
流動食　유동식
流動性知能　유동성 지능
利用料　이용료
レクリエーション　레크에이션
レム睡眠　렘수면
聾　농 [귀머거리]
老化　노화
老眼　노안
老人性うつ病　노인성 우울증
老人性難聴　노인성 난청
老人保健施設　노인보건시설

老年認知症　노년치매
老齢基礎年金　노령기초연금
老齢年金　노령연금
老齢福祉年金　노령복지연금
ロールプレイ　롤 플레이

3. スペイン語（Spanish）

IQ　conciente de la inteligencia；índice intelectual
ICIDH　Clasificación Internacional de Deficiencias, Discapacidades y Minusvalías：CIDDM
ICF　Clasificación Internacional del Funcionamiento：CIF
ICD　Clasificación Internacional de Enfermedades：CIE
アクティビティ　actividad
アセスメント　evaluación
アテトーシス　atetosis
アテトーゼ　atetosis
アドボカシー　abogacia；defensa
アルツハイマー型認知症　demencia senil del tipo del Alzheimer：DSTA
アルツハイマー病　enfermedad de Alzheimer
安全管理　control de seguridad
罨法　fomentar
安眠　sueño profundo
安眠援助　ayuda para el sueño tranquilo
安楽　comodidad
安楽な体位　posición cómoda
意識障害　disturbio de la conciencia
維持期リハビリテーション　rehabilitación en la etapa crónica
萎縮　atrofia
移乗動作　movimiento de la transferencia
移送費　costo del transporte
遺族基礎年金　pensión básica del sobreviviente
移動　tranferencia
移動介護　cuidado de tranferencia
移動関連福祉用具　herramientas de ayuda relacionadas con traslación
移動トイレ　retrete portátil
移動浴槽　bañera portable；bañera portátil
衣服　ropa
衣服着脱　cambio de ropa
衣料障害　debilidad a los materiales de ropa
医療ソーシャルワーカー　asistente social médico
医療保険制度　sistema del seguro médico
インスリン　insulina
インテーク　entrevista de admisión
インフォーマル　informal
陰部清拭　limpieza de los órganos genitales
陰部洗浄　cuidado perineal；limpieza del área genital
インペアメント　impedimento
うつ病　depresión
運営適正化委員会　comité para la administración apropiada
運動器の機能向上　mejoramiento de la función del movimiento
運動失調　ataxia
運動障害　incapacidad de movimiento
運動療法　ejercicio terapéutico
エアーパッド　cojin de aire
エアーマット　colchón de aire
エイジズム　edadismo
エイズ　síndrome adquirido de la inmunodeficiencia：SIDA
栄養　nutrición
栄養改善　mejora de la nutrición；mejoramiento nutricional
栄養管理　administración alimenticia
栄養士　nutricionista
栄養所要量　requisito alimenticio
栄養素　nutrientes
腋窩温　temperatura axilar
壊死　necrosis
ADL　actividades de la vida diaria：AVD
NPO　organización sin fines de lucro
MRSA　methicillin-resistant staphylococcus aureus
MMSE　mini-examen del estado mental
MMT　prueba manual del músculo
嚥下　deglución
嚥下困難　dificultad para deglutir
嚥下性肺炎　neumonía por aspiración
嚥下補助剤　suplemento de la deglución
エンゲル係数　coeficiente de Engel
円座　colchoneta redonda；amortiguador del recorte
エンパワメント　capacitación；atribución de poder
応益負担　cuota conforme a beneficio recibido
嘔気　náusea
応急手当　primeros auxilios en emergencia
嘔吐　vómito
応能負担　principios de cuota conforme a solvencia
起き上がり　el levantarse
おむつ　pañal
おむつカバー　cubierta del pañal
おむつ交換　cambio de pañal
おむつ外し　retiro de pañal
臥位　decúbito；posición acostada
介護　cuidado a largo plazo
介護過程　proceso del cuidado a largo plazo
介護技術　técnica de cuidado a largo plazo
介護休業　baja por cuidado de la familia
介護給付　ventaja del cuidado a largo plazo
介護計画　plan del cuidado a largo plazo
介護サービス計画　plan del servicio del cuidado a largo plazo
介護支援専門員　administrador del cuidado
介護指導　dirección del cuidado a largo plazo

介護者　cuidador
介護職員　trbajador del cuidado
介護ニーズ　necesidades del cuidado a largo plazo
介護認定審査会　Junnta de Certificacion del cuidado a largo plazo
介護福祉　bienestar del cuidado
介護福祉士　trabajador certificado del cuidado
介護福祉士国家試験　examinación nacional del trabajador certificado del cuidado
介護福祉士登録　registro de trabajador certificado del cuidado
介護負担　carga del cuidado a largo plazo
介護報酬　honorario del cuidado a largo plazo
介護保険　seguro de cuidado a largo plazo
介護保険事業計画　plan del proyecto del Seguro de cuidado de largo plazo
介護保険審査会　junta de ajuste sobre el certificado del seguro de cuidado
介護保険制度　sistema del seguro de cuidado a largo plazo
介護保険認定調査　encuesta para la certificación de la necesidad del cuidado a larago plazo
介護保険法　Ley de seguro del cuidado a largo plazo
介護目標　meta del cuidado a largo plazo
介護用具　herramientas para el cuidado a largo plazo
介護予防　prevención de la necesidad del cuidado a largo plazo
介護予防事業　trabajo de la prevención del cuidado a largo plazo
介護療養型医療施設　instalación para el cuidado médico a largo plazo
介護老人福祉施設　instalación del bienestar para el cuidado de los ancianos a largo plazo
介護老人保健施設　instalación de la salud para el cuidado de los ancianos a largo plazo
介護労働者　trabajador del cuidado
介助　ayuda
疥癬　sarna
回想法　terapia de la reminiscencia
階段　escaleras
階段昇降　subir y bajar de escaleras
回復期リハビリテーション　rehabilitación en la fase de recuperación
潰瘍　úlcera
かかりつけ医　doctor primario
核家族　familia nuclear
家計　presupuesto doméstico
家事　tareas domésticas
家政　economía domestica
家政婦　empleada doméstica
家族　familia
家族会　grupo del esfuerzo personal para las familias

家族介護　cuidado por la familia
家族介護者　cuidador familiar
家族関係　relación familiar
合併症　complicación
寡婦　viuda
紙おむつ　pañal de papel
過用症候群　síndrome por sobreuso
加齢　envejecimiento
癌　cáncer
感音難聴　sordera sensorineural
感覚機能　función sensorial
換気　ventilación
環境整備　mantenimiento ambiental
看護　oficio de enfermera ; cuidado de enfermería
肝硬変　cirrosis del hígado
看護師　enfermera
関節　articulación
関節可動域　rango de movimiento articular
関節リウマチ　artritis reumatoide
感染　infección
感染菌　bacteria
感染症　enfermedad infecciosa
感染予防　prevención de la infección
浣腸　enema
観念失行　apraxia ideacional
管理栄養士　nutricionista registrado
緩和ケア　cuidado paliativo
記憶障害　desorden de la memoria
着替え　cambio de ropa
気管　tráquea
危険防止　prevención de riesgo
起座位　posición sentada
義歯　diente postizo
義肢装具士　protésico
基礎代謝　metabolismo básico
機能維持　mantenimiento funcional
機能訓練　entrenamiento funcional
機能障害　desorden funcional
記銘力　retención de memoria
虐待　abuso
ギャッチベッド　cama de Gatch
救急救命士　técnico médico de emergencia
仰臥位　posición supina
共感　empatía
虚弱　físicamente débil
起立性低血圧　hipotensión ortostática
記録　registro
筋萎縮　atrofia muscular
緊急連絡先　dirección en caso de emergencia
金銭管理　administración del dinero
苦情解決　solución de quejas
くも膜下出血　hemorragia subaracnoidea
クリティカルパス　maneras de la trayectoria crítica

日本語	スペイン語
グループホーム	hogar de grupo
グループリビング	convivencia en grupo
グループレクリエーション	recreación en grupo
グループワーク	trabajo en grupo
車いす	silla de ruedas
車いすからベッド	de silla de ruedas a cama
車いすの移動	movimiento en silla de ruedas
車いすの介助	asistencia de silla de ruedas
クロックポジション	posición del reloj
ケア	cuidado
ケアカンファレンス	conferencia sobre el cuidado
ケアチーム	equipo del cuidado
ケアハウス	casa de cuidado
ケアプラン	plan del cuidado
ケアマネジメント	administración del cuidado a largo plazo
ケアマネジャー	administrador del cuidado
ケアワーク	trabajo del cuidado
経管栄養	alimentación de tubo
頸髄損傷	lesión cervical
傾聴	el escuchar
契約	contrato
劇薬	droga peligrosa
下血	melena
ケースカンファレンス	conferencia del caso
ケースワーク	trabajo del caso
血圧	presión arterial
下痢	diarrea
幻覚	alucinación
健康	salud
健康観察	observación de la salud
健康保険	seguro médico
言語障害	desorden de la lengua
言語聴覚士	terapeuta de la audiencia de la lengua ; logopeda
見当識障害	desorden de la orientación
権利擁護	defensa para los derechos
公益事業	proyecto de servicio público
公益法人	corporación de la ventaja pública ; corporación de servicios públicos
構音障害	desorden de la articulación
後期高齢者	ancianos de 75 años o más
抗菌・防臭素材	material antibacteriano y desodorisante
口腔機能の向上	mejora de la función oral
口腔ケア	cuidado médico oral
合計特殊出生率	indice de fertilidad total : IFT
高血圧	hipertensión
拘縮	contracción
拘縮予防	prevención de la contracción
公証人	notario público
公正証書	acta notarial
抗生物質	antibióticos
拘束	retención
後天性免疫不全症候群	sindrome adquirido de la inmunodeficiencia : SIDA
高齢化	envejecimiento de la poblacion
高齢期障害	desordenes seniles
高齢者	persona vieja
高齢社会	población anciana
高齢者虐待	abuso de los ancianos
高齢者虐待防止法	ley de la prevención de abuso a los ancianos
高齢者世帯	hogar envejecido
声かけ	estímulo verbal
誤嚥	mala deglucion
誤嚥性肺炎	pulmonía de la aspiración ; pulmonía de la mala deglución
呼吸	respiración
呼吸機能障害	desorden funcional respiratorio
国際疾病分類	Clasificación Internacional de Enfermedades : CIE
国際障害分類	Clasificación Internacional de Deficiencias, Discapacidades y Minusvalías : CIDDM
国際生活機能分類	Clasificación Internacional del Funcionamiento, de la Discapacidad y de la Salud : CIF
国際標準化機構	Organización Internacional para la Estandarización : ISO
骨折	fractura
骨粗鬆症	osteoporosis
言葉かけ	estímulo verbal
個別介護	cuidado individual
コミュニケーション	comunicación
コミュニケーションエイド	ayuda de la comunicación
コレステロール	colesterol
献立	menú
座位	posición sentada
再アセスメント	revaloración
在宅介護	cuidado casero
在宅看護	cuidados de la salud casera
在宅ケア	cuidado casero
作業療法	terapia ocupacional
作業療法士	terapeuta ocupacional
サービス担当者会議	reunión del personal de servicio
サポートシステム	sistema de apoyo
残存機能	función residual
散髪	corte de pelo
紫外線遮蔽素材	material de proteccion contra los rayos ultravioletas
歯科衛生士	higienista dental
視覚障害	discapacidad visual
視覚障害者	impedido visualmente
弛緩	flacidez ; relajación
止血	homeostasis

思考障害　desorden del pensamiento	少子高齢化　baja natalidad y envejecimiento de la población
自己覚知　autoconciencia	
自己決定　autodeterminación	静脈栄養法　nutrición parenteral
自己実現　autorealización	職業的リハビリテーション　rehabilitación vocacional
脂質異常症　dislipidemia	食事　comida
自傷行為　automutilación	食事介護　cuidado para comer
自助具　dispositivo para autoayuda	食事介助　cuidado de qpoyo para comer
死生観　vista de la vida y de la muerte	食事動作　movimiento de la consumición
施設介護　cuidado a largo plazo en establecimiento	食事療法　terapia dietética
自尊心　amor propio	褥瘡　úlcera por presión
肢体不自由　lisiado	褥瘡予防　prevención de la úlcera por presión
実技試験　examen de la práctica	食中毒　intoxicación alimentaria
失禁　incontinencia	食品衛生　saneamiento del alimento
失語　afasia	植物状態　estado vegetativo
シーツ交換　cambio de sabanas	植物性食品　alimento del origen vegetal
実支出　gastos Actuales	食欲　apetito
実収入　ingresos actuales	食欲不振　anorexia
失認　agnosia	ショートステイ　estancia corta para el cuidado a largo plazo
実務経験証明書　certificado de práctica del trabajo	
自動運動　movimiento activo	初老期認知症　demencia presenil
児童期障害　desordenes en etapa de la ninez	自立　independencia
自閉症　autismo	自立支援　apoyo para la independencia
社会資源　recursos sociales	自立度　grado de vida independiente
社会的不利　desventaja social	視力低下　debilitamiento de la vista
社会福祉　asistencia social	事例検討　estudio de caso
社会福祉士　asistente social certificado	心気症　hipocondría
社会福祉事業　proyecto de la asistencia social	人工呼吸　respiración artificial
社会保険　seguro social	身上監護　tutela personal
社会保障　seguridad Social	心身症　enfermedad psicosomática
社会保障審議会　Consejo de la Seguridad Social	振戦　temblor
視野狭窄　restricción del campo de visión	心臓弁膜症　enfermedad cardíaca valvular
視野障害　defecto del campo de visión	身体介護　cuidado físico
シャワー浴　baño de ducha	身体機能　función física
収益事業　negocio ventajoso	信頼関係　relación de confianza
従属人口　población dependiente	推奨量　ingestas recomendadas de energía y nutrients
住宅改修　renovación de la casa	
終末期　etapa terminal	水分バランス　balance de agua
終末期介護　cuidado terminal	水分補給　rehidratación
主治医　doctor primario	水疱　blister ; ampolla
主治医意見書　juicio del médico encargado	睡眠　sueño
手段的日常生活動作　actividades instrumentales de la vida diaria : AIVD	頭痛　dolor de cabeza
	ストレス　estrés
出血　hemorragia	ストレッチャー　camilla
守秘義務　deber de confidencialidad	ストレングス視点　perspectiva de la fuerza
手浴　baño de la mano	スーパーバイザー　supervisor
手話　lenguaje de señas	スーパーバイジー　supervisado
除圧　descompresión	スーパービジョン　supervisión
障害　inhabilidad : impedimento	スピリチュアルケア　cuidado espiritual
障害基礎年金　pensión de inhabilidad básica	生活援助　apoyo de las tareas domésticos
障害の受容　aceptación de la inhabilidad	生活環境　ambiente del alrededor
小規模多機能型居宅介護　pequeños servicios multifuncionales del cuidado casero	生活習慣病　enfermedad relacionada con el modo de vida
少子化　natalidad decreciente	生活の質　calidad de vida

日本語	スペイン語
生活扶助	subsidio social a los indigentes
生活歴	historia de vida
清潔	limpieza
清拭	baño de esponja
精神科ソーシャルワーカー	asistente social psiquiátrico
精神障害	desorden psiquiátrico
精神障害者	gente con desorden psiquiátrico
精神保健福祉士	asistente social psiquiátrico certificado
成年後見制度	sistema de la tutela de adultos
整髪	preparación del pelo
生命の延長	extensión de la vida
生命倫理	bioética
整容	higiehe personal
世界保健機関	Organización Mundial de la Salud : OMS
脊髄損傷	lesión de la médula espinal
脊椎圧迫骨折	fractura por compresión vertebral
世帯	unidad familiar
摂食	toma de comida ; toma de alimentos
摂食障害	desorden alimenticio
セミファーラー位	posición del semi-Flower
セルフケア	autocuidado
セルフヘルプグループ	grupo del esfuerzo personal ; grupo de autoayuda
繊維	fibra
全援助	ayuda total
洗顔	limpiamiento de la cara ; el lavarse la cara
洗剤	detergente
洗浄	lavado
染色体異常	cromosoma anormal
全人格的ケア	cuidado personal total
全身清拭	baño de esponja
全身浴	baño completo
尖足	pie equino
洗濯	lavado de ropa
洗髪	lavado de cabeza
せん妄	delirio
総入れ歯	dentadura postiza
躁うつ病	psicosis maniacodepresiva
早期発見	detección temprana
装具	ortosis
掃除	limpieza
喪失体験	experiencia perdida
側臥位	posición lateral
足浴	lavado de pies
咀嚼	masticación
ソーシャルワーカー	asistente social
措置制度	remedios institucionales
措置費	costo de los remedios institucionales
体位変換	cambio de posición
体温	temperatura corporal
体温測定	medición de la temperatura corporal
退行	regresión
帯状疱疹	herpes zóster
大腿四頭筋	músculo femoral de cuadriceps
大腸癌	cáncer de colon
代読	asistencia de lectura
代筆	asistencia en escritura
代理電話	asistencia en teléfono
ダウン症候群	síndrome de Down
立ち上がり	levantarse
脱臼	dislocación
脱水症	deshidratación
他動運動	movimiento pasivo
ターミナルケア	cuidado terminal
短下肢装具	ortesis corto de extremidades inferiores
端座位	posición sentada
チアノーゼ	cianosis
地域包括支援センター	centro de cuidado comprensivo de la comunidad"
地域密着サービス	servicios de base comunitaria
チェーンストークス呼吸	respiración de Cheyne-Stokes
蓄尿障害	disturbio de la colección urinaria
知的障害	deficiente mental : DM
知的障害者	mentalmente retardado
知能	inteligencia
知能指数	cociente de inteligencia
痴呆	demencia
痴呆性老人	demencia senil
痴呆性老人の日常生活自立度	grado de la independencia de vida diaria para los ancianos con demencia
チームアプローチ	acercamiento de equipo
チームケア	cuidado de equipo
着脱	verstir y desvestir
聴覚障害	desorden auditivo
長寿社会	sociedad de la longevidad
調整交付金	subsidios del ajuste
重複障害	inhabilidades múltiples
腸閉塞	íleo
調理	cocinar
調理方法	receta
聴力レベル	nivel auditivo
直接援助技術	trabajo social directo
対麻痺	paraplejia
通所介護	servicio del día ; cuidado ambulatorio
通所リハビリテーション	rehabilitación ambulatoria
杖	bastón
杖歩行	paso con bastón
手洗い	lavarse las manos
低血圧	hipotensión
低血糖	hipoglucemia
T字杖	bastón en T
摘便	extracción del taburete ; extracción de heces
手すり	barandilla

スペイン語

日本語	Español
手引き	introducción ; guía
伝音難聴	sordera conductora
点字	Braille
電動車いす	silla de ruedas eléctrica
電動ベッド	cama eléctrica
動悸	palpitación
統合失調症	esquizofrenia
透析	diálisis
疼痛	dolor
糖尿病	diabetes
動脈硬化	arteriosclerasis
特殊寝台	cama especializada
特殊浴槽	baño especializado
特別治療食	dieta terapéutica especial
特別養護老人ホーム	hogar geriátrico del bienestar para los ancianos
読話	lectura labial
吐血	hematemesis
徒手筋力テスト	prueba manual del músculo : PMM
独居	vida solitaria
内部障害	desorden de órganos internos
難聴	pérdida auditiva
難病	enfermedades incurables
ニーズ	necesidades
日常生活活動	actividades de la vida diaria : AVD
日内変動	variación circadiana
入眠	inicio del sueño
入浴	baño
尿	orina
尿意	uresiestesia
尿器	botella de orina
尿失禁	incontinencia urinaria
尿路感染	infección de zona urinaria
認知症	demencia
認知症高齢者	ancianos con demencia
認知症高齢者の日常生活自立度	grado de la independencia de vida diaria de los ancianos con demencia
認知症対応型共同生活介護	cuidado en el hogar del grupo para los ancianos con demencia
認知症対応型通所介護	cuidado ambulatorio para los pacientes con demencia
寝返り	vuelco
寝たきり	postrado en la cama
寝たきり度	grado del postrado en cama
熱傷	quemadura
寝床	lugar para dormir
年金	pensión
脳血管障害	desorden cerebrovascular
脳血管性認知症	demencia cerebrovascular
脳血栓症	trombosis cerebral
脳梗塞	infarto cerebral
脳死	muerte cerebral
脳出血	hemorragia cerebral
脳性麻痺	parálisis cerebral : PC
脳塞栓	embolia cerebral
能力低下	incapacidad ; bajada del nivel de capacidad
ノーマライゼーション	normalización
ノンレム睡眠	sueño NREM ; sueño sin movimiento rápido de los ojos
肺炎	neumonía
徘徊	merodeo
肺癌	cancer pulmonal
肺気腫	enfisema pulmonar
バイキング食	bufé
バイスティックの7原則	7 principios de Biestek
排泄	excreción
排泄介助	cuidado de la excreción
バイタルサイン	signos vitales
排尿	micción
排尿困難	dificultad urinaria
排尿障害	desorden urinario
排便	defecación
排便障害	desorden de la defecación
廃用萎縮	atrofia por desuso
廃用症候群	síndrome del desuso
パーキンソン病	enfermedad de Parkinson
白杖	bastón blanco
白内障	catarata
長谷川式簡易認知症スケール改訂版	Demencia de Hasegawa Escala-Revisada
バックサポート	ayuda trasera
発達障害	desorden de desarrollo
発熱	fiebre
バリアフリー	sin barreras
バルンカテーテル	catéter del globo
半身浴	baño de asiento
半調理	comida situado a mitad del camino ; comida medio preparada
BMI	índice de masa corporal : IMC
被害妄想	delirio de persecución
非言語的コミュニケーション	comunicación no verbal
ビタミン	vitamina
筆記試験	examen escrito
被保険者	los asegurados
肥満	obesidad
秘密保持	confidencialidad
氷枕	almohadilla del hielo
氷嚢	bolso de hielo
日和見感染	infección oportunista
貧血	anemia
頻便	defecación frecuente
ファーラー位	posición de Fowler
フェイスシート	hoja de la cara
フォローアップ	seguimiento
腹臥位	posición boca abajo

日本語	Español	日本語	Español
副作用	efecto secundario	麻痺	parálisis
福祉	bienestar	ミキサー食	alimento del mezclador ; alimento preparado por el liquador
福祉機器	implementos de ayuda para el bienestar	ミネラル	mineral
腹式呼吸	respiración abdominal	脈拍	pulso
福祉事務所	oficina de la asistencia social	メタボリック症候群	síndrome metabólico
福祉用具	implementos de ayuda para el bienestar	滅菌	esterilización
福祉用具貸与	alquiler de implementos de ayuda para el bienestar	妄想	ilusión
フットサポート	soporte para los pies	燃え尽き症候群	síndrome de burnout
部分援助	ayuda parcial	モニタリング	seguimiento
部分清拭	baño parcial de la cama	問題行動	conducta problemática
部分浴	baño parcial	夜間せん妄	delirio de noche
プライバシー	privacidad	薬剤	droga
プライマリ・ケア	atención primaria	薬剤管理	control de medicinas ; administración de medicinas
プロフィール	perfil	薬剤師	farmacéutico
平均寿命	promedio de la vida	薬物療法	farmacoterapia
平均余命	esperanza media de vida	有料老人ホーム	hogar residencial privado
ベッド	cama	ユニットケア	cuidado de la unidad
ベッドから車いす	de la cama a la silla de ruedas	ユニバーサルファッション	diseño universal en la moda
ベッドメーキング	arreglo de la cama	要援護高齢者	Ancianos necesitados de apoyo
便器	retrete	要介護	necesidad del cuidado a largo plazo
便失禁	incontinencia fecal	要介護者	el necesitado del cuidado a largo plazo
便秘	estreñimiento	要介護度	etapa de la necesidad del cuidado a largo plazo
片麻痺	hemiplejía	要介護認定	certificación de la necesidad de largo plazo del cuidado
保育士	enfermera de niños	養護老人ホーム	hogar residencial para los ancianos
防炎素材	material ignífugo	要支援	necesidad de largo plazo de la ayuda
防汚素材	material anti-incrustante	要支援者	el necesitado de la ayuda de largo plazo
訪問介護	servicio del cuidado a domicilio	要支援認定	certificación de la necesidad de largo plazo de la ayuda
訪問看護	servicio de enfermería a domicilio	腰痛症	lumbago
訪問看護ステーション	estación de servicio de enfermería a domicilio	腰痛体操	ejercicio lumbago
訪問入浴介護	visita para cuidado de baño	腰痛予防	prevención del lumbago
訪問リハビリテーション	visita para rehabilitación	抑制	inhibición
保健師	enfermera de salud pública	浴槽	tina de baño
保険者	asegurador	予防給付	ventaja preventiva ; ventaja para la prevencion
保健所	centro de salud público	四脚杖	bastón de cuatro pies
保険料	prima de suguro	ライフサイクル	ciclo vital
歩行	paso	ライフスタイル	estilo de vida
歩行器	caminante ; andador	ライフレビュー	revisión de la vida
歩行練習	entrenamiento del paso	ラポール	relación
ポジショニング	colocación	理学療法士	terapeuta físico ; fisioterapeuta
補足給付	ventaja suplementaria	立位	posición levantada
ポータブルトイレ	retrete portátil	利尿剤	diurético
ポータブル浴槽	baño portable ; bañera portátil	リハビリテーション	rehabilitación
補聴器	prótesis de oído	リハビリテーション医学	medicina de la rehabilitación
発疹	erupción	リハビリテーション介護	cuidado de largo plazo rehabilitativo
発赤	rojez		
ボディメカニクス	mecánicas del cuerpo	留置カテーテル	catéter dejado en un órgano
ホームヘルパー	ayudante a domicilio		
ボランティア	voluntario		
ホルモン	hormona		
マット	colchón		
松葉杖	muleta		

スペイン語

流動食　dieta de liquidos
流動性知能　inteligencia fluida
利用料　costo del uso
レクリエーション　recreacion
レム睡眠　sueño REM ; sueño con movimiento rápido de los ojos
聾　sordera
老化　senilidad
老眼　presbiopía ; presbicia
老人性うつ病　depresión senil
老人性難聴　sordera senil
老人保健施設　instalación de la salud para los ancianos
老年認知症　demencia senil
老齢基礎年金　pensión básica de la vejez
老齢年金　pensión de vejez
老齢福祉年金　pensión de la vejez del bienestar
ロールプレイ　juego del papel

4．タガログ語（Tagalog）

IQ　katalinuhang kusyente
ICIDH　Pandaigdigang Klasipikasyon ng may Kapansanan at Inutil
ICF　Pandaigdigang Klasipikasyon ng Pagganap, Kapansanan at Kalusugan
ICD　Pandaigdigang Klasipikasyon ng mga sakit
アクティビティ　aktibidad；gawain
アセスメント　tasasyon
アテトーシス　athetosis
アテトーゼ　athetosis
アドボカシー　adbokasiya
アルツハイマー型認知症　Sakit sa Pagkalimot dahilan sa Katandaan
アルツハイマー病　Sakit sa Pagkalimot ng mga bagay na kailan lang nangyayari
安全管理　ligtas na pamamahala
罨法　pomentuhan
安眠　mahimbing na pagtulog
安眠援助　suporta para sa mahimbing na tulog
安楽　kaginhawaan
安楽な体位　maginhawang posisyon
意識障害　kapansanan sa katinuan
維持期リハビリテーション　rehabilitasyon para sa malalang karamdaman
萎縮　pagkatuyo ng kalamnan
移乗動作　galaw sa paglipat
移送費　bayad sa transportasyon
遺族基礎年金　pensyon para sa naulila
移動　paggalaw
移動介助　tamang galaw sa pangangalaga
移動関連福祉用具　kagamitang kaagapay sa paggalaw
移動トイレ　mabitbit na kubeta
移動浴槽　mabitbit na banyera
衣服　damit
衣服着脱　pagpalit ng damit
衣料障害　pinsala sa balat sanhi ng kasuotan
医療ソーシャルワーカー　medical social worker
医療保険制度　sistema ng pangkalusugang kasegurohan
インスリン　insyulin
インテーク　nakain at nainom
インフォーマル　di pormal
陰部清拭　paghuhugas；paglilinis ng ari ng babae at lalaki
陰部洗浄　paglilinis sa ari ng lalaki o babae
インペアメント　kapansanan
うつ病　kapighatian；kalungkutan
運営適正化委員会　komite sa tamang pamamahala ng alokasyon

運動器の機能向上　pagpapabuti sa tungkulin ng katawan
運動失調　pagkasira ng pandinig
運動障害　kawalan ng kakayahan sa paggalaw
運動療法　terapiyutikong ehersisyo
エアーパッド　sapin na may hangin
エアーマット　air mat
エイジズム　di makatarungang pakikitungo sa matatanda
エイズ　AIDS
栄養　nutrisyon
栄養改善　pagpapabuti ng nutrisyon
栄養管理　pamamahala sa nutrisyon
栄養士　dietician
栄養所要量　kinakailangang nutrisyon
栄養素　masustansyang pagkain
腋窩温　pagkuha ng temperatura sa kili-kili
壊死　nekrosis
ADL　araw-araw na gawain
NPO　di pamahalaang samahan
MRSA　klase ng bakterya na lumalaban sa meticillin na nagdudulot ng iba't-ibang impeksyon na mahirap lunasan
MMSE　pagsusuri sa estado ng pag-iisip
MMT　manwal na pagsusuri ng kalamnan
嚥下　paglunok
嚥下困難　hirap sa paglunok
嚥下性肺炎　pamamaga sa daanan ng hangin sa baga
嚥下補助剤　suplemento para sa madaling paglunok
エンゲル係数　ang saligan sa pag-aaral sa kita ng pamilya na pantustos sa pagkain
円座　pabilog na almohadon
エンパワメント　pagbibigay kapangyarihan
応益負担　bayad sa kasegurohang lunas sa kagipuran
嘔気　pagduwal
応急手当　pangunahing lunas sa kagipitan
嘔吐　pagsusuka
応能負担　prinsipyo sa kakayanan ng pagbayad
起き上がり　pagbangon
おむつ　dayaper；lampin
おむつカバー　takip sa diaper o lampin
おむつ交換　pagpalit ng dayaper；lampin
おむつ外し　pagtanggal ng diaper o lampin
臥位　nakahiga
介護　pangangalaga
介護過程　proseso ng pangangalaga
介護技術　paraan ng pangangalaga
介護休業　pagpaalam para sa pangalaga sa pamilya
介護給付　benepisyo sa pangangalaga

介護計画　plano sa pag-aalaga
介護サービス計画　plano sa serbisyo ng pangangalaga
介護支援専門員　tagapamahala sa tamang pangangalaga
介護指導　patnubay sa pangangalaga
介護者　tagapangalaga
介護職員　mga kawani na tagapangalaga
介護ニーズ　kinakailangang pangangalaga
介護認定審査会　kapulungan na nagbibigay sertipiko para sa pangangalaga
介護福祉　kapakanan ng pangangalaga
介護福祉士　sertipikado ; lisensyadong tagapangalaga ng kalusugan
介護福祉士国家試験　pambansang pagsusuri para sa sertipikado ; lisensyadong tagapangalaga ng kalusugan
介護福祉士登録　pagtatala ng CCW
介護負担　pasanin sa pangangalaga
介護報酬　bayad sa pangangalaga
介護保険　insyurans para sa pangangalaga
介護保険事業計画　plano sa proyekto ng kasegurohan
介護保険審査会　kapulungan na nagsusuri sa kasegurohan para sa pangangalaga
介護保険制度　sistema ng kasegurohan sa pangangalaga
介護保険認定調査　sertipikadong pagsusuri sa nangangailangan ng pangangalaga
介護保険法　batas ng kasegurohan sa pangangalaga
介護目標　layunin ng pangangalaga
介護用具　kagamitan sa pangangalaga
介護予防　pang ampat na pangangalaga
介護予防事業　pang ampat na trabaho para sa pangmatagalang pangangalaga
介護療養型医療施設　kagamitan sa pangangalaga ng kalusugan
介護老人福祉施設　institusyon na tagapangalaga para sa kapakanan ng matatanda
介護老人保健施設　institusyon na tagapangalaga para sa kalusugan ng matatanda
介護労働者　tagapangalaga sa institusyon
介助　pag-alalay
疥癬　galis
回想法　paggamot sa pamamagitan ng pagbabalik tanaw sa nakaraan
階段　hagdan
階段昇降　akyat at panaog sa hagdan
回復期リハビリテーション　rehabilitasyon na makapagpagaling
潰瘍　ulser
かかりつけ医　family doctor
核家族　maliit na pamilya
家計　badyet para sa pamamahay
家事　gawaing-bahay

家政　pamamahala sa gawaing-bahay
家政婦　tagapangalaga ng bahay
家族　pamilya
家族会　grupo na tumutulong sa pamilya
家族介護　pangangalaga ng matanda sa tahanan
家族介護者　tagapangalaga ng pamilya
家族関係　relasyon sa pamilya
合併症　pagluwa ng dugo
寡婦　biyudo ; biyuda
紙おむつ　disposable dayaper
過敏症侯群　kondisyon sanhi ng sobrang paggamit
加齢　pagtanda
癌　kanser
感音難聴　pagkabingi sanhi ng pagkasira ng vestibular nerve
感覚機能　tungkulin na pandamdam
換気　pagpasok ng hangin
環境整備　proteksiyon sa kalikasan
看護　pangangalaga
肝硬変　pamamaga ng atay
看護師　kursong Nars
関節　kasukasuan
関節可動域　pagitan ng paggalaw
関節リウマチ　rayuma
感染　impeksyon
感染菌　bakterya
感染症　nakakahawang sakit
感染予防　pagpigil sa impeksyon
浣腸　labatiba
観念失行　ideational apraxia
管理栄養士　rehistradong dietician
緩和ケア　pampatighaw na pangangalaga
記憶障害　kapansanan sa memorya
着替え　pagpalit ng damit
気管　lalagukan
危険防止　pagpigil sa panganib
起座位　pagbangon
義歯　pustiso
義肢装具士　dalubhasa sa paggawa ng artipisyal na parte ng katawan
基礎代謝　basal metabolism
機能維持　mapanatili ang kakayahan
機能訓練　isinasagawang pagsasanay
機能障害　kapansanan
記銘力　abilidad sa paggunita
虐待　abuso
ギャッチベッド　gatch bed
救急救命士　tekniko na nagliligtas ng buhay sa kagipitan
仰臥位　nakatihaya
共感　pakikiramay
虚弱　mahinang pangangatawan
起立性低血圧　pagbaba ng presyon dahilan sa

pagbangon
記録　talaan
筋萎縮　pagkatuyot ng kalamnan
緊急連絡先　numero para sa emergency na tawag
金銭管理　pamamahala sa pera
苦情解決　pamamaraan sa pagharap ng mga reklamo at hinaing
くも膜下出血　pagdurugo sa pagitan at himaymay na bumabalot sa utak
クリティカルパス　critical path
グループホーム　grupong bahay
グループリビング　grupong pamumuhay
グループレクリエーション　grupong libangan
グループワーク　grupong gawain
車いす　upuang de gulong
車いすからベッド　mula sa wheelchair patungo sa kama
車いすの移動　paggalaw gamit ang wheelchair
車いすの介助　pag-alalay sa paggamit ng upuang de gulong
クロックポジション　posisyon ng orasan
ケア　pangangalaga
ケアカンファレンス　komperensya sa pangangalaga
ケアチーム　kuponan ng mga nangangalaga
ケアハウス　tahanan ng matanda na walang kapansanan
ケアプラン　plano sa pag-aalaga
ケアマネジメント　pamamahala ng pangangalaga
ケアマネジャー　tagapamahala sa tamang pangangalaga
ケアワーク　pangangalaga na gawain
経管栄養　pagpapakain sa pamamagitan ng tubo
頸髄損傷　pinsala sa cervical cord
傾聴　aktibong pakikinig
契約　kasunduan
劇薬　mapanganib na gamot
下血　pagtatae na may dugo
ケースカンファレンス　pagpupulong sa kalagayan
ケースワーク　kalagayan ng gawain
血圧　presyon ng dugo
下痢　pagtatae
幻覚　kinikinita
健康　kalusugan
健康観察　obserbasyon ng kalusugan
健康保険　kaseguruhan pangkalusugan
言語障害　kapansanan sa pananalita
言語聴覚士　dalubhasa sa paggamot ng kapansanan sa pananalita at pandinig
見当識障害　kapansanan sa pagkalito
権利擁護　pagtatanggol sa karapatan
公益事業　pampublikong kagamitan
公益法人　pampublikong korporasyon
構音障害　kapansanan sa pagbigkas ng salita

後期高齢者　matandang matanda
抗菌・防臭素材　pamatay ng mikrobyo
口腔機能の向上　pagpapabuti ng pananalita
口腔ケア　pangangalaga sa bibig
合計特殊出生率　kabuuang bilang ng taong may kakahayang manganak
高血圧　mataas na presyon ng dugo；alta presyon
拘縮　paninigas ng kalamnan
拘縮予防　pagpigil sa paninigas ng kalamnan
公証人　notaryong pampubliko
公正証書　na-notaryong kasulatan
抗生物質　antibayotikong gamot na panlaban sa bakterya at impeksyon
拘束　pagsaway
後天性免疫不全症候群　acquired immune deficiency syndrome：AIDS
高齢化　populasyon ng mga matatanda
高齢期障害　mga kapansanan sanhi ng katandaan
高齢者　matanda
高齢社会　lipunan ng matatanda
高齢者虐待　pag-abuso sa mga matatanda
高齢者虐待防止法　batas ng pagpigil sa pag-aabuso ng matatanda
高齢者世帯　matandang sambahayan
声かけ　pagtawag；pagsambit
誤嚥　nabilaukan；nasamid
誤嚥性肺炎　aspiration pneumonia
呼吸　paghinga
呼吸機能障害　karamdaman sa paghinga
国際疾病分類　pandaigdigang Klasipikasyon ng mga sakit
国際障害分類　pandaigdigang Klasipikasyon ng may Kapansanan at Inutil
国際生活機能分類　pandaigdigang Klasipikasyon ng pagganap, Kapansanan at Kalusugan
国際標準化機構　pandaigdigang organisasyon para sa pamantayan ng teknikal at di teknikal na kalakalan
骨折　nabalian ng buto
骨粗鬆症　sakit sa buto sanhi ng kakulangan ng calcium
言葉かけ　pangangalaga sa komunikasyon
個別介護　pangangalaga sa bawat isa
コミュニケーション　komunikasyon
コミュニケーションエイド　pantulong sa komunikasyon
コレステロール　kolesterol
献立　putahe
座位　nakaupo
再アセスメント　muling tasasyon
在宅介護　pangangalaga sa tahanan
在宅看護　pangangalaga sa tahanan
在宅ケア　pangangalaga sa tahanan

作業療法　terapeutika sa pamamagitan ng trabaho
作業療法士　taong gumagawa ng terapeutika sa pamamagitan ng trabaho
サービス担当者会議　pulong ng mga kawani na nagbibigay serbisyo
サポートシステム　sistema ng pagsuporta
残存機能　natitirang tungkulin
散髪　paggupit ng buhok
紫外線遮蔽素材　pantakip sa ultraviolet rays
歯科衛生士　tagalinis ng ngipin
視覚障害　kapansanan sa paningin
視覚障害者　taong bulag
弛緩　malambot
止血　pagtigil ng pagdurugo
思考障害　karamdaman sa pag-iisip
自己覚知　pagkakilala sa sarili
自己決定　sariling determinasyon
自己実現　pag-unawa sa sarili
脂質異常症　karamdaman sa lipido sanhi ng pagtaas ng kolesterol at tryglycerides
自傷行為　pananakit sa sarili
自助具　kagamitang pantulong sa sarili
死生観　pananaw sa buhay at kamatayan
施設介護　pangangalaga sa loob ng institusyon
自尊心　pagpapahalaga sa sarili ; tiwala sa sarili
肢体不自由　pisikal na kapansanan
実技試験　pagsusulit sa kahusayan
失禁　di mapigilang paglabas ng ihi
失語　karamdaman sa komunikasyon o pag intindi
シーツ交換　pagpalit ng sapin ng kama
実支出　kabuuang gastos
実収入　kabuuang kita
失認　agnosia
実務経験証明書　sertipiko ng pagsasanay sa pangangalaga
自動運動　maliksing paggalaw
児童期障害　karamdaman mula pagkabata
自閉症　autism
社会資源　pinagkukunan ng yaman ng lipunan
社会の不利　kapansanan
社会福祉　kapakanan ng lipunan
社会福祉士　sertipikadong manggagawa sa lipunan
社会福祉事業　trabaho para sa kapakanan ng lipunan
社会保険　panlipunang kasegurohan
社会保障　panlipunang seguridad
社会保障審議会　sangguniang ng panlipunang kaligtasan
視野狭窄　hadlang sa paningin
視野障害　depekto sa paningin
シャワー浴　pagligo gamit ang shower
収益事業　kumikitang kabuhayan
従属人口　malayang populasyon
住宅改修　repormang pambahay

終末期　pinakamalubhang antas ng karamdaman
終末期介護　pangangalaga sa may malubhang karamdaman
主治医　personal na doktor ; doktor ng pamilya
主治医意見書　pangunahing doctor na nagpasya sa pangangalaga
手段的日常生活活動　may kinalaman sa pang araw-araw na gawain
出血　pagdurugo
守秘義務　tungkuling kompidensyal
手浴　paghugas ng kamay
手話　pakikipag-usap sa pamamagitan ng senyas
除圧　pagbabawas sa presyon ng hangin
障害　kapansanan
障害基礎年金　pangunahing pensyon sa pagkainutil
障害の受容　pagtanggap sa pagkainutil
小規模多機能型居宅介護　small multi-functional satellite home care service
少子化　pagbaba ng bilang sa panganganak
少子高齢化　pagbaba ng bilang ng panganganak at pagtaas ng populasyon ng matatanda
静脈栄養法　pagpapakain gamit ang swero
職業のリハビリテーション　bokasyonal na rehabilitasyon
食事　pagkain
食事介護　pag alalay sa pagkain
食事介助　pag-alalay sa pagpapakain
食事動作　galaw sa pagkain
食事療法　paggamot sa pamamagitan ng diyeta
褥瘡　pressure ulcer
褥瘡予防　pagpigil sa pagkakaroon ng pressure ulcer
食中毒　pagkalason sa pagkain
食品衛生　kalinisan sa pagkain
植物状態　pagkaratay sa kama sanhi ng malubhang pagkasira sa utak
植物性食品　pagkaing gulay
食欲　gana
食欲不振　kawalan ng gana sa pagkain sanhi ng sobrang pagdiyeta
ショートステイ　panandaliang pamamalagi
初老期認知症　maagang pagkaroon ng dementia
自立　kalayaan
自立支援　suporta para sa kakayanan
自立度　antas ng malayang pamumuhay
視力低下　paglabo ng paningin
事例検討　pag-aaral sa kalagayan
心気症　labis na pagkabahala sa karamdamang guni-guni lamang
人工呼吸　makina na sumusuporta sa paghinga
身上監護　personal na tagapangalaga
心身症　sakit na nagpapabago sa pisyolohiya o dahilan sa sikolohiyang tensyon

日本語	タガログ語
振戦	panginginig
心臓弁膜症	vulvular sakit sa puso
身体介護	pangangalaga sa sarili
身体機能	pisikal na gawain
信頼関係	mabuting relasyon
推奨量	ipinapayong pagdidiyeta
水分バランス	balanse sa tubig
水分補給	pagdagdag ng tubig sa katawan
水疱	paltos
睡眠	pagtulog
頭痛	sakit sa ulo
ストレス	pag-alala sanhi ng problema
ストレッチャー	stretcher
ストレングス視点	matibay na pananaw
スーパーバイザー	tagapangasiwa
スーパーバイジー	mangasiwa
スーパービジョン	pangangasiwa
スピリチュアルケア	ispirituwal na pangangalaga
生活援助	suporta sa pamumuhay
生活環境	pamumuhay sa kapaligiran
生活習慣病	mga karamdamang may kaugnayan sa uri ng pamumuhay
生活の質	kalidad ng pamumuhay
生活扶助	tulong pangkabuhayan
生活歴	kasaysayan ng buhay
清潔	kalinisan
清拭	pagpunas ng katawan sa higaan ; kama
精神科ソーシャルワーカー	social worker para sa may kapansanan sa pag iisip
精神障害	sakit sa pag-iisip
精神障害者	taong may kapansanan sa pag-iisip
精神保健福祉士	sertipikadong social worker para sa may kapansanan sa pag-iisip
成年後見制度	sistema sa pag-alaga sa taong may sapat na gulang
整髪	pag-ayos ng buhok
生命の延長	pampahaba ng buhay
生命倫理	bayoetiko
整容	lugar para sa pag ayos ng sarili
世界保健機関	pandaigdigang organisasyon sa kalusugan
脊髄損傷	pinsala sa gulugod
脊椎圧迫骨折	napinsalang gulugod sanhi ng sobrang puwersa sa likod
世帯	buong pamilya
摂食	nakain
摂食障害	hirap sa pagkain
セミファーラー位	nakahilig
セルフケア	pangangalaga sa sarili
セルフヘルプグループ	self-help group : SHG
繊維	hibla
全援助	kabuuang tulong
洗顔	paglinis ng mukha
洗剤	sabong panlaba
洗浄	paghuhugas
染色体異常	di-normal na chromosome
全人格的ケア	kabuuang pangangalaga sa sarili
全身清拭	pagpunas ng buong katawan sa higaan ; kama
全身浴	pagligo ng buong katawan sa loob ng banyera
尖足	patiyad
洗濯	paglalaba
洗髪	paghugas ng buhok
せん妄	deliryo
総入れ歯	pustiso ang buong ngipin
躁うつ病	kapansanan sa pag-iisip sanhi ng sobrang kalungkutan
早期発見	maagang pagtutop
装具	kasangkapan
掃除	paglilinis
喪失体験	walang karanasan
側臥位	higa na nakatagilid
足浴	paghugas ng paa
咀嚼	pagnguya
ソーシャルワーカー	social worker
措置制度	pamamaraan ng hakbang
措置費	halaga sa pamamaraan ng hakbang
体位変換	pagpalit ng posisyon
体温	temperatura ng katawan
体温測定	pagkuha sa temperatura ng katawan
退行	pag-urong
帯状疱疹	herpes
大腿四頭筋	kalamnan sa hita
大腸癌	kanser sa colon
代読	halili sa pagbasa
代筆	pagsulat ng liham
代理電話	halili sa telepono
ダウン症候群	Down syndrome
立ち上がり	pagtayo
脱臼	pagkalinsad
脱水症	kawalan ng tubig sa katawan
他動運動	maluwag na galaw
ターミナルケア	pangangalaga sa may malubhang karamdaman
短下肢装具	SLB [suhay sa maikling paa]
端座位	nakaupo sa kama
チアノーゼ	cyanosis
地域包括支援センター	sentro ng komunidad na may konprehensibong pangangalaga
地域密着サービス	serbisyong pangangalaga na nakabase sa komunidad
チェーンストークス呼吸	Cheyne-sokes breathing
蓄尿障害	bagabag sa pagkolekta ng ihi
知的障害	kakulangan sa pag-iisip
知的障害者	taong may kakulangan sa pag-iisip
知能	katalinuhan

知能指数　IQ
痴呆　sakit sa pagkalimot
痴呆性老人　makakalimuting matanda
痴呆性老人の日常生活自立度　antas ng malayang pamumuhay ng mga matandang may dementia
チームアプローチ　pakikitungo ng pangkat
チームケア　pangkat ng nangangalaga
着脱　pagbihis at paghubad ng damit
聴覚障害　kapansanan sa pandinig
長寿社会　samahan ng mga matatanda
調整交付金　pagsasaayos ng tulong
重複障害　maraming kapansanan
腸閉塞　balakid sa bituka
調理　pagluluto
調理方法　resipe
聴力レベル　antas ng pandinig
直接援助技術　tuwirang suportang teknikal
対麻痺　paralisa sa ibabang bahagi ng katawan
通所介護　serbisyong pang-araw
通所リハビリテーション　pangangalagang pang-araw
杖　tungkod
杖歩行　tungkod
手洗い　paghugas ng kamay
低血圧　pagbaba ng presyon ng dugo
低血糖　pagbaba ng blood sugar sa dugo
T字杖　hugis T na tungkod
摘便　pagsusuri ng tae
手すり　sanggalan ; hawakan sa paglakad
手引き　paggabay gamit ang kamay
伝音難聴　pagkabingi
点字　Braille
電動車いす　de-kuryenteng wheelchair
電動ベッド　de-kuryenteng kama
動悸　pagbilis ng pintig ng puso
統合失調症　schizophrenia
透析　dayalisis
疼痛　masakit
糖尿病　diyabetes
動脈硬化　paninikip o pagbara ng daanan ng dugo
特殊寝台　gatch bed
特殊浴槽　di pangkaraniwang paliguan
特別治療食　espesyal na terapiyutikong diyeta
特別養護老人ホーム　tahanan para sa kapakanan ng matanda
読話　nagsasalitang mag-isa
吐血　pagsusuka ng dugo galing sa GIT
徒手筋力テスト　manwal na pagsusuri ng kalamnan
独居　malungkot na buhay
内部障害　karamdaman sa loob ng bahagi ng katawan
難聴　pagkawala ng pandinig
難病　walang lunas na karamdaman
ニーズ　pangangailangan
日常生活活動　pang araw- araw na gawain

日内変動　siklo sa pagbabago ng pisyolohiya at gawi ng tao
入眠　nakatulog
入浴　pagligo
尿　ihi
尿意　naiihi
尿器　botelyang may hawakan para sa pag-ihi
尿失禁　di mapigilang paglabas ng ihi
尿路感染　impeksiyon sa ihi
認知症　sakit sa pagkalimot
認知症高齢者　makakalimuting matanda
認知症高齢者の日常生活自立度　antas ng malayang pamumuhay ng mga matandang may dementia
認知症対応型共同生活介護　bahay na nangangalaga sa mga malilimuting matanda
認知症対応型通所介護　pang-araw na pangangalaga sa taong ulyanin
寝返り　paggulong papunta sa kabilang posisyon
寝たきり　nakaratay sa kama
寝たきり度　antas ng pagkaratay sa kama
熱傷　pagkapaso
寝床　kama
年金　pensiyon
脳血管障害　karamdaman sa bahagi ng utak
脳血管性認知症　pagkakaroon ng dementia sanhi ng pagkasira ng ugat na nag uugnay sa utak at puso
脳血栓症　pamumuo ng dugo sa ugat ng cerebral
脳梗塞　pagkaharang sa pagbibigay ng dugo sa utak
脳死　pagtigil sa lahat ng galaw ng utak
脳出血　pagdurugo sa cerebral
脳性麻痺　pagkawala ng kontrol sa galaw sanhi ng pagkasira ng bahagi ng utak
脳塞栓　pagbabara ng ugat sa cerebral
能力低下　kapansanan
ノーマライゼーション　pagbabalik sa normal
ノンレム睡眠　hindi mabilis na paggalaw ng mata
肺炎　pulmonya
徘徊　pagala gala
肺癌　kanser sa baga
肺気腫　pagkasira sa daanan ng hangin sa baga
バイキング食　buffet
バイスティックの7原則　pitong prinsipyo ni Biestek
排泄　pagdudumi
排泄介助　pag-aalalay sa pagdumi
バイタルサイン　vital sign
排尿　pag-ihi
排尿困難　hirap sa pag-ihi
排尿障害　karamdaman sa pag-ihi
排便　pagtae
排便障害　karamdaman sa pagbawas
廃用萎縮　kawalan ng silbi ng kalamnan sanhi ng di paggamit
廃用症候群　di makakilos sanhi ng karamdaman

パーキンソン病　Parkinson's disease
白杖　tungkod na ginagamit ng mga bulag
白内障　katarata
長谷川式簡易認知症スケール改訂版　HDS-R [siyam (9) na tanong para sa pagsusuri ng matandang may dementia]
バックサポート　suporta sa likod
発達障害　namumuong karamdaman
発熱　lagnat
バリアフリー　walang hadlang
バルンカテーテル　balloon catheter
半身浴　pagligo na di binabasa ang ulo
半調理　kalagitnaan ng pagkain
BMI　indikador para malaman ang timbang at taas sa pamamagitan ng kalkulasyon
被害妄想　paranoya
非言語的コミュニケーション　di pasalitang komunikasyon
ビタミン　bitamin
筆記試験　nakasulat na pagsusuri
被保険者　ang nagseguro
肥満　labis na katabaan
秘密保持　pagkakompidensyal
氷枕　unan na may yelo
氷嚢　ice bag
日和見感染　nakakasamang impeksyon
貧血　anemya o kakulangan sa dugo
頻便　madalas na pagtatae
ファーラー位　nakaupong nakasandal
フェイスシート　pamunas para sa mukha
フォローアップ　sundan
腹臥位　nakadapa
副作用　masamang epekto
福祉　kapakanan
福祉機器　kagamitan para sa kapakanan
腹式呼吸　paghinga sa tiyan
福祉事務所　opisina ng panlipunanng kapakanan
福祉用具　tulong para sa lipunan
福祉用具貸与　pag-upa ng mga kagamitang kaagapay para sa kapakanan
浮腫　pamamaga
フットサポート　suporta sa paa
部分援助　kaunting suporta ; alalay
部分清拭　pagpunas sa bahagi ng katawan sa kama
部分浴　paghuhugas sa bahagi ng katawan
プライバシー　pribado
プライマリ・ケア　pangunahing pangangalaga
プロフィール　profile
平均寿命　haba ng buhay
平均余命　karaniwang haba ng buhay
ベッド　kama
ベッドから車いす　mula kama papuntang wheelchair
ベッドメーキング　pagpalit ng sapin sa kama

便器　arinola
便失禁　di mapigilang pagdumi
便秘　tibi
片麻痺　kalahati ng katawan na paralisado
保育士　sertipikadong guro ng pre-school
防炎素材　kagamitang di nasusunog ng apoy
防汚素材　kagamitang pangontra-dumi
訪問介護　tulong sa gawaing bahay
訪問看護　nars na bumibisita sa bahay
訪問看護ステーション　estasyon ng bumibisitang nars
訪問入浴介護　bumibisita para magpaligo
訪問リハビリテーション　bumibisita para sa rehabilitasyon
保健師　pampublikong nars
保険者　nagseseguro
保健所　sentro ng pampublikong kalusugan
保険料　uri ng bayad sa nagseseguro
歩行　paglakad
歩行器　kagamitan sa paglakad
歩行練習　pagsasanay sa paglalakad
ポジショニング　pagpoposisyon
補足給付　karagdagang benepisyo
ポータブルトイレ　mabitbit na kubeta
ポータブル浴槽　mabitbit na banyera
補聴器　tulong pandinig
発疹　butlig-butlig
発赤　pamumula
ボディメカニクス　body mechanics
ホームヘルパー　katulong sa bahay
ボランティア　boluntaryo
ホルモン　hormone
マット　banig
松葉杖　tungkod
麻痺　paralisado
ミキサー食　blended food
ミネラル　mineral
脈拍　pulso
メタボリック症候群　metabolic syndrome
滅菌　isterilisasyon
妄想　guni-guni
燃え尽き症候群　pagkayamot
モニタリング　pagmonitor
問題行動　problemadong pag-uugali
夜間せん妄　deliryo sa gabi
薬剤　gamot
薬剤管理　pamamahala ng mga gamot
薬剤師　parmaseutiko
薬物療法　pharmacotherapy
有料老人ホーム　pribadong tahanan para sa matatanda
ユニットケア　yunit na pangangalaga
ユニバーサルファッション　pandaigdigang uso
要援護高齢者　matandang nangangailangan ng tulong
要介護　nangangailangan ng pangangalga

タガログ語

要介護者　taong nangangailangan ng pangangalaga
要介護度　taas yugto sa pangangailangan ng matagalang pangangalaga
要介護認定　sertipikasyon para sa pangangailangan ng matagalang pangangalaga
養護老人ホーム　tahanan para sa matatanda
要支援　kailangan na tulong
要支援者　taong nangangailangan ng suporta
要支援認定　sertipikasyon sa kinakailangang tulong
腰痛症　pananakit sa ibabang bahagi ng likod
腰痛体操　ehersisyo para sa may sakit sa ibabang bahagi ng likod
腰痛予防　pag-iwas sa pananakit ng ibabang bahagi ng likod
抑制　pagsaway
浴槽　banyera
予防給付　pang-ampat na benepisyo
四脚杖　tungkod na may apat na paa
ライフサイクル　siklo ng buhay
ライフスタイル　istilo ng pamumuhay
ライフレビュー　paggunita ng buhay
ラポール　mabuting relasyon
理学療法士　physical therapist
立位　patayong posisyon
利尿剤　pampaihi
リハビリテーション　rehabilitasyon
リハビリテーション医学　gamot pangrehabilitasyon
リハビリテーション介護　rehabilitasyong pangangalaga
留置カテーテル　indwelling catheter
流動食　likidong diyeta
流動性知能　kabutihan ng tubig
利用料　halaga ng paggamit
レクリエーション　libangan
レム睡眠　mabilis na paggalaw ng mata habang natutulog
聾　pagkabingi
老化　katandaan
老眼　pagkalabo ng paningin
老人性うつ病　kalungkutan ng mga matatanda
老人性難聴　pagkabingi sanhi ng katandaan
老人保健施設　mga kagamitan para sa kalusugan ng mga matatanda
老年認知症　sakit sa pagkalimot sanhi ng katandaan
老齢基礎年金　pangunahing pensyon ng mga matatanda
老齢年金　pensyon ng mga matatanda
老齢福祉年金　pensyon para sa kapakanan ng mga matatanda
ロールプレイ　pagsasadula

5．中国語（Chinese）

IQ　智商
ICIDH　国际残损、残疾和残障分类
ICF　国际功能、残疾和健康分类
ICD　国际疾病分类
アクティビティ　活动
アセスメント　评估
アテトーシス　手足徐动症
アテトーゼ　手足徐动症
アドボカシー　主张；辩护；维护权利
アルツハイマー型認知症　阿尔茨海默型老年痴呆症；阿尔茨海默氏症痴呆
アルツハイマー病　阿尔茨海默病
安全管理　安全管理
罨法　罨法
安眠　安眠
安眠援助　辅助安眠
安楽　舒适
安楽な体位　舒适的姿势；舒适体位
意識障害　意识障碍
維持期リハビリテーション　维持期康复
萎縮　萎缩
移乗動作　移乘动作
移送費　转送费
遺族基礎年金　遗属基本养老金
移動　转移；移动
移動介護　移动介护
移動関連福祉用具　助行器
移動トイレ　移动式厕所
移動浴槽　移动式浴缸
衣服　衣服
衣服着脱　穿脱衣服；衣服穿脱
衣料障害　衣料过敏
医療ソーシャルワーカー　医疗社会工作者
医療保険制度　医疗保险制度
インスリン　胰岛素
インテーク　受理；面试
インフォーマル　非正式的
陰部清拭　擦洗阴部
陰部洗浄　清洗阴部
インペアメント　功能障碍
うつ病　抑郁症
運営適正化委員会　投诉处理委员会；合理化运营指导委员会
運動器の機能向上　改善人体运动器官的功能
運動失調　运动失调
運動障害　运动障碍
運動療法　运动疗法
エアーパッド　空气睡垫
エアーマット　空气垫
エイジズム　老年歧视

エイズ　获得性免疫缺陷综合征；后天性免疫缺陷症候群
栄養　营养
栄養改善　营养改善
栄養管理　营养管理
栄養士　营养师
栄養所要量　营养所需量；推荐膳食供给量
栄養素　营养素
腋窩温　腋下体温
壊死　坏死
ADL　日常生活能力
NPO　非营利组织
MRSA　耐甲氧西林金黄色葡萄球菌
MMSE　简易智能量表
MMT　徒手肌力测试
嚥下　吞咽
嚥下困難　吞咽困难
嚥下性肺炎　吸入性肺炎
嚥下補助食　下咽防噎辅助剂
エンゲル係数　恩格尔系数
円座　圆形坐垫
エンパワメント　赋权；授权
応益負担　根据费用支出负担
嘔気　恶心；想吐
応急手当　急救措施
嘔吐　呕吐
応能負担　根据支付能力负担
起き上がり　坐起来；站起来；起床
おむつ　尿布
おむつカバー　尿布套；尿布罩
おむつ交換　换尿布
おむつ外し　去除尿布
臥位　卧位
介護　介护；护理；照料
介護過程　介护过程
介護技術　介护技术
介護休業　介护休假
介護給付　介护补助
介護計画　介护计划
介護サービス計画　介护服务计划
介護支援専門員　介护支援专门员
介護指導　介护指导
介護者　提供护理的人；介护者
介護職員　介护工作人员；介护职员
介護ニーズ　介护需求
介護認定審査会　介护评定审查会
介護福祉　介护福利
介護福祉士　介护福利士
介護福祉士国家試験　介护福利士全国统一考试
介護福祉士登録　介护福利士注册
介護負担　介护压力；介护负担

中国語

介護報酬	介护报酬	浣腸	灌肠
介護保険	介护保险	観念失行	观念性失用
介護保険事業計画	介护保险事业计划	管理栄養士	注册营养师
介護保険審査会	介护保险审查会	緩和ケア	安宁疗护
介護保険制度	介护保险制度	記憶障害	记忆障碍
介護保険認定調査	介护保险评定调查	着替え	换衣服
介護保険法	介护保险法	気管	气管
介護目標	介护目标	危険防止	防止危险
介護用具	介护用具	起座位	直立姿势
介護予防	介护预防	義歯	义齿；假牙
介護予防事業	介护预防事业	義肢装具士	假肢安装矫正师
介護療養型医療施設	介护疗养型医疗机构	基礎代謝	基础代谢
介護老人福祉施設	老年人介护福利机构	機能維持	机能维持
介護老人保健施設	老年人介护保健机构	機能訓練	机能训练
介護労働者	以介护为工作来提供介护的人；介护劳动者	機能障害	机能障碍
介助	帮助他人起居；搀扶；辅助	記銘力	铭记能力
疥癬	疥癣	虐待	虐待
回想法	怀旧疗法	ギャッチベッド	盖奇士床；活动靠背床
階段	楼梯；台阶	救急救命士	急救救护员
階段昇降	上下楼梯；上下台阶	仰臥位	仰卧位
回復期リハビリテーション	恢复期康复	共感	共鸣
潰瘍	溃疡	虚弱	虚弱
かかりつけ医	经常就诊的医生	起立性低血圧	起立性低血压
核家族	核心家庭	記録	记录
家計	家庭收支；家庭理财	筋萎縮	肌肉萎缩
家事	家务事；家务	緊急連絡先	紧急联络方式
家政	家政	金銭管理	金钱管理
家政婦	家政服务员	苦情解決	解决投诉
家族	家属；家庭；家人	くも膜下出血	蛛网膜下腔出血
家族会	家属自助会	クリティカルパス	医疗关键路径
家族介護	由家人提供介护；家庭介护	グループホーム	集体生活之家
家族介護者	为家人提供介护的家庭成员；家庭介护者	グループリビング	集体生活
家族関係	家庭关系	グループレクリエーション	集体文娱活动
合併症	并发症	グループワーク	小组工作；团体工作
寡婦	寡妇	車いす	轮椅
紙おむつ	纸尿裤	車いすからベッド	从轮椅移到床上
過用症候群	过度使用综合征	車いすの移動	使用轮椅移动
加齢	年龄增长；老化	車いすの介助	使用轮椅时的辅助
癌	癌症	クロックポジション	钟点方位辨物方法
感音難聴	感音神经性重听	ケア	护理；照顾
感覚機能	感觉功能	ケアカンファレンス	护理会议
換気	换气	ケアチーム	护理团队
環境整備	完善环境	ケアハウス	老人公寓
看護	看护；护理	ケアプラン	护理计划
肝硬変	肝硬化	ケアマネジメント	护理管理
看護師	护士	ケアマネジャー	介护支援专门员
関節	关节	ケアワーク	护理工作；照顾工作
関節可動域	关节可活动度	経管栄養	胃管喂食
関節リウマチ	类风湿性关节炎	頸髄損傷	颈髓损伤
感染	感染；传染	傾聴	倾听
感染菌	感染菌	契約	契约；合同
感染症	传染病	劇薬	烈性药
感染予防	预防传染	下血	便血；肛门出血

ケースカンファレンス	个案会议	再アセスメント	重新评估
ケースワーク	个案工作	在宅介護	居家介护
血圧	血压	在宅看護	居家看护；居家护理
下痢	腹泻	在宅ケア	居家照顾
幻覚	幻觉	作業療法	作业疗法
健康	健康	作業療法士	作业疗法师
健康観察	健康观察	サービス担当者会議	服务负责人会议
健康保険	健康保险	サポートシステム	支援体系
言語障害	语言障碍	残存機能	残余机能
言語聴覚士	语言听力治疗师	散髪	理发
見当識障害	判断障碍	紫外線遮蔽素材	紫外线遮蔽材料
権利擁護	维护权利	歯科衛生士	牙科保健师
公益事業	公益事业	視覚障害	视力残疾；视觉障碍
公益法人	公益法人	視覚障害者	视力残疾人；视力障碍者
構音障害	构音障碍	弛緩	松弛；松散
後期高齢者	75岁以上的老年人	止血	止血
抗菌・防臭素材	抗菌・防臭材料	思考障害	思考障碍
口腔機能の向上	改善口腔功能	自己覚知	援助者的自我评价；援助者的自我认知
口腔ケア	口腔护理	自己決定	自主决定
合計特殊出生率	总和生育率	自己実現	自我实现
高血圧	高血压	脂質異常症	高脂血症
拘縮	拘挛	自傷行為	自伤行为
拘縮予防	拘挛预防	自助具	自助器具
公証人	公证人	死生観	生死观
公正証書	公证书	施設介護	机构介护
抗生物質	抗生素	自尊心	自尊心
拘束	限制；束缚；拘束	肢体不自由	肢体残疾
後天性免疫不全症候群	获得性免疫缺陷综合征；艾滋病	実技試験	实际操作考试
高齢化	老龄化	失禁	失禁
高齢期障害	老龄期障碍	失語	失语
高齢者	老年人；老人	シーツ交換	换床单
高齢社会	老龄社会	実支出	实际支出
高齢者虐待	虐待老人	実収入	实际收入
高齢者虐待防止法	防止虐待老人法	失認	失认
高齢者世帯	老年人家庭	実務経験証明書	实际工作经验证明书
声かけ	打招呼	自動運動	自主运动
誤嚥	误咽；误吞	児童期障害	儿童期障碍
誤嚥性肺炎	吸入性肺炎	自閉症	自闭症
呼吸	呼吸	社会資源	社会资源
呼吸機能障害	呼吸机能障碍	社会的不利	不利于社会
国際疾病分類	国际疾病分类	社会福祉	社会福利
国際障害分類	国际残损、残疾和残障分类	社会福祉士	社会福祉士
国際生活機能分類	国际功能、残疾和健康分类	社会福祉事業	社会福利事业
国際標準化機構	国际标准化组织	社会保険	社会保险
骨折	骨折	社会保障	社会保障
骨粗鬆症	骨质疏松症	社会保障審議会	社会保障审议会
言葉かけ	言语鼓励	視野狭窄	可视范围狭窄
個別介護	个别介护	視障害	视野障碍
コミュニケーション	沟通；交流	シャワー浴	淋浴
コミュニケーションエイド	沟通器械；沟通工具	収益事業	营利事业
コレステロール	胆固醇	従属人口	被抚养人口
献立	食谱	住宅改修	住房整修
座位	坐姿	終末期	末期；临终期

中国語

日本語	中国語	日本語	中国語
終末期介護	末期介护；临终期介护	ストレッチャー	担架车
主治医	主治医生	ストレングス視点	优势观点；强项观点
主治医意見書	主治医生意见书	スーパーバイザー	督导员
手段的日常生活活動	工具性日常生活活动	スーパーバイジー	被督导者
出血	出血	スーパービジョン	督导
守秘義務	保密义务	スピリチュアルケア	灵性照顾；精神关爱
手浴	手浴	生活援助	生活援助
手話	手语	生活環境	生活环境
除圧	减压	生活習慣病	生活习惯病
障害	残疾；障碍	生活の質	生活质量
障害基礎年金	伤残基本养老金	生活扶助	生活扶助；生活救济
障害の受容	接受伤残事实	生活歴	生活经历
小規模多機能型居宅介護	小规模多功能型居家介护	清潔	清洁
少子化	少子化	清拭	擦拭
少子高齢化	少子老龄化	精神科ソーシャルワーカー	精神科社会工作者
静脈栄養法	静脉注射营养法	精神障害	精神障碍
職業的リハビリテーション	职业康复	精神障害者	精神病患者
食事	进餐；用餐；饮食	精神保健福祉士	精神保健福祉士
食事介護	进餐介护	成年後見制度	成年人监护制度
食事介助	进餐辅助	整髪	理发；梳理头发
食事動作	进餐动作	生命の延長	生命的延长；延长生命
食事療法	饮食疗法	生命倫理	生命伦理
褥瘡	褥疮	整容	整理面容；修饰外表
褥瘡予防	预防褥疮	世界保健機関	世界卫生组织
食中毒	食物中毒	脊髄損傷	脊髓损伤
食品衛生	食品卫生	脊椎圧迫骨折	脊椎压迫骨折
植物状態	植物状态	世帯	家庭
植物性食品	植物性食品	摂食	摄食
食欲	食欲	摂食障害	摄食障碍
食欲不振	食欲不振	セミファーラー位	半斜坡卧位
ショートステイ	短期入所；短期居住	セルフケア	自我护理
初老期認知症	早老性痴呆	セルフヘルプグループ	自助团体
自立	自立	繊維	纤维
自立支援	自立支援；自立援助	全援助	全面援助
自立度	自立度；自立程度	洗顔	洗脸
視力低下	视力下降	洗剤	洗涤剂
事例検討	个案讨论	洗浄	洗净
心気症	疑病症	染色体異常	染色体异常
人工呼吸	人工呼吸	全人格的ケア	全面的个人照顾
身上監護	个人监护	全身清拭	擦拭全身
心身症	心身疾病	全身浴	全身浴
振戦	震颤	尖足	下垂足
心臓弁膜症	心脏瓣膜病	洗濯	洗衣服
身体介護	身体介护	洗髪	洗头
身体機能	身体机能	せん妄	妄想；幻觉
信頼関係	信赖关系	総入れ歯	全口义齿
推奨量	推荐摄食量	躁うつ病	躁郁症
水分バランス	水分平衡	早期発見	早期发现
水分補給	补充水分	装具	肢体矫正辅助用具
水疱	水疱	掃除	扫除
睡眠	睡眠	喪失体験	丧失体验
頭痛	头痛	側臥位	侧卧姿
ストレス	压力	足浴	足浴

咀嚼　咀嚼
ソーシャルワーカー　社会工作者
措置制度　措置制度
措置費　措置費
体位変換　变换姿势
体温　体温
体温測定　测量体温
退行　退化
帯状疱疹　带状疱疹
大腿四頭筋　股四头肌
大腸癌　大肠癌
代読　代读
代筆　代笔
代理電話　代理打电话
ダウン症候群　唐氏综合征
立ち上がり　起身
脱白　脱白
脱水症　脱水症
他動運動　被动运动
ターミナルケア　临终关怀；临终护理
短下肢装具　踝足矫正辅助用具
端座位　端坐姿
チアノーゼ　发绀；青紫
地域包括支援センター　地区综合援助中心
地域密着サービス　紧贴社区的服务
チェーンストークス呼吸　潮式呼吸
蓄尿障害　蓄尿障碍
知的障害　智力残疾
知的障害者　智力残疾人
知能　智力
知能指数　智商
痴呆　痴呆
痴呆性老人　痴呆症老人
痴呆性老人の日常生活自立度　痴呆症老人的日常生活自立度
チームアプローチ　组队工作法
チームケア　团队护理
着脱　穿脱衣服
聴覚障害　听觉障碍
長寿社会　长寿社会
調整交付金　调整补助金
重複障害　多种残疾
腸閉塞　肠梗阻
調理　烹饪
調理方法　烹饪方法
聴力レベル　听力水平
直接援助技術　直接援助技术
対麻痺　截瘫
通所介護　日间机构介护；日托介护
通所リハビリテーション　日间机构康复；日托康复
杖　手杖
杖歩行　拄拐走步；使用手杖走路
手洗い　洗手

低血圧　低血压
低血糖　低血糖
T字杖　T字手杖
摘便　采便
手すり　扶手
手引き　引路
伝音難聴　传导性重听
点字　盲文
電動車いす　电动轮椅
電動ベッド　电动床
動悸　心悸
統合失調症　精神分裂症
透析　透析
疼痛　疼痛
糖尿病　糖尿病
動脈硬化　动脉硬化
特殊寝台　特殊床
特殊浴槽　特殊浴缸
特別治療食　特殊治疗食物
特別養護老人ホーム　特别养护老人院
読話　读唇语
吐血　吐血；呕血
徒手筋力テスト　徒手肌力测试
独居　独居
内部障害　身体内部残疾
難聴　重听
難病　难治之症
ニーズ　需求
日常生活活動　日常生活活动
日内変動　昼夜节律
入眠　入睡
入浴　入浴；洗澡；淋浴
尿　尿
尿意　尿意
尿器　泌尿设备
尿失禁　尿失禁
尿路感染　尿路感染
認知症　痴呆症；失智症
認知症高齢者　失智症老年人
認知症高齢者の日常生活自立度　失智症老年人的日常生活自立度
認知症対応型共同生活介護　失智症対应型集体生活介护
認知症対応型通所介護　失智症対应型日间机构介护
寝返り　换睡姿；翻身
寝たきり　卧床不起
寝たきり度　卧床不起的程度
熱傷　烫伤；烧伤
寝床　床；被窝儿
年金　养老金；年金
脳血管障害　脑血管障碍
脳血管性認知症　脑血管性失智症
脳血栓症　脑血栓
脳梗塞　脑栓塞

中国語

脳死　脳死	福祉　福利
脳出血　脳出血	福祉機器　福利器械
脳性麻痺　脳瘫	腹式呼吸　腹式呼吸
脳塞栓　脳梗塞	福祉事務所　福利事务所
能力低下　能力下降；能力低下	福祉用具　福利用具
ノーマライゼーション　常态化；正常化；正规化	福祉用具貸与　福利用具出租
ノンレム睡眠　非快动眼睡眠	浮腫　浮肿
肺炎　肺炎	フットサポート　脚踏
徘徊　徘徊	部分援助　部分援助
肺癌　肺癌	部分清拭　部分擦拭
肺気腫　肺气肿	部分浴　部分浴
バイキング食　自助餐	プライバシー　个人隐私
バイスティックの7原則　贝斯提克的七大原则	プライマリ・ケア　初级护理；初级保健护理
排泄　排泄	プロフィール　人物简介；简况
排泄介助　排泄辅助	平均寿命　平均寿命
バイタルサイン　生命体征	平均余命　平均剩余寿命
排尿　排尿	ベッド　床
排尿困難　排尿困难	ベッドから車いす　从床移乘到轮椅
排尿障害　排尿障碍	ベッドメーキング　铺床法；铺床
排便　排便	便器　便器；马桶
排便障害　排便障碍	便失禁　大便失禁
廃用萎縮　废用性萎缩	便秘　便秘
廃用症候群　废用综合征	片麻痺　偏瘫
パーキンソン病　帕金森氏病	保育士　注册儿童保育员
白杖　盲杖	防炎素材　防燃材料；防火材料
白内障　白内障	防汚素材　防污材料
長谷川式簡易認知症スケール改訂版　长谷川式简易痴呆症量表修订版	訪問介護　上门介护；访问介护
	訪問看護　上门看护；访问看护
バックサポート　护背	訪問看護ステーション　上门看护工作站；访问看护工作站
発達障害　发育障碍	
発熱　发烧	訪問入浴介護　上门沐浴介护；家庭入浴介护
バリアフリー　无障碍	訪問リハビリテーション　上门康复；访问康复
バルンカテーテル　气囊导管	保健師　保健师
半身浴　半身浴	保険者　保险人
半調理　半烹饪	保健所　保健所
BMI　身体质量指数	保険料　保险费
被害妄想　被害妄想症	歩行　歩行；走路
非言語的コミュニケーション　非言语性沟通	歩行器　歩行器
ビタミン　维生素	歩行練習　歩行练习
筆記試験　笔试	ポジショニング　定位；体位保持
被保険者　被保险人	補足給付　差额补贴
肥満　肥胖	ポータブルトイレ　便携式马桶
秘密保持　保密	ポータブル浴槽　便携式浴缸
氷枕　冰枕	補聴器　助听器
氷嚢　冰袋	発疹　皮疹；发疹
日和見感染　机会感染	発赤　发红
貧血　贫血	ボディメカニクス　人体力学
頻便　便频	ホームヘルパー　家庭护理服务员
ファーラー位　斜坡卧位	ボランティア　志愿者
フェイスシート　个人基本情况表	ホルモン　激素
フォローアップ　随访；回访	マット　垫子
腹臥位　俯卧位	松葉杖　拐杖
副作用　副作用	麻痺　麻痹；瘫痪

ミキサー食　半流食
ミネラル　矿物质
脈拍　脉搏
メタボリック症候群　代谢综合征
滅菌　灭菌
妄想　幻想；胡思乱想；妄想
燃え尽き症候群　心身耗竭综合征
モニタリング　監測
問題行動　问题行为
夜間せん妄　夜间妄想
薬剤　药剂
薬剤管理　药剂管理
薬剤師　药剂师
薬物療法　药物疗法
有料老人ホーム　收费养老院
ユニットケア　单元照顾；单元护理
ユニバーサルファッション　通用时装
要援護高齢者　需要援助护理的老年人
要介護　需要介护
要介護者　需要介护的人
要介護度　需要介护等级
要介護認定　需要介护评定
養護老人ホーム　养护老人院
要支援　需要支援
要支援者　需要支援服务的人
要支援認定　需要支援程度评定
腰痛症　腰痛
腰痛体操　缓解腰痛的体操
腰痛予防　预防腰痛
抑制　抑制
浴槽　浴缸
予防給付　预防补助
四脚杖　四支点杖；四支点拐杖
ライフサイクル　生命周期
ライフスタイル　生活方式
ライフレビュー　生命回顾
ラポール　友好和信赖关系；亲和感；默契
理学療法士　理疗师
立位　站姿
利尿剤　利尿剂
リハビリテーション　康复
リハビリテーション医学　康复医学
リハビリテーション介護　康复介护
留置カテーテル　留置导管
流動食　流食
流動性知能　液化智力
利用料　使用费
レクリエーション　文娱
レム睡眠　快动眼睡眠
聾　耳聋
老化　老化；衰老
老眼　老花眼
老人性うつ病　老年性抑郁症

老人性難聴　老年性重听
老人保健施設　老年人保健机构
老年認知症　老年失智症
老齢基礎年金　基本养老金
老齢年金　养老金
老齢福祉年金　福利养老金
ロールプレイ　角色扮演

中国語

6. ドイツ語 (German)

IQ　Intelligenzquotient [M]
ICIDH　Internationale Klassifikation [F] der Schädigungen, Behinderungen, Beeinträchtigungen
ICF　Internationale Klassifikation [F] der Funktionsfähigkeit, Behinderung und Gesundheit
ICD　Internationale Klassifikation [F] der Krankheiten
アクティビティ　Aktivität [F]
アセスント　Beurteilung [F]
アテトーシス　Athetose [F]
アテトーゼ　Athetose [F]
アドボカシー　Advokatur [F]
アルツハイマー型認知症　Demenz [F] bei Alzheimer-Krankheit
アルツハイマー病　Alzheimer-Krankheit [F]
安全管理　Sicherheitskontrolle [F]
罨法　Umschlag [M]
安眠　guter Schlaf [M]
安眠援助　Einschlafhilfe [F]
安楽　Komfort [M]
安楽な体位　komfortable Position [F]
意識障害　Bewusstseinsstörung [F]
維持期リハビリテーション　Langzeitrehabilitation [F]
萎縮　Atrophie [F]
移乗動作　Transfer [M]
移送費　Transportkosten [Pl]
遺族基礎年金　Hinterbliebenengrundrente [F]
移動　Mobilität [F]
移動介護　Mobilitätshilfe [F]
移動関連福祉用具　Beweglichkeitshilfen [Pl]
移動トイレ　Toilettenstuhl [M]
移動浴槽　mobile Badewanne [F]
衣服　Kleidung [F]
衣服着脱　Kleidung [F] wechseln
衣料障害　Hautreizung [F] durch Kleidung
医療ソーシャルワーカー　medizinische/r Sozialarbeiter/in
医療保険制度　Krankenversicherungssystem [N]
インスリン　Insulin [N]
インテーク　Aufnahmebefragung [F]
インフォーマル　informell
陰部清拭　Genitalhygiene [F]
陰部洗浄　Genitalspülung [F]
インペアメント　Beeinträchtigung [F]
うつ病　Depression [F]
運営適正化委員会　Pflegeaufsichtsrat [M]
運動器の機能向上　Beweglichkeitssteigerung [F]
運動失調　Ataxie [F]
運動障害　motorische Störung [F]
運動療法　Sporttherapie [F]
エアーパッド　Wechseldruckmatratze [F]

エアーマット　Luftmatratze [F]
エイジズム　Altersdiskriminierung [F]
エイズ　Aids [N]
栄養　Ernährung [F]
栄養改善　Ernährungsverbesserung [F]
栄養管理　Ernährungsverwaltung [N]
栄養士　Ernährungsspezialist/in
栄養所要量　empfohlene Tagesdosis [F] ; recommended dietary allowance : RDA
栄養素　Nährstoff [M]
腋窩温　Achselhöhlentemperatur [F]
壊死　Nekrose [F]
ADL　Aktivitäten [Pl] des täglichen Lebens : ATL
NPO　gemeinnützige Organisation [F]
MRSA　Methicillinresistenter Staphylococcus aureus [M]
MMSE　Mini-Mental-Status-Test [M]
MMT　Manueller Muskeltest [M]
嚥下　Schlucken [N]
嚥下困難　Schluckbeschwerden [Pl]
嚥下性肺炎　Aspirationspneumonie [F]
嚥下補助剤　Verdickungsmittel [N]
エンゲル係数　Engelscher Koeffizient [M]
円座　Sitzring [M]
エンパワメント　Empowerment [N]
応益負担　Äquivalenz [F]
嘔気　Übelkeit [F]
応急手当　Erste Hilfe [F]
嘔吐　Erbrechen [N]
応能負担　Leistungsfähigkeit [F]
起き上がり　Aufstehen [N]
おむつ　Windeln [Pl]
おむつカバー　Wäscheschutz [M]
おむつ交換　Windelwechsel [M]
おむつ外し　Toilettenpositioning [N]
臥位　Liegeposition [F]
介護　Pflege [F]
介護過程　Pflegeprozess [M]
介護技術　Pflegetechnik [F]
介護休業　Pflegeurlaub [M]
介護給付　Pflegeleistung [F]
介護計画　Pflegeplan [M]
介護サービス計画　Pflegedienstplan [M]
介護支援専門員　Care Manager [M]
介護指導　Pflegeleitung [F]
介護者　Pfleger/in
介護職員　Pflegepersonal [N]
介護ニーズ　Pflegebedarf [M]
介護認定審査会　Begutachtungskommission [F] der Pflegebedürftigkeit

| 介護福祉 Pflegefürsorge〔F〕
| 介護福祉士 Altenpfleger/in
| 介護福祉士国家試験 Staatsexamen〔N〕für Altenpfleger/in
| 介護福祉士登録 Register〔N〕zugelassener Altenpfleger/in
| 介護負担 Pflegebelastung〔F〕
| 介護報酬 Pflegegebühr〔F〕
| 介護保険 Pflegeversicherung〔F〕
| 介護保険事業計画 Business-Plan〔M〕zur Pflegeversicherung
| 介護保険審査会 Kommission〔F〕zur Begutachtungs von Pflegeausprüchen
| 介護保険制度 Pflegeversicherungssystem〔N〕
| 介護保険認定調査 Feststellung〔F〕des Pflegebedürftigkeitsgrades
| 介護保険法 Pflegeversicherungsgesetz〔N〕
| 介護目標 Pflegeziel〔N〕
| 介護用具 Pflegehilfsmittel〔N〕
| 介護予防 Pflegeprävention〔F〕
| 介護予防事業 Unternehmen〔N〕für Pflegeprävention
| 介護療養型医療施設 geriatrisches Krankenhaus〔N〕
| 介護老人福祉施設 Altenpflegeheim〔N〕
| 介護老人保健施設 geriatrische Pflegeeinrichtung〔F〕
| 介護労働者 Pflegearbeiter/in
| 介助 Versorgung〔F〕
| 疥癬 Scabies〔F〕
| 回想法 Reminiszenztherapie〔F〕
| 階段 Treppe〔F〕
| 階段昇降 Treppensteigen〔N〕
| 回復期リハビリテーション Rehabilitation〔F〕in der Rekonvaleszenzphase
| 潰瘍 Geschwür〔N〕
| かかりつけ医 Hausarzt/ärztin
| 核家族 Kernfamilie〔F〕
| 家計 Wirtschaft〔F〕
| 家事 Hauswirtschaft〔F〕
| 家政 Hauswirtschaft〔F〕
| 家政婦 Hauswirtschaftsgehilfin〔F〕
| 家族 Familie〔F〕
| 家族会 Selbsthilfegruppe〔F〕für Familien
| 家族介護 Pflege〔F〕durch Familienangehörige
| 家族介護者 familiäre Pflegekraft〔F〕
| 家族関係 Familienverwandtschaft〔F〕
| 合併症 Komplikation〔F〕
| 寡婦 Witwe〔F〕
| 紙おむつ Papierwindel〔F〕
| 過用症候群 Überbelastungssyndrom〔N〕
| 加齢 Alterung〔F〕
| 癌 Krebs〔M〕
| 感音難聴 sensoneurale Taubheit〔F〕
| 感覚機能 sensorische Funktion〔F〕
| 換気 Ventilation〔F〕

環境整備 Umgebungsgestaltung〔F〕
看護 Krankenpflege〔F〕
肝硬変 Leberzirrhose〔F〕
看護師 Krankenpfleger/in；Krankenschwester〔F〕
関節 Gelenk〔N〕
関節可動域 Bewegungsexkursion〔F〕
関節リウマチ Gelenkrheumatismus〔M〕
感染 Infektion〔F〕
感染菌 Infektionskeime〔Pl〕
感染症 Infektionskrankheit〔F〕
感染予防 Infektionsprävention〔F〕
浣腸 Klystier〔N〕
観念失行 ideatorische Apraxie〔F〕
管理栄養士 staatlich geprüfte Diätistin〔F〕
緩和ケア Palliativpflege〔F〕
記憶障害 Gedächtnisschwäche〔F〕
着替え Kleidungswechsel
気管 Trachea〔F〕
危険防止 Risikoprävention〔F〕
起座位 Sitzhaltung〔F〕
義歯 Zahnersatz〔M〕
義肢装具士 Prothetiker und Orthetiker〔F〕
基礎代謝 Grundumsatz〔M〕
機能維持 Funktionserhalt〔M〕
機能訓練 funktionale Training〔N〕
機能障害 Funktionsstörung〔F〕
記銘力 Kurzzeitgedächtnis〔N〕
虐待 Misshandlung〔F〕
ギャッチベッド Krankenhausbett〔N〕
救急救命士 Rettungssanitäter/in
仰臥位 Rückenlage〔F〕
共感 Empathie〔F〕
虚弱 Gebrechlichkeit〔F〕
起立性低血圧 orthostatische Hypotonie〔F〕
記録 Akte〔F〕
筋萎縮 Muskelatrophie〔F〕
緊急連絡先 Notfallkontaktadresse〔F〕
金銭管理 Budgetmanagement〔N〕
苦情解決 Abwicklung〔F〕
くも膜下出血 Subarachnoidalblutung〔F〕
クリティカルパス klinischer Behandlungsweg〔M〕
グループホーム betreute Wohngemeinschaft〔F〕
グループリビング Senioren-Wohngemeinschaft〔F〕
グループレクリエーション Gruppenerholung〔F〕
グループワーク Gruppenarbeit〔F〕
車椅子 Rollstuhl〔M〕
車いすからベッド Transfer〔M〕vom Rollstuhl zum Bett
車いすの移動 Bewegung〔F〕im Rollstuhl
車いすの介助 Rollstuhl-Assistenz〔F〕
クロックポジション Uhrzeigerposition〔F〕
ケア Pflege〔F〕
ケアカンファレンス Pflegebesprechung〔F〕

ドイツ語

ケアチーム　Pflegeteam〔N〕
ケアハウス　Pflegeheim〔N〕
ケアプラン　Pflegeplan〔M〕
ケアマネジメント　Pflegemanagement〔N〕
ケアマネジャー　Pflegemanager/in
ケアワーク　Pflegearbeit〔F〕
経管栄養　Katheterernährung〔F〕
頸髄損傷　Rückenmarksverletzung〔F〕
傾聴　aktives Zuhören〔N〕
契約　Vertrag〔M〕
劇薬　stark wirkendes Medikament〔N〕
下血　Melaena〔F〕
ケースカンファレンス　Fallbesprechung〔F〕
ケースワーク　Einzelfallhilfe〔F〕
血圧　Blutdruck〔M〕
下痢　Abführmittel〔N〕
幻覚　Halluzination〔F〕
健康　Gesundheit〔F〕
健康観察　Gesundheitsbeobachtung〔F〕
健康保険　Krankenversicherung〔F〕
言語障害　Sprachstörung〔F〕
言語聴覚士　Logopäde/Logopädin
見当識障害　Disorientierung〔F〕
権利擁護　Advokatur〔F〕
公益事業　gemeinnütziges Unternehmen〔N〕
公益法人　gemeinnützige Körperschaft〔F〕
構音障害　Artikulationsstörung〔F〕
後期高齢者　ältere Senioren〔Pl〕〔Bezeichnung für Senioren über 75〕
抗菌・防臭素材　antibakterielles, desodorierendes Material〔N〕
口腔機能の向上　Verbesserung oraler Funktionen〔F〕
口腔ケア　Mundhöhlenpflege〔F〕
合計特殊出生率　zusammengefasste Fertilitätsrate〔F〕
高血圧　Hypertonie〔F〕
拘縮　Kontraktur〔F〕
拘縮予防　Kontrakturprophylaxe〔F〕
公証人　Notar〔M〕
公正証書　notarielle Urkunde〔F〕
抗生物質　Antibiotikum〔N〕
拘束　Fixierung〔F〕
後天性免疫不全症候群　erworbenes Immunschwächesyndrom〔N〕
高齢化　Vergreisung〔F〕
高齢期障害　Altersstörung〔F〕
高齢者　Senioren〔Pl〕
高齢社会　vergreisende Gesellschaft〔F〕
高齢者虐待　Seniorenmisshandlung〔F〕
高齢者虐待防止法　Gesetz〔N〕zur Vorbeugung von Seniorenmisshandlung
高齢者世帯　Seniorenhaushalt〔M〕
声かけ　〈mündliche〉Ermutigung〔F〕

誤嚥　Aspiration〔F〕
誤嚥性肺炎　Aspirationspneumonie〔F〕
呼吸　Atmung〔F〕
呼吸機能障害　Atemfunktionsstörung〔F〕
国際疾病分類　Internationale Klassifikation〔F〕der Krankheiten : ICD
国際障害分類　International Classification of Impairments, Disabilities and Handicaps : ICIDH
国際生活機能分類　Internationale Klassifikation〔F〕der Funktionsfähigkeit, Behinderung und Gesundheit : ICF
国際標準化機構　Internationale Standardisierungsorganisation〔F〕
骨折　Fraktur〔F〕
骨粗鬆症　Osteoporose〔F〕
言葉かけ　mündliche Ermutigung〔F〕
個別介護　individuelle Pflege〔F〕
コミュニケーション　Kommunikation〔F〕
コミュニケーションエイド　Kommunikationshilfe〔F〕
コレステロール　Cholesterin〔N〕
献立　Menü〔N〕
座位　Sitzhaltung〔F〕
再アセスメント　Reevaluation〔F〕
在宅介護　häusliche Pflege〔F〕
在宅看護　häusliche Krankenpflege〔F〕
在宅ケア　häusliche Pflege〔F〕
作業療法　Arbeitstherapie〔F〕
作業療法士　Arbeitstherapeut/in
サービス担当者会議　Pflegepersonalversammlung〔F〕
サポートシステム　Unterstützungssystem〔N〕
残存機能　Restfunktion〔F〕
散髪　Haarschnitt〔M〕
紫外線遮蔽素材　UV-Schutzmaterial〔N〕
歯科衛生士　Dentalhygieniker/in
視覚障害　Sehstörung〔F〕
視覚障害者　Sehbehinderte〔M・F〕
弛緩　Erschlaffung〔F〕
止血　Hämostase〔F〕
思考障害　Denkstörung〔F〕
自己覚知　Selbstwahrnehmung〔F〕
自己決定　Selbstbestimmung〔F〕
自己実現　Selbstverwirklichung〔F〕
脂質異常症　Fettstoffwechselstörung〔F〕
自傷行為　selbstverletzendes Verhalten〔N〕
自助具　Selbsthilfegerät〔N〕
死生観　Einstellung〔F〕zu Leben und Tod〔F〕
施設介護　Einrichtungspflege〔F〕
自尊心　Selbstachtung〔F〕
肢体不自由　körperliche Behinderung〔F〕
実技試験　praktische Prüfung〔F〕
失禁　Inkontinenz〔F〕
失語　Aphasie〔F〕
シーツ交換　Bettwäschewechsel〔M〕

実支出	Nettoausgaben [Pl]
実収入	Nettoeinkommen [N]
失認	Agnosie [F]
実務経験証明書	Arbeitszeugnis [M]
自動運動	aktive Bewegung [F]
児童期障害	Kindheitsstörung [F]
自閉症	Autismus [M]
社会資源	soziale Ressourcen [Pl]
社会的不利	soziale Beeinträchtigung [F]
社会福祉	soziale Wohlfahrt [F]
社会福祉士	Sozialarbeiter/in
社会福祉事業	Wohlfahrtspflege [F]
社会保険	Sozialversicherung [F]
社会保障	soziale Sicherung [F]
社会保障審議会	Sozialversicherungsbeirat [M]
視野狭窄	Gesichtsfeld-Beschränkung [F]
視野障害	Gesichtsfeldstörung [F]
シャワー浴	Dusche [F]
収益事業	gewinnbringendes-orientiertes Unternehmen [N]
従属人口	abhängiger Bevölkerungsanteil [M]
住宅改修	barrierefreier Wohnungsumbau [M]
終末期	Lebensende [N]
終末期介護	Sterbebegleitung [F]
主治医	Hausarzt [M]
主治医意見書	ärztliches Attest [N]
手段的日常生活活動	instrumentelle Aktivitäten [Pl] des täglichen Lebens : IATL
出血	Blutung [F]
守秘義務	Schweigepflicht [F]
手浴	Handbad [N]
手話	Gebärdensprache [F]
除圧	Druckverminderung [F]
障害	Behinderung [F]
障害基礎年金	Behindertengrundrente [F]
障害の受容	Behinderungsakzeptanz [F]
小規模多機能型居宅介護	leichte allgemeine häusliche Pflege [F]
少子化	Geburtenrückgang [M]
少子高齢化	Geburtenrückgang [M] und Überalterung [F]
静脈栄養法	parenterale Ernährung [F]
職業的リハビリテーション	berufliche Rehabilitation [F]
食事	Mahlzeit [F]
食事介護	Nahrungsdarreichung [F]
食事介助	Esshilfe [F]
食事動作	Nahrungsaufnahme [F]
食事療法	Ernährungstherapie [F]
褥瘡	Dekubitus [M]
褥瘡予防	Dekubitusprophylaxe [F]
食中毒	Lebensmittelvergiftung [F]
食品衛生	Lebensmittelhygiene [F]
植物状態	Wachkoma [N]
植物性食品	pflanzliche Nahrungsmittel [N]
食欲	Appetit [M]
食欲不振	Appetitlosigkeit [F]
ショートステイ	Kurzzeitpflege [F]
初老期認知症	präsenile Demenz [F]
自立	Unabhängigkeit [F]
自立支援	Selbständigkeitshilfe [F]
自立度	Unabhängigkeitsgrad [M]
視力低下	Verlust [M] des Sehvermögens
事例検討	Fallstudie [F]
心気症	Hypochondrie [F]
人工呼吸	künstliche Atmung [F]
身上監護	Vormundschaft [F]
心身症	psychosomatische Krankheit [F]
振戦	Tremor [M]
心臓弁膜症	Herzklappenfehler [M]
身体介護	Körperpflege [F]
身体機能	physische Funktion [F]
信頼関係	Vertrauensbeziehung [F]
推奨量	empfohlene Tagesdosis [F] : RDA
水分バランス	Flüssigkeitshaushalt [M]
水分補給	Rehydration Wasserzufuhr [F]
水疱	Blase [F]
睡眠	Schlaf [M]
頭痛	Kopfschmerz [M]
ストレス	Stress [M]
ストレッチャー	Stretcher [M]
ストレングス視点	Empowermentphilosophie [F]
スーパーバイザー	Pflegedienstleitung [F]
スーパーバイジー	Pflegeverantwortlicher [M]
スーパービジョン	Supervision [F]
スピリチュアルケア	Spiritual Care [F]
生活援助	Haushaltshilfe [F]
生活環境	Lebensumgebung [F]
生活習慣病	Zivilisationskrankheit [F]
生活の質	Lebensqualität [F]
生活扶助	Lebenshilfe [F]
生活歴	Lebensgeschichte [F]
清潔	Sauberkeit [F]
清拭	Waschen [Pl] im Bett
精神科ソーシャルワーカー	psychiatrische/r Sozialarbeiter/in
精神障害	psychische Erkrankung [F]
精神障害者	geistig Behinderte [Pl]
精神保健福祉士	psychiatrische/r Sozialarbeiter/in
成年後見制度	Betreuungssystem [N]
整髪	Haare schneiden
生命の延長	Lebensverlängerung [F]
生命倫理	Bioethik [F]
整容	Körperpflege [F]
世界保健機関	Weltgesundheitsorganisation [F]
脊髄損傷	Rückenmarksverletzung [F]
脊椎圧迫骨折	Wirbelkompressionsfraktur [F]

ドイツ語

世帯　Haushalt〔M〕
摂食　Nahrungsaufnahme〔F〕
摂食障害　Essstörung〔F〕
セミファーラー位　Semi-Fowler-Lagerung〔F〕
セルフケア　Selbstfürsorge〔F〕
セルフヘルプグループ　Selbsthilfegruppe〔F〕
繊維　Faser〔F〕
全援助　Vollpflege〔F〕
洗顔　Gesichtsreinigung〔F〕
洗剤　Waschmittel〔N〕
洗浄　Spülung〔F〕
染色体異常　Chromosomabweichung〔F〕
全人格的ケア　Rundumversorgung〔F〕
全身清拭　Ganzkörperwäsche〔F〕im Bett
全身浴　Ganzkörperbad〔N〕
尖足　Spitzfuß〔M〕
洗濯　Wäsche〔F〕
洗髪　Haarwäsche〔F〕
せん妄　Delirium〔N〕
総入れ歯　Gebiß〔N〕
躁うつ病　bipolare Störung〔F〕
早期発見　Früherkennung〔F〕
装具　Orthese〔F〕
掃除　Gebäudereinigung〔F〕
喪失体験　Verlusterfahrung〔F〕
側臥位　Seitenlage〔F〕
足浴　Fußbad〔N〕
咀嚼　Kauen〔N〕
ソーシャルワーカー　Sozialarbeiter/in
措置制度　Maßnahmesystem〔N〕
措置費　Maßnahmekosten〔Pl〕
体位変換　Lagewechsel〔M〕
体温　Körpertemperatur〔F〕
体温測定　Messung〔F〕der Körpertemperatur
退行　Regression〔F〕
帯状疱疹　Gürtelrose〔F〕
大腿四頭筋　vierköpfiger Schenkelstrecker〔M〕
大腸癌　Dickdarmkrebs〔M〕
代読　Vorlesen〔N〕
代筆　Hilfe〔F〕beim Schreiben
代理電話　Hilfe〔F〕beim Telefonieren
ダウン症候群　Down-Syndrom〔N〕
立ち上がり　Aufstehen〔N〕〔aus dem Sitzen〕
脱臼　Luxation〔F〕
脱水症　Dehydration〔F〕
他動運動　passive Bewegung〔F〕
ターミナルケア　Sterbebegleitung〔F〕
短下肢装具　Unterschinkelorthese〔F〕
端座位　Sitzhaltung〔F〕
チアノーゼ　Zyanose〔F〕
地域包括支援センター　〔eigentlich : allgemeines regionales Pflegezentrum〔N〕, heute meist〕Pflegestützpunkt〔M〕

地域密着サービス　regionaler Pflegedienst〔M〕
チェーンストークス呼吸　Cheyne-Stokes-Atmen〔N〕
蓄尿障害　Harnspeicherstörung〔F〕
知的障害　geistige Behinderung〔F〕
知的障害者　geistig Behinderter〔M〕
知能　Intelligenz〔F〕
知能指数　Intelligenzquotient〔M〕
痴呆　Demenz〔F〕
痴呆性老人　demenzkranke Senioren〔Pl〕
痴呆性老人の日常生活自立度　Unabhängigkeitsgrad〔M〕altersdementer Menschen
チームアプローチ　teamorientierter-Ansatz〔M〕
チームケア　Teampflege〔F〕
着脱　An- und Ausziehen〔N〕
聴覚障害　Schwerhörigkeit〔F〕
長寿社会　Langlebigkeitsgesellschaft〔F〕
調整交付金　Ausgleichssubvention〔F〕
重複障害　mehrfache Behinderung〔F〕
腸閉塞　Darmverschluss〔M〕
調理　Kochen〔N〕
調理方法　Kochrezept〔N〕
聴力レベル　Hörvermögen〔N〕
直接援助技術　direkte soziale Arbeit〔F〕
対麻痺　Paraplegie〔F〕
通所介護　Tagespflege〔F〕
通所リハビリテーション　ambulante Rehabilitation〔F〕
杖　Stock〔M〕
杖歩行　Gehen〔N〕am Stock
手洗い　Händewaschen〔N〕
低血圧　Hypotonie〔F〕
低血糖　Hypoglykämie〔F〕
T字杖　Gehstock〔M〕mit T-Griff
摘便　digitales Ausräumen〔N〕
手すり　Geländer〔N〕
手引き　Anleitung〔F〕
伝音難聴　Hörsturz〔M〕
点字　Blindenschrift〔F〕
電動車いす　Elektrorollstuhl〔M〕
電動ベッド　elektrisches Bett〔N〕
動悸　Palpitation〔F〕
統合失調症　Schizophrenie〔F〕
透析　Dialyse〔F〕
疼痛　Schmerz〔M〕
糖尿病　Zuckerkrankheit F〕
動脈硬化　Arteriosklerose〔F〕
特殊寝台　Pflegebett〔N〕
特殊浴槽　Pflegebadewanne〔F〕
特別治療食　therapeutische Diät〔F〕
特別養護老人ホーム　Spezialaltenpflegeheim〔N〕
読話　Lippenlesen〔N〕
吐血　Hämatemesis〔F〕
徒手筋力テスト　manueller Muskeltest〔M〕: MMT
独居　Alleinleben〔N〕

内部障害　Innenstörung〔F〕
難聴　Schwerhörigkeit〔F〕
難病　unheilbare Krankheit〔F〕
ニーズ　Bedarf〔M〕
日常生活活動　Aktivitäten〔Pl〕des täglichen Lebens：ATL
日内変動　Circadianik〔F〕
入眠　Einschlafen〔N〕
入浴　Baden〔N〕
尿　Urin〔M〕
尿意　Harndrang〔M〕
尿器　Urinflaschenhalterung〔F〕
尿失禁　Harninkontinenz〔F〕
尿路感染　Harnwegsinfekt〔M〕
認知症　Demenz〔F〕
認知症高齢者　Altersdemente〔Pl〕
認知症高齢者の日常生活自立度　Grad〔M〕der Unabhängigkeit Altersdementer
認知症対応型共同生活介護　betreute Wohngemeinschaft〔F〕für Demenzkranke
認知症対応型通所介護　Tagespflege〔F〕für Demenzkranke
寝返り　sich wälzen im Schlaf
寝たきり　bettlägerig
寝たきり度　Grad〔M〕der Bettlägerigkeit
熱傷　Verbrennung〔F〕
寝床　Schlafstätte〔F〕
年金　Rente〔F〕
脳血管障害　zerebrovaskuläre Störung〔F〕
脳血管性認知症　zerebrovaskuläre Demenz〔F〕
脳血栓症　Hirnthrombose〔F〕
脳梗塞　Zerebralinfarkt〔M〕
脳死　Hirntod〔M〕
脳出血　Hirnblutung〔F〕
脳性麻痺　zerebrale Lähmung〔F〕
脳塞栓　Hirnembolie〔F〕
能力低下　Leistungsrückgang〔M〕
ノーマライゼーション　Normalisierung〔F〕
ノンレム睡眠　NREM-Schlaf〔M〕
肺炎　Pneumonie〔F〕
徘徊　Herumwandern〔N〕
肺癌　Lungenkrebs〔M〕
肺気腫　Lungenemphysem〔N〕
バイキング食　Büfett〔N〕
バイスティックの7原則　die Sieben Grundsätze Biesteks〔Pl〕
排泄　Ausscheidung〔F〕
排泄介助　Toilettenhilfe〔F〕
バイタルサイン　Vitalparameter〔M〕
排尿　Harnlassen〔N〕
排尿困難　Dysurie〔F〕
排尿障害　Miktionsbeschwerde〔F〕
排便　Kotentleerung〔F〕

排便障害　Darmentleerungsstörung〔F〕
廃用萎縮　Inaktivitätsatrophie〔F〕
廃用症候群　Abnutzungssyndrom〔N〕
パーキンソン病　Parkinson-Krankheit〔F〕
白杖　Blindenstock〔M〕
白内障　Katarakt〔F〕
長谷川式簡易認知症スケール改訂版　überarbeitete Hasegawa-Demenz-Skala〔F〕：HDSR
バックサポート　Rückenstütze〔F〕
発達障害　Entwicklungsstörung〔F〕
発熱　Fieber〔N〕
バリアフリー　barrierefrei
バルンカテーテル　Ballonkatheter〔M〕
半身浴　Sitzbad〔N〕
半調理　vorgekochtes Gericht〔N〕
BMI　Body Mass Index〔M〕
被害妄想　Verfolgungswahn〔M〕
非言語的コミュニケーション　nonverbale Kommunikation〔F〕
ビタミン　Vitamin〔M〕
筆記試験　schriftliche Prüfung〔F〕
被保険者　Versicherte〔F・M〕
肥満　Adipositas〔F〕
秘密保持　Schweigepflicht〔F〕
氷枕　Eisbeutel〔M〕
氷嚢　Eisbeutel〔M〕
日和見感染　opportunistische Infektion〔F〕
貧血　Anämie〔F〕
頻便　Pollakikoprose〔F〕
ファーラー位　Fowler-Körperlage〔F〕
フェイスシート　Deckblatt〔N〕
フォローアップ　Fortsetzung〔F〕
腹臥位　Bauchlage〔F〕
副作用　Nebenwirkung〔F〕
福祉　Wohlfahrt〔F〕
福祉機器　Hilfsmittel〔N/Pl〕für Menschen mit Behinderungen
腹式呼吸　Bauchatmung〔F〕
福祉事務所　Sozialamt〔N〕
福祉用具　therapeutische Hilfsmittel〔Pl〕
福祉用具貸与　Vermietung〔F〕therapeutischer Hilfsmittel
浮腫　Ödem〔N〕
フットサポート　Fußstütze〔F〕
部分援助　Teilunterstützung〔F〕
部分清拭　Teilwaschen〔Pl〕im Bett
部分浴　Teilbad〔N〕
プライバシー　Privatsphäre〔F〕
プライマリ・ケア　ärztliche Grundversorgung〔F〕
プロフィール　Persönlichkeitsprofil〔F〕
平均寿命　durchschnittliche Lebenserwartung〔F〕
平均余命　durchschnittliche weitere Lebenserwartung〔F〕

ドイツ語

ベッド　Bett〔N〕
ベッドから車いす　Transfer〔M〕vom Bett in den Rollstuhl
ベッドメーキング　Bettmachen〔N〕
便器　Nachttopf〔M〕
便失禁　Stuhlinkontinenz〔F〕
便秘　Verstopfung〔F〕
片麻痺　Hemiplegie〔F〕
保育士　Kinderpfleger/in
防炎素材　Feuerschutzmaterial〔N〕
防汚素材　schmutzabweisendes Material〔N〕
訪問介護　ambulante Pflege〔F〕
訪問看護　ambulante Krankenpflege〔F〕
訪問看護ステーション　ambulante Krankenpflegestation〔F〕
訪問入浴介護　ambulante Badepflege〔F〕
訪問リハビリテーション　ambulante Rehabilitation〔F〕
保健師　Gesundheitspfleger/in
保険者　Versicherer〔M〕
保健所　Gesundheitsamt〔N〕
保険料　Versicherungsbeitrag〔M〕
歩行　Gang〔M〕
歩行器　Gehgestell〔N〕
歩行練習　Gehtraining〔N〕
ポジショニング　Positionsunterstützung〔F〕
補足給付　Ergänzungsleistung〔F〕
ポータブルトイレ　Toilettenstuhl〔M〕
ポータブル浴槽　mobile Badewanne〔F〕
補聴器　Hörapparat〔M〕
発疹　Hautausschlag〔M〕
発赤　Ausschlag〔M〕
ボディメカニクス　Körpermechanik〔F〕
ホームヘルパー　Homehelper〔M〕
ボランティア　Freiwillige/r
ホルモン　Hormon〔N〕
マット　Matte〔F〕
松葉杖　Krücke〔F〕
麻痺　Lähmung〔F〕
ミキサー食　Breikost〔F〕
ミネラル　Mineral〔N〕
脈拍　Puls〔M〕
メタボリック症候群　metabolisches Syndrom〔N〕
滅菌　Sterilisation〔F〕
妄想　Wahnvorstellung〔F〕
燃え尽き症候群　Burnout-Syndrom〔N〕
モニタリング　Monitoring〔N〕
問題行動　problematisches Verhalten〔N〕
夜間せん妄　nächtliches Delirium〔N〕
薬剤　Medikament〔N〕
薬剤管理　Medikationsmanagement〔N〕
薬剤師　Apotheker/in
薬物療法　Medikamententherapie〔F〕
有料老人ホーム　privates〔gebührenpflichtiges〕 Altenheim〔N〕
ユニットケア　Gruppenpflege〔F〕
ユニバーサルファッション　universal Fashion〔F〕
要援護高齢者　unterstützungsbedürftige/r Senior/in
要介護　Pflegebedürftigkeit〔F〕
要介護者　Pflegebedürftige/r
要介護度　Pflegestufe〔F〕
要介護認定　Anerkennung〔F〕der Pflegebedürftigkeit
養護老人ホーム　Altenheim〔N〕
要支援　Hilfsbedürftigkeit〔F〕
要支援者　Hilfsbedürftige/r
要支援認定　Anerkennung〔F〕der Hilfebedürftigkeit
腰痛症　Lumbago〔F〕
腰痛体操　Rückengymnastik〔F〕
腰痛予防　Lumbago-Prophylaxe〔F〕
抑制　Fixierung〔F〕
浴槽　Badewanne〔F〕
予防給付　Versicherungsleistungen〔F〕zur Gesundheitsprävention
四脚杖　Vierfußgehhilfe〔F〕
ライフサイクル　Lebenszyklus〔M〕
ライフスタイル　Lebensstil〔M〕
ライフレビュー　Lebensrückblick〔M〕
ラポール　Rapport〔M〕
理学療法士　Physiotherapeut/in
立位　Stehhaltung〔F〕
利尿剤　Diuretica〔Pl〕
リハビリテーション　Rehabilitation〔F〕
リハビリテーション医学　Rehabilitationsmedizin〔F〕
リハビリテーション介護　rehabilitative Pflege〔F〕
留置カテーテル　Dauerkatheter〔M〕
流動食　Flüssignahrung〔F〕
流動性知能　fluide Intelligenz〔F〕
利用料　Nutzungskosten〔Pl〕
レクリエーション　Erholung〔F〕
レム睡眠　REM-Schlaf〔M〕
聾　Taubheit〔F〕
老化　Altern〔N〕
老眼　Presbyopie〔F〕
老人性うつ病　senile Depression〔F〕
老人性難聴　senile Schwerhörigkeit〔F〕
老人保健施設　geriatrisches Pflegeheim〔N〕
老年認知症　senile Demenz〔F〕
老齢基礎年金　Altersgrundrente〔F〕
老齢年金　Altersrente〔F〕
老齢福祉年金　Alterssozialrente〔F〕
ロールプレイ　Rollenspiel〔N〕

7. ヒンディー語 (Hindi)

IQ आई.क्यू
ICIDH आई.सी.आई.डी.एच
ICF आई.सी.एफ
ICD आई.सी.डी
アクティビティ क्रिया- प्रक्रिया
アセスメント मूल्यांकन
アテトーシス हाथ की अनैच्छिक गतियाँ
アテトーゼ हाथ की अनैच्छिक गतियाँ
アドボカシー वकालत
アルツハイマー型認知症 अल्ज़ाइमर प्रकार का मनोभ्रंश
アルツハイマー病 अल्ज़ाइमर रोग
安全管理 सुरक्षा प्रबन्धन
罨法 सिकाई
安眠 चैन की नींद
安眠援助 गहरी नींद का अवलम्बन
安楽 आराम
安楽な体位 आरामदायक स्थिति
意識障害 चेतना में बाधा
維持期リハビリテーション परवर्ती काल में शारीरिक
　क्रियाकलाप का पुनर्संचालन
萎縮 अपक्षय
移乗動作 स्थान परिवर्तन
移送費 परिवहन शुल्क
遺族基礎年金 उत्तरजीवी की मूल पेंशन
移動 चलना; चलना फिरना
移動介護 अंग संचालन सेवा
移動関連福祉用具 अंग संचालन संबंधी तकनीकी उपकरण
移動トイレ कमोड; पोर्टेबल टॉयलेट
移動浴槽 पोर्टेबल बाथ टब; वहनीय स्नानकुंड
衣服 वस्त्र
衣服着脱 वस्त्र परिवर्तन
衣料障害 वस्त्र संबंधी संकट
医療ソーシャルワーカー चिकित्सीय सामाजिक कार्यकर्ता
医療保険制度 स्वास्थ्य बीमा पद्धति
インスリン इन्सुलिन
インテーク [भोजनादि का] अंतर्ग्रहण
インフォーマル अनौपचारिक
陰部清拭 जननांग शौच
陰部洗浄 गुप्तांग शुचिता की देखभाल
インペアメント जीर्णता
うつ病 मानसिक अवसाद
運営適正化委員会 आवंटन संबंधी प्रशासन समिति
運動器の機能向上 व्यायाम उपकरणों में सुधार
運動失調 गतिभंग; गतिविभ्रम
運動障害 अंग संचालन में अवरोध
運動療法 उपचारार्थ व्यायाम
エアーパッド एयर पैड
エアーマット एयर मैट
エイジズム आयु के आधार पर भेदभाव
エイズ एड्स

栄養 पोषण
栄養改善 पौष्टिकता में सुधार
栄養管理 पौष्टिकता प्रबंधन
栄養士 आहार विशेषज्ञ
栄養所要量 पौष्टिकता आवश्यकता
栄養素 पोषक तत्व
腋窩温 कक्ष/बगल/काँख का तापमान
壊死 तंतु वा कोशिका क्षय
ADL दैनिक गतिविधियां!
NPO एन.पी.ओ.
MRSA एम. आर. एस.ए
MMSE एम.एम.एस.ई
MMT मैन्युल मांसपेशी परीक्षण : एम.एम.टी
嚥下 निगलन
嚥下困難 निगलने में कठिनाई
嚥下性肺炎 च्यूषण न्यूमोनिया
嚥下補助剤 निगलने में संपूरक
エンゲル係数 एंगेल्ज़ गुणांक
円座 गोल आसन
エンパワメント सशक्तीकरण
応益負担 [वृद्ध द्वारा] प्रदत्त लाभांश
嘔気 मितली ; उबकाई
応急手当 आपातकालीन प्राथमिक चिकित्सा
嘔吐 वमन ; उलटी
応能負担 भुगतान क्षमता संबंधी सिद्धांत
起き上がり उठना
おむつ डायपर
おむつカバー डायपर कवर
おむつ交換 डायपर बदलना
おむつ外し डायपर हटाना
臥位 शयित ; लेटा हुआ
介護 दीर्घकालीन सेवा
介護過程 दीर्घकालीन सेवा प्रक्रिया
介護技術 दीर्घकालीन सेवा तकनीक
介護休業 परिवार देखभाल के लिए अवकाश
介護給付 दीर्घकालीन सेवा लाभ
介護計画 सेवा योजना
介護サービス計画 दीर्घकालीन सेवा योजना
介護支援専門員 सेवा प्रबंधन
介護指導 दीर्घकालीन सेवा हेतु मार्गदर्शन
介護者 सेवाकर्ता
介護職員 सेवा श्रमिक
介護ニーズ दीर्घकालीन सेवा संबंधी आवश्यकताएँ
介護認定審査会 दीर्घकालीन सेवा संबंधी आवश्यकता
　प्रमाणन परिषद्
介護福祉 सेवा कल्याण
介護福祉士 प्रमाणित सेवा कार्यकर्ता
介護福祉士国家試験 प्रमाणित सेवा कार्यकर्ता राष्ट्रीय
　परीक्षा
介護福祉士登録 प्रमाणित सेवा कर्ता का पंजीकरण

介護負担	दीर्घकालीन सेवा भार	感染	संक्रमण
介護報酬	दीर्घकालीन सेवा शुल्क	感染菌	जीवाणु
介護保険	दीर्घकालीन सेवा बीमा	感染症	संक्रामक रोग
介護保険事業計画	दीर्घकालीन सेवा बीमा परियोजना रूपरेखा	感染予防	संक्रमण निवारण
		浣腸	एनीमा, गुदावस्ति
介護保険審査会	दीर्घकालीन सेवा बीमा समीक्षा परिषद्	観念失行	क्रिया-कलापों की योजना बनाने में असमर्थता का मानसिक विकार
介護保険制度	दीर्घकालीन सेवा बीमा पद्धति		
介護保険認定調査	दीर्घवधि देखभाल बीमा योग्यता आकलन	管理栄養士	पंजीकृत आहार विशेषज्ञ
		緩和ケア	रोग उपशामक सेवा
介護保険法	दीर्घकालीन सेवा बीमा नियम	記憶障害	स्मृति विकार
介護目標	दीर्घकालीन सेवा बीमा उद्देश्य	着替え	वस्त्र
介護用具	दीर्घकालीन सेवा बीमा उपकरण	気管	श्वास नली
介護予防	दीर्घकालीन निवारक सेवा	危険防止	संकट निवारण
介護予防事業	दीर्घकालीन सेवा निवारक कार्य	起座位	आसन्न ; बैठने की अवस्था
介護療養型医療施設	दीर्घकालीन स्वास्थ्य सेवा सुविधा	義歯	कृत्रिम दाँत
介護老人福祉施設	वृद्ध हेतु दीर्घकालीन कल्याण संस्था	義肢装具士	कृत्रिम अंगों की अभावपूर्ति व कृत्रिम अंगों का विशेषज्ञ
介護老人保健施設	वृद्ध हेतु दीर्घकालीन स्वास्थ्य संस्था		
介護労働者	दीर्घकालीन सेवा कर्त्ता	基礎代謝	आधारभूत चयापचय
介助	सहायता	機能維持	कार्यात्मक रखरखाव
疥癬	खुजली	機能訓練	कार्यात्मक प्रशिक्षण
回想法	संस्मरण चिकित्सा	機能障害	जीर्णता
階段	सीढ़ियाँ ; जीना	記銘力	स्मरण शक्ति
階段昇降	सीढ़ियाँ चढ़ना-उतरना	虐待	दुर्व्यवहार
回復期リハビリテーション	स्वास्थ्य लाभ काल में पुनर्संचालन	ギャッチベッド	गैच बेड
		救急救命士	आपतकालीन जीवन रक्षक तक्नीशियन
潰瘍	व्रण, फोड़ा	仰臥位	चित, पीठ के बल लेटने की अवस्था ; शवासन
かかりつけ医	प्राथमिक चिकित्सक	共感	परानुभूति ; समानुभूति
核家族	एकक परिवार	虚弱	शारीरिक दुर्बलता
家計	घरेलू बजट	起立性低血圧	स्थिर दशा में खड़े रहने से उत्पन्न निम्न रक्त चाप
家事	गृह संचालन		
家政	गृह संचालन प्रबंधन	記録	अंकन ; रेकॉर्ड
家政婦	गृह प्रबंधक	筋萎縮	मांसपेशीय क्षीणता
家族	परिवार	緊急連絡先	आपतकालीन संपर्क सूत्र
家族会	परिवारों का संगठन	金銭管理	धन प्रबंधन
家族介護	दीर्घकालीन पारिवारिक सेवा	苦情解決	शिकायत निवारण प्रक्रिया
家族介護者	पारिवारिक सेवा कर्त्ता	くも膜下出血	अधोजाल तानिक रक्तस्राव
家族関係	पारिवारिक संबंध	クリティカルパス	क्रिटिकल पाथ
合併症	थूक में खून आना	グループホーム	सामूहिक गृह
寡婦	विधवा	グループリビング	सामूहिक जीवन
紙おむつ	पेपर डाइपर ; काग़ज़ की लंगोट	グループレクリエーション	सामूहिक मनोरंजन
過用症候群	अति प्रयोग संलक्षण	グループワーク	सामाजिक समूह-कार्य
加齢	जीर्णन	車いす	व्हील चेयर
癌	कैंसर	車いすからベッド	व्हील चेयर से शैया
感音難聴	संवेदी श्रवण तंत्रिका में चोट से उत्पन्न बधिरता	車いすの移動	व्हील चेयर से आना जाना
感覚機能	अनुभूति विषयक कार्य	車いすの介助	व्हील चेयर हेतु सहायता
換気	संवातन ; वायु संचालन	クロックポジション	क्लॉक पोज़ीशन
環境整備	पर्यावरणीय संरक्षण	ケア	सेवा
看護	परिचर्या, नर्सिंग	ケアカンファレンス	सेवा सम्मेलन ; केयर कान्फ्रेंस
肝硬変	यकृत [जिगर] का कठोर हो जाना	ケアチーム	सेवा दल
看護師	परिचारिका ; नर्स	ケアハウス	सेवा सदन
関節	जोड़ ; संधि	ケアプラン	सेवा योजना
関節可動域	अंग संचालन सीमा	ケアマネジメント	सेवा प्रबंधन
関節リウマチ	गठियावात	ケアマネジャー	सेवा प्रबंधक

日本語	ヒンディー語
ケアワーク	सेवा कार्य
経管栄養	नली द्वारा आहार देना
頸髄損傷	ग्रीवा-रज्जु की चोट
傾聴	क्रियाशील श्रवण
契約	अनुबंध
劇薬	घातक औषधि
下血	मल में ख़ून आना
ケースカンファレンス	केस कान्फ़्रेंस
ケースワーク	केस वर्क
血圧	रक्त चाप
下痢	अतिसार
幻覚	निर्मूल भ्रम
健康	स्वास्थ्य
健康観察	स्वास्थ्य निरीक्षण
健康保険	स्वास्थ्य बीमा
言語障害	भाषा विकार
言語聴覚士	भाषा श्रवण चिकित्सक
見当識障害	स्थिति भ्रांति
権利擁護	अधिकारों की पैरवी
公益事業	लोकोपयोगिता
公益法人	लोकहित नियम
構音障害	उच्चारण संबंधी विकार
後期高齢者	अति वृद्ध
抗菌・防臭素材	प्रतिजीव दुर्गंधनाशक पदार्थ
口腔機能の向上	मौखिक क्रिया में सुधार
口腔ケア	मौखिक स्वास्थ्य सेवा
合計特殊出生率	कुल प्रजनन दर
高血圧	उच्च रक्त चाप
拘縮	अस्थाई अकड़न
拘縮予防	संकुचन निवारण
公証人	सार्वजनिक विपत्र प्रमाणक
公正証書	विपत्र प्रमाणक विलेख
抗生物質	जीवाणुनाशक
拘束	नियंत्रण
後天性免疫不全症候群	एड्स
高齢化	वृद्ध जनसंख्या में वृद्धि
高齢期障害	वृद्धावस्था के विकार
高齢者	वृद्ध व्यक्ति
高齢社会	वृद्ध समाज
高齢者虐待	वृद्धों के प्रति दुर्व्यवहार
高齢者虐待防止法	वृद्ध के प्रति दुर्व्यवहार निवारण नियम
高齢者世帯	वृद्ध बहुल परिवार
声かけ	वार्तालाप द्वारा सेवा
誤嚥	आहार निगलने में कठिनाई
誤嚥性肺炎	चूषण न्यूमोनिया
呼吸	श्वास प्रश्वास क्रिया
呼吸機能障害	श्वसन कार्यात्मक विकार
国際疾病分類	रोगों का अंतर्राष्ट्रीय वर्गीकरण
国際障害分類	जीनता: अक्षमताओं व बाधाओं का अंतर्राष्ट्रीय वर्गीकरण
国際生活機能分類	अंतर्राष्ट्रीय क्रियात्मकता: अक्षमता एवं स्वास्थ्य वर्गीकरण
国際標準化機構	मानकीकरण अंतर्राष्ट्रीय संगठन
骨折	अस्थि भंग
骨粗鬆症	अस्थि न्यूनता
言葉かけ	वाक सेवा
個別介護	व्यक्तिगत सेवा
コミュニケーション	संचार: कम्यूनिकेशन
コミュニケーションエイド	वार्तालाप [संचरण] में सहायक उपकरण
コレステロール	कोलेस्ट्रॉल: वसा समान पदार्थ
献立	व्यंजन सूची; मेन्यू
座位	बैठने की स्थिति
再アセスメント	पुनर्मूल्यांकन
在宅介護	दीर्घकालीन गृह सेवा
在宅看護	गृह स्वास्थ्य परिचर्या सेवा
在宅ケア	गृह सेवा
作業療法	व्यावसायिक उपचार
作業療法士	व्यावसायिक चिकित्सक
サービス担当者会議	सेवा कर्मचारी सभा
サポートシステム	सहारा देनेवाला व्यक्ति तन्त्र
残存機能	अवशिष्ट क्रियाकलाप
散髪	बाल कटाना
紫外線遮蔽素材	परा-बैंगनी किरण आवरण सामग्री
歯科衛生士	दंत शुचिता विशेषज्ञ
視覚障害	दृष्टिहीनता
視覚障害者	नेत्रहीन
弛緩	झुर्रीदार: शिथिल
止血	रक्त परिसंचरण में अवरोध
思考障害	चिंतन विकार
自己覚知	स्व-जागरूकता
自己決定	स्व-निर्णय
自己実現	स्व-कार्यान्वयन
脂質異常症	रक्त में वसा की अति
自傷行為	आत्म अंग भंग; आत्म-विकृति
自助具	स्व-सहायता उपकरण
死生観	जीवन मृत्यु के प्रति दृष्टिकोण
施設介護	संस्थानिक दीर्घकालीन सेवा
自尊心	आत्मसम्मान
肢体不自由	अपंग
実技試験	प्रायोगिक परीक्षा
失禁	मूत्र आदि रोकने में अवरोध; नियंत्रण असमर्थता
失語	वाचाघात
シーツ交換	चादर बदलना
実支出	वास्तविक व्यय
実収入	वास्तविक आमदनी
失認	इंद्रियों के संकेत पहचानने में असमर्थता
実務経験証明書	सेवा अनुभव का प्रमाण पत्र
自動運動	सक्रिय गति
児童期障害	शैशवकालीन विकार
自閉症	स्वलीनता
社会資源	सामाजिक संसाधन
社会的不利	परिस्थितिक बाधा: असुविधा
社会福祉	समाज कल्याण
社会福祉士	प्रमाणित सामाजिक कार्यकर्ता
社会福祉事業	समाज कल्याण कार्य

ヒンディー語

社会保険	सामाजिक बीमा
社会保障	सामाजिक सुरक्षा
社会保障審議会	समाज सुरक्षा परिषद्
視野狭窄	दृष्टिक्षेत्र प्रतिबंध
視野障害	दृष्टिक्षेत्र विकार
シャワー浴	शावर बाथ ; फव्वारा-स्नान
収益事業	लाभार्जन का व्यवसाय
従属人口	आश्रित जनसंख्या
住宅改修	घरेलू हेतु घर में परिवर्तन
終末期	मरणावस्था ; [जीवन का] अंतिम काल
終末期介護	अंतकालीन सेवा
主治医	प्राथमिक चिकित्सक
主治医意見書	दीर्घकालीन सेवा के बारे में प्राथमिक चिकित्सक का निर्णय
手段的日常生活活動	दैनिक जीवन के औपकरणिक क्रियाकलाप ; आई. ए. डी. एल.
出血	रक्त स्राव
守秘義務	गोपनीयता का कर्तव्य
手浴	हस्त प्रक्षालन
手話	(बधिरों के लिए) सांकेतिक भाषा
除圧	विसंपीड़न, चाप मुक्त करना
障害	विकलांगता
障害基礎年金	विकलांग हेतु मूल पेंशन
障害の受容	विकलांगता की स्वस्वीकृति
小規模多機能型居宅介護	बहुक्रियात्मक लघु गृह सेवा
少子化	गिरती जन्मदर
少子高齢化	जन्मदर में कमी व वृद्ध जनसंख्या में वृद्धि
静脈栄養法	अन्त: शिरा पोषण
職業のリハビリテーション	व्यवसायिक पुनर्वास
食事	भोजन ; आहार
食事介護	आहार देने में दीर्घकालीन सेवा
食事介助	आहार देने में सहायक सेवा
食事動作	भोजन संबंधी क्रिया
食事療法	पोषण चिकित्सा
褥瘡	शय्या व्रण ; लंबे समय तक शय्याग्रस्त रहने से बनने वाले ज़ख्म
褥瘡予防	शय्या व्रण निवारण
食中毒	दूषित या विषाक्त भोजन खाने से उत्पन्न स्थिति
食品衛生	भोजन स्वच्छता
植物状態	वनस्पति-समान अवस्था
植物性食品	शाकाहार
食欲	क्षुधा
食欲不振	भूख न लगना
ショートステイ	दीर्घकालीन सेवा के लिए अस्थाई निवास
初老期認知症	जरापूर्व मनोभ्रंश
自立	स्वतंत्रता
自立支援	स्वतंत्रता अवलंबन
自立度	स्वतंत्र जीवन का स्तर
視力低下	दृष्टि क्षीणता
事例検討	वस्तुपरक/व्यक्ति अध्ययन ; केस स्टडी
心気症	रोगभ्रांति
人工呼吸	कृत्रिम श्वसन
身上監護	व्यक्तिगत अभिभावकता
心身症	मनोकाय रोग
振戦	कंपन
心臓弁膜症	हृत्कपाट संबंधी रोग ; हृत्कपाटीय रोग
身体介護	शारीरिक दीर्घ सेवा
身体機能	शारीरिक क्रियाकलाप संबंधी योग्यता
信頼関係	सौहार्द संबंध
推奨量	निर्देशित आहार मात्रा
水分バランス	जल संतुलन
水分補給	[शरीर में] पुनः जल पहुँचाना ; जलापूर्ति
水疱	छाला ; फफोला
睡眠	निद्रा
頭痛	सिरदर्द
ストレス	तनाव
ストレッチャー	स्ट्रेचर
ストレングス視点	स्वशक्ति संज्ञान [प्रविधि]
スーパーバイザー	निरीक्षक
スーパーバイジー	निरीक्षित व्यक्ति
スーパービジョン	निरीक्षण
スピリチュアルケア	आध्यात्मिक सेवा
生活援助	जीवन रक्षक अवलंबन
生活環境	पारिस्थितकीय परिवेश
生活習慣病	जीवन शैली संबंधित रोग
生活の質	जीवन की गुणवत्ता
生活扶助	जीविकोपार्जन सहायता
生活歴	जीवन वृत
清潔	स्वच्छता
清拭	शय्या स्नान
精神科ソーシャルワーカー	मनोचिकित्सीय सामाजिक कार्यकर्ता
精神障害	मनोरोग ; मनोविकार
精神障害者	मनोरोगी ; मनोविकृत व्यक्ति
精神保健福祉士	प्रमाणित मनोचिकित्सीय सामाजिक कार्यकर्ता
成年後見制度	वयस्क संरक्षण पद्धति
整髪	केश प्रसाधन
生命の延長	जीवन अवधि वर्धन
生命倫理	जैवनैतिकता
整容	व्यक्तिगत स्वच्छता
世界保健機関	विश्व स्वास्थ्य संगठन
脊髄損傷	रीढ़ की हड्डी की चोट
脊椎圧迫骨折	दबा से होने वाला कशेरु का भंग
世帯	गृहस्थी ; कुटुम्ब
摂食	आहार अंतर्ग्रहण
摂食障害	आहार अंतर्ग्रहण विकार
セミファーラー位	सेमी फाउलर पोज़ीशन
セルフケア	स्वसेवा
セルフヘルプグループ	स्व-सहायता समूह
繊維	रेशा
全援助	संपूर्ण सहायता
洗顔	मुख प्रक्षालन/मुँह धोना
洗剤	कपड़े धोने का साबुन ; शोधक
洗浄	धुलाई
染色体異常	असामान्य गुणसूत्र

全人格的ケア　पूर्ण व्यक्तिगत सेवा	聴覚障害　श्रवण विकार
全身清拭　शय्या में संपूर्ण शरीर का स्नान	長寿社会　दीर्घायु समाज
全身浴　संपूर्ण स्नान	調整交付金　समायोजन अनुदान
尖足　ड्राप फुट ; पैर का लटक जाना	重複障害　विविध विकलांगताएँ
洗濯　वस्त्रों की धुलाई	腸閉塞　आन्त्रशूल
洗髪　शैम्पू	調理　पाचन क्रिया
せん妄　घ्सन्निपात आदि जनितघ् मानसिक उन्माद	調理方法　पाक प्रविधि
総入れ歯　कृत्रिम दंतावली	聴力レベル　श्रवणस्तर
躁うつ病　मानसिक अवसाद जनित मनोविक्षिप्ति	直接援助技術　साक्षात् सामाजिक कार्य
早期発見　आरंभिक अवस्था में [रोग का] पता चलना	対麻痺　अधरांगघात
装具　विकलांगी उपकरण	通所介護　दिवसीय सेवा
掃除　सफाई ; झाड़-पोंछ	通所リハビリテーション　दिवसीय सेवा
喪失体験　[प्रियजन के] खोने का अनुभव	杖　छड़ी
側臥位　करवट में लेटना	杖歩行　छड़ी की सहायता से चलना
足浴　पद प्रक्षालन	手洗い　हस्त प्रक्षालन
咀嚼　चवर्ण ; चबाने की क्रिया	低血圧　निम्न रक्तचाप
ソーシャルワーカー　सामाजिक कार्यकर्ता	低血糖　अल्प मधुमयता
措置制度　कल्याण स्थापन पद्धति	T字杖　T [आकार की] छड़ी
措置費　कल्याण स्थापन लागत	摘便　[बाह्य उपकरण द्वारा] मल उत्सर्जन
体位変換　स्तिथि परिवर्तन	手すり　रेलिंग, जंगला
体温　शरीर का तापमान	手引き　हाथ पकड़ कर मार्ग दर्शन करना
体温測定　तापमान लेना	伝音難聴　ध्वनि संचरण संबंधी बाधा मूलक बधिरता
退行　प्रतिक्रमण	点字　ब्रेल
帯状疱疹　विसर्पिका ; त्वचा रोग	電動車いす　विद्युत व्हील चेयर
大腿四頭筋　चतुर्भुजी जंघापेशी	電動ベッド　विद्युत शय्या
大腸癌　वृहदान्त्र कैंसर	動悸　धड़कन ; स्पंदन
代読　अक्षम व्यक्ति के लिए पढ़ना	統合失調症　खंडित मानसिकता ; विक्षिप्तता रोग
代筆　अक्षम व्यक्ति की ओर से लिखना	透析　डायलेसिस
代理電話　अक्षम व्यक्ति की ओर से फोन करना	疼痛　पीड़ा
ダウン症候群　डाउन संलक्षण	糖尿病　मधुमेह
立ち上がり　खड़ा होना, उत्थान	動脈硬化　धमनियों का मोटा हो जाना
脱臼　संधिच्युति	特殊寝台　विशिष्ट शय्या
脱水症　शरीर में पानी की कमी	特殊浴槽　विशिष्ट स्नान-कुंड
他動運動　व्यक्ति या उपकरण की सहायता से व्यायाम करना	特別治療食　उपचारार्थ विशेषाहार
ターミナルケア　अंतकालीन सेवा	特別養護老人ホーム　वरिष्ठ नागरिक [हेतु] कल्याण गृह
短下肢装具　ए. एफ.ओ. [पैरों के लिए] विकलांगी उपकरण	読話　ओष्ठपठन
端座位　बैठने की स्थिति	吐血　रक्त वमन
チアノーゼ　श्यावता	徒手筋力テスト　शारीरिक बल परीक्षण ; एम. एम. टी.
地域包括支援センター　समुदाय समग्र सेवा केन्द्र	独居　एकाकी जीवन
地域密着サービス　समुदाय आधारित सेवा	内部障害　आंतरिक अंग विकार
チェーンストークス呼吸　चाइन-स्टोक्स श्वसन	難聴　श्रवण क्षीणता
蓄尿障害　मूत्र संग्रह में बाधा	難病　असाध्य रोग
知的障害　बुद्धि ह्रास ; मानसिक मंदन	ニーズ　आवश्यकताएँ
知的障害者　मंद बुद्धि व्यक्ति	日常生活活動　दैनिक जीवन क्रियाकलाप
知能　बुद्धि	日内変動　जीव चक्रीय परिवर्तन
知能指数　बुद्धि लब्धि	入眠　निद्रा में जाना ; सो जाना
痴呆　मनोभ्रंश	入浴　स्नान
痴呆性老人　मनोभ्रष्ट वृद्ध	尿　मूत्र
痴呆性老人の日常生活自立度　मनोभ्रष्ट वृद्ध का स्वावलंबन स्तर	尿意　पेशाब करने का सामान्य आवेग
	尿器　शय्या मूत्रपात्र
チームアプローチ　टीम अप्रोच ; सामूहिक उपक्रम	尿失禁　मूत्र-नियंत्रण असमर्थता
チームケア　सामूहिक सेवा	尿路感染　मूत्र नलिका संक्रमण
着脱　वस्त्र पहनना व उतारना	認知症　मनोभ्रंश

ヒンディ語

認知症高齢者	मनोभष्ट वृद्ध	非言語的コミュニケーション	अशाब्दिक वार्तालाप
認知症高齢者の日常生活自立度	विक्षिप्त वृद्ध का स्वतंत्रता/आत्मनिर्भता स्तर	ビタミン	विटामिन
		筆記試験	लिखित परीक्षा
認知症対応型共同生活介護	मनोभष्ट वृद्ध रोगी हेतु सामूहिक गृह	被保険者	बीमाकृत व्यक्ति
		肥満	मोटापा
認知症対応型通所介護	मनोभष्ट हेतु दिवसीय सेवा	秘密保持	गोपनीयता
寝返り	करवट बदलना	氷枕	बर्फ का तकिया
寝たきり	शय्याग्रस्त	氷嚢	बर्फ की थैली
寝たきり度	शय्याग्रस्त होने की मात्रा	日和見感染	अवसरवादी संक्रमण
熱傷	जलने का घाव ; प्रदाह	貧血	लालरक्त कोशिकाओं की कमी ; रक्त-अल्पता
寝床	शय्या ; बिस्तर	頻便	बारंबार मलोत्सर्ग
年金	पेंशन	ファーラー位	फाउलर पोजीशन
脳血管障害	प्रमस्तिष्कीय वाहिका विकार	フェイスシート	फेसशीट
脳血管性認知症	प्रमस्तिष्कीय वाहिका मनोभ्रंश	フォローアップ	क्रियान्वयन
脳血栓症	प्रमस्तिष्कीय शिरावरोध	腹臥位	अधोमुख आसन ; पेट के बल लेटना
脳梗塞	प्रमस्तिष्कीय संक्रमण	副作用	नकारात्मक प्रभाव
脳死	मस्तिष्क निष्क्रियता	福祉	कल्याण
脳出血	प्रमस्तिष्कीय रक्त स्राव	福祉機器	कल्याण उपकरण
脳性麻痺	मस्तिष्कीय पक्षाघात ; सी. पी.	腹式呼吸	उदरीय श्वसन
脳塞栓	प्रमस्तिष्कीय रक्तवाहिनी अवरोध	福祉事務所	समाज कल्याण कार्यालय
能力低下	अपंगता ; विकलांगता	福祉用具	कल्याण संबंधी सामग्री
ノーマライゼーション	सामान्यीकरण	福祉用具貸与	भाड़ा कृत कल्याण उपकरण
ノンレム睡眠	नॉन रैपिड निद्रा [एन.आर.ई.एम.]	浮腫	शोध ; सूजन
肺炎	निमोनिया, फुप्फुस प्रदाह	フットサポート	पादावलंबन
徘徊	निरुद्देश्य इधर उधर घूमना	部分介助	सीमित सहयोग/सहायता
肺癌	फेफड़े का कैंसर	部分清拭	आंशिक शय्या स्नान
肺気腫	फुप्फुसीय वातस्फीति	部分浴	आंशिक स्नान
バイキング食	वाइकिंग आहार	プライバシー	गोपनीयता ; व्यक्तिगत जीवन
バイスティックの7原則	बाइस्टेक के सात सिद्धांत	プライマリ・ケア	प्राथमिक सेवा
排泄	मलमूत्र त्याग	プロフィール	रूपरेखा ; प्रोफाइल
排泄介助	मलत्याग में सहायता	平均寿命	औसत जीवन अवधि
バイタルサイン	जीवन चिह्न	平均余命	औसत जीवन प्रत्याशा
排尿	मूत्र त्याग	ベッド	शय्या
排尿困難	मूत्र त्याग में कठिनाई	ベッドから車いす	शय्या से व्हीलचेयर
排尿障害	मूत्र संबंधी विकार	ベッドメーキング	बिस्तर बिछाना
排便	मल त्याग	便器	शय्या मलपात्र
排便障害	मल त्याग विकार	便失禁	मलनिरोध असमर्थता
廃用萎縮	अनुपयोग जनित अस्थि या मांसपेशीय अपक्षय	便秘	कब्ज
廃用症候群	अव्यवहार	片麻痺	पक्षाघात
パーキンソン病	पार्किन्संज रोग [अंग कंपन]	保育士	प्रमाणित परिचर्या कार्यकर्ता
白杖	सफेद छड़ी	防炎素材	अग्नि रोधक पदार्थ
白内障	मोतियाबिंद	防汚素材	मैल रोधक पदार्थ
長谷川式簡易認知症スケール改訂版	हासेगावा मनोभ्रंश मापदंड-संशोधित [एच डी एस-आर]	訪問介護	गृह-सहायता
		訪問看護	गृहागमन परिचर्या
バックサポート	पृष्ठ अवलंबन ; बैक सपोर्ट	訪問看護ステーション	आगंतुक परिचारिका केन्द्र
発達障害	बालावस्था में होने वाले विकार	訪問入浴介護	आगंतुक परिचारिका द्वारा स्नान सेवा
発熱	ज्वर	訪問リハビリテーション	गृह सेवा पुनर्वास
バリアフリー	बाधा मुक्त	保健師	लोक स्वास्थ्य परिचारिकी
バルンカテーテル	बैलून कैथिटर	保険者	बीमा कर्ता
半身浴	अर्ध शरीर स्नान	保健所	लोक स्वास्थ्य केंद्र
半調理	अधपका भोजन	保険料	बीमा किश्त
BMI	बी.एम.आई.	歩行	चाल
被害妄想	उत्पीड़न की भांति	歩行器	वॉकर ; चलने में सहायक उपकरण

歩行練習　चाल प्रशिक्षण	立位　खड़े होने की स्थिति
ポジショニング　स्थिति निर्धारित करना	利尿剤　मूत्रवर्धक औषधि
補足給付　पूरक लाभ	リハビリテーション　पुनर्वास ; पुनर्संचालन
ポータブルトイレ　पोर्टेबल टॉयलेट ; वहनीय शौचालय	リハビリテーション医学　पुनर्संचालन औषधि
ポータブル浴槽　वहनीय स्नान कुंड	リハビリテーション介護　पुनर्संचालन हेतु दीर्घकालीन सेवा
補聴器　श्रवण साधन ; हियरिंग एड	留置カテーテル　स्थाई कैथिटर
発疹　चिती, दाने	流動食　तरल आहार
発赤　लाली	流動性知能　अस्थिर बौद्धिकता
ボディメカニクス　बॉडी मैकेनिक्स, शरीर यांत्रिकी	利用料　उपयोग शुल्क
ホームヘルパー　गृह-सहायक	レクリエーション　मनोरंजन
ボランティア　स्वयं सेवक	レム睡眠　रैपिड आई निद्रा
ホルモン　अंतःस्राव ; हार्मोन	聾　बधिरता ; बहरापन
マット　चटाई	老化　बुढ़ापा आना
松葉杖　बैसाखी	老眼　जराजन्य दूरदृष्टि
麻痺　पक्षाघात ; लकवा	老人性うつ病　जराजन्य मनोभ्रंश
ミキサー食　अर्ध द्रवित आहार	老人性難聴　जराजन्य बधिरता
ミネラル　खनिज	老人保健施設　वृद्ध-स्वास्थ्य सुविधा
脈拍　नाड़ी	老年認知症　जराजन्य मनोभ्रंश
メタボリック症候群　उपापचय संलक्षण	老齢基礎年金　वृद्धावस्था मूल पेंशन
滅菌　बंध्याकरण	老齢年金　वृद्धावस्था पेंशन
妄想　भ्रांति	老齢福祉年金　वृद्धावस्था कल्याण पेंशन
燃え尽き症候群　शक्ति क्षय संलक्षण	ロールプレイ　रोलप्ले ; अभिनय
モニタリング　निरीक्षण	
問題行動　समस्याजनक व्यवहार	
夜間せん妄　रात्रि प्रलाप	
薬剤　औषधि	
薬剤管理　औषधि प्रबंधन	
薬剤師　औषधि विक्रेता ; केमिस्ट	
薬物療法　औषधि उपचार	
有料老人ホーム　गैर-सरकारी वृद्ध सेवासदन	
ユニットケア　यूनिट केयर	
ユニバーサルファッション　सार्वजनीन फैशन	
要援護高齢者　सहायतार्थी वृद्ध	
要介護　दीर्घकालीन सेवा की आवश्यकता	
要介護者　दीर्घकालीन सेवा प्रार्थी	
要介護度　दीर्घकालीन सेवा की आवश्यकता अवस्था	
要介護認定　दीर्घकालीन सेवा की आवश्यकता का प्रमाणन	
養護老人ホーム　वृद्धाश्रम	
要支援　दीर्घकालीन सहायता की आवश्यकता	
要支援者　दीर्घकालीन सहायतार्थी	
要支援認定　सहायता आवश्यकता का प्रमाणन	
腰痛症　कटिवात	
腰痛体操　कमर दर्द उपचार हेतु व्यायाम	
腰痛予防　कमर दर्द निवारण	
抑制　संयम ; नियंत्रण	
浴槽　स्नान कुंड ; बाथटब	
予防給付　निवारक-लाभ	
四脚杖　चतुष्क छड़ी	
ライフサイクル　जीवन चक्र	
ライフスタイル　जीवन शैली	
ライフレビュー　जीवन पुनरावलोकन	
ラポール　सौहार्द संबंध	
理学療法士　भौतिक चिकित्सक	

ヒンディ語

8．フランス語 (French)

IQ　quotient intellectuel : Q.I.
ICIDH　Classification Internationale des Déficiences, des Incapacités et du Handicap : CIDIH
ICF　Classification Internationale du Fonctionnement, du handicap et de la santé : CIF
ICD　Classification Internationale des Maladies : CIM
アクティビティ　activité
アセスメント　évaluation
アテトーシス　athétose
アテトーゼ　athétose
アドボカシー　plaidoyer
アルツハイマー型認知症　démence sénile du type Alzheimer : DSTA
アルツハイマー病　maladie d'Alzheimer
安全管理　gestion de sécurité
罨法　fomentation
安眠　sommeil tranquille
安眠援助　soutien pour sommeil tranquille
安楽　confort
安楽な体位　position confortable
意識障害　troubles de la conscience
維持期リハビリテーション　rééducation à se maintenir
萎縮　atrophie
移乗動作　mouvements du déplacement
移送費　frais de transport
遺族基礎年金　pension de base de réversion
移動　déplacement
移動介護　aide de déplacement
移動関連福祉用具　équipement sociaux pour déplacements
移動トイレ　toilettes mobile
移動浴槽　baignoire mobile
衣服　vêtements
衣服着脱　changement de vêtements
衣料障害　irritation vestimentaire
医療ソーシャルワーカー　assistant medico-social
医療保険制度　régimes d'assurance maladie
インスリン　insuline
インテーク　entretien
インフォーマル　informel
陰部清拭　hygiène génitale
陰部洗浄　soin génital
インペアメント　déficience
うつ病　dépression
運営適正化委員会　Comité de Résolution des Plaintes
運動器の機能向上　amélioration des fonctions motrices
運動失調　ataxie
運動障害　troubles motrices
運動療法　thérapeutique par les exercices physiques
エアーパッド　matelas à air

エアーマット　matelas pneumatique
エイジズム　âgisme
エイズ　SIDA
栄養　nutrition
栄養改善　amélioration nutritionnelle
栄養管理　gestion nutritionnelle
栄養士　diététicien
栄養所要量　besoins nutritionnels
栄養素　nutriment
腋窩温　température axillaire
壊死　nécrose
ADL　Activités de la vie quotidienne : ADLVQ
NPO　organisme sans but lucratif
MRSA　staphylocoque doré résistant à la méthicilline : SDRM
MMSE　mini-examen de l'état mental : MEEM
MMT　bilan musculaire
嚥下　déglutition
嚥下困難　difficulté de déglutition
嚥下性肺炎　pneumonie par déglutition
嚥下補助剤　épaississant
エンゲル係数　coefficient d'Engel
円座　tapis circulaire
エンパワメント　autonomisation
応益負担　principe de bénéfice reçu
嘔気　nausée
応急手当　soins de premiers secours
嘔吐　vomissement
応能負担　principe de capacité de paiement
起き上がり　lever
おむつ　couche
おむつカバー　protection de couche
おむつ交換　changement des couches
おむつ外し　retrait de couche
臥位　position couchée
介護　soins de longue durée
介護過程　processus des soins de longue durée
介護技術　techniques des soins
介護休業　congé pour les soins familials
介護給付　prestation pour les soins de longue durée
介護計画　plan des soins
介護サービス計画　plan des services pour les soins de longue durée
介護支援専門員　responsable des soins de longue durée
介護指導　direction des soins de longue durée
介護者　soignant
介護職員　employé des soins
介護ニーズ　besoins des soins de longue durée
介護認定審査会　Comité de l'évaluation des Soins de

介護福祉　aide sociale pour les soins de longue durée
介護福祉士　agent des soins certifié
介護福祉士国家試験　Examen National de Certification pour les Agents des Soins
介護福祉士登録　Registre des Agents des Soins Certifiés
介護負担　charge des soins
介護報酬　rémunération des soins de longue durée
介護保険　Assurance des Soins de Longue Durée
介護保険事業計画　Plan des Soins de Longue Durée
介護保険審査会　Comité de Révision de l'Assurance des Soins de Longue Durée
介護保険制度　Système d'Assurance des Soins de Longue Durée
介護保険認定調査　études pour l'évaluation de l'Assurance des Soins de Longue Durée
介護保険法　Loi de l'Assurance des Soins de Longue Durée
介護目標　but des soins
介護用具　équipements pour les soins
介護予防　prévention des soins de longue durée
介護予防事業　plan de la prevention des soins de longue durée
介護療養型医療施設　établissement hospitalier pour les soins de longue durée
介護老人福祉施設　établissement social pour les soins de longue durée
介護老人保健施設　établissement médico-social pour les soins de longue durée
介護労働者　agent des soins
介助　aide
疥癬　gale
回想法　thérapie de réminiscence
階段　escalier
階段昇降　marche d'escalier
回復期リハビリテーション　rééducation de convalescence
潰瘍　ulcère
かかりつけ医　docteur en charge
核家族　famille nucléaire
家計　budget familial
家事　entretien ménager
家政　ménage
家政婦　femme de ménage
家族　famille
家族会　groupe d'entraide familial
家族介護　soins donnés par la famille
家族介護者　soignant de la famille
家族関係　relation familiale
合併症　complications
寡婦　veuve

Longue Durée

紙おむつ　couche en papier
過剰症候群　syndrome de surutilisation
加齢　vieillissement
癌　cancer
感音難聴　surdité neurosensorielle
感覚機能　fonction sensorielle
換気　ventilation
環境整備　aménagement de l'environnement
看護　sciences infirmières
肝硬変　cirrhose du foie
看護師　infirmier
関節　articulation
関節可動域　portée de mouvement
関節リウマチ　polyarthrite rhumatoïde
感染　infection
感染菌　bactérie
感染症　maladie infectieuse
感染予防　prévention de l'infection
浣腸　lavement
観念失行　apraxie idéatoire
管理栄養士　diététicien certifié
緩和ケア　soin palliatif
記憶障害　troubles de la mémoire
着替え　changement de vêtements
気管　trachée
危険防止　prévention de risque
起座位　position assise
義歯　dent artificielle
義肢装具士　prothésiste et orthésiste : PO
基礎代謝　métabolisme basique
機能維持　entretien fonctionnel
機能訓練　entraînement fonctionnel
機能障害　troubles fonctionnels
記銘力　rétention de mémoire
虐待　maltraitance
ギャッチベッド　lit de Gatch
救急救命士　technicien d'urgence médicale : TUM
仰臥位　position couché allongé
共感　empathie
虚弱　faiblesse physique
起立性低血圧　hypotension orthostatique
記録　données
筋萎縮　atrophie musculaire
緊急連絡先　coordonées en cas d'urgence
金銭管理　gestion de portefeuille
苦情解決　résolution des griefs et des plaintes
くも膜下出血　hémorragie méningée
クリティカルパス　carte clinique
グループホーム　foyer du petit groupe
グループリビング　vie de groupe
グループレクリエーション　récréation en groupe
グループワーク　activités en groupe
車いす　fauteuil roulant

フランス語

車いすからベッド	transfert du fauteuil roulant au lit
車いすの移動	déplacement en fauteuil roulant
車いすの介助	aide pour le fauteuil roulant
クロックポジション	position horloge
ケア	soins
ケアカンファレンス	conférence des soins
ケアチーム	équipe des soins
ケアハウス	maison des soins
ケアプラン	plan des soins
ケアマネジメント	gestion des soins
ケアマネジャー	responsable des soins
ケアワーク	travail des soins
経管栄養	gavage
頸髄損傷	blessure de la moelle épinière cervicale
傾聴	écoute thérapeutique
契約	contrat
劇薬	médecine drastique
下血	méléna
ケースカンファレンス	étude du cas en groupe
ケースワーク	entrerien
血圧	pression sanguine
下痢	diarrhée
幻覚	hallucination
健康	santé
健康観察	observation de santé
健康保険	assurance maladie
言語障害	troubles du langage
言語聴覚士	orthophoniste
見当識障害	désorientation
権利擁護	plaidoyer des droits de l'homme
公益事業	utilité publique
公益法人	administration de prestations publiques
構音障害	troubles de l'articulation
後期高齢者	personne âgée de plus de 75 ans
抗菌・防臭素材	matériaux antibactérien et désodorisant
口腔機能の向上	amélioration des fonctions orales
口腔ケア	soins de la santé buccale
合計特殊出生率	taux de fertilité total : TFT
高血圧	hypertension artérielle
拘縮	contracture
拘縮予防	prévention des contractures
公証人	notaire
公正証書	acte notarial
抗生物質	antibiotique
拘束	contention
後天性免疫不全症候群	Syndrome d'immunodéficience acquise : SIDA
高齢化	population vieillissante
高齢期障害	troubles du vieillissement
高齢者	personne âgée
高齢社会	société vieillissante
高齢者虐待	maltraitance sur personne âgée
高齢者虐待防止法	Loi pour la Prévention des Maltraitances sur Personnes Agées
高齢者世帯	ménage des personnes âgées
声かけ	encouragement verbal
誤嚥	aspiration pulmonaire
誤嚥性肺炎	pneumonie par aspiration
呼吸	respiration
呼吸機能障害	troubles des fonctions respiratoires
国際疾病分類	Classification Internationale des Maladies : CIM
国際障害分類	Classification Internationale des Déficiences, des Incapacités et du Handicap : CIDIH
国際生活機能分類	Classification Internationale du Fonctionnement, du handicap et de la santé : CIF
国際標準化機構	Organisation Internationale de Normalisation : ISO
骨折	fracture
骨粗鬆症	ostéoporose
言葉かけ	encouragement verbal
個別介護	soins individualisés
コミュニケーション	communication
コミュニケーションエイド	aide à la communication
コレステロール	cholestérol
献立	menu
座位	position assise
再アセスメント	réévaluation
在宅介護	soins à domicile
在宅看護	infirmier à domicile
在宅ケア	soins à domicile
作業療法	ergothérapie
作業療法士	ergothérapeute
サービス担当者会議	réunion des personnels en charge
サポートシステム	réseau des soutiens
残存機能	fonction résiduelle
散髪	coupe des cheveux
紫外線遮蔽素材	matériaux de protection contre les ultraviolets
歯科衛生士	hygiéniste dentaire
視覚障害	troubles de la vue
視覚障害者	déficient visuel
弛緩	flasque
止血	hémostase
思考障害	troubles de la pensée
自己覚知	conscience de soi
自己決定	autodétermination
自己実現	réalisation de soi-même
脂質異常症	dyslipidémie
自傷行為	Automutilation
自助具	matériaux adaptés
死生観	façon de voir la vie et la mort
施設介護	soins aux établissements
自尊心	estime de soi
肢体不自由	infirme

実技試験　Examen de Pratique Professionnelle
失禁　incontinence
失語　aphasie
シーツ交換　changement de draps
実支出　dépenses effectuées
実収入　revenu réel
失認　agnosie
実務経験証明書　preuve d'expérience professionnelle
自動運動　mouvement actif
児童期障害　troubles de l'enfance
自閉症　autisme
社会資源　ressources sociales
社会的不利　désavantage social
社会福祉　aide sociale
社会福祉士　agent des services sociaux certifié
社会福祉事業　services sociaux
社会保険　assurance sociale
社会保障　Sécurité Sociale
社会保障審議会　Conseil Consultatif de la Sécurité Sociale
視野狭窄　restriction du champ visuel
視野障害　défaut de champ visuel
シャワー浴　douche
収益事業　exploitation rentable
従属人口　population dépendante
住宅改修　rénovation de la maison
終末期　phase terminale
終末期介護　soins palliatifs
主治医　médecin en charge
主治医意見書　note du médecin
手段的日常生活活動　activité instrumentale de la vie quotidienne
出血　saignement
守秘義務　devoir de confidentialité
手浴　manuluve
手話　langage des signes
除圧　décompression
障害　déficiences et incapacités
障害基礎年金　Pension de base pour personnes handicapées
障害の受容　acceptation des déficiences et incapacités
小規模多機能型居宅介護　services des soins à domiciles multifonctionnels à petite échelle
少子化　baisse de la natalité
少子高齢化　baisse de la natalité et vieillissement de la population
静脈栄養法　alimentation parentérale
職業的リハビリテーション　rééducation professionnel
食事　repas
食事介護　aide du repas
食事介助　aide à l'alimentation
食事動作　manières de manger

食事療法　régime alimentaire
褥瘡　escarre de décubitus
褥瘡予防　prévention de l'escarre de décubitus
食中毒　intoxication alimentaire
食品衛生　hygiène alimentaire
植物状態　état végétatif
植物性食品　nourriture végétale
食欲　appétit
食欲不振　perte d'appétit
ショートステイ　l'accueil de jour
初老期認知症　démence présénile
自立　indépendance
自立支援　aide à l'indépendance
自立度　niveau d'indépendance
視力低下　perte de la vue
事例検討　étude de cas
心気症　hypochondrie
人工呼吸　respiration artificielle
身上監護　tutelle
心身症　maladie psychosomatique
振戦　tremblement
心臓弁膜症　valvulopathie
身体介護　soins physiques
身体機能　fonction physique
信頼関係　rapport de confiance
推奨量　apports alimentaires recommandés
水分バランス　équilibre électrolytique dans le corps
水分補給　réhydratation
水疱　cloque
睡眠　sommeil
頭痛　mal de tête
ストレス　stress
ストレッチャー　civière
ストレングス視点　perspective de forces
スーパーバイザー　superviseur
スーパーバイジー　supervisé
スーパービジョン　supervision
スピリチュアルケア　soins spirituels
生活援助　aide à domicile
生活環境　conditions de vie
生活習慣病　maladie liée au style de vie
生活の質　qualité de vie
生活扶助　assistance pour besoins quotidiens
生活歴　historique
清潔　propreté
清拭　toilette
精神科ソーシャルワーカー　assistant social de service psychiatrique
精神障害　troubles psychiatriques
精神障害者　déficient mental
精神保健福祉士　assistant social de service psychiatrique certifié
成年後見制度　système de tutelle pour adultes

フランス語

整髪　coiffure	他動運動　exercice passif
生命の延長　extension l'espérance de vie	ターミナルケア　soins palliatifs
生命倫理　bioéthique	短下肢装具　orthèse cheville-pied
整容　hygiène personnelle	端座位　position assis redressé
世界保健機関　Organisation Mondiale de la Santé : OMS	チアノーゼ　cyanose
脊髄損傷　blessure de la moelle épinière	地域包括支援センター　centre local des soins globaux
脊椎圧迫骨折　fracture ou compression de la colonne vertébrale	地域密着サービス　service local des soins
	チェーンストークス呼吸　dyspnée de Cheyne-Stokes
世帯　ménage	蓄尿障害　troubles de la poche à urine
摂食　prise de nourriture	知的障害　troubles intellectuels
摂食障害　troubles de l'alimentation	知的障害者　déficient intellectuel
セミファーラー位　position de demi-Fowler	知能　intelligence
セルフケア　autosoins	知能指数　quotient intellectuel : Q.I.
セルフヘルプグループ　groupe d'entraide	痴呆　démence
繊維　fibre	痴呆性老人　personne âgée démentielle
全援助　assistance totale	痴呆性老人の日常生活自立度　niveau d'indépendance de la personne âgée démentielle
洗顔　toilette	
洗剤　détergent	チームアプローチ　approche en équipe
洗浄　lavage	チームケア　soins en équipe
染色体異常　aberration chromosomique	着脱　changement de vêtements
全人格的ケア　soins personnels complets	聴覚障害　troubles de l'audition
全身清拭　toilette complet	長寿社会　société de longévité
全身浴　bain complet	調整交付金　subvention d'ajustement
尖足　pied tombant	重複障害　infirmités multiples
洗濯　lessive	腸閉塞　occlusion intestinale
洗髪　shampooing	調理　cuisine
せん妄　délire	調理方法　recette de cuisine
総入れ歯　dentition complète	聴力レベル　niveau d'audition
躁うつ病　psychose maniacodépressive	直接援助技術　pratique de travail social direct
早期発見　détection précoce	対麻痺　paraplégie
装具　orthèse	通所介護　service de jour
掃除　nettoyage	通所リハビリテーション　rééducation aux établissements
喪失体験　expérience de perte	
側臥位　décubitus latéral	杖　canne
足浴　pédiluve	杖歩行　déplacement avec canne
咀嚼　mastication	手洗い　lavage des mains
ソーシャルワーカー　assistant social	低血圧　hypotension artérielle
措置制度　système d'affectation des patients	低血糖　hypoglycémie
措置費　coûts d'affectation des patients	T字杖　canne en T
体位変換　changement de position	摘便　extraction des selles
体温　température corporelle	手すり　main courante
体温測定　mesure de la température corporelle	手引き　accompangement à la main
退行　régression	伝音難聴　surdité de transmission
帯状疱疹　zona	点字　Braille
大腿四頭筋　muscle quadriceps crural	電動車いす　fauteuil roulant électrique
大腸癌　cancer du colon	電動ベッド　lit à réglages électriques
代読　assistance de lecture	動悸　palpitation
代筆　allographe	統合失調症　schizophrénie
代理電話　assistance téléphonique	透析　dialyse
ダウン症候群　trisomie 21	疼痛　douleur
立ち上がり　debout	糖尿病　diabète
脱臼　luxation	動脈硬化　artériosclérose
脱水症　déshydratation	特殊寝台　lit spécialisé

特殊浴槽　baignoire spécialisée
特別治療食　régime thérapeutique spécial
特別養護老人ホーム　maison de retraite avec soins intensifs
読話　lecture labiale
吐血　hématémèse
徒手筋力テスト　bilan musculaire
独居　vie seul
内部障害　troubles internes
難聴　perte auditive
難病　maladie incurable
ニーズ　besoins
日常生活活動　activités de la vie quotidienne : ADLVQ
日内変動　variation circadienne
入眠　s'endormir
入浴　bain
尿　urine
尿意　désir d'uriner
尿器　bouteille d'urine
尿失禁　incontinence urinaire
尿路感染　infection urinaire
認知症　démence
認知症高齢者　personne âgée démentielle
認知症高齢者の日常生活自立度　niveau d'indépendance de la personne âgée démentielle
認知症対応型共同生活介護　soins pour la vie en groupe avec les déments
認知症対応型通所介護　service des soins pour les déments
寝返り　roulement
寝たきり　grabataire
寝たきり度　niveau grabataire
熱傷　brûlure
寝床　lit
年金　retraite
脳血管障害　trouble cérébrovasculaire
脳血管性認知症　démence cérébrovasculaire
脳血栓症　thrombose cérébrale
脳梗塞　infarctus cérébral
脳死　mort cérébrale
脳出血　hémorragie cérébrale
脳性麻痺　infirmité motrice cérébrale : IMC
脳塞栓　embolie cérébrale
能力低下　incapacité
ノーマライゼーション　normalisation
ノンレム睡眠　sommeil lent
肺炎　pneumonie
徘徊　vagabondage
肺癌　cancer du poumon
肺気腫　emphysème pulmonaire
バイキング食　buffet
バイスティックの7原則　les 7 principes de Biestek
排泄　excrétion

排泄介助　aide de l' excrétion
バイタルサイン　signe vital
排尿　urination
排尿困難　difficulté d'urination
排尿障害　troubles urinaires
排便　défécation
排便障害　dyschézie
廃用萎縮　atrophie par inaction
廃用症候群　syndrome d'inaction
パーキンソン病　maladie de Parkinson
白杖　canne blanche
白内障　cataracte
長谷川式簡易認知症スケール改訂版　mesure révisée de la démence d'Hasegawa
バックサポート　soutien dorsal
発達障害　troubles du développement
発熱　fièvre
バリアフリー　accès facile
バルンカテーテル　cathéter de Fogarty
半身浴　bain moitié du corps
半調理　plat à moitié préparé
BMI　indice de masse corporelle : IMC
被害妄想　délire de persécution
非言語的コミュニケーション　communication non verbale
ビタミン　vitamine
筆記試験　examen écrit
被保険者　l'assuré
肥満　obésité
秘密保持　confidentialité
氷枕　coussin glacé
氷嚢　vessie de glace
日和見感染　infection opportuniste
貧血　anémie
頻便　défécation fréquente
ファーラー位　position de Fowler
フェイスシート　dossier du patient
フォローアップ　suivi
腹臥位　procubitus
副作用　effet secondaire
福祉　aide sociale
福祉機器　équipements pour l'aide sociale
腹式呼吸　respiration abdominale
福祉事務所　agence sociale
福祉用具　équipements sociaux
福祉用具貸与　location d'équipements sociaux
浮腫　œdème
フットサポート　repose-pied
部分援助　aide partielle
部分清拭　toilette partielle
部分浴　bain partiel
プライバシー　vie privée
プライマリ・ケア　soins primaires

フランス語

日本語	Français
プロフィール	profil
平均寿命	espérance de vie moyenne
平均余命	espérance de vie
ベッド	lit
ベッドから車いす	transfert du lit au fauteuil roulant
ベッドメーキング	faire le lit
便器	bassin hygiénique
便失禁	incontinence fécale
便秘	constipation
片麻痺	hémiplégie
保育士	éducateur certifié pour les jeunes enfants
防炎素材	matériaux ignifugé
防汚素材	matériaux non salissant
訪問介護	soins à domicile
訪問看護	soins de la santé à domicile
訪問看護ステーション	infirmier visiteur
訪問入浴介護	soins de bain à domicile
訪問リハビリテーション	soins de la rééducation à domicile
保健師	infirmier de la santé publique
保険者	l'assureur
保健所	centre de la santé publique
保険料	cotisation d'assurance
歩行	démarche
歩行器	cadre de marche
歩行練習	entraînement à la marche
ポジショニング	posture passive
補足給付	prestation supplémentaire
ポータブルトイレ	toilettes portables
ポータブル浴槽	baignoire portable
補聴器	aide auditive
発疹	éruption
発赤	rougeur
ボディメカニクス	mécanisme corporel
ホームヘルパー	aide à domicile
ボランティア	bénévole
ホルモン	hormone
マット	tapis
松葉杖	béquille
麻痺	paralysie
ミキサー食	régime au mixeur
ミネラル	minéral
脈拍	pouls
メタボリック症候群	syndrome métabolique
滅菌	stérilisation
妄想	illusion sensorielle
燃え尽き症候群	syndrome d'épuisement professionnel
モニタリング	monitorage
問題行動	comportement à problème
夜間せん妄	délire nocturne
薬剤	médication
薬剤管理	gestion de médication
薬剤師	pharmacien
薬物療法	pharmacothérapie
有料老人ホーム	maison de retraite privée
ユニットケア	soins par petit groupe
ユニバーサルファッション	mode universelle
要援護高齢者	personne âgée nécessitant une assistance
要介護	soins necessaries de longue durée
要介護者	bénéficiare des soins de longue durée
要介護度	niveaux de classification des soins de longue durée
要介護認定	certificat des soins necessaires de longue durée
養護老人ホーム	maison de retraite
要支援	assistance nécessaire de longue durée
要支援者	bénéficiaire d'assistance de longue durée
要支援認定	certificat d'assistance nécessaire de longue durée
腰痛症	lumbago
腰痛体操	exercice pour lumbago
腰痛予防	prévention du lumbago
抑制	contention
浴槽	baignoire
予防給付	prestation préventive
四脚杖	canne tétrapode
ライフサイクル	cycle de vie
ライフスタイル	style de vie
ライフレビュー	examen rétrospectif de la vie
ラポール	rapport
理学療法士	physiothérapeute
立位	position debout
利尿剤	diurétique
リハビリテーション	rééducation
リハビリテーション医学	médecine de réadaptation
リハビリテーション介護	soins de rééducation
留置カテーテル	sonde à demeure
流動食	régime liquide
流動性知能	intelligence fluide
利用料	coûts d'utilisation
レクリエーション	récréation
レム睡眠	sommeil paradoxal
聾	surdité
老化	vieillissement
老眼	presbytie
老人性うつ病	dépression sénile
老人性難聴	surdité sénile
老人保健施設	établissement médico-social pour les personnes âgées
老年認知症	démence sénile
老齢基礎年金	pension de vieillesse de base
老齢年金	pension de vieillesse
老齢福祉年金	pension d'aide sociale de vieillesse
ロールプレイ	jeu de rôle

9．ベトナム語（Vietnamese）

IQ　chỉ số thông minh	エアーパッド　miếng đệm
ICIDH　phân loại khuyết tật : ICIDH	エアーマット　nệm hơi
ICF　Bảng phân loại Quốc tế về chức năng khuyết tật và sức khỏe	エイジズム　sự phân biệt đối xử với người già
ICD　phân loại căn bệnh nhiễm : ICED	エイズ　bệnh Sida : AIDS
アクティビティ　sự vận động ; hoạt động	栄養　dinh dưỡng
アセスメント　sự đánh giá	栄養改善　cải thiện dinh dưỡng
アテトーシス　chứng hoạt động không chủ đích của tay và chân	栄養管理　quản lý chế độ dinh dưỡng
アテトーゼ　chứng hoạt động không chủ đích của tay và chân	栄養士　nhà sinh dưỡng
	栄養所要量　lượng chất dinh dưỡng cần
アドボカシー　sự hỗ trợ	栄養素　chất dinh dưỡng
アルツハイマー型認知症　chứng mất trí Alzheimer	腋窩温　nhiệt độ vùng nách
アルツハイマー病　bệnh Alzheimer	壊死　hoại tử
安全管理　giám sát an toàn	ADL　hoạt động sinh hoạt hằng ngày
罨法　chườm nóng	NPO　NPO
安眠　ngon giấc	MRSA　MRSA
安眠援助　hỗ trợ ngủ ngon giấc	MMSE　kiểm tra MMSE
安楽　thoải mái	MMT　kiểm tra MMT nhận định mức độ bại liệt
安楽な体位　điểm đặt vị trí cơ thể cho thoải mái	嚥下　nuốt
意識障害　khuyết tật nhận thức	嚥下困難　khó nuốt
維持期リハビリテーション　tập vật lý trị liệu thời kỳ duy trì	嚥下性肺炎　viêm phổi do thức ăn đi vào cuống phổi
	嚥下補助剤　thuốc hỗ trợ đưa thức ăn xuống dạ dày
萎縮　sự teo	エンゲル係数　hệ số Engel
移乗動作　di chuyển bằng máy móc	円座　tấm đệm tròn
移送費　chi phí di chuyển	エンパワメント　sự trao quyền
遺族基礎年金　tiền trợ cấp cơ bản cho thân nhân	応益負担　chi phí người bệnh cần chi trả
移動　sự di chuyển	嘔気　sự nôn mửa
移動介護　sự săn sóc khi di chuyển	応急手当　chăm sóc ứng cứu
移動関連福祉用具　những dụng cụ di chuyển phúc lợi xã hội	嘔吐　làm cho nôn mửa
	応能負担　trả thuế theo khả năng
移動トイレ　toilet di động	起き上がり　ngồi dậy
移動浴槽　bồn tắm di động	おむつ　tả lót
衣服　trang phục	おむつカバー　cái bọc tả lót
衣服着脱　cởi bỏ trang phục	おむつ交換　thay tả lót
衣料障害　dị ứng trang phục	おむつ外し　tháo tả lót
医療ソーシャルワーカー　nhân viên xã hội của bệnh viện	臥位　tư thế nằm
	介護　sự săn sóc
医療保険制度　chế độ bảo hiểm chữa bệnh	介護過程　quá trình săn sóc
インスリン　insulin	介護技術　kỹ thuật săn sóc
インテーク　hấp thụ	介護休業　nghỉ phép theo chế độ săn sóc người nhà
インフォーマル　không chính thức	介護給付　trợ cấp săn sóc
陰部清拭　lau âm hộ	介護計画　kế hoạch săn sóc
陰部洗浄　rửa âm hộ	介護サービス計画　kế hoạch phục vụ săn sóc bệnh nhân
インペアメント　thương tật ; khuyết tật	介護支援専門員　chuyên viên hỗ trợ săn sóc
うつ病　bệnh trầm uất	介護指導　chỉ đạo săn sóc
運営適正化委員会　Ủy ban chuẩn hóa hành chính	介護者　người săn sóc
運動器の機能向上　nâng cao chức năng máy tập thể dục	介護職員　nhân viên săn sóc
	介護ニーズ　nhu cầu săn sóc
運動失調　sự mất điều hòa vận động	介護認定審査会　Hội thẩm định mức độ săn sóc
運動障害　thiếu năng vận động	介護福祉　ngành săn sóc phúc lợi xã hội
運動療法　phương pháp vận động trị liệu	介護福祉士　chuyên viên săn sóc phúc lợi

ベトナム語

介護福祉士国家試験　kỳ thi quốc gia chuyên viên săn sóc phúc lợi
介護福祉士登録　sự đăng ký chuyên viên săn sóc phúc lợi
介護負担　gánh nặng săn sóc
介護報酬　thù lao săn sóc
介護保険　bảo hiểm săn sóc
介護保険事業計画　chương trình sự nghiệp bảo hiểm săn sóc
介護保険審査会　hội thẩm định bảo hiểm săn sóc
介護保険制度　chế độ bảo hiểm săn sóc
介護保険認定調査　điều tra nhận định
介護保険法　luật bảo hiểm săn sóc
介護目標　mục tiêu săn sóc
介護用具　dụng cụ săn sóc
介護予防　săn sóc phòng ngừa
介護予防事業　công cuộc dự phòng cho săn sóc
介護療養型医療施設　cơ sở điều trị săn sóc
介護老人福祉施設　cơ sở săn sóc phúc lợi người già
介護老人保健施設　cơ sở bảo hiểm săn sóc người già
介護労働者　người săn sóc
介助　hỗ trợ săn sóc
疥癬　ghẻ lở
回想法　phương pháp hồi tưởng
階段　cầu thang bộ
階段昇降　thăng và giảm cấp săn sóc
回復期リハビリテーション　tập vật lý trị liệu trong giai đoạn hồi phục
潰瘍　bị loét
かかりつけ医　bác sỹ thường khám cho mình
核家族　gia đình hạt nhân
家計　kinh tế gia đình
家事　việc nhà
家政　người quản lý gia đình
家政婦　người trông coi gia đình
家族　gia đình
家族会　Hội tương trợ của những gia đình
家族介護　săn sóc tại gia
家族介護者　người thân săn sóc bệnh nhân
家族関係　mối quan hệ gia đình
合併症　biến chứng
寡婦　góa phụ
紙おむつ　tã lót giấy
過症侯群　triệu chứng của chứng lạm dụng
加齢　thêm tuổi
癌　ung thư
感音難聴　bệnh điếc
感覚機能　chức năng cảm nhận
換気　sự thay đổi không khí
環境整備　môi trường thiết bị
看護　y tá
肝硬変　bệnh xơ gan
看護師　chuyên viên y tá
関節　khớp

関節可動域　phạm vi cử động khớp
関節リウマチ　bệnh thấp khớp
感染　truyền nhiễm
感染菌　vi khuẩn lây bệnh
感染症　chứng lây nhiễm
感染予防　phòng chống lây nhiễm
浣腸　súc ruột
観念失行　rối loạn hành động
管理栄養士　chuyên viên dinh dưỡng
緩和ケア　sự chăm sóc nhẹ nhàng
記憶障害　sự mất trí nhớ
着替え　thay đổi trang phục
気管　khí quản
危険防止　phòng ngừa hiểm nguy
起座位　vị trí đứng
義歯　răng giả
義肢装具士　nhân viên hỗ trợ gắn tay chân giả
基礎代謝　trao đổi chất cơ bản
機能維持　chức năng duy trì
機能訓練　tập vật lý trị liệu
機能障害　khuyết tật chức năng
記銘力　khả năng nhớ
虐待　sự ngược đãi
ギャッチベッド　giường điều khiển tự động
救急救命士　chuyên viên cứu hộ
仰臥位　tư thế nằm ngửa
共感　đồng cảm
虚弱　sự suy nhược
起立性低血圧　hạ huyết áp khi đứng lên
記録　ký lục ; sự ghi lại
筋萎縮　sự teo cơ
緊急連絡先　nơi liên lạc khi khẩn cấp
金銭管理　quản lý tiền bạc
苦情解決　giải quyết than phiền khách hàng
くも膜下出血　chảy máu dưới nhện
クリティカルパス　đường tới hạn [phân khúc dễ phát sinh vấn đề và tốn thời gian nhất trong 1 dự án]
グループホーム　nhóm gia đình
グループリビング　sinh hoạt theo nhóm của người già
グループレクリエーション　giải trí theo nhóm
グループワーク　làm việc theo nhóm xã hội
車いす　xe lăn
車いすからベッド　di chuyển từ xe lăn lên giường
車いすの移動　di chuyển bằng xe lăn
車いすの介助　sự hỗ trợ cho xe lăn
クロックポジション　chốt khóa
ケア　sự chăm sóc
ケアカンファレンス　hội thảo về chăm sóc
ケアチーム　Đội chăm sóc
ケアハウス　Nhà chăm sóc
ケアプラン　kế hoạch chăm sóc
ケアマネジメント　quản trị phục vụ chăm sóc
ケアマネジャー　quản lý phục vụ chăm sóc

日本語	ベトナム語	日本語	ベトナム語
ケアワーク	công tác chăm sóc		khuyết tật và sức khỏe
経管栄養	ống thức ăn	国際標準化機構	ISO ; Cơ quan chuẩn hóa quốc tế
頸髄損傷	chấn thương đốt sống cổ	骨折	gãy xương
傾聴	tạo kỹ năng lắng nghe cho bệnh nhân	骨粗鬆症	chứng loãng xương
契約	hợp đồng	言葉かけ	bắt chuyện với..
劇薬	loại thuốc nguy hiểm	個別介護	điều dưỡng săn sóc cá biệt
下血	sự chảy máu hậu môn	コミュニケーション	sự giao tiếp
ケースカンファレンス	cuộc họp phân định nhiệm vụ phương hướng	コミュニケーションエイド	sự giúp đỡ trong giao tiếp
ケースワーク	nhiệm vụ và phương hướng công việc	コレステロール	chất béo cholesterol
		献立	thực đơn
血圧	huyết áp	座位	tư thế ngồi
下痢	sự tiêu chảy	再アセスメント	tái định giá
幻覚	ảo giác	在宅介護	săn sóc tại nhà
健康	sức khỏe	在宅看護	sự điều dưỡng tại nhà
健康観察	theo dõi sức khỏe	在宅ケア	sự chăm sóc tại nhà
健康保険	bảo hiểm sức khỏe	作業療法	phương pháp trị liệu bằng lao động
言語障害	thiểu năng ngôn ngữ	作業療法士	bác sỹ chuyên khoa tác nghiệp phương pháp trị liệu
言語聴覚士	chuyên viên ngôn ngữ và thính giác	サービス担当者会議	buổi họp nhân viên phụ trách dịch vụ
見当識障害	khuyết tật định hướng nhận thức	サポートシステム	hệ thống hỗ trợ
権利擁護	bảo hộ quyền lợi	残存機能	chức năng còn tồn tại
公益事業	Công ty công ích	散髪	cắt tóc
公益法人	Công ty công ích tư cách pháp nhân	紫外線遮蔽素材	chất liệu ngăn tia cực tím
構音障害	thiểu năng phát âm	歯科衛生士	chuyên viên vệ sinh răng miệng
後期高齢者	giai đoạn cuối người cao tuổi	視覚障害	khuyết tật thị lực
抗菌・防臭素材	chất liệu khánh khuẩn và tránh mùi	視覚障害者	người khuyết tật thị giác
口腔機能の向上	khắc phục các chức năng khoang miệng	弛緩	nới lỏng
口腔ケア	sự săn sóc răng miệng	止血	cầm máu
合計特殊出生率	tổng hợp tỷ lệ sinh hiếm	思考障害	tâm thần phân liệt
高血圧	cao huyết áp	自己覚知	sự tự nhận thức
拘縮	sự co cứng ; co rút	自己決定	tự quyết
拘縮予防	phòng tránh co cứng	自己実現	sự thể hiện
公証人	người công chứng	脂質異常症	chứng rối loạn mỡ trong máu
公正証書	hồ sơ công chứng	自傷行為	hành vi tự gây thương tích
抗生物質	thuốc kháng sinh	自助具	dụng cụ tự hỗ trợ
拘束	sự kiềm chế	死生観	quan điểm sinh tử
後天性免疫不全症候群	bệnh Sida ; AIDS ; bệnh thiếu miễn dịch tổng hợp	施設介護	cơ sở săn sóc
高齢化	cao tuổi hóa	自尊心	lòng tự tôn
高齢期障害	khuyết tật vào giai đoạn tuổi cao	肢体不自由	cơ thể bị khuyết tật
高齢者	người cao tuổi	実技試験	thi thực hành
高齢社会	xã hội người cao tuổi	失禁	mất chức năng điều khiển hành vi
高齢者虐待	ngược đãi người cao tuổi	失語	bị câm
高齢者虐待防止法	Luật phòng chống ngược đãi người cao tuổi	シーツ交換	thay đổi bọc nệm
高齢者世帯	hộ gia đình người cao tuổi	実支出	thực chi
声かけ	bắt chuyện với.	実収入	thực thu
誤嚥	sự nuốt nhầm	失認	sự mất nhận thức
誤嚥性肺炎	viêm phổi do hít nhầm	実務経験証明書	giấy chứng nhận lý lịch nghề nghiệp
呼吸	hô hấp	自動運動	sự tự vận động
呼吸機能障害	khuyết tật chức năng hô hấp	児童期障害	khuyết tật từ thời thơ ấu
国際疾病分類	ICED ; phân loại căn bệnh nhiễm	自閉症	chứng tự kỷ
国際障害分類	ICIDH ; phân loại khuyết tật	社会資源	tài nguyên xã hội
国際生活機能分類	Bảng phân loại Quốc tế về khả năng	社会の不利	sự bất lợi mang tính xã hội
		社会福祉	phúc lợi xã hội

ベトナム語

社会福祉士　chuyên viên phúc lợi xã hội	心気症　chứng nghi bịnh
社会福祉事業　sự nghiệp phúc lợi xã hội	人工呼吸　hô hấp nhân tạo
社会保険　bảo hiểm xã hội	身上監護　giám sát nhân thân [người khuyết tật]
社会保障　sự bảo hộ xã hội	心身症　bệnh tinh thần
社会保障審議会　Hội đồng xét duyệt bảo hộ xã hội	振戦　bệnh run
視野狭窄　giảm thị lực	心臓弁膜症　bệnh van tim
視野障害　khuyết tật thị lực	身体介護　sự săn sóc cơ thể
シャワー浴　tắm vòi sen	身体機能　chức năng cơ thể
収益事業　sự nghiệp thu lợi	信頼関係　mối quan hệ tin cậy
従属人口　dân số phụ thuộc	推奨量　lượng dinh dưỡng khuyến cáo RDA
住宅改修　sửa sang nhà cửa	水分バランス　cán cân lượng nước
終末期　giai đoạn cuối	水分補給　bổ sung nước cho cơ thể
終末期介護　sự săn sóc bệnh nhân giai đoạn cuối	水疱　bị rộp da
主治医　bác sỹ phụ trách	睡眠　ngủ
主治医意見書　sổ ý kiến bác sỹ điều trị chính	頭痛　đau đầu
手段的日常生活動　phương tiện sử dụng sinh hoạt hàng ngày	ストレス　căng thẳng
	ストレッチャー　người bị căng thẳng
出血　sự chảy máu	ストレングス視点　quan điểm giải quyết vấn đề bằng cách khai thác tiềm năng và điểm mạnh của bệnh nhân
守秘義務　nghĩa vụ bảo vệ bí mật	
手浴　tắm bằng tay	スーパーバイザー　người giám sát
手話　hội thoại bằng tay	スーパーバイジー　người thực hiện săn sóc đã được người giám sát cung cấp kiến thức chuyên môn
除圧　trừ [giảm] áp	
障害　khuyết tật	
障害基礎年金　tiền hưu trí cơ bản cho người khuyết tật	スーパービジョン　sự trông nom
	スピリチュアルケア　sự chăm sóc tinh thần
障害の受容　chấp nhận sự khuyết tật	生活援助　viện trợ cuộc sống
小規模多機能型居宅介護　sự săn sóc tại nhà đa chức năng quy mô nhỏ	生活環境　môi trường sinh hoạt
	生活習慣病　căn bệnh từ thói quen sinh hoạt
少子化　tình trạng trẻ con ít đi	生活の質　chất lượng cuộc sống
少子高齢化　Tình trạng hiếm muộn trẻ em nhiều người già	生活扶助　trợ giúp cuộc sống
	生活歴　quá trình sinh hoạt
静脈栄養法　phương pháp cung cấp dinh dưỡng cho tĩnh mạch	清潔　sự sạch sẽ
	清拭　dùng khăn lau sạch cơ thể
職業のリハビリテーション　vật lý trị liệu cho mỗi ngành nghề	精神科ソーシャルワーカー　nhân viên xã hội khoa Thần kinh
食事　bữa ăn	
食事介護　săn sóc bữa ăn	精神障害　rối loạn thần kinh
食事介助　hỗ trợ săn sóc ăn uống	精神障害者　người bị rối loạn thần kinh
食事動作　hành vi ăn uống	精神保健福祉士　nhân viên bảo hiểm phúc lợi về bệnh thần kinh
食事療法　phương pháp trị liệu bằng thức ăn	
褥瘡　tình trạng da bị thối [vì nằm mãi một tư thế]	成年後見制度　Chế độ bảo hộ dành cho người lớn
褥瘡予防　phòng ngừa thối loét vì nằm liệt giường	整髪　làm tóc
	生命の延長　sự kéo dài sinh mệnh
食中毒　sự trúng thực	生命倫理　lý luận về sinh mệnh
食品衛生　thức ăn vệ sinh	整容　ăn mặc gọn gàng
植物状態　tình trạng thực vật	世界保健機関　Tổ chức Y tế thế giới
植物性食品　thức ăn thực vật	脊髄損傷　tổn thương dây thần kinh cột sống
食欲　thèm ăn	脊椎圧迫骨折　sự gãy xương cột sống người già
食欲不振　không thèm ăn	
ショートステイ　ở lại săn sóc trong một thời gian ngắn	世帯　hộ gia đình
	摂食　hấp thụ thức ăn
初老期認知症　chứng mất trí khi mới về già	摂食障害　khuyết tật hấp thụ thức ăn
自立　tự lập	セミファーラー位　tư thế ngồi từ 15~30độ
自立支援　hỗ trợ tự lập	セルフケア　tự chăm sóc
自立度　mức độ tự lập	セルフヘルプグループ　nhóm tự chăm sóc
視力低下　thị lực kém	
事例検討　tham khảo tiền lệ	繊維　sợi quang

全援助　sự hỗ trợ chăm sóc toàn bộ	痴呆性老人の日常生活自立度　mức độ tự lập trong cuộc sống thường ngày của người già bị mất trí
洗顔　rửa mặt	
洗剤　bột giặt	チームアプローチ　đội tiếp cận
洗浄　sự giặt giũ	チームケア　đội chăm sóc
染色体異常　rối loạn nhiễm sắc thể	着脱　sự mặc và cởi trang phục
全人格のケア　sự chăm sóc riêng	聴覚障害　khuyết tật thính giác
全身清拭　lau sạch toàn thân	長寿社会　xã hội có người già tuổi thọ cao
全身浴　tắm toàn thân	調整交付金　sự điều chỉnh tiền trợ cấp
尖足　mũi chân bị dị tật đi bằng đầu ngón chân	重複障害　đa khuyết tật
洗濯　giặt giũ	腸閉塞　sự tắt đường ruột
洗髪　gội đầu	調理　nấu nướng
せん妄　mê sảng	調理方法　phương pháp nấu nướng
総入れ歯　răng giả toàn bộ	聴力レベル　khả năng nghe
躁うつ病　chứng vui buồn thất thường	直接援助技術　kỹ thuật hỗ trợ trực tiếp
早期発見　sự phát hiện sớm	対麻痺　toàn thân bất toại
装具　dụng cụ	通所介護　săn sóc đi về trong ngày
掃除　lau dọn	通所リハビリテーション　cơ sở vật lý trị liệu đi về trong ngày
喪失体験　trải nghiệm của sự mất mát	
側臥位　tư thế nằm nghiêng một bên	杖　cây gậy
足浴　tắm chân	杖歩行　đi nạng
咀嚼　nhai nát	手洗い　rửa tay
ソーシャルワーカー　nhân viên xã hội	低血圧　huyết áp thấp
措置制度　chế độ thẩm định người sử dụng phúc lợi xã hội	低血糖　giảm glucoza huyết
措置費　chi phí sự thẩm định	T字杖　gậy chữ T
体位変換　thay đổi tư thế nằm	摘便　lấy phân [bằng ngón tay]
体温　thân nhiệt	手すり　tay cầm
体温測定　đo thân nhiệt	手引き　sách hướng dẫn
退行　thoái lui	伝音難聴　điếc dẫn truyền
帯状疱疹　bệnh zona	点字　chữ nổi
大腿四頭筋　bốn đầu cơ đùi	電動車いす　xe lăn điều khiển tự động
大腸癌　ung thư đại tràng	電動ベッド　giường điều khiển tự động
代読　đọc thay	動悸　tim đập nhanh
代筆　viết thay	統合失調症　chứng tâm thần phân liệt
代理電話　gọi điện thoại thay	透析　sự thẩm tách
ダウン症候群　triệu chứng bệnh down	疼痛　đau nhức
立ち上がり　đứng dậy	糖尿病　DM ; bệnh tiểu đường
脱臼　trật khớp	動脈硬化　xơ cứng động mạch
脱水症　chứng mất nước	特殊寝台　giường ngủ đặc thù
他動運動　các hoạt động khác	特殊浴槽　bồn tắm đặc thù
ターミナルケア　chăm sóc giai đoạn cuối	特別治療食　thức ăn trị liệu đặc biệt
短下肢装具　thiết bị nối chân ngắn	特別養護老人ホーム　nhà dưỡng lão đặc biệt
端座位　tư thế ngồi trên giường	読話　kể chuyện
チアノーゼ　chứng xanh tím	吐血　thổ huyết
地域包括支援センター　Trung tâm hỗ trợ tổng quát	徒手筋力テスト　kiểm tra MMT nhận định mức độ bại liệt
地域密着サービス　sự phục vụ chăm sóc theo suốt	独居　sống một mình
チェーンストークス呼吸　hô hấp kiểu chetne-stokes	内部障害　khuyết tật nội tạng
蓄尿障害　khuyết tật bọng đái	難聴　bệnh điếc
知的障害　thiểu năng trí tuệ	難病　bệnh nan y
知的障害者　người bị thiểu năng trí tuệ	ニーズ　nhu cầu
知能　sự thông minh	日常生活活動　hoạt động sinh hoạt hằng ngày
知能指数　chỉ số thông minh	日内変動　sự biến động trong ngày
痴呆　chứng mất trí	入眠　ngủ thiếp đi
痴呆性老人　chứng mất trí ở người già	入浴　tắm rửa

ベトナム語

405

尿　nước tiểu	発熱　phát sốt
尿意　mắc tiểu	バリアフリー　tạo sự thuận lợi cho người khuyết tất tham gia hoạt động cộng đồng mà không có sự trở ngại
尿器　bình đựng nước tiểu	
尿失禁　đái dầm	バルンカテーテル　ống thông đường tiểu bình cầu
尿路感染　lây nhiễm qua ống niệu	半身浴　tắm nửa người
認知症　chứng mất trí	半調理　xử lý sơ qua thức ăn
認知症高齢者　chứng mất trí ở người cao tuổi	BMI　chỉ số BMI
認知症高齢者の日常生活自立度　mức độ tự lập trong cuộc sống hằng ngày của người cao tuổi bị chứng mất trí	被害妄想　sự hành hạ ảo tưởng
	非言語的コミュニケーション　sự giao tiếp phi ngôn ngữ
認知症対応型共同生活介護　Sự sống chung và săn sóc người mất trí	ビタミン　vitamin
	筆記試験　thi viết
認知症対応型通所介護　sự săn sóc đi về trong ngày dành cho người mất trí	被保険者　người được bảo hiểm
	肥満　béo phì
寝返り　lật mình khi ngủ	秘密保持　giữ bí mật
寝たきり　mê man liệt giường	氷枕　cái gối chườm bằng nước đá
寝たきり度　mức độ nằm liệt giường	氷囊　túi chườm bằng nước đá
熱傷　vết bỏng	日和見感染　nhiễm bệnh do cơ thể yếu [thường ở người già]
寝床　giường nằm	
年金　tiền hưu trí	貧血　thiếu máu
脳血管障害　người khuyết tật rối loạn mạch máu não	頻便　đại tiện nhiều lần trong ngày
脳血管性認知症　mất trí do yếu tố mạch máu não	ファーラー位　tư thế ngồi thẳng góc 45 độ
脳梗塞　nhồi máu não	フェイスシート　phiếu điều tra dư luận
脳死　não chết	フォローアップ　sự hỗ trợ
脳出血　xuất huyết não	腹臥位　tư thế nằm nghiêng một bên
脳性麻痺　liệt não	副作用　tác dụng phụ
脳塞栓　tắc động mạch não	福祉　phúc lợi xã hội
能力低下　thiếu năng	福祉機器　dụng cụ máy móc phúc lợi
ノーマライゼーション　sự tiêu chuẩn hóa	腹式呼吸　thở bằng bụng
ノンレム睡眠　giấc ngủ NREM	福祉事務所　văn phòng phúc lợi xã hội
肺炎　viêm phổi	福祉用具　dụng cụ phúc lợi
徘徊　đi lăng văng	福祉用具貸与　cho mượn dụng cụ phúc lợi xã hội
肺癌　ung thư phổi	浮腫　bệnh phù
肺気腫　khí thủng phổi	フットサポート　hỗ trợ chân
バイキング食　ăn buffe	部分援助　hỗ trợ từng phần
バイスティックの7原則　7 nguyên tắc của biestek	部分清拭　vệ sinh cục bộ
排泄　đi ngoài	部分浴　tắm cục bộ
排泄介助　sự giúp đỡ đi ngoài	プライバシー　riêng tư
バイタルサイン　dấu hiệu sự sống	プライマリ・ケア　chăm sóc cơ bản
排尿　tiểu tiện	プロフィール　lý lịch
排尿困難　khó đi tiểu	平均寿命　tuổi thọ bình quân
排尿障害　khuyết tật tiểu tiện	平均余命　dự báo thời gian sống trung bình
排便　đại tiện	ベッド　giường nằm
排便障害　khuyết tật đại tiện	ベッドから車いす　từ giường xuống xe lăn
廃用萎縮　sự teo dần khả năng hoạt động	ベッドメーキング　trải giường
廃用症候群　hội chứng đeo mang vật dụng trên mình	便器　bồn cầu
パーキンソン病　bệnh parkinson	便失禁　không cầm được đại tiện
白杖　gậy màu trắng	便秘　táo bón
白内障　bệnh đục thủy tinh thể	片麻痺　tê nửa người
長谷川式簡易認知症スケール改訂版　phiên bản mới của phương pháp xác định đơn giản bệnh mất trí Hasegawa	保育士　nhân viên giữ trẻ
	防炎素材　chất liệu phòng chống cháy
	防汚素材　chất liệu chống bẩn
バックサポート　hỗ trợ từ phía sau	訪問介護　việc đến nhà săn sóc
発達障害　khuyết tật phát triển	訪問看護　y tá đến nhà chăm sóc

訪問看護ステーション　điểm đến săn sóc của y tá
訪問入浴介護　y tá đến nhà săn sóc tắm gội
訪問リハビリテーション　đến nhà hướng dẫn tập vật lý trị liệu
保健師　chuyên gia sức khỏe
保険者　người tham gia bảo hiểm
保健所　cơ sở y tế
保険料　phí bảo hiểm
歩行　đi bộ
歩行器　thiết bị tập đi
歩行練習　tập đi
ポジショニング　đặt vào vị trí
補足給付　chu cấp hỗ trợ
ポータブルトイレ　toitet di động
ポータブル浴槽　bồn tắm di động
補聴器　thiết bị trợ thính
発疹　phát ban
発赤　phát đỏ ở da do viêm mạch máu
ボディメカニクス　kỹ thuật nâng đỡ người bệnh
ホームヘルパー　người giúp việc nhà
ボランティア　nhà từ thiện
ホルモン　hormone
マット　chiếu
松葉杖　cây nạng gỗ
麻痺　tê liệt
ミキサー食　thức ăn xay
ミネラル　chất khoáng
脈拍　mạch
メタボリック症候群　triệu chứng bệnh do thói quen sinh hoạt
滅菌　sự tiệt trùng
妄想　hoang tưởng
燃え尽き症候群　triệu chứng mỏi mệt đuối sức
モニタリング　sự định phân
問題行動　hành vi rắc rối
夜間せん妄　mê sảng
薬剤　thuốc thang
薬剤管理　quản lý thuốc men
薬剤師　dược sỹ
薬物療法　phương pháp dùng thuốc để cải thiện các triệu chứng bệnh thần kinh
有料老人ホーム　nhà dưỡng lão thu phí
ユニットケア　xếp bệnh nhân thành nhóm nhỏ để chăm sóc
ユニバーサルファッション　trang phục phổ biến
要援護高齢者　người cao tuổi cần hỗ trợ chăm sóc
要介護　cần sự săn sóc
要介護者　người cần sự săn sóc
要介護度　mức độ cần săn sóc
要介護認定　nhận định cần sự săn sóc
養護老人ホーム　nhà dưỡng lão
要支援　cần sự hỗ trợ
要支援者　người cần sự hỗ trợ
要支援認定　nhận định cần sự hỗ trợ

腰痛症　bệnh đau lưng
腰痛体操　bài thể dục cho đau lưng
腰痛予防　phòng bệnh đau lưng
抑制　sự kiềm chế
浴槽　bồn tắm
予防給付　trợ cấp phòng bệnh
四脚杖　gậy chống có 4 chân
ライフサイクル　chu kỳ trong cuộc sống
ライフスタイル　cách sống
ライフレビュー　hồi tưởng cuộc sống
ラポール　tình trạng dung hòa tinh thần
理学療法士　bác sỹ chuyên khoa phương pháp vật lý
立位　vị trí đứng
利尿剤　thuốc lợi tiểu
リハビリテーション　tập vật lý trị liệu
リハビリテーション医学　y học vật lý trị liệu
リハビリテーション介護　sự săn sóc vật lý trị liệu
留置カテーテル　ống thông đường tiểu đặt trong
流動食　thức ăn lỏng
流動性知能　khả năng học hỏi rút kinh nghiệm
利用者　phí sử dụng
レクリエーション　sự tiêu khiển
レム睡眠　kiểu ngủ REM
聾　bệnh điếc
老化　lão hóa
老眼　viễn thị
老人性うつ病　bệnh trầm uất ở người già
老人性難聴　bệnh điếc ở người già
老人保健施設　cơ sở bảo hiểm người già
老年認知症　chứng mất trí khi về già
老齢基礎年金　tiền hưu trí cơ bản cho người già
老齢年金　tiền hưu trí người già
老齢福祉年金　tiền hưu trí phúc lợi người già
ロールプレイ　phương pháp điều trị bằng cách sắm vai role-play

ベトナム語

10. ポルトガル語 (Portuguese)

IQ　quociente de inteligencia
ICIDH　Classificação internacional das deficiências, incapacidades e desvantagens
ICF　Classificação Internacional de funcionalidade, incapacidade e saúde
ICD　Classificação internacional das doenças : CID [os médicos usam a sigla CID9]
アクティビティ　atividade
アセスメント　avaliação
アテトーシス　atetose
アテトーゼ　atetose
アドボカシー　advocacia
アルツハイマー型認知症　demência senil do tipo Alzheimer
アルツハイマー病　doença de Alzheimer
安全管理　controle de segunça
罨法　cataplasma [uso do frio e calor no corpo como tratamento]
安眠　sono tranquilo
安眠援助　suporte para um sono tranquilo
安楽　conforto
安楽な体位　posição confortável
意識障害　distúrbio de consciência
維持期リハビリテーション　reabilitação no estágio crônico
萎縮　Atrofia
移乗動作　movimento de transferência
移送費　custo do transporte
遺族基礎年金　pensão anual basica
移動　movimento
移動介護　assistencia e cuidado durante o movimento
移動関連福祉用具　técnicas de implantação do bem-estar social relacionadas ao movimento de transferencia
移動トイレ　toalete portátil
移動浴槽　banheira portátil
衣服　vestimenta
衣服着脱　troca de roupas
衣料障害　vestimentas para portadores de deficiencias
医療ソーシャルワーカー　médico assistente social
医療保険制度　sistema de seguro saúde
インスリン　insulina
インテーク　admissão
インフォーマル　informal
陰部清拭　limpeza dos órgãos genitais
陰部洗浄　toalete perineal
インペアメント　dificultado
うつ病　depressão
運営適正化委員会　comitê de administração para alocação apropriada

運動器の機能向上　melhoria nos equipamentos de exercícios
運動失調　ataxia
運動障害　déficits de movimentos
運動療法　execício terapêutico
エアーパッド　almofada contendo ar
エアーマット　colchão contendo ar
エイジズム　ageism [palavra criada por Robert Neil Butler para] discriminação em relação aos idosos
エイズ　síndrome da imunudeficiência adquirida : SIDA
栄養　nutrição
栄養改善　melhoria nutricional
栄養管理　administração nutricional
栄養士　nutricionista
栄養所要量　requisição nutricional
栄養素　nutriente
腋窩温　temperatura axilar
壊死　necrose
ADL　atividades de vida diária
NPO　organização sem fins lucrativos
MRSA　staphylococcus aureus resistente à meticilina [batéria ultra resistente]
MMSE　mini exame do estado mental
MMT　teste muscular manual
嚥下　deglutição
嚥下困難　dificuldade de deglutição
嚥下性肺炎　pneumonia aspirativa
嚥下補助剤　suplemento para auxiliar a deglutição
エンゲル係数　coeficiente de Engel [Para cálculo de despesas domiciliares]
円座　capacho [forma circular]
エンパワメント　poder
応益負担　beneficios a serem pagos
嘔気　náusea
応急手当　primeiros socorros em emergência
嘔吐　vômito
応能負担　disposição a ser paga
起き上がり　levantar-se
おむつ　fralda
おむつカバー　capa da fralda
おむつ交換　troca de fralda
おむつ外し　remoção da fralda
臥位　repousar
介護　cuidados prolongados
介護過程　procedimentos em cuidados prolongados
介護技術　técnicas em cuidados prolongados
介護休業　periodo sem cuidados prolongados
介護給付　beneficios em cuidados prolongados
介護計画　planejamento de cuidados prolongados

介護サービス計画　plano e serviços em cuidados prolongados
介護支援専門員　administrador de cuidados
介護指導　guia em cuidados prolongados
介護者　cuidador
介護職員　cuidador profissional
介護ニーズ　necessidades em cuidados prolongados
介護認定審査会　certificado de inspeção e autorização para cuidados prolongados
介護福祉　bem-estar e cuidados prolongados
介護福祉士　administrador de cuidados prolongados
介護福祉士国家試験　exame nacional para profissionais de cuidados prolongados
介護福祉士登録　registro de cuidador profissional
介護負担　encargos em cuidados prolongados
介護報酬　despesas em cuidados prolongados
介護保険　seguro de cuidados prolongados
介護保険事業計画　plano de seguro em cuidados prolongados
介護保険審査会　inspeção do seguro de cuidados prolongados
介護保険制度　sistema de seguro para cuidados prolongados
介護保険認定調査　investigacao para autorizacao de seguro em cuidados prolongados
介護保険法　lei de seguros em cuidados prolongados
介護目標　objetivos dos cuidados prolongados
介護用具　equipamentos em cuidados prolongados
介護予防　prevenção em cuidados prolongados
介護予防事業　trabalho de prevenção em cuidados prolongados
介護療養型医療施設　instituição de saúde para cuidados prolongados
介護老人福祉施設　instituição de bem estar em cuidados prolongados para idosos
介護老人保健施設　instituição de saúde em cuidados prolongados para idosos
介護労働者　profissionais de cuidados prolongados
介助　assistência
疥癬　sarna
回想法　terapia da reflexão
階段　escada
階段昇降　subir e descer escadas
回復期リハビリテーション　fase de recuperação na reabilitação
潰瘍　úlcera
かかりつけ医　médico encarregado
核家族　núcleo familiar
家計　orçamento domestico
家事　afazeres domésticos
家政　economia doméstica
家政婦　empregada doméstica
家族　família

家族会　grupo de auto-ajuda para famílias
家族介護　cuidados prolongados em família
家族介護者　cuidador da família
家族関係　relacionamento familiar
合併症　complicações
寡婦　viúva
紙おむつ　fralda papel
過用症候群　síndrome causada pelo uso excessivo
加齢　envelhecimento
癌　Câncer
感音難聴　surdez neuro-sensorial
感覚機能　função sensorial
換気　ventilação
環境整備　manutenção do meio ambiente
看護　enfermeiro/a
肝硬変　cirrose hepática
看護師　enfermeira
関節　articulação
関節可動域　nível ou grau de mobilidade articular
関節リウマチ　artrite reumatóide
感染　infecção
感染菌　bactéria infecciosa
感染症　doença infecciosa
感染予防　prevenção de infecção
浣腸　enema [introdução de líquido no ânus para lavagem, purgação ou administração de medicamentos]
観念失行　apraxia ideomotora
管理栄養士　responsável pelo gerenciamento nutricional
緩和ケア　cuidado paliativo
記憶障害　deficit de memória
着替え　troca de roupas
気管　traquéia
危険防止　prevenção de riscos
起座位　posição no leito
義歯　prótese dentaria
義肢装具士　usuario de prótese e órtese
基礎代謝　metabolismo basal
機能維持　manutenção funcional
機能訓練　treino funcional
機能障害　perda funcional
記銘力　Capacidade de registrar
虐待　abuso e maus tratos
ギャッチベッド　cama hospitalar
救急救命士　paramédico [técnico em salvar vidas em casos de emergência]
仰臥位　posição supina
共感　empatia
虚弱　fisicamente fraco
起立性低血圧　hipotensão ortostática
記録　registro
筋萎縮　atrofia muscular

ポルトガル語

緊急連絡先　contato em caso de emergência
金銭管理　administração financeira
苦情解決　resolução de dúvidas e queixas
くも膜下出血　hemorragia subaracnóide
クリティカルパス　decisão crítica
グループホーム　grupo do lar
グループリビング　grupo de vida diária
グループレクリエーション　grupo recreacional
グループワーク　grupo de trabalho social
車いす　cadeira de rodas
車いすからベッド　da cadeira de rodas para o leito
車いすの移動　movimento com a cadeira de rodas
車いすの介助　assistência em cadeira de rodas
クロックポジション　posição de relógio
ケア　cuidados
ケアカンファレンス　conferência sobre cuidados
ケアチーム　grupo de cuidados
ケアハウス　casa de repouso
ケアプラン　plano de cuidados
ケアマネジメント　administração dos cuidados
ケアマネジャー　administrador de cuidados
ケアワーク　cuidados no trabalho
経管栄養　alimentação por sonda
頸髄損傷　lesão da coluna cervical
傾聴　escuta atenta
契約　contrato
劇薬　Droga perigosa
下血　melena [fezes pastosas de cor escura e cheiro fétido]
ケースカンファレンス　caso para conferência
ケースワーク　relato de caso
血圧　pressão sanguinea
下痢　diarréia
幻覚　alucinação
健康　saúde
健康観察　observação da saúde
健康保険　seguro saúde
言語障害　disfasia
言語聴覚士　fonoaudiólogo
見当識障害　desorientação
権利擁護　direitos reivindicados
公益事業　economia e utilidade pública
公益法人　corporacao de beneficio público
構音障害　déficit na articulação da palavras
後期高齢者　terceira idade
抗菌・防臭素材　material estéril e inodoro
口腔機能の向上　melhoria na função oral
口腔ケア　cuidados da saúde bucal
合計特殊出生率　taxa de fertilidade total
高血圧　hipertensão
拘縮　contratura
拘縮予防　prevenção das contraturas
公証人　notoriedade pública

公正証書　ato notório
抗生物質　antibiótico
拘束　limitação, restrição
後天性免疫不全症候群　síndrome da imunodeficiência adquirida：AIDS
高齢化　envelhecimento populacional
高齢期障害　doenças geriátricas
高齢者　pessoa idosa
高齢社会　sociedade da terceira idade
高齢者虐待　abuso e maus tratos em idosos
高齢者虐待防止法　lei de prevenção contra abusos de idosos
高齢者世帯　lar do idoso
声かけ　cuidados na comunicação
誤嚥　má deglutição
誤嚥性肺炎　pneumonia por aspiração
呼吸　respiração
呼吸機能障害　disfunção respiratória
国際疾病分類　Classificação Internacional das Doenças
国際障害分類　Classificação Internacional das Deficiências, Incapacidades e Desvantagens
国際生活機能分類　Classificação Internacional de Funcionalidade, Incapacidade e Saúde
国際標準化機構　Organização Internacional para Padronização
骨折　fratura
骨粗鬆症　osteoporose
言葉かけ　cuidados no discurso
個別介護　cuidados individuais
コミュニケーション　comunicação
コミュニケーションエイド　apoio comunicativo
コレステロール　colesterol
献立　cardápio
座位　posição sentado
再アセスメント　reavaliação
在宅介護　serviços domiciliares de cuidados prolongados
在宅看護　enfermagem domiciliares
在宅ケア　cuidados domiciliares
作業療法　terapia ocupacional
作業療法士　terapeuta ocupacional
サービス担当者会議　reunião do grupo de serviço
サポートシステム　sistema de apoio
残存機能　função residual
散髪　corte de cabelo
紫外線遮蔽素材　protetor contra raio ultravioleta
歯科衛生士　higiene dental
視覚障害　deficiência visual
視覚障害者　cego
弛緩　flácido
止血　hemostasia
思考障害　distúrbio de pensamento

自己覚知　auto-avaliação
自己決定　autodeterminação
自己実現　auto-realização
脂質異常症　dislipidemia
自傷行為　auto mutilação
自助具　equipamento de autonomia
死生観　ponto de vista sobre vida e morte
施設介護　instituto para cuidados prolongados
自尊心　auto-estima
肢体不自由　portador de deficiência motora
実技試験　exame prático
失禁　incontinência
失語　afasia
シーツ交換　troca de lençóis
実支出　despesas atuais
実収入　renda atual
失認　agnosia
実務経験証明書　certificado de prática para cuidadores
自動運動　movimento ativo
児童期障害　desordens da infância e juventude
自閉症　autismo
社会資源　recurso social
社会的不利　deficiência social
社会福祉　bem-estar social
社会福祉士　assistente social
社会福祉事業　trabalho da assistência social
社会保険　seguro social
社会保障　seguridade social
社会保障審議会　Conselho de Seguridade Social
視野狭窄　restrição do campo visual
視野障害　déficit no campo visual
シャワー浴　banho de chuveiro
収益事業　negócio lucrativo
従属人口　população dependente
住宅改修　reforma do lar
終末期　estágio terminal
終末期介護　cuidados prolongados em pacientes na fase terminal
主治医　médico encarregado
主治医意見書　julgamento por escrito do médico encarregado em cuidados prolongados
手段的日常生活活動　instrumentos para atividades de vida diária
出血　sangramento
守秘義務　direitos de confidencialidade
手浴　lavagem das mãos
手話　linguagem de sinais
除圧　descompressão
障害　deficiência
障害基礎年金　pensão básica para deficientes
障害の受容　aceitação das incapacidades
小規模多機能型居宅介護　pequena casa de serviços e cuidados multifuncionais

少子化　redução da taxa de natalidade
少子高齢化　baixa taxa de natalidade e envelhecimento populacional
静脈栄養法　nutrição parenteral
職業的リハビリテーション　reabilitação vocacional
食事　refeição
食事介護　refeição em cuidados prolongados
食事介助　assistência alimentar
食事動作　movimento alimentar
食事療法　dieta terapêutica
褥瘡　úlcera de decúbito ou pressão
褥瘡予防　prevenção de úlceras de pressão
食中毒　envenenamento alimentar
食品衛生　saneamento alimentar
植物状態　estado vegetativo
植物性食品　alimento de origem vegetal
食欲　apetite
食欲不振　anorexia
ショートステイ　estadia curta permanência para cuidados prolongados
初老期認知症　demência pré-senil
自立　independência
自立支援　suporte para indepedência
自立度　grau de vida independente
視力低下　baixa acuidade visual
事例検討　estudo de caso
心気症　hipocondria
人工呼吸　respiração artificial
身上監護　tutor pessoal
心身症　doença psicossomática
振戦　tremor
心臓弁膜症　doença cardiovalvar
身体介護　cuidados prolongados individuais
身体機能　capacidade física
信頼関係　relação de confiança [harmonia]
推奨量　nutrientes diários recomendados
水分バランス　balanço hídrico
水分補給　reidratação
水疱　cluster
睡眠　sono
頭痛　dor de cabeça
ストレス　estresse
ストレッチャー　maca
ストレングス視点　persperctiva de força
スーパーバイザー　supervisor
スーパーバイジー　supervisão
スーパービジョン　supervisão
スピリチュアルケア　cuidados espirituais
生活援助　suporte vital
生活環境　circunstancias da vida
生活習慣病　doenças relacionados ao estilo de vida
生活の質　qualidade de vida
生活扶助　assistência de vida

ポルトガル語

| 生活歴 histórico de vida
| 清潔 higiene
| 清拭 banho no leito
| 精神科ソーシャルワーカー trabalho de assistente social em psquiatria
| 精神障害 doença psiquiátrica
| 精神障害者 paciente psiquiátrico
| 精神保健福祉士 certificado de psiquiatra assistente social
| 成年後見制度 sistema de tutoria de adultos
| 整髪 cabeleleiro
| 生命の延長 expectativa de vida
| 生命倫理 bioética
| 整容 melhoria da aparência estética
| 世界保健機関 Organização Mundial da Saúde : OMS
| 脊髄損傷 lesão da medula espinhal
| 脊椎圧迫骨折 fratura por compressão de vértebra
| 世帯 lar
| 摂食 ingestão de alimento
| 摂食障害 dificuldade na ingestão de alimento
| セミファーラー位 semi deitado [30 graus]
| セルフケア auto cuidado
| セルフヘルプグループ grupo de auto-ajuda
| 繊維 fibra
| 全援助 assitência financeira
| 洗顔 limpeza facial
| 洗剤 detergente
| 洗浄 lavagem
| 染色体異常 anormalidade cromossômica
| 全人格的ケア cuidado totalmente personalizado
| 全身清拭 banho do corpo inteiro no leito
| 全身浴 banho de todo o corpo
| 尖足 pé equino
| 洗濯 lavanderia
| 洗髪 shampoo
| せん妄 delírio
| 総入れ歯 prótese dentaria total
| 躁うつ病 Transtorno bipolar do Humor
| 早期発見 detecção precoce
| 装具 órteses
| 掃除 limpeza
| 喪失体験 perda da experiência pessoal
| 側臥位 decúbito lateral
| 足浴 banho dos pés
| 咀嚼 mastigação
| ソーシャルワーカー assistente social
| 措置制度 sistema das ações básicas em bem-estar
| 措置費 custos das ações em bem-estar
| 体位変換 mudança de posição
| 体温 temperatura corporal
| 体温測定 medida de temperatura corporal
| 退行 regressão
| 帯状疱疹 herpes zoster

| 大腿四頭筋 músculo quadríceps femural
| 大腸癌 câncer de cólon
| 代読 leitura ; assistência a leitura
| 代筆 secretário
| 代理電話 telefonia ; assistência telefônica
| ダウン症候群 síndrome de Down
| 立ち上がり ficar em pé
| 脱臼 deslocamento
| 脱水症 desidratação
| 他動運動 movimento passivo
| ターミナルケア cuidados terminais
| 短下肢装具 braçadeira curta para as pernas
| 端座位 da posição sentado para o leito
| チアノーゼ cianose
| 地域包括支援センター centro de cuidados da comunidade
| 地域密着サービス serviço de cuidados baseados na comunidade local
| チェーンストークス呼吸 respiração do tipo Cheyne-Stokes
| 蓄尿障害 distúrbio urinário
| 知的障害 incapacidade mental
| 知的障害者 portador de incapacidade mental
| 知能 inteligência
| 知能指数 quociente de inteligência
| 痴呆 demência
| 痴呆性老人 idoso portador de demência
| 痴呆性老人の日常生活自立度 grau de independência em vida diária para os idosos com demência
| チームアプローチ grupo de abordagem
| チームケア grupo de cuidados
| 着脱 vestir e tirar roupa
| 聴覚障害 déficit auditivo
| 長寿社会 sociedade com perspectivas de longevidade
| 調整交付金 ajuste subsidiário
| 重複障害 múltiplas incapacidades
| 腸閉塞 obstrução intestinal
| 調理 preparo de alimentos
| 調理方法 método para preparo de alimentos
| 聴力レベル capacidade auditiva
| 直接援助技術 técnica de assistencia social direta
| 対麻痺 paraplegia
| 通所介護 serviço dia
| 通所リハビリテーション cuidados diários
| 杖 bengala
| 杖歩行 deambular com a bengala
| 手洗い lavar as mãos
| 低血圧 hipotensão
| 低血糖 hipoglicemia
| T字杖 bengala em "T"
| 摘便 desimpactação
| 手すり corrimão
| 手引き guia

伝音難聴　perda auditiva condutiva
点字　escrita em braille
電動車いす　caldeira de rodas elétrica
電動ベッド　cama elétrica
動悸　palpitação
統合失調症　esquizofrenia
透析　diálise
疼痛　dor
糖尿病　diabetes mellitus：DM
動脈硬化　arterosclerose
特殊寝台　cama especial
特殊浴槽　banheira especial
特別治療食　dieta terapêutica especial
特別養護老人ホーム　instituição para cuidados
　　intensivos para idosos
読話　leitura de lábios
吐血　hematêmese [vômito de sangue]
徒手筋力テスト　teste muscular manual
独居　vida solitária
内部障害　deficiência interna
難聴　dificuldade auditiva
難病　doença incurável
ニーズ　necessidades
日常生活活動　atividades de vida diária
日内変動　ritmo circadiano
入眠　iniciar o sono
入浴　iniciar o banho
尿　urina
尿意　urgencia miccional
尿器　equipamento para urinar
尿失禁　incontinência urinária
尿路感染　infecção do trato urinário
認知症　demência
認知症高齢者　idoso portador de demência
認知症高齢者の日常生活自立度　grau de
　　independência em vida diária para os idosos
　　portadores de demência
認知症対応型共同生活介護　grupo de pessoas
　　portadoras de demência
認知症対応型通所介護　suporte para cuidados
　　relativos a demência [em instituições]
寝返り　rolar-se
寝たきり　acamado
寝たきり度　grau de pacientes acamados
熱傷　queimados
寝床　cama
年金　pensão；anuidade
脳血管障害　doença cerebrovascular
脳血管性認知症　demência por lesão
　　cerebrovascular
脳血栓症　trombose cerebral
脳梗塞　infarto cerebral
脳死　morte cerebral

脳出血　hemorragia cerebral
脳性麻痺　paralisia cerebral：PC
脳塞栓　embolia cerebral
能力低下　inabilidade
ノーマライゼーション　normalização
ノンレム睡眠　sono REM；sono rapid eye moviment
肺炎　pneumonia
徘徊　vagar sem rumo definido
肺癌　câncer de pulmão
肺気腫　enfisema pulmonar
バイキング食　buffet [disposição variada de pratos]
バイスティックの7原則　7 princípios de Biesteck
排泄　excreção
排泄介助　auxílio na excreção
バイタルサイン　sinais vitais
排尿　micção
排尿困難　dificuldade em urinar
排尿障害　distúrbio miccional
排便　defecar
排便障害　disquesia [doença do tracto intestinal]
廃用萎縮　atrofia por desuso
廃用症候群　síndrome causada pelo desuso
パーキンソン病　doença de Parkinson
白杖　bengala branca
白内障　catarata
長谷川式簡易認知症スケール改訂版　escala revisada
　　de demência de Hasegawa
バックサポート　suporte de costas
発達障害　distúrbio no desenvolvimento
発熱　febre
バリアフリー　sem barreiras
バルンカテーテル　balão do catéter
半身浴　banho parcial do corpo
半調理　comida semi cozida
BMI　índice de massa corporal：IMC
被害妄想　delírio persecutório
非言語的コミュニケーション　comunicação não verbal
ビタミン　vitamina
筆記試験　exame escrito
被保険者　segurado
肥満　obesidade
秘密保持　confidencial
氷枕　travesseiro de gelo
氷嚢　bolsa de gelo
日和見感染　infecção oportunista
貧血　anemia
頻便　defecações frequentes
ファーラー位　posição de Fowler
フェイスシート　papel para face
フォローアップ　follow up
腹臥位　posição prona
副作用　efeito colateral
福祉　bem-estar

ポルトガル語

日本語	Português
福祉機器	utensílios para o bem-estar
腹式呼吸	respiração abdominal
福祉事務所	escritório de bem-estar social
福祉用具	equipamentos para bem-estar
福祉用具貸与	aluguel de equipamentos em bem-estar
浮腫	edema
フットサポート	suporte para os pés
部分援助	assistência parcial
部分清拭	banho parcial no leito
部分浴	banho parcial
プライバシー	privacidade
プライマリ・ケア	cuidados primários
プロフィール	perfil
平均寿命	expectativa de vida
平均余命	média da expectativa de vida
ベッド	cama
ベッドから車いす	do leito para cadeira de rodas
ベッドメーキング	preparação do leito
便器	vaso sanitário
便失禁	incontinência fecal
便秘	constipação
片麻痺	hemiplegia
保育士	enfermeira
防炎素材	material contra incêndio
防汚素材	material anti-aderente
訪問介護	cuidados domiciliares
訪問看護	visita da enfermagem
訪問看護ステーション	visita do posto de enfermagem
訪問入浴介護	visita e cuidados com o banho
訪問リハビリテーション	visita da reabilitação
保健師	enfermeira de saúde pública
保険者	seguradora
保健所	centro de saúde pública
保険料	valor do seguro
歩行	caminhada
歩行器	andador
歩行練習	treino de marcha
ポジショニング	posicionamento
補足給付	benefício suplementário
ポータブルトイレ	banheiro portátil
ポータブル浴槽	banheiro portátil
補聴器	aparelho auditivo
発疹	erupção cutânea
発赤	rubor cutâneo
ボディメカニクス	mecânica corporal
ホームヘルパー	ajudante do lar
ボランティア	voluntário
ホルモン	hormônio
マット	colchão
松葉杖	muleta
麻痺	paralisia
ミキサー食	liquidificador
ミネラル	minerais
脈拍	pulsação
メタボリック症候群	síndrome metabólica
滅菌	esterilização
妄想	desilusão
燃え尽き症候群	síndrome burn out [distúbrio psiquiátrico]
モニタリング	monitoramento
問題行動	distúrbio de comportamento
夜間せん妄	delírio noturno
薬剤	droga
薬剤管理	controle de medicamentos
薬剤師	farmacêutico
薬物療法	farmacoterapia
有料老人ホーム	residência privada para idosos
ユニットケア	unidade de cuidados
ユニバーサルファッション	forma universal
要援護高齢者	assistente para necessidade dos idosos
要介護	necessidades em cuidados prolongados
要介護者	encarregado das necessidades relacionadas aos cuidados prolongados
要介護度	níveis relacionados as necessidades em cuidados prolongados
要介護認定	autorizacao requerida para graduacao de necessidades em cuidados prolongados
養護老人ホーム	residência para idosos [com serviço de enfermagem]
要支援	auxilio as necessidades em cuidados prolongados
要支援者	assistente de ajuda em cuidados prolongados
要支援認定	certifcado de necessidades em cuidados prolongados
腰痛症	lumbago ou lombalgia
腰痛体操	exercícios para lombalgia
腰痛予防	prevenção da lombalgia
抑制	inibição
浴槽	banheira
予防給付	benefícios preventivos
四脚杖	bengala de quatro apoios
ライフサイクル	ciclo de vida
ライフスタイル	estilo de vida
ライフレビュー	revisão da vida
ラポール	harmonia
理学療法士	fisioterapeuta
立位	posição em pé
利尿剤	diurético
リハビリテーション	reabilitação
リハビリテーション医学	medicina de reabilitação
リハビリテーション介護	reabilitação em cuidados prolongados
留置カテーテル	catéter alojado
流動食	dieta líquida
流動性知能	inteligência
利用料	custo de uso

レクリエーション　recreação
レム睡眠　movimento rápido dos olhos no sono REM
聾　surdez sensorineural
老化　senescência
老眼　presbiopia
老人性うつ病　depressão senil
老人性難聴　surdez senil
老人保健施設　instituição de saúde geriátrico
老年認知症　demência senil
老齢基礎年金　pensão básica do idoso
老齢年金　pensão do idoso
老齢福祉年金　pensão de bem-estar para idoso
ロールプレイ　jogo de papeis；jogos RPG

ポルトガル語

引用・参考文献一覧

青木務編『福祉・住環境用語辞典ハンドブック』保育社，2003．
秋元美世・芝野松次郎・森本佳樹・ほか編『現代社会福祉辞典』有斐閣，2003．
秋山美栄子編著『介護の用語と英語』NOVA，2006．
足立正樹編著『各国の社会保障』法律文化社，2003．
米国ナースの労働環境と患者編『患者の安全を守る‐医療・看護の労働環境の変革』日本評論社，2006．
飯島渉・澤田ゆかり著『高まる生活リスク‐社会保障と医療』岩波書店，2010．
池上直己訳『MDS 2.1‐施設ケアアセスメントマニュアル改訂版』医学書院，2005．
一番ケ瀬康子・井上千津子・中島紀恵子・ほか編『介護ハンドブック』光生館，1991．
伊藤善典著『ブレア政権の医療福祉改革‐市場機能の活用と社会的排除への取組み』ミネルヴァ書房，2006．
井部俊子・開原成允・京極高宣・前沢政次編『在宅医療辞典』中央法規出版，2009．
林春植・宣賢奎・住居広士編著『韓国介護保険制度の創設と展開‐介護保障の国際的視点』ミネルヴァ書房，2010．
上田敏・大川弥生編著『リハビリテーション医学大辞典』医歯薬出版，1996．
内薗耕二・小坂樹徳監修『看護学大辞典（第5版）』メヂカルフレンド社，2002．
大田仁史・三好春樹監修『実用介護事典』講談社，2005．
大森正集編著『介護職・福祉職のための医学用語辞典』中央法規出版，2006．
小田兼三著『コミュニティケアの社会福祉学‐イギリスと日本の地域福祉』勁草書房，2002．
小田兼三著『現代イギリス社会福祉研究‐日本からみた理論・政策・実践と課題』川島書店，1993．
小田兼三・桑原洋子・谷勝英・ほか編著『現代福祉学レキシコン（第2版）』雄山閣，1998．
介護福祉用語研究会編『必携介護福祉用語の解説』建帛社，2001．
金沢美智監修『福祉住環境コーディネーター基本用語辞典』エクスナレッジ，2007．
川上正夫・辻和男編著『実用介護・福祉・ケア用語辞典（2006年版）』土屋書店，2006．
木下康仁著『改革進むオーストラリアの高齢者ケア』東信堂，2007．
京極高宣著『社会福祉学小辞典（第2版）』ミネルヴァ書房，2004．
郡司篤晃著『医療と福祉における市場の役割と限界‐イギリスの経験と日本の課題』聖学院大学出版会，2004．
小池五郎・福場博保編著『栄養学事典』朝倉書店，1992．
小山剛監修『介護支援専門員基本用語辞典（第2版）』エクスナレッジ，2008．
近藤克則著『「医療費抑制の時代」を超えて‐イギリスの医療・福祉改革』医学書院，2004．
最新医学大辞典編集委員会編『最新医学大辞典（第3版）』医歯薬出版，2005．
坂本忠次・住居広士編著『介護保険の経済と財政‐新時代の介護保険のあり方』勁草書房，2006．

島津淳・高橋信幸・内藤佳津雄・ほか編著『介護保険辞典（新版）』中央法規出版，2002．
社会福祉辞典編集委員会編『社会福祉辞典』大月書店，2002．
庄司洋子・武川正吾・木下康仁・ほか編著『福祉社会事典』弘文社，1999．
シリーズ21世紀の社会福祉編集委員会編『社会福祉基本用語集（七訂版）』ミネルヴァ書房，2009．
新村出編著『広辞苑（第六版）』岩波書店，2008．
杉本敏夫・南 武志・和田謙一郎・ほか編著『ケアマネジメント用語辞典（改訂版）』ミネルヴァ書房，2007．
鈴木幸雄編著『介護福祉用語辞典ハンドブック』保育社，2003．
硯川真旬編著『国民福祉辞典』金芳堂，2006．
住居広士編『医療介護とは何か - 医療と介護の共同保険時代』金原出版，2004．
生活福祉研究機構編『イギリスの実践にみるコミュニティ・ケアとケアマネジメント』中央法規出版，1998．
袖井孝子・陳立行編著『転換期中国における社会保障と社会福祉』明石書店，2008．
染谷俶子著『オーストラリアの高齢者福祉 - 豊かな国の豊かな老後』中央法規出版，1999．
竹内孝仁編著『図解リハビリテーション事典』廣川書店，1987．
武久洋三監・山口典考著『早わかりリハビリテーション用語・略語・英和辞典』ナツメ社，2011．
田中雅子監修『介護福祉士基本用語辞典』エクスナレッジ，2007．
田端光美著『イギリス地域福祉の形成と展開』有斐閣，2003．
中央法規出版編集部編『介護福祉用語辞典（四訂版）』中央法規出版，2007．
寺出浩司監修『介護・社会福祉用語辞典 新星出版社，2005．
内閣官房「部局課名・官職名英訳名称一覧」(ww.cas.go.jp/jp/seisaku/hourei/name.pdf，2011)．
中村磐男・池弘子・牛津信忠・ほか監修『標準社会福祉用語辞典』秀和システム，2006．
中村永司著『英国と日本における医療福祉とソーシャルワーク』ミネルヴァ書房，2006．
仲村優一・小島蓉子・トムソン，LH編『社会福祉英和・和英用語辞典』誠信書房，1981．
那須宋一監修『老年学事典』ミネルヴァ書房，1989．
南山堂編『南山堂医学大辞典（第19版）』南山堂，2006．
二木立著『21世紀初頭の医療と介護 - 幻想の「抜本改革」を超えて』勁草書房，2001．
二木立著『「世界一」の医療費抑制政策を見直す時期』勁草書房，1994．
日本介護福祉士会監修『介護職のための実務用語集（改訂版）』エルゼビア・ジャパン，2003．
日本看護協会著『高齢者への質の高いケアをめざして』日本看護協会，1996．
日本在宅ケア学会監修『在宅ケア事典』中央法規出版，2007．
日本社会福祉実践理論学会編『社会福祉実践基本用語辞典』川島書店，2004．
日本地域福祉学会編『地域福祉事典（新版）』中央法規出版，2006．

橋本篤孝編著『介護・医療・福祉小辞典』法律文化社，2004.
平岡公一著『イギリスの社会福祉と政策研究-イギリスモデルの持続と変化』ミネルヴァ書房，2003.
福地義之助著『長寿社会総合講座〈10〉高齢化対策の国際比較』第一法規出版，1993.
舟場正富・斎藤香里著『介護財政の国際的展開-イギリス・ドイツ・日本の現状と課題』ミネルヴァ書房，2003.
見藤隆子・小玉香津子・菱沼典子編著『看護学事典』日本看護協会出版会，2003.
宮原伸二編『福祉医療用語辞典』創元社，2006.
村川浩一編著『介護保険・保健福祉辞典（新版）』ジャパンインターナショナル総合研究所，2003.
森岡清美・塩原勉・本間康平編著『新社会学辞典』有斐閣，1993.
山縣文治・柏女霊峰編著『社会福祉用語辞典（第7版）』ミネルヴァ書房，2009.
「用語事典」編集委員会編『イラストでみる介護福祉用語事典（第3版）』福祉教育カレッジ，2006.
古川孝順・川村佐和子・白澤政和編著『社会福祉士・介護福祉士のための用語辞典（第2版）』誠信書房，2006.
吉川春寿・芦田淳編著『総合栄養学事典（第4版新装版）』同文書院，2004.
吉田聡編『福祉・介護・リハビリ英語小事典』英文社，2008.
吉田宏岳監修『介護福祉学習辞典（第2版）』医歯薬出版，2007.
吉本光一・小松真編著『介護・福祉・医療用語集（改訂版）』エルゼビア・ジャパン，2008.
和田攻・南裕子・小峰光博編著『看護大事典』医学書院，2002.
Barker RL: The Social Work Dictionary: 5th Edition. NASW Press, 2003.
Birren JE and Schaie KW: Handbook of the Psychology of Aging. Academic Press Limited, 1996.
Colman AM: Dictionary of Psychology. Oxford University Press, 2009.
Davies M: The Blackwell Encyclopedia of Social Work. Blackwell Publishing Ltd., 2000.
DiGiovanna AG: Human Aging: Biological Perspectives. McGraw-Hill, Inc., 1994.
Editors of the American Heritage Dictionaries: The American Heritage Dictionary of the English Language. Houghton Mifflin Company, 2000.
Evashwick C: The Continuum of Long-Term Care. Delmar Publishers, 1996.
Ferrini AF and Ferrini RL: Health in the Later Years. Brown Benchmark, 1992.
Gelfand DE: The Aging Network-Programs and Services. Springer Publishing Company, 1993.
Hafen B, Karren KJ, Frandsen KJ, et al: Mind/Body Health: The Effects of Attitude, Emotions, and Relationships. Allyn & Bacon, 1996.

Kandel J: The Encyclopedia of Elder Care. Facts on File, 2009.
Koff TH and Park RW: Aging Public Policy-Bounding the Generations. Baywood Publishing Company, Inc., 1993.
Matcha DA: The Sociology of Aging-A Social Problems Perspective. Allyn & Bacon, 1997.
Merriam-Webster: Merriam-Webster's Collegiate Dictionary. Merriam-Webster Inc., 2009.
Mezey MD: The Encyclopedia of Elder Care: The Comprehensive Resource on Geriatric and Social Care. Prometheus, 2004.
Moody HR: Aging: Concepts and Controversies. Pine Forge Press, 1994.
Morris JN, Murphy K and Nonemaker S: Minimum Data Set 2.0. Health Care Financing Administration, 1995.
Romaine-Davis A, Boondas J and Lenihan A: Encyclopedia of Home Care for the Elderly. Greenwood Press, 1995.
World Health Organization: International Classification of Impairments, Disabilities and Handicaps. World Health Organization, 1980.

― 翻訳・校閲協力者 ―

インドネシア語
　アエプ・サエフル・バッフリ（Aep Saeful Bachri, インドネシア教育大学, 首都大学東京大学院留学生）

オーストラリア英語
　中島　美幸（Miyuki Nakashima, 通訳・知識）
　ショーン・リチャーズ（Sean Richards, 元クイーンズランド工科大学）

スペイン語
　サンディ・ガリドー（Sandy Garrido, Keiro Nursing Home）
　ニコル・ファハルド（Nicole Fajardo, 新見公立短期大学留学生）

タガログ語
　大本　和子（Kazuko Ohmoto, ミンダナオ国際大学客員教授）
　ロサリンダ・ピネダ（Rosalinda Pineda, ミンダナオ国際大学非常勤講師）
　メリー・ヤップ（Mary Yap, Keiro Intermediate Care Facility）
　エレン・ランゾ（Ellen Lanzo, ミンダナオ国際大学教員）
　ルース・レスマ（Ruth Resma, 日本フィリピンボランティア協会マリナオン・ドミトリー所長）

中国語
　汪　明軍（Ming-jun Wang, オウ　メイグン, 元岡山大学大学院環境学研究科留学生）
　楊　洋（Yang Yang, ヤン　ヤン, 広島大学大学院総合科学研究科留学生）

ドイツ語
　フベルトス・ドライヤー（Hubertus Dreyer, 東京芸術大学, 日本大学, 千葉商科大学非常勤講師）

ヒンディ語
　シュシャマ・ジェーン（Sushama Jain, ジャワハルラール・ネルー大学教授）
　シュルティ・デシュパンデ（Shruti Deshpande, 元岡山大学インド系国費留学生）

フランス語
　大庭　三枝（Mie Oba, 福山市立大学教育学部准教授）

ベトナム語
　フイン・トロン・ヒエン（Huynh Trong Hien, 広島大学大学院文学研究科ベトナム系国費留学生）

ポルトガル語
　ジュディッチ・平（Judpth Taira, 岡山大学大学院脳神経外科留学生）
　ダグラス・森（Douglas Mori, 県立広島大学留学生）

　　　　　　　　　　　　　　　　　　　　　　　　　　　　（五十音順）

― 協 力 者 ―

網代　正孝　（NPO法人・日本フィリピンボランティア協会会長）
有村　大士　（日本子ども家庭総合研究所研究員）
石田　博嗣　（特定非営利活動法人・日本ケアワーク研究会）
今泉　敏　　（県立広島大学保健福祉学部長）
大塚　忠廣　（特別養護老人ホーム蓬莱荘施設長・全国老人福祉施設協議会在宅委員長）
岡本　幸治　（特定非営利活動法人・日印友好協会理事長）
影山　佳奈　（県立広島大学保健福祉学専攻大学院）
狩谷　明美　（県立広島大学保健福祉学部准教授）
河村　純　　（閃利株式会社代表取締役）
笠原　幸子　（四天王寺大学短期大学部教授）
國定　美香　（県立広島大学保健福祉学部准教授）
塩川　満久　（県立広島大学保健福祉学部准教授）
棚田　裕二　（特定非営利活動法人・日本ケアワーク研究会）
束村　康文　（認定NPO法人・ブリッジ　エーシア　ジャパン）
中井　聡　　（NPO法人・日本フィリピンボランティア協会事務局長）
花田　達紀　（県立広島大学保健福祉学部人間福祉学科）
ベルンハルト・キルフェル　（Bernhard Kirfel, ケルン大学教授）
日高　久志　（邑南町, 福祉事務所所長補佐）
日髙　正巳　（兵庫医療大学リハビリテーション学部教授）
プラシャンテ・パルデシ（Prashant Pardeshi, 国立国語研究所教授）
増田　雅暢　（岡山県立大学保健福祉学部教授）
松本　百合美（新見公立短期大学講師）
妙見　幸子　（詩人）
吉田　繁子　（倉敷芸術科学大学大学院人間文化研究科教授）
レイシャル・バロナ・伊藤　（Rachel Valona-Ito）
山岡　喜美子（宇部フロンティア大学人間社会学部教授）

(五十音順)

― 協 力 団 体 ―

岡山県介護福祉研究会／株式会社・誠和／閃利・株式会社／中国四国介護福祉学会／特定非営利活動法人・日本ケアワーク研究会

(五十音順)

―編　者―

住居　広士　　（Hiroshi Sumii，県立広島大学大学院教授，日本学術会議連携会員）
澤田　如　　　（Yuki Sawada，日本福祉大学健康社会研究センター客員研究員）

―執　筆　者―

明渡　陽子　　（Yoko Akedo，大妻女子大学教授）
アンスガール・シュトラッケ‐メアテス
　　　　　　　（Ansgar Stracke-Mertes，ドイツ・ベルギー高齢福祉研究所長）
林　春植　　　（Choon-Seek Rim，イム　チュンシク，韓南大学教授・韓国老人福祉学
　　　　　　　　会名誉会長）
齋藤　香里　　（Kaori Saito，千葉商科大学講師）
澤田　如　　　（Yuki Sawada，日本福祉大学健康社会研究センター客員研究員）
住居　広士　　（Hiroshi Sumii，県立広島大学大学院教授・日本学術会議連携会員）
宣　賢奎　　　（Hyeon-Kyu Seon，ソン　ヒョンギュ，共栄大学教授）
張　天民　　　（Tianmin Zhang，チョウ　テンミン，中国政法大学副教授）
杜　鵬　　　　（Peng Du，ト　ホウ，中国人民大学老年学研究所所長・教授）
三原　博光　　（Hiromitsu Mihara，県立広島大学教授）

（五十音順）

― 編者紹介 ―

住居　広士（Hiroshi Sumii）

1982年	鳥取大学医学部医学卒業
1987年	岡山大学大学院医学研究科修了（医学博士）
1993年	岡山県立大学短期大学部助教授
1998年	ミシガン大学老年医学センター留学（文部省在外研究員）
2000年	広島県立保健福祉大学教授
2005年	県立広島大学保健福祉学部人間福祉学科教授
現　在	県立広島大学大学院保健福祉学専攻教授、医学博士、社会福祉士、介護福祉士、日本学術会議連携会員、日本介護福祉学会事務局長、日本保健福祉学会理事、日本在宅ケア学会理事、日本社会福祉系学会連合委員等、その他多数。

〈主要著書・論文〉

『介護モデルの理論と実践』（単著、大学教育出版、1998）、『アメリカ社会保障の光と陰』（編訳、大学教育出版、2000）、『介護保険入門書』（編著、インデックス出版、2002）、『要介護認定とは何か』（単著、一橋出版、2004）、『介護保険における介護サービスの標準化と専門性』（単著、大学教育出版、2007）、『高齢者に対する支援と介護保険制度』（共編者、ミネルヴァ書房、2009）、『介護福祉用語辞典』（編著、ミネルヴァ書房、2009）、その他多数。

澤田　如（Yuki Sawada）

1996年	南カリフォルニア大学心理学部卒業
2000年	南カリフォルニア大学老年学スクール修士課程修了（老年学修士）、Keiro ICF, Social Services Dept. Manager
2006年	日本福祉大学　COE研究員
2010年	日本福祉大学大学院社会福祉学研究科社会福祉学専攻博士後期課程修了（社会福祉学博士）
現　在	日本福祉大学健康社会研究センター客員研究所員

〈主要著書・論文〉

「米国のナーシングホームにおけるケアの質マネジメントシステム―文献レビューと現場経験をもとに―」（共著、病院管理第43巻3号、2007）、「米国のナーシングホームにおけるケアの質マネジメントシステム―行政監査と施設レベルの取組みに焦点をあてて―」（共著、日本医療・病院管理学会誌第45巻1号、2008）、『福祉社会開発学―理論・政策・実際，第7章第3節　施設ケアプログラムの評価』（共著、ミネルヴァ書房、2008）、「介護サービスに関する情報公表制度の日米比較」（共著、社会福祉学第50巻1号、2009）、『アメリカ高齢者ケアの光と陰』（単著、大学教育出版、2012）、その他多数。

国際介護保険用語辞典 ―介護保険の国際化―

2012年2月28日　初版第1刷発行

- ■編 著 者──住居広士／澤田　如
- ■発 行 者──佐藤　守
- ■発 行 所──株式会社 大学教育出版
  　　　　　　〒700-0953　岡山市南区西市855-4
  　　　　　　電話(086)244-1268代　FAX(086)246-0294
- ■印刷製本──サンコー印刷㈱
- ■ＤＴＰ──ティーボーンデザイン事務所

"International Dictionary of Long-Term Care Insurance Terms: Globalization of Long-Term Care Insurance" by Hiroshi Sumii & Yuki Sawada
Copyright © 2012 by Hiroshi Sumii & Yuki Sawada. All rights reserved.

本書のコピー・スキャン・デジタル化等の無断複製は著作権法上での例外を除き禁じられています。本書を代行業者等の第三者に依頼してスキャンやデジタル化することは、たとえ個人や家庭内での利用でも著作権法違反です。

ISBN978-4-86429-119-4